D0400655

Guatemala, Belize & Yucatán

Conner Gorry, Lucas Vidgen, Danny Palmerlee

Contents

YUCATÁN PENINSULA,
TABASCO & CHIAPAS
p309

BELIZE
p201

GUATEMALA
p53

Destination
Guatemala, Belize & Yucatán

Whether you crave pyramids buried by jungles, adrenaline-flushing river trips to grand, crumbling cities, remote rebel villages or spooky caves dripping with stalactites, this destination is for you. Sprinkled liberally with outdoor and off-the-beaten-track adventures, Guatemala, Belize and the Yucatán Peninsula are a superb combination of culture and natural wonders.

As intricate and electrifying as the textiles piled high in its markets, La Ruta Maya (the Mayan Route) beckons modern travelers to explore the Western Hemisphere's greatest ancient civilization. Comprised of Guatemala, Belize and a handful of southern Mexican states, this exciting multicultural route fosters wanderlust with its traditional customs, phenomenal Mayan sites, hedonistic beaches, ace diving, huffing volcanoes and frisky wildlife.

La Ruta Maya was a plan designed to develop tourism as an economic alternative to environmentally unsustainable practices, while ensuring minimal impact on the land and the Maya's heritage. The fruits – a few sour, but mostly sweet – are evident everywhere you travel, with large tracts of rain forest open to hikers, archaeological sites being discovered and uncovered regularly and palpable Mayan culture throughout. The region is fast becoming a traveler's favorite.

Bargaining over a beautiful *huipil* in the market at Chichicastenango or gazing upon the electric waters of the Caribbean lapping below the ruins at Tulum can be both transforming and addictive. You've got the guide, now come get hooked on all things Maya.

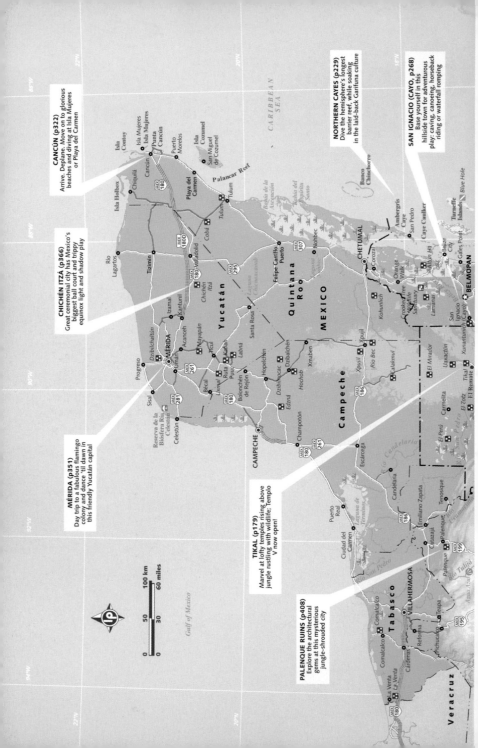

CANCÚN (p322)
Arrive. Deplane. Move on to glorious beaches and diving at Isla Mujeres or Playa del Carmen

NORTHERN CAYES (p229)
Dive the hemisphere's longest barrier reef, while soaking in the laid-back Garifuna culture

SAN IGNACIO (CAYO, p268)
Base yourself in this hillside town for adventurous play: caving, canoeing, horseback riding or waterfall romping

CHICHÉN ITZÁ (p366)
Great ceremonial city has Mexico's biggest ball court and trippy equinox light and shadow play

MÉRIDA (p351)
Day trip to a fabulous flamingo colony and dance 'til dawn in this friendly Yucatán capital

TIKAL (p179)
Marvel at lofty temples rising above jungle rustling with wildlife; Templo V now open!

PALENQUE RUINS (p408)
Explore the architectural gems at this mysterious jungle-shrouded city

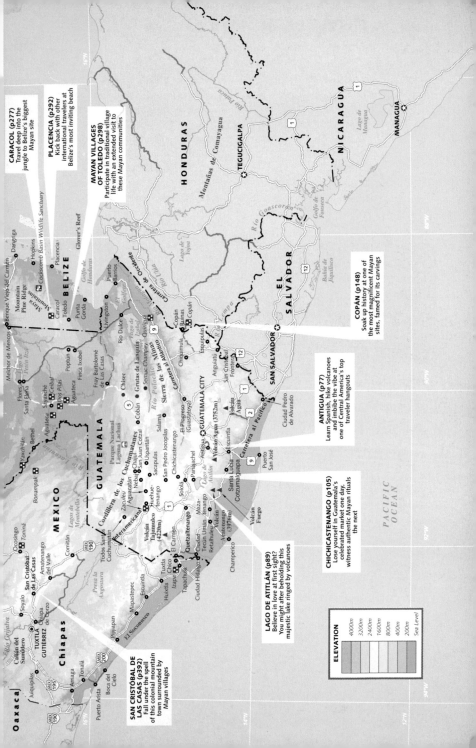

CARACOL (p277)
Travel deep into the jungle to Belize's biggest Mayan site

PLACENCIA (p292)
Kick back with other international travelers at Belize's most inviting beach

MAYAN VILLAGES OF TOLEDO (p298)
Participate in traditional village life with an extended visit to these Mayan communities

COPÁN (p148)
Soak up history at one of the most magnificent Mayan sites, famed for its carvings

ANTIGUA (p77)
Learn Spanish, hike volcanoes and imbibe the vibe at one of Central America's top traveler hangouts

CHICHICASTENANGO (p105)
Lose yourself in Guatemala's celebrated market one day, witness authentic Mayan rituals the next

LAGO DE ATITLÁN (p89)
Believe in love at first sight? You might after beholding this majestic lake ringed by volcanoes

SAN CRISTÓBAL DE LAS CASAS (p392)
Fall under the spell of this colonial mountain town surrounded by Mayan villages

ELEVATION

4000m
3200m
2400m
1600m
800m
400m
200m
Sea Level

Piercing the jungle canopy, the magnificent pyramids of **Tikal** (p179) in northern Guatemala testify to the grandeur of Mayan civilization. A border hop away in Chiapas sprawls the exquisite city of **Palenque** (p406), with magnificent views. Fabulously restored **Chichén Itzá** (p366) in the Yucatán is famous for its 'time temples' that produce a psychedelic light show on the equinoxes, while the ruins at **Tulum** (p342) are known for their inviting setting overlooking a Caribbean beach. For hieroglyphs and stelae, **Quiriguá** (p154) in southeastern Guatemala is the place to go. While kicking around here, don't miss the outstanding ruins at **Copán** (p151) nearby in Honduras. Belize's most important Mayan site is **Caracol** (p277) where you can witness archaeology in action.

JEFFREY N. BECOM

Detail on a Mayan temple, Chichén Itzá (p366)

Templo del Gran Jaguar (p182), Tikal

ERIC L WHEATER

El Castillo (p368), also known as the Pyramid of Kukulcán, Chichén Itzá

JOHN ELK

JON DAVISON

El Palacio (p410) in Palenque

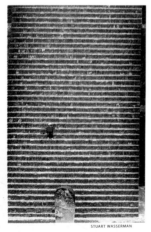

STUART WASSERMAN

Steps of a pyramid in Tikal
(p179)

The Templo de los Guerreros (Temple of the Warriors), part of the Grupo de las Mil Columnas (p369),
Chichén Itzá

JON DAVISON

For some alone time with the ancient Maya, check out **Cobá** (p345), where you might have a pyramid to yourself. Travelers are raving about the caves at **Actun Tunichil Muknal** (p273), and **Hopkins** (p288) has great barrier reef diving without the crowds. Guatemala's entire Petén region is dotted with remote sites including towering **El Mirador** (p190), unrestored **El Perú** (p189) and picturesque **Yaxhá** (p189). A river trip to visit **Ceibal** (p188), **Aguateca** (p189) or **Dos Pilas** (p189) proves it's the journey more than the destination that counts. Delve deep into the Mexican rain forest to discover the ruins at **Calakmul** (p254), where archaeologists are uncovering an ancient city bigger than Tikal.

JOHN ELK III

Temple of the Jaguar (Structure N10-9, p255), one of the unrestored ruins at Lamanai

Stone carving of Chan Muwan II, Bonampak (p414)

JEFFREY N. BECOM

Edificio 33 (p416), the best-preserved temple at Yaxchilán

JON DAVISO

Charming **San Cristóbal de Las Casas** (p392) in Chiapas is within striking distance of several intriguing Mayan mountain towns like **San Juan Chamula** (p401) and **Ocosingo** (p403). The famous market towns of **Chichicastenango** (p105) and **Sololá** (p104) in Guatemala are stupefying, and traditional rituals are well preserved in the villages dotting the shores of **Lago de Atitlán** (p89). Tourist crowds aside, **Antigua** (p77), that colonial gem, still pulses with Mayan energy. Many foreigners study Spanish here or in **Quetzaltenango** (p111). Studying Mayan languages or weaving is popular in these towns and in several mainly Mayan communities like **Todos Santos Cuchumatán** (p126) and **Nebaj** (p110). In Belize, the beautifully located indigenous villages of **Toledo** (p299) welcome travelers into the heart of modern Mayan and Garifuna life, accommodating their explorations of the natural and cultural wonders there.

The busy and colorful market (p106) at Chichicastenango

ANDREW MARSHALL & LEANNE WALKER

RYAN FOX

Girl using a *kaperraj* (p105) as head covering

Group of Mayan men in the back of a pickup truck, Guatemala

KRAIG LIEB

Belize is bursting with tropical fish, birds and beasts: diving the marine reserves around The **Cayes** (p229, p287) means manta rays and reef sharks, and loads of wildlife and hundreds of bird species flutter around the **Cockscomb Basin Wildlife Sanctuary** (p290). The **Community Baboon Sanctuary** (p248) is the only place in the world you can see the endangered black howler monkey and **Gales Point** (p281) has manatees and breeding hawksbill turtles in abundance. In Guatemala, the jungle around **Tikal** (p179) jumps with monkeys, toucans and coatis, while nearby **Biotopo Cerro Cahuí** (p177) is home to ocelots, monkeys, armadillos and varied bird species. Further afield is **Parque Nacional Laguna del Tigre** (p190) where you'll glimpse scarlet macaws, white tortoises and crocodiles. Divers of all stripes consider **Cozumel** (p337) among the world's best scuba diving destinations for its abundant fish and coral. For an unforgettable flamingo fix, the Yucatán's **Reserva de la Biósfera Ría Celestún** (p365) is tops, with the **Reserva de la Biosfera Ría Lagartos** (p374) running a close second.

A green iguana, Belize

LUKE HUNTER

A tamandua or three-toed anteater, Belize

TOM BOYDE

MARK WEBSTER

Belize is home to the jaguar

TOM BOYDEN

A red-lored Amazon parrot, Belize

MARK WEBSTER

A green moray eel, Belize

A flock of flamingoes take flight over Río Lagartos (p374)

SCOTT DOGGETT

Hiking one of Guatemala's 30 volcanoes like **Volcán Agua** (p83) or **Tajumulco** (p115) are popular trips. Chugging over the rugged **Cuchumatanes** (p127) from **Huehuetenango** (p122) to **Cobán** (p137) is spectacular, as are the terraced pools of **Semuc Champey** (p143). The reef off **Isla Mujeres** (p331) in the Yucatán is a travelers' favorite and a boat trip through Chiapas' **Cañón del Sumidero** (p391) is a rush. Lose yourself in the dense jungle surrounding spectacular **Laguna Miramar** (p405) or kick back on the shores of the multicolored **Lagunas de Montebello** (p417). From the laid-back **Cayes** (p229, p287) you can visit Belize's barrier reef or head south to the isolated beaches of **Hopkins** (p288).

Playa del Carmen (p339)

JON DAVISON

Elephant ear sponge in Belize's barrier reef (p229, p287)

MARK WEBSTER

Lago de Atitlán (p89) with Volcán Tolimán and Volcán Atitlán

RICHARD I'ANSO

Getting Started

'Something for everyone' might be the tagline here. Sling a hammock and swat jungle bugs, or honeymoon at Francis Ford Coppola's lux resort; scuba dive or study Spanish; rent a jeep or paddle a canoe – here, anything is possible, with options for every budget. Unless you want to glimpse rare horned guans in the wild or are traveling during Semana Santa, little advance planning is necessary. Jungle treks, specialist dives, Spanish school, even volunteer gigs, are possible to arrange once you arrive, so don't hold back if you've got the urge to get up and go. Bus transport and river passage between the countries covered in this book are frequent and mostly well-coordinated, but always check visa requirements ahead of time if border crossings are in your travel plans (see p452).

See p438 for climate charts

WHEN TO GO

Varied topography means there isn't a bad time to travel here. If you're freezing in the highlands, you can head to the beach or if jungle mud bogs you down, you can get high and dry in the Yucatán. By and large, variabilities in temperature are more connected to altitude and location, while seasons are delineated by how wet you'll get.

The time to beat the crowds and find cheaper airfares is during *invierno* (winter rainy season), running roughly from May to November. Expect afternoon downpours for a couple of hours and higher humidity (especially in lowland areas). Uninterrupted days of rain and flooding do occur, but with lower frequency. Highland areas in Guatemala and Chiapas are chilly and damp – especially at night – during *invierno*. The entire Caribbean coast braces itself for hurricane season (June to November), with the worst storms blowing through in October and November.

DON'T LEAVE HOME WITHOUT...

- Checking the visa situation (p196, p304 & p428).
- Checking travel advisory warnings (p439).
- Warm clothes for chilly highland nights – at least a sweater or light jacket and a pair of warm-ish pants (eg denim).
- A flashlight (torch) for exploring caves, ruins and your room when the electricity fails (as it often does).
- A mosquito net, if you plan an extended jungle adventure or will be sleeping in cheap rooms without screens.
- Insect repellent containing DEET (p467) for wet-season travels. You may want to take medication against malaria, too (p465).
- A towel, for rooms without one.
- An alarm clock for those early-morning departures.
- Diving or snorkeling gear.
- A small Spanish-English dictionary and/or Lonely Planet's *Latin American Spanish phrasebook*.
- Water purifier or iodine tablets; drinking bottled water (especially on longer trips) is detrimental to your budget and the environment (where do you think all those plastic bottles go?). For more on traveling and minding the environment in your travels, see p17.

The *verano* (summer, dry season) falls between November and May and is a blessing of warm, comfortable days in the highlands and a curse of sweltering heat in the lowlands. This is also peak tourist season, when prices are up and vacancies down – particularly around Christmas, New Year's and Easter (Semana Santa), when locals and foreigners alike descend on popular regional destinations; the situation intensifies during Semana Santa, when you need to book ahead for rooms and transportation. A secondary high season lasts from June to August, when throngs of North Americans and Europeans are kicking about.

School holidays here, like anywhere in the world, will swell park, beach and recreational-area crowds.

For more specific details on festivals in each country, see p193 (Guatemala), p302 (Belize) and p425 (Mexico). For information on holidays, see p194 (Guatemala), p303 (Belize) and p426 (Mexico).

COSTS & MONEY

Truly an equitable destination, there are options to please all budgets here. With its US$4 rooms and US$3 set meals, Guatemala is shoestringer paradise; it's completely realistic to spend under US$15 a day here without too much hardship. Double your eating and sleeping budget to US$30 and you'll enjoy comfortable accommodations (private bath, hot water!), plus at least two decent meals daily. On the other end of the spectrum is Belize, where rock-bottom rooms on the cayes go for around US$10 and a fried-chicken sandwich is US$5. Jump up to a beachside cabaña (with bath and snapper to sup on) and you're looking at twice the price. Budget travelers should bank on US$20 to US$30 a day in Belize, at least double that for more comfortable, mid-range arrangements. Cost-wise, Southern Mexico generally falls between Guatemala and Belize.

> Many ATMs in the region only accept personal identification codes (PIN) of four digits; double check with your bank before traveling.

Always account for expenses like transportation, museum/site admission, checking email, shopping and nights out. This is a good region to consider a splurge, as spending even a little more can net a lot more value. See p57, p205 and p314 for approximate daily expenses and sample costs.

Carrying a combination of traveler's checks (in US dollars is easiest) and credit/debit cards works well. While all but the smallest towns in Guatemala and southern Mexico have ATMs accepting MasterCard/Cirrus cards, and Belize recently leapt into the 21st century by installing ATMs countrywide, you shouldn't rely solely on plastic. MasterCard and Visa are the most widely accepted; American Express somewhat less so. Changing money as you jump around the countries covered in this book is straightforward. See the Regional Directory (p443) for more on money, plus the individual country Directories (Guatemala p194; Belize p303; Mexico p426).

READING UP
Books

Learned and careful, yet readable and well illustrated, *The Maya*, by Michael D Coe, is probably the best single-volume account of the ancient Maya story. Coe's *Breaking the Maya Code* tells the fascinating story of the modern decipherment of ancient Mayan writing, and his *Reading the Maya Glyphs* will help you to actually read ancient inscriptions.

Sylvanus G Morley's classic 1940s tome, *The Ancient Maya*, has been updated for contemporary readers by Robert J Sharer. The first half of the nearly 900-page book treats the Maya story chronologically; the second half discusses different aspects of their culture.

The Blood of Kings: Dynasty & Ritual in Maya Art, by Linda Schele and Mary Ellen Miller, is an intriguingly illustrated guide to the art and culture of the ancient Maya, with particular emphasis on sacrifices, bloodletting, the ball game, torture of captives and other gory aspects of Mayan culture. Schele, who died in 1998, was one of the world's most eminent Mayanists. Any of her several books will prove illuminating.

Chronicle of the Maya Kings and Queens, by Simon Martin and Nikolai Grube, tells in superbly illustrated detail the histories of 11 of the most important Mayan city-states and their rulers.

Maya Cosmos – Three Thousand Years of the Shaman's Path, by David Freidel, Linda Schele and Joy Parker, traces Maya creation myths from the past to the present with a dose of lively personal experience.

More visually oriented travelers will enjoy Mary Ellen Miller's *Maya Art & Architecture*, with superb illustrations of giant temples, intricately painted ceramics and more.

Two beautiful books explaining the techniques, meanings and relevance of Mayan weaving are *The Maya Textile Tradition*, edited by Margot Blum Schevil, and *Maya of Guatemala – Life and Dress* by Carmen L Pettersen.

Ronald Wright's *Time Among the Maya* is a tale of travels through the Maya region – Guatemala, Mexico, Belize and Honduras – delving into the glorious past and exploited present of the Maya people. Wright travels to many of the places you'll visit, and his book is a fascinating on-the-road read, even though written in the troubled 1980s.

MINDING YOUR MS, BZS & QS

Employing simple money-saving strategies can make a big difference in your budget, freeing up finances to take a special side trip, prolong your foreign odyssey or splurge on an exotic meal or lux lodging. Consider these tried and true tips:

- Trundle along in second-class local buses rather than first-class, air-con coaches or shuttles and save big (500% in some cases!).
- Cross borders with as little of the currency of the country you're leaving as possible, so you won't lose in the exchange back to dollars or to the currency of the country you're entering.
- Slow down. The slower you travel, the less transport you use per day, the less entrance fees per day, and the longer you have to figure out the cheap deals in a town.
- Visiting in the off-season means the possibility of cheaper airfares and lower hotel prices.
- Soloists don't get a break on room costs, with a single often costing more than half a double: if you're traveling alone, hook up with others to defray costs; bunks in dorm rooms (US$3 to US$10) are usually the best deal for solo travelers.
- If you're traveling in a group, note that it's often more expensive to stay in a hostel than share a good-value, cheap hotel room.
- Look for the *menú del día* in restaurants: these two- or three-course set meals are cheap and filling. Eating at street stalls or having a picnic is even cheaper.
- Over longer trips, using a water filter will prove cheaper than buying bottled water – and more environmentally friendly too.
- A ticket to enter Tikal after 3pm is also good for the next day; if arriving late at other big sites, wait until the following morning to enter, maximizing your visit to price-of-admission ratio.
- Many archaeological sites and museums in Mexico are free on Sunday.
- Base your Belize dive vacation in mellow, budget-friendly Hopkins, where you have access to all the same sites as from pricier Ambergris Caye or crowded Caye Caulker.

John L Stephens' *Incidents of Travel in Central America, Chiapas and Yucatan* (1841) and *Incidents of Travel in Yucatan* (1843) are tried-and-true classics. Beautifully illustrated by Frederick Catherwood, these are more the stuff of explorers than travelers. Indeed, they introduced the world to many Mayan archeological sites when they were first published and are now the only evidence we have for some features of the sites that have been lost, destroyed or stolen.

Websites

Lanic Guatemala, Belize or Mexico (http://lanic.utexas.edu/la/ca/guatemala; http://lanic.utexas.edu/la/ca/belize; http://lanic.utexas.edu/la/mexico) For links, nothing rivals the University of Texas' comprehensive site, divided by category and updated regularly.

Mesoweb (www.mesoweb.com) Head here for late-breaking news on archaeological discoveries and digs; includes updates on site access, historical theories and hieroglyphic interpretations.

Mostly Maya (www.mostlymaya.com) This comprehensive, ad-free site is traveler-written, with loads of intriguing links and practical information you'll actually use (eg how to get to the Belize City airport for cheap or where to buy over-the-counter chloroquine).

Mundo Maya Online (www.mayadiscovery.com) Bilingual virtual magazine of the region covers everything from waterfall hikes in Chiapas to reading stelae in Quiriguá.

Planeta.com (www.planeta.com) Ron Mader's award-winning ecotourism site covers green themes galore, plus travel trends and current events of ecological import.

MUST-SEE MOVIES

Kicking back with a movie made in or about where you'll be traveling can be a powerful motivator and educator. While movies shot in Belize are all about location, location, location, those taking place in southern Mexico or Guatemala usually tackle important human rights or political issues. Try one of the following for a taste.

La Hija del Puma (The Daughter of the Puma, 1995), directed by Ulf Hultberg, is a powerful film based on a true story about a Quiché Maya girl who survives the army massacre of her fellow villagers and sees her brother captured. She escapes to Mexico but returns to Guatemala in search of her brother. Available in Spanish with English, Swedish or Danish subtitles.

Gregory Nava's tragic film, *El Norte* (The North, 1984) brings home not only the tragedy of Guatemala's civil war but also the illusory nature of many Guatemalans' 'American Dream', as it follows an orphaned brother and sister north to the USA to look for a living.

Discovering Dominga (2002), by Patricia Flynn, is the heart-wrenching documentary about Denise Becker (aka Dominga Sic Ruiz), a survivor

---

JUNGLE BUMMER *Conner Gorry*

I don't know how many hours we walked through the Guatemalan jungle that first day en route to El Mirador (p190), but it was almost dark when our guide called a halt. We collapsed, covered in mud, almost hallucinating with exhaustion. Or was that hunger? The beasts were certainly ravenous and it was only when we heard the first thwack, thwack, crash! that we realized our trio of pack mules would eat an entire young sapodilla tree every day of the multiday trek. Tender branches also fell to the machete for hammock slinging, bushwhacking and campfires. When I started adding up all those trees, felled purely for our tourist jaunt into the jungle, I was appalled (and put in mind of the horror stories from the Inca Trail leading to Peru's Machu Picchu, where decades of careless tourism has left its mark). When our guide chucked the tuna and tomato cans into the forest, we became proactive, successfully convincing him we should pack out our garbage. Alas, those damn asses had nothing else to eat but trees.

OUR FAVORITE FESTIVALS

A riot of music, dancing and fireworks, festivals in this part of the world (especially Guatemala) are so commonplace, you won't have to hunt for them – they'll find you. Still, some of the fiestas are so spectacular, they're worth a little extra planning. For more details on each country's events, see p193 (Guatemala), p303 (Belize) and p425 (Mexico).

- Fiesta de El Cristo de Esquipulas, January 15, Esquipulas (p147)
- Vernal Equinox, March 20 or 21, Chichén Itzá (p366)
- Carnaval, February or March, Mérida (p354) & San Juan Chamula (p401)
- Semana Santa (Easter Week), March or April, Antigua (p84) & Santiago Atitlán (p98)
- Lobster Festival, late June/early July, Placencia, Caye Caulker & San Pedro (p302)
- Rabin Ajau Folkloric Festival, late July/early August, Cobán (p139)
- El Día de Todos los Santos (All Saints' Day), November 1, Todos Santos Cuchumatán (p126)
- Feria del Barrilete Gigante (Giant Kite Festival), November 1, Santiago Sacatepéquez & Sumpango (not covered in this book)
- Día de Muertos (Day of the Dead), November 2, cemeteries throughout Mexico (p425)
- Garifuna Settlement Day, November 19, Dangriga & Hopkins (p295)
- Fiesta de Santo Tomás, December 13–21, Chichicastenango (p108)

---

of the 1982 massacre in the Guatemalan village of Río Negro where 70 women and 107 children were murdered. In English with occasional Spanish subtitles, Denise's search for her past, identity and parents' remains is a moving personal testimony about the brutal civil war.

Sweat, blood, tears and bugs: the Belizean jungle is a nasty place, especially for the family trying to carve out utopia in *Mosquito Coast* (1986), starring Harrison Ford and River Phoenix.

RESPONSIBLE TRAVEL

This region has witnessed more than 500 years of outside interference and influence, 36 years of civil war (Guatemala), episodic armed insurgency (Chiapas), devastating hurricanes (the Yucatán and Belize) and refugee movements throughout. Furthermore, Maya ruins that remained buried for generations are being discovered, exposed, picked over and eroded. Deforestation, prostitution, drug running and capital flight are reaching (sometimes surpassing) crisis proportions. Throw tourism into this complex mix and the picture can darken further.

So what can you do? A lot. Knowing where to spend your money and spending it wisely is the key. Don't simply accept ecotourism as a buzzword, but educate yourself; actually practice and preach low-impact tourism. Being aware and using common sense will go a long way towards protecting gains and promoting the future of the physical and cultural landscapes that you visit. For ideas on how to meet locals, see p34.

MINDFUL TIPS

- Ask before taking someone's photo. Ever had a camera thrust in your face? Not nice. Always ask, especially before photographing indigenous people.
- Learn the lingo. Take Spanish classes before or during the trip, pick up some Maya or indigenous phrases and use them. Even just a 'hello' shows respect. See the Language chapter (p470).

■ Never litter. Sure the locals do it, but you're not local. Pack out all trash when camping. Put cigarette butts in ashtrays or trashcans. Don't toss garbage from bus windows; carry a small plastic bag for bus-trip garbage and share it around.

At www.stopftaa.org or www.alcaabajo.cu, learn why the Free Trade Area of the Americas (FTAA; ALCA in Spanish) is under attack by activists, social scientists and trade, labor and indigenous groups.

■ Buy locally. Drink the national bottled water, not the one Coca-Cola makes. Ditto for beer or candy bars. Seek out community-owned tourist services like Internet cafés and tour groups.

■ Buy directly from craftspeople or artisan cooperatives. More money goes to the creative mind behind the wares this way.

■ Don't eat shellfish out of season. Lobster or conch caught out of season shouldn't be on the menu, or in your belly. Never eat turtle or any endangered species.

■ Respect local traditions. Dress appropriately when visiting churches and shrines and consider the effect your presence may have on local rituals or ceremonies.

■ Hands off the antiquities. No rubbing at the ruins, flash photography in underground tunnels or touching ritual pots or remains. Respect signage at all ruins.

■ Leave wild things where they are. Don't collect or purchase souvenirs made from endangered plants or animals, including coral, turtle shell and orchids.

■ Be a bus buddy. When it fills up (and it will), give up your seat to an elderly passenger or a mom. If you're sitting, offer to take bags from someone left standing.

■ Ask yourself the hard questions. Would I (mis)behave this way at home? Should I really bury my used toilet paper? Where does the nasty sewage from this lovely cabaña go? (If the answer is to the lake, ocean or woods, consider relocating).

■ Volunteer. There are scads of worthy causes around (see p196 and p214).

The local needs versus conservation debate is complex: learn more, in English or Spanish, at the Capise (Centro de Análisis Político e Investigaciones Sociales y Economicas) website www.capise.org/eng /documents/index.html.

■ Share the wealth. Also try to patronize businesses not listed in this book, thereby spreading your money around the community. What you discover will likely be refreshingly tourist free!

■ Brace the cold. Don't take hot showers if water is heated by wood fire, especially in rural areas.

■ Make showers short and sweet. Water is a limited resource, especially in the Yucatán, so keep showers short. Never let a faucet run.

■ Remember the three tenets of ecotourism, that special brand of tourism that provides for conservation measures, involves the local community in a meaningful way and is both profitable and sustainable.

WEB RESOURCES

Planeta.com (www.planeta.com) Ron Mader's outstanding ecotourism website.

TIES (www.ecotourism.org) Links to businesses devoted to ecotourism.

Tourism Concern (www.tourismconcern.org.uk) UK-based organization dedicated to promoting ethical tourism.

Transitions Abroad (www.transitionsabroad.com) Website of the eponymous magazine focusing on immersion and responsible travel.

BOOKS

For more on how not to dent the lands we visit (as well as listings of ecotour groups), read *The Good Alternative Travel Guide* or Mark Mann's outstanding *The Community Tourism Guide*.

Itineraries

CLASSIC ROUTES

SURF & TURF
10 to 14 Days / Cancún to Antigua

Sun yourself in **Cancún** (p322) or hipper **Isla Mujeres** (p331) for a spell before heading south to the dazzling ruins of **Tulum** (p342), perched over a beach, where you can grab a sand-floor cabaña for a night or two. At **Chetumal** (p349), cross into northern Belize for some swinging wildlife at the **Crooked Tree Wildlife Sanctuary** (p251), detouring to the famous **Altun Ha** ruins (p249) or ripping along the croc-filled waters of the New River en route to the ruins at **Lamanai** (p254). A bus-boat combo takes you to purgatorial **Belize City** (p216), before landing in the heavenly cayes: **Caye Caulker** (p233) for the budget crowd or **Ambergris Caye** (p239) for more organized comfort. Head west to popular **San Ignacio** (Cayo; p268), with a side trip to **Caracol** (p277), Belize's biggest Mayan site, before crossing into Guatemala, where **Tikal** (p179) awaits. Camp, sling a hammock or take a room at the ruins, beholding the sunrise over the jungle and its wild inhabitants as they wake. For a hardcore option, travel south over-land visiting **Poptún** (p168), **Río Dulce** (p155) and **Lívingston** (p162), or fly straight to **Guatemala City** (p65) and visit charming **Antigua** (p77). Check the calendar and catch Technicolor market days in **Chichicastenango** (p105) or **Sololá** (p104), near stunning **Lago de Atitlán** (p89).

This 1275km smorgasbord trip samples the best of land and sea. Though it's a lot of ground to cover in two weeks, taking one flight will allow you downtime in towns of your choice. With three weeks, there are many variations possible: explore Lago de Atitlán in earnest, dive in Cozumel or make a side trip to Palenque.

MAYAN HEARTLAND   Two Weeks to One Month / Cancún to Tikal

Take advantage of cheap airfares to **Cancún** (p322), allowing you quality beach time, or to **Mérida** (p351) for some good day trips such as wildlife watching at the **Reserva de la Biósfera Ría Celestún** (p365). From either city it's a quick trip to see the monumental ruins (including Mexico's largest ball court) at **Chichén Itzá** (p366). More ruins await west at **Uxmal** (p358); it's then just a scenic hop to the architectural gems and stunning caves on **Ruta Puuc** (p362). You might get hooked and hang around the delightful pirate city of **Campeche** (p375), a World Heritage Site, or hightail it directly to the money shot: **Palenque** (p406), one of Mexico's Mayan treasures. From here, the ancient and modern Maya meet in a string of traditional towns that carry you by road into Guatemala: colonial **San Cristóbal de Las Casas** (p392), bustling **Huehuetenango** (p122) and orderly **Quetzaltenango** (Xela, p111). Spend several days exploring the surrounding areas of these cities or push straight on to the wonderful lakeside villages of **Lago de Atitlán** (p89) or to colonial **Antigua** (p77), where volcano hikes, kayaking and cycling are all possibilities. From nearby **Guatemala City** (p65), catch a flight to the diminutive island town of **Flores** (p169) to visit the remnants of a great civilization at **Tikal** (p179).

A primer on the great achievements of the ancient Maya, combined with the living traditions of today, this route is ideal for first timers to the region. It gives a taste of both Guatemala and Mexico, providing variety for your travel diet. Make it in two weeks or a month; either way this trip covers about 1500km.

ROADS LESS TRAVELED

JUNGLE BOOGIE   Two to Three Weeks / San Cristóbal de Las Casas to Flores

Starting at graceful **San Cristóbal de Las Casas** (p392), head over to **Ocosingo** (p403), taking a day jaunt to the jungle-backed Mayan ruins of **Toniná** (p404). An exciting trip through mountainous river valleys and Zapatista strongholds takes you to remote **Laguna Miramar** (p405), an exquisite rainforest lake where howler monkeys greet the dawn. Return to Ocosingo and jog north to the thundering **Agua Azul** (p406) waterfalls. North of Ocosingo is **Palenque** (p406), arguably the most beautifully proportioned of all Mayan cities, tucked photogenically in the jungle. A fascinating trip follows the Mexico–Guatemala border southeast on the Río Usumacinta to **Bonampak** (p414) and **Yaxchilán** (p415), two more fine Mayan sites situated in dense forest with prolific wildlife. An adventurous river passage into Guatemala is also possible on the **Río San Pedro** (p386) or **Río de la Pasión** (p187). The latter is the gateway to several other secluded jungle sites, including **Ceibal** (p188) and **Aguateca** (p189). Leaving the rivers behind, good minor roads lead to **Flores** (p169) and the temples hidden amid the rainforest canopy that define **Tikal** (p179). Archaeological sites hiding deep in the jungle here include **El Perú** (p189), home to scarlet macaws; **El Zotz** (p189), famed for its bat population, and the trailhead for a killer 36km trek to Tikal; and **El Mirador** (p190), which has the highest (known) temple in the Mayan world. Though rewarding, getting this far off the beaten path takes time and stamina.

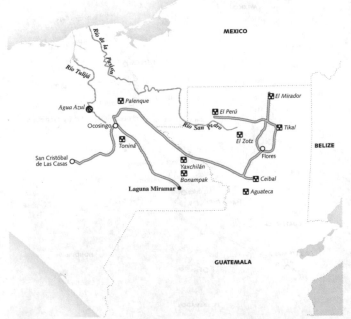

Revolution, ruins and rainforest: this adventurous two- to three-week, 645km trip combines stellar natural settings with ancient and contemporary culture in Mexico and Guatemala, and is a dandy for would-be explorers and travel junkies. Take advantage of the hikes delving into the greatest stands of virgin forest north of the Amazon, but don't forget the insect repellent!

GUATEMALA TO BELIZE: THE BACKDOOR
10 to 14 Days

After surviving **Guatemala City** (p65), check out **Antigua** (p77), chilling long enough to climb a volcano, learn Spanish or hook up with other travelers before hopping a bus or shuttle east to **Copán Ruinas** (p151) across the border in Honduras. A visit to the archaeological site, one of the Mayan world's greatest city-sites, and justly famous for its carvings, is almost compulsory. Afterwards, you can soak in hot springs or tube down a river. If you like your sculptures beautiful *and* big, however, nearby **Quiriguá** (p154) in Guatemala, with its 10m stelae, is the ticket. If you're in this area around January 15, do not miss the pilgrimage to see the Black Christ at **Esquipulas** (p146). Hugging the shores of **Lago de Izabal** (p155) is **Río Dulce** (p155), setting-off point for the jungle-fringed river passage to funky **Lívingston** (p162). From this reggae-infused beach town, catch a boat to untouristed **Punta Gorda** (p296) in multi-culti Belize, with its lively mix of Mayan, Creole and Garifuna flavors. Stick around and get to know the traditional villages and friendly folk of **Toledo** (p298) with a little jungle exploration thrown in, or pick your way north to the halcyon coastal towns of **Placencia** (p292), **Hopkins** (p288) or **Dangriga** (p284). From the latter, you can dive or snorkel the unspoiled reefs around **Glover's Reef** (p288), where dolphins and manatees frolic. While in this neck of the woods, don't miss **Gales Point** (p281), with hawksbill turtles in big numbers and a manatee or two, and the **Cockscomb Basin Wildlife Sanctuary** (p290), with some of Belize's best wildlife watching. More spectacular diving (including the famous **Blue Hole**, p247) is waiting at the many **cayes** (p229) just off the coast near **Belize City** (p216).

A sweet blend of culture and natural wonders, this 1070km trip through Mayan ruins and coastal towns promises an intimate look at local life. Up the ante: travel exclusively by chicken bus, lingering beyond the 10 to 14 days it would take on first-class buses or by car.

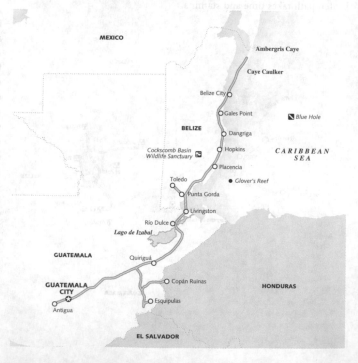

TAILORED TRIPS

NATURAL WONDERS   Two Weeks to Two Months / Ambergris Caye to Antigua

Explore the world's second-largest barrier reef from **Ambergris Caye** (p239) off the coast of Belize. Once you tire of sharks and rays, head west for some horseback riding or river tubing in the **Mountain Pine Ridge Forest Reserve** (p276), reprovisioning and partying in **San Ignacio** (Cayo, p268). Push over to **Flores** (p169) in Guatemala, where you can arrange multiday treks into the rainforest or, if time is short, head immediately to the temples of **Tikal** (p179). Stay overnight at the ruins or in nearby **El Remate** (p177).

The truly inspiring route south from here is via the riverside town of **Sayaxché** (p187), near a group of intriguing Mayan sites: **Ceibal** (p188), **Aguateca** (p189) and **Dos Pilas** (p189). The road south leads to **Cobán** (p137), jumping-off point for natural wonders such as jungle-ringed **Laguna Lachuá** (p143), the **Grutas de Lanquín** (p142) and the turquoise pools of **Semuc Champey** (p143). From here, head south to **Antigua** (p77), where you can hike (and bike) up **Volcán Acatenango** (p83) or do a peddle-and-paddle tour to **Lago de Atitlán** (p89).

You can augment this itinerary by doing good: volunteer to rehabilitate monkeys in **El Petén** (p171) or plant trees in **Belize** (p212). For more volunteer opportunities, see p446.

HIGHLAND FLING   10 Days / Guatemala City to Quetzaltenango

For a heavy dose of Mayan culture, spectacular scenery and riotous markets, give this well-traveled itinerary a whirl.

From **Guatemala City** (p65), head to cozy **Antigua** (p77) to enjoy the country's finest colonial architecture and the tourist and language-student scene. Climb a volcano or two before moving on to **Panajachel** (p91) on volcano-ringed **Lago de Atitlán** (p89). Love or hate this classic Gringo Trail town, it's a handy base for boat trips to some of the more traditional Mayan villages around the lake, including **Santiago Atitlán** (p98), **San Pedro La Laguna** (p100), **San Marcos La Laguna** (p102) and **Santa Cruz La Laguna** (p103). You shouldn't miss the market in **Chichicastenango** (p105). If you have the time, detour north to **Nebaj** (p110), where you'll find great walking and a strong Mayan way of life amid stunning scenery.

From Chichicastenango, follow the Interamerican Hwy west to **Quetzaltenango** (Xela, p111), with a host of intriguing villages, markets and natural wonders nearby. From Quetzaltenango, you can head into Mexico, perhaps via **Todos Santos Cuchumatán** (p125), a fascinating Mayan mountain town with great walking possibilities.

The Authors

CONNER GORRY
Coordinating Author

Gotta love that Gap Year: after earning a BA in Latin American Studies, Conner hit the road camping, backpacking and chicken bussing around Central America, eventually landing in Guatemala with the civil war raging. Super Mayan hospitality; camping on the shores of Semuc Champey – who wouldn't love it? One set of Peace Accords and an International Policy degree later, she returned to experience the country anew and venture farther off the beaten track. In addition to coordinating this edition of *Guatemala, Belize & Yucatán*, she wrote the first edition of *Guatemala*, among other regional titles.

My Favorite Trip

Surrounded by that kicking Verapaz scenery, I chugged from Cobán (p137) on a chicken bus towards Fray (p144). As the weekend fiesta wound down, I hopped on an even stinkier old bus for the dirt-road haul to Poptún (p168) and legendary Finca Ixobel (p168). Cool place, but I was making tracks for Tikal (p179), already loving the jungle-ruins combo. Hooking up with another solo traveler, we arranged for a guide to take us on the 120km-round-trip trek to El Mirador (p190), with the tallest temple in the Mayan world. Mud around our knees, ticks in our armpits, mosquitoes up to our eyeballs, a two-meter rattlesnake and more wacky wildlife were just the start. But on top of La Danta, beholding 360 degrees of virgin rainforest – where not a manmade sound could be heard, nor structure seen – I knew this travel memory would last me a lifetime.

LUCAS VIDGEN
Belize & Guatemala

Lucas started wandering away from his mother in shopping malls when he was five and has never really stopped. Since then he has lived, traveled and worked in more than 20 countries. He's been rambling around Latin America for years now, trying (and failing) to manage his *frijol* habit sensibly. A keen scuba diver and avid beach bum, Lucas was well suited to the rigors of Belizean life. Time spent in Guatemala gave him a chance to download highly dubious archaeological theories on anybody who was awake.

DANNY PALMERLEE
Yucatán Peninsula, Tabasco & Chiapas

Danny first traveled to Mexico in 1991 and has been obsessed with the country ever since. He has written about Mexico for the *San Francisco Chronicle* and is the coordinating author of Lonely Planet's *Mexico's Pacific Coast*. Though he spends much of his time working and traveling in South America, he always returns to Mexico to devour the food, comb the beaches and stock up on *norteño* music.

CONTRIBUTING AUTHORS

Dr Allen J Christenson wrote the Ancient Mayan Culture chapter. He earned his PhD in Pre-Columbian Art History at the University of Texas at Austin, and now works in the Humanities, Classics and Comparative Literature department of Brigham Young University in Provo, Utah. He is the author of *Art and Society in a Highland Maya Community* on the art and culture of Santiago Atitlán, Guatemala, published in 2001, as well as a translation of the great K'iche'-Maya epic, the *Popol Vuh*, published in 2003.

Dr David Goldberg wrote the Health chapter. He completed his training in internal medicine and infectious disease at Columbia-Presbyterian Medical Center in New York City, where he also served as voluntary faculty. At present, he is an infectious-diseases specialist in Scarsdale, NY, and the editor-in-chief of www.mdtravelhealth.com.

Snapshots

CURRENT EVENTS

Get the latest: the *Washington Post* (www .washingtonpost.com) and the *Guardian* (www .guardian.co.uk) both have free online archives with more Mexican and Central American coverage than most papers.

Recent affairs here are like traveling through the Mayan highlands in the back of a pickup: bumping along with the overloaded truck threatening to career off the edge, the up-and-down adventure suddenly turns beautiful, providential even, with a placid, sun-studded valley peeking around the corner.

Perhaps most inspiring was the discovery in 2004 of ceremonial jade objects and giant carved masks at Cival, in Guatemala (see boxed text on p169), proving the existence of a great civilization here. This little-known site, which once housed an estimated 10,000 people, is reversing previously held theories about the sophistication of Preclassic Mayan society.

In December 2003, a sigh of communal relief was heaved with the election of former Guatemala City Mayor Oscar Berger as Guatemala's new president. Not only did he defeat Ríos Montt, the former dictator in control at the time of the Civil War's worst atrocities, he has made conciliatory overtures vis-à-vis the peace process, including naming Nobel Peace Prize winner Rigoberta Menchú his 'goodwill ambassador to the peace accords.' For his part, Ríos Montt lost immunity in January 2004 and was placed under house arrest a month later, pending charges connected to the murder of a journalist. In other criminal news, Guatemalan authorities chased former president Alfonso Portillo from El Salvador to Mexico, charging him with looting some US$500,000 from the country's coffers while in power (2000–4); the vice president and two other officials were also reportedly involved in the scam.

'I make the laws of Congress, I approve the budget of Congress, so I am already President': Ríos Montt speaking to reporters during his 2003 Presidential campaign.

Berger's victory breathed new life into the floundering 1996 Peace Accords that ended the traumatic 36-year civil war and offered hope to the Maya majority. Both the United Nations and the Interamerican Human Rights Commission reported very negatively in 2002 and 2003 on the state of indigenous rights, women's rights and human rights in Guatemala. Activists campaigning for such rights were often the victims of threats, attacks and murders, adding to the burgeoning crime rate. Speaking of which, crime against tourists continued to alarm, with attacks against hikers on various volcanoes being the most common.

Another set of accords falling flat were the San Andrés Accords. Designed to legislate indigenous rights in Chiapas as a step towards peace talks between the government and the Ejército Zapatista de Liberación Nacional (EZLN; Zapatista Nacional Liberation Army), the diluted document eventually passed by congress was rejected by indigenous leaders. Nevertheless, the Zapatistas are forging ahead with their autonomous governance program and in August 2003 established five independent municipalities in southern Chiapas. The cause continues to garner major support from the international left and global grassroots organizations; travelers will notice the difference in San Cristóbal de Las Casas, with its hip, socially conscious vibe and worldly flavors.

On issues of environmental import, deforestation tops the list. Resettled refugees, oil exploration and logging interests are all part of the problem. The refugee-conservation connection is a strong, often inharmonious, one. Clashes between conservation organizations and refugees occupying reserve land continued in both Chiapas and Guatemala, where the goals for protecting land and providing for people are increasingly irreconcilable. In Belize, the controversial Chalillo Dam Project was given the green light in February 2004.

In national elections in Belize, Said Musa of the People's United Party won a second term as prime minister, while the country continued to post record-breaking tourist numbers into 2004. Partial credit for the Belize boom goes to the sadistic *Temptation Island* reality television series that beamed into homes worldwide from 2001 to 2003.

HISTORY
Archaic Period (Up to 2000 BC)

It's accepted that the indigenous inhabitants of the Americas arrived from Siberia. It seems they came sometime between 60,000 and 8000 BC (the last ice age). These early inhabitants hunted mammoths, fished and gathered wild foods until the hot, dry period that followed the ice age scorched the mammoths' natural pastureland. Those beasts died out, nuts and berries became scarce, and the primitive inhabitants were forced into creating other means for survival. They invented agriculture, in which maize (corn) became king, using techniques still practiced today.

Preclassic Period (2000 BC–AD 250)

Even at the beginning of the Early Preclassic period, people here spoke an early form of the Mayan language and architectural advances weren't far behind. Cave dwelling and huddling under palm fronds were out and the *na*, or thatched Mayan hut, was in; some 4000 years later, this ancient architecture is still common throughout much of the region. When a family member died, burial took place right there in the living room, with the deceased attaining the rank of honored ancestor.

Without question, the most significant event of this period occurred about 1000 BC, not in the traditional Mayan lands, but in nearby Tabasco and Veracruz, Mexico, when the mysterious Olmec people developed a hieroglyphic writing system, along with what is known as the Vague Year calendar of 365 days (see p50).

Although aspects of Olmec culture lived on among their neighbors, paving the way for the later accomplishments of Mayan art, architecture and science (Abaj Takalik, p129, in Guatemala, offers a taste of this) the Olmecs themselves disappeared; historians assume they were trampled by waves of invaders.

From 800 to 300 BC, known as the Middle Preclassic Period, rich villages already existed in Honduras' Copán Valley and trade routes flourished, with coastal peoples exchanging ever-important salt for high-landers' tool-grade obsidian. There was a brisk trade in ceramic pots and villages were founded at Tikal.

Improved agricultural techniques led to surpluses, an accumulation of wealth, class divisions and monumental construction projects, particularly temples. The first temples were modest affairs, consisting of raised-earth platforms topped by a thatch-roofed shelter. The local potentate was buried beneath the shelter. In the lowlands, where limestone was abundant, the Maya began to build platform temples from stone. As each succeeding local potentate had to have a bigger temple, more and larger platforms were put over other platforms, forming huge step pyramids with a *na*-style shelter on top. The potentate was buried deep within the stack of platforms. More and more pyramids were built around large plazas, and the stage was set for the flourishing of Classic Mayan civilization.

¡Ya Basta! (Enough is Enough!) is the Zapatista battle cry and you'll see souvenir hawkers peddling Zapa gear and travelers sporting t-shirts with the slogan throughout southern Mexico and beyond.

DID YOU KNOW?

The People's United Party's Said Musa was the first prime minister to be re-elected to consecutive terms since Belizean independence in 1981.

Popol Vuh, called the Maya bible, is a sacred book containing the Maya creation story, along with many insights into Mayan cosmology.

Classic Period (AD 250–900)

Armies from Teotihuacán (near modern Mexico City) conquered the Mayan highlands, but were eventually absorbed into Mayan daily life. The Esperanza culture, a blend of Mexican and Mayan elements, was born of this conquest and acculturation.

It was during this period that the Maya produced the Western Hemisphere's most brilliant ancient civilization. From Copán in modern-day Honduras to Mexico's Yucatán Peninsula, they constructed great ceremonial and cultural centers including Quiriguá and Tikal in Guatemala, Caracol in Belize, and Yaxchilán and Chichén Itzá in Mexico. Mayan astronomers developed the elaborate Long Count calendar.

At its peak, most Mayan lands of the Late Classic Period were ruled as a network of independent, but interdependent, city-states. Each city-state had its noble house, headed by a king who was the social, political and religious focus of the city's life. He also led his soldiers into battle against rival cities, capturing prisoners for use in human sacrifices.

By the end of the period, conflict was up, trade was down and the great Mayan cities of Tikal, Yaxchilán, Copán, Quiriguá, Piedras Negras and Caracol reverted to little more than villages. The focus of Mayan civilization shifted to northern Yucatán, where a new civilization developed at Chichén Itzá, Uxmal and Labná.

Postclassic Period (900–1524)

Why Classic Mayan civilization suddenly collapsed is still a matter of debate. The basis for most theories is unsustainability precipitated by overpopulation that taxed the food supply and exhausted fertile farmland. Devastating droughts around 810, 860 and 910, each of several years' duration, may have signaled the beginning of the end. Regardless of what eventually toppled the great civilization, these trials sufficiently weakened the society so that they fell prey to the next wave of invaders from central Mexico.

The warlike Toltecs of Tula (near Mexico City) conquered Teotihuacán, then marched and sailed eastward to Yucatán. They were regular practitioners of human sacrifice, leaving fear and destruction in their wake. Legend has it that the Toltecs were led by a fair-haired, bearded king named Quetzalcóatl (Kukulcán or Plumed Serpent), who established himself in Yucatán at Uucil-abnal (Chichén Itzá). The story went that he would one day return from the direction of the rising sun. The culture at Uucil-abnal flourished after the late 10th century, when all of the great buildings were constructed, but by 1200 the city was abandoned.

After the abandonment of Toltec Uucil-abnal, the site was occupied by a people called the Itzáes. Probably of Mayan race, the Itzáes had lived among the Putún Maya, near Champotón in Campeche, until the early 13th century. Forced by other invaders to leave their traditional homeland, they headed southeast into El Petén to the lake that became known as Petén Itzá after their arrival. Some continued to Belize, later making their way north along the coast and into northern Yucatán, where they settled at Uucil-abnal. The Itzá leader styled himself Kukulcán, after Quetzalcóatl, recycling lots of other Toltec lore along with the name. But the Itzáes strengthened the belief in sacred cenotes (the natural limestone caves that provided the Maya with their water supply on the riverless plains of the northern Yucatán Peninsula), and they even named their new home Chichén Itzá (Mouth of the Well of the Itzáes).

The Itzáes were overthrown by the Cocomes, based in the city of Mayapán to the west of Chichén Itzá. Claiming descent from Kukulcán (who supposedly founded Mayapán), the Cocom group ruled a fractious collection of Yucatecan city-states from the late 12th to mid-15th centuries. They were in turn overthrown by a subject people called the Xiú, from Uxmal. For the next century, until the coming of the conquistadors, northern Yucatán smoldered with battles and power struggles among its city-states.

Your best introduction to this part of the world is Michael D Coe's The Maya.

Spanish Conquest

The Spaniards, of course, arrived with Christopher Columbus in 1492, establishing their main bases on the islands of Santo Domingo (Hispaniola, now Haiti and the Dominican Republic) and Cuba. Trading, slaving and exploring expeditions sailing from Cuba were led by Francisco Hernández de Córdoba in 1517 and Juan de Grijalva in 1518. When these expeditions attempted to penetrate inland from Mexico's Gulf Coast, they were driven back by hostile natives.

In 1518 the governor of Cuba, Diego Velásquez, petitioned Hernán Cortés to lead a new expedition westward. As Cortés gathered ships and men, Velásquez became uneasy about the spiraling costs and Cortés' loyalty, so he canceled the expedition. Cortés ignored the governor and set sail on February 15, 1519, with 11 ships, 550 men and 16 horses.

Landing first at Cozumel, off the Yucatán, Cortés and company were joined by Jerónimo de Aguilar, a Spaniard who had been shipwrecked there several years earlier. With Aguilar acting as translator and guide, Cortés' force moved west along the coast to Tabasco. After defeating an indigenous group there, the expedition headed inland, winning battles and Christian converts as it went.

At this time, central Mexico was dominated by the Aztec empire from its capital of Tenochtitlán. The Aztecs, like many other Mesoamerican cultures, believed that Quetzalcóatl (Kukulcán), the fair-skinned god, would one day return from the east. By chance, Cortés' arrival coincided with their prophecies of Quetzalcóatl's return. Fearful of angering these strangers who might be gods, the Aztecs allowed the small Spanish force into the capital rather than slaughtering them outright.

A good travelogue of the modern scene is Time Among the Maya *by Richard Wright.*

Big mistake. Infighting and a smallpox epidemic devastated the Aztecs and Cortés went on to conquer central Mexico, after which he turned his attentions to the Yucatán.

Colonial Period (1530–1821)

YUCATÁN

Despite rabid political infighting among the Yucatecan Maya, conquest by the Spaniards was difficult. The Spanish monarch commissioned Francisco de Montejo (El Adelantado, the Pioneer) with the task, and he set out from Spain in 1527 accompanied by his son, also named Francisco de Montejo (El Mozo, the Lad). Landing first at Cozumel off the Caribbean coast, then at Xel-Há on the mainland, the Montejos discovered that the local people were not interested in being conquered. The Maya sent the foreigners packing.

The father-and-son team then sailed around the peninsula, conquered Tabasco (1530) and established their base near Campeche, which could easily be supplied with provisions, arms and troops from New Spain (central Mexico). They pushed inland to conquer, but after four long, difficult years, were forced to retreat, returning to Mexico City with tails between their legs.

With dad's support, the younger Montejo took up the cause anew, returning to Campeche in 1540 with his redundantly named cousin,

Francisco de Montejo. The two Franciscos pressed inland with speed and success, allying themselves with the Xiús against the Cocomes, defeating the Cocomes and gaining the Xiús as converts to Christianity.

The Montejos founded Mérida in 1542 and within four years had almost all of Yucatán subjugated to Spanish rule. The once proud and independent Maya became peons, working for Spanish masters without hope of deliverance except in heaven. The attitude of the conquerors toward the indigenous peoples is graphically depicted in the reliefs on the facade of the Montejo mansion in Mérida: In one scene, armor-clad conquistadors are shown with their feet holding down ugly, hairy, club-wielding savages.

Quite to the contrary, the Maya were learned and cultured, recording much information about their history, customs and ceremonies in beautiful 'painted books' made of beaten-bark paper. These 'codices' must have numbered in the hundreds when the conquistadors and missionary friars first arrived in Mayan lands. Unfortunately, the Franciscans ordered the priceless books to be destroyed, considering them a threat to the domination of Christianity in the region. While only a handful of the painted books survive, they provide valuable insight into ancient Mayan life.

Among those Franciscans directly responsible for the book burning was Friar Diego de Landa, who, in July of 1562 at Maní (near present-day Ticul in Yucatán), ordered the destruction of 27 'hieroglyphic rolls' and 5000 idols. Landa went on to become Bishop of Mérida from 1573 until his death in 1579.

Ironically, it was Friar Diego de Landa who wrote the most important book on Mayan customs and practices – the source (albeit secondary) for much of what we know about the Maya. Landa's book, *Relación de las Cosas de Yucatán*, was written about 1565. It covers virtually every aspect of Mayan life, from Mayan houses, food, drink, and wedding and funeral customs to the calendar and the counting system.

The Maya of Belize, thanks to their bellicose reputation and the jungle-choked terrain to which they retreated, escaped much of the brutality visited upon other indigenous groups. Indeed, the first real Spanish presence was not felt in Belize until the 1600s, when pirates were the Europeans to fear.

CHIAPAS & GUATEMALA

The conquest of Chiapas and Guatemala fell to Pedro de Alvarado (1485–1541), a clever but cruel soldier who had been Cortés' lieutenant at the conquest of Tenochtitlán. Cortés dispatched Alvarado in 1523, and his armies roared through Chiapas and the highland kingdoms of the K'iche' and Cakchiquel Maya, crushing them with their firearms and horsepower, superior technology both. The Mayan lands were divided into large estates, or *encomiendas*, and the Maya living there were mercilessly enslaved by the invaders-cum-landowners. Refusal to work the land meant death.

Things improved, if only slightly, with the coming of the Catholic Church and Dominican friar Bartolomé de Las Casas in particular. Though forced labor was still the rule, Las Casas successfully stemmed the worst of the violence by appealing to Carlos V of Spain with his *A Very Brief Account of the Destruction of the Indies*. This influential tract was born of the near genocide of indigenous groups Las Casas witnessed in Cuba and Hispaniola. By controlling the most brutal practices, preaching pacifism and extending relative respect to traditional practices and beliefs, the Church won many converts, becoming extremely powerful in Guatemala fairly quickly.

Detailed, firsthand accounts of the Spaniards' arrival and domination are found in *True History of the Conquest of New Spain* by one of Cortés' soldiers, Bernal Díaz del Castillo.

Look for Friar Diego de Landa's book in English as *Yucatán Before and After the Conquest*. You can buy it in many shops at archaeological sites in Yucatán and Guatemala.

Not all of Guatemala succumbed with such alacrity, however. The last region of Mayan sovereignty was the city-state of Tayasal, in Guatemala's department of El Petén. The intrepid Cortés visited Tayasal in 1524, while on his way to conquer Honduras, but did not make war against King Canek, who greeted him peacefully. In the late 17th century, however, the Spanish decided to bring this last surviving Mayan state within the Spanish empire; in 1697 Tayasal fell, some 2000 years after the founding of the first important Mayan city-states.

Independence

During the colonial period, society in Spain's New World holdings was rigidly and precisely stratified. Old World Spaniards were at the very top; next were the criollos, people born in the New World of Spanish stock; below them were the mestizos or ladinos, people of mixed Spanish and indigenous blood; and at the bottom were the Maya and black slaves. Only the European-born Spaniards had real power – a fact deeply resented by the criollos, who took it out on the ladinos, who in turn exploited the indigenous population who, as you read this, still struggle on the lowest rungs of the socioeconomic ladder.

Napoleon's conquests in Europe disrupted the power structure and destabilized the Spanish empire's foundations. When the French emperor deposed Spain's King Ferdinand VII and put his brother Joseph Bonaparte on the Spanish throne (1808), criollos in many New World colonies took the opportunity to rise in revolt. By 1821, both Mexico and Guatemala had proclaimed their independence.

Independent Mexico, with Chiapas and Yucatán on board, briefly annexed Guatemala. In 1823, Guatemala not only reasserted its independence, it led the formation of the United Provinces of Central America, which included Guatemala, El Salvador, Nicaragua, Honduras and Costa Rica. Their union, torn by civil strife from the beginning, lasted only until 1840 before breaking up into its constituent states.

Though independence brought new prosperity to the criollos, it worsened the lot of the Maya. The end of Spanish rule meant that the Crown's few liberal safeguards, which had afforded indigenous communities minimal protection from the most extreme forms of exploitation, were abandoned. Mayan claims to ancestral lands were largely ignored and huge plantations were created for the cultivation of tobacco, sugar cane and *henequen* (agave rope fiber). The Maya, though legally free, were enslaved by debt peonage to the great landowners.

The Modern Republics

Historically, the fate of these countries has been hitched to the political and economic interests of others: first Europe and the Catholic Church, and more recently, the United States. The ruling classes (of Spanish or mestizo descent, a historic fact that remains unchallenged today) continued to subjugate indigenous and black slave populations, thus consolidating economic power. Even when driven to revolt, as in the War of the Castes in Yucatán (p314) or that which brought Rafael Carrera to power in Guatemala (p58), the poor masses were unable to level the playing field.

The task became more difficult still when the United States began to exert direct pressure on the region. Although the Yucatán retained some semblance of independence from both the Mexican and US governments, Guatemala fell into a deepening spiral of instability. When Colonel Jacobo Arbenz came to power and began agrarian reforms using

DID YOU KNOW?

An estimated one million Guatemalans were displaced during the 36-year civil war.

DID YOU KNOW?

Belize was called British Honduras until 1973 and, though now a fully independent country, is still a part of the British Commonwealth.

expropriated land from the United Fruit Company, the US sent in the CIA to arrange his ouster. Today, some believe the US flexes similar hegemonic muscles through the North American Free Trade Agreement (Nafta), to which Mexico is a signatory, and the Central American Free Trade Agreement (Cafta), which Guatemala was slated to join in mid-2004; these agreements are the blueprints for the controversial Free Trade Area of the Americas (FTAA).

Oppression of the indigenous masses created a cycle of violence from which the region is still not free. The 36-year civil war in Guatemala only ended in 1996 and the Zapatistas took up arms for the indigenous cause in 1994 in Chiapas. That there are untapped oil reserves in Chiapas makes it a political and military hot spot. However, smoldering hope has been rekindled through indigenous organizations and leadership by powerful figures like Nobel Prize winner Rigoberta Menchú.

From conquest to today, Belize has remained just below the radar and regional issues generally have more immediacy than foreign influence. The border dispute with Guatemala, a sore that festered since Belizean independence, was only settled in 2002 and is still subject to referenda in both countries.

PEOPLE
Multiculturalism
This region enjoys an extraordinary cultural mix, richly seasoning the travel flavors you'll encounter. With its Mayan majority, Guatemala boasts the largest indigenous population in Central America and you'll mingle with them everywhere. In Mexico, about 1.5 million Maya call the Yucatán home and another 900,000 or so live in Chiapas.

Belize is a modern mosaic of Creole (mixed black and European), mestizo (indigenous and European), Maya and Garifuna (descended from Caribbean islanders and shipwrecked/escaped slaves). These last, sometimes called Black Caribs, also inhabit Lívingston, a popular stop-over on the Guatemalan Caribbean coast.

Mayan refugees fleeing the civil war in Guatemala bled over borders to Chiapas, Belize and Yucatán, some choosing to stay despite the 1996 Peace Accords; this means you'll meet many native Spanish speakers near the Guatemala-Belize border.

Lifestyle
Exciting is the travel day you're welcomed into a home to break tortillas with a Mayan family. Imagine a group of small one-room houses made of brick, concrete blocks or traditional *bajareque* (a construction of stones, wooden poles and mud), with roofs of tin, tiles or thatch, arranged around a communal courtyard. Chickens dart back and forth and a woman may be weaving on a backstrap loom tied to a tree. Ducking to enter – most Maya are diminutive – your eyes adjust to the dark, earthen-floor interior. There will likely be few possessions and little adornment, maybe an outdated calendar or a picture of the Alps clipped from a magazine.

Thus live most of the Maya majority. Things look quite different in bigger towns and cities, of course, where more resources are available. Sizable, comfortable homes might have two floors and a garden, plus fences and security alarms, as you enter fancier, wealthier barrios.

Legislation aimed at protecting traditional customs in areas with large indigenous populations was passed in Guatemala in 1996 and Mexico in 2002. While many of the provisions of the Guatemalan Peace Accords

DID YOU KNOW?
The Western Institute for Security Cooperation is a US institution that has trained over 60,000 Latin American soldiers, including individuals implicated in the murder of Bishop Gerardi and the Ocosingo massacre.

DID YOU KNOW?
Rigoberta Menchú was the first indigenous person to receive the Nobel Prize, as well as the youngest, at the ripe old age of 33.

SLIP ME SOME SKIN, BROTHER *Lucas Vidgen*

The Belizean handshake comes in a bewildering variety of forms and, unless you're meeting your bank manager, may not even closely resemble what you are accustomed to.

The foundation of all streetside hand-based greetings in Belize is the gentle horizontal fist punch, as used by many sporting celebrities mid-game. This one is particularly effective if you meet someone on the street who wants to shake your hand, but you don't want to commit emotionally. Give them a tap, they'll be happy and you can be on your way. The punch on its own is also quite acceptable for greeting people who you already know, and for farewelling people who you've been talking to for a while. It's a casual gesture that implies familiarity.

From here things start to get complicated. Many Belizeans shake hands in the soul-brother, thumbs upward style, but convert their shake for tourists to the more conventional thumbs downward, meeting-your-girlfriend's-father style. It takes a keen eye to glean what your shake partner has in mind, and a certain speed of reflex to adjust to changing conditions.

However you start, this will not be the end. From the initial shake, there is often a slide into the monkey grip, grabbing fingertips posture. Pressure here should be firm, but not hard. Make sure your nails are properly trimmed before attempting this.

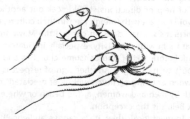

From here all sorts of slaphappy nonsense can ensue, but a perfectly legitimate maneuver at this point is to segue into the gentle punch (see step 1), and once that's completed, you can actually start the conversation.

ILLUSTRATIONS BY HAYDEN FOELL

remain unfulfilled, in Mexico the Law of Linguistic Rights recognizes indigenous tongues as national languages. In Chiapas, radio broadcasts in local languages promote women's and indigenous rights, often relating to topics like health and education, two pressing issues for the region's Maya.

While protecting traditional culture is a goal, it doesn't mean you won't see young toughs in Metallica t-shirts and grannies wearing Nikes. Here, it's not a rejection of traditional culture as often as an adaptation to fit local needs and aesthetics. Witness the synthetic color dyes now used in some traditional weaving and the use of Coca Cola as an offering in Catholic churches. One area where you may witness an outright rejection of global culture is in Chiapas, where the indigenous movement is strongly linked to antiglobalization campaigns like those protesting the World Trade Organization (WTO) and the Free Trade Area of the Americas (FTAA).

Gender roles are generally rigid; women may have jobs to increase family income, but they're rarely in decision-making positions and they're still responsible for cooking, cleaning and childcare. Gays and lesbians, while more visible in Guatemala City and Cancún, remain largely marginalized or silenced.

RELIGION

Like almost everywhere in Latin America, religion here combines ancient and contemporary themes. Roman Catholicism remains a formidable force throughout the region. The majority of Guatemalans claim Catholicism as

MEETING LOCALS ALONG LA RUTA MAYA

Trying out the local language is a sure way to make new friends. Besides, greetings are a requirement of polite interchange, here – a simple *buenos días* (good morning) or *buenas tardes* (good afternoon) when entering a store or boarding a bus starts everything off on a good note. Avoid using the term *indio/a* (Indian) to refer to a Mayan person as it carries racist undertones; the preferred term is *indígena*. Where spoken language fails – your Spanish skills may molder in off-the-beaten-track areas where many Maya speak only their indigenous tongue – body language takes over.

Slowing down is one of the best ways to increase your chances of meeting locals. You'll notice a more relaxed pace among the rarely rushed Maya, who take time to savor conversations and interactions. Adjusting to the local cadence will serve you well. An invitation into a Mayan home is an honor for a foreigner and you'll share in a cultural experience not readily available to outsiders. If you have time to prepare for the visit, bring a gift: baseball caps, notebooks, crayons, colored chalk, a cheap day pack, radio or watch, or a calendar with images from your home country will be greatly appreciated; homestay students might want to bring small gifts, too.

Male travelers in need of help or directions should seek out another male to ask, as many Mayan women prefer to avoid contact with foreign men; in their culture, talking with strange men is not something that a virtuous woman does. In general the Maya are a fairly private people, and outsiders need to treat them with sensitivity, especially in Guatemalan regions traumatized by the civil war. Always ask before taking photos (some churches and ceremonial sites specifically forbid it; always respect such signage). Another sign of respect is shown through the way you dress: modest attire when entering a church will be appreciated (no tank tops) and shorts are usually only worn, both by men and women, at the beach or where there are lots of foreign tourists. Most of laid-back Belize is the exception.

Buses are a great place to meet locals (hey, it's a captive audience!) and sharing road snacks or headphones is an instant icebreaker. Children, too, thaw things quickly and travelers with children have a great advantage, as the wee ones will bring smiles and open doors that remain closed to the rest of us. Still, the tried and true way to meet people no matter where you travel is to volunteer in the local community. This area is ripe with opportunities (see p446).

their religion, as do three out of five Belizeans. In the Yucatán, the percentage hovers around 85%, and is a whopping 90% for Mexico countrywide.

But Catholicism among the Maya has never fit the traditional mold. The missionaries who brought Catholicism to the Maya in the 16th century permitted aspects of the animistic, shamanistic Maya religion to continue alongside Christian rites and beliefs. Often the savvy missionaries simply grafted Catholic ideas and deities onto pre-Hispanic religions. Even today, Catholicism here is still fused with ancient tenets. A fantastic example is Maximón in Santiago Atitlán (p99), a syncretic deity that foreigners are welcome to worship (for some cigarettes or rum, his favorite treats). Traditional beliefs are so ingrained that ailing Maya often consult shaman healers instead of medical doctors. The use of folk remedies, too, is strongly linked to ancient religious practices and is widespread in Mayan areas.

For a moving look at the discipline, art and soul that goes into Mayan healing practices, see the documentary *Sastun: My Apprenticeship with a Maya Healer* (2002) by Guido Verweyen.

A relatively new arrival on the religious scene is evangelical Protestant sects, many Pentecostal. These churches, including the Mormons, Seventh-Day Adventists and Jehovah's Witnesses, are winning converts rapidly. Between 30% and 40% of Guatemalans are evangelicals and you'll see these solid, new churches in even the smallest village. Likely, the evening service will be rocking with testimonials, screaming preachers and gospel music. You'll probably run into boys and girls with white shirts and name tags spreading the Mormon word – engage at your own risk. In southeastern Mexico, especially, the Protestant presence is strong and millions have converted since missionaries arrived in the 1970s. In Chiapas, coexistence hasn't always been peaceful, with strife between Protestants and Catholics breaking out in and around San Juan Chamula (p401) – a town rife with quirky religious observances.

ARTS
Music

Music is a mainstay here and the streets, plazas and buses are alive with audio accompaniment. From marimba teams to dreadlocked drummers

---

MODERN MAYAN RITUALS

One of the most exhilarating parts of traveling in this region is the opportunity to witness ancient Mayan rites in caves, hilltop sites and shrines. While visitors are welcome at all the places below, it's imperative to maintain decorum and respect when observing these practices that are so integral to Mayan life. Assume you cannot take pictures unless explicitly given permission and do not touch altars or otherwise disturb the *mise-en-scène*. Please also see tips for responsible travel (p17) and the individual entries for these sites. As travel ambassadors, we are each responsible for fostering goodwill between cultures.

Pascual Abaj (p107) Sacrifices and offerings made to a stone-faced idol.

Costumbrista sacred sites (p110) Let your guide introduce you to folks practicing non-Christian Mayan rites in beautiful Nebaj.

Laguna Chicabal (p122) Mysterious lakeside site has charged rituals and great camping.

El Baúl (p130) Wax-stained head doused in alcoholic offerings is reached via a 5km hike.

K'umarcaaj (p109) An important prayer site, this tunnel at the former K'iche' capital is strewn with candles, flowers and incense.

Actun Tunichil Muknal (p273) Skeletal remains and pottery artifacts fill this cave of ancient, but not modern, worship; access is for the adventurous.

Grutas de Balankanché (p370) Ancient ceremonial caves with abundant ritual objects and offerings; photo exhibit of the modern Ch'a Chaac ceremony.

Shrine to Maximón, San Simón or Rilaj Maam (p99) Effulgent effigy, crowded with offerings; receives devotees daily in festive surroundings.

and mariachi bands (violinists, trumpeters, guitarists and a singer, all dressed in 'cowboy' costume), you'll hear it all. Marimbas are particularly popular in Guatemala's highlands and on Mexico's Gulf Coast, and reggae rules in Belize and the Caribbean coast. Each country has its particular musical style and instruments; see individual Arts sections for more.

Architecture
MAYAN ARCHITECTURE

Ancient Mayan architecture is a mixed bag of incredible accomplishments and severe limitations. The great buildings are both impressive and beautiful, with intricately patterned facades, delicate 'combs' on temple roofs, and sinuous carvings. But these magnificent structures, in sophisticated urban centers such as Tikal, El Mirador, Palenque and Copán, were created without beasts of burden (except for humans) or the luxury of the wheel. Nor did Mayan builders ever devise the arch; instead, they used what is known as a corbeled arch, consisting of two walls leaning toward one another, nearly meeting at the top and surmounted by a capstone. This creates a triangular rather than rounded arch, and does not make for much strength nor allow any great width (notice the long, narrow halls as you explore temples). Instead, the building's foundations and substructure needed to be very strong. Once structures were completed, experts hypothesize, they were covered with stucco and painted red with a mixture of hematite and, most probably, water.

Much of the Mayan sites' architectural how and why remains a mystery. For example, while we know the Maya habitually built one temple on top of another, we have little idea how they actually erected these symbols of power. All the limestone used to construct the great Mayan cities had to be moved and set in place by hand – an engineering feat that must have demanded astronomical amounts of human labor.

Cosmology played a central role in Mayan life and every major architectural work had a celestial plan. Temples were aligned so as to enhance celestial observation, whether of the sun, moon or certain stars and planets, especially Venus. For example, openings might be aligned to frame a celestial body at an exact point in its course on a certain day of a specific year. This was accomplished at the Palacio del Gobernador (Governor's Palace; p360) at Uxmal, which is aligned so that from the main doorway, Venus would have been visible exactly on top of a small mound some 3.5km away, in the year AD 750. At Chichén Itzá, the observatory building called El Caracol (p369) was aligned in order to sight Venus exactly in the year AD 1000, and the alignment of El Castillo (p368) catches the sun and makes a shadow of the sacred sky serpent descending into the earth on the vernal equinox (March 21) each year. The serpent is formed perfectly only on that day, and it descends during a period of only 34 minutes. An incredible accomplishment by folks who didn't even have wheel technology, don't you think?

COLONIAL ARCHITECTURE

During the colonial period, churches, convents, mansions and palaces were built in the Spanish styles of the day: chiefly Renaissance, baroque and neoclassical. But while the architectural concepts were European inspired, the labor used to realize them was strictly indigenous. As revolts were frequent, church walls were thick and high to protect the upper classes from the wrath of the indigenous people.

If you're into churches of note, check out La Merced in Antigua (p82), the Basilica at Esquipulas (p147), the church at San Andrés Xequl (p120),

DID YOU KNOW?

The El Tigre pyramid (p190) in Guatemala exemplifies the grandeur of the potentate's temple. More than 60m high, it is believed to be the largest ever built by the Maya.

the San Cristóbal Cathedral (p393) or the church at San Juan Chamula (p402). Most of the churches you'll see throughout the region are plain, however, belying the richness of the religious pageantry that takes place inside, including many half-Mayan, half-Catholic processions, rituals, decorations and attire.

Towns in the region worth a visit to admire colonial architecture include San Cristóbal de Las Casas (p392), Campeche (p375) and Antigua (p77). The last two are Unesco World Heritage Sites (whc.unesco.org).

Weaving

Your eyes will hurt beholding the *traje* (traditional clothing) Mayan women wear, weave, trade and sell. Indescribably beautiful, the intricate designs and vibrant colors of these textiles make them the most awe-inspiring manifestation of Mayan culture.

Wildly expressive, these weavings are distinguished by electrifying hues and thick, fanciful embroidery. Painstaking love and care goes into the creation of these garments, especially the long sleeveless tunic worn by women called a *huipil*. Often entire *huipiles* are covered in a multicolored web of stylized animal, human, plant and mythological shapes that can take months to complete. Each garment identifies the village from which its wearer hails (the Spanish colonists allotted each village a different design in order to distinguish their inhabitants from each other), and within the village style there can be variations according to social status, as well as individual creative touches that make each garment unique.

Along with the *huipil*, other colorful garments in use since pre-Hispanic times include the *tocoyal*, a woven head-covering often decorated with bright tassels; the *corte* (*enredo* in Mexico), a piece of material 7m or 10m long that is used as a wraparound skirt; and the *faja*, a long, woven waist sash that can be folded to hold what other people might put in pockets. Mayan men's garments owe more to Spanish influence and the church's objection to nudity; shirts, hats and *calzones*, long baggy shorts that evolved into full-length pants in most regions, were introduced in colonial times.

Materials and techniques are changing, but the pre-Hispanic backstrap loom is still widely used. The warp (long) threads are stretched between two horizontal bars, one of which is fixed to a post or tree, while the other is attached to a strap that goes round the weaver's lower back. The weft (cross) threads are then woven in. Throughout the Guatemalan highlands and Chiapas you'll see women weaving on these outside their homes. Nowadays, some *huipiles* and *fajas* are machine made.

Some of the most colorful, intricate and eye-catching designs are found in Sololá (p104), Santiago Atitlán (p98), Nebaj (p110), Zunil (p120) and Todos Santos Cuchumatán (p125) in Guatemala, and in and around San Cristóbal de Las Casas (p392) in Chiapas. See the boxed text on p105.

ENVIRONMENT
The Land

This region is a delightful combination of mountains, jungles and coast, with a few fertile plains thrown in. Hot, humid, tropical lowlands covered by dense (but shrinking) forests cover most of the Yucatán and Belize, spreading south and west into El Petén in northern Guatemala and extending into Chiapas, Mexico. At the confluence of the three countries is a massive biosphere reserve, protecting 2,941,325 hectares (7,265,073 acres) of rainforest. For a detailed list of reserves and protected areas in each country, see those individual chapters.

For fine weaving, visit Museo Ixchel in Guatemala City (p70) or the Nim Po't shop in Antigua (p88). You can buy *huipiles* and quilts at their website www.nimpot.com.

In markets, expect to pay US$8 to US$10 for embroidered *huipiles*, US$18 to US$25 for woven ones. Buying directly from the artisan or a cooperative is a good idea.

Where the trees end, the mountains take over, giving rise to the Sierra Madre de Chiapas (1000m to 2500m) and turning into the Cordillera de los Cuchumatanes in Guatemala (the highest peak measures 4220m). Both mountain ranges are flanked by highlands. In addition, the Guatemalan highlands are strung with a chain of 30 volcanoes, some active, beckoning hikers and the people who rob them (see p90 and p439). Fertile plains run in a band from the Guatemalan Pacific coast north through Chiapas, an area known as El Soconusco.

Wildlife

One of the sexiest attractions here is the abundance and variety of wildlife, with plenty of opportunities to view exotic species in their natural habitat. Whether it's land or marine animals you wish to see, the richest areas for wildlife watching are Belize, the northern department of El Petén in Guatemala and the southeastern slice of Mexico.

ANIMALS

Is that a longbilled gnatwren I hear or a Montezuma oropendula? Head to Bird Songs of the Yucatan Peninsula (http://biology.queensu.ca/~mennilld/Mexico.html) to listen to melodies collected in this region.

Mammals you have a very good chance of seeing in the wild include coatis and spider and howler monkeys. The endangered black howler monkey is only found in Belize, but easily spotted at the Bermudian Landing Community Baboon Sanctuary (p248). Deeper in the jungle, you have a chance of seeing – or more likely hearing – bigger beasts like peccaries (an irascible type of wild pig that can weigh 30kg or more) and tapirs. Deer are plentiful in Yucatán, especially on menus. The big cats – jaguars, ocelots, margays, jaguarundi and pumas – are more commonly seen in cages than in the wild these days, though you'll probably see prints on extended jungle hikes.

The variety of birds here is awesome, especially in the Yucatán, where 537 species have been recorded. You'd be lucky to glimpse the nearly extinct quetzal (try the Biotopo del Quetzal, p137), but macaws, parrots, toucans and big, bawdy ocellated turkeys abound. Wading birds such as egrets, herons, white ibis and flamingos are also easily spotted. Thousands of flamingos inhabit the mangroves near the Ría Lagartos Biosphere Reserve (p374) in eastern Yucatán; head here in May at the start of the rainy season to partake of the stunning sight.

This region does not want for reptiles – good, bad and ugly. Of the last, there are the ubiquitous iguanas, some up to a meter long, that sun themselves on Yucatán temples. Sea turtles, those ever-smiling stewards of the sea, are found in the waters of all three countries. These majestic animals and their eggs are protected by law, and while there are some legal methods for taking them, menu items featuring turtles or eggs are best avoided. Take a river trip up to Lamanai in Belize (p254) or along Río Dulce in Guatemala (p166) and you're bound to see a crocodile. Keep in mind that dense forests like those in the Reserva de la Biósfera Calakmul (p380) and engulfing the El Mirador ruins in the Petén region (p190) harbor venomous snakes like the coral and fer-de-lance, while tropical rattlesnakes are found in drier areas.

Rainforest Remedies: 100 Healing Herbs of Belize, by Dr Michael Balick with Rosita Arvigo, is among the most detailed guides to the Maya's natural pharmacy.

Marine creatures you can see, especially in the rich waters off Belize, include manatees (sea cows), dolphins, sharks of all sorts, including whale sharks, and an incredible variety of coral.

PLANTS

The number and variety of forests here foster the region's incredible biodiversity. Coastal mangrove forest, dense low-growing deciduous forest, rain forest, cloud forest and quintessential jungle – with its multilayered canopy, climbing vegetation and epiphytes (air plants) – are all part of the complex ecosystems here.

In addition to palms of all sorts, tropical fruit trees – such as mango, avocado and papaya, plus the sacred ceiba and sapodilla – cover many lowland areas. Orchid lovers will delight in the 550 species found in Guatemala.

Environmental Issues

Deforestation is a problem of grand proportions. In Guatemala's El Petén for instance, 120 sq km of forest is cut down annually. At this rate, the virgin forest there, together with adjoining forest in Belize and Mexico (the largest continuous forest north of the Amazon), will be completely demolished by the year 2025. In all three countries, the destruction begins with the cutting of logging or oil roads, followed by the resettling of worker's and farming families in the cleared area, and the cattle ranchers that arrive on their coat tails.

Gigantic, joint conservation projects like the tripartite biosphere reserve straddling the Guatemala–Belize–Mexico border were created, in part, as a way to stem this destruction. In fact, such cooperation between governments and nongovernmental organizations like Conservation International (CI), with the seal of approval of Unesco, is aimed at creating a 'green corridor', or 'greenway', of protected lands across national borders. Eventually this would become part of the Paseo Pantera (Path of the Panther), a greenway project that aims to link threatened habitats from Mexico to Colombia.

Sounds great, but making the dream a reality is much more complicated. Many Guatemalan refugees fleeing terrifying civil-war violence resettled in areas of El Petén, and are now considered illegal squatters occupying protected land by conservation organizations. This has led to violent clashes, including the burning of a CI research station and murder of a local conservationist. Poor people needing land (and trees) are often in direct conflict with conservation organizations that want to preserve that same land. Things are most volatile in the Reserva de la Biósfera Montes Azules (p405) in Chiapas and Reserva de la Biósfera Maya (p190), where bioprospecting – the collecting, cataloging and exporting of medicinal plants – is a project goal.

Belize, a country with an admirable conservation record, is forging ahead with the contentious Chalillo Dam Project. This massive project will dam the Macal River, flooding 1000 hectares of primary forest. Many environmentalists are concerned about the effects this may have on wildlife habitat and undiscovered Mayan sites. That the foundation where the dam is to be built is no stranger to seismic tremors worries the 12,000 people living downriver. On the flip side, proponents point to the benefits an increased energy supply means for Belize, specifically a decreased reliance on Mexico for their energy needs.

FOOD & DRINK

If you want food that will tingle your palate's imagination long after your trip is over, go to Thailand because you won't find much memorable food here. The exception is in the Yucatán, which has staples and specialties of Mayan origin and local ingenuity (see p321). Otherwise, there's just not much variety, which partly explains why eateries specializing in international-traveler food are so popular in towns with an international-traveler scene. Belize is awash in these types of places, and you won't have to search there if (when!) that banana pancake or pesto craving hits.

Les D Beletsky's *Belize & Northern Guatemala: The Ecotravellers' Wildlife Guide* provides detailed, almost encyclopedic information on the area's flora and fauna.

It's estimated that 15,000 to 30,000 plant species, many with pharmaceutical applications, are found in Chiapas, making it one of the most sought-after bioprospecting areas.

Staples & Specialties

Tortillas: know them, love them, because you'll be eating them daily. These thin, round patties of pressed corn dough are cooked on griddles and found throughout the region. Wrapped around or topped with various foods (eg ground beef, cheese, hard-boiled eggs, beans), these little tasties will fill you up fast. When you run out, just ask for more.

Black beans (*frijoles*; fri-*hoh*-les) are another staple with which you will become very familiar. Nutritious and toothsome, these are served boiled, fried, refried, in soups, slathered on tortillas or alongside them. In Belize, the beans may be black, navy or pinto and are usually cooked together with rice and coconut milk. Seafood is a staple in the coastal towns of Belize, where you'll find snapper year round and lobster and conch in season.

Hot sauce can make the difference between mediocre and savory meals and restaurants usually have bottles on the table; Marie Sharp's famous hot sauce will always accompany you at Belizean meals. Chilies (peppers) are consumed in hundreds of ways, particularly in Mexico. Chili eaters should learn to distinguish between the super spicy *habaneros*, the sorta spicy *serranos* or the varyingly spicy *poblanos*. If you're unsure, ask if the chili you're about to eat is *picante* (spicy hot) or *muy picante* (very spicy hot), 'spicy' being a relative term.

Specialties from around the region include turkey and venison in the Yucatán; a seafood and coconut stew called *tapado*, particular to Guatemala's Caribbean coast; and 'boil-up,' a Garifuna-inspired dish of beef or chicken stewed with root vegetables found in Belize.

Food to think about twice before eating include salads and fruit, which can spell trouble if improperly washed or cut with a dirty knife; there's a reason 'Montezuma's revenge' is synonymous with traveler's diarrhea in these parts. Anything on the endangered, nay threatened, species list should be avoided, like turtles and their eggs, armadillo, agouti and iguana. Even deer and rabbit are no-nos in Guatemala, and lobster and conch should not be consumed out of season.

MEALS

Depending on where you wake, you'll be looking at local breakfast, international breakfast or a choice of the two. In Mexico, the typical morning meal is coffee and *pan dulce* (sweet rolls) in Guatemala, it's a meal to get you through hard labor: eggs, rice, beans, fried plantains, coffee and mountains of tortillas. Wherever there are tourists, you'll likely have a broad choice of bacon, eggs and omelettes, pancakes, fruit juice, and cold cereals like corn flakes or granola/muesli with yogurt.

Lunch is the big meal of the day and your choices will be greatest between noon and 2pm. Fixed-price meals of several courses, called *comida corrida* in Mexico and *almuerzo* or *menú del día* in Guatemala, are filling and cheap; the options and prices for the day are usually posted by the door. In simpler places, you can expect a soup and main course with chicken or fish and potatoes or rice. Fancier places might augment this with ceviche (raw seafood marinated in lime juice), salad, dessert or coffee. Ordering à la carte is always an option, albeit more expensive.

Hardly worth describing at length, dinner is usually a simpler version of lunch (or, in rural Guatemala, a repeat of breakfast), served between 7pm and 9pm. Latecomers will be disappointed as food runs out and kitchens close, so dine out early. Coastal tourist towns like Cancún and the Belizean Cayes run a little later.

Drinks

As you travel around this generally hot region having fabulous adventures, it's important to keep hydrated, drinking lots of fluids even if you don't feel thirsty. Heat exhaustion is no fun and you wouldn't be the first visitor to collapse at Tikal because of it. Bottled or purified water is widely available, but consider toting a water filter to cut costs and minimize plastic waste.

The Pacific coastal plain of Chiapas and Guatemala is coffee country, producing excellent beans, including those typed as Maragogipes and Guatemalan Antigua. Coffee is available everywhere: strong and flavorful in Mexico, surprisingly weak and sugary in Guatemala. Sadly, instant coffee, a luxury item, is popular. Java junkies off the Gringo Trail will want to tote a heating coil, bandana or sock and coffee grounds to keep their buzz going.

Tea drinkers will be pleased by the herbals available, including decent *té de manzanilla* (chamomile), but probably disappointed by *té negro* (black tea); carry your own if tea is your thing.

Among the greatest gastronomic treats in this part of the world are the drinks made from fruits and/or vegetables. *Jugos* (juices), flavored waters (*aguas frescas* in Mexico, *aguas de frutas* in Guatemala) and *licuados* (shakes) are available everywhere and pack both flavor and nutrition. Basic *licuados* are blended fruit with either water or milk and sugar; raw egg, ice, vanilla or nutmeg might also be added. *Aguas frescas* are made by mixing fruit juice, or a syrup made from mashed grains or seeds, with sugar and water. Look for the big, glass jars swimming with *agua fresca de arroz* (rice water), for example, with its sweet, nutty taste.

Beer is by far the most common alcoholic beverage, though *ron* (rum), tequila and *aguardiente* (sugarcane firewater) run a close second. Light lagers dominate, but you will find some quality dark beers like Negra Modelo (Mexico) and Moza (Guatemala). Wine is available, especially in Mexico, which has a few national wineries like the high-profile Pedro Domecq, but in Belize and Guatemala you will find prices and selection less attractive. In all but the highest-brow places, you'll have to specify that you want your red at room temperature and your white chilled. Famous liqueurs from Mexico including Controy (orange liqueur, a knock-off Cointreau) and Kahlúa (coffee-flavored liqueur), plus tequila and mezcal (made from the maguey plant), are also sold widely.

The True History of Chocolate (2000), by Mayanists Sophie and Michael D Coe, is the first and last word on that delight for which we have the Maya to thank.

Where to Eat & Drink

Your simplest meals will be taken in cafés, *cafeterías* (literally 'coffee shop', the term refers to any informal restaurant with waiter service), market stalls and *comedores* (local joints serving wholesome, filling food without much ado). At best, you'll find home cooking at good prices, especially around lunchtime, when the big, fixed meal of the day goes for US$3 or less. The surroundings will probably be sparse, but clean; if not, head elsewhere.

You can hit the bars any day of the week (some close Sunday), usually starting at around 10am; last call falls sometime between 10pm and 11pm, except in larger touristy towns, which keep longer hours. In Guatemala and Mexico, especially, the local watering hole is called a *cantina*, a place for hard drinking and, sometimes, whoring. Not recommended for solo female travelers, *cantinas* can be a lot of fun if the drunks are happy rather than mean. Use your traveler's sense in these places.

Vegetarians & Vegans

This is a friendly part of the world for vegetarians as the eggs-beans-tortilla combination is ubiquitous and fairly nutritious. If you eat seafood, so much the better. If you say '*soy vegetariano/a*', most restaurants will gladly hook up a vegetarian plate of the staples, plus whatever nonmeat items are on hand. Strict vegetarians should take care with soups, which may have been made with meat stock or had pieces of meat extracted just before being served. Refried beans are another danger, as lard is usually the default fry medium. Picnic fixings and simple raw meals can be prepared in any hostel: hit the market for fruits, nuts and veggies. This is one of the best alternatives for vegans (also look for accommodation with kitchen facilities) determined to eat well and according to their dietary preferences. International restaurants and those specifically for vegetarians exist in places with lots of tourist traffic (eg Antigua, the Cayes, Cancún) and are worth seeking out, if only for a change of pace.

The ancient Maya used hot chilies as a painkiller and smoking bowls of them were set out as a weapon in war.

Whining & Dining

Fussy children should stay home. Just kidding! Seriously, though, little travelers will probably find themselves having to adjust to different foods; children-tailored menus and food are rare indeed. Boxed UHT and powdered milk, for example, are way more common in Guatemala than fresh milk, and while these are a sufficient substitute, they *do* taste different. Parents can do their part by explaining the reasoning behind unfamiliar food products (boxed milk, for example, is less perishable and great for the more than 2 billion people without refrigerators or electricity), embracing adventurous eating with their children as part of the travel experience and carrying a stash of goodies to sate appetites on long bus trips or if weird food becomes overwhelming. The usual international fast-food chains are here, plus some local variations, if all else fails.

Ancient Mayan Culture Dr Allen J Christenson

The foundations of the Maya world-view date back more than 2000 years and core elements of their beliefs and rituals continue to be practiced in many traditional Maya communities. It is a part of who the Maya are, and significant numbers of them have held to their unique perspective on the world despite the Spanish conquest in the sixteenth century and the many years of pressure that followed to abandon their traditional faith.

Ruth Bunzel, who worked as an anthropologist in the Maya town of Chichicastenango, Guatemala, in the early 1930s, once asked why the people of the town continued to pray and worship in the old ways. An elder told her, 'This rite and custom belongs to the first people, our mothers and fathers... This belongs to them; we are the embodiment of their rites and ceremonies... It is our name and destiny to repeat and perpetuate these ceremonies before the world.' A priest of the traditional Maya religion in the town of Santiago Atitlán, Guatemala, expressed a similar thought decades later: 'Our ancient mothers and fathers are still with us. We all know them, they visit us in our dreams, they are still very powerful. They are the soul of the town... These first people live because I live. I carry their blood. I remember, and so they are not forgotten.'

> For a lively discussion of Maya religion and the creation, pick up a copy of *Maya Cosmos* by David Freidel, Linda Schele and Joy Parker.

THE CREATION STORY

The ancient Maya patterned their lives according to precedents set by their first ancestors. Nearly all aspects of Maya faith begin with their view of the creation, when the gods and divine forebears established the world at the beginning of time. From their hieroglyphic texts and art carved on stone monuments and buildings, or painted on pottery, we can now piece together much of the Maya view of the creation, even down to the precise date of the beginning of creation.

In AD 775, a Maya lord with the high-sounding name of K'ak' Tiliw Chan Yoat (Fire Burning Sky Lightning God) set up an immense stone monument in the center of his city, Quiriguá. The unimaginative archaeologists who discovered the stone called it simply Stela C. This monument bears the longest single hieroglyphic description of the creation, noting that it took place on the day 13.0.0.0.0, 4 Ahaw, 8 Kumk'u, a date corresponding to August 13, 3114 BC on our calendar.

WORLD-TREE & XIBALBÁ

For the Maya, the sky, the surface of the earth and the mysterious 'unseen world' beneath the earth called Xibalbá (shee-bahl-*bah*) were all one great, unified structure. At the center, transcending each of the three layers of the cosmos was a World-Tree, the first life to emerge out of the primordial chaos of creation. The Maya often linked this sacred World-Tree with the towering ceiba, which grows throughout the Maya world. A unique feature of the ceiba is the fact that its branches grow straight out from the trunk, forming a cruciform shape. Such cross-like trees appear frequently in the art of the Maya, particularly in the famous Group of the Cross panels and sarcophagus lid of Pakal at Palenque (p408). In the 16th century, Christian missionary friars arrived and required the Maya to venerate the cross; this Christian symbol soon became linked with the World-Tree in the eyes of the Maya, an association that continues today.

This date appears over and over in other inscriptions throughout the Maya world.

On that day the creator gods set three stones, or mountains, in the dark waters that once covered the primordial world. These three stones formed a cosmic hearth at the center of the universe. The gods then struck divine new fire by means of lightning, which charged the world with life.

This account of the creation is echoed in the first chapters of the *Popol Vuh*, a book compiled by members of the Maya nobility soon after the Spanish Conquest, many centuries after the erection of Quiriguá Stela C. Although this book was written in their native Maya language, its authors used European letters rather than the more terse hieroglyphic script. Thus, we have a fuller account of how they conceived the first creation:

The most recent and accurate English translations of the *Popol Vuh* are *Popol Vuh: The Sacred Book of the Maya*, translated by Allen Christenson, and *Popol Vuh*, translated by Dennis Tedlock.

> This is the account of when all is still silent and placid. All is silent and calm. Hushed and empty is the womb of the sky. These then are the first words, the first speech. There is not yet one person, one animal, bird, fish, crab, tree, rock, hollow, canyon, meadow, or forest. All alone the sky exists. The face of the earth has not yet appeared. Alone lies the expanse of the sea, along with the womb of all the sky. There is not yet anything gathered together. All is at rest. Nothing stirs. All is languid, at rest in the sky. Only the expanse of the water, only the tranquil sea lies alone. All lies placid and silent in the darkness, in the night.

> All alone are the Framer and the Shaper, Sovereign and Quetzal Serpent, They Who Have Borne Children and They Who Have Begotten Sons. Luminous they are in the water, wrapped in feathers… They are great sages, great possessors of knowledge. Thus surely there is the sky. There is also Heart of Sky [a lightning god], which is said to be the name of the god…

For an incredibly beautiful and searchable collection of photographs of painted vases, monuments and other works of ancient Maya art, visit the Kerr Archives at www.famsi.org.

> Then they called forth the mountains from the water. Straightaway the great mountains came to be. It was merely their spirit essence, their miraculous power, that brought about the conception of the mountains.

The Maya saw this pattern of creation all around them. In the night sky, the three brightest stars in the constellation of Orion's Belt were thought of as the cosmic hearth at the center of the universe. On a clear night in the crisp mountain air of the Maya highlands, one can even see what looks like a wisp of smoke within these stars, although it is really only a far-distant string of stars within the M-4 Nebula.

MAYA CITIES AS THE CENTER OF CREATION

The ancient Maya often chose to build their communities in such a way that they reflect sacred geography. One of the earliest Maya centers was Kaminaljuyú, a massive site now buried beneath the sprawling

ANONYMOUS

The authors of the *Popol Vuh* did not sign their names, likely because doing so would have endangered their lives. The *Popol Vuh* contains devout descriptions of the ancient Maya gods and deified ancestors that would have offended the Spanish authorities who ruled Guatemala at the time. Those found in possession of the book were often tortured or killed.

capital of Guatemala City. Kaminaljuyú was settled by at least 1000 BC along the shores of a lake that no longer exists, surrounded by three volcanoes. The ancient capital of the highland, Tz'utujil-Maya, located across a small bay from the modern city of Santiago Atitlán, was also built along the shores of a lake, at the point where three great volcanoes came together. The people of Santiago claim that they live at the r'muxux jab', r'muxux uliw ('navel of the rain, navel of the earth'), the place where the first three mountains of creation emerged from Lake Atitlán, which they believe to be a remnant of the primordial sea that once covered everything.

Because the ancient Maya of the eastern lowlands didn't have real mountains as symbols of the creation, they built them instead in the form of plaza-temple complexes, impressive examples of which may be seen at Tikal (p179), Palenque (p408) and Copán (p148). In hieroglyphic inscriptions, the large open-air plazas at the center of Maya cities were often called nab' (sea) or lakam ja' (great water). Rising above these plastered stone spaces were massive pyramid-temples, often oriented in groups of three, representing the first mountains to emerge out of the 'waters' of the plaza. The tiny elevated sanctuaries of these temples served as portals into the abodes of gods that lived within. Offerings were burned on these plazas, as if the flames were struck in the midst of immense three-stone hearths. Only an elite few were allowed to enter these small inner sanctuaries, while the majority of the populace observed from the plaza below. The architecture of ancient Maya centers thus replicated sacred geography to form an elaborate stage on which rituals could be carried out that charged their world with regenerative power.

A good introduction to the art of the Maya world is Mary Ellen Miller's *Maya Art and Architecture*.

THE CREATION OF HUMANKIND

According to the *Popol Vuh*, the purpose of creation was to give form and shape to beings who would 'remember' the gods through ritual. The Maya take their roles in life very seriously, believing that people exist as mediators between this world and that of the gods. If they don't carry out the proper prayers and ceremonies at just the right time and place, the universe will come to an abrupt end.

For a complete overview of Maya cities and culture from the point of view of an eminent archaeologist, try *The Ancient Maya* by Robert J. Sharer.

The Maya don't see their gods as either perfect or immortal. The gods made three attempts at creating people powerful enough to maintain the world before finally getting it right on the fourth. On the first attempt the gods made deer, birds and other animals, but when the gods called upon the animals to pronounce the names of their creators, they only squawked and grunted and roared. Not being able to speak properly to honor the gods, they were deemed unworthy and condemned to be eaten.

FLATLANDS *Dr Allen J Christenson*

When I first visited the ruins of Tikal in the 1970s, the twin-prop airplanes that ferried tourists there were not equipped with global-positioning instruments as they are now. During one flight, the pilot got a little lost over the Petén jungle with its sea of unbroken green forest. He asked us passengers over the intercom to help him look out for the tops of the ancient temples at Tikal. These just barely cleared the 45m jungle canopy and could be seen from kilometers away. He later told me that pilots would love to have at least one real hill to help orient them.

The second attempt was a person made out of mud. At first, the mud person spoke, 'but without knowledge and understanding' and soon he fell apart and dissolved back into the mud.

The gods' third attempt resulted in people carved from wood. These were a bit better, but still not perfect. They could speak, walk around, and even began to populate the world with their children. But they didn't 'possess their hearts nor their minds. They did not remember their Framer or their Shaper. They walked without purpose,' and so were also destroyed – this time being attacked by their own dogs and ground up on their own grinding stones. The *Popol Vuh* says that the survivors of these wooden people are the chattering monkeys that inhabit the trees of their forests.

The gods finally got it right when they discovered maize, from which they made the flesh of mankind:

> Thus their frame and shape were given expression by our first Mother and our first Father. Their flesh was merely yellow ears of maize and white ears of maize...

> People they came to be. They were able to speak and converse. They were able to look and listen. They were able to walk and hold things with their hands. They were excellent and chosen people. Their faces were manly in appearance. They had their breath, therefore they became. They were able to see as well, for straightaway their vision came to them.

> Perfect was their sight, and perfect was their knowledge of everything beneath the sky. If they gazed about them, looking intently, they beheld that which was in the sky and that which was upon the earth. Instantly they were able to behold everything... Thus their knowledge became full. Their vision passed beyond the trees and the rocks, beyond the lakes and the seas, beyond the mountains and the valleys. Truly they were very esteemed people.

THE PEOPLE OF MAIZE

In nearly all of their languages, the Maya refer to themselves as 'true people' and consider themselves literally of a different flesh than those who do not eat maize. (Foreigners, who eat bread, are deemed 'wheat people.') This mythic connection between maize and human flesh influenced birth rituals in the Maya world for centuries. Soon after the conquest, a Spanish priest noted that when a male child was born, the Maya burned blood shed from its severed umbilical cord and passed an ear of maize through the smoke. The seeds from this ear were then planted in the child's name in a specific area of his field. Parents used the maize from this small patch of land to feed the child until he was old enough to plant for himself, saying that thus 'he not only ate by the sweat of his brow but of his own blood as well.'

Even today, traditionalist mothers in the highlands place an ear of maize into the palm of their newborns, and eat only dishes made from maize while breastfeeding to ensure that the child grows 'true flesh.' Once the child is weaned, he or she is given only food prepared with maize for several months.

No self-respecting Maya raised in the traditional way would eat a meal that didn't include maize. Women do not let grains of maize fall on the ground or into an open fire. If it happens accidentally, the woman will gently pick up the grains and apologize to them. The Maya love to talk and laugh, but are generally silent during meals. A elder once explained, 'for us tortillas are like the Catholic sacramental bread, it is the flesh of god. You don't laugh or speak when taking the flesh of god into your body. The young people are beginning to forget this. They will someday regret it.'

KINGSHIP

For the Mayan, creation wasn't a one-time event. They constantly repeated the primordial events through ceremonies timed to the sacred calendar. They saw the universe as a living thing that, just like any living thing, grows old, weakens and ultimately passes away. Everything, including the gods, needed to be periodically recharged with life-bearing power or the world would slip back into the darkness and chaos that existed before the world began. Maya kings were seen as the mediators to this renewal. In countless wall carvings and paintings, monumental stone stelae, altars and painted pottery, the Maya depicted their kings dressed as gods, repeating the actions of the deity at the time of creation.

A common theme was the king dressed as the Maize God himself, bearing a huge pack on his back containing the sacred bits and pieces that make up the world, while dancing them into existence. These rituals were done at very specific seasons of the year, timed to match calendric dates when the gods first performed them. For the Maya, these ceremonies were not merely symbolic of the rebirth of the cosmos, but a genuine creative act in which time folded inward on itself to reveal the actions of the divine creators in the primordial world.

In Maya theology, the Maize God is the most sacred of the creator deities because he gives his very flesh in order for human beings to live. But this sacrifice must be repaid. The Maya as 'true people' felt an obligation to the cosmos to compensate for the loss of divine life, not because the gods were cruel, but because gods cannot rebirth themselves and need the intercession of human beings. Maya kings stood as the intermediaries between their subjects and the gods. A king was thus required to periodically give that which was most precious: his own blood, which was believed to contain the essence of godhood itself. Generally, this meant that members of the royal family bled themselves with stingray spines or stone lancets. Males did their bloodletting from the genital area, literally birthing gods from the penis. Women most often drew blood from their tongues. This royal blood was collected on sheets of bark paper and then burned to release its divine essence, opening a portal to the other world and allowing the gods to emerge into new life. At times of crisis, such as the end of a calendar cycle, or upon the death of a king and the succession of another, the sacrifice had to be greater to compensate for the loss of divine life. This generally involved obtaining noble or royal captives through warfare against a neighboring Maya state in order to sacrifice them. If this were not done, the Maya believed that the universe itself would cease to exist.

The beauty of Maya religion is that these great visions of creation mirror every-day events in the lives of the people. When a woman rises before dawn to prepare food for her family, she replicates the actions of the creators at the beginning of time. The darkness that surrounds her is reminiscent of the gloom of the primordial world. When she lights the three-stone hearth on the floor of her home, she is once again striking the

DID YOU KNOW?

Like ancient Greece, there was no unified Maya empire. Each city had its own royal family and its own patron gods.

DID YOU KNOW?

Commoners among the Maya were usually safe from warfare violence simply because their blood was not divine. It was the blood of nobility or royalty that was needed to rebirth the world new fire that generates life. The grains of maize that she cooks and then forms into tortillas are literally the flesh of the Maize God, who nourishes and rebuilds the bodies of her family members.

HIEROGLYPHIC WRITING

During the Classic period, the Maya lowlands were divided into two major linguistic groups. In the Yucatán Peninsula and Belize people spoke Yucatec, and in the eastern highlands and Motagua Valley of Guatemala they spoke a language related to Chol. People in El Petén likely spoke both languages, as this was where the linguistic regions overlapped. Yucatec and Chol were similar – about as similar as Spanish and Italian – a fact that facilitated trade and cultural exchange.

In addition, the entire region was unified by a single hieroglyphic writing system. In recent years, scholars have suggested that the written language throughout the Maya world was a form of Chol. Thus, no matter what the scribe spoke among his neighbors, he wrote with Cholan words – an international language something like Latin in the Middle Ages or French in the days of Louis XIV.

More than 1500 years prior to the Spanish conquest, the Maya developed a sophisticated hieroglyphic script capable of recording complex literary compositions, on folded screen codices made of bark paper or deer skin, as well as texts incised on more durable stone or wood. The importance of preserving written records was a hallmark of Maya culture, as witnessed by the thousands of known hieroglyphic inscriptions, many more of which are still being discovered in the jungles of southern Mexico and northern Central America. The sophisticated Maya hieroglyphic script is partly phonetic (glyphs representing sounds tied to the spoken language), and partly logographic (glyphs representing entire words), making it capable of recording any idea that could be thought or spoken.

Most of the people who lived on the American continents prior to the arrival of Europeans lacked a written script. Even in Mesoamerica, where there was a long tradition of hieroglyphic writing among some of the ancient cultures of the region, such as the Maya and Zapotecs, other neighboring cultures preserved their history and theology principally through the spoken word, passed from generation to generation. This was true even of highly sophisticated cultures such as the Aztecs, whose painted texts relied primarily on a rebus (or picture form) of writing, incapable of recording abstract ideas phonetically.

Ancient Maya scribes were among the most honored members of their society. They were often important representatives of the royal family, and as such were believed to carry the seeds of divinity within their blood. Among the titles given to artists and scribes in Classic-period Maya inscriptions were *itz'aat* ('sage') and *miyaatz* ('wise one'). In an important royal tomb at Tikal (Burial 116), an incised bone depicts a deified scribe's hand emerging from the gullet of an open-mouthed dragon. In Classic Maya art, the open jaws represent a portal that leads from this world to the world of the gods. In his or her hand is a calligraphic paintbrush used to both write and illustrate the ancient Maya codex books. The message of this incised bone is that the activities of the scribe come closest to those of the gods themselves, who paint the realities of this world as divine artists.

COUNTING SYSTEM

The Maya way of counting was elegantly simple. Dots were used to count from one to four; a horizontal bar signified five; a bar with one dot above it was six, a bar with two dots was seven, etc. Two bars signified 10, three bars 15. Nineteen, the highest common number was three bars stacked up and topped by four dots.

The Maya didn't use a decimal system (base 10), but rather a vigesimal system, a system with base 20. The late Mayanist Linda Schele used to suggest this was because they wore sandals, and thus counted not only their fingers but toes as well. This is a likely explanation since the number 20 in nearly all Maya languages means 'person.'

To signify larger sums, the Maya used positional numbers – a fairly sophisticated system similar to the one we use today and much more advanced than the crude additive numbers used in the Roman Empire. In positional numbers, the position of a sign, as well as the sign's value, determine the number. For example, in our decimal system the number 23 is made up of two signs: a 2 in the 'tens' position and a 3 in the 'ones' position; two tens plus three ones equals 23.

In the Maya system, positions of increasing value went not right to left (as ours do) but from bottom to top. So the bottom position showed values from one to 19 (remember that this is a base-20 system, so three bars and four dots in this lowest position would equal 19); the next position up showed multiples of 20 (for example, four dots at this position would equal 80); the next position represents multiples of 400; the next, multiples of 8000, etc. By adding more positions one could count as high as needed.

DID YOU KNOW?

The Maya likely used the counting system from day to day by writing on the ground, the tip of the finger creating a dot, and using the edge of the hand to make a bar.

Left: Bars and dots formed the basis of the Mayan counting system

Such positional numbers depend upon the use of zero, a concept that the Maya developed. The zero in Maya numbering was represented by a stylized picture of a shell or some other object – but never a bar or a dot.

CALENDAR SYSTEM

The Maya counting system was used by merchants and others who had to add up many things, but its most important use – and the one you will most often encounter during your travels – was in writing calendar dates. The ancient Maya calendar was a way of interpreting the order of the universe itself. The movement of the sun, moon and stars was not simply a handy way of measuring the passage of time, but they were living beings that influenced the world in fundamentally important ways.

The days and years were conceived as being carried by gods, each with definite personalities and spheres of influence that colored the experience of those who lived them. Even today, the Maya refer to days as 'he.' Priests carefully watched the sky for the appearance of celestial bodies that would determine the time to plant and harvest crops, celebrate certain ceremonies or go to war. The regular rotation of the heavens served as a comforting contrast to the chaos that characterizes our imperfect human world. Most Maya cities were constructed in strict accordance with these celestial movements.

In some ways, the ancient Maya calendar – still used in certain parts of the region – is more accurate than the Gregorian calendar we use today. Without sophisticated technology, Maya astronomers were able to ascertain the length of the solar year as 365.2420 days (a 17.28-seconds-per-year discrepancy from the true average length of 365.2422 days). The Gregorian calendar year works out to be 365.2425 days. Thus the Maya year count is 1/10,000 closer to the truth than our own modern calendar.

The Mayan Calendar System

TRUDI CANAVAN

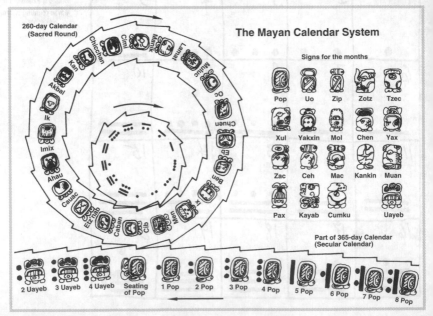

The Mayan Calendar System

260-day Calendar (Sacred Round)

Signs for the months

Pop   Uo   Zip   Zotz   Tzec

Xul   Yakxin   Mol   Chen   Yax

Zac   Ceh   Mac   Kankin   Muan

Pax   Kayab   Cumku   Uayeb

Part of 365-day Calendar (Secular Calendar)

2 Uayeb   3 Uayeb   4 Uayeb   Seating of Pop   1 Pop   2 Pop   3 Pop   4 Pop   5 Pop   6 Pop   7 Pop   8 Pop

Maya astronomers were able to pinpoint eclipses with uncanny accuracy, a skill that was unknown among the brightest scholars in contemporary Medieval Europe. The Maya lunar cycle was a mere seven minutes off today's sophisticated technological calculations. They calculated the Venus cycle at 583.92 days. By dropping four days every 61 Venus years and eight days at the end of 300 Venus years, the Maya lost less than a day in accuracy in 1000 years!

To translate a date using the Mayan calendar, visit the Mayan Date Calculator at www.halfmoon .org. This site also has a hieroglyphic translator, ancient games and virtual walk-throughs of archaeological sites.

More than a millennium after the Maya developed their remarkably accurate solar calendar, Pope Gregory XIII declared that the day following October 4, 1582 would be October 15, 1582 to make up for a ten-day error that had accumulated over the years. This became the Gregorian Calendar that is standard today.

There were actually three calendars used by the ancient Maya. The first was a period of 260 days, known as the Tzolkin, likely based on the 9 months it takes for a human fetus to develop prior to birth. Traditionalist Maya priests in highland Guatemala still undergo a 260-day period of training before they are 'reborn' as priests worthy to interpret the ancient calendar on behalf of petitioners. The second Maya calendar system was a solar year of 365 days, called the Haab. Both the Tzolkin and Haab were measured in endlessly repeating cycles. When meshed together, a total of 18,980 day-name permutations are possible (a period of 52 solar years) called the Calendar Round.

Though fascinating in its complexity, the Calendar Round has its limitations, the greatest being that it only goes for 52 years. After that, it starts again, and so provides no way for Maya ceremony planners (or modern historians) to distinguish a day in this 52 year Calendar Round cycle from the identically named day in the next cycle, or a dozen cycles later. Thus, the Maya developed a third calendar system we call the Long Count, which pinpoints a date based on the number of days it takes place after the day of creation. This refers to a great cycle of days, counted from the creation, the moment when the present age of the world began (August 13, 3114 BC).

Let's look at an example: the Maya Long Count date corresponding to Saturday April 10, 2004, is 12.19.11.3.3, 12 Akbal 4 Men. The first number, 12, of this Long Count date represents how many *baktuns* (400 x 360 days or 144,000 days) have passed since the day of creation (thus 12 x 144,000 = 1,728,000 days). The second number, 19, represents the number of *katuns* (20 x 360 or 7200 days) that have passed, thus adding another 19 x 7200 = 136,800 days. The third number, 11, is the number of *tuns* (360 days), or 3960 days. The fourth number, 3, is the number of *uinals* (20 days), or 60 days. Finally, the fifth number, 3, is the number of whole days. Adding each of these numbers gives us the sum of 1,728,000 + 36,800 + 3960 + 60 + 3 = 1,868,823 days since the day of creation. To further nail down this date, although it isn't really necessary, the Maya added the Tzolkin date (12 Akbal) and the Haab date (4 Men). If that weren't precise enough, the Maya would also often mention the dates from various planetary cycles, which lord of the night was in place, and so on.

The ancient Maya believed that the Great Cycle of the present age would last for 13 *baktun* cycles in all (each *baktun* lasting 144,000 days), which according to our calendar will end on December 23, AD 2012. The Maya saw the end of large cycles of time as a kind of death, and these times were thus fraught with peril. But both death and life must dance together on the cosmic stage for the succession of days to continue, and so the Maya conducted ceremonies to periodically 'rebirth' the world and keep the endless march of time going.

The Maya never expected the end of this Great Cycle to be the last word for the cosmos, since the world regularly undergoes death and rebirth. Cobá Stela 1 actually records a period of time equivalent to approximately 41,341,050,000,000,000,000,000,000,000 of our years! (In comparison, the Big Bang that is said to have formed our universe is estimated to have occurred a mere 15,000,000,000 years ago.)

It is important to remember that to the Maya, time was not a continuum but a cycle, and even this incomprehensibly large cycle of years would be repeated, over and over, infinitely, in infinitely larger cycles. In effect, the Mayan 'clock' has an unlimited number of gear wheels, and they keep ticking around and around, forever.

Guatemala

RICHARD I'ANSON

Guatemala

Guatemala is one of those rare destinations that rewards even the most jaded traveler – a place where the indigenous culture perseveres, and where no superlatives can accurately capture the grandeur of the landscape. In the highlands it seems there's always a volcano looming over your shoulder, and beautiful lakes large and small are scattered among pine, cloud and rain forests all over the country. This fabulous geography means travelers can hike, bike, dive, ride, cave, kayak and play at outdoor adventure activities *ad infinitum*.

Wildlife-watching is popular too, especially in the rain forests of the northern Petén region. The Petén also holds the awesome temples of Tikal, towering above its jungle canopy. Tikal has no real peer among Classic Mayan cities and is a must-see for any visitor. Harder-to-reach Mayan sites such as El Mirador can be even more exciting because getting to them is an adventure in its own right.

Studying Spanish has long served as a traveler's gateway to Guatemalan life, and there are now language schools in almost every town where travelers like to linger. Whether you prefer the international scene of Antigua or the mountain seclusion of Todos Santos, odds are there's a school and setting for you.

The most striking feature of Guatemala is its people. A visit to the raucous, colorful markets in towns such as Chichicastenango or Sololá will give you a feel for the palpable living culture of Guatemala's indigenous population. You'll rarely receive a brusque reception from any Guatemalan, and with their infectiously amicable and helpful demeanor, it's the Guatemalans themselves who really make traveling in Guatemala special.

FAST FACTS

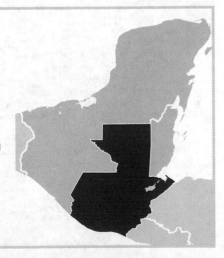

- **Area** 109,000 sq km (slightly smaller than the US state of Louisiana, a bit bigger than England)
- **Capital** Guatemala City
- **Country Code** ☎ 502
- **Departure Tax** US$30 by air
- **Languages** Spanish, Mayan languages
- **Money** quetzals, US dollars readily accepted (US$1 = Q8.10)
- **Phrases (slang)** *vecha* (beer), *pachanga* (party), Chapín (Guatemalan)
- **Population** 11.2 million
- **Visas** North American and most European citizens need only a valid passport

GUATEMALA

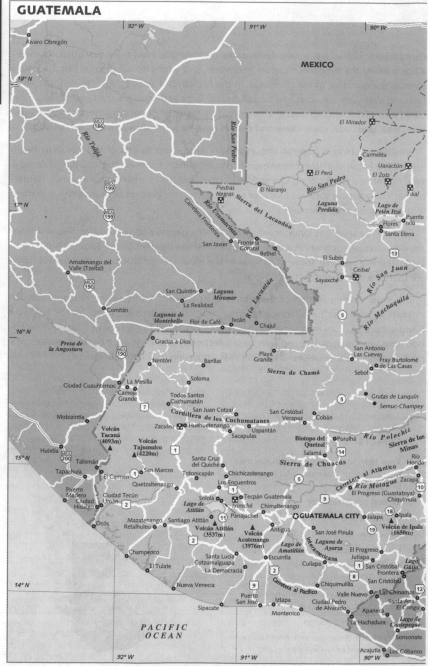

MEXICO

Álvaro Obregón

18° N

Río Tulijá

MEX 186

17° N

MEX 199

MEX 199

El Mirador

Carmelita

El Perú
Uaxactún
El Zotz

Tikal

Piedras
Negras
El Naranjo
Sierra del Lacandón
Río San Pedro
Laguna
Perdida
Lago de
Petén Itzá

Río Usumacinta
Carretera Fronteriza
San Javier
Frontera
Corozal
Bethel
El Subín
Puente
Ixlú
Flores
Santa Elena

Amatenango del
Valle (Tzeltal)

16° N

MEX 190

MEX 190

San Quintín
La Realidad
Laguna
Miramar
Ixcán
Chajul
Río Lacantún
Ceibal
Sayaxché
Río San Juan
Río Machaquilá
13

Comitán

Lagunas de
Montebello
Flor de Café
5

Presa de
la Angostura

Gracias a Dios

Nentón
Barillas
Playa
Grande
Sierra de Chamá
San Antonio
Las Cuevas
Fray Bartolomé
de Las Casas
Sebol

Ciudad Cuauhtémoc
La Mesilla
Camoja
Grande
Soloma
Todos Santos
Cuchumatán
San Juan Cotzal
San Cristóbal
Verapaz
Cobán
Grutas de Lanquín
Semuc-Champey

Motozintla

1
Cordillera de los Cuchumatanes
Zaculeu Huehuetenango
Uspantán
Sacapulas
5
Biotopo del
Quetzal
Purulhá
Salamá
Sierra de las
Minas
Río Polochic

15° N

Volcán
Tacaná
(4093m)

Volcán
Tajumulco
(4220m)

1

Santa Cruz
del Quiché
Chichicastenango
Sierra de Chuacús
14
Río
Hondo

Huixtla
MEX 200
Talismán

El Carmen
San Marcos
Totonicapán
Los Encuentros
5
Carretera al Atlántico
Río Motagua
Zacapa
10

Tapachula

Quetzaltenango
1
Tecpán Guatemala
Ixïmché
El Progreso (Guastatoya)
9
Chiquimula

Puerto
Madero
Ciudad
Hidalgo
Ciudad Tecún
Umán
2
Sololá
Lago de
Atitlán
Panajachel
Chimaltenango
GUATEMALA CITY
Jalapa
18
Ipala

Ocós
Mazatenango
Retalhuleu
Santiago Atitlán
11
Volcán Atitlán
(3537m)
2
Volcán
Acatenango
(3976m)
Antigua
Escuintla
San José Pinula
Lago de
Amatitlán
Laguna de
Ayarza
19
Volcán de Ipala
(1650m)

Champerico
El Tulate
Santa Lucía
Cotzumalguapa
La Democracia
Cuilapa
El Progreso
Jutiapa
1
San Cristóbal
Frontera
Lago
Güija

14° N
Nueva Venecia
2
Chiquimulilla
8
San Cristóbal
12

Sípacate
Puerto
San José
9
Iztapa
Monterrico
Carretera al Pacífico
Valle Nuevo
Ciudad Pedro
de Alvarado
Las Chinamas
Santa Ana
El Congo
Apaneca
La Hachadura
Lago de
Coatepeque
Sonsonate
Acajutla
Los Cóbanos

PACIFIC
OCEAN

Interamericana

92° W
91° W
90° W

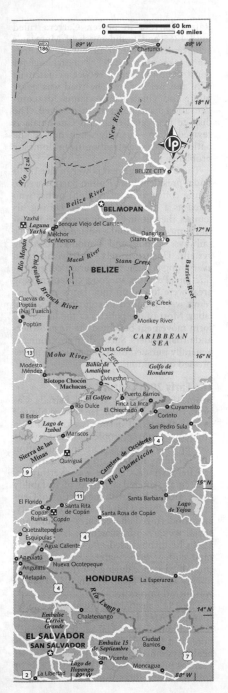

HIGHLIGHTS

- Speed down a jungle-fringed tropical river to the fascinating Caribbean enclave of **Lívingston** (p162).
- Marvel at lofty temples rising above a jungle full of wildlife at **Tikal** (p179).
- Study Spanish, climb volcanoes and visit indigenous villages around **Quetzaltenango** (p111), Guatemala's clean, orderly second city.
- Explore spectacular caves and cool off in the gorgeous turquoise lagoons at the **Grutas de Lanquín** (p142) and **Semuc Champey** (p143).
- Chill out in a pyramid hut for a few days in the tranquil little village of **San Marcos La Laguna** (p102) on the shores of the mighty Lago de Atitlán.

ITINERARIES

- **Ten days** Start in Antigua, move on to Panajachel on Lago de Atitlán, then the highlands towns Chichicastenango and Quetzaltenango.
- **One month** Add on Quiriguá, Lívingston, the Río Dulce (river) to Río Dulce town, then Finca Ixobel, Flores, Tikal and remote Mayan sites such as Yaxhá and Uaxactún. From Flores head to Sayaxché, then Cobán, the Grutas de Lanquín and Semuc Champey.

HOW MUCH?

- **Three-hour 2nd-class bus ride** US$2
- **A week of Spanish classes with homestay in Antigua** US$140-150
- **Admission to Tikal** US$6.50
- **One hour of Internet** US$1-2
- **Comfortable lakeside double with bathroom on Lago de Atitlán** US$26

LONELY PLANET INDEX

- **Gallon of gas (petrol)** US$2.25
- **Liter of bottled water** US$0.60
- **Bottle of Gallo (beer)** US$1.50
- **Souvenir T-shirt** US$6
- **Chuchito (corn dough filled with spicy meat and served in a corn husk)** US$0.50

CLIMATE & WHEN TO GO

The *invierno* (rainy season) in winter lasts from mid-May to mid-October, and on into November and even December in the north and east of the country. In the lowland jungles of El Petén, the mud at this time will be a downer, guaranteed. Humidity increases during the rainy season, too.

The highlands get very cold and damp during the rainy season – you can expect daily showers (downpours in the north) at the very least. The *verano* (dry season) in summer runs November to May, meaning sweltering heat in El Petén and along the coasts and comfortably warm days in the highlands.

The peak tourist season is from Christmas to Easter. Things become acute around Christmas, New Year's and Easter, when Guatemalans travel and many places are booked out. A second high season runs June to August when throngs of foreigners arrive to study Spanish and to travel.

For climate charts see p438.

HISTORY

From conquistadors and earthquakes to death squads and guerrilla cadres, Guatemalans have been locked in a centuries-long struggle for tranquility and equality.

The country's history since independence in 1847 has been one of struggle between the forces of left and right. Both sides have bolstered the social and economic elite and done little for the people of the countryside, mostly Maya.

The 19th Century

Early in Guatemala's republican history, the liberals, who had been the first to advocate independence, opposed the interests of elite conservatives, who included large landowners and the Church.

During the short existence of the United Provinces of Central America, liberal president Francisco Morazán (1830–39) instituted reforms aimed at correcting three persistent problems: the overwhelming power of the Church; the division of society into a Hispanic upper class and an Indian lower class; and the region's impotence in world markets.

Unpopular economic policies, heavy taxes and an 1837 cholera epidemic led to an Indian uprising that brought conservative

Rafael Carrera to power. Carrera ruled until 1865 and undid much of Morazán's achievements. His government allowed Britain to take control of Belize in exchange for construction of a road between Guatemala City and Belize City. The road was never built, and Guatemala's claims for compensation have never been resolved. The dispute between Belize and Guatemala is revived often – usually when one of the nations needs a distraction from domestic problems.

The liberals regained power in the 1870s under president Justo Rufino Barrios, a rich, young coffee *finca* (plantation) owner who ruled as a dictator (1873–79). During his tenure, the country made great strides toward modernization, constructing roads, railways, schools and a modern banking system. Unsurprisingly, Barrios also did everything possible to encourage coffee production. Peasants in good coffee-growing areas were forced off their lands and many Maya were required to contribute seasonal labor. Most of the policies of the liberal reform movement benefited the *finca* owners and urban traders. Succeeding governments generally pursued the same policies and repressed opposition.

The Early 20th Century

From 1898 to 1920, Manuel Estrada Cabrera ruled as a dictator. He fancied himself as an enlightened despot, seeking to turn Guatemala into a 'tropical Athens,' while looting the treasury, ignoring education and spending millions on the military.

After Estrada Cabrera was overthrown, Guatemala entered a period of instability that ended in 1931 with the election of General Jorge Ubico. Ubico insisted on honesty, and modernized the country's health and social welfare infrastructure. In the early 1940s he dispossessed and exiled the German coffee *finca* owners. He assumed a pro-Allied stance during World War II, but openly admired Spain's Franco. In 1944 he was forced into exile.

The 1945 elections brought philosopher Juan José Arévalo to power. Arévalo established the nation's social-security system, a bureau of Indian affairs, a modern public-health system and liberal labor laws. His six years as president saw 25 coup attempts by conservative military forces.

Arévalo was succeeded in 1951 by Colonel Jacobo Arbenz Guzmán, who looked to break up estates and foster high productivity on small farms. But the USA supported the interests of large companies such as United Fruit, and in 1954 orchestrated an invasion from Honduras led by two exiled Guatemalan military officers. Arbenz Guzmán was forced to step down and land reform never took place. Violence, oppression and disenfranchisement ensued, fueling the formation of guerrilla groups and fomenting discord.

Civil War

During the 1960s and '70s, economic inequality, surging urban migration and the developing union movement pushed oppression to new heights. Amnesty International estimates that 50,000 to 60,000 people were killed during the political violence of the 1970s. Furthermore, the 1976 earthquake killed about 22,000 people and left one million homeless. Most of the aid sent to help people in need never reached them.

In 1982 President José Efraín Ríos Montt initiated a 'scorched earth' policy, that exterminated the populations of more than 400 villages. Ríos Montt, an evangelical Christian, was acting in the name of anti-insurgency, stabilization and anti-communism. An estimated 15,000 people, mostly Maya men, were tortured and massacred; 100,000 refugees fled to Mexico. In response, four guerrilla organizations united to form the URNG (Unidad Revolucionaria Nacional Guatemalteca, ie Guatemalan National Revolutionary Unity).

In August 1983 Ríos Montt was deposed in a coup led by General Oscar Humberto Mejía Victores, but the abuses continued. It was estimated that over 100 political assassinations and 40 abductions occurred every month under the new ruler. The USA suspended military aid to the government, leading to the 1985 election of civilian Christian Democrat Marco Vinicio Cerezo Arévalo – but not before the military secured control of the countryside and immunity from prosecution.

The 1990s

Cerezo Arévalo was succeeded by Jorge Serrano Elías (1990–93), who reopened dialogue with the URNG. The talks collapsed, Serrano's popularity declined, and he came to depend more on the army for support. On May 25, 1993, Serrano carried out an *autogolpe* (installing himself as dictator), suspended the constitution and ruled by decree. Though supported by the military, he was deposed and forced into exile. Congress elected Ramiro de León Carpio, the Solicitor for Human Rights and an outspoken critic of the army, to complete Serrano's term.

In March 1995 the USA announced a further suspension of aid due to the government's failure to investigate the murder or disappearance of, among others, Michael Devine, who had operated Finca Ixobel in Poptún, and URNG leader Efraín Bámaca Velásquez, whose wife, US attorney Jennifer Harbury, had been conducting a protest since his disappearance in 1992. Eventually it was revealed that Velásquez had been murdered. Claims of CIA involvement in both these murders were declared unfounded by the US government.

In 1996 Álvaro Enrique Arzú Irigoyen of the middle-right PAN (Partido de Avanzada Nacional) was elected. In December he and the URNG signed peace accords ending the 36-year civil war, in which an estimated 200,000 Guatemalans were killed, one million left homeless and untold thousands 'disappeared.'

The accords called for accountability for the armed forces' human-rights violations and resettlement of one million refugees. They also addressed the identity and rights of indigenous peoples, health care, education and other basic social services, women's rights, the abolition of obligatory military service and the incorporation of ex-guerrillas into civilian life.

It has been a rocky road since the war's end. Bishop Juan Gerardi, coordinator of the Guatemalan Archbishop's Human Rights Office (ODHAG), was beaten to death outside his home in 1998, two days after detailing the military's human-rights violations during the civil war. (Three suspects were finally arrested for the murder in January 2000, but they were released on appeal in 2002).

The greatest challenge to peace stems from inequities in the power structure. It's estimated that 70% of the country's arable land is owned by less than 3% of the population. According to a UN report, the top 20% of the population has an income 30 times greater than the bottom 20%. On an encouraging note, the country's Maya population has mobilized politically since the signing of the peace accords.

Discrimination against indigenous people, deeply ingrained in society, results in poverty and misery for most of the population. How the need for economic and social reforms is met may be the most important factor in creating a true and lasting peace.

Guatemala Today

In November 1999 Guatemala held its first peacetime elections in nearly 40 years. In a runoff, conservative and admitted murderer Alfonso Portillo of the FRG (Frente Republicano Guatemalteco) defeated Oscar Berger of the incumbent PAN. Also disturbing to human-rights observers was that Ríos Montt, who became the leader of Congress, also ran on the FRG ticket and advised Portillo. Portillo vowed to clean up the judicial system, crack down on crime, tax the rich and respect human rights. He paid compensation in 2001 to the families of 226 men, women and children killed by soldiers and paramilitaries, but implementation of the Peace Accords stalled before going into reverse.

In 2002 the UN representative for Indian peoples, after an 11-day Guatemalan tour, stated that 60% of Guatemalan Maya were still marginalized by discrimination and violence. International organizations from the European Parliament to the Interamerican Human Rights Commission criticized the state of human rights in Guatemala. Human rights workers were subjected to threats and killings by perpetrators acting with seeming impunity. Portillo failed to carry out a promise to disband the presidential guard (whose soldiers killed Bishop Gerardi and whose chief had ordered the 1990 killing of Myrna Mack, a Guatemalan anthropologist who had been documenting army violence against rural Maya) and he doubled the defense budget, taking it beyond the maximum level fixed in the Peace Accords.

Lawlessness and violent crime have increased horrifyingly. The US 'decertified' Guatemala – meaning it no longer considered it an ally in the battle against the drugs trade – in 2002. The same year Amnesty International reported that criminals were colluding with sectors of the police, military and local affiliates of multinational corporations to flout human rights. According to police figures, 3630 people died violently in 2002. Lynchings were not uncommon as people increasingly took the law into their own hands.

National anticorruption prosecutor Karen Fischer fled the country in 2003 after receiving death threats when she investigated Panamanian bank accounts allegedly opened for Portillo. Ríos Montt himself was named FRG candidate for the late-2003 presidential elections, and given the go-ahead by the country's constitutional court – despite a constitutional ban on presidents who had in the past taken power by coup (which Ríos Montt did in 1982). The FRG showed its colors blatantly in the run-up to the election by making sizable 'compensation' payments to former members of the Patrullas de Autodefensa Civil (PACs; Civil Defense Patrols), who had carried out many atrocities during the civil war.

Although less extreme, right-winger Oscar Berger, of the Gran Alianza Nacional, emerged victorious and appointed indigenous activist Rigoberta Menchú (see the boxed text, p91) as a 'Goodwill Ambassador' to the government, many Guatemalans feel that true democracy is still a long way off. At the time of writing, the signing of the Central American Free Trade Agreement (Cafta) looks to be a certainty despite massive protests in Guatemala and the rest of the region.

Berger has done his bit for tourist safety, at least, by increasing the Tourist Police force from 325 to 800 members and raising its budget to about US$250,000.

THE CULTURE
The National Psyche

You'll be amazed when you first reach Guatemala by just how helpful, polite and unhurried Guatemalans are. Everyone has time to stop and chat and explain what you want to know. This is apparent even if you've just crossed the border from Mexico, which doesn't exactly rush things itself. Most Guatemalans like to get to know other people without haste, feeling for common ground, rather than making blunt assertions and engaging in contradictory dialectic. Some observers explain this mild manner as a reaction to centuries of repression and violence by the ruling class, but whatever the truth of that, it makes most Guatemalans a pleasure to meet.

What goes on behind this outward politeness is harder to encapsulate. Few Guatemalans exhibit the stress, worry and hurry of the 'developed' nations, but this isn't because they don't have to worry about money or employment. They are a long-suffering people who don't expect wealth or good government but make the best of what comes their way – friendship, their family, a good meal, good company. Families, on the whole, are strong and religion, too, is a source of great strength to most Guatemalans – whether the orthodox Catholicism of the ladinos (people of mixed Indian and European parentage), the animist-Catholic syncretism of the traditional Maya, or the evangelical Protestantism of increasing numbers of converts. People's faith gives them hope, not only of better things in the afterlife but also of improvements in the here and now.

Some say that Guatemala has no middle class, just a ruling class and an exploited class. It's true that Guatemala has a small, rich, ladino ruling elite whose main goal seems to be to maintain wealth and power at almost any cost. It also has an indigenous Maya population, comprising more than half the people in the country, that tends to be poor, poorly educated and poorly provided for and has always been kept in a secondary role by the ruling elite. The Maya villagers' strengths lie in their family and community ties and traditions. Those who do break out of the poverty cycle, through business or education, do not turn their backs on their communities.

There is also a large group of working-class and middle-class ladinos, typically Catholic and family-oriented but with aspirations influenced by education, TV, international popular music and North America and maybe by liberal ideas of equality, and social tolerance. This segment of society has its bohemian/student/artist circles whose overlap with educated, forward-looking Mayans may hold the greatest hope for progress toward an equitable society.

Lifestyle

Despite modernizing influences – cable TV, education, contact with foreign travelers, international popular music, time spent as migrant workers in the USA – traditional family ties remain strong at all levels of society. Extended-family groups gather for weekend meals and holidays. Old-fashioned gender roles are strong, too: many women have jobs to increase the family income but relatively few have positions of much responsibility. Homosexuality is barely recognized: only in Guatemala City is there anything approaching an open gay scene, and that is pretty much for men only.

Traveling in Guatemala you will encounter a much wider cross-section of Guatemalans than many Guatemalans ever do, as they live within relatively narrow worlds. The Guatemalans you'll meet will also tend to be among the most worldly and open-minded, as a result of their contact with tourists. If you spend time studying Spanish or work on one of the many volunteer projects, you stand an even higher chance of meeting Guatemalans who are interested in learning, in other cultures, in human rights, in music and the arts, in improving the position of women, the indigenous and the poor. Guatemala has a broad web of people, often young, with these kinds of concerns, and you only need peel away a layer or two of the onion to uncover them.

Still, the predominant lifestyle factor of most Guatemalans remains poverty. The official national minimum wage is only US$130 a month in urban areas and US$120 in rural areas. A typical teacher earns around US$180 a month. Poverty is most prevalent in rural, indigenous areas, especially the highlands. Wealth, industry and commerce are concentrated overwhelmingly in sprawling, polluted Guatemala City, home to about 18% of its people.

Population

Of the 11.2 million people counted by Guatemala's 2002 census, some 50% to 60% are indigenous; nearly all are Maya groups but there is also a very small population of non-Maya indigenous people called the Chinka' (Xinca) in the southeastern corner of the country. The rest of Guatemala's population are nearly all ladinos, ie descended from both Maya and European (mostly

Spanish) settlers. There are also a few thousand Garifuna (descended from Caribbean islanders, indigenous Central Americans and shipwrecked African slaves) around the Caribbean town of Lívingston.

The Maya are spread throughout the country but are most densely concentrated in the highlands, which are home to the four biggest Maya groups: the K'iche' (Quiché), Mam, Q'eqchi' (Kekchí) and Kaqchiquel (Cakchiquel). Mayan languages are still the way most Maya communicate, with approximately 20 separate (and often mutually unintelligible) Mayan languages spoken in different regions of the country. It's language that primarily defines which Maya people someone belongs to. Though many Mayans speak some Spanish, it's always a second language, and there are many who don't speak any Spanish.

The overall population is densest in the highland strip from Guatemala City to Quetzaltenango, the country's two biggest cities. Some 40% of the population lives in towns and cities, and 44% are aged under 15.

RELIGION

Roman Catholicism is Guatemala's predominant religion, but not the only one. Since the 1980s evangelical Protestant sects, most of them rabidly Pentecostal, have surged in popularity, and now an estimated 30% of Guatemalans are Protestant.

Catholicism never wiped out the traditional Mayan religion. Many aspects of Catholicism easily blended with Mayan beliefs, and the Maya still bring offerings and make sacrifices at many ancient places of worship. Various saints hold double meanings; often the saint's Catholic identity was superimposed over a pre-Hispanic deity or saint: Maximón in Santiago Atitlán and San Simón in Zunil are examples.

ARTS

The Maya of Guatemala still make various traditional handicrafts. Weavings, embroidery and other textile arts are among the most striking, as well as basketry, ceramics and wood carving.

A number of well-known Maya painters work in a primitivist style depicting scenes from daily life. Known as Tz'utujil oil painting, this genre is typified by vibrant colors and is centered in Lago de Atitlán.

Accomplished artists of this style include Rafael González y González, Pedro Rafael González Chavajay and Mariano González Chavajay. Visit the Arte Maya website at www.artemaya.com.

Music is a very important part of Guatemalan society, and it is a source of pride that the marimba, a xylophone-type instrument, may have been invented here, or imported and refined by African slaves. The Maya also play traditional instruments including the *chirimía* (of Arabic origin and related to the oboe) and reed flute.

Guatemalan writer Miguel Ángel Asturias won the Nobel Prize for Literature in 1967. Best known for his thinly veiled vilification of Latin American dictators in *El Señor Presidente,* Asturias also wrote poetry (collected in *Sien de Alondra,* published in English as *Temple of the Lark*). Other celebrated writers include poet Luis Cardoza y Aragón and short-story master Augusto Monterroso.

The Spanish colonial structures in Antigua and ancient Mayan ruins are impressive works of architecture. Interestingly, Mayan embellishments can be found on many colonial buildings (such as the lotus flowers adorning Antigua's La Merced) – an enduring testament to the Maya laborers forced to carry out European architectural concepts.

ENVIRONMENT
Land

Consisting primarily of mountainous forest highlands and jungle plains, Guatemala covers an area of 109,000 sq km. The western highlands hold 30 volcanoes, reaching heights of 3800m in the Cordillera de los Cuchumatanes northwest of Huehuetenango.

The Pacific Slope holds rich coffee, cacao, fruit and sugar plantations. Down along the shore the volcanic slope meets the sea, yielding vast, sweltering beaches of black volcanic sand.

Guatemala City lies at an altitude of around 1500m. To the north, the Alta Verapaz highlands gradually give way to El Petén, whose climate and topography is similar to the Yucatán: hot and humid or hot and dry. Southeast of El Petén is the banana-rich valley of the Río Motagua, which is dry in some areas, moist in others.

Guatemala is at the confluence of three tectonic plates, resulting in earthquakes and volcanic eruptions. Its dynamic geology includes a tremendous system of above-ground and subterranean caves. This type of karst terrain riddles the Verapaces region and has made Guatemala a popular spelunking destination.

Wildlife
ANIMALS
The country's abundance of animals includes 250 species of mammal, 600 bird species, 200 species of reptile and amphibian and numerous butterflies and other insects.

The national bird, the resplendent quetzal, is often used to symbolize Guatemala. The male sports a bright red breast, brilliant blue-green across the rest of the body and a spot of bright white on the underside of the long tail. The female, alas, is decidedly less dramatic.

Other colorful birds include toucans, macaws and parrots. Boasting the ocellated turkey (or 'Petén turkey'), a large, multicolored bird reminiscent of a peacock, Tikal is a birding hot spot, with some 300 tropical and migratory species sighted to date. Several woodpecker species, nine types of hummingbirds and four trogon species are just the beginning of the list. Also in the area are large white herons, hawks, warblers, kingfishers, harpy eagles (rare) and many others.

Although Guatemala's forests host several mammal and reptile species, many remain difficult to observe. Still, visitors to Tikal can enjoy the antics of the omnipresent pizotes (coatis) and might spy howler and spider monkeys. Other mammals deeper in the forest include jaguars, ocelots, pumas, peccaries, agoutis, opossums, tapirs, kinkajous, *tepezcuintles* (pacas), white-tailed and red brocket deer, armadillos and very large rattlesnakes. Reptiles and amphibians elsewhere include at least three species of sea turtle (leatherback, *tortuga negra* and olive ridley) and two species of crocodile. Manatees also frequent the waters around Río Dulce.

PLANTS
Guatemala has over 8000 plant species in 19 different ecosystems, ranging from coastal mangrove forests and mountainous interior pine forests to high cloud forests. In addition, El Petén supports a variety of trees, including mahogany, cedar, ramón and sapodilla.

The national flower, the *monja blanca* (white nun orchid), is said to have been picked so much that it is now rare in the wild. Nevertheless, the country is home to around 600 species of orchid – a third of them endemic.

Guatemala also has the perfect climate for *xate* (*sha*-tay), a low-growing palm that thrives in El Petén and is prized in the developed world as flower-arrangement filler.

National Parks & Reserves
Guatemala has 92 protected areas, including biosphere reserves, national parks, protected biotopes, wildlife refuges and private nature reserves, amounting to 28% of the national territory. Many of the protected areas are remote and hard for the independent traveler to reach; the table shows those that are easiest to reach and/or most interesting to visitors (but excludes volcanoes, nearly all of which are protected, and areas of mainly archaeological interest).

Environmental Issues
Environmental consciousness is not enormously developed in Guatemala, as vast amounts of garbage strewn across the country will quickly tell you. Despite the impressive list of parks and protected areas, genuine protection for those areas is harder to achieve, partly because of official collusion to ignore the regulations and partly because of pressure from poor Guatemalans in need of land. Deforestation is a problem in many areas, especially El Petén, where jungle is being felled at an alarming rate for timber, cattle ranches, oil pipelines, clandestine airstrips, new settlements and maize fields.

On the Pacific side of the country, land is mostly agricultural or given over to industrial interests. The forests remaining are not long for this world, as local communities cut down the trees for heating and cooking.

Nevertheless a number of Guatemalan organizations are doing valiant work to protect their country's environment and biodiversity. The following are good resources for finding out more about Guatemala's natural and protected areas:

Alianza Verde (Map p172; www.alianzaverde.org; Parque Central, Flores, El Petén) Association organizations, businesses and people involved in conservation and tourism in the Petén; provides information services such as Destination Petén magazine, the website www.peten.net, and

GUATEMALA

GUATEMALA'S NATIONAL PARKS

Protected Area	Features	Activities	Best Time to Visit	Page
Reserva de Biósfera Maya	vast 21,000-sq-km area stretching across northern Petén; includes 4 national parks	jungle treks, wildlife-watching	any, but Nov-May drier	p190
Reserva de Biósfera Sierra de las Minas	cloud-forest reserve of great biodiversity; key quetzal habitat	hiking, wildlife-watching	any	p159
Parque Nacional Tikal	diverse jungle wildlife among Guatemala's most magnificent Mayan ruins	wildlife-watching; seeing Mayan city	any, but Nov-May drier	p179
Parque Nacional Laguna del Tigre	remote, large park within Reserva de Biósfera Maya; freshwater wetlands, Petén flora and fauna	spotting wildlife including scarlet macaws, monkeys, crocodiles; visiting El Perú archaeological site, volunteer opportunities at Las Guaca-mayas biological station	any, but Nov-May drier	p190
Parque Nacional Mirador-Río Azul	national park within Reserva de Biósfera Maya; Petén flora and fauna	jungle treks to El Mirador archaeological site	any, but Nov-May drier	p190
Parque Nacional Río Dulce	beautiful jungle-lined lower Río Dulce between Lago de Izabal and the Caribbean; manatee refuge	boat trips	any	p166
Parque Nacional Laguna Lachuá	circular, jungle-surrounded, turquoise lake, 220m deep; many fish, occasional jaguars and tapir	camping, swimming, guided walks	any	p143
Parque Nacional Grutas de Lanquín	large cave system 61 km from Cobán	visiting caves, swimming, seeing bats; visiting nearby Semuc Champey lagoons and waterfalls	any	p142
Biotopo del Quetzal	easy-access cloud-forest reserve; howler monkeys, birds	nature trails, bird watching, possible quetzal sightings	any	p137
Biotopo Cerro Cahuí	forest reserve beside Lago de Petén de Itzá; Petén wildlife including monkeys	walking trails	any	p177
Biotopo San Miguel La Palotada	adjoins Parque Nacional Tikal; dense Petén forest with millions of bats	jungle walks, visits to El Zotz archaeological site and bat caves	any, but Nov-May drier	p189
Refugio de Vida Silvestre Petexbatún	lake near Sayaxché; waterbirds	boat trips, fishing, visiting several archaeological sites	any	p189
Refugio de Vida Silvestre Bocas del Polochic	delta of Río Polochic at western end of Lago de Izabal; Guatemala's 2nd-largest freshwater wetlands	bird-watching (more than 300 species), howler monkey observation	any	p159
Reserva Natural Monterrico	Pacific beaches and wetlands; birdlife, turtles	boat tours, bird- and turtle-watching	Jun-Nov (turtle nesting)	p133
Área de Protección Especial de Punta de Manabique	large Caribbean wetland reserve; beaches, mangroves, lagoons, birds, crocodiles, possible manatee sightings	boat trips, wildlife-watching, fishing, beach	any	p133

Cincap, the Centro de Información Sobre la Naturaleza, Cultura y Artesanía de Petén, in Flores.

Arcas (Asociación de Rescate y Conservación de Vida Silvestre; ☎ /fax 5476-6001; www.rds.org.gt/arcas; 21a Calle 9-44A, Zona 11, Mariscal, Guatemala City) NGO working with volunteers in sea turtle conservation and rehabilitation of Petén wildlife (see also Flores, p169; Monterrico, p133).

Asociación Ak' Tenamit (☎ 2254-1560, 2254-3346 in Guatemala City, 5908-3392 in Río Dulce; www.aktenamit .org; 11a Av A9-39, Zona 2, Guatemala City) Mayan-run NGO working to reduce poverty and promote conservation and ecotourism in the rain forests of eastern Guatemala.

Cecon (Centro de Estudios Conservacionistas de la Universidad de San Carlos; Map p66-7; ☎ 2361-5450, 2331-0904; www.usac.edu.gt/cecon/INDEX%20CECON.htm; Av La Reforma 0-63, Zona 10, Guatemala City) Manages six public biotopos and one *reserva natural*.

Conap (Consejo Nacional de Áreas Protegidas; Map p66-7; ☎ 2238-0000, 2253-5579; conap.online.fr; Edificio IPM, 5a Av 6-06, Zona 1, Guatemala City) The government arm in charge of protected areas.

Fundación Defensores de la Naturaleza (Map p66-7; ☎ 5440-8138, 5445-0332; www.defensores.org.gt; 7a Av 7-09, Zona 13, Guatemala City) NGO that owns and administers several protected areas.

ProPetén (Map p172; ☎ 7926-1370, 7926-1141; www .propeten.org; Calle Central, Flores, Petén) Works in conservation in Parque Nacional Laguna del Tigre.

Proyecto EcoQuetzal (☎ /fax 7952-1047; bidaspeq@ guate.net; 2a Calle 14-36, Zona 1, Cobán, Alta Verapaz) Works in forest conservation and ecotourism.

FOOD & DRINK

Guatemalan food is basic; try to develop a taste for corn *tortillas* before your trip. Maintaining a vegetarian diet is challenging but not impossible. A good source for vegetarian food is Chinese restaurants, present in all the cities and some large towns.

Breakfast is eaten anytime between 6am and 10am, and lunch between noon and 2pm. *La cena* (dinner) is a lighter version of lunch, usually eaten between 7pm and 9pm. In rural areas, sit down no later than 8pm to avoid disappointment.

Mostly you will encounter *bistec* (tough grilled or fried beef), *pollo asado* (grilled chicken), *chuletas de puerco* (pork chops) and lighter fare such as *hamburguesas* (hamburgers) and *salchichas* (sausages similar to hot dogs). Of the simpler food, *frijoles con arroz* (beans and rice) is cheapest and often best. A few Mexican standards such as enchiladas, guacamole and tamales (boiled or steamed cornmeal filled with meat and

wrapped in a banana leaf) are usually available as well. In El Petén you may come across such native meats as *mojarra* (perch), *tepzcuintle* (paca), armadillo, *venado* (deer) and *pavo silvestre* (wild turkey), although conservation-minded travelers will probably want to avoid them

In the tourist towns you can find delicious brewed coffee, but everywhere else it's the weak, sweet instant variety. Sweetened fruit juice mixed with water (ask if it's purified) is popular and refreshing. Soft drinks are available everywhere. Delicious *limonadas* are made with lime juice, water and sugar; *naranjadas* are the same thing made with orange juice. *Jamaica* (hah-*my*-cah) is a refreshing juice made from hibiscus flowers. The three Guatemalan beers are Gallo (the most popular), Moza and Dorado.

Guatemala grows plenty of sugarcane and makes rum – the dark Ron Zacapa Centenario is said to be the best. Ron Botrán Añejo, another dark rum, is also good. Venado is a light, locally produced rum. Then there's Quetzalteca Especial, a white firewater made of sugarcane.

GUATEMALA CITY

eeeww get out!

pop 2 million

Guatemala's capital city, the largest urban agglomeration in Central America, spreads across a flattened mountain range run through by deep ravines. Its huge, chaotic market bursts with dazzling smells, sounds and colors. Rickety buses chug along in clouds of diesel, trolling for ever more passengers, and street urchins eke out a tenuous existence in the city's poverty-stricken outlying areas.

The city's few interesting sights can be seen in a day or two. Many travelers skip 'Guate' altogether, preferring to make Antigua their base. Still, you may need to get acquainted with the capital, as it's a transportation and service hub.

ORIENTATION

Guatemala City, like all Guatemalan towns, is laid out according to a logical grid system. Avenidas run north–south, calles east–west. Streets are usually numbered from north and west (lowest) to south and east (highest). However, Guatemala City is divided

GUATEMALA CITY

0   500 m
0   0.3 mile

Enlargement 1

0   100 m

See Enlargement 1

To Elibra Cruz Roja
(350m), Mapa en
Relieve (1.25km)

To Ethelbut
(100m)

Parque Concordia
(Parque Gomez
Carrillo)

ZONA 1

ZONA 3

Centro
Civico

Cuatro
Grades Norte

Av Elena

Av Elena

Av Centroamérica

Diagonal 1 (Av Bolívar)

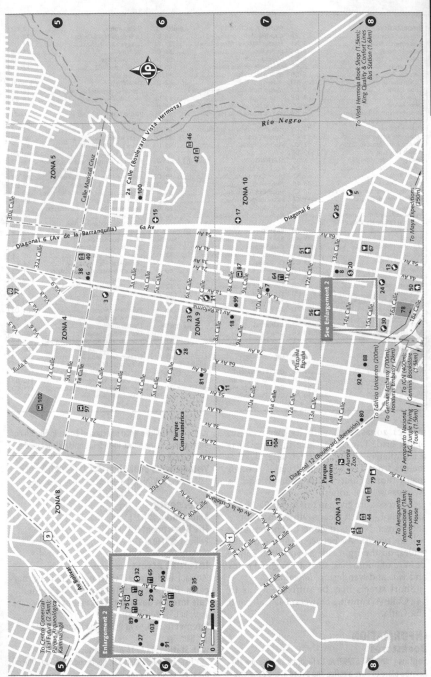

Río Negro

ZONA 5

ZONA 10

ZONA 4

ZONA 9

ZONA 8

ZONA 13

Parque Centroamérica

Parque Aurora

La Aurora Zoo

Plazuela España

To Vista Hermosa Book Shop (1.5km);
King Quality & Confort Lines
Bus Station (1.6km)

To Maya Expeditions (250m)

To Edificio Unicentro (200m)

To Germán Embassy (700m);
Honduras Embassy (2km)

To IGN (400m);
Géminis Bookstore (1.5km)

To Aeropuerto Nacional,
TAG, Jungle Flying
Tours (1.5km)

To Aeropuerto
Internacional (1km);
Aeropuerto Guest
House

To Centro Comercial
Tikal Futura (2.5km);
Parque Arqueológico
Kaminaljuyú

Diagonal 6 (Av de la Barranquilla)

Calle Mariscal Cruz

2a Calle (Boulevard Vista Hermosa)

6a Av

Av la Reforma

Diagonal 6

Diagonal 12 (Boulevard Liberación)

Av Bolívar

Av de la Castellana

Ruta 8

See Enlargement 2

Enlargement 2

0   100 m

into 21 zonas, each with its own version of the grid. Thus, 14a Calle in Zona 10 is a completely different street several kilometers from 14a Calle in Zona 1, though major thoroughfares such as 6a Av and 7a Av cross several zones.

Addresses are given in this form: '9a Av 15-12, Zona 1,' which means '9th Avenue above 15th Street, No 12, in Zone 1.' The building will be on 9th Av between 15th and 16th Calles, on the right side as you walk south. Beware of anomalies, such as diagonal *rutas* and *vías* and wandering *diagonales*.

Short streets may be suffixed 'A,' as in 14a Calle A, running between 14a Calle and 15a Calle.

INFORMATION
Bookstores
Sophos (☎ 2334-67797; Av La Reforma 13-89, Zona 10) Relaxed place to have a coffee and a read in the Zona Viva

(Lively Zone), with a good selection of books in English on Guatemala and the Maya, including Lonely Planet guides, and maps.

Vista Hermosa Book Shop (☎ 2369-1003; 2a Calle 18-50, Zona 15) This has a similar selection to Sophos.

Emergency
Ambulance (☎ 123)
Fire Department (☎ 123)
Police (☎ 110 or 120)

Internet Access
Zona 1 is thronged with inexpensive cybercafés. Elsewhere, rates tend to be higher.
Café Internet Navigator (14a Calle east of 6a Av, Zona 1; per hr US$0.80; 🕐 8am-8pm)
Internet (Local 5, 6a Av 9-27, Zona 1; per hr US$0.65; 🕐 8am-7pm)
Web Station (2a Av 14-63, Zona 10; per hr US$2.60; 🕐 10am-midnight Mon-Sat, noon-midnight Sun) One of the cheapest in the Zona Viva.

Medical Services

Guatemala City has many private hospitals and clinics. Two recommended ones, both with some English-speaking doctors, are **Hospital Herrera Llerandi** (☎ 2334-5959, emergencies 2334-5955; 6a Av 8-71, Zona 10) and **Hospital Centro Médico** (☎ 2332-3555, 2334-2157; 6a Av 3-47, Zona 10).

Public hospitals and clinics provide free consultations but can be very busy; to reduce waiting time, try to be there before 7am. One of the best is **Hospital General San Juan de Dios** (☎ 2253-0443/7; 1a Av at 10a Calle, Zona 1).

Farmacia del Ejecutivo (☎ 2238-1447; 7a Av 15-01, Zona 1; ☯ 24hr) accepts Visa and Master-Card.

Money

Take normal safety precautions when using ATMs here.

American Express (☎ 2331-7422; Centro Comercial Montufar, 12a Calle 0-93, Zona 9; ☯ 8am-5pm Mon-Fri, 8am-noon Sat) In an office of Clark Tours.

Credomatic (☯ 8am-7pm Mon-Fri, 9am-1pm Sat) In Edificio Testa, gives cash advances on Visa and MasterCard; take your passport.

Edificio Testa (cnr 5a Av & 11a Calle, Zona 1) Has Visa, MasterCard and American Express ATMs.

Other Visa ATM locations include the corner of 5a Av and 6a Calle, Zona 1 (opposite Parque Centenario); 2a Av south of 13a Calle, Zona 10; Edificio Unicentro, 18a Calle 5-56, Zona 10; and Guatemala City Marriott Hotel, at 7a Av 15-45, Zona 9.

You can change US dollars cash at:

Banco Agromercantil (8a Calle, Zona 1; ☯ 9am-7pm Mon-Fri, 9am-1pm Sat) Facing Parque Centenario.

Banco Uno (☎ 2366-2191; Edificio Unicentro, 18a Calle 5-56, Zona 10) Changes cash euros into quetzals.

Lloyds TSB (14a Calle 3-51, Zona 10) Changes euro traveler's checks.

At the airport, **Banquetzal** (☯ 6am-9pm), in the arrivals hall, changes US cash and American Express traveler's checks into quetzals and has a MasterCard and American Express ATM. There's a Visa ATM by the exit doors. **Banquetzal** (☯ 6am-8pm Mon-Fri, 6am-6pm Sat & Sun) on the departures level also has currency exchange services and a MasterCard ATM.

Post

Main Post Office (7a Av 11-67, Zona 1; ☯ 8:30am-5pm Mon-Fri, 8:30am-1pm Sat) In the huge pink Palacio de Correos. There's a small post office at the airport.

Tourist Information

Main Tourist Office (☎ 2331-1333, 2331-1347; informacion@inguat.gob.gt; 7a Av 1-17, Zona 4; ☯ 8am-4pm Mon-Fri) In the lobby of the Inguat (Guatemalan Tourism Institute) headquarters in the Centro Cívico. The office has limited hand-out material but staff are extremely helpful. Inguat has further tourist offices at:

Aeropuerto Internacional La Aurora (☎ 2331-4256; ☯ 6am-9pm) In the arrivals hall.

Palacio Nacional de la Cultura (☎ 2253-0748; 6a Calle, Zona 1; ☯ 9-11:45am & 2-4:45pm Mon-Fri, 9-10:45am & 2-3:45pm Sat & Sun) Facing Parque Central.

DANGERS & ANNOYANCES

Street crime, including armed robbery, has increased in recent years. Use normal urban precautions: don't walk down the street with your wallet bulging out of your back pocket and avoid walking downtown alone late at night. Work out your route before you start so you're not standing on corners looking lost or peering at a map. It's safe to walk downtown in the early evening, as long as you stick to streets with plenty of lighting and people. Stay alert and leave your valuables in your hotel. Incidents of robbery increase around the 15th and at the end of each month, when workers get paid.

The area around 18a Calle in Zona 1 has many bus stations and even more lowlife and hustlers, the worst blackspots being the intersections with 4a, 6a and 9a Avs. This part of town (also a red-light district) is notoriously dangerous at night; if you are arriving by bus at night or must go to 18a Calle at night, take a taxi.

The more affluent sections of the city – Zona 9 and Zona 10, for example – are much safer. The Zona Viva in Zona 10 has police patrols at night. But even here, going in pairs is better than alone.

All buses are the turf of adroit pickpockets. Some armed robberies happen on buses, too, though mainly in outlying zones.

Never try to resist if you are confronted by a robber.

SIGHTS
Zona 1
PARQUE CENTRAL (PLAZA MAYOR)

Most of the city's notable sights are in Zona 1 near the Plaza Mayor, which is bounded by 6a and 8a Calles and 6a and 7a Avs.

Every town in the New World had a plaza for military exercises, ceremonies and reviews. On the plaza's north side would be the *palacio de gobierno,* or colonial government headquarters. On another side, preferably east, was a church (or cathedral). The other sides of the square could hold additional civic buildings or imposing mansions. Plaza Mayor is a good example of this classic town plan.

Visit on Sunday when locals stroll, play in the fountains, gossip, neck and groove to salsa music. Otherwise, try for lunchtime or late afternoon.

PALACIO NACIONAL

On Plaza Mayor's north side is the magnificent **Palacio Nacional de la Cultura** (☎ 2253-0748; 6a Calle; ☽ 9-11:45am & 2-4:45pm Mon-Fri, 9-10:45am & 2-3:45pm Sat & Sun), built at enormous cost by dictator/president Jorge Ubico (1931–44). It is the third palace to stand here, and is currently being restored to house a Guatemalan-history museum.

Free tours take you through a labyrinth of gleaming brass, polished wood, carved stone and frescoed arches (painted by Alberto Gálvez Suárez). Notable features include the 2000kg gold, the bronze and Bohemian-crystal chandelier in the reception salon and two Moorish-style courtyards.

MERCADO CENTRAL

Until it was destroyed by the earthquake of 1976, the **central market** (9a Av btwn 6a & 8a Calles; ☽ 7am-6pm Mon-Sat, 6am-noon Sun) was where locals bought food and other necessities. Reconstructed in the late 1970s, the new market specializes in touristy items and handicrafts, but there are better places to buy crafts. Vegetables, daily needs and super cheap *comedores* (eateries) are on the lowest level.

MUSEO NACIONAL DE HISTORIA

The **National History Museum** (☎ 2253-6149; 9a Calle 9-70; admission US$1.30; ☽ 8:30am-4pm Mon-Fri) is a jumble of historical relics with an emphasis on photography and portraits.

Zona 2

Zona 2 is north of Zona 1. Though mostly a middle-class residential district, its northern end holds the large **Parque Minerva**, which is surrounded by golf courses, sports grounds and the Universidad Mariano Gálvez.

Minerva – the goddess of wisdom, technical skill and invention – was a favorite of President Manuel Estrada Cabrera. Her park is a placid place, good for walking among the eucalyptus trees and sipping a cool drink. Watch out for pickpockets and purse snatchers.

The prime sight here is the **Mapa en Relieve** (Relief Map; admission US$2; ☽ 9am-5pm), a huge relief map of Guatemala. Constructed in 1904 under the direction of Francisco Vela, the map shows the country at a scale of 1:10,000, but the height of the mountainous terrain has been exaggerated to 1:2000 for dramatic effect. The Mapa en Relieve and Parque Minerva are 2km north of Plaza Mayor along 6a Av, but that street is one-way heading south. To get there take bus No V-21 northbound on 7a Av just north or south of the Parque Central.

Civic Center Area

The Centro Cívico complex, constructed during the 1950s and '60s, lies around the junction of Zonas 1, 4 and 5. Here you'll find the **Palacio de Justicia** (Palace of Justice), city hall, the Inguat headquarters and the Banco del Quetzal building, which bears high-relief murals by Dagoberto Vásquez depicting the history of his homeland. City hall holds a huge mosaic by Carlos Mérida.

Across the street from the Centro Cívico on a hilltop is **Centro Cultural Miguel Ángel Asturias** (p74), which holds the national theater, a chamber theater, an open-air theater and a small museum of old armaments.

Zona 10

East of Av La Reforma, the posh Zona 10 holds two of the city's most important museums, both in large new buildings at the Universidad Francisco Marroquín.

Museo Ixchel del Traje Indígena (☎ 2331-3634/8; 6a Calle Final; admission US$2.50; ☽ 9am-5pm Mon-Fri, 9am-1pm Sat) is named for Ixchel, wife of Maya sky god Itzamná and goddess of the moon, women, reproduction and textiles, among other things. Photographs and exhibits of indigenous costumes, textiles and other crafts show the incredible richness of traditional highland art.

Behind the museum is **Museo Popol Vuh** (☎ 2361-2301; www.popolvuh.ufm.edu; 6a Calle Final; adult/student with ID/child US$2.50/1/0.75; ☽ 9am-5pm Mon-Fri, 9am-1pm Sat), where well-chosen polychrome pottery, figurines, incense burners, burial urns, carved masks and traditional

Hotel los Volcanes
16 street 8-00 Zones 13 aurora 1
info @ hostallosvolcanes.com

textiles fill several exhibit rooms. Other rooms hold colonial paintings and wood and silver objects. A faithful copy of the Dresden Codex, one of the precious 'painted books' of the Maya, is among the most interesting pieces. This is an important collection, especially given its precolonial emphasis.

The Universidad de San Carlos has a large, lush **Jardín Botánico** (Botanical Garden; Calle Mariscal Cruz 1-56; admission US$1.30; ⏰ 8am-3:30pm Mon-Fri) on the northern edge of Zona 10. The admission includes the university's **Museo de Historia Natural** (Natural History Museum) at the site.

Zona 13

The major attraction in the city's southern reaches is **Parque Aurora**, with its zoo, children's playground, fairgrounds and several museums. The Moorish-looking **Museo Nacional de Arqueología y Etnología** (☎ 5472-0489; Sala 5, Finca La Aurora; admission US$4; ⏰ 9am-4pm Tue-Fri, 9am-noon & 1:30-4pm Sat & Sun) has a collection of Mayan artifacts from all over Guatemala, including stone carvings, jade, ceramics, statues, stelae and a tomb. Exhibits in the ethnology section highlight the various indigenous peoples and languages in Guatemala, with emphasis on traditional costumes, dances and implements of daily life.

Facing it is **Museo Nacional de Arte Moderno** (☎ 5472-0467; Sala 6, Finca La Aurora; admission US$1.30; ⏰ 9am-4pm Tue-Fri, 9am-noon & 2-4pm Sat & Sun), which holds a collection of 20th-century Guatemalan art.

Several hundred meters to the east of these museums is the city's official handicrafts market, the **Mercado de Artesanías** – see Shopping, p74 for details.

La Aurora Zoo (☎ 5472-0894; adult/child US$1.30/0.65; ⏰ 9am-5pm Tue-Sun) is not badly kept, and the lovely, parklike grounds alone are worth the admission fee.

Zona 7

Parque Arqueológico Kaminaljuyú (☎ 2253-1570; 11a Calle just west of 23a Av, Zona 7; admission US$3.25; ⏰ 9am-4pm), with remnants of one of the first important cities in the Maya region, is some 4km west of the city center. At its peak from about 400 BC to AD 100, ancient Kaminaljuyú had thousands of inhabitants and scores of temples built on earth mounds, and probably dominated much of highland Guatemala. Large-scale carvings found here

---

GAY & LESBIAN GUATEMALA CITY

Don't get too excited about this heading – while there are a couple of places worthy of mention for men, there is nothing much for women.

Pandora's Box (☎ 2332-2823; Ruta 3 No 3-08, Zona 4; ⏰ 9pm-1am Fri & Sat, 8am-1pm Sun) This place has been hosting Guatemala's gay crowd since the '70s. Modernized a few years ago, it has two dance floors, a rooftop patio and a relaxed atmosphere with a mainly under-30 crowd. There's no entry charge. Zona 4 isn't the best section of the city, so don't go a-wandering unaccompanied or late at night.

Ephebus (☎ 2253-4119; 4a Calle 5-30, Zona 1; ⏰ 9pm-3am Thu-Sat) This well-established gay disco-bar is in a former private house near the city center, often with strippers.

El Encuentro (☎ 2230-4459; Local 229, Centro Capitol, 6a Av 12-51, Zona 1; ⏰ 5pm-midnight Mon-Sat) This quiet bar in the back of a noisy downtown mall is another gay meeting place.

---

were the forerunners of Classic Maya carving, and Kaminaljuyú had a literate elite before anywhere else in the Maya world. The city fell into ruin before being reoccupied around AD 400 by invaders from Teotihuacán in central Mexico, who rebuilt it in Teotihuacán's '*talud-tablero*' style, with buildings stepped in alternating *tablero* (vertical) and *talud* (sloping) sections. Unfortunately most of Kaminaljuyú has been covered by urban sprawl: the *parque arqueológico* is but a small portion of the ancient city and even here the remnants consist chiefly of grassy mounds. The best carvings from the site are in the Museo Nacional de Arqueología y Etnología (left).

You can get there by bus No 35 from 4a Av, Zona 1, but check that the bus is going to the '*ruinas de Kaminaljuyú*' ('kah-mih-nahl-huh-*yuh*') – not all do. A taxi from Zona 1 costs around US$3.50.

SLEEPING
Budget

Budget travelers tend to head straight for Zona 1. Prices in Guate are higher than in the rest of the country, but there are a few bargains. Keep street noise in mind as you look for a room.

Hotel Spring (☎ 2230-2858; hotelspring@hotmail .com; 8a Av 12-65; s/d/tr with shared bathroom US$12/17/ 22, with private bathroom US$17/22/26; **P** **▣**) The Spring combines sunny patios and 43 tall, spacious, clean rooms with fair prices, although the rooms with shared bathroom are often full. All rooms have cable TV. It's worth booking ahead. A cafeteria serves meals from 6:30am to 1:30pm; Internet access is available until 3pm.

Hotel Fenix (☎ 2251-6625; 7a Av 15-81; s or d US$6, with private bathroom & TV US$10) This is one of the best budget bets in town, with a friendly atmosphere, clean rooms and good security, despite the somewhat dodgy locale. The rooms upstairs are quieter. The hotel has a café and spacious hangout areas.

Pensión Meza (☎ 2232-3177; 10a Calle 10-17; dm US$4, s/d/q US$6/7/4, d with bathroom US$12) A savvy traveler's gathering ground, it boasts a book exchange, a ping pong table and a big notice board. Rooms are dilapidated but come with mostly firm beds.

Mid-Range

Hotel Pan American (☎ 2232-6807/8/9; www.hotel panamerican.com; 9a Calle 5-63, Zona 1; s/d/tr/q US$54/60/ 65/70; **P** **▣**) Guatemala City's luxury hotel before WWII, the Pan American is one of the few hotels in the city with any air of history. In the fine, tall Art Deco lobby, a tinkling fountain and colorful weavings provide colonial and Mayan touches. The 52 rooms follow the same themes and sport attractively tiled floors, cable TV, telephone, private bathroom (with tub) and fan. Avoid rooms facing the noisy street.

Hotel Casa Santa Clara (☎ 2339-1811; www.hotel casasantaclara.com; 12a Calle 4-51, Zona 10; s/d/tr US$75/ 80/90; **P** **▣**) This charming 14-room hotel offers many of the same comforts as the Zona Viva giants a block or two or away, but with much more personalized attention and intimate atmosphere. Reading lamps, cable TV, phone, fan, wooden furnishings and attractive paintings and prints of Guatemalan life give the amply sized rooms comfort and character, and there's a garden restaurant/ café out front. Book ahead.

Hotel Royal Palace (☎ 2232-5125, 2220-8970; www .hotelroyalpalace.com; 6a Av 12-66, Zona 1; s & d US$55; **P** **▨**) Right at the heart of bustling 6a Av, this is an old colonial hotel that's had a major facelift. Rooms are large, sparkling clean and wheelchair accessible, with good wooden

furniture and flowery bedspreads. They have fans and white-tile floors, except on the 4th floor, which is carpeted, air-conditioned and costs US$67. Exterior rooms mostly have small balconies, but interior ones avoid street noise. Facilities include a restaurant, bar, gym, sauna and free airport transfers.

Eco Hotel los Próceres (☎ 2337-3250; ecopro ceres@hotmail.com; 18a Calle 3-03, Zona 10; s/d/tr US$35/ 45/59; **P** **▨**) The 20 brightly decorated, air-conditioned rooms, each with attractive tiled bathroom, phone, clock, cable TV and wooden furniture, are very good value for the location on the edge of the Zona Viva. Rates include a light breakfast.

Aeropuerto Guest House (☎ 2332-3086; www .hotelaeropuerto.centroamerica.com; 15a Calle A 7-32; s/d US$25/30, with private bathroom US$30/35; **P** **▣**) Just 350m from the airport door, this guesthouse has nine comfy rooms and a friendly atmosphere. English is spoken, and it offers luggage storage and cable TV in the living room.

Top End

Radisson Hotel & Suites (☎ 2332-9797, US ☎ +1-800-333-3333; www.radissonguatemala.com; 1a Av 12-46, Zona 10; ste US$117; **P** **▨** **▣** **▧**) The Radisson boasts a floor for women (with beauty salon and pink towels!) and one for families. The 99 suites vary widely in size and facilities but not in price. All have kitchen, safe, minibar and big windows with views that get better the higher you go. Free Internet, coffee and snacks are available on all floors, and the rooms have US$5-a-day data ports. Other facilities include restaurant, bar, business center, gym and sauna.

EATING

Cheap eats are easily found, particularly in Zona 1, as fast-food and snack shops abound. Fine dining focuses on Zona 10.

Zona 1

Café Sebastián (☎ 2232-1646; 5a Calle 6-81; set lunch US$2; ☯ lunch Mon-Fri) An inexpensive little spot with just five tables, in the street behind the Palacio Nacional de la Cultura, Café Sebastián makes a great lunchtime retreat from the noise and heat of the city. Cool jazz plays and the jolly color scheme makes you feel good. The set lunch (eg soup followed by beef stroganoff with rice, melon, guacamole and *tortillas*) is good value.

Restaurante Altuna (☎ 2232-0669; 5a Av 12-31; mains US$9-13; 🕑 lunch Tue-Sun, dinner Tue-Sat) This large, classy restaurant has the atmosphere of a private club, with tables in several rooms off a skylit patio. Specialties are seafood and Spanish dishes; service is both professional and welcoming.

Café-Restaurante Hamburgo (☎ 2238-4029; 15a Calle 5-34; set lunch or dinner US$2.25-3.25; 🕑 breakfast, lunch & dinner) This bustling spot facing the south side of Parque Concordia serves good Guatemalan food, with chefs at work along one side and orange-aproned waitresses scurrying about. At weekends a marimba adds atmosphere.

Bar-Restaurante Europa (☎ 2253-4929; Local 201, Edificio Testa, 11a Calle 5-16; mains US$2.50-5; 🕑 breakfast, lunch & dinner Mon-Sat) The Europa is a comfortable, relaxed, 11-table restaurant, bar and gathering place for locals and foreigners alike (the bar stays open until midnight). It has good-value food – try chicken cordon bleu for dinner, or eggs, hash browns, bacon and toast for breakfast.

Hotel Pan American (☎ 2232-6807; 9a Calle 5-63; breakfast US$6-10, lunch US$8-12; 🕑 breakfast, lunch & dinner) The restaurant at this venerable hotel (opposite) is high on ambiance, with highly experienced waitstaff sporting traditional Mayan regalia. The food (Guatemalan, Italian and North American) is fine, if slightly overpriced.

Zona 4
Cuatro Grados Norte (Vía 5 btwn Rutas 1 & 3) This is the name for a two-block pedestrianized strip of restaurants and cafés with sidewalk tables and relaxed café society, inaugurated in 2002 and the only place of its kind in the city. It's conveniently close to the main Inguat tourist office and gets lively in the evening. You can choose from a dozen or so establishments, some of which double as galleries, bookstores or music venues.

Del Paseo (☎ 2385-9047; Vía 5 1-81, Cuatro Grados Nte; dishes US$5-8.50) This spacious, artsy, Mediterranean-style bistro is one of Cuatro Grados Norte's most popular spots. Relaxed jazz plays in the background unless there's a live band (try your luck on Thursday from 9pm). You might select roast chicken breast with tropical fruits and grated coconut – or how about spinach-and-ricotta filo pastry parcels? Wine goes for US$3 a glass.

Zona 10
Hacienda Real (☎ 2333-5408; 13a Calle 1-10; steaks US$9.75-18; 🕑 lunch & dinner) For carnivores, nowhere beats the Hacienda Real, where the service is good but the atmosphere relaxed as you dine by candlelight around the fountain in the patio or under a wooden roof. Guatemalan steaks cost US$9.75 to US$12.25, imported ones are dearer. The entrance is on 1a Av.

Tamarindos (☎ 2360-2815; 11a Calle 2-19A; meals around US$15-20 incl drinks; 🕑 lunch Mon-Fri, dinner Mon-Sat) A chic and delicious Thai and Italian restaurant with a Guatemalan twist. The four-cheese gnocchi is irresistible, the vegetarian pad Thai blends a thousand flavors. The stylish decor recalls New York – but the prices are Guatemalan.

San Martín & Company (13a Calle 1-62; items US$2-4; 🕑 breakfast, lunch & dinner Mon-Sat) Cool and clean, with ceiling fans inside and a small terrace outside, this Zona Viva café and bakery is great at any time of day. For breakfast try a scrumptious omelet and croissant (the former arrives inside the latter). Later there are tempting and original sandwiches, soups and salads. The entrance is on 2a Av.

Tre Fratelli (☎ 2366-2678; 2a Av 13-25; pasta & pizza US$5-10; 🕑 lunch & dinner) For good Italian food and a fun atmosphere, don't miss this large Zona Viva restaurant. It's immensely popular with all comers, thanks to an unmatchable recipe of good food in ample portions, thumping background music, sparkling lights and sports on TV.

Ta'Contento (cnr 14a Calle & 2a Av; around US$1 per taco) One of the few places you can eat for under US$5 in the Zona Viva, bright Ta'Contento serves up a big variety of tacos with lots of Mexican sauces.

DRINKING
Zona 1
Staggering from bar to bar along the darkened streets of Zona 1 is not recommended, but fortunately there's a clutch of good drinking places all within half a block of each other just south of the Parque Central.

Las Cien Puertas (Pasaje Aycinena 8-44, 9a Calle 6-45) This super-hip (but not studiously so) little watering hole is a gathering place for all manner of local creative types – and a few travelers. Tasty snacks such as tacos and *quesadillas* (pastry filled with, most commonly, potato or cheese and beans) are served.

Cafe Kumbala (Pasaje Aycinena 8-51) Across the arcade, this is a neater bar with a big screen showing mellow music videos and, sometimes, movies.

El Portal (Portal del Comercio, 6a Av; ☾ 10am-10pm Mon-Sat) This atmospheric old drinking den serves fine draft beer (around US$2 a mug) and free tapas. Ché Guevara was once a patron. Sit at the long wooden bar or one of the wooden tables. To find it, enter the Portal del Comercio arcade from 6a Av, a few steps south of the Parque Central.

Zona 10
El Establo (14a Calle 5-08) This mellow watering hole attracts both foreigners and locals with its pub-style layout, three-sided, brass-topped bar, good pub food and enormous range of music spun by the German owners. Not cheap, though, at US$3 a Gallo.

ENTERTAINMENT
Wining and dining the night away in the Zona Viva is what many visitors do. Otherwise, consider taking in a movie at one of the multiscreen cinema complexes such as **Cines Tikal Futura** (Centro Comercial Tikal Futura, Calz Roosevelt 22-43, Zona 11) or **Cines Próceres** (Centro Comercial Los Próceres, 16a Calle, Zona 10). Tickets cost between US$2 and US$4. Or check out the cultural events at **Centro Cultural Miguel Ángel Asturias** (☎ 2232-4042/3/4/5; 24a Calle 3-81, Zona 1). You'll find movie (and other) listings in *Prensa Libre* newspaper. The Ministerio de Cultura y Deportes publishes a monthly what's-on bulletin, available free at the Palacio Nacional de la Cultura (p70).

Music
La Bodeguita del Centro (☎ 2230-2976; 12a Calle 3-55, Zona 1) There's a hopping, creative local scene in Guatemala City, and this large, bohemian hangout is one of the best places to connect with it. Posters featuring the likes of Ché, Marley, Lennon, Victor Jara, Van Gogh and Pablo Neruda cover the walls from floor to ceiling. There's live music of some kind almost every night from Tuesday to Saturday, usually starting at 9pm, plus occasional poetry readings, films or forums. Food and drinks are served.

Blue Town Cafe Bar (11a Calle 4-51, Zona 1) Nearby is this youthful spot with live bands.

TrovaJazz (Vía 6 No 3-55, Zona 4) Jazz and folk fans should look into what's happening here.

La Leyenda (12a Calle 4-80; ☾ 4pm-midnight Mon-Thu, 4pm-3am Fri & Sat) This friendly neighborhood bar is a good place for a few quiet drinks during the week. Young folk singers play acoustically on the small stage on weekends.

Nightclubs
Zona 10 has a bunch of clubs attracting 20-something local crowds along 13a Calle and adjacent streets such as 1a Av. For salsa and merengue, head for **Mr Jerry** (☎ 2368-0101; 13a Calle 1-26, Zona 10).

SHOPPING
If you're firmly committed to Zona 1, check out the **Mercado Central** (p70). Otherwise, the sleepy, official **Mercado de Artesanías** (☎ 5472-0208; cnr 5a Calle & 11a Av, Zona 13; ☾ 9:30am-6pm), just off the access road to the airport near the museums and zoo, sells similar goods in less crowded conditions.

For fashion boutiques, electronic goods and other First-World paraphernalia, head for the large shopping malls such as **Centro Comercial Los Próceres** (16a Calle, Zona 10) or **Centro Comercial Tikal Futura** (Calz Roosevelt 22-43, Zona 11). For a more everyday Guatemalan experience, take a walk along 6a Av between 8a and 16a Calles in Zona 1. This street is always choked with street stalls noisily hawking everything from cheap, copied CDs to shoes, underwear and overalls.

GETTING THERE & AWAY
Air
Guatemala City's **Aeropuerto La Aurora** (☎ 2334-7680/9, 2331-7241/3) is the country's major airport. All international flights land and take off here. At the time of writing, the only scheduled domestic flights were between Guatemala City and Flores – a route operated daily by five airlines.

Tickets to Flores cost around US$90/125 one-way/round-trip with Grupo TACA (one hour, four flights daily), US$90/112 with Tikal Airlines (45 minutes, one flight daily), and around US$70/100 with Racsa, Jungle Flying Tours, TAG and Inter. Some travel agents, especially in Antigua, offer large discounts from these prices.

Note that Grupo TACA and Tikal Airlines go from the Aeropuerto Internacional (the main terminal on the west side of the La Aurora runways, entered from 11a Av), while other domestic carriers use the Aeropuerto Nacional (the east side of the aerodrome, entered from Av Hincapié).

Bus

Buses from Guatemala City run all over Guatemala and into Mexico, Belize, Honduras, El Salvador and beyond. Most bus companies have their own terminals, many of which are in Zona 1. The Terminal de Autobuses, in Zona 4, is used only by some 2nd-class buses. Here are details of services to domestic and international destinations:

Antigua (US$0.65, 1¼hr, 45km, departs every few minutes, 5am-9pm) Departs from the lot at 18a Calle and 4a Av, Zona 1. See also p76.

Belize City, Belize Take a bus to Flores/Santa Elena and an onward bus from there.

Biotopo del Quetzal (US$4, 3½hr, 156km); Escobar y Monja Blanca (☎ 2238-1409; 8a Av 15-16, Zona 1; departs hourly, 4am-5pm, via El Rancho and Purulhá)

Chetumal, Mexico Take a bus to Flores/Santa Elena, where daily buses depart for Chetumal; see p175.

Chichicastenango (US$1.55, 3hr, 145km, departs every 15-20min, 5am-5pm) Departs from the Terminal de Autobuses. Some buses also depart from the corner of 20a Calle and Av Bolívar, Zona 1.

Chiquimula (US$2.60, 3hr, 170km); Rutas Orientales (☎ 2253-7282; 19 Calle 8-18, Zona 1; departs every 30min, 4:30am-6pm); Transportes Guerra (☎ 2238-2917; 19a Calle 8-39, Zona 1; departs every 30min, 7am-6pm)

Ciudad Pedro de Alvarado/La Hachadura, El Salvador border Take a bus to Taxisco; some of these continue to the border; otherwise change at Taxisco. Buses to Taxisco (US$2, 2hr) leave the Terminal de Autobuses every half an hour, 5am to 4pm. Buses leave Taxisco for the border about every 15min until about 5pm.

Ciudad Tecún Umán/Ciudad Hidalgo, Mexican border (US$5.25, 6hr, 250km); Fortaleza del Sur (☎ 2230-3390; 19a Calle 8-70, Zona 1; departs 20 times daily, 12:15am-6:30pm)

Cobán (US$4.25, 4½hr, 213km); Escobar y Monja Blanca (☎ 2238-1409; 8a Av 15-16, Zona 1; departs hourly, 4am-5pm) Buses stop at El Rancho and the Biotopo del Quetzal.

Copán, Honduras (US$35, 5hr, 238km); Hedman Alas (☎ 2362-5072/3/4; 2a Av 8-73, Zona 10; departs daily, 5am) First-class buses, which continue to San Pedro Sula and La Ceiba. It's cheaper, and slower, to take a bus to Chiquimula, then another to the border at El Florido, then another on to Copán.

El Carmen/Talismán, Mexican border (US$5.75, 7hr, 290km); Fortaleza del Sur (☎ 2230-3390; 19a Calle 8-70, Zona 1; departs 20 times daily, 12:15am-6:30pm)

Escuintla (US$1.25, 1hr, 57km) Various companies run about every 15min, 5am-6pm, from the Terminal de Autobuses.

Esquipulas (US$4, 4½hr, 222km); Rutas Orientales (☎ 2253-7282; 19 Calle 8-18, Zona 1; departs every 30min, 4:30am-6pm)

Flores/Santa Elena (8-10hr, 500km); Fuente del Norte (☎ 2251-3817; 17a Calle 8-46, Zona 1; departs 18 times daily, US$9-17); Línea Dorada (☎ 2232-5506, 5201-2710; 16a Calle 10-03, Zona 1; US$12-23, departs at 10am, 9pm, 10pm & 10:30pm)

Huehuetenango (5hr, 266km); Los Halcones (☎ 2238-1929; 7a Av 15-27, Zona 1; US$4, departs at 7am, 2pm & 5pm); Transportes Velásquez (☎ 2221-1084; 20a Calle 1-37, Zona 1; US$2.60) All go by the Interamericana.

La Democracia (US$1.50, 2hr, 92km); Chatía Gomerana (every 30min, 6am-4:30pm) Stops at Escuintla. Departs from the Terminal de Autobuses.

La Mesilla/Ciudad Cuauhtémoc, Mexican border (US$5.25, 8hr, 345km); Transportes Velásquez (☎ 2221-1084; 20a Calle 1-37, Zona 1; every 2hr, 5:30am-1:30pm) From Ciudad Cuauhtémoc there are fairly frequent buses and vans on to Comitán and San Cristóbal de Las Casas.

Lívingston See Puerto Barrios and Río Dulce; from either place, you can reach Lívingston by boat (p165).

Melchor de Mencos, Belize border (US$10.50, 11hr, 600km); Fuente del Norte (☎ 2251-3817; 17a Calle 8-46, Zona 1; departs 4 times daily) There's a special Maya de Oro service, US$17, at 10:30pm every two days.

Monterrico Take a bus to Taxisco, change there for a bus to La Avellana, and from La Avellana take a boat (p135).

Nebaj Take a bus to Santa Cruz del Quiché, and another from there.

Panajachel (US$2.10, 3½hr, 150km); Transportes Rébuli (☎ 2230-2748; 21a Calle 1-34, Zona 1; departs hourly, 7am-4pm) There's a Pullman service, US$3.25, at 9:30am.

Poptún (US$7-10.50, 6-7hr, 387km) Take a Fuente del Norte bus headed to Flores.

Puerto Barrios (US$5.25, 5hr, 295km); Litegua (☎ 2232-7578; 15a Calle 10-40, Zona 1; departs 16 times daily 5am-5pm)

Puerto San José (US$2, 2½hr, 90km) Via Escuintla. Various companies run about every 15min, 5am-6pm, from the Terminal de Autobuses.

Quetzaltenango (US$4, 4hr, 205km); Transportes Álamo (☎ 2251-4838; 21a Calle 0-14, Zona 1; departs 6 times daily, 8am-5:30pm); Líneas América (☎ 2232-1432; 2a Av 18-47, Zona 1; departs 7 times daily, 5am-7:30pm); Transportes Galgos (☎ 2253-4868; 7a Av 19-44, Zona 1; departs 7 times daily, 5:30am-7pm); Transportes Marquensita (☎ 2230-0067; 1a Av 21-31, Zona 1; departs 8 times daily, 6:30am-5pm) All these are Pullman services.

Quiriguá Take a Puerto Barrios bus. (For details on getting from the highway to the Quiriguá ruins, see p155.)

Retalhuleu (US$4, 3hr, 196km); Fortaleza del Sur (☎ 2230-3390; 19 Calle 8-70, Zona 1; departs 20 times daily, 12:15am-6:30pm)

Río Dulce (US$5.25, 6hr, 280km); Litegua (☎ 2232-7578, 15a Calle 10-40, Zona 1; departs 6am, 9am, 11:30am & 1pm) Flores-bound buses stop at Río Dulce too.

Salamá (US$2-2.50, 3hr, 150km); Transportes Dulce María (☎ 2253-4318; 17a Calle 11-32, Zona 1; departs every 30min, 5am-5pm)

San Salvador, El Salvador (5-6hr, 240km); Melva Internacional (☎ 2331-0874; 3a Av 1-38, Zona 9; via the border at Valle Nuevo/Las Chinamas; US$8, departs hourly, 5am-4pm; and *especiales*, US$10, at 6:45am, 9am and 3pm); Tica Bus (☎ 2331-4279, 2361-1773; 11a Calle 2-74, Zona 9; US$9.50, departs at 1pm); King Quality & Confort Lines (☎ 2369-0404/56; 18a Av 1-96, Zona 15; US$19.50, luxury bus departs 6:30am, 8am, 2pm and 3:30pm); Pullmantur (☎ 2367-4746; Holiday Inn, 1a Av 13-22, Zona 10; US$28/45 *ejecutiva/primera clase*, luxury bus departs at 7am, 8:30am Sunday, & 3pm)

Santa Cruz del Quiché (US$2.10, 3½hr, 163km, departs every 15-20min, 5am-5pm) Departs from the Terminal de Autobuses. Some buses also depart from the corner of 20a Calle and Av Bolívar, Zona 1.

Santa Elena See Flores/Santa Elena.

Santa Lucía Cotzumalguapa Take a bus to Escuintla and another from there.

Santiago Atitlán (US$2.60, 4hr, 165km) Buses from the Atitlán and Esmeralda companies depart hourly 4am-2pm from the corner of 20a Calle and 8a Av, Zona 1.

Sayaxché Fuente del Norte (☎ 2251-3817; 17a Calle 8-46, Zona 1) Via Río Dulce and Flores (departs at 4pm, US$10.50, and 7pm, US$13, 11hr, 560km) Via Cobán (US$10.50, 10hr, 420km, departs 5:30pm)

Tapachula, Mexico (6-7hr, 290km); Transportes Galgos (☎ 2253-4868, 2232-3661; 7a Av 19-44, Zona 1; US$21.50, departs 7:30am & 2pm); Línea Dorada (☎ 2232-5506; 16a Calle 10-03, Zona 1; US$18, departs 8am); Tica Bus (☎ 2331-4279; 11a Calle 2-74, Zona 9; US$17.50, departs noon)

Taxisco (US$2, 2hr, every 30min 5am-4pm) Departs from Terminal de Autobuses.

Tecpán (US$1, 2hr, 92km); Veloz Poaquileña (cnr 20a Calle & Av Bolívar, Zona 1; departs every 30min, 5:30am-7pm)

Tegucigalpa, Honduras (US$52, 12hr, 700km); Hedman Alas (☎ 2362-5072/3/4; 2a Av 8-73, Zona 10; departs 5am)

Tikal Take a bus to Flores/Santa Elena, and onward transport from there.

Shuttle Minibus

Shuttle services from Guatemala City to popular destinations, such as Panajachel and Chichicastenango (both around US$20), are offered by travel agencies in Antigua, including **Sin Fronteras** (☎ 7832-1017; www.sinfront .com; 5a Av Nte 15A, Antigua). See p81 for more details.

GETTING AROUND
To/From the Airport

Aeropuerto La Aurora is in Zona 13, in the southern part of the city, 10 to 15 minutes from Zona 1 by taxi, half an hour by bus.

Taxis wait outside the airport's arrivals exit. Official fares are posted on signs (US$6 to US$7 to Zona 9 or 10, US$8 to Zona 1, US$25 to Antigua) but in reality you may have to pay a bit more. Be sure to establish the destination and price before getting in. Prices for taxis to the airport, hailed on the street, are likely to be lower – around US$6 from Zona 1.

For the city bus, cross the road outside the arrivals exit and climb the steps. At the top, with your back to the terminal building, walk to the left down the approach road (about 100m), then turn right to the bus stop. Buses No 83 'Terminal' and No 83 'Bolívar' go to the Parque Central in Zona 1, passing through Zonas 9 and 4 en route; you can get off at any corner along the way. No 83 'Terminal' goes up 7a Av through Zonas 9, 4 and 1; No 83 'Bolívar' goes via Av Bolívar and then 5a Av. Both run about every 15 minutes, 6am to 9pm, and cost US$0.15. Going from the city center to the airport, No 83 'Aeropuerto' goes south through Zona 1 on 10a Av, south through Zonas 4 and 9 on 6a Av, passes by the west end of La Aurora Zoo and the Zona 13 museums, and stops outside the international terminal. It then continues southward passing close to all the Zona 13 guesthouses.

Door-to-door shuttle minibuses run from the airport to any address in Antigua (usually US$10 per person, one hour). Look for signs in the airport exit hall or people holding up 'Antigua Shuttle' signs. The first shuttle leaves for Antigua about 7am and the last around 8pm or 9pm.

Bus

If you spend any time in Guatemala City, especially Zona 1, its buses will become a major feature of your existence as they roar along, belching great clouds of black smoke. Still, buses are cheap (US$0.15 per ride; pay the driver as you get on), frequent and, though often very crowded, useful.

To get from Zona 1 to Zona 10, take bus No 82 or 101 southbound on 10a Av between 8a and 13a Calles. These buses swing west to travel south down 6a Av for 1km or so before swinging southeast along Ruta 6 (Zona 4), then south along Av La Reforma. For the main Inguat tourist office, get off on 6a Av at 22a Calle (Zona 1) and walk east along 22a Calle, then south down the far (east) side of 7a Av.

Traveling north to Zona 1, bus Nos 82 and 101 go along Av La Reforma then 7a Av, Zona 4 (passing right by Inguat) and 9a Av, Zona 1.

Going by city bus, the best way to Zona 1 from the Terminal de Autobuses in Zona 4 is to walk a few blocks east to 7a Av and catch any bus going north (such as No 83). The same holds true in reverse if you want to get to the terminal by city bus.

Car
Most major rental companies have offices both at Aeropuerto La Aurora (in the arrivals area) and in Zona 9 or 10. Companies include:

Ahorrent (www.ahorrent.com) Airport (☎ 2362-8921/2); Zona 9 (☎ 2361-5661; Blvd Liberación 4-83)
Avis (www.avisenlinea.com) Airport (☎ 2331-0017); Zona 9 (☎ 2339-3249; 6a Av 7-64)
Dollar (www.dollarguatemala.com) Airport (☎ 2339-4724); Zona 10 (☎ 2332-7525; Av La Reforma 8-33)
Hertz (www.hertz.com.gt) Airport (☎ 2331-1711, 2339-2631); Holiday Inn (☎ 2332-2555); Hotel Real Inter-Continental Guatemala (☎ 2379-4444); Westin Camino Real (☎ 2368-0107)

Taxi
Plenty of taxis cruise most parts of the city. Fares are negotiable – always establish your destination and fare before getting in. Zona 1 to Zona 10, or vice versa, costs around US$4 to US$5. If you want to phone for a taxi, **Taxi Amarillo Express** (☎ 2332-1515, 5470-1515) has metered cabs that often work out cheaper than others.

ANTIGUA

Dirty, stinky, 1 odd, great shopping

pop 40,000
Nestled between three volcanoes, Antigua Guatemala is almost impossibly cute… cobbled streets, mustard and ochre colored houses with colonial fittings, the leafy central park…did they get somebody *in* to do all this stuff? Antigua's profusion of language schools, fine restaurants and happening bars has made it a magnet for language students and lovers of the high life, and there's always a sizable gringo population. Some people love it, some hate it, but you'd be silly to miss it.

The most exciting time to visit Antigua is during Semana Santa, especially Good Friday. It takes planning (reserve hotels at least four months in advance), as this is the busiest week of the year.

Antigua is cold after sunset, especially between September and March, so bring warm clothes, a sleeping bag or a blanket. Antigua residents are known by the nickname *panza verde* (green belly), as they are said to eat lots of avocados, which grow abundantly here.

HISTORY
Antigua was founded on March 10, 1543, and served as the colonial capital for 233 years. The capital was transferred to Guatemala City in 1776, after Antigua was razed in the earthquake of 1773. The town was slowly rebuilt, retaining much of its traditional character. In 1944 the Legislative Assembly declared Antigua a national monument, and in 1979 Unesco declared it a World Heritage Site.

Most of Antigua's buildings were constructed during the 17th and 18th centuries, when the city was a rich Spanish outpost and the Catholic church was powerful. Many handsome, sturdy colonial buildings remain, and several impressive ruins have been preserved and are open to the public. *Antigua Guatemala: The City and its Heritage*, by long-time Antigua resident Elizabeth Bell, describes all the city's important buildings and museums, and neatly encapsulates Antigua's history and fiestas.

ORIENTATION
Volcán Agua is southeast of the city and visible from most points; Volcán Acatenango is to the west; and Volcán Fuego (Fire) – easily recognizable by its plume of smoke and red glow – is to the southwest. These three volcanoes (which appear on the city's coat of arms) provide easy reference points.

Antigua's streets use a modified version of Guatemala City's numbering system (see Orientation, p65). In Antigua, compass points are added to the avenidas and calles. Calles run east–west, so 4a Calle west of Parque Central is 4a Calle Pte, whereas

GUATEMALA

ANTIGUA

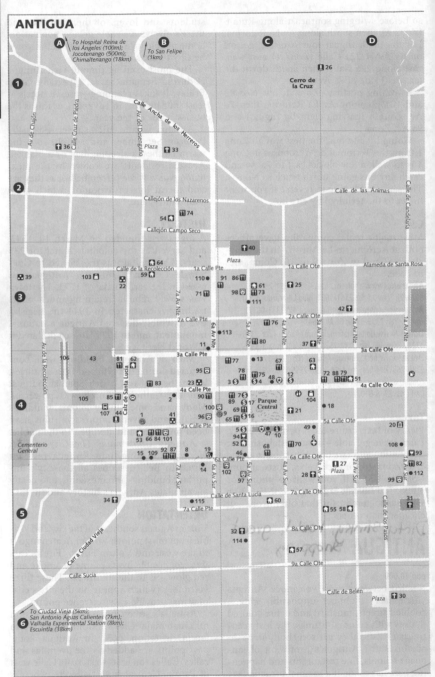

To Hospital Reina de
los Ángeles (100m);
Jocotenango (500m);
Chimaltenango (18km)

To San Felipe
(1km)

Cerro de
la Cruz

26

Av de Chajón

Calle Cruz de Piedra

Calle Ancha de los Herreros

Av del Desengaño

Plaza

36

33

Calle de las Ánimas

Calle de Candelaria

Callejón de los Nazarenos

54   74

Callejón Campo Seco

40

Plaza

64

Calle de la Recolección   1a Calle Pte   1a Calle Ote

Alameda de Santa Rosa

39   103   59   110   91   86   25

22   71   98   61   73

111

42

2a Calle Pte   76   2a Calle Ote

3a Av Nte

2a Av Nte

1a Av Nte

6a Av Nte

5a Av Nte

4a Av Nte

113   80   37   3a Calle Ote

11

Av de la Recolección

3a Calle Pte   77   13   67   63

106   81   62   95   78   72 88 79

43   83   23   3   75   48   51

105   85   4a Calle Pte   4a Calle Ote

107   44   90   89   5   104

1   41   100   69   17 Parque   21   18

53 66 84 101   96   65   16 Central

15   109   92 87   8   19   94   47 10   49   20

14   52   46   68   6 70   108

102   97   6a Calle Pte   28   27 Plaza   93

Calz de Santa Lucía

Cementerio
General

Carr a Ciudad Vieja

34   115   Calle de Santa Lucía   60   55 58   31

7a Calle Pte   7a Calle Ote

32   8a Calle Ote   82

114   57   99   112

9a Calle Ote

Calle Sucia

Calle de Belén

Plaza   30

To Ciudad Vieja (5km);
San Antonio Aguas Calientes (7km);
Valhalla Experimental Station (8km);
Escuintla (38km)

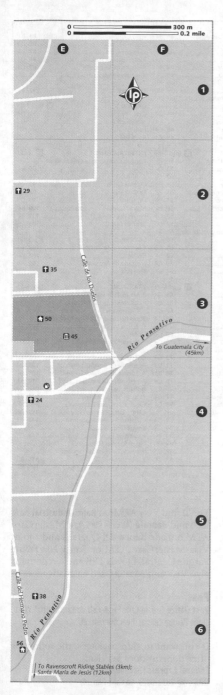

0   300 m
0   0.2 mile

To Guatemala City
(45km)

Río Pensativo

Calle de los Duelos

Calle del Hermano Pedro

Río Pensativo

To Ravenscroft Riding Stables (3km);
Santa María de Jesús (12km)

4a Calle east of Parque Central is 4a Calle Oriente; avenidas run north–south, so 3a Avenida north of Parque Central is 3a Avenida Norte and 3a Avenida south of Parque Central is 3a Avenida Sur.

Most buses arrive at the Terminal de Autobuses, a large open lot just west of the market.

INFORMATION
Bookstores
El Cofre (6a Calle Pte 26) Second-hand books, mainly in English.
Hamlin y White (☎ 7832-7075; 4a Calle Ote 12A) New and used books in several languages, including many Lonely Planet titles.
Rainbow Reading Room (7a Av Sur 8) Thousands of used books in English and Spanish for sale, rent or trade.

Emergency
Formal reports to the police about a crime or loss have to be made to the **Policía Nacional Civil** (National Civil Police; ☎ 7832-0251; Palacio de los Capitanes, Parque Central), but go first to the **Policía Municipal de Turismo** (Municipal Tourism Police; ☎ 7832-7290; Palacio del Ayuntamiento, 4a Av Nte; ⊙ 24hr). They will go with you to the National Civil Police and assist with the formalities.

Internet Access
Antigua is awash in affordable Internet services. See p81 for Internet telephone services. The best places for Internet price (around $1 per hour), connection quality and/or convenience, include:
Aló Internet (5a Calle Pte 28)
Conexion (☎ 7832-3768; Centro Comercial La Fuente, 4a Calle Ote 14; ⊙ 8:30am-7:30pm) All-purpose communications center. It's US$2 an hour to hook up your laptop, and there are CD-burning services.
El Cofre (6a Calle Pte 26)
Enlaces (☎ 7832-5555; 6a Av Nte 1; ⊙ 8am-7:30pm Mon-Sat, 8am-1pm Sun) Good connections, smoking and nonsmoking areas.
Enlínea (5a Av Sur 12)
Funky Monkey (Pasaje El Corregidor, 5a Av Sur 6)

Medical Services
Hospital Nacional Pedro de Betancourth (☎ 7832-2801) in San Felipe, 2km north of the center, has emergency service. If possible, you're better off going to one of the private hospitals such as **Hospital Reina de los Ángeles** (☎ 7832-2258; Calle Ancha de los Herreros 59).

Casa de los Nahuales (☎ 7832-0068; 3a Av Sur 6) offers alternative medical and spiritual services including Mayan horoscopes, massages, aromatherapy and Bach flower remedies.

Money

The following, all on or near Parque Central, change US dollars (cash and traveler's checks):

Banco del Quetzal (4a Calle Pon; ☼ 8:30am-7pm Mon-Fri, 9am-1pm Sat & Sun) Facing Parque Central.

Credomatic (Portal del Comercio; ☼ 9am-7pm Mon-Fri, 9am-1pm Sat)

Lloyds TSB (cnr 4a Calle Ote & 4a Av Nte; ☼ 9am-3:30pm Mon-Fri, 9:30am-12:30pm Sat)

You'll find Visa ATMs at **Banco Industrial** (5a Av Sur 4) and **Bancafé** (4a Calle Pte 22), a MasterCard ATM outside Banco del Quetzal, and a joint Visa/MasterCard ATM on 5a Av Nte facing Parque Central. Lloyds TSB and Credomatic give Visa and MasterCard cash advances.

Post

Post Office (cnr 4a Calle Pte & Calz de Santa Lucía) West of the Parque Central, near the market.

If you want to ship packages, the following offer door-to-door service:

Federal Express (2a Calle Pon 3)

UPS (☎ 7832-0073; 6a Calle Pon 34)

Telephone

Many businesses, including several cybercafés, offer cut-rate international calls. Some of these are by Internet telephone – very cheap, but line quality is unpredictable. Try:

Conexion (☎ 7832-3768; Centro Comercial La Fuente, 4a Calle Ote 14; ⏰ 8:30am-7:30pm) Charges US$0.40 a minute to the USA or Canada and US$0.80 to Europe.

Funky Monkey (Pasaje El Corregidor, 5a Av Sur 6) Offers Internet calls anywhere in the world for between US$0.15 and US$0.40 a minute.

Guatemala Ventures (☎ /fax 7832-3383; 1a Av Sur 15) Rents cell phones on which you can call the USA for US$0.10 a minute or Europe for US$0.20, for US$10 a week (with a US$50 deposit).

Western Union Kall Shop (6a Av Sur 12; ⏰ 8:30am-6pm Mon-Fri, 8:30am-4pm Sat) You pay US$0.45 a minute to call the USA or Canada, US$0.65 to Mexico, Central America or Europe, US$0.75 to South America and US$0.90 to anywhere else.

Tourist Information

Inguat (☎ 7832-0763; Palacio de los Capitanes, Parque Central; ⏰ 8am-12:30pm & 2:30-5pm Mon-Fri, 9am-12:30pm & 2:30-5pm Sat & Sun) Has free city maps, bus information and schedules of Semana Santa events and is very helpful.

Travel Agencies

Everywhere you turn in Antigua, you will see travel agencies offering tours to interesting sites around Antigua and elsewhere in Guatemala, international flights, shuttle minibuses and more. Reputable agencies include:

LAX Travel (☎ /fax 7832-1621, 7832-2674; laxantigua@intelnet.net.gt; 3a Calle Pte 12) An international flight specialist.

Sin Fronteras (☎ 7832-1017; www.sinfront.com; 5a Av Nte 15A) Sells one-way international air tickets; issues student and youth cards for US$8; sells International Travel Maps; runs tours to Cuba, among other destinations.

STA Travel (☎ 7832-3985; istranti@intelnet.net.gt; 6a Calle Pte 25) Offers student and teacher airfares and a change-of-date and lost-ticket replacement service for tickets issued by student/youth travel agencies.

Vision Travel & Information Services (☎ 7832-3293, 7832-1962/5; www.guatemalainfo.com; Casa de Mito, 3a Av Nte 3) Tours ranging from Tikal to local coffee *fincas* are offered, as are shuttle services and many guidebooks.

Voyageur Tours (☎ 7832-4237; www.travel.net.gt; Centro Comercial La Fuente, 4a Calle Ote 14) Operates good-value shuttle minibus services.

Volunteering

Proyecto Mosaico Guatemala (☎ /fax 7832-0955; www.promosaico.org; Casa de Mito, 3a Av Nte 3; ⏰ 2-4pm Mon-Fri) is a nonprofit organization providing volunteers and resources to over 60 projects in Guatemala. Its center here has information and matches volunteers with projects. They're very interested in people with medical experience but there's work (from one week to one year) doing jobs as varied as carpentry, teaching, environmental protection, helping HIV-positive kids and organic farming. You need to be over 18 and fit.

AmeriSpan Guatemala (☎ 7832-0164; www.amerispan.com; 6a Av Nte 40A) can also hook you up with volunteer opportunities all over Guatemala. It charges a US$60 registration fee.

DANGERS & ANNOYANCES

Antigua isn't quite as mellow as it seems; be wary at night. Armed robberies (and worse) have occurred on Cerro de la Cruz, on Volcán Pacaya and at the cemetery, which should be considered off limits unless you're escorted by the Tourist Police. Crime against tourists has dropped precipitously since the formation of this agency.

SIGHTS
Parque Central

The gathering place for locals and visitors alike, on most days the plaza is lined with villagers selling handicrafts to tourists; on Sunday it's mobbed and the streets on the east and west sides are closed to traffic. Things are cheapest late Sunday afternoon, when the peddling is winding down.

The plaza's famous fountain was built in 1738. At night, mariachi or marimba bands play in the park.

PALACIO DE LOS CAPITANES

Begun in 1558, the Captain-Generals' Palace was the governmental center of all Central America from Chiapas to Costa Rica until 1773. The stately, double-arcaded façade, which proudly lines the southern side of Parque Central, was added in the early 1760s. Today the palace houses Inguat, the national police and the office of the governor of Sacatepéquez department.

CATEDRAL DE SANTIAGO

On Parque Central's east side, the cathedral was founded in 1542. It was damaged by earthquakes many times, badly ruined in 1773 and only partially rebuilt between 1780 and 1820. In the 16th and early 17th centuries, Antigua's churches had lavish baroque interiors, but most – including this one – lost this richness during post-earthquake rebuilding. Inside, a crypt contains the bones of Bernal Díaz del Castillo, historian of the Spanish conquest, who died in 1581. If the front entrance is closed, you can enter at the rear or on the south side.

PALACIO DEL AYUNTAMIENTO

The City Hall, on the north side of the park, dates mostly from 1743. In addition to town offices, it houses **Museo de Santiago** (☎ 7832-2868; admission US$1.30; ⏰ 9am-4pm Tue-Fri, 9am-noon & 2-4pm Sat & Sun), in the former town jail, exhibiting furnishings, artifacts and weapons from colonial times. Next door is **Museo del Libro Antiguo** (Old Book Museum; ☎ 7832-5511; admission US$1.30; ⏰ same as Museo de Santiago), with exhibits of colonial printing and binding, including a replica of Guatemala's first printing press, which began work here in the 1660s.

UNIVERSIDAD DE SAN CARLOS

The San Carlos University, now in Guatemala City, was founded in Antigua in 1676; what used to be its main building (built in 1763), half a block east of the park, houses **Museo de Arte Colonial** (☎ 7832-0429; 5a Calle Ote 5; admission US$3.25; ⏰ same as Museo de Santiago), with some expressive sculptures of saints and paintings by leading Mexican artists of the era, including Miguel Cabrera and Juan de Correa.

Churches

Once glorious in their gilded baroque finery, Antigua's churches have suffered indignities from both nature and humankind. Rebuilding after earthquakes gave the churches thicker walls, lower towers and belfries, and bland interiors. Still, they are impressive. In addition to those noted below, you'll find many others scattered around town.

IGLESIA Y CONVENTO DE NUESTRA SEÑORA DE LA MERCED

At the north end of 5a Av is Antigua's most striking colonial church. Construction began in 1548 and improvements continued until 1717, when the church was ruined by earthquakes. Reconstruction was completed in 1767, but in 1773 earthquake struck again and the convent was destroyed. Repairs to the church were made from 1850 to 1855; its baroque facade dates from this period. Inside the **monastery ruins** (admission US$0.40; ⏰ 9am-6:30pm) is a fountain 27m in diameter – possibly the largest in Central America.

IGLESIA DE SAN FRANCISCO

The town's next most notable church, at the east end of 8a Calle, dates from the mid-16th century, but little of the original building remains. Rebuilding and restoration over the centuries have produced a handsome structure; reinforced concrete added in 1961 protected the church from suffering serious damage in the 1976 earthquake. All that remains of the original church is the Chapel of Hermano Pedro, resting place of Hermano Pedro de San José Betancourt, a Franciscan monk who founded a hospital for the poor and died here in 1667. He's Guatemala's most venerated local Christian figure, and was made a saint in 2002 when Pope John Paul II visited Guatemala.

LAS CAPUCHINAS

The Iglesia y Convento de Nuestra Señora del Pilar de Zaragoza, usually called **Las Capuchinas** (cnr 2a Av Nte & 2a Calle Ote; adult/student US$4/2; ⏰ 9am-5pm), was founded in 1736 by nuns from Madrid. Destroyed repeatedly by earthquakes, it is now a museum, with exhibits on religious life in colonial times. The building has an unusual structure of 18 concentric cells around a circular patio.

IGLESIA Y CONVENTO DE LA RECOLECCIÓN

A massive ruin at the west end of 1a Calle Pte, the **Iglesia y Convento de la Recolección** (Av de la Recolección; adult/student US$4/2; ⏰ 9am-5pm), is among Antigua's most impressive monuments. Built between 1701 and 1708, it was destroyed in the 1773 earthquake.

Near La Recolección, **Colegio de San Jerónimo** (cnr Calz de Santa Lucía & 1a Calle Pon; adult/student US$4/2; ⏰ 9am-5pm) – also called the Real Aduana – was built in 1757 by friars of the Merced order. Because it did not have royal authorization, it was taken over by Spain's Carlos III in 1761. In 1765 it was designated for use as the Royal Customhouse, but was destroyed in the 1773 earthquake.

Casa Popenoe

This beautiful **colonial mansion** (☎ 7832-3087; 1a Av Sur 2; admission US$1.30; ⏰ 2-4pm, Mon-Sat) was built in 1636 by Don Luis de las Infantas Mendoza. After the 1773 earthquake, the house stood desolate for 150 years until it was bought by agricultural scientist William Popenoe and his wife Dorothy. Their painstaking, authentic restoration yields a fascinating glimpse of how a royal official lived in 17th-century Antigua.

Monumento a Landívar

At the west end of 5a Calle Pte is the Landívar Monument, a structure of five colonial-style arches set in a little park. The poetry of Rafael Landívar, an 18th-century Jesuit priest, is esteemed as the colonial period's best, even though he wrote much of it in Italy after the Jesuits' expulsion from Guatemala.

Market

At the west end of 4a Calle Pte, across Calz de Santa Lucía, sprawls the market – chaotic, colorful and always bustling. The frenzied mornings are the best time to come. Official market days are Monday, Thursday and Saturday.

Cerro de la Cruz

On the town's northeast side is the Hill of the Cross, offering fine views over Antigua and south toward Volcán Agua. Don't come here without a Tourist Police escort (p79) – it's famous for muggers. The Tourist Police was formed because of robberies at Cerro de la Cruz; reportedly no crime against tourists has taken place on the hill since.

ACTIVITIES

Two professional, established and friendly outfits offering a wide range of activities are **Old Town Outfitters** (☎ /fax 7832-4171; www.bike guatemala.com; 5a Av Sur 12C), which also rents and sells camping equipment, and **Guatemala Ventures/Mayan Bike Tours** (☎ /fax 7832-3383; www .guatemalaventures.com; 1a Av Sur 15).

Climbing the Volcanoes

Get reliable safety advice before you climb. Check with your embassy in Guatemala City or with Inguat in Antigua. If you decide to go, make sure you're with reputable guides, arranged through an established agency. Wear adequate footwear (volcanic rock can shred shoes), warm clothing and in the rainy season, some sort of rain gear. Carry snacks, water and a flashlight.

Volcán Agua, at 3766m, looms over Antigua, south of town. Various outfitters in Antigua can furnish details about the climb. Santa María de Jesús is the tiny village that lies in the shadow of the volcano. The main plaza is also the bus terminal. **Comedor & Hospedaje El Oasis**, a tidy little pensión, offers meals and beds.

You could also climb the other two volcanoes near Antigua: **Volcán Acatenango** and **Volcán Fuego**. Various companies offer guided tours. **Guatemala Ventures/Mayan Bike Tours** (left) offers hike/bike tours on Acatenango, while **Old Town Outfitters** (left) will take you up any volcano.

Cycling

Old Town Outfitters (left) rents quality bikes with gloves, helmets and maps for US$13/20 per half/whole day. It also does a great range of mountain-bike tours at all levels of difficulty, from the gentle Sip & Cycle Coffee Tour (US$25) or the exhilarating one-day Cielo Grande Ridge Ride (US$45) to the two-day Pedal & Paddle Tour (US$140 to US$175), which includes kayaking and hiking at Lago de Atitlán.

Guatemala Ventures/Mayan Bike Tours (left) also rents good mountain bikes for US$1.50 an hour, and offers some tempting bike tours from intermediate to expert levels. It does hike-and-bike tours to Volcán Acatenango (US$49 to US$109, one or two days) and bike-and-kayak trips to Lago de Atitlán and Monterrico (both two days, US$129).

Horseback Riding

Ravenscroft Riding Stables (☎ 7832-6229 afternoons; 2a Av Sur 3, San Juan del Obispo), 3km south of Antigua on the road to Santa María de Jesús, offers English-style riding, with scenic rides of three, four or five hours in the valleys and hills around Antigua, for US$15 per hour per person. You need to be fairly fit. Reservations and information are available through the **Hotel San Jorge** (☎ 7832-3132; 4a Av Sur 13) – see p85. You can reach the stables on a bus bound for Santa María de Jesús.

Guatemala Ventures/Mayan Bike Tours (left) offers half-day rides on trails around Volcán Agua for US$69.

White-Water Rafting

Area Verde Expeditions (☎ /fax 7832 3383, US ☎ / fax +1-719-583 8929; mayanbike@guate.net; 1a Av Sur 15) is in the Hotel Villa San Francisco. The company offers a variety of one- to five-day rafting tours year-round.

Maya Expeditions, represented in Antigua by **Sin Fronteras** (☎ 7832 1017, ☎ /fax 7832 2674; 3a Calle Pte 12), also leads a variety of day trips and multiday tours on several rivers.

COURSES

Antigua is world-famous for its many Spanish-language schools. Prices, teacher quality and student satisfaction vary greatly, so shop around. Ask for references and talk to ex-students. **Inguat** (p81) has a list of reputable schools, including:

Academia de Español Sevilla (☎ /fax 7832-5101; www.sevillantigua.com; 1a Av Sur 8) This school has a good, free activity program & offers a shared student house as an accommodations option.

Academia de Español Tecún Umán (☎ /fax 7832-2792; www.escuelatecun.com; 6a Calle Pte 34A) Also has a school on Lago de Atitlán.

Casa de Lenguas Guatemala (☎ 7832-4846; guatemala@casadelenguas.com; 6a Av Nte 40) This school has group classes (US$65 a week) as well as individual classes (US$95).

Centro Lingüístico La Unión (☎ /fax 7832-7337; www.launion.conexion.com; 1a Av Sur 21) Many classes take place in the school's pretty patio; gives discounts for good test results!

Christian Spanish Academy (☎ 7832-3922; www.learncsa.com; 6a Av Nte 15) Very professional outfit where students get to report on teachers weekly.

Escuela de Español San José el Viejo (☎ 7832-3028; www.sanjoseelviejo.com; 5a Av Sur 34) Professional, 30-teacher school with pool, superb gardens, tennis court and own tasteful accommodations.

Ixchel Spanish School (☎ /fax 7832-7137; www.ixchelschool.com; 3a Av Sur 6) Comfortable, welcoming school with enjoyable group activities and lush garden.

Proyecto Lingüístico Francisco Marroquín (☎ /fax 7832-2886; www.plfm-antigua.org; 7a Calle Pte 31) Antigua's oldest Spanish school, founded in 1971; run by a nonprofit foundation working to preserve Maya languages and culture, and courses in some of these are also available.

Classes start Mondays at most schools, though you can usually be placed with a teacher any day of the week. The busiest seasons are January and April to August; some schools request advance reservations for these times. Instruction is usually one on one and costs between US$65 to US$115 per week for four hours of classes daily, five days a week. You can enroll for up to 10 hours a day of instruction. Most schools offer room and board with local families, where you'll usually have your own room with shared bathrooms for around US$55 per week (including three meals daily except Sunday). Homestays are supposed to promote the 'total immersion' concept of language learning, but often there are several foreigners staying with one family, often with separate mealtimes for students and the family. Make a point of inquiring about such details if you really want to be totally immersed.

TOURS

Elizabeth Bell, author of books on Antigua, leads three-hour cultural walking tours of the town (in English and/or Spanish) on Tuesday, Wednesday, Friday and Saturday at 9:30am. On Mondays and Thursdays, tours are led by her colleague Roberto Spillari and start at 2pm. The cost is US$18 (US$15 for Spanish students and project volunteers). Reservations are advised and can be made at **Antigua Tours** (☎ /fax 7832-5821; www.antiguatours.net; Portal de Santo Domingo, 3a Calle Ote 28), inside the Casa Santo Domingo Hotel. **Vision Travel** and **Sin Fronteras** (see p81 for both) also offer daily city walking tours, visiting a variety of convents, ruins and museums. All these firms also do interesting tours of assorted villages and coffee or macadamia plantations for US$20 to US$30.

Numerous travel agencies offer tours to further-flung places including Tikal, Copán, Río Dulce, the Cobán area, Monterrico, Chichicastenango, Guatemala City and Panajachel. Two-day trips to Tikal, flying from Guatemala City to Flores and back, cost between US$150 and US$300, largely depending on where you stay. A hectic one-day Tikal round-trip costs US$150 to US$180. Two-day land tours to Copán (some also including Quiriguá and Río Dulce) are between US$115 and US$150.

On long-distance tours, be sure what you are paying for – some of the cheaper 'tours' simply amount to shuttling you to Guatemala City then popping you on a public bus.

FESTIVALS & EVENTS

Antigua really comes alive in **Semana Santa**, when hundreds of people dress in robes of deep-purple to accompany the most revered sculptural images from the city's churches in daily street processions remembering Christ's Crucifixion. Dense clouds of incense envelop the parades and the streets are covered in breathtakingly elaborate *alfombras* (carpets) of colored sawdust and flower petals.

The fervor and the crowds peak on Good Friday, when an early-morning procession departs from La Merced church and a late-afternoon one leaves from the Escuela de Cristo church. There may also be an enactment of the Crucifixion in the Parque Central. Have ironclad Antigua room reservations well in advance of Semana Santa, or plan to stay in Guatemala City or another town and commute to the festivities.

Processions, *velaciones* (vigils) and other events are held every weekend through Lent, the 40-day period prior to Semana Santa. Antigua's tourist office has schedules of everything, and the booklet *Lent and Holy Week in Antigua*, by Elizabeth Bell, gives explanations.

On a secular note, beware of pickpockets. It seems that Guatemala City's entire population of pickpockets decamps to Antigua for Semana Santa.

SLEEPING
Budget
Yellow House (☎ 7832-6646; main@granjaguar.com; 1a Calle Pte 24; s/d US$6.50/13; ☒ ▣) This popular little newcomer, run by a local couple, has a particularly friendly atmosphere. Rooms are simple, clean and nonsmoking, with comfy beds, wooden furniture, pastel walls and big mosquito-netted windows. The shared bathrooms are immaculate. Rates include breakfast, use of the guest kitchen, unlimited free Internet use and drinking water.

Posada Juma Ocag (☎ 7832-3109; Calz de Santa Lucía 13; s/d/tr US$13/13/18) This place has everything you could want in a budget hotel. The seven spotless, comfortable rooms have high-quality mattresses and traditional appointments including wrought-iron bedspreads, reading lamps and handmade mirrors. Each room has a private hot shower; there's also a rooftop patio and well-tended little garden. It's peaceful, despite the location on a busy street.

Internacional Mochilero Guesthouse (☎ 7832-0520; 1a Calle Pte 33; dm/s/d US$5/6/9, s/d/tr with private

bathroom US$16; ▣) Rooms are small but mattresses are firm. Open-air kitchen.

Mid-Range
Some of Antigua's mid-range hotels allow you to wallow in the city's colonial charms for a moderate outlay of cash. Most rates below include breakfast.

Hotel Quinta de las Flores (☎ 7832-3721; www.quintadelasflores; Calle del Hermano Pedro 6; s/d/tr/q US$54/67/76/120; ℗ ▣) This is a special place, aptly named for its flowers. The large, beautiful gardens are tastefully strewn with old paraphernalia like carts and boats and incorporate fountains, a play area, pool, sitting areas and restaurant. There are eight large, luxurious rooms, most with fireplace, plus five rustic-style, two-story houses each with two bedrooms, a kitchen and living room. Considerable discounts are offered for stays by the week.

Posada Asjemenou (☎ 7832-2670; 5a Av Nte 31; s/d/tr US$20/26/32, with private bathroom US$26/33/40) Just north of the Arco de Santa Catalina, the Asjemenou is built around two patios, the front one being a lovely grassy courtyard with a fountain. Rooms are sizable and clean, with drinking water provided and little safe boxes built into the wall.

Hotel La Sin Ventura (☎ 7832-0581, 7832-4888; www.lasinventura.com; 5a Av Sur 8; s/d/tr US$20/35/50) This friendly place sports 34 sparkling-clean rooms, in a color combination of yellow, blue and white. It's just half a block from the Parque Central – the views from the small roof terrace are superb. One-bed doubles cost just US$25, but these, like the singles, are on the lowest, and darkest, of the three floors.

Posada San Sebastián (☎ /fax 7832-2621, 7832-6952; snsebast@hotmail.com; 3a Av Nte 4; s/d/tr US$45/60/70) Staying here is like spending the night in a museum. Each of the nine terracotta-tiled rooms is unique and richly packed with fascinating Guatemalan antiques. All have hot-water bathroom and cable TV, and you have use of a kitchen, roof terrace and a pretty little courtyard garden.

Hotel San Jorge (☎ /fax 7832-3132; 4a Av Sur 13; s/d/tr US$39/46/53; ℗) Though in a modern building, this hotel has a rustic reception area and all 14 rooms share a long balcony and overlook a beautiful flower-filled garden, complete with tinkling fountain and chirping birds. The rooms have a fireplace, cable TV, pretty tiles and private bathroom with tub. Guests can use the swimming pool of the posh Hotel Antigua nearby for US$6.50. The English-speaking local host is very welcoming.

Hotel Posada Los Búcaros (☎ /fax 7832-2346; www .hotelosbucaros.com; 7a Av Nte 94; s/d/tr US$25/30/40; P) This hotel in the northwest of town provides 13 plain but well-kept rooms, many of them with wood-beam roofs and red-tile floors. It's set around two patios and guests have the use of a sitting room with fireplace and a large, clean, equipped kitchen with free coffee. There's free Guatemala City airport pickup.

A few more good options:

Hotel Santa Clara (☎ /fax 7832-0342; 2a Av Sur 20; s/ d/tr/q US$22/30/35/40) In a quiet area south of the center.

Hotel Aurora (☎ /fax 7832-0217, 7832-5155; www .hotelauroraantigua.com; 4a Calle Ote 16; s/d/tr/q US$48/ 55/62/70; P) A beautiful old-fashioned place with rooms around a grassy courtyard graced by a fountain.

Hotel Posada Landívar (☎ /fax 7832-2962; posada _landivar@hotmail.com; 5a Calle Pte 23; s/d/tr US$20/ 26/32; P) All rooms have hot-water bathrooms, and there is drinking water, baggage storage and a little roof garden.

Hotel Posada San Pedro (☎ 7832-3594; 3a Av Sur 15; s/d US$22/30) Rooms are inviting, with nice tiled bathrooms. Its two terraces have great views.

Top End

Casa Santo Domingo Hotel (☎ 7832-0140; www .casasantodomingo.com.gt; 3a Calle Ote 28; s/d/tr Mon-Fri US$122/122/140, Sat & Sun US$144/144/162; P ☐ ☒) This wonderful luxury hotel is set amid the beautiful remains of the Santo Domingo monastery. The 97 rooms and suites are of an international five-star standard, but the public spaces are wonderfully colonial, dotted with antiques and archaeological relics, and including a large swimming pool, fine restaurant, shops and three museums. The Dominican friars never had it so good. A fine place to spend a lot of money.

Another luxurious spot is **La Casa de la Música** (☎ 7832-3684; www.lacasadelamusica.centra merica.com; 7a Calle Pte 3; s US$36-54, d US$42-90), a charming, five-room, kid-friendly B&B with patios, fountains, triple volcano views and a fabulous breakfast.

EATING

Within 10 minutes' walk of the Parque Central, you can dine well and inexpensively on international and Guatemalan food. Small restaurants north of the bus station on Calz de Santa Lucía do good-value set lunches for around US$2.50.

Guatemalan & Latin American Cuisine

La Posada de Don Rodrigo (☎ 7832-0291; 5a Av Nte 17; plato chapín US$11) The indoor/outdoor restaurant in this hotel is one of the city's most charming and popular places for lunch or dinner, to the strains of a live marimba. Order the house favorite, *plato chapín*, a platter of Guatemalan specialties.

Cafe La Escudilla (4a Av Nte 4; pasta US$2.50-3.25, meat US$3.50-5.50; ☽ breakfast, lunch & dinner) Hugely popular with travelers and language students, La Escudilla is an inexpensive patio restaurant with tinkling fountain, lush foliage and some tables under the open sky. The food is simple but well prepared and there are plenty of vegetarian options, as well as economical breakfasts and a one-course set lunch or dinner for under US$2.40.

Tacool (☎ 7832-0287; 6a Av Nte 35B; 4 tacos US$3.25; ☽ lunch & dinner) Savor Antigua's best tacos in Tacool's two cozy upstairs rooms, one lounge-style.

Restaurante Doña Luisa Xicotencatl (☎ 7832-2578; 4a Calle Ote 12; sandwiches & breakfast dishes US$3-4; ☽ breakfast, lunch & dinner) Probably Antigua's best-known restaurant, this is a place to enjoy the colonial patio ambiance over breakfast or a light meal. The bakery here sells many kinds of breads, including whole grain.

La Fonda de la Calle Real (mains US$5-8.50) 3a Calle Pte (☎ 7832-0507; 3a Calle Pte 7; ☽ lunch & dinner) 5a Av Nte (☎ 7832-2629; 5a Av Nte 5; ☽ lunch & dinner) 5a Av Nte (☎ 7832-3749; 5a Av Nte 12; ☽ breakfast, lunch & dinner) This restaurant with three spacious branches, all in appealing colonial style, has a good, varied menu ranging from generous salads and sandwiches (US$3) to grilled meats (up to US$8.50). The specialty *caldo real*, a hearty chicken soup, makes a good meal.

Texas Restaurante (7a Av Nte 18; meals US$4) Possibly the best Tex-Mex food in town, with regular beer 'n' burrito-type meal deals and a very tasty breakfast taco.

Fridas (☎ 7832-0504; 5a Av Nte 29; snacks US$2.50-4, mains US$6-8; ☽ lunch & dinner) Dedicated to Ms Kahlo, this bright bar-cum-restaurant serves tasty, if not cheap, Mexican fare and is always busy.

Perú Café (☎ 7832-2147; 5a Calle Pte 15B; mains US$4-6.50; ☽ lunch & dinner Wed-Mon) You can enjoy Peruvian specialties at this pretty patio restaurant. The excellent *causas* are like burgers with layers of mashed potato instead of bread; *ají de gallina* is chicken in yellow chili sauce with baked potatoes, parmesan and rice.

International Cuisine

La Cocina de Lola (2a Calle Pte 3; mains US$7.50-11; lunch & dinner Tue-Sun) This relaxed and pretty Spanish restaurant, with rooms around a patio, specializes in fish, seafood and paella. The food is delicious and the service excellent. Some days there are lunch deals such as paella and *sangría* (a cold drink of wine and fruit) for two at US$12.

Mi Destino (1a Av Sur 17; mains US$2-2.50) This casual café run by a collection of happy-go-lucky young Guatemalans serves a variety of good-value eats – try the *quesadillas* or the Greek salad with chicken breast.

Rainbow Cafe (7a Av Sur 8; mains US$4-6; breakfast, lunch & dinner) Fill up from an eclectic range of all-day breakfasts, curries, stir-fries, Cajun chicken, guacamole etc, and enjoy the relaxed patio atmosphere. The Rainbow has a bookstore and travel agency on the premises.

La Fuente (4a Calle Ote 14; mains US$4; breakfast & lunch, until 7pm) Another pretty courtyard restaurant, tranquil La Fuente has lots of vegetarian selections, good breakfasts and desserts.

Restaurante La Estrella (☎ 7832-7264; 4a Calle Pte 3; mains US$2.50-4; lunch & dinner) An efficient, friendly, economical Chinese restaurant, the Estrella has several tofu options.

Jardín Bavaria (7a Av Nte 49; breakfast US$2.20, mains US$2.20-4.50; 7am-1am Mon-Sat, 9am-3pm Sun high season; 1pm-1am Mon-Sat, 9am-3pm Sun low season) A bar/restaurant with a verdant patio and spacious roof terrace, offering a mixed Guatemalan/German menu.

Queso y Vino (☎ 7832-7785; 5a Av Nte 32A; salads US$3-10, pizzas from US$4.50; lunch & dinner Wed-Mon) This popular little spot is a fine choice for Italian food. There is a wide range of pizzas, pastas, sauces and cheeses, plus Chilean wines and Spanish reds to wash them down.

Caffé Mediterráneo (☎ 7832-7180; 6a Calle Pte 6A; mains US$5-6; lunch & dinner Mon & Wed-Sun) A refined little restaurant with just seven tables spaced around a large room, Caffé Mediterráneo serves well-prepared Italian food.

Tre Fratelli (☎ 7832-7730; 6a Calle Pte 30; pizza & pasta US$5-10; lunch & dinner) Antigua's branch of one of Guatemala City's best restaurants

has the same animated atmosphere and a pretty, verdant courtyard. The food is quality Italian, with fish, chicken and steaks for US$9 to US$11.

Café Flor (4a Av Sur 1; mains US$4-8; lunch & dinner) The Flor makes a good stab at Thai, Indonesian and Chinese food. Dishes come in generous quantity.

Cafe Beijing (5a Calle Pte 15C; mains US$4-6) Perú Café's neighbor, another pretty courtyard restaurant, has food from all over Asia. There are plenty of vegetarian options and a set lunch of soup, fried rice and salad costs US$3 to US$4.

Café Rocío (☎ 7832-1871; 6a Av Nte 34; mains US$5-7; breakfast, lunch & dinner) Another pan-Asian locale, and with a romantic little garden area, this restaurant offers you gado-gado (an Indonesian vegetarian dish with peanut sauce), Thai satay, yellow Thai curry and a range of tofu dishes.

Restaurante Las Palmas (☎ 7832-0376; 6a Av Nte 14; mains US$4-6) Twinkling lights and gentle guitar music make this a popular romantic dinner spot. The staples are chicken, seafood, steaks and pasta – try the fettuccine with goat's cheese, shrimp, herbs and garlic.

Recommended spots for breakfast and pastries are:

Bagel Barn (5a Calle Pte 2; bagels US$2-3.25; breakfast, lunch & dinner)

Café Condesa (Portal del Comercio 4; light meals & snacks US$2.50-5) The Sunday buffet, from 10am to 2pm, a lavish spread for US$7, is an Antigua institution.

La Repostería (Calz de Santa Lucía Portal 13; snacks US$0.35)

Panificadora Colombia (4a Calle Pte 34; coffee & croissant US$1.80) Good for breakfast before the 7am Pullman bus to Panajachel.

Cookies Etc (3a Av Nte 7; breakfasts & sandwiches US$1.30-2; breakfast, lunch & dinner)

La Cenicienta Pasteles (5a Av Nte 7) Serves a range of tempting cakes at US$1 a slice.

DRINKING

Antigua's bar scene has bounced back after many establishments were closed down in 2001 and 2002 by a mayor trying to smarten up the city's image. You can choose from a bunch of buzzing drinking places, except on Sunday, when no alcohol is served after 8pm. Many people roll in from Guatemala City for a spot of Antigua-style revelry on Friday and Saturday.

Riki's Bar (4a Av Nte 4; ☽ until midnight) Behind Cafe La Escudilla is the hippest bar in town, packed every evening with Antigua's young, international scene of locals, travelers and language students. For quieter moments, slip through to the low-key Paris Bar in the rear.

Monoloco (5a Av Sur 6, Pasaje El Corregidor) The 'Crazy Monkey' can be the funnest bar in Antigua, with a real party atmosphere. It's a two-level place (semi-open-air upstairs, with benches and long tables), with sports on TV and good-value food.

Café Sky (1a Av Sur 15) A very popular place for sunset drinks on the rooftop above Guatemala Ventures/Mayan Bike Tours.

Perú Café (5a Calle Pte 15B; ☽ 6pm-midnight Wed-Mon) The lounge here has chilled electronic background music, often with a DJ or live music Wednesday to Friday.

ENTERTAINMENT
Theater & Concerts
Proyecto Cultural El Sitio (☎ 7832-3037; www.elsitiocultural.org; 5a Calle Pte 15) This arts center has lots going on, from music, dance and theater events (including plays in English) to exhibition openings most Saturdays. Stop by to check the schedule.

Classical concerts happen in the **Museo de Arte Colonial** (see p82) and the **Antiguo Colegio de la Compañía de Jesús** (6a Av Nte btwn 3a & 4a Calles).

Cinema & TV
Several cinema houses show a wide range of Latin American, art-house and general-release movies, some in English, some in Spanish, usually for US$1.25 to US$2. Check the programs of the following:

Bagel Barn (opposite) Café with movies at 8pm.

Cafe 2000 (☎ 7832-2981; 6a Av Nte 2) Free movies on a big screen.

Cinema Bistro (5a Av Sur 14) Four screenings a day, three films each time; movie-and-meal deals US$4 to US$5.

Maya Moon (6a Av Nte 1A) Three screens each show three films a day.

Mi Destino (1a Av Sur 17) This is a café, too, and the nightly movies are free with any consumption.

Proyecto Cultural El Sitio (see Theater & Concerts above) Movies usually on Tuesday evening.

For North American and European sports on TV, check the programs posted at **Cafe 2000** (above) and **Monoloco** (above).

Writer Elizabeth Bell gives a fascinating one-hour English-language slide show (US$3) about Antigua called *Behind the Walls* at 6pm on Tuesday at the **Christian Spanish Academy** (p84).

Dancing
La Casbah (☎ 7832-2640; 5a Av Nte 30; admission US$2.50-4 incl 1 drink; ☽ 9pm-1am Mon-Sat) This two-level disco near the Santa Catalina arch has a warm atmosphere, is gay friendly and quite a party most nights – especially on Thursday (ladies' night), when women who arrive before 11pm get two drinks free.

Torero's Discoteque (Av de la Recolección) After a few drinks at weekends, emboldened salsa lovers head out here, west of the market, for a local experience.

You can learn to salsa at several places including **Latinos** (1a Av Sur 22) and **Salsa Buena** (6a Calle Pte 19). Ask around for the current hot spot.

SHOPPING
Nim Po't (www.nimpot.com; 5a Av Nte 29) This place boasts a huge collection of Maya dress, as well as hundreds of masks and other woodcarvings. The sprawling space is packed with *huipiles* (long, woven, white, sleeveless tunics with colorful embroidery), *cortes* (pieces of material used as wraparound skirts), *fajas* (waist sashes) and more, all arranged according to region, so it makes for a fascinating visit. Shoppers will pay more here than in any market, though the selection is huge.

Colibri (4a Calle Ote) This shop has beautiful basketwork from El Petén and top-quality woven fabric from a Mayan women's cooperative. Prices are moderate.

Mercado de Artesanías (Handicrafts Market; 4a Calle Pte; ☽ 8am-8pm) At the west end of town by the main market, this sells masses of Guatemalan handicrafts – mostly not top quality but plenty of colorful variety in masks, blankets, jewelry, purses and so on.

Casa del Tejido Antiguo (www.casadeltejido.com; 1a Calle Pte 51; admission US$0.70; ☽ 9am-5:30pm Mon-Sat) This is another intriguing place for textiles, like a museum, market and workshop rolled into one.

GETTING THERE & AROUND
Bus
Buses to Guatemala City, Ciudad Vieja and San Miguel Dueñas arrive and depart from

a street just south of the market. Buses to Chimaltenango, Escuintla, San Antonio Aguas Calientes and Santa María de Jesús go from the street outside the west side of the market. If you're heading out to local villages, it's best to go early in the morning and return by mid-afternoon, as bus services drop off dramatically as evening approaches.

To reach highland towns such as Chichicastenango, Quetzaltenango, Huehuetenango or Panajachel (except for the one direct daily bus to Panajachel – see below), take one of the frequent buses to Chimaltenango, on the Interamericana, and catch an onward bus from there. Making connections in Chimaltenango is easy, as many friendly folks will jump to your aid as you alight from one bus looking for another. Stay alert and don't leave your pack unattended, as bag slashing is not unheard of in Chimal. Alternatively you can take a bus from Antigua heading toward Guatemala City, get off at San Lucas Sacatepéquez and change buses there – this takes a little longer, but you'll be boarding closer to the capital so you're more likely to get a seat.

Chimaltenango (US$0.30, 30min, 19km) Buses every 15 minutes, 5am to 7pm.

Ciudad Vieja (US$0.15, 15min, 7km) Take a San Miguel Dueñas bus.

Escuintla (US$0.65, 1hr, 39km) Sixteen buses daily, 5:30am to 5pm.

Guatemala City (US$0.65, 1¼hr, 45km) Buses every few minutes, 6am to 7pm.

Panajachel (US$4.50, 2½hr, 146km) One Pullman bus daily, 7am, departs from **El Condor Expeditions** (☎ 5498-9812; 4a Calle Pte 34).

San Antonio Aguas Calientes (US$0.15, 30min, 9km) Buses every 20 minutes, 6:30am to 7pm.

San Miguel Dueñas (US$0.20, 30min, 10km) Buses every few minutes, 6am to 7pm (placards just say 'Dueñas').

Santa María de Jesús (US$0.15, 30min, 12km) Buses every 45 minutes, 6am to 7:30pm.

Shuttle Minibus

Numerous travel agencies offer frequent and convenient shuttle services to places including Guatemala City, La Aurora International Airport, Panajachel and Chichi. They also go less frequently (usually on weekends) to places further afield such as Río Dulce, Copán Ruinas (Honduras) and Monterrico. These services cost a lot more than ordinary buses, but they are comfortable and convenient, with door-to-door service on both ends. Typical one-way prices are: Guatemala City (US$7 to US$10), Chichicastenango (US$10 to US$12), Panajachel (US$10 to US$12), Copán (Honduras, US$15 to US$25), Monterrico (US$9 to US$15), Río Dulce (US$25 to US$40) and Quetzaltenango (US$25).

Pin down shuttle operators about departure times and whether their trip requires a minimum number of passengers. Be careful of 'shuttles' to Flores or Tikal. This service may just consist of taking you to Guatemala City and putting you on a public bus there.

Taxi

Taxis wait where the Guatemala City buses stop, also west of the market and on the eastern side of Parque Central. A ride in town costs around US$1.60. A taxi to/from Guatemala City usually costs US$30 (US$40 after midnight).

THE HIGHLANDS – LAGO DE ATITLÁN

Guatemala's most dramatic region is the highlands, which stretches from Antigua to the Mexican border northwest of Huehuetenango. Here the verdant hills sport emerald-green grass, cornfields and towering stands of pine, and every town and village has a story.

The traditional values and customs of Guatemala's indigenous peoples are strongest in the highlands. Mayan dialects are the first language, Spanish a distant second. The age-old culture based on maize is still alive; a sturdy cottage set in the midst of a thriving *milpa* (cornfield) is a common sight. And on every road you'll see men, women and children carrying burdens of *leña* (firewood), to be used for heating and cooking.

One of the most spectacular locales in Central America, Lago de Atitlán is a caldera (collapsed volcanic cone) filled with shimmering waters to a depth of more than 320m. The lake covers 128 sq km and is surrounded by colorful hills. Three powerful volcanoes – Volcán Tolimán (3158m), Volcán Atitlán

GUATEMALA

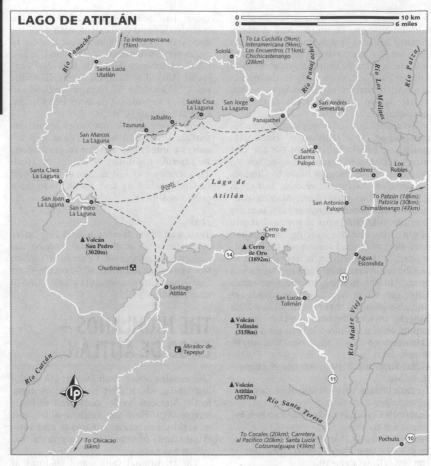

LAGO DE ATITLÁN

(3537m) and Volcán San Pedro (3020m) – loom over the landscape.

If you visit during the rainy season, May to October, be prepared for some dreary days; the region's lush vegetation comes from abundant rain.

This section starts in Panajachel and works clockwise around the lake. The lake is three hours by bus from either Guatemala City or Antigua.

Dangers & Annoyances

Though most visitors never experience any trouble, there have been incidents of robbery, rape and murder in the highlands. These have occurred on volcano trails, on the outskirts of Chichicastenango, at desolate spots along roads, and, with disturbing frequency, on mountain and lakeside trails in the Atitlán area, including robberies by gangs with machetes on Volcán Atitlán, armed robbers on the hike to Santa Cruz and machete-wielding robbers near San Juan.

Use caution and common sense. Don't roam at night, and before traveling in the highlands, contact your embassy or consulate in Guatemala City for information on the current situation and advice. Don't rely on local authorities, as they may downplay the dangers. Encouragingly, Lago de Atitlán is one of the government's 'red zone' areas, where the tourist police presence has been reinforced in recent years.

RIGOBERTA MENCHÚ TUM

Rigoberta Menchú was born in 1959 near Uspantán in the Guatemalan highlands and lived the life of a typical young Mayan woman until the late 1970s, when the country's civil war affected her tragically and drove her into the left-wing guerrilla camp. Her father, mother and brother were killed in the slaughter carried out by the Guatemalan military in the name of 'pacification' of the countryside and repression of communism.

Menchú fled to exile in Mexico, where her story, *I, Rigoberta Menchú: An Indian Woman in Guatemala*, based on a series of interviews, was published and translated throughout the world, bringing the plight of Guatemala's indigenous population to international attention. In 1992 Rigoberta Menchú was awarded the Nobel Prize for Peace. The Rigoberta Menchú Tum Foundation, which she founded with the US$1.2 million Nobel Prize money, works for conflict resolution, plurality and human, indigenous and women's rights in Guatemala and internationally.

Anthropologist David Stoll's book, *Rigoberta Menchú and the Story of All Poor Guatemalans* (1999), contested the truth of many aspects of Menchú's book, but has not seriously dented her reputation.

In 1999, before a Spanish court, the Rigoberta Menchú Tum Foundation formally accused former dictators General Oscar Humberto Mejía Victores (1983–86) and Efraín Ríos Montt (1982–83) of genocide. Menchú pressed for extradition proceedings, unsuccessful as of writing. Menchú was still living in exile in Mexico, saying that she would not return to Guatemala unless true peace took hold in her country. In 2004, incoming President Oscar Berger invited Menchú to serve as the 'goodwill ambassador to the peace accords.'

Getting There & Away
THE HIGHLANDS
The curvy Interamericana, also known as Centroamérica 1 (CA-1), passes through the highlands between Guatemala City and the Mexican border at La Mesilla. Driving the 266km between Guatemala City and Huehuetenango can take five hours, but the scenery is beautiful. The lower Carretera al Pacífico (CA-2), via Escuintla and Retalhuleu, is straighter and faster; it's the better route if you're trying to reach Mexico as quickly as possible.

CA-1 is thick with bus traffic. As most places you'll want to reach are off the Interamericana, you may find yourself waiting at junctions such as Los Encuentros (for Panajachel and Chichicastenango) and Cuatro Caminos (for Quetzaltenango) to connect with a bus or pickup. Travel is easiest on market days and in the morning. By mid- or late afternoon, buses may be scarce, and short-distance local traffic stops by dinnertime. On remote routes, you'll probably be relying more on pickups than buses for transport.

LAGO DE ATITLÁN
Following CA-1 32km west from Chimaltenango, you'll reach the turnoff for the back road to Lago de Atitlán via Patzicía and Patzún. The area around these two towns was notable for high levels of bandit activity in the past, so stay on the Interamericana to Tecpán Guatemala, the starting point for a visit to the ruined Kaqchiquel capital of Iximché (p104).

Another 40km west along the Interamericana from Tecpán is the **Los Encuentros** junction. A nascent town serves people waiting to catch buses. The road to the right heads north to Chichicastenango and Santa Cruz del Quiché. From the Interamericana a road to the left descends 12km to Sololá and another 8km to Panajachel, on the shores of Lago de Atitlán.

If you are not on a direct bus, you can get off at Los Encuentros and catch another bus or minibus, or flag a pickup, from here down to Panajachel or up to Chichicastenango; it's a half-hour ride to either place.

PANAJACHEL
pop 14,000 / elevation 1560m
Nicknamed Gringotenango (Place of the Foreigners) by locals and foreigners alike, Pana is one of Guatemala's oldest tourist hangouts. In the 1960s and '70s, it was crowded with laid-back travelers in semi-permanent exile. When the civil war made Panajachel dangerous in the late '70s and '80s, many moved on. But the town's tourist industry is booming again and has spread to lakeside villages.

PANAJACHEL

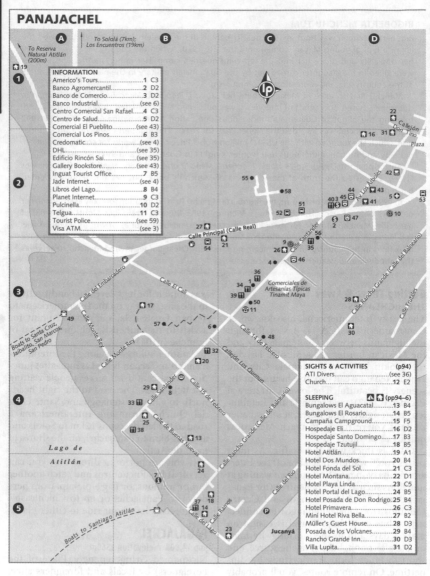

INFORMATION

Americo's Tours	1 C3
Banco Agromercantil	2 D2
Banco de Comercio	3 D2
Banco Industrial	(see 6)
Centro Comercial San Rafael	4 C3
Centro de Salud	5 D2
Comercial El Pueblito	(see 43)
Comercial Los Pinos	6 B3
Credomatic	(see 4)
DHL	(see 35)
Edificio Rincón Sai	(see 35)
Gallery Bookstore	(see 43)
Inguat Tourist Office	7 B5
Jade Internet	(see 4)
Libros del Lago	8 B4
Planet Internet	9 C3
Pulcinella	10 D2
Telgua	11 C3
Tourist Police	(see 59)
Visa ATM	(see 3)

To Sololá (7km);
Los Encuentros (19km)

To Reserva
Natural Atitlán
(200m)

Calle Principal (Calle Real)

Calle del Embarcadero

Calle El Caj

Comerciales de
Artesanías Típicas
Tinamit Maya

Boats to Santa Cruz,
Jaibalito, San Marcos,
San Pedro

Calle Monte Rey

Calle Santander

Calle 14 de Febrero

Callejón Los Quenun

Calle 15 de Febrero

Calle de Buenas Nuevas

Calle Rancho Grande (Calle del Balneario)

Lago de
Atitlán

Calle del Rio

Calle Ramos

Calle del Lago

Boats to Santiago Atitlán

Jucanyá

SIGHTS & ACTIVITIES (p94)

ATI Divers	(see 36)
Church	12 E2

SLEEPING (pp99–6)

Bungalows El Aguacatal	13 B4
Bungalows El Rosario	14 B5
Campaña Campground	15 F5
Hospedaje Eli	16 D2
Hospedaje Santo Domingo	17 B3
Hospedaje Tzutujil	18 B5
Hotel Atitlán	19 A1
Hotel Dos Mundos	20 B4
Hotel Fonda del Sol	21 C3
Hotel Montana	22 D1
Hotel Playa Linda	23 C5
Hotel Portal del Lago	24 B5
Hotel Posada de Don Rodrigo	25 B4
Hotel Primavera	26 C3
Mini Hotel Riva Bella	27 B2
Müller's Guest House	28 D3
Posada de los Volcanes	29 B4
Rancho Grande Inn	30 D3
Villa Lupita	31 D2

Several different cultures mingle on Panajachel's dusty streets. Ladinos and gringos control the tourist industry, while the Kaqchiquel and Tz'utujil Maya from surrounding villages come to sell their handicrafts to tourists. The town itself is a small, unattractive place that has developed haphazardly, but you need only go down to the lakeshore to understand why Pana attracts so many visitors.

Information
BOOKSTORES
Gallery Bookstore (Comercial El Pueblito, Av Los Árboles)
Sells and exchanges used books, and sells a few new ones including some Lonely Planet guides.

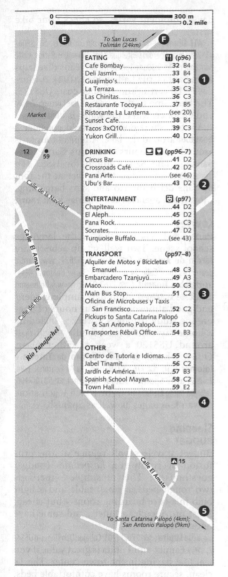

EATING 🍴 (p96)	
Cafe Bombay..........................32 B4	
Deli Jasmín............................33 B4	
Guajimbo's............................34 C3	
La Terraza.............................35 C3	
Las Chinitas..........................36 C3	
Restaurante Tocoyal..............37 B5	
Ristorante La Lanterna.......(see 20)	
Sunset Cafe..........................38 B4	
Tacos 3xQ10.........................39 C3	
Yukon Grill...........................40 D2	
DRINKING 🖥️ 🍷 (pp96–7)	
Circus Bar............................41 D2	
Crossroads Café....................42 D2	
Pana Arte........................(see 46)	
Ubu's Bar.............................43 D2	
ENTERTAINMENT 🎭 (p97)	
Chapiteau.............................44 C3	
El Aleph...............................45 C3	
Pana Rock............................46 C3	
Socrates...............................47 D2	
Turquoise Buffalo................(see 43)	
TRANSPORT (pp97–8)	
Alquiler de Motos y Bicicletas	
Emanuel............................48 C3	
Embarcadero Tzanjuyú...........49 A3	
Maco...................................50 C3	
Main Bus Stop.......................51 C2	
Oficina de Microbuses y Taxis	
San Francisco.....................52 C2	
Pickups to Santa Catarina Palopó	
& San Antonio Palopó.........53 C2	
Transportes Rébuli Office........54 B3	
OTHER	
Centro de Tutoría e Idiomas....55 C2	
Jabel Tinamit........................56 C2	
Jardín de América..................57 B3	
Spanish School Mayan............58 C2	
Town Hall.............................59 E2	

Libros del Lago (Calle Santander) An excellent stock of books in English and other tongues on Guatemala, the Maya and Mesoamerica, plus maps, English and Latin American literature in English, and guidebooks.

EMERGENCY

The English-speaking **tourist police** (☎ 7762-1120; Municipalidad, Calle Principal) has its principal office in the town hall. It also has a **branch** (🕙 9am-5pm) underneath Inguat (below).

INTERNET ACCESS

As you would expect, Pana has plenty of places to check your email and surf the Web. The standard price is US$1.30 an hour; typical hours are 9am to 10pm, perhaps slightly shorter on Sunday.

Jade Internet (Centro Comercial San Rafael, Calle Santander)

Gallery Bookstore (Comercial El Pueblito, Av Los Árboles) See opposite.

Planet Internet (Calle Santander)

Pulcinella (Calle Principal 0-62)

MEDICAL SERVICES

The nearest hospital is at Sololá.

Centro de Salud (Clinic; Calle Principal; 🕙 8am-6pm Mon-Fri, 8am-1pm Sat)

MONEY

Americo's Tours (☎ 7762-2021; Calle Santander) Does Visa and MasterCard cash advances but charges 10% commission.

Banco Agromercantil (cnr Calles Principal & Santander; 🕙 9am-6pm Mon-Fri, 9am-1pm Sat) Changes US-dollar cash and traveler's checks, and has a MasterCard ATM.

Banco de Comercio (Calle Principal; 🕙 9am-5pm Mon-Fri, 9am-1pm Sat) Changes US-dollar cash and traveler's checks.

Banco Industrial (Comercial Los Pinos, Calle Santander) Has Visa ATM.

Circus Bar (Av Los Árboles) Changes euros (p96).

Credomatic (Centro Comercial San Rafael, Calle Santander) Visa and MasterCard cash advances and changes US-dollar cash.

POST

DHL (Edificio Rincón Sai, Calle Santander)

Post Office (cnr Calles Santander & 15 de Febrero)

TELEPHONE

Some cybercafés and travel agencies on Calle Santander offer moderately cheap phone calls – around US$0.70 a minute to North or Central America, US$1.30 a minute to Europe. Try **Jade Internet** or **Planet Internet** (above for both).

TOURIST INFORMATION

Inguat (☎ 7762-1392, ☎ /fax 7762-1106; Calle del Lago; 🕙 9am-5pm) By the lakeside. There's little material available but staff can answer straightforward questions.

HOW ATITLÁN WAS BORN

The first volcanoes in the Atitlán region emerged 150,000 years ago, but today's landscape has its origins in the massive Los Chocoyos eruption of 85,000 years ago, which blew volcanic ash as far as Florida and Panama. The quantity of magma expelled from below the earth's crust caused the surface terrain to collapse, forming a huge, roughly circular hollow that soon filled with water – the Lago de Atitlán. Smaller volcanoes rose out of the lake's southern waters thousands of years later: Volcán San Pedro (today 3020m above sea level) about 60,000 years ago, followed by Volcán Atitlán (3537m) and Volcán Tolimán (3158m) some 40,000 to 30,000 years ago. These reduced the lake's surface area but at the same time created the dramatic volcano vistas that make Atitlán what it is. The lake today is around 300m deep and has a surface area of 128 sq km. Its water level fluctuates curiously from year to year.

Sights & Activities

Reserva Natural Atitlán (☎ 7762-2565; admission US$3; 8am-5pm) is down the spur leading to Hotel Atitlán and makes a good full-day or half-day trip. The well-designed nature reserve has trails, an interpretive center, butterfly farm, small shade coffee plantation, lots of monkeys and an aviary.

Museo Lacustre Atitlán (Hotel Posada de Don Rodrigo, Calle Santander; admission US$4.50; ☽ 8am-6pm Sun-Fri, 8am-7pm Sat) has fascinating displays on the history of the Atitlán region and the volcanic eruptions that created its majestic landscape, and a collection of ancient Mayan artifacts recovered from the lake.

Lago de Atitlán offers phenomenal **hiking and biking**. You can walk from Panajachel to Santa Catarina in about an hour, continuing to San Antonio in about another hour; it takes only half as long by bicycle, on hilly roads, or take a bike by boat to Santiago, San Pedro or another village to start a tour of the lake. There have been many serious incidents involving armed bandits on isolated trails in this area (see Dangers & Annoyances, p90) and seek reliable local advice before heading out.

Several places along Calle Santander rent bicycles; rates start at around US$6.50 per day. Equipment varies, so check your bike first.

ATI Divers (☎ 7762-2621, out of hours ☎ 5706-4117; laiguanaperdida@itelgua.com; Plaza Los Patios, Calle Santander; ☽ 9:30am-1pm Mon-Sat) leads dive trips from Santa Cruz La Laguna (p104). A four-day PADI certification course costs US$175. The best time to dive here is between May and October, when the water is clear.

Visitors short on time should consider a **boat tour** around the lake. A typical tour lasts around seven hours and visits San Pedro, Santiago and San Antonio for US$7. To arrange a tour, head to the pier at the foot of Calle del Balneario and start bargaining. Most travel agencies also arrange boat tours.

Courses

Panajachel has a niche in the language school scene. Two well-set-up schools are **Jardín de América** (☎ /fax 7762-2637; www.jardin deamerica.com; Calle 14 de Febrero, 3a Av Peatonal 4-44) and **Jabel Tinamit** (☎ 7762-0238; www.jabeltinamit .com; Calle Santander). Both have ample gardens and good atmospheres. Four hours of one-on-one study five days a week – including a homestay with a local family – will cost around US$120 a week at either place. Other schools include **Centro de Tutoría e Idiomas** (CTI; ☎ 7762-0259/1005; 2a Av Peatonal 1-84, Zona 2) and **Spanish School Mayan** (☎ 5810-7196; Callejón Santa Elena), both of which teach Mayan languages as well as Spanish.

Sleeping

BUDGET

Budget travelers will rejoice at the profusion of family-run *hospedajes* (budget guesthouses). They're simple – perhaps two rough beds, a small table and a light bulb in a bare boarding room – but cheap. Most provide clean toilets, and some have hot showers.

Villa Lupita (☎ 7762-1201; Callejón Don Tino; s/d US$4/7; **P**) Family-run Lupita is great value if you feel like staying in the town center. The 18 clean, secure rooms have comfortable beds, reading lamps and colorful carpets, and there's free coffee and drinking water. The shared hot-water bathrooms are clean, and the roof terrace affords good views.

Hospedaje Tzutujil (☎ 7762-0102; down laneway off Calle del Balneario; s/d with private bathroom & cable TV US$5/9) Definitely in the running for the best deal in town, this place has clean, modern rooms. Upstairs rooms all have fantastic mountain views. Let's hope the current renovations don't extend to the price list.

Hospedaje Santo Domingo (☎ 7762-0236; Calle Monte Rey; s/d US$3/4.50, s/d/tr with private bathroom US$9/13/16) This amicable, tranquil place has a variety of rooms. The cheapest are very basic wood-plank affairs, but there are also better shared-bathroom doubles for US$7 in a newer, two-story block. There's a great grassy hangout area here.

Campaña Campground (☎ 7762-2479; Carr a Santa Catarina Palopó; per person US$4) About 1km out of town on the road to Santa Catarina Palopó, amenities here include a kitchen, book exchange, luggage storage and pickup from Panajachel.

The following places offer good deals on doubles:

Hospedaje Eli (☎ 7762-0148; End of Callejón El Pozo; s/d US$4.50/6.50, d with private bathroom US$8)

Hotel Fonda del Sol (☎ 7762-1162; h_fondadelsol@ hotmail.com; Calle Principal near bus stop; s/d with shared bathroom US$5/10; P)

MID-RANGE

Mid-range lodgings are busiest on weekends; from Sunday to Thursday you may get a discount. All these places provide private bathrooms with hot showers.

Hotel Dos Mundos (☎ 7762-2078, 7762-2140; dos mundos@atitlan.com; Calle Santander 4-72; s/d/tr US$50/ 55/60; P ☒) Italian-owned Dos Mundos has a great location toward the lake end of Calle Santander, but its installations are set well away from the street. The 22 bungalows, all with terracotta floors, woven bedspreads, Italian fittings, cable TV and at least one double and one single bed, are set around tropical gardens with a large pool. Also here are a good Italian restaurant (p96), an in-house travel agency and a clean-cut continental-style bar fronting the street.

Hotel Primavera (☎ 7762-2052; www.primavera titlan.com; Calle Santander; s/d/tr US$20/30/40) The 10 rooms, nine of them upstairs above a green garden-patio, are clean, uncluttered and appealing, with Spanish-tile floors and cypress-wood fittings. Rates go up about 50% for July, August, Semana Santa and the Christmas-New Year holidays.

Posada de los Volcanes (☎ 7762-0244; www.pos adadelosvolcanes.com; Calle Santander 5-51; s/d/tr/q US$25/ 30/40/50) This is a comfortable little hotel with 12 rooms on four floors. Some have

two double beds, some have one; all are brightened by paintings and mirrors.

Hotel Playa Linda (☎ 7762-0097; akennedy@gua .gbm.net; Calle del Lago; s/d/tr/q with lake view US$40/ 40/50/60, s/d/tr without view US$30/40/50; P) The Playa Linda has 17 assorted rooms, mostly good-sized, and welcoming owners and staff. Six rooms have large private balconies with tables, chairs and wonderful lake views; all rooms have private bathroom, most have fireplaces and some have TV. Rates go up US$5 on Friday and Saturday, and by around 50% (with view) or around 35% (without view) for July, August, Semana Santa and the Christmas-New Year holidays.

Müller's Guest House (☎ /fax 7762-2442; atmuller@ amigonet.gt; Calle Rancho Grande; s/d/tr US$35/45/55; P) Just three attractive rooms with wood floors and ceilings and white-tiled bathrooms, around well-tended gardens, comprise the accommodations here. But there's plenty of comfortable communal space, and rates include breakfast.

Rancho Grande Inn (☎ 7762-1554, 7762-2255; www .ranchograndeinn.com; Calle Rancho Grande; d US$40-70; P ☒) Founded in the 1940s, the Rancho Grande has a dozen varied rooms, suites and cabañas in perfectly maintained German country-style villas, all in a tropical Guatemalan setting with bright green lawns and a large pool. Some rooms sleep up to five people (US$115). All have TV, phone and carpets, and rates include a filling, delicious breakfast featuring pancakes and homegrown honey and coffee.

Hotel Montana (☎ 7762-0326; fax 7762-2180; Callejón Don Tino; s/d/tr US$16/31/43; P) Down a narrow street near the church, the Montana has 23 clean, bright rooms with cable TV ranged along a fine, green, parking courtyard full of birdsong.

A few places offer self-contained bungalows, which are good if you're traveling with a family or large group:

Bungalows El Rosario (☎ 7762-1491; Calle del Lago; s/d/tr/q US$13/26/33/39; P)

Mini Hotel Riva Bella (☎ 7762-1348; fax 7762-1353; Calle Principal 2-21; s/d/tr/q US$27/32/37/43; P)

Bungalows El Aguacatal (☎ 7762-1482; fax 5476-1582; Calle de Buenas Nuevas; s/d/tr/q US$26/26/45/45, with kitchen US$33/33/58/58; P)

TOP END

Hotel Atitlán (☎ /fax 7762-1416/29/41; www.hotel atitlan.com; Finca San Buenaventura; s/d/tr US$132/132/147;

(P ▢ 🕮) Pana's loveliest hotel is on the lakeshore 1.5km northwest of the town center. It's a rambling, three-story, semicolonial-style affair surrounded by large and gorgeous gardens. Inside are gleaming tile floors, antique woodcarvings and exquisite handicraft decorations. The patio has views across the swimming pools to the lake. The 65 rooms all have lake-facing balconies, and the hotel has a restaurant, bar and an outstanding gift shop. Rates include breakfast.

Another fine top-end hotel is **Hotel Posada de Don Rodrigo** (☎ 7762-2326/29; chotelera@c.netgt; Calle Santander; s/d/tr US$85/95/105; P 🕮), with good-sized rooms, fireplaces and big beds.

Eating

BUDGET

Deli Jasmín (☎ 7762-2586; lower Calle Santander; items US$2-3.50; 🕑 breakfast, lunch & dinner Wed-Mon) This tranquil garden restaurant serves a great range of healthy foods and drinks to the strains of soft classical music. Breakfast is served all day, and you can buy wholewheat or pita bread, hummus or mango chutney to take away.

Yukon Grill (Calle Principal; burgers from US$3; 🕑 breakfast, lunch & dinner) The Krazy Kanuk on the grill here serves up the best burgers in town, if not the country. The beef is flown in from Alaska, the fries are crispy fresh and the coleslaw – mmm, just right.

Las Chinitas (Plaza Los Patios, Calle Santander; mains or set lunch US$3-6) Las Chinitas serves up unbelievably delicious, moderately priced food. Try the Malaysian curry with coconut milk or the satay, both with rice, tropical salad and your choice of tofu, tempeh, chicken, pork or prawns.

Guajimbo's (Calle Santander; mains US$4-6) This Uruguayan grill is one of Pana's best eateries, serving up generous meat and chicken dishes with vegetables, salad, garlic bread and either rice or boiled potatoes. You won't leave hungry. Try the *chivita Hernandarias*, tenderloin cooked with bacon, mozzarella, peppers and olives. There are vegetarian dishes too, good-value breakfasts and bottomless cups of coffee for US$0.70.

Cafe Bombay (☎ 7762-0611; Calle Santander; dishes around US$2.50-4; 🕑 dinner Mon, lunch & dinner Tue-Sun) Little streetside Bombay turns out all sorts of inexpensive but carefully prepared vegetarian and vegan goodies ranging from a plate of hummus, mushroom paté,

olives and pita bread to stir-fry veggies with brown rice and ginger-soy-cashew sauce.

Tacos 3xQ10 (Calle Santander; 3 tacos US$1.30) Wanna live like the locals? Load up on Gallo, then head down for some tasty taco action. Try the yummy *hawaiiano*, with chicken, onion, chili and pineapple.

MID-RANGE

Sunset Cafe (cnr Calles Santander & del Lago; mains US$4-6; 🕑 breakfast, lunch & dinner) This open-air eatery has a great lake vista and serves meat, fish and vegetarian dishes. With a bar and live music nightly, it can get quite chirpy at weekends and holidays.

Ristorante La Lanterna (Hotel Dos Mundos, Calle Santander 4-72; mains US$4.50-6.50; 🕑 breakfast, lunch & dinner) This is a good, authentic Italian restaurant with both inside and garden tables; you're welcome to use the swimming pool if you eat here.

La Terraza (☎ 7762-0041; Edificio Rincón Sai, Calle Santander; mains US$5-10) This airy upstairs terrace restaurant has Asian, French and Mexican offerings on its wide-ranging and reliable menu.

Restaurante Tocoyal (Calle del Lago; mains US$8-11; 🕑 breakfast & lunch Sun-Fri; breakfast, lunch & dinner Sat) The Tocoyal is a cut above the other Calle del Lago eateries. Staples are meat, chicken and fish, but there are cheaper vegetarian dishes and *chiles rellenos* (stuffed chilies).

Hotel Porta del Lago (☎ 7762-1555; cnr Calle Rancho Grande & Calle de Buenas Nuevas; breakfast/dinner buffet US$5.75/11.50) This luxury hotel offers lavish Sunday buffets when it's fully occupied, which usually happens on weekends and holidays.

TOP END

Hotel Atitlán (☎ 7762-1416/029/41; Finca San Buenaventura; lunch or dinner buffet US$15) This hotel on the northern outskirts of town (p95) has a beautiful restaurant with some outdoor tables and magnificent lake views. If you come to eat here, you can use the swimming pool and gardens for free. The Sunday breakfast buffet is US$9. Lunch or dinner buffets are offered when occupancy is high; call ahead. Otherwise, ample set meals are available for similar prices.

Drinking

Circus Bar (Av Los Árboles; 🕑 noon-midnight) The best thing about this place is the double swing doors, so you can go busting in like a real cowboy. Yeehar! Following closely is the huge list of imported liquors, US$2 Bloody Marys, good pizza and live music most nights.

Pana Arte (Calle Santander) This is a good place to start, continue or finish your night, with a seemingly endless happy hour (two mixed drinks for under US$2). Besides, it's good to hear Guns 'n' Roses again…or is it?

Ubu's Bar (Comercial El Pueblito, Av Los Árboles) A lounge-style spot good for more laid-back guzzling.

If your beverage is coffee, make for **Crossroads Café** (Calle del Campanario 0-27; coffee US$0.80-1; ☉ 9am-1pm & 4-8pm Tue-Sat), where the friendly North American host has worked in coffee around the world. Try his espresso or the good café con leche made with local organic beans.

Entertainment

DANCING

Socrates (Calle Principal) Opposite the start of Av Los Árboles, this large disco-bar plays thumping Latin pop, highly popular with the Guatemalan teens and 20-somethings who descend on Pana at weekends and holidays (and a smattering of gringos).

After the music stops at the Circus Bar, many folk simply cross the street to **Chapiteau** (Av Los Árboles), a disco-bar with billiards upstairs. A couple of doors down is **El Aleph** (Av Los Árboles), with occasional trance and hip-hop DJ sessions or live music. Both stay open till 3am.

MUSIC

Pana Rock (Calle Santander) This bar hosts varied live music from about 7pm to midnight nightly. The band might just be playing Marley, Lennon and Eagles covers, but it can be fun, often with quite a crowd of gringos and young Guatemalans.

Sunset Cafe (cnr Calles Santander & del Lago; ☉ 11am-midnight) For sunset (and later) drinks overlooking the lake, head for this popular place with great views, food (opposite), a bar and live music nightly.

CINEMA

Turquoise Buffalo (Comercial El Pueblito, Av Los Árboles; admission US$2) The Buffalo shows two movies nightly. Earlier in the day you can choose your own film if there are at least two of you.

Shopping

One of Guatemala's most extensive handicrafts markets is the **Comerciales de Artesanías Típicas Tinamit Maya** (☉ 7am-7pm), selling traditional clothing, jade, leather items, woodcarvings and more. You can get good deals if you're patient and bargain.

Getting There & Away

BOAT

Passenger boats depart from the public beach at the foot of Calle del Balneario. The big, slow ferries have largely been discontinued in favor of fast, frequent lanchas (small motorboats). Boats stop running around 4:30pm.

One-way passage anywhere on Lago de Atitlán costs US$1.30 to US$2, but prepare to pay more. Generally, foreigners end up paying around US$2.50. One way to keep the cost down is to ignore all middlemen (or boys as the case may be) and negotiate the fare directly with the captain.

The main route goes counterclockwise around the lake, stopping in Santa Cruz La Laguna (15 minutes), Jaibalito, Tzununá, San Marcos La Laguna (30 minutes), San Juan La Laguna and San Pedro La Laguna (40 minutes). After departing Panajachel from the Calle del Balneario dock, the boats stop at another dock at the foot of Calle del Embarcadero before heading out (or vice versa, when arriving at Panajachel).

Try to get your traveling done in the morning before the southeasterly wind whips up, making it a tough crossing for small boats plying the lakeside villages. This is particularly true between November and February.

BUS

The town's main bus stop is where Calles Santander and Real meet. Rébuli buses depart from the **Transportes Rébuli office** (Calle Real).

Antigua (US$4.50, 2½hr, 146km) A direct Pullman bus leaves from the Rébuli office at 10:45am, Monday to Saturday. Or take a Guatemala City bus and change at Chimaltenango.

Chichicastenango (US$1.30, 1½hr, 37km) About eight buses run daily, 7am to 4pm. Or take any bus heading to Los Encuentros and change buses there.

Ciudad Tecún Umán (Mexican border) By the Pacific route (210km), take a bus to Cocales and change there; by the highland route (210km), take a bus to Quetzaltenango and change there.

Cocales, Carr al Pacífico (US$1, 2½hr, 70km) Eight buses daily, 6:30am to 2:30pm.

Guatemala City (US$2.10, 3½hr, 150km) Transportes Rébuli goes 10 times daily, 5am to 2:30pm. Or take a bus to Los Encuentros and change there.

Huehuetenango (3½hr, 140km) Take a bus to Los Encuentros and wait there for a bus bound for Huehue or La Mesilla. Or catch a bus heading to Quetzaltenango, alight at Cuatro Caminos and change buses there. There are buses at least hourly from these junctions.

La Mesilla, Mexican border (6hr, 225km) See Huehuetenango in this list.

Los Encuentros (US$0.70, 35min, 20km) Take any bus heading toward Guatemala City, Chichicastenango, Quetzaltenango or the Interamericana.

Quetzaltenango (US$1.55, 2½hr, 90km) Six buses daily, 5am to 4pm. Or take a bus to Los Encuentros and change there.

San Lucas Tolimán (US$1, 1½hr, 28km) There's a bus at 4pm, or you can take any bus heading for Cocales, get off at the San Lucas turnoff and walk about 1km into town.

Santa Catarina Palopó (US$0.40, 20min, 4km) There are daily buses, or get a pickup at the corner of Calles Real and El Amate.

Sololá (US$0.20, 20min, 8km) There are frequent direct local buses. Or take any bus heading to Guatemala City, Chichicastenango, Quetzaltenango or Los Encuentros.

CAR & MOTORCYCLE

Alquiler de Motos y Bicicletas Emanuel (☎ 7762-2790; Calle 14 de Febrero; ☯ 8am-6pm Mon-Fri, 8am-1pm Sun) and **Maco** (☎ 7762-0883; Calle Santander) both rent motorbikes for around US$6/23/30 per one/eight/24 hours. Emanuel also offers better, modern, automatic machines for US$9/45/58. Maco also has cars for US$39/61/250 per eight hours/day/week.

SHUTTLE MINIBUS & TAXI

Tourist shuttle buses take half the time of buses, for several times the price. You can book at a number of travel agencies on Calle Santander. The **Oficina de Microbuses y Taxis San Francisco booth** (Calle Principal), near the corner of Calle Santander, also sells shuttle bus seats (or can call you a taxi). Despite impressive advertised lists of departures, real shuttle schedules depend on how many customers there are, so try to establish a firm departure time before parting with money.

Typical fares are: Antigua (US$10), Chichicastenango (US$7 to US$8), Guatemala City (US$20), La Mesilla (US$35), Quetzaltenango (US$20) and Ciudad Tecún Umán (US$35).

On Chichicastenango's market days, Thursday and Sunday, shuttles run from Panajachel to Chichi for US$4/7 one-way/round-trip.

SANTIAGO ATITLÁN

South across the lake from Panajachel, on the shore of a lagoon squeezed between the volcanoes of Tolimán and San Pedro, lies Santiago Atitlán. Though the most visited village outside Panajachel, it clings to the traditional lifestyle and clothing of the Tz'utujil Maya. The best days to visit are market days (Friday and Sunday, with a lesser market on Tuesday).

Santiago reveres Maximón (see the boxed text, opposite), who is paraded around during Semana Santa. The rest of the year, Maximón resides with a caretaker, receiving offerings. Local children will take you to see him for a small tip.

As you disembark, children greet you selling clay whistles and little embroidered strips of cloth. They can act as guides, find you a taxi or lead you to a hotel, for a tip.

Boats to Santiago from Pana take about an hour; from San Pedro La Laguna 20 minutes.

Orientation & Information

The street straight ahead from the dock leads up to the town center. Every tourist walks up and down this street, so it's lined with craft shops and art galleries. A short distance from the dock you'll see a small **Oficina de Información Turística** (☯ 9am-5pm), run by local guide Martín Tzina Sicay. Martín can set you up with guided trips to most places of interest in the area and put you in touch with almost anyone in Santiago, as well as provide straightforward information and a useful town map (US$0.30).

You'll find a lot of fascinating information about Santiago, in English, at www.santiagoatitlan.com.

Santiago has a **post office**, a **Telgua** fax/telephone office and a **bank** where you can change US dollars and traveler's checks.

Sights & Activities

At the top of the slope is the main square, flanked by the town office and a massive centuries-old **church**. Within are wooden statues of the saints, each of whom gets new handmade clothes every year. On the carved

A GOD IS A GOD IS A GOD

The Spanish called him San Simón, the ladinos named him Maximón (mah-shee-*mohn*) and the Maya know him as Rilaj Maam (ree-lah-*mahm*). By any name, he's a deity revered throughout the Guatemalan highlands. Assumed to be a combination of Maya gods, Pedro de Alvarado (the Spanish conquistador of Guatemala) and the biblical Judas, San Simón is an effigy to which Guatemalans of every stripe go to make offerings and ask for blessings. The effigy is usually housed by a member of a *cofradía* (Mayan religious brotherhood), moving from one place to another from year to year, a custom anthropologists believe was established to maintain the local balance of power. The name, shape and ceremonies associated with this deity vary from town to town, but a visit will be memorable no matter where you encounter him. For a small fee, photography is usually permitted, and offerings of cigarettes, liquor or candles are always appreciated.

In Santiago Atitlán, Maximón is a wooden figure draped in colorful silk scarves and smoking a fat cigar. Locals guard and worship him, singing and managing the offerings made to him (including your US$0.25 entry fee). His favorite gifts are Payaso cigarettes and Venado rum, but he often has to settle for the cheaper firewater Quetzalteca Especial. Fruits and gaudy, flashing electric lights decorate his chamber; effigies of Jesus Christ and Christian saints lie or stand on either side of Maximón and his guardians. Fires may be burning in the courtyard outside as offerings are made to him.

In Nahualá, between Los Encuentros and Quetzaltenango, the Maximón effigy is à la Picasso: a simple wooden box with a cigarette protruding from it. Still, the same offerings are made and the same sort of blessings asked for. In Zunil, near Quetzaltenango, the deity is called San Simón but is similar to Santiago's Maximón in custom and form.

San Jorge La Laguna on Lake Atitlán is a very spiritual place for the highland Maya; here they worship Rilaj Maam. It is possible that the first effigy was made near here, carved from the *palo de pito* tree that spoke to the ancient shamans and told them to preserve their culture, language and traditions by carving Rilaj Maam (*palo de pito* flowers can be smoked to induce hallucinations). The effigy in San Jorge looks like a joker, with an absurdly long tongue.

In San Andrés Itzapa near Antigua, Rilaj Maam has a permanent home, and is brought out on October 28 and paraded about in an unparalleled pagan festival. This is an all-night, hedonistic party where cosmic dancers grab the staff of Rilaj Maam to harness his power and receive magical visions. San Andrés is less than 10km south of Chimaltenango, so you can easily make the party from Antigua.

pulpit are figures of corn (from which humans were formed, according to Mayan religion), as well as a literate quetzal bird and Yum-Kax, the Maya god of corn. A similar carving is on the back of the priest's chair.

There are several rewarding **day hikes** around Santiago. Unfortunately, owing to robberies and attacks on tourists in the Atitlán area, it's highly advisable to go with a guide and tourist police escort. **Martín Tzina Sicay** (opposite) will take you with two tourist police up any of the three **volcanoes** (US$78 per group); to the **Mirador de Tepepul**, about 4km south of Santiago (US$26 for two); or to **Cerro de Oro** some 8km northeast (US$26 for two). Walking to San Pedro La Laguna is not recommended, unless the security situation improves.

Dolores Ratzan Pablo is an accomplished guide specializing in **Mayan ceremonies**. This charming, funny Tz'utujil woman can introduce you to the wonders of Mayan birthing and healing ceremonies or take you to weaving demonstrations and art galleries. Dolores speaks English, Spanish, Kaqchiquel and, of course, Tz'utujil. Tours typically last between one and three hours, for US$15 an hour. Contact her through the **Posada de Santiago** (p100) or **Oficina de Información Turística** (opposite).

Sleeping & Eating

Hotel Chi-Nim-Yá (☎ 7721-7131; s/d US$3/6, with private bathroom US$5/10) This simple hotel is 30m to the left from the first crossroads as you walk up from the dock. The 22 rooms, around a central courtyard, are bare and clean, with concrete floors. The nicest is No 6 on the upper floor, which is large and airy, with lots of windows and lake views.

Hotel & Restaurant Bambú (☎ 7721-7333; www
.ecobambu.com; s/d/tr with private bathroom US$39/48/54;
P) The Bambú is a fine hotel with lovely
lakeside gardens, 600m from the dock.
Walk to the left along a path through lakeside vegetable gardens: the hotel's large
grass-roofed restaurant building is visible
from the dock. The 10 spacious rooms are
in grass- or bamboo-roofed buildings, with
cypress-wood fittings, colorful paint and
earthy tile floors. The excellent restaurant,
with big picture windows, serves an international array of very well-prepared pasta,
meat, seafood and vegetarian main dishes
for US$6 to US$11. For those with vehicles,
the hotel has an entrance from the Cerro de
Oro road on the edge of Santiago.

Posada de Santiago (☎ 7721-7366, 7721-7167; www
.posadadesantiago.com; s/d/tr US$38/50/60, ste US$60-70;
P) This is another of the most charming
hotels around Lago de Atitlán. Seven cottages and two suites, all with stone walls,
fireplaces, porches, hammocks and folk art,
are set around beautiful gardens stretching
up from the lake. There are also a few
budget rooms for US$11 per person, shar-
ing hot-water bathrooms. The restaurant
has well-prepared Asian, continental and
American food and a very cozy ambiance.
The Posada can set you up with hikes and
biking trips. It's 1.5km from the dock; walk
up the street ahead all the way to its end,
turn left, go to the end of the street, and
turn right onto a paved road which almost
immediately becomes dirt. Alternatively
you can arrange for the Posada to pick you
up by *lancha* at the Santiago dock (US$3 to
US$4) or at Panajachel (US$20).

El Pescador (set lunch US$4) Two blocks up the
street straight ahead from the dock, this is
a good, clean restaurant with big windows,
white-shirted waiters and neatly laid tables.
A typical *menú del día* might bring you
chicken, rice, salad, guacamole, tortillas and
a drink.

There are plenty of cheap **comedores** above
the market next to the plaza.

Getting There & Away

Subject to change (of course!), boats leave
Santiago for San Pedro La Laguna (US$1.30,
45 minutes) at 7am, 9am, 10am, 11am, noon,
1pm, 2pm, 3:30pm and 5pm. Pickups to San
Pedro, Cerro de Oro and San Lucas Tolimán start outside the **Hotel Chi-Nim-Yá** (p99).

Buses to Guatemala City (US$2.60, four
hours) leave about hourly, 4am to 2pm, from
the main plaza. See p91 for details of transport from Panajachel.

SAN PEDRO LA LAGUNA

San Pedro is the most popular lakeside town
among budget travelers thanks to its super-
cheap accommodations, super-cheap language schools and hip gringo scene. You'll
see coffee being picked and spread out to
dry on wide platforms at the beginning of
the dry season.

Orientation & Information

San Pedro has two docks. The one on the
south side of town serves boats going to/
from Santiago Atitlán. Another dock, around
on the east side of town, serves boats going
to/from Pana. At either, walk uphill to reach
the center of town. Alternatively, from the
Santiago dock, you can take your first right
past the Hospedaje Tika'aaj and follow the
beaten path for about 15 minutes to the
other side of town. Along this path are
several *hospedajes* and simple eateries. To
work your way across this lower area from
the Panajachel dock, turn left immediately
before Hotel Mansión del Lago, then right
opposite Casa Elena, then left at the top of
that street.

You can change US-dollar cash and traveler's checks at **Banrural** (🕑 8:30am-5pm Mon-
Fri, 9am-1pm Sat), in the town center. There's
Internet access at **D'Noz** (p102), **Casa Verde
Internet** and the **Internet Cafe**, just up the
street from the Panajachel dock, and **Plan-
etoutreach** above Restaurant Tin-Tin. The
typical rate is US$1 an hour. You can call
North America/Europe for US$0.65/0.90 at
D'Noz, or anywhere in the world for US$0.65
a minute at **Hotel Mansión del Lago**, 100m further up the street.

Sights & Activities

Looming above the village, San Pedro volcano almost asks to be climbed by anyone
with a bit of energy and an adventurous
spirit. Unfortunately the trails have been the
scene of robberies, and without a dramatic
improvement in the situation we suggest
that you do not climb the volcano without
a responsible guide who can convince you
that the risk when you go will be minimal.
Excursion Big Foot, 50m to the left at the first

crossroads up from the Panajachel dock, has a track record of responsibility in this respect and goes at 6am when there are at least four people, charging US$4 each. The ascent is through fields of maize, beans and squash, followed by primary cloud forest. You'll be back in San Pedro about 1pm. Take water, snacks, a hat and sun block.

Thermal Waters (☎ 5206-9658), right on the lakeshore between the two docks, has individual open-air, solar-heated pools with great views. Reservations are a good idea; the cost is US$3 per person. Antonio from California, the eccentric horticulturist inventor who built and operates Thermal Waters, also runs an organic vegetarian restaurant and a sweat lodge here.

Several **walks** between San Pedro and neighboring villages make terrific day trips, but please read Dangers & Annoyances on p90 and seek reliable local advice before starting out. You can walk west to San Juan La Laguna (30 minutes), San Pablo La Laguna (1½ hours), San Marcos (three hours), Jaibalito (five hours) and, finally, Santa Cruz (all day). From the last three you can easily hail a *lancha* back to San Pedro until around 3pm.

Courses

The standard price for four hours of one-on-one classes, five days a week, is US$50 to US$55. Accommodations with a local family, with three meals daily (except Sunday), usually cost US$40. Schools can also organize other accommodations options. Schools include:

Casa Rosario (☎ 5613-6401; www.casarosario.com) Run by respected brothers and teachers Samuel and Vicente Cumes, it holds classes in gardens near the lake. The office is along the first street to the left as you walk up from Santiago dock.

San Pedro Spanish School (☎ 7721-8176; www.san pedrospanishschool.org) Well-organized school on the street between the two docks, with classes held under shelters in artistically designed gardens; consistently gets good reviews.

Sleeping

In many places in San Pedro, it's possible to negotiate deals for longer stays and during the off-season. For longer stays, it's also possible to rent a room or an entire house in town. Ask around.

Hotel Restaurant Maritza (s/d US$3/6) From the Pana dock, go 200m to the right from the crossroads just below Hotel Mansión del Lago to reach this basic family-run place, with four small rooms and a garden overlooking the lake. The price includes use of a kitchen and hot showers.

Casa Elena (☎ 5310-9243; 7a Av 8-61, Zona 2; s/d US$2/4, with private bathroom US$4/8) Go 200m to the left from the Hotel Mansión del Lago corner to find Casa Elena, which has good, clean rooms, some of them large with big windows overlooking the lake. The Elena has its own dock.

Hotel Xocomil (s/d US$2/4) This is up the lane opposite Casa Elena. It has quiet rooms around a cement courtyard. To reach further cheapies, continue along 7a Av past Casa Elena and take the second path to the right (after Hotel Mansión del Lago). The path soon passes the very basic **Posada Casa Domingo** (s/d US$2/4) and comes out at the better **Posada Xetawal** (6a Calle B 7-22, Zona 2; s/d US$3/4), which has clean, large rooms with firm beds, hot showers and a kitchen for guests.

Hospedaje the Island (7a Av A 6-11, Zona 2; s/d US$2/4) Turn right at the Xetawal, then left along a wider street after 100m to reach this place with reasonably sized, bare, clean rooms.

After Hospedaje the Island, the street wanders along past a few language schools and travelers' eateries to reach another cluster of accommodations nearer to the Santiago dock.

Hotelito El Amanecer Sak'cari (☎ 5812-1113, 7721-8096; 7a Av 2-12, Zona 2; s/d US$5/8; P) On the left just after San Pedro Spanish School, the Sak'cari has clean, tangerine-colored rooms with private bathroom. Eastward lake views from the 10 front rooms make it a little special.

Hospedaje Tika'aaj (7a Av, Zona 2; s/d/tr US$2/4/5) This popular budget place is 150m along the street past the Sak'cari. Rooms are generic, but the hammocks around the gardens help create a relaxed atmosphere. The shared showers have hot water.

Past Hospedaje Tika'aaj, 7a Av ends at Calle Principal, the street running up from the Santiago dock toward the town center.

Hospedaje Villasol (☎ 7721-8009; cnr 7a Av & Calle Principal; s/d US$3/5, with private bathroom US$5/8; P) The 45 rooms here, just 200m from the Santiago dock, are bare but clean; those with bathroom look onto a grassy courtyard.

Hotel San Francisco (☎ 7721-8016; 5a Av 2-32, Zona 3; s or d US$2.50, s or d with private bathroom US$6) Most rooms at this popular place have a small terrace with lake view. All have a kitchen, which makes it a good deal for language students not staying with families. To find it, go 80m up Calle Principal from Hospedaje Villasol, then along the street to the left.

Eating

Arriving at San Pedro's Panajachel dock, you can't miss travelers' favorite **Restaurante Nick's Place** (breakfasts US$1.60, mains US$2.50) straight in front of you, serving generous portions inside or out on its terrace overlooking the lake. Upstairs above Nick's is another popular hangout, **D'Noz**, with a global menu, free movies, a big bar, board games and lending library.

Clark's Café Luna Azul (breakfast US$2-2.50, lunch US$2.50-3.50; ☺ breakfast & lunch) The Luna Azul has no serious rivals for the accolade of Guatemala's best three-egg omelet and hash-brown breakfast for under US$2. You can see it from the Panajachel dock, and most arriving boats will drop you there if you ask. Otherwise go 300m to the right from the crossroads just below Hotel Mansión del Lago, then 50m down a stone-paved path to the right, then left along an earth path through a cornfield.

The following restaurants are on the path between the two docks.

Vaya Vos Serves Middle Eastern food and pizza. The happy hour is a ripper (7pm to midnight), there's live music some nights and it stays open until 3am.

Café Munchies Set in a lovely garden and serving healthy, wholefood-type meals (curries, stir-fries and tofu burritos) for around US$3. This is a great place to meet other travelers.

Cafe Arte On the road leading uphill from the Santiago dock, it is a good, inexpensive café that serves meat, fish and vegetarian dishes. The Arte is operated by the family of internationally known primitivist artist, Pedro Rafael González Chavajay; his paintings, and those of his students, are exhibited here.

Entertainment

El Otro Lado (7a Av, Zona 2) This is the nocturnal hotspot, with a bar, lounge and roof garden, two nightly happy hours, cocktails from US$1.30, nightly movies, darts, board games, big-screen TV with English-language

news and sports, and techno and trance to gyrate to. You couldn't ask for much more.

D'Noz (above Restaurante Nick's, left) Shows movies nightly.

Alegre Lounge Just up the street from D'Noz, you can dance to salsa and merengue and watch more TV.

Getting There & Away

Passenger boats come here from Panajachel (p97) and Santiago Atitlán (p100). Boats from San Pedro to Santiago (US$1.30, 45 minutes) leave hourly from 6am to 2pm. The last *lancha* from San Pedro to San Marcos, Jaibalito, Santa Cruz and Panajachel usually leaves around 5pm.

San Pedro is connected by paved roads to Santiago Atitlán (18km, a route served by pickups) and to the Interamericana at Km 148 (about 20km west of Los Encuentros). A paved branch heads off the San Pedro-Interamericana road and runs along the northwest side of the lake from Santa Clara to San Marcos. Veloz San Pedro buses leave for Quetzaltenango (US$2, 2½ hours) from San Pedro's Catholic parish church, up in the town center, at 4:45am, 6am and 7am.

SAN MARCOS LA LAGUNA

San Marcos is a peaceful place with houses set among shady coffee trees near the shore. Some believe it has a special spiritual vibe, so it's not surprising that it has become a center for meditation, holistic therapies, massage, Reiki and other spiritually oriented activities. It's certainly a tranquil place for anyone to kick back and distance the everyday world for a spell. Lago de Atitlán is beautiful and clean here, with several little docks you can swim from.

The town's greatest claim to fame is the meditation center **Las Pirámides** (☎ 5205-7302, 5205-7151; www.laspiramides.com.gt), on the path heading inland from Posada Schumann. Every structure on the property is built in a pyramid shape and oriented to the four cardinal points. Among the many physical (eg yoga, massage) and metaphysical (eg Tarot readings, channeling) offerings is a one-month lunar meditation course that begins every full moon and covers four elements of human development (physical, mental, emotional and spiritual). Most sessions are held in English. Nonguests can come here for meditation (5pm to 6pm) or Hatha yoga (7am to 8:30am) sessions Monday to Saturday (US$4).

Accommodations are available for US$12/11/10 per day by the day/week/month. This includes the meditation course, use of the sauna and access to a fascinating multilingual library. A restaurant serves vegetarian fare. The best chance to get a space is just prior to the full moon. Las Pirámides has a private dock; all the *lancheros* know it and can drop you here.

Sleeping & Eating

Hotel La Paz (☎ 5702-9168; per person US$5) Along a side path off the track behind Posada Schumann, the mellow La Paz has rambling grounds holding two doubles and five dormitory-style rooms. All are in bungalows of traditional *bajareque* (a stone, bamboo and mud construction) with thatch roofs, and some have loft beds. Antiques, art works, the organic gardens and vegetarian restaurant, the traditional Mayan sauna and the music and book room all contribute to making this a special place. You can join Hatha yoga sessions (US$2) in a special pavilion at 8am.

Aaculaax (niecolass@hotmail.com; per person US$7-11) An ecological fantasy come true, the new, German-owned Aaculaax is a five- to 10-minute walk to the left (west) along the lakeside path from the Posada Schumann dock. It's built around the living rock of the hillside, also using lots of recycled glass and plastic. Each of the seven double rooms is unique, with terrace, lake views, private hot-water bathroom and compost toilets; four have kitchens. A bar and restaurant should be open by the time you get there.

Hotel Jinava (www.jinava.de; s/d/tr US$13/13/20) The Jinava rambles up lovely hillside gardens from its own little beach on the western edge of San Marcos. Five pretty rooms in tile-roofed *casitas* have hot-water bathroom, small terrace, tile floors and ethnic textiles. The restaurant/bar serves an eclectic menu running from burritos (US$2.40) to Thai curry (US$5.25). *Lancheros* should be able to drop you at the Jinava's own dock; otherwise walk up past Posada Schumann to the main street, then go about 250m up to the left.

Hotel El Unicornio (www.hotelunicornio.com; s/d US$5/9) A favorite with the budget-conscious,

El Unicornio has eight rooms in small, thatch-roofed, A-frame bungalows among verdant gardens, sharing hot showers, nice hangout areas, a sauna and an equipped kitchen. To get there turn left past Hotel La Paz, or walk along the lakeside path and turn right after Las Pirámides.

A couple of *comedores* around the plaza sell tasty, good-value Guatemalan standards.

Il Forno (☼ dinner) Serves delicious pizzas cooked in its wood-fired oven. To get there follow the signs from the main path to the dock.

Il Giardino (☎ 5804-0186; mains US$2.75-5.25) This excellent vegetarian restaurant, owned by a Costa Rican/Italian couple, is set in a tranquil, spacious garden reached just before Hotel Paco Real. Main dishes include pizzas, spaghetti and fondues. The burritos with salsa and melted mozzarella are a treat.

Getting There & Away

You can drive to San Marcos from the Interamericana; the turnoff is at Km 148. See Sights & Activities (p100) if you're interested in walking, but read Dangers & Annoyances (p192) as well. The walk or drive between Santa Clara La Laguna and San Marcos is incredible.

See Panajachel (p97) for information on passenger boats. The last dependable boat back to Jaibalito, Santa Cruz and Panajachel usually goes about 5pm.

JAIBALITO

Accessible only by boat or on foot, Jaibalito hosts Guatemala's most magical hotel, **La Casa del Mundo Hotel & Cafe** (☎ 5218-5332, 5204-5558; www.lacasadelmundo.com; s US$10-20, d US$13-20, d or tr with bathroom US$25-43; ✗). Perched on a secluded cliff, it has gorgeous gardens, swimming holes and a hot tub overhanging the lake. All rooms have views and are impeccably outfitted with comfortable beds, *típico* fabrics and fresh flowers. The restaurant is fantastic. You can rent kayaks or bikes here. Reservations are advisable.

Jaibalito is a 20-minute *lancha* ride from Panajachel or San Pedro. There is a public dock in the center of the village, and La Casa del Mundo has pier.

SANTA CRUZ LA LAGUNA

Another peaceful lakeside village, Santa Cruz features a vibe somewhere between

San Pedro's party scene and the spiritual feel of San Marcos. The main part of the village is uphill from the dock; the hotels are lakeside.

Activities

ATI Divers (☎ 7762-2646; santacruz@guate.net) offers a four-day PADI open-water diving certification course (US$175), as well as a PADI high-altitude courses and fun dives. It's based at **La Iguana Perdida hotel** (below).

ATI Divers also organize the annual garbage cleanup of the lake, during which several tons of trash are collected. This event, typically held in September, is a great opportunity to give something back to the community and make new friends.

Sleeping & Eating

Casa Rosa Hotel (☎ 5390-4702, 5416-1251; la_casa _rosa@hotmail.com; dm US$5, s US$10-15, d US$19-29) With gardens running down to the lake but a little removed from the action of the other hotels, Casa Rosa is a quiet place with clean, plain rooms, with shared or private bathroom, and also stone-and-wood bungalows costing a bit more. There's good food in the restaurant, which so far is the only part of the establishment to have electricity. Spanish classes are available and there's a sauna in the well-maintained gardens.

La Iguana Perdida (☎ 7762-2621, 5706-4117; la iguanaperdida@itelgua.com; dm US$3, s US$6-10, d US$8-15, tr US$12-16) This place has a fun atmosphere and a variety of accommodations from an open-air dorm to a triple with private terrace. There's no electricity and the showers in the bathrooms (all shared) are lovely and cold! Meals are served family-style, with everyone eating together; a three-course dinner is US$5.50. There is always a vegetarian choice, and everything is on the honor system – your tab is totaled up when you leave. Don't miss the Saturday night cross-dressing, fire and music barbecues.

Arca de Noé (thearca@yahoo.com; dm US$3.50, s/d with shared bathroom US$6/10, with private bathroom US$20/21.75) Recommended for its excellent food and the beautiful lake views from its dense, colorful gardens.

SOLOLÁ

pop 9000

Sololá lies along trade routes between the *tierra caliente* (Pacific Slope 'hot lands') and *tierra fría* (the chilly highlands). All the traders meet here, and Sololá's Friday **market** is one of the highlands' best. The plaza next to the cathedral comes ablaze with the colorful costumes of people from a dozen surrounding villages, and displays of meat, vegetables, fruit, housewares and clothing occupy every available space.

Every Sunday morning the officers of the *cofradías* parade ceremoniously to the cathedral for their devotions. On other days, Sololá sleeps.

It's a pleasant walk from Sololá down to the lake, whether on the highway to Panajachel (9km) or on the path to Santa Cruz La Laguna (10km).

TECPÁN

Founded as a Spanish military base during the conquest, Tecpán today is a somewhat dusty town with a couple of small hotels. The ruins of the Kaqchiquel Maya capital, Iximché (ish-im-*chey*) make it worth a visit for history fans.

Iximché

Set on a flat promontory surrounded by cliffs, Iximché (founded in the late 15th century) was easily defended against attack by the hostile K'iche' Maya. When the conquistadors arrived in 1524, the Kaqchiquel formed an alliance with them against the K'iche' and the Tz'utujil. The Spaniards set up headquarters next door to the Kaqchiquel capital at Tecpán, but Spanish demands for gold and other loot soured the alliance; the Kaqchiquel were defeated in the ensuing battles.

The **archaeological site** (admission US$3.25; ☪ 8am-4:30pm) has a small museum, four ceremonial plazas surrounded by grass-covered temple structures and ball courts. Some structures have been cleaned and maintained; on a few, the original plaster coating still exists, and traces of the original paint are visible.

Tecpán has a couple of basic **hotels** and **eateries**. Veloz Poaquileña runs buses to Guatemala City (US$1, two hours) every 30 minutes, 5:30am to 7pm, from in front of the church.

Entering Tecpán, you'll see signs for the unpaved road leading less than 6km south to Iximché. Go in the morning so you can return to the highway by early afternoon, before bus traffic dwindles.

TRADITIONAL CLOTHING

Anyone visiting the Highlands can delight in the beautiful *traje indígena,* traditional clothing of the Maya. The styles, patterns and colors used by each village – originally devised by the Spanish colonists to distinguish one village from another – are unique, and each garment is the creation of its weaver, with subtle individual differences.

Women's *tocoyal* (head coverings) are elaborate bands of cloth up to several meters long, wound around the head and often decorated with tassels, pom-poms and silver ornaments. In some places they are now only worn on ceremonial occasions and for tourist photos.

Women's *huipiles* (tunics) are worn proudly every day. Though some machine-made fabrics are now being used, many *huipiles* are still made completely by hand. The white blouse is woven on a backstrap loom, then decorated with appliqué and embroidery designs and motifs common to the weaver's village.

Cortes (refajos) are pieces of cloth 7m to 10m long that are wrapped around the body. Traditionally, girls wear theirs above the knee, married women at the knee and old women below the knee, though the style can differ markedly from region to region.

Both men and women wear *fajas,* long strips of backstrap-loom-woven cloth wrapped around the midriff as belts. When they're wrapped with folds upward like a cummerbund, the folds serve as pockets.

Tzutes (for men) or *kaperraj* (for women) are the all-purpose cloths carried by local people and used as head coverings, baby slings, produce sacks, basket covers and shawls. There are also shawls for women called *perraj.*

Caïtes or *xajáp* (sandals) complete the traditional outfit.

THE HIGHLANDS – QUICHÉ

The road to Quiché leaves the Interamericana at Los Encuentros, winding its way north through pine forests and cornfields, down into a steep valley and up the other side. Women sit in front of roadside cottages weaving gorgeous pieces of cloth on their simple backstrap looms.

The department of Quiché is famous mostly for the town of Chichicastenango, with its bustling Thursday and Sunday markets. Further to the north is Santa Cruz del Quiché, the departmental capital; on its outskirts lie the ruins of K'umarcaaj (or Gumarcaah), also called Utatlán, the last capital city of the K'iche' Maya.

See p89 for details on the highlands.

CHICHICASTENANGO

pop 23,000 / elevation 2030m

Surrounded by valleys, with nearby mountains looming overhead, Chichicastenango seems isolated from the rest of Guatemala. When its narrow cobbled streets and red-tiled roofs are enveloped in mists, it seems magical.

Chichi is a beautiful, fascinating place with shamanistic undertones despite gaggles of camera-toting tour groups. Masheños (citizens of Chichicastenango) are famous for their adherence to pre-Christian religious beliefs and ceremonies. You can readily see versions of these old rites in and around the church of Santo Tomás and at the shrine of Pascual Abaj on the outskirts of town.

Chichi has always been an important trading town, and its Sunday and Thursday markets remain fabulous. If you have a choice of days, come on Sunday, when the *cofradías* often hold processions.

History

Once called Chaviar, this was an important Kaqchiquel trading town long before the Spanish conquest. Just prior to the conquistadors' arrival, the Kaqchiquel and the K'iche' (based at K'umarcaaj) went to war. The Kaqchiquel abandoned Chaviar and moved to Iximché, which was easier to defend. The conquistadors conquered K'umarcaaj, and many of its residents fled to Chaviar, which they renamed Chugüilá (Above the Nettles) and Tziguan Tinamit (Surrounded by Canyons). These names are still used by the K'iche' Maya, although

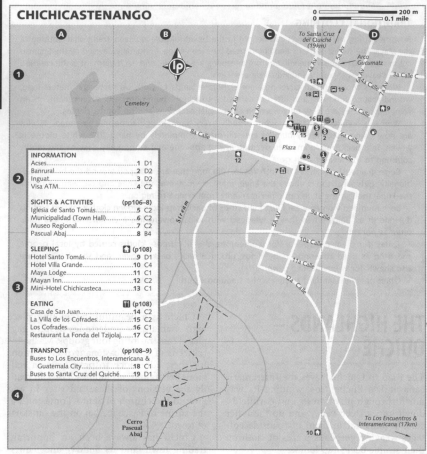

CHICHICASTENANGO

0 ——— 200 m
0 ——— 0.1 mile

To Santa Cruz
del Quiché
(19km)

Arco
Gucumatz

Cemetery

Plaza

Stream

Cerro
Pascual
Abaj

To Los Encuentros &
Interamericana (17km)

INFORMATION	
Acses..1	D1
Banrural......................................2	D2
Inguat...3	D2
Visa ATM....................................4	C2

SIGHTS & ACTIVITIES	(pp106–8)
Iglesia de Santo Tomás...............5	C2
Municipalidad (Town Hall)..........6	C2
Museo Regional..........................7	C2
Pascual Abaj..............................8	B4

SLEEPING	(p108)
Hotel Santo Tomás......................9	D1
Hotel Villa Grande.....................10	C4
Maya Lodge...............................11	C1
Mayan Inn.................................12	C2
Mini-Hotel Chichicasteca...........13	C1

EATING	(p108)
Casa de San Juan.......................14	C2
La Villa de los Cofrades.............15	C2
Los Cofrades.............................16	C1
Restaurant La Fonda del Tzijolaj...17	C2

TRANSPORT	(pp108–9)
Buses to Los Encuentros, Interamericana &	
Guatemala City.......................18	C1
Buses to Santa Cruz del Quiché.....19	D1

everyone else calls the place Chichicaste-nango, a foreign name given it by the con-quistadors' Mexican allies.

Information

Inguat (7a Calle 5-43; ☺ 8am-noon Mon, Tue, Fri, 2-6pm Wed, 10am-6pm Sat, 8am-6pm Sun) occasionally keeps to its posted hour; otherwise, try directing questions to staff at the museum on the plaza or one of the hotels. You'll find the **Mayan Inn** (p108) the most helpful and best informed.

Most banks change US-dollar cash and traveler's checks, including **Banrural** (6a Calle; ☺ 9am-5pm Sun-Fri, 9am-1pm Sat), east of 5a Av, which has a MasterCard ATM. There's also a **Visa ATM** (cnr 5a Av & 6a Calle).

Acses (6a Calle), east of 5a Av, charges US$1.60 an hour for Internet use. The **post office** (7a Av 8-47) is 3½ blocks south of Hotel Santo Tomás on the road into town.

The cemetery on the town's western edge is a decidedly unsavory place to wander, even in groups. There have been several reports of tourists robbed at gunpoint.

Sights
MARKET

Maya traders from outlying villages come to Chichi on Wednesday and Saturday evenings in preparation for one of Guatemala's largest indigenous markets. You'll see them carrying bundles of long poles up the narrow, cobbled streets to the square, then laying down their loads and spreading out blankets to cook dinner and sleep in the arcades surrounding the square.

Just after dawn on Sunday and Thursday, the poles are erected into stalls, which are hung with cloth, furnished with tables and piled with goods. In general, the tourist-oriented stalls sell carved-wood masks, garments and lengths of embroidered cloth; these stalls are around the market's outer edges in the most visible areas. Behind them, the center of the square is devoted to locals' needs: vegetables and fruit, baked goods, macaroni, soap, clothing, spices, sewing notions and toys. Cheap cookshops provide lunch for buyers and sellers alike.

Most stalls are taken down by late afternoon, and prices are best just before the market breaks up.

Arriving in town the day before the market to pin down a room is highly recommended. In this way, too, you'll be up early for the action. Otherwise you can always come by bus on market day itself, or by shuttle bus (p109 for details).

IGLESIA DE SANTO TOMÁS

Though dedicated to the Catholic faith, this simple **church** (cnr 5a Av & 8a Calle), dating from about 1540, is more often the scene of rituals that are only slightly Catholic and more distinctly Mayan. The front steps of the church serve much the same purpose as did the great flights of stairs leading up to Mayan pyramids. For much of the day (especially on Sunday), the steps smolder with copal incense, while *chuchkajaues* (mother-fathers) – indigenous prayer leaders – swing censers containing *estoraque* (balsam) incense and chant magic words in honor of the ancient Mayan calendar and their ancestors.

It's customary for the front steps and door of the church to be used only by important church officials and by the *chuchkajaues,* so you should go around to the right and enter by the side door.

Inside, the floor of the church may be spread with pine boughs and dotted with offerings of corn, flowers and bottles of liquor; candles are everywhere. The candles and offerings are in remembrance of the ancestors, many of whom are buried beneath the church floor. Photography is not permitted in the church.

MUSEO REGIONAL

In the arcade facing the square's south side is the **Museo Regional** (5a Av 4-47; admission US$0.15; 8am-noon & 2-4pm Tue, Wed, Fri, Sat, 8am-4pm Thu, 8am-2pm Sun), which holds exhibits of ancient clay pots and figurines, flint and obsidian arrowheads and spearheads, copper axe heads, metates and a jade collection.

SHRINE OF PASCUAL ABAJ

Before you have been in Chichi very long, some village lad will offer to guide you (for a tip) to a pine-clad hilltop on the town's outskirts to have a look at Pascual Abaj (Sacrifice Stone), the local shrine to Huyup Tak'ah, the Mayan earth god. Said to be hundreds – perhaps thousands – of years old, the stone-faced idol has suffered numerous indignities at the hands of outsiders, but locals still revere it. *Chuchkajaues* come here regularly to offer incense, food, cigarettes, flowers, liquor and Coca-Cola to the earth god. They may even sacrifice a chicken – all to express their thanks and hope for the earth's continuing fertility. The site also offers nice views of the town and valley.

Tourists have been robbed walking to Pascual Abaj – the best plan is to go in a large group. To get there, walk downhill on 5a Av from the main plaza, turn right into 9a Calle and follow this as it winds downhill. At the bottom of the hill, bear left along a path and head up through either of the **morerías** (ceremonial mask workshops, worth a visit on the way up or way back) that are signposted here. From the back of either *morería,* follow the path uphill through the trees to the top of the hill. You'll find the idol in its rocky, smoke-blackened shrine in a clearing. The squat stone crosses nearby have much significance for the Maya, only one of which pertains to Christ. The area is littered with past offerings.

Festivals & Events

December 7 is **Quema del Diablo,** the Burning of the Devil, when residents burn their garbage in the streets to release the evil spirits within. Highlights include a marimba band and a daring fireworks display that has observers running for cover. The following day is the Feast of the Immaculate Conception; don't miss the early morning dance of the giant cartoon characters in the plaza.

The **Fiesta de Santo Tomás** starts on December 13 and culminates on December 21, when pairs of brave (or crazy) men fly about at high speeds suspended from a pole.

Sleeping

As Chichi has few accommodations, arrive early on Wednesday or Saturday if you want to secure a room before market day.

Mini-Hotel Chichicasteca (☎ 7756-2111; 5a Calle 4-42; s/d US$5/9) This hotel's adequately clean rooms with bare brick walls and shared bathrooms are a decent budget choice.

Maya Lodge (☎ 7756-1167; 6a Calle A 4-08; s/d/tr US$25/31/39; P) Located right on the main plaza, this hotel has a bit of colonial atmosphere. The 10 wood-ceilinged rooms, three with fireplace and all with hot-water bathroom, are set along a pillared patio and adorned with woven rugs and Maya-style bedspreads. The hotel has parking and a restaurant.

Hotel Villa Grande (☎ 7756-1053; www.villasde guatemala.com; s/d US$37/43, ste s/d/tr US$49/61/71; P 🛋) This modern, 75-room hotel is 1km south of the center, in low tile-roofed buildings set into a hillside. The walk to or from town can make a nice stroll, though it might not be the safest at night. The Villa Grande has good views, a swimming pool and a restaurant, but the regular rooms are rather stark, and half of them look out on nothing but a rear wall. The suites all have patio, sitting area, fireplace and large bathroom.

Mayan Inn (☎ 7756-1176; www.mayaninn.com.gt; 8a Calle A 1-91; s/d/tr US$80/92/110) A lovely old inn on a quiet street, the Mayan Inn was founded in 1932 by Alfred S Clark of Clark Tours and is the best hotel in town. It has grown to include several restored colonial houses, their courtyards planted with tropical flora and their walls covered with bright indigenous textiles. Not all of the 30 rooms are equally charming, so look before choosing. Each has a fireplace and interesting antique furnishings. The bathrooms (many with tubs) may be old-fashioned, but they are decently maintained. A staff member is assigned to answer your questions and serve you in the dining room (right), as well as to look after your room – there are no door locks.

Hotel Santo Tomás (☎ 7756-1316; hst@itelgua.com; 7a Av 5-32; s/d/tr US$82/97/119; P 🛋) Colonial in architecture and decoration but modern in construction and facilities, the Santo Tomás is very attractive and a favorite with tour operators. Each of the 73 rooms has private bathroom (with tub) and fireplace; all are grouped around pretty courtyards with colonial fountains. There's a swimming pool, Jacuzzi and a good bar and dining room.

Eating

On Sunday and Thursday, eating at the **cookshops** set up in the center of the market is the cheapest way to go. Don't be deterred by the fried-food stalls crowding the fringe – dive in to the center for wholesome fare. On other days, look for the little *comedores* near the post office on the road into town.

Casa de San Juan (4a Av, main plaza; dishes US$1-3) The San Juan is one of the few eateries in town with style – art on the walls and the tables, jugs of lilies, wrought-iron chairs – and its food is great too, ranging from burgers and tortillas to a *churrasco* (steak) or a *plato vegetariano*.

La Villa de los Cofrades (6a Calle A; dishes US$2.50-4) You can't beat this location in the arcade on the north side of the plaza. This is a fine café for breakfast, crepes or larger meals, and a throw of backgammon.

Restaurant La Fonda del Tzijolaj (Centro Comercial Santo Tomás; breakfast US$2-3.50, lunch or dinner US$3.50-6) Upstairs overlooking the plaza, this restaurant combines reasonable food with low-ish prices.

Los Cofrades (cnr 6a Calle & 5a Av; 2-course lunch or dinner US$4.50-6.50) This bright upstairs restaurant (enter from 6a Calle) with excellent food has tables out on the balcony and inside between brick arches. The set lunch or dinner is substantial; simpler fare is available too.

Mayan Inn (8a Calle A 1-91; set breakfast/lunch/dinner US$6/12/12) The three dining rooms at Chichi's classiest hotel have beamed ceilings, red-tiled floors, colonial-style tables and chairs, and decorations of colorful local cloth. Waiters wear traditional costumes evolved from the dress of Spanish colonial farmers: colorful headdress, sash, black embroidered tunic, half-length trousers and squeaky leather sandals called *caïtes*. The food may not be as stellar as the costuming, however.

Getting There & Away

BUS

Buses heading south to Los Encuentros, Panajachel, Quetzaltenango, Guatemala City and all other points reached from the

JEFFREY N. BECOM

An *alfombra* (carpet of dyed sawdust) for the Easter procession during Semana Santa (p84)

RICHARD I'ANSON

Masks for sale at the Sunday market (p106) in Chichicastenango

The colorful church of San Andrés Xequl (p120)

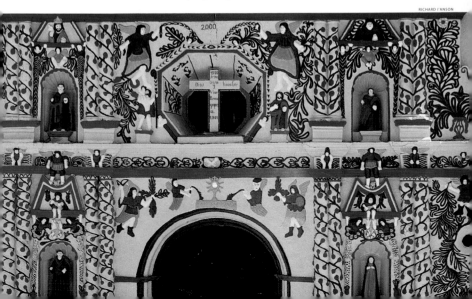

RICHARD I'ANSON

RICHARD I'ANSON

Lago de Atitlán (p89) at sunset

CHRIS BAR...

Río Cahabón flowing near Semuc Champey (p143)

View over Sololá (p104) with Lago de Atitlán and Volcán San Pedro

RICHARD I'AN...

Interamericana normally arrive and depart from the corner of 5a Calle and 5a Av. Buses heading north to Santa Cruz del Quiché stop half a block downhill on the same street (5a Av). On market days, however, buses to or from the south may stop at the corner of 7a Av and 9a Calle, to avoid the congested central streets.

Antigua (3½hr, 108km) Take any bus heading for Guatemala City and change at Chimaltenango.

Guatemala City (US$1.55, 3hr, 145km) Buses run every 20 minutes, 4am to 5pm.

Los Encuentros (US$0.65, 30min, 17km) Take any bus heading south for Guatemala City, Panajachel, Quetzaltenango and so on.

Nebaj (103km) Take a bus to Santa Cruz del Quiché and change there.

Panajachel (US$1.30, 1½hr, 37km) About eight buses run daily, 5am to 2pm, or take any southbound bus and change at Los Encuentros.

Quetzaltenango (US$1.50, 3hr, 94km) Seven buses run daily, mostly in the morning, or take any southbound bus and change at Los Encuentros.

Santa Cruz del Quiché (US$0.40, 30min, 19km) Buses go every 20 minutes, 5am to 8pm.

SHUTTLE BUS

On market days, shuttle buses arrive mid-morning en masse, bringing tourists from Panajachel, Antigua, Guatemala City and Quetzaltenango. They depart around 2pm. If you're looking to leave Chichi, you can usually catch a ride out on one of these.

SANTA CRUZ DEL QUICHÉ

pop 13,000 / elevation 2020m

The capital of the department, Santa Cruz, usually called 'El Quiché' or simply 'Quiché', is 19km north of Chichicastenango. The small, dusty town is quieter and more typical of the Guatemalan countryside than Chichi. Few tourists come here, but those who do are treated well. The main market day is Saturday.

K'umarcaaj

The **ruins** (admission US$1.30; 8am-5pm) of the ancient K'iche' Maya capital are 3km west of El Quiché. Start out of town along 10a Calle and ask the way frequently. No signs mark the way and no buses ply the route. A taxi there and back from the bus station, including waiting time, costs around US$8. Consider yourself lucky if you succeed in hitching a ride with other travelers.

The kingdom of Quiché was established in Late Postclassic times (about the 14th century) from a mixture of indigenous people and Mexican invaders. Around 1400, King Gucumatz founded his capital here and conquered many neighboring cities, eventually extending his borders to Huehuetenango, Sacapulas, Rabinal and Cobán, even coming to influence the peoples of the Soconusco region in Mexico.

Pedro de Alvarado led his Spanish conquistadors into Guatemala in 1524, and it was the K'iche', under their king, Tecún Umán, who organized the defense of the territory. Alvarado won the decisive battle fought near Quetzaltenango on February 12, 1524. The defeated K'iche' invited the victor to visit their capital, where they secretly planned to kill him. Smelling a rat, Alvarado enlisted the aid of his Mexican auxiliaries and the anti-K'iche' Kaqchiquel, and together they captured the K'iche' leaders, burnt them alive and destroyed K'umarcaaj.

The history is more interesting than the ruined city, of which little remains but a few grass-covered mounds. Still, the site – shaded by tall trees and surrounded by defensive ravines – is a beautiful place for a picnic. It's also used by locals as a religious ritual site; a long tunnel beneath the plaza is a favorite spot for prayers and chicken sacrifices.

Sleeping & Eating

Hotel San Pascual (7755-1107; 7a Calle 0-43, Zona 1; s/d US$5/10, with private bathroom US$8/13; P) Between the bus station and plaza, this is a clean and friendly hotel with plants in its two courtyards.

Hotel Rey K'iche (7755-0827; 8a Calle 0-39, Zona 5; s/d/tr US$11/19/27; P) Also between the bus station and the plaza, the Rey K'iche has 24 good, clean, modern rooms with brick and/or whitewash walls, cable TV and hot-water bathroom. There's free drinking water, and a decent restaurant open 24 hours daily.

El Torito (3a Av 4-35, Zona 1; set lunch US$3) A real bull's head and several imitations gaze down on diners here, one block west of the plaza. The good-value set lunch will normally bring you soup and a meat dish with *tortillas*. The house specialty, filet mignon, is US$5.50.

Getting There & Away

Many buses from Guatemala City to Chichicastenango continue to El Quiché. The last bus from El Quiché headed south to Chichicastenango and Los Encuentros leaves midafternoon.

El Quiché is the jumping-off point for the somewhat remote reaches of northern Quiché, which extend all the way to the Mexican border. Departures from the bus station include:

Chichicastenango (US$0.40, 30min, 19km) Take any bus heading for Guatemala City.

Guatemala City (US$2.10, 3½hr, 163km) Buses run every 20 minutes, 3am to 5pm.

Los Encuentros (US$0.80, 1hr, 36km) Take any bus heading for Guatemala City.

Nebaj (US$1.70, 2½hr, 75km) There are eight departures daily between approximately 8:30am and 5pm.

Sacapulas (US$1, 1hr, 45km) Buses go about every hour, 8:30am to 5pm; or take any bus heading for Nebaj or Uspantán.

Uspantán (US$2, 3hr, 75km) Buses go at approximately 9:30am, 10:30am, 1:30pm, 3pm and 3:30pm.

SACAPULAS TO COBÁN

Heading east out of Sacapulas, the road meanders up sadly deforested slopes before reaching the village of **Uspantán** (population 3500). Rigoberta Menchú, the 1992 Nobel Peace Prize laureate, grew up a five-hour walk from Uspantán (see the boxed text on p91). Be aware that Menchú is not universally loved around here.

If you're headed to Cobán by bus, you'll be spending the night in Uspantán, as the two daily eastbound buses leave at 3am and 5am (US$1.30, 4½ hours); these buses fill up fast, so get to the stop at least half an hour early. Note that it can get very cold here.

Pensión Galindo (5a Calle 2-09; s/d US$3/6), about three blocks from the plaza, has a dozen tiny, clean rooms round a neat little patio open to the stars. Banrural on the plaza will change US dollars.

Along with the Huehue to Sacapulas leg of the same highway (see East toward Cobán under Around Huehuetenango, p127), the Uspantán to Cobán road is one of the most gorgeous rides in Guatemala. Sit on the right for views.

NEBAJ

pop 11,000 / elevation 1900m

High among the Cuchumatanes are the Ixil Maya villages of Nebaj, Chajul and Cotzal, which form the famous Triángulo Ixil (Ixil Triangle). The scenery is breathtaking and the local people, removed from modern influences, proudly preserve their ancient way of life. They make excellent handicrafts, mostly textiles, and the Nebaj women wear beautiful *huipiles.*

Nebaj's remote location has been both a blessing and a curse. The Spaniards found it difficult to conquer, and they laid waste to the area when they finally did. In more recent times, guerrilla forces made the area a base of operations, drawing strong measures from the army to dislodge them, particularly during the short, brutal reign of Ríos Montt. The few surviving inhabitants of these villages either fled into Mexico or were herded into 'strategic hamlets.' Refugees are still making their way back home here.

Travelers come to Nebaj for the scenery, local culture, excellent handicrafts, market (Thursday and Sunday) and, during the second week in August, the annual festival honoring La Virgen de la Asunción.

Information

Bancafé (2a Av 46; ⊙ 9am-4pm Mon-Fri, 9am-1pm Sat), one block east from the northeast corner of the Parque, then half a block north, changes US-dollar cash and traveler's checks and has a Visa ATM. The **post office** (5a Av 4-37) is one block north of the Parque. **Centro de Internet Cámara de Comercio** (2a Av; ⊙ 8am-9pm), in the same block as Bancafé, charges US$0.50 per 20 minutes online.

Trekking Ixil (below) sells a very useful booklet, *Trekking en la Región Ixil* (US$2), full of maps and information on village walks.

There's a heap of fascinating and helpful information about Nebaj in Spanish at www .nebaj.org. If you can't understand Spanish, the maps and listings are still useful.

Hiking

Trekking Ixil (☎ 5418-3940; 3a Calle, Zona 1), in the El Descanso building, offers hikes with informative young local guides. Like the other enterprises in this building, a portion of its profits goes to a lending library for children and young adults. Short one-day hikes, costing US$5.25 for one person, plus US$2.60 for each extra person, go to **Las Cataratas** (a series of waterfalls on the Río Las Cataratas north of town), or around town with visits to the **sacred sites** of the *costumbristas* (people who still practice pre-Christian Maya rites). Multiday treks, from US$6.50 per person plus US$2.50 per additional person, pass through the stunning surrounding countryside with stops in small villages.

Las Cataratas is actually easy enough to reach on your own: walk 1.3km past Hotel Ilebal Tenam along the Chajul road, to a bridge over a small river. Immediately before the bridge, turn left (north) onto a gravel road and follow the river. Walking downriver for 45 minutes to an hour, you'll pass several small waterfalls before reaching a larger waterfall about 25m high.

Sleeping & Eating

Hotel Ixil (☎ 7756-0036; 10a Calle, Zona 4; per person US$3) Hotel Ixil is a friendly budget spot with bare, clean rooms with shared hot-water bathrooms, around two courtyards. Rooms sleep up to four. Buses from the south come into town up 5a Av and almost pass the door.

Anexo Hotel Ixil (☎ 7756-0036; cnr 2a Av & 9a Calle, Zona 5; s/d US$7/13; **P**) This is the best place in town, just one block south of the bus station. The clean, bright, good-sized rooms, on two levels around a garden courtyard with parking, have cable TV and private hot-water bathroom. Good breakfasts cost US$2.50.

Hotel Villa Nebaj (Av 15 de Septiembre) When completed, this larger, mid-range hotel under construction two blocks from the Parque, will likely provide the most comfortable lodgings in town.

El Descanso (☎ 5418-3940; 3a Calle, Zona 1; items US$2-3.25; ☺ 6am-10pm) A two-floor café with bar and lounge areas, good music and board games, serving everything from salads to sandwiches to *churrascos*.

Restaurante Maya-Inca (☎ 7756-0058; 5a Calle 1-90; lunch or dinner US$3; ☺ breakfast, lunch & dinner) This is a very clean little restaurant 1½ blocks east of the Parque. Your US$3 dinner could be Peruvian *papas rellenas* (baked potatoes with a minced-meat, raisin and egg filling), accompanied by beans, avocado, soup, a drink, bread, butter, jam, fruit salad and honey. Large and excellent breakfasts cost US$2.30. Also here is a room with quality weavings done by widows of the Triángulo Ixil.

Getting There & Away

About eight daily buses run to/from Santa Cruz del Quiché (US$1.70, 2½ hours) via Sacapulas (US$1, 1½ hours). The best time to get one is between 5am and 8am, and the last departure may be no later than noon. There's an 11pm bus all the way to Guatemala City via Chichicastenango.

To head west to Huehuetenango or east to Cobán, change at Sacapulas. It's a matter of luck whether you make Cobán in one day from Nebaj.

WESTERN HIGHLANDS

The areas around Quetzaltenango, Totonicapán and Huehuetenango are more mountainous and less frequented by tourists than regions closer to Guatemala City. The scenery here is just as beautiful and the indigenous culture just as fascinating. Travelers going to and from the border post at La Mesilla find these towns welcome breaks, and the area offers some interesting excursion possibilities.

See The Highlands – Lago de Atitlán (p89) for introductory information on the highlands.

CUATRO CAMINOS

Heading westward from Los Encuentros, the Interamericana twists and turns ever higher into the mountains, bringing increasingly dramatic scenery and cooler temperatures. After 59km you come to the important highway junction known as Cuatro Caminos (Four Roads), where you can continue north (straight on) to Huehuetenango (77km), turn east to Totonicapán (12km) or turn southwest to Quetzaltenango (Xela) (13km). Buses pass through Cuatro Caminos about every half hour from 6am to 6pm, on their way between Totonicapán and Quetzaltenango.

QUETZALTENANGO (XELA)

pop 119,000 / elevation 2335m

Almost everyone calls Quetzaltenango by its K'iche' Maya name: Xelajú, or simply Xela (*shay*-lah). Not as frantic as the capital, and not as gringofied as Antigua, Xela sits somewhere in the middle and is many travelers' favorite Guatemalan city. The commercial center of southwestern Guatemala, it's the country's second-largest city and the center of the K'iche' Maya people.

Xela's good selection of hotels makes it an excellent base for day trips to hot springs, lakes and traditional villages. In

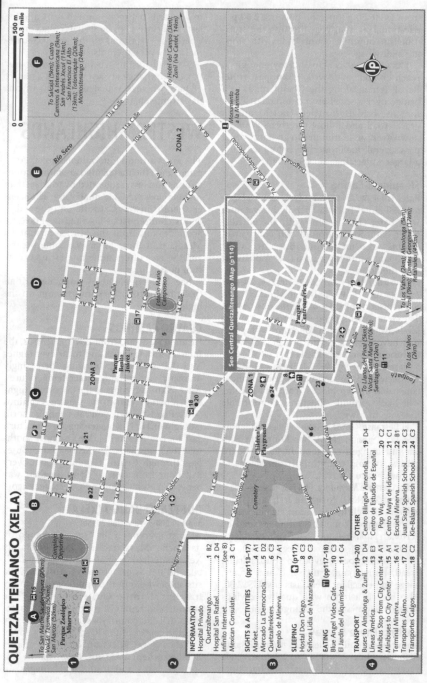

recent years, Xela has built a reputation for its Spanish schools.

History

Quetzaltenango came under the sway of the K'iche' Maya of K'umarcaaj in the 14th century. Before that it had been a Mam Maya town. See K'umarcaaj (p109) for more on this period.

With the mid-19th-century formation of the Federation of Central America, Quetzaltenango initially decided on federation with Chiapas and Mexico. Later, the city switched alliances and joined the Central American Federation, becoming an integral part of Guatemala in 1840.

The late-19th-century coffee boom augmented Quetzaltenango's wealth. The city prospered until 1902, when a dual calamity, an earthquake and a volcanic eruption, brought mass destruction. At the intersection of the roads to the Pacific Slope, Mexico and Guatemala City, today it's again busy with commerce.

Orientation

The heart of Xela is the Parque Centroamérica, shaded by old trees, graced with neoclassical monuments and surrounded by the city's important buildings.

The main bus station is Terminal Minerva on 7a Calle, Zona 3, on the western outskirts and next to one of the city's main markets. City bus Nos 2, 6 and 10 run between Terminal Minerva and Parque Centroamérica – look for 'Terminal' and 'Parque' signs in the front windows of the buses.

Information

BOOKSTORES

El Libro Abierto (Map p114; 15a Av A 1-56, Zona 1) Great selection of books in English and Spanish on Guatemala and the Maya, plus Lonely Planet guides, fiction, dictionaries, language textbooks and maps; will buy used books.

Vrisa Bookshop (Map p114; 15a Av 3-64, Zona 1) Excellent range of second-hand books in English.

EMERGENCY

Bomberos (Firefighters; ☎ 7761-2002)
Cruz Roja (Red Cross; ☎ 7761-2746)
Policía Municipal (☎ 7761-5805)

INTERNET ACCESS

Email access here is some of the cheapest in Guatemala at around US$0.80 to US$0.90

an hour. These are just some of the places available:

Celas Maya (Map p114; 6a Calle 14-55, Zona 1) Language school with public Internet room; lots of computers (p115).
Infinito Internet (Map p112; 7a Calle 15-16, Zona 1)
S@turno Internet (Map p114; 15a Av 3-51, Zona 1) Scanning and printing services available here too.

INTERNET RESOURCES

Xela Pages (www.xelapages.com) is packed with information, though not all is fully up-to-date.

MEDICAL SERVICES

Hospital Privado Quetzaltenango (Map p112; ☎ 7761-4381, Calle Rodolfo Robles 23-51)
Hospital San Rafael (Map p112; ☎ 7761-4414, 7761-2956, 9a Calle 10-41, Zona 1) Has 24-hour emergency service.

MONEY

Parque Centroamérica is the place for banks. A MasterCard ATM and a Visa ATM are on the west side of the plaza.

Banco de Occidente (Map p114; ☽ 8:30am-7pm Mon-Fri, 8:30am-1:30pm Sat) In the beautiful building on the north side of the plaza, changes US-dollar cash and traveler's checks and gives advances on Visa card.

POST

DHL (Map p114; cnr 12a Av & 1a Calle)
Main Post Office (Map p114; 4a Calle 15-07, Zona 1)

TELEPHONE

You'll find plenty of card phones outside **Telgua** (Map p114; cnr 15a Av & 4a Calle). Several places offer international telephone services, including:

Infinito Internet (Map p112; 7a Calle 15-16, Zona 1) US$0.20/0.25/0.40 a minute to USA/Canada/Europe.
Megatel (Map p114; 1a Calle 14-35, Zona 1; ☽ 8am-8pm Mon-Sat, 8am-6pm Sun) US$0.45/0.55/0.60 a minute to USA/Canada/Europe.

TOURIST INFORMATION

Inguat (Map p114; ☎ /fax 7761-4931; ☽ 8am-1pm & 2-5pm Mon-Fri, 8am-1pm Sat) Next door to the Museo de Historia Natural, at the southern end of Parque Centroamérica. It offers free maps and information about the town and the area in Spanish, English and Italian.

Sights & Activities

PARQUE CENTROAMÉRICA   Map p114

This plaza and its surrounding buildings are pretty much all there is to see in Xela

GUATEMALA

CENTRAL QUETZALTENANGO (XELA)

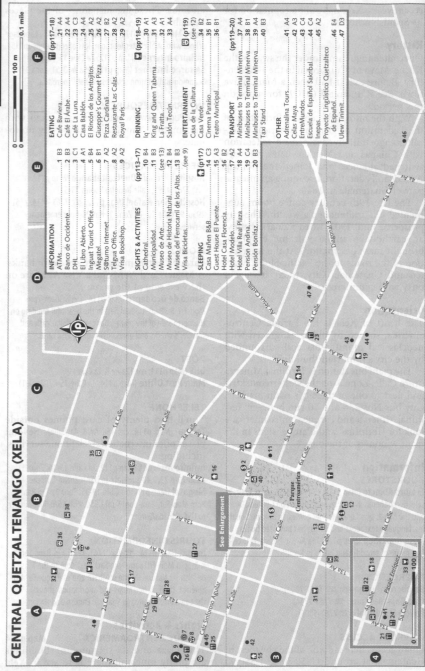

INFORMATION	
ATMs....................................	1 B3
Banco de Occidente...............	2 B3
DHL.....................................	3 C1
El Libro Abierto.....................	4 A1
Inguat Tourist Office..............	5 B4
Megatel................................	6 B1
Søturno Internet....................	7 A2
Telgua Office........................	8 A2
Vrisa Bookshop.....................	9 A2

SIGHTS & ACTIVITIES	(pp113–17)
Cathedral.............................	10 B4
Municipalidad.......................	11 B3
Museo de Arte.......................	(see 13)
Museo de Historia Natural......	12 B4
Museo del Ferrocarril de los Altos..	13 B3
Vrisa Bicicletas.....................	(see 9)

SLEEPING	(p117)
Casa Mañen B&B...................	14 C3
Guest House El Puente...........	15 A3
Hotel Casa Florencia..............	16 B2
Hotel Modelo........................	17 A2
Hotel Villa Real Plaza............	18 A4
Pensión Andina.....................	19 C4
Pensión Bonifaz....................	20 B3

EATING	(pp117–18)
Café Baviera.........................	21 A4
Café El Árabe........................	22 A4
Café La Luna........................	23 C3
Casa Babilón.........................	24 A4
El Rincón de los Antojitos......	25 A2
Giuseppe's Gourmet Pizza......	26 A2
Pizza Cardinali......................	27 B2
Restaurante Las Calas............	28 A2
Royal Paris...........................	29 A2

DRINKING	(pp118–19)
Iq'.......................................	30 A1
King and Queen Taberna........	31 A3
La Fratta..............................	32 A1
Salón Tecún.........................	33 A4

ENTERTAINMENT	(p119)
Casa de la Cultura.................	(see 12)
Casa Verde...........................	34 B2
Cinema Paraíso.....................	35 B1
Teatro Municipal...................	36 B1

TRANSPORT	(pp119–20)
Minibuses to Terminal Minerva..	37 A4
Minibuses to Terminal Minerva..	38 B1
Minibuses to Terminal Minerva..	39 A4
Taxi Stand...........................	40 B3

OTHER	
Adrenalina Tours...................	41 A4
Celas Maya..........................	42 A3
EntreMundos........................	43 C4
Escuela de Español Sakribal....	44 C4
Inepas.................................	45 A2
Proyecto Lingüístico Quetzalteco de Español....	46 E4
Ulew Tinimit.........................	47 D3

proper. At its southeast end, the Casa de la Cultura holds the **Museo de Historia Natural** (admission US$0.80; 8am-noon & 2-6pm Mon-Fri, 9am-1pm Sat), which has exhibits on the Maya, the liberal revolution in Central American politics and the Estado de Los Altos, of which Quetzaltenango was the capital. Marimbas, weaving, taxidermy and other local lore also claim places here.

The once-crumbling **cathedral** has been rebuilt in the last few decades and was still being renovated at the time of writing. Up the block, the **Municipalidad** (Town Hall) follows the grandiose neoclassical style so favored as a symbol of culture in this wild mountain country. On the plaza's northwest side, the palatial **Pasaje Enríquez**, between 4a and 5a Calles, was built to be lined with elegant shops, but has declined with grungy dignity.

At the plaza's southwest corner, the **Museo del Ferrocarril de los Altos** (admission US$0.80; 8am-noon & 2-6pm Mon-Fri, 9am-1pm Sat) focuses on the railroad that once connected Xela and Retalhuleu. Upstairs you'll find the **Museo de Arte** (admission US$0.80; 8am-noon & 2-6pm Mon-Fri, 9am-1pm Sat) exhibiting mostly modern art, along with schools of art, dance and marimba.

OTHER SIGHTS

Walk north on 14a Av to 1a Calle to see the impressive neoclassical **Teatro Municipal** (Map p114), which hosts regular performing-arts productions, from international dance recitals to the crowning of La Señorita Quetzaltenango (see Entertainment, p119).

Check out **Mercado La Democracia** (Map p112; 1a Calle, Zona 3), 10 blocks north of Parque Centroamérica, for the hustle of a real Guatemalan city market.

About 3km northwest of Parque Centroamérica, near the Terminal Minerva bus station and another big market, is the **Parque Zoológico Minerva** (Map p112; admission free; 9am-5pm Tue-Sun), a zoo-park with a few monkeys, coyotes, raccoons, deer, Barbary sheep and a sad, solitary lion. Outside the zoo on an island in the middle of 4a Calle stands the neoclassical **Templo de Minerva** (Map p112), built by dictator Estrada Cabrera to honor the Roman goddess of education and to inspire Guatemalans to new heights of learning.

CYCLING

Cycling is a excellent way to explore the surrounding countryside or commute to

Spanish class. Fuentes Georginas, San Andrés Xequl and the steam vents at Los Vahos – see Around Quetzaltenango (Xela), later – are all attainable day trips. **Vrisa Bicicletas** (Map p114; 15a Av 3-64, Zona 1) rents mountain and town bikes for US$3.50/9.50 a day/week.

HIKING

Volcán Tajumulco (4220m) is the highest point in Central America and a challenging two-day hike from Quetzaltenango. Volcán Santiaguito (2488m) and Volcán Santa María (3772m) can also be ascended.

Quetzaltrekkers (Map p112; 7761-5865; www .quetzaltrekkers.org; Casa Argentina's, Diagonal 12 8-37, Zona 1) This well-run outfit specializes in volcano ascents and other hikes, sometimes camping along the way. Two-day Tajumulco trips (US$40) start every Saturday. Quetzaltrekkers also offers full-moon ascents of Santa María (US$13) and unusual two-day Santiaguito trips (US$50) starting from the ghost town of El Palmar Viejo, south of the mountain. A three-day Quetzaltenango–Lago de Atitlán trek, starting every Saturday, is US$65. Prices include transport, food, equipment and guide (usually a foreign volunteer). Quetzaltrekkers is a nonprofit organization that exists to fund the Escuela de la Calle, a free school in a poor neighborhood of Xela, and a dormitory for street children.

Courses

In recent years, Xela has become well known for its Spanish-language schools. Unlike Antigua, it is not overrun with foreigners, but it does have a small student social scene. See www.xelapages.com/schools .htm for information on many of the schools here.

Most of the Spanish schools participate in social-action programs with the local K'iche' people and provide an opportunity for students to get involved. The standard price is US$110/125 per week for four/five hours of instruction per day, Monday to Friday, including room and board with a local family, or around US$80/95 per week without homestay. Some schools charge up to 20% more tuition during the high season (June through August), and many require nonrefundable registration fees. College students may be able to take classes for academic credit.

The following are among the many reputable schools:

Celas Maya (Map p114; ☎ /fax 7761-4342; www.celas maya.edu.gt; 6a Calle 14-55, Zona 1) Set around a pleasant garden-courtyard; also offers classes in K'iche'.

Centro Bilingüe Amerindia (CBA; Map p112; ☎ 7761-1613; www.xelapages.com/cba; 7a Av 9-05, Zona 1) Classes in Mayan languages as well.

Centro de Estudios de Español Pop Wuj (Map p112; ☎ /fax 7761-8286; www.pop-wuj.org; 1a Calle 17-72, Zona 1) Pop Wuj's profits go to development projects in nearby villages, in which students can participate. The school also offers medical and social-work, specialist-language programs. There is a party at the end of each week.

Centro Maya de Idiomas (CMI; Map p112; ☎ 7767-0352; www.centromaya.org; 21a Av 5-69, Zona 3) Spanish, K'iche', Mam, Q'anjob'al and Tz'utujil classes. A Maya teachers' cooperative, it charges slightly more than most other schools, sponsors female indigenous university students and has an English-language program for village children.

Escuela de Español Sakribal (Map p114; ☎ /fax 7763-0717; www.sakribal.com; 6a Calle 7-42, Zona 1) Founded and directed by women.

Escuela Minerva (Map p112; ☎ /fax 7767-4427; www .xelapages.com/minerva; 24 Av 4-39) Warm, welcoming staff here and plenty of activities; recommended.

Inepas (Map p114; Instituto de Estudios de Español y Participación en Ayuda Social; ☎ 7765-1308; www .inepas.org; 15a Av 4-59 Zone 1) Offers a range of cheap accommodations other than living with a family, and organizes worthy projects in which students are invited to participate.

Juan Sisay Spanish School (Map p112; ☎ /fax 7765-1318; www.juansisay.com; 15a Av 8-38, Zona 1) Named for the Tz'utujil artist from Lake Atitlán, this is a teachers' collective involved in worthy projects.

Kie-Balam Spanish School (Map p112; ☎ 7761-1636; www.super-highway.net/users/moebius; Diagonal 12 No 4-46, Zona 1) This school can set up internships in community literacy projects and rural libraries.

Proyecto Lingüístico Quetzalteco de Español (Map p114; ☎ /fax 7763-1061; www.hermandad.com; 5a Calle 2-42, Zona 1) This very professional and politically minded school also runs the Escuela de la Montaña, a language school with a maximum enrollment of eight on an organic coffee *finca* in the mountains near Xela, where participation in local culture and volunteering are strongly encouraged.

Ulew Tinimit (Map p114; ☎ /fax 7761-6242; www .intworkshop.com/spanishschool; 7a Av 3-18, Zona 1) Mayan language classes also offered.

Volunteering

Xela has several organizations that need volunteers. The **Asociación Hogar Nuevos Horizontes** (☎ 5210-5055; 3a Calle 6-51, Zona 1), **La Escuela de la Calle** (☎ 7761-152123, Avenida A 2-36, Zona 1) and **Red International** are all based in Quetzaltenango.

EntreMundos (Map p114; ☎ 7761-2179; www.entre mundos.org; El Espacio, 6a Calle 7-31, Zona 1) is a forum for social projects in Xela. Its website has details on over 100 nonprofit projects all over Guatemala, many of which need volunteers, and its magazine, *EntreMundos*, comes out every couple of months with articles and ads about volunteer opportunities.

Tours

Adrenalina Tours (Map p114; ☎ 7761-4509; www .adrenalinatours.com; Pasaje Enríquez, Zona 1) is a professional, knowledgeable and amiable outfit that provides a range of trips in the Xela area. A half-day tour to Zunil and Fuentes Georginas costs US$12 per person (minimum two); a fascinating all-day outing to El Palmar Viejo, Abaj Takalik and a coffee/rubber/sugarcane *finca* is US$42. It also rents out camping gear, offers horseback riding to San Andrés Xecul and other places, and does a range of volcano trips.

Inepas (left) does day tours to Fuentes Georginas, San Francisco El Alto (US$25 per person) and other spots, plus camping trips of two or three days to Volcáns Santa María and Santiaguito. Inepas co-founder **Thierry Roquet** (☎ 7761-5057; www.mayaexplor .com) offers his own adventure and thematic tours and still works with Inepas on its longer and large-group trips. Between the two outfits, there are English-, Spanish- and French-speaking guides.

Quetzalventures (☎ 7761-4520; www.quetzalven tures.com) offers a range of Guatemala-wide tours focusing on the country's classic destinations – some involving camping and jungle hiking, others more luxurious. One-week trips are mostly in the US$800 range. It can also arrange Spanish classes and volunteer opportunities. Profits go to community projects.

Festivals & Events

Xela's big annual party is the **Feria de la Virgen del Rosario**, also called the Feria Centroamericana de Independencia, in the week from September 15. Residents kick up their heels at a fairground on the city's perimeter and there's plenty of entertainment in the Parque Centroamérica too. The prizes in the **Juegos Florales Centroamericanos**, an international Spanish-language literary competition hosted by the city, are awarded at this time too.

Sleeping

BUDGET

Cheap accommodations are scattered around the central area, with a concentration just north of Parque Centroamérica.

Guest House El Puente (Map p114; 15a Av 6-75; per person US$3-5) Formerly a language school, this simple old place has a lovely green garden to sit out in. Rates depend on the number of beds in each room; a double is US$10. There are two hot-water bathrooms shared between the half-dozen rooms.

Pension Andina (Map p114; ☎ 7761-4012; 8a Av 6-07; s/d with private bathroom US$6/10) It doesn't look like much from the outside (except maybe a parking lot), but the Andina has a beautiful plant-filled patio, spotless rooms and scorching hot water.

Hostal Don Diego (Map p112; ☎ 7761-6497; don diegoxela@hotmail.com; 7a Calle 15-20; dm/s US$5/6) This friendly place has a large, sociable courtyard area and small rooms with shared bathrooms. Rates include a small breakfast and half an hour online at Infinito Internet next door. It offers reduced rates for weekly or monthly stays, with or without kitchen use.

MID-RANGE

Casa Mañen B&B (Map p114; ☎ 7765-0786; www.come seeit.com; 9a Av 4-11; s/d US$67/80, ste US$122) Most tourist towns in Guatemala have at least one hotel fit for honeymooning couples – a quiet place with romantic atmosphere, comfortably outfitted rooms and tranquil gardens. In Xela, Casa Mañen is it. All nine rooms have traditional appointments (hand-woven woolen rugs, bed throws and wall hangings), hand-carved furniture, tiled floors, TV and private hot-water bathroom, even toweling dressing gowns folded on the beds. Upstairs units have balconies and views, there's a roof terrace, and the breakfast is great.

Pensión Bonifaz (Map p114; ☎ 7765-1111; boni faz@intel.net.gt; 4a Calle 10-50, Zona 1; s/d/tr US$55/68/77; P) Though a bit on the stuffy side, this four-star hotel near the northeast corner of Parque Centroamérica is Xela's best known. Some of the 73 comfortably old-fashioned rooms have cable TV and phone; all have private bathrooms, some with tubs.

The 30 rooms in the original colonial-style building are preferable to those in the adjoining, modernized building. The hotel has a cheery bar and a good dining room (p118).

Hotel del Campo (☎ 7763-1665; Km 224, Cam a Cantel; s/d/tr US$37/47/57; P 🏊) This is Xela's largest and most modern hotel. Its 96 rooms have showers and TV and are decorated in natural wood and red brick, and there's an all-weather swimming pool. Rooms on the lowest floor can be dark, so get a room numbered in the 50s. The hotel is 4.5km (a 10-minute drive) east of the town center, off the main road between Quetzaltenango and Cuatro Caminos; watch for signs for the hotel and for the road to Cantel.

Hotel Modelo (Map p114; ☎ 7761-2529, 7763-0216; 14a Av A 2-31, Zona 1; s/d/tr/q US$30/34/37/40; P) This friendly, family-run hotel has good, wood-floored rooms with bathroom, cable TV and phone. Some are along a pretty patio at one side but tend to be noisier because they front the street.

Hotel Villa Real Plaza (Map p114; ☎ 7761-4045; 4a Calle 12-22, Zona 1; s/d/tr US$43/49/55; P) Only half a block west of Parque Centroamérica, this is a comfortable hotel with young, vivacious management. The 60 large, airy rooms all have bathroom, cable TV, phone and false chimney. There's a courtyard restaurant, bar and sauna.

Hotel Casa Florencia (Map p114; ☎ 7761-2326; www .hotelcasaflorencia.com; 12a Av A 3-61, Zona 1; s/d/tr US$25/38/43; P) This hotel, just a few steps up the hill from the plaza, is run by a pleasant *señora* who keeps everything spotless. There are nine spacious rooms, all with bathroom, cable TV and carpet, but mostly without an exterior window. Breakfast is available in the dining room.

For long-term stays, an option is renting an apartment. Read all the fine print and know the terms for deposits, gas and electricity charges before plunking down your cash.

Señora Lidia de Mazariegos (Map p112; ☎ 7761-2166; silvia@hotmail.com; 4a Calle 15-34; apt per week/month US$59/179) Rents fully furnished apartments with cable TV and free gas for the first month.

Eating

Quetzaltenango has a broad selection of places to eat. Cheapest are the food stalls around the small market to the left of the

Casa de la Cultura, where snacks and substantial main-course plates are sold for US$1 or less.

BUDGET

El Jardín del Alquimista (Map p112; 13a Av D16-53; snacks US$1, meals US$2.50; ☽ breakfast, lunch & dinner) A 10-minute slog up the hill at the south end of town brings you to this vegetarian/vegan restaurant, which offers dishes from around the world. Most ingredients are organic and grown on the premises. It has delicious homemade desserts and the view's not bad, either. Part of the profits go to grassroots ecological groups

Salón Tecún (Map p114; Pasaje Enríquez, Zona 1; burgers, salads, sandwiches US$2.25-3.25; ☽ breakfast, lunch & dinner) The Tecún, consistently Xela's busiest bar (right), serves good food, too. The pizzas (US$4 to US$5) are fine.

El Rincón de los Antojitos (Map p114; ☎ 7765-1308; 15a Av 4-59; mains US$3.25-4.50; ☽ breakfast, lunch & dinner) This is a tiny but popular spot with good Guatemalan and French food, including a variety of vegetarian dishes. The specialties include *pepián* (chicken or pork in a special sesame sauce, a typical indigenous Guatemalan dish) and chicken in mushroom-and-cream sauce. It offers a range of cheeses and wines. From 3pm to 6pm only hot drinks are served – the idea is to use the place as a student study space.

Restaurante Las Calas (Map p114; 14a Av A 3-21; mains US$4-5; ☽ breakfast, lunch & dinner Mon-Sat) An artistic sort of place with lilies growing in the patio, lily-theme art on the walls and a gallery in the back. It offers satisfying portions of chicken, fish or beef, creatively prepared and served with a unique *salsa picante*, as well as paella and cheaper vegetarian dishes.

Café La Luna (Map p114; 8a Av 4-11; cake, salad or sandwich US$2; ☽ breakfast, lunch & dinner Mon-Fri, dinner Sat & Sun) A comfortable, relaxed place to hang out, drink coffee, write letters and socialize.

Also recommended:

Hotel Modelo (14a Av A 2-31; set lunch or dinner US$4.50) For a variety of international fare (p117).

Casa Mañen B&B (9a Av 4-11) For breakfast (p117).

Blue Angel Video Cafe (Map p112; 7a Calle, Zona 1) For excellent food and an awesome tea selection.

MID-RANGE

Café El Árabe (Map p114; ☎ 7761-7889; 4a Calle 12-22, Zona 1; mains US$4-9) Fans of Middle Eastern food will be thrilled to find such an authentic place here, just off Parque Centroamérica. The Arabic bread is made on the premises and the ingredients for all dishes are lovely and fresh. You can fill up on meat dishes but there are plenty of vegetarian choices. The falafel and dips are wonderful.

Pizza Cardinali (Map p114; ☎ 7761-0924; 14a Av 3-41, Zona 1; pasta, pizzas, meat & fish mains US$6.50-7.50) This Italian-owned restaurant has Mediterranean-style decor to conjure the ambiance. The menu of pastas, pizza and dishes like *scaloppine* is equally authentic. *Ravioli al ricotta* is a tasty choice. Portions are large, the wine is good and classical music helps the digestion.

Royal París (Map p114; 14a Av A 3-06, Zona 1; mains US$6-8; ☽ 11am-3pm & 6-11pm Mon-Sat, noon-11pm Sun) This classy French restaurant, in a long upstairs room with cool jazz in the background and a few balcony tables, is just the place for a splurge. It's good on fish and meat – try the *sabroso de res al roquefort* (steak fillet with blue cheese). There's plenty of wine (from US$4.50 a half-liter) and you can start with soup (US$2.50), salad (US$3.50), snails (US$5) or baked Camembert (US$5), rounding things off with a crepe (US$1.50).

Casa Babilón (Map p114; cnr 5a Calle & 13a Av; mains US$3-9) There's French influence, too, at this smaller eatery, where good *churrascos* are served simply with fried mushrooms and garlic bread. Or choose more economical burgers, tacos or sandwiches. French wine starts at US$19 a bottle, but there's Italian too, from US$1.50 a glass.

Pensión Bonifaz (Map p114; 4a Calle 10-50, Zona 1; mains US$8-9) The dining room of this hotel (p117) is the best in town. This is where the local social set comes to dine and be seen. Food is good, and prices, though high by Guatemalan standards, are not outrageous. Two courses might run to US$15.

Other recommended options:

Cafe Baviera (Map p114; 5a Calle 13-14; crepes, croissants, soups, salads US$2-3; ☽ 7am-8:30pm)

Giuseppe's Gourmet Pizza (Map p114; 15a Av 3-68; medium pizza US$6-9; ☽ noon-10pm) A local favorite for yummy, filling Italian.

Drinking

Salón Tecún (Map p114; Pasaje Enríquez, Zona 1; ☽ 8am-1am) Busy all day and night with a healthy crowd of Guatemalans and foreigners, the Tecún claims to be the country's longest-running bar (since 1935). Don't miss it.

King and Queen Taberna (Map p114; 7a Calle 13-27, Zona 1) Popular with a language student/volunteer crowd, this is a fine place for a few beers and a snack.

Iq' (Map p114; 14a Av A 1-37) This long, thin bar plays good rock music and specializes in varied beers and Middle Eastern and Greek snacks such as *baklava*.

La Fratta (Map p114; 14a Av A A-80) The salsa hotspot on Wednesday night until about 1am, with rock other nights and a two-drinks-for-one student deal on Thursday.

Entertainment
Casa Verde (Map p114; ☎ /fax 7763-0271; www.spanish gua.com/casaverde.html; 12a Av 1-40, Zona 1; ☺ 4pm-midnight Tue-Sat) A happening venue for concerts, theater, poetry readings, films and open-mike nights. Thursday night features salsa dancing and there's *trova* (Latin American protest folk) on Friday night. Casa Verde also has billiards, chess, backgammon and other games, and a restaurant/bar.

Cultural performances are presented at the beautiful **Teatro Municipal** (Map p114; 1a Calle) and the **Casa de la Cultura** (Map p114; ☎ 7761-6427) on Parque Centroamérica.

Videos are shown every night at the **Blue Angel Video Cafe** (Map p112; 7a Calle, Zona 1); see opposite. Also showing nightly videos is **Cinema Paraíso** (Map p114; ☎ 5408-1963; 1a Calle 12-20, Zona 1; admission US$1.30), which is a café, too.

Getting There & Away
For 2nd-class buses head out to the **Terminal Minerva** (Map p112), in the west of town. Buses leave frequently for many highlands destinations. Leaving or entering town, some buses make a stop east of the center at the Rotonda, a traffic circle on Calz Independencia, marked by the Monumento a la Marimba. Getting off here when you're coming into Xela saves the 10 or 15 minutes it will take your bus to cross town to Terminal Minerva.

First-class companies operating between Quetzaltenango and Guatemala City have their own terminals (see the list).

All the following buses depart from Terminal Minerva, unless otherwise indicated.

Almolonga (for Los Vahos; US$0.25, 15min, 6km) Buses every 15 minutes, 5:30am to 5pm, with a stop for additional passengers at the corner of 9a Av and 10a Calle.

Antigua (170km) Take any bus heading to Guatemala City by the Interamericana and change at Chimaltenango.

Chichicastenango (US$1.20, 3hr, 94km) Buses at 5am, 6am, 9:30am, 10:45am, 11am, 1pm, 2pm and 3:30pm. If you don't get one of these, take a bus heading to Guatemala City by the Interamericana and change at Los Encuentros.

Ciudad Tecún Umán (Mexican border; US$2, 3½hr, 129km) Hourly buses, 5am to 2pm.

Cuatro Caminos (US$0.25, 30min, 11km) Take any bus for Huehuetenango, Momostenango, Totonicapán, San Francisco El Alto etc.

El Carmen/Talismán (Mexican border) Take a bus to Coatepeque (US$1.45, 2 hours, every half hour) and get a direct bus to El Carmen. From Coatepeque it's two hours to El Carmen (US$1.65).

Guatemala City (US$4, 4hr, 205km); Transportes Álamo (Map p112; ☎ 7761-7117; 4a Calle 14-04, Zona 3; 5 daily 4:30am-2:30pm); Líneas América (Map p112; ☎ 7761-2063; 7a Av 3-33, Zona 2; 7 daily 5:15am-8pm); Autobuses Galgos (Map p112; ☎ 7761-2248; Calle Rodolfo Robles 17-43, Zona 1; 5-8 daily 3am-4:15pm) Cheaper 2nd-class buses go from Terminal Minerva every half-hour, 3am to 4:30pm, but they make many stops and take longer.

Huehuetenango (US$1, 2hr, 90km) Buses every half hour, 5am to 5:30pm.

La Mesilla (Mexican border; US$1.55, 3½hr, 170km) Buses at 5am, 6am, 7am, 8am, 1pm and 4pm. Or take a bus to Huehuetenango and change there.

Momostenango (US$0.50, 1¼hr, 26km) Buses about every 30 minutes, 6am to 5pm.

Panajachel (US$1.55, 2½hr, 90km) Buses at 5am, 6am, 8am, 10am, noon and 3pm. Or take any bus for Guatemala City via the Interamericana and change at Los Encuentros.

Retalhuleu (US$1, 1hr, 46km) Buses every 30 minutes, 4:30am to 6pm; look for 'Reu' on the bus – 'Retalhuleu' won't be spelled out.

San Andrés Xecul (US$0.25, 40min) Buses every hour or two, 6am to 3pm; or take any bus to San Francisco El Alto or Totonicapán, get out at the Esso station at the Morería junction and flag a pickup.

San Francisco El Alto (US$0.25, 1hr, 15km) Buses about every 15 minutes, 6am to 6pm.

San Martín Sacatepéquez (San Martín Chile Verde; US$0.40, 45min, 22km) Various companies have buses that leave when full. Placards may say 'Colomba' or 'El Rincón.' Minibuses also serve this route.

Totonicapán (US$0.40, 1hr, 22km) Buses every 20 minutes, 6am to 5pm, departing from the Rotonda on Calzada Independencia. Placards generally say 'Toto.'

Zunil (US$0.25, 20min, 10km) Buses every half hour, 7am to 7pm, with an additional stop at the corner of 9a Av and 10a Calle, southeast of Parque Centroamérica.

SHUTTLE MINIBUS
Adrenalina Tours (p116) runs shuttles services to many destinations including Guatemala City (US$36), Antigua (US$32), Ciudad Tecún

Umán (US$30), Chichicastenango (US$23), Panajachel (US$23), Monterrico (US$60) and La Mesilla (US$50). Prices assume a minimum of two people; there's 20% off for four people.

Getting Around

Inguat has information on city bus routes. There's a **taxi stand** (Map p114) on the north end of Parque Centroamérica; the cab fare between Terminal Minerva and the city center is around US$3.

AROUND QUETZALTENANGO (XELA)

The beautiful volcanic countryside around Quetzaltenango makes for exciting day trips. The natural steam baths at Los Vahos are primitive and the hot springs at Fuentes Georginas are idyllic.

Feast your eyes and soul on the wild church at San Andrés Xequl, hike to the shores of Laguna Chicabal from Xela, or simply hop on a bus and explore the myriad traditional villages that pepper this region. Market days in surrounding towns include Sunday in Momostenango and Monday in Zunil.

Los Vahos

Hikers will enjoy a trip to the rough-and-ready sauna/steam baths at **Los Vahos** (The Vapors; admission US$2; 🕑 8am-6pm), about 3.5km from Parque Centroamérica. To get there take a bus headed for Almolonga and ask to get out at the road to Los Vahos, which is marked with a small sign reading 'A Los Vahos.' From here it's a 2.3km uphill walk (around 1½ hours) to Los Vahos. The views are remarkable.

San Andrés Xequl

About 11km northwest of Xela is San Andrés Xequl. Surrounded by fertile hills, this small town boasts a bizarre church. Technicolor saints, angels, flowers and climbing vines share space with whimsical tigers and monkeys on its shocking-yellow facade. The village has no visitor facilities.

The annual festival is November 29 and 30 – a good time to visit. The easiest way to get here is by taking any northbound bus from Xela and alighting at the Esso station at the Morería crossroads and hailing a pickup or walking the 3km uphill. Buses returning to Xela line up at the edge of the plaza and depart until about 5pm.

Zunil

pop 6000 / elevation 2076m

Zunil, founded in 1529, is a pretty agricultural market town in a lush valley framed by steep hills and dominated by a towering volcano. As you approach from Quetzaltenango, you'll see it framed as if in a picture, with its white colonial church gleaming above the red-tiled and rusted-tin roofs of the low houses. The cultivated plots, divided by stone fences, are irrigated by canals; you'll see the indigenous farmers scooping water from the canals with a shovel-like instrument and throwing it over their plants. Women wash clothes near the river bridge, in pools of hot water that emerge from the rocks.

SIGHTS

Zunil boasts a particularly pretty **church**; the ornate facade, with eight pairs of serpentine columns, is echoed inside by a richly worked silver altar. On market day (Monday), the plaza in front of the church is bright with the predominantly red traditional garb of locals buying and selling goods.

Half a block downhill from the church plaza, the **Cooperativa Santa Ana** (🕑 7:30am-6pm) is a handicrafts cooperative in which over 500 local women participate. Handicrafts are displayed and sold here, and weaving lessons are offered.

While you're in Zunil, visit the image of **San Simón**, an effigy of a local Maya hero venerated as a (non-Catholic) saint. The effigy is moved each year to a different house; ask anyone where to find San Simón. You'll be charged a few quetzals to visit him and take pictures – see the boxed text (p99).

The **Festival of San Simón** is held each year on October 28, after which the image is moved to a new house. The **Festival of Santa Catarina Alejandrí**, official patron saint of Zunil, is celebrated on November 25.

GETTING THERE & AWAY

From Zunil, which is 10km from Quetzaltenango, you can continue to Fuentes Georginas (8km), return to Quetzaltenango via the Cantel road (16km), or alternatively, take highway 9S down through ever-lusher countryside to El Zarco junction on the Carretera al Pacífico. Buses depart Zunil for Xela (US$0.25, every half hour from 7am to 7pm, 20 minutes) from the main road beside the bridge.

Fuentes Georginas

This is the prettiest natural **spa** (admission US$1.30; ☺ 8am-5pm Mon-Sat, 8am-4pm Sun) in Guatemala. Here, pools of varying temperatures are fed by hot sulfur springs and framed by a high wall of tropical vegetation. A massive landslide destroyed several structures (including the primary bathing pool) in 1998 and crushed the Greek goddess that previously gazed upon the pools. After restoration, spa regulars realized the landslide had opened a new vent. As a result, the water is hotter than ever. Though the setting is intensely tropical, the mountain air keeps it deliciously cool all day.

The site has a restaurant and three sheltered picnic tables with cooking grills (bring your own fuel). Down the valley are seven rustic **cottages** (s/d/tr/q US$12/16/20/24), each with a shower, a BBQ area and a fireplace to ward off the mountain chill at night (wood and matches are provided; US$3.25 for extra wood). Included in the price is access to the pools all day and night. Trails here lead to Volcán Zunil (three hours each way) and Volcán Santo Tomás (five hours each way). Going with a guide is essential – they're available (ask at the restaurant) for US$10 for either trip, regardless of group size.

GETTING THERE & AWAY

Take any bus to Zunil, where pickups wait to take you 8km uphill to the springs (30 minutes). Negotiate the price – they'll probably tell you it's US$4.50 round-trip, but when you arrive at the top they'll say it's US$4.50 each way. If there are many people in the group, they may charge US$1 per person. Unless you want to walk back down the hill, arrange a time for the driver to return.

You can walk from Zunil to Fuentes Georginas in about two hours. Hitchhiking is not good on the Fuentes Georginas access road, especially on weekends.

If you're driving, walking or hitching, go uphill from Zunil's plaza on the Cantel road (about 60m), turn right and go downhill 100m to a road on the left marked 'Turicentro Fuentes Georginas, 8km.' This road, near the bus stop on the Quetzaltenango–Retalhuleu road (note that there are three different bus stops in Zunil), heads off into the mountains – the baths are 9km from Zunil's plaza.

Momostenango

pop 8000 / elevation 2200m

Thirty-five kilometers from Quetzaltenango, Momostenango is Guatemala's famous center for *chamarras* (thick, heavy woolen blankets). The villagers also make ponchos and other woolen garments. As you enter the plaza, you'll see signs inviting you to watch blankets being made and purchase the finished products. The best time to do this is market day (Sunday); haggle like mad. A basic good blanket costs around US$13, perhaps twice as much for an extra-heavy 'matrimonial.'

Momostenango is also noted for its adherence to the ancient Mayan calendar and traditional rites. Ceremonies coordinated with the important dates of the calendar take place in the hills about 2km west of the plaza. It's not easy to witness these rites, though **Rigoberto Itzep Chanchavac** (below) hosts ceremonial workshops.

INFORMATION

Bancafé (1a Calle, Zona 2; ☺ 9am-4pm Mon-Fri, 9am-1pm Sun), a block south of the plaza, changes US-dollar cash and traveler's checks and has a Visa ATM.

The **post office** is across the park on the eastern corner. Medical services are available at the **hospital** (cnr 1a Calle & 3a Av) near the bus stop.

SIGHTS & ACTIVITIES

Los Riscos (The Crags) are peculiar geological formations on the edge of town – the eroded pumice spires rise into the air like something from *Star Trek*. To get there, head downtown on 3a Av, Zona 2, from beside Kikotemal shop, which is two blocks east along 1a Calle from Bancafé. Turn right after 100m at the bottom of the hill, go left at a fork (signed 'A Los Riscos'), then after 100m turn right along 2a Calle and walk 300m to Los Riscos.

Takiliben May Wajshakib Batz (☎ 7736-5537; misionmaya@yahoo.com.mx; 3a Av A 6-85, Zona 3), at the entrance to Momostenango, teaches classes in Mayan ceremonies. Its director, Rigoberto Itzep Chanchavac, is a Maya priest who does horoscopes (US$5) and private consultations and hosts ceremonial workshops. His **tuj** (traditional Mayan sauna; per person US$10; ☺ Tue & Thu 3-6pm) requires advance bookings.

FESTIVALS & EVENTS
Picturesque *diablo* (devil) **dances** are held in the plaza a few times a year, notably on Christmas Eve and New Year's Eve. The homemade devil costumes can get quite campy and elaborate: All have masks and cardboard wings, and some go the whole hog with fake-fur suits and heavily sequined outfits. Dance groups gather in the plaza with a five- to 13-piece band. They are at their best around 3pm, but the festivities go late into the night. The annual fair, **Octava de Santiago**, is celebrated from July 28 to August 2.

SLEEPING & EATING
Accommodations are very basic.

Posada de Doña Pelagia (☎ 7736-5175; 2a Av 2-88, Zona 1; s/d US$2/3) Just off the second of Momos' twin plazas, this has small rooms off a small, open-air patio. Some are moderately clean, some are grubby. A shower, hot or cold, is US$0.65.

Hospedaje y Comedor Paclom (2a Av & 1a Calle, Zona 2; d US$7) A block uphill from the first plaza, this has serviceable rooms facing a courtyard crammed with plants and birds.

Comedor Aracely (2a Av 3-02, Zona 1) Down the street from the church, this friendly eatery is one of the better cheapies.

GETTING THERE & AWAY
You can get buses to Momostenango from Quetzaltenango's Terminal Minerva, or Cuatro Caminos. They run about every half hour, with the last one back to Quetzaltenango normally leaving Momos at 4:30pm.

Laguna Chicabal
This magical lake is nestled in a crater of Volcán Chicabal (2712m). Billed as the 'Center of Maya-Mam Cosmovision,' it's an intensely sacred place and a hotbed for Mayan ceremonies. Mayan priests come from all over to make offerings here, especially around May 3. Visitors are definitely not welcome at this time, so do not visit Laguna Chicabal the first week of May.

The lake is a two-hour hike from San Martín Chile Verde (also known as San Martín Sacatepéquez), a friendly village about 25km from Xela and notable for the traditional dress worn by the village men. To get to the lake, head down from the highway toward town and look for the sign on your right (you can't miss it). Hike 45 minutes uphill through fields and past houses until you crest the hill. Continue hiking downhill for 15 minutes to the ranger station, where you pay a US$2 entrance fee. From here, it's another 30 minutes uphill to a *mirador* (lookout point) and then a whopping 615 steep steps down to the edge of the lake. Start early for the best visibility; clouds and mist envelop the volcano and crater by early afternoon.

The thick vegetation ringing the lake hides picnic tables and sublime **campsites**. Treat the lake with the utmost respect.

Xelajú buses leave Quetzaltenango every 30 minutes until 4pm for San Martín Chile Verde; hail a pickup to get back.

HUEHUETENANGO
pop 40,000 / elevation 1902m
Separated from the capital by mountains and a twisting road, Huehuetenango has that self-sufficient air exuded by many mountain towns. Coffee growing, mining, sheep raising, light manufacturing and agriculture are the region's main activities.

The lively market is filled daily with traders who come down from the Cuchumatanes. Surprisingly, the market area is about the only place you'll see traditional costumes in this town, as most of its citizens are ladinos wearing modern clothes.

For travelers, Huehue (*way*-way) is usually a leg on the journey to or from Mexico, and the logical place to spend your first night in Guatemala. The town is the perfect staging area for forays deeper into the Cuchumatanes or through the highlands on back roads.

History
Huehuetenango was a Mam Maya region until the 15th century, when the K'iche', expanding from their capital K'umarcaaj, pushed them out. Many Mam fled into neighboring Chiapas, Mexico, which still has a large Mam population near its border with Guatemala. In the late 15th century, the weakness of K'iche' rule brought about civil war, which engulfed the highlands and provided a chance for Mam independence. The turmoil was still unresolved in 1525 when Gonzalo de Alvarado, brother of Pedro, arrived to conquer Zaculeu, the Mam capital, for Spain.

HUEHUETENANGO

0   200 m
0   0.1 mile

To Chiantla (4km);
El Mirador (12km);
Todos Santos
Cuchumatán (40km)

Río La Villa

1a Calle

2a Calle

Parque
Central

Market

School

3a Calle

4a Calle

To Zaculeu
(3.5km)

To Hotel Cascata, Hotel California &
Main Bus Station (2km); Tabarini (2km);
Interamericana (4km)

5a Calle

6a Calle

Hotel Gobernador	12	C1
Hotel San Luis de la Sierra	13	A2
Hotel Zaculeu	14	B1

EATING		(pp124–5)
Café Bougambilias	15	C2
La Cabaña del Café	16	B1
La Fonda	17	B1
Mi Tierra	18	B2
Restaurante Las Brasas	19	C1

DRINKING		(p125)
Zafarrancho	20	B2

INFORMATION		
Bancafé	1	B2
Banco Industrial	2	B1
Centro de Información Turística	3	C1
Hotel La Sexta	4	B2
Interhuehue	5	B2
Mexican Consulate	6	C2
Visa ATM	(see 2)	

SIGHTS & ACTIVITIES	(pp123–4)
Church	7 C2
Town Hall	8 B1
Xinabajul Spanish Academy	9 B1

SLEEPING		(p124)
Hotel Casa Blanca	10	B2
Hotel Central	11	B1

TRANSPORT	(p125)
Buses from Main Bus Station	21 C2
Buses to Main Bus Station	22 B2
Buses to Zaculeu	23 A2
Los Halcones Bus Station	24 B2
Taxis	25 C2

Orientation & Information

The town center is 4km northeast of the Interamericana and the bus station is off the road linking the two, about 2km from each. Almost every service of interest to tourists is in Zona 1, within a few blocks of the Parque Central.

Huehue's helpful, English-speaking **Centro de Información Turística** (☎ 5694-9354; Edificio de Gobernación de Zona 1, 2a Calle; ⏰ 8am-noon & 1:30-5pm Mon-Fri) can provide information on the city and the whole Huehuetenango department, which stretches to the Mexican borders north and west.

Bancafé (cnr 6a Av & 3a Calle; ⏰ 9am-7pm Mon-Fri, 9am-1pm Sat) changes US-dollar cash and traveler's checks. There are Visa ATMs at Bancafé and Banco Industrial, a block further north.

The **post office** (2a Calle 3-54; ⏰ 8:30am-5:30pm Mon-Fri, 9am-1pm Sat) is half a block east of the Parque. **Hotel La Sexta** (6a Av 4-29) offers calls to North America for US$0.65 a minute or to Europe for US$0.80.

Interhuehue (3a Calle 6-65B; ⏰ 9am-12:30pm & 2-6pm) charges US$0.90 an hour for Internet access.

The **Mexican consulate** (5a Av 4-11; ⏰ 9am-noon, 3-5pm Mon-Fri) is in the same building as the Farmacia del Cid.

Sights

PARQUE CENTRAL

Huehuetenango's main plaza is shaded by old trees and surrounded by the town's imposing buildings: the Municipalidad (with its band shell on the upper floor) and the huge colonial church. The plaza has its own little relief map of Huehuetenango department.

ZACULEU

With ravines on three sides, the Late Postclassic religious center Zaculeu ('White Earth' in the Mam language) occupies a strategic defensive location that served its Mam Maya inhabitants well. It finally failed, however, in 1525 when Gonzalo de Alvarado and his conquistadors laid siege to the site for two months. Starvation ultimately defeated the Mam.

The park-like Zaculeu **archaeological zone** (admission US$3.25; ⏰ 8am-6pm), about 200 sq meters, is 4km west of Huehuetenango's main plaza. Cold soft drinks and snacks are available. A small **museum** at the site holds, among other things, skulls and grave goods found in a tomb beneath Estructura 1, the tallest structure at the site.

Restoration by the United Fruit Company in the 1940s has left Zaculeu's pyramids, ball courts and ceremonial platforms covered by a thick coat of graying plaster. Some of the restoration methods were not authentic to the buildings, but the work goes further than others in making the site look as it might have to the Mam priests and worshipers when it was still an active religious center. What is missing, however, is the painted decoration, which was applied to the wet plaster as in frescoes. The buildings show a great deal of Mexican influence.

Buses to Zaculeu (US$0.15, 20 minutes) leave about every 30 minutes, 7am to 6pm, from in front of the school at the corner of 2a Calle and 7a Av. A taxi from the town center costs US$2.50 one-way (US$3.25 from the bus station). One hour is plenty of time to look around the site and museum.

EL MIRADOR
This lookout point is in the Cuchumatanes overlooking Huehuetenango, 12km from town (one hour by bus). On a sunny day it offers a great view of the entire region and many volcanoes. A beautiful poem, *A Los Cuchumatanes*, is mounted on plaques here. Any bus from Huehue heading for Todos Santos, Soloma or Barrillas comes past here.

Courses
Xinabajul Spanish Academy (☎ /fax 7964-1518; 6a Av 0-69) offers one-to-one Spanish courses and homestays with local families.

Festivals & Events
Special events in Huehue include the **Fiestas Julias** (July 13 to 20), honoring La Virgen del Carmen, Huehue's patron saint, and the **Fiestas de Concepción** (December 5 and 6), honoring the Virgen de Concepción.

Sleeping
BUDGET
Hotel Central (☎ 7764-1202; 5a Av 1-33; s/d/tr/q US$3/4/6/7) This cheapie has 10 largish, simple and well-used rooms with shared bathroom. Most are around a pillared, wooden interior balcony, giving the place a sliver of charm.

Hotel Gobernador (☎ /fax 7769-0765; 4a Av 1-45; s/d/tr US$4/6/8, with private bathroom US$6/9/13) This is a solid budget choice, but compare a few rooms before choosing, as some are airier and less damp and dingy than others. The shared showers are hot and strong.

MID-RANGE
Hotel Casa Blanca (☎ 7769-0777/8/9; 7a Av 3-41; s/d/tr US$24/30/35; **P**) This bright, pleasant hotel is the best in the city center. The 15 rooms all come with private hot-water bathroom, phone and cable TV, and there are two flowery patios, two restaurants (below) and parking.

Hotel Zaculeu (☎ 7764-1086; fax 7764-1575; 5a Av 1-14; s/d/tr/q ground floor US$15/22/26/29, upstairs US$28/36/45/54; **P**) Half a block north of the plaza, the colonial-style Zaculeu has a lovely garden courtyard, a good restaurant serving breakfast and dinner, laundry service and 37 large rooms, all with private hot-water bathroom, drinking water and TV. Ground-floor rooms are darker and some are damp-affected, unfortunately including some of those around the plant-filled front patio, which is the prettiest area.

Hotel San Luis de la Sierra (☎ 7764-9216/7/8, ☎ /fax 7764-9219; 2a Calle 7-00; s/d US$20/28; **P**) The clean, medium-sized rooms here have pine furniture, TV, hot-water bathroom and nice touches like fan, reading lamp and shampoo. There's a restaurant, too.

There are plenty of hotels near the bus station: leave the east side of the station between the Díaz Álvarez and Transportes Fronterizos offices, and walk left up the street outside to come out on 3a Av, Zona 5. Within 300m or so in each direction here there's a total of at least seven hotels.

Try **Hotel California** (☎ 7769-0500; 3a Av 4-25; s US$9, s/d with private bathroom US$16/32) or **Hotel Cascata** (☎ 7764-1188; Lote 4 4-42; s/d US$8/16, with private bathroom US$12/26).

Eating
Hotel Casa Blanca (7a Av 3-41; set lunch US$2.50; ☯ breakfast, lunch & dinner) For lovely surroundings, you can't beat the two restaurants at this classy hotel, one indoors, the other in the garden. Breakfasts cost US$2 to US$3.50 (on Sunday, from 8am to 11am, it's a big buffet for US$3.25), burgers and croissants are around US$2, and steaks (try filet mignon or cordon bleu) are around US$5.

Mi Tierra (4a Calle 6-46; mains US$3-5; ☺ breakfast, lunch & dinner) An informal café/restaurant/cybercafé with Antigua-like ambiance that serves local and foreign dishes. Breakfast features croissants, muffins, omelets, hash browns, eggs, bacon, pancakes, *tortillas*, juices and good coffee. Dinner choices range from baked potatoes to fajitas or *puyaso* (dinner dish).

Restaurante Las Brasas (4a Av 1-36; mains US$4.50-6; ☺ breakfast, lunch & dinner) Half a block from the Parque Central, this is one of Huehue's best restaurants. The specialties are Chinese food and steaks, but the pizzas are truly *grande* – one small and a salad makes a feast for two people.

Cafe Bougambilias (5a Av north of 4a Calle; breakfast US$2) One of three *comedores* in a line along the southern part of the Parque, the Bougambilias has a team of busy cooks preparing food on the ground floor, while the two upper floors have tables with views over the park and plenty of fresh air. It's good for all meals, with large serves of straightforward food.

La Fonda (2a Calle 5-35; mains US$3-5; ☺ breakfast, lunch & dinner) A few steps from the Parque Central, this clean, reliable place serves varied Guatemalan and international fare, including good-value pizzas.

La Cabaña del Café (2a Calle 6-50; dishes US$2-3; ☺ breakfast, lunch & dinner) Espresso…donuts…cocktails. The food's OK, too.

Drinking

Zafarrancho (4a Calle 6-42) Although downtown Huehue has few bright after-dark spots, an exception is this bar with free tapas, next to Mi Tierra restaurant. Ché and Zapatista photos contribute to its slightly underground feel.

Getting There & Away

A taxi between the bus terminal and town center costs around US$2.50. The bus terminal is in Zona 4, 2km southwest of the plaza along 6a Calle. For city buses from the bus station to the town center, leave the east side of the bus station through the gap between the Díaz Álvarez and Transportes Fronterizos offices. At night until 11pm and after 2am, 'Centro' buses (US$0.15) go intermittently from the street outside; in daylight hours, cross this street and walk through the covered market opposite to a second

street, where 'Centro' buses (US$0.10) depart every few minutes. To return to the bus station from the center, catch the buses outside **Barbería Wilson** (6a Av 2-22).

Buses serving this terminal include the following:
Antigua (230km) Take a Guatemala City bus and change at Chimaltenango.
Cobán (142km) No direct service. Transportes Mejía has a bus from Aguacatán, east of Huehuetenango, to Cobán at 6:30am Tuesday and Saturday, via Sacapulas and Uspantán. In general your best bet is to use whatever buses, pickups or other transport you can find to get to Uspantán, spend the night there and catch the 3am or 5am bus on to Cobán. See Sacapulas to Cobán (p110) for more transportation information. If you start very early you *might* get to Cobán in one day from Huehue.
Cuatro Caminos (US$1, 1½hr, 77km) Take any bus heading for Guatemala City or Quetzaltenango.
Guatemala City (5hr, 266km) Los Halcones Pullman buses (US$4) leave at 4:30am, 7am and 2pm from their town-center terminal on 7a Av; from the main terminal, around 20 buses (US$2.50 to US$4) leave between 2am and 4pm by Transportes El Condor, Díaz Álvarez and Transportes Velásquez.
La Mesilla (Mexican border; US$1, 2hr, 84km) At least 20 buses, 5:45am to 6:30pm, by various companies.
Nebaj (68km) Take a bus to Sacapulas, or a bus to Aguacatán and a pickup on to Sacapulas, then another bus from Sacapulas to Nebaj (p111).
Panajachel (159km) Take a Guatemala City bus and change at Los Encuentros.
Quetzaltenango (US$1, 2hr, 90km) At least 14 departures, 6am to 2:30pm, by various companies.
Sacapulas (US$2, 2½hr, 42km) Buses at 11:30am (Rutas García) and 12:45pm (Transportes Rivas).
Soloma (US$1.80, 3hr, 70km) About 16 buses daily, 2am to 10pm, by Transportes Josué and Autobuses del Norte.
Todos Santos Cuchumatán (US$1.30, 3hr, 40km) Buses at approximately 3:45am, 5:30am, 11:30am, 12:45pm, 1:30pm, 1:45pm, 2pm, 2:45pm and 3:45pm by Flor de María, Mendoza, Pérez, Todosanterita, Concepcionerita and Chicoyera; some buses do not run Saturday.

AROUND HUEHUETENANGO
Todos Santos Cuchumatán
pop 3000 / elevation 2450m

If you're interested in contemporary but traditional Mayan life and dramatic mountain scenery, put the small town of Todos Santos Cuchumatán on your itinerary. Todos Santos lies in the bottom of a deep valley, 40km northwest of Huehuetenango, and the last 1¼ hours of the approach by bus are down a bone-shaking dirt road that leaves the paved Huehuetenango–Soloma road after a 1½-hour climb up from Huehue.

Saturday is market day, with a smaller market on Wednesday. Hiking is excellent in the local hills.

If you're coming to Todos Santos in winter, bring warm clothes.

The **post office** and **Banrural** (◷ 8:30am-5pm Mon-Fri, 8am-noon Sat) are on the central plaza. The bank changes US-dollar cash and traveler's checks.

Todos Santos Internet (◷ 9am-9pm; per hr US$1.60) is 30m off the main street, 400m back toward Huehue from the church.

COURSES

Todos Santos' three language schools are controlled by villagers and make major contributions to community projects: funding a library, medicines, school materials and scholarships for village kids to go to high school in Huehue.

They are:

Academia Hispano Maya Opposite Hotelito Todos Santos.
El Proyecto Lingüístico (elproyecto1@hotmail.com) On the main street.
Nuevo Amanecer (escuela_linguistica@yahoo.com) 150m down the main street, opposite the church.

The standard weekly price for 25 hours' one-on-one Spanish tuition, with lodging and meals in a village home, is US$115. Included are guided walks, seminars on local life and issues, movies, and saunas. All three schools also offer classes in Mam and in Mayan weaving (weaving costs around US$1 an hour or US$35 for a week's course). Individual language classes cost US$4 an hour. The schools can put you in touch with volunteer work in reforestation and English teaching.

FESTIVALS & EVENTS

Todos Santos is famous for the annual horse races held on November 1 (El Día de Todos los Santos), the culmination of a week of festivities and an all-night male dancing and *aguardiente* (cane liquor) drinking spree on the eve of the races. Traditional foods are served throughout the day, and there are mask dances.

SLEEPING & EATING

Hotelito Todos Santos (s/d US$4/7, with private bathroom US$5/9) Along a side street that goes off

to the left a few meters up the hill beside the plaza, this has Todos Santos' most comfortable rooms – bare but clean, with tile floors and firm beds. Three of the four rooms with private bath open onto the street, separate from the main part of the hotel upstairs. The hotel has a casual café, sinks for washing clothes, and hot water.

Hotel Casa Familiar (dm/s/d US$2/3/6) About 50m up the hill from the plaza, this place has bare wooden rooms adorned with past travelers' graffiti, and hot shared showers. The rooms are clean and have plenty of blankets, windows and fine views. There's a sauna, too, and a restaurant where chicken dishes cost around US$2.60 and *mosh* (granola and banana) US$1.60.

You can arrange **rooms with families** (per person US$2-2.50, with 3 meals US$4.50) through the language schools irrespective of whether you are studying. You'll get your own bedroom, and share bathroom and meals with the family. A week's full board should cost US$25.

Comedor Martita (opposite Hotel Mam; meals around US$2.25) This simple, family-run *comedor* (a basic, cheap eatery) serves the best food in town, prepared with fresh ingredients by friendly hosts. You walk through the kitchen to get to the eating area, which has a nice view over the town and valley. A typical meal might be boiled chicken, rice, vegetables, beans, a *refresco* (soft drink) and coffee.

Cafe Ixcanac (also called Restaurante Tzolkin; pizzas US$4-4.50) On the main street 200m east of church, the pizzas here aren't bad. Cheaper salads, sandwiches and breakfasts are served, too.

ENTERTAINMENT

All the language schools show movies on Guatemalan, Mayan and Latin American themes in the evening, with a small charge (usually US$0.65) for nonstudents. The English-language documentaries *Todos Santos* and *Todos Santos: The Survivors*, made in the 1980s by Olivia Carrescia, are particularly fascinating to see here on the spot. They detail the traditional life of Todos Santos and the devastation and terror of the civil war when, by some accounts, 2000 people were killed in the area.

GETTING THERE & AWAY

Half-a-dozen buses leave for Huehuetenango (US$1.30, three hours) between 4:45am and

6:30am, then usually three others between noon and 1pm.

East Toward Cobán

The road from Huehuetenango to Cobán is rarely traveled, often rugged and always inspiring. It can take two days of challenging travel and several transfers to make the 150km trip by bus, but it's well worth it for the views and tableaux of highland life. Adventurous types craving more can continue the odyssey via the Cobán to Poptún route.

Starting high in the Cuchumatanes Mountains, you climb out of Huehuetenango en route to **Aguacatán**, from where you'll have panoramic views of pine-pocked slopes and fertile valleys below. The road then snakes down through the Río Blanco valley to **Sacapulas**, along the Río Negro. This makes a good stopover. For more on the eastward continuation of this route, see Sacapulas to Cobán (p110). Nebaj is reachable on this route by hopping off in Uspantán.

La Mesilla & the Mexican Border

Four kilometers separate the Mexican and Guatemalan immigration posts at La Mesilla/Ciudad Cuauhtémoc, and you'll have to drive, walk, hitch or take a collective taxi (US$0.50) between them. The strip in La Mesilla leading to the border post has a variety of services including a police station, post office and a Banrural.

Moneychangers at the border give a good rate if you're exchanging your dollars for their pesos or quetzals, a terrible rate if you want dollars for your pesos or quetzals.

If you get marooned in La Mesilla, try **Hotel Mily's** (d US$15), which has rooms with fan, cable TV and private hot-water bathroom; bargaining may be in order here. Further down the hill is the super-basic **Hotel El Pobre Simón** (per person US$2).

With an early start from Huehuetenango (or from Comitán or San Cristóbal de Las Casas in Mexico), you should have no trouble getting through this border and well on into Mexico (or Guatemala) in one day. During daylight hours, fairly frequent buses and combis run from Ciudad Cuauhtémoc to Comitán (US$3 to US$4, 1¼ hours) and San Cristóbal (US$7, 2½ hours). From La Mesilla buses leave for Huehuetenango (US$1, two hours) at least 20 times between 5:45am and 6pm.

THE PACIFIC SLOPE

Guatemala's steamy Pacific Slope is lush and tropical, with rich, volcanic soil good for growing coffee at higher elevations, and palm-oil seeds and sugarcane lower down. Along the coast, the temperature and humidity are uncomfortably high – day and night, rainy season and dry – and endless stretches of dark, volcanic sand remind the visitor that beautiful beaches are not Guatemala's strong suit.

The Carretera al Pacífico (CA-2) runs from the border crossings at Ciudad Hidalgo/Ciudad Tecún Umán and Talismán/El Carmen to Guatemala City. The 275km between the Mexican border at Tecún Umán and Guatemala City takes about four hours by car, five by bus – much less than the Interamericana between La Mesilla and Guatemala.

Most towns along the CA-2 are muggy and chaotic, and most beach villages hot and dilapidated. However, Retalhuleu, a logical stopping place if you're coming from Mexico, is pleasant and fun. Nearby is the active archaeological dig at Abaj Takalik. East of Retalhuleu, the pre-Olmec stone carvings at Santa Lucía Cotzumalguapa and La Democracia are unique.

The small beach village of Monterrico, with its wildlife preservation project and nature reserve, is buzzing with foreigners. Otherwise, the port town of Iztapa and its beach resort of Likín are fine if you gotta get to the beach.

CIUDAD TECÚN UMÁN/CIUDAD HIDALGO

This is the preferable and busier of the two Pacific Slope border crossings; a bridge links Ciudad Tecún Umán (Guatemala) with Ciudad Hidalgo (Mexico). The border is open 24 hours a day, and banks change dollars and traveler's checks. Several basic hotels and restaurants are available, but there's no real point in lingering here.

Minibuses and buses depart until about 6pm along the CA-2 to Coatepeque, Retalhuleu, Mazatenango, Escuintla and Guatemala City. Direct buses to Quetzaltenango (US$2, 3½ hours) leave until about 2pm. If you don't find a bus to your destination, take one to Coatepeque or, better still,

Retalhuleu, and change buses there. On the Mexican side, buses run from Ciudad Hidalgo to the city of Tapachula (US$1.25, 45 minutes) every 20 minutes, 7am to 7:30pm.

EL CARMEN/TALISMÁN

A bridge across the Río Suchiate connects El Carmen with Talismán (Mexico). The border is open 24 hours daily, but it's generally easier and more convenient to cross at Tecún Umán. There are few services at El Carmen, and those are very basic. Most buses between here and the rest of Guatemala go via Ciudad Tecún Umán, 39km south. On the way to Ciudad Tecún Umán, most stop at Malacatán on the road to San Marcos and Quetzaltenango road, so you could try looking for a bus to Quetzaltenango there, but it's more dependable to change at Coatepeque (US$1.65, two hours from El Carmen) or Retalhuleu.

On the Mexican side, minibuses run frequently between Talismán and Tapachula (US$0.80, 30 minutes) until about 10pm.

RETALHULEU

pop 40,000

The Pacific Slope is a rich agricultural region, and Retalhuleu – known simply as Reu (ray-oo) to most Guatemalans – is its clean, attractive capital. The balmy tropical air and laid-back attitude are restful, and the region's wealthy coffee traders come here to relax – splashing in the pool at Hotel Posada de Don José or sipping a drink in the bar. Tourists are something of a curiosity in Reu and are treated well.

Orientation & Information

The town center is 4km southwest of the CA-2, along Calzada Las Palmas, a grand boulevard lined with towering palms. The bus terminal is on 10a Calle between 7a and 8a Avs, northeast of the plaza. To find the plaza, walk toward the twin church towers.

There is no official tourist office, but people in the Municipalidad (Town Hall), on 6a Av facing the east side of the church, do their best to help.

Banco Industrial (cnr 6a Calle & 5a Av; ✆ 9am-7pm Mon-Fri, 10am-2pm Sat) changes US-dollar cash and traveler's checks and gives cash advances on Visa cards. It also has a Visa ATM. **Banco Agromercantil** (5a Av), facing the plaza, changes US-dollar cash and traveler's checks and has a MasterCard ATM.

Internet (cnr 5a Calle & 6a Av) charges US$1.30 for an hour online.

Sights & Activities

Museo de Arqueología y Etnología (6a Av 5-68; admission US$1.30; ✆ 8am-5:30pm Tue-Sat, 9am-noon Sun) is a small museum of archaeological relics. Upstairs are historical photos and a mural showing locations of 33 archaeological sites in Retalhuleu department.

You can **swim** at the Colonial hotel (out on the CA-2) even if you're not staying there. Cost is US$2 and there's a poolside bar.

Sleeping & Eating

Hotel América (✆ 7771-1154; 8a Av 9-32, Zona 1; s/d US$11/15) A good-value cheaper place just down the street from the bus terminal, the América has spotless rooms with private bathroom, fan and TV.

Hotel Posada de Don José (✆ 7771-0963; donjose@ infovia.com.gt; 5a Calle 3-67, Zona 1; s/d US$35/42; ✖ ☎) Two blocks northwest of the plaza, this is the nicest place in town. The 25 rooms, nearly all with air-con, are on two levels surrounding the large swimming pool, and the town's best restaurant (chicken, fish and steaks US$5.50 to US$8.50) is set beneath an arcade beside the pool. Rooms have TV, telephone and private bathroom. The hotel has a less attractive annex a block along the street.

Hotel Astor (✆ 7771-0475; hotelastor@terra.com.gt; 5a Calle 4-60, Zona 1; s/d/tr US$20/35/41; ✖ ☎) Also close to the plaza, this hotel, remodeled a few years ago, has a charming courtyard with a smaller pool and 26 very clean rooms, each with air-con, ceiling fan, phone, TV and hot-water bathroom. The upstairs rooms are new, but those downstairs around the courtyard have more atmosphere. Cocktails can be had in the hotel's air-conditioned **Bar La Carreta**.

Cafetería La Luna (5a Av 4-97; lunch dishes incl 1 drink US$2.90) Opposite the west corner of the plaza, this is a town favorite.

Italo's Pizza (5a Av; small pizzas US$3.50-4) Half a block from the plaza, it does reasonable pizzas.

Getting There & Away

Most buses traveling along the CA-2 detour into Reu. Departures include:

Champerico (US$0.40, 1hr, 38km) Buses every few minutes, 6am to 7pm.

Ciudad Tecún Umán (Mexican border; US$1.65, 1½hr, 78km) Buses every 20 minutes, 5am to 10pm.

Guatemala City (US$4, 3hr, 196km) Buses every 15 minutes, 2am to 8:30pm.

Quetzaltenango (US$1, 1hr, 46km) Buses every 30 minutes, 4am to 6pm.

Santa Lucía Cotzumalguapa (US$1.70, 2hr, 97km) Some Escuintla or Guatemala City-bound buses may drop you at Santa Lucía; otherwise get a bus to Mazatenango ('Mazate') and change there.

Local buses go to El Asintal (for Abaj Takalik; see right).

AROUND RETALHULEU
Xocomil & Xetulul

If you have children along, or simply if the heat is getting to you, head out to **Parque Acuático Xocomil** (☎ 7772-5763; Carr CITO Km 180.5; adult/child US$9.75/6.50; ☯ 9am-4pm Thu-Sun), a huge water park in the Disneyland vein, but with a distinct Guatemalan theme. Xocomil is at San Martín Zapotitlán on the Quetzaltenango road, about 12km north of Reu. Among the 10 water slides, two swimming pools and two wave pools are recreations of the Maya monuments from Tikal, Copán and Quiriguá. Visitors can bob along a river through canyons flanked with ancient temples and Mayan masks spewing water from the nose and mouth. Three real volcanoes – Santiaguito, Zunil and Santa María – can be seen from the grounds. Xocomil is very well executed and maintained, and the kids love it.

Next door on the same road is the even more impressive **Parque de Diversiones Xetulul** (☎ 5449-5480; adult/child US$26/13; ☯ 10am-6pm Thu-Sun), a theme park with representations of a Tikal pyramid, historical Guatemalan buildings and famous buildings from many European cities, plus restaurants and many first-class rides. You need an extra US$6.50 ticket for the rides.

These two attractions are both run by Irtra, the Instituto de Recreación de los Trabajadores de la Empresa Privada de Guatemala (Guatemalan Private Enterprise Workers' Recreation Institute). Between them, Xocomil and Xetulul comprise the most popular tourist attraction in Guatemala, with over a million visitors a year.

Any bus heading from Retalhuleu toward Quetzaltenango will drop you at Xocomil or Xetulul.

Abaj Takalik

Thirty kilometers west of Retalhuleu is the active archaeological dig at **Abaj Takalik** (ah-*bah*-tah-kah-*leek*), which is K'iche' for 'standing stone.' Large 'Olmecoid' stone heads discovered here date the site as one of the earliest in the Mayan realm. The site has yet to be restored and prettified, so don't expect a Chichén Itzá or Tikal, but if you want to see archaeology as it's done, pay a visit. This site is believed to be one of the few places where the Olmec and Maya lived together.

To reach Abaj Takalik by public transport, catch a bus from Retalhuleu to El Asintal (US$0.15, 30 minutes), which is 12km northwest of Reu and 5km north of the CA-2. The buses leave from a bus station on 5a Av A, 800m southwest of Reu plaza, about every half hour, 6am to 6pm. Pickups at El Asintal provide transport on to Abaj Takalik, 4km further by paved road. You'll be shown around by a volunteer guide, who you should probably tip.

Champerico

Built as a coffee-shipping point during the late 19th century, Champerico, 38km to the southwest of Retalhuleu, is a tawdry, sweltering, dilapidated place that sees few tourists. Despite this ickiness, it's one of the easiest beaches to access on a day trip from Xela, and beach-starved foreigners still try their luck here. Beware of strong waves and an undertow if you go in the ocean, and stay in the main, central part of the beach – if you stray too far in either direction you put yourself at risk from impoverished, potentially desperate shack dwellers who live toward the ends of the beach. Tourists have been victims of violent armed robberies here. Most beachgoers come on day trips, but there are several restaurants and cheap hotels; **Hotel Neptuno** (☎ 7773-7206; s/d US$ 4/7), on the beachfront, is the best bet. The last bus back to Retalhuleu goes about 6:30pm.

SANTA LUCÍA COTZUMALGUAPA
pop 24,000 / elevation 356m

About 100km to the east of Retalhuleu is the unexciting but historically important town of Santa Lucía Cotzumalguapa. In the

GUATEMALA

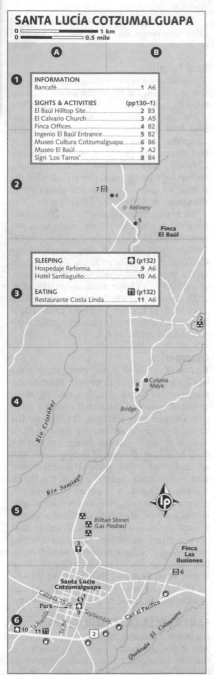

SANTA LUCÍA COTZUMALGUAPA

0 |=======| 1 km
0 |=======| 0.5 mile

Ⓐ   Ⓑ

Ⓐ (row 1)

| INFORMATION | |
| Bancafé | 1 A6 |

SIGHTS & ACTIVITIES	(pp130–1)
El Baúl Hilltop Site	2 B3
El Calvario Church	3 A5
Finca Offices	4 B2
Ingenio El Baúl Entrance	5 B2
Museo Cultura Cotzumalguapa	6 B6
Museo El Baúl	7 A2
Sign 'Los Tarros'	8 B4

Ⓑ (row 2)
7 🏛
● 4
◆ Refinery
● 5
Finca
El Baúl

Ⓒ (row 3)

SLEEPING	🛏 (p132)
Hospedaje Reforma	9 A6
Hotel Santiaguito	10 A6

| EATING | 🍴 (p132) |
| Restaurante Costa Linda | 11 A6 |

2 🏛

8 ● ● Colonia
        Maya

Río Cristóbal

Bridge

Río Santiago

ⒾⓅ

Bilbao Stones
(Las Piedras)

3 🏛
Finca
Las
Ilusiones

🏛 6

Santa Lucía
Cotzumalguapa

Calzada 15 de
Park
12 Avenida
11 🍴
Septiembre
3a AV
Carr al Pacífico
Quebrada El Colmenero

sugarcane fields and *fincas* near town stand great stone heads carved with grotesque faces and fine relief scenes. Who carved these objects, and why, remains a mystery.

The people are descended from the Pipil, an Indian culture known to have historic, linguistic and cultural links with the Nahuatl-speaking peoples of central Mexico. In early Classic times, the Pipil grew cacao, the currency of the time. They were obsessed with the Mayan/Aztec ball game and with the rites and mysteries of death. Pipil art, unlike the flowery, almost romantic Mayan style, is cold and severe, but it's finely done. How these 'Mexicans' ended up in the midst of Maya territory remains unexplained.

Orientation & Information

Santa Lucía Cotzumalguapa is northwest of the CA-2. In its main square, several blocks from the highway, are copies of some of the region's famous carved stones. A few basic hotels and restaurants are available in town.

Of the three archaeological sites, the hilltop site at El Baúl is by far the most interesting. Taxi drivers in the main square will take you round all three sites for about US$12. In this hot and muggy climate, riding at least part of the way is a very good idea. If you do it all on foot and by bus, pack a lunch; the hilltop site at El Baúl is perfect for a picnic.

Bancafé (cnr 4a Av & 4a Calle), a block north of the plaza, changes US-dollar cash and traveler's checks and has a Visa ATM.

El Baúl Hilltop Site

This site has the additional fascination of being an active place of pagan worship for local people. Maya people regularly (especially on weekends) make offerings, light fires and candles and sacrifice chickens here. They won't mind if you visit as well, and may be happy to pose with the idols for photographs, in exchange for a small 'contribution.'

To get there you leave town northward on the road passing El Calvario church. From the intersection just past the church, go 2.7km to a fork in the road just beyond a bridge; the fork is marked by a sign saying 'Los Tarros.' Take the right-hand fork, passing a settlement called Colonia Maya on your right. After you have gone 1.5km from the Los Tarros sign, a dirt track crosses the road – turn right here, between two concrete posts. Ahead now is a low mound topped by three large trees: this is the hilltop site. After about 250m, fork right between two more identical concrete posts and follow this track round in front of the mound to its end after some 150m; take the path up on to the mound, which is actually a great ruined temple platform that has not been restored.

Of the two stones here, the great, grotesque, half-buried head is the most striking, with its elaborate headdress, beak-like nose and 'blind' eyes with big bags underneath. The head is stained with wax from candles, splashes of liquor and other drinks, and with the smoke and ashes of incense fires, all part of worship. People have been coming here to pay homage for more than 1400 years.

The other stone is a relief carving of a figure with an elaborate headdress, possibly a fire god, surrounded by circular motifs that may be date glyphs.

Museo El Baúl

This **museum** (admission free; ☉ 8am-4pm Mon-Fri, 8am-noon Sat) is about 2.8km on foot, or 5km by vehicle, from the hilltop site. In a vehicle, return to the fork with the Los Tarros sign. Take the other fork this time (what would be the left fork as you come from Santa Lucía), and follow the paved road 3km to the Finca El Baúl offices. Buses trundle along this road every few hours, shuttling workers between the refinery and the town center. (If you're on foot, you can walk from the hilltop site back to the crossroads with the paved road and straight across it, continuing on the dirt track. This will eventually bring you to the asphalt road that leads to the *finca* headquarters. When you reach the road, turn right.)

Approaching the *finca* headquarters (6km from Santa Lucía's main square), you cross a bridge at a curve. Continue uphill and you will see the entrance on the left, marked by a guard post and a sign 'Ingenio El Baúl Bienvenidos.' Tell the guards that you would like to visit the *museo*, and you should be admitted. Pass the sugar refinery buildings to arrive at the museum on the right. This comprises a very fine open-air collection of Pipil stone sculpture collected from around Finca El Baúl's sugarcane fields. A large stone jaguar faces you at the entrance. Other figures include four humans or monkeys with arms folded across

their chests, a grinning, blank-eyed head reminiscent of the one at the hilltop site, carvings of skulls, and at the back a stela showing a personage wearing an animal headdress standing over a similarly attired figure on the ground, seemingly winner and loser of a ball game. Unfortunately, nothing is labeled.

Museo Cultura Cotzumalguapa

This indoor **museum** (US$1.30; ☉ 8am-4pm Mon-Fri, 8am-noon Sat) is at the headquarters of another sugarcane plantation, Finca Las Ilusiones. About 1.5km east of the town center on the CA-2, shortly before an Esso station on the left (not to be confused with other Esso stations on the right), take a side track 400m to the left (north) to find it. The collection here, of sculptures found around Las Ilusiones lands, has some explanatory material and you'll probably be shown around by the caretaker. It includes a reconstruction of a sacrificial altar with the original stones, and photos of some fine stelae that were removed to the Dahlem Museum in Berlin in 1880. The most impressive exhibit, Monumento 21, is actually a glass-fiber copy of a stone that still stands in the fields of Finca Bilbao (part of Las Ilusiones' plantations), depicting what may be a shaman holding a sort of puppet on the left, a ball-game player in the middle with a knife in one hand, and a king or priest on the right holding what may be a heart. Another copy of this stone, along with one of Monumento 19, lie on the ground across the street from the museum. Along the road just before the bridge to the *finca* house are copies of some of the sculptures from Museo El Baúl.

Bilbao Stones

Monumento 21, whose copy is in the Museo Cultura Cotzumalguapa, still stands with three other fine sculpted stones dotted about the Finca Bilbao cane fields to the northeast of El Calvario church, on the north edge of Santa Lucía town. In the past, tourists have regularly visited *las piedras* (the stones), often guided through the tall cane by local boys. Unfortunately locals say it is now dangerous for tourists to go into these fields, because of recent assaults. So unless you receive convincing information to the contrary, we don't recommend it.

Sleeping & Eating

Hospedaje Reforma (4a Av 4-71; s/d US$4/7) A block off the main plaza, this last-resort cheapie has dark, cell-like rooms (some with hay beds!). The rooms around the courtyard are better, but are only rented by the hour.

Hotel Santiaguito (☎ 7882-5435/6/7; fax 7882-2287; Carr al Pacífico Km 90.4; s/d/tr US$33/46/53; Ⓟ Ⓧ Ⓡ) On the highway on the west edge of town, the Santiaguito is fairly lavish for Guatemala's Pacific Slope, with spacious tree-shaded grounds and a nice swimming pool. The pool is open to nonguests for US$2.60. The large rooms have TV, phone, air-con and private bathroom. The restaurant serves three meals for US$3 to US$9.

Restaurante Costa Linda On the highway, this is a friendly and clean place serving tasty meat and seafood at reasonable prices.

Getting There & Away

As the CA-2 now bypasses Santa Lucía, lots of buses don't come into town. Coming to Santa Lucía from the east, you'll almost certainly need to change buses at Escuintla (US$0.50, 30 minutes). From the west you will probably have to change at Mazatenango (US$1.30, 1¼ hours). At Cocales, 23km west of Santa Lucía, a road down from Lago de Atitlán meets the CA-2, providing a route to or from the highlands. Eight buses daily run from Cocales to Panajachel (US$1, 2½ hours, 70km), between about 6am and 2pm.

LA DEMOCRACIA

pop 4200 / elevation 165m

South of Siquinalá, 9.5km along the road to Puerto San José, is La Democracia, a nondescript Pacific Slope town that's always hot. Like Santa Lucía Cotzumalguapa, La Democracia is in the midst of a region populated from early times (according to some archaeologists) by cultures with mysterious connections to Mexico's Gulf Coast.

At the Monte Alto archaeological site, on the outskirts of La Democracia, huge basalt heads have been found. Though cruder, the heads resemble those carved by the Olmec near Veracruz several thousand years ago.

Today these heads are arranged around La Democracia's main plaza. As you come into town from the highway, follow signs to the museum, which will lead you left, then left again, and left yet again.

Facing the plaza, along with the church and the modest Palacio Municipal, is the small, modern **Museo Regional de Arqueología** (admission US$1.30; ☉ 8am-noon & 2-6pm), which exhibits some fascinating archaeological finds. The star of the show is an exquisite jade mask.

La Democracia has no places to stay and only a few basic and ill-supplied eateries; it's best to bring your own food and buy drinks at the plaza.

The Chatía Gomerana company runs buses every half hour, 6am to 4:30pm, from Guatemala City's Terminal de Autobuses to La Democracia (US$1.50, two hours) via Escuintla. From Santa Lucía Cotzumalguapa, catch a bus 8km east to Siquinalá (8km) and change there.

ESCUINTLA

Surrounded by rich, green foliage, Escuintla should be a relaxed tropical idyll. It's actually a dilapidated industrial city that's important to the Pacific Slope's economy but not to travelers, except to change buses. Inhabited by Pipils before the conquest, it's now solidly ladino.

Bancafé (cnr 4a Av & 12a Calle; ☉ 9am-6pm Mon-Fri, 9am-1pm Sat), two blocks north of the bus station, changes US-dollar cash and traveler's checks and has a Visa ATM. Escuintla has some marginal hotels and restaurants. If stranded, try **Hotel Costa Sur** (☎ 7888-1819; 12a Calle 4-13; s/d US$11/16), a couple of doors from Bancafé, which has well-used, but tolerable rooms with TV and fan but no hot water.

The main bus station is in the southern part of town, just off 4a Av, its entrance marked by a Scott 77 fuel station. Buses go to Antigua (US$0.65, one hour) about every half hour, 5:30am to 4:30pm. Buses for Guatemala City (US$1.25, 1½ hours) go about every 20 minutes from the street outside, 5am to 6pm. Buses to Puerto San José (US$0.80, 45 minutes), some continuing to Iztapa, have similar frequency. Buses coming along the CA-2 may drop you in the north of town, meaning a sweaty walk through the hectic town center to reach the main terminal.

IZTAPA

Iztapa was Guatemala's first Pacific port, used by Pedro de Alvarado in the 16th century. When Puerto San José was built in

1853, Iztapa's reign came to an end, and the city relaxed into a tropical torpor from which it has never really emerged. The town has a post office but no bank.

Iztapa has gained renown as one of the world's premier **deep-sea fishing** spots. World records have been set here and enthusiasts can go for marlin, sharks and yellowfin tuna, among others. November through June is typically the best time to angle for sailfish.

From the US, **B&B Worldwide Fishing Adventures** (☎ +1-541-296-3962; www.wheretofish.com; 14161/2 E 10th Pl, The Dalles, OR), **Artmarina** (☎ +1-305-663-3553; www.artmarina.com; 1390 South Dixie Hwy Suite 2221, Miami, FL) and **Fishing International** (☎ +1-707-542-4242; www.fishinginternational.com; 184 S 4th St, Santa Rosa, CA) run all-inclusive deep-sea fishing tours to Iztapa. It is also possible to contract local boat owners for fishing trips, though equipment and comfort may be nonexistent and 'catch and release' could prove a foreign concept. The boat owners hang out at the edge of the Río María Linda – bargain hard. Yellowfin tuna will likely be out of reach for the local boats, as these fish inhabit the waters some 17km from Iztapa.

Should you want to stay, the **Sol y Playa Tropical** (☎ 7881-4365/6; 1a Calle 5-48; s/d/tr US$12/22/28; 🏊) has tolerable rooms with fan and private bathroom on two floors around a swimming pool. On the beach, **Rancho Maracaibo** (r US$2.50) has very basic cabañas, with a bed and reed mat on the floor.

The bonus of Iztapa is that you can catch a Transportes Pacífico bus from the market in Zona 4 in Guatemala City all the way here (US$2, three hours). They leave about every half hour, 5am to 6pm, traveling via Escuintla and Puerto San José. The last bus heading back from Iztapa goes around 5pm. You can reach Monterrico by paved road from Iztapa: follow the street 1km east from Club Cervecero bar, where the buses terminate, and get a boat across the river to Pueblo Viejo (US$0.30 per person in passenger *lanchas*; US$2.20 per vehicle, including passengers, on the vehicle ferry). From the far side buses leave for the pretty ride to Monterrico (US$0.80, one hour) at 8am, 11:30am, 2pm, 4pm and 6pm.

MONTERRICO

The coastal area around Monterrico is a totally different Guatemala. Life here is imbued with a sultry, tropical flavor that's more relaxed and inviting than anywhere else on the Pacific Slope. The architecture, too, is different; wooden slat walls and thatched roofs prevail over the cement walls and corrugated-tin roofs common elsewhere.

Monterrico is probably the best spot in Guatemala for a weekend beach break. Quiet on weekdays, on weekends and holidays it teems with families. It's also popular with foreigners, especially those studying Spanish.

A few small, inexpensive hotels front the beach, which is dramatic here; powerful surf and riptides collide at odd angles. Swim with caution – there have been drownings. Behind the beach, on the other side of town, is a large network of mangrove swamps and canals, part of the 190km Canal de Chiquimulilla. Also in the area are a large wildlife reserve and a center for the hatching and release of sea turtles and caimans.

Orientation & Information

From where you alight from the La Avellana boat, it's about 1km to the beach and the hotels. You pass through the village en route. From the *embarcadero* (jetty) walk straight ahead and then turn left. Pickups (US$0.25) meet scheduled boats or *lanchas*.

If you come by bus from Pueblo Viejo, from the stop walk about 300m toward the beach on Calle Principal. At the beach, head left to reach the cluster of hotels.

The village has a **post office** (Calle Principal) but no bank.

Sights & Activities

A big attraction here is the **Reserva Natural Monterrico** (sometimes called the Biotopo Monterrico-Hawaii), a 20km-long nature reserve of coastal mangrove swamps filled with bird and aquatic life.

Canals lace the swamps, connecting 25 lagoons hidden among the mangroves. **Boat tours**, passing through the mangrove swamps and visiting several lagoons, take around 1½ to two hours and cost US$5.25 per passenger. Sunrise is the best time for wildlife. If you have binoculars, bring them for bird-watching, which is best in January and February.

To arrange a boat tour, stop by the Cecon-run **Tortugario Monterrico visitors center** (admission US$1.20; 🕐 8am-noon & 2-5pm), just a short walk east down the beach and back a block from the Monterrico hotels (left, if you're facing the sea). Several endangered species of animals are raised here, including leatherback, olive ridley and green sea turtles, caimans and iguanas. There's an interesting interpretive trail and a little museum with pickled displays in bottles.

Reserva Natural Hawaii is operated by Arcas (Asociación de Rescate y Conservación de Vida Silvestre, Wildlife Rescue & Conservation Association; www.arcasguatemala.com) and comprises a sea-turtle hatchery with some caimans, 8km east along the beach from Monterrico. Volunteers are welcome year-round, but the real sea-turtle nesting season is from June to November, with August and September being the peak months. Volunteers are charged US$50 a week for a room, with meals extra and homestay options with local families. A bus (US$0.50, 30 minutes) leaves the Monterrico jetty at 6am, 11am, 1:30pm and 3:30pm (and 6:30pm except Saturday) for the bumpy ride to the reserve. Pickups also operate on this route charging US$3.25 per person.

Sleeping & Eating

Monterrico has several simple hotels, most of which are on the beach; the majority have restaurants serving whatever is fresh from the sea that day. Many accommodations offer discounts for stays of three nights or more. Reserve for weekends if you want to avoid a long, hot walk on the scalding sand asking for vacancies. Weekend prices are given here.

Johnny's (☎ 5206-4702, 7762-0015; johnnys@backpack americas.com; dm US$4.50, s or d US$16, with private bathroom US$18, bungalows for 4 US$51; P ⚑ ⚏) This is the first substantial place you come to heading left from Calle Principal. It's popular with backpackers and is a favorite of vacationing Guatemalan families, particularly for the attractive bungalows, each with two bedrooms, living room, private bathroom and fully equipped kitchen. Every pair of bungalows shares a BBQ and small swimming pool. There's also a larger, general swimming pool. The rooms are not glamorous but have fans and screened windows. The bar/restaurant overlooks the sea and is a popular hangout; the food is not gourmet but there are plenty of choices and imaginative *licuados* (fresh fruit drinks) and other long, cool drinks. Meals are US$3.50 to US$11.75.

Hotel Pez de Oro (☎ 5204-5249, ☎ /fax 2368-3684; s/d/tr US$30/40/50; P ⚏) Further down the beach with a palm-shaded garden, this is Monterrico's most upscale hotel. Italian-owned, it has 11 pleasant, solid bungalows, each with fan, mosquito nets and a hammock on the porch. The private bathrooms are more inviting than elsewhere in the village. The excellent restaurant, with big sea views, serves up great Italian food and fish and seafood dishes. Pastas go from US$5.25, whole fish from US$5.80.

Other good options:

El Kaiman (☎ 5517-9285, 5617-9880; per person US$7; P ⚏) The best rooms are upstairs, though they're all a bit shabby.

Eco Beach Place (☎ 5611-6637; ecobeachplace@ hotmail.com; d/tr US$20/24; P ⚏) The four rooms are well kept and nicely decorated, with private bathroom, mosquito net and fan.

Going in the opposite direction from these hotels, heading right from Calle Principal, are more options.

Café del Sol (☎ 5810-0821; www.cafe-del-sol.com; d/tr Fri & Sat from US$18/24, s/d/tr Sun-Thu from US$11/ 13/16; P ⚏) This Swiss- and Guatemalan-owned place has a warm, family atmosphere. You'll recognize it by the yellow paint, the expansive terrace and the tall palm trees. Most of the nine rooms are on the ground level, some beachside, and others behind the main building, close to the pool. All have private bathroom, mosquito net and fan. The restaurant's menu has some original dishes; try risotto with funghi (US$4) or fish fillet with tomatoes, peppers and olives (US$7; delicious). Eat on the terrace or in the big *palapa* (thatched, palm-leaf-roofed shelter with open sides) dining area.

From the beach, turn left at the first alley after Calle Principal.

Taberna El Pelicano (mains US$8) This place garners good reviews for the international fare prepared by its Swiss chef.

There are many simple seafood restaurants on Calle Principal.

El Divino Maestro On the right as you head away from the beach, this is a good choice; try its *caldo de mariscos* (seafood stew; US$4).

Drinking

El Animal Desconicido (⏲ 8pm-late Thu-Sat) This is a real popular nightspot, both for its French owner's wide-ranging taste in music and for its decor, in which bright, orange walls collide with moons, stars, suns, skeletons, iguanas and shells. Best from 11pm, it's on the beach near Hotel El Delfín.

Getting There & Away
There are two ways to get to Monterrico. Best is to get to La Avellana, from where boats and car ferries depart for Monterrico – enabling you to get a taste for the relaxing and interesting launch trips on the area's waterways. The Cubanita company runs a handful of direct buses to/from Guatemala City (US$2.60, four hours, 124km), leaving the capital's Zona 4 Terminal de Autobuses at 10:30am, 12:30pm and 2:30pm, and starting back from La Avellana at 4pm and 6pm. Be sure to ask the driver about the route before you start your journey. Alternatively you reach La Avellana by changing buses at Taxisco on the CA-2. Buses operate half-hourly from 5am to 4pm between Guatemala City and Taxisco (US$1.50, 3½ hours) and roughly hourly from 7am to 6pm between Taxisco and La Avellana (US$0.50, 40 minutes). A taxi between Taxisco and La Avellana costs around US$4.

From La Avellana, catch a *lancha* or car ferry to Monterrico. The collective *lanchas* charge US$0.40 per passenger for the half-hour trip along the Canal de Chiquimulilla. They start at 4:30am and run more or less every half hour or hour until late afternoon; from Monterrico they leave at 3:30am, 5:30am, 7am, 8am, 9am, 10:30am, noon, 1pm, 2:30pm and 4pm. You can always pay more and charter your own boat. The car ferry costs US$6.50 per vehicle.

The second, longer route to Monterrico is via Iztapa and Pueblo Viejo. Only a few buses a day link Pueblo Viejo and Monterrico – they leave Monterrico for Pueblo Viejo (US$0.80, one hour) at 5:30am, 7:30am, 11am, 12:30pm, 2pm and 3pm.

Shuttle buses also serve La Avellana. You can take a round-trip from Antigua, coming on one day and returning the next, for around US$9 one-way. From Antigua it's a 2½-hour trip. **Voyageur Tours** (p81) comes to La Avellana three or four times weekly in the low season, daily in peak periods, with a minimum of three passengers. On Saturday and Sunday, it picks up in Monterrico (not La Avellana) from outside Proyecto Lingüístico Monterrico at 3pm for the round-trip.

It charges only US$6.50 from Monterrico to Antigua, so it's best not to buy a round-trip ticket in Antigua; Voyageur Tours will take you on to Guatemala City (US$11) if you wish. Other shuttle services also make the Antigua–Monterrico trip.

CENTRAL & EASTERN GUATEMALA

North and east of Guatemala City is a land of varied topography, from the misty, pine-covered mountains of Alta Verapaz to the hot, dry-tropic climate of the Río Motagua valley. The Carretera al Atlántico (CA-9) climbs northeast out of the capital before descending from the relative cool of the mountains to the dry heat of valleys, where dinosaurs once roamed.

Reached from this highway are many intriguing destinations, including the beautiful highland scenery around Cobán; the paleontology museum at Estanzuela; and the great basilica at Esquipulas, famous throughout Central America. The CA-9 ends at Puerto Barrios, Guatemala's Caribbean port, from where you can take a boat to far-flung Lívingston, peopled by the Garifuna. A quick detour into Honduras takes you to some of the most impressive ruins in the Mayan world, at Copán.

Salamá and Cobán are easily accessible along a smooth, fast, asphalt road that winds up from the hot, dry valley passing through long stretches of coffee-growing country and wonderful mountain scenery. Along the way to Cobán is one of Guatemala's premier nature reserves, the Biotopo del Quetzal. Beyond Cobán, along rough roads, are the country's most famous caverns, the Grutas de Lanquín, and the beautiful pools and cascades of Semuc Champey.

Minibuses now ply the mostly paved route north from Cobán to Flores, El Petén, a journey that can be done in five or six hours. However, you can still take back roads to El Petén if you're addicted to chicken buses and pickups.

SALAMÁ
pop 11,000 / elevation 940m
Hwy 17, also marked CA-14, leaves the CA-9 at El Rancho, 84km from Guatemala

City. It heads west through dry, desert-like lowlands, then turns north and ascends into the forested hills. After 47km is the turnoff for Salamá.

Before the Spanish conquest, the mountainous departments of Baja Verapaz and Alta Verapaz were populated by the Rabinal Maya, noted for their warlike habits and merciless victories. They battled the powerful K'iche' Maya for a century but were never conquered.

When the conquistadors arrived, they too had trouble defeating the Rabinals. It was Fray Bartolomé de Las Casas who had convinced the Spanish authorities to try peace where war had failed. Armed with an edict that forbade Spanish soldiers from entering the region for five years, the friar and his brethren pursued their religious mission and succeeded in pacifying and converting the Rabinals. Their homeland was renamed Verapaz (True Peace) and is now divided into Baja Verapaz, with its capital at Salamá, and Alta Verapaz, centered on Cobán. The Rabinal have remained among the most dedicated and true to ancient Maya customs, and there are many intriguing villages to visit in this part of Guatemala, including Rabinal itself.

Information

Bancafé (🕐 9am-5pm Mon-Fri, 9am-1pm Sat) on the south side of the plaza (opposite the church) changes cash and traveler's checks and has a Visa and MasterCard ATM. Internet access (US$1.30 an hour) is available at **Telgua**, across the street from Hotel Tezulutlán (right). A **police station** is one block west of the plaza; opposite is a **tourist office** (🕐 9am-1pm Mon-Fri). **Cafe Deli-Donas** (right) has useful giveaway maps of the town.

Sights

Attractive Salamá has some reminders of colonial rule. The main plaza boasts an ornate colonial **church** with gold-encrusted altars and a carved pulpit. Be sure to check out Jesus lying in a glass coffin with cotton bunting in his stigmata and droplets of blood seeping from his hairline. His thick mascara and the silver lamé pillow where he rests his head complete the scene. The Salamá **market** is impressive for its colorful, local bustle, particularly on Sunday.

Tours

EcoVerapaz (☎ 7940-0146, 5610-3821; 8a Av 7-12, Zona 1) has local, trained naturalists offering interesting tours throughout Baja Verapaz including caving, birding, hiking, horseback riding and orchid trips. It also goes to Rabinal (opposite) to check out the museum and crafts. Guides speak some English. One-day tours start at US$25 per person for a group of 10 or more, US$40 per person for a group of five.

Sleeping & Eating

Hotel San Ignacio (☎ 7940-0186; 4a Calle 7-09; s/d/tr US$7/9/15) This clean, family-run place has a big *palapa* sitting area overlooking the street. The bright, fresh rooms are upstairs and have hot-water bathrooms.

Hotel Real Legendario (☎ 7940-0501; 8a Av 3-57, Zona 1; s/d/tr US$9/15/18) Three blocks east of the plaza, you'll recognize this one by the stands of bamboo in the car park. The clean, secure rooms have fan, private hot bathroom and cable TV.

Hotel Tezulutlán (☎ /fax 7940-0141; s/d US$10/11; P) This hotel, just east of the plaza and behind the Texaco fuel station, has five rooms around a leafy garden courtyard. All have cable TV and private hot-water bathroom.

Cafe Deli-Donas (15a Calle 6-61; cakes US$1.30, sandwiches US$1.45, licuados US$0.90) This popular little café is just a few doors south of the plaza. Light meals, sweets and Salamá's best coffee are served daily. The cheesecake is delectable!

Restaurante El Balcón de los Recuerdos (8a Av 6-28; mains US$4-6.50; 🕐 breakfast, lunch & dinner Mon-Sat) This restaurant, a half block west of the plaza on the road to La Cumbre, is spacious, fan-cooled and has a central fountain. Here you can choose from a typical list of grilled meats, fish, prawns and seafood soup.

Getting There & Away

Buses for Guatemala City (US$2.10 to US$2.60, three hours, 151km) depart hourly between 3am and 8pm from in front of Cafe Deli-Donas. There is a Pullman at 4am – arrive early for a seat. Buses coming from Guatemala City continue west from Salamá to Rabinal (US$1, 40 minutes, 19km) and then 15km further along to Cubulco. Buses for Cobán leave from in front of the Municipalidad (east side of the plaza) about every 30 minutes from early morning to 4pm.

AROUND SALAMÁ

Ten kilometers along the road to Salamá from the Cobán highway, you come to the turnoff for **San Jerónimo**. Behind the town's beautiful church, a former sugar mill is now a **museum** (admission free; 🕑 8am-4pm Mon-Fri, 10am-noon & 1-4pm Sat & Sun) with a decent collection of unlabeled artifacts and photographs. On the town plaza are some large stones carved in ancient times.

Nine kilometers west of Salamá along Hwy 5 is **San Miguel Chicaj**, known for its weaving and traditional fiesta (September 25 to 29). Continue along the same road another 10km to reach the colonial town of **Rabinal**, founded in 1537 by Fray Bartolomé de Las Casas as a base for proselytizing. Rabinal has gained fame as a center for pottery making (look for the hand-painted chocolate cups) and citrus growing. Rabinal is also known for its adherence to pre-Columbian traditions. Try to make the annual fiesta of Saint Peter, between January 19 and 25 (things reach a fever pitch on January 21), or Corpus Christi. Market day is Sunday. Two small hotels, **Pensión Motagua** and **Hospedaje Caballeros**, can put you up.

BIOTOPO DEL QUETZAL

Along the main highway (CA-14), 34km north of the turnoff for Salamá, is the Biotopo Mario Dary Rivera reserve, commonly called the **Biotopo del Quetzal** (admission US$3.25; 🕑 7am-4pm); it's at Km 161, near the village of Purulhá (no services). The ride along here is sobering: Entire hillsides are deforested and covered in huge sheets of black plastic meant to optimize growing conditions for *xate*.

If you hope to see a quetzal, Guatemala's national bird, you'll likely be disappointed – the birds are rare and elusive, and their habitat is almost destroyed. The best time to see them is between February and September, in the early morning or early evening. However, it's still worth a visit to explore their lush, high-altitude cloud-forest habitat. If you're really keen to see one in the wild, contact **Proyecto EcoQuetzal** (p140) in Cobán.

Two well-maintained trails wind through the reserve past several waterfalls, most of which cascade into swimmable pools. Deep in the forest is Xiu Ua Li Che (Grandfather Tree), some 450 years old.

Trail maps in English and Spanish are sold at the visitors center for US$0.70. They contain a checklist of 87 birds commonly seen here. Other animals include spider monkeys and tigrillos (similar to ocelots).

As well as the visitors center, the reserve has a drinks stand and a camping and barbecue area. The ruling on camping changes often. Check by contacting **Cecon** (see Environmental Issues, p63), which administers this and other *biotopos*.

Services in the area include:

Hotel Restaurant Ram Tzul (☎ 5908-4066, in Guatemala City ☎ 2335-1805; ramtzul@internet.net.gt; CA-14 Km 158; s/d/tr US$ 4/8/12, with private hot-water bathroom US$13/13/20, s/d bungalows US$20/38; 🅟) This eye-catching, tall, thatched-roof hotel is about 2.5km before the *biotopo* entrance if you're coming from Guatemala City. It has a bar/restaurant where main dishes cost US$3 to US$4. The hotel property includes waterfalls and swimming spots.

Biotopín Restaurant (CA-14 Km 160.5) A half-kilometer before the *biotopo* entrance, this restaurant has decent meals at good prices.

Any bus to/from Guatemala City will set you down at the park entrance. Heading in the other direction, it's best to flag down a bus or microbus to El Rancho and change there for your next destination. The road between the *biotopo* and Cobán is good – smooth and fast (though curving). As you ascend into the evergreen forests, you'll still see tropical flowers here and there.

COBÁN

pop 20,000 / elevation 1320m

Cobán is fast becoming a travelers' favorite. It's a smallish, relaxed town with a multitude of activities and adventures on offer in the surrounding countryside, including the awesome Semuc Champey and Grutas de Lanquín.

Cobán was once a stronghold of the Rabinal Maya. In the 19th century, German immigrants moved in, founding vast coffee and cardamom *fincas*. The era of German cultural and economic domination ended during WWII, when the USA prevailed upon the Guatemalan government to deport the powerful *finca* owners, many of whom supported the Nazis.

Today Cobán is a pleasant town, despite the chilly, rainy weather. You can count on sunny days in Cobán for only about three

COBÁN

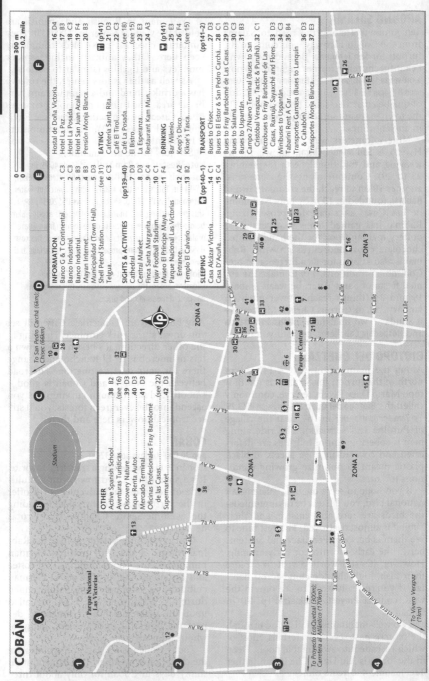

300 m
0.2 mile

weeks in April. In the midst of the 'dry' season (January to March), it can be misty and rainy or bright and marvelously clear.

Guatemala's most impressive indigenous festival, the folkloric festival of Rabin Ajau, takes place in late July or early August.

Orientation & Information

Most services of interest to travelers are within a few blocks of *el parque* (the plaza), which was undergoing extensive renovations in 2003. Unfortunately there were no signs that the Soviet boom-era style gazebo (known locally as *el kiosko* and to travelers as 'that big ugly orange thing blocking my view of the church') was going to get knocked down. We live in hope.

The heart of Cobán is built on a rise, so unless what you're looking for is in the dead center, you'll be trudging uphill and down.

A tourist office is planned for the remodeled plaza. Meanwhile, you can speak to the tourism people in the **Municipalidad** (Town Hall; ☎ 7952-1305, 7951-1148) where some switched-on young staff work in an office behind the police office. **Casa D'Acuña** (p140) can also give you loads of information.

The **post office** (cnr 2a Av & 3a Calle) is a block from the plaza.

Mayan Internet (6a Av 2-28; per hr US$1.50; ☯ 8:30am-8pm Mon-Sat, 2:30-9pm Sun), with fast connections, is 500m west of the plaza.

The following banks are good for changing US-dollar cash and traveler's checks:
Banco Industrial 1a Calle (1a Calle 4-36); 7a Av (cnr 1a Calle & 7a Av) Has a Visa ATM.
Banco G & T Continental (1a Calle) Opposite Hotel La Posada; has a MasterCard ATM.

Sights & Activities
TEMPLO EL CALVARIO

You'll get a fine view over town from this church atop a long flight of stairs at the north end of 7a Av, Zona 1. Indigenous people leave offerings at shrines and crosses in front of the church. You can walk behind the church to enter the side gate of the Parque Nacional Las Victorias.

PARQUE NACIONAL LAS VICTORIAS

This forested 0.82-sq-km **national park** (admission US$0.80; ☯ 8am-4:30pm, walking trails 9am-3pm), right in town, has ponds, BBQ, picnic areas, camping grounds (p140), children's play areas, a lookout point and kilometers

of trails. The entrance is at 11a Av and 3a Calle, Zona 1.

VIVERO VERAPAZ

Orchid lovers mustn't miss a chance to see the many thousands of species at this famous **nursery** (☎ 7952-1133; Carr Antigua de Entrada a Cobán; admission US$1.30; ☯ 9am-noon & 2-4pm). The rare *monja blanca*, or white nun orchid (Guatemala's national flower), grows here, as do hundreds of miniature orchid species. The national orchid show is held here each December.

Vivero Verapaz is about 2km from the town center – a 40-minute walk southwest from the plaza. You can hire a taxi for around US$2.

FINCA SANTA MARGARITA

This working **coffee farm** (☎ 7951-3067; 3a Calle 4-12, Zona 2; admission US$2; ☯ guided tours 8am-12:30pm & 1:30-5pm Mon-Fri, 8am-noon Sat) offers guided tours of its operation. From propagation and planting to roasting and exporting, the 45-minute tour will tell you all you ever wanted to know about these powerful beans. At tour's end, you're treated to a cup of coffee and can purchase beans straight from the roaster for US$2.60 to US$5 a pound (0.45kg). The talented guide speaks English and Spanish.

MUSEO EL PRÍNCIPE MAYA

This private **museum** (☎ 7952-1541; 6a Av 4-26, Zona 3; admission US$1.30; ☯ 9am-6pm Mon-Sat) features a collection of pre-Columbian artifacts, with an emphasis on jewelry, other body adornments and pottery. The displays are well designed and maintained.

Courses

Active Spanish School (☎ 7952-1432; www.guatemala365.com; 3a Calle 6-12, Zona 1), run by the dynamic Nirma Macz, can provide one-on-one teaching in Spanish and Q'eqchi'. Cost for 20 hours' tuition a week and a homestay with a local family including all meals is US$100.

Tours

Aventuras Turísticas (☎ /fax 7951-4213; aventurasturisticas@terra.com; 3a Calle 2-38, Zona 3), in the Hostal de Doña Victoria, leads tours to Laguna Lachuá, the Grutas de Lanquín, Semuc Champey, Tikal and Ceibal, and will customize itineraries. It employs French-, English- and Spanish-speaking guides.

Casa D'Acuña (☎ 7951-0484; fax 7951-0482; 4a Calle 3-11, Zona 2) offers its own tours to Semuc Champey, the Grutas de Lanquín and other places further afield. Its guides are excellent (see Sleeping, below.)

Discovery Nature (☎ 7951-0811; 3a Calle 1-46) operates out of Posada Don Matalbatz. This outfit offers day and overnight trips to La- guna Lachuá, excursions to other fantastic places around Cobán and rafting trips.

Proyecto EcoQuetzal (☎ /fax 7952-1047; bida speq@guate.net; 2a Calle 14-36, Zona 1; ☻ 8:30am-1pm & 2-5:30pm Mon-Fri) is an innovative project of- fering 'ethnotourism' trips in which partici- pants hike to nearby villages in the cloud forest and stay with a Q'eqchi' Maya family. To maximize the experience, travelers are encouraged to learn some Q'eqchi' words and stay with their host family for at least two days. For US$42 you'll get a guide for three days, lodging for two nights and six meals. Your guide will take you on hikes to interesting spots. The men of the fam- ily are the guides, providing an alternative, sustainable way to make a living.

Reservations are required at least one day in advance. The project also rents boots, sleeping bags and binoculars at reasonable prices. Participants should speak at least a little Spanish. With a month's notice, this outfit also offers quetzal-viewing platforms.

Sleeping
BUDGET

Casa D'Acuña (☎ 7951-0482, 7951-0484; uisa@amigo .net.gt; 4a Calle 3-11, Zona 2; dm/d US$6/13) This clean, comfortable European-style hostel has four dorms (each with four beds) and two pri- vate doubles, all with shared bathroom with good hot showers. Also here is a fabulous restaurant (opposite), a gift shop, laundry service and reasonably priced local tours.

Hostal San Juan Acala (☎ 7952-1528; 6a Av 2-50, Zona 3; dm US$3.50) This place usually has a place free in the eight-bed dorm, with comfy beds and homely handicraft-style decorations. The showers are warm and good.

Hotel La Paz (☎ 7952-1358; 6a Av 2-19, Zona 1; s US$4, s/d with private bathroom US$6/10; ☐) This cheerful, clean hotel, 1½ blocks north and two blocks west of the plaza, is an excellent deal. It has many flowers and a good cafe- teria next door. It claims to have hot water.

Camping (per person per night US$2.50) is avail- able at Parque Nacional Las Victorias, right in town (p139). Facilities include water and toilets but no showers.

MID-RANGE

Hostal de Doña Victoria (☎ /fax 7951-4213/4; 3a Calle 2-38, Zona 3; s/d US$20/26/54, low season US$12/20/26; ☐) This lovely hotel, in a restored man- sion more than 400 years old, is jam-packed with eye-catching decorations varying from an old copper coffee machine to wooden masks and antique religious statues. Eight brightly painted comfortable rooms with private bathroom and TV surround a cen- tral courtyard with lush plants and a bar/ restaurant.

Hotel La Posada (☎ 7952-1495, 7951-0588; la posada@c.net.gt; 1a Calle 4-12, Zona 2; s/d US$33/45/54) Just off the plaza, this colonial-style hotel is Cobán's best, though streetside rooms suffer from traffic noise. Its colonnaded porches are dripping with tropical flowers and furnished with easy chairs and ham- mocks from which to enjoy the mountain views. The rooms have nice old furniture, fireplaces and wall hangings of local weav- ing, and private bathroom. Television costs US$3.50 daily. It has a restaurant and café (opposite).

Pensión Monja Blanca (☎ 7952-1712, 7951-0531; www.sitio.de/hotelmonjablanca; 2a Calle 6-30, Zona 2; s/d US$7/14, with private hot-water bathroom US$13/26) Run by a sweet older couple, this place is peaceful despite being on busy 2a Calle. After walking through two courtyards, you come to a lush garden packed with fruit and hibiscus trees around which the spot- less rooms are arranged. Each room is fur- nished with two good-quality single beds with folksy covers and cable TV. This is a good place for solo women travelers.

Casa Alcázar Victoria (☎ 7952-1143; fax 7952-1389; 1a Av 5-34; s/d US$20/26/54; ☐) This attractive new hotel, about 600m north of the plaza, is owned by the same people as the Doña Vic- toria, but it's a different type of place. Set on two levels around a large interior patio, the building is a tasteful modern version of old colonial style. Local weddings and parties are held here, so it's best to ask before you take a room if the patio will be used for a function during your stay. Rooms come with private hot-water bathroom and have pretty furnishings. There is a restaurant.

Quetzaltenango (p111)

Festival participants dressed as conquistadors, Chichicastenango (p105)

Iglesia y Convento de Nuestra Señora de la Merced (p82), Antigua

The Semana Santa parade (p84) in Antigua

ALFREDO MAIQU

Colonial house facade in Guatemala City (p65)

Antigua (p77)

ALFREDO MAIQUEZ

ERIC L WHEATER

Antigua (p77)

ALFREDO MAIQ

Flowers floating in bowl of water, Antigua (p77)

Vivero Verapaz (s & d US$32) The orchid nursery (p139) has three nice, quiet, fully equipped cabañas for rent.

Eating

Most of Cobán's hotels have their own restaurants.

El Bistro (4a Calle 3-11; fish, steak & chicken mains US$8.50-13; ☺ breakfast, lunch & dinner) The restaurant at Casa D'Acuña whips up authentic Italian and other European-style dishes, served in an attractive oasis of tranquility to background classical music. In addition to protein-oriented main meals, there is a range of pastas (US$4 to US$5.25), salads, homemade breads, cakes and outstanding desserts.

Café La Posada (1a Calle 4-12, Zona 2; snacks under US$4; ☺ lunch & dinner) This café has tables on a verandah overlooking the square and a comfortable sitting room inside with couches, coffee tables and a fireplace. All the usual café fare is served. Snacks comprise nachos, *tortillas*, sandwiches, burgers, tacos, *tostadas*, fruit salad etc.

Café El Tirol (Oficinas Profesionales Fray Bartolomé de Las Casas; 1a Calle 3-13; breakfasts US$2-4; ☺ Mon-Sat) Another good central café, the Tirol claims to have Cobán's ' best coffee' (we disagree) and offers several types of hot chocolate. It's a cozy little place in which to enjoy breakfasts, pastries and light meals, with a pleasant terrace away from the traffic.

La Esperanza (2nd fl, 1a Calle 3-66, Zona 3; buffet US$2.50) Don't get excited – the buffet is strictly a one-plate-only affair, but this clean and modern café *does* have the best espresso machine in town, and a range of silly cakes baked in the downstairs bakery.

Cafetería Santa Rita (1a Calle; lunch US$3) Small, tidy and popular with locals, this eatery on the south side of the plaza offers good, simple Guatemalan breakfasts, lunches and dinners.

Restaurant Kam Mun (1a Calle 8-12, Zona 2; mains US$5-11) You'll find Chinese fare served in a nice, clean atmosphere here, 500m west of the plaza. Enjoy your meal surrounded by Chinese dragons, Buddhas and floral paintings.

In the evening, **food trucks** park around the plaza and offer some of the cheapest dining in town. As always, the one to go for will have the largest crowd of locals hanging around and chomping down.

Drinking

Cobán has several places where you can get down and boogie.

Bar Milenio (3a Av 1-11, Zona 4) Milenio has a bar, food, a pool table and mixed-music disco.

Kikoe's Tasca (2a Av, Zona 2; ☺ 5pm-midnight) Near Casa D'Acuña, this is a bar in the Bavarian vein. Cocktails, beer and bar food are served.

Keop's (3a Calle 4-71, Zona 3; admission US$4.50) This is a popular disco. Wear your best gear.

Getting There & Away

The highway connecting Cobán with Guatemala City and the Carretera al Atlántico is the most-traveled route between Cobán and the outside world. The road north through Chisec to Sayaxché and Flores has almost all been paved in recent years, providing much easier access than before to El Petén. The off-the-beaten-track routes west to Huehuetenango and northeast to Fray Bartolomé de Las Casas and Poptún remain almost completely unpaved and still a bit of an adventure. Always double-check bus departure times, especially for less frequently served destinations. Tourism staff at the Municipalidad try to keep up with the frequent schedule changes and display bus details in the foyer.

A few buses depart from a sort of terminal, southeast of the stadium, called Campo 2 or Terminal Nuevo (New Bus Station). Buses to Guatemala City, Salamá, Lanquín and other destinations leave from completely different terminals and stops, most near the Mercado Terminal market (stops are shown on our Cobán map). Minibuses, known as microbuses, are replacing (or are additional to) chicken buses on many routes. Many buses do a circuit of the plaza before leaving town and stop outside Oficinas Profesionales Fray Bartolomé de Las Casas.

Biotopo del Quetzal (US$0.65, 1¼hr, 58km) Any bus heading for Guatemala City will drop you at the entrance to the *biotopo*.

Chisec (US$1.95, 2hr, 66km) Ten buses a day leave from the corner of 1a Av and 2a Calle between 6am and 5pm.

El Estor (US$4, 7hr, 166km) This route via Tactic and Panzós is unsafe and not recommended (see El Estor, p158). If the situation changes, you'll find buses departing from outside the Injav football stadium six times daily between 5am and 1pm.

Flores (5-6hr, 224km) Go to Sayaxché and take an onward bus or minibus from there.

Fray Bartolomé de Las Casas (US$2.60, 3hr, 121km) Via Chisec, which isn't covered in this book; US$2.20, 4hr, 101km via San Pedro Carchá). Several buses daily from 5am to 3:30pm depart from the corner of 2a Calle and 3a Av, opposite Inque Renta Autos. Buses might just say 'Las Casas.' Microbuses leave from 2a Calle and 1a Av right by Mercado Terminal.

Guatemala City (US$3.25-4.50, 4-5hr, 213km) Transportes Monja Blanca (☎ 7951-3571; 2a Calle 3-77, Zona 4) Has buses leaving for Guatemala City every half-hour from 2am to 6am, then hourly until 5pm.

Lanquín (US$1.30-1.95, 2½-3hr, 61km) Buses depart at 5am and 6am from in front of the Dispensa Familiar supermarket just east of the plaza, and at 5:30am, 7am, 8am, 9am, 11am and 1pm from Transportes Gamasa (cnr 3a Calle & 2a Av), next to Restaurant Los Camarones. Do check these times as they seem to be fluid. There are also assorted *micros* with no fixed timetable from the same stop.

Playa Grande (for Laguna Lachuá; US$5.25, 4hr, 141km) Buses depart daily at 5am and 11am from Mercado Terminal; there are also microbuses. Playa Grande is sometimes called Cantabal.

Puerto Barrios (6½hr, 335km) Take any bus headed to Guatemala City and change at El Rancho junction.

Río Dulce (6½hr, 318km) Take any bus headed to Guatemala City and change at El Rancho junction. You may have to transfer again at La Ruidosa junction, 169km past El Rancho, but there is plenty of transport going through to Río Dulce and on to Flores.

Salamá (US$1.80, 1½hr, 57km) Frequent minivans leave from the corner of 3a Calle & 2a Av opposite the Transportes Gamasa office, or take any bus to Guatemala City & change at La Cumbre.

Sayaxché (US$5.50, 4hr, 184 km) Buses at 6am and noon, and microbuses from early until 1pm, leave from Mercado Terminal.

Uspantán (US$3.50, 4½hr, 94km) Buses depart at 10am and noon from the Shell station on 1a Calle near 7a Av. Microbuses go from the corner of 2a Calle and 3a Av, with a stop at Oficinas Profesionales Fray Bartolomé de Las Casas.

AROUND COBÁN

Cobán (indeed all of Alta Verapaz) is becoming a hot destination for adventure travel. Not only does the area hold scores of villages where you can find traditional Mayan culture in some of its purest extant form, it also harbors caves, waterfalls, pristine lagoons and many other undiscovered natural wonders.

San Juan Chamelco

About 16km southeast of Cobán is the village of San Juan Chamelco, with swimming at Balneario Chio. The **church** here, which may have been the first in Alta Verapaz, sits atop a small rise and has awesome views of the villages below. Mass is still held here in Spanish (Sunday 5pm) and Q'eqchi' (Sunday 7am and 9:30am).

In **Aldea Chajaneb**, only 12km from Cobán, **Don Jerónimo's** (☎ 5308-2255; www.dearbrutus.com/donjeronimo; s/d US$25/45) rents comfortable, simple bungalows. The price includes three ample, delicious vegetarian meals fresh from the garden. Many activities, including tours to caves and the mountains and inner tubing on the Río Sotzil, are offered.

Buses to San Juan Chamelco leave from 4a Calle, Zona 3, in Cobán. To reach Don Jerónimo's, take a bus or pickup from San Juan Chamelco toward Chamil and ask the driver to let you off at Don Jerónimo's. When you get off, take the footpath to the left for 300m, cross the bridge and it's the first house on the right. Alternatively, hire a taxi from Cobán (US$6.50).

Grutas de Lanquín

The best excursion from Cobán is to the caves near Lanquín, a pretty village 61km east. If you get this far, make sure to visit Semuc Champey as well.

The **Grutas de Lanquín** (admission US$2.60; ⏰ 8am-4pm) are a short distance northwest of the village and extend several kilometers into the earth. There is a ticket office here. The caves have lights, but bring a powerful flashlight anyway. You'll also need shoes with good traction, as it's slippery inside.

Though the first few hundred meters of cavern have been equipped with a walkway and electric lights, most of this subterranean system is untouched. If you're a neophyte spelunker, think twice about wandering too far – the entire extent of this cave has yet to be explored, let alone mapped. Aside from funky stalactites and stalagmites, these caves are crammed with bats; at sunset they fly out of the mouth of the cave in dense, sky-obscuring formations. The river here gushes from the cave in clean, cool torrents; search out the hot pockets near the shore.

Camping is permitted near the cave entrance. Between Lanquín and the caves, **El Recreo** (☎ 7952-2160; d US$4-7, s/d/tr with private bathroom US$19/25/31; P ⏰) has large gardens, two swimming pools and a restaurant.

The sublimely located **El Retiro** (dm US$4-5, d US$9-13) is about 500m along the road beyond Rabin Itzam. *Palapa* buildings look down over green fields to a beautiful, wide river – the same one that flows out from the Lanquín caves. It's safe to swim, even inner tube, if you're a confident swimmer. Attention to detail in every respect makes this a backpackers' paradise. Excellent vegetarian food (three-course dinners US$4.50) is available in the hammock-lined restaurant.

The bright, clean **Comedor Shalom**, near Rabin Itzam, is good for a meal. A plate of chicken, rice and salad costs US$1.55.

Tours to the Grutas de Lanquín and Semuc Champey, offered in Cobán for US$35 per person (p139), are the easiest way to visit these places. Tours take about two hours to reach Lanquín from Cobán; the price includes a packed lunch. If you're driving on your own, you'll need a 4WD vehicle.

Buses operate several times daily between Cobán and Lanquín, continuing to Cahabón. Buses leave Lanquín to return to Cobán at 3am, 4am, 5:30am and 1pm, and there are assorted microbuses with no fixed timetable. Since the last reliable return bus departs so early, it's best to stay the night.

Semuc Champey

Nine kilometers south of Lanquín, along a rough, bumpy, slow road, is **Semuc Champey** (admission US$2.60), famed for its great natural limestone bridge 300m long, on top of which is a stepped series of pools of cool, flowing river water, good for swimming. The water is from the Río Cahabón, and much more of it passes underground beneath the bridge. Though this bit of paradise is difficult to reach, the beauty of its setting and the perfection of the pools, ranging from turquoise to emerald green, make it all worthwhile.

If you're visiting on a tour, some guides will take you down a rope ladder from the lowest pool to the river, which gushes out from the rocks below.

It's possible to **camp** at Semuc Champey, but be sure to pitch a tent only in the upper areas, as flash floods are common. It's risky to leave anything unattended, as it might get stolen. The place now has 24-hour security, but you must bring all camping needs with you.

Las Marías (dm US$2, private r per person US$4) is a newish, rustic, laid-back place by the road 1km short of Semuc Champey. There are a couple of dorm rooms and three private rooms, all in wooden buildings in a verdant setting. Cool drinks and vegetarian food are available (full dinner US$2.60). You can swim in nearby Río Cahabón.

Pickups run from the plaza in Lanquín to Semuc Champey – your chances of catching one are better in the early morning and on market days (Sunday, Monday and Thursday). If there are a lot of local people traveling, expect to pay US$0.65; otherwise, it's US$1.95. The walk is long and hot.

PARQUE NACIONAL LAGUNA LACHUÁ

This **park** (admission US$5.25; camping per tent US$3.25, bunk per person US$7.75) is renowned for the perfectly round, pristine turquoise lake (220m deep) for which it was named. Until recently, this Guatemalan gem was rarely visited by travelers because it was an active, violent area during the civil war and the road was in pathetic disrepair. A new road (though unpaved most of the way from Chisec) means you can get to the park entrance from Cobán in four hours by bus. Take a Playa Grande (Cantabal) bus from Cobán via Chisec and ask the driver to leave you at the park entrance, from where it's about a 4km walk to the lake. Overnight visitors can use the cooking facilities, so come prepared with food and drink.

The Cobán tour outfits offer two-day/one-night trips for US$90 per person.

Outside the park, about 7km southwest of the park entrance, is **Finca Chipantún** (www .chipantun.com, www.cybercoban.com; camping/bed per person US$1.30/4), 4 sq km of private land bordering the Río Chixoy (Negro). Apart from accommodations, there is horse riding, forest trails, river trips, kayaking and bird- and wildlife-watching. The owners can take you by boat on the Río Negro to El Peyan, a magical gorge. Meals cost US$2.50 to US$4.

Proyecto EcoQuetzal (p140) does jungle hikes to the Río Ikbolay in the Laguna Lachuá vicinity.

BACKDOOR PETÉN ROUTES

The **Cobán to Poptún** route via Fray Bartolomé de Las Casas used to be a desolate dirt road. Nowadays plenty of buses and pickups ply the now-decent roads. This route is a great opportunity for you to get off the Gringo Trail and into the heart of Guatemala.

The hospitable town of **Fray Bartolomé de Las Casas**, often referred to as Las Casas, is sizable for the middle of nowhere. You can't make it from Cobán to Poptún in one shot, so you'll be spending the night here. **Banrural**, just off the plaza, changes US dollars and traveler's checks. The **post office** and **police station** are nearby. The **Municipalidad** is on the plaza.

The friendly **Hotel y Restaurante Bartolo** (s/d with private bathroom US$4/8; 🗨), behind the plaza, has the best accommodations in town. The restaurant serves good food for US$2 a plate.

One daily bus departs from the plaza at 3am for Poptún (US$4, five to six hours, 100km). Buses for Cobán leave hourly between 4am and 4pm. Some go via Chisec (US$2, 3½ hours; not covered in this book). Others take the slower route via San Pedro Carchá.

Another backdoor trip you could take goes from Cobán to Sayaxché and Ceibal. See Getting There & Away, p141. You can also go via Raxrujá (many services), west of Fray Bartolomé de Las Casas. One bus daily leaves Fray for Sayaxché at 10am (4½ hours, 117km).

RÍO HONDO

Río Hondo (Deep River) lies at the junction of the CA-9 and CA-10, 42km east of El Rancho junction and 126km from Guatemala City. The center of town is northeast of the highway junction.

Río Hondo motels are used as weekend resorts by locals and Guatemala City residents, so they may be full on weekends. All are modern, with well-equipped bungalows (with cable TV and private bathroom), spacious grounds and good restaurants.

The following motels are all near one another at Km 126 on the CA-9.

Hotel Santa Cruz (☎ 7934-7112; fax 7934-7075; s/d/tr with air-con US$14/27/39; 🅿 🗙 🗨) Cheapest and the lowest-key of the three, the Santa Cruz has rooms in duplex bungalows, with fan or air-con, spread over a large area with plenty of foliage. Its popular **restaurant** (breakfasts US$2-4, 3-course lunches US$4.50) is cheaper than the other motels.

Hotel El Atlántico (☎ 7934-7160; fax 7934-7041; s/d/tr US$18/36/42; 🅿 🗙 🗨) This place has 58 large bungalows set in spacious grounds and is the most attractive for the price.

Hotel Nuevo Pasabién (☎ 7934-7201; pasabien@ infovia.com.gt; s/d/tr US$20/39/42; 🅿 🗙 🗨) On the north side of the highway, this establishment has large rooms with big windows. It's a good choice for travelers with children who can enjoy the three pools with all manner of fancy slides.

Valle Dorado (☎ 2220-8840, 7933-1111; www .valledorado.com; Carr al Atlántico Km 149) This large complex 14km past the CA-10 junction and 23km from the other Río Hondo hotels, includes an **aquatic park** (adult/child on weekends US$6/5, weekdays US$5/4; 🕒 8:30am-5:30pm) with giant pools, waterslides, toboggans and other entertainment. Make reservations on weekends.

ESTANZUELA
pop 10,000

Traveling south from Río Hondo along the CA-10 takes you to the midst of the Río Motagua valley, a hot 'dry tropic' area that once supported a great number and variety of dinosaurs. Three kilometers south of the CA-9, you will see a small monument on the right (west) side of the road commemorating the terrible earthquake of February 4, 1976.

Less than 2km south of the monument is the small town of Estanzuela, with its **Museo de Paleontología, Arqueología y Geología Ingeniero Roberto Woolfolk Sarvia** (☎ 7941-4981; admission free; 🕒 9am-5pm). This interesting museum holds bones of dinosaurs, a giant ground sloth some 30,000 years old and a prehistoric whale. Also on display are early Mayan artifacts. To get there, go 1km west from the highway directly through town, following the small, blue 'museo' signs.

CHIQUIMULA
pop 24,000 / elevation 370m

Capital of its namesake department, Chiquimula lies in a tobacco-growing and mining region on the CA-10, 32km south of the CA-9. Though small, it's a major market town for eastern Guatemala. It's also a transportation point and overnight stop for those en route to Copán in Honduras; this is the reason most travelers stop here. Among other things, Chiquimula is known for its sweltering climate, decent budget hotels and the flower-packed central plaza, wired for sound and pumping out nonstop Guate pop.

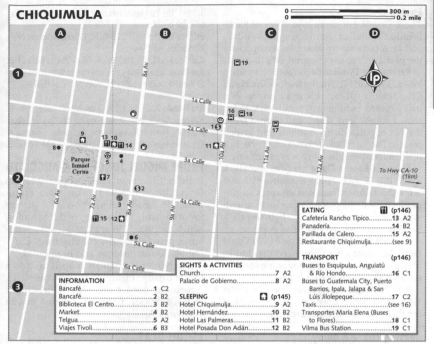

CHIQUIMULA

INFORMATION	
Bancafé..1	C2
Bancafé..2	B2
Biblioteca El Centro....................3	B2
Market...4	B2
Telgua...5	A2
Viajes Tivoli................................6	B3

SIGHTS & ACTIVITIES	
Church..7	A2
Palacio de Gobierno....................8	A2

SLEEPING 🏠 (p145)	
Hotel Chiquimulja.......................9	A2
Hotel Hernández.......................10	B2
Hotel Las Palmeras....................11	B2
Hotel Posada Don Adán.............12	B2

EATING 🍴 (p146)	
Cafetería Rancho Típico.............13	A2
Panadería...................................14	B2
Parillada de Calero.....................15	A2
Restaurante Chiquimulja.......(see 9)	

TRANSPORT (p146)	
Buses to Esquipulas, Anguiatú	
& Río Hondo..........................16	C1
Buses to Guatemala City, Puerto	
Barrios, Ipala, Jalapa & San	
Lúis Jilolepeque......................17	C2
Taxis......................................(see 16)	
Transportes María Elena (Buses	
to Flores)...............................18	C1
Vilma Bus Station......................19	C1

Orientation & Information

Though very hot, Chiquimula is easy to get around on foot.

The **post office** (10a Av btwn 1a & 2a Calles) is in an alley around the side of the building opposite the bus station. **Telgua** (3a Calle) is a few doors downhill from Parque Ismael Cerna. Check your email at **Biblioteca El Centro** (cnr 4a Calle & 8a Av; per hr US$1.30; ⏰ 8am-7pm Mon-Fri, 8am-6pm Sat & Sun). The busy **market** is right by Telgua.

Many banks will change US-dollar cash and traveler's checks. Both branches of **Bancafé** (Hotel Victoria cnr 2a Calle & 10a Av, Zona 1; Comercial Centro El Punto, cnr 4a Calle & 8a Av, Zona 1) have Visa ATMs.

Viajes Tivoli (☎ 7942-4915, 7942-4933; fax 7942-2258; 8a Av 4-71, Zona 1) can help you with travel arrangements.

Sleeping

Hotel Hernández (☎ 7942-0708; 3a Calle 7-41, Zona 1; s/d US$4/6, with private hot-water bathroom US$8/13; 🎐 🖳) In the block to the northeast of the plaza, this is the pick of the bunch. It's clean, pleasant and friendly; the owner speaks English, Spanish and a little French. The sprawling property has a sparkling swimming pool and plenty of greenery. The rooms all have fans and good beds. Overlooking the pool are some rooms with air-con for US$13/20.

Hotel Posada Don Adán (☎ 7942-3924; 8a Av 4-30, Zona 1; s/d/tr US$16/24/32; 🅿 🎐) Run by a friendly, efficient *señora* and her polite husband, Adán, this place is spotless. The spacious rooms have private hot-water bathroom, cable TV, fan and air-con.

Hotel Las Palmeras (☎ 7942-4647; 10a Av 2-00; s/d US$4/7, with air-con US$7/13; 🅿 🎐) This clean, family-run hotel has 30 rooms with private bathroom, cable TV, air-con or fan, and good beds. There's a place to do your laundry, a terrace, and a few splashes of color – pink on one level, blue on another.

Hotel Chiquimulja (☎ 7942-0387; 3a Calle 6-51; s/d US$8/16, with air-con US$9/18; 🅿 🎐) This hotel is on the north side of the *parque*. Despite some remodeling and bright bed covers, these rooms with private bathroom and TV seem a bit run-down, but don't miss the fantastic *palapa*-style restaurant out back.

Eating

There's a string of cheap *comedores* an 8a Av behind the market. At night, snack vendors and taco carts set up along 7a Av opposite the plaza, selling the cheapest eats in town.

Restaurante Chiquimujla (3a Calle 6-51; breakfasts US$2-3.25, mains US$4-7) Out the back of the Hotel Chiquimulja (p145), this is an impressive, palm-roofed building on two levels. Relax with a lovely, long drink and choose from the list of pasta dishes, prawns and grilled meats. The *parillada* (platter) for two is a real heartstopper, in more ways than one.

Cafetería Rancho Típico (3a Calle; limonadas & licuados US$1.20, snacks US$0.65-2, breakfasts US$0.80-4) A few doors down from Restaurante Chiquimulja, the Rancho prepares good drinks with lots of ice and serves varied light meals – hamburgers, tostadas, enchiladas etc.

Parillada de Calero (7a Av 4-83; meals US$8) You'd better like meat if you come here. Big chunks of it, char-grilled. Closest they come to vegetarian dishes is chicken. Or fries.

The **Panadería bakery** next door to Hotel Hernández (p145) opens at 5:30am – perfect for that predawn bus departure.

Getting There & Away

Several companies operate buses to Guatemala City and Puerto Barrios; all of them arrive and depart from the bus station area on 11a Av, between 1a and 2a Calles. Ipala and San Lúis Jilotepeque microbuses and the Jalapa bus also go from here. Minibuses to Esquipulas, Río Hondo and Anguiatú and buses to Flores arrive and depart a block away, on 10a Av between 1a and 2a Calles. **Vilma** (☎ 7942-2064), which operates buses to El Florido, the border crossing on the way to Copán, has its own bus station a couple of blocks north.

Agua Caliente (Honduras border) Take a minibus to Esquipulas and change there.

Anguiatú (El Salvador border; US$1.20, 1hr, 54km) Hourly minibuses, 5am to 5:30pm.

El Florido (Honduras border; US$1.20, 1½hr, 58km) Chicken buses depart from the Vilma bus station half-hourly, 5:30am to 4:30pm.

Esquipulas (US$1.20, 45min, 52km) Minibuses run every 10 minutes, 4am to 8pm. Sit on the left for the best views of the basilica.

Flores (US$7, 7-8 hours, 385km) Transportes María Elena (☎ 7942-3420; 6am, 10am & 3pm)

Guatemala City (US$3.25, 3hr, 169km) Rutas Orientales and other companies depart at least hourly, 3am to 3:30pm. The 3am bus leaves from the plaza, the rest leave from the bus station.

Puerto Barrios (US$3.25, 4½hr, 192km) Buses run every 30 minutes, 4am to 6pm.

Quiriguá (US$2.10, 2hr, 103km) Take a Puerto Barrios bus.

Río Dulce Take a Flores bus, or a Puerto Barrios bus to La Ruidosa junction (US$3.25, three hours, 144km) and change there.

Río Hondo (US$1.35, 32km) There are minibuses every half hour, 5am to 6pm. Or take any bus heading for Guatemala City, Flores or Puerto Barrios. On Sunday, Guatemala City buses won't let you on for Río Hondo – take a minibus.

PADRE MIGUEL JUNCTION & ANGUIATÚ

Between Chiquimula and Esquipulas (35km from Chiquimula and 14km from Esquipulas), Padre Miguel junction is the turnoff for Anguiatú, the border of El Salvador, which is 19km (30 minutes) away. Minibuses pass frequently, coming from Chiquimula, Quezaltepeque and Esquipulas.

The border at Anguiatú is open from 6am to 7pm daily. Plenty of trucks cross here. Across the border there are hourly buses to San Salvador, passing through Metapán and Santa Ana.

ESQUIPULAS

From Chiquimula the CA-10 goes south into the mountains, where it's cooler and a bit more comfortable. After an hour's ride through pretty country, the highway descends into a valley ringed by mountains. Halfway down the slope, about 1km from town, a *mirador* provides a good view. As soon as you catch sight of the place you'll see the reason for coming: the great Basílica de Esquipulas that towers above the town, its whiteness shining in the sun.

History

This town may have been a place of pilgrimage even before the conquest. Legend has it that Esquipulas takes its name from a Maya lord who ruled this region when the Spanish arrived.

With the arrival of the friars, a church was built, and in 1595 an image of Christ carved from black wood was installed. The steady flow of pilgrims to Esquipulas became a flood after 1737, when Pedro Pardo de Figueroa, Archbishop of Guatemala, came here on pilgrimage and went away cured of a chronic ailment. Delighted with this development, the prelate commissioned a huge new church to be built on the site. It was finished in 1758 and the pilgrimage trade has been the town's livelihood ever since.

Esquipulas is assured a place in modern history, too. Beginning here in 1986, President Vinicio Cerezo Arévalo brokered agreements with the other Central American leaders on economic cooperation and conflict resolution. These became the seeds of the Guatemalan Peace Accords, which were finally signed in 1996.

Orientation & Information

The basilica is the center of everything. Most of the good cheap hotels are within a block or two, as are numerous small restaurants. The highway does not enter town; 11a Calle, also sometimes called Doble Vía Quirio Cataño, comes in from the highway and is the town's 'main drag.'

The **post office** (6a Av 2-15) is about 10 blocks north of the center. **Telgua** (cnr 5a Av & 9a Calle) has plenty of card phones. Check your email at **Global.com** (3a Av; per hr US$1.55), opposite Banco Internacional.

A number of banks change US-dollar cash and traveler's checks. **Banco Internacional** (3a Av 8-87, Zona 1) changes both, gives cash advances on Visa and MasterCard, is the town's American Express agent and has a Visa ATM.

January 15 is the annual **Cristo de Esquipulas festival**, with mobs of devout pilgrims coming from all over the region to worship at the altar of El Cristo Negro.

Basilica

A massive pile of stone that has resisted earthquakes for almost 250 years, the basilica is approached through a pretty park and up a flight of steps. The impressive facade and towers are floodlit at night.

Inside, the devout approach El Cristo Negro (the Black Christ) with extreme reverence, many on their knees. Incense, the murmur of prayers and the scuffle of sandaled feet fill the air. When throngs of pilgrims are here, you must enter the church from the side to get a close view of the famous image. Shuffling along quickly, you may get a good glimpse before being shoved onward by the press of the crowd. On Sunday, religious holidays and (especially) during the festival, the press of devotees is intense. Otherwise, you may have the place to yourself.

Sleeping

Esquipulas has an abundance of accommodations. On holidays and during the annual festival, every hotel in town is filled, whatever the price; weekends are fairly busy as well, with prices substantially higher. On nonfestival weekdays, ask for a *descuento* (discount). For cheap rooms, look in the streets immediately north of the basilica.

Pensión Santa Rosa (☎ 7943-2908; cnr 10a Calle & 1a Av, Zona 1; s/d US$4/8, with private hot-water bathroom US$5/10) Typical of the small backstreet places, this family-run pension has rooms off a big concrete courtyard. The **Hotel San Carlos II** next door is similar, as is the **Pensión La Favorita** and several others on this street.

Hotel Payaquí (☎ 7943-2025; fax 7943-1371; s/d/tr US$23/45/58; 🏠 🛗 P) This large, attractive hotel has 55 rooms, all with private bathroom, cable TV, telephone and fridge. Prices quoted above include air-con. During the week, the same rooms go for US$18/36/54 while rooms without air-con are US$12/24/36. It has two restaurants (below).

Hotel El Gran Chortí (☎ 7943-1148; fax 7943-1551; Carr Internacional a Honduras Km 222; s/d US$46/61, ste for 4 US$92; P 🏠 🛗) One kilometer west of the church on the road to Chiquimula, this hotel has a lobby floor composed of a hectare of black marble; behind it a serpentine swimming pool is set amid lawns, gardens and umbrella-shaded café tables. There's a games room and a good restaurant, bar and cafeteria. The rooms have all comforts.

The following are fine mid-range choices, with decent restaurants:

Hotel Legendario (☎ 7943-1824/5; www.porta hotels.com; cnr 3a Av & 9a C, Zona 1; s/d/tr US$38/44/51; P 🛗)

Hotel Posada del Cristo Negro (☎ 7943-1482; fax 7943-1829; Carr Internacional a Honduras Km 224; s/d/tr/q US$17/22/33/39; P 🏠 🛗)

Eating

Restaurants are slightly more expensive here than in other parts of Guatemala. Budget restaurants are clustered at the north end of the park, where hungry pilgrims can find them readily. Most eateries open from 6:30am until 9pm or 10pm daily.

Restaurant Payaquí (whole chickens US$10.50, ¼ chicken with trimmings US$3.25, other mains US$5.25-7) This is a bright and clean cafeteria with big windows looking out onto the park. Prices are reasonable, and there's a good selection. Breakfasts are US$1.55 to US$2.60.

Restaurante La Frontera (breakfasts US$2-4, mains US$4-10) Opposite the park, this restaurant is attached to Hotel Las Cúpulas. It is a spacious, clean place serving up a good variety of rice, chicken, meat, fish and seafood dishes for good prices.

The street running north opposite the church, 3a Av, has several eateries including **Restaurante Calle Real** (breakfasts US$2-4, mains US$4-6), which is large, clean and well priced.

The *comedor* attached to the **Pensión Santa Rosa** (cnr 10a Calle & 1a Av, Zona 1) has good set lunches for under US$3.

Getting There & Away

Buses to Guatemala City arrive and depart from the **Rutas Orientales bus station** (☎ 7943-1366; cnr 11a Calle & 1a Av), near the entrance to town. Minibuses to **Agua Caliente** (Honduras) arrive and depart across the street; taxis also wait here, charging the same as the minibuses, once they have five passengers.

Minibuses to Chiquimula and to Anguiatú depart from the east end of 11a Calle; you will probably see them hawking for passengers along the main street.

Agua Caliente (Honduras border; US$1.30, 30min, 10km) Minibuses run every half hour, 6am to 5pm.

Anguiatú (El Salvador border; US$1, 1hr, 33km) Minibuses run every half hour, 6am to 6pm.

Chiquimula (US$1, 45min, 52km) Minibuses run every 15 minutes, 5am to 6pm.

Flores (US$7.75, 8-10hr, 437km) Transportes María Elena (☎ 7943-0448; 4am, 8am & 1pm) Buses depart from east of the basilica, amid the market.

Guatemala City (US$4, 4hr, 222km) Rutas Orientales *servicio especial* buses depart at 6:30am, 7:30am, 1:30pm and 3pm; ordinary buses depart every half hour, 4:30am to 6pm.

COPÁN SITE (HONDURAS)

The ancient city of **Copán** (admission US$10; ⏰ 8am-4pm) is one of the most outstanding Mayan achievements, ranking in splendor with Tikal, Chichén Itzá and Uxmal. To fully appreciate Mayan art and culture, you must visit here.

There are two Copáns: the town and the ruins. The town (confusingly named Copán Ruinas) is 12km to the east of the Guatemala–Honduras border. The actual ruins are 1km further east.

History

PRE-COLUMBIAN

Ceramic evidence indicates that people have been living in the Copán valley since around 1400 BC. Graves showing Olmec influence have been dated to around 900–600 BC.

In the 5th century AD a mysterious king named Mah K'ina Yax K'uk' Mo' (Great Sun Lord Quetzal Macaw) came to power and ruled from 426 to 435. He was revered by later kings as the semidivine founder of the city. His dynasty ruled throughout Copán's florescence during the Classic period (AD 250–900).

Among the greatest of Copán's kings was Smoke Imix (Smoke Jaguar; 628–95), the 12th king, who built Copán into a major military and commercial power.

Smoke Imix was succeeded by Uaxaclahun Ubak K'awil (18 Rabbit; 695–738), who pursued further military conquest. In a war with King Cauac Sky from Quiriguá, 18 Rabbit was captured and beheaded. He was succeeded by Smoke Monkey (738–49), whose short reign left little mark on Copán.

Smoke Monkey's son Smoke Shell (749–63) was, however, one of Copán's greatest builders. He commissioned the Escalinata de los Jeroglíficos (Hieroglyphic Stairway), which chronicles the achievements of the dynasty from its establishment until 755. It's the longest inscription ever discovered in the Maya lands.

Yax Pac (Sunrise or First Dawn; 763–820), Smoke Shell's successor and the 16th king, continued the beautification of Copán. The final occupant of the throne, U Cit Tok', became ruler in 822, but it is unknown when he died.

Near the end of Copán's heyday, the population grew exponentially, straining agricultural resources. Ultimately, Copán was no longer self-sufficient and had to import food. The urban core expanded into the fertile lowlands, forcing agricultural and residential areas onto the steep valley walls. Widespread deforestation resulted in massive erosion, further decimating food production and causing chronic flooding.

Skeletal remains dating from Copán's final years show marked evidence of malnutrition, infectious diseases and decreased lifespans.

Agriculturists probably continued to live in the devastated valley for another couple of hundred years. By around the year 1200, even the farmers had departed and the city of Copán was reclaimed by jungle.

TODAY

The history of Copán continues to unfold. The remains of 3450 structures have been found in the 24 sq km surrounding the Grupo Principal (Principal Group), most of them within 500m of it. Within 135 sq km of the ruins, 4509 structures have been detected. These discoveries indicate that at Copán's peak, the valley had over 27,500 inhabitants – a population not reached again until the 1980s.

Archaeologists continue to make new discoveries in the Grupo Principal. Five phases of building have been identified; the final phase, dating from 650 to 820, is what we see today. Buried underneath these ruins are more layers, which archaeologists are exploring by means of tunnels. This is how the Templo Rosalila was found.

Information

Admission does not include entry to the two **excavation tunnels** (admission US$12; ⊙ 8am-3:30pm).

The **Museo de Escultura** (Museum of Sculpture; admission US$5; ⊙ 8am-3:40pm) exhibits many original stelae and an awesome replica of the Rosalila temple.

A **Sendero Natural** (Nature Trail), entering the forest several hundred meters from the visitors center, passes by a small ball court.

Pick up a copy of the booklet *History Carved in Stone: A guide to the archaeological park of the ruins of Copán*, available at the visitors center for US$4, or hire a guide, who can help to explain the ruins and bring them to life. Guides cost US$20 regardless of group size.

Grupo Principal

The Principal Group is 400m beyond the visitors center, along a path through shady avenues of trees. The ruins themselves have been numbered for easy identification; see the Copán map (p150).

STELAE OF THE GRAN PLAZA

The path leads to the **Gran Plaza** (Great Plaza; Plaza de las Estelas) and the huge, intricately carved stelae portraying the rulers of Copán. Most of Copán's best stelae date from AD 613 to 738.

Many of the stelae on the Gran Plaza portray King 18 Rabbit. Perhaps the most beautiful is **Stela A** (AD 731) – the original is now in the Museo de Escultura; the one outdoors is a reproduction. Nearby are **Stela B** (731), depicting 18 Rabbit upon the throne; and **Stela C** (782), with a turtle-shaped altar in front and figures on both sides. **Stela E** (614), erected on top of Estructura 1 (Structure 1) on the west side of the plaza, is among the oldest.

On the east side of the plaza is **Stela F** (721), more lyrically designed than other stelae here: the robes of the main figure flow around to the other side of the stone, where there are glyphs. **Altar G** (800), showing twin serpent heads, is among the last monuments carved at Copán. **Stela H** (730) may depict a queen or princess rather than a king. **Stela J**, to the east, resembles the stelae of Quiriguá – it's covered in glyphs, not human figures. South of the Gran Plaza, across the Plaza Central, is the **Juego de Pelota** (Ball Court; 731), the second largest in Central America.

ESCALINATA DE LOS JEROGLÍFICOS

South of the ball court is Copán's most famous monument, the **Hieroglyphic Stairway** (743). The flight of 63 steps bears a history – in several thousand glyphs – of the royal house of Copán. The story is still not completely understood because the stairway was partially ruined and the stones jumbled.

At the base of the stairway is **Stela M** (756), bearing a figure in a feathered cloak; glyphs describe the solar eclipse of that year. The altar in front shows a plumed serpent with a human head emerging from its jaws.

Beside the stairway, a tunnel leads to the tomb of a nobleman, which held a treasure trove of painted pottery and beautiful carved-jade objects, now housed in Honduran museums.

ACRÓPOLIS

The flight of steps to the south of the Escalinata de los Jeroglíficos mounts the **Templo de Las Inscripciones** (Temple of the Inscriptions). At the top the walls are carved with hieroglyphs. In the Patio Occidental, be sure to see **Altar Q** (776), among the most famous sculptures here. Carved around its sides are the 16 great kings of Copán, ending with its creator, Yax Pac.

COPÁN

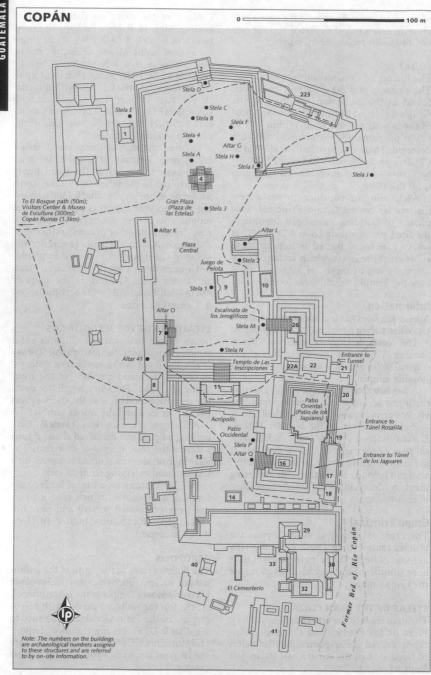

0   100 m

2

223

Stela D

Stela E

Stela C

Stela B

Stela F

1

Stela 4

Altar G

Stela A

Stela H

3

Stela I

4

Stela J

To El Bosque path (50m);
Visitors Center & Museo
de Escultura (300m);
Copán Ruinas (1.3km)

Gran Plaza
(Plaza de
las Estelas)

Stela 3

Altar K

6

Altar L

Plaza
Central

Juego de
Pelota

Stela 2

Stela 1

9

10

Altar O

Escalinata de
los Jeroglíficos

7

Stela M

26

Altar 41

Stela N

Entrance to
Tunnel

Templo de Las
Inscripciones

22A

22

21

8

11

20

Acrópolis
Patio
Occidental

Patio
Oriental
(Patio de los
Jaguares)

Entrance to
Túnel Rosalila

19

Stela P

Altar Q

Entrance to Túnel
de los Jaguares

13

16

17

14

18

29

33

30

40

El Cementerio

32

41

Note: The numbers on the buildings
are archaeological numbers assigned
to these structures and are referred
to by on-site information.

Former Bed of Río Copán

Both the Patios Oriental and Occidental hold a variety of fascinating stelae and sculptured heads. To see the most elaborate relief carving, climb Estructura 22; this was the **Templo de Meditación** (Temple of Meditation).

Túnel Rosalila

The Rosalila Tunnel exposes the Rosalila temple below Estructura 16; the carvings are remarkably crisp and vivid, especially the Sun God mask looming over the doorway, considered by some scholars to be the best-preserved stucco edifice in the Mayan world. Under the Rosalila temple is Templo Margarita, built 150 years earlier.

Túnel de los Jaguares

This tunnel shows the Tumba Galindo (Galindo Tomb), below Estructura 17 in the southern part of the Patio Oriental. It's less dramatic, with burial tombs and niches for offerings. Bones, obsidian knives and beads were found here, and archaeologists date the tomb's antebase mask to AD 540. The decorative macaw mask here is incredible.

El Bosque & Las Sepulturas

Las Sepulturas, once connected to the Gran Plaza by a causeway, may have been the residential area where rich and powerful nobles lived. One luxurious residential compound may have housed 250 people in 40 or 50 buildings arranged around 11 courtyards. The principal structure, the **Palacio de los Bacabs** (Palace of the Officials), had outer walls carved with full-size figures of 10 males in feathered headdresses; inside was a huge hieroglyphic bench.

The walk to get to El Bosque is the real reason for visiting it – one hour through foliage dense with birds, though there isn't much to see at the site itself, save for a small ball court. Still, it's a powerful experience to walk on the thoroughfares of an ancient Mayan city.

COPÁN RUINAS

pop 6000

Copán Ruinas, often simply called Copán, across the border in Honduras, is a beautiful town paved in cobblestone and lined with white adobe buildings with red-tile roofs. An aura of timeless harmony permeates the air. Copán has become a prime tourist destination, but this hasn't disrupted the town's integrity.

Orientation & Information

A **tourist office** (www.copanhonduras.org; ☽ 11am-7pm) is half a block to the east of the Parque Central.

Banco de Occidente (☽ 8:30am-4:30pm Mon-Fri, 8:30am-noon Sat) changes US-dollar cash, traveler's checks and Guatemalan quetzals, and gives cash advances. **Banco Credomatic** has a Visa and MasterCard ATM.

Email services cost around US$1 an hour; **Copán Net** is one block south and one block west of the Parque Central.

For visa matters, a Honduran **immigration office** (☽ 7am-4:30pm Mon-Fri) is inside the Palacio Municipal on the Parque Central.

Sights & Activities

Museo de Arqueología Maya (admission US$2; ☽ 8am-4pm Mon-Sat) is well worth a visit, containing the original Stela B portraying King 18 Rabbit. Other exhibits include painted pottery, carved jade, Mayan glyphs, a calendar round and the Tumba del Brujo, the tomb of a shaman who died around AD 700 and was buried with many items under the Plaza de los Jaguares.

Casa K'inich (admission free; ☽ 8am-noon, 1-5pm Mon-Sat), inside the artisan market, is an interactive museum for kids about the Maya.

Sleeping

Café ViaVia (☎ 651-4652; www.viaviacafe; dm/s/d US$4/10/12) This European-style hotel has spotless rooms with private bathroom, tiled floors and great beds. One room functions as a dormitory with six beds. There are hammocks and a small garden.

Hostel Iguana Azul (☎ 651-4620; www.todomundo.com/iguanaazul; dm/s/d US$5/7/11) This funky place has eight comfy bunk beds in two rooms, with shared bathrooms, in a colonial-style ranch home. Three private rooms sleep two and there's a pretty garden.

Hotel La Posada (☎ 651-4070; laposada@hotelmarinacopan.com; s/d/tr US$15/25/30) This tranquil, good-value place has comfortable rooms

---

CALLING COPÁN

The Honduras telephone country code is ☎ 504. Honduras has no area or city codes. When dialing a number in Copán Ruinas, you dial the international access code (usually 00), then 504, then the local number.

COPÁN RUINAS

0 —————— 200 m
0 —————— 0.1 mile

INFORMATION
Banco Credomatic.........................1 B2
Banco de Occidente......................2 B2
Copán Net....................................3 B3
Immigration Office....................(see 4)
Palacio Municipal (City Hall)........4 B2
Tourist Office...............................5 B2

SIGHTS & ACTIVITIES   (p151)
Artisan Market..........................(see 6)
Casa K'inich................................6 B2
Church.......................................7 B2
Museo de Arqueología Maya......8 B2

To Agua Caliente
Hot Springs
(23km)

To Ruins (1km); Hacienda
& Cine El Jaral (11km);
Santa Rita de
Copán (9km);
La Entrada
(61km)

Sendero
Peatonal

Soccer
Field

Quebrada Sesesmil

To Guatemala
Border (12km)

Bridge

Parque
Central

To River
(200m)

To River (100m)

SLEEPING   (pp151-2)
Café ViaVia..................................9 A2
Hostel Iguana Azul...................(see 13)
Hotel La Posada.........................10 B2
Hotel Marina Copán....................11 B2
Hotel Plaza Copán......................12 B2
La Casa de Café B&B..................13 A3

EATING   (pp151-2)
Café Velchez............................(see 11)
Café ViaVia..............................(see 9)
Carnitas Nia Lola......................14 B3
Churrrasquería Momos..............15 B2
Food Market.............................16 B2
Glifo's.....................................(see 11)
La Casa de Todo.......................17 C2
LLama del Bosque.....................18 A2
Tunkul Bar...............................(see 9)

DRINKING   (p152)
Bar Jaguar Venado...................(see 11)

TRANSPORT   (pp153-4)
Hedman Alas Bus Terminal........19 B1
Minibuses & Pickup Trucks to
    the Border..........................20 B1
Monarcas Travel.......................21 B1

with private bathroom, fan and TV, set around two leafy patios.

La Casa de Café (☎ 651-4620; www.todomundo .com/casadecafe; s/d/tr incl breakfast US$35/45/53) This classy B&B has loads of character in a beautiful setting: the garden area with tables and hammocks has a view over cornfields to the mountains. The 10 rooms with private bathrooms have wooden ceilings and other nice touches.

Hotel Plaza Copán (☎ 651-4274; www.hotelplaza copan.com; s/d/tr US$46/52/58; P ☒ ☒) Rooms here are flash and have good beds, cable TV and telephone, plus some extras like private balconies and church views. Each room differs so look around before choosing.

Hotel Marina Copán (☎ 651-4070/1/2; www.hotel marinacopan.hn; s/d/tr US$87/99/111; P ☒ ☒) The top hotel in town has all the top-end amenities like a spa, sauna and gym. Rooms are spacious and there's a restaurant/bar in an attractive, wooden, jungle-inspired building.

Eating
Tunkul Bar (mains US$2.65-6; ☾ lunch & dinner) One of Copán's main gathering spots, two blocks

east of the plaza, this attractive covered-patio bar/restaurant has good food, decent music and a book exchange. There's a good variety of meat and vegetarian meals.

Café ViaVia (breakfast US$1.40-2.35, daily specials US$5, other mains US$3-5; ☾ breakfast, lunch & dinner) This terrific restaurant next door to the Tunkul Bar (opposite) has tables overlooking the street and a replica of Altar Q behind the bar. Its stab at world food with a vegetarian bias works.

Carnitas Nia Lola (mains US$3-6.20; ☾ breakfast, lunch & dinner) This open-air restaurant two blocks south of the plaza has a beautiful view over corn and tobacco fields toward the mountains. It's a relaxing place with simple and economical food; the specialties are charcoal-grilled chicken and beef.

Glifo's (breakfasts US$1.70-4.25, mains US$8-13; ☾ breakfast, lunch & dinner) Some say this is the best place to eat in town; the menu includes some fancy dishes with a traditional Mayan twist. It's at Hotel Marina Copán (left), on the plaza. **Café Velchez**, next door, has the only cappuccino machine in town and excellent cakes.

Churrasquería Momos (small meals US$2) Half a block south of the plaza, this place is the hot local favorite. *Pinchos* (shish kebabs) served with salad and rice are recommended.

Llama del Bosque (breakfast US$1.76-3.53, mains US$2-4; ☺ breakfast, lunch & dinner) This large, popular place offers a good selection of Honduran meals and snacks; its *anafre* (fondue cooked in a clay pot) is especially tasty.

La Casa de Todo (pastas US$3; ☺ breakfast, lunch & dinner) This cafeteria has a pretty garden, with handcrafted wooden tables and chairs, where light meals and snacks are served.

Drinking

The **Tunkul Bar** and the bar in **Carnitas Nia Lola** (opposite) are happening spots in the evening. You might also try the bar in the **Café ViaVia** (opposite). **Bar Jaguar Venado**, in Hotel Marina Copán (opposite), has live marimba music on weekends from 5pm to 8pm.

Getting There & Away

Several Antigua travel agencies offer weekend trips to Copán (US$125), which may include stops at other places, including Quiriguá. All-inclusive day trips from Antigua to Copán (US$90) are very rushed. Check with agencies in Antigua (p81).

BUS

It's 227km (five hours) from Guatemala City to El Florido, the Guatemalan village on the Honduran border.

Hedman Alas (☎ 651-4106) runs direct 1st-class services daily between Copán Ruinas and Guatemala City (US$35), leaving from Copán Ruinas at 1pm and 5:30pm and Guatemala City at 5am. Coming from other places, you have to take a bus to Chiquimula

(p144) and then change there to get to the border.

Minivans depart for Copán Ruinas from the Honduran side of the border regularly throughout the day. They should charge around US$1.50 for the 30-minute ride and may take you on to the ruins after a stop in town. If not, the *sendero peatonal* (footpath) alongside the road makes for a pretty 20-minute walk.

Minibuses and pickups from Copán Ruinas to Guatemala depart every 40 minutes (or when full), 6am to 6pm, and charge around US$1.50. On the Guatemala side, buses to Chiquimula (US$1.20, 1½ hours) leave the border hourly from 5:30am to 11:30am, then hourly from noon to 4pm.

CAR

You *could* visit the ruins as a day trip from Guatemala City by car, but it's exhausting and far too harried. From Río Hondo, Chiquimula or Esquipulas, it still takes a full day to get to Copán, tour the ruins and return. It's better to spend at least one night in Copán Ruinas if you can.

If you're driving a rented car, you must present the Guatemalan customs authorities at the border with a letter of permission to enter Honduras, written on the rental company's letterhead, and signed and sealed by the appropriate company official. If you don't have such a letter, you'll have to leave your car at El Florido and continue to Copán by public transport.

SHUTTLE MINIBUS

Monarcas Travel (☎ 651-4361; www.mayabus.com) runs a shuttle between Copán Ruinas and Antigua. In Copán it cooperates with Copán

---

CROSSING INTO HONDURAS

The Guatemalan village of El Florido is 1.2km west of the border. At the border are a branch of **Banrural** (☺ 7am-6pm Mon-Sat) and the Vilma bus office. The border crossing is open from 6am to 7pm but closes to vehicles at 6pm.

Money-changers on both sides of the border change Guatemalan quetzals for Honduran lempiras, or either for US dollars. Usually they're offering a decent rate because the exchange rate is posted in the Honduran immigration office. There's no bank on the Honduran side of the border.

If you're only planning to go to Copán for a few days, tell the Honduran immigration officers and you'll receive a separate piece of paper with a three-day stamp that you have to produce upon crossing back into Guatemala. With such a permit you cannot go further than the ruins and you must leave Honduras by the same route. If you want to travel further in Honduras, you'll need a 30- or 90-day stamp.

Tours. Scheduled shuttles (minimum four passengers) leave for Antigua (US$15, six hours) at 2pm daily and can drop you in Guatemala City. Shuttles leave Antigua at 4am and Guatemala City at 5am. Copán Tours also runs shuttles to Río Dulce and Panajachel.

QUIRIGUÁ

Quiriguá's archaeological zone is famed for its intricately carved stelae – gigantic sandstone monoliths up to 10.5m tall – that rise like ancient sentinels in a quiet tropical park. Visiting the ruins is easy if you have your own transportation, more difficult if you're traveling by bus. From the Río Hondo junction, it's 67km along

QUIRIGUÁ

the Carretera al Atlántico to Los Amates, which has a couple of hotels, a restaurant and a bank. The village of Quiriguá is 1.5km east of **Los Amates**, and the turnoff to the ruins is 1.5km further east again. Following the access road south from the Carretera al Atlántico, it's 3.4km through banana groves to the archaeological site.

History

Quiriguá's history parallels that of Copán, of which it was a dependency during much of the Classic period. The location lent itself to the carving of giant stelae. Beds of brown sandstone in the nearby Río Motagua had cleavage planes suitable for cutting large pieces; though soft when first cut, the sandstone dried hard. With Copán's expert artisans for guidance, Quiriguá's stonecarvers were ready for greatness. All they needed was a leader to inspire them – and to pay for the carving.

That leader was Cauac Sky (AD 725–84), who sought Quiriguá's independence from Copán. In a war with his former suzerain, Cauac Sky took Copán's King 18 Rabbit prisoner in 737 and beheaded him soon after. Independent at last, Cauac Sky called up the stonecutters and for the next 38 years they turned out giant stelae and zoomorphs dedicated to his glory.

In the early 1900s the United Fruit Company bought all the land around Quiriguá and turned it into banana groves. In 1981 Unesco declared Quiriguá a World Heritage Site.

Ruins

It's hot and there are mosquitoes everywhere, but the park-like **archaeological zone** (admission US$3.25; 7:30am-5pm) is unforgettable. The giant stelae on the Gran Plaza are awe-inspiring despite their worn condition.

Stelae A, C, D, E, F, H and J, were built during the reign of Cauac Sky and carved with his image. Stela E is the largest Mayan stela known, standing 8m above ground, with about another 3m buried in the earth. It weighs almost 60,000 kg. Note the elaborate headdresses; the beards on some figures (an oddity in Mayan art and life); the staffs of office held in the kings' hands; and the glyphs on the stelae's sides.

At the far end of the plaza is the **Acrópolis**. At its base are several zoomorphs, blocks of stone carved to resemble real and mythic creatures. Frogs, tortoises, serpents and jaguars were favorite subjects in these superb works of art, imagination and mythic significance.

A *tienda* (small shop) near the entrance sells cold drinks and snacks, but you'd be better off bringing a picnic.

Sleeping & Eating

Hotel y Restaurante Royal (☎ 7947-3639; per person US$4, s/d with private bathroom US$7/13) In the center of the village of Quiriguá, 700m south of the CA-9, this is bright, clean and quiet. Of the 13 rooms, six have private hot-water bathroom. The restaurant serves meat and vegetarian meals. Most guests here are international travelers in town to visit the archaeological site.

Hotel y Restaurante Santa Mónica (☎ 7947-3602; Carr al Atlántico Km 200; s/d/tr US$6/13/18) Behind the Texaco station at Los Amates, this hotel has eight reasonable rooms with private cold-water bathroom and fan. Meals cost US$4.50.

Parrillada del Atlántico (mains US$5-8) This steakhouse, about 100m east of the Texaco station, is probably the best restaurant in the area.

Getting There & Away

Buses running Guatemala City–Puerto Barrios, Guatemala City–Flores, Esquipulas–Flores or Chiquimula–Flores will drop you off or pick you up at the turnoff to Quiriguá town. Better yet, they'll drop you at the turnoff to the archaeological site if you ask.

The transportation center in this area is Morales, about 40km northeast of Quiriguá. It's not pretty, but it's where the bus for Río Dulce (US$1.95, two hours) originates. If a seat isn't important, skip Morales and wait at Ruidosa junction for the Río Dulce bus.

Getting Around

From the turnoff on the highway, it's 3.4km to the archaeological site. Buses and pickups provide transportation between the turnoff and the site for US$0.25 each way. If you don't see one, don't fret; it's a nice walk on a dirt road through banana plantations to get there.

If you're staying in Quiriguá or Los Amates and walking to and from the archaeological site, take the short cut along the railway line from the village through banana fields, crossing the access road near the site entrance.

LAGO DE IZABAL

Guatemala's largest lake is starting to register on travelers' radars. Most visitors stay at Río Dulce village, north of the bridge where the CA-13, the road to Flores and Tikal, crosses the lake's east end. East of this bridge is the beautiful Río Dulce, which opens into El Golfete before flowing into the Caribbean at Lívingston; a river trip is one of the highlights of a visit to eastern Guatemala. Other lake highlights include El Castillo de San Felipe (p157) and the Bocas del Polochic river delta (p159).

Río Dulce

East of Quiriguá at Km 245, on the Carretera al Atlántico (near the town of Morales), is La Ruidosa junction, where the CA-13 turns north en route to Flores. About 34km up CA-13 from the junction, the road crosses the Río Dulce, an outlet of Lago de Izabal. Straddling the river are a pair of villages: Río Dulce, sometimes called Fronteras, on the bridge's north side, and El Relleno on the south side. Both harbor a sizable population of foreign yachties.

The minute you step from the bus, there are people wanting to put you on a motorboat to Lívingston. This may be exactly what you want to do. Or you could spend some days relaxing around the lake. For details of Río Dulce boat trips, see p166.

ORIENTATION & INFORMATION

All the places listed below are on the north side of the bridge. Get off near the Río Bravo Restaurant, or you'll be checking the length of what is purported to be Central America's longest bridge – a steamy 30-minute walk.

Tijax Express, in the little lane between the river and the Fuente del Norte office, is Río Dulce's unofficial tourist information center. Bus, *lancha*, hotel and other important travel details are available here. It's open every day and English is spoken. There are two similar places nearby, **Otitours** and **Atitrans**. You can book *lanchas*, tours, sailing trips and shuttles with all three.

If you need to change cash or traveler's checks, hit one of the four air-conditioned banks in town, all on the main road. **Banco**

Industrial (⏰ 9am-5pm) has a Visa ATM. **Banrural** has Visa and MasterCard ATMs. **Banco Agromercantil** will give cash advances on credit cards if there is a problem with the ATMs.

Cap't Nemo's Communications (☎ 7930-5174; www.mayaparadise.com; ⏰ 7am-8pm Mon-Sat, 9am-2pm Sun), beside Bruno's on the river, offers email (US$3.25 an hour) and international phone and radiophone calls. **Tijax Express**, **Hacienda Tijax** and **Hotel Backpacker's** (right for the latter two) are hooked up too, all charging US$3 an hour.

The website www.mayaparadise.com has loads of information about Río Dulce.

You can rent bicycles for US$2 an hour from a *tienda* next door to Tijax Express.

TOURS

Aventuras Vacacionales (☎ /fax 7832-5938; www .sailing.conexion.com; Centro Comercial María, 4a Calle Pte 17, Antigua) runs fun sailing trips on the sailboat *Las Sirenas* from Río Dulce to the Belize reefs and islands (US$325 to US$360, seven days) and through the Parque Nacional Río Dulce to Lago Izabal (US$135 to US$165, four days). Its office is in Antigua but you can hook up with it in Río Dulce. It makes the Belize and lake trips in alternate weeks.

SLEEPING & EATING

Casa Perico (☎ 5909-0721, VHF channel 68; dm/r US$5.25/ 6.50) This is another great riverside jungle hideaway, fine for chilling out for a couple of days, 10 minutes downstream from Río Dulce by *lancha*. Sleep beneath the vast *palapa* roof in the dorm above the bar/ restaurant/sitting area, or in rooms at the rear. It's run by four Swiss guys who cook up great food (dinner US$4 to US$5). They'll pick up/drop off from/to Río Dulce for free; interim trips are US$1.30 round-trip.

Bruno's (☎ 7930-5175; www.mayaparadise; dm US$5; r per person US$10, with private bathroom US$20-23; Ⓟ ⌧ ⛵) A path leads down from the northwest end of the bridge to this riverside hangout for yachties needing to get some land under their feet. All rooms are clean and comfortable and look out to the river. The cheapest have a sink, fan and shared bathroom. There are four rooms with private hot-water bathroom and air-con. There are also bungalows, and an air-con apartment with two bedrooms (sleeps eight), costing US$24 per person. There's plenty of

space to kick back here – poolside is highly recommended.

Las Brisas Hotel (☎ 7930-5124; s/d per person with shared bathroom US$6, s/d/tr with private bathroom US$10/13/20; ⌧) This hotel is opposite Tijax Express. All rooms are clean enough and have three beds and fans. Three rooms have private bathroom and air-con (US$45). It's a bit exposed to pedestrian traffic.

Hospedaje Golding (☎ 7930-5123; Carr a San Felipe; r per person US$4, with private bathroom US$7) A yellow building with no sign, just off the main road, this is another simple place, but its brightly colored upstairs rooms have a bit of a view.

Hotel Backpacker's (☎ 7930-5169; casaguatemal@ guate.net; dm US$4, s/d US$8/16, with private bathroom US$10/20) Across the bridge, this is run by Casa Guatemala and the orphans it serves. The hotel has a restaurant and bar right on the water and offers *lancha*, laundry, phone, fax and email services (US$5.15 an hour). If you're coming by *lancha* or bus, ask the driver to let you off here to spare yourself the walk across the bridge.

Hacienda Tijax (☎ 7930-5505/7; VHF channel 09; www.tijax.com; camping per person US$2.60, s US$8-60, d US$12-60; Ⓟ ⛵) This 200-hectare hacienda, two minutes' boat ride across the cove from the Río Bravo restaurant, is a special place to stay. Activities include horseback riding, hiking, birding, sailboat trips and tours around the rubber plantation. Access is by boat or by a road that turns off the highway about 1km north of the village. The folks here speak Spanish, English, Dutch, French and Italian, and they'll pick you up from across the river; ask at the Tijax Express office. There's a restaurant, and day passes are US$1.30. Some travelers might be uncomfortable with the isolation of this place.

Hotel Catamaran (☎ 7930-5494/5; www.hotelcata maran.com; s/d/tr from US$52/62/74; ⌧ ⛵) This upmarket place occupies a tropical island, roughly five minutes by *lancha* beyond the Tijax. It has 34 rustic wooden bungalows (most built over the water), a fancy restaurant, sports bar, tennis court and swimming pool.

Restaurant Río Bravo (breakfasts US$1.70-3, mojarra US$9, pizzas US$4.50-9.25) The best place to eat in town, Río Bravo has an open-air deck over the lake. It has a good variety of seafood, ceviche (marinated seafood) and pasta dishes, and a full bar.

Bruno's (breakfasts US$2.60-4, large mojarra US$7.75) Nearby, this open-air place right beside the water is a restaurant/sports bar with satellite TV and video; its floating dock makes it popular with yachties.

Cafetería La Carreta (breakfasts US$1.55, mixed dish of prawns, mojarra & crab US$10) A bright and clean *palapa*-style restaurant off the highway on the road toward San Felipe, this is consistently recommended by locals.

Hacienda Tijax (mains US$4.25-13) This fine restaurant has a wide range of dishes, a full bar and good coffee.

GETTING THERE & AWAY

Beginning at 7am, 14 Fuente del Norte buses a day head north to Poptún (US$3.90, two hours, 99km) and Flores (US$6.50, four hours, 208km). The 12:30pm, 7:30pm, 9:30pm and 11:30pm buses continue all the way to Melchor de Mencos (US$10) on the Belize border. With good connections you can get to Tikal (279km) in a snappy six hours. At least 17 buses daily go to Guatemala City (US$5.25, six hours, 280km) with Fuente del Norte and Litegua. Linea Dorada/Fuente del Norte has 1st-class buses departing at 1:30pm for Guatemala City and 2:30pm for Flores (both US$15.60). This shaves up to an hour off the journey times.

To get to Puerto Barrios, take any bus heading for Guatemala City and change at La Ruidosa.

Fuente del Norte buses leave for El Estor (US$1.30, 1½ hours, 43km) from the Pollolandia restaurant at the San Felipe and El Estor turnoff in the middle of town, hourly from 7am to 4pm.

Atitrans' shuttle minibus operates from its office on the highway to Antigua (US$37), Copán Ruinas (US$30) and Guatemala City (US$30), with a minimum of four passengers in each case. **Otitours** and **Tijax Express** (p155) offer much the same.

Colectivo lanchas ('taxi boat') go down the Río Dulce (from the new dock) to Lívingston. They usually require eight to 10 people and charge US$10 per person. The trip is beautiful and there are often several tour-like halts along the way (p164). If everyone wants to get there as fast as possible, it takes one hour without any stops. Boats usually leave from 9am to about 2pm.

El Castillo de San Felipe

The fortress and castle of **San Felipe de Lara** (admission US$1.30; ⏲ 8am-5pm), about 3km west of the bridge, was built in 1652 to keep pirates from looting the villages and commercial caravans of Izabal. Though it deterred the buccaneers a bit, a pirate force captured and burned the fortress in 1686. By the end of the next century, pirates had disappeared from the Caribbean and the fort's sturdy walls served as a prison. Eventually the fortress was abandoned and became a ruin. The present fort was reconstructed in 1956.

Today the castle is protected as a park and is one of the lake's principal tourist attractions. In addition to the fort itself, the site has a large park with barbecue/picnic areas, and you can swim in the lake.

Near the castle, **Hotel Don Humberto** (☎ /fax 7930-5051; s/d/tr US$5/10/15; **P**) has simple but clean rooms of varying sizes, with private bathroom. If the restaurant here isn't open, try **Cafetería Don Miguel**, next to the castle entrance.

Nearby, the fancier **Viñas del Lago** (☎ 7930-5053; www.infivia.com.gt/hotelvinasdellago; s US$21-60, d US$ 31-70, tr US$40-80; **P** 🏊 🐾) has 18 clean, spacious rooms, all with private hot-water bathroom, air-con and TV. The grounds are large and there's a restaurant (mains US$7.75 to US$10.50) with views of Lago de Izabal.

San Felipe is on the lakeshore, 3km west of Río Dulce. It's a beautiful 45-minute walk between the two, or *colectivo* pickups can provide transportation for US$0.35, running about every half hour. In Río Dulce it stops on the corner of the highway and the road to El Estor, across from the Pollolandia restaurant; in San Felipe it stops in front of Hotel Don Humberto.

Boats coming from Lívingston will drop you in San Felipe if you ask them. The Río Dulce boat trips usually come to El Castillo, allowing you to get out and visit the castle. Or you can come over from Río Dulce by private launch for US$5.

Finca El Paraíso

On the lake's north side, between San Felipe and El Estor, the **Finca El Paraíso** (☎ 7949-7122, 2230-3028; admission US$1.30) is a popular day trip from Río Dulce and other places around the lake. At the *finca*, which is a working ranch, you can walk to an incredibly beautiful spot in the jungle where a wide, hot waterfall drops about 12m into a clear, deep pool. You can bathe in the hot water, swim in the cool pool or duck under an overhanging promontory and enjoy a jungle-style sauna. Also on the *finca* are several interesting caves and good hiking. You can rent bungalows (doubles US$25).

The *finca* is on the Río Dulce–El Estor bus route, about one hour (US$0.90) from Río Dulce and 30 minutes (US$0.60) from El Estor. The last bus in either direction passes at around 4:30pm to 5pm.

El Estor

The major settlement on the northern shore is El Estor. The nickel mines a few kilometers to the northwest closed in 1980, but are set to reopen as world nickel stocks run low. A friendly, somnolent, little town with a lovely setting, El Estor is the jumping-off point for the Bocas del Polochic, a highly biodiverse wildlife reserve at the west end of the lake. The town is also a staging post on a possible route between Río Dulce and Lanquín.

ORIENTATION & INFORMATION

El Estor is an easily negotiable town. Buses from Río Dulce terminate at Tienda Cobanerita on the corner of 3a Calle and 4a Av. Walk one block west from here along 3a Calle to find the Parque Central, on whose east side is **Café Portal** (☎ 5818-0843; eloydam@hotmail.com; 5a Av 2-65; 🕑 6:30am-10pm), providing excellent information, tours and transport service. Local tourism businesses have put together a fine website about the area, **El Estor** (www.ecoturismoelestor.com).

Banrural (cnr 3a Calle & 6a Av; 🕑 8:30am-5pm Mon-Fri, 9am-1pm Sat) changes US dollars and American Express traveler's checks. The **municipal police** (cnr 1a Calle & 5a Av) is near the lakeshore.

The **Asociación Feminina Q'eqchi'** sells clothes, blankets and accessories made from traditional cloth woven by the association's members. To find it go two blocks north along 5a Av from the Parque Central, then two blocks west. All profits benefit the women involved in the program.

SLEEPING & EATING

Hotel Vista al Lago (☎ 7949-7205; vistalago@intelnett.com; 6a Av 1-13; s/d/tr US$10/18/23) Overlooking the lake, as its name implies, this hotel is inviting and clean. Built between 1815 and 1825, the wooden building was once a general store owned by an Englishman and a Dutchman; 'the store' gave the town of El Estor its name. The 21 rooms are small and clean, with fans. Get one upstairs at the front if you can. The friendly owners can arrange tours and guides.

Restaurante Típico Chaabil (☎ 7949-7272; west end 3a Calle; rooms per person US$7; Ⓟ) The four sizable rooms behind this excellent restaurant are attractive, wooden and almost brand-new. Two, with bunks, hold up to five people each. The upper two have beds, and all have private bathroom. The restaurant itself, on a lovely lakeside terrace, does great food ranging from large breakfasts for US$2 to *tapado* (a rich stew made from fish, shrimp, shellfish, coconut milk and plantain, spiced with coriander) for US$9. You can have *mojarra* from the lake fried, grilled or steamed in garlic, escabeche or salsa for US$4 to US$7.

Hotel Villela (☎ 7949-7214; 6a Av 2-06; s/d US$5/9) The rooms are less attractive than the neat lawn and trees they're set around, but some are airier and brighter than others. All have fan and private bathroom.

The Chaabil apart, the best place to look for food is around the Parque Central, where **Café Portal** and **Restaurante Hugo's** both serve a broad range of fare with some vegetarian options. Mains are around US$3 to US$4 at either.

GETTING THERE & AWAY

See Río Dulce (p157) for information on buses from there. The schedule from El Estor to Río Dulce is hourly, 6am to 4pm.

The road west from El Estor to Panzós and Tucurú to Tactic, south of Cobán, has a bad reputation for highway holdups and robberies, especially around Tucurú, and we do not recommend it. You can, however, get to Grutas de Lanquín by taking the truck that leaves El Estor's Parque Central at 9am for Cahabón (US$2, four to five hours), and then a bus or pickup straight on from Cahabón to Lanquín the same day. This route is not recommended in the reverse direction because the truck leaves Cahabón about 4am, meaning you have to spend the preceding night in impoverished Cahabón, where things can get dodgy after dark.

There are no public boat services between El Estor and other lake destinations. Private *lanchas* can be contracted, though this can be pricey. Ask at your hotel.

Refugio de Vida Silvestre Bocas del Polochic & Reserva de Biósfera Sierra de las Minas

The **Bocas del Polochic Wildlife Reserve** covers the delta of the Río Polochic, which provides most of Lago de Izabal's water. A visit here provides great bird-watching and howler-monkey observation. The reserve supports more than 300 species of birds; the migration seasons are September to October and April to May. You may well see alligators and, if you're very lucky, glimpse a manatee. **Café Portal** (opposite) can set up early-morning trips with local boatmen (US$32 for two people plus US$13 for each extra person for 3½ hours). The reserve is managed by the Fundación Defensores de la Naturaleza, whose research station, the **Estación Científica Selempim**, just south of the Bocas del Polochic reserve, in the **Reserva de Biósfera Sierra de las Minas**, is open for ecotouristic visits. Contact Defensores' El Estor **office** (☎ 5815-1736; www.defensores.org.gt; cnr 5a Av & 2a C) for bookings and further information. You can get to the station on a local launch service leaving El Estor at 11am on Monday, Wednesday and Saturday (US$6.50 round-trip, 1¼ hours each way) or by special hire (US$65 to US$90 per boatload), and stay in attractive wood-and-thatch cabañas (US$6.50 per person) or camp (US$4 for two people). Meals are available for US$2 or you can use the Estación Científica's kitchen (US$2.50 for campers). To explore the reserve you can rent canoes (US$2 an hour) or bicycles (US$3.25 a day), take boat trips (US$20 to US$32) or walk trails.

Mariscos

Mariscos is the principal town on the lake's south side. Ferries from here used to be the main access to El Estor and the north side of the lake, but since a road was built from Río Dulce to El Estor, Mariscos has taken a back seat. As a result, **Denny's Beach** (☎ 5302-8121; VHF channel 63; www.mayaparadise com; camping per tent US$4, hammocks US$2, cabañas per person US$5-10), 10 minutes by boat from Mariscos, is a good place to get away from it all. It offers tours, hiking and swimming,

and hosts full-moon parties. When you arrive in Mariscos, radio Denny's to pick you up. Otherwise, hitch a ride with a *cayuco* (dugout canoe) at the market for US$1.30 or go to Shop-n-Go and hire a speedboat for US$13 (fine if you're a group).

PUERTO BARRIOS

pop 35,000

Heading east from La Ruidosa junction toward Puerto Barrios, the country becomes even more lush, tropical and humid. The powerful United Fruit Company owned vast plantations in the Río Motagua valley. It constructed railways to ship produce to the coast, and built Puerto Barrios early in the 20th century to put that produce onto ships sailing for New Orleans and New York. Laid out as a company town, Puerto Barrios has long, wide streets arranged neatly on a grid. Many of its Caribbean-style wood-frame houses are on stilts.

For foreign visitors Puerto Barrios remains little more than a place to get a boat across the Bahía de Amatique to Punta Gorda (Belize), the Garifuna enclave Lívingston or the Punta de Manabique wetland reserve.

Orientation & Information

Because of its spacious layout, you must walk or ride further in Puerto Barrios to get from place to place. It's 800m from the bus terminals in the town center to the Muelle Municipal (Municipal Boat Dock) at the end of 12a Calle, from where passenger boats depart.

El Muñecón, at the intersection of 8a Av, 14a Calle and Calz Justo Rufino Barrios, is a statue of a dock worker; it's a useful landmark.

Bancafé (cnr 13a Calle & 7a Av; ☽ 9am-7pm Mon-Fri, 9am-1pm Sat) and **Banco Industrial** (7a Av btwn 7a & 8a Calles; ☽ 9am-5pm Mon-Fri, 9am-1pm Sat) change US-dollar cash and traveler's checks and have Visa ATMs. **Banrural** (8a Av btwn 9a & 10a Calles; ☽ 8:30am-5pm Mon-Fri, 9am-1pm Sat) changes cash dollars only and has a MasterCard ATM.

The **immigration office** (cnr 12a Calle & 3a Av; ☽ 24hr) is a block in from the Muelle Municipal. Come here for your entry or exit stamp if you're arriving from or leaving for Belize. If you're heading to Honduras, you get your exit stamp at another immigration office on the road to the border (see the boxed text, p162).

PUERTO BARRIOS

0 |————————| 300 m
0 |————————| 0.2 mile

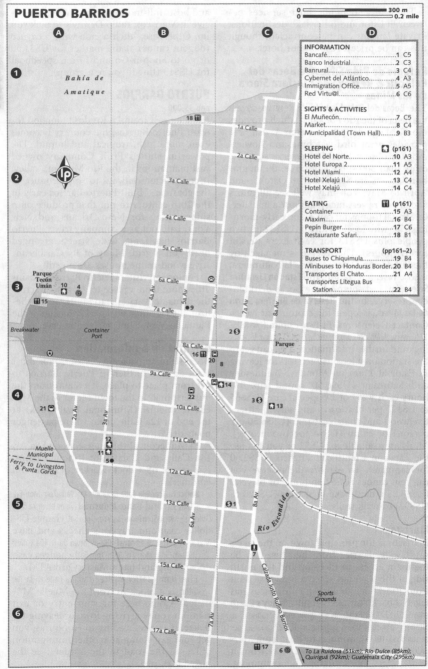

INFORMATION
Bancafé.....................................1 C5
Banco Industrial.......................2 C3
Banrural...................................3 C4
Cybernet del Atlántico.............4 A3
Immigration Office...................5 A5
Red Virtu@l..............................6 C6

SIGHTS & ACTIVITIES
El Muñecón..............................7 C5
Market......................................8 C4
Municipalidad (Town Hall).......9 B3

SLEEPING 🛏 (p161)
Hotel del Norte......................10 A3
Hotel Europa 2.......................11 A5
Hotel Miami...........................12 A4
Hotel Xelajú II........................13 C4
Hotel Xelajú...........................14 C4

EATING 🍴 (p161)
Container................................15 A3
Maxim.....................................16 B4
Pepín Burger..........................17 C6
Restaurante Safari.................18 B1

TRANSPORT (pp161–2)
Buses to Chiquimula..............19 B4
Minibuses to Honduras Border.20 B4
Transportes El Chato..............21 A4
Transportes Litegua Bus
    Station...............................22 B4

Bahía de
Amatique

1a Calle
2a Calle
3a Calle
4a Calle
5a Calle
6a Calle
7a Calle

Parque
Tecún
Umán

Breakwater

Container
Port

8a Calle
Parque

9a Calle

10a Calle

11a Calle

12a Calle

13a Calle

14a Calle

15a Calle

16a Calle

17a Calle

Muelle
Municipal
Ferry to Livingston
& Punta Gorda

4a AV
5a AV
6a AV
7a AV
8a AV
2a AV
3a AV
6a AV
7a AV
8a AV

Río Escondido

Calzada Justo Rufino Barrios

Sports
Grounds

To La Ruidosa (51km); Río Dulce (85km);
Quiriguá (92km); Guatemala City (295km)

Go online at **Cybernet del Atlántico** (7a Calle), west of 2a Av, or **Red Virtu@l** (cnr 17a Calle & Calz Justo Rufino Barrios; 8am-9:30pm), US$1.30 an hour at each.

Sleeping

Hotel del Norte (7948-2116; fax 7948-0087; west end 7a Calle; s/d US$11/16, s with air-con US$16-20, d with air-con US$26-33; P) The century-old Hotel del Norte is in a class by itself. A large, classically tropical wooden construction with corridors wide enough to run a banana train through, its weathered and warped frame is redolent of history. In the airy dining room overlooking the Bahía de Amatique, you can almost hear the echoing conversation of bygone banana moguls and smell their pungent cigars. All rooms have private bathroom and are kept very clean, though some floors have an interesting tilt. There's a swimming pool beside the sea. Meals are served with old-fashioned refinement by white-jacketed waiters, though the food isn't always up to the same standard.

Hotel Xelajú (7948-0482; 9a Calle btwn 6a & 7a Avs; s/d/tr US$5/7/9, with private bathroom US$7/11/16) The Xelajú is right in the town center, facing the market, but it's secure: no rooms are let after 10pm and *señoritas de clubes nocturnos* are not allowed. It has clean fan-cooled rooms and its own generator for when the electricity fails.

More decent budget choices, with good clean rooms, are:

Hotel Miami (7948-0537; s/d US$6/12, with air-con US$10/20; P)

Hotel Europa 2 (7948-1292; 3a Av btwn 11a & 12a Calles; s/d US$7/11; P)

Hotel Xelajú II (7948-1117; 8a Av btwn 9a & 10a Calles; s/d/tr US$5/7/9, with private bathroom US$11/11/16)

Eating

Restaurante Safari (7948-0563; 5a Av; seafood US$6.50-10; lunch & dinner) The town's most enjoyable restaurant is on a thatch-roofed, open-air platform right over the water about 1km north of the town center. Locals and visitors alike love to catch the sea breezes here. Excellent seafood of all kinds – including that great Garifuna casserole, *tapado* – is the specialty; chicken and meat dishes are less expensive (US$3 to US$6).

Maxim (7948-2258; cnr 6a Av & 8a Calle; mains US$4-6) Whirring fans provide the breezes at this busy and enjoyable Chinese place opposite the market. The food is well prepared and comes in generous quantities, beneath a big Taiwanese flag.

Pepín Burger (17a Calle btwn 8a & 9a Avs; fajitas US$1.80; closed Tue) Come here for great fajitas and good-value burgers, chicken and flour *tortillas* on an open-air upstairs terrace.

Container At the west end of 7a Calle, this is the oddest café in town – made from two shipping containers, with fine bay views.

Getting There & Away

BOAT

Boats depart from the Muelle Municipal at the end of 12a Calle.

A ferry (US$1.30, 1½ hours) departs for Lívingston every day at 10am and 5pm. From Lívingston it leaves for Puerto Barrios at 5am and 2pm. Get to the dock 30 to 45 minutes early to make sure you get a seat.

Smaller, faster *lanchas* depart from both sides whenever there are a dozen passengers; they take 30 minutes and cost US$3.25.

Most of the movement from Lívingston to Puerto Barrios is in the morning, returning in the afternoon. From Lívingston your last chance may be the 2pm ferry, especially during the low season when fewer travelers are shuttling back and forth.

A *lancha* of **Transportes El Chato** (7948-5525; 1a Av btwn 10a & 11a Calle) departs from the Muelle Municipal at 10am daily for **Punta Gorda**, Belize (US$15.50, one hour), arriving in time for the noon bus from Punta Gorda to Belize City. Tickets are sold at El Chato's office, which is 1½ blocks from the *muelle* (pier). Before boarding you also need to get your exit stamp at the nearby immigration office (see Orientation & Information, p159). The return boat leaves Punta Gorda at 4pm.

BUS & MINIBUS

Transportes Litegua (7948-1172; cnr 6a Av & 9a Calle) leaves for Guatemala City (US$5.25, five to six hours, 295km), via Quiriguá and Río Hondo, 15 times between 1am and noon and at 4pm. *Directo* services avoid a half-hour detour into Morales.

Buses for Chiquimula (US$2.50, 4½ hours, 192km), also via Quiriguá, leave every half hour, 4am to 4pm, from the east side of the 6a Av/9a Calle corner.

For Río Dulce take a Chiquimula bus to La Ruidosa junction (US$0.65, 50 minutes)

GETTING TO THE HONDURAS BORDER

Minibuses leave for the Honduras frontier (US$1.30, 1¼ hours) every 20 minutes, 5:30am to 6pm, from 6a Av outside the market. The paved road to the border turns off the CA-9 at Entre Ríos, 13km south of Puerto Barrios. Buses and minibuses going in all directions wait for passengers at Entre Ríos, making the trip from the border fairly easily, whichever direction you are traveling in.

Minibuses from Puerto Barrios stop en route to the border at Guatemalan immigration, where you have to pay US$1.30 for an exit stamp. Honduran entry formalities may leave you US$1 lighter. Pickups shuttle between the border and the small Honduran town of Corinto for about US$1 (or you can walk for about 15 minutes). From Corinto buses leave for Omoa and Puerto Cortés (US$2, two hours) about every two hours.

---

and change to a bus or minibus (US$0.65, 35 minutes) there.

TAXI

A cab between the market area and the Muelle Municipal, Hotel del Norte or Restaurante Safari costs around US$2.50.

PUNTA DE MANABIQUE

The Punta de Manabique promontory, which separates the Bahía de Manabique from the open sea, along with the coast and hinterland all the way southeast to the Honduran frontier comprise an ecologically fascinating, sparsely populated wetland area. Access to the area is not cheap, but attractions include pristine Caribbean beaches; boats trips through mangrove forests; lagoons and waterways; bird-watching; fishing with locals; and crocodile and possible manatee sightings. To visit, get in touch – a week in advance, if possible – with the NGO involved in the reserve's management, **Fundary** (Fundación Mario Dary; ☎ 7948-0435; manabique@intelnet .net.gt; 17a C btwn 5a & 6a Avs, Puerto Barrios; Guatemala City ☎ 2232-3230; fundary@intelnet.net.gt).

Fundary is helping to develop several ecotouristic possibilities in the reserve. It offers accommodation for groups of two to four people at the **Estación Biológica Julio Obiols** (1/2/3 nights per person US$65/90/115) at the small community of Cabo Tres Puntas on the north side of the promontory, near a lovely beach. The price includes transport from Puerto Barrios or Lívingston and meals. At **Estero Lagarto**, villagers will provide a fresh fish lunch (US$3.25) or take you on a boat trip through the lagoons and mangroves (US$6.50 per person). Ask for Ingris, who lives by the school. Accommodations in local homes may be available here for about US$6.50 per person. A visitors center offering information and meals is under construction at **Santa Isabel** on the Canal de los Ingleses, a waterway connecting the Bahía de Manabique with the open sea, with canoe trips along the canal available – also fishing with locals and demonstrations of the local charcoal-making process.

If you want to organize your own transport, a *lancha* from Puerto Barrios or Lívingston will cost between US$65 and US$125 round-trip depending on the deal you strike. A small boat (four passengers) to Estero Lagarto might be US$50.

LÍVINGSTON

pop 6000

As you come ashore in Lívingston, which is reachable only by boat, you'll meet black Guatemalans who speak Spanish and their traditional Garifuna language; some also speak the musical English of Belize and the islands. Lívingston is an interesting anomaly, with a laid-back, Belizean way of life, groves of coconut palms, gaily painted wooden buildings and an economy based on fishing and tourism.

The Garinagu (plural of Garifuna; see boxed text, p295) people of Lívingston and southern Belize are the descendants of Africans brought to the New World as slaves. They trace their roots to the Honduran island of Roatán, where they were settled by the British after the Garifuna revolt on the Caribbean island of St Vincent in 1795. From Roatán the Garifuna spread out along the Caribbean coast from Belize to Nicaragua. Intermarrying with Carib Indians as well as with Maya and shipwrecked sailors of other races, they've developed a distinct culture and language incorporating African, Indian and European elements.

Beaches here are largely disappointing, as the jungle comes to the water's edge, and the beaches are frequently clogged with

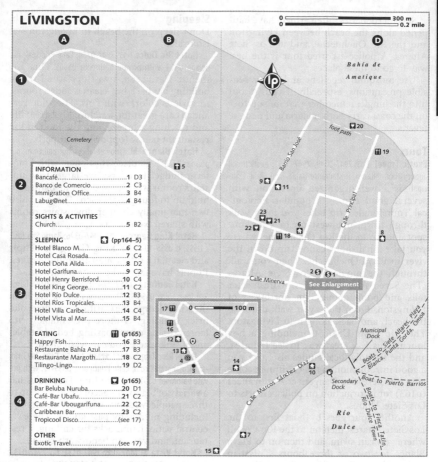

LÍVINGSTON

0 — 300 m
0 — 0.2 mile

*Bahía de
Amatique*

Cemetery

Barrio San José

foot path

20

19

Calle Principal

5

9
11

23
21
22
18
6

8

Calle Minerva

See Enlargement

2 **1**

17 **** 0 — 100 m

16

12 ****
13 ****
4 ****
3

14

Calle Marcos Sánchez Díaz

10

Municipal
Dock

Secondary
Dock

Boats to Siete Altares, Playa
Blanca, Punta Gorda, Omoa

Boat to Puerto Barrios

Boats to Finca Tatín,
Río Dulce Town

*Río
Dulce*

7

15 ****

INFORMATION	
Bancafé.........................1	D3
Banco de Comercio..........2	C3
Immigration Office............3	B4
Labug@net......................4	B4

SIGHTS & ACTIVITIES	
Church............................5	B2

SLEEPING	(pp164–5)
Hotel Blanco M.................6	C2
Hotel Casa Rosada...........7	C4
Hotel Doña Alida.............8	D2
Hotel Garifuna.................9	C2
Hotel Henry Berrisford......10	C4
Hotel King George...........11	C2
Hotel Río Dulce..............12	B3
Hotel Ríos Tropicales.......13	B4
Hotel Villa Caribe............14	C4
Hotel Vista al Mar...........15	B4

EATING	(p165)
Happy Fish.....................16	B3
Restaurante Bahía Azul......17	B3
Restaurante Margoth.........18	C2
Tilingo-Lingo..................19	D2

DRINKING	(p165)
Bar Beluba Nuruba...........20	D1
Café-Bar Ubafu...............21	C2
Café-Bar Ubougarifuna......22	C2
Caribbean Bar.................23	C2
Tropicool Disco............(see 17)	

OTHER	
Exotic Travel...............(see 17)	

vegetation and are unsafe for swimming due to contaminated water. Safe swimming is possible at Los Siete Altares (p166).

Orientation & Information

After half an hour you will know where everything is. Email services are offered by **Labug@net** (Calle Principal; per 30min/hr US$2/3.25) and at the **Happy Fish restaurant** (Calle Principal; per 30min/1hr US$1.30/2.60).

Banco de Comercio (Calle Principal; ☾ 9am-5pm Mon-Fri, 9am-1pm Sat) and **Bancafé** (Calle Principal; ☾ same as Banco de Comercio) change US-dollar cash and traveler's checks. Several private businesses do, too.

Laundry service is available at **Hotel Casa Rosada** (p164).

The **immigration office** (Calle Principal; ☾ 6am-7pm) issues entry and exit stamps for travelers arriving/going direct from/to Belize or Honduras. Outside its normal hours, you can knock at any time.

The best beach in the area is **Playa Blanca**, around 12km from Lívingston. This is privately owned (admission US$2) and you need a boat to get there – see Tours, p164.

Dangers & Annoyances

Lívingston has its edgy aspects and a few hustlers operate here, trying to sweet-talk tourists into 'lending' money, or paying up front for tours that don't happen etc. Take care with anyone who strikes up conversation for no obvious reason on the street or elsewhere.

Several robberies, often armed, have happened along the beach between Lívingston and the Río Quehueche, and at Los Siete Altares. A police-escorted tour is the best way to go to these places.

Use mosquito repellent and other sensible precautions, especially if you go out into the jungle; remember that mosquitoes on the coast carry both malaria and dengue fever.

Tours

Exotic Travel (☎ 7947-0049, 7947-0151; exotictravel agency@hotmail.com; Restaurante Bahía Azul, Calle Principal) is a well-organized operation with several good trips. Its popular Ecological Tour/Jungle Trip takes you for a walk through town, out west up to a lookout spot and on to the Río Quehueche, where you take a half-hour canoe trip down the river to Playa Quehueche. Then you walk through the jungle to Los Siete Altares (The Seven Altars), a series of freshwater falls and pools about 5km northwest of Lívingston. From there you walk down to the beach and back along it to Lívingston. The trip costs US$6.50 including a box lunch. This is a great way to see the area, and the friendly local guides also give you a good introduction to the Garifuna people who live here. See Dangers & Annoyances (p163) for information on police escorts to Los Siete Altares.

Another tour goes by boat first to the Los Siete Altares, then on to the Río Cocolí where you can swim, and then on to Playa Blanca for two or three hours. This trip goes with a minimum of six people and costs US$13.

Exotic Travel also offers day trips to the Cayos Sapodillas (or Zapotillas), well off the coast of southern Belize, where there is great snorkeling (US$40 plus US$10 to enter the cayes), and to Punta de Manabique for US$13 per person. A minimum of six people is needed for each of these trips. See p156 for tour company details.

Festivals & Events

During **Semana Santa**, Lívingston is packed with merrymakers. **Garifuna** national day is celebrated on November 26 with a variety of cultural events. The day of the **Virgin of Guadalupe**, Mexico's patron saint, is celebrated on December 12.

Sleeping

Don't sleep on the beach in Lívingston – it isn't safe.

Hotel Río Dulce (☎ 7947-0764; Calle Principal; per person US$4, with private bathroom US$6) This authentic Caribbean, two-story wood-frame building has bare-but-clean wooden rooms, in various colors, with fans. The wide verandahs are great for watching the street life and catching a breeze, and the food in the restaurant below (opposite) is superb.

Hotel Blanco M (snoweblanco@hotmail.com; per person US$6) This place is popular with long-term budget travelers; five large, bare upstairs rooms with fan and private bathroom hold up to four people each. There are also two marginally cheaper downstairs rooms with shared bathroom.

Hotel King George (☎ 7947-0326; Barrio San José; s US$5, d US$5-10) The King George is simple and clean, if a little rough around the edges. Rooms have fan and private bathroom.

Hotel Garífuna (☎ 7947-0183; fax 7947-0184; Barrio San José; s/d/tr US$6/9/11) Across the street from the King George, the Garífuna, another solid brick building, is more presentable, with larger rooms even boasting bedside tables and a sink where you can wash clothes.

Hotel Ríos Tropicales (☎ 7947-0158, 5494-7093; rios -tropico@hotmail.com; Calle Principal; r US$9-12, with private bathroom US$14-16) The Ríos Tropicales has a variety of big rooms accommodating up to three people, with bits of homey decoration including murals by past guests. There's a central patio, hammocks for chilling, a restaurant, and you can hand-wash clothes.

Hotel Vista al Mar (☎ 7947-0131; fax 7947-0134; Calle Marcos Sánchez Díaz; s/d/tr US$8/12/18, with private bathroom US$13/20/26) Just down the street from the Casa Rosada, the Vista al Mar has six quite spacious wooden bungalows, three with private bathroom. It rents bicycles and canoes, offers laundry service and accepts credit cards. It will install mosquito nets if you ask, which may be a good thing as the stream at the back is pretty slow moving.

Hotel Casa Rosada (☎ 7947-0303; info@hotelcasa rosada.com; Calle Marcos Sánchez Díaz; r US$20) The Casa Rosada (Pink House) is an attractive place to stay right on the river, 500m upstream from the main dock; it has its own pier where boats will drop you if you ask. Neat little riverside gardens, a gazebo on the dock and one of the best restaurants in town (opposite) all contribute to a relaxed, friendly ambiance. The rooms are well kept, thatch-roofed, wooden bungalows with fans, screens, mosquito nets and folksy, hand-painted furniture. The shared bathrooms are very clean. Also available are a laundry service and tours.

Hotel Doña Alida (☎/fax 7947-0027; d US$11-24, tr US$40-45; ⊠) In a great position just above the sea, a few blocks from the center of town, the Doña Alida has a variety of good, clean, mostly breezy rooms and bungalows, and has its own restaurant.

Hotel Villa Caribe (☎ 2334-1818; www.villasde guatemala.com; Calle Principal; s/d/tr US$63/75/88; ⊠) The 45-room Villa Caribe is a luxurious anomaly among Livingston's laid-back, low-priced lodgings. Modern but still Caribbean in style, it has many conveniences and comforts, including extensive tropical gardens, a big swimming pool and a large poolside bar. Rooms are fairly large, with modern bathrooms, ceiling fans and little balconies overlooking the gardens and river mouth.

Eating

Food in Livingston is relatively expensive because most of it (except fish and coconuts) must be brought in by boat. There's fine seafood here and some unusual flavors for Guatemala, including coconut and curry; *tapado* is the delicious local specialty. A potent potable is made by slicing off the top of a green coconut and mixing in a healthy dose of rum – these *coco locos* hit the spot.

Tilingo-Lingo (Calle Principal; mains US$3.25-6.50) Down at the seaward end of the main street, this great little place serves up a fine array of well-concocted international flavors, among them curries, pasta, fish, *tapado* and Spanish omelet.

Hotel Río Dulce (Calle Principal; mains US$3.50-9) The owner here has been chef at Antigua's famed Panza Verde and produces superb Italian and international food. Try the Bombay prawns (curried with bananas, peanuts and cream) or *pasta alle vongole* (in a sauce of white wine, clams, garlic and parsley). There are burgers, sandwiches and Garifuna-style rice and beans for tighter budgets.

Hotel Casa Rosada (Calle Marcos Sánchez Díaz; mains US$5.75-9.75) The open-air restaurant at this riverside hotel serves carefully prepared food in neat, breezy surroundings. All three meals are available. Dinner is served between 7pm and 7:30pm, but you need to

order it by 6pm. We recommend the *tapado* and the garlic shrimp.

Hotel Villa Caribe (Calle Principal; dinner around US$15) This is Livingston's most expensive restaurant (left). The price brings you a good, complete dinner with drinks.

Listed below are more options for reasonable fish and seafood meals:

Happy Fish (☎ 7947-0661; www.happyfishresort.com; Calle Principal; mains US$3.50-7)

Restaurante Margoth (mains US$4-7) Reasonable prices and good portions but haphazard service.

Restaurante Bahía Azul (Calle Principal; mains US$5-7)

Drinking

A handful of bars down on the beach to the left of the end of Calle Principal pull in travelers and locals after about 10pm or 11pm. It's very dark down here, so take care. In vogue is **Bar Beluba Nuruba**, which has a small dance floor and a few tables on the sand.

A traditional Garifuna band is composed of three large drums, a turtle shell, some maracas and a big conch shell, producing throbbing, haunting rhythms and melodies. The chanted words are like a litany, with responses often taken up by the audience. Punta is the Garifuna dance; it's got a lot of gyrating hip movements. Several places around town have live Garifuna music though schedules are unpredictable. Probably most dependable is **Café-Bar Ubafu**, supposedly with music and dancing nightly, but liveliest on weekends. Across the street, **Café-Bar Ubougarífuna** is a popular gathering spot. Next door, the **Caribbean Bar** is more of a mainstream disco.

Diners at the **Hotel Villa Caribe** (left) can enjoy a Garifuna show nightly at 7pm. **Restaurante Bahía Azul** (above) has live Garifuna music on weekends and sometimes on other evenings. **Tropicool Disco** next door has more mainstream pop to dance to.

Getting There & Away

Frequent boats come downriver from Río Dulce (p157) and across the bay from Puerto Barrios (p161). There are also international boats from Honduras and Belize.

Exotic Travel (opposite) operates international boat routes to Omoa, Honduras (US$35, 2½ hours) and Punta Gorda, Belize (US$16, 1¼ hours), both leaving at 7am on Tuesday and Friday. For both trips you must book by 5pm the day before, and get your exit stamp from immigration in Lívingston (p163) the day before, too. In Punta Gorda, the boat connects with a bus to Placencia and Belize City. The boat waits for this bus to arrive from Placencia before it sets off back for Lívingston from Punta Gorda at about 10:30am. In Omoa the boat docks near the bus stop where you can catch a bus to Puerto Cortés. Change there and again at San Pedro Sula to reach La Ceiba (the cheapest gateway to Honduras' Bay Islands) – but you might not make the 3pm boat from La Ceiba to Roatán island the same day. You can also reach Omoa by taking a ferry or *lancha* to Puerto Barrios then continuing overland (p161), but you're unlikely to get there any earlier. The boat from Omoa to Lívingston leaves about 10:30am, Tuesday and Friday.

The travel agency at the **Happy Fish** (p165) offers private trips to Punta Gorda for US$100 per boat, and shuttle services to Omoa, La Ceiba, Copán and San Pedro Sula, all in Honduras.

AROUND LÍVINGSTON
Río Dulce Cruises
Lívingston is the starting point for boat rides on the Río Dulce. Passengers enjoy the jungle scenery, swim, picnic, and explore the Biotopo Chocón Machacas, 12km west along the river.

Almost anyone in Lívingston can tell you who's organizing trips upriver. Exotic Travel makes trips daily, as do La Casa Rosada hotel and the Happy Fish restaurant. Many travelers use these tours as one-way transport to Río Dulce, paying around US$10. If you want to return to Lívingston the cost is US$15 to US$18. It's a beautiful ride through lush scenery, with several places to stop on the way.

Or you can simply walk to the dock and arrange a trip, thereby supporting the many local boat captains.

Shortly after you leave Lívingston headed upriver, you'll enter a steep-walled gorge called **Cueva de la Vaca**, its walls hung with great tangles of jungle foliage and bromeliads. Tropical birdcalls fill the air. Just beyond is **La Pintada**, a graffiti-covered rock escarpment. Further on, a **thermal spring** forces sulfurous water out at the base of the cliff, providing a delightful place for a swim.

Emerging from the gorge, the river eventually widens into **El Golfete**, a lake-like body of water that presages the even vaster Lago de Izabal.

On the north shore of El Golfete is the **Biotopo Chocón Machacas** (admission US$2.50), a 7600-hectare reserve established to protect the river and mangrove swamps and the manatees that inhabit the waters. A network of 'water trails' provides ways to see the reserve's flora and fauna. A nature trail begins at the visitors center, winding its way through forests of mahogany, palms and rich tropical foliage. Jaguars and tapirs live in the reserve, though seeing one is unlikely. The walrus-like manatees are even more elusive. These huge mammals can weigh up to a tonne, yet glide effortlessly beneath the river.

From El Golfete and the nature reserve, the boats continue upriver to the village of Río Dulce, where the road into El Petén crosses the river, and to El Castillo de San Felipe on Lago de Izabal (p157).

Los Siete Altares
The Seven Altars is a series of freshwater falls and pools about 5km (1½-hour walk) northwest of Lívingston, along the shore of Bahía de Amatique. It's a good place for a picnic and swim, but the falls can be disappointing in the dry season.

See Tours on p164 for details on getting here – note that the poor security situation means you will need a police escort.

Finca Tatin
This wonderful B&B is at the confluence of the Ríos Dulce and Tatin, about 10km from Lívingston. **Finca Tatin** (☎ 5902-0831; www .fincatatin.centramerica.com; per person US$8-11.50) was built by husband-wife team Carlos and Claudia Simonini. It's a great place for experiencing the forest, and four-hour guided walks and kayak trips through the jungle are offered, some visiting local Q'eqchi' villages. The wood-and-thatch accommodations range from dormitories to bungalows with private bathroom. Room rates include breakfast; other good meals, with vegetarian options, are served (lunch US$3.50, dinner US$4.50). There are trails, waterfalls and endless river tributaries that you can explore with one of the *cayucos* available for guest use. Ask for suggestions on area camping, but note that this is not a place for phobics of bugs or creeping fauna.

Lanchas traveling between Río Dulce and Lívingston (or vice-versa) will drop you here. It costs around US$4 from Lívingston, 20 minutes away. Or the *finca* may be able to send its own *lancha* to pick you up at Lívingston (US$5 per person, minimum two people).

EL PETÉN

In the dense jungle cover of Guatemala's vast northeastern department of El Petén, you may hear the squawk of parrots, the chatter of monkeys and the rustlings of strange animals moving through the bush. The landscape here is utterly different from that found in Guatemala's cool mountainous highlands or steamy Pacific Slope.

The monumental ceremonial center at Tikal is among the most impressive Mayan archaeological sites. Though it is possible to visit Tikal on a single-day excursion by plane from Guatemala City or Belize City, travelers are strongly encouraged to stay at least one night, whether in Flores, El Remate or Tikal itself. A day trip simply cannot do the place justice. The ruins of Uaxactún and Ceibal aren't as easily accessible, which makes them more exciting to visit. Several dozen other great Mayan cities hidden in El Petén, previously only accessible to archaeologists (or artifact poachers) with aircraft, are now open for limited tourism.

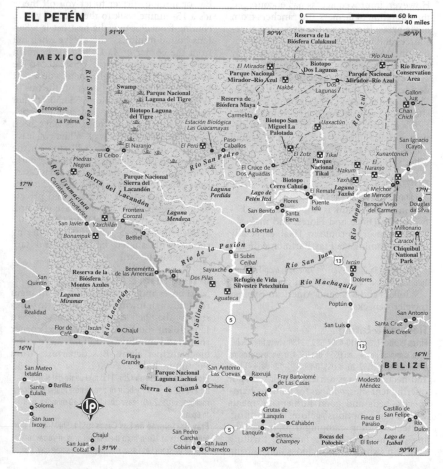

EL PETÉN

In 1990 the Guatemalan government established the one-million-hectare Maya Biosphere Reserve, which includes most of northern El Petén. The Guatemalan reserve adjoins the vast Reserva de la Biósfera Calakmul in Mexico and the Río Bravo Conservation Area in Belize – forming a multinational reserve of over two million hectares.

Many travelers linger in Poptún, a small town 113km southeast of Santa Elena that has been a popular backpacker layover for many years.

Getting There & Around

The roads leading into El Petén have now all been paved, so travel is fast and smooth. However, improved access has encouraged the migration of farmers and ranchers from other areas, increasing the pressure on resources and leading to even more deforestation in a region whose forests were already disappearing at an alarming rate.

The Guatemalan government long ago decided to develop the adjoining towns of Flores, Santa Elena and San Benito, on the shores of Lago de Petén Itzá, into the region's tourism base. Here you'll find an airport, hotels and other services. A few small hotels and restaurants are right at Tikal, but other services there remain limited.

POPTÚN

pop 8000 / elevation 540m

Diminutive Poptún is about halfway between Río Dulce and Flores, and makes a good stopover en route to Tikal, especially if you're coming via Fray Bartolomé de Las Casas.

Bancafé (5a Calle 7-98; 9am-5pm Mon-Fri, 9am-1pm Sat) has a Visa ATM and changes cash US dollars and Visa and American Express traveler's checks.

Sleeping & Eating

Finca Ixobel (5410-4307, 5892-3188; www.fincaixobel.com; camping per person US$3, dm US$4, treehouses, rooms & bungalows s US$7-20, d US$10-29; P Q) This 160-hectare *finca* is a friendly, relaxed spot offering tent sites, *palapas* for hanging hammocks, beds and good homemade meals with veggie options galore. Swimming, horseback riding, camping trips, inner tubing on the river and a famous, thrilling cave trip (which even includes bodysurfing

rapids) are all organized on a daily basis for a reasonable charge.

Meals here are excellent, including the eat-all-you-like buffet dinner for US$3.25 (salads, garlic bread, drinks) or US$6.50 (with a main dish, too). You can cook in the campground if you bring your own supplies. After 9pm many people move on to the pool bar, where reasonably priced cocktails and other drinks are served.

Volunteer opportunities exist for bilingual English-Spanish speakers; volunteers get free room and board. If you want to help and hang out for six weeks minimum, ask about volunteering.

The turnoff for the *finca* is marked on Hwy 13. In the daytime, you can ask the bus or minibus driver to let you off there; it's a 15-minute walk to the *finca*. If you're coming from Poptún, the best bet is a San Luís-bound minibus – these leave when full from the corner of 4a Calle and the main road in town and charge US$0.50 for the 10-minute trip. At night, or if you don't feel like making the walk, get off the bus in Poptún and take a taxi for US$2.50. It's not advisable to walk to the *finca* at night – it's an isolated spot and robberies have been known to occur on the way. When you leave Finca Ixobel, most buses will stop on the highway to pick you up, but not after dark.

In Poptún town, **Hotel Posada de los Castellanos** (7927-7222; cnr 4a Calle & 7a Av; s/d/tr US$5/6/8) has clean rooms with fan and private bathroom, arranged around a courtyard. Round the corner is **Hotel Izalco** (7927-7372; 4a Calle 7-11; s/d US$4/5, upstairs US$4/6), offering rooms with shared bathroom and fan. Splurge for the fan!

Getting There & Away

Most buses and minibuses stop on the main road through town; Fuente del Norte buses stop by the Shell station; minibuses to San Luís, 16km south, go from the next corner south; and minibuses to Flores start half a block further along. Bus departures from Poptún include:

Flores/Santa Elena (2hr, 113km) Fuente del Norte buses (US$2) go every hour or two almost round the clock; minibuses (US$2.60) leave about every 30 minutes, 6am to 6pm.

Fray Bartolomé de Las Casas (US$4, 5hr, 100km) One bus departs at 10am from the market area. If you want to push on from Las Casas to Lanquín the same day, try

RESERVA DE BIÓSFERA MAYA

The Maya Biosphere Reserve, occupying 21,000 sq km stretching right across the north of El Petén, is part of the Unesco world biosphere reserve network, which recognizes that the many human demands on this planet's land require innovative strategies if nature is to be conserved. In this vein, the Maya reserve is split into three spheres. Along its southern fringe is a buffer zone where economic activities are permitted, supposedly within a framework of environmental protection.

The main part of the reserve is divided into a multiple-use zone composed of tropical forest and supposedly dedicated to the sustainable harvest of *xate* ferns, chicle gum and timber; and eight core areas (all national parks and protected biotopes) for scientific research, conservation of the natural environment and/or archaeological sites, and tightly controlled ecological and cultural tourism. Unfortunately the theory is prettier than the reality: the forest is still being ravaged by people illegally harvesting timber on a massive scale, looters desecrating Mayan tombs and tourists (no matter how conscientious) negatively impacting the fragile ecosystem. Even some core areas have been subject to illegal settlements by land-hungry peasants from further south. In 1998 the environmental organization Conservation International had a camp in the reserve burned down by angry settlers. At least two conservationists who have spoken out about abuses in the reserve have been shot dead. The buffer zone is rapidly changing from a forested landscape with scattered agricultural patches to an agricultural landscape with scattered forest patches.

Meanwhile the remaining forests of southern Petén are falling at an alarming rate to the machetes of subsistence farmers. Sections of forest are felled and burned off, crops are grown for a few seasons until the fragile jungle soil is exhausted, and then the farmer moves deeper into the forest to slash and burn new fields. Cattle ranchers, also slashing and burning the forest in order to make pasture, have also contributed to the damage, as have resettled refugees and urban Guatemalans moving from the cities to El Petén in their endless struggle to make a living.

---

getting a Guatemala City–bound bus as far as Modesto Méndez (also called Cadenas), 60km south on Hwy 13, and change there to a westbound bus or minibus to Las Casas.
Guatemala City (US$7-10.50, 6-7hr, 387km) Fuente del Norte buses go about every half hour, 5:30am to midnight.
Río Dulce (US$3.25-4, 2hr, 99km) Fuente del Norte buses go about every half hour, 5:30am to midnight.

FLORES & SANTA ELENA

pop Flores 2000, Santa Elena 25,000 / elevation 110m

Flores is built on an island in Lago de Petén Itzá. A causeway connects it to the lakeshore town of Santa Elena; adjoining Santa Elena to the west is San Benito (population 22,000). Flores' main claim to fame is its proximity to Tikal and many people base themselves here for that reason, although El Remate (p177), halfway between the two, is gaining in popularity, particularly among budget travelers.

As the departmental capital, Flores is a dignified place. Its church, small government building and municipal basketball court surround the plaza, which sits atop a hill in the island's center. The narrow streets are lined with charming, red-roofed houses. Santa Elena is a disorganized town of dusty unpaved streets, and San Benito is even more chaotic.

The three towns form one large settlement, usually referred to simply as 'Flores.' All have numerous restaurants and small hotels.

History

Flores was founded on a *petén* (island) by the Itzáes after their expulsion from Chichén Itzá. They named the place Tayasal. Hernán Cortés peaceably dropped in on King Canek of Tayasal in 1524 on his way to Honduras. Only in March 1697 did the Spaniards finally bring Tayasal's Maya forcibly under their control.

At the time of the conquest, Flores was perhaps the last major functioning Mayan ceremonial center; it was covered in pyramids and temples, with idols everywhere. The God-fearing Spanish soldiers destroyed these buildings, and no trace remains.

Tayasal's Maya fled into the jungle and may have started anew, giving rise to stories of a 'lost' Mayan city; some believe this is El Mirador, near the Guatemala–Mexico border.

GUATEMALA

SANTA ELENA

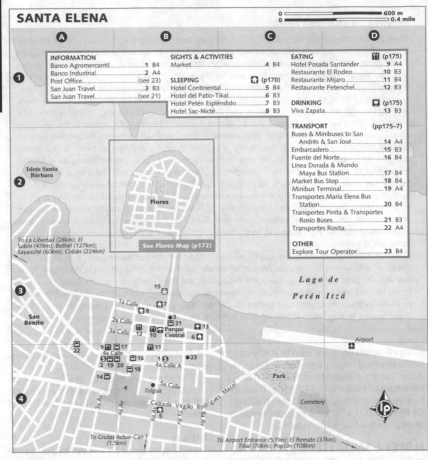

0 —————— 600 m
0 —————— 0.4 mile

A   **B**   **C**   **D**

INFORMATION
Banco Agromercantil....................1 B4
Banco Industrial............................2 A4
Post Office.............................(see 23)
San Juan Travel............................3 B3
San Juan Travel......................(see 21)

SIGHTS & ACTIVITIES
Market...4 B4

SLEEPING   (p170)
Hotel Continental........................5 B4
Hotel del Patio-Tikal...................6 B3
Hotel Petén Espléndido.............7 B3
Hotel Sac-Nicté.............................8 B3

EATING   (p175)
Hotel Posada Santander.............9 A4
Restaurante El Rodeo................10 B3
Restaurante Mijaro....................11 B4
Restaurante Petenchel..............12 B3

DRINKING   (p175)
Viva Zapata................................13 B3

TRANSPORT   (pp175–7)
Buses & Minibuses to San
   Andrés & San José.................14 A4
Embarcadero..............................15 B3
Fuente del Norte........................16 B4
Línea Dorada & Mundo
   Maya Bus Station...................17 B4
Market Bus Stop.........................18 B4
Minibus Terminal.......................19 A4
Transportes María Elena Bus
   Station....................................20 B4
Transportes Pinita & Transportes
   Rosio Buses.............................21 B3
Transportes Rosita.....................22 A4

OTHER
Explore Tour Operator..............23 B4

Islote Santa
Bárbara

Flores

See Flores Map (p172)

To La Libertad (28km); El
Subín (47km); Bethel (127km);
Sayaxché (60km); Cobán (224km)

*Lago de
Petén Itzá*

1a Calle
2a Calle
3a Calle

Parque
Central

4a Calle

4a Calle A

5a Calle
Telgua

Calzada
Virgilio Rodríguez Macal

3a Av
4a Av
6a Av
7a Av
8a Av

San
Benito

Airport

Park

Cemetery

To Grutas Actun-Can
(1.5km)

To Airport Entrance (500m); El Remate (37km);
Tikal (70km); Poptún (108km)

Orientation

The airport is on the eastern outskirts of Santa Elena, 2km from the 500m causeway connecting Santa Elena and Flores. Long-distance buses drop passengers on or just off Santa Elena's main drag, 4a Calle.

Information

AIRLINE OFFICES

Contact numbers at Flores airport:
Inter/Grupo TACA (☎ 7926-1238/0295/0650)
Jungle Flying Tours (☎ 7926-0292)
Maya Island Air (☎ 7926-3386)
Racsa (☎ 7926-0596/1477, 2332-1831)
TAG (☎ 7926-0653)
Tikal Airlines (Tikal Jets; ☎ 7926-0386/3823)
Tropic Air (☎ 7926-0348)

EMERGENCY

Policía Nacional (☎ 7926-1365)
Hospital San Benito (☎ 7926-1459)

INTERNET ACCESS

Flores.Net (Map p172; Av Barrios, Flores; per hr US$1.30)
Internet Petén (Map p172; Calle Centroamérica, Flores; ☻ 8am-10pm; per hr US$1.60)

MONEY

At the airport, **Banquetzal** (Map p170; ☻ 7am-noon & 2-5pm) changes US-dollar cash and traveler's checks. **Banrural** (Map p172), just off the Parque Central in Flores, changes US-dollar cash and traveler's checks.

Other banks are on 4a Calle in Santa Elena. The following all change cash US dollars and at least American Express US-dollar traveler's checks:

Banco Agromercantil (Map p170; 🕓 9am-6pm Mon-Fri, 9am-1pm Sat) Has MasterCard ATM.

Banco Industrial (Map p170; 🕓 9am-7pm Mon-Fri, 10am-2pm Sat) Has Visa ATM.

Many travel agencies and places to stay will change cash US dollars, and sometimes traveler's checks, at poor rates. **San Juan Travel** (right) will also change Belize dollars and Mexican pesos and give Visa, MasterCard, Diner's Club and American Express cash advances.

POST

There are **post offices** (Flores Map p172; Av Barrios; Santa Elena Map p170; 4a Calle, east of 7a Av).

TELEPHONE & FAX

Martsam Travel (Map p172; ☎ /fax 7926-3225; www .martsam.com; Calle Centroamérica, Flores) offers domestic and international telephone and fax services.

TOURIST INFORMATION

Inguat (Airport Map p170; ☎ 7926-0533; 🕓 7am-noon & 3-6pm; Flores Map p172; ☎ 7926-0669; Parque Central; 🕓 8am-12:30pm & 1:30-4pm) has helpful tourist information.

Cincap (Map p172; Parque Central, Flores; ☎ 7926-0718; mercadeo@peten.net; 🕓 9am-noon & 2-9pm) has interesting displays on archaeological sites, conservation areas and the local way of life in El Petén. It also sells handicrafts from the region and has an information desk where you can ask about visits to some of the remoter natural and archaeological sites.

Cincap is run by **Asociación Alianza Verde** (☎ /fax 7926-0718; www.alianzaverde.org), which is dedicated to sustainable, responsible and low-impact tourism in the Maya Biosphere Reserve. It publishes *Destination Petén* magazine and runs the website www.peten.net.

TRAVEL AGENCIES

Several travel agencies in Flores and Santa Elena offer trips to archaeological sites, as well as shuttle minibuses and other services. Several hotels can book you on tours, shuttles, buses and flights.

Martsam Travel (Map p172; ☎ /fax 7926-3225; www .martsam.com; Calle Centroamérica, Flores) A well-established, well-organized agency with a wide range of services.

San Juan Travel (☎ 7926-0041/2, 7926-2146; sanjuant@internetdetelgua.com.gt); Santa Elena (Map p170; 2a Calle); Flores (Map p172; Playa Sur) Provides various shuttles and tours, including the most regular service to Tikal and Palenque.

Volunteering

Estación Biológica Las Guacamayas, in the Parque Nacional Laguna del Tigre, and the rehabilitation center at **Arcas** (p63) both offer the chance of volunteer work with wildlife. At Las Guacamayas you pay US$7.75 a day for the first two weeks, US$7 a day the third week and US$6.50 a day the fourth week, and provide your own food. If you're interested, contact **ProPetén** (Proyecto Petenero para un Bosque Sostenible; Map p172; ☎ 7926-1370, 7926-1141; www.propeten.org; Calle Central, Flores; 🕓 9am-5pm Mon-Fri), the Guatemalan NGO that owns the station. At Arcas you pay US$100 a week including food.

Courses

Ixchel Spanish Academy (Map p172; ☎ 7926-0346, ☎ /fax 7926-3225; info@martsam.com; Calle Central, Flores) offers four hours of one-on-one tuition five days a week for US$110, or US$175 including a week's lodging and meals in a local home.

Tours

Many travel agencies in Flores offer day tours to the more accessible archaeological sites such as Tikal, Uaxactún, Yaxhá and Ceibal. Day trips to these places with guide and lunch cost US$40 to US$60 with agencies such as **Martsam Travel** and **San Juan Travel** (above). They're cheaper (US$25 to US$40) with **Ecomaya** (Map p172; ☎ 7926-3202; www.ecomaya.com; Calle Centroamérica, Flores) and **Explore Tour Operator** (Map p170; ☎ 7926-2375; www .exploreguate.com; cnr 4a Calle & 7a Av, Santa Elena).

Ecomaya, which is a joint venture of several community-based businesses, and Martsam also offer more demanding hiking-and-camping 'eco-trails' and 'eco-tours' to exciting, remoter archaeological sites such as Nakum, El Perú, El Zotz, El Mirador, Nakbé, Wakná and La Muralla, working with Comités Comunitarios de Ecoturismo (Community Ecotourism Committees), which provide guides to these sites deep in the Petén jungles.

Sample prices per person for two-/four-/five-plus people, normally including food,

FLORES

0 ————— 200 m
0 ————— 0.1 mile

Boats to San Miguel
Boats to Arcas

Calle Unión

Avenida Libertad

Av La Reforma

Parque
Central

Calle 10 de Noviembre

Calle 30 de Junio

Callejón San Pedrito

Callejón El Crucero

Av Barrios

Calle Central

Av Santa Ana

Callejón El
Rosario

Callejón Las
Palmas

Calle Centroamérica

Playa Sur

*Lago de
Petén Itzá*

To Santa Elena
(400m)

water, sleeping gear and Spanish-speaking guide, are:

El Zotz & Tikal 2 days US$148/125/116, 3 days US$192/147/133

El Perú 2 days US$213/120/108, 3 days US$247/146/133

El Mirador 5 days US$391/343/322

El Mirador–Nakbé–La Muralla 7 days US$494/444/405

Estación Biológica Las Guacamayas 3 days US$574/371/330

Grutas Actun-Can

The limestone cave of **Actun-Can** (La Cueva de la Serpiente, Cave of the Serpent; admission US$1.30; ☉ 8am-5pm) holds no serpents, but the cave-keeper may give you the rundown on the cave formations, which suggest animals,

humans and various scenes. Bring a flash-light and adequate shoes – it can be slippery. Exploring the cave takes 30 to 45 minutes.

Actun-Can makes a good goal for a long walk from Santa Elena. Head south on 6a Av past the Telgua office. About 1km from the center of Santa Elena, turn left, go 300m and turn right at the electricity generating plant. Go another 1km to the site. A taxi costs US$2.

Sleeping
FLORES   Map p172
Hotel Mirador del Lago (☎ 7926-3276; s/d/tr US$7/ 10/16) With a waterside position on the east side of the island, this is good value.

The clean, blue-painted rooms have a fan, good beds, hot-water bathroom and mosquito-netted windows. There's a good roof terrace above. Hotel Mirador del Lago II, opposite, has 13 more rooms of the same type.

Hotel La Hospedaje Doña Goya (☎ 7926-3538; Calle Unión; s/d/tr US$7/11/13, with private bathroom US$8/13/16) This family-room guesthouse is one of the best budget choices in town and often full as a result. The beds are comfortable, the water's hot and there's a roof terrace with a palm-thatched shelter from

which to enjoy lake views. There is a safe for valuables too.

Hotel Petenchel (☎ 7926-3359; s/d/tr US$8/11/13) This is solid value, with clean rooms with private hot-water bathroom, ceiling fan and comfortable beds. A small courtyard jammed with plants provides a little character; some rooms are dark, however.

Hotel La Canoa (☎ 7926-0852/53; s/d/tr US$8/11/16) This dependable budget place has bare-but-clean, decent-sized, fan-cooled rooms with hot-water bathroom. Upstairs rooms are airier, and downstairs triples can be crowded. Two rooms with shared bathroom cost US$4 per person.

Hotel La Mesa de los Mayas (☎ /fax 7926-1240; mesamayas@hotmail.com; Av La Reforma; s/d/tr US$10/18/25, with air-con US$12/25/35; 🅿) This is a lovely place, very clean and well kept. All 20 rooms have TV, cerise walls, colorful bedspreads, reading lamp, hot-water bathroom and fan.

Hotel Villa del Lago (☎ /fax 7926-0629; hotelvilla delago@itelgua.com; s or d US$25; 🅿) Beside the lake on the east side of the island, this is a fine, clean place to stay. Its once drab exterior now sports a classical facade more in keeping with the quality of the 18 rooms. Prices depend on whether they have air-conditioning (most do) and lake view (four do). All have private hot-water bathroom, fan, cable TV and tiled floors. Breakfast is available, there's a breezy upstairs terrace, and they can do your laundry, exchange books and book flights.

Hotel Casona de la Isla (☎ 7926-0593; www .corpetur.com; Calle 30 de Junio; s US$30-33, d US$36-41; 🅿 🅿) This is a romantic place with a pool with waterfall and an open-air restaurant/ bar overlooking the lake. All 27 rooms have private bathroom, cable TV, phone, air-con, fan and cane furniture. Rooms 31, 303 and 304 have windows facing right out to the lake and gorgeous sunsets.

Hotel Isla de Flores (☎ 7926-0614; www.jungle lodge.guate.com; Av La Reforma; s/d US$36/41; 🅿) This clean and attractive hotel has large rooms well equipped with cable TV, air-con, ceiling fan, telephone and private hot-water bathroom with tub. Many rooms have little balconies with a view of the lake. Breakfast is available.

Hotel Petén (☎ 7926-0692; www.corpetur.com; Calle 30 de Junio; s/d/tr US$38/45/58; 🅿 🖥 🅿) This hotel on the western shore of the island has a small courtyard with tropical plants, a pleasant lakeside terrace and restaurant, and a small indoor swimming pool. The 19 comfy-if-plain rooms all have private bathroom, air-con and fan: try to get one on the top floor with a lake view; the interior rooms can be a little gloomy.

Two budget hotels with respectable, fan-cooled rooms are:

Hotel Casa del Lacandón (☎ 7926-4359; Calle Unión; s/d US$8/9)

Hotel Itzá 2 (☎ 7926-3654; Av La Reforma; s/d/tr with private bathroom US$9/9/12)

SANTA ELENA   Map p170

Hotel Continental (☎ 7926-0095; 6a Av; s/d US$4/8, with fan, private bathroom & TV US$7/12, with air-con, private bathroom & TV US$13/18; P ☒) A 51-room hotel south of Calz Virgilio Rodríguez Macal, with friendly reception staff, the Continental provides a range of rooms on three floors along a courtyard painted in vaguely refreshing shades of blue and green. The rooms with private bath are good and clean, but there's no hot water.

Hotel Sac-Nicté (☎ 7926-0092, 7926-1731; 1a Calle; s/d/tr US$7/8/10, upstairs US$7/11/13) The rooms here are tolerably clean and will do in a pinch. They all have private bathroom and fan, and the rooms upstairs have small balconies from which you might just glimpse the lake. They will pick you up for free from the airport, where they have a desk.

Hotel del Patio-Tikal (☎ 7926-0104; www.hoteldel patio.com.gt; cnr 8a Av & 2a Calle; s/d/tr US$61/61/70; ☒ ☒) This looks severe from outside but is actually a colonial-style hotel with a pretty courtyard. Its 21 rooms all have air-con and ceiling fan, cable TV, telephone and private bathroom, and there's a restaurant and pool.

Hotel Petén Espléndido (☎ 7926-0880; www .petenesplendido.com; 1a Calle 5-01; s/d US$98/122; P ☒ ☒) This glitzy waterside fun palace may have the only elevator in all of El Petén. Its amenities include a lakeside pool, poolside bar, a restaurant that is lakeside, poolside and barside all at once, and a free airport shuttle. The 62 spotless rooms have air-con, fan, cable TV, safe, phone, computer jacks and little balconies, and are wheelchair accessible. Staff sport garish tropical shirts and some of them speak English, Italian or German.

Eating

On the menu at many places, there is a variety of local game, including *tepescuintle* (agouti, a rabbit-sized jungle rodent), *venado* (venison), armadillo, *pavo silvestre* (wild turkey) and *pescado blanco* (white fish). You may want to avoid dishes that may soon jump from the menu to the endangered species list.

FLORES   Map p172

Food stalls (Parque Central; tacos & burritos US$0.70 each) At the breezy northwest corner of the plaza, these are a good place to dine cheap on *antojitos* (snacks).

La Luna (☎ 7926-3346; cnr Calle 30 de Junio & Calle 10 de Noviembre; mains US$6.50-10; ☒ lunch & dinner Mon-Sat) In a class by itself, this very popular restaurant cultivates a classic tropical ambiance, with potted palms to catch the breeze from the whirling overhead fans. The food is continental and delectable, with innovative chicken, fish and beef dishes. There are also good pasta and vegetarian options, such as falafel, salad and rice, for US$4 to US$5.

Café-Bar Las Puertas (☎ 7926-1061; cnr Calle Central & Av Santa Ana; meat, fish & seafood mains US$8-9; ☒ breakfast, lunch & dinner Mon-Sat) This popular restaurant and bar has good, if pricey, food. It's an arty sort of place with walls painted Jackson Pollock–style, and a hangout for an interesting mix of people. There's live music some nights (mainly weekends). The *camarones a la orientall* (prawns served with vegetables and rice) are a treat. For something cheaper it has 10 ways of doing spaghetti and nine types of salad; round it off with a crepe (US$2). Breakfasts (US$2.50) are good here, too.

Hotel Posada del Peregrino (Av La Reforma 3; plato del día US$2.20) The restaurant here serves great food at good prices. The *plato del día* is usually meat or chicken with rice, salad, *tortillas* and a soft drink. Other main dishes go for US$3.25 to US$4.50, breakfasts are US$2.50 to US$3.25, and a liter jug of beer is just US$2.40.

Capitán Tortuga (Calle 30 de Junio; mains US$3.50-7) A long, barn-like place stretching down to a small lakeside terrace, 'Captain Turtle' serves large plates of a wide variety of tasty food – pizzas, steaks, chicken, pasta, salads, sandwiches, tacos – at medium prices. Big tour groups turn up here from time to time.

Naomi's Café (☎ /fax 7926-3225; Calle Centroamérica; sandwiches, salads & breakfasts US$2-2.75; ⏲ breakfast, lunch & dinner) You can get breakfast here before that early departure, and inexpensive snacks at any time of day. It has Internet and sells guidebooks, too.

Restaurant El Barco (☎ 7926-0346; Playa Sur; antojitos, salads & sandwiches US$2.25-2.75, chicken & steaks US$4.50-7) On a boat moored on the island's southern shore, El Barco does good food in a Tex-Mex vein. The *tacos hawaiianas* are yummy.

Also recommended are:

Restaurante Peche's (Playa Sur; mains US$2.50-3.25; ⏲ breakfast, lunch & dinner) Inexpensive plates of meat, rice, *tortillas* and salad, open for early breakfast.

Restaurante El Gran Jacal (Calle Centroamérica; chicken & meat US$4.50-7.75)

Pizzería Picasso (pizza US$4-5; ⏲ lunch & dinner Tue-Sun) Reasonable pizzas and pasta at fair prices.

Restaurante La Unión (Calle Unión; mains US$3-5) What's special here is the location, right on the water with terrific views.

SANTA ELENA   **Map p170**

Restaurante Mijaro (4a Calle; mains US$3.50-4.25) Cool off at this friendly *comedor* on the main street, which has fans not only inside but also in its little thatch-roofed garden area. It does good, long *limonadas* and snacks like sandwiches and burgers (US$1.30 to US$2) as well as weightier food.

Hotel Posada Santander (4a Calle; breakfast around US$1.50, lunch US$2.50) This budget hotel has a clean upstairs restaurant serving good-value set meals.

Other recommendations:

Restaurante El Rodeo (cnr 2a Calle & 5a Av) Often recommended by locals.

Restaurante Petenchel In the next block of 2a Calle; also popular.

Drinking

Flores doesn't exactly jive at night but there are a couple of places to hang out.

Viva Zapata (Map p172; cnr 2a Calle & 8a Av Santa Elena; ⏲ 7pm-midnight Sun-Wed, 7pm-3am Thu-Sat) Just across the bridge in Santa Elena, this church-turned-nightclub has mellow karaoke action during the week and full on disco frenzy at weekends.

The terrace overlooking the lake at **Restaurante La Unión** (above; Calle Unión) is a magnificent spot to watch the sun go down over a Cuba libre (US$1) or a pina colada (US$2).

If you are hankering to hear some reggae, try the little patio-bar **El Trópico** (Map p172; Playa Sur).

Restaurants such as **La Luna**, **Las Puertas** and **El Barco** (opposite and left) are places you can go just for a drink if you like, and Las Puertas has live music, often jazz, some nights (most often weekends).

Entertainment

Mayan Princess Café (Map p172; cnr Calle 10 de Noviembre & Av La Reforma) shows free movies in the evening if the customers want them. There are also nightly **films** in a house on Calle Central opposite Las Puertas (see Eating, opposite).

Locals gather in the cool of the evening for long drinks, snacks and relaxation in Flores' **Parque Central**, where a marimba ensemble plays some nights.

Getting There & Away

AIR

The airport at Santa Elena is usually called Flores airport and sometimes Tikal airport. Five airlines fly daily from and back to Guatemala City. Tikal Airlines (Tikal Jets), Jungle Flying Tours, Racsa and TAG all make this one-hour flight in the morning, arriving between 7am and 8am, and starting back at 4:30pm or 5pm. Inter of Grupo TACA makes two round-trip flights daily, arriving at Flores at 7am and 5:30pm and starting back half an hour later in each case. One-way/round-trip tickets from the airlines cost US$56/100 with Racsa, US$65/90 with Jungle Flying Tours, US$70/100 with TAG, US$89/112 with Tikal Airlines and US$90/124 with Inter, but you may get discounts at travel agencies. Four days a week, Inter of Grupo TACA makes an extra morning flight from Guatemala City to Flores and on to Cancún, Mexico, returning in the afternoon. The one-way/round-trip fare from Flores to Cancún is US$207/316. Two Belizean airlines, **Tropic Air** (in Guatemala ☎ 7926-0348, in Belize ☎ 226-2012; www.tropicair.com) and **Maya Island Air** (in Guatemala ☎ 7926-3386, in Belize ☎ 223-1140; www.mayaairways.com), fly twice a day each from and to Belize City, both charging US$88 each way for the one-hour trip.

BUS & MINIBUS

In Santa Elena, buses of **Fuente del Norte** (Map p170; ☎ 7926-0517), **Transportes María Elena**,

Línea Dorada/Mundo Maya (Map p170; ☎ 7926-1788, 7926-0528) and **Transportes Rosita** (Map p170; ☎ 7926-1245) all stop at their own ticket offices on 4a Calle. Línea Dorada/Mundo Maya has a second office in **Flores** (Map p172; ☎ 7926-3649; Playa Sur), where its buses also pick up passengers.

The bus stop in Santa Elena's crowded market area, off the south side of 4a Calle, is used by the chicken buses of Transportes Pinita and Transportes Rosío. Minibuses to El Remate, Melchor de Mencos, Poptún, El Naranjo and Sayaxché have their own yard on 4a Calle just west of the market entrance. Buses and minibuses to San Andrés and San José go from 5a Calle just west of the market. Buses of **San Juan Travel** (Map p170; ☎ 7926-0041/2, 7926-2146) leave from its office on 2a Calle, Santa Elena.

Bus and minibus departures include:

Belize City (4-5hr, 220km); Línea Dorada/Mundo Maya (US$15.50, 2 daily, 5am & 7am, returns 2pm & 5pm); San Juan Travel (US$20, 1 daily, 5am, returns 9:30am & 4:30pm) These buses to Belize City all connect with boats to Caye Caulker and Ambergris Caye. It's cheaper but slower from Flores to take local buses to the border and on from it.

Bethel, Mexico border (US$3.25, 4hr, 127km); Fuente del Norte (1 daily, 5am, returns 4pm) Pinita (4 daily, 5am, 8am, noon & 1pm, returns 5am, noon & 2pm) Mexico border.

Carmelita (US$3.25, 3hr, 80km); Pinita (1 daily, 1pm, returns 5am)

Chetumal, Mexico (7-8hr, 350km); Línea Dorada/Mundo Maya (US$22, 2 daily 5am & 7am, returns 6:30am & 2pm); San Juan Travel (contact Posada Chaktemal, ☎ 7832-0727/ 6348; US$25, 1 daily 5am return 9:30am & 4:30pm) Check Belize visa regulations before you set off.

Cobán (US$6.50, 6hr, 245km); Rosío (1 daily, 10:30am) Leaves the market bus stop. You could also take a bus or minibus to Sayaxché, from where a bus leaves for Cobán at 10am. See also Shuttle Minibus, right.

El Naranjo (Río San Pedro; US$3.25, 4hr, 151km, minibuses every hour, 5am-6pm, buses 5 daily, 5am, 7am, 11am, 2pm & 3pm) Buses leave from the market.

El Remate (US$2, 40min, 29km, minibuses hourly, 6am-1pm) Alternatively, buses and minibuses to/from Melchor de Mencos will drop you at Puente Ixlú junction, 2km south of El Remate.

Esquipulas (US$10.50, 10hr, 440km); Transportes María Elena (US$7.75, 9hr, 3 daily, 6am, 10am & 2pm) Goes via Chiquimula.

Fray Bartolomé de Las Casas (US$4.50, 5hr, 178km); Transportes Rosío (10:30am) Leaves from the market.

Guatemala City (8-10hr, 500km); Línea Dorada/Mundo Maya (deluxe US$28, 2 daily, 10am & 9pm; economy US$14.50, 1 daily, 10pm); Transportes Rosita (US$6.50-9.75, 2 daily, 7pm & 8pm); Fuente del Norte (US$9-10.50, 29 daily, 3:30am-11pm) Fuente price exceptions are: the 10am and 9pm buses cost US$17, and the 2pm, 8pm and 10pm departures cost US$13.

La Técnica, Mexico border Pinita (US$4, 5hr, 140km, 2 daily, 5am & 1pm, returns 4am & 11am)

Melchor de Mencos, Belize border (2hr, 100km); minibuses (US$2.60, hourly, 5am-6pm); Transportes Rosita (US$1.30, 5 daily, 5am, 11am, 2pm, 4pm & 6pm); Pinita (US$2, 1 daily 8am)

Palenque (Mexico) See Shuttle Minibus, below.

Poptún (2hr, 113km, every 30min, 5am-6pm); Fuente del Norte (US$2); minibus (US$2.60) The buses are Guatemala City-bound.

Puerto Barrios Take a Guatemala City-bound Fuente del Norte bus and change at La Ruidosa junction, south of Río Dulce.

Río Dulce (4½hr, 212km); Fuente del Norte (US$6.50); Línea Dorada (US$10.50/19.50 economy/deluxe) Take a Guatemala City-bound bus.

San Andrés (US$0.50, 30min, 20km, hourly, 5am-5pm)

San José (US$0.50, 45min, 25km, hourly, 5am-5pm)

Sayaxché (US$1.30, 1½hr, 60km); minibuses (every 30min, 5am-6pm); Pinita (3 daily 11am, 2pm & 2:30pm)

Tikal See Shuttle Minibus, below.

SHUTTLE MINIBUS

Mundo Maya (Map p170; ☎ 7926-1788, 7926-0528) and **San Juan Travel** (p171) operate shuttle minibuses to Tikal (US$2.50/5 one-way/round-trip, 1¼ hours each way). San Juan leaves hourly from 5am to 10am and usually at 2pm. Mundo Maya goes at 5am and 8:30am and some days at 3:30pm. Most hotels and travel agencies can book these shuttles for you and the vehicles will pick you up where you're staying. Round-trips leave Tikal at 12:30pm, 2pm, 3pm, 4pm, 5pm and 6pm with San Juan and at 2pm and 5pm with Mundo Maya. If you know which round-trip you plan to be on, ask your driver to hold a seat for you or arrange a seat in a colleague's minibus. If you stay overnight in Tikal and want to return to Flores by minibus, it's a good idea to reserve a seat with one of the drivers when they arrive in the morning. Outside the normal timetable, you can rent a whole minibus for US$30.

Martsam Travel (p171) runs shuttles to Cobán (US$25 per person, five to six hours) for a minimum of four people. It also does a

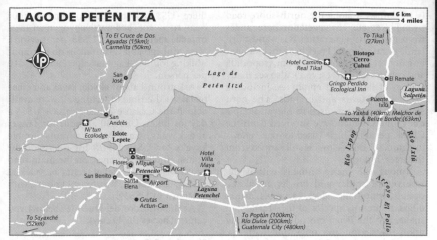

LAGO DE PETÉN ITZÁ

0 — 6 km
0 — 4 miles

To El Cruce de Dos
Aguadas (15km);
Carmelita (50km)

To Tikal
(27km)

Hotel Camino
Real Tikal

Biotopo
Cerro
Cahuí

San
José

*Lago de
Petén Itzá*

Gringo Perdido
Ecological Inn

El Remate

*Laguna
Salpetén*

Puente
Ixlú

To Yaxhá (40km); Melchor de
Mencos & Belize Border (63km)

San
Andrés

Ni'tun
Ecolodge

Islote
Lepete

San
Miguel

Petencito

Arcas

Hotel
Villa
Maya

San
Flores

San Benito

Santa
Elena

Airport

*Laguna
Petenchel*

Grutas
Actun-Can

Río Ixpop

Río Ixlú

Arroyo El Pollo

To Sayaxché
(52km)

To Poptún (100km);
Río Dulce (200km);
Guatemala City (480km)

US$90 trip to Palenque, Mexico, visiting the outstanding Maya ruins at Yaxchilán and Bonampak en route. San Juan Travel does a more basic Palenque minibus-boat-minibus shuttle (US$30, eight hours, leaving 5am). On the Palenque run (in either direction) make sure you get a ticket, receipt or other documentation that proves you have paid for the whole trip from Flores to Palenque or vice-versa. Occasionally travelers find that the driver waiting on the far side of the Río Usumacinta to take them on to their destination attempts to extract an extra payment.

Getting Around

A taxi from the airport to Santa Elena or Flores costs US$1.30. Yellow local buses (US$0.15) shuttle between 6a Av in Santa Elena and the north end of the causeway in Flores. **Martsam Travel** (p171) rents mountain bikes with helmets for US$2.60 an hour and 125cc motorbikes at US$14.25/32.50/36.50 for two/eight/24 hours.

BOAT

Lanchas ferrying passengers between Santa Elena and Flores depart from both ends of the causeway (US$0.15, five minutes). Motor launches making tours around Lago de Petén Itzá depart from the Santa Elena end. *Colectivo* boats to San Andrés and San José, villages across the lake, depart from San Benito, on the west side of Santa Elena and alongside the Hotel

Santana in Flores (US$0.40 if the boat is full, US$8 for one passenger). You can also contract the *lancheros* for lake tours – bargain hard.

EL REMATE

Once little more than a few thatched huts 29km northeast of Santa Elena on the Tikal road, El Remate keeps on growing, thanks to the tourist trade. Halfway between Flores and Tikal, it allows you to be closer to Tikal but still on the lake.

El Remate is known for its wood carving. Several handicrafts shops on the lakeshore opposite La Mansión del Pájaro Serpiente sell local handicrafts and rent canoes, rafts and kayaks.

El Remate begins 1km beyond Puente Ixlú (also called El Cruce), the village where the road to Melchor de Mencos on the Belize border diverges from the Tikal road. El Remate is strung along the Tikal road for 1km to another junction, where an unpaved road branches west along the north shore of Lago de Petén Itzá to the Biotopo Cerro Cahuí and beyond. Several places to stay and eat are dotted along this road, which continues all the way to the villages of San José and San Andrés near the west end of the lake, making it possible to go all the way around the lake by road.

Biotopo Cerro Cahuí

The entrance to this 6.5-sq-km subtropical **forest reserve** (admission US$2.50; 6:30am-dusk)

is 1.75km west along the north-shore road from El Remate. The vegetation here ranges from *guamil* (regenerating slash-and-burn land) to rain forest. Trees here include mahogany, cedar, ramón, broom, sapodilla and cohune palm trees; you'll also see many species of lianas and epiphytes, including bromeliads, ferns and orchids. The hard sapodilla wood was used in Mayan temple door lintels, which have survived from the Classic period. Chicle (used to make chewing gum, see box below) is still sapped from the trees' innards.

Among the many animals within the reserve are spider and howler monkeys, ocelots, white-tailed deer, raccoons, armadillos, numerous species of fish, turtle and snake, and the Petén crocodile. Depending upon the season and migration patterns, you might see kingfishers, ducks, herons, hawks, parrots, toucans, woodpeckers and the beautiful ocellated (Petén) turkey, which resembles a peacock.

A network of loop trails starts at the road and goes uphill, affording a view of the lake and Lagunas Salpetén and Petenchel. A trail map is at the entrance.

The admission fee includes the right to **camp** or **sling your hammock** under small thatch shelters inside the entrance. There are toilets and showers, but El Remate is the closest place to get supplies.

Activities

Most El Remate accommodations can book you on five-hour **horseback rides** to Laguna Salpetén and a small archaeological site

there (US$16.50 per person), or two-hour boat trips for **bird-watching** or nocturnal **crocodile spotting** (each US$8 per person). Casa Mobego and Casa Yaikán do five-hour walking tours to Laguna Salpetén for US$10 per person.

Ask around about **bicycle**, **kayak** and **canoe rental**. At the time of writing all were available at the Casa de Doña Tonita – US$4 a day for bikes, US$1.30 an hour for canoes and kayaks. Casa Mobego rents double kayaks for US$3.25/4/8 for one/two/four hours. Hotel Las Sirenas, on the main road south of Posada Ixchel, rents bicycles at US$2/3.25/4.50 for two/four/24 hours, with a deposit of US$39.

At the Mirador del Duende (below) you can **rent horses** (US$10 a day).

Sleeping & Eating

Hotel La Mansión del Pájaro Serpiente (☎ 5702-9434, Flores airport office ☎ /fax 7926-4264; s/d/tr US$30/40/65; ⌘) Just north of the Mirador del Duende, this American-owned establishment has the loveliest rooms and grounds in El Remate. The 11 rooms, in bungalows dotted about beautiful hillside gardens and all with lake views, sport colorful textiles, tile floors, fans and netted windows, and each has a sitting room and hot-water bathroom as well as a bedroom. There's a gorgeous pool, too, with hammocks under *palapa* shelters nearby, and a reasonably priced restaurant/bar.

Mirador del Duende (☎ 5707-1093, 5806-2231; camping per person US$3, bungalows US$5) One of the first places you encounter as you enter El

---

CHICLE & CHEWING GUM

Chicle, a pinkish to reddish-brown gum, is actually the coagulated milky sap, or latex, of the sapodilla tree *(Achras zapota)*, a tropical evergreen native to the Yucatán Peninsula and Central America. *Chicleros* (chicle workers) enter the forests and cut large V-shaped gashes in the sapodillas' trunks, as high up as 9m. The sap runs from the wounds and down the trunk into a container at the base. After being boiled, it is shaped into blocks for shipping. The cuts often kill the tree, and thus chicle harvesting tends to result in the serious depletion of sapodilla forests. Even if the tree survives the first round of cuts, a typical tree used for harvesting chicle has a life span of just 10 years.

First used as a substitute for natural rubber (to which the sapodilla is related), by about 1890 chicle was best known as the main ingredient in chewing gum.

As a result of war research for a rubber substitute during the 1940s, synthetic substitutes were developed for chicle. Now chewing gum is made mostly from these synthetic substitutes. However, in the northern reaches of the Petén, *chicleros* still live in the forest for months at a time harvesting the sap for gum. To check out some real chicle gum, visit www.junglegum.com.

Remate, this has great lake views and quirky bungalows that are almost completely open to the air. You can sling your hammock here for US$3, too. Healthy, economical vegetarian food is served and the owner boasts that this is a 'mosquito-free zone,' thanks to breezes off the lake.

Hotel Camino Real Tikal (☎ 7926-0204/09, 2333-3000; www.caminorealtikal.com.gt; s & d US$134; P ⊠ ⊛) Two kilometers further along the lake is the luxury Camino Real, the fanciest hotel in El Petén, with 72 air-con rooms with balconies, lake views and all the comforts. Two restaurants, a bar and a coffee shop keep guests happy, as do the Tikal and Cerro Cahuí tours, swimming pool, kayaking, sailing, windsurfing and beach sports. This hotel is rather remote; check out its special packages, which include airport transfers.

Las Orquideas (pasta US$3.25-5, fish & pizza US$7-9.50) Las Orquideas has a genial Italian owner-chef cooking up genuine Italian fare, with tempting desserts, too.

Mon Ami (mains US$3.25-4.25, crepes US$2) Further along the north-shore road (1200m from the main Tikal road), Mon Ami serves good French and Guatemalan food in a peaceful palm-thatched, open-walled area. Try the *carne al vino* with rice and tomato salad, or the big *ensalada francesa*.

Among the simple *comedores* along the main road, **Restaurante Cahuí** (mains US$3.25), 60m south of Posada Ixchel, stands out for its rustic wooden terrace overlooking the lake. The food is straightforward and inexpensive; meat or chicken main dishes include rice, salad and *tortillas*. Spaghetti and salads cost a little less.

Getting There & Around

El Remate is linked to Flores by a public minibus service (see Bus & Minibus, p175).

A minibus leaves El Remate at 5:30am for Tikal, starting back from Tikal at 2pm (US$4 round-trip). Any El Remate accommodations can make reservations, or you can catch one of the shuttles passing through from Flores to get to Tikal, normally charging US$2.50 per person.

For taxis, ask at your hotel; a one-way ride to Tikal or Flores costs about US$15.

For Melchor de Mencos on the Belize border, get a minibus or bus from Puente Ixlú, 2km south of El Remate.

TIKAL

Towering pyramids pierce the jungle's green canopy and catch the sun. Howler monkeys swing noisily through the branches of ancient trees as brightly colored parrots and toucans dart from perch to perch amid a cacophony of squawks. When the complex warbling song of some mysterious jungle bird tapers off, the buzz of tree frogs fills the background and it will dawn on you that this is indeed hallowed ground.

Certainly the most striking feature of **Tikal** (☎ 2361-1399; admission US$6.50; ⊙ 6am-6pm) is its steep-sided temples, rising to heights of more than 44m. But Tikal is different from Copán, Chichén Itzá, Uxmal and most other great Mayan sites because it is deep in the jungle. Its many plazas have been cleared of trees and vines, its temples uncovered and partially restored, but as you walk from one building to another you pass beneath the dense rain-forest canopy. Rich, loamy smells of earth and vegetation, a peaceful air and animal noises all contribute to an experience not offered by other Mayan sites.

You can visit Tikal in a day trip from Flores or El Remate. You can even make a literally flying visit from Guatemala City in one day, using the daily flights between there and Flores airport. But you'll get more out of Tikal if you spend a night here, enabling you to visit the ruins twice and to be here in the late afternoon and early morning, when other tourists are rare and wildlife more active.

History

Tikal is set on a low hill above the surrounding swampy ground – maybe why the Maya settled here around 700 BC. Another reason was the abundance of flint, used to make clubs, spearheads, arrowheads and knives. Flint could also be exported in exchange for other goods. Within 200 years, the Maya of Tikal had begun to build stone ceremonial structures, and by 200 BC a complex of buildings stood on the site of the North Acropolis.

CLASSIC PERIOD

The Gran Plaza was beginning to assume its present shape and extent two thousand years ago. By the dawn of the Early Classic period, about AD 250, Tikal had become an

TIKAL

important, heavily populated religious, cultural and commercial city. King Yax Moch Xoc, whose reign began around AD 230, founded the ruling dynasty.

Under the reign of King Great Jaguar Paw (who ruled in the mid-4th century), Tikal adopted a new, brutal method of warfare used by rulers of Teotihuacán in central Mexico. Rather than meeting their adversaries in hand-to-hand combat, the army of Tikal encircled their enemy and killed them by throwing spears. This first use of 'air power' among the Maya of Petén enabled Tikal to conquer Uaxactún and become the dominant kingdom in the region.

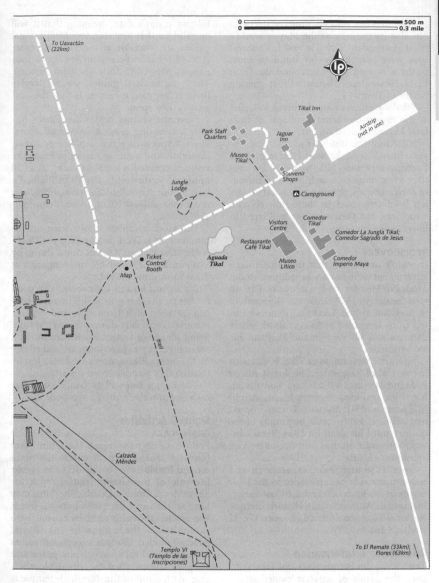

By the middle of the Classic period, in the mid-6th century, Tikal sprawled over 30 sq km and had a population of perhaps 100,000. In 553, Lord Water ascended to the throne of Caracol (p277), and by 562, using the same warfare methods learned from Tikal, conquered and sacrificed Tikal's king. Tikal and other Petén kingdoms suffered under Caracol's rule until the late 7th century.

TIKAL'S RENAISSANCE

Around 700 a powerful king named Moon Double Comb (682–734), also called Ah Cacau (Lord Chocolate), 26th successor of Yax Moch Xoc, ascended Tikal's throne.

He restored not only its military strength, but also its primacy as the Mayan world's most resplendent city. He and his successors were responsible for building most of the surviving temples around the Gran Plaza. He was buried beneath the staggering height of Templo I.

Tikal's greatness waned around 900, part of the mysterious general collapse of lowland Mayan civilization.

No doubt the Itzáes, who occupied Tayasal (now Flores), knew of Tikal in the Late Postclassic period (1200 to 1530). Perhaps they even came to worship at the shrines of their old gods. Spanish missionary friars left brief references to these junglebound structures, but their writings moldered in libraries for centuries.

REDISCOVERY
It wasn't until 1848 that the Guatemalan government sent out an expedition, under Modesto Méndez and Ambrosio Tut, to visit the site. In 1877 Dr Gustav Bernoulli of Switzerland visited Tikal and removed lintels from Templos I and IV to Basel, where they are still on view in the Museum für Völkerkunde.

Scientific exploration of Tikal began with the arrival of English archaeologist Alfred P Maudslay in 1881; others continuing his work included Teobert Maler, Alfred M Tozzer and RE Merwin. Tozzer worked tirelessly at Tikal from the beginning of the century until his death in 1954. Tikal's inscriptions were studied and deciphered by Sylvanus G Morley.

Since 1956 archaeological research and restoration has been carried out by the University of Pennsylvania and the Guatemalan Instituto de Antropología e Historia. Parque Nacional Tikal was declared a Unesco World Heritage Site in 1979.

Orientation & Information
The 550-sq-km Parque Nacional Tikal contains thousands of separate ruined structures. The central area of the city occupied about 16 sq km, with more than 4000 structures.

The road from Flores enters the national park 17km south of the ruins. The gate opens at 6am. Here you must pay the entrance fee; if you enter after about 3pm, your ticket should be stamped with the following day's date, meaning that it will be valid for that next day, too. Multilingual guides are available at the visitors center (US$40 for a half-day tour for up to four people, plus US$5 for each extra person). These authorized guides always display their accreditation carnet, listing the languages they speak.

Near the visitors center are Tikal's hotels, a camping area, a few small *comedores*, a tiny post office, a police post, two museums and a disused airstrip. From the visitors' center it's a 1.5km walk (20 to 30 minutes) southwest to the Gran Plaza. To visit all the major building complexes, you must walk at least 10km, so wear comfortable shoes.

For more complete information on the monuments at Tikal, pick up a copy of *Tikal – A Handbook of the Ancient Maya Ruins*, by William R Coe, available in Flores and at Tikal for around US$14.

It's a good idea to wear shoes with good rubber treads that grip well. The ruins here can be very slick from rain and organic material, especially during the wet season. Bring plenty of water, as dehydration is a real danger if you're walking around all day in the heat. Please don't feed the *pisotes* (coatis) that wander about the site.

The Jaguar Inn will exchange US-dollar cash and traveler's checks at a poor rate.

Sights & Activities
GRAN PLAZA
Follow the signs to reach the Gran Plaza (Great Plaza). The path enters the plaza around **Templo I**, the Templo del Gran Jaguar (Temple of the Grand Jaguar), built for King Moon Double Comb. The king may have worked out the plans himself, but it was erected above his tomb by his son, who succeeded to the throne in 734. Burial goods included 180 jade objects, 90 pieces of bone carved with hieroglyphs, pearls and stingray spines, used for ritual bloodletting. At the top of the 44m-high temple is a small enclosure of three rooms covered by a corbelled arch. The lofty roof comb was originally adorned with reliefs and bright paint, perhaps symbolizing the 13 realms of the Mayan heaven.

Since at least two people tumbled to their deaths, the stairs up Templo I have been closed. Don't fret: the views from **Templo II** just across the way are nearly as awe-inspiring. Templo II was once almost as high as Templo I, but now measures 38m without its roof comb.

The **Acrópolis del Norte** (North Acropolis), while not as impressive as the twin temples, is of great significance. Archaeologists have uncovered about 100 structures, with evidence of occupation as far back as 400 BC. The Maya rebuilt on top of older structures, and the many layers, combined with the elaborate burials, added sanctity and power to their temples. Look for the two huge, powerful wall masks, uncovered from an earlier structure. The final version of the acropolis, as it stood around AD 800, had more than 12 temples atop a vast platform, many of them the work of King Moon Double Comb.

On the plaza side of the Acrópolis del Norte are two rows of stelae. Though hardly as impressive as those at Copán or Quiriguá, these served the same purpose: to record the great deeds of the kings of Tikal, to sanctify their memory and to add 'power' to the surrounding temples and plazas.

ACRÓPOLIS CENTRAL

On the south side of the Gran Plaza, this maze of courtyards, little rooms and small temples is thought by some to have been a residential palace for Tikal's nobility. Others believe the tiny rooms may have been used for sacred rites, as graffiti found within suggests. Over the centuries the room configuration was repeatedly changed, indicating perhaps that this 'palace' was in fact a residence changed to accommodate different groups of relatives. A century ago, one part of the acropolis, called Palacio de Maler, provided lodgings for archaeologist Teobert Maler when he worked at Tikal.

PLAZA OESTE

The West Plaza is north of Templo II. On its north side is a large Late Classic temple. To the south, across the Calzada Tozzer (Tozzer Causeway), is Templo III, 55m high. Yet to be uncovered, it allows you to see a temple the way the last Tikal Maya and first explorers saw them. The causeway leading to Templo IV was one of several sacred ways built among the complexes, no doubt for astronomical as well as aesthetic reasons.

ACRÓPOLIS DEL SUR & TEMPLO V

Due south of the Gran Plaza is the South Acropolis. Excavation has just begun on this two-hectare mass of masonry. The palaces on top are from Late Classic times, but earlier constructions probably go back a thousand years.

Templo V, just east of the Acrópolis del Sur, is 58m high and was built around AD 700. Unlike the other great temples, this one has rounded corners and one tiny room at the top. The room is less than 1m deep, but its walls are up to 4.5m thick. Restoration of this temple started in 1991 and was completed in 2004. It's now open to the public via a wooden stairway to the top.

PLAZA DE LOS SIETE TEMPLOS

The Plaza of the Seven Temples is on the other side of the Acrópolis del Sur. The little temples, clustered together, were built in Late Classic times, though the structures beneath go back at least a millennium. Note the skull and crossbones on the central temple (the one with the stela and altar in front). On the plaza's north side is an unusual triple ball court; another, larger version in the same design stands just south of Templo I.

EL MUNDO PERDIDO

About 400m southwest of the Gran Plaza is El Mundo Perdido (The Lost World), a complex of 38 structures surrounding a huge pyramid. Unlike the rest of Tikal, where Late Classic construction overlays earlier work, El Mundo Perdido holds buildings of many different periods. The large pyramid is thought to be Preclassic with some later repairs and renovations, the Templo del Talud-Tablero (Temple of the Three Rooms) is an Early Classic structure, and the Templo de las Calaveras (Temple of the Skulls) is Late Classic.

The pyramid, 32m high and 80m along its base, had huge masks flanking each stairway but no temple structure at the top. Each side displays a slightly different architectural style. Tunnels dug by archaeologists reveal four similar pyramids beneath the outer face; the earliest (Structure 5C-54 Sub 2B) dates from 700 BC, making the pyramid the oldest Mayan structure in Tikal.

TEMPLO IV & COMPLEJO N

Complex N, near Templo IV, is an example of the 'twin-temple' complexes popular during the Late Classic period. These complexes are thought to have commemorated the completion of a *katun*, or 20-year cycle, in the Mayan calendar. This one was built in 711 by King Moon Double Comb to mark the 14th *katun* of Baktun 9. The king is portrayed on Stela 16, one of Tikal's finest.

Templo IV, at 64m, is Tikal's highest building. It was completed about 741, in the reign of King Moon Double Comb's son. A series of steep wooden steps and ladders take you to the top.

TEMPLO DE LAS INSCRIPCIONES (TEMPLO VI)

Compared to Copán or Quiriguá, Tikal sports relatively few inscriptions. The exception is this temple, 1.2km southeast of the Gran Plaza. On the rear of the 12m-high roof comb is a long inscription; the sides and cornice of the roof comb bear glyphs as well. The inscriptions give us the date AD 766. Stela 21 and Altar 9, standing before the temple, date from 736. Badly damaged, the stela has now been repaired.

NORTHERN COMPLEXES

About 1km north of the Gran Plaza is **Complejo P**. Like Complejo N, it's a Late Classic twin-temple complex that probably commemorated the end of a *katun*. **Complejo M**, next to it, was partially torn down by Late Classic Maya to provide material for the causeway – now named after Alfred Maudslay – that runs southwest to Templo IV.

Complejos Q and **R**, about 300m due north of the Gran Plaza, are Late Classic twin-pyramid complexes. Complejo Q is perhaps the best example of the twin-temple type, as it has been mostly restored. Stela 22 and Altar 10 are excellent examples of Late Classic Tikal relief carving, dated 771.

WARNING

The Templo VI is remote and there have been incidents of robbery and rape of single travelers and couples in the past. Though safety has been greatly improved at Tikal, ask a guard before you make the trek out here, or come in a group.

Complejo O, due west of these complexes on the west side of the Calzada Maler, has an uncarved stela and altar in its north enclosure. The point of stelae was to record happenings – why did this one remain uncarved?

MUSEUMS

Tikal has two museums. The **Museo Lítico** (Museum of Stone; admission free; ⊗ 9am-noon & 1-4:30pm Mon-Fri, 9am-4pm Sat & Sun), the larger of the two, is in the visitors center. It houses a number of stelae and carved stones from the ruins. The photographs taken by Maudslay and Maler of the jungle-covered temples in various stages of discovery in the late 19th century are particularly striking.

The **Museo Tikal** or **Museo Cerámico** (Museum of Ceramics; admission US$1.30; ⊗ 9am-5pm Mon-Fri, 9am-4pm Sat & Sun) is near the Jaguar Inn. It has some fascinating exhibits, including the burial goods of King Moon Double Comb, carved jade, inscribed bones, shells, stelae, ceramics and other items recovered from the excavations.

BIRD-WATCHING

Around 300 bird species (migratory and endemic) have been recorded at Tikal. Early morning is the best time for bird-watching; even amateurs will have their share of sightings. Bring binoculars, tread quietly and be patient and you'll probably see some of the following birds:

- tody motmots, four trogon species and royal flycatchers around the Templo de las Inscripciones
- two oriole species, keel-billed toucans and collared aracaris in El Mundo Perdido
- great curassows, three species of woodpecker, crested guans, plain chachalacas and three tanager species around Complejo P
- three kingfisher species, jacanas, blue herons, two sandpiper species and great kiskadees at the Aguada Tikal (Tikal Reservoir) near the entrance; tiger herons in the huge ceiba tree along the entrance path
- red-capped and white-collared manakins near Complejo Q; emerald toucanets near Complejo R.

TRAILS

The Sendero Benilj'a'a, a 3km trail with three sections, begins in front of the Jungle

EUREKA!!

Two gigantic, menacing looking masks and 120 precious jade objects found in Guatemala's northern Petén region are changing the world's understanding of Mayan civilization. Dug out by archaeologists between 2001 and 2004 under the auspices of the National Geographic Society, the discoveries at the ancient city of Cival point to a complex society of 10,000 that flourished at about 150 BC, during the Preclassic period. The only problem is that the elaborate stucco carvings and ritual jade, plus the architectural layout of the ancient city, are usually associated with the Classic period. Not anymore, say experts, who agree that the finds at Cival mean the trajectory of the Mayan civilization and chronology of its development may have to be rolled back several hundred years. Archaeologists surmise that Cival, which was mysteriously abandoned, was the biggest city of the Preclassic period.

Lodge. Ruta Monte Medio and Ruta Monte Medio Alto (both one hour) are accessible year-round. Ruta Monte Bajo (35 minutes) is accessible only in summer. A short interpretive trail called El Misterio de la Vida Maya (The Mystery of Maya Life) leads to the Gran Plaza.

Tours

All the hotels can arrange guided tours of the ruins, as well as tours to other places in the region.

At the national park entrance, you can take a fairly expensive one-hour treetop tour through the forest by harness attached to a series of cables linking trees up to 300m apart, at **Tikal Canopy Tour** (☎ 5412-7252; US$25; ☼ 7am-5pm).

Sleeping & Eating

Most hotels are booked in advance by tour groups. In recent years travelers have logged numerous complaints of price gouging, unacceptable accommodations and 'lost' reservations at these hotels. And the value you get compared to hotels in the rest of the country is laughable. It may be best to stay in Flores or El Remate and visit Tikal on day trips or on a tour.

On the other hand, staying at Tikal enables you to relax and savor the dawn and dusk, when most of the jungle fauna can be observed.

There's no need to make reservations if you want to stay at Tikal's **campground** (per person US$4, cabañas per person US$6.50) opposite the visitors center. This is a large, grassy area with a clean bathroom block, plenty of space for tents, *palapa* shelters for hanging hammocks, and tiny cabañas.

Jungle Lodge (☎ 7926-0519, 2361-4098; www.jungle lodge.guate.com; s/d US$26/31, with private bathroom US$54/72; P ☼) The largest and most attractive of the hotels was built originally to house archaeologists excavating and restoring Tikal. It has 34 decent rooms in duplex bungalows, each with ceiling fan, private hot-water bathroom and two double beds. In an older section are 12 much-less-attractive rooms with shared bathroom. There is a swimming pool, large garden grounds, and a restaurant/bar with breakfast for US$5 and lunch or dinner for US$10.

Tikal Inn (☎ 7926-1917/50/53, ☎ /fax 7926-0065; hoteltikalinn@itelgua.com; s/d US$57/81 incl dinner & breakfast; P ☼) This is the second most attractive place to stay. It has 17 rooms in the main building, as well as bungalows, which are slightly nicer, plus gardens, a swimming pool and restaurant. The accommodations are simple but clean and quite large, all with private hot-water bathroom and ceiling fan. The rooms in the main building go down to US$37/54 when they decide it isn't high season. The electricity only operates from 6pm to 10pm.

As you arrive in Tikal, look on the right-hand side of the road to find the little **comedores** (☼ breakfast, lunch & dinner). Comedor Tikal seems to be the most popular. These places offer rustic and agreeable surroundings and are run by local people serving huge plates of fairly tasty food at low prices. Chicken or meat dishes cost around US$4.50, pasta and burgers a little less.

Picnic tables beneath shelters are located just off Tikal's Gran Plaza, with soft-drink and water peddlers standing by, but no food is sold. If you want to spend all day at the ruins without having to make the 20- to

30-minute walk back to the *comedores*, carry food and water with you.

Getting There & Away
For details of transport to and from Flores and Santa Elena, see p175. Coming from Belize, you could consider taking a taxi from the border to Tikal for around US$40. Otherwise get a bus to Puente Ixlú, sometimes called El Cruce, and switch to a northbound minibus or bus for the remaining 36km to Tikal. Note that there is little northbound traffic after lunch. Heading from Tikal to Belize, start early in the morning and get off at Puente Ixlú to catch a bus or minibus eastward. Be wary of shuttles to Belize advertised at Tikal: these have been known to detour to Flores to pick up passengers!

UAXACTÚN
Uaxactún (wah-shahk-*toon*), 23km north of Tikal along a poor, unpaved road through the jungle, was Tikal's political and military rival in Late Preclassic times. It was eventually conquered by Tikal's King Great Jaguar Paw in the mid-4th century, and was subservient to its great southern sister for centuries thereafter.

Villagers in Uaxactún live in houses lined up along the airstrip. They make a living by collecting chicle, *pimienta* (allspice) and *xate* from the surrounding forest.

Ruins
The pyramids at Uaxactún have been uncovered and stabilized to prevent further deterioration; they were not restored. White mortar is the mark of the repair crews, who patched cracks to keep out water and roots. Much of the work on the famous Templo E-VII-Sub was done by Earthwatch volunteers in 1974.

Turn right from the airstrip to reach Grupos E and H, a 15-minute walk. Perhaps the most significant temple here is E-VII-Sub, among the earliest intact temples excavated, with foundations going back perhaps to 2000 BC. It lay beneath much larger structures, which have been stripped away. On its flat top are sockets for poles that would have supported a wood-and-thatch temple.

About 20 minutes' walk to the northwest of the runway are Grupos A and B.

At Grupo A, early excavators sponsored by Andrew Carnegie cut into the temple sides indiscriminately, looking for graves, occasionally using dynamite. This destroyed many temples, which are now being reconstructed.

If you are visiting Uaxactún from Tikal, no fee is charged. But if you are going to Uaxactún without stopping to visit Tikal, you still have to pass through the Parque Nacional Tikal and will have to pay a US$2 Uaxactún-only fee at the park entrance.

Tours to Uaxactún can be arranged at hotels in Tikal. The **Jungle Lodge** (p185) has a trip departing daily at 8am and returning at 1pm, costing US$60 for one to four people.

Sleeping & Eating
Campamento, Hotel & Restaurante El Chiclero (in San Benito ☎ /fax 7926-1095; camping US$5, s/d US$12/15) On the north side of the airstrip, this has 10 small and very basic rooms with good mattresses and mosquito-netted ceilings and windows, and does the best food in town (US$6 for soup and a main course with rice). Accommodations prices are very negotiable. Also here is a small museum with shelves full of Mayan pottery from Uaxactún and around. The owners can organize trips to more remote sites such as El Mirador, Xultún, Río Azul, Nakbe and La Muralla.

Aldana's Lodge (camping per person US$2, r per person US$3.25) To the right off the street leading to Grupos B and A, this has cheaper accommodations and also offers tours to other sites, but has erratic water supplies. Camping using their equipment costs US$2.50 per person.

A few basic **comedores** also provide food.

Getting There & Away
A Pinita bus supposedly leaves Santa Elena for Uaxactún (US$2.50) at 1pm, passing through Tikal about 3pm to 3:30pm, and starting back for Santa Elena from Uaxactún at 6pm. But its schedule is rubbery and it can arrive in Tikal any time up to about 5pm and in Uaxactún up to about 6:30pm. During the rainy season (May to October, sometimes extending into November), the road from Tikal to Uaxactún can become pretty muddy: locals say it is always passable but a 4WD vehicle might be needed during the wet.

If you're driving, the last chance to fill your fuel tank as you come from the south is at Puente Ixlú, just south of El Remate. A taxi from El Remate to Uaxactún and back, including waiting time, should cost about US$40; bargain hard.

From Uaxactún, unpaved roads lead to other ruins at El Zotz (about 30km southwest), Xultún (35km northeast) and Río Azul (100km northeast).

EASTWARD TO BELIZE

It's 100km from Flores to Melchor de Mencos, the Guatemalan town on the border with Belize. See p175 for information on bus services to the border and also on more expensive services going right through to Belize City and Chetumal, Mexico.

The road to the border diverges from the Flores–Tikal road at **Puente Ixlú** (also called El Cruce), 27km from Flores. It continues paved until about 25km short of the border. The stretch between Puente Ixlú and the border has been the scene of a few highway robberies.

There should be no fees at the border for entering or leaving Guatemala, and none for entering Belize. But travelers leaving Belize usually have to pay a US$13.75 departure tax.

There are money-changers at the border with whom you can change sufficient funds for immediate needs. Taxis run between the border and the nearest town in Belize, Benque Viejo del Carmen (3km away), for around U$0.50 per person. Bus services operate from Benque to Belize City (US$3, three hours) about every half hour from 11am to 4pm.

EL PETÉN TO CHIAPAS & TABASCO (MEXICO)
Via Bethel/La Técnica & Frontera Corozal

The only route with regular transport connections is via Bethel or La Técnica on the eastern (Guatemalan) bank of the Río Usumacinta and Frontera Corozal on the Mexican bank. See p175 for details of bus services to and from Bethel and La Técnica and shuttle minibus services all the way through to Palenque. Guatemalan immigration is in Bethel: bus drivers to La Técnica will normally stop and wait for you to do the formalities in Bethel.

It's cheaper and quicker from La Técnica than from Bethel, but crossing at La Técnica means a longer bus journey on the Guatemalan side. Minibuses leave Frontera Corozal for Palenque at about 5am, 10am, noon and 3pm (US$5, three hours).

If you want to stay in the Usumacinta area, perhaps to visit the Mayan ruins at Yaxchilán on the Mexican side of the river, the riverside **Posada Maya** (☎ 5801-1799/1800; s/d/tr US$9/18/28), 1km outside Bethel, has a great location and comfortable, thatched bungalows, plus tent and hammock shelters. Boats from Bethel to Yaxchilán cost between US$11 and US$22 per person for four to 12 people, round-trip.

Other Routes

You can also cross into Mexico by boat down the Río de la Pasión from Sayaxché to Benemérito de las Américas, or down the Río San Pedro from \ to La Palma. But there are no regular passenger services on either river and you will probably have to rent a boat privately for around US$80 on the Río San Pedro or US$100-plus on the Río de la Pasión. Both trips take around four hours.

La Palma has transport connections with Tenosique, Tabasco, from where minibuses leave for Palenque up to 5:30pm. Benemérito has good bus and minibus connections with Palenque. Both Sayaxché and El Naranjo have bus and minibus connections with Flores (p175).

A possible alternative on the Río San Pedro route is to take a boat from El Naranjo only as far as El Ceibo, on the border, for around US$30. From El Ceibo there are a few bus services to Tenosique (US$2.50, 1½ hours), the last one leaving about 5:30pm. Mexico has no immigration facilities at Benemérito or El Ceibo – you have to get your passport stamped at Frontera Corozal or Tenosique, or failing that, Palenque.

El Naranjo, Tenosique and Benemérito all have a few basic accommodations.

SAYAXCHÉ

Sayaxché, on the south bank of the Río de la Pasión, 61km southwest of Flores, is the closest town to nine or 10 scattered Mayan archaeological sites, including Ceibal, Aguateca, Dos Pilas, Tamarindito and Altar de Sacrificios. Otherwise, for travelers it's little more than a transportation halt between Flores and Cobán.

Minibuses and buses from Santa Elena stop on the north bank of the Río de la Pasión. Frequent ferries (pedestrians/cars US$0.15/2) carry you across to the town.

Banoro (9am-4pm Mon-Fri, 10am-1pm Sat), just up the main street from Hotel Guayacán, changes US-dollar cash and traveler's checks.

Hotel Guayacán (☎ 7926-6111; s or d downstairs with fan US$17, upstairs with air-con US$20; P) Right on the south bank of the river in Sayaxché, the Guayacán is the best place in town, with good rooms equipped with solid wooden beds and tile floors. It also has the best restaurant, on a terrace overlooking the river. Chicken, fish or meat with salad and fries costs US$4 to US$6.

El Botanero (mains around US$3.50) Directly behind Hotel Mayapán on the next street up the hill, this is a dark, funky place full of atmosphere, with stools and tables hewn from tree trunks. It serves a variety of beef, chicken and seafood dishes and it's a good place to kick back and have a beer.

Restaurant Yaxkin, a couple of doors from Hotel Mayapán, is typical of the few other eateries in town: basic, family-run and inexpensive.

Getting There & Away

Hwy 5 from Flores to Sayaxché is now all paved except the first 20km or so out of Flores. The road south from Sayaxché to Cobán is now also all paved except for one stretch of about 20km. See p175 for details of transportation from there. The return schedule is similar.

Southbound from Sayaxché, buses and minibuses leave at 5am, 6am, 10am and 3pm for Cobán (US$5.25, five hours). Most if not all of these go via Raxrujá and Sebol, not via Chisec. Other minibuses and buses go just to Raxrujá (US$2.60), about hourly from 7am to 3pm. For Chisec (not covered in this book), you can change in Raxrujá or at San Antonio Las Cuevas. Vehicles may start from the southern riverbank or they may start from the Texaco station opposite Hotel Guayacán.

For river transport talk to any of the boatmen on the riverbank or to **Servicio de Lanchas Don Pedro** (☎ /fax 7928-6109), run by the experienced and affable Pedro Mendéz, with an office on the riverbank where you can arrange transportation and guides to any of the area sites, for slightly higher prices than in most other boats.

A trip all the way down the Río de la Pasión to Benemérito de las Américas (Mexico), with stops at the ruins of Altar de Sacrificios and Guatemalan immigration at Pipiles, should cost between US$100 and US$150.

Ceibal

Unimportant during the Classic period, Ceibal grew rapidly thereafter, attaining a population of perhaps 10,000 by AD 900. Much of the growth may have been due to immigration from what is now Chiapas, in Mexico, because the art and culture of Ceibal seems to have changed markedly during this period. The Postclassic period saw the decline of Ceibal, after which its low ruined temples were quickly covered by thick jungle.

Ceibal is not one of the most impressive Mayan sites, but the journey there is among the most memorable. A two-hour voyage on the jungle-bound Río de la Pasión brings you to a primitive dock. After landing you clamber up a rocky path beneath gigantic trees and vines to reach the archaeological zone.

Smallish temples, many still (or again) covered with jungle, surround two principal plazas. In front of a few temples, and standing seemingly alone on jungle paths, are magnificent, intact stelae. Exploring the site takes about two hours.

See p171 for tours to Ceibal. Otherwise, talk to any of the boatmen in Sayaxché. They charge around US$30 for one person plus US$3 for each extra person, round-trip including waiting time. You should hire a guide to see the site, as some of the finest stelae are off the plazas in the jungle. Most *lancheros*, conveniently, also serve as guides.

If you wish, you can get to Ceibal cheaper by land: get any bus, minibus or pickup heading south from Sayaxché on highway 5 (toward Raxrujá and Chisec) and get off after 9km at Paraíso (US$0.25), from which a dirt track leads 8km east to Ceibal. You may have to walk the last 8km. In the rainy season this stretch may not be passable.

LAGUNA PETEXBATÚN ARCHAEOLOGICAL SITES

Laguna Petexbatún is a 6km-long lake to the southwest of Sayaxché approached by an hour's *lancha* ride up the Río Petexbatún, a tributary of the Río de la Pasión, from Sayaxché.

If you have limited time and funds, **Aguateca**, just off the far-south end of the lake, is the easiest reached of the sites and the most immediately impressive. The ruins are on a hilltop, defended by cliffs facing the lake and by a ravine. There are two main groups, both in process of restoration: the Grupo del Palacio where the ruler lived, and the Plaza Mayor (Main Plaza) to its south, where glass-fiber copies of several stelae showing finely attired rulers stand beside the fallen originals. The rangers are usually happy to let people camp at Aguateca (bring supplies with you). They might even be willing to show you the way overland to Dos Pilas (11km northwest). Howler monkeys are much in evidence early and late in the day. The archaeological highlight of the partly excavated and cleared **Dos Pilas** site is a hieroglyphic stairway with five 6m-wide steps, each with two rows of superbly preserved glyphs, climbing to the base of the royal palace near the main plaza.

REMOTE MAYAN SITES

Several sites of interest to archaeology buffs and adventurous travelers are open for limited tourism. Few can be visited without a guide, but many businesses in Flores and Santa Elena offer trips to sites deep in the jungle. Few of these tours offer anything approaching comfort, and you should be prepared for basic conditions.

Yaxhá

This beautiful and quite large Classic Mayan **ceremonial site** (US$1.30; ☺ 6am-5pm) is 11km north of the Puente Ixlú–Melchor de Mencos road, from a turning 32km from Puente Ixlú and 33km from Melchor de Mencos. The access road is unpaved. Yaxhá's setting, on a hill overlooking two sizable lakes – Laguna Yaxhá and Laguna Sacnab – makes it particularly worth visiting. It takes about 1½ hours to wander around the main groups of ruins, which are gradually being cleared and restored, though many mounds

are still under vegetation. The high point (literally), towering above all else, is **Templo 216** in the Acrópolis Este (Eastern Acrópolis), which affords magnificent views in every direction. On an island near the far (south) shore of Laguna Yaxhá is a separate, Late Postclassic archaeological site, Topoxté, whose dense covering of ruined temples and dwellings may date back to the Itzá culture that occupied Flores island at the time the Spanish came.

On the northern lakeshore below the Yaxhá ruins is **Campamento Yaxhá**, where you can camp for free on raised platforms with thatched roofs and where you might be able to find a boatman to take you over to Topoxté. On the southern shore, 250m off the approach road, is the excellent **Campamento Ecológico El Sombrero** (☎ 5800-0179; sombrero@guate.net; s/d/tr US$18/29/44, with private bathroom US$29/40/55; Ⓟ), which has good-sized, neat and clean rooms in mosquito-netted bungalows overlooking the lake. There's a good restaurant here, with a small library on local archaeology, and *lancha* tours to Topoxté are offered (US$20 for up to three people, US$26 for four to nine people) as well as horseback riding and day trips to Nakum and El Naranjo, other Classic period sites to the north and northeast of Yaxhá.

Don't swim in the lakes by the way – there are crocodiles!

Agencies in Flores (p171) and El Remate offer organized trips to Yaxhá, some combined with Nakum and/or Tikal. To get there independently you could get a Melchor de Mencos–bound bus or minibus as far as the Yaxhá turnoff (and be prepared to walk the 11km to the site), or find a taxi in El Remate, Puente Ixlú (about US$30 round-trip) or elsewhere.

Other Sites

El Zotz is about 25km west of Tikal. Zotz means 'bat,' and you'll encounter plenty on a trek to this archaeological site in the **Biotopo San Miguel La Palotada**. Among the many unexcavated mounds and ruins is Devil's Pyramid, which is so tall that you can see the temples of Tikal from its summit. Trips to El Zotz can be extended to include a trek to Tikal.

El Perú, 62km northwest from Flores, lies along La Ruta Guacamaya (Scarlet Macaw

Trail) in the **Parque Nacional Laguna del Tigre**. The trek starts in Paso Caballos and continues by boat along the Río San Pedro. Several important structures here have been dated to between AD 300 and 900. Archaeologists believe El Perú was an important commercial center.

Río Azul is small but important, just over 80km northeast of Tikal and within the **Parque Nacional Mirador – Río Azul**. The biggest attractions you will find here are the vibrant cave paintings that adorn the tombs sprinkled throughout the site. It is accessible by vehicle.

El Mirador is buried within the furthest reaches of the Petén jungle, just 7km from the Mexican border, deep within the **Reserva de Biósfera Maya**. A trip here involves an arduous 60km trek in primitive conditions. The metropolis at El Mirador flourished between 150 BC and AD 150, when it was abandoned for mysterious reasons. The site holds the tallest pyramid ever built in the Mayan world: El Tigre is over 60m high, and its base covers 18,000 sq meters. Its twin, La Danta (Tapir), though technically smaller, soars higher because it's built on a rise. There are hundreds of buildings at El Mirador, but almost everything is still hidden beneath the jungle.

This trip is not for the faint of heart. For more on this incredible site, see the September 1987 *National Geographic* article, 'An Early Maya Metropolis Uncovered: El Mirador.' This is the most thorough mainstream investigative report ever written about the site.

GUATEMALA DIRECTORY

ACCOMMODATIONS

Guatemalan accommodations range from luxury hotels to budget hotels to ultra-budget guesthouses called *hospedajes, casas de huéspedes* or *pensiones*.

A 'matrimonial' is generally a room with a double bed, whereas a double is a twin (ie two single beds).

Budget doubles under about US$10 are generally small, dark and not particularly clean. Nor may the security be the best in such places. An exception is the low-priced dormitories that exist alongside other rooms in generally better establishments. A typical US$20 double should be clean, sizable and airy, with a private bathroom, TV and, in hot parts of the country, a fan.

Mid-range rooms are always comfortable: private hot-water bathroom, TV, decent beds, fan and/or air-con are standard. Good mid-range hotels have attractive public areas such as dining rooms, bars and swimming pools. In hot regions the rooms may be attractive wooden bungalows with thatch roofs, verandahs and hammocks; in cooler areas they may be in beautiful, old, colonial-style houses with antique furnishings and lovely patios. The smaller the establishment, the better the attention to guests is likely to be. Many B&Bs in Guatemala fit this description.

Guatemala City's international-class business-oriented hotels, Antigua's very finest hostelries and a few resort hotels elsewhere constitute nearly the whole top-end accommodations in the country.

Room rates often go up in touristy places during Semana Santa (Easter Week), Christmas-New Year's and July and August. Semana Santa is the major Guatemalan holiday week of the year, and prices can rise by anything from 30% to 100%. At these times, advance reservations are a very good idea.

Room rates are subject to two taxes: 12% IVA (value-added tax) and 10% to pay for the activities of Inguat. All prices in this book include both taxes, though some of the more expensive hotels forget to include them when they quote their prices.

ACTIVITIES

Guatemala's **volcanoes** are irresistible challenges, and many can be climbed in one day from Antigua or Quetzaltenango. There's further great hill country in the Ixil Triangle and the Cuchumatanes mountains north of Huehuetenango, especially around Todos Santos. Lago de Atitlán is surrounded by spectacular trails, although robberies here have made some routes inadvisable. **Treks** of several days are perfectly feasible and agencies in Antigua, Quetzaltenango and Nebaj can guide you. In the Petén jungles, treks to **remote archaeological sites** such as El Mirador and El Perú offer an exciting challenge.

There is probably no better way to experience the Guatemalan highlands than by

bicycle. Antigua (especially), Panajachel and Quetzaltenango are the best launching points, with agencies offering trips and/or equipment.

Guatemala attracts **cavers** from all around the world. The limestone area around Cobán is particularly riddled with cave systems – Lanquín's are among those open for tourist visits. There are also exciting caves to visit from Finca Ixobel, located near Poptún.

Few national parks and reserves have many tourist facilities, but they do have lots of **wildlife- and bird-watching**. Fine bird-watching locales in the Petén jungles include Tikal, El Mirador, Cerro Cahuí, Laguna Petexbatún and (for scarlet macaws) Las Guacamayas biological station. Elsewhere the wetlands of Bocas del Polochic, Punta de Manabique and Monterrico, the Río Dulce and Laguna Lachuá national parks and the Biotopo del Quetzal also provide lots of avian variety. Mammals are more elusive, but you should see several species at Tikal. Monkey fans will also be happy at the Reserva Natural Atitlán (Panajachel), the Bocas del Polochic and Biotopo Cerro Cahuí.

Opportunities for a **gallop, trot** or even a **horse trek** are on the rise. Antigua, Quetzaltenango, El Remate, Salamá and Río Dulce all have stables.

You can **dive** inside a volcanic caldera at Lago de Atitlán, **raft** the white waters of the Río Cahabón near Lanquín, **sail** from the yacht haven of Río Dulce, and **canoe** or **kayak** the waterways of Monterrico, Lívingston, the Bocas del Polochic or Punta de Manabique.

BOOKS

Lonely Planet publishes a range of books relating to Guatemala – from the richly detailed *Guatemala* guide to the beautiful *Watching Wildlife Central America* and the more practical *Read This First: Central and South America, Healthy Travel Central and South America* and *Latin American Spanish Phrasebook*.

Guatemalan Journey, by Stephen Benz, is one to enjoy while you're in Guatemala. It casts an honest and funny modern traveler's eye on the country. So does Anthony Daniels' *Sweet Waist of America* (also published as *South of the Border: Guatemalan Days*),

where the medic author pinpoints some of the country's quirky contradictions.

In *Sacred Monkey River*, Christopher Shaw explores by canoe the jungle-clad basin of the Río Usumacinta, a cradle of ancient Maya civilization along the Mexico-Guatemala border – a great read.

Bird of Life, Bird of Death, by Jonathan Evan Maslow (subtitled 'A naturalist's journey through a land of political turmoil'), tells of the author's searches for the resplendent quetzal (the 'bird of life'), which he found increasingly endangered, while the *zopilote* (vulture), the 'bird of death,' flourished.

BUSINESS HOURS

Guatemalan shops and businesses are generally open from 8am to noon and 2pm to 6pm, Monday to Saturday, but there are many variations. Banks typically open 9am to 5pm Monday to Friday (again with variations), and 9am to 1pm Saturday. Government offices usually open 8am to 4pm, Monday to Friday. Official business is always better conducted in the morning.

General meal times are breakfast between 6am and 10am, lunch from noon to 2pm, and dinner 7pm to 9pm, often a bit earlier in rural areas.

COURSES

Guatemala is celebrated for its many language schools. A spot of study here is a great way not only to learn Spanish but also to meet locals and get an inside angle on the culture.

Guatemalan language schools are a lot cheaper than those in Mexico, but few people go away disappointed. There are so many schools, it's essential to check out a few before choosing. It's not hard to see whether a school is professional and well organized, or whether its teachers are qualified and experienced.

Antigua (p84), with its lively students' and travelers' social scene, is the most popular place to study, with about 75 schools. Quetzaltenango (p115), the second-most popular, perhaps attracts a more serious type of student. San Pedro La Laguna (p101) and Panajachel (p94), on the Lago de Atitlán, both have a handful of language schools, and if you'd like to learn Spanish while hanging out in a remote mountain town, there are schools in Todos Santos (p125). On average schools charge US$110 to US$120 for four hours of one-on-one classes, five days a week, plus accommodation with a local family.

You can start any day at many schools, any week at all of them, and study for as long as you like. All decent schools offer a variety of elective activities, from salsa classes to movies to volcano hikes. Many schools offer classes in Mayan languages as well as Spanish.

DANGERS & ANNOYANCES

No one could pretend that Guatemala is a safe country – there are just too many stories of robbery (often armed) for that. Rapes and murders of tourists have also happened, but the two most frequently reported types of nasty incident involving tourists are highway robbery, when a vehicle is stopped and its occupants relieved of their belongings, and robberies on walking trails. For a scary litany of recent incidents, visit the website of the US embassy in Guatemala City (http://usembassy.state .gov/guatemala) and click on 'Recent Crime Incidents Involving Foreigners.' Marginally less alarming information is on the US Department of State's website (http://travel .state.gov/travel_warnings.html) and the UK Foreign and Commonwealth Office site (www.fco.gov.uk).

Vehicles carrying tourists, such as shuttle minibuses and buses along heavily touristed routes, seem to be a prime target for highway robbery. On this basis, some people argue that chicken buses are the most risk-free way to travel, but these are certainly not exempt from holdups. No road in the country is free of risk, but most frequently mentioned are the Interamericana (CA-1) between the Antigua and Panajachel turnoffs and near the El Salvador border, the CA-2 near the El Salvador and Mexican borders, and the CA-13 between the Belize border and the Puente Ixlú (El Cruce) junction.

Robberies against tourists on walking trails tend to occur in isolated spots on well-known walks. Some trails around Lago de Atitlán (p90) and near Lívingston (p163) are particularly notorious. Although foreigners climbing the volcanoes around Antigua sometimes used to

be robbed and even raped or murdered, recent tourist-safety measures have reduced the problem dramatically (p81). The Tikal archaeological site, Pacaya volcano and Cerro de la Cruz (Antigua), all the scenes of several incidents not so long ago, have become (for now) safer because of increased police and ranger presence designed to protect tourism.

Another danger category is pickpocketing, bag snatching, bag slitting and the like in crowded bus stations, buses, streets and markets, but also in empty, dark city streets.

Hiking on active volcanoes obviously has an element of risk – get the latest story before you head out. In the wet season, go up volcanoes in the morning before rain and possible thunderstorms set in. In 2002 a Canadian tourist was killed by lightning on Pacaya volcano.

There have been a few bizarre incidents in which foreign visitors have been unjustly suspected of malicious designs against Guatemalan children. In 2000 a Japanese tourist photographing a child, and his driver, were killed in Todos Santos by crowds inflamed by rumors of satanists at large in the area. A woman taking photographs of children in a town near Cobán was nearly murdered by a hysterical crowd apparently afraid that she wanted children's organs for transplant operations. Be careful not to put yourself in any situation that might be misinterpreted.

Any crowd can be volatile, especially when alcohol is involved or at times of political tension.

It is impossible to remove the element of risk from traveling in Guatemala, but it is possible to reduce the danger by always staying alert to the behavior of other people around you. For more information, refer to Dangers and Annoyances in the regional directory (p439).

DISABLED TRAVELERS

Guatemala is not the easiest country to negotiate with a disability. Although many sidewalks in Antigua have ramps and cute little inlaid tiles depicting a wheelchair, the streets are cobblestone, so the ramps are anything but smooth and the streets worse!

Many hotels in Guatemala are old converted houses with rooms around a courtyard that are wheelchair accessible. The most expensive hotels have facilities such as wheelchair ramps, elevators and accessible toilets.

Transitions (☎ 7832-4261; transitions@guate.net; Colonia Candelaría 80, Antigua) is an organization aiming to increase awareness and access for disabled persons in Guatemala.

EMBASSIES & CONSULATES
Guatemalan Embassies & Consulates
You'll find a full listing of Guatemala's embassies and consulates at www.minex.gob.gt/sistemaprotocolo/protocolos/cmisiones.asp. The following listings are for embassies unless noted:

Australia Contact the Guatemalan embassy in Tokyo.

Belize (☎ 223-3150; 8 A St, Belize City)

Canada (☎ 613-233-7237; embassy1@embaguate.canada.com; 130 Albert St, Suite 1010, Ottawa, Ontario K1P 5G4). Also consulate in Vancouver.

El Salvador (☎ 271-2225; 15 Av Nte, No. 135, San Salvador)

Honduras (☎ 232-1580; Calle Arturo López Rodezno No 2421 Colonia Las Minitas, Tegucigalpa)

France (☎ 01 42 27 78 63; embfrancia@minex.gob.gt; 73 rue de Courcelles, 75008, Paris)

Germany (☎ 030-206-4363; embalemania@minex.gob.gt; Joachim-Karnatz-Allee 45-47 Ecke Paulstrasse, 10557 Berlin Tiergarten, Berlin)

Japan (☎ 813-380-01830; No 38 Kowa Building, 9th Floor, Room 905, 4-12-24, Nishi-Azabu, Tokyo)

Mexico Mexico City (☎ 55-5540-7520; embmexico@minex.gob.gt; Av Explanada 1025, Lomas de Chapultepec, 11000); consulate, Chetumal (☎ 983-23045; Av Independencia 326); consulate, Ciudad Hidalgo, Chiapas (☎ 962-80184; 5a Calle Ote s/n entre 1a & 3a Nte); consulate, Comitán (☎ 963-20491; fax 963-22669; 1a Calle Sur Pte 26); consulate, Tapachula (☎ 962-56380; 3a Av Nte 85)

Netherlands (☎ 070-302 0253; embpaisesbajos@minex.gob.gt; Javastraat 44, 2585AP, The Hague)

New Zealand Contact the Guatemalan embassy in Tokyo.

Spain (☎ 91 344 1417; embespaña@minex.gob.gt; Calle Rafael Salgado 3, 100 derecha, 28036, Madrid)

UK (☎ 020-7351 3042; www.embaguatelondon.bt internet.co.uk; 13 Fawcett St, SW10 9HN, London)

USA Washington DC (☎ 202-745-4952/53/54; www.guatemala-embassy.org; 2220 R St NW, 20008); consulates in Los Angeles (www.guatemala-consulate.org), San Francisco (www.sfconsulguate.org), Chicago, Houston, Miami and New York.

Embassies & Consulates in Guatemala
Canada (☎ 2333-4348; www.dfait-maeci.gc.ca/guatemala; 8th floor, Edificio Edyma Plaza, 13a Calle 8-44, Zona 10, Guatemala City)

Germany (☎ 2364-6700; embalemana@intelnet.net.gt; Edificio Plaza Marítima, 20a Calle 6-20, Zona 10, Guatemala City)

UK (☎ 2367-5425/6/7/8/9; embassy@intelnett.com; 11th Floor, Torre Internacional, 16a Calle 00-55, Zona 10, Guatemala City)

USA (☎ 2331-1541 to 2331-1555; usembassy.state.gov/guatemala; Av La Reforma 7-01, Zona 10, Guatemala City)

FESTIVALS & EVENTS
The following are events of national significance:

El Cristo de Esquipulas (January 15) This super-devout festival in Esquipulas brings pilgrims from all over Central America to catch a glimpse of the Black Jesus housed in the Basilica.

Semana Santa (Holy Week, the week leading up to Easter Sunday) Statues of Jesus and Mary are carried through the streets of towns all around the country, followed by devout, sometimes fervent crowds, to mark Christ's crucifixion. The processions walk over and destroy *alfombras*, elaborate carpets of colored sawdust and flower petals. The week peaks on Good Friday.

Fiesta de la Virgen de la Asunción (Peaking on August 15) This is celebrated with folk dances and parades in Tactic, Sololá and Guatemala City.

Día de Todos los Santos (All Saints' Day, November 1) Sees giant-kite festivals in Santiago Sacatepéquez and Sumpango, near Antigua, and the renowned drunken horse races in Todos Santos.

Quema del Diablo (December 7) The Burning of the Devil starts at around 6pm throughout the country, when everyone takes to the streets with their old garbage, physical and psychic, to stoke huge bonfires of trash. This is followed by impressive fireworks displays.

GAY & LESBIAN TRAVELERS
Few places in Latin America are outwardly gay friendly, and Guatemala is no different. Technically homosexuality is legal for persons 18 years and older, but the reality can be another story, with harassment and violence occurring against gays. Don't even consider testing the tolerance for homosexual public displays of affection here.

Though Antigua has a palatable – if subdued – scene, affection and action are still kept behind closeted doors; the chief exception being the gay-friendly club La Casbah. In Guatemala City, Pandora's Box and Ephebus are the current faves. In large part, though, gays traveling in Guatemala will find themselves keeping it low key and pushing the twin beds together.

The websites **The Gully** (www.thegully.com) and **Gay.com** (www.gay.com) have some articles and information relevant to Guatemala. The best site, **Gay Guatemala** (www.gayguatemala.com), is in Spanish.

HOLIDAYS

The main Guatemalan holiday periods are Semana Santa (Easter Week), Christmas-New Year's and July and August. During Semana Santa room prices rise in many places and it's advisable to book accommodations and transport in advance.

Guatemalan public holidays are:

New Year's Day January 1
Easter (Holy Thursday to Easter Sunday inclusive) March/April
Labor Day May 1
Army Day June 30
Assumption Day (Día de la Asunción) August 15
Independence Day September 15
Revolution Day October 20
All Saints' Day November 1
Christmas Eve afternoon December 24
Christmas Day December 25
New Year's Eve afternoon December 31

INTERNET ACCESS

Most medium-size towns have cybercafés with fairly reliable connections. Internet cafés typically charge between US$1 and US$1.50 an hour.

If you really want to travel with a laptop, consider using a local Internet service provider (ISP), unless you use an international server with access numbers in Guatemala such as AOL or CompuServe. A good bet for a Guatemalan ISP is **Conexion** (p79) in Antigua, which charges US$7.75/18/36/62 for five/24/72/unlimited hours online a month, plus a US$3.25 setup fee.

INTERNET RESOURCES

Gringo's Guide (www.thegringosguide.com) Useful info on the country's main travel destinations.
Guatemala (www.mayaspirit.com.gt) Moderately interesting official site of Inguat, the national tourism institute.
Lanic Guatemala (lanic.utexas.edu/la/ca/guatemala) The University of Texas' magnificent set of Guatemala links.

La Ruta Maya Online (www.larutamayaonline.com) Reasonably useful mixed bag.
LonelyPlanet.com (www.lonelyplanet.com) Succinct summaries on Guatemala travel; the popular Thorn Tree bulletin board; travel news; and the Subwwway section with links to the most useful travel resources elsewhere on the Web.

MAPS

The *Mapa Turístico Guatemala*, produced locally by Intelimapas, tends to be the most up-to-date on the state of Guatemala's roads, many of which have been newly paved in recent years. It also includes plans of many cities. Inguat's *Mapa Vial Turístico* is another worthwhile map. Guatemala City, Antigua, Panajachel and Quetzaltenango all have bookstores selling some of these maps – see the relevant city sections.

MONEY

You will find *cajeros automáticos* (ATMs; cash machines) for Visa/Plus System cards in all but the smallest towns, and there are MasterCard/Cirrus ATMs in many places, too, so one of these cards is the best basis for your supplies of cash in Guatemala. In addition many banks give cash advances on Visa cards, and some on MasterCard. You can pay for many purchases with these and with American Express cards.

If you don't have one of these cards, a combination of American Express US-dollar traveler's checks and a limited amount of cash US dollars is the way to go. Take some of these as a backup even if you do have a card.

Some towns suffer from change shortages – always try to carry a stash of small bills.

Currency

Guatemala's currency, the quetzal (Q, 'ket-sahl'), has been fairly stable at around Q8=US$1 for several years. The quetzal is divided into 100 centavos.

Exchanging Money

Banks all over the country change cash US dollars, and many change US-dollar traveler's checks too. American Express is easily the most recognized brand.

In many places you can make payments with cash dollars, and a few places will accept traveler's checks. Currencies other than the US dollar are virtually useless in any form, although a small handful of places will now change cash euros.

Banks generally give the best exchange rates on both cash and traveler's checks. If you can't find an open bank you can often change cash (and occasionally checks) in travel agencies, hotels or shops.

POST

The Guatemalan postal service was privatized in 1999. Generally, letters take eight to 10 days to travel to the US and Canada, and 10 to 12 days to reach Europe. Almost every city and town (but not villages) has a post office where you can buy stamps and send mail. A letter sent to North America costs around US$0.40 and to anywhere else around US$0.50.

The Guatemalan mail system no longer holds poste restante or general-delivery mail. The easiest and most reliable way to receive mail is through a private address. It is important to address mail clearly: the last lines should read 'Guatemala, Centro América.'

TELEPHONE

Guatemala has no area or city codes. Calling from other countries, you just dial the international access code (☎ 00 in most countries), then the Guatemala country code (☎ 502), then the eight-digit local number. Calling within Guatemala, just dial the eight-digit local number. The international access code from Guatemala is ☎ 00.

Many towns and cities frequented by tourists have privately run call offices where you can make local and international calls for reasonable rates. If the telephone connection is by Internet, the rates can be very cheap (eg US$0.15 a minute to the USA, US$0.30 to Europe), but line quality is unpredictable. Calling from a hotel is the most expensive way of telephoning, but you *can* just make a quick call to get your party to call you back there.

A number of companies provide public-phone services. The most common street phones, found all over Guatemala, are those of Telgua, for which you need to buy a *tarjeta telefónica de Telgua* (Telgua phone card) from shops, kiosks and the like. Card sales points may advertise the fact with red signs saying *Ladatel De*

Venta Aquí. The cards come in denominations of 20, 30 and 50 quetzals: you slot them into a Telgua phone and dial your number; the display will tell you how much time you have left. The second-most common street phones are those of Telefónica, which require a Telefónica card, also sold by shops and kiosks. Telefónica cards are not meant to be inserted into the phone, but simply bear codes to be keyed in and instructions to be followed. In our experience Telgua is cheaper than Telefónica for local calls (about US$0.01 per minute against US$0.05) and for calls to Europe (about US$1 a minute against US$1.60), but Telefónica is cheaper for calls to the USA (about US$0.20 a minute against US$0.50 with Telgua).

Unless it's an emergency, don't use the black phones placed strategically in tourist towns that say 'Press 2 to call the United States free!' This is a bait-and-switch scam: you put the call on your credit card and return home to find you have paid between US$8 and US$20 per minute.

Telgua street phones bear instructions to dial ☎ 147110 for domestic collect calls and ☎ 147120 for international collect calls. The latter number is usually successful for the USA and Canada, less so for the rest of the world. International collect calls using País Directo (Home Country Direct) services and North American calling cards are usually impossible from street phones but can usually be made from hotel or private phones. País Directo numbers include:

USA (MCI) (☎ 9999189)
USA (AT&T) (☎ 9999190)
USA (Sprint) (☎ 9999195)
Canada (☎ 9999198)
UK (☎ 9999044)

Cell phones are widely used. If you want to rent one in Guatemala, try **Guatemala Ventures** (p81) in Antigua or **Digital Mundo Celular** (Map pp66-7; ☎ 5614-2731; 13a Calle 8-16, Zona 1, Guatemala City).

TOURIST INFORMATION

Guatemala's national tourism institute, **Inguat** (www.mayaspirit.com.gt), has information offices in Guatemala City, Antigua, Panajachel, Quetzaltenango and Flores; a few other towns have departmental, municipal or private-enterprise, tourist-information offices (see city sections for details). Inguat operates a free, 24-hour tourist-information-and-assistance line: ☎ 1-801-464-8281.

The Guatemalan embassies in the USA, Germany, France, Italy, Spain and the UK can provide some tourist information. In the USA you can call ☎ 888-464-8281.

VISAS

Citizens of the USA, Canada, EU countries, Norway, Switzerland, Australia, New Zealand, Israel and Japan are among those who do not need visas for tourist visits to Guatemala. On entry into Guatemala you will normally be given a 90-day stay (the number 90 will be written in the stamp in your passport). This can normally be extended for a further 90 days at the **Departamento de Extranjería** (Foreigners' Office; Map pp66-7; ☎ 2361-8476/9, 2331-1333; 7a Av 1-17, Zona 4, Guatemala City; ⊗ 8am-2:30pm Mon-Fri), on the 2nd floor of the Inguat headquarters. For an extension, take with you *one* of the following:

- a credit card with a photocopy of both of its sides
- an air ticket out of Guatemala with photocopy
- US$500 worth of traveler's checks.

The extension will normally be issued in the afternoon of the working day after the day you apply.

Citizens of Iceland, South Africa and Eastern European countries are among those who do need visas to visit Guatemala. Inquire at a Guatemalan embassy well in advance of travel.

Visa regulations are subject to change and it's always worth checking them with a Guatemalan embassy before you go.

If you have been in Guatemala for your original 90 days and a 90-day extension, you must leave the country for 72 hours, after which you can return to Guatemala to start the process all over again. Some foreigners have been repeating this cycle for years.

The procedure for obtaining a work permit is quite involved. See http://pubweb .fdbl.com/ihp8/global/media85.nsf/public -country-briefs/guatemala for more info. You don't need a work permit for volunteer work.

WOMEN TRAVELERS

Women should encounter no special problems traveling in Guatemala. In fact solo women will be pleasantly surprised by how gracious and helpful most locals are. The primary thing you can do to make it easy for yourself while traveling here is to dress modestly. Specifically, shorts should be worn only at the beach, not in town, and especially not in the highlands. Skirts should be at or below the knee. Wear a bra, as going braless is considered provocative. Many local women swim with T-shirts over their swimsuits; in places where they do this, you may want to follow suit to avoid stares.

Women traveling alone can expect plenty of attempts by men to talk to them. Often they are just curious and not out for a foreign conquest. Consider the situation and circumstances (on a bus is one thing, on a barstool another) and stay confident. Try to sit next to women or children on the bus if that makes you more comfortable. Local women rarely initiate conversations, but usually have lots of interesting things to say once the ball is rolling.

Nasty rumors about Western women kidnapping Guatemalan children for a variety of sordid ends have all but died down. Still, women travelers should be cautious around children, especially indigenous children.

The possibility of rape and assault does exist. Use your normal traveler's caution: avoid walking alone in isolated places or through city streets late at night, and don't hitchhike.

WORK

Some travelers find work in bars, restaurants and accommodations in Antigua, Panajachel or Quetzaltenango, but the wages are just survival pay.

If you really want to get to the heart of Guatemalan matters and you've altruistic leanings, consider volunteer work. Volunteering is rewarding and exposes foreigners to the rich and varied local culture typically out of reach for the average traveler. Opportunities abound, from caring for abandoned animals and children to tending fields. Travelers with specific skills, such as nurses, doctors or teachers, are particularly encouraged to investigate volunteering in Guatemala.

Four excellent sources of information on volunteer opportunities are **Proyecto Mosaico Guatemala** (p81) and **AmeriSpan Guatemala**, (p81) both in Antigua, and **EntreMundos** (p116) in Quetzaltenango. Many language schools have close links to volunteer projects and can introduce you to the world of volunteering. A few well-established organizations are mentioned under Courses headings in this chapter. Also check the Regional Directory (p439) for more organizations and tips.

TRANSPORTATION IN GUATEMALA

GETTING THERE & AWAY
Air
Guatemala City's Aeropuerto La Aurora (GUA) is the country's major international airport. The only other airport with international flights (from Cancún, Mexico and Belize City) is Flores (FRS). The Guatemalan national airline Aviateca is part of the regional Grupo TACA, along with El Salvador's TACA, Costa Rica's Lacsa and Nicaragua's Nica.

Airlines flying to and from Guatemala:

American Airlines (www.aa.com; ☎ 2337-1177; airline code AA; hubs Dallas & Miami)
Aviateca (see Grupo TACA)
Continental Airlines (www.continental.com; ☎ 2366-9985; airline code CO; hub Houston)
Copa Airlines (www.copaair.com; ☎ 2385-5500; airline code CM; hub Panama City)
Cubana (www.cubana.cu; ☎ 2367-2288/89/90; airline code CU; hub Havana)
Delta Airlines (www.delta.com; ☎ 2337-0642; from the US ☎ 1-800-300-0005; airline code DL; hub Atlanta)
Grupo TACA (www.taca.com; ☎ 5470-8222; airline code TA; hub San Salvador)
Iberia (www.iberia.com; ☎ 2331-1012; airline code IB; hub Madrid)
Inter (see Grupo TACA)
Lacsa (see Grupo TACA)
Maya Island Air (www.mayaairways.com; ☎ 7926-3386; airline code MW; hub Belize City)
Mexicana (www.mexicana.com; ☎ 2333-6001; airline code MX; hub Mexico City)
TACA (see Grupo TACA)
Tropic Air (www.tropicair.com; ☎ 7926-0348; airline code PM; hub Belize City)

United Airlines (www.united.com; ☎ 2336-9923/4/5/6; airline code UA; hub Los Angeles)

Land
Bus is the most common way to enter Guatemala, though you can also do so by river or sea. Try to cross borders as early in the day as possible. Onward transportation tends to wind down in the afternoon and border areas are not always the safest places to hang around late in the day. You'll find more detail on the services mentioned here in the destination sections of this book. There is no departure tax when you leave Guatemala by land.

BUS
Several international bus routes connect Guatemala with Mexico, Belize, El Salvador and Honduras and beyond (p455). When traveling between Guatemala and neighboring countries, you will often have the choice of a direct, 1st-class bus or a series of 'chicken buses' (with lots of rowdy, live-animal cargo). The latter option usually takes longer but is always cheaper and more interesting. International bus destinations from Guatemala City include: Belize City, El Carmen/Talismán (Mexican border), El Florido/Copán Ruinas (Honduras), La Mesilla/Ciudad Cuauhtémoc (Mexican border), Managua, San Salvador (El Salvador), Tapachula (Mexico) and Tecún Umán/Ciudad Hidalgo (Mexican border).

CAR & MOTORCYCLE
The mountain of paperwork and liability involved in driving into Guatemala deters most travelers. You will need the following documents, all clear and consistent, to enter Guatemala with a car:
* current and valid registration
* proof of ownership (if you don't own the car, you'll need a notarized letter of authorization from the owner that you are allowed to take it)
* your current and valid driver's license or an International Driving Permit (IDP), issued by the automobile association in your home country
* temporary import permit available free at the border and good for a maximum of 30 days.

Insurance from foreign countries is not recognized by Guatemala, forcing you to purchase a policy locally. Most border posts and nearby towns have offices selling liability policies. To deter foreigners from selling cars in Guatemala, the authorities make you exit the country with the vehicle you used to enter it. Don't be the designated driver when crossing borders if you don't own the car, because you and it will not be allowed to leave Guatemala without each other.

Sea & River

On the Caribbean coast, boats leave Punta Gorda (Belize) for Puerto Barrios and Lívingston. Passage from Omoa (Honduras) to Lívingston is also possible, though it may be difficult to arrange in low season. Generally, sea passage is easiest to and from Puerto Barrios, as this is an active transit point. No car ferries are available.

Three river crossings connect Chiapas, Mexico, to El Petén, Guatemala. These are good alternatives for travelers visiting Palenque and Tikal in one trip. All involve a combination of bus and boat travel (see p453 for details).

If arriving or departing by river or sea, make sure you get your exit and entry stamps at the appropriate immigration offices in both countries.

GETTING AROUND
Air

The only scheduled internal flights at the time of writing were between Guatemala City and Flores, a route operated daily by five companies with one-way/round-trip fares ranging between US$70/100 and US$90/125 (see p74 for details). A departure tax of five quetzals (about US$0.65) has to be paid in cash at check-in for these flights.

Bicycle

Bikes for rent are available in a few places. The most professional outfits include **Old Town Outfitters** (p83) and **Guatemala Ventures/ Mayan Bike Tours** (p83) in Antigua, and **Vrisa Bicicleta** (p115) in Quetzaltenango.

Boat

The Caribbean town of Lívingston is only reachable by boat across the Bahía de Amatique from Puerto Barrios, or down the Río Dulce from the town of Río Dulce –

both great trips. The other place where boats come into play is the Lago de Atitlán, where fast fiberglass *lanchas* zip across the waters between one village and another. See destination sections for details.

Bus, Minibus & Pickup

Buses go almost everywhere in Guatemala – most travelers do most of their traveling on them. The majority are ancient school buses from the US and Canada, and it's not unusual for a local family of five to squeeze into seats that were originally designed for two child-sized bottoms. Many travelers know these vehicles as 'chicken buses' after the live cargo accompanying many passengers. They are frequent, crowded and cheap: expect to pay US$1 (or less!) for an hour of travel.

Chicken buses will stop anywhere, for anyone. Helpers will yell '*hay lugares!*' ('eye loo-*gar*-ays'), which literally means 'there are places.' Never mind that the space they refer to may be no more than a sliver of air between dozens of locals mashed against one another. (Tall travelers will be especially challenged on these buses.) These same helpers will also yell their bus's destination in voices of varying hilarity and cadence; just listen for the song of your town. To catch a chicken bus, simply stand beside the road with your arm out parallel to the ground.

Some routes, especially between big cities, are served by more comfortable buses with the luxury of one seat per person. The best buses are labeled Pullman, *especial* or *primera clase*. Occasionally these may have bathrooms, televisions and even food service.

For a few of the better services, you can buy tickets in advance, and this is generally worth doing as it ensures that you get a place.

In general more buses leave in the morning (some as early as 3am) than the afternoon. Bus traffic drops off precipitously after about 4pm; night buses are rare and not generally recommended. An exception is Línea Dorada's overnight *especial* from Guatemala City to Flores, which has not experienced any trouble of note in several years.

Distances in Guatemala are not huge and you won't often ride for more than four hours at a time. On a typical four-hour bus trip, you'll cover 175km to 200km for US$3.50 to US$4.

On some shorter routes, minibuses (usually called microbuses) are replacing chicken buses. These are operated on the same cram-'em-all-in principles and can be even more uncomfortable because they have less legroom. Where neither buses nor minibuses roam, *picop* (pickup) trucks serve as de facto buses: you hail and pay them as if they were the genuine article.

SHUTTLE MINIBUS
Shuttle minibuses run by travel agencies provide comfortable and quick transport along the main routes plied by tourists. You'll find these heavily advertised wherever they are offered. They're much more expensive than buses (anywhere between five and 15 times as expensive), but more convenient: they usually offer a door-to-door service. The most popular shuttle routes include Guatemala City airport–Antigua, Antigua–Panajachel, Panajachel–Chichicastenango and Flores–Tikal.

Car & Motorcycle
DRIVING LICENSE
You can drive in Guatemala with your home-country driver's license or with an IDP.

FUEL & SPARE PARTS
Gasoline (petrol) and diesel are widely available. Motor parts may be hard to find, especially for modern vehicles with sophisticated electronics and emissions-control systems. Old Toyota pickups are ubiquitous, though, so parts and mechanics will be more widely available.

HIRE
You can rent cars in Guatemala City, Antigua, Quetzaltenango, Huehuetenango, Cobán and Flores. A four-door, five-seat, five-gear, air-con vehicle such as a Mitsubishi Lancer will normally cost around US$50 a day including insurance and unlimited kilometers. The smallest cars start at around US$40 a day. Discounts may apply if you rent for three days or more.

To rent a car or motorcycle you need to show your passport, driver's license and a major credit card. Usually the person renting the vehicle must be 25 years or older.

Insurance policies accompanying rental cars may not protect you from loss or theft, in which case you could be liable for hundreds or even thousands of dollars in damages. Be careful where you park, especially in Guatemala City and at night.

Guatemala has both international and local rental car companies. You will find details of some major players on p77. Motorcycles are available for rent in Guatemala City, Antigua, Panajachel and Quetzaltenango. Safety gear such as a helmet and gloves are highly recommended.

ROAD RULES
Guatemalan driving etiquette will probably be very different from what you're used to back home: passing on blind curves, ceding the right of way to vehicles coming uphill on narrow passes and deafening honking for no apparent reason are just the start. Expect few road signs and no indication from other drivers of what they are about to do. A vehicle coming uphill always has the right of way. *Tumulos* are speed bumps which are generously (sometimes oddly) placed throughout the country, usually on the main drag through a town. Use of seat belts is obligatory, but generally not practiced.

Driving at night is a bad idea for many reasons, not the least of which are armed bandits and drunk drivers.

Every driver involved in an accident that results in injury or death is taken into custody until a judge determines responsibility.

Hitching
Hitchhiking in the strict sense of the word is not practiced in Guatemala because it is not safe. However, where the bus services are sporadic or nonexistent, pickup trucks and other vehicles serve as supplemental forms of public transport. If you stand beside the road with your arm out, someone will stop. You are expected to pay the driver as if it were a bus and the fare will be similar. This is a safe and reliable system used by locals and travelers, and the only inconvenience you're likely to encounter is full-to-overflowing vehicles.

Local Transportation
Public transportation within towns and cities and to nearby villages is chiefly provided by aged, polluting, crowded and loud buses.

They're useful to travelers chiefly in the more spread-out cities such as Guatemala City, Quetzaltenango and Huehuetenango. Quetzaltenango has a lovely fleet of quiet, smooth, comfortable, modern minibuses (operating alongside the usual ancient city buses).

Taxis are fairly plentiful in most significant towns. A 10-minute ride will normally cost you about US$3. They don't use meters, so you must agree on the fare before you set off – best to do it before you get in, in fact. Taxis will also often take you to out-of-town archaeological sites and other places for reasonable round-trip fares, including waiting time while you look round.

Belize

MARK WEBSTER

Belize

CONTENTS

BELIZE

Picture it: The breeze is coming off the Caribbean, making the palm trees sway. You're on the beach, body tired from diving the Technicolor reef, swimming with manta rays and all sorts of exotic fish. In front of you the water is crystal clear, turquoise like you've only seen in tourist posters. The air is filling with the smell of grilled lobster from the barbecue down the beach. Somewhere in the distance somebody puts on another reggae CD. Some locals walk past, chatting in the soft patter of Kriol, recognizable but at the same time utterly foreign. Welcome to Belize.

It's not all lying around soaking up rays, though – Belize is a small country, but packed with things to do. Out west there are caves to explore and rivers to raft. Down south you can get down with the Garifuna, surely the funkiest dancers in all of Central America. The jungle is dotted with important Mayan sites, many of which you'll probably have to yourself. There are national parks all over the place, where you can look for wildlife, go hiking or just have a swim in a natural rock pool.

When your major city doesn't even have 60,000 inhabitants it sounds a bit odd talking about getting off the beaten track, but there are some great little coastal towns for doing just that. Belize is an independent traveler's dream. An efficient network of buses making frequent runs in all directions means that it's easy to get from point to point without much waiting around or advance planning.

FAST FACTS

- **Area** 23,000 sq km (slightly larger than Wales or Massachusetts)
- **Capital** Belmopan (but Belize City is the major city)
- **Country Code** ☎ 501
- **Departure Tax** US$3.75 by sea, US$18 by land, US$35 by air
- **Languages** English, Spanish, Kriol, Garifuna
- **Money** Belize dollars; US dollars accepted everywhere; US$1=BZ$2, or slightly more if you can get it
- **Phrases** *aarait?* (an all-purpose hello/how's it going type greeting), *right now* (some time soon, or possibly later), *for real* (seriously)
- **Population** 266,440
- **Visas** North American and most European citizens need only a valid passport. Swiss nationals need a visa

BELIZE

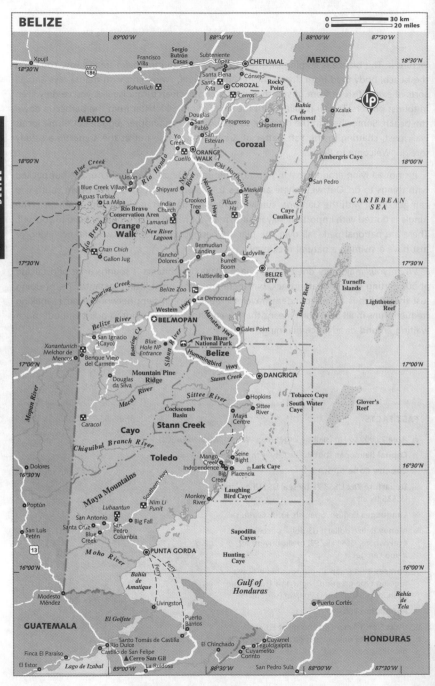

BELIZE

0 —————— 30 km
0 —————— 20 miles

MEXICO

Xpujil

MEX 186

Francisco Villa

Sergio Butrón Casas

Subteniente López

Santa Elena

Kohunlich

Santa Rita

CHETUMAL

MEXICO

18°30'N

89°00'W   88°30'W   88°00'W   87°30'W

Consejo

COROZAL

Cerros

Rocky Point

Bahía de Chetumal

Xcalak

18°30'N

MEXICO

Douglas
San Pablo

Progresso

Shipstern

Corozal

Blue Creek

Yo Creek

San Estevan

Maskall

Ambergris Caye

18°00'N

La Unión

ORANGE WALK

Cuello

Old Northern Hwy

San Pedro

18°00'N

Blue Creek Village

Shipyard

Rio Hondo

New River

Northern Hwy

CARIBBEAN SEA

Aguas Turbias

La Milpa

Indian Church

Crooked Tree

Altun Ha

Caye Caulker

Rio Bravo Conservation Area

Lamanai

Río Bravo

Orange Walk

New River Lagoon

Bermudian Landing

Ladyville

17°30'N

Chan Chich

Gallon Jug

Rancho Dolores

Burrell Boom

BELIZE CITY

Turneffe Islands

17°30'N

Labouring Creek

Hattieville

Barrier Reef

Lighthouse Reef

Belize River

Belize Zoo

La Democracia

Xunantunich

Melchor de Mencos

San Ignacio (Cayo)

BELMOPAN

Western Hwy

Manatee Hwy

Gales Point

17°00'N

Benque Viejo del Carmen

Blue Hole NP Entrance

Roaring Ck

Sibun River

Five Blues National Park

Belize

Hummingbird Hwy

17°00'N

Mopan River

Douglas da Silva

Mountain Pine Ridge

Macal River

Stann Creek

DANGRIGA

Tobacco Caye

Caracol

Cayo

Cockscomb Basin

Stann Creek

Sittee River

Hopkins

Sittee River

Maya Centre

South Water Caye

Glover's Reef

Chiquibul Branch River

Toledo

Dolores

16°30'N

Poptún

Maya Mountains

Lubaantun

Southern Hwy

Nim Li Punit

Mango Creek

Independence

Big Creek

Seine Bight

Placencia

Lark Caye

16°30'N

San Luis Petén

San Antonio

Santa Cruz

Blue Creek

San Pedro Columbia

Big Fall

Monkey River

Laughing Bird Caye

13

Moho River

PUNTA GORDA

Sapodilla Cayes

Hunting Caye

16°00'N

Modesto Méndez

Bahía de Amatique

Ferry

Gulf of Honduras

Bahía de Tela

16°00'N

GUATEMALA

El Golfete

Livingston

Puerto Barrios

Puerto Cortés

Finca El Paraíso

Santo Tomás de Castilla

Río Dulce

El Chinchado

Cuyamel

Tegucigalpita

HONDURAS

El Estor

Castillo de San Felipe

Lago de Izabal

Cerro San Gil

La Ruidosa

San Pedro Sula

Cuyamelito

Corinto

89°00'W   88°30'W   88°00'W   87°30'W

HIGHLIGHTS

- Snorkel or dive Belize's mighty **barrier reef** (p230).
- Experience the tranquility of the Mayan temples of **Lamanai** (p254), **Caracol** (p276) and **Lubaantun** (p300), which are often deserted enough to provide a memorable atmosphere.
- Witness Belize's fascinating cultural mix at the mostly Garifuna towns of **Hopkins** (p288) and **Dangriga** (p284).
- Satisfy your thirst for adventure in the area around **San Ignacio** (p268).
- Get off the well-worn trail, and into some beautiful jungle villages in the **Toledo District** (p298).

ITINERARIES

- **Three days** San Ignacio on the first day, then the northern cayes (via Belize City), then Altun Ha, on a day trip from Belize City.
- **One week** Follow the above, but take in the Belize Zoo en route from San Ignacio to Belize City. After Altun Ha, head to Placencia or Hopkins.
- **Two weeks** Add on a week in the Toledo district.
- **One month** Take you time with all the above, and add a dive course or some sailing to your northern cayes trip. See the southern cayes and take a boat ride up the New River to Lamanai.

CLIMATE & WHEN TO GO

The busy winter season occurs from mid-December to April, and a second peak is from June through August. The dry season (November to May) is the best time to travel; however, in summer (July to November) prices are lower and lodgings on the cayes are easier to find.

Belize is typically hot and humid day and night for most of the year. Rainfall is lightest in the north, heaviest in the south. The southern rain forests receive over 160 inches (4m) of rainfall annually, helping to make the south the country's most humid region.

An exception to Belize's low-lying topography and hot, sticky climate can be found in the Maya Mountains, which traverse western and southern Belize at elevations approaching 3300ft (around 1000m). The mountains enjoy a more pleasant climate

than the lowlands – comfortably warm during the day, cooling off a bit at night. But even here the forests are lush, well watered and humid year-round.

For climate charts see p438.

Hurricanes

While hurricane season officially lasts from June to November, Belize has traditionally been struck by its most damaging hurricanes in September and November. Spookily, the most extreme hurricanes happened in years ending with '1': the hurricane of 1931 (before they were named), Hurricane Hattie in 1961, and, most recently, Hurricane Iris in 2001.

Hurricane Iris struck southern Belize in October 2001, bringing profound damage to Placencia, Monkey River and the Mayan villages around Toledo, with winds in excess of 150mph (242km/h), causing an estimated US$250 million in damages. Luckily there was plenty of warning, and with the tragic exception of those on a houseboat that wasn't evacuated, there was very little loss of life.

If you are in Belize when a hurricane threatens, the best advice is to head inland. If this isn't possible, you should shelter in the sturdiest concrete building you can find, as far away as possible from the coast and away from windows. Hurricanes usually take a while to reach the Central American shore and are well reported as they make

---

HOW MUCH?

- **Three-hour 2nd-class bus ride** US$5
- **PADI open water dive certification** US$350
- **Admission to national parks** US$5–7.50
- **Hour of Internet access** US$2
- **Comfortable beachfront cabaña with bathroom, Placencia** US$60

LP INDEX

- **Gallon of gas (petrol)** US$3.80
- **Liter of bottled water** US$0.75
- **Bottle of Belikin beer** US$1.50
- **Souvenir T-shirt** US$8
- **Small bottle of seaweed punch from street vendor** US$1.50

their way across the Caribbean – it's likely that there will be plenty of time to seek shelter should you have the misfortune of being involved in one.

HISTORY
The Maya

Belize's most important ancient culture is that of the Maya, a people whose descendants live on in the country today. The earliest evidence of the Maya can be found at the ruins of Cuello in the Orange Walk District, thought to be in existence from 1000 BC. The heyday of Mayan civilization, known as the Classic period, was from AD 250–900 – sometimes further broken down into Early Classic (AD 250–600) and Late Classic (AD 600–900). During the Classic period there were Mayan centers in Altun Ha, Lubaantun, El Pilar, Xunantunich and Caracol.

The Maya could be loosely grouped into three classes: the rulers, who inherited their positions; traders, who plied wares such as cocoa, cotton, honey and precious stones by land and sea; and farmers, the majority group, who grew corn, beans, rice and squash and kept turkey as game meat.

The Belize shoreline was a major trading center and widely inhabited by the Maya during the Classic period. Maya dug the channel at Bacalar Chico (between present-day Ambergris Caye and Mexico) 1500 years ago. Creating this shortcut to the mainland, effectively opening up a lucrative trade route, was one of the first acts that separated Belize from Mexico's Yucatán Peninsula.

Overall, the Mayan culture mysteriously declined after AD 900. Most historians attribute the decline to food shortages, probably brought on by climate changes. While the population certainly declined, there were still Mayan settlements existing when the Spanish first came to Belize in the 17th century. In Lamanai, for example, there are ruins of a Catholic church, evidence that there were plenty of Maya to convert. Many Maya accepted early conversion in Lamanai, but then rejected it in the 1640s.

As the Spanish forayed into Belize, many Maya in the coastal regions retreated inland. They remained entrenched in the jungles of western Belize and often skirmished with Spanish and British settlers as the Europeans tried to gain more control of the region.

European Settlement

The region probably had its first contact with Europe in the early 16th century, when the Spanish began to inhabit the Central American region. The Spanish were interested in Belize for its large quantity of logwood – a wood valuable as a dye in Europe – and claimed Belize as its territory. But because of its fierce Maya and inhospitable terrain, Belize was never a priority for the Spaniards, who were more interested in the gold and silver that could be more easily taken from neighboring Honduras and Mexico.

The Baymen

Shipments of gold and silver past the Belizean coastline piqued the interest of British pirates, known as Baymen because they spent most of their time in the Bay of Honduras. They found the convoluted coastline of Belize an ideal place to play hide-and-seek with Spanish transport ships.

The pirating business began to dry up around 1670 when Spain asked the British to crack down on their marauding citizens through the Treaty of Madrid. The Baymen looked west and realized that there was a fortune to be made inland by pulling valuable logwood from the forests. In 1673, through the Treaty of Paris, the Spanish allowed the Baymen to log in a prescribed portion of Belize, in hope of containing them to a specific area, keeping the rest of Central America for Spain. Such logging became the primary economic base for the British in Belize, and remained so for nearly a century.

Slavery

Logwood also brought slavery to Belize as the Baymen began to discover that mining logwood was much more labor-intensive than pirating. The first record of slaves in Belize (brought from Africa via the Caribbean) was in 1725, and by 1790 slaves made up 75% of Belize's registered population (the Maya weren't included in the census), while 10% were European and the rest were freed slaves or free settlers of mixed ancestry. The British abolished slavery throughout the British Empire in 1833, mainly because the industrial revolution created a need for a wage-earning labor force to purchase goods. In Belize, however, the former slaves were required to remain indentured to their former owners until 1838. Beyond this point former slaves were not allowed to own land, perpetuating a system in which freed slaves remained dependent on land owners. No compensation was offered to the former slaves, although former slave owners were compensated for their loss of 'property.'

British Colonization

Although Spain still considered Belize to be its territory, it gave the Baymen, and thereby the British, more and more control of the land by way of successive treaties throughout the 18th century.

As British economic interests in the Caribbean increased, so too did British involvement in Belize. In the 1780s the British actively protected the former pirates' logging interests, at the same time assuring Spain that Belize was indeed a Spanish possession. This was a fiction. By this time, Belize was already British by tradition and sympathy.

The Battle of St George's Caye, on September 10, 1798, was the last attempt by Spain to protect its interests in Belize. From that point on Belize was under British rule, although it didn't formally become a Crown colony until 1871.

The Baymen were an independent, unruly bunch and were slow to cooperate with either Spain or the British government. In the early days of the settlement, Britain didn't provide much governmental structure, and the Baymen brought it upon themselves to create a democratic system by which their settlement was run. Burnaby's Code was enacted in 1765 and continued to be the primary structure until 1840, when Britain put an executive council in place. The code was a practical one with 12 articles and regulations. Most involved rules against stealing servants and property, but within the code, systems for levying and collecting taxes, settling disputes and determining punishments (usually fines) were also established.

The Mahogany Trade

Logwood continued to be the primary economic force in Belize until the late 18th century. At that point, synthetic dyes and suppliers of logwood from other parts of the world lessened demand, and the economy took a tumble. The Baymen quickly turned their attention from one forest product to another as the demand for mahogany matched the region's ample supply. The mahogany industry flourished until the mid-19th century, but it collapsed as well when African sources of the wood brought fierce price competition.

War of the Castes

Though it happened north in the Yucatán Peninsula, the War of the Castes (1847–1901, between the Maya of the Yucatán Peninsula and the Spanish and mestizos who controlled the area) was important in the development and settlement of Belize. For Belizeans, the war presented a trade boom in arms, ammunition and other supplies sold to the Maya rebels in the Yucatán.

More profoundly, the war also brought a flood of refugees to Belize, especially in the northern areas – what are now the Corozal and Orange Walk Districts – and in the northern cayes of Ambergris and Caulker. First came the Spanish and mestizo lieutenants, driven out by the wrath of the Maya; then came the Maya themselves when the Spanish regained control of the Yucatán. The Mayan refugees brought new farming skills that were of great value in expanding the horizons and economic viability of Belizean society.

The 20th Century

The first half of the 20th century was a difficult time in Belize, and misrule by the British led to the country's agitation for independence. Belize sent troops to fight for the British in WWI, but because of their race, they were relegated to labor camps. This humiliation brought on rioting and unrest and contributed to the sentiment that Britain did not have the best interests of Belize's citizenry at heart. The economy worsened during the Great Depression and WWII, leading popular sentiment toward independence. This feeling was fueled in 1947 when India gained independence.

Independence

Democratic institutions and political parties were established over the years following 1947, and self-government eventually became a reality in 1962. Coincidentally and symbolically, in the early 1960s Belizeans switched to the Central American

BELIZE

CULTURE OF COLONIZATION

Most Belizeans believe that British colonization has had its ups and downs. The up side includes a better system for social welfare including socialized medicine, mandatory education, a fairly clean record on human rights and a system that acknowledges laborers' rights, at least for native Belizeans. Many Belizeans will admit that at least on these counts they are far better off than neighboring countries that were colonized by the Spanish. On the down side, Belizean activists feel they are fighting a system of institutionalized complacency – citizens feel powerless to effect change, even in their immediate communities.

Over the past 20 years Belizeans have been struggling to reintegrate their native culture. As with many colonized areas, diminished emphasis is placed on pre-existing traditions, arts and culture. Instead, imported ideas and products are seen to be of more value than what is produced domestically. US consumer imports are hugely popular (accounting for nearly half of the country's total imports) and much of the popular culture is imported directly from the States. In Belize's art scene, local goods are not revered as they are in neighboring Mexico and Guatemala. Indeed many Belizeans have had to leave their country to make their fortunes, sending money home to support a family. Luckily these attitudes seem to be changing, especially as Belize welcomes the 21st century, with a surge in popularity of Belizean art and culture, and the fact that some lucrative industries (such as tourism) are now attracting Belizean investment.

standard of driving on the right. This was brought about partially because Hurricane Hattie had wiped out the lefty cars that remained on the road. In 1973 the name of the country was officially changed from British Honduras to Belize. On September 21, 1981, Belize officially became an independent nation, but it remains a member of the British Commonwealth.

Many educated (and especially older) Belizeans will tell you that the widespread corruption and nepotism in Belize today are a result of the country becoming independent too early, before democratic institutions had a chance to take hold. It's a compelling argument, and one that's likely to ruffle a few feathers if you decide to take it for a spin.

Belizean independence was not celebrated by neighboring Guatemala, which had long claimed Belize as part of its national territory. The Guatemalans threatened war, but British troops stationed in Belize kept the territorial dispute to a diplomatic squabble. In 1992, a new Guatemalan government signed a treaty recognizing Belize's independence but not relinquishing claim to some 7500 sq miles of land. Intermittent border flare-ups continued. Tension eased somewhat in 2002 when the two countries signed an agreement over the disputed land and Caribbean fishing rights, but then picked up when Belize threatened to expel two Guatemalan settlements it claimed were on the wrong side of the border. The

agreement depends on ratification by voters in both countries, which, at the time of writing, hadn't happened yet. So far, Belize refuses to let any land go, but has stated that it is willing to explore options for allowing Guatemala expanded access to the sea.

After Independence, the ruling People's Unity Party (PUP) split over the issue of relations with Cuba and Nicaragua. Some felt that Belize's warm relations with these leftist governments were endangering diplomatic ties with the USA. Two years later, with the PUP still divided, the conservative United Democratic Party swept into office with a program of harsh economic rationalism. Control of the country has see-sawed between these two major parties ever since.

Beyond Independence

In 1992, Belize (often used as a staging post for drug smuggling between South or Central America and the US) stepped up its efforts in the War Against Drugs and introduced a raft of legislation designed to reduce drug smuggling and gang related violence – one particularly controversial law made it illegal to wear gang 'colors' on the streets.

In 1994, Guatemala (perhaps seeking distraction from domestic troubles) revived its claim on Belize, stating that it had never formally recognized the latter as an independent state, and claiming half of southern Belize as Guatemalan territory.

Current Affairs

The latest political news has all been scandal and intrigue, with President Musa implicated in a series of corruption exposés, leaving him scrambling to reshuffle his cabinet and causing him to give up various portfolios. Despite this, Musa's PUP made history in March 2003 by becoming the first Belizean government to win a second term in office.

THE CULTURE
The National Psyche

Belizeans have elevated 'taking it easy' to an art form (where else will you be told that checkout time is 'Whatever time you like'?). Shopkeepers will close early if they feel they've made enough money for the day and hammock swinging is pretty much a national pastime.

Widespread corruption in the middle and upper levels of government has left most Belizeans with a healthy cynicism when it comes to politicians. The woeful state of the economy and huge gap between rich and poor doesn't make them think much better of the private sector.

Lifestyle

With compulsory education and a relatively stable democracy, you would expect Belize to be doing alright by its citizens. Unfortunately, this isn't the case. The country has never been rich, and a reliance on agriculture, fishing and, lately, the tourism industry hasn't done much to change that. As a result, many Belizeans live in very basic circumstances. New houses are often made from cinder-block boxes; old ones from warped and rotting wood which has seen much better days. It is estimated that one third of the population live below the poverty line – which should be grim, but it ain't. Above all, the folk here know how to have a good time – check out any karaoke bar on a Friday night and you'll see enough Belikin beer consumption and smiling faces to know that, for some at least, things aren't as bad as they look on paper.

Population

For such a tiny country, Belize enjoys a fabulous, improbable ethnic diversity. Creoles – descendants of the African slaves and British pirates who first settled here to exploit the country's forest riches – are by far the dominant cultural group in Belize, even though they make up less than a third (30%) of the population. Racially mixed and proud of it, Creoles speak a fascinating, unique language that was long thought simply to be a dialect of English. For more on Kriol, see the boxed text.

Almost one half (44%) of Belize's people are mestizos, or persons of mixed European and Central American indigenous ancestry, some of whose ancestors immigrated from Yucatán during the 19th century.

The Maya of Belize make up about 11% of the population and are divided into three linguistic groups. The Yucatec live in the north near the Yucatán border, the Mopan live in western Belize around the border town of Benque Viejo del Carmen, and the Kekchi inhabit far southern Belize in and around Punta Gorda. In recent years, political refugees coming in from Guatemala and El Salvador have added to Belize's Maya population.

Southern Belize is the home of the Garinagu (plural of Garifuna), who account for around 7% of the population (for more on the Garinagu see the boxed text on p295) The Garinagu are of South American indigenous and African descent. They look more African than indigenous, but they speak a language that's much more indigenous than African and their unique culture combines aspects of both peoples. Other ethnic groups in Belize include small populations of Europeans, Mennonites (see Who Are Those White Guys in the Overalls? on p267), East Indians, Chinese, Lebanese and North Americans.

SPORTS

Like any Central American country worth its stripes, Belize is a soccer playing nation. The Regent Insurance Cup competition runs from February to July and the Prime Minister's Cup starts in August. Check newspapers for details – the **MCC grounds** (Map p217; ☎ 223-4415; Newtown Barracks Rd) in Belize City is your best bet for seeing a semi-pro game.

You'll probably find that the sport of choice for the kids is basketball. If you're up for it, you can easily jump in on a game – it's a great way to meet locals and keep warm on those chilly Caribbean afternoons.

BELIZE

TAAKIN EENA KRIOL

For a long time, the prevailing (ie colonial) view was that the language that the Creole peoples of the Caribbean speak was simply a dialect of English, and a lazy and inferior one at that.

Serious linguistic studies have discovered, however, that Kriol (as it is called among native speakers) bears the characteristics of a separate language – a unique, consistent grammar (that is based more on West African grammars than English) and a vocabulary independent of English (while Kriol uses many loan words from English, it also loans from Spanish, Miskitu and African languages as well as having its own, unique words).

English speakers can generally understand spoken Kriol, if it is spoken slowly enough, but if you listen to two Kriol speakers having a heated discussion, chances are you'll be very lost, very quickly. KREM (96.5 FM) is a good place to hear a mix of Kriol and English, as the early morning talkback callers often start off speaking English, then segue into Kriol as they get more excited about the topic.

Writers have begun to publish books, plays and poetry either partially or entirely in Kriol, and the newspaper the *Reporter* publishes a column in Kriol on Sunday titled 'Weh wi gat fi seh' (What we've got to say). Below are some basic words and phrases to get you started. For further information, look for the *Kriol Glossary an Spellin Gide* in bookstores and check out www .kriol.org.bz.

What's going on?	Weh di go aan?	How long?	Da how lang?
(a greeting, often		How far?	Da how faa ih deh?
used in place of		My name is...	Ah nayhn...
'hello' or 'what's up')		I am going to Belmopan	Ah gwain da Belmopan
What is your name?	Da weh (da) yu	I am hot	Ah hat
	naym?	I am very hot	Ah hat hat/Ah hat bad
Good morning	Gud maanin	I am thirsty	Ah tosti
Good afternoon	Gud aftanoon	I am hungry	Ah hongri
How are you?	Da how yu di du?		
Fine, thank you	Aarait	Do you speak Creole/	Yoo kud taak Kriol/
I'll see you later	Ah wahn si yu layta	Spanish/English?	Spanish/Inglish?
Until next time	Si yu neks taim	I know a little Spanish	Ah noa wahn lee bit
Goodbye	Bai		a Spanish
		Speak slowly, please	Pleez taak sloa
Yes	Yay	I don't understand you	Ah noh andastan yu
No	No/noh	I understand you	Ah andastan yu
Maybe	Maybi	Do you understand me?	Yoo di andastan mi?
I am sorry	Ah sari	Would you say it again,	Seh ahn agen noh,
Thank you	Tenk yu	please?	pleez?
You're welcome/	Ih aarait (aalrait)	What's that?	Da weh dat?
It's okay		Would you write it	Rait ahn dong noh,
It doesn't matter	Ih noh matta	down, please?	pleez?
I know	Ah noa	What does that	Da weh da werd
I don't know	Ah noh noa	word mean?	deh meen?
I think so	Ah tink soh	How do you say...	Da how yu seh...
I don't think so	Ah noh tink soh	in Kriol?	eena Kriol?

Cricket is also played, mostly in the Orange Walk and Cayo Districts, but there are fairly regular games in season (15 January to 31 August) at the old BDF cricket pitch in Ladyville, 10 miles (16km) northwest of Belize City. Check Friday's *Amandala* for details.

RELIGION

Belize's mixture of religions follows its ethnic composition. Roman Catholics and Protestants (mainly Anglicans and Methodists, but also Mennonites, Seventh Day Adventists and Jehovah's Witnesses) prevail, but Belize's tradition of tolerance has welcomed Buddhists, Hindus and Muslims. Mayan communities continue to practice traditional Mayan rites, usually blended with Catholicism. Garifuna customs, which went through a long period of decline, are making a comeback as more initiatives are launched to involve young people in the culture.

ARTS

Music is by far the most popular art form in Belize, from the ubiquitous karaoke bars to the reggae-soaked cayes and the ribcage-rattling tunes pumped out on every bus in the country. Styles are much more Caribbean than Latin – after a few weeks you'll be an expert on marimba, calypso, soca, steel drums and, quite possibly, reggae.

Punta rock is the official musical style of Belize. Its origins are from the music of the Garifuna – drum heavy with plenty of call and response. This music is designed to get your hips moving. Aziatic has blended punta with R&B, jazz and pop to create what some are now calling punta pop.

Brukdown, another Belizean style, was developed by Creoles working in logging camps during the 18th and 19th centuries. It involves an accordion, banjo, harmonica and a percussion instrument – traditionally a pig's jawbone is used, the teeth rattled with a stick. Wilfred Peters' Boom and Chime band is perhaps the best-known of the brukdown artists.

Although he hasn't lived in Belize since he was a child, Jamal Shyne Barrow is perhaps Belize's best-known musician. Barrow was a promising rapper, a protégé of Sean 'P Diddy' Combs, until his participation in a 1999 New York nightclub shooting involving Combs and then-girlfriend Jennifer Lopez. Barrow is currently serving out a 10-year sentence for opening fire in the nightclub.

ENVIRONMENT
The Land
Belize is mostly tropical lowland, typically hot and humid for most of the year.

Victoria Peak, in Cockscomb Basin Wildlife Sanctuary, and Doyle's Delight, in Toledo near Belize's southern border, vie for highest peak status – both are around 3680ft (1104m). Doyle's Delight is said to be about 13ft (3.9m) taller than Victoria Peak, but Victoria Peak is more visible and the popular favorite for tallest mountain status.

The country's coastline and northern coastal plain are largely covered in mangrove swamp, which indistinctly defines the line between land and sea. Offshore, the limestone bedrock extends eastward into the Caribbean for several kilometers at a depth of about 16.4ft (5m). At the eastern extent of this shelf is the longest barrier reef in the Western Hemisphere, and second longest in the world (behind Australia's Great Barrier Reef).

Wildlife
PLANTS
Belize is covered in lush tropical forests containing huge ceiba trees as well as mahogany (the national tree), guanacaste and cohune palms, all festooned with orchids, bromeliads and other epiphytes and lianas vines. The shorelines of both the mainland and the islands are cloaked in dense mangrove. Fruit trees abound all over the country – the most common being cashew, coconut, custard apple, guava, mango, papaya, banana, pineapple and mammee.

ANIMALS
Baird's tapir is Belize's national animal. The gibnut or paca (*tepezcuintle* in Spanish), a rabbit-size burrowing rodent, is abundant (and tasty!). Other tropical animals include the jaguar, ocelot, howler monkey, spider monkey, peccary, vulture, stork and anteater.

There are 60 species of snake in the forests and waters of Belize, but only a handful are dangerous: boa constrictor, fer-de-lance, coral snake, and the tropical rattlesnake.

Two types of crocodile call Belize home – the American crocodile, which lives in freshwater and saltwater, and Morelet's croc, which only lives in freshwater.

Belize is a birder's paradise, with over 500 species having been spotted. Hummingbirds, keel-billed toucans and woodpeckers lead the list, as well as many kinds of parrots and macaws.

The seas are home to turtles, lobsters, manatees, and a mind-boggling variety of fish.

National Parks
Nearly 40% of land in Belize is protected, either by national organizations or private

NATIONAL PARKS OF BELIZE

Protected Area	Features	Activities	Best Time to Visit	Page
Bacalar Chico National Park and Marine Reserve	lagoons, sink holes; mangroveforests, savannahs, semi-deciduous forest; Mayan sites; sea turtle, grouper, jaguar and puma habitat	snorkeling, diving, walking trails	year-round	p232
Belize Barrier Reef Reserve System	World Heritage–listed coral reef, habitat for marine turtles, manatees and the American marine crocodile	snorkeling, diving	year-round	p230
Blue Hole National Monument	spectacular 400ft- (122m-) deep circular marine sinkhole	diving, snorkeling	year-round	p232
Blue Hole National Park	jaguar, ocelot and jaguarundi habitat, caves, Mayan artifacts	hiking, wildlife spotting, swimming	year-round, but the Blue Hole gets muddy after heavy rain	p282
Burdon Canal Nature Reserve	canal weaving through the back swamps of Belize City	boat ride, bird and wildlife spotting	year-round	p282
Chiquibul National Park	Doyle's Delight, the highest point in Belize (3675ft, 1120m), caves; Maya sites; keel-billedmotmot, scarlet macaws	bird-watching, cave exploration	year-round	p276
Cockscomb Basin Wildlife Sanctuary	128,000 acres of lush jungle, home to all five of Belize's native cats and Victoria Peak	hiking, bird-watching, swimming, kayaking	Jun/Jul for wildlife Dec for birds	p290
Community Baboon Sanctuary	black howler monkey sanctuary	walking trails, wildlife spotting	year-round	p248

trusts. Much of the Maya Mountain forest south of San Ignacio is protected as the Mountain Pine Ridge Forest Reserve (p276) and Chiquibul National Park (p276). The Río Bravo Conservation Area (p252) is Belize's largest private reserve – 260,000 acres containing 392 species of birds, 200 species of trees, 70 species of mammals and 12 endangered animal species. There are smaller parks and reserves, including marine reserves, throughout the country. See the table on above.

Environmental Issues

Belize takes environmental issues quite seriously, and much has been done to protect the endangered species that live within its borders. Species under threat include the hawksbill, green and leatherback sea tur-

tles, the Morelet's and American crocodiles, the scarlet macaw, the jabiru stork and the manatee. Clearing forest for farmland is becoming a concern, leading to loss of habitat, soil erosion and salination of waterways.

Other concerns include water pollution from sewage, industrial effluents and agricultural runoff. The most recent environmental kerfuffle centered on the building of the Chalillo Dam on the Macal River. The project caused a rift between environmental NGOs, some arguing against the loss of habitat for the scarlet macaw, others arguing in favor as the hydroelectricity generated could go some way to easing Belize's dependence on Mexican electricity (which constitutes 50%, and growing, of their supply) and reducing associated brownouts

NATIONAL PARKS OF BELIZE

Protected Area	Features	Activities	Best Time to Visit	Page
Crooked Tree Wildlife Sanctuary	home to thousands of native and migratory birds	bird-watching, lagoon tours	Apr–May & Nov for jabiru storks; greatest concentration of birds is around Apr; boat tours are better in Mar when the water level is higher	p250
Five Blues National Park	caves, lakes, bats, hawks	swimming, boating, cave exploration	year-round	p284
Glover's Reef Marine Reserve	mangrove, cayes, littoral thicket, sea grass beds, coral reef, grouper and shark habitat	snorkeling, diving	year-round	p288
Gra Gra Lagoon National Park	recently established reserve with extensive mangroves	boat rides, night tours, bird and wildlife spotting	year-round	p286
Guanacaste National Park	the most accessible of Belize's national parks, well-maintained and compact at 50 acres	swimming, 2 miles of trails	year-round	p265
Half Moon Caye Natural Monument	World Heritage–listed marine zone; home to red-footed boobies, turtles and the magnificent frigate bird	diving, bird and wildlife spotting	boobies nest from mid-Dec–Aug; young appear around Mar; calmest weather for diving is around May	p247
Hol Chan & Shark Ray Alley	nurse shark and stingray habitat	snorkeling, underwater photography, diving	year-round	p229
Mountain Pine Ridge Forest Reserve	caves, waterfalls, Mayan sites	bird-watching, swimming, horseback riding, kayaking	roads get muddy from Jul–Feb; rain peaks in Sep & Oct	p276
Shipstern Nature Reserve	mangrove, subtropical moist forest and semi-deciduous forest, forest trails	bird-watching, wildlife viewing, hiking	year-round	p261

and blackouts. The case went all the way to Britain's Privy Council, where it was ruled (3 to 2) that construction should go ahead.

Also in the Cayo District, the fabulous Mountain Pine Ridge area has lately been decimated by the southern pine beetle, which has destroyed 90% of the pine forest (see boxed text, p280). Plans are in place to replant the pines that have been destroyed, but it is projected that this will take at least 25 years.

Another challenge is lethal yellowing, a fatal disease of coconut palms that has destroyed millions of trees in the Caribbean region over the past 40 years. It reached Belize from the Yucatán in 1992 and rapidly spread down the coast. Only some of the more remote cayes have remained

unaffected by the infestation. The disease, caused by an organism called phytoplasma, is spread by insects known as plant-hoppers. Coconut palms die within three to six months of infection. There is no cure for the disease, but healthy trees can be injected with a vaccine every three to four months to keep the bacteria at bay. Unfortunately, the vaccine is prohibitively expensive, so treatment isn't possible in all parts of the country. Some people claim to have spared their trees from destruction by nailing rusty nails into the trunks. Another solution is the planting of resistant varieties of coconut, namely Mayalan Dwarfs, which take 40 years to reach maturity, and the Mapan Hybrid, faster growing but not always true breeding.

CONSERVATION & ENVIRONMENT GROUPS

A number of groups are working hard to protect Belize's natural beauty. Below are some organizations that place volunteers in conservation projects:

Belize Audubon Society (www.belizeaudubon.org) Assisting in the main office or in education and field programs. Volunteer birders are always required for the Christmas bird count.

Belize Zoo and Tropical Education Center (TEC) (p262; www.belizezoo.org) Motivated, knowledgeable volunteers sought to work in the zoo and education and outreach programs in the TEC.

Earthwatch International (www.earthwatch.org) Specializes in scientific research. Paying volunteers are teamed with professional scientists in the field. Most projects are 10 to 14 days, but some are longer.

Explorations in Travel (www.volunteertravel.com) Places volunteers in wildlife rescue/rehabilitation centers, monkey sanctuaries and ecotourism projects.

Monkey Bay Wildlife Sanctuary (www.monkeybay belize.org) Monkey Bay's programs provide opportunities in conservation and community service. Also has many links to other conservation organizations in Belize.

Oceanic Society (www.oceanic-society.org) The Oceanic Society has a field station out on Blackbird Caye (see p247) where paying volunteers can help with natural history research, documenting the diverse wildlife in the area.

Plenty International (www.plenty.org) Opportunities for working with grass roots organizations, such as cooperative trade workshops and organic gardening/sustainable agriculture. Most placements in the Toledo District.

Programme for Belize (www.pfbelize.org) Manages the 260,000-acre Río Bravo Conservation and Management area; volunteer opportunities are occasionally available, both in conservation and archaeology.

ProWorld Service Corps (www.proworldsc.org) Much like a privately run Peace Corps, ProWorld organizes small-scale, sustainable projects in health care, education, conservation, appropriate technology and construction among others.

Trekforce Expeditions (www.trekforce.org.uk) Offers two programs; one of about two months in the rain forest doing construction or trail building; and one of about five months, which adds rural teaching and language learning.

World Challenge Expeditions (www.world-challenge .co.uk) Teaching and conservation placements in several areas of Belize, for three or six months. Teaching placements are in rural schools; conservation placements could be at a marine reserve or at a visitors center in a national park.

FOOD & DRINK

Being a young, small, somewhat isolated and relatively poor country, Belize never developed an elaborate native cuisine. Recipes in Belize are mostly borrowed – from the UK, the Caribbean, Mexico and the USA. Even so, there is some good food to be had, especially the fresh-fish options available in seaside locales. Each community has its own local favorites. In the north and west you'll find more Central American dishes on menus. For some of the top eats in the country, see the boxed text on opposite.

Belizeans usually eat their large meal in the afternoon, so later in the day you may find that restaurants have run out of, or are no longer serving, their traditional menu items.

Breakfast is generally served between 7am and 10am, lunch from noon to about 3pm and dinner starts anywhere around 6pm and usually wraps up around 9pm or 10pm.

With exactly one exception, you won't see chain fast food in Belize, which is a refreshing change from other developing countries. In fact, 'fast' and 'food' are not words that go together much in this country, so be patient and treat mealtimes as leisure time.

Staples & Specialties

Beans and rice prevail on Belizean menus and plates. They come in two varieties: 'rice and beans,' wherein the rice and beans are cooked together, and 'stew beans with rice,' where beans in a soupy stew are served in a bowl, and rice is served separately on a plate. Each variation is usually served with chicken, beef, pork or fish. For garnish, sometimes you will get coleslaw, potato or fried plantain. Both varieties of rice and beans are flavored with coconut milk.

Meals are not usually very spicy, but the popular Marie Sharp's hot sauces are at virtually every table to liven things up if you need it (see the boxed text, p283).

Some restaurants serve wild game such as armadillo, venison and the guinea-pig-like gibnut (also called 'paca').

Garifuna dishes sometimes appear on restaurant menus, but there are few Garifuna restaurants in the country. If you have a chance to try a Garifuna meal you shouldn't pass it up. The dish you'll see most commonly on menus is 'boil-up,' a stew made of root vegetables and fish or pig tail. Less common is *alabundiga*, a dish of grated green bananas, coconut cream, spices, boiled potato and peppers served with fried fish fillet (often snapper) and rice. Similar to alabundiga but without the

---

NOW THAT'S GOOD EATIN'

Whoever said that Belizean food was bland? If traveling is the stuff *you* do to fill in time between meals, here are a few not-to-be-missed experiences to tell the folks back home about:

- **Bird's Isle Restaurant** (p226) Belize City; boil-up, a traditional Belizean dish, is a big stodgy plate of potato, yam, bell peppers, tomatoes, fish, egg and (if you're lucky) pig's tail.
- **Dave's Bar & Grill** (p237), Caye Caulker; line up for Dave's secret marinade.
- **Dit's Restaurant** (p226) Belize City; have the stewed chicken with rice and beans, but don't forget a slice of that coconut pie!
- **Le Café Kela** (p260) Corozal; try the Fillet St Moritz, fish topped with pistachios, olives and other goodies.
- **Muscovy Blues** (p295) Placencia; don't miss the Cuban chicken.
- **Neria's** (p226) Belize City; Neria's is the place to try gibnut.
- **Radisson Fort George Hotel** (p225) Belize City; don't miss the Sunday night seafood buffet.

---

vegetables, *tapu* is shredded green banana, cooked in coconut milk and spices, served with fish.

Mayan meals are hard to come by unless you're in the villages of southern Belize. *Caldo* – a stew usually made with chicken (sometimes beef or pork), corn and root vegetables – is the most common.

Mexican snacks, such as tacos, *salabutes* and tostadas – all a variation on the fried tortilla, meat and cheese theme – are often available as midday snacks from food carts or small cafés. Mexican soups, such as *chirmole* (chicken with a chili-chocolate sauce) and *escabeche* (chicken with lime and onions), commonly appear on menus.

In the beach towns of San Pedro, Caye Caulker and Placencia, you'll have no problems lining up a variety of meals – from banana pancakes to cheese quesadillas to burgers and, of course, the best and freshest seafood around. Reef fish are always on the menu. Lobster is available from mid-June to mid-February (to discourage poaching, don't order it the rest of the year) and it's always the most expensive item on the menu. Conch season begins when lobster season ends. This large snail-like sea creature has a chewy consistency, much like calamari, and is often prepared in ceviche or conch fritters. Seafood is barbecued, steamed or stewed. A common preparation is 'Creole-style,' where seafood, peppers, onions and tomatoes are stewed together.

Vegetarian items are not hard to come by in most of Belize, but if you're camping, visiting rural areas or taking part in a beach barbecue you should make your requirements known well before setting off. Be prepared for rice, beans and tortillas. Stew beans are often prepared with ham or bacon, so you might want to double-check base ingredients before ordering.

Drinks

Delicious and refreshing fruit juices are available throughout Belize. Most commonly served are orange, papaya and mango, but you'll also see watermelon, soursop and grapefruit juices on the menu.

Brewed coffee or espresso drinks are a rarity here, so when you find them, be sure to enjoy. Coffee is often of the instant variety. Tea and Milo are readily available.

Because of refrigeration issues, fresh milk is not always available in restaurants; instead, canned condensed milk or reconstituted powdered milk will be served.

Belikin is the native beer of Belize (the main temple of Altun Ha is pictured on each bottle) and you'll be hard-pressed to find any other beer on the menu, except in the resorts. Fear not, the Belikin is always cold and refreshing. Most commonly served is Belikin Regular, a lager, but Belikin recently began brewing a lower calorie, lower alcohol beer, called Lighthouse Lager. It's lighter mostly because it comes in a smaller bottle, but it has quickly become popular all over the country. Belikin Stout is also available in the same bottles as Belikin Regular; the only way to identify which is which is to check the bottle tops: Stout tops are blue, regular are green. Cost is usually around

BELIZE

US$1.50 a bottle, although this can vary from place to place.

Rum is prevalent in Belize. One Barrel, a thick, spicy concoction, was recently judged the best rum in the Caribbean. Coconut rum is also enjoyed throughout the country. Special rum punches made with delicious fresh fruit juices are usually on the menu at upscale bars. Although probably not indigenous to Belize, the national drink, according to Belize bartenders, is a coconut rum–pineapple juice concoction known as the 'panty-ripper' or 'brief-ripper,' depending on your gender.

Middle-class Belizeans have recently begun discovering wine. Red wines imported from Australia are usually the best-priced wines on the menu, although it is possible to get reasonably priced Californian and Chilean wines as well.

BELIZE CITY

pop 54,000
Ramshackle, colorful and alive with Caribbean-style hustle and bustle, Belize City is a great place to explore. Here, unlike in more tourist-oriented areas, you'll have a good opportunity to meet Belizeans going about their everyday lives.

In the past, travelers to Belize joked that the best thing to do in Belize City was to leave. Stories of street crime and harassment have caused many to skip the city altogether and head straight to a safe haven in the cayes or the Cayo District. Much has been done to make the streets safer and visitors to the city need only practice the sort of precautions they would in any major city.

Belize City isn't a picture-postcard seaside village. It's a mostly gritty seaside city and one with a fascinating native and colonial past that is apparent everywhere you look. In the center of town, business, Belizean-style, is conducted in Victorian buildings situated along narrow streets. Gingerbread detailing competes with less-graceful window bars on residential clapboard houses. Glimpses of the sea or the river surprise you at the end of most streets, and frigate birds cruise serenely overhead.

As the center of Belize, the city has a style and energy that you won't find elsewhere in the country, amid a cultural blend that you'll find nowhere else in Central America. It attracts a large concentration of high-achievers and a dense concentration of the many ethnicities that blend together to create Belize's vibrant, evolving culture. This is where the country is run, where policy is shaped, where the innovations in business and culture are created.

HISTORY

Originally the nation's capital, Belize City was built on the site of a Mayan fishing village. Popular lore has it built on a landfill of mahogany chips and rum bottles, both ingredients generated by the Baymen (British pirates) in the 18th century. It was the first European settlement on mainland Belize, and became Belize's official seat of government after Spanish forces invaded St George's Caye in 1779. (The Baymen won St George's Caye back in 1798, but it was never to be the capital again.) Belize City served as a trading post for loggers, who would spend months in the bush, then return to the city to get paid and to spend their wages on rum and relaxation.

During its tenure as capital, the city endured a multitude of disasters, including fires, epidemics and – most profoundly – hurricanes.

After Hurricane Hattie ravaged the city in 1961, the government moved inland to Belmopan, the country's current capital. That said, the prime minister still lives in Belize City, and most events and announcements of nationwide significance still originate here, usually from the conference rooms of the Radisson Fort George Hotel.

ORIENTATION

Haulover Creek, a branch of the Belize River, runs through the middle of the city, separating the commercial center (bounded by Albert, Regent, King and Orange Sts) from the slightly more genteel residential and hotel district of Fort George to the northeast. Hotels and guesthouses are found on both sides of Haulover Creek.

The Swing Bridge joins Albert St with Queen St, which runs through the Fort George district. The Belize Marine Terminal, used by motor launches traveling to Caye Caulker and Ambergris Caye, is at the north end of the bridge.

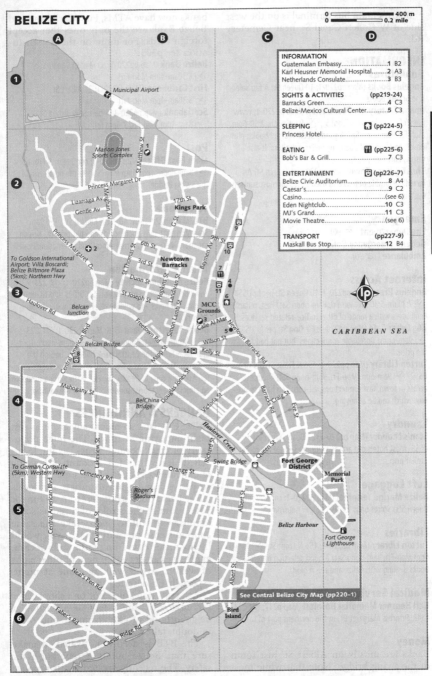

BELIZE CITY

	0 ――――― 400 m
	0 ――――― 0.2 mile

INFORMATION

Guatemalan Embassy	1 B2
Karl Heusner Memorial Hospital	2 A3
Netherlands Consulate	3 B3

SIGHTS & ACTIVITIES (pp219–24)

Barracks Green	4 C3
Belize-Mexico Cultural Center	5 C3

SLEEPING (pp224–5)

Princess Hotel	6 C3

EATING (pp225–6)

Bob's Bar & Grill	7 C3

ENTERTAINMENT (pp226–7)

Belize Civic Auditorium	8 A4
Caesar's	9 C2
Casino	(see 6)
Eden Nightclub	10 C3
MJ's Grand	11 C3
Movie Theatre	(see 6)

TRANSPORT (pp227–9)

Maskall Bus Stop	12 B4

BELIZE

Municipal Airport

Marion Jones
Sports Complex

Princess Margaret Dr

Lizarraga Av

Gentle Av

Meighan Av

Princess Margaret Dr

St Matthew St

17th St
Kings Park

G St

9th St

Baymen Av

6th St

St Thomas St

3rd St

Dunn St

St Joseph St

Hopkins St

Landivar St

Simon Lamb St

**Newtown
Barracks**

To Goldson International
Airport; Villa Boscardi;
Belize Biltmore Plaza
(5km); Northern Hwy

Haulover Rd

Belcan
Junction

Belcan Bridge

Freetown Rd

Mopp St

**MCC
Grounds**

Calle Al Mar

Newtown Barracks Rd

Wilson St

Kelly St

CARIBBEAN SEA

Central American Blvd

Mahogany St

BelChina
Bridge

Douglas Jones St

Victoria St

Barracks Craig St

Eva St

To German Consulate
(5km); Western Hwy

Lakeview St

Cemetery Rd

Roger's
Stadium

Orange St

Richard St

Haulover Creek

Swing Bridge

Queen St

**Fort George
District**

Memorial
Park

Currasow St

Neal's Pen Rd

Albert St

Albert St

Belize Harbour

Fort George
Lighthouse

Faber's Rd

Caesar Ridge Rd

**Bird
Island**

See Central Belize City Map (pp220–1)

Belize's main bus terminal is on the west side of W Collett Canal St, near Cemetery Rd.

INFORMATION

Bookstores

Angelus Books (Map pp220-1; 10 Queen St) A fair selection of new books.

Image Factory Art Foundation (Map pp220-1; www .imagefactory.bz; 81 N Front St; ☺ 9am-noon, 2:30-6pm Mon-Fri; 9am-noon Sat) A good selection of art books, plus novels and books of poetry by Belizean writers. It also displays art (see p222).

Thrift & Book Town (Map pp220-1; 4 Church St) An incredible jumble of new and used books on most subjects; upstairs.

Emergency

Fire Department (☎ 90)
General Emergency/Police (☎ 911)
Ambulance (☎ 90)

Internet Access

Angelus Press (Map pp220-1; 10 Queen St; per hr US$4; ☺ 7:30am-5:30pm Mon-Fri; 8am-noon Sat) Fast, reliable computers with a range of other, office-related services.

KGs Cyber Café (Map pp220-1; 60 King St; per hr US$3; ☺ 9am-6pm) Unreliable connections, but not bad for the price.

Turton Library (Map pp220-1; 156 N Front St; per hr US$2; ☺ 9am-5pm Mon-Fri, 9am-noon Sat) Cheapest access in town, fast connections, air-con. You have to pre-pay, which can be annoying.

Laundry

Stan's Laundry (Map pp220-1; 22 Dean St; per load US$5) Most hotels can arrange laundry service for you at similar prices.

Left Luggage

Belize Marine Terminal (Map pp220-1; cnr N Front & Queen Sts) Stores bags for US$1/5 per hour/day.

Libraries

Turton Library (Map pp220-1; 156 N Front St; ☺ 9am-5pm Mon-Fri, 9am-noon Sat) A good selection of reference books dealing with Belize and the region.

Medical Services

Karl Heusner Memorial Hospital (Map p217; ☎ 223-1548; Princess Margaret Dr) In the northern part of town.

Money

Banks are mostly on Albert St, just south of the swing bridge. Note that while most banks now have ATMs, First Caribbean and Belize Bank are the only ones that accept foreign cards. For more on the ATM situation see p303.

Belize Bank (Map pp220-1; 60 Market Square; ☺ 8:30am-4pm Mon-Fri)

First Caribbean (Map pp220-1; 21 Albert St; ☺ 8:30am-4pm Mon-Fri)

Scotiabank (Map pp220-1; Albert St & Bishop St; ☺ 8am-1pm Mon-Fri, 3-6pm Fri)

Post

Main Post Office (Map pp220-1; cnr Queen & Front Sts; ☺ 8am-noon, 1pm-5pm Mon-Sat) At the north end of the Swing Bridge.

Telephone

BTL (Map pp220-1; cnr Albert & Church Sts; ☺ 9am-5pm Mon-Sat) Sells phone cards and has private, air-con cabañas where you can make local and international calls.

Tourist Information

Belize Audubon Society (Map pp220-1; ☎ 223-5004; www.belizeaudubon.org; 12 Fort St) Offers information on national parks and wildlife reserves throughout the country.

Belize Tourism Board (BTB; Map pp220-1; ☎ 223-1913; btbb@btl.net; Gabourel Lane; ☺ 8am-noon, 1pm-5pm Mon-Fri) In the Central bank building, behind the museum. The staff has a few maps and can be vaguely useful. Ask for a copy of *Destination Belize* (free) for a rundown on almost every tourist service offered in the country.

DANGERS & ANNOYANCES

Belize City isn't so much dangerous as just plain annoying at times. The huge popularity of crack cocaine ('rock' as the locals call it) leads to a fair amount of begging and incidences of petty (and sometimes not so petty) crime against tourists and locals alike. That said, it's not necessary to run for your room at the stroke of dusk, as some doomsayers will tell you. Take the same commonsense precautions that you would in any major city. Don't flash wads of cash, expensive camera equipment or other signs of wealth. Avoid walking alone at night, especially on deserted streets.

Ask your hotel operator or a shopkeeper for advice on the safety of a particular neighborhood or establishment, and when in doubt, take a cab.

The BTB is deeply motivated to make sure that Belize builds a reputation for safety. The recently created tourism police force patrol heavily touristed areas, and must have a fairly heavy hand – everybody becomes very polite and courteous when they're around. Additionally, the regular municipal police force has developed a higher profile over the past few years. If you're hassled or scammed, report any incidents to the BTB so its staff will be aware of trouble spots and patterns.

SIGHTS

Central Belize City   Map pp220-1

The **Swing Bridge** is the heart and soul of Belize City and usually opens at 5:30am and 5:30pm daily. Almost everyone passes through this part of town on a daily basis. The bridge, a product of Liverpool's ironworks, was built in 1923 and is the only remaining working bridge of its type in the world. Its operators manually rotate the bridge open, just long enough to let tall boats pass and to bring most of the traffic in the city center to a halt. It's quite a procedure, and if you're in the right place at the right time, you might even get to help out.

Nearby on Regent St, is the **Court House** (cnr Regent & Church Sts), built in 1926 as the headquarters for Belize's colonial administrators. It still serves municipal administrative and judicial functions.

Along the waterfront street called Southern Foreshore is the **Bliss Institute** (☼ 8am-4pm Mon-Fri), Belize City's prime cultural institution. Baron Bliss was an Englishman with a happy name and a Portuguese title who came here on his yacht to fish. He seems to have fallen in love with Belize without ever having set foot on shore. When he died – not too long after his arrival – he left the bulk of his wealth in trust to the people of Belize. Income from the trust has paid for roads, market buildings, schools, cultural centers and many other worthwhile projects over the years.

The Bliss Institute is home to the **National Arts Council**, which stages periodic exhibits, concerts and theatrical works. Also inside is a small display of artifacts from the Mayan archaeological site at Caracol.

The **House of Culture** (☎ 227-3050; admission US$5; ☼ 8:30am-4:30pm Mon-Fri), built in 1814, is one of the oldest buildings in Belize City. It sustained severe damage from the hurricane of 1931 and Hurricane Hattie in 1961. Formerly called the Government House, this

was the residence of the governor-general until Belize attained independence within the British Commonwealth in 1981. This is also the spot where, on September 21 of that year, the Belizean flag was raised to signify independence from Britain. Today it holds the tableware and furniture once used at the residence, along with exhibits of historic photographs (including those of visits to Belize by Marcus Garvey and Mohammed Ali (then called Cassius Clay) and occasional special exhibits.

Right on the shore, **Albert Park** gets nice sea breezes and has a well-maintained playground. Albert St ends at a footbridge that leads to **Bird Island**, a small recreation area with a basketball court and a restaurant (see Eating, p226) that serves meals, snacks and cool drinks.

St John's Cathedral (cnr Albert & Regents Sts) is the oldest Anglican church in Central America, built in 1812 with bricks brought from Europe as ballast. It's often under renovation because of weather and termite damage. Notable inside is the ancient pipe organ and the Baymen-era tombstones offering a sad history of Belize's early days and the toll taken on the city's early settlers. A block southwest of the cathedral is **Yarborough Cemetery** where you'll see the graves of less prominent early citizens – an even more turbulent narrative of Belize, dating back to 1781.

Fort George District   Map pp220-1

Many sights are across the Swing Bridge, including the **Maritime Museum** (adult/student US$4/2; ☼ 7am-5pm). If you're a visual learner instead of a reader this might not be good value for you – the exhibits consist of dusty dioramas and skeletons and rather static photos, but the signage and text covering wildlife, boats, fishing and other sea-related topics is lively and informative.

Northeast of here is the city's quaint wooden **central police headquarters** (cnr Queen St & New Rd). At the end of Queen St, the old Belize prison is now the **Museum of Belize** (Garbourel Lane; admission US$5; ☼ 9am-5pm Mon-Fri, 9am-1pm Sat). Each window in the building represents one cell in the old prison – and you thought your room was cramped! The top floor of the museum features rotating exhibitions on Mayan life while the ground floor focuses on the history of different towns in Belize.

CENTRAL BELIZE CITY

Ⓐ **Ⓑ** **Ⓒ** **Ⓓ**

INFORMATION
Angelus Books.............................(see 1)
Angelus Press...................................1 F3
Atlantic Bank Limited.........................2 E4
Belize Audubon Society.....................3 G4
Belize Bank..4 E3
Belize Tourism Board.........................5 G2
Belize Tourism Industry Association..6 G3
BTL Telephone Office.........................7 E4
Canadian Consulate...........................8 F3
FedEx..(see 30)
First Caribbean Bank..........................9 E3
French Consulate..............................10 E1
Honduras Embassy.............................11 G3
Image Factory Art Foundation.........12 F3
Italian Consular Agency....................13 E4
KGs Cyber Café..................................14 E4
Main Post Office...............................15 E4
Mexican Embassy..............................16 H3
National Arts Council.....................(see 24)
Programme for Belize........................17 E4
Scotiabank..18 E4
Stan's Laundry...................................19 E5
Thrift & Book Town...........................20 E4
Turton Library...................................21 F3
US Embassy.......................................22 G3

SIGHTS & ACTIVITIES   (pp219–24)
Baron Bliss Tomb...............................23 H5
Bliss Institute....................................24 F4
Catholic Church................................25 E3
Central Police Headquarters............26 F3
Commercial Center............................27 F3
Court House......................................28 F4
Ghane Clock Tower............................29 F1
Hindu Temple...................................30 E5
House of Culture...............................31 E6
Hugh Parkey's Belize Dive
    Connection..................................32 H4
Maritime Museum.........................(see 64)
Methodist Church.............................33 E5
Methodist Church.............................34 F1
Musuem of Belize.............................35 G2
Paslow Building..............................(see 15)
Playground.......................................36 E6
St John's Cathedral...........................37 E6

SLEEPING   (pp224–5)
Belcove Hotel...................................38 E3
Bellevue Hotel...................................39 F4
Chateau Caribbean Hotel.................40 H4
Colton House.....................................41 H4
Coningsby Inn....................................42 E5
Downtown Guest House....................43 G2
Freddie's Guest House.......................44 F1
Great House......................................45 H4
Isabel Guest House............................46 E3
Radisson Fort George Hotel..............47 H4
Seaside Guest House.........................48 F4
Three Sisters Guest House.................49 G1

EATING   (pp225–6)
Big Daddie's...................................(see 27)
Bird's Isle Restaurant........................50 E6
Brodie's...51 E4
Dit's Restaurant................................52 E4
Jambel's..53 F4
Neria's...54 F2
Pete's Pastries...................................55 G2
Riverside Patio..................................56 F3
Ro-Mars...57 E4
Smokey Mermaid...........................(see 45)
St George's Dining Room.............(see 47)
Wet Lizard..58 G4

DRINKING   (p226)
Moon Clusters Coffee House............59 F2

SHOPPING   (p227)
National Handicrafts Centre..............60 G4
Sing's...61 E4

TRANSPORT   (pp227–9)
American Airlines..............................62 F2
Batty Brothers Bus Station (Northern & Western
    Transport-am buses)....................63 D3
Belize Marine Terminal......................64 F3
Caye Caulker Water Taxi Association...(see 64)
Continental Airlines...........................65 E5
Fuel Station.......................................66 C3
James Bus Station..............................67 C3
MacFadzean's....................................68 D3
Novelo's Bus Station (Northern & Western
    Transport-pm buses)....................69 C3
Ritchie's Bus Station......................(see 67)
Russell's Bus Service..........................70 D4
TACA Airlines................................(see 73)
Taxi Stand...71 E4
Urbina's Bus Station......................(see 67)
Venus Bus Station (Southern Transport-all
    buses, Northern Transport-pm buses)..72 C3
Z-Line Bus Station.........................(see 72)

OTHER
American Express Travel Service........73 E4
S & L Travel.......................................74 F3

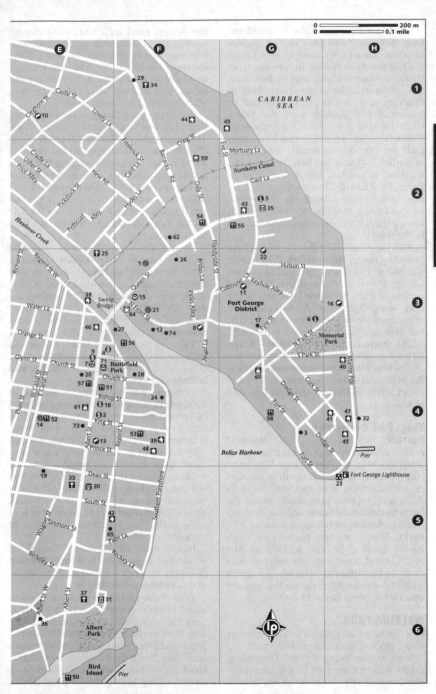

South on Gabourel Lane is the **US embassy** (cnr Gabourel Lane & Hutson St). The original structure has an interesting history. Originally, it was built in 1866 in New England. It was dismantled and sent to Belize on a freighter as ballast, then reassembled in this very spot. It was privately owned by American PW Shufeldt until the 1930s, when he sold it to the US government. It has taken its licks – several hurricanes and, even more profoundly, generations of termites – but it has been restored and repaired as needed. (Read *Our Man in Belize*, by Richard Timothy Conroy, for a description of the damage Hurricane Hattie did to this building in 1961.) This is among the last wooden embassy structures in the world.

A string of seaside sights are east of here including breezy **Memorial Park**, the Chateau Caribbean Hotel and the Radisson Fort George Hotel. At the southern tip of the peninsula is the **Baron Bliss Tomb** next to the Fort George lighthouse. A small park here offers good views of the water and the city; kids will enjoy the playground at the back.

The **Image Factory Art Foundation** (☎ 223-4151; www.imagefactory.bz; 81 N Front St; admission free; ☷ 9am-noon, 2:30-6pm Mon-Fri; 9am-noon Sat), near the Marine Terminal, displays work by Belizean artists and has an excellent selection of books.

Kings Park & Newtown Barracks   Map p217

A nice seaside stroll of smaller houses is along Eve St in the Fort George District to Newtown Barracks, a bit north of the city center. When Eve St merges with Barracks Rd, a wide modern promenade passes the **Belize-Mexico Cultural Center** and the Princess Hotel to **Barracks Green** (also known as BTL Park). This is where Charles Lindbergh landed *Spirit of St Louis* in 1927 as part of a Central American promotional tour extolling the virtues of air travel. The streets west of Barracks Rd make up the modern upscale Newtown Barracks District.

WALKING TOUR

In a few hours it's possible to take in many of the city's sights and sounds by foot.

Start at the Swing Bridge. Depending on the season there may be a collection of wooden sailboats racked up at the base of the bridge, piled high with small dugout canoes. They belong to local fisherfolk, usually from the north, who come to ply the waters of the south. For each canoe there's an angler, so it makes for a crowded trip out to sea, and an even more crowded return when the catch has been good.

From the Swing Bridge, walk south along Regent St, one block inland from the shore. The large, modern **Commercial Center (1)**, to the left, just off the Swing Bridge, replaced a ramshackle market dating from 1820. The ground floor holds a food market; offices and shops are above. This market hasn't really caught on with the vendors yet and you'll find more and better wares for sale on the sidewalks around the market than in its interior.

As you start down Regent St, you can't miss the prominent **Court House (2**; p219), across from **Battlefield Park**. Always busy with vendors, loungers, con artists and other slice-of-life segments of Belize City society, the park offers shade in the sweltering midday heat, and a near constant sideshow as mini dramas are played out.

Turn left just past the Court House and walk one long block to the waterfront street, called Southern Foreshore, to find the **Bliss Institute (3**; p219).

Continue walking south to the end of Southern Foreshore, once the neighborhood of Belize's most prominent citizens, then over to Regent St and south to the **House of Culture (4**; p219). When you are finished with the exhibits inside, take a few moments to sit in the shady gardens.

Down beyond the House of Culture you will come to pleasant **Albert Park** (p219), and over the pedestrian bridge at the end of Albert St, **Bird Island** (p219). Jump over here for a terrific lunch or fresh fruit juice in mellow surroundings.

Inland from the House of Culture, at Albert and Regent Sts, is **St John's Cathedral (5**; p219). A block southwest of the cathedral is **Yarborough Cemetery (6**; p219).

Walk back to the Swing Bridge north along historic Albert St, which has long been the city's main commercial thoroughfare. Note the little **Hindu temple (7)** between South and Dean Sts, a testament to Belize's small but lively East Indian community. Head left for two blocks on any of the side streets – King St might be a good choice,

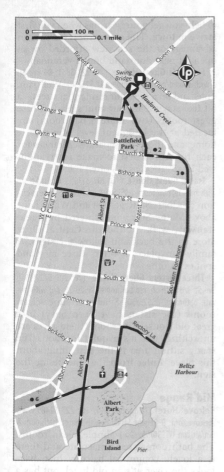

TOURS

From Belize City you can book tours to all the country's major sites.

Tours can be arranged through your hotel or by contacting one of the tour operators listed below. Sites can be visited in combinations depending on their proximity to one another. Altun Ha (p249), Crooked Tree (p250) and the Baboon Sanctuary (p248) are often packaged as a combination. These are within easiest reach of Belize City, and an early morning tour of any of these sites is a good option if you're leaving Belize on an afternoon flight. The Belize Zoo (p262) is also a good quick trip, but day trips can be arranged all the way west to Xunantunich (p274) or south to the jaguar reserve at Cockscomb Basin Wildlife Sanctuary (p290). Prices range from US$60 to US$150 per person per tour, depending on distance and number of stops. Other day-trip options from Belize City include a canal trip to Gales Point (p281), dive or snorkeling tours out to the reef, or the La-manai River Trip (US$80).

Day trips to Tikal (p179; reached by air), in Guatemala, can be arranged through **Maya Island Air** (☎ 223-1140; www.mayaairways.com) and **Tropic Air** (☎ 226-2012; www.tropicair.com).

Many of the taxi drivers in town also serve as tour operators, and they are likely to present you with their business card and give you a sales pitch as you enter their cab. These cabbies/tour guides can be quite knowledgeable and personable and may suit you well if you want a customized tour of Belize, probably for about US$100 per day. They're also a good window into the day-to-day life of Belizeans, and are more likely to offer candid information and firsthand recommendations than tour leaders in more structured groups. Cabbies are known to the hotel staff, if you feel you need a personal recommendation. Also, always make sure your cabby has a BTB license.

S & L Travel (Map pp220-1; ☎ 227-7593; www.sltravel belize.com; 91 N Front St) A reliable travel agency which organizes the trips mentioned in this section, as well as further afield, such as Mountain Pine Ridge (p276) and Tikal (Guatemala, p179).

American Express Travel Service (Map pp220-1; ☎ 227-0755; bzadventure@btl.net; 41 Albert St) Arranges tours all over the country and offers mail holding services for card holders. A day trip to Altun Ha costs US$50 per person including entrance fee, guide and transport.

because you can pop into **Dit's Restaurant** (**8**; p226) for another slice of coconut pie – to view the Southside Canal, one of the few remaining canals in Belize City. The canals used to carry waste to the sea via Haulover Creek. Enclosed toilets, called 'long drops,' were suspended over the canals for comfort and privacy. Luckily, the canals no longer serve as sewers, but still provide drainage for the city streets.

Make your way back to the swing bridge, and cross it. To the right at the north end is the **Maritime Museum** (**9**; p219), but more interesting than the museum is the crowd waiting to head out to the islands – a lively mix of students, commuters, merchants, families and, of course, fellow travelers.

Belize Audubon Society (Map pp220-1; ☎ 223-5004; www.belizeaudubon.org; 12 Fort St) Offers presentations on bird-watching and environmental awareness the second Tuesday of each month at 7:30pm in the Maritime Museum. The organization also leads nature walks in Belize City and sponsors other nature-related activities; call for a schedule of events.

Hugh Parkey's Belize Dive Connection (Map pp220-1; ☎ 223-4526; www.belizediving.com) On the pier at the Radisson Fort George Hotel; specializes in dive trips but also arranges inland excursions.

FESTIVALS
The **Belize International Film Festival** (www .belizefilmfestival.com) is generally held in Belize City in early March. The festival highlights work by Belizean and Caribbean film makers, and films from all over the world.

SLEEPING
A 7% lodging tax (due to rise to 9% in mid-2005) will be added to the cost of your room. In addition, some hotels will tack on a service charge, often around 10%. Prices listed here (and throughout this chapter) are base prices, exclusive of tax and service charge; when settling on the cost of a room, be sure to ask about additional charges.

Budget   Map pp220-1
The BTB keeps an eye on the city's lowest-budget lodgings and occasionally shuts down those it deems unworthy. Travelers on a tight budget should call first to make sure the place they're thinking of staying is still open for business.

Downtown Guest House (☎ 223-2057; 5 Eve St; s/d with shared bathroom US$8/15) Friendlier, quieter and cleaner than the other rock-bottom options in town, the Downtown attracts an interesting mix of backpackers and traveling Belizeans. They also have a book exchange (US$1) and balconies at the front (for people watching) and back (for a little more privacy).

Seaside Guest House (☎ 227-8339; www.seaside belize.com; 3 Prince St; dm US$12, s/d/tr/q US$21/32/40/48; 🖳) The Seaside has been around for many years. Formerly operated by Friends Services International, a Quaker service organization, it has been sold to new owners who appear to be carrying on the tradition of offering good, helpful service and a safe, happy haven for travelers. You'll feel looked after here, and the staff is more than willing

to help you get your bearings when you first arrive in town. The new owners have taken advantage of the sea view afforded by an open lot next door and built a verandah.

Freddie's Guest House (☎ 223-3851; 86 Eve St; d with shared/private bathroom US$25/30) Well run, quiet and on a pleasant residential street – a bit like staying at your aunt's place. Three guest rooms (two share a bathroom) are located at the basement level of a private home, and there are separate entrances for each room. It's best to make reservations well in advance, as it's often full.

Isabel Guest House (☎ 207-3139; 3 Albert St; s/d with private bathroom US$25/30) At the intersection of Albert St, Regent St and Water Lane above Matus Store, but entered by a rear stairway; walk around the Central Drug Store to the back and follow the signs. A family-run place, it offers three airy and spotless rooms.

Three Sisters Guest House (☎ 203-5729; 55b Eve St; s/d with shared bathroom US$20/25, s/d with private bathroom US$25/30) Spacious, super-clean rooms (the sisters have been busy) in a great old house. The rooms themselves are unexciting, but it's a quiet location. The shady sitting area is the best thing about this place. Enter from the lane beside the sign.

Mid-Range
Belcove Hotel (Map pp220-1; ☎ 227-5248; www .belcove.com; 9 Regent St W; d with shared bathroom & fan/air-con US$30/55; 🗷) Simple, clean rooms. The bathrooms are immaculate and there is a lovely communal balcony that overlooks the river. It's an old hotel, but has a friendly, family-style management, remodeled rooms, comfortable beds and tiled bathrooms. Its atmospheric riverside location, on the banks of Haulover Creek overlooking the Swing Bridge, will help you imagine what it was like in Belize City 100 years ago. A member of the tourist police is stationed at the top of the street and the Belcove has a security guard who will help make sure you make it in the door safe and sound. Next door is Marlin's, a rough-and-tumble fishermen's bar, worth a visit if you're staying here.

Coningsby Inn (Map pp220-1; ☎ 227-1566; 75 Regent St; r with fan US$46, s/d with air-con from US$54/59) Centrally located in a modern building, this new motel offers 10 modern, comfortable rooms with some eccentric decorations. There is a nice common area with a big-mouth bass that you can play with all you like. The dog isn't as vicious as it looks.

Colton House (Map pp220-1; ☎ 203-4666; www .coltonhouse.com; 9 Cork St; s/d US$55/65, with TV & kitchenette US$65/75; **P** **X** **X**) Wanna play Caribbean merchant for a day? This is the place to do it. This place has the works – polished boards, four-poster beds, wickerwork fans. Catch the sea breeze in the double swing seat out on the wide verandah… only thing missing is the gin and tonics. The six rooms all have private entrances and are decorated roughly in the style of this 1928 colonial wooden house. They're also named after the kids who grew up there. Sonia's room is the one with the fridge, microwave, toaster and coffee maker.

Chateau Caribbean Hotel (Map pp220-1; ☎ 223-0800; www.chateaucaribbean.com; 6 Marine Pde; s/d US$79/89; **X**) Flanked by the sea and Memorial Park, this was once a gracious old Belizean mansion and then a hospital. Rooms in the annex are modern and simple; the ones in the original building have a delightfully run-down feeling to them. The bar and dining room, also in the original building, offer beautiful Caribbean views.

Bellevue Hotel (Map pp220-1; ☎ 227-7051; fins@ btl.net; 5 Southern Foreshore; r with fan/air-con US$30/55; **X** **X**) In the city center on the waterfront, not far from the Bliss Institute. The hotel's unimpressive facade hides a modern interior with 35 comfortable TV-equipped rooms. Amenities include a restaurant and bar.

Villa Boscardi (Map p217; ☎ 223-1691; www .villaboscardi.com; 6043 Manatee Dr, Buttonwood Bay; s/d with breakfast US$59/69) Located in a quiet suburb between Belize City and the airport, this is a small, charming retreat converted from a family home. Built with all Belizean materials, the rooms are simple, chic and comfortable. There is one private bungalow with a king-size bed; the other four rooms – two with king beds, two with queen – are on the ground floor of the house (the owners live upstairs). Guests have kitchen and laundry access. On weekdays, a courtesy shuttle service is available.

Top End

Great House (Map pp220-1; ☎ 223-3400; www.great housebelize.com; 13 Cork St; s/d US$110/120; **X**) A beautiful old colonial home that has been converted into a hotel, the Great House has

12 good-sized, tastefully decorated rooms with wide balconies.

Princess Hotel (Map p217; ☎ 223-2670; www.prin cessbelize.com; Newtown Barracks Rd; s/d from US$100/120; **X** **X**) Northeast of the city center in the King's Park neighborhood, this 120-room hotel was formerly the Fiesta Inn Belize and before that the Ramada Royal Reef. It has a marina, cinema and casino and undistinguished but serviceable rooms.

Radisson Fort George Hotel (Map pp220-1; ☎ 223-3333; www.radissonbelize.com; 2 Marine Pde; s/d from US$160/170; **X** **□** **X** **P**) The Belize Radisson manages to avoid the blandness of its international counterparts by using local woods, furnishings and decorations. Many rooms have great sea views. Besides a couple of good restaurants and a bar, the Fort George has its own dock used by fishing boats and cruise vessels.

Belize Biltmore Plaza (Map p217; ☎ 223-2302; www.belizebiltmore.com; Mile 3 Northern Hwy; r US$89-125; **P** **X** **□** **X**) Three and a half miles (4.5km) north of the city center on the way to Ladyville and Goldson International Airport, the Biltmore is a fairly standard top-end affair; comfortable, quiet and clean. But if you get the feeling that you're stuck in the middle of nowhere, it's because you are.

EATING

Belize City's restaurants present a well-rounded introduction to Belizean cuisine, as well as options for reasonable and tasty foreign meals. The basic and ubiquitous Belizean dish of rice and beans with stewed chicken is inexpensive and usually delicious. Lobster (when in season) and shrimp will be at the high end of the price spectrum. Conch (when in season), snapper and other fish fillets are good, moderately priced choices.

Wet Lizard (Map pp220-1; Fort St; lunch US$7.50, dinner from US$15; ☺ lunch & dinner Tue-Sat) Housed in a beautiful old wooden building down on the waterfront, this is the best restaurant in town outside of the five-star hotels. Sip a cool drink on the wide, breezy verandahs as you admire the river views and watch sun-scorched tourists returning from the cayes. Located right next to the Tourist Village (aka Hell on Earth), they cater mainly to cruise ship passengers. Still – a menu that offers Greek salad, pita bread sandwiches and plenty of seafood options isn't to be sneezed at, especially in this town.

Bob's Bar & Grill (Map p217; 164 Newtown Barracks Rd; meals US$10-15; ☺ lunch & dinner Mon-Sat) It has a lovely balcony overlooking the sea (and some ugly apartments). Bob dishes out a good range of Caribbean, seafood, pasta and steaks. There's also an air-con dining room decorated in ye olde fisherman style from the Hemmingway school. Happy hour is 5pm to 7pm.

Dit's Restaurant (Map pp220-1; 50 King St; mains US$5, burgers US$2; ☺ breakfast, lunch & dinner) A homey place with a loyal local clientele. It offers huge portions at low prices. Home-made cakes and pies make a good dessert at US$1 per slice.

Jambel's (Map pp220-1; 2-B King St; mains from US$10; ☺ lunch & dinner) This place specializes in Jamaican/Belizean food. The leafy courtyard is a favorite with travelers, and the menu features plenty of funky seafood dishes, soups and salads. Draft beer is available.

Bird's Isle Restaurant (Map pp220-1; Bird Island; mains US$5-12; ☺ lunch & dinner Mon-Sat) Set in a shady *palapa* (thatched, palm-leaf–roofed shelter with open sides) in a parklike setting, this is a great lunchtime spot, popular with local office workers, although there are more mosquitoes here than you'll find at the in-town spots. If you're lucky you'll be able to catch a basketball game at the neighboring court. They serve enormous glasses of fruit juice for US$2, boil-up and barbecue ribs on weekends and all the standards during the week.

Neria's (Map pp220-1; cnr Queen & Daly Sts; dishes around US$5; ☺ breakfast, lunch & dinner) Offers up consistently good Caribbean-Creole cooking, friendly service and decent prices. The chicken is delicious, but there are always more interesting options on the menu (such as stewed cow foot, gibnut and deer).

Big Daddie's (Map pp220-1; 2nd fl, Commercial Center; breakfast US$3.50, lunch US$3-5; ☺ breakfast & lunch) Serves hearty meals at low prices. Lunch is served cafeteria-style starting at 11am and lasting until the food is gone. Breakfasts of fry jacks, eggs, beans and bacon are US$3.50, burgers about US$2.

Riverside Patio (Map pp220-1; ☺ breakfast & lunch) On the riverside, next to Commercial Center, this is a great place for a few beers as the sun goes down. The patio gets just enough of a breeze to make it a comfortable spot any time of the day. They also serve fried fish with… rice and beans!

Pete's Pastries (Map pp220-1; 41 Queen St; ☺ lunch) Near Handyside St, Pete's serves good pies (fruit or meat), cakes and tarts. A slice and a soft drink cost US$1. You might try the famous cow-foot soup, served on Saturday only.

St George's Dining Room (Map pp220-1; mains US$20, buffet US$18; ☺ lunch & dinner) At the Radisson Fort George Hotel, St George's offers a broad à la carte menu as well as buffet dinners and theme nights.

Smokey Mermaid (Map pp220-1; mains US$10-20; ☺ breakfast, lunch & dinner) Downstairs at the Great House hotel, Smokey Mermaid is less formal than St George's Dining Room. Its terraced patio with bubbling fountain is a lovely place to relax at the end of the day. The menu offers plenty to choose from in the way of Caribbean cuisine and burgers.

Brodie's (Map pp220-1; 2 Albert St) and **Ro-Mars** (Map pp220-1; 27 Albert St) are good places to load up on groceries and other supplies.

DRINKING

Moon Clusters Coffee House (Map pp220-1; 25 Daly St; ☺ 8am-6pm) The coolest café in town, serving up six types of espresso, frappuccino and snacks. The Attitude Adjuster (five shots of espresso) is not recommended for those with heart conditions. Smoking is allowed on the balcony only.

Friday happy hours at the **Belize Biltmore Plaza** (p225) or the **Radisson Fort George Hotel** (p225) offer a microcosm of the Belize City social life.

ENTERTAINMENT

Cultural events, such as performances of the Belize National Dance Company, are mostly held at the **Bliss Institute** (p219). Notices of performances are posted all over town.

Belize Civic Auditorium (Map p217; ☎ 227-2051; Central American Blvd) When touring acts come through town they'll usually play here for the younger set, then play one of the hotels to a more sedate or older group. You can call the Civic Auditorium to see what's on, but posters announcing major events are usually hung all over town (including at hotels and guesthouses), so you probably won't have to work that hard.

Princess Hotel & Casino (Map p217; ☎ 223-2670; www.princessbelize.com; Newtown Barracks Rd) The Princess has a number of entertainment venues that have come under some criticism for not being welcoming to locals, an unusual practice for Belize City hotels. There is a casino here with 400 slot machines, several gaming tables and a floor show with Russian dancing girls kicking it up daily around midnight. Nonguests must show US$100 or a foreign passport to enter. Cash is converted to tokens at the door. Also on the premises is a **movie theater** (☎ 223-7162) showing first(ish)-run films. Movies usually start at 6pm and 9pm, with matinees at 3pm on Saturday and Sunday. Also here is Belize's only bowling alley (unless you count coconut bowling in Placencia). For accommodation details see p225.

The following venues can get very happening on Friday and Saturday nights. Note that the bar and nightclub scene in Belize City changes rapidly, so take this info with a grain of salt and ask around to get the freshest information on the hot spots.

Caesar's (Map p217; Newtown Barracks Rd) A good place to start your night, Caesar's caters to a mostly Latino crowd – the music and the action on the small dance floor testify to this. The crowd starts turning up at about 10:30pm.

Eden Nightclub (Map p217; 190 Newtown Barracks Rd; admission US$5) Just south of Caesar's, the Eden is a bigger place playing classic pop remixes and other commercial dance tracks. It's fairly empty until about 11:30pm.

MJ's Grand (Map p217; 170 Newtown Barracks Rd) If there's a pop concert going on, it's likely to be here. Other nights, they specialize in Latin breakbeats. Not a great place to go if fluorescent paint jobs and black lights give you the jitters. This place is open the latest, but people tend to come later, too. If you're waiting for the action to start, you can hang out on the verandah out front which doubles as a karaoke bar.

SHOPPING

National Handicrafts Centre (Map pp220-1; 3 Fort St; 8am-4pm Mon-Sat) This is ground zero for Belizean souvenirs, carrying the work of 540 Belizean craftspeople, and it's often a stop for tour buses routed through the city (although prices are still reasonable). Things to buy include ironwood carvings, slate carvings, rosewood bowls, jewelry carved from *cohune* palms, original oil paintings by Belizean artists, Mayan jipijapa baskets, some Mayan textiles and the

usual souvenir knickknacks. Information on events going on around the city is usually posted on the door.

Sing's (Map pp220-1; Albert St; 9am-6pm Mon-Fri, 9am-noon Sat) Sing's sells a wide range of souvenirs (including almost any Belikin paraphernalia you could ever possibly want) at better prices.

Visa and MasterCard are accepted at both of the above.

GETTING THERE & AWAY
Air

Belize City's municipal airport (TZA) is 1.5 miles (2.5km) north of the city center, on the shore. You can depart for domestic flights from the international terminal, but this is always about US$15 more expensive than flying from the municipal airport.

Local Belizean airlines include **Maya Island Air** (Belize City ☎ 223-1140, US & Canada ☎ 1800-225-6732; www.mayaairways.com) and **Tropic Air** (☎ 226-2012, US & Canada ☎ 1800-422-3435; www.tropicair.com).

There are two main air routes: Belize City–Caye Caulker–San Pedro–Corozal; and Belize City–Dangriga–Placencia–Punta Gorda. Fares and duration are similar on both airlines, and there are frequent (ie hourly) departures on most routes.

Caye Caulker (US$26, 20min)
Corozal (US$61, 45min) You have to connect with another flight in San Pedro
Dangriga (US$30, 15min)
Placencia (US$59, 35min)
Punta Gorda (US$76, 1hr)
San Pedro (US$26, 20min)

Boat

Fast motor launches zoom between Belize City, Caye Caulker and Ambergris Caye frequently every day.

The **Belize Marine Terminal** (Map pp220-1; ☎ 203-1969; N Front St), at the north end of the Swing Bridge in Belize City, is the main dock for boats to the northern cayes.

The efficient **Caye Caulker Water Taxi Association** (☎ 203-1969; www.cayecaulkerwatertaxi.com; Marine Terminal) operates fast, frequent launches between Belize City, Caye Caulker and San Pedro on Ambergris Caye, with stops on request at Caye Chapel and St George's Caye.

Boats leave Belize City's Marine Terminal for Caye Caulker (one-way US$9, round-trip US$15; 30 to 45 minutes) at 8am, 9am,

BELIZE

10:30am, noon, 1:30pm, 3pm, 4:30pm and 5:30pm.

Boats leave Belize City for San Pedro (one-way US$14, round-trip US$25, 45 minutes to an hour) at 9am, noon and 3pm.

Bus

Novelo's (Map pp220-1; ☎ 207-2025; novelos@btl.net; West Collet Canal) now has a near monopoly on the Belizean bus scene. It has taken over Batty Brothers, Northern Transports and Z-Line, but these companies still use their old names (which are still painted on their buses). All enquiries about these (and in fact any bus services in Belize) should be directed to Novelo's.

Below is a list of most of the places where you might want to go. Note that while local buses are marginally cheaper, express buses are generally much comfier and faster.

Belmopan (local/express US$3.50/5, 1hr) Half-hourly departures.

Benque Viejo del Carmen (local/express US$5.50/7, 3hr) Half-hourly departures.

Chetumal (Mexico) (local/express US$4.50/6, 4hr)

Corozal (local/express US$4/4.50, 3hr) Hourly departures.

Dangriga (local/express US$5/7, 3-4hr) Regular departures.

Orange Walk (local/express US$2.50/3, 2hr) Hourly departures.

Placencia (local/express US$10/13, 4hr) Regular departures.

Punta Gorda (local/express US$11/13, 8-10hr) Regular departures.

San Ignacio (local/express US$5/7, 3hr) Half-hourly departures.

Other bus companies operating out of Belize City include :

Russell's Bus Service (Map pp220-1; Cairo St; ⊗ 2 per day Mon-Sat) For Bermudian Landing.

MacFadzean's (Map pp220-1; Mosul & Orange Sts; ⊗ 2 daily Mon-Sat) For Bermudian Landing.

Jex Bus (Map pp220-1; Regent St W & Pound Yard; ⊗ 10:30am & 4:30pm Mon-Sat) For Crooked Tree.

Southern Transport (Map pp220-1; Magazine Rd; ⊗ 7am-5pm) For the Hummingbird Hwy, Southern Hwy and Coastal Rd to Dangriga, Placencia and Punta Gorda.

James Bus (Map pp220-1; ☎ 702-2049; Shell station, Cemetery Rd, at Collet Canal; ⊗ 7am, 9am, 10am & 3pm) For Punta Gorda via Belmopan and Dangriga.

GUATEMALA

Luxurious **Linea Dorada/Mundo Maya** (☎ 223-0457; Marine Terminal) buses leave from the Marine Terminal daily at 10am and go all the way to Flores, Guatemala with a pause for border formalities. If you're planning on hoofing it through Cayo District without stopping, the US$15 fare is a worthwhile investment in terms of time (four to five hours) and the quality of the buses. Tickets are available from Mundo Maya in the Marine Terminal.

San Juan Travel (☎ 223-6186; Marine Terminal) also has comfortable coaches to Flores (US$20, five hours), leaving from the Marine Terminal at 9am and 4pm daily.

You can connect with both of these services in San Ignacio, in Cayo District. The slower, cheaper option is to catch a regular bus to San Ignacio and continue on local transport from there. See p272 for details.

Car

Car hire in Belize is expensive (see p306 for details). If you still want to be in the driver's seat, here are a few reliable rental companies with offices at the international airport. They can also arrange to deliver a car to your hotel at no extra cost.

Avis (☎ 225-2385; www.avis.com)

Budget (☎ 223-2435; www.budget.com)

Thrifty (☎ 225-2436; www.thrifty.com)

GETTING AROUND
To/From the Airport

The taxi fare to or from the international airport is US$20. You might want to approach other passengers about sharing a cab to the city center.

It takes about half an hour to walk from the air terminal 2 miles (3km) out the access road to the Northern Hwy, where it's easy to catch a bus going either north or south.

Car & Motorcycle

Parking is rarely a problem in the city. Make sure you don't park where the curb is painted with a red stripe – the cash-starved government has a fast moving army of parking inspectors out there. Often when you park you will be approached by somebody offering to wash your car, and also 'look after it.' This little protection racket is hard to avoid – you could save yourself the US$2.50 and stand firm, but then who wants to return to find a flat tire (or worse)? The city is small enough to walk around, anyway – the best bet is to leave the car at the hotel (and don't forget to tip the parking-lot guard).

A couple of main streets can get you out of town. To reach the Western Hwy (which leads to the turnoffs for the Hummingbird and Manatee Hwys) you must exit via Cemetery Rd, which bisects a fantastic, huge, ramshackle cemetery. (Most of the graves are above the ground because of the high water table and frequent flooding – it's a good reminder to drive safe.)

Taxi

Trips by taxi within Belize City (including to and from Municipal Airport) cost US$2.50 for one person, US$6 for two or three and US$8 for four. Be aware that if you phone for a cab instead of hailing one on the street, the price may go up, as it will if you're going outside the city center, or traveling at night (this last being an unofficial policy popular among many drivers). Secure the price in advance with your driver and, if in doubt, check with hotel staff about what the cost should be before setting out.

THE NORTHERN CAYES

Belize's 180-mile-long barrier reef, the longest in the Western Hemisphere, is the eastern edge of the limestone shelf that underlies most of the Mayan lands. To the west of the reef the sea is very shallow – usually not much more than 15ft (around 5m) deep – allowing for numerous islands called cayes (pronounced 'keys') to bask in warm waters.

Of the dozens of cayes, large and small, that dot the blue waters of the Caribbean off the Belizean coast, the two most popular with travelers are Caye Caulker and Ambergris Caye. Caulker is commonly thought of as the low-budget island, where hotels and restaurants are less expensive than on resort-conscious Ambergris, though with Caulker's booming popularity, its residents are fighting to keep the distinction.

Both islands have an appealing, laid-back Belizean atmosphere. Other common denominators include unbelievably blue water offshore, fresh seafood at every meal, grass shacks for all comfort levels, a party atmosphere when you're ready for one and a spectacular sunrise and sunset delivered daily.

No one's in a hurry here, and everyone is friendly. Island residents include Creoles, mestizos and a few transplanted North Americans and Europeans. They operate lobster- and conch-fishing boats, hotels, little eateries and island businesses supplying the few things necessary in a benevolent tropical climate. One of the delights of these cayes, indeed of all of Belize, is that the locals enjoy their natural treasures as much as visitors do. They'll keep an eye out for you and are genuinely concerned with your enjoying their home/island. Somehow, folks on both islands have managed to avoid becoming jaded.

Comparing costs to other Central American destinations, you'll be in for some sticker shock, but when compared to other Caribbean destinations, Belize's island delights are quite reasonable.

These cayes aren't so much about lounging on the beach – Placencia's for that. Visitors here tend to stay active and scheduled during the day, but return home smiling and ready for more fun.

DIVE & SNORKEL SITES

Many consider the Shark Ray Neighborhoods and Hol Chan Marine Reserve to be must-see spots, so they can get very crowded. Later in this section is an assortment of other, less frequented sites.

Shark Ray Neighborhoods

Most visitors to Belize agree that a visit to one of the shark and stingray habitats off Caye Caulker (called Shark Ray Village) or Ambergris (Shark Ray Alley) is quite an exhilarating experience, especially if you're new to snorkeling. Although frowned upon by environmentalists (see Considerations for Responsible Diving, p436), these tours are very popular. Read the arguments and be aware of the impact you will make.

Encouraged by chum (fishy snacks) from tour operators, nurse sharks and southern stingrays have been tamed to the extent that they'll swim up to boats and around the legs of snorkelers. As you arrive on the scene at one of these spots, the animals will rush your boat, anxious to see what kind of snacks are on offer. You're welcome to stay in the boat for this, but most adventurous visitors jump in the water to see the animals up close.

BEST OF CAYE DIVING

It's best to be flexible about where you want to go. Rather than request a specific site, let your dive operator know what you would like to see or do, and they'll do their best to accommodate you under the current conditions.

Dive masters usually choose the site based on weather conditions. On stormy or windy days you are likely to stay within the reef where the water is calmer and the visibility is better. Another variable is the price of fuel, which can fluctuate dramatically. In order to keep prices consistent and competitive, dive operators usually frequent sites closer in to San Pedro when the price of gas is high.

An old-timer rule of thumb is that if you can see the waves breaking over the reef from the shore, stay inside of it. Of course, you may not have the luxury if you've only got a week or two on the islands.

Site names can be confusing, since dive shops, and even dive masters, sometimes have different names for the same sites. However, the sites are usually named for the landmark closest to them. So, for example, you'll have Victoria Tunnels across from the Victoria House. One of the most popular sites is Tacklebox, named for the former Tacklebox Bar, where Sharks Bar is now.

Formations to be seen on the local dives are similar – you'll see the terms cuts, canyons, tunnels and caverns in the name of some of the sites. Canyons or cuts are deep, dramatic grooves cut into the coral by the surf. Caverns or tunnels are created when coral formations on either side of the canyons grow together – they're known in dive vernacular as 'swim-throughs.' Swimming through and between these formations alongside schools of colorful fish can be an extraordinary experience.

Sea life off the cayes ranges from tiny nudibranchs, banded coral shrimps, brittle staffs, tube worms and tunicates living in coral crevices to large animals like groupers and sharks, which are best seen near cuts with strong currents. Several varieties of sharks ply these waters, so you're sure to see a nurse shark and probably will see a reef shark. There are also lemontips and hammerheads. Oceanic white tips are sometimes spotted by lucky divers and snorkelers.

Best to See Large Animals
Sites near cuts are usually good for seeing large, hungry fish, which are attracted to the area by the current and the variety of tasty marine life that comes into the cuts. These include Mata Cut and Punta Azul.

Best for Coral-Viewing
Tuffy Cut maintains a terrific variety of coral, including staghorn, elkhorn, brain, lettuce and gorgonian fans.

Best to See Turtles
You'll have a good chance of seeing turtles around Tacklebox during March and April.

Best Wreck Diving
Amigos Wreck is a 60ft tug boat intentionally sunk to provide a marine habitat. Living in and around it are several nurse sharks and moray eels. Between Coral Garden Canyons and Sandbox Canyons, it's the only wreck on the local reef. This is a popular dive site because the variety of marine life you'll see here is a sure thing. Sure thing, too, are the crowds.

Some of the sharks and rays are tame enough to be held, so you'll be able to pet them (the rays feel like velvet, the sharks like sandpaper) and even cradle them in your arms for a photo op. Nurse sharks eat by suction (hence the name) and will make a huge slurp when they get too close to the surface when sucking up their food.

There is some danger associated with these creatures. Always keep in mind that they are wild animals – treat them with respect and follow the directions of your tour guide.

See p235 for details of trips out of Caye Caulker and p241 for trips out of Ambergris Caye.

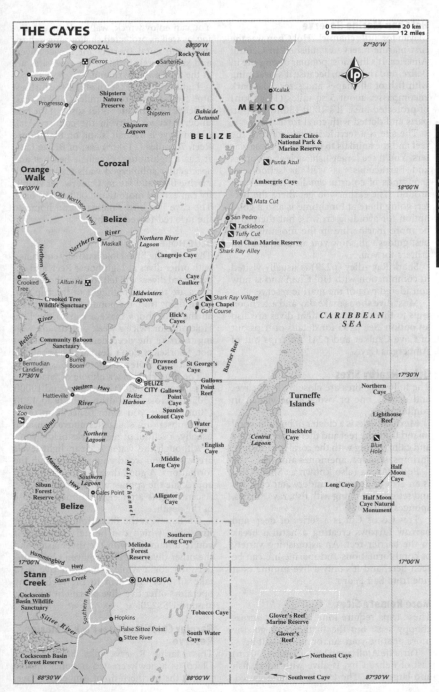

THE CAYES

0 —————— 20 km
0 —————— 12 miles

88°30'W

COROZAL

Cerros

Rocky Point

88°00'W

Sarteneja

Louisville

Progresso

Shipstern
Nature
Preserve

Shipstern

Bahía de
Chetumal

Xcalak

MEXICO

BELIZE

Shipstern
Lagoon

Bacalar Chico
National Park &
Marine Reserve

Orange
Walk

18°00'N

Corozal

Punta Azul

Ambergris Caye

Old Northern Hwy

Belize

River

Maskall

Northern River
Lagoon

Mata Cut

San Pedro
Tacklebox
Tuffy Cut
Hol Chan Marine Reserve
Shark Ray Alley

Crooked
Tree

Altun Ha

Cangrejo Caye

Midwinters
Lagoon

Caye
Caulker

Ferry

Shark Ray Village
Caye Chapel
Golf Course

CARIBBEAN
SEA

Crooked Tree
Wildlife Sanctuary

Belize River

Hick's
Cayes

Community Baboon
Sanctuary

Burrell
Boom

Ladyville

Bermudian
Landing

17°30'N

Western Hwy

Drowned
Cayes

St George's
Caye

Barrier Reef

Hattieville

BELIZE
CITY

Gallows
Point Reef

Northern
Caye

Turneffe
Islands

Belize
Zoo

River

Belize
Harbour

Gallows
Point
Caye
Spanish
Lookout Caye

Water
Caye

Central
Lagoon

Blackbird
Caye

Lighthouse
Reef

Blue
Hole

Sibun

Northern
Lagoon

English
Caye

Mamatee

Southern
Lagoon

Gales Point

Belize

Middle
Long Caye

Long Caye

Half
Moon
Caye

Sibun
Forest
Reserve

Main Channel

Alligator
Caye

Half Moon
Caye Natural
Monument

Hummingbird Hwy

17°00'N

Melinda
Forest
Reserve

Southern
Long Caye

Stann
Creek

Stann Creek

DANGRIGA

Cockscomb
Basin Wildlife
Sanctuary

Southern Hwy

Sittee River

Hopkins

False Sittee Point
Sittee River

Tobacco Caye

South Water
Caye

Glover's Reef
Marine Reserve

Glover's
Reef

Cockscomb Basin
Forest Reserve

Northeast Caye

88°30'W

88°00'W

Southwest Caye

87°30'W

BELIZE

Hol Chan Marine Reserve

Mayan for 'little channel,' Hol Chan was the first marine reserve established in Central America. It's the most popular diving site in Belize, and rightly so, because it's swarming with fish of all shapes and sizes. The park encompasses about 5 sq miles (13 sq km) of protected area. It's 100ft (30m) deep in parts and dotted with coral formations.

The site is a terrific introduction to the reef and the animals to be seen in these waters. You'll see larger fish such as groupers and barracudas, as well as schools of thousands of colorful smaller fish darting around. The earlier you get there the better; going there at lunchtime is also a good option for avoiding crowds, but there will be more marine life in the morning. The best guides will show you around and find critters for you.

Shark Ray Alley (p229) is usually visited in combination with Hol Chan and is now considered part of the marine reserve.

Most dive shops make day and afternoon trips to these sites, and night dives are also an option. See p235 for details of trips out of Caye Caulker and p241 for trips out of Ambergris Caye.

Other Nearby Sites

The following sites are close by both cayes and usually one or two will be visited in combination.

Mexico Rocks is a cluster of boulder coral inland from the reef and therefore protected and calm. Living with the coral are lobsters, shrimps, scallops, anemones and eels.

Punta Arena (also known as Small Cut) is an area of dramatic underwater canyons and sea caves teeming with fish, rays, turtles, sponges and coral.

Tres Cocos Cut is a series of deep and narrow furrows creating a natural break in the barrier reef. An astonishing variety of coral formations and marine life can be seen here, and it's only a five-minute boat ride from San Pedro.

More Remote Sites

These trips require long boat rides across choppy seas, but the further you go, the more pristine your surroundings will be.

Turneffe Atoll (see p246), 19 miles (30km) east of Belize City, is alive with coral, fish and large rays. The terrain is quite varied.

You can enjoy wreck, wall and current diving, as well as protected shallow areas abundant with coral (perfect for novice divers and snorkelers). Most of the dive sites are at the atoll's southern end.

Lighthouse Reef (see p247) is the furthest atoll from the shore, 62 miles (100km) east of Belize City. Its sites offer some of the best underwater visibility in the country. Half Moon Caye is a small island on Lighthouse Reef, 70 miles (113km) east of Belize City. It has a lighthouse, excellent beaches and spectacular submerged walls teeming with marine flora and fauna. Underwater visibility can extend more than 200ft (60m) here. The caye is a bird sanctuary and home to the rare red-footed booby.

BLUE HOLE

The trip to the Blue Hole is usually combined with other dives at Lighthouse Reef, and experienced divers will tell you that those other dives are the real highlight of the trip out. But judging from the popularity of this trip – all the dive shops make a run to the Blue Hole once or twice a week – plenty are willing to make the deep descent, gimmick or not. Snorkelers don't despair: The shallows around Blue Hole are interesting as well.

The Blue Hole is a sinkhole of vivid blue water around 400ft (122m) deep and 1000ft (305m) across. You drop quickly to 130ft (40m), where you swim beneath an overhang, observing stalactites above you and, usually, a school of reef sharks below you.

Although the water is clear, light levels are low as you wend your way through the formations. A good dive light is essential to appreciate the sponge and invertebrate life. Ascent begins after eight minutes because of the depth.

On day trips the Blue Hole will be your first dive, which can be nerve-racking if you're unfamiliar with the divemaster and the other divers or if you haven't been underwater for a while. An alternative is to take an overnight trip to the reef. Many operators offer five-dive overnight trips for around US$220.

Bacalar Chico National Park & Marine Reserve

This Marine Reserve (aka Boca Bacalar Chico) is a newly created national marine park at the northern tip of Ambergris Caye.

The park, accessed through a channel dug 1500 years ago by sea-trading Maya, has a nature trail and a Mayan site to explore on land and pristine coral and plentiful marine life under the sea. It's intended to be developed as an alternative to the increasingly crowded Hol Chan Marine Reserve, but its distance, about 90 minutes from San Pedro, has kept the tours from developing. To arrange a trip to the site, ask at your hotel or contact San Pedro's **Bacalar Chico National Park & Marine Reserve office** (☎ 226-2247; Carabeña St, San Pedro), west of Pescador Dr. Bacalar Chico can also be visited from Corozal (see p260).

CAYE CAULKER
pop 800

Caye Caulker remains a magnet for budget travelers. It's long been part of a classic route that involves Tulum in Mexico and Tikal and Antigua in Guatemala. Proud of this heritage, Caulker retains the shacky, low-rent charms that have drawn travelers here for near on 20 years. There is a tradition of sitting and staying a while. Lately, however, a couple of upscale resorts have cropped up.

Even though it's a hanging-out kind of place, there are some activities available to keep those who are used to covering a lot of territory from going stir crazy. Guesthouses are basic and haven't seen many improvements beyond what is required by the BTB. Hotels don't have restaurants or pleasant grounds; instead, visitors take to the village for entertainment. This, and the fact that it's tiny, makes for more of a traveling community. Water is the name of the game here; snorkel tours are the most common day-trips. It is possible to plan inland tours from Caulker, but there is much less movement back and forth to the mainland than from Ambergris Caye.

Caulker is actually two islands now: Hurricane Hattie carved 'the Split' through the island just north of the village. It's a popular swimming area now. North of the Split is mostly undeveloped land, although much of it has been parceled and sold off to long-term Caulker residents. There is talk of developing it for tourism some day, but part of the north island was recently declared a nature reserve.

Caye Caulker is a place of unpaved 'streets.' The town government has carefully placed 'Go Slow' and 'Stop' signs at the appropriate places, even though there are usually no vehicles in sight and everyone on Caulker naturally goes slow and stops frequently. Virtually constant sea breezes keep the island comfortable, even in Belize's sultry heat. If the wind dies, the heat immediately becomes noticeable, and sand flies and mosquitoes may become pesky.

You'll share the streets with tame, good-sized iguanas fairly tolerant of the paparazzi – a nice couple live in the cemetery. Many gardens and paths on the island have borders of conch shells, and every house has its catchment, or large cistern, to gather rainwater for drinking.

History

Caye Caulker was a fishing settlement and popular in the days of the British buccaneers as a place to stop for water and to work on their boats. Like Ambergris Caye, it grew in population with the War of the Castes, and is known mainly as a mestizo island. It was purchased in 1870 by Luciano Reyes, whose descendants live on the island. Reyes parceled the land out to a handful of families, who sub-parceled them to their growing families as the years went by. In fact, to this day, descendants of those first land owners still live in the general vicinities of those original parcels. Caye Caulker remains a fishing village, although tourism and guiding is becoming increasingly important for the economy.

Caulker was one of the first islands to establish a fishermen's cooperative in the 1960s, allowing them to receive fair prices for the lobster and other sea life pulled from their waters.

Orientation

Approaching Caye Caulker from Belize City, you glide along the eastern shore, where dozens of wooden docks jut out to give moorings to boats. Off to the east, about a mile (1.6km) away, the barrier reef is marked by a thin white line of surf.

Caye Caulker lies some 20 miles (32km) northeast of Belize City and 15 miles (24km) south of San Pedro. The island is about 4 miles (6.5km) long and only about 650 yards (600m) wide at its widest point. Mangrove covers much of the shore and coconut palms provide shade. The village is on the southern portion of the island.

BELIZE

BELIZE

CAYE CAULKER

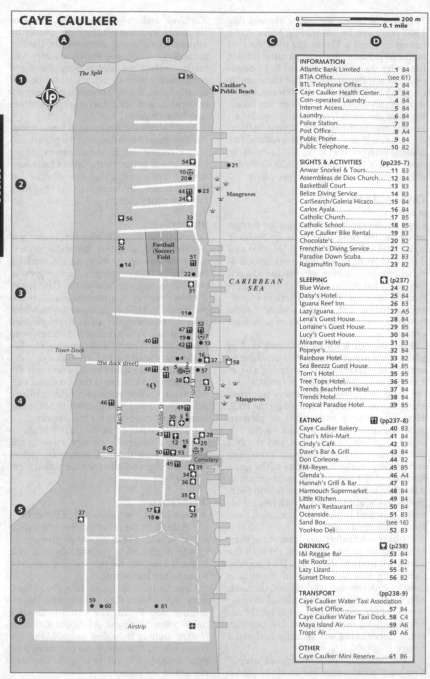

0 — 200 m
0 — 0.1 mile

The Split

Caulker's
Public Beach

Mangroves

Football
(Soccer)
Field

CARIBBEAN
SEA

Town Dock

(the dock street)

Back St

Middle St

Front St

Mangroves

Cemetery

Airstrip

INFORMATION	
Atlantic Bank Limited	1 B4
BTIA Office	(see 61)
BTL Telephone Office	2 B4
Caye Caulker Health Center	3 B4
Coin-operated Laundry	4 B4
Internet Access	5 B4
Laundry	6 B4
Police Station	7 B3
Post Office	8 A4
Public Phone	9 B4
Public Telephone	10 B2

SIGHTS & ACTIVITIES	(pp235-7)
Anwar Snorkel & Tours	11 B4
Assembleas de Dios Church	12 B4
Basketball Court	13 B3
Belize Diving Service	14 B3
CariSearch/Galeria Hicaco	15 B4
Carlos Ayala	16 B4
Catholic Church	17 B5
Catholic School	18 B5
Caye Caulker Bike Rental	19 B3
Chocolate's	20 B2
Frenchie's Diving Service	21 C2
Paradise Down Scuba	22 B3
Ragamuffin Tours	23 B2

SLEEPING	(p237)
Blue Wave	24 B2
Daisy's Hotel	25 B4
Iguana Reef Inn	26 B3
Lazy Iguana	27 A5
Lena's Guest House	28 B4
Lorraine's Guest House	29 B5
Lucy's Guest House	30 B4
Miramar Hotel	31 B3
Popeye's	32 B4
Rainbow Hotel	33 B2
Sea Beezzz Guest House	34 B5
Tom's Hotel	35 B5
Tree Tops Hotel	36 B5
Trends Beachfront Hotel	37 B4
Trends Hotel	38 B4
Tropical Paradise Hotel	39 B5

EATING	(pp237-8)
Caye Caulker Bakery	40 B3
Chan's Mini-Mart	41 B4
Cindy's Café	42 B3
Dave's Bar & Grill	43 B4
Don Corleone	44 B2
FM-Reyes	45 B5
Glenda's	46 A4
Hannah's Grill & Bar	47 B3
Harmouch Supermarket	48 B4
Little Kitchen	49 B4
Marin's Restaurant	50 B4
Oceanside	51 B3
Sand Box	(see 16)
YooHoo Deli	52 B3

DRINKING	(p238)
I&I Reggae Bar	53 B4
Idle Rootz	54 B2
Lazy Lizard	55 B1
Sunset Disco	56 B2

TRANSPORT	(pp238-9)
Caye Caulker Water Taxi Association	
Ticket Office	57 B4
Caye Caulker Water Taxi Dock	58 C4
Maya Island Air	59 A6
Tropic Air	60 A6

OTHER	
Caye Caulker Mini Reserve	61 B6

Caulker has been growing and is now a village with Front, Middle and Back Streets. What was previously known as Back St is now Middle St, and Way Back St (formerly no more than a path) has been promoted to Back St. The dock street runs east–west through the center of the village.

North of the dock is where most of the action and nightlife is. Budget travelers looking for a more social environment usually settle here. The south side is quieter – cheaper, more traditional restaurants and hotels are located here. Secluded beachside hotels are available south of the cemetery, mostly accessed by a beach path.

Most of the tourist facilities were once on the east side of the village, but that's changed, with a few hotels and a restaurant cropping up 'to the back.' Here you'll get lovely sunsets and seclusion, but you'll pay with a longer walk into civilization and extra bugs. This area is ironically referred to as the suburbs and considered to be the territory of 'nonlocal' residents.

Information

Caye Caulker has a few websites, including www.gocayecaulker.com and www.cayecaulker.org. They are helpful for planning what to do and provide some descriptive information on many of the island's guesthouses, restaurants and tours. You can leave your luggage at the Caye Caulker Water Taxi office as you look for a place to stay. Other useful businesses include:

Atlantic Bank Limited (Middle St; ☺ 8am-2pm Mon-Fri, 8:30am-noon Sat) Does cash advances on Visa cards.

Belize Tourism Industry Association (☎ 220-4079) On the site of the Caye Caulker Mini Reserve. You can get information on the island's flora and fauna, then put your new knowledge to work as you stroll along a short interpretive trail. Hours for the visitors center are irregular, but the trail is always open.

Internet access (per hr US$5) On the dock street.

Post office (Back St; ☺ 8am-noon, 1-5pm Mon-Fri) Three blocks south of the dock street.

Activities

The surf breaks on the barrier reef and is easily visible from the eastern shore of Caye Caulker. Don't attempt to swim out to it – the local boaters speed their powerful craft through these waters and are completely heedless of swimmers. Swim only in protected areas.

Beachgoers will find the water warm, clear and blue, but will not find much in the way of beach. Though there's lots of sand, it doesn't seem to arrange itself in nice, long, wide stretches along the shore. Most of your sunbathing will be on docks or in deck chairs at your hotel. Caulker's public beach, north of the village at the Split, is tiny, crowded and nothing special.

Plenty of people offer gear for rent – snorkeling gear and beach floats each cost around US$5 per day, sit-on **sea kayaks** US$20 per half day, and a Hobie Cat **sailboat** US$10 per hour.

A short boat ride takes you out to the reef to enjoy some of the world's most exciting **snorkeling**, **diving** and **fishing**. Boat trips are big business on the island, so you have many operators to choose from. Virtually all of the island residents are trustworthy boaters, but it is still good to discuss price, number of people on the boat (they can become crowded), duration, areas to be visited and the seaworthiness of the boat. Boat and motor should be in good condition. Even sailboats should have motors in case of emergency (the weather can change quickly here).

DIVING

Common dives made from Caye Caulker include two-tank dives to the local reef; two-tank dives in the Hol Chan area (see p232); three dives off Turneffe (see p246), and trips to the Blue Hole (see p232) and Shark Ray Village (p229). Two-tank dives with gear included range from US$55 to US$90; three-tank dives should cost between US$95 and US$165, all depending on the distance to the site. Prices are roughly the same from each dive operator, but there may be differences in level of service, quality of equipment and quantity and quality of meals. Check with other divers, and inspect boats and equipment before choosing your dive operators. Following are some recommended outfits:

Belize Diving Service (☎ 226-0217; www.belizedivingservices.com)

Frenchie's Diving Service (☎ 226-0234; www.frenchiesdiving.com; Front St)

Paradise Down Scuba (☎ 226-0437; www.paradisedown.com; Front St)

SNORKELING

The most popular trips are to Hol Chan and Shark Ray Alley. They cost around US$35

SNORKELING TIPS

Snorkeling around the Northern Cayes can be rewarding even to the greenest snorkeler. Following are some tips for spotting underwater wildlife.

Trying to cover a lot of ground is fun because the flippers give you superhuman speed, but if you want to commune with a fish, you'll need to stay still and blend in. When you get to a spot that looks promising, stay still. If you don't seem threatening, the animals will come out to have a look at you. Be patient, often it takes time for your eyes to adjust. Learn to look for the fish: It's a primary responsibility of some of them to maintain camouflage, so you need to look carefully. It's a good idea to stick with a guide when you start out, as they'll be able to point out animals and show you where to look for them. Once you know what to look for, it becomes easier to spot things. It is immensely rewarding when you find something on your own. Your best bet is to seek out areas of coral that are unbroken, healthy and colorful – fish are attracted to the nutrients of live, healthy coral.

Inspect your gear carefully before you check it out. Just like a rental car, you're responsible for any dents or scratches, so it's best to be aware of the condition of your equipment before you head out. Look for broken or chipped flippers and broken straps on your mask, and make sure the seal is good around your mask. Your mask should fit snugly on your face; your nose and forehead should not come in contact with the mask lens if you press on it.

for a full day or US$20 for a half day, after factoring in cost for gear rental and entry fee. Full-day tours include a stop in San Pedro for lunch. The best guides will get in the water with you to point out interesting coral formations. They also know where to find the best critters, since many of the animals have territories and favorite spots.

Also available are snorkeling trips combined with **manatee watching** for around US$38. Be sure to bring a sun hat, as this involves a lot of waiting and bubble-watching. Another short excursion typically offered is to a shark- and ray-viewing point off the reef at Caye Caulker. For snorkeling or manatee-watching tours, try the following:

Anwar Snorkel & Tours (☎ 226-0327; Front St)

Carlos Ayala (☎ 226-0058; Front St) Highly recommended.

Chocolate's (☎ 226-0151; Front St) Specializes in manatee tours.

SAILING

A handful of sailboats take travelers out to the various sites. Ask other visitors to the island for recommendations for tours. Or check by the boat dock before 10am or in the evening to speak to the boat skippers themselves.

Raggamuffin Tours (☎ 226-0348; www.raggamuffintours.com) offers sunset cruises for around US$20 per person (2½ to three hours including snacks) and three- to four-day tours to the Blue Hole (from US$250 per person

depending on group size). The star of their show, however, is a three-day, two-night trip to Placencia, stopping to camp on beautiful Rendezvous and Tobacco Cayes. There are plenty of opportunities for snorkeling and fishing along the way, and the price (US$250 per person) includes all gear and meals along the way. This trip leaves on Tuesday and Friday to connect with the *Gulf Cruza* to Honduras (see p296). All above trips need a minimum of eight people and have a maximum limit of 15. Ragamuffin also arranges boat charters in the low season for around US$400 per day with crew.

Tours

Most of the tour operators are clustered on either side of Front St north of the dock street. There is little to no difference in prices among tour operators. In fact, most work closely together consolidating tours on slow days and juggling overflow during busier seasons. You may be gently touted on your way up and down the street.

A variety of inland trips can be arranged from the cayes. The most popular is the Altun Ha river trip, which stops at Maruba Resort for lunch, swimming and horseback riding for US$60. This can be arranged through Carlos Ayala, Chocolate's, Anwar Snorkel & Tours (p235) or your hotel.

Nature, bird-watching and mangrove tours can be arranged through the **Caye Caulker Mini Reserve** (☎ 220-4079). The cost is

US$15 per person in groups or US$25 for one person.

Sleeping
Hotels surrounded by trees, with some grounds, or on the beach cost slightly more than those without such amenities. The rates listed below do not include room tax.

BUDGET
Miramar Hotel (☎ 226-0157; s/d US$10/12.50) Spacious, plain wooden rooms with a great balcony for sea-gazing.

Lucy's Guest House (☎ 226-0110; s/d with shared bathroom US$10/20) Lucy's isn't on the shore, but it has some trees and gardens, as well as porches off the bungalows for hanging hammocks.

Daisy's Hotel (☎ 226-0150; r US$13.50) Spacious, but very basic. Try to get an upstairs room where the ventilation is better.

Blue Wave (☎ 206-0114; r with shared/private bathroom US$18/25) A reasonable deal – clean rooms with fan set in a big old wooden building.

Lena's Guest House (☎ 226-0106; r with bathroom US$25) A good budget deal right on the water, offering homely doubles.

Lorraines Guest House (☎ 226-0002; r with shared/private bathroom US$15/25) Basic cabañas with linoleum floors. A bit stuffy, but the price is good for this close to the beach.

MID-RANGE & TOP END
Tree Tops Hotel (☎ 226-0240; www.treetopsbelize.com; r from US$38) Tidy and friendly, this place is a gem. Each of its four bright rooms has a fridge and TV.

Tom's Hotel (☎ 226-0102; toms@btl.net; r with shared/private bathroom US$19/29) Well-kept white buildings on the beach. The rooms are nothing to get excited about, but the location is good.

Popeye's (☎ 226-0032; www.popeyesbeachresort.com; r US$50, 4-person ste US$80) Reasonable rooms with a great beachfront atmosphere. Coffee in the hammocks watching the sunrise is a great way to start the day.

Tropical Paradise Hotel (☎ 226-0124; www.tropicalparadise.bz; r with fan/air-con US$30/35, cabañas US$45) Cramped rooms and modern, well-equipped cabañas. Amenities include a good restaurant and bar and a big dock for boats or sunning.

Sea Beezzz Guest House (☎ 226-0176; www.seabeezzz.com; r US$45) A solid two-story house on the shore with a nice patio garden in front. It's safe, secure and comfortable, and it offers hot water in the private showers as well as dining-room service for all three meals.

Rainbow Hotel (☎ 226-0123; s/d with fan US$28/32, with air-con US$43/50) Just north of the boat docks, in a two-story concrete building. The rooms are plain but clean. In addition, two kitchen-equipped apartments rent for US$150 for up to four people.

Lazy Iguana (☎ 226-0320; www.lazyiguana.net; r from US$85) Caye Caulker's only B&B is a homey affair, with comfortable rooms and a great rooftop area for sunset watching.

Iguana Reef Inn (☎ 226-0213; www.iguanareefinn.com; r from US$87) Some will say it's not the 'real' Caye Caulker, but plenty of others will welcome the amenities offered at the island's most upscale accommodations. Solidly built and chicly decorated, the most expensive hotel on the island is also one of the best values. Rooms are spacious and comfortable, beds are big, decor is chic but subdued, and service is friendly and efficient. Set back from the center of town you'll avoid foot traffic and noise, but still be minutes away from Front St.

Trends (☎ 226-0094; www.trendsbze.com; r from US$30) This happy, turquoise building beckons you from the dock, and even if you don't stay here, it's a nice greeting to what lies in store for you on Caye Caulker. The pink-trimmed building has gracious porches with sea views and the location can't be beat for its birds-eye view of the dock area. They also have another, not quite so welcoming place on Front St.

Eating
You'll find prices higher here than on the mainland, though not as high as the restaurants in San Pedro. Seafood is your best bet.

Do your part to avoid illegal lobster fishing: Don't order lobster outside its mid-June to mid-February season, and complain if you are served a 'short' (a lobster below the legal harvest size, which is 4 ounces for a tail).

Glenda's (☿ breakfast Mon-Fri) On the island's west side, this is the in spot for breakfast: eggs, bacon or ham, bread and coffee for US$3. Get there early, as they usually run out of menu items – and interest – around 9am.

Dave's Bar & Grill (meals US$10-15; ☿ lunch & dinner) A relaxed (read barefoot waiters) indoor and outdoor place serving all your grilled favorites at prices slightly lower than the beachside joints. This is one of the few places in Belize where you're likely to have to wait for a table, but after one taste of Dave's special barbecue sauce, you'll be glad you did.

Tropical Paradise Hotel (mains US$8-14; ☺ breakfast, lunch & dinner) This mid-range hotel (p237) has a restaurant that is busy all day because it serves the island's most consistently good food in big portions at decent prices. The light, cheerful dining room serves a good range of fresh food, including curried shrimp or lobster for US$12 and many lower-priced items.

Hannah's Grill & Bar (meals US$5-12; ☺ lunch & dinner) Offers good local dishes and seafood at reasonable prices from a leafy balcony overlooking Front St.

Oceanside (meals US$6-12; ☺ dinner) Caye Caulker's fast lane, this place has good, cheap standard menu items prepared with care and doled out in generous portions. The space, however, is more for drinking and making new friends than it is for dinner, so if you're after quiet or romance (with someone you already know), choose elsewhere. It often hosts live bands.

Don Corleone (pasta around US$15; ☺ lunch & dinner) Caulker's Italian restaurant serves up 'meals that you can't refuse,' including big, aromatic plates of pasta and seafood.

Sand Box (☺ breakfast, lunch & dinner) Serving delicious food (and gallons of Belikin), this is the island's most popular place to dine. For dinner, the specials board may include fish with spicy banana chutney (US$7) or the less expensive barbecued chicken or pastas (including vegetarian lasagna). The food's good, but it will come quicker if you ask at the side of the bar for your menu. Atmospheric touches include barstools with names engraved in them, sand floors and illuminated glass buoys, but the best decor is the clientele. This is the island's unofficial seat of government and where you will meet Caye Caulker's characters and eavesdrop on some island gossip.

Marin's Restaurant (☺ lunch & dinner) Hearty Belizean fare and seafood dishes priced around US$5.

Little Kitchen (☺ lunch & dinner) Slightly cheaper than Marin's Restaurant.

The **Caye Caulker Bakery** (Middle St) is the place to pick up fresh bread, rolls and similar goodies. Other picnic supplies are available at **Harmouch Supermarket** and **Chan's Mini-Mart**. For box lunches (US$3 to US$5) try the **YooHoo Deli** (Front St) near the police station, or **FM-Reyes**, next to the Tropical Paradise Hotel. If you're leaving early in the morning for a tour, it's best to organize a meal the day before.

Drinking & Entertainment

Lazy Lizard (the Split) Mainly serves beer to swimmers and other hangers-about, but it has some menu items as well. The faithful stay here until long after dark.

I & I Reggae Bar This is the happening reggae bar, and its construction resembles an adult jungle gym. The main structure is a three-level tree house, with swings for chairs and a good sound system. There's a putting green and a makeshift weight machine on the ground floor, and a slab on the main floor that serves as the platform for body shots.

Sunset Disco (admission US$5) On the west side of the island, Sunset has weekend dances and a rooftop bar with snacks. Don't turn up before midnight.

Of the multitude of happy hours, **Idle Rootz** has the best atmosphere. It's a breezy place with mellow grooves and it offers two rum drinks for US$2.50 from 6pm to 8pm.

Getting There & Away

AIR

Maya Island Air (☎ 226-0012) and **Tropic Air** (☎ 226-0040) offer regular flights to and from Caye Caulker and Ambergris Caye (US$26) and from either caye to the Belize City airports (international terminal US$47, municipal US$26).

BOAT

The Caye Caulker Water Taxi Association runs boats from Caulker to Belize City and Ambergris Caye. Water taxis also run to St George's Caye (p246) and to Caye Chapel (p246).

Boats to Belize City (US$9 one-way, US$15 round-trip) run every hour or two until 4pm.

Boats to San Pedro on Ambergris Caye (US$9 one-way, US$15 round-trip; 20 to 30 minutes) run every hour or two until 3:30pm.

Getting Around

Caulker is so small that most people walk everywhere. If need be, you can use the golf-cart taxi service, which costs US$3 for a one-way trip anywhere on the island.

AMBERGRIS CAYE & SAN PEDRO

pop 2000

The largest of Belize's cayes, Ambergris (am-*ber*-gris, sometimes am-*ber*-jis) lies 36 miles (58km) north of Belize City. It's about 25 miles (40km) long, and its northern side almost adjoins Mexican territory.

Most of the island's population lives in the town of San Pedro, near the southern tip, and, in fact, the entire island is often referred to as San Pedro. The barrier reef is only half a mile (0.8km) offshore here. In the morning, before the workday noises begin, stand on one of the docks on the town's east side – you can hear the low bass roar of the surf breaking over the reef.

More than half the tourists who visit Belize fly straight to San Pedro and use it as their base for excursions elsewhere. Even so, San Pedro is certainly no Cancún, though there has been some small-scale development in recent years.

Ambergris has an engaging, laid-back atmosphere. You'll see plenty of 'no shirt, no shoes – no problem!' signs. San Pedro has sandy streets, lots of Caribbean-style wooden buildings (some on stilts) and few people who bother to wear shoes. Everyone is friendly, and, for the most part, each visitor is welcomed as a person, not a source of income.

That said, Belizeans and travelers do have a love-hate relationship with San Pedro. Some think it's too crowded and overrun by foreign intruders, but the island has willingly taken on tourism and gracefully handles crowds.

The crowds it draws are people passionate about being in the water. Water sports are the name of the game on Ambergris. The streets of San Pedro tend to be deserted in early afternoon, filling up again after the diving and snorkeling boats return in late afternoon. Then visitors relax and rejuvenate for the evening's festivities. In addition, tours and attractions are accessible, safe and well managed here.

It may be too settled and 'resorty' for some, and indeed if your motivation is purely to make your money last, this may not be the place for you. But think about it – there are under 700 hotel rooms on the island – that's one hotel in Cancún – so when put in perspective, it's still pretty relaxed on old Ambergris Caye.

History

Ambergris Caye started life as a Mayan trading post and part of the Yucatán Peninsula. Mayans dug the narrow channel at Bacalar Chico (only a mile long and little more than a canoe's width across) around 1500 years ago, separating Ambergris from Mexico and opening up a better trade route to mainland Belize. As with the Maya on the mainland, the inhabitants here gradually relocated to the bush as contact with the Europeans became more frequent. The Baymen likely gave the island its seafaring name in the 17th century and, according to lore, used the coves, alongside French and Dutch pirates, as hideouts when ambushing Spanish ships. European contact with Ambergris declined when the Baymen turned from pirating to logging in the mid-18th century.

Ambergris wasn't significantly populated until the War of the Castes in the Yucatán first forced mestizos, then Maya, across Bacalar Chico and onto the island. San Pedro (named for Peter, the patron saint of fishermen) was founded in 1848. While fisherfolk lived in relative peace on the island, its ownership was bandied about by wealthy British mainlanders who intended to farm the land but never quite made a go of it. The land was in foreclosure in 1873 when it was purchased by James Hume Blake. The Blake family converted much of the island to a coconut plantation, conscripting many of the islanders to work the land by demanding rent from them to stay in their homes. This coconut business thrived through the 1930s, but by the 1950s it had been all but destroyed by a series of hurricanes that hit the island. The 1960s formally broke the Blake family stronghold on Ambergris Caye when the Belize government forced a purchase of Ambergris Caye and redistributed the land to the islanders.

While the coconut industry declined, the island's lobster industry began to develop. Before the 1920s, the area's spiny lobsters were considered a nuisance because they ruined fishing nets. The market for these

BELIZE

BELIZE

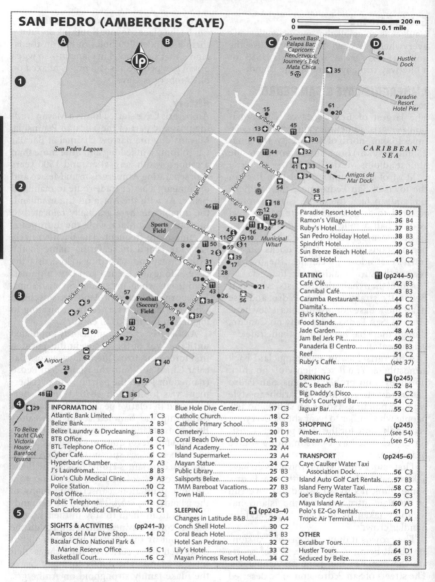

SAN PEDRO (AMBERGRIS CAYE)

0 ———— 200 m
0 ———— 0.1 mile

To Sweet Basil;
Palapa Bar;
Capricorn;
Rendezvous;
Journey's End;
Mata Chica

Hustler Dock

Paradise Resort Hotel Pier

CARIBBEAN SEA

San Pedro Lagoon

Caribeña St

Pescador Dr

Angel Coral Dr

Pelican St

Ambergris St

Amigos del Mar Dock

Buccaneer St

Sports Field

Black Coral St

Almond St

Chicken St

Esmeralda St

Lion St

Coconut Dr

Football (Soccer) Field

Barrier Reef Dr

Tarpon St

Municipal Wharf

Airport

To Belize
Yacht Club;
Victoria
House;
Barefoot
Iguana

INFORMATION		
Atlantic Bank Limited	1	C3
Belize Bank	2	B3
Belize Laundry & Drycleaning	3	B3
BTB Office	4	C2
BTL Telephone Office	5	C1
Cyber Café	6	C2
Hyperbaric Chamber	7	A3
J's Laundromat	8	B3
Lion's Club Medical Clinic	9	A3
Police Station	10	C2
Post Office	11	C2
Public Telephone	12	C2
San Carlos Medical Clinic	13	C1

SIGHTS & ACTIVITIES	(pp241–3)	
Amigos del Mar Dive Shop	14	D2
Bacalar Chico National Park & Marine Reserve Office	15	C1
Basketball Court	16	C2

Blue Hole Dive Center	17	C3
Catholic Church	18	C2
Catholic Primary School	19	B3
Cemetery	20	D1
Coral Beach Dive Club Dock	21	C3
Island Academy	22	A4
Island Supermarket	23	A4
Mayan Statue	24	C2
Public Library	25	B3
Sailsports Belize	26	C3
TMM Bareboat Vacations	27	B3
Town Hall	28	C2

SLEEPING	(pp243–4)	
Changes in Latitude B&B	29	A4
Conch Shell Hotel	30	C2
Coral Beach Hotel	31	B3
Hotel San Pedrano	32	C2
Lily's Hotel	33	C2
Mayan Princess Resort Hotel	34	C2

Paradise Resort Hotel	35	D1
Ramon's Village	36	B4
Ruby's Hotel	37	B3
San Pedro Holiday Hotel	38	B3
Spindrift Hotel	39	C3
Sun Breeze Beach Hotel	40	B4
Tomas Hotel	41	C2

EATING	(pp244–5)	
Café Olé	42	B3
Cannibal Café	43	B3
Caramba Restaurant	44	C2
Diamita's	45	C1
Elvi's Kitchen	46	B2
Food Stands	47	C2
Jade Garden	48	A4
Jam Bel Jerk Pit	49	C2
Panadería El Centro	50	B3
Reef	51	C3
Ruby's Caffe	(see 37)	

DRINKING	(p245)	
BC's Beach Bar	52	B4
Big Daddy's Disco	53	C2
Fido's Courtyard Bar	54	C2
Jaguar Bar	55	C2

SHOPPING	(p245)	
Amber	(see 54)	
Belizean Arts	(see 54)	

TRANSPORT	(pp245–6)	
Caye Caulker Water Taxi Association Dock	56	C3
Island Auto Golf Cart Rentals	57	B3
Island Ferry Water Taxi	58	C2
Joe's Bicycle Rentals	59	C3
Maya Island Air	60	A3
Polo's EZ-Go Rentals	61	D1
Tropic Air Terminal	62	A4

OTHER		
Excalibur Tours	63	B3
Hustler Tours	64	D1
Seduced by Belize	65	B3

shellfish skyrocketed once refrigerated ships came to the island and were able to transport the fresh catch to the mainland.

The lobster catchers of San Pedro formed cooperatives to eliminate price-fixing by the key players in the industry and eventually built a freezer plant on their island, making lobster fishing a viable means of income for the islanders. This brought people off the coconut plantations and into their boats, further dooming the coconut industry.

Inevitably, the waters close to Ambergris Caye became fished out, and San Pedranos were forced to go further out to sea for their catch. The resulting loss of product and profit led to the rise of the tourism industry on San Pedro, as fisherfolk began to see the value of augmenting their income by acting as tour, fish and dive guides for the smattering of travelers who began visiting the island. The lobster industry peaked in 1984, with 184,000lb of lobster fished out of the waters. In 1992–93 the yield was 18,000lb. The government created a lobster season to help sustain the industry, and while the 2001 season was one of the worst in recent history, recent years have shown steady improvements.

Orientation

Most of San Pedro's services are walking distance from each other in the town center, within half a mile of the airstrip, but to reach the hotels and resorts to the south and north of the center you'll need to use wheeled or water transportation.

San Pedro has three main north–south streets, which used to be called Front St (to the east), Middle St and Back St (to the west). Now these streets have tourist-class names – Barrier Reef Dr, Pescador Dr and Angel Coral Dr – but some islanders still use the old names.

The river at the north end of Pescador Dr is as far as you can go by car. From there, you can cross by hand-drawn ferry to reach a bike and golf-cart trail that runs north to Journey's End resort. Most take the road only as far as **Sweet Basil** (☎ 226-3870) for lunch, or the Palapa Bar for drinks, before heading back to San Pedro.

The far north resorts are accessed by water taxi.

Information

LAUNDRY

Several Laundromats lie at the southern end of Pescador Dr, among them Belize Laundry & Dry Cleaning and J's Laundromat.

MEDICAL SERVICES

San Carlos Medical Clinic, Pharmacy & Pathology Lab (☎ 226-2918; Pescador Dr) Just south of Caribeña St, treats ailments and does blood tests.

Lion's Club Medical Clinic Across the street from the Maya Island Air terminal at the airport. Right next door is the island's hyperbaric chamber for diving accidents.

MONEY

You can change money easily in San Pedro, and US cash and traveler's checks are accepted in most establishments. Major banks are as follows:

Atlantic Bank Limited (Barrier Reef Dr; 🕑 8am-noon, 1-3pm Mon, Tue, Thu; 8am-1pm Wed; 8am-1pm, 3-6pm Fri; 8:30am-noon Sat)

Belize Bank (🕑 8am-3pm Mon-Thu; 8am-1pm, 3-6pm Fri; 8:30am-noon Sat)

POST & INTERNET ACCESS

Post office (Buccaneer St; 🕑 8am-noon, 1-5pm Mon-Thu, until 4:30pm Fri) Off Barrier Reef Dr.

Cyber Café (25 Barrier Reef Dr; per 5min US$0.75, per hr US$10) Provides customers with free cookies and coffee while they're using the equipment.

TOURIST INFORMATION

BTB office (Barrier Reef Dr) Opposite the basketball court. Tourist information is also available on the caye's own Web site: www.ambergriscaye.com.

Activities

Ambergris is good for all water sports: scuba diving, snorkeling, sailboarding, boating, swimming, deep-sea fishing and sunbathing. Many island hotels have their own dive shops, which rent equipment, provide instruction and organize diving excursions (for possible dive sites see p229). In fact, just about any local can put you in touch with someone organizing water-sports trips. Snorkeling and picnicking excursions cost about US$40. The going rental rate for a snorkel, mask and fins is US$8. Hire a fishing boat for US$165 a day (deep-sea fishing for US$650 a day for six people). Recommended operators include the following:

Amigos del Mar Dive Shop (☎ 226-2706; www.amigosdive.com) On the dock east of Lily's Restaurant, rents scuba and snorkeling gear and leads diving and fishing trips.

Blue Hole Dive Center (☎ 226-2982; www.bluedive.com) Offers a variety of snorkeling and diving trips, including overnight excursions, and is known for the competence and professionalism of its staff. A boat, guide and equipment for a two-tank dive costs around US$70. A diving certification course runs about US$350.

Coral Beach Dive Club (☎ 226-2013; coralbeach@btl.net) Arranges a variety of trips, including overnight boat excursions on its Offshore Express. It's not the island's fanciest dive operation, but it gets high marks from experienced divers.

SAILBOARDING & SAILING

Sailsports Belize (☎ 226-4488; www.sailsportsbelize.com) Rents sailboards for US$20 per hour and sailboats for US$45 per hour; lessons are available. They are also the first in Belize to offer kite surfing (US$150 for three hours). You must show your PASA card before they will rent you gear and let you go on your own. Lessons are available.

TMM Bareboat Vacations (☎ 226-3026; www.sailtmm.com) Charters sailboats (cats and monohulls) for extended trips. Prices start at US$1850 per week. Skippers, cooks and provisioning are extra. You must have proven sailing experience before they will let you take a boat out, and you must stay inside the reef, unless you hire a skipper. TMM has a marina in Placencia, making a one-way trip a possibility.

MANATEE-WATCHING
The best manatee-watching (US$75) is south of Ambergris Caye and Caye Caulker, in a habitat off Swallow Caye. Trips out to this site usually include a few snorkel stops along with the manatee viewing. If you're planning to spend time on Caye Caulker as well as San Pedro, this trip might be better done from Caye Caulker, since the location is closer, and you'll pay less and spend less time getting to and from the sites.

SWIMMING
While sandy beaches are plentiful, sea grass at the waterline makes entry from the shore not terribly pleasant, so you'll mostly be swimming from piers.

All beaches are public, and most waterside hotels and resorts are generous with their lounge chairs on slow days. The pier at Ramon's Village (see p244) is a great spot for swimming. Another good spot is the beach in front of the Banana Beach Lodge. Current from a cut in the reef has created an area here where there is less beach grass than elsewhere in the area.

Tours
BOAT TOURS
The **Winnie Estelle** (☎ 226-2394; www.ambergriscaye.com/winnieestelle), a 66ft island trader moored at the Paradise Resort Hotel pier, goes out on snorkeling trips (Tuesday, Thursday, Sunday) to Caye Caulker (US$55 per person).

The **Reef Seeker** (☎ 226-2014) glass-bottom boat, based at the San Pedro Holiday Hotel, makes daily reef trips for US$25 per adult

(half price for kids). The aptly named *Rum Punch II*, a wooden sailboat, runs sunset cocktail cruises for US$20 (book at tour agents in town).

The diving operators on p241 organize diving tours to the Blue Hole National Monument (p232) and Half Moon Caye (p232) for around US$220 for a three-tank dive, including lunch and equipment.

MAINLAND TOURS
Many visitors to Belize use San Pedro as their base and make excursions by plane or boat to other parts of the country. Following is a selection of tours to the mainland that are offered from San Pedro.

Altun Ha (p249), the closest ruin from the cayes, is one of the most popular stops on day trips from San Pedro. If you have one day and wish to see a wide sample of mainland attractions, you can choose an Altun Ha trip paired with a couple of other stops (US$75).

One trip pairs Altun Ha with a stop at Maruba Resort, accessed by a river boat. The long pause at Maruba can be filled with lunch, then swimming or horseback riding (at extra cost). Lunch is pricey at the nearby spa, and if you're watching your budget, it's OK to bring a packed lunch.

If you're interested in seeing some wildlife and moving at a quicker pace, you might combine Altun Ha with a trip to the Community Baboon Sanctuary at Bermudian Landing (p248) or the Crooked Tree Wildlife Sanctuary (p251), or both. The Belize Zoo (see p262) and Altun Ha are also packaged together, but it's a long drive between the two.

Altun Ha is lovely, but there isn't the detail, significance and architectural variety as Lamanai (see p254). If you want a closer look at Mayan history and ruins, consider the Lamanai River Trip (US$125), which takes you up the Lamanai River (lots of bird and croc spotting), past the Mennonite village of Shipyard, and to the ruins of Lamanai – a large and important trading post that flourished during the Late Pre-Classic Mayan era. This is a great tour, but it makes for a long day trip in a variety of vehicles – ocean boat, then van, then river boat, then back again.

Another option is one of the excellent **cave-tubing** adventures that are offered by

Ian Anderson's Caves Branch Adventure Company (US$90 to US$125 – see p282). Tours combine a tube float and a tour of a cave, where you will see pottery shards and other evidence of the ancient Maya. At some point your guide will ask that you turn off all head lamps and flashlights, and the group will spend a few spooky moments in total darkness. For those craving an extra dose of adrenaline, try the Black Hole Drop.

Half-day tours to Altun Ha, the Community Baboon Sanctuary and the Belize Zoo can also be arranged for US$45.

Maya Island Air (☎ 226-2435; www.mayaislandair .com) and **Tropic Air** (☎ 226-2012; www.tropicair.com) offer trips (by air) to the Tikal ruins (p179) in Guatemala.

Tours all the way west to San Ignacio (p268), Xunantunich (p274) and to the Mountain Pine Ridge (p276) are also on the menus of San Pedro tour operators. You will spend most of your time getting to and from these sites from San Pedro, and it's recommended that you spend a few days in the region instead of trying to visit from the cayes.

Your hotel or the following tour operators offer all of these trips on a near-daily basis.

Excalibur Tours (☎ 226-3235; www.ambergriscaye.com /excalibur; Barrier Reef Dr)
Hustler Tours (☎ 226-4137; www.scubadivingbelize .net)
Seaduced by Belize (☎ 226-3221; www.ambergriscaye .com/seaduced)

Sleeping

Wherever you stay, you'll never be more than a minute's walk from the water. All but the cheapest hotels accept major credit cards, usually for a 5% surcharge. Listed below are summer, off-peak rates. Rates usually rise 15% to 20% November through May, although some hotels may consider June through August high season as well, since it coincides with summer break for North American schools.

Competition for guests on San Pedro is fierce, and taxi drivers are often rewarded commissions for bringing guests to hotels. Often this commission is tacked on to the cost of your room, so you're likely to save money if you make reservations in advance or show up unescorted. You'll also avoid being taken on a lodging tour of the island

if you tell your cab driver that you have reservations. Most hotels on the island now have a 24-hour cancellation policy to dissuade reservation pirating by cab drivers.

BUDGET

Ruby's Hotel (☎ 226-2063; www.ambergriscaye.com /rubys; Barrier Reef Dr; s/d with shared bathroom US$12/16, with private bathroom US$20/40) Right on the water, Ruby's attracts return visitors year after year. Five of the nine rooms have a private shower. The choice waterfront rooms must be reserved in advance.

Tomas Hotel (☎ 226-2061; Barrier Reef Dr; r US$25) Very good value. Ramshackle on the outside, this family-run place offers eight light, airy rooms with private bathroom (some with tub).

Hotel San Pedrano (☎ 226-2054; sanpedrano@btl .net; Barrier Reef Dr at Caribeña St; s/d with fan US$20/25) Six rooms, all with private bathroom and three with air-con. Most rooms don't have ocean views, but you can always sit out on the wraparound porch.

Conch Shell Hotel (☎ 226-2062; Caribeña St; s/d with private bathroom US$25/50) Good rooms right on the beach, but the price doubles in high season, making it slightly less attractive.

MID-RANGE

Note that some of these hotels charge an additional 10% or 15% for service.

Changes in Latitude B&B (☎ /fax 226-2986; www .ambergriscaye.com/latitudes; Coconut Dr; s/d 60/65; 🖳) Just north of the Belize Yacht Club, this trim two-story guesthouse offers six ground-floor rooms with private bathroom and air-con. It's just a short block inland from the beach and has a nice garden area.

Coral Beach Hotel (☎ 226-2013; www.coralbeach hotel.com; Barrier Reef Dr; s/d from US$50/57) A simple diver's hotel offering fan and air-con rooms. Good-value dive packages are available.

Lily's Hotel (☎ 206-2059; www.ambergriscaye.com /lilys; Caribeña St; s/d from US$45/55) Facing the sea, off the east end of Caribeña St, with 10 clean, pleasant rooms with air-con; several (especially those on the top floor) have good sea views.

San Pedro Holiday Hotel (☎ 226-2014, www.san pedroholiday.com; Barrier Reef Dr; s/d from US$85/95) In the south part of the town center, the rooms here are in three cheery, pink and white wooden buildings, all facing the sea. The rooms are basic (with air-con, ceiling fans and patios), and the walls can be thin. What you're really paying for is the location – if you want to be on the beach in the thick of things, this is your place.

Spindrift Hotel (☎ 226-2174; www.ambergriscaye .com/spindrift; Buccaneer St at Barrier Reef Dr; r from US$50) A good location right in the center of town on the beach. It's a modern concrete affair with 30 rooms of various sizes. Each of the small rooms has one double bed, a ceiling fan and a view of the street. Larger ones have two double beds, air-con and sea views. Several apartments are also available (US$110).

Paradise Resort Hotel (☎ 226-2083; www.amber griscaye.com/paradiseresort; Barrier Reef Dr; s/d cabañas from US$80/90, s/d from US$100/110) Set on sandy, shady grounds right on the beach. They have a bar and deli on the premises. Rooms with kitchenette cost US$10 extra.

Mayan Princess Resort Hotel (☎ 226-2778; www.ambergriscaye.com/mayanprin; Barrier Reef Dr; s/d US$90/110) A modern condominium building in the town center on the beach. Suites have kitchenettes, air-con and cable TV.

Sun Breeze Beach Hotel (☎ 226-2191; www.sun breeze.net; s/d from US$100/110; 🍴) Across Coconut Dr from the airport, this is a generic two-story concrete building with a sandy inner court and swimming pool opening toward the beach. Shady tiled porticos set with easy chairs are great for lounging. Each of the 34 air-con rooms has two double beds, cable TV and private bathroom.

Belize Yacht Club (☎ 226-2777; www.belizeyacht club.com; Coconut Dr; units from US$140; 🍴) South of the airport, Belize Yacht Club has several two-story Spanish-style buildings arranged around a swimming pool and set amid lawns stretching down to the beach. Its air-con one- to three-bedroom units have full kitchens, balconies and sea views.

TOP END

Ramon's Village (☎ 226-2071; www.ramons.com; Coconut Dr; r from US$150; 😼 🍴) Right on the seafront south of town, Ramon's offers 60 rooms in two-story cabañas, thatched Ta-hitian-style, facing a good beach and a nice dock for swimming. A dive shop, excursion boats, jet skis, sailboards, lounge chairs for sunbathing, a swimming pool… This place has everything. This is among the island's best places to stay.

Journey's End (☎ 226-2108; www.journeysend resort.com; r US$120, cabañas from US$200) A large,

all-inclusive-style resort on a northern nar-row strip of the island. It's popular with divers and families and bills its offering 'a barefoot adventure.' There is also a three-bedroom villa for US$492 a night.

Victoria House (☎ 226-2067; www.ambergriscaye .com/victoriahouse; r from US$135, houses from US$220; 😼 🍴) An elegant resort hotel 2 miles (3km) south of the airport, on the beach. The beach, the lawns and the 31 rooms are beautifully kept, and amenities include a dining room, bar and dive shop. A variety of tasteful accommodations are available, up to the Casa Azul, a four-bedroom, two-story house with its own swimming pool, which goes for a cool US$1150 a night in low sea-son. Here you're away from it all, but San Pedro is a quick 10-minute bike, shuttle van or golf cart ride away (use of bikes is free for hotel guests; golf carts can be rented).

Mata Chica (☎ 220-5010; www.matachica.com; villas US$190-490; 😼) At the north end of Amber-gris, this is perhaps the chicest place on the island, with its 11 luxurious thatch-roofed villas, each decorated in a tropical-fruit theme. You can also visit for dinner at Mambo Café, Mata Chica's restaurant (see opposite).

Eating

Several small cafés in the center of town serve cheap, simple meals. The best places for low-budget feasting are the stands in front of the park, where you can pick up a plate of stewed chicken with beans and rice, barbecue and other delicacies for about US$2.

Elvi's Kitchen (Pescador Dr; meals US$5-30) Hotel staff will recommend this place near Am-bergris St, for seafood and traditional Belizean dishes. You can have just a ham-burger or a full lobster dinner with wine. Mixed drinks are available but expensive. Be sure to ask about items not priced on the menu – they're sometimes out of scale and you may get a surprise.

Café Olé (meals US$8; 😼 breakfast, lunch & dinner) Across from the airport, it has a deli offer-ing olive oils, cheeses and wine. It serves excellent espresso coffee.

Caramba Restaurant (Pescador Dr; meals US$5) Serves reasonably priced seafood and Mexi-can dishes and offers a free rum punch on arrival!

Diamita's (meals US$3.50; 😼 breakfast & lunch) Has a simple menu of well-priced items. Beware the large coffee – it's truly large.

Ruby's Caffe (Barrier Reef Dr; snacks from US$3, meals from US$5) Next to Ruby's Hotel, this is a tiny place with good cakes and pastries but unpredictable hours.

Panadería El Centro (cnr Buccaneer St & Pescador Dr; from US$1.50) For simpler take-out pastries and bread.

Reef (Pescador Dr; meals US$5-7) This is the place if you're yearning for traditional Belizean fare at traditional prices. It has a thatched roof with sand-covered floors (between Pelican and Caribeña Sts).

Jade Garden (Coconut Dr; meals US$5-$18; ☺ dinner) A 10-minute walk south of the airport. San Pedro's Chinese restaurant has a long menu.

Jam Bel Jerk Pit (meals from US$6.50) Next to Big Daddy's Disco, it serves spicy hot Jamaican dishes at reasonable prices. It also has a nice rooftop patio.

Cannibal Café (cnr Barrier Reef Dr & Black Coral St; meals US$7; ☺ breakfast, lunch & dinner) This beachside café serves moderately priced breakfasts, lunches and early dinners.

The latest thing in fine dining is to take a moonlight water-taxi ride up to one of the resort restaurants at the island's north end. Meals are usually pricey (US$30 to US$40 for mains), but menus are often unusual and feature excellent seafood preparations. Mata Chica's **Mambo Café** (☎ 220-5010; www .matachica.com/mambo.html) has a Mediterranean flair, **Rendezvous** (☎ 226-3426; www.ambergriscaye .com/rendezvous) is pan-Asian and **Capricorn** (☎ 226-2809; www.ambergriscaye.com/capricorn) has been described as nouvelle.

Drinking & Entertainment

Sipping, sitting, talking and dancing are parts of everyday life on Ambergris. Many hotels have comfortable bars, often with sand floors, thatched roofs and reggae music.

Fido's Courtyard (Barrier Reef Dr) This bar, near Pelican St, is the landlubbers' favorite, with live music most nights.

Big Daddy's Disco Right next to San Pedro's church, this is a hot nightspot, often featuring live reggae, especially during winter.

Jaguar Bar Across Barrier Reef Dr from Big Daddy's, this jungle-themed bar is often closed off-season, but it rocks in winter.

Barefoot Iguana (Coconut Dr) This relative newcomer, south of the airstrip, is giving the older establishments a run for their money.

BC's Beach Bar On the beach in a *palapa* between Ramon's Village and the Sea Breeze Beach Hotel, BC's stays open late and is usually filled with sun-crisped expatriates enjoying Jimmy Buffett on the jukebox. The Sunday afternoon barbecue is a hot ticket. It starts at noon and continues until the food runs out, usually around 2:30pm.

Shopping

Plenty of gift shops in the hotels and on Barrier Reef Dr sell key chains, T-shirts and beachwear.

Belizean Arts (☎ 226-3019; Fido's Courtyard) One of the best shopping spots, it sells ceramics, woodcarvings and paintings alongside affordable and tasteful knickknacks.

Amber (☎ 226-3101; Fido's Courtyard) Sells handmade jewelry produced on the island.

Getting There & Away

AIR

Both **Maya Island Air** (☎ 226-2435; www.mayais landair.com) and rival **Tropic Air** (☎ 226-2012; www .tropicair.com) offer several flights daily between San Pedro and the Belize City airports (international US$47, municipal US$26) and to Corozal (US$35).

BOAT

The **Caye Caulker Water Taxi Association** (☎ 226-0992) runs boats between San Pedro, Caye Caulker and Belize City. Boats to Belize City via Caye Caulker leave from the Caye Caulker Water Taxi Association Dock in San Pedro at 8am, 9:30am, 11:30am and 2:30pm (also 4:30pm on weekends and holidays). Boats leave Belize City for San Pedro at 9am, noon and 3pm. Cost is US$14 one-way, US$25 round-trip. Boats leave Caye Caulker for San Pedro at 7am, 8:30am, 10am, 1pm and 4pm; fare is US$9 each way, US$15 round-trip.

Thunderbolt Travels (Belize City ☎ 226-2904) departs San Pedro daily at 3pm for Corozal, making the return trip at 7am. One-way fares are US$22.50.

Getting Around

You can walk into town from the airport in 10 minutes or less, and the walk from the boat docks is even shorter. A taxi ride from the airport costs US$2.50 to any place in town, US$5 to the hotels south of town.

San Pedranos get around on foot or by bicycle, golf cart, pickup truck or minivan.

BELIZE

You can rent golf carts at **Polo's EZ-Go Rentals** (☎ 226-3542), at the northern end of Barrier Reef Dr, or at **Island Auto Golf Cart Rentals** (☎ 226-2790), on Coconut Dr across from the airstrip. Golf carts rent for US$13 per hour, US$60 per day. Rent bikes at Polo's EZ-Go or **Joe's Bicycle Rentals** (☎ 226-4371); rates are around US$6 for half a day, US$10 for 24 hours.

The **Island Ferry** (☎ 226-3231) operates an Ambergris-only water-taxi service north and south from the Fido's Courtyard dock.

OTHER CAYES

Though Ambergris and Caulker are the most easily accessible and popular cayes, it is possible to arrange visits to the others. Serious divers are the usual customers at camps and resorts on the smaller cayes. Often a special flight or boat charter is necessary to reach these cayes; you can make arrangements for transportation when you book your lodgings. Most booking offices are in Belize City, as the smaller cayes have infrequent mail service and no telephones (only radios).

Caye Chapel

Caye Chapel Island Resort (☎ 226-8250; www .belizegolf.cc; villa per person from US$229; 💥 ⚑) Just south of Caye Caulker, this private 265-acre island holds an 18-hole golf course and a superdeluxe corporate retreat center (room rates include meals and unlimited golfing). The golf course is open to the public (by reservation only) when there are no retreaters. Cost is US$200 for the day which includes unlimited golf, golf cart, clubs, poolside Caribbean lunch and use of the resort's swimming pool complex, hot tub and private beach. Boat transportation to the island can be arranged in advance with boats going to or from San Pedro or Caye Caulker.

St George's Caye

Nine miles (14km) offshore of Belize City, St George's Caye was the Belize settlement's first capital (1650–1784) and site of the decisive 1798 battle between British settlers and a Spanish invasion force. Today it holds vacation homes for the Belize elite and two resorts perfect for those looking to get away from it all: **St George's Lodge** (☎ /fax 220-4444, US ☎ +1-800-678-6871; www.gooddiving.com; s/d US$247/255), a 10-room,

six-cottage resort with a staggering array of dive packages, and **Pleasure Island Resort** (☎ 209-4020; www.stgeorgescayepleasure.bz; r low/high season US$55/85; 💥 ⚑), which is more family-oriented, but an extremely good deal for this part of the world.

Gallows Point Caye

Belcove Island Lodge (☎ 227-3054; www.belcove .com; s/d US$155/200) This is the only lodge on this caye, so if it's tranquility you're after, this may be the place – chances are you'll have the lodge to yourself. The rooms are on the top floor of an old wooden house; downstairs is the timber-lined and fishing-net–adorned dining room. This is by far the most rustic of the accommodations on the smaller cayes – the perfect place to indulge your Caribbean castaway fantasies (if you ever had any, that is). Activities include glass-bottom boat tours (US$70 full day) and manatee/dolphin watching (US$70 per day). Room rates include three meals and transfers.

Spanish Lookout Caye

Spanish Bay Resort (no phone; www.sirenian.org /spanishbay.html; weekly packages relaxation/snorkeling/ diving US$715/900/1190) Incredibly peaceful and secluded, this resort shares the small caye with the Earthwatch Marine Research station. The resort has recently been taken over by Belize-based Hugh Parkey's Belize Dive Connection, so the dive operation should be world class, and there are many fantastic sites close by. Kayaks are available for guests to go paddling through the mangroves, where you stand a pretty good chance of seeing manatees. Accommodation is in rustic wooden cabañas built out over startlingly clear water. Stargazing from the balconies at night is truly a memorable experience.

Turneffe Islands

This coral atoll 19 miles (30km) east of Belize City is a magnet for divers and fishers. Divers will find walls and wrecks to explore and rewarding sites for all experience levels. Fishing enthusiasts are attracted by the flats, which are ideal for saltwater fly-fishing.

Turneffe Flats Lodge (☎ 220-2046; www.tflats .com; weekly packages diving/fishing US$1495/2495; 💥) Although it gained fame as a fishing retreat with expert guides, this lodge offers dive trips which are often far less crowded than on other resorts (because most of the other guests are out fishing). Accommodation is in spacious terracotta-tiled duplex apartments, each with balcony and dramatic views of the waves crashing on the nearby reef. This lodge donates 1% of revenues to conservation and sustainability of sensitive areas like the Turneffe Flats.

Blackbird Caye Resort (☎ 223-2772; www.black birdresort.com; weekly packages diving/snorkeling US$1395/ 1250; ⊠) Blackbird offers fishing and diving as well, but is popular with snorkelers as they have two dedicated snorkeling boats trip per day. Accommodation is in separate, roomy cabañas with stereo systems (radio reception is dodgy, so bring some CDs).

Oceanic Society (☎ 220-4256; www.oceanic-society .org; weekly snorkel package US$1450) The Society has a field station about five minutes' walk from Blackbird Caye Resort. Accommodations here are more basic, but perfectly comfortable, in wooden beachfront cabañas. The snorkeling package includes trips to Soldiers and Lighthouse Reef. The Society also accepts volunteers on a paying basis to help with natural history research, documenting the incredibly diverse wildlife (manatees, crocodiles, bottle-nosed dolphins and hawksbill sea turtles among others) that call the Turneffe Islands their home. Incredibly, the Turneffe Islands form the only atoll in Belize with no environmental protection, and part of the Society's work is to gather data that will rectify this situation.

Turneffe Island Lodge (☎ 220-4011; www.turneffe lodge.com; weekly packages beachcombing/diving/fishing from US$1400/1462/3045; ⊠ ⊠) Definitely the fanciest of the Turneffe Islands resorts, this place offers everything including gorgeous cabañas with screened porches (where your morning coffee will be delivered), wooden floorboards and indoor and outdoor showers. Their proximity to the famous 'Elbow' dive site means that they go there several times a week, and some of the best Tarpon fishing is a three-minute boat ride away.

Lighthouse Reef
NORTHERN CAYE
Lighthouse Reef Resort (☎ 223-1205, US ☎ +1-800-423-3114; www.scubabelize.com; ⊠) The only resort on the Lighthouse Reef was undergoing a change of ownership at time of writing, so details are sketchy, but this place is definitely in the 'luxury' category and has its own airstrip to bring guests out

to the closest resort to the Blue Hole and many other fabulous dive sites. It should be open again by the time you read this and prices will probably be around US$1500 for weekly dive packages.

HALF MOON CAYE
This caye in Lighthouse Reef is protected as the **Half Moon Caye Natural Monument** (admission US$5). Standing less than 10ft (3m) above sea level, the caye's 45 acres (18 hectares) hold two distinct ecosystems. To the west is lush vegetation fertilized by the droppings of thousands of seabirds, including some 4000 red-footed boobies, the wonderfully named magnificent frigate bird and some 98 other bird species; the east side has less vegetation but more coconut palms. Loggerhead and hawksbill turtles, both endangered, lay their eggs on the southern beaches.

A nature trail weaves through the southern part of the island to an observation platform that brings viewers eye level with nesting boobies and frigate birds. Along the path you'll see thousands of seashells, many inhabited by hermit crabs (unnerving when you first notice them moving!). Accommodations are unavailable, but camping is allowed in designated areas and showers and toilets are provided. Organized boat trips (mostly from Caye Caulker and Ambergis Caye) stop at Half Moon Caye and the nearby Blue Hole.

BLUE HOLE
Also within Lighthouse Reef, the Blue Hole is the country's best-known dive site and often appears in tourist brochures touting Belize's marine wonders. See p232 for details.

NORTHERN BELIZE

The northern Belize most commonly seen by visitors is farmland. Vast sugarcane fields grow alongside the paved, swift Northern Hwy, and off on the side roads. Mennonites, Maya and mestizos tend efficient multipurpose farms. Head deeper into the region and you will hit jungle in the hilly west and mangrove swamp along the convoluted Caribbean shoreline.

Orange Walk and Corozal are the region's two major towns. Orange Walk is the commercial center for area farming as well as the starting point for river tours to Lamanai, a Mayan ruin site known for its historical interest and for the exotic river journey that most travelers take to reach it.

The Crooked Tree Wildlife Sanctuary, midway between Orange Walk and Belize City, is an excellent place for birdwatching, as is Shipstern Nature Reserve, south of Sarteneja on the large peninsula southeast of Corozal.

Corozal is Belize's northernmost town of appreciable size and is a gateway for travelers going to and from Mexico's Yucatán Peninsula.

The north has several significant biosphere reserves. Largest is the Río Bravo Conservation and Management Area, a giant preserve of tropical forests, rivers, ponds and Mayan archaeological sites in the western part of the Orange Walk District.

While sugar extraction and processing is by far the number one industry here, most of this land was settled not by farmers looking for lush pastures, but by refugees fleeing war in the Yucatán. The War of the Castes began in 1847 and lumbered on in a series of bloody battles until 1901. One of the war's main points of contention involved the caste system, essentially a class system that shoved the indigenous Maya to the bottom of the socio-economic ladder under Spanish and later British rule.

A treaty ratified in 1897 defined Belize's northwestern border. The number of Caste War settlers, along with the area's proximity to Mexico, gives northern Belize a unique Spanish influence.

COMMUNITY BABOON SANCTUARY

No real baboons inhabit Belize, but Belizeans use that name for the country's indigenous black howler monkeys. 'Howler' is definitely a good name for these beasts, being that squealy grunter monkeys was probably thought to be unacceptable at the time of naming. Though howler monkeys live throughout Central and South America, the endangered black howler exists only in Belize.

The **Community Baboon Sanctuary** (☎ 220-2181; admission US$5; ☼ 8am-5pm), in the village of Bermudian Landing, is unique in that it's completely voluntary. This grassroots conservation initiative is fully dependent on the cooperation of private landowners. Led by US zoologist Robert Horwich, a small group of local Creole farmers signed an agreement in 1985 that would protect the howler monkeys' habitat where it butted up against their lands.

To date, 160 landowners from the eight villages surrounding the 20-sq-mile (52-sq-km) sanctuary have voluntarily pledged to protect riparian forest and maintain forest buffer zones around their farmland in order to keep the large monkey habitat in the middle intact.

Managing the Sanctuary

The sanctuary garnered some of its first monies from the World Wildlife Fund and went into a management association with the Belize Audubon Society.

Initially, councils set up to manage the sanctuary, made up of men elected from surrounding villages, were riddled with conflict. Hot tempers led to bad, ineffective management and, for a while, it seemed the sanctuary was in trouble.

That's when the women stepped in. Led by Jesse Young, the local Women's Conservation Group took over full management of the sanctuary in the late 1990s. Since then, the group has procured funding from national groups like Programme for Belize and Protected Areas Conservation Trust. They now have a computer, phone, fax, a small restaurant and some money to invest in the upkeep of the sanctuary. Partial support for the sanctuary comes from outside funding, but a lot of it comes from travelers who, the hope is, will continue to support the economies of the surrounding villages by buying local baked goods and crafts, paying for guides, homestays and admission to the sanctuary.

The Sanctuary Today

The result of so much community cooperation is a thriving broadleaf-forest habitat where a growing population of howlers feed, sleep and – at dawn and dusk – howl (loudly and unmistakably). Black howlers are vegetarians and spend most of the daylight hours cruising the treetops in groups of four to eight, led by a dominant male. Various fruits, flowers, leaves and other tidbits keep them happy. As long as visitors keep to small groups and stay quiet and respectful of the habitat, the monkeys don't seem to mind humans lurking below.

At the sanctuary's small museum and visitors center, you can learn all about the black howler and the 200 other species of wildlife found in the reserve. A guided nature walk is included with your price of admission.

Tours of the villages surrounding the sanctuary are available for US$20, as are canoe trips and night hikes.

For more information about the reserve, check with the **Belize Audubon Society** (Map pp220-1; ☎ 223-5004; www.belizeaudubon.org; 12 Fort St) in Belize City.

Sleeping & Eating

There's a basic restaurant at the reserve and both hotels offer a good selection of meals.

Howler Monkey Resort (☎ 220-2158; www.howler monkeylodge.bz; s/d/tr US$15/25/35) This place has wonderful cabañas with just the right mix of luxury and roughin' it. The grounds sweep down to the river and all sorts of canoeing and crocodile-watching activities are available.

Nature Resort (☎ 223-3668; naturer@btl.net; s/d US$30/35) Basic but comfortable cabañas right next to the visitors center. More-expensive cabañas with private bathroom and kitchenette are available.

Camping (per person US$5); superbasic **rooms** (s/d US$5/7.50) where you must bring bedding and shower with a bucket or in the river; and village **homestays** (US$12.50) can be arranged at the visitors center.

Getting There & Away

The Community Baboon Sanctuary lies 26 miles (42km) west of Belize City in the village of Bermudian Landing – an easy day trip from Belize City or the cayes. You can book an organized tour or arrange for a taxi in Belize City (round-trip taxi fare will be about US$70).

If you are driving, turn west off the Northern Hwy at the Burrell Boom turnoff (Mile 13). From there it's another 12 miles (20km) of dirt road to the sanctuary. Note that if you're heading to western Belize after visiting the sanctuary, you'll save time by taking the 8-mile (13km) cut from Burrell Boom south to Hattieville on the Western Hwy, avoiding Belize City traffic.

Russell's and MacFadzean's operate buses to Bermudian Landing, but the schedules are such that it is necessary to spend the night and leave early in the morning.

Another option is to catch one of the frequent Northern Transport buses heading to the Mexican border; get off at Burrell Boom and hitch the 13 miles (8km) into the sanctuary. Any passing pickup will give you a ride if they're heading that way, but beware – this route doesn't see much traffic.

ALTUN HA

Northern Belize's most famous Mayan ruin is **Altun Ha** (admission US$5; ⏰ 9am-5pm), 34 miles (55km) north of Belize City along the Old Northern Hwy. The site is near the village of Rockstone Pond, 10 miles (16km) south of Maskall.

Altun Ha (Mayan for 'rockstone pond') was undoubtedly a small (population about 3000) but rich and important Mayan trading town, with agriculture also playing an essential role in its economy. Altun Ha had formed as a community by at least 600 BC, perhaps even several centuries earlier, and the town flourished until the mysterious collapse of Classic Mayan civilization around AD 900. Most temples you will see date from Late Classic times, though burials indicate that Altun Ha's merchants were trading with Teotihuacán in Preclassic times.

Of the grass-covered temples arranged around the two plazas here, the largest and most important is the **Temple of the Masonry Altars** (Structure B-4), in Plaza B. The restored structure you see dates from the first half of the 7th century and takes its name from altars on which copal was burned and beautifully carved jade pieces were smashed in sacrifice. Excavation of the structure in 1968 revealed many burial sites of important officials. Most of the burial sites had been looted or desecrated, but two were intact. Among the jade objects found in one of these was a unique mask sculpture portraying Kinich Ahau, the Mayan sun god; as of now, this is the largest well-carved jade object ever uncovered from a Mayan archaeological site. (Look for the jade head illustration in the corner of Belizean banknotes.)

In Plaza A, Structure A-1 is sometimes called the **Temple of the Green Tomb**. Deep within it was discovered the tomb of a priest-king dating from around AD 600. Tropical humidity had destroyed the king's garments and the paper of the Mayan

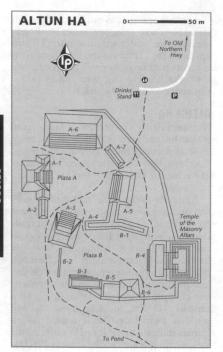

ALTUN HA   0 ▭▬▬ 50 m

To Old Northern Hwy

Drinks Stand

A-6
A-7
A-1
Plaza A
A-2   A-3
A-4   A-5
B-1
Temple of the Masonry Altars
Plaza B   B-4
B-2
B-3   B-5
B-6

To Pond

'painted book' that was buried with him, but many riches were intact: shell necklaces, pottery, pearls, stingray spines used in bloodletting rites, jade beads and pendants, and ceremonial flints.

Modern toilets and a drinks stand are on site.

Sleeping & Eating

Camping, though not strictly legal, is sometimes permitted; ask at the site.

Mayan Wells Restaurant (☎ 221-2039) On the road to Altun Ha, 1.5 miles (2.4km) from the ruins, this is a popular stop for lunch or refreshments. Traditional Belizean lunches of rice, beans and stewed chicken are served for US$5 in a pleasant outdoor setting. **Camping** (US$5) is allowed on the premises; bathroom and shower facilities are available.

Getting There & Away

The easiest way to visit Altun Ha is on one of the many tours running daily from Belize City (p223) or San Pedro on Ambergris Caye (p242).

To get there in your own vehicle, take the Northern Hwy 19 miles (31km) northwest from Belize City to the town of Sand Hill, where the highway divides – the new paved highway continues northwest and the old one heads northeast to the ruins. The old road is narrow and potholed, passing through jungle and the occasional village. The ruins are about 2 miles (3km) west off the road, 10.5 miles (17km) from the junction. Note that the Old Northern Hwy is not busy; a breakdown could be problematic, and hitchhiking is usually disappointing.

If you're firmly committed to public transportation, you can catch an afternoon bus departing from Douglas Jones St (see Map p217) for the town of Maskall, north of Altun Ha.

CROOKED TREE

pop 693

Midway between Belize City and Orange Walk is the turnoff to the fishing and farming village of Crooked Tree and the Crooked Tree Wildlife Sanctuary.

While the village's real drawcard is the abundance of wildlife, it's a mellow, pretty little place that serves well as a spot to hang out and relax for a few days.

The story goes that this small village got its name when logwood cutters in the 18th century floated up the Belize River through Black Creek to a giant lagoon marked by a tree that seemingly grew in every direction. These 'crooked trees' still grow around the lagoon.

Until the causeway to the Northern Hwy was built in 1984, the only way to get to Crooked Tree was by boat, so it's no wonder life here centers on the lagoon, a natural reservoir whose water level fluctuates with the rains.

Other than the lagoon and its birds, the big draw here is the annual **Cashew Festival**, held on the first weekend in May, to celebrate the cashew nuts harvested from the village's bounty of cashew trees. Soils here are supposedly perfect for growing the sweet fruit upon which the cashew nut grows. During the festival, cashews are parched, cracked and roasted, or turned into cashew cake, cashew jelly, cashew juice, cashew wine and cashew-you-name-it. The festival features live music, storytelling and lots of eating. The harvest season continues into July.

BELIZE

Crooked Tree Wildlife Sanctuary

In 1984 the Belize Audubon Society was successful in having 5 sq miles (12 sq km) around the village declared a **wildlife sanctuary** (admission US$4; 8am-4pm) principally because of the area's wealth of migrant and resident birds. A small visitors center right at the entrance to town can give you information and a map of Crooked Tree.

Migrating birds flock to the rivers, swamps and lagoons here each year during the dry season (December to May). The best time of year for wildlife-watching is in May, when the water in the lagoon drops to its lowest level and the animals must come further out into the open to reach their food supply.

Bird-watchers, don your binoculars and telephoto lens and get ready to witness an orgy of ornithological bliss. Herons, ducks, kites, egrets, ospreys, kingfishers and hawks are just a smattering of the 275 bird species seen here. Jabiru storks grace the area, eating fish, shells and snakes, and nesting in winter. With a wingspan of up to 8ft (2.5m), the jabiru is the largest flying bird in the Western Hemisphere. Habitat destruction throughout its range had the jabiru on the brink of extinction, but protected wetlands in Belize have given it a shot at survival. Crooked Tree sees the country's highest concentration of these magnificent birds.

Black howler monkeys, Morelet's crocodiles, coatis, iguanas and turtles also live among the mango and cashew trees at Crooked Tree.

Day trips to Crooked Tree are possible, but it's best to stay the night so you can be here at dawn, when the birds are most active. Trails weave through the village and you can spot plenty of species on your own, but you'll get further and see much more on a guided boat tour. In fact, for those interested in viewing birds and other wildlife, a guided nature tour of this sanctuary is among the most rewarding experiences in Belize.

Tours cost US$60 to US$70 for groups of four (less per person for larger groups) and usually include a boat trip through the lagoon, a walk along the elevated boardwalk and viewing time atop the observation towers. Arrangements can be made through the visitors center or your hotel. More information can be obtained from the **Belize Audubon Society** (Map p220-1; 223-5004; www .belizeaudubon.org; 12 Fort St) in Belize City.

The hotels in Crooked Tree can also arrange day trips to Altun Ha (p249; US$35 per person), the Community Baboon Sanctuary (p248; US$40 per person) or Lamanai (p254; US$75 per person).

Sleeping & Eating

Sam Tillett's Hotel & Tour (220-7026, samhotel@btl .net; s with shared bathroom US$15, s/d with private bathroom US$25/35) Well-appointed rooms are set in a tidy central location. There's a good *palapa* dining room with meals available, and possibly the friendliest Doberman on Earth. Sam's bird tours are in demand – he's known throughout the country as the 'king of birds.'

Paradise Inn (225-7044; s/d with private bathroom US$37/48) The Crawford family, owners of the inn, also enjoy a considerable reputation among birders. The inn rents simple cabañas with nice lagoon views and the restaurant gets high marks with travelers. Breakfast is US$3, lunch US$4, dinner US$7.

Bird's Eye View Lodge (225-7027; www.birds eyeviewlodge.com; dm US$15, s/d with private bathroom from US$40/60) This is in Crooked Tree village facing the lagoon. The rooms are tidy if somewhat lacking in character. Meals are available.

Private rooms (s/d US$10/15) These can be easily arranged. The map of the village provided by the visitors center shows the location of some of them – ask which are currently operating.

Getting There & Away

The road to Crooked Tree village is 33 miles (53km) up the Northern Hwy from Belize City, 25 miles (40km) south of Orange Walk. The village is 3.5 miles (5.5km) west of the highway via a causeway over Crooked Tree Lagoon.

If you want to take a bus round-trip to Crooked Tree, you'll have to spend the night there. Jex Bus (p228) offers service daily departing Belize City for Crooked Tree village at 10:30am and 4:30pm Monday to Saturday; return trips leave Crooked Tree at 6:30am and 7am. A Batty Brothers bus (Map pp220-1) leaves Belize City at 4pm and departs Crooked Tree at 6am.

If you start early from Belize City, Corozal or Orange Walk, you can bus to Crooked Tree Junction and then walk the 3.5 miles (5.5km) to the village (about an hour).

CHAN CHICH LODGE

In western Orange Walk District, **Chan Chich Lodge** (☎ 223-4419; www.chanchich.com; s/d from US$140/165) is truly a destination unto itself; in fact, many of its visitors take a charter from Belize City and spend their entire trip here. Its setting is incredible: Thatched cabañas share space with partially excavated ruins in the central plaza of a Mayan archaeological site. The lodge offers guided walks and activities throughout the day, and nine miles (15km) of trails invite independent exploration. While you may not see jaguars during your visit, you'll definitely feel their presence, and you are likely to see coatis, warries, deer, howler and spider monkeys and an array of bird life. Resident ornithologists have identified more than 350 bird species here. One of Belize's first eco-lodges, Chan Chich remains among the most luxurious, though it maintains a casual, shorts-and-T-shirt atmosphere.

Each of the 12 cabañas has a private bathroom, fan, two queen-size beds, a verandah and bottled water. No more than 32 guests (mostly families and couples) stay here at one time, which keeps it uncrowded and helps maintain the truism that you're really in the middle of nowhere.

The lodge lies between the settlement of Gallon Jug and the Guatemalan border. It's best reached by chartered plane from Belize City (about US$210 per person round-trip), though you can also drive in on an all-weather road (130 miles/210km, 3½ hours from Belize City).

Gallon Jug

One of the activities available from Chan Chich is a tour of Gallon Jug, a small village essentially fabricated in 1986. Like most of the land surrounding Chan Chich, Gallon Jug is owned by Barry Bowen, the Belikin beer brewer and Coca-Cola distributor often described rather overtly as 'the richest man in Belize.' Of his 130,000-acre (52,000-hectare) parcel of tropical rain forest, Bowen set aside 3000 acres (1214 hectares) for experimental farming under the name of Gallon Jug Agro-Industries. The sense of organization and intention here is hard to ignore; everything growing in the manicured and orderly fields is deliberate and very controlled. Projects to date include growing corn, soybean, sugarcane, cacao and organic coffee beans. Another program hopes to raise the quality of local beef by artificially inseminating local cows with the sperm of imported English Hereford cattle. Ask at Chan Chich if you are interested in touring Gallon Jug.

RÍO BRAVO CONSERVATION AREA

Protecting 260,000 acres (105,200 hectares) of tropical forest and its inhabitants, the Río Bravo Conservation and Management Area (RBCMA) encompasses a whopping 4.6% of Belize's total land. Owned and managed by the private, nonprofit **Programme for Belize** (PFB; Map pp220-1; ☎ 227-5616; www.pfbelize .org; 1 Eyre St, Belize City), the RBCMA supports a myriad of forest types along with astonishing biodiversity in plant, bird and animal life – including 392 bird species (more than half of the total species count in Belize), 380 tree species and 70 species of mammal, including all five of Belize's cats (jaguar, jaguarundi, ocelot, puma and margay). In fact, Río Bravo is said to have the largest concentration of jaguars in all of Central America. Some 50 species of bat live here, along with a creepy-crawly array of spiders and scorpions. If you're looking for true, wild tropical rain forest, this is the place to come.

In addition to the wealth of plant and animal life here, over 60 Mayan sites have been discovered on the land. The preeminent site is **La Milpa**, the third-largest Mayan site in Belize, believed to have been founded in the Late Preclassic period. Archaeologists from Boston University are conducting ongoing excavations at the site.

Though none of the RBCMA's funding comes from the government, the reserve is set up as a sort of national park whose goals are ecosystem protection, along with research and sustainable-development projects. The long-term goal of PFB is to create a sustainable reserve that generates income without upsetting the integrity of the land. Projects to date include agro-forestry (tree reproduction and sustainable logging), micro-propagation of orchids, carbon sequestration and community development in villages traditionally dependent on reserve lands. Tourism accounts for a sizeable chunk of funding, and thousands of visitors – including local and international school groups – come each year to learn about the ecosystem, conservation and environmental awareness.

History

Archaeologists figure Maya lived in the area as early as 800 BC. When Spanish expeditions first came through what is now the RBCMA in the early 17th century, the Maya were still accessing the same riverine trade routes, though by then their population, like at other inland Mayan sites, had been seriously depleted.

By the mid-18th century, mahogany logging camps dominated the area, and the loggers – Baymen – were continually attacked by the Maya who resented the woodcutters' presence. Logging companies fought hard against Mayan resistance, and the industry eventually won.

By the mid-19th century, the Belize Estate and Produce Company (BEC) owned almost all of the land in northwestern Belize. The company carried out major extractions of mahogany and Mexican cedar, which they would float through the river system out to the coast. With the advent of rail systems and logging trucks, operations flourished until over-cutting and a moody market finally prompted BEC to stop cutting trees.

In addition to logging, intensive chicle tapping by *chicleros* (who extracted chide from sapodilla trees) took place throughout the 20th century. The chicle was exported and used to make chewing gum (including Chiclets) until synthetic gums proved cheaper. (You can still see slash scars on chicle trees throughout the RBCMA.) See the box on p178 for more information on chicle.

Belizean businessman Barry Bowen purchased the land in the mid-1980s. He quickly sold off massive chunks to Yalbac Ranch (owned by a Texan cattle farmer) and to Coca-Cola Foods. Meanwhile the Massachusetts Audubon Society was looking for a reserve for migrating birds. Coke donated 42,000 acres (1700 hectares) to support the initiative, and Programme for Belize was created to manage the land. Coke had plans to develop citrus farms throughout what is now the RBCMA, but outcries from environmentalists prompted Coke to reconsider. In 1992, Coke donated another 52,000 acres to PFB through the Nature Conservancy. Bowen also donated some land and PFB bought the rest, bringing today's total to 260,000 acres (105,200 hectares).

Sleeping

It's a long trek out here, so most visitors who come to Río Bravo stay overnight at one of the two field stations in the reserve. Hill Bank Field Station is used primarily for school groups, while most independent travelers will stay at La Milpa Field Station,

---

NOW WE'VE DUG IT UP, LET'S BURY IT AGAIN!

In the bad old days, archaeology was all about getting in there, digging up as much as possible and carrying the loot off to some foreign museum (or auction house). The field has become a lot more conservation-minded lately, and an interesting debate has developed.

It's all got to do with erosion and the way that some sites are literally falling apart due to exposure to wind, rain and weather in general. Originally, these structures would have been covered in stucco, the stones thus protected from the elements. After falling into disuse, many sites have been covered by soil, which acts as a natural shield. Now, having been excavated, they lie exposed and every year takes its toll. Some archaeologists and conservationists are calling for structures to be buried again once they have been examined for archaeological purposes. Others argue that, without tourist revenue, governments will not be able to afford even what meager resources they now contribute to excavation projects.

Ironically, tourism has played a part in some of the major archaeological finds in this century. The hugely popular (and much maligned) sound and light shows that are installed at some of the more popular ruins are pretty much the only time that anybody does any kind of heavy work around the ruins, and there are many stories of lighting technicians falling through roofs and into previously undiscovered chambers.

Either way, regardless of whether you're a traveler, archaeologist or conservationist, the argument raises some interesting questions: What are the ruins for? Are they just tourist eye candy, or should they be left solely to people studying them for academic reasons? And if we are going to bury them again, who exactly *is* allowed to dig them up?

which also puts up educational and research groups.

La Milpa Field Station (cabañas per person US$95) On the road to Gallon Jug and Chan Chich, it has an education center, on-site medicinal trail, access to hiking trails and the nearby La Milpa archaeological site. Visiting and transportation arrangements must be made in advance through **Programme for Belize** (Map pp220-1; ☎ 227-5616; www.pfbelize.org) in Belize City. Meals and two guided tours are included in the cost of a cabaña.

LAMANAI

By far the most impressive site in this part of the country is Lamanai, in its own archaeological reserve on the New River Lagoon near the small settlement of Indian Church. Though much of the site remains unexcavated and unrestored, the trip to Lamanai, by motorboat up the New River, is an adventure in itself.

Take a sun hat, sunblock, insect repellent, shoes (rather than sandals), lunch and a beverage.

History

As with most sites in northern Belize, Lamanai ('Submerged Crocodile,' the original Mayan name of the place) was occupied as early as 1500 BC, with the first stone buildings appearing between 800 and 600 BC. Lamanai flourished in Late Preclassic times, growing into a major ceremonial center with immense temples long before most other Mayan sites.

Unlike many other sites, Maya lived here until the coming of the Spanish in the 16th century. The ruined indigenous church (actually two of them) nearby attests to the fact that there were Maya here for the Spanish friars to convert. Convert them they did, but by 1640 the Maya had reverted to their ancient forms of worship. British interests later built a sugar mill, now in ruins, at Indian Church. The archaeological site was excavated by David Pendergast in the 1970s and '80s.

Sights

Landing at **Lamanai** (admission US$2.50; ⏱ 9am-5pm), you'll sign the visitor's book, visit the museum and pay the admission fee. The museum exhibits some figurative flint stones, beautiful examples of pottery and obsidian and jade jewelry. From the museum, you'll wander into the dense jungle, past gigantic guanacaste, ceiba and ramón (breadnut) trees, strangler figs, allspice, epiphytes and examples of Belize's national flower, the black orchid. In the canopy overhead you might see (or hear) one of the groups of resident howler monkeys. A tour of the ruins takes 90 minutes minimum, more comfortably two or three hours. The time you'll spend at the sight depends on your guide and the size of the group. If you want to stay longer, just ask your guide for a little extra time.

To the north along a jungle path, **Structure N9-56** (The Mask Temple), built and modified between 200 BC and AD 1300, has a huge stylized mask of a man in a crocodile-mouth headdress 13ft (4m) high emblazoned on its southwest face. Archaeologists have dug deep into this structure (from the platform level, high on the east side) to look for burials and to document the several earlier structures that lie beneath. To date, they've found a tomb containing the remains of a man adorned with shell and jade jewelry. Nearby, the remains of a woman found in a second tomb suggest a succession of leaders – perhaps a husband and wife, or brother and sister.

Near this structure are a small temple and a copy of a ruined stela that once stood on the temple's front face. Apparently some worshipers built a fire at the base of the limestone stela and later doused the fire with water. The hot, stone stela, cooled too quickly by the water, broke and toppled.

Structure N10-43, the tallest temple on the site, is a massive building rising 125ft (33m) above the jungle canopy. Other buildings along La Ruta Maya are taller and in better shape, but this one was built well before the others; its construction began in about 100 BC. Excavations show that the grand ceremonial temple was constructed on a site that was primarily residential, indicating a rather dramatic shift in power to this part of the community. In today's terms, this equates to a palace being built in the middle of a working-class neighborhood. Over the next few years, you'll likely witness excavation work happening at this structure.

Not far from N10-43 is Lamanai's **ball court**; it's smallish compared to those at other Mayan sites, but it boasts one of the largest ball-court markers found anywhere.

A ceremonial vessel containing liquid mercury was found beneath the marker. The mercury probably came from Guatemala, but like much else in the Mayan world, it remains a mystery.

East of the ball court, the Late Classic **Stela 9** represents Lord Smoking Shell. The date depicted on the stela celebrates the conclusion of the *tun* (year), as well as the anniversary of the lord's reign. The remains of five children – ranging in age from newborn to eight – were found buried beneath the stela. Archaeologists believe the burial must have been highly significant, since offerings are not usually associated with the dedication of monuments.

Part of a complex of residential buildings, this Early Classic temple, **Structure N10-9** (Temple of the Jaguar), has a succession of modifications that attests to the Maya at Lamanai's longevity and perseverance in traditional ways, even after European influence. Archaeologists have found evidence that the community here continued to thrive at a time when other Mayan cities were already in rapid decline.

Tours

Most visitors opt to reach Lamanai on a spectacular boat ride up the New River from the Tower Hill toll bridge south of Orange Walk. On this trip, available only as part of an organized tour, you motor 1½ hours upriver, between riverbanks crowded with dense jungle vegetation. En route, your skipper/guide points out the many local birds and will almost certainly spot a crocodile or two. Along the way you pass the Mennonite community at Shipyard. Finally you come to New River Lagoon – a long, broad expanse of water that can be choppy during the frequent rainstorms – and the boat dock at Lamanai.

The Novelo brothers (Antonio and Herminio) have excellent reputations as guides and naturalists. Their company, **Jungle River Tours** (☎ 302-2293; lamanaimayatour@btl.net; 20 Lovers' Lane, Orange Walk), near the southeast corner of the central park, offers excursions to Lamanai for US$40 per person (minimum of four persons), which includes lunch, beverages and the guided tour along the river and at the ruins. The tour group meets at 9am at the office in Orange Walk and returns at 4pm. Reservations required.

Reyes & Sons (☎ 322-3327) will pick you up from your hotel in Orange Walk at 9am (Caribbean Time). The boat ride and guided tour costs US$25 per person, or you can pay another US$10 and have a good lunch, admission and drinks thrown in.

Sleeping & Eating

Lamanai Outpost Lodge (☎ 223-3578; www.lamanai .com; s/d US$110/130) Perched on a hillside sloping down to the lagoon, the well-kept lodge, bar and open-air dining room enjoy panoramic views. Guests stay in one of 18 thatch-roof bungalows, each with fan, private bathroom and verandah. The archaeological zone is a five-minute boat ride to the south.

Archaeologists, ornithologists, botanists and naturalists in residence at the lodge lead tours and provide information and programs for guests. Activities include river excursions (the nighttime spotlight safari is a highlight), wildlife walks and tours of Lamanai.

Meals cost US$9 for breakfast, US$15 for lunch and US$25 for dinner. Multiday, all-inclusive packages are available, as are education-adventure programs that allow guests to participate in archaeological or jungle-habitat research. Transfers from Belize City can be arranged by land or air.

Getting There & Away

Though the river voyage is much more convenient and enjoyable, Lamanai can be reached by road (36 miles/58km) from Orange Walk via Yo Creek and San Felipe. Bus service from Orange Walk is available but limited (it's primarily for village people coming to town for marketing); buses depart Orange Walk on Tuesday at 3pm and Thursday at 4pm.

It's possible to get an early Batty Brothers bus (Map p220-1, US$2.50) from Belize City to Orange Walk, get out at the Tower Hill toll bridge and be in time for the morning departure of the boats to Lamanai. In the evening you can catch a return bus to Belize City at the bridge or, preferably, in Orange Walk.

ORANGE WALK

pop 13,480

The agricultural and social center of northern Belize, Orange Walk is 58 miles (94km) north of Belize City. The town serves the

BELIZE

region's farmers (including many Mennonites), some of whom grow citrus fruits and papaya. The name of the game here, however, is sugarcane and its byproducts – sugar, molasses and rum.

Orange Walk is not highly developed for tourism, but does have a few modest hotels and good restaurants. Another option, if you are spending a few days in the region, is to base yourself in Corozal about 41 miles (66km) north. Buses between the two towns are plentiful.

History

British mahogany cutters in Belize (then British Honduras) helped make Orange Walk one of Belize's first settlements. The loggers shipped raw mahogany out of Orange Walk, along the New River to Corozal Bay and eventually to Belize City. When mahogany exports started to decline, the residents turned to corn farming and tapping sapodilla trees for chicle, which was exported and used for making chewing gum and rubber (see box on p178).

Orange Walk's first real population 'boom' happened in the 1850s when refugees fleeing Yucatán's War of the Castes began spilling over to settle in British Honduras. The indigenous Maya were already resentful of British and Spanish encroachment and had spent the majority of the 19th century defending their lands. The War of the Castes (1847–1901) simply fueled the cause.

The ruins of two British forts in Orange Walk – Fort Mundy and Fort Cairnes – serve as unfortunate reminders of the often horrific conflict. In 1872, the British garrison held off a final attack by the Icaiche Maya by killing their leader and severely weakening their army's power. This battle stands as the last armed resistance by Maya peoples in Belize. Today, an old flagpole in front of Orange Walk's town hall is the only remnant of Fort Cairnes, while Independence Plaza marks the site of Fort Mundy.

Orientation & Information

Orange Walk's new **House of Culture** (Main St; admission free; ☺ 10am-6pm Tue-Fri, 8am-1pm Sat), next to the bridge, has some great old photographs of the town, plus information about local cultures and exhibits from local Mayan sites.

The Northern Hwy, called Queen Victoria Ave in town, serves as the main road. The center of town is shady Central Park, on the east side of Queen Victoria Ave. The town hospital is in the northern outskirts, readily visible on the west side of the Northern Hwy.

Archaeological Sites

CUELLO

Close to Orange Walk and with a 3000-year history, Cuello (*kway*-yo) is the earliest-known settled community in the Maya world, although there's unfortunately little to show for it. The Maya of Cuello were excellent pottery makers and prolific farmers, and though archaeologists have found plenty here, only Structure 350, a nine-tiered, stepped pyramid, will draw your interest.

The site is on private property owned by the **Cuello Brothers Distillery** (☎ 322-2141; San Antonio Rd, aka Yo Creek Rd), 2.5 miles (4km) west of Orange Walk (take Bakers St out of town). The distillery, on the left (south) side of the road, is unmarked except for a gate; the site is through and beyond it. It's free to explore, but ask permission at the distillery gate. A taxi to Cuello from Orange Walk will cost about US$12 round-trip.

NOHMUL

'Great Mound' in Mayan, Nohmul (*noh-mool*) was a much more important site than Cuello. The vast site covers more than 7 sq miles (18 sq km), though most of it is now overgrown by grass and sugarcane. Though the ruins themselves aren't exactly spectacular, the view from Structure 2, a lofty acropolis and the site's tallest building, is. You can see clear across the Orange Walk District, over endless fields of cane.

From the north edge of Orange Walk, drive 9.6 miles (15.5km) north on the Northern Hwy to the village of San Jose. On the north end of the village look for the sign directing you 1.3 miles (2km) west to Nohmul. The site is owned by Steven Itzab, who lives in the northern part of San Pablo village, opposite the water tower. Stop at Itzab's house for permission to visit; a guide will be sent with you.

Getting to the site is tricky without a car, though you could take a bus to San Jose, and walk the dirt road. A taxi from Orange Walk will cost about US$15 round-trip.

Sleeping

If you're staying on Main St, make sure you get a room away from the front – the street gets noisy early and stays that way all day.

Lamanai Riverside Retreat (☎ 302-3955; Lamanai Alley; r US$25) Good, basic cabañas facing the river. The restaurant/bar is the best place in town to be when the sun goes down, and is worth a visit even if you're not staying here. A crocodile can occasionally be seen cruising in the river out the front and boats to Lamanai can pick you up directly from here.

St Christopher's Hotel (☎ 322-2420; rowbze@btl .net; 10 Main St; r with fan/air-con US$30/45) Simple, relatively quiet and decently priced. Rooms have cable TV and private bathrooms with good hot water. Riverside rooms (US$50) are the most attractive.

Hotel D*Victoria (☎ 302-2518; 40 Queen Victoria Ave; s/d with fan US$23/30, with air-con US$38/43; ✗ ≈ P) An ageing but serviceable hotel with firm beds and good showers. There are hammocks set up out the back under shady *palapas* by the good sized swimming pool.

Akihoto Hotel (☎ 302-0185; 22 Queen Victoria Ave; r US$12.50-30) A newish place, the Akihito's cheaper rooms are serviceable concrete boxes with spotless shared bathrooms (and scorching hot water). The more expensive rooms have air-con, private bathrooms and cable TV.

Hotel Mi Amor (☎ 302-2031; 19 Queen Victoria Ave; r US$24) This place manages to be both over-the-top and shabby at the same time. Rooms have private bathrooms and fans. A noisy disco is on the ground floor.

Eating

Lamanai Riverside Retreat (☎ 302-3955; Lamanai Alley; meals US$8-13; ✗ lunch & dinner) The restaurant here is probably the best in town in terms of location and menu. The grilled lobster (US$10) is a particular bargain, and the breezes coming off the river may have you knocking back the Belikins for far longer than originally planned.

Fort Mundy Bar & Grill (meals US$5-6; ✗ lunch & dinner) Set in a park below the House of Culture, this open-air restaurant has daily specials like cow-foot soup (and less exotic items) and converts into a karaoke jam on weekends.

Juanita's (Santa Ana St; meals from US$2.50; ✗ breakfast, lunch & dinner) Near the Shell fuel station, this is a simple place with tasty local fare at low prices.

Orange Walk has several Chinese restaurants. **Happy Valley** (32 Main St; meals US$3-6; ✗ breakfast, lunch & dinner) is popular for drinks (it can't be the loud pop music, surely) and its standard range of Chinese meals. They also serve good-value breakfasts from 7:30am.

Diner (34 Clark St; meals from US$5; ✗ breakfast, lunch & dinner) This is the favorite local hangout. It's a bit off the beaten track but worth it for its creative menu and cool, leafy setting. Go north and turn left just before the hospital, then bear right (follow the signs) and go about a quarter mile (400m).

Mercy's Place (52 Queen Victoria Ave; burritos US$3; ✗ lunch & dinner) This hole-in-the-wall taco and burrito joint is hugely popular with the locals. It could be a bit dodgy for those with unaccustomed stomachs, however.

Getting There & Away

Buses run hourly to Belize City and Corozal, and additional southbound runs in the early morning and northbound runs in late afternoon accommodate work and school schedules. All services use the bus stop on Queen Victoria Ave at St Peter St. By bus, it takes about two hours to reach Belize City (US$2.50, 58 miles/92km) and an hour to get to Corozal (US$2, 41 miles/66km). It's also possible to reach Lamanai from here (see p225).

COROZAL

pop 8,000

This breezy seaside town definitely has a Caribbean vibe – if the wind is right, you can walk all over town accompanied by a reggae soundtrack. Corozal is a prosperous farming town blessed with fertile land and a favorable climate for agriculture (sugarcane is the area's leading crop).

It's a popular stop with travelers busing their way to or from Mexico, and many choose to base here when exploring northern Belize. Two Mayan ruins vie for attention here, and if you've been traveling inland, Corozal offers a welcome respite from the heat. Parkland runs all along the waterfront and there are many places to jump in the water and cool off.

Due to its proximity to Mexico and settlement by the War of the Castes refugees, Spanish is the predominant language here,

BELIZE

though most residents also speak English and Kriol. A small North American expatriate community centers on the retirement developments in Consejo Shores, south of Tony's Inn.

History

Corozal's Mayan history is long and important. On the town's northern outskirts are the ruins of a Mayan ceremonial center once called Chetumal, now called Santa Rita. This center controlled trade routes from the coast along modern-day Mexico's Río Hondo and Belize's New River.

Unlike most Mayan sites, Santa Rita's structures were not elevated, so most of the ruins lie buried beneath the town of Corozal. Across the bay, Cerros was also a substantial coastal trade center and is one of the most important Late Preclassic sites discovered in Belize. Today the Cerros Maya Archaeological Reserve covers 53 acres of land overlooking Bahía de Chetumal.

Maya have been living in the Corozal area since about 1500 BC (modern Corozal dates from only 1849). When refugees from the War of the Castes in the Yucatán fled across the border to a safe haven in British-controlled Belize, they were still exposed to random attacks by indigenous Maya. The refugees built Fort Barlee for protection and founded a town and named it Corozal after the Spanish word for cohune palm, which is a strong symbol of fertility. Today the post office complex sits on the fort's foundation. A colorful mural by Belizean-Mexican artist Manual Villamor depicting Corozal's history enlivens the lobby of the town hall. (If the town hall is closed, which it often is, you can still see the mural by peeking through the window).

For years Corozal had the look of a typical Caribbean town, with adobe and thatched-roof homes. Then Hurricane Janet roared through in 1955 and blew away many of the old wooden buildings on stilts. Much of Corozal's wood and cinderblock architecture dates from the late 1950s.

A sugar refinery located in Libertad, just a few miles south of Corozal, was closed in 1985 after falling victim to declining sugar prices. Though the ministry of the sugar industry toys with the idea of reactivating the Libertad refinery, it sits like an industrial skeleton, and the town of Libertad is a veritable ghost town. The Corozal economy is still based on sugar, however, with many of its residents involved in farming cane, all of which is now processed in Orange Walk.

Orientation & Information

Though founded by the Maya, Corozal is now arranged around a town square in the traditional style of a Mexican town. You can walk easily to any place in town.

The main road is 7th Ave, which briefly skirts the sea before veering inland through town. The old town market and customhouse has recently been converted to a museum and houses the **BTB office** (www.corozal.bz; 9am-4:30pm Mon-Fri, 9am-noon Sat).

Other useful businesses include:

Belize Bank (8am-1pm Mon-Thu, 8am-1pm & 3-6pm Fri) On the north side of the plaza, it has an ATM that accepts Visa and MasterCard. They also offer currency exchange, as do various *casas de cambio* around town.

Shikar Systems (per hr US$2.50; 9am-5pm Mon-Sat) Internet services.

Archaeological Sites

SANTA RITA

Called Chetumal by the Maya, this coastal city sat astride important trade routes from the coast to two major rivers – modern Mexico's Río Honda and modern Belize's New River. These rivers were vital to the local Maya, but also proved essential to residents as far off as Petén in Guatemala. Trade items included honey, vanilla and cacao. Because of its position at the two river mouths, Santa Rita had its share of wealth. It was an important site, believed to have been established in 2000 BC, though its heyday was during the Postclassic period, which meant the Maya occupied the site when Spanish explorers arrived.

Despite its prominence, however, there isn't much of the city left to see. Excavations in the early 20th century found jade and pottery artifacts, most of which were dispersed to museums, and the site's important frescoes have long been destroyed. Much of Santa Rita lies buried beneath the town site of Corozal. When Corozal expanded from a tiny village into a bustling town, many of the covered mounds became road fill and the stones of the ancient temples were used for building house foundations.

Santa Rita's one restored **Mayan temple** (admission free) is in a small, tidy park just

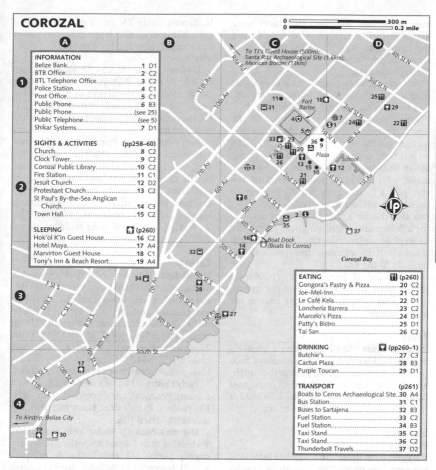

COROZAL

INFORMATION
Belize Bank	1 D1
BTB Office	2 C2
BTL Telephone Office	3 C2
Police Station	4 C1
Post Office	5 C1
Public Phone	6 B3
Public Phone	(see 25)
Public Telephone	(see 5)
Shikar Systems	7 D1

SIGHTS & ACTIVITIES (pp258–60)
Church	8 C2
Clock Tower	9 C2
Corozal Public Library	10 C2
Fire Station	11 C1
Jesuit Church	12 D2
Protestant Church	13 C2
St Paul's By-the-Sea Anglican Church	14 C3
Town Hall	15 C2

SLEEPING (p260)
Hok'ol K'in Guest House	16 C2
Hotel Maya	17 A4
Marvirton Guest House	18 C1
Tony's Inn & Beach Resort	19 A4

EATING (p260)
Gongora's Pastry & Pizza	20 C2
Joe-Mel-Inn	21 C2
Le Café Kela	22 D1
Lonchería Barrera	23 C2
Marcelo's Pizza	24 D1
Patty's Bistro	25 D1
Tai San	26 C2

DRINKING (pp260–1)
Butchie's	27 C3
Cactus Plaza	28 B3
Purple Toucan	29 D1

TRANSPORT (p261)
Boats to Cerros Archaeological Site	30 A4
Bus Station	31 C1
Buses to Sartajena	32 B3
Fuel Station	33 C2
Fuel Station	34 B3
Taxi Stand	35 C2
Taxi Stand	36 C2
Thunderbolt Travels	37 D2

To TJ's Guest House (500m);
Santa Rita Archaeological Site (1.6km);
Mexican Border (13km)

Fort
Barlee

Plaza

School

Corozal Bay

Boat Dock
(Boats to Cerros)

To Airstrip; Belize City

over half a mile (1km) northwest of the bus terminal in Corozal. Go north on the main highway just under half a mile (800m) and bear right just before the statue. After about another 100 yards (90m) turn left and go straight for about two-tenths of a mile (320m) to the site. The 'hill' on the right is actually a temple. There is no visitors center, but an old guy on a bicycle may be around to give you a detailed (and mostly accurate) history of the site for a small fee.

CERROS

This **site** (8am-5pm) was an important coastal trade center that flourished in Late Preclassic times. Today, the site is at the heart of the sprawling **Cerros Maya Archaeological Reserve** sitting on a peninsula overlooking Bahía de Chetumal. Its proximity to the New River made it a valuable trade center for Lamanai especially, and it acted as a major gateway into other inland Mayan communities. Unlike at other Mayan sites, little subsequent construction from the Classic and Postclassic periods covers the original structures here. Thus, the site has given archaeologists important insights into Mayan Preclassic architecture.

Climb **Structure 4**, a temple more than 65ft (20m) high, for stunning panoramic views. Though the site is still mostly a mass of grass-covered mounds, the center has been cleared and consolidated, and it's easy to see how the plaza structures were designed to fit together. Also notable are the canals that ring the site, which have remained mysteriously clear of vegetation through the ages.

You can drive to Cerros via a rough dirt road that's only accessible in the dry season. Ask in town for specific directions.

Many people opt to take a boat to the site. A few guides specialize in **boat trips** that include guided tours of the site. They can be arranged through your hotel, or contact **Stefan Moerman** (☎ 402-2833; tours for 1-4 people US$60), who conducts guided tours of the site, plus a boat trip on the New River to search for manatees and crocodiles. You can also charter a boat (US$50) or arrange for a fisherman to take you over to the site to explore independently. The boat trip takes about 15 minutes; then you walk 10 minutes to the site.

Tony's Inn & Beach Resort (p260) arranges tours to Cerros (US$60 per group, up to three people, US$20 per person for larger groups).

Tours

Stefan Moerman (☎ 402-2833) runs a snorkeling and bird-watching tour to Bacalar Chico (p232), a national marine park at the northern tip of Ambergris Caye. Tours cost US$200 for one to two people, US$250 for three to four, US$300 for five to six.

Sleeping

BUDGET

Marvirton Guest House (☎ 422-3365; 16 2nd St N; s/d with private bathroom US$17/40) This small family-style guesthouse is quiet and clean with wide balconies that are perfect for people watching.

Hotel Maya (☎ 422-2082; www.hotelmaya.net; r with bathroom US$30, with air-con & TV US$43) On 7th Ave (the main road) between 9th and 10th Sts S, Hotel Maya is the longtime budget favorite. Good, cheap meals are served in the adjoining eatery.

MID-RANGE

Hok'ol K'in Guest House (☎ 422-3329; www.corozal .net; cnr 4th St S & 4th Ave; s/d US$35/48) Given the Mayan name for 'rising sun,' this modern hotel is the best value in town. The comfortable rooms are designed to catch sea breezes, and each has two double beds, a

bathroom, cable TV and a patio, complete with hammock. The large common room has a sink, fridge and bookshelf full of tradable books.

TJ's Guest House (☎ 422-0150; www.corozal.bz/tj; 2nd N St; s/d with fan US$15/20, with air-con US$40/50; 🖳 🖭) North of the action in town, TJ's is small but tidy; the modern rooms have TV. Meals are available in the attached restaurant and bar.

Tony's Inn & Beach Resort (☎ 422-2055; www .tonysinn.com; s/d from US$40/50) This popular resort, about a mile (1.6km) south of the plaza on the shore road, has landscaped grounds and lawn chairs set to enjoy the view of the bay. It also offers its own swimming lagoon, cable TV, restaurant and bar. The 26 rooms, in a motel-style building, come with fan or air-con.

Eating

Le Café Kela (37 1st Ave; meals US$4-8; ☾ breakfast, lunch & dinner) This café blends traditional Belizean dishes with French cuisine. Here you will find the best crepes in Belize. Belizean dishes, pastas and crepes are around US$4; steak and seafood cost US$6 to US$8. With 24-hour notice you can get a traditional cassoulet (US$4.50). There are only five tables, so come early or make a reservation.

Patty's Bistro (13 4th Ave N; meals US$3-5; ☾ lunch & dinner) Practically wallpapered with Belikin posters, Patty's does saucy burritos, big steaks and fried fish.

Marcelo's Pizza (25 4th Ave; meals from US$2.50; ☾ breakfast, lunch & dinner) Marcelo's sells very cheesy pizzas (to match the decor, perhaps?), burgers and Belizean dishes in sweet air-con luxury.

Tai San (Park St; meals from US$4) Between 1st and 2nd Sts S, this is the favored Chinese restaurant.

Joe-Mel-Inn (cnr 4th Ave & 2nd St S; meals US$5; ☾ lunch) Serves terrific Belizean food.

Lonchería Barrera (dishes US$3.50; ☾ lunch & dinner) Off the west corner of the square; offers delicious Mexican dishes at unbeatable prices.

Drinking

Cactus Plaza (6th St) A lively spot for drinks. Most of the action happens on the sidewalk out front.

Purple Toucan (4th Ave) Probably the seediest joint in town, this is midway between bar, disco and pool hall. The beer garden out the back is OK for a drink or two.

Butchies (1st Ave) An open air *palapa* on the beachfront that sells drinks and food and has a beat-up old pool table.

Getting There & Away
AIR
Corozal has its own airstrip (CZL) south of the town center, reached by taxi (US$4). It is only an airstrip, with no shelter or services, so there's no point in arriving too early for your flight. Taxis meet all incoming flights.

Maya Island Air (☎ 422-2874) and **Tropic Air** (☎ 422-0356) each have three flights daily between Corozal and San Pedro (US$30 one-way, 20 minutes). From San Pedro you connect with flights to Belize City and onward to other parts of the country.

BOAT
Thunderbolt Travels (Belize City ☎ 226-2904) departs Corozal daily at 7am from the town wharf for San Pedro (Ambergris Caye), and can stop en route to Sarteneja. It makes the return trip at 3pm. One-way fares are US$22.50, US$15 to Sarteneja.

BUS
Corozal is eight miles (13km) to the south of the border-crossing point at Santa Elena/Subteniente López. Most of the frequent buses that travel between Chetumal (Mexico) and Belize City stop at Corozal (around US$2). Otherwise, hitch a ride or hire a taxi (expensive at US$12) to get to Santa Elena. Buses running Corozal–Chetumal will wait for you to complete border formalities. You'll have to pay an exit fee of around US$18 to leave Belize.

Buses leave Corozal from the main bus terminal and head south via Orange Walk (US$2, 41 miles/66km) for Belize City (US$4.50) at least every hour from 4am to 7:30pm, with extra buses in the morning. Likewise, buses run from Belize City to Corozal hourly (2¼ to 2¾ hours, 96 miles/155km), with extra runs in the afternoon to accommodate work and school schedules.

One bus per day leaves for Sartajena (via Orange Walk) from outside the immigration office. It takes three hours and costs US$4. Buy tickets on board.

SARTENEJA
Sarteneja is a tiny traditional fishing village (population 1600) east of Corozal. It is not an easy place to get to, which means it doesn't make it onto many itineraries – a great option for travelers who really want to get away from it all. In town there's not much to do but gaze at the turquoise sea and make friends with the townspeople, although it's possible to arrange boating and fishing trips. The name Sarteneja (sar-ten-*eh*-ha) comes from the Mayan 'Tzaten-a-Ha,' which means 'water between the rocks,' a phrase that describes some of the old sinkholes, or cenotes, used by the Maya as water wells.

Shipstern Nature Reserve
This huge **nature reserve** (admission US$5; ☺ 8am-5pm), 3 miles south of Sarteneja is owned by the International Tropical Conservation Foundation, based in Switzerland, and under the management of the **Belize Audubon Society** (Map pp220-1; ☎ 223-5004; www.belizeaudubon .org; 12 Fort St, Belize City). The park covers approximately 22,000 acres (9000 hectares) of hardwood forest, saline lagoons, savannah wetlands and mangrove swamps. Some 250 bird species are known to exist in the reserve, and coatis, peccaries, tamanduas and other wild creatures put in frequent appearances. You might even see jaguar tracks.

The entrance fee includes a visit to the small museum, a 45-minute guided nature walk and a tour of the butterfly breeding farm. Because of the profusion of wildlife and dense unmarked trails, you must have a tour guide to go further into the reserve. Guides charge US$2.50 per hour and usually provide excellent insight into the reserve's flora and fauna. You can also take an all-day tour that includes a boat trip, birding and hiking (US$50 per person), and you can arrange for overnight trips deep within the reserve. While this remote area is light on tourists (don't be surprised if you're the only one around), it's unmistakably heavy with mosquitoes; bug spray, long sleeves and pants are recommended.

Sleeping & Eating
Both of the following sleeping options have restaurants that serve meals to their guests.

Fernando's Seaside Guesthouse (☎ 423-2085; N Front St; r US$30) Fernando's has three rooms, each with a sparkling private bathroom and fan.

Krisami's Bayview Lodge (☎ 423-2283; www
.krisamis.com; r US$60) Down the road from
Fernando's, Krisami's rents modern, tiled
cabañas with private bathrooms.

Richie's (meals around US$4; ☽ dinner) In a *pal-
apa* south of Fernando's, the official hours
here are 3pm to 11pm, but Richie will cook
for you at other times by special arrangement. Meals include stewed chicken, rice
and beans, and various Mexican dishes.

Getting There & Away

Sarteneja is 40 miles (64km) northeast of
Orange Walk, where the road starts in the
north part of town at the bridge near the
village bus station. The road will take you
through the village of San Estevan and the
Mennonite community of Little Belize.
At Mile 23, veer right to reach Sarteneja
and Shipstern. The left road will take you
through Progresso to Copper Bank. Village
buses run from Orange Walk to Sarteneja
and Copper Bank from Monday to Saturday. The Thunderbolt Travels (p261) can
drop you at Sarteneja for US$15. A charter
boat from Corozal to Sarteneja will take 45
minutes and cost US$75.

WESTERN BELIZE

As you travel west from Belize City, the
topography takes a dramatic and refreshing turn. Way in the distance, the purple-
hued, jagged crags of the Maya Mountains
seem to suddenly bloom out of the flat land.
This is the Cayo District – western Belize –
where the country's highland peaks rise to
over 3000ft (900m). This beautiful, unspoiled
mountain terrain is dotted with waterfalls,
caves and Mayan ruins, and is teeming with
wild orchids, colorful parrots, keel-billed
toucans and other exotic flora and fauna –
prime territory for adventure seekers.

For much of its existence, the Cayo District was considered (especially in terms of
tourism) to be a last frontier, a patch of impenetrable jungle way out west. Though the
Western Hwy was built in the 1930s, paving
wasn't completed until the 1980s, when the
first lodge-owners bought land and started
their endless wrestles with the jungle. The
district's cultural mix – Spanish-speaking
mestizos, Maya, Creoles, Garinagu, Chinese, Lebanese, and British, Canadian and
American expats – does wonders to keep
things interesting.

Belmopan, the nation's sleepy capital, is
perhaps more helpfully regarded as a de
facto transportation hub, with buses stopping here before sliding south down the
Hummingbird Hwy, or winding along the
Western Hwy to San Ignacio and the Guatemalan border.

San Ignacio, the beating heart of the Cayo
District and an undeniable ecotourism hub,
is surrounded by rivers, lush broadleaf rain
forest and, oddly, pine forest. This is a place
where you can be pampered at a high-end
jungle lodge or get grimy and dirty climbing through a cave.

Throughout the reign of the Mayan
Empire, the Cayo District hummed with
powerful kingdoms and ceremonial centers. Take an adventurous visit to the ancient
metropolis of Caracol, or check out easy-to-
access sites like Xunantunich, El Pilar and
Cahal Pech.

The area's numerous and popular forest
lodges make great base camps for your explorations of the region.

Getting There & Around

Buses run at least hourly from Belize City
along the Western Hwy to Benque Viejo del
Carmen at the Guatemalan border. They
will drop you anywhere along the highway
upon request. Reaching sights off the highway, however, involves your own transport
(see p272 for details of hiring a car) or,
more commonly, being part of the numerous tours (p269) of the region.

DOWN THE WESTERN HIGHWAY

Heading west from Belize City along Cemetery Rd, you'll pass right through the middle of Lords Ridge Cemetery and soon find
yourself headed out of town on the Western
Hwy. In 15 miles (25km) you'll pass Hattieville, founded in 1961 after Hurricane
Hattie wreaked destruction on Belize City,
and in another 13 miles (21km) you'll come
to the Belize Zoo.

Belize Zoo

The well-presented **Belize Zoo & Tropical Education Centre** (☎ 220-8004; www.belizezoo.org; Western
Hwy, Mile 29; adult/student US$7.50/3.75; ☽ 8:30am-4:30pm
closed public holidays) owes its existence to a documentary film entitled *Path of the Raingods*

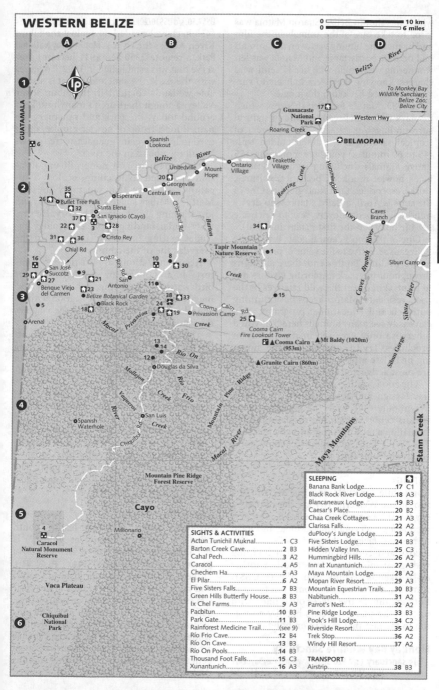

WESTERN BELIZE

0 ———— 10 km
0 ———— 6 miles

BELIZE

To Monkey Bay
Wildlife Sanctuary;
Belize Zoo;
Belize City

GUATEMALA

Belize River

Guanacaste
National Park 17

Western Hwy

Roaring Creek

BELMOPAN

Spanish
Lookout

Belize River

Unitedville Mount Hope
20 Georgeville Ontario Village Teakettle Village

35
26 Bullet Tree Falls
32 Esperanza Central Farm
37 Santa Elena
22 San Ignacio (Cayo)
3 28
31 36 Cristo Rey

Chial Rd

16
San José
Succotz
29 27
9
Benque Viejo
del Carmen 23 21 San Antonio
Belize Botanical Garden
18 Black Rock
5 Arenal

10 8
30
2 34
Tapir Mountain
Nature Reserve 1

Caves Branch

Sibun Camp

Creek

38 33
24 19
7 Privassion Camp
11 Cooma Cairn Rd
25 15

Cooma Cairn
Fire Lookout Tower
Cooma Cairn (953m) Mt Baldy (1020m)

13 14
12 Rio On
Douglas da Silva Granite Cairn (860m)

Mollejon
Rio Frio

Vaqueros San Luis
Spanish Waterhole
Chiquibul Rd Creek
Macal River Maya Mountains

Stann Creek

**Mountain Pine Ridge
Forest Reserve**

Cayo

4
**Caracol
Natural Monument
Reserve**

Millionario

Vaca Plateau

**Chiquibul
National Park**

SIGHTS & ACTIVITIES

Actun Tunichil Muknal	1 C3
Barton Creek Cave	2 B3
Cahal Pech	3 A2
Caracol	4 A5
Chechem Ha	5 A3
El Pilar	6 A2
Five Sisters Falls	7 B3
Green Hills Butterfly House	8 B3
Ix Chel Farms	9 A3
Pacbitun	10 B3
Park Gate	11 B3
Rainforest Medicine Trail	(see 9)
Río Frio Cave	12 B4
Río On Cave	13 B3
Rio On Pools	14 B3
Thousand Foot Falls	15 C3
Xunantunich	16 A3

SLEEPING

Banana Bank Lodge	17 C1
Black Rock River Lodge	18 A3
Blancaneaux Lodge	19 B3
Caesar's Place	20 B2
Chaa Creek Cottages	21 A3
Clarissa Falls	22 A2
duPlooy's Jungle Lodge	23 A3
Five Sisters Lodge	24 B3
Hidden Valley Inn	25 C3
Hummingbird Hills	26 A2
Inn at Xunantunich	27 A3
Maya Mountain Lodge	28 A2
Mopan River Resort	29 A3
Mountain Equestrian Trails	30 B3
Nabitunich	31 A2
Parrot's Nest	32 A2
Pine Ridge Lodge	33 B3
Pook's Hill Lodge	34 C2
Riverside Resort	35 A2
Trek Stop	36 A3
Windy Hill Resort	37 A2

TRANSPORT

Airstrip	38 B3

which was shot in Belize. Sharon Matola was hired to take care of the animals in the film and by the time filming was over, the animals had become partly tame and Matola was left wondering what to do with her 17 semi-wild charges, knowing they were unlikely to survive if released back into the jungle.

In 1983, Matola founded this zoo, which displays native Belizean wildlife in natural surroundings on 29 acres (12 hectares) of tropical savannah. On a self-guided tour (45 to 60 minutes) you'll see more than 125 native animals, including jaguars, ocelots, black howler monkeys, peccaries, vultures, storks, crocodiles, tapirs and gibnuts. One of the stars is April, a Baird's tapir who draws hundreds of people every year to celebrate her birthday (on the first Friday in April).

One of the zoo's central goals is to make Belizeans sensitive to the value of preserving native wildlife. To this end, there are signs throughout the park imploring visitors not to hunt, skin or eat the wild relatives of the zoo's residents. Matola keeps busy running outreach and educational programs. You can easily see many animals here that you'd otherwise only ever see in movies or on brochures. Try to come early in the morning or in late afternoon, when the animals are most active and the tourists scarce.

The zoo is on the north side of the highway (a sign marks the turnoff). It's just a five-minute walk from the highway to the visitors center, which has displays and information about the programs and animals. The 'Wild Ting' gift shop has some good books and souvenirs.

EATING

Competing for customers just west of the zoo on the Western Hwy are **Cheer's** (Western Hwy, Mile 31.3; ☺ breakfast, lunch & dinner), a breezy, tiled *palapa* serving international and local dishes and **Amigo's** (Western Hwy, Mile 32.6; 💻), a cozy and comfortable wooden building with great mountain views and live music on weekends. Happy hour (beers US$1, rum drinks US$1.25) is from 5pm to 7pm. Both are fun, festive places often filled with just-off-the-plane travelers happily adjusting to the fact that they're on holiday.

Monkey Bay Wildlife Sanctuary

This **sanctuary** (☎ 820-3032; www.monkeybaybelize .org; Western Hwy, Mile 31.5; campsite per person US$5, dm

US$7.50, s/d US$10/20) stretches across 1070 acres (433 hectares) nestled up against the Sibun River. Across the river is **Monkey Bay National Park**, a remote 2250 acre (911 hectare) preserve that was established in 1992. Together with the park, the sanctuary creates a sizeable wetlands corridor in the Sibun River Valley. Though there aren't many monkeys around today, the park and sanctuary are named for a troop of howler monkeys that used to live in a giant guanacaste tree growing along a bend in the river.

The sanctuary is a nonprofit organization dedicated to teaching 'ecology education,' a phrase that sanctuary founder Matthew Miller suggests goes way beyond just learning about natural history. He says truly understanding a place's ecology includes getting intricately involved in the everyday life of the community.

Accommodations are rustic but comfortable and make an excellent base for bird-watching, canoeing, fishing and hiking around the nearby Cox Lagoon with its abundant wildlife ('If you don't see a jaguar, the jaguar probably sees you').

There's plenty to do here, but the star attraction of this place is that it's the starting point for a three-day **hike** along the Indian Creek Trail, through a green corridor, taking in the Sibun River and Indian Creek, Maya caves, the Manatee Forest Reserve and ending in the Five Blues National Park (see p284). Jungle hammocks (with mosquito nets) are provided, or you can bring a tent. Guides are employed from local villages. This trail has only recently been opened and is sure to become hugely popular. The trail entrance fee is US$20 and guides cost US$35 per group for three days.

Jaguar Paw Resort

Six miles down a dirt road leading south from the highway (turnoff at Mile 37) is the **Jaguar Paw Resort** (☎ 820-3023; www.jaguar paw.com; r low/high season US$125/140; 🅿 😽 😹). Stone paths weave through lush rain forest and banana trees down to the crystal clear Caves Branch River and a huge nearby cave. This is possibly the most fabulous of all jungle lodges in Belize – a near perfect blend of wilderness and luxury. The sixteen cabañas are all individually (and somewhat energetically) decorated and the dining room is decked out in Mayan themes. Dishes served are mostly cosmopolitan, with a few Belizean faves thrown in to keep the rice 'n' beans fiends happy (from US$10).

Guanacaste National Park

Further west down the highway, at the junction with the Hummingbird Hwy, this small (52-acre or 21-hectare) **nature reserve** (Map p263; admission US$2.50; 🕒 8am-4:30pm), around the confluence of Roaring Creek and the Belize River, is named for a giant guanacaste tree on its southwest edge. Somehow, possibly thanks to the odd shape of its trunk, the tree survived the axes of canoe makers and still rises majestically in its jungle habitat. Festooned with bromeliads, epiphytes and ferns, the great tree supports a whole ecosystem of its own.

The guanacaste, or tubroos tree, is the national tree of Costa Rica (in Belize that honor goes to the mahogany) and is one of Central America's largest trees. Its light wood was used by the Maya to make dugout canoes. The tree is identifiable by its wide, straight trunk and broad, flat seed pods that coil up into what looks like a giant, shriveled ear (you'll see fallen 'ears' on trails throughout Belize).

A hike along the park's two miles (3.2km) of trails will introduce you to the abundant local trees (including the guanacaste) and colorful birds. Birding gets even better here in winter, when migrating birds fleeing North America come here for warmth. After your hike, you can head down to the river for a dip in the park's good, deep swimming hole.

On the north side of the Western Hwy (turn off near Guanacaste National Park) is **Banana Bank Lodge** (Map p263; ☎ 820-2020; www.bananabank .com; Western Hwy, Mile 46; s/d from US$85/100; ❈ ♨) This wonderful lodge on the north side of the Western Hwy sits on an isolated bluff overlooking the Belize River and is reached by hand-operated ferry. Lush green pastures and modern stables house some 135 horses, all of which are loved and in good condition. Each of the thatched cabañas here has a private bathroom and a unique two-bedroom design. All are decorated with local art, including the work of lodge owner Carolyn Carr. A giant telescope lets you search for planets in the starry skies, and the lodge's 'zoo' includes two spider monkeys and Tika, the Carr's pet jaguar

who appears in most of Belize's tourist brochures. Horseback tours are available at the lodge's equestrian center, and the lodge offers a variety of tours around the country. Discounts are available for longer stays – check the website for details.

Getting There & Around

Buses running (at least hourly) along the Western Hwy will drop you at the zoo or by Guanacaste National Park upon request.

BELMOPAN

pop 8100

Travelers arriving in Belize's capital are faced with that most basic of all existential questions: what am I doing here? Thankfully, the town provides a ready answer: changing buses.

In 1961, Hurricane Hattie all but destroyed Belize City. Perhaps it was government paranoia or just proactive planning, but certain that killer hurricanes would come again and that Belize City could never be secure from their ensuing destruction, the government decided to move. Many people were skeptical when in 1971 it declared its intention to build a model capital city in the geographic center of the country – a small place nobody went to, called Belmopan.

During its first decade Belmopan was a lonely place. Weeds grew through cracks in the streets, a few bureaucrats dozed in new offices, and insects provided most of the town's traffic. The capital has been slow to come to life but the gradually growing population is friendly and content. Most of the government ministries are based here, and a few embassies liven the place up (including the British High Commission, although the US embassy is still in Belize City). With the vision of Belmopan as a government hub, a grand new National Assembly was built to resemble a Mayan temple and plaza. It was supposed to house the government offices, but the buildings, together looking something like a drab college campus of concrete bunkers, provide insufficient space. The result is a variety of government offices lacking uniformity and spread throughout town. Belmopan is also home to the national police academy training center, and if you strike a match in Belize, it'll probably be the Toucan brand, made right here in Belmopan.

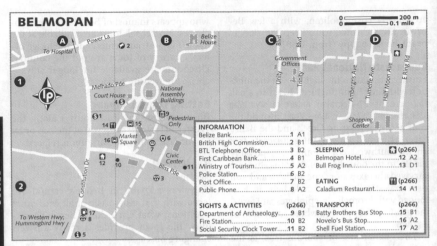

BELMOPAN

0 _____ 200 m
0 _____ 0.1 mile

INFORMATION	
Belize Bank...................................1	A1
British High Commission............2	B1
BTL Telephone Office................3	B2
First Caribbean Bank.................4	B1
Ministry of Tourism...................5	A2
Police Station............................6	B2
Post Office.................................7	B2
Public Phone.............................8	A2

SIGHTS & ACTIVITIES	(p266)
Department of Archaeology......9	B1
Fire Station..............................10	B2
Social Security Clock Tower.....11	B2

SLEEPING	🏠 (p266)
Belmopan Hotel.......................12	A2
Bull Frog Inn............................13	D1

EATING	🍴 (p266)
Caladium Restaurant...............14	A1

TRANSPORT	(p266)
Batty Brothers Bus Stop.........15	B1
Novelo's Bus Stop...................16	A2
Shell Fuel Station....................17	A2

Though the majority of the workforce is employed by the government, most people opt to commute from Belize City rather than move into Belmopan's quiet suburbia. This is most noticeable at the end of a working day, when the mass exodus of government workers catching buses out of town makes the otherwise slow capital come to life.

Orientation & Information

Belmopan, just under 2.5 miles (4km) south of the Western Hwy and about a mile east of the Hummingbird Hwy, is a small place easily negotiated on foot. The regional bus lines stop at Market Square, which is near the post office, police station, market and telephone office.

Sleeping & Eating

Belmopan is a town for bureaucrats and diplomats, not one for budget travelers.

Bull Frog Inn (☎ 602-8597; www.belizex.com/bull -frog-inn.htm; 25 Half Moon Ave; s/d US$60/70; 🌐) With 14 rooms, the Bull Frog is Belmopan's nicest place to stay. Its cheerful rooms each have a bathroom and cable TV. The restaurant at the inn is one of the town's best; dinners are around US$7, breakfast and lunch US$3 to US$4.

Belmopan Hotel (☎ 822-2130; 2 Bliss Pde; s/d US$45/50; 🌐 🍴) This 20-room hotel is convenient to the Market Square bus terminal. Its restaurant is open for all three meals and the outdoor pool offers refreshing

respite from Belmopan's heat. Rooms are spacious though dark and worn and come with cable TV.

Caladium Restaurant (Market Square; meals from US$4; 🕑 breakfast, lunch & dinner) Located just opposite the bus station, Caladium offers daily specials.

Another option for food is the market, which features plenty of snack carts selling tasty, low-cost munchies.

Getting There & Away

Thanks to its location near a major highway intersection, Belmopan is a stop for virtually all buses operating along the Western and Hummingbird Hwys. That makes it easy to get in and out of the city. Buses leave every half hour from 5:30am to 6:30pm for Belize City (local bus US$3.50, express bus US$5, one hour), every half hour from 5am to 10:30pm for San Ignacio (local bus US$1.50, express bus US$2, two hours) and hourly from 8am to 6pm for Dangriga (US$6, two to three hours).

BELMOPAN TO SAN IGNACIO

The Western Hwy continues west through the Cayo District, climbing slowly to higher altitudes through lush farming country. Tiny country towns with odd names such as Teakettle Village, Ontario Village, Mount Hope and Unitedville appear along the way. Mayan ruins are everywhere, even in the small mounds on the sides of the road, like the ones currently being excavated at **Baking**

WHO ARE THOSE WHITE GUYS IN THE OVERALLS?

They're the Mennonites – hardcore Anabaptists whose ancestors left Holland back in the 16th century. Persecuted because of their rigid religious beliefs, they settled first in Germany, then moved to Prussia (where there is still a large community), Canada (likewise), and Pennsylvania in the US.

In 1959, 3000 Mennonites arrived in Belize from Guatemala (where they outstayed their welcome by refusing to serve in the military) and started to establish communities in Northern Belize. Mennonite communities exist all the way down to Paraguay.

Mennonites tend to relocate for two reasons – mainly persecution, but also because of religious differences within the group. Different interpretations of their doctrine (often involving what level of technology and involvement with society is acceptable) lead to splits within groups. One lot stays, one goes off to found a new community.

Mennonites believe in simple living, relying on a strict interpretation of the Christian Bible. If it's not in the Bible and your parents didn't do it, chances are you won't be doing it either. If you're male, you build your house, farm your land and fang around in your horse and buggy. Have some kids, work hard, maybe build your coffin before you die. Women's roles are largely restricted to breeding and feeding, with some housework and light yard work thrown in. Imagine.

The idea is to do things as simply *as is practical*. Nowadays, there may be some Mennonites who have only ever left town under horsepower, but most are quite comfortable with the idea that if you have to go from Paraguay to Canada (as a surprising number do), it's OK to catch a plane.

The Mennonites have a biblical work ethic, excelling in farming and woodworking. It is estimated that 90% of all poultry products in Belize come from Mennonite farms. No wonder everybody else is so laid back – the Mennonites are doing all the work!

Mennonites do not pay income tax (an idea popular with most people but few governments) or do military service (ditto). Traditionally, they do not get involved with politics beyond the village level, although one Mennonite recently ran for election in Belmopan, but being that his constituency consists mainly of ardent nonvoters, you can imagine how he fared.

There are Moderates, however, and as you can imagine within a group that keeps splitting, a huge range of opinion. There are even Progressive Mennonites (www.mennolink.org was almost inevitable) – timber and poultry merchants who have swapped the horse and buggy for sports cars, cell phones and mansions that would make Scarface weep with envy.

The four main Mennonite Communities in Belize today are: Shipyard near Orange Walk, Springfield near Belmopan, Spanish Lookout in the Cayo District and Pine Hill outside of Punta Gorda.

Some Mennonites are quite friendly and don't mind a good chat (it *is* one of their major forms of entertainment, after all). Others think that non-Mennonites are the spawn of Satan's evil plan and should be shunned at all costs. Many are stand-offish and just want to be left alone (that's how they got here in the first place, remember), so give them some respect and ask permission if you want to take a photo. Try to save questions about plumbing for at least a few minutes into the conversation.

A simple hello is never out of order (unless you're a smelly backpacker addressing one of the bonneted womenfolk), or if you speak Low German, you could drop a *goo(de)ndach* and get the ball rolling that way.

Pot near the village of Mount Hope. At Teakettle Village, a dirt road leading to the south of the Western Hwy skirts the Roaring Creek and the mostly impenetrable Tapir Mountain Nature Reserve. This is the road guides take to Actun Tunichil Muknal (p273), a popular cave tour out of San Ignacio. North of the Western Hwy is the town of Spanish Lookout, a prosperous Mennonite community.

Teakettle Village

A dirt road leading off the Western Hwy from Teakettle Village leads six miles (10km) to **Pook's Hill Lodge** (Map p263; ☎ 820-2017; www .pookshillbelize.com; high season s/d US$104/108). This 300-acre estate is nestled in wilderness beside the Tapir Mountain Nature Reserve.

The main lodge surrounds a small Mayan plaza, and the round, thatch and stucco cabañas sport wraparound windows and immaculate tile bathrooms. Breakfast costs US$7, lunch US$9, dinner US$18. River swimming and forest hiking are free, and horseback riding, river tubing and mountain biking are available for a reasonable charge. The lodge is very popular with birders, and rare species such as the spectacled owl and emerald toucanette have been spotted on the grounds. Tours can be arranged to all the Mountain Pine Ridge and Cayo attractions at rates similar to those charged in San Ignacio. You can also walk from here to nearby Actun Tunichil Muknal cave (p273). Pook's Hill is around 12 miles (20km) southwest of Belmopan.

Georgeville

Continuing west down the highway, around Georgeville you will come to **Caesar's Place** (Map p263; ☎ 822-2341; www.blackrocklodge.com/cae sars/guesthouse.htm; Western Hwy, Mile 60; campsite US$7.50, s/d US$40/50) Rooms are well appointed, with a hot-water shower, fan and private bathroom, and decorated with local handicrafts. The bar has a blues and jazz band on the first Saturday of every month and RV hookups are available. Caesar also runs one of the country's best gift shops, with a wide selection of Belizean souvenirs and Guatemalan handicrafts at good prices.

Chiquibul Road

At Mile 61, Chiquibul Rd turns south off the highway and heads toward Mountain Pine Ridge – you'll take this road if you're headed straight from Belize City to one of the Mountain Pine Ridge lodges (p279). Up the road are several points of interest.

Biologists Jan Meerman and Tineke Boomsma (the same duo who founded Belize's first butterfly farm at Shipstern Nature Reserve) raise a staggering variety of butterfly species at **Green Hills Butterfly House** (Map p263; ☎ 820-4017; www.biological-diversity.info/greenhills .htm; Chiquibul Rd, Mile 8; admission US$5; ☯ 8am-4pm). The insects bred here are exported to butterfly houses all over the world. Knowledgeable guides will walk you through the farm, explaining the butterfly's life cycle.

Mountain Equestrian Trails (MET; Map p263; ☎ 820-4041; www.metbelize.com; Chiquibul Rd, Mile 8; high season s/d US$100/120; breakfast/lunch/dinner per person US$5/10/12) is technically just outside the Mountain Pine Ridge Forest Reserve, but its topography is broadleaf tropical forest with nary a pine tree in site. Horseback riding is the specialty at this lovely jungle lodge sitting on 150 acres of rolling greenery. Accommodations are in spacious cabañas with private bathroom and kerosene lamps – there's no electricity. They can arrange tours throughout the area, but the horses draw most guests. Packages are available, as are half-day (US$60) and full-day (US$85 with lunch) rides. You can reach MET by taking the Chiquibul Rd from Georgeville off the Western Hwy, or via the Cristo Rey Rd from San Ignacio. Call for directions or to arrange transfers.

Two cave systems accessed via Chiquibul Rd – Barton Creek Cave (p273) and Actun Tunichil Muknal (p273) – can be explored on guided tours, usually undertaken from San Ignacio (p269).

SAN IGNACIO (CAYO) & SANTA ELENA

pop San Ignacio 13,300, Santa Elena 3600

Fairly teeming with Guatemala-bound travelers, archaeologists, peace corps workers and other thrill seekers, San Ignacio is a pretty little town and a prosperous farming and holiday center in the lovely, tropical Macal River valley.

San Ignacio is also called El Cayo, or simply Cayo – 'the island' in Spanish – for its remote island-like isolation deep in the Macal River Valley. The Macal and Mopan Rivers flow together at Branch Mouth near San Ignacio; together they become the Belize River, which roughly follows the highway east to Belmopan and veers north for a while before spilling into Haulover Creek and the Belize Harbour at Belize City.

Long before roads drove in to San Ignacio, river transportation served an important role. San Ignacio's place at the confluence made it a watery hub for boats carrying mahogany and chicle crops down the river to the coast. Once logging and chicle-tapping fizzled out and roads made access easier, the town and its surrounding areas shifted to agriculture and cattle ranching.

Together with neighboring Santa Elena across the river, this is the chief population center of the Cayo District. That said, it's still a small, slightly grungy town continually redefining itself as tourism takes hold. By day, it's a relaxed, even quiet place. By night, the jungle rocks to music from the town's bars and restaurants.

GREG JOHNSTON

The Blue Hole (p247) at Lighthouse Reef

Purple tunicates on the barrier reef in Belize

MARK WEBSTER

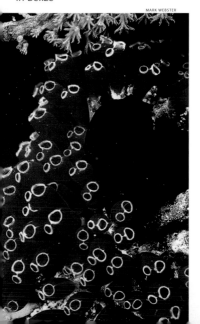

MARK WEBSTER

A flamingo tongue near Turneffe Islands (p246)

MARK WEBSTER

A nurse shark at Amigos Wreck (p230)

DOUG MCKINLAY

A boat off Ambergris Caye (p239)

JOHN ELK III

Sunrise over New River, seen from
Lamanai Outpost Lodge (p255)

TOM BOYDEN

Sea kayaking on the Belize barrier
reef

A palm tree–covered caye off the coast of
Belize

GREG JOHNS

There's not much sight-seeing to do in town, but San Ignacio makes a good base if you're planning to explore the Mountain Pine Ridge, or if you want to arrange tours on one of Cayo's outdoor adventures such as horseback treks, canoe trips on the rivers and creeks, caving, touring the region's Mayan ruins and hiking in the tropical forests.

San Ignacio, with its selection of hotels and restaurants, is also the logical place to spend the night before or after you cross the Guatemalan border, which is just 9 miles (14km) west.

Orientation

San Ignacio sits in a valley of seven hills on the west bank of the Macal River; Santa Elena is to the east over the Hawkesworth Bridge, San Ignacio's landmark suspension bridge. The town's two bridges are usually both one-way – the newer, northernmost bridge leads traffic into San Ignacio, while Hawkesworth Bridge leads traffic out of town. During the rainy season, however, the new bridge often floods, and traffic is diverted to Hawkesworth Bridge. Burns Ave is the town's main street. Everything in town is accessible on foot.

Information

The town's traditional information exchange is **Eva's Restaurant & Bar** (22 Burns Ave; Internet access per 15/60min US$2.50/$9.50). There is a small BTB office in the market square.

Tradewinds (per hr US$3; ☒ 7am-11pm Mon-Sat, 10am-8pm Sun) has Internet access. The **Green Dragon** (Hudson St) has similar prices.

Belize Bank (Burns Ave; ☒ 8am-1pm Mon-Fri, 3-6pm Fri) changes traveler's checks, as do restaurants and hotels. **Atlantic Bank** is also on Burns Ave.

The **post office** (☒ 8am-noon, 1-5pm Mon-Fri; 8am-1pm Sat) is on the upper floor of Government House, near the bridge.

The basic San Ignacio Hospital is up the hill off Waight's Ave, west of the center. Across the river in Santa Elena is the Hospital La Loma Luz.

Tours

Lodges in Cayo District operate their own tours and excursions on foot, by canoe and on horseback, but you can also take similar excursions using a cheap hotel in San Ignacio as your base. Every hotel and most restaurants in town will want to sign you up. Compare offerings and talk to other travelers before making your choice.

Many guides and tour operators advertise their services at **Eva's Restaurant & Bar** (22 Burns Ave) or at nearby shops on Burns Ave. Drop by and see what's available. To be assured the best tour for your money, sign on only with a licensed tour operator. Always check to see if entrance fees and lunch are included in the tour price – you don't want to get caught short, or hungry!

Easy Rider (☎ 824-3734), a stable on the outskirts of town, will pick you up in San Ignacio and take you on a horseback excursion into the jungle for US$40 per person, lunch included. Shorter rides can be had for US$25. Bookings can be made at Arts & Crafts of Central America, next to Eva's on Burns Ave.

Tours can be arranged through the **Maya Mountain Lodge** (Map p263; ☎ 824-2164; www.mayamountain.com), even if you're not a guest. Another reputable operator is **International Archaeological Tours** (☎ 824-3991; www.belizeweb.com/iat; West St) near Martha's Guest House.

Following are some of the widely offered tours in and around San Ignacio, along with some sample prices:

- Voyages by boat or canoe along the Macal, Mopan and Belize Rivers; favorite goals on the Macal River include the Rainforest Medicine Trail at Ix Chel Farm and the butterfly farm at Chaa Creek (US$30).
- A trip to the Mountain Pine Ridge area, which usually includes a picnic and a swim in the pools at Río On, a walk to Thousand Foot (Hidden Valley) Falls and a tour of the Río Frio Caves (US$50).
- An overland trip to the Mayan ruins at Caracol with quick stops at the above Mountain Pine Ridge sites (US$65).
- Cave tours to Chechem Ha, Barton Creek Cave or Actun Tunichil Muknal – Mayan ceremonial caves where you'll see pottery shards, skulls and other evidence of the Maya (US$25 to US$60).
- An excursion to Tikal (Guatemala), either for the day or overnight (from US$65).

Sleeping
BUDGET
J&R's Guest House (☎ 824-2502; 20 Far West St; per person US$10) A modern home with a family atmosphere. Rooms have cable TV, there's

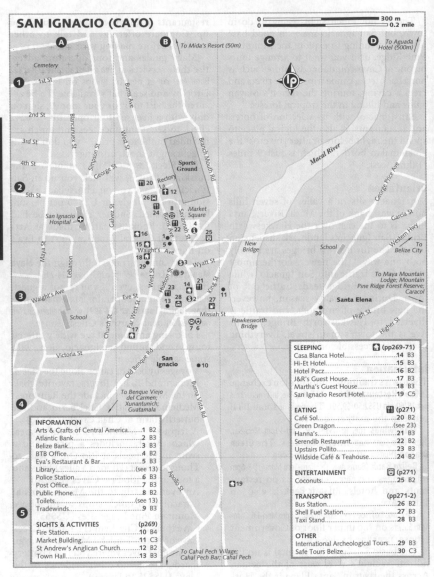

SAN IGNACIO (CAYO)

To Mida's Resort (50m)

To Aguada Hotel (500m)

Cemetery

1st St

2nd St

3rd St

4th St

5th St

Burns Ave

Blancaneux St

West St

Simpson St

George St

Sports Ground

Rectory Ln

Branch Mouth Rd

Macal River

George Price Ave

Garcia St

Western Hwy

To Belize City

San Ignacio Hospital

Maya St

Lebanon

Galvez St

Savannah St

Burns Ave

Market Square

New Bridge

School

To Maya Mountain Lodge; Mountain Pine Ridge Forest Reserve; Caracol

Waight's Ave

Waight's Ave

Hudson St

West St

Wyatt St

Knile St

Santa Elena

School

Eve St

Far West St

Church St

Missiah St

Hawkesworth Bridge

High St

Higher St

Victoria St

Old Benque Rd

San Ignacio

To Benque Viejo del Carmen; Xunantunich; Guatamala

Buena Vista Rd

Apollo St

To Cahal Pech Village; Cahal Pech Bar; Cahal Pech

INFORMATION
Arts & Crafts of Central America.......**1** B2
Atlantic Bank.................................**2** B3
Belize Bank..................................**3** B3
BTB Office....................................**4** B2
Eva's Restaurant & Bar...................**5** B3
Library....................................(see 13)
Police Station..............................**6** B3
Post Office..................................**7** B3
Public Phone................................**8** B2
Toilets....................................(see 13)
Tradewinds..................................**9** B3

SIGHTS & ACTIVITIES   (p269)
Fire Station.................................**10** B4
Market Building............................**11** C3
St Andrew's Anglican Church.........**12** B2
Town Hall...................................**13** B3

SLEEPING   (pp269-71)
Casa Blanca Hotel.........................**14** B3
Hi-Et Hotel..................................**15** B3
Hotel Pacz..................................**16** B2
J&R's Guest House.........................**17** B3
Martha's Guest House.....................**18** B3
San Ignacio Resort Hotel................**19** C5

EATING   (p271)
Café Sol....................................**20** B2
Green Dragon............................(see 23)
Hanna's.....................................**21** B3
Serendib Restaurant......................**22** B2
Upstairs Pollito...........................**23** B3
Wildside Café & Teahouse..............**24** B2

ENTERTAINMENT   (p271)
Coconuts....................................**25** B2

TRANSPORT   (pp271-2)
Bus Station.................................**26** B2
Shell Fuel Station.........................**27** B3
Taxi Stand..................................**28** B3

OTHER
International Archeological Tours.....**29** B3
Safe Tours Belize..........................**30** C3

---

a nice little balcony out the front and a front yard full of hummingbirds.

Hi-Et Hotel (☎ 824-2828; 12 West St; s/d US$10/ 12.50) At Waight's Ave, this is a rickety old house with thinly partitioned rooms, clean beds and shared bathrooms.

Hotel Pacz (☎ 824-4538; 402 Far West St; r with shared/ private bathroom US$18/23) Popular with visiting

archaeological groups, this place is clean and friendly, if a little heavy on the 1970s-style brown tile work.

MID-RANGE
Casa Blanca Hotel (☎ 824-2080; www.casablancaguest house.com; 10 Burns Ave; s/d with fan US$20/25, with air-con US$38/45) This place won the BTB's 'best small

hotel in Belize' award for 2003, and gets rave reviews from travelers. It's a homey place, where you can use the kitchen and hang out in the lounge room. Rooms are fair sized, and spotless.

Martha's Guest House (☎ 824-3647; www.marthas belize.com; 10 West St; r with shared bathroom US$27, s/d with private bathroom US$35/40; **P**) A modern home with a family atmosphere. Some rooms have cable TV. Amenities include a Laundromat (US$5 per load) and a ground-floor café serving good food.

San Ignacio Resort Hotel (☎ 824-2034; www.san ignaciobelize.com; Buena Vista Rd; s/d US$95/130; **P** **⚄** **⚄**) About half a mile (1km) uphill from Government House, Cayo town's only real resort has 25 basic rooms with time-worn bathrooms. Queen Elizabeth had a luncheon here in 1994 on her trip to Belize, followed by a nap in room 31. The hotel has a restaurant (with stunning views), bar, disco and iguana hatchery (bet you weren't expecting *that* one). Salsa lessons are available and Thursday is karaoke night.

Mida's Resort (☎ 824-3172; www.midasbelize.com; campsite per person US$4, s/d US$27/34) Tidy, well-constructed cabañas set on shady grounds that slope down to the river. Breakfast is served and the bar stays open for as long as you keep drinking.

Cahal Pech Village (☎ 824-3740; www.cahalpech .com; Branch Mouth Rd; cabaña/r US$42/53; **⚄**) About 1.5 miles (2.5km) uphill (south) from the town center, Cahal Pech Village has a large thatched main building surrounded by 14 small thatched cabañas. Perched atop Cahal Pech Hill, the cabañas enjoy fine views of the town and valley, and are a much better deal than the rooms. Without a car the walk to and from town can get tedious and on Saturday night the road can get downright treacherous with traffic running to and from the Cahal Pech bar.

Aguada Hotel (☎ 804-3609; www.aguadahotel .com; 1 Aguada St, Santa Elena; r from US$30; **⚄** **⚄** **⚄**) Santa Elena's best hotel has modern, comfortable rooms with dashes of style. There's a fishing pond on the grounds and the restaurant serves three meals.

Maya Mountain Lodge (Map p263; ☎ 824-2164; www.mayamountain.com; 9 Cristo Rey Rd; r from US$49) Just over 1.5 miles (3.5km) south of San Ignacio, on the Cristo Rey Rd, Maya Mountain Lodge is a good choice. Six rooms and eight thatched cottages all with fan and

private bathroom with hot water. Delicious meals are served in the verandah restaurant. The owners are walking encyclopedias of Belizean jungle lore. In fact, they pioneered many of the tours that are widely offered throughout the region.

Eating

Martha's Guest House (10 West St; meals US$2-11; ☯ breakfast, lunch & dinner) The popular terrace café at this guesthouse (left) serves up breakfast for US$4 to US$5, pizzas for US$9 to US$11 and sandwiches for US$2 to US$3.

Upstairs Pollito (Hudson St; meals US$4-6) A popular spot with travelers for cheap, good eats.

Wildside Café & Teahouse (Burns Ave; meals from US$4; ☯ breakfast, lunch & dinner) A casual, mostly outdoor eatery serving only vegetarian food with a good range of herbal teas from the local jungle. Try the Belizean pizza (US$4).

Green Dragon (Hudson St; meals from US$5; ☯ lunch & dinner) Serves sandwiches and tapas in their shady rear courtyard, and the best coffee in town, if not the region.

Café Sol (West St; meals around US$5; ☯ lunch & dinner) The most imaginative menu in town, with plenty of vegetarian options.

Serendib Restaurant (Burns Ave; meals US$3.50-10; ☯ lunch & dinner) This place serves – of all things – Sri Lankan dishes (and pretty good ones, too). The service is friendly, and the prices aren't bad.

Hanna's (5 Burns Ave; meals US$4.50-6; ☯ breakfast, lunch & dinner) This is a good choice for Indian, Belizean and vegetarian dishes.

Entertainment

Coconuts (10 Savannah St) This is the most happening bar in town. Reggae bands play from 9pm to midnight Thursday to Saturday.

Cahal Pech About 2 miles south of town, at the top of Cahal Pech Hill, this bar sometimes schedules weekend dances.

Benque Viejo del Carmen, the small town just east of the Guatemala border, often holds weekend dances attracting people from all over the country. Ask in San Ignacio to see if anything's on for the weekend.

Getting There & Away

Buses run to and from Belize City (standard US$5, express US$7, 72 miles/110km), plus Belmopan (two hours, local US$1.50, express US$2, 23 miles/35km) and Benque Viejo del Carmen (US$1, 8 miles/13km), nearly every half hour.

The taxi stand for the Cayo Taxi Drivers Association is located on the traffic circle opposite Government House. Rates can be surprisingly high for short trips out of town (a trip of a few miles can easily cost US$5 to US$10), but a jitney cab ride to Benque Viejo del Carmen costs US$2.

Safe Tours Belize (☎ 824-4262; dcpil@yahoo.com; Western Hwy), across the Hawkesworth Bridge in Santa Elena, rents reliable vehicles. Rental rates are US$82 per day for 4WD Isuzu Troopers, and US$110 per day for full-size passenger vans. Rates include tax, insurance, unlimited mileage and air-con. They take a credit card imprint as deposit, which you'll get back when you return the vehicle. Be sure to note existing damage before you drive away, otherwise you might get charged for it later.

GUATEMALA
Luxurious **Linea Dorada/Mundo Maya** (Belize City ☎ 223-0457) and **San Juan Travel** (Belize City ☎ 223-6186) buses pass through Cayo on the way to Flores, Guatemala with a pause for border formalities. Call the offices direct or stop in at **Eva's Restaurant & Bar** (22 Burns Ave) to arrange a ticket.

Otherwise, you can catch a bus or jitney cab to Benque Viejo del Carmen, then head onwards into Guatemala (see p275 for details of border formalities).

AROUND SAN IGNACIO
Archaeological Sites
Two Mayan ruin sites make good excursions from San Ignacio. Cahal Pech is right on the edge of town, while El Pilar is a short distance to the northwest. The nearby ruins of Caracol and Pacbitun are covered on p277, while the ruins of Xunantunich are covered on p274.

CAHAL PECH
Sitting on the top of a hill overlooking San Ignacio, **Cahal Pech** (Map p263; admission US$5; ◷ 6am-6:30pm) is Mopan and Yucatec Mayan for 'Tick City.' It earned the nickname in the 1950s when the site was surrounded by pasture whose cows were riddled with ticks.

Cahal Pech (kah-*hahl*-pech) was a city of some importance from 900 BC to AD 800. The 34 buildings here are spread over 6 acres (2.4 hectares) and grouped around seven plazas. **Plaza B**, about 500ft (150m) from the museum building and parking area, is the site's largest plaza and also the most impressive. It is surrounded by some of the site's most significant buildings. Off Plaza A, **Structure A-1** is the site's tallest pyramid.

Cahal Pech is about a mile (less than 2km) from San Ignacio. A small visitors center explains some of the history. If you are walking, head up Buena Vista Rd (near the Hawkesworth Bridge); the uphill hike will take you about 45 minutes. You might want to bring water and a picnic lunch and enjoy the views from the hilltop. Otherwise, catch a taxi or a jitney cab from San Ignacio.

EL PILAR
About 12 miles (19km) northwest of San Ignacio, 7 miles (11km) northwest of Bullet Tree Falls, the Mayan archaeological site of **El Pilar** (Map p263; admission free; ◷ daylight), which is Spanish for 'watering basin,' is perched high above the Belize River. El Pilar was occupied for 15 centuries, from the Middle Preclassic (about 500 BC) through the Late Classic (about AD 1000) periods. Long before political borders, El Pilar stretched into modern-day Pilar Poniente in Guatemala, and the two countries are now working in partnership to preserve the area.

With 25 plazas and 70 major structures, the city was more than three times the size of Xunantunich. Despite ongoing excavations since 1993, El Pilar has been left largely uncleared. While seeing El Pilar's greatness requires a certain amount of imagination, six archaeological and nature trails meander among the jungle-covered mounds and make exploration worthwhile.

Though you can explore El Pilar on your own, there is no public transportation to the site, so you'll need a car, tour guide (p269) or taxi.

Caves
The fascinating activity of cave exploration is relatively new in Belize and cave excavation is even newer. A series of limestone cave systems throughout western Belize is believed to have been used by the ancient Maya for rituals, ceremonies, sacrificial

offerings and burials. Archaeologists say caves throughout the region were believed by the Maya to be gateways to Xibalbá, a nine-tiered underworld where gods resided (p43). As such, findings include hundreds of pottery vessels, remnants of food, fire and even human remains.

Considering this context, a new breed of archaeology – called spelioarchaeology – has been born. And it's an exciting time to be in Belize. The folks who explore caves have a few things in common: They're adventurous, athletic and relentlessly curious. You don't have to be a spelioarchaeologist (hell, you don't even have to be able to say it) to explore these caves, but you do have to go on tours (see p269). Caves are extremely sensitive and are being dangerously exposed to tourism overload. You can help by not disturbing artifacts and cave formations, and by not going on tours with groups larger than eight people.

In addition to the fascinating Mayan cave history, you'll be awed by the geomorphological structures of the caves themselves, where undulating flowstone decorates the walls, stalactites and stalagmites grow like ancient trees, bats flit in and out of ceiling nooks and darkness prevails.

ACTUN TUNICHIL MUKNAL

Undoubtedly one of the most incredible and adventurous tours you can take in Belize, the trip to Tunichil Muknal (toon-*itch*-all muk-*nahl*; Map p263) is an unforgettable journey on the edge of the remote **Tapir Mountain Nature Reserve**. The trip starts with an easy 45-minute hike through trails and creeks (your feet will be wet all day) to the cave opening, a spectacularly wide, misty mouth surrounded by lush jungle. You'll then don your helmet, complete with headlamp, follow your guide into the cave (starting with a frosty plunge into a 20ft-deep pool), and then hike, climb, twist and turn your way through the cave.

Giant shimmering flowstone rock formations compete for your attention with thick calcium-carbonate stalactites dripping from the ceiling. Phallic-looking stalagmites grow up from the cave floor. Later, you'll follow your guide up into a massive opening, where you'll see hundreds of pottery vessels and shards, along with human remains. One of the most shocking displays is the calcite-encrusted remains of a woman, the cave's namesake – Actun Tunichil Muknal means 'Cave of the Stone Sepulcher.'

Actun Tunichil Muknal was first 'discovered' in the 1970s, but it wasn't fully investigated until Jaime Awe, a Belizean archaeologist, started poking around Belize's caves in the early 1990s. Only then did anyone even fathom the scope of the cave's significance. From 1996 to 2000, researchers found more than 200 pottery pieces and 14 skeletal remains. Only a few of these artifacts have been removed, keeping the cave something of a living natural museum.

In 1993, a crew for the National Geographic video series 'Journey to the Underworld' filmed scenes in Tunichil Muknal. It garnered even more attention when another crew, this time from *National Geographic Adventure* followed Awe into the cave and published a story in the magazine's July/August 2001 edition.

While all this attention is good for archaeotourism in Belize, it may prove not so good for the integrity of the cave. In an effort to keep wear and tear to a minimum, only two tour operators are allowed to bring groups into the cave. The guides know the cave's history and fragility, but they are also under renewed pressure to keep up with tourist demand.

BARTON CREEK CAVE

One of the more popular day trips offered out of San Ignacio (p269) is the canoe or tube float through Barton Creek Cave (Map p263) off the Chiquibul Rd. The cave holds spooky skulls, bones and pottery shards. Ten ledges above the river, along with artifacts such as *ollas* (large jars), suggest that this was a place of important rituals. Some 28 sets of human remains found in the cave leave archaeologists wondering if the bodies were sacrificial offerings or just burials that played some part of ancestor worship.

On the trip, you'll canoe or ride an inner tube about a mile through the cave, looking at the formations and remaining artifacts.

CHECHEM HA

Antonio Morales' dog was busy chasing down a gibnut when it seemingly disappeared into a rock wall on Morales' property. Dumbfounded, Morales pressed into the 'wall' and discovered it was actually a cave mouth, and inside he found 96 pieces of priceless Mayan artifacts. Morales, who has been farming this land with his family since the 1940s, could have sold the artifacts, or hoarded them and kept the cave a secret, but he knew his find was too important to keep buried. He contacted the government and now, along with his wife Lea, graciously hosts archaeology field camps and travelers. His son William conducts most of the tours through the cave, and the experience is a family affair.

Chechem Ha (Map p263) is a mix of the word 'Chechemex' (a poisonwood tree named by a Maya tribe for its strength and hardiness) and the Mayan word 'ha,' meaning water. The Morales' lush property boasts creeks and waterfalls.

The cave, which measures about 820ft (250m) long, was used by the Maya for food storage and rituals. Today it features narrow passages that wind past intact ceremonial pots to a stela at the end of the tunnel. Bring good shoes, water and a flashlight. The tour takes about 90 minutes. Later, you can hike down to **Vaca Falls** for a swim in the river.

Bullet Tree Falls

Three miles (5km) northwest of San Ignacio, this charming little village is the perfect staging post for trips to El Pilar, seven miles (10km) further up the road. *Colectivo* taxis to Bullet Tree are available from San Ignacio. Private taxis should cost around US$8, with taxis to the site costing another US$8 one-way.

Parrot's Nest (Map p263; ☎ 820-4058; www.parrot-nest.com; s/d US$40/50) A 10-minute walk from town, this place is aptly named. Guests stay in treehouse-like thatched cabañas built high on stilts. Bathrooms are mostly shared, and there's electricity all the time. The site is beautiful, surrounded by the river on three sides. Hiking, canoeing and horseback riding are available, and shuttles to San Ignacio can be arranged.

Riverside Resort (Map p263; ☎ 820-4007; www.riversidelodge belize.com; r with fan/air-con US$40/60) Offers modern cabañas with balconies overlooking the river and artwork by local artists in the rooms. The restaurant/bar is in a huge shady *palapa*. They serve Belizean dishes, pizza and an artery-clogging full English breakfast (US$7.50).

Hummingbird Hills (Map p263; ☎ 614-4699; www.hummingbirdhills.com; cabañas from US$30) A working tree farm with bamboo and wood cottages and tree houses set in lush grounds. To get there, take a left just before the bridge and continue for a third of a mile (500m).

SAN IGNACIO TO GUATEMALA

From San Ignacio it's another 9 miles (16km) southwest down the Western Hwy to the Guatemala border.

Xunantunich

Belize's most accessible Mayan site of significance, **Xunantunich** (Map p263; admission US$5; ☽ 9am-5pm) is reached via a free hand-cranked ferry crossing at San José Succotz, on the Western Hwy about 7 miles (12km) southwest of San Ignacio. From the ferry, which comes and goes on demand, it's a hot walk of a mile (2km) uphill to the ruins.

Set on a leveled hilltop overlooking the Mopan River, Xunantunich (soo-*nahn*-too-neech), built mainly between AD 600 and 1000, controlled the riverside track that led from the hinterlands of Tikal down to the Caribbean. During the Classic period, a ceremonial center flourished here. When Caracol and Naranjo (Guatemala) collapsed around AD 800–50, the much smaller Xunantunich – whose population never topped 10,000 – remained partially inhabited. Archaeologists have uncovered evidence that an earthquake damaged the city badly about AD 900, after which the place may have been largely abandoned.

The site's dominant structure, **El Castillo** (Structure A-6), rises 130ft (40m) above the jungle floor. Climb to the top of the temple and marvel at the spectacular 360-degree view.

El Castillo underwent two distinct construction phases, the first of which produced the spectacular friezes that encircle the exterior walls. The second phase, oddly, covered up much of the artwork. The temple's west frieze was excavated in 1933 and today is buried behind a fiberglass replica. Work to uncover the temple's east side is ongoing. The name Xunantunich, meaning 'Stone Maiden,' comes from an old story that a maiden appeared one night, then mysteriously dissolved into the stone of El Castillo.

Guides can be hired for a one-hour tour for US$15, but the site can easily be navi-

XUNANTUNICH

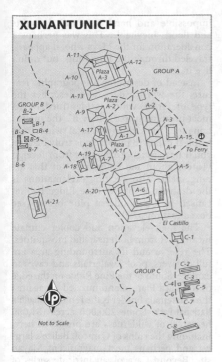

GROUP A

GROUP B

El Castillo

GROUP C

Not to Scale

To Ferry

gated independently. The **Inn at Xunantunich** (Map p263; ☎ 804-3739; www.discovercayo.com; r with fan/air-con from US$25/58), across the road, is a good stop for lunch and refreshments. Rooms are modern and comfortable and they offer a range of tours.

Buses between San Ignacio and Benque Viejo del Carmen will drop you at the ferry for the fare of US$0.50. Jitney taxis shuttling the same route cost US$1.50. Ferry hours are 8am to noon and 1pm to 5pm; crossing is on demand and free for both foot passengers and cars.

Benque Viejo del Carmen

A sleepy town 1 mile (1.6km) east of the border, this town stirs from its normal tropical somnolence in mid-July, when the **Benque Festival** brings three days of music and revelry.

Mopan River Resort (Map p263; ☎ 823-3272; www.mopanriverresort.com; Riverside North; weekly packages from US$1198) Definitely one of the best options in the area – the grounds are beautiful and the thatch roof cabañas have gorgeous hardwood furniture and are decorated with

local handicrafts. Packages are truly all-inclusive; they provided transfers from the airport, meals, cocktails, daily guided tours (including Tikal) – even marimba bands!

CROSSING THE BORDER

Cross early in the morning to have the best chance of catching buses onward. Get your passport (and, if applicable, your car papers) stamped at the Belizean station, then cross into Guatemala at Melchor de Mencos. The border station is supposedly open 24 hours a day, but most travelers try to cross during daylight hours. If you need a Guatemalan visa (see p196), obtain it before you reach the border. Guatemalan tourist cards (US$5) are obtainable at the border. Be prepared to pay a US$18 departure tax when crossing the border.

Two banks at the border will change money, but the itinerant moneychangers often give you a better deal – for US cash. The rates for exchanging Belizean dollars to Guatemalan quetzals and vice versa are poor. Use up your local currency before you get to the border, then change hard foreign currency, preferably US dollars.

Both Transportes Pinita and Transportes Rosalita buses westward to Santa Elena and Flores, in Guatemala (US$3), depart town early in the morning. Sometimes more comfortable – and more expensive – minibuses (US$10 per person) are available; many travelers feel this is money well spent.

To go on to Tikal, get off the bus at El Cruce (Puente Ixlu), 22 miles (36km) east of Flores, and wait for another bus, minibus or obliging car or truck to take you the final 21 miles (35km) north to Tikal. Note that the flow of traffic from El Cruce to Tikal drops dramatically after lunch.

Sleeping

Windy Hill Resort (Map p263; ☎ 824-2017; www .windyhillresort.com; Western Hwy, Mile 67; 2-night packages s/d from US$860/980; 🐾) About 1.5 miles (2.5 km) west of San Ignacio on the Western Hwy, this has all the facilities: swimming pool, horse riding, nature trail, canoes ready for a paddle on the Mopan River and a full program of tours. The two-day package includes the Belize Zoo, Guanacaste Park, Xunantunich Maya Ruins, Mountain Pine Ridge Forest Reserve, Hidden Valley Falls, Río Frio Cave and Río On Pools.

BELIZE

Clarissa Falls (Map p263; ☎ 824-3916; www.clarissa-falls.com; campsite per person US$7.50, dm/cabaña US$15/65) The rooms are not special (although the restaurant, open 7am to 7pm, is quite good), but the location is superb – right next to the small, wide Clarissa Falls. They can drop you at San José Succotz and you can tube (US$10) or kayak (US$20) back down. The turnoff is at Mile 70, Western Hwy, then another mile down a dirt road.

Trek Stop (Map p263; ☎ 823-2265; www.thetrekstop.com; Western Hwy, Mile 71; s/d US$10/20) Six miles (10km) west of San Ignacio, this is ideal for backpackers and a good staging point for the Xunantunich ferry, half a mile (800m) away. It's set in a leafy forest and offers basic wooden cabañas with shared solar showers. It's a five-minute walk to the river. Nature trails are on the site, as is the **Tropical Wings Nature Center**, which houses an interpretive center and a small butterfly farm. The latest addition is a nine hole Frisbee golf course. Fore! Meals are available as is tube (US$7.50) and kayak (US$20) rental, with pick up and drop off.

Nabitunich (Map p263; ☎ 823-2096; rudyjuan@btl.net; Western Hwy, Mile 71; s/d US$20/40) Simple but clean cottages on well-kept grounds, with a great view of Xunantunich on the nearby hilltop. Horseback tours to Xunantunich are available from around US$20, more if you dawdle or spend more than two hours at the site.

MOUNTAIN PINE RIDGE AREA

South of the Western Hwy, the land begins to climb toward the heights of the Maya Mountains, whose arcing crest forms the border separating the Cayo District from the Stann Creek District to the east and the Toledo District to the south. From San Ignacio, it's about 9 to 13 miles (15km to 21km) to the park gate, depending on which route you take.

In the heart of this highland area – the land of macaws, mahogany, mangoes and jaguars – over 300 sq miles (777 sq km) of tropical pine forest has been set aside as the **Mountain Pine Ridge Forest Reserve**. Unlike the tropical broadleaf forests so prevalent in Belize, whose shallow soil base sits on limestone, much of the Mountain Pine Ridge's soil sits on a superficial level of red clay, beneath which lies solid granite. This infertile soil base makes agriculture almost impossible and harsh seasonal droughts and floods inevitable. This was perhaps a consideration for the Maya who, it appears, traveled through the Pine Ridge but didn't live in it.

Instead of describing a topographic feature, the word 'ridge' here describes the type of forest, which is identified by its most prominent tree – here it's the mountain pine. The sudden and total switch from tropical palms to pine trees is truly bizarre; you'll hear much exclaiming from foreign visitors about the incongruity of this arrangement. Also eliciting exclamations is the destruction of the Pine Ridge habitat caused by the southern pine beetle (see boxed text on p280).

The high elevation and cooler climate mean relief from both heat and mosquitoes. The reserve and its surrounding area are full of rivers, pools, waterfalls and caves to explore. South of the Pine Ridge on the edge of the Vaca Plateau and nuzzled up against the Guatemala border is the remote **Chiquibul National Park**. Some 200,000 acres (81,000 hectares) of wilderness are protected here, including the ruins of Caracol, Belize's largest and perhaps most magnificent Mayan site. Beyond Caracol, an intricate series of karst caves is believed to be the biggest in the Western Hemisphere. The area was not noted by modern researchers until the 1970s and, because of difficult access, most of the cave system remains unexplored.

When visiting the Mountain Pine Ridge and Chiquibul National Park, keep in mind that except for a small presence of forestry workers in the village of Douglas da Silva, staff at the area lodges, a few archaeologists, occasional British troops on training exercises and a smattering of illegal squatters from Guatemala, this massive area is mostly uninhabited.

Rainforest Medicine Trail

Formerly called the Pantí Medicine Trail, this herbal-cure research center is at **Ix Chel Farms** (Map p263; self-guided tour US$5; ☉ 8am-noon, 1-5pm), 8 miles (13km) southwest of San Ignacio up Chial Rd.

Dr Eligio Pantí, who died in 1996 at age 103, was a healer in San Antonio village who used traditional Mayan herb cures. Dr Rosita Arvigo, a North American, studied medicinal plants with Dr Pantí, then began several projects to spread the wisdom of traditional healing methods and to preserve the rain forest habitats, which harbor an incredible 4000 plant species.

One of her projects was the establishment of the Rainforest Medicine Trail, a self-guiding path among the jungle's natural cures. At the farm's shop you can buy Rainforest Remedies – herbal cures drawn from the farm's resources and marketed by the Ix Chel Tropical Research Foundation.

Waterfalls & Caves

With the exception of Five Sisters Falls, all of the sites listed below are free to explore.

One of the region's much-touted aquatic highlights is **Thousand Foot Falls** (Hidden Valley Falls; Map p263). Access it by turning off the Chiquibul Rd onto Cooma Cairn Rd and following it for 9 miles (14km). Hiking trails surround the falls, and a viewing platform at the top of the cascade is a great spot for catching a Mountain Pine Ridge vista. Despite the name, the falls actually are around 1600ft (488m) high and, despite the height, the thin long stream of falling water isn't that spectacular. Still it's a beautiful, lush spot to hike around and shows a good example of the blending forest ecosystems.

The shorter, fatter **Five Sisters Falls** (Map p263; admission around US$2.50) are accessible by an outdoor elevator ride from Five Sisters Lodge (p279). The five falls cascade over a short drop-off and gather in a tranquil pool. Travelers and locals alike visit this site.

At **Río On Pools** (Map p263) small waterfalls connect a series of pools that the river has carved out of granite boulders. The natural pools are refreshing and the smooth slabs of granite rock are perfect for stretching out to dry off. A picnic area and outhouse are the only amenities here.

Less than a mile (2km) from Douglas da Silva is one of the most popular Pine Ridge attractions. **Río Frio Cave** (Map p263), a large, easily accessed cavern, was part of a cave system used by the Maya to bury their dead. The river gurgles through the sizeable cave, keeping it cool while you explore, looking at the interesting rock formations. Energetic types can take the easy **Río Frio Nature Trail**, a 45-minute jaunt through the forest, with some good vantage points of the surrounding area. The site has an outhouse and picnic tables. This, along with the Río

On Pools, is usually included on Mountain Pine Ridge tours out of San Ignacio (p269).

Pacbitun

Mayan for 'Stones Set in Earth,' Pacbitun (pahk-be-*toon*; Map p263) is a small archaeological site, approximately 12 miles (20km) south of San Ignacio via Cristo Rey Rd, near the village of San Antonio. The site seems to have been occupied continuously through most of Mayan history, from 900 BC to AD 900. Archaeologists began work here only in 1971, when they uncovered more than 20 pyramids, eight stelae and several raised irrigation channels. Today only lofty **Plaza A** has been uncovered and partially consolidated. Structures 1 and 2, on the east and west sides of the plaza, respectively, are worth a look. Within them archaeologists discovered the graves of Maya women of nobility, buried – interestingly – with a variety of musical instruments, perhaps played at their funerals. Pacbitun is on private land; you can visit by yourself, but you should ask permission from Mr Tzal, whose property you'll pass on the road to the ruins.

Caracol

Some 50 miles (80km) south of San Ignacio and 26 miles (42km) south of Douglas da Silva via Chiquibul Rd lies **Caracol** (Map p263; admission US$7.50; 8am-4pm), a vast Mayan city hidden deep in the jungle of Chiquibul National Park. Following a rugged road, this trip takes about three hours (each way) from San Ignacio.

Sitting high on a plateau 500ft (152m) above sea level, the site – the largest in Belize – is massive, with evidence of 37 miles (60km) of internal roadways and transportation routes. It is estimated that, at its height, Caracol's population topped 150,000 – more than half of Belize's population today. Why such an enormous city developed here, in the middle of the jungle and far from an accessible water source, is one of the big questions that leave archaeologists scratching their heads.

Once you've traveled the long road to Caracol, you'll get to the site's main gate and **visitors center**. The site is staffed by guides who will show you around for free (you can tip at your discretion). Keep in mind when

BELIZE

touring here that it would take archaeologists several lifetimes to excavate a site this size; an imagination and sense of adventure are essential. There are toilets, but no other services, so be sure to have food, water and, if you're driving, a spare tire.

MAYAN HISTORY

A small population lived at Caracol in the Late Preclassic and Early Classic periods (300 BC to AD 550), but it wasn't until after a series of wars with Tikal and Naranjo (Guatemala) in the Late Classic period that Caracol flourished. A ball court marker (called Altar 21) dedicated in AD 633 by Lord K'an II suggests that his father, 'Lord Water,' defeated Tikal in AD 562 and Naranjo in AD 556. This is an exciting discovery that indicates Caracol could have rivaled (or surpassed) the size and power of Tikal.

Residents of Caracol came from all levels of society, from poor farmers to royalty, though its population was probably dominated by a large middle class.

At its height, the metropolis would have surpassed modern-day Belize City's size and bustle.

EXCAVATION HISTORY

The ruins were first stumbled upon in 1938 by a mahogany logger named Rosa Mai. That year, commissioner of archaeology AH Anderson named the site Caracol (Spanish for snail), perhaps because of all the snail shells found in the soil. Since then, various excavations have brought the site (slowly) to what you see today.

A four-year (2000–04) loan from the International Development Bank has given the Tourism Development Project (TDP) a surge in funding that will allow excavations to continue year-round. More money from Taiwanese investors will go to improving the road in to Caracol. Leading the TDP are Drs Jaime Awe and Allan Moore, Belizean archaeologists who suggest that this is the most exciting time in Caracol's modern history and that in the not-too-distant future, the site could rival Guatemala's Tikal.

SIGHTS

A system of trails meanders through Caracol, but Plazas A and B around the Central Acropolis are the most excavated. The big highlight here is **Caana** (Sky-Palace) in Plaza B, Caracol's tallest structure at 141ft (43m) and the tallest human-made structure in Belize. Caana underwent many construction phases until its completion in about AD 800. There are stone 'beds' throughout the middle portion. High steps narrowing up to the top probably led to the royal family's compound, where Structure B-19 was found to house Caracol's largest and most elaborate tomb (containing a woman's remains). You can climb to the top of Caana and feast upon one of the most magnificent views in all of Belize. Other than the occasional patch-farm fire, it's jungle as far as the eye can see.

The **Temple of the Wooden Lintel**, in Plaza A, was built with zapote wooden crossbeams, which dates the building to the 1st century AD and means it was one of the oldest and longest-used buildings at Caracol. Excavations here revealed a cache containing 684 grams of liquid mercury.

The neat and extensively excavated **ball court** is the site of Altar 21, the marker commemorating Caracol's defeat of Tikal. Nearby, an elite group likely lived in the **Central Acropolis**, 'downtown Caracol.' A royal tomb found here contained four sets of human remains, along with more than 20 pottery vessels. Another elite residential area, the **South Acropolis**, is worth a look, as are the reservoirs (which caught rainwater) and causeways.

You can sign up for a tour (US$50 to US$75 per person) in San Ignacio (p269) or at one of the lodges. Those who opt to visit Caracol on their own can reach it on a long day trip in a 4WD or high-clearance vehicle; check road conditions before you go. See p272 for car hire outfits. No services are available at the site, so bring your own food, water and motor fuel.

Sleeping

The forests and mountains of the greater Mountain Pine Ridge area are dotted with small inns, lodges and ranches offering accommodations, meals, hiking, horseback trips, caving, swimming, bird-watching and similar outdoor activities.

Standard room rates are listed below, but most of the lodges also offer money-saving packages that include lodging, meals and tours. It never hurts to ask if discounts and specials are available.

Unless you have your own transportation, you'll have to depend on taxis or the hospitality of your lodge hosts to transport you between San Ignacio and the lodges. Sometimes the lodges will shuttle you at no extra cost; sometimes they will arrange a taxi for you. See the map on p263 for a general idea of the location of the following lodges. If you decide to drive in on your own, your lodge will provide you with exact directions.

MOUNTAIN PINE RIDGE LODGES

Although you can sometimes show up unannounced and find a room, these are small, popular places, so it's best to write or call for reservations as far in advance as possible.

The Mountain Pine Ridge lodges are served by the Blancaneaux Lodge airstrip; charter flights are arranged by the lodge.

Blancaneaux Lodge (Map p263; ☎ 824-4912; www .blancaneaux.com; s/d from US$110/150; ✂ 🖳 🐾) Offers 14 rooms in thatched cabañas and luxury villas overlooking waterfalls deep in the Mountain Pine Ridge reserve. Formerly a private writing retreat for the resort's owner, director Francis Ford Coppola, the lodge features beautiful tiled bathrooms, open-air living rooms (in the villas) and a decor filled with handicrafts from Belize, Guatemala, Mexico and Thailand. The restaurant serves Italian cuisine and wines from California's Napa Valley.

Five Sisters Lodge (Map p263; ☎ 820-4005; www .fivesisterslodge.com; s/d US$45/55, cabaña from US$60/75, ste from US$105) West of Blancaneaux, Five Sisters is named for the five waterfalls that cascade through the property. A hydro-powered tram runs guests down to the river for swimming and sunbathing. Breakfast and lunch cost US$6 and dinner US$17.50.

Pine Ridge Lodge (Map p263; ☎ 606-4557; www .pineridgelodge.com; cottages low/high season US$59/79) Spacious, well-maintained cottages with private bathrooms. The restaurant serves lunch (US$7.50) and dinner (US$19.50).

Hidden Valley Inn (Map p263; ☎ 822-3320; www .hiddenvalleyinn.com; s/d from US$120/135; 🖳 🐾) Luxurious without being over the top. Cabañas are beautifully decorated and very comfortable. The property sits on 7200 acres of private reserve, with 90 miles of hiking and mountain-biking trails. The inn is popular with birders, but the grounds also have access to a staggering array of waterfalls, lakes and other natural attractions.

MACAL RIVER LODGES

Several lodges, some quite famous, lie along the Macal River, reached by Chial Rd. If you drive in yourself, your host lodge will give you exact directions.

Chaa Creek Cottages (Map p263; ☎ 824-2037; www .chaacreek.com; s/d from US$130/150, ste US$180) The most luxurious of the Cayo lodges, right on the bank of the Macal River next to Ix Chel Farm and the Rainforest Medicine Trail. Its beautifully kept thatch-roofed cottages are set in tropical gardens and richly decorated with Mayan textiles and local crafts; all have fan and private bathroom. A state-of-the-art spa has recently been added. Breakfast costs US$10, a box lunch is US$8 and dinner is US$26. Chaa Creek also operates **Macal River Camp** (tent per night US$50), a budget alternative offering platformed safari-style tents; rates include meals, and bathrooms are shared. Guests at Macal River Camp have access to the grounds at Chaa Creek Cottages.

duPlooy's Jungle Lodge (Map p263; ☎ 824-3101; www.duplooys.com; s/d from US$40/50) Set largely on a fairly steep hill, the rooms look out over the tree canopy and are accessed by a board-walk, giving the place a treehouse appeal. Guests can enjoy swimming in the Macal River or sunbathing on the resort's white, sandy beach. Three levels of accommodations are available. Rooms in the Pink House have fan and shared bathroom, and standard bungalows and rooms in the Jungle Lodge have fans and private bathrooms. High-end bungalows are also available. Meal packages cost US$35 per day for three meals.

Black Rock River Lodge (Map p263; ☎ 824-2341; www.blackrocklodge.com; cabaña s/d with shared bathroom US$40/50, with private bathroom from US$56/66) This simple, remote place has thatched-roof cottages with solar electricity and solar-heated hot water. It's not a sit-around-the-pool type of resort (in fact there is no pool) – people come here to do things, and is are a great range of activities on offer, including canoeing, horseback riding, caving, birding and hiking. Check the website for more info. For directions, ask at Caesar's Place, near Georgeville on the Western Hwy (p268).

Getting There & Away

There is no public transportation in this area. See p269 for tour details. Blancaneaux Lodge (left) arranges charter flights to their nearby airstrip. If you're staying at one of

BELIZE

THE SOUTHERN PINE BEETLE'S PATH OF DESTRUCTION

Like a thief in the night or a snake in the grass, a tiny beetle no longer than 0.2 inches (6mm) is devastating Belize's Mountain Pine Ridge forest. Take a look around and you'll see that the pine trees, which are supposed to be green, are now a sickly, fiery hue of red, or they've already fallen dead. The culprit for this mess is the tiny southern pine beetle *(Dendroctonus frontalis)*, which has destroyed more than 90% of the Pine Ridge forest.

The beetles, which only live up to a month, possess sophisticated 'semiochemical' communication systems that they use to move onto a host material – in this case, pine trees – where they feed, mate and reproduce. In her lifetime, a female can produce up to 150 eggs. The beetle in Belize is one of five bark beetles destroying pine forests in the Americas. Extreme weather conditions (such as hurricanes) contribute to the problem and, while the beetles are almost impossible to eradicate, certain methods can be used to slow their path of destruction.

A well-managed forest should be able to survive a pine beetle attack. Sanitation salvaging (removing infested trees), selective logging (creating forest buffer zones) and spraying of insecticides can help control the problem. In Belize, critics say, government cutbacks in forestry, slow response and lax management meant that this approach happened too late.

While today's infestation already promises to annihilate the pine forest trees – a major catastrophe in itself – it's the other ramifications that have resident environmentalists concerned. The ecological changes in the forest affect the Macal River watershed, which supplies residents living along the Macal and Belize Rivers (including Belize City) with freshwater. Soil erosion on an already shallow soil base threatens river flow and wildlife habitat, and the dry, unstable trees make massive wildfires almost a certainty.

While the Forestry Department has major plans underway to replant trees and salvage whatever it can of the remaining forest, it will take at least 25 years for the forest to recover if, in fact, it can.

the lodges listed on p279, they can arrange transfers from San Ignacio (which could be free or US$20) or anywhere else in the country (which will be a lot more expensive). If you're driving yourself, note that roads into the Mountain Pine Ridge area are few. The most important are (from east to west) Chiquibul Rd, which intersects the Western Hwy at Mile 61, near Georgeville, about 6 miles (10km) east of San Ignacio; Cristo Rey Rd, which turns south off the Western Hwy in Santa Elena (across the river from San Ignacio); and Chial Rd, a rough, unpaved road that turns south off the Western Hwy about 5 miles (8km) southwest of San Ignacio or roughly 2 miles (3km) northeast of Benque Viejo del Carmen.

Of these, Chiquibul Rd penetrates deepest into the mountains; the unpaved but graded road runs all the way through the forest reserve and continues south as far as the Caracol archaeological site. About 2.5 miles (4km) south of the Río On Pools is the forestry settlement of **Douglas da Silva**. While there's little to do here, it's a good idea to stop by the ranger's station if you are planning on going further south into

the Chiquibul National Park. The roads in the area may sometimes be impassable between May and late October. Always check with tour operators in San Ignacio about road conditions; you don't want to drive deep into the jungle only to be turned back.

At the entrance to the reserve, a park ranger stops all vehicles and registers names and license plates. This is to control illegal activity and to keep track of who is in the area in case of accidents or bad weather.

SOUTHERN BELIZE

If you want to explore off the tourist track, this is the place. Southern Belize, encompassing the districts of Stann Creek and Toledo, presents the country's most diverse topography, including an extensive limestone cave system off the Hummingbird Hwy, the Maya Mountains running through the middle of the area, and miles of virgin rain forest in the south. Within the region are Cockscomb Basin Wildlife Sanctuary (p290) and the lovely and remote ruins of Toledo – Lubaantun (p300) and Nim Li Punit (p300).

Out to sea, the barrier reef continues to stretch its way down the coastline, and the further south you get the fewer other humans you'll have to share it with. Off Dangriga, Tobacco and South Water Cayes and Glover's Reef (p288) offer divers and snorkelers nearly virgin reef to explore. From Placencia (p292) divers and snorkelers can access Gladden Spit, where it's possible to see migrating whale sharks when the season is right, and Laughing Bird Caye, an area with diverse undersea life. Off Punta Gorda (p296) are the Sapodilla and Snake Cayes, still largely undiscovered and teeming with marine life.

There are three major towns in the region – Dangriga (p284), a lively seaside town and the center of Garifuna culture in Belize; Placencia (p292), the region's biggest draw, attracting beach-loving travelers for whom life in the cayes is just too hectic; and Punta Gorda (p296), Belize's southernmost town, largely untraveled (but on the brink of discovery) – and a fascinating mix of Creole, ladino and Mayan cultures.

The Southezrn Hwy, only partially paved and perpetually under construction, carries travelers through the region. The further south you travel, the more remote and wild the landscape becomes, the fewer travelers you'll see, and the more adventurous you will be.

MANATEE HIGHWAY TO GALES POINT

The mostly unpaved Manatee (or Coastal) Hwy goes southeast from the Western Hwy at Mile 30, at the village of La Democracia, a short distance past the Belize Zoo. Keep your eyes peeled for a gas station on the south side of the road, as this is where you'll turn.

This was long considered the shortcut to Dangriga, but the Hummingbird Hwy takes about the same amount of time now that it's been paved, and when the weather is rainy the unpaved Manatee Hwy will take a bit longer. If you're driving south and back, going one direction on Hummingbird and the other direction on Manatee is a nice way to break up the trip. The landscape is much different than what you'll see elsewhere in Belize. Orange dirt roads wind through lush farmland, approaching and then passing through limestone formations that rise sharply up from the fields, much like coral rises sharply from the sandy bottom of the sea.

GALES POINT

Gales Point is a sleepy Creole town built along 2.5 miles of narrow peninsula jutting into Belize's southern lagoon. This area has a couple of superlative distinctions. One, it has the highest concentration of Western Manatees in the Caribbean. Two, it's the primary breeding ground for 60% of the hawksbill turtles in Belize. There's only one road in and out of the town, and you'll find that you get to know the townspeople pretty quickly.

Tours
MANATEE WATCHING
Manatees are attracted to the region for the warm freshwater spring located 200 yards (182m) off the point. They can be seen around the spring and grazing on the sea grass that grows in the lagoon. Manatee tours can be arranged at the Manatee Lodge (see p282); a two-hour tour costs US$55 for one or two people. Manatee watching can be combined with other activities offered by the lodge, such as a southern lagoon or river tour, a jungle hike or a visit to one of the nearby caves. A half-day tour combining one of the above activities with manatee watching costs US$140 for one or two people. A full-day tour is US$185 and includes a choice of two activities, plus the manatees.

TURTLE TOURS
Hawksbill, which are protected, as well as loggerhead and green sea turtles, which aren't yet protected in Belize, lay their eggs on 21 miles (34km) of beach across the lagoon from Gales Point.

The action happens from May to November each year. Turtles work hard to hide their nests (they lay about 150 to 200 eggs), but a good eye (or nose if you're a raccoon or a skunk) can find them. This is not for everyone; it's buggy, muddy work, with lots of exposure to the elements and, obviously, you're not guaranteed a turtle sighting. Though definitely not a soft adventure, it's a rewarding experience for those willing to roll up their sleeves and get up close and participatory with nature. Part of the US$175 (for one or two people) tour fee goes to local conservation efforts. Bookings can be made through Manatee Lodge (see below).

SNORKELING TOURS
Snorkeling tours of the reef can be arranged at Manatee Lodge for US$275 for one or two people – you'll take a 10-minute boat ride east on the Bar River, which connects the southern lagoon to the Caribbean Sea. Cockscomb Basin (p290) is also within reasonable day-trip distance.

Sleeping & Eating
Manatee Lodge (☎ 220-8040; www.manateelodge.com; r up to 4 people US$85; meal package per day US$35) Located at the tip of the Gales Point peninsula, this is a peaceful spot on a pleasant piece of land and the center of activity for visitors to the area. The grassy grounds stretch out to the water on three sides, and a long dock is offered for swimming. There are 10 spacious and comfortable rooms with good, modern bathrooms. Larger rooms are available for groups. The restaurant is excellent and serves large portions. Meals are based on traditional Belizean dishes and made with fresh ingredients and plenty of green vegetables. All-inclusive packages are available for longer stays. Check the website for details.

John Moore's Lodging (☎ 220-8040; r US$14) Basic rooms can be rented at Manatee Lodge where John leads tours.

A few local restaurants such as **Gentle's Cool Spot**, **Carol's Caribbean Cuisine**, and **Mrs T's Kitchen** will prepare meals for around US$4. For upscale dining head to the Manatee Lodge.

Getting There & Away
Manatee Hwy (also known as the Coastal Route) is the road you'll take if you're driving to Gales Point. The turnoff is 23 miles (37km) from the Western Hwy, 15 miles (24km) north of the Hummingbird Hwy junction.

A 5pm Southern Transport bus leaves Belize City and travels the Manatee Hwy to Dangriga, arriving at the Gales Point junction around 6:30pm. From Dangriga, the Manatee Hwy/Coastal Route bus leaves at 5am and arrives at the Gales Point junction at 6am.

It's also possible to get there by boat from Belize City through a network of canals and Burdon Canal Nature Reserve. Arrangements can be made through Manatee Lodge; the price will be around US$175 for up to four passengers. The trip takes you through a riverine mangrove area and the location where *Mosquito Coast* was filmed.

HUMMINGBIRD HIGHWAY
Heading south from Belmopan, the Hummingbird Hwy stretches 49 miles (79km) to the junction of the Southern Hwy and the turnoff to Dangriga. It's a gorgeous and dramatic drive over the Maya Mountains and through foothills and valleys of citrus plantations – probably the most scenic and varied route in Belize. Mile counters on the Hummingbird Hwy run from Mile 55 at the Western Hwy junction to Mile 0 at Dangriga city limits. At Mile 16 (39 miles from Belmopan) you'll crest the hills at a spot aptly named Over the Top, also known as Hummingbird Gap.

At the southern end of the highway you'll go over a few one-lane bridges. This is evidence of an old railway line that ran through the valley in the early 20th century. It fell out of use when the banana industry declined.

Past Five Blues National Park, the Hummingbird Hwy crosses several rivers that empty out of the Maya Mountains to the south. You'll pass through plantations of citrus, cacao and bananas before coming to the junction of the Southern Hwy and the road into Dangriga.

Blue Hole National Park & St Herman's Cave
The **Blue Hole** focus of the like-named **national park** (admission US$4; ☺ 8am-4pm) is a cenote (a water-filled limestone sinkhole) formed when the roof caved in on a portion of one of the underwater rivers of the Sibun River tributaries. The cenote is 328ft (98.4m) in diameter and 108ft (33m) deep. A set of stairs leads into the recession to a swimming hole that is 25ft (7.6m) deep and the glowing sapphire blue that inspired its name. The river dips back underground through a spooky echo- and bat-filled chamber. A popular stop on the Hummingbird Hwy for visitors and locals, its subterranean cooling systems makes for a refreshing dip, even on

LOOKING FOR SOME HOT STUFF?

While in Belize, you'll find that you never eat alone. Your table and your meal are always enlivened by Marie Sharp's inimitable presence.

Sharp got into the hot-sauce business in 1981, and it happened by chance, as kitchen-table operations often do. She worked as an executive secretary at a citrus plant and, with her husband, ran a family farm in her spare time. One season she found herself with a surplus of habanero peppers when a buyer backed out of purchasing them after harvest. Sharp hated to see them go to waste, so she decided to figure out something to do with the peppers.

Working in the evening in her kitchen, she blended the excess habaneros into a mash and began to experiment with various concoctions. She found that other bottled hot sauces were often watery, tasteless and sometimes too hot to be flavorful. She wanted a sauce that would specifically complement Belizean cuisine, and one that didn't contain artificial ingredients. She came up with some interesting blends and took them around to her friends and family for taste-testing. By far, the favorite was one that used carrots as a thickener and blended the peppers with onions and garlic.

Once she had her formula, she embarked on a guerilla marketing campaign. She carried samples of the sauce, along with corn chips and refried beans, door-to-door to shopkeepers all over Belize. When the proprietors liked what they tasted, Marie asked them to put the sauce on the their shelves and agreed to take back the bottles that didn't sell. The sauce, then bottled under the brand name Melinda, which was the name of Sharp's ranch, caught on and was soon not only on store shelves but also on restaurant tables all over the country.

Marie worked at bottling the sauces from her kitchen for three years, finally bringing in a couple of workers to help her mix up the zealously guarded formula. She continued to work on modifications for her sauce, eventually hybridizing her own red habanero pepper – a mix of scotch bonnet and Jamaican red peppers – which contributes to the distinctive color of the sauce. Seeds were distributed to her producers with strict instructions on how to grow and maintain the hybrid. She opened her own factory in 1986 with two three-burner stoves and six women to look after her pots, and moved to her current factory in 1998 (see p285 for details on tours).

Her business suffered a setback in 1991, when she was forced to break ties with her US distributor for allegedly bottling other, lesser-quality products under the Melinda name. Rather than commit to a protracted court battle, Sharp signed off the Melinda name to the distributor and began bottling her top-secret formula under her own name.

Today, one half of all Marie Sharp's hot sauce is distributed to stores and restaurants in Belize, while the other half is exported to the US and Japan. She employs a workforce of 20, mostly women, who can package 1000 cases (12,000 bottles) of hot sauce in eight hours and are able to produce one shipping container full of sauce in a month.

In addition to hot sauces – which come in regular, mild, hot, fiery hot and XXX – Sharp also produces jams and chutneys made from mango and papaya, and a tamarind steak sauce that Sharp proudly claims is far superior to sauces made with raisins.

Her company now serves as an example for small businesses in Belize and elsewhere. Sharp is committed to creating industry for Belizeans; her jams and fruit sauces are often created from locally grown fruit that is too small for export and would usually go to waste.

Sharp notes proudly that the folks running the X-ray machines at the airport have told her that bottles of her sauce are the most common item in the bags of departing vacationers. Those who can't carry enough can find the sauce in specialty shops in the US and Japan, or order online from www.firegirl.com.

the hottest days. It becomes murky and less inviting after rain.

The visitors center is about 11 miles (18km) south of Belmopan on the Hummingbird Hwy (Mile 44). At the center is the trailhead to **St Herman's Cave**, a large cavern used by the Maya during the Classic period. This is one of the few caves in Belize that you can visit independently, although a guide is required if you wish to venture in further than half a mile. A flashlight is a must. Also here is an observation tower and

3-mile (4.8km) network of trails, including a nature walk.

The trail to the Blue Hole itself starts at a parking area about a mile further down the highway. (Break-ins are not unheard of here, so be cautious with your belongings.) You don't have to stop at the visitors center if you're just going for a swim; an attendant is posted at the trail to the Blue Hole to collect your money. Most visitors are content just to have a dip in the water and a peek in the cave; however, guides can be arranged at the visitors center to point out the special features of the cave or to help you out with nature spotting.

Between the two entrances, a road on the left leads to **Ian Anderson's Caves Branch Adventure Company & Jungle Camp** (☎ 822-2800; www .cavesbranch.com; Hummingbird Hwy, Mile 41.5; campsite per person US$5, dm US$15, cabaña from US$78) featuring adventure tours to caves on a privately owned estate. Day trips cost US$75 to US$105 per person and require various levels of activity – you can choose a leisurely tube float down the Caves Branch River or go for a harder adventure where you will hike, climb and even rappel to reach your destination. Packages and multiday cave expeditions (including Ian's Bad Ass Adventures) are available. A good balance of adventure and comfort makes this jungle lodge popular with honeymooners and families.

The jungle has been cleared just enough to allow room for the buildings, giving the grounds an exotic feel. There are three classes of rooms: dorm rooms containing seven bunks each, bungalows built two to a building, and deluxe jungle suites with living rooms and private bathrooms. The shared bathroom facilities here are the best in Belize.

On the premises you will hear howler monkeys in the middle of the night and see keep-billed toucans in the trees. The management keeps dogs as pets, so there's little chance of running into any sort of ferocious animal, but there has been evidence that jaguars are present in the wilderness around the lodge.

Five Blues National Park

Twenty-two miles (36km) south of Belmopan is the turnoff to **Five Blues National Park** (admission US$4; ☉ 8am-4pm), a primitive community-managed reserve surrounding five (blue) lakes. Turn left (north) off the highway and you'll see a visitors center, where you'll be asked to pay an entry fee. Be sure to pick up a map from the attendant, as the park's features – a series of nature walks, a diving platform and a couple of small caves – are not clearly marked. The park is about 4 miles (6.5km) from the visitors center down a rough road, and it's difficult to reach without your own transportation.

DANGRIGA
pop 8,800

Once called Stann Creek Town, Dangriga is the largest town in southern Belize. It's much smaller than Belize City and, consequently, a friendlier and quieter place.

Most travelers coming through Dangriga spend one night and move on, catching the bus to Placencia or a launch out to the popular diving and fishing spots off Glover's Reef and Tobacco Caye, and most come away not thinking much of the place. Indeed, to the naked eye there's not much to see. Looking, listening and talking is the way you get to know Dangriga. Wander the streets in the early morning or late afternoon, hang out in the restaurants and talk to people. You'll walk with the blue sea always out of the corner of your eye, the ocean breeze on your skin, and Garifuna drumming and the unfamiliar cadence of Garifuna language in your ears.

Early evening or mid-morning are the best times for exploring; that's when you'll meet the fisherfolk in from their early hours of work or catch the townspeople as they relax and visit along the streets in the evening.

Orientation & Information

Stann Creek empties into the Gulf of Honduras at the center of town. Dangriga's main street is called St Vincent St south of the creek and Commerce St to the north. The bus station is at the southern end of St Vincent St just north of the Shell fuel station. The airstrip is a mile (2km) north of the center, near the Pelican Beach Resort.

First Caribbean Bank (☉ 8am-1pm Mon-Thu, 8am-4:30pm Fri) has a Visa ATM.

You can have your clothes washed and check your email at the same time at **Val's Laundry** (1 Sharp St). A load costs US$4, as does an hour on the Internet.

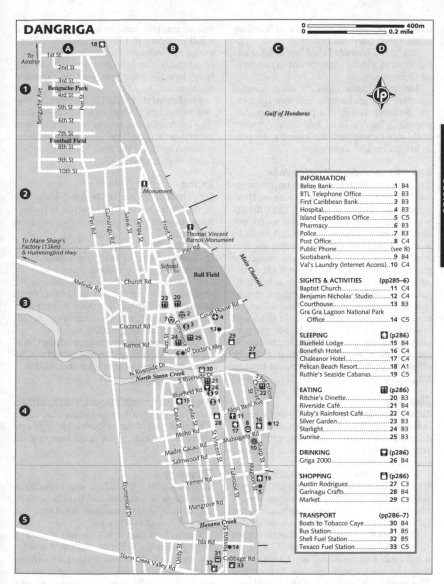

DANGRIGA

0 — 400m
0 — 0.2 mile

To Airstrip

1st St
2nd St
3rd St
4th St
5th St
6th St
7th St
8th St
9th St
10th St

Benguche Ave
Benguche Park
Pen St
Football Field

Gulf of Honduras

Monument

Pen Rd
Gumaragu Rd
Sawai St
Yampa St
Front St

Thomas Vincent
Ramos Monument

Pier Rd

To Marie Sharp's
Factory (13km)
& Hummingbird Hwy

School
Ball Field

Main Channel

Melinda Rd
Church Rd

23 20
7 2
9 3
24 25
6 5

Commerce St
Plum St

Court House Rd
4
13

Coconut Rd
Ramos Rd

Doctor's Alley

29

27

N Riverside Dr
North Stann Creek
S Riverside Dr

30
21
26
9
1

15
Bluefield Rd
Cedar St

S Foreshore
Chatuye St

Alejo Beni Ave

28
17
8
16
12

Canal St
Moho Rd

St Vincent St

Madre Cacao Rd
Salmwood Rd

Mahogany Rd
10

Sharp St

Yemeri Rd
Ecumenical Dr
Mangrove Rd

Tubroose St
Magoon St

19
5

Havana Creek

Isla Rd

31
32
14
Cabbage Rd
33

Stann Creek Valley Rd
Unity St
Havana St

INFORMATION	
Belize Bank	1 B4
BTL Telephone Office	2 B3
First Caribbean Bank	3 B3
Hospital	4 B3
Island Expeditions Office	5 C5
Pharmacy	6 B3
Police	7 B3
Post Office	8 C4
Public Phone	(see 8)
Scotiabank	9 B4
Val's Laundry (Internet Access)	10 C4

SIGHTS & ACTIVITIES	(pp285–6)
Baptist Church	11 C4
Benjamin Nicholas' Studio	12 C4
Courthouse	13 B3
Gra Gra Lagoon National Park Office	14 C5

SLEEPING	(p286)
Bluefield Lodge	15 B4
Bonefish Hotel	16 C4
Chaleanor Hotel	17 C4
Pelican Beach Resort	18 A1
Ruthie's Seaside Cabanas	19 C5

EATING	(p286)
Ritchie's Dinette	20 B3
Riverside Café	21 B4
Ruby's Rainforest Café	22 C4
Silver Garden	23 B3
Starlight	24 B3
Sunrise	25 B3

DRINKING	(p286)
Griga 2000	26 B4

SHOPPING	(p286)
Austin Rodriguez	27 C3
Garinagu Crafts	28 B4
Market	29 C3

TRANSPORT	(pp286–7)
Boats to Tobacco Caye	30 B4
Bus Station	31 B5
Shell Fuel Station	32 B5
Texaco Fuel Station	33 C5

BELIZE

Tours & Activities

Eight miles (13km) northwest of town on Melinda Rd is **Marie Sharp's Factory** (☎ 520-2087; admission free; ☼ 7am-noon, 1-4pm), the source of Belize's beloved hot sauce (see box on p283). The primary ingredients are habanero peppers and carrots, purchased from local farmers. Casual tours, often led by Marie herself, are offered during business hours, and the shop sells hot sauce and jams at outlet prices.

Pelican Beach Resort (☎ 522-2044; www.pelican beachbelize.com), Dangriga's upmarket hotel, can also arrange cultural tours and education packages (such as talks by historians, meals in Garifuna houses, drumming and dancing) for people interested in learning more about Garifuna culture.

Ask at the **Riverside Café** (S Riverside Dr) about fishing and snorkeling trips out to the cayes or treks inland.

Benjamin Nicholas, Belize's most famous painter, lives and works in Dangriga near the Bonefish Hotel. His paintings are displayed in banks, hotel lobbies and public buildings throughout the country. Stop in at his studio and have a look.

GRA GRA LAGOON NATIONAL PARK
This recently established **nature reserve** (admission US$5; 🕗 8am-5pm), 2 miles south of Dangriga, was originally used by local fishers when the seas were too rough to go out and as a natural harbor to protect boats in storms. It features extensive mangrove formations (the name means 'white mangrove patch' in Garifuna). The lagoon itself measures 1194 acres and the reserve is home to manatees, raccoons, pumas, jaguars, crocodiles and migratory birds. The park offers bird-watching, canoe tours, night tours and crocodile watching. Tours (US$40 per person, two hours) are conducted by traditional inhabitants of the area. Call or stop by the **office** (☎ 502-0043; 6 Havana St, Dangriga) to arrange transport.

Sleeping

Ruthie's Seaside Cabañas (☎ 522-3184; cnr Magoon St & Yemeri Rd; s/d US$20/30) Clean and comfy cabañas with private bathroom, right on the seaside. Ruthie cooks dinner and breakfast on request, too.

Bluefield Lodge (☎ 522-2742; bluefield@btl.net; 6 Bluefield Rd; s/d with shared bathroom US$13/15, with private bathroom US$16/18) With a homey atmosphere close to the center of town, the seven tidy rooms with fan here are a good deal.

Chaleanor Hotel (☎ 522-2587; chaleanor@btl.net; 35 Magoon St; s/d with shared bathroom US$10/15, s/d/tr with private bathroom US$25/35/45) Clean, comfortable rooms with private bathrooms. The rooftop offers views of the Caribbean. The rooms with shared bathroom are at the side.

Pelican Beach Resort (☎ 522-2044; www.pelican beachbelize.com; s/d with fan from US$51/70, with air-con US$73/92) At the north end of town, this is Dangriga's upmarket hotel. It's on the waterfront and some of the beautiful mahogany-lined rooms have ocean views. It boasts a

restaurant, bar, sand beach, boat dock and a full program of tours to area sites. Nonguests are welcome to use the beach, which is probably the best in town. The Friday **happy hour** (🕗 5:30-7:30pm) features Garifuna drummers.

Bonefish Hotel (☎ 522-2243; www.bluemarlinlodge .com/bonefish.html; 15 Mahogany Rd; s/d from US$50/55; 🕄) Ten bunkerlike rooms with fan, TV and private bathroom. The hotel caters to divers and also operates the Blue Marlin Lodge on South Water Caye.

Eating

Ruby's Rainforest Café (cnr S Riverside Dr & S Foreshore Dr; 🕗 breakfast & dinner) Probably the best place to eat in town – the service is great and the food fresh.

Ritchie's Dinette (Commerce St; meals US$4-6; 🕗 breakfast, lunch & dinner) The locals favor Ritchie's for Belizean food.

Riverside Café (S Riverside Dr; meals US$5-7; 🕗 breakfast, lunch & dinner) Just east of the North Stann Creek Bridge, this place is riding on its laurels a bit, but they serve up decent meals at moderate prices.

Most of the other restaurants along Commerce St are Chinese: **Sunrise**, **Starlight** and **Silver Garden** serve full meals for about US$6.

Drinking

Griga 2000 (St Vincent St) Just south of the bridge, this club (known locally as 'the club') gets a bit of a crowd for midweek karaoke sessions, but things really start jumping on weekends.

Shopping

Garínagu Crafts (☎ 522-2596; 44 St Vincent St) A wide range of Garifuna handicrafts, including drums, dolls, maracas, paintings and dolls at reasonable prices.

Austin Rodriguez (🕗 10am-7pm) Under a large *palapa* behind the market, Austin is *the* man to talk to if you want a Garifuna drum – you can see the various stages of production in his open air workshop, and buy directly from him.

Getting There & Away

Maya Island Air (Belize City ☎ 223-1140; www.mayaair ways.com) and **Tropic Air** (Belize City ☎ 226-2012; www .tropicair.com) serve Dangriga on flights also stopping at Placencia, Punta Gorda and Belize City.

Buses to Belize City (US$5/7 standard/express, 107 miles/161km) via Belmopan leave regularly from the bus station and take about 4½ hours. Get an express – it's worth it.

Water taxis are available from outside Ritchie's Dinette. The only real use they serve (unless you're going in for a US$200-plus private hire) are as collective rides out to Tobacco Caye. All other Cayes listed here offer transfers as part of the accommodation price.

The **Riverside Café** (S Riverside Dr) serves as the unofficial water-taxi terminal where you can arrange trips out to the southern cayes with local fishers or tradespeople. It's best to stop in by 10am to find out when boats will be leaving.

THE SOUTHERN CAYES

Tobacco Caye, South Water Caye and the resorts of Glover's Reef are accessed by boat from Dangriga. Their distance from Belize City has kept casual visitors away, protecting the reef from much human impact. Dolphins, manta rays and manatees are commonly sighted, and the quantity and variety of coral on display is incredible. Good snorkeling and diving can be had right off the shore from the cayes, and the major dive sites can be reached from all accommodations listed in this section.

Tobacco Caye

Tiny Tobacco Caye is a 5-acre (2-hectare) island catering to travelers on a low-to-moderate budget, located off Dangriga at the northern tip of the South Water Caye Marine Reserve. Diving, fishing, snorkeling and hammocking are the favorite pastimes here. One of the best things about this little hideout is that there is good snorkeling to be done right off the shore. The island can be circumnavigated in less than 20 minutes, and while some of the islanders run fishing boats, tourism is the prime motivation. There is nothing here by way of shops or services, except what is offered through the handful of hotels. If you're expecting a full-service luxury-resort experience, look elsewhere. If you're looking for somewhere to get away from it all, this is the way to go. Here it's about old guesthouses, run by families who have lived on the island for years. The caye is pretty much fully developed, but

you can usually find a quiet spot. It was hit hard by Hurricane Mitch in October 1998, but it's bounced back well.

Passage to Tobacco Caye can be arranged in Dangriga along the river near the Riverside Café. Cost will be approximately US$15 one-way.

ACTIVITIES

Reef's End Lodge (☎ 520-5037; www.reefsendlodge .com) Runs the only dive shop on the island – local dives cost US$30 per tank and PADI open water certification costs US$350. They also arrange dive trips to South Water Caye, Glover's Reef, Turneffe and the Blue Hole. Full equipment hire costs US$25 for all dives. Snorkeling gear rents for US$7.50 per day.

SLEEPING & EATING

Rates listed below include three meals. The island has no restaurants, but the Tobacco Caye Lodge has a bar – an ideal place for watching the sunset.

Ocean's Edge (☎ 614-9632; oceansedge@btl.net; s/d US$45/90) Good-sized wooden cabañas with tiled floors and private bathrooms. There's a big raised wooden deck (for guests' use only) out over the water that's perfect for sunrise and fish viewing.

Tobacco Caye Lodge (☎ 520-5033; www.tclodge belize.com; s/d US$80/120) New cabañas with private bathrooms and hammocks on the balcony. Rates include snorkeling gear.

Lana's (☎ 520-5036; s/d US$40/80) Slightly run down, but homey. Lana's a great cook, and the home-style meals she serves up make up for a lot.

Gaviota's (☎ 509-5032; s/d US$35/60) Basic wooden rooms with linoleum floors. It's not a bad deal for the price.

Reef's End Lodge (☎ 520-5037; www.reefsend lodge.com; s/d US$65/130) Reasonable rooms and a fantastic dining room built out over the water. There's also a honeymoon cabaña for US$180.

South Water Caye

Five miles south of Tobacco Caye is South Water Caye, a much more exclusive island, with excellent snorkeling, sandy beaches and palm trees that survived the yellowing leaf blight.

Pelican's Pouch (☎ 522-2044; www.southwater caye.com; s/d US$130/195, cabaña s/d US$173/220) The

Pelican refuses to over-develop their side of the island and the basic but very comfortable cabañas are well spaced, giving an air of seclusion. The Heron's Hideaway cabaña is probably the pick of the bunch, with a big porch and two hammocks overlooking the surf crashing onto the reef.

Blue Marlin Lodge (☎ 522-2243; www.bluemarlin lodge.com; weekly packages per person vacation/fishing/diving US$1250/2495/1595) Rates listed are for double occupancy – single is slightly more expensive. Accommodation is in rooms, concrete igloos (weird, but comfy) or cozy beachfront cabañas. Waterskiing is also available for US$50/80 for half /full day.

International Zoological Expeditions (US ☎ +1-800-548-5843; www.ize2belize.com; per person for 1/7/9 days US$150/945/1080) Beautiful wooden cottages with one, two or three bedrooms and private bathrooms and the swingin'est bar on the island.

Passage to South Water Caye is usually arranged through the resorts, although it's possible (but pricey at over US$100 one-way) to pick up a boat at the Riverside Café in Dangriga.

Glover's Reef

Named for the pirate John Glover, Glover's Reef holds a handful of secluded lodges.

Glover's Atoll Resort (☎ 520-5016; www.glovers .com.bz; campsite/dm/cabaña per week US$100/150/200) On **Northeast Caye**, Glover's offers budget accommodations on a 9-acre (3.6-hectare) atoll about 20 miles (32km) from the mainland. Facilities are rustic, but the 360-degree Caribbean view can't be beat. It's a good deal for budget travelers, but extras – water, food, equipment – can add up. Call or email to arrange a boat ride, which is included in the price of the accommodation.

Southwest Caye

Isla Marisol (☎ 520-2056; www.islamarisol.com; weekly packages snorkeling/diving/fishing US$1400/2000/3000) Seclusion is the keyword out on Southwest Caye. This place offers sturdy, comfortable cabañas, a highly recommended dive shop and is located near some of the region's top dive sites.

Island Expeditions (US ☎ +1-800-667-1630; www .islandexpeditions.com; weekly packages from US$1388) On the other side of Southwest Caye, this ecologically-minded operation offers snorkeling, sailing, windsurfing and educational expeditions on the surrounding reef. Accommodation is in comfortable army-style tents with beds and shared solar showers. This is not a luxury resort – it's much more a get-back-to-nature kind of setup.

Long Caye

Slickrock Adventures (US ☎ +1-800-390-5715; www .slickrock.com; weekly packages from US$1895) Basic, breezy cabañas with a view of one of Belize's few surfable breaks (although the waves are much better suited to sea kayaking). This place is definitely for the adventurous – each day you can learn a different water sport (sea and sea kayaking, windsurfing and snorkeling) from trained instructors, then decide what you want to do with the rest of your week. Scuba diving is available from the Off The Wall dive shop (see following).

Off the Wall (☎ 614-6348; www.offthewallbelize .com; weekly packages relaxation/diving/fishing US$1300/1600/1900) Just down the beach from Slickrock, this is a small, family-run operation that focuses mainly on diving. The reasons for diving out here are that the groups are small, there's over 800 patch reefs just offshore and the waters are literally swimming (sorry) with sharks, groupers, turtles and rays.

HOPKINS

pop 1100

The words 'hi' and 'hello' fly thick and fast as you walk along either of the two streets in this mainly Garifuna fishing village. The village is 4 miles (7km) east of the Southern Hwy and was settled in 1942 by the inhabitants of Newtown, a nearby Garifuna settlement that was destroyed by a hurricane. It was eventually named for Frederick Charles Hopkins, a Catholic priest who drowned in the waters off the village site in 1923, but for a while the settlement was known as Yugada, which in Garifuna means 'village by the sea.' The town was leveled by Hurricane Hattie in 1961, but this time the villagers stuck around and rebuilt. The town stretches about 2 miles (3.2km) along a road that runs parallel to the sea.

Although there's a good travelers' scene here, it's fairly low-key. There are a number of bars and restaurants in the area, so while you can make your own party if you wish, it's probably not a good idea to come here looking for one. Instead you'll find friendly folks, quiet surroundings, sea views and easy access to inland tours. Not to mention quick access to some of the best diving in Belize; Glover's Reef is a mere half hour by boat. Lighthouse Reef and the Blue Hole are the same distance from here as they are from Ambergris. Dolphins and manatees are spotted regularly from the beach.

Travelers appreciate this as a place to retreat and be part of another world for a while. There are lots of young families around, and at dusk the main road becomes a promenade for school-age kids and adults out enjoying the breeze.

This is a good base if you wish to do some independent explorations. You can kayak offshore, on the Sittee River or to the freshwater lagoon just north of the village. The Sittee River is also a popular destination with anglers and those looking to live on the river for a few days. Because Hopkins is away from the highway, it's easy and relaxing to use bikes to explore the area. You're within half an hour's drive of Cockscomb Basin Wildlife Sanctuary, where you can hike on your own or sign on with a tour.

Orientation & Information

South of town is a cluster of resorts catering to higher-end active travelers. This group and the village seem to mix well, and travelers staying in Hopkins often head south to splurge on dinner or drinks.

Scooters can be rented from the All Seasons Guesthouse (right) for US$38 per day.

Speedy Internet access is provided by **Windschief** (per hr US$4), on the beach, south of Ransom's.

Activities

Under the Sun (☎ 523-7127, US ☎ +1-800-285-6967; www.underthesunbelize.com) Offers a variety of sailing and land-based packages, but the standout is the Lodge Hopper's special, eight days and seven nights of cruising the Caribbean on your own 18ft Catamaran, with plenty of stops for snorkeling, fishing, diving, kayaking and hammocking. Instruction is provided for novice sailors or you can tag along in the support boat. Accommodations are in lodges out on the smaller cayes, and food, accommodation, sailboats, guide, support boat and (if necessary) transfers to and from Dangriga are included in the price of US$1985 per person.

Windschief rents windsurfers for US$10/30 per hour/day and can arrange private lessons for US$30 per hour.

Dive trips are offered by Hamanasi Resort (see p290). Options include Southern Barrier Reef (two tanks US$76), Glover's Reef (three tanks US$126), Turneffe Islands (three tanks US$126), Lighthouse Reef & Blue Hole (three tanks US$187).

Lebeha (☎ 608-3143), at the north end of the village, should be your first stop if you are interested in learning more about Garifuna culture. Primarily set up as an education and culture center for local kids, they have drumming most nights from 7pm, and offer private/group lessons for US$13/25 per hour.

Sleeping

IN TOWN

Ransoms (no phone; www.members.tripod.com/~cabana belize; s/d US$15/30) Oozing with charm and bustling with plant life, this place is a real bargain. The cabaña at the back is rustic and funky, equipped with kitchen and private bathroom – you could hole up here for a few days or a couple of months. There are a couple of well-decorated basic, comfortable rooms in the main building, too.

Tipple Tree Beya (☎ 520-7006; www.tippletree.net; campsite per person US$5, r with shared/private bathroom from US$20/33) This place, sturdily built with natural, unpainted planks on a beautiful stretch of beach, rents attractive rooms with coffeemakers and refrigerators, and one beach cabaña with a kitchen. The owners have a wealth of knowledge about the region and are willing to help you make the most of your stay.

Hopkins Inn (☎ 523-7013; www.hopkinsinn.com; s/d US$40/50) Near the center of town, this place has tiled cabañas with full bathroom, refrigerator, coffeemaker and fan. Breakfast is served in your cabaña. A catamaran is available for guests' use (US$30 per day) and there are free bikes. One cabaña has a private bedroom and a sitting area with a foldout couch; it's ideal for families.

All Seasons Guesthouse (☎ 614-3328; www.all seasonsbelize.com; r US$43) This modern guesthouse offers homey, spotless rooms with private bathroom and coffeemaker. There's a breezy upstairs sitting area with sea views.

Yagudah Inn (☎ 523-7089; campsite per person US$7.50; s/d US$10/15) Open year-round, this place offers spacious, airy rooms with shared bathroom in a block set back from the beach.

OUT OF TOWN

One mile south of Hopkins is a cluster of high-end resorts catering to divers with an interest in inland tours. Water buffs are finding that this is a good alternative to the resort atmosphere of San Pedro. You'll still get comfort and all the luxury you're willing to pay for, but in addition you'll have quick access to inland sites and culture. The resorts are arranged around False Sittee Point and are well planned for seclusion.

Hamanasi Dive & Adventure Resort (☎ 520-7073; www.hamanasi.com; low season r US$140-200; 🔀 🖭) This resort is a mile south of Hopkins on the Hopkins/Sittee River Rd (continue straight where the road veers). Hamanasi, its name derived from the Garifuna name for almond tree, is a gorgeous luxury property on 400ft (120m) of beachfront. There are eight rooms in two buildings in addition to four secluded tree-house–style honeymoon cabañas. Some rooms have two bedrooms. Hamanasi bills itself as an adventure hotel, although it primarily serves divers with an interest in land-based activities. There's a large pool, and bicycles are available to guests at no charge.

Jaguar Reef Lodge (☎ 520-7040; www.jaguarreef .com; r from US$120; 🔀 🖭) This place consistently gets good reviews from the travel press, though it's not as exotic as its neighbors. The cabañas are arranged on spacious grounds and solidly built, with a conservative, familiar design that you would find in Hawaiian or Mexican resorts. It's good for families or wary adventurers.

Beaches & Dreams (☎ 523-7078; www.beaches anddreams.com; r from US$75) This smaller-scale resort offers casual, down-to-earth elegance and personal service. Rooms are in octagonal cabañas, arranged along a private beach with a view of False Sittee Point. Kayaks and bikes are offered free of charge.

Eating & Drinking

The resorts out of town all have fine restaurants. Most restaurants in town serve good, inexpensive seafood and Belizean dishes, including gibnut. Try **Iris's**, the **Watering Hole** or **Innie's** (all 🕑 breakfast, lunch & dinner).

King Kassava in the middle of town is the place to go for beer, pool and reggae music.

Getting There & Away

The Hopkins turnoff is at Mile 15 of the Southern Hwy; the town is another 4 miles east. Buses that travel the Hopkins and Sittee River roads leave Placencia at 5:30am and 7am (US$4, two hours) and Dangriga at noon and 5:30pm (US$2, one hour). Any bus traveling the Southern Hwy will stop at the Hopkins or Sittee River junctions; you'll need to walk or hitch your way into the village (4 miles/7km).

SITTEE RIVER

Another small coastal village where you can get away from it all is Sittee River. **Glover's Atoll Bunkhouse** (☎ 520-5016; www.glovers.com.bz /glover2; dm US$8, d with private bathroom US$29) is where the boat to Glover's Reef picks up passengers.

Toucan Sittee (☎ 523-7039; www.toucansittee.info; dm US$10; r with shared/private bathroom from US$20/48), next door to Glover's Atoll, is the more gracious of the two, offering good-value riverside rooms as well as two apartments.

COCKSCOMB BASIN WILDLIFE SANCTUARY

Almost halfway between Dangriga and Independence is the village of Maya Centre, where a track runs 6 miles (10km) west to the **Cockscomb Basin Wildlife Sanctuary** (admission US$5; 🕑 7:30am-4:30pm). It's sometimes called the Jaguar Reserve and is a prime place for wildlife watching.

The varied topography and lush tropical forest within the 98,000-acre (39,000-hectare) sanctuary make it an ideal habitat for a wide variety of native Belizean fauna. Several species of wildcats – including jaguarundis, jaguars, pumas, ocelots and margays – inhabit the reserve. Among the other resident animals, many the prey of these fierce cats, are agoutis, anteaters, armadillos, Baird's tapirs, brocket deer, coatis, kinkajous, otters, pacas, peccaries and the weasel-like tayras. Snakes here include boa constrictors and the deadly poisonous fer-de-lance. There are birds galore – over 290 species have been spotted here – including toucans, parrots and, if the time is right, the rare scarlet macaw. The best wildlife spotting can be done early in the morning.

Recently, eight jaguars have been tracked in the park, evidence that the population is healthy and growing enough to coax the animal closer to human population centers. Chances are slim to none that you'll see one of these stealthy creatures, but you will see evidence of their presence – perhaps a track or two, or remains from their evening meal.

You are quite likely to meet up with a community of howler monkeys, relocated from Burrell Boom and thriving in the basin.

Cockscomb first became a protected area in 1984, and the jaguar sanctuary was created in 1986 by American Alan Rabinowitz. Controversial was the relocation of a village of Maya who were living off the land in the basin. Many of the Maya relocated from the park now live in Maya Centre and work in the park as tour guides, attendants or maintenance workers.

In the early days of the camp, jaguars were captured and tagged (Rabinowitz' original traps are displayed on the premises). Nowadays jaguars are tracked by infrared cameras placed throughout the basin – a much less intrusive way to keep track. On the drive into the park you can stop and see the remains of a plane crash that Rabinowitz survived while he was working in the area.

Loggers also lived in this area way back when, pulling mahogany, cedar and other trees from the basin. The logging camps have long since been reclaimed by the jungle, but they still appear on some maps. Their names – Go to Hell, Leave If You Can – reflect the difficulty of the work and the terrain. Artifacts left by the loggers are on display near the visitors center.

No public transportation to the reserve is available. A taxi from Maya Center will cost about US$12.

Information & Sleeping

Visitor facilities at the reserve include a **campsite** (per person US$2.50), several dorm-style **cabañas** (per person US$18, kitchen use per person US$1) with solar electricity, and a visitors center.

For information, or to book a cabaña, contact the **Belize Audubon Society** (Map pp220-1; ☎ 223-5004; www.belizeaudubon.org; 12 Fort St, Belize City), or the **Cockscomb Basin Wildlife Sanctuary** (PO Box 90, Dangriga).

At the start of the road into the reserve, in Maya Centre, are the **Tutzil Nah Cottages** (☎ 520-3044; www.mayacenter.com; Southern Hwy, Mile 14; s/d US$15/24), two well made and pretty

cottages with shared bathrooms (cold-water showers), each containing two rooms. They can also arrange tours in the preserve and around the country, the best of which must be a four-hour kayak drift/paddle down the river through the preserve (US$70 per person).

Activities

Cockscomb has a nicely maintained 12-mile (20km) network of trails, varying in length, terrain and degree of difficulty. Most of the walks are flat along the bottom of the basin. The longest is about 2.5 miles (4km), but many of the trails intertwine to form longer walks. The walk through the lush forest is a pretty one, and though you cannot be assured of seeing a jaguar, you will certainly enjoy seeing many of the hundreds of other species of birds, plants and animals in this rich environment.

There is a **self-guided trail** that loops together the Curassow Trail and the Rubber Tree Tail and returns along the River Path. Along the way you'll see evidence of the Mayan settlement that was abandoned in 1983. The Mayas, who practiced slash-and-burn farming, once grew plantains, sugarcane, cassava and cocoa here. Along the path is a sacred ceiba tree as well as epiphytes, bromeliads, ironwood (ziracote), strangler figs, cohune palms and rubber trees.

The **River Path** (0.3 miles/0.5km) and the **Wari Loop** (0.9 miles/1.5km) are good early-morning bets for seeing a wide variety of birds. Jaguar tracks are often spotted on the **Gibnut Loop** (0.9 miles/1.5km) and the short BYCC Express, which breaks from the Wari Loop to the road. The **Antelope Loop** (2.2 miles/3.5km) rises and falls through a variety of terrain and vegetation and offers a good sample of the geological features within the basin.

The **Waterfall Trail** (1.9 miles/3km) is one of the most popular trails. Hikers who are willing to endure some steep bits are rewarded with a lovely waterfall and swimming hole at the end. **Ben's Bluff** (2.5 miles/4km) is the steepest and most strenuous trail, but will afford you a view of the entire basin. It's named for one of the original members of the Cockscomb Jaguar Sanctuary Project, who would make this climb daily to listen for signals from the radio transmitters that had been attached to the jaguars.

PLACENCIA

pop 600

Perched at the southern tip of a long, narrow, sandy peninsula, Placencia is 'the caye you can drive to.' Not too long ago, the only practical way to get here was by boat from the mainland. Now a road runs all the way down the peninsula and an airstrip lies just north of town. But Placencia still has the wonderful laid-back ambience of the cayes, along with varied accommodations and friendly local people. Long considered a backpacker's hideout, lately it's becoming one of Belize's worst-kept secrets. Getting in and out via the long, bumpy road can be trying; if you're a traveler who likes to cover a lot of ground, you may feel marooned here.

But it's not such a bad place to be stuck. It's home to some of the best beaches in Belize and has a fun party atmosphere. The beaches attract an international crowd looking for sun and sand, and low-key pastimes, such as swimming, sunbathing and lazing about, are the preferred 'activities' for many visitors. The food is great and the people are friendly; you'll get to know everyone pretty quickly here as you walk up and down the narrow sidewalk.

There is a well-worn track of tour options in the area, out to Laughing Bird Caye and down to the Monkey River. Travelers also make the long day trip down to Lubaantun (p300) and Nim Li Punit (p300), near Punta Gorda.

Placencia has seen a lot of development over a short space of time, which has brought its own problems. As one local put it, 'Placencia used to be a sleepy little fishing village, now it's a fishy little sleeping village'. Relax, but don't let your guard down completely.

As on the cayes, plenty of activities are available here, including water sports and excursions to many points of interest both onshore and off. Unlike most of the cayes, however, Placencia has good sandy beaches on its east side.

Orientation & Information

The town owes its layout to years gone by, when all commerce and activity was carried out by boat so streets were of little use. The village's main north–south 'street' is actually a narrow concrete footpath about 3ft (1m) wide that threads its way among simple wood-frame houses (some on stilts) and beachfront lodges. An unpaved road skirts the town to the west, ending at the peninsula's southern tip, which is the bus stop.

An easy walk takes you anywhere in town. From the airstrip, it's about half a mile (0.8km) south to the village and a mile (1.6km) further to the peninsula's southern tip. North of the airstrip, past various resorts scattered along the coast, lie the villages of Seine Bight and Maya Beach, both of which are struggling to develop their own tourism infrastructures. Seine Bight is a mostly Garifuna village, whereas Maya Beach is a popular retirement spot for North Americans. The resorts there are basically the same.

The village has no central landmark or town square. At its south end you'll find the wharf, fuel station, bus stop and icehouse. **Atlantic Bank** (⊙ 9am-2pm Mon-Thu; 9am-noon, 1-4pm Fri) is also on the south end of town. You can check your email at the **Purple Space Monkey Internet Café** (⊙ 7am-midnight; per hr US$5). They also have a two-for-one book exchange and an espresso machine – a rare sight in southern Belize.

Laundry service (per load US$5) is available from most of the hotels and guesthouses.

Diving

The barrier reef is 20 miles (32km) offshore from Placencia, and there's little boat traffic beyond the tour boats beating a wake between the village and the reef (45 minutes from dock to plunge). The reef is wider here than in points north, with plenty of dramatic walls, canyons and swim-throughs. In addition to the fanciful coral formations is the myriad of sea life living here relatively undisturbed. For those craving charismatic macro-fauna, there is the **Shark Hole** about 38 miles (61km) from Placencia. This formation was an underwater cave many moons ago, but part of the ceiling collapsed, forming an entrance for fish, sharks and, now, interested divers. The entrance is at a depth of 42ft (12.6m).

Glover's Reef (p288) is a popular site for divers and takes about 2½ hours to reach from Placencia.

Whale sharks can be seen at **Gladden Spit** and **Silk Cayes Marine Reserve**, north of Placencia, up to 10 days after the full moon, April through June. What attracts the whale sharks is the same thing that attracts divers and snorkelers – lots of species of fish. Only, the whale sharks aren't interested in seeing the fish, they're interested in the eggs of the fish, which spawn in great quantity after the full moon.

Inner-reef dives are better for beginning divers, since the water is calmer; there's plenty of marine life to see. Outer-reef dives present a more dramatic landscape of walls and canyons.

DIVE OPERATORS

Seahorse Diving (☎ 523-3166; www.belizescuba.com) and **Advanced Diving Services** (☎ 523-4037; www .beautifulbelize.com/advanceddiving) offer dive trips to the local reef, usually around Laughing Bird Caye. North of the village, **Rum Point Inn**, **Robert's Grove** and the **Nautical Inn** also have highly professional dive shops.

Two-tank dives cost around US$75, trips to the Shark Hole US$100, and whale-shark expeditions US$150. Certification is offered for US$300, including four open-water dives. Intervals on these dives are usually off one of the cayes. Inner-reef stops include Laughing Bird or Moho Cayes; outer-reef stops include Ranguana Caye and the Silk Cayes. Trips to Glover's Reef cost around US$100. Plan on an additional US$35 for gear.

Tours

Vying to sign up customers for tours of the region are **Ocean Motion Guide Service** (☎ 523-3363) and **Nite Wind Guide Service** (☎ 523-3487), both operating out of small offices near the boat dock, **Cool Running** (☎ 523-3134), on the main road, and **Kitty's Place** (☎ 523-3227; www .kittysplace.com), about 1.5 miles (2.5km) north of the village (p294).

Some of the tours available from Placencia, along with ballpark prices are as follows:

- Snorkeling or sea kayaking around Laughing Bird, Ranguana or Silk Cayes. Usually includes a beach barbecue (US$35 to US$40). Diving these areas costs around US$90, equipment included.
- Bird-watching and a tube float in the Cockscomb Basin Wildlife Sanctuary (US$60).
- A trip up the Monkey River, which includes a short sea cruise south to the river's mouth, then nature watching and a walk through Monkey River Village (US$40).

- A long day trip to the Mayan ruins of Nim Li Punit or Lubaantun, possibly with a stop at Blue Creek caves (US$70).

Toadal Adventures at Deb & Dave's Last Resort (see p294) offers four-day kayaking trips around Silk Caye, Hatchet Caye and Little Water Caye, with camping on Silk Caye. These trips require about four hours of paddling per day (unless you are keen to do more). The price (US$895) is all-inclusive and includes a night's accommodation before and after the trip at Westwind hotel (see p294). Toadal Adventures also offers some inland tours.

Programme for Belize (Map pp220-1; ☎ 227-5616; www.pfbelize.org; 1 Eyre St, Belize City) offers a trip to the forests surrounding the village of Red Bank to see a seasonal population of scarlet macaws, an increasingly rare site in Central America. Otherwise, inquire at hotels or guide services in Placencia.

Sailing Belize (☎ 523-3138; www.sailingbelize .com) offers day sailing on a 52ft ketch for US$120 per person. Activities include snorkeling, fishing, wildlife watching and kayaking. Lunch, snacks and drinks are included. They also do live-aboard charters with crew and provisioning for US$250 to US$300 per person per day.

Cayescape Tours (☎ 523-3587), operating out of Sugar Reef (see p296), has customized motor boat tours from US$150 per day. Fuel, food, drinks and equipment (for snorkeling or diving) cost extra.

TMM Bareboat Vacations (see p242) has a marina in Placencia where you can start or finish your sailing charter.

Sleeping

Placencia has lodgings in all price ranges. Budget and mid-range accommodations are in the village (you're likely to get a beachside cabaña, but your neighbor will be just a couple of feet away); top-end places are mostly north along the beach.

BUDGET

Manatee Inn (☎ 523-4083; www.manateeinn.com; s/d US$35/40) Clean and breezy wooden rooms in a two-story building set back from the beach. Rooms are simply but tastefully decorated. A four-person apartment rents for US$70. Rumor has it that this is where the Belikin calendar girls stay when they're in town on photo shoots, a piece of information which may or may not be of interest to you.

Westwind (☎ 523-3255; westwind@btl.net; r from US$40) Simple, no-nonsense rooms with a cheery atmosphere. Rooms at the front cost US$15 more and have big windows looking out onto the sea.

Deb & Dave's Last Resort (☎ 523-3207; www .toadaladventure.com; r US$22) Basic wooden rooms with shared bathroom set in a leafy garden. There are good screened sitting areas, and it's on the lagoon side of the peninsula, so it stays quieter than the beach places.

Lydia's Guest House (☎ 523-3117; lydias@btl.net; s/d US$31/46) Basic, spacious rooms with clean shared bathrooms. Some rooms have sea views, and kitchen facilities are available.

Julia & Lawrence Guesthouse (☎ 522-3185; cabañas US$27) This guesthouse is central and clean. It's in a congested part of the village; rooms with shared bathroom are in an older back building, and newer higher-end rooms have sea views.

MID-RANGE

Harry's Cozy Cabañas (☎ 523-3155; www.placencia .com/members/harrys.html; s/d US$60/70) Truly cozy cabañas on the south side of the peninsula, with hot water, screened balconies and kitchens. There's a funky common sitting area under the shade of the 'tree of knowledge' (actually a governor plum tree).

Ranguana Lodge (☎ 523-3112; www.ranguana belize.com; cabañas from US$65) These are attractive, good-sized mahogany cabañas with private shower, but they're packed tightly together. Each room has a fan, refrigerator, coffeemaker and balcony. The more expensive rooms have beach views.

Seaspray Hotel (☎ 523-3148; www.seasprayhotel .com; s/d from US$23/25, cabañas with kitchenette US$60) Right in the village center on the beach, this is the backpacker favorite. Seaspray has accommodations with shared or private bathroom (and hot water). The more expensive rooms are larger and have porches and sea views, and there's one deluxe cabaña on the beach. The variety of rooms offered assures that you'll meet travelers from all over and all budgets.

TOP END

The lodgings north of the village tend to be more expensive destination-style resorts, but they're very satisfying, with tropical-isle ambience. All offer various water sports, activities and local excursions.

Soulshine (☎ 523-4078; www.soulshine.com; s/d US$125/155) The only resort in the actual town, Soulshine is also one of the best on the peninsula. Accommodation is in big thatch-roofed duplex cabañas with kitchenette, some with separate bedroom and living room. The grounds are leafy and dotted with *palapas* with hammocks strung up underneath them. There is a day spa on the premises with a variety of treatments (US$50 to US$150) including seaweed wraps and many treatments using local herbs. There is excellent snorkeling right off the dock out the back.

Kitty's Place (☎ 523-3227; www.kittysplace.com; s/d US$35/40, cabañas from US$125/135) One and a half miles (2.5km) north of the village, this Caribbean Victorian beachfront lodge is the longtime favorite for high-end travelers. Guests return year after year, and you'll find lots of personal recommendations and superlatives for this place. There are a variety of rooms to choose from, the best being the beachfront cabaña suites with separate sleeping areas, tiled floors and gracious verandahs. In the standard category the garden rooms are the way to go – the landscaping is lush, lovely and private, and there's a nice deck for bird-watching. Kitty's also owns French Louie Caye, a private island that can be rented for US$300 per night, with accommodation in a simple, furnished wooden house.

Nautical Inn (☎ 523-3595; www.nauticalinnbelize .com; Seine Bight; s/d from US$139/159; 🛇 🏊) The folks at this small, modern resort are equipped for all adventures. They provide independent-minded guests with free use of bikes, snorkels, sailboats and kayaks and run daily diving expeditions and coastal tours. There are 12 comfortable rooms, and the menu offers meals ranging from southwestern US to Continental cuisine. If the buildings seem out of place, it's because the entire hotel was shipped down from Florida and assembled here back when building materials were harder to come by. There's a swimming pool and a pleasant deck and beach area. Meal packages and weekly rates are available.

Green Parrot (☎ 523-2488; www.greenparrot-belize .com; Maya Beach; cabañas from US$145) This place has six split-level, mahogany cabañas with loft bedrooms, kitchenettes and living rooms with foldout couches. Two honeymoon cabañas are set off from the rest of the resort so you'll have your own stretch of beach and an open-air shower.

Rum Point Inn (☎ 523-3239; www.rumpoint.com; cabañas US$165, ste US$189; ☒ ☒) Open since 1974, Placencia's oldest resort is about 1.5 miles (2.5km) north of the village. Guests can stay in mushroom-shaped stucco cabañas, designed with numerous small screened windows for optimum ventilation. For the more modest, there are more conventional cabañas, winding through thick gardens and sandy walkways. Meal packages are available for US$56 more per person. Amenities include a library and massage center and use of bikes, snorkel gear and kayaks.

Inn at Robert's Grove (☎ 523-3565; www.roberts grove.com; r from US$169; ☒ ☒) Just north of Rum Point Inn, this inn has modern and spacious rooms, beautiful grounds, rooftop hot tubs and a tennis court. Shiny and new, this innovative place has shaken up the establishment by offering world-class service, but still staying in touch with the culture and feel of Belize. It's popular with Belize's elite. A dive shop is on site, and tours to all local attractions can be arranged. The restaurant is excellent and meal plans are available for US$55 per day.

Luba Hati (☎ 523-3403; www.lubahati.com; weekly packages from US$1135; ☒) North of the Inn at Robert's Grove, Luba Hati has subtly decorated, terracotta-tiled rooms in a semicircular building set in lush grounds. This is a great place to get away from it all, while still having a sense that you're in Belize. The menu at the restaurant is particularly imaginative, serving nouveau Belizean food. Kayaks, catamarans, windsurfers and bikes are available for guests' use.

Eating

Muscovy Blues (meals US$5-10; ☒ breakfast, lunch & dinner) Some interesting variations on Creole and Cuban food are on offer here. This is also the only place in the village serving draft beer. Happy hour is 6pm to 7pm.

DeThatch (☒ breakfast, lunch & dinner) The latest hotspot, in the north of town, is a small bar on the beach serving drinks and some meals. Fish burritos cost US$3.50.

Trattoria Placencia (☒ dinner Mon-Sat) Homemade fettuccine with delicious fresh sauces right on the beachfront. The smoked chicken with cream and broccoli fettuccine (US$11) satisfies about four cravings at once.

La Dolce Vita (mains US$10; ☒ lunch & dinner) Upstairs from the supermarket in the main part of the village. Serves up authentic Italian pastas and mains cooked by an authentic Italian chef.

Daisy's Ice Cream Parlor (meals US$7-10; ☒ breakfast, lunch & dinner) In the center of town, west off the central pathway, Daisy's serves meals as well as desserts and has a pleasant patio area. Burgers cost US$2.

BJ's (meals US$4-6; ☒ breakfast, lunch & dinner) Just south of the football field off the road into town, this is a good stop for low-priced Belizean food and friendly service.

THE GARINAGU

Southern Belize is the home of the Garinagu (the plural form of Garifuna), people of mixed South American indigenous and African heritage, who inhabited the island of St Vincent in the 17th century. By the end of the 18th century, British colonizers had brought the independent-minded Garinagu under their control and transported them from one island to another in an effort to subdue them.

In the early 19th century, oppression and wandering finally brought many of the Garinagu to southern Belize. The most memorable migration took place late in 1832, when on November 19, a large number of Garinagu reached Belize from Honduras in dugout canoes. The event is celebrated annually in Belize as Garifuna Settlement Day.

The Garinagu, who account for less than 7% of Belize's population, look more African than indigenous, but they speak a language that's much more indigenous than African, and their unique culture combines aspects of both peoples.

Many of the citizens of Dangriga, chief town of the Stann Creek District, are Garifuna. Dangriga is the place to be on Garifuna Settlement Day, as the town explodes in a frenzy of dancing, drinking and celebration of the Garinagu heritage.

BELIZE

Omar's Fast Food (meals US$3-8; 😋 breakfast, lunch & dinner) On the beach, just south of St John Church, Omar's has home-made food at low prices. Try the cheap, good burritos or higher-priced menu items like conch steak.

Drinking

With a little forward planning and some steely discipline you can hit five (yes, count them: five) consecutive hours of happy hour (rum drinks US$1), starting at 3pm and ending at 8pm, which should leave you nice and hammered for dinner.

Start off at **Jungle Juice** (happy hour 😋 3-5pm), 500m north of the village on the road out of town; then hit the **Pickled Parrot** (happy hour 😋 5-6pm), on the path between the supermarket and the beach; wander over to **Sugar Reef** (happy hour 😋 6-7pm), on the road heading to the marina, west out of the village; and end up at the **Tipsy Tuna** (happy hour 😋 7-8pm), on the beach. All these places stay open until around midnight most nights, serve food and have occasional live music.

Getting There & Away

AIR

Maya Island Air (📞 523-3475) and **Tropic Air** (📞 523-3410) offer daily flights linking Placencia with Belize City (US$59) and Dangriga (US$34) to the north and Punta Gorda (US$35) to the south. The village begins half a mile (0.8km) south of the airstrip; taxis meet most flights (US$3 into town).

BOAT

Being that most buses *leave* Placencia ridiculously early, the quickest (and most enjoyable) way out of town is on the **Hokey Pokey Water Taxi** (US$5), which departs Placencia at 10am for Mango Creek, and departs Mango Creek at 2:30pm for the return trip. It's a 15-minute zip through the mangroves. At Mango Creek, walk five minutes up the main street, turn left at the gas station and wait in front of Sherl's Restaurant. Buses to Punta Gorda (US$9) and Belize City (US$19) roll in at about 11am. Many boats will do a charter run to and from Mango Creek for US$20 for up to six persons.

Gulf Cruza (📞 603-7787) makes a Placencia–Big Creek–Puerto Cortés (Honduras) run

on Friday, leaving Placencia at 9:30am, arriving at Puerto Cortés at 1:30pm. Cost is US$50 Placencia–Puerto Cortés. The boat takes passengers only, no vehicles.

BUS

Novelo's runs two buses from Belize City to Placencia (standard US$10, express US$13, 161 miles/243km) via Dangriga. Buses return to Belize City at 5am and 6am.

Getting Around

G 'n' G bike rentals (📞 614-7911) rents bikes for US$12.50 per day. Taxis from the airport into town should cost around US$3, US$5 to Seine Bight and US$7 to Maya Beach.

PUNTA GORDA

pop 4330

The Southern Hwy ends at Punta Gorda, the southernmost town in Belize. Rainfall and humidity are at their highest and the jungle at its lushest here in the Toledo District. Prepare yourself for at least a short downpour almost daily and some sultry weather in between.

'Sleepy' is an understatement for this southern seafront town. People here are so laidback they can't even be bothered calling the town by its full name – all over Belize it's known simply as PG.

The town was originally founded for the Garinagu who emigrated from Honduras in 1832. In 1866, after the US Civil War, some Confederate veterans received land grants from the British government and founded a settlement here, but it didn't endure.

Though still predominantly Garifuna, PG is also home to the typical bewildering variety of Belizean citizenry: Creoles, Kekchi Maya, and expat Americans, Brits, Canadians, Chinese and East Indians.

Fishing was the town's major livelihood for almost two centuries, but now farming is important as well. Tourism is building, as PG is the base for excursions inland to the Mayan archaeological sites at Lubaantun and Nim Li Punit, to the Mayan villages of San Pedro Columbia and San Antonio, and to Blue Creek Cave.

Orientation & Information

The town center is a triangular park with a bandstand and a distinctive blue-and-white clock tower.

PUNTA GORDA

INFORMATION
Belize Bank...1 C2
BTL Telephone Office......................2 D2
District Government Offices.....(see 6)
Dr Maria Luz Legra Clinic.............3 C2
PG's Pharmacy...................................4 C2
Police Office.......................................5 D2
Post Office..6 C2
Public Phone......................................7 D1
Punta Gorda Laundry Service.....8 C2
Toledo Ecotourism Association..(see 9)
Toledo Visitors' Information
    Center (BTIA).................................9 C2

EATING   🍴 (p298)
Cafeteria El Cafe............................21 D1
Earth Runnins..................................22 C1
Emery Restaurant...........................23 D1
Verde's Restaurant.........................24 C2

DRINKING   🍺 (p298)
PG Sports Bar...................................25 C2

SHOPPING   🛍 (p298)
Fajina Craft Center.........................26 C2

SIGHTS & ACTIVITIES
Church..10 B3
Clock Tower......................................11 C2
Customs & Immigration.............12 D2
Fire Station.......................................13 C1
Town Board Offices.......................14 B1
Volleyball Gym................................15 B1

TRANSPORT   (p298)
Bus Station.......................................27 A4
Charter Boat Dock.........................28 C1
Customs Dock..................................29 D2
Maya Island Air Terminal............30 B1
Paco's Boat Charter Service
    (Olympic Bar)..............................31 C3
Requena's Charter Services........32 D2
Texaco Fuel Station........................33 D1
Tropic Air Terminal...............(see 30)

SLEEPING   🛏 (pp297–8)
Nature's Way Guest House..........16 B3
Pallavi's Hotel..................................17 C1
Sea Front Inn...................................18 D1
St Charles Inn..................................19 C1
Traveller's Inn.................................20 A4

Gulf of Honduras

Nature's Way Guest House (right) is the
unofficial information center for travelers.
Toledo Visitors' Information Center (☎ 722-2531;
www.southernbelize.com; ◷ 9am-1pm Mon-Wed, Fri &
Sat) shares office space on Front St with the
Toledo Ecotourism Association (see p298).
There's usually somebody around.

Belize Bank (cnr Main & Queen Sts; ◷ 8am-1pm
Mon-Thu, 8am-4:30pm Fri) is across from the town
square.

The **Punta Gorda Laundry Service** (2 Prince St)
charges US$1.50 per pound.

Sleeping
Punta Gorda's lodging is resolutely budget-
class, with only a few places rising above
basic shelter.

Nature's Way Guest House (☎ 722-2119; 65 Front
St; s/d/tr with shared bathroom US$10/15/20) One of
the better budget hotels in Belize. There's
a shady courtyard with plenty of hammock
action and excellent breakfasts (tofu available) for US$3.50.

St Charles Inn (☎ 722-2149; 23 King St; s/d
US$15/20) Dinky little motel-style rooms with
private bathroom, but an excellent verandah for chilling out on.

Pallavi's Hotel (☎ 722-2414; 19 N Main St; d US$15)
Pallavi's has reasonable rooms and a restaurant downstairs.

Sea Front Inn (☎ 722-2300; www.seafrontinn
.com; s/d US$65/81) North of the town center
on Front St, this is the town's newest hotel.
It's a fascinating arrangement of wood and

BELIZE

stone, towering above the rest of the town's buildings. Breakfast (US$3 to US$6) in the 3rd-floor dining room, with its fantastic sea views, is open to nonguests as well.

Traveller's Inn (☎ 702-2568; s/d US$40/107; ☒ ℗) At the southern end of José María Núñez St, next to the bus station. Traveller's Inn has modern, if stodgy, rooms with private bathrooms and cable TV; breakfast is included.

Eating & Drinking
Emery Restaurant (Main St; meals US$6-8) Daily fresh-fish specials, good Mexican food and quite possibly the best fried chicken to be had in all of Belize.

Waluco's (meals from US$5; ☱ lunch & dinner Wed-Sat, dinner Tue) If you're wondering where everybody is on a Sunday, they're probably out here, 1.5 miles north of town – swimming off the pier, eating barbecue and knocking back a few Belikins under a big breezy *palapa*.

Earth Runnins (11 Main Middle St; ☱ breakfast, lunch & dinner Wed-Mon) Good cheap food with plenty of vegetarian options. Happy hour is from 5pm to 7pm – cocktails are US$2, local beers US$1.25.

Cafeteria El Café (North St; meals US$4-6; ☱ breakfast & lunch) A tidy place.

Verde's Restaurant (Main St; meals US$5) Standard Belizean family cooking and good breakfasts.

PG Sports Bar (cnr Main & Prince Sts) A good bet for live music on weekends. It's a good-sized, fairly standard bar, incongruously enhanced by a staggering collection of US sports photos and posters.

Shopping
Fajina Craft Center (Front St; ☱ 8am-11am Mon, Wed, Fri, Sat) Next door to the post office, this is a good place to pick up local Mayan handicrafts such as jipijapa baskets, slate carvings and embroidered shirts, dresses and hangings.

Saturday is the main market day, when villagers come to town to buy, sell and barbecue. It's a fascinating and colorful mix-up.

Getting There & Away
Punta Gorda is served daily by **Maya Island Air** (www.mayaairways.com) and **Tropic Air** (www.tropic air.com). Flights to Belize City cost US$76. Ticket offices are at the airport. If you plan to fly out of PG, be at the airstrip at least

15 minutes before departure time, as the planes sometimes leave early.

Requena's Charter Services (☎ 722-2070; 12 Front St), operates the *Mariestela*, with boats departing from Punta Gorda daily at 9am for Puerto Barrios (Guatemala), and departing Puerto Barrios' public pier at 2pm for the return to PG. Tickets cost US$10 one-way. Requena's also has boats to Livingston (Guatemala) on Tuesday and Friday at 10am.

James Bus (p228) offers one run daily each way between Belize City and Punta Gorda (standard US$11, express US$13, 202 miles/305km); Southern Transport (p228) offers four runs daily in each direction.

AROUND PUNTA GORDA
Toledo Ecotourism Association
The **Toledo Ecotourism Association** (TEA; ☎ 722-2096; Front St, Punta Gorda; www.ecoclub.com/toledo) runs a Village Guesthouse and Ecotrail Program that takes participants to any of eight traditional Mopan Maya, Kekchi Maya, and Garifuna villages.

This is probably the least-appreciated tourism possibility in the whole of Belize. The villages are gorgeous. Accommodations are simple (mostly without electricity, all with cold showers and shared bathrooms) and the villagers are friendly without being overly so. You can participate in village life as much as you like – if you want to go wandering around on your own, that's fine, but if you want to take part in day-to-day life, folks are generally very welcoming. Accommodation costs US$10 per night and three meals go for US$10.

More than 80% of the fees collected stays with the villagers, helping them to achieve a sustainable, ecofriendly economy as an alternative to slash-and-burn agriculture. Another goal is to sustain and preserve the culture and heritage of the villages by offering another form of income to them.

The usual tours offered include a village tour (often by a woman in the village, a rare opportunity to get a female perspective on village life) and jungle tours to nearby caves, ruins, lakes or waterfalls (see the individual village descriptions, opposite). Craft lessons, evening performances or storytelling can also be arranged.

Guests are invited into village homes for their meals. It's unlikely that the family will join you while you eat, instead they'll go about their family business while you're there. Some find this disconcerting, but if you are prepared, you will find that it's a great opportunity to ask questions and learn more about village and home life. Meals usually consist of tortillas and *caldo* – a stew made of root vegetables and meat, usually chicken, although in Barranco you might luck onto some traditional Garifuna food.

You can book at the office (and pay a US$5 administrative fee which supports the office facilities) or you can simply rock into town on your own steam. In the unlikely event that the guesthouse is full, you're sure to be offered a bed somewhere. Transport is problematic – see p300. Be aware that each village guesthouse is run independently, and your experience and service may differ. Let the organizers at TEA know if you have special interests or needs and they'll help you choose the village that will be the most satisfying for you.

THE VILLAGES

Landscapes vary in the region, but there is usually a river or a stream at the heart of each village. Surrounding the villages are waterfalls, caves and Mayan ruins that can be best experienced with a local guide. Family homes in the villages are usually one- or two-room thatched-roof huts with wooden plank walls and dirt floors. Local government in the villages is a meld of the ancient *alcalde* system, where a leader is elected by majority and makes all the major decisions for the village, and a village-council system, where the decision making is shared. The villages were established as early as the 1850s, mostly by Maya fleeing oppression in Guatemala to settle in Belize. For more information about individual villages, check www.southernbelize.com/tea.

San Antonio village is probably the best-known and most-visited Mayan village in Toledo, possibly the country. The population is 1000 to 3000, depending on who you talk to. The village is arranged on roads winding through foothills. It's picture-postcard imagery, complete with brightly dressed villagers, thatched-roof buildings, roaming livestock, a church built from stones taken from Mayan ruins and stained-glass windows from a church in St Louis, Missouri. This is the most developed of the Mayan villages of Toledo, with electricity, a village

telephone and running water. The Mopan Maya of San Antonio are descended from former inhabitants of the Guatemalan village of San Luís Petén, just across the border. Bells in the church are said to have been taken from the village of San Luís Petén when the settlers fled oppression there in the mid-19th century.

If you are here during a festival, your visit will be much more memorable. The **Feast of San Luís**, a harvest festival where the famous deer dance is performed, is celebrated here in late summer.

Santa Cruz and **Santa Elena** are Mopan Maya villages with a combined population of about 500. These are near Río Blanco Falls (which has one of the best swimming holes in the whole country) and Uxbenka ruins. The ruins are not open to the public, but you can visit them with a guide from one of the villages.

Pueblo Viejo ('old town' in Spanish) is home to about 700 Mopan Mayas. It was the first settlement of the Mopan Mayas who fled Guatemala to settle in Toledo. There is a waterfall close to the village, and a road into Guatemala is being built from here.

San Miguel is a Kekchi village of 400 people, near the Southern Hwy close to the turnoff to the Lubaantun ruins.

San José is a Mopan village known for practicing organic farming methods. It's located in the foothills near the Guatemalan border, and the rain forest surrounding it is said to be the most pristine in Toledo. There are jungle hikes to Gibnut cave and a 200ft sinkhole.

Blue Creek, formerly called Río Blanco, is a village of 280. Approximately half are Kekchi, half Mopan. It gets plenty of traffic because it's the site of the Blue Creek Rainforest Preserve, which attracts visitors for its great swimming hole, canopy walk and cave.

Laguna, about 10 miles (16km) west of Punta Gorda, is just off the main road and quick and easy to get to. It has one of the best guesthouse facilities of all the villages: a two-story structure with outdoor showers. Laguna is home to about 300 Kekchi Maya villagers. Its namesake lagoon is a two-hour walk through the wetlands of **Aguas Calientes Wildlife Sanctuary**, a great area for bird-watching. (Note that this area floods in the wet season and the trails can be impassable.)

Barranco is the only Garifuna village located south of Punta Gorda on the coast, and the southernmost inhabited point in Belize. It can be accessed by sea from PG in about 20 minutes; by dirt road the trip takes 45 minutes. The population of Barranco is about 150 and dwindling. You'll find lots of women, children and elderly folks staying put, while the men of working age head for the cities and better economic opportunity. Villagers here are proud of their home and recognize that their lifestyle is rare and disappearing. The village now supports itself by fishing, but in the past the area was heavily farmed; you'll see evidence of farming and plenty of fruit trees as you wander around.

GETTING THERE & AWAY

The trickiest part of the program is transportation. Most choose to catch a village bus that comes into Punta Gorda on market days, usually Monday, Wednesday, Friday and Saturday, although schedules vary for individual villages. Village buses are brightly painted school buses that make regular runs into Punta Gorda to allow the villagers to visit the market to sell wares and buy supplies.

The buses drive in from the villages early in the morning and park at the town square or on surrounding streets until midday, when villagers are ready to make their return trip. In the abstract, it sounds confusing, but when you get there it will become fairly straightforward – townspeople will help you find the bus and make sure you're in the right place at the right time to visit the villages. Check with **TEA** (☎ 722-2096; Front St; www.ecoclub.com/toledo) in Punta Gorda for the most current bus schedules.

It is also possible to arrange for a taxi to take you to the villages; the price will be around US$50 to US$75 depending on the distance. Hitchhiking is a common way to get around. This should be done with extreme caution and travelers, especially women, shouldn't hitch alone, but most feel comfortable hitching in groups around here.

On your return, you'll have to be prepared to get up early in the morning – the further from PG the village is, the earlier you'll have to leave. Luckily everyone in your village will be aware of your presence, so you'll have plenty of help making your connection.

Blue Creek Rain Forest Preserve & Cave

About 12 miles (20km) south of San Antonio lies the village of Blue Creek, and beyond it the **rain forest preserve** (☼ 8am-5pm) and **Blue Creek Cave**. It's less than a mile (1.6km) hike into the site along a marked trail – you'll enjoy the rain forest around you and the pools, channels, caves and refreshingly cool waters of the creek system. Accommodation is best arranged through TEA Guesthouse in Blue Creek.

Lubaantun

The Mayan ruins at **Lubaantun** (Fallen Stones), 1 mile (1.6km) northwest of the village of San Pedro Columbia, have been excavated to some extent but not restored. The many temples are still mostly covered with jungle, so you will have to use your imagination to envisage the great city that once thrived here. In its heyday, the merchants of Lubaantun traded with people on the cayes, in Mexico and Guatemala, and perhaps beyond.

Archaeologists have found evidence that Lubaantun flourished until the late 8th century AD, after which little was built. The site covers a square mile (3 sq km) and holds the only ruins in Belize with curved stone corners. Of its 18 plazas, only the three most important – **Plazas III to V** – have been cleared. **Plaza IV**, the most important of all, is built along a ridge of hills and surrounded by the site's most impressive buildings: Structures 10, 12 and 33. A visitors center on the site exhibits Mayan pottery and other artifacts.

See left for information about getting to Lubaantun.

Nim Li Punit

About 24 miles (38km) northwest of Punta Gorda, just west of the Southern Hwy, stand the ruins of **Nim Li Punit** (Big Hat; admission US$5; ☼ 8am-5pm). Named for the headgear worn by the richly clad figure on Stela 14, Nim Li Punit may have been a tributary city to larger, more powerful Lubaantun.

The South Group of structures was the city's ceremonial center and is of the most interest. The plaza has been cleared, but the structures surrounding it are largely unre-

DOUG MCKINLAY

Ambergris Caye (p239)

Waterfront accommodations in Caye Caulker
(p233)

ANDREW MARSHALL & LEANNE WALKER

JOHN ELK III

A boat making the trip along New
River from Orange Walk (p255) to
Lamanai (p254)

Long Caye (p288)

MARK WEBSTER

The jungle around Punta Gorda (p296)

GREG JOHNSTON

ANDREW MARSHALL & LEANNE WA

The Mayan ruins of Altun Ha (p249)

Tropical flora near Lamanai (p254)

LUKE HU

stored. Have a look at the stelae, especially Stela 14, one of the longest Mayan stela yet discovered at 33ft (10m), and Stela 15, which dates from AD 721 and is the oldest work recovered here so far.

See opposite for advice about reaching Nim Li Punit.

BELIZE DIRECTORY

ACCOMMODATIONS

Lodgings in Belize are generally more expensive and of lower comfort than in neighboring countries. Some have great charm and are well worth the cost; most are just places to stay. On the coast there are plenty of cabañas to choose from, although they are nearly always more expensive than staying in hotels. Many hotels offer single rooms (from US$10), but a lot charge simply for the room (starting at US$20), so if you are a solo traveler and you really want to save money it is a good idea to hook up with someone else. The YHA is non-existent in Belize, but there are a few places around offering dorm-style accommodation from around US$10. A cabaña will generally sleep 2 people, but family ones are also available. Usually it houses a double bed, but can also be two singles.

ACTIVITIES

Snorkeling, diving, fishing, sailing and all manner of other water sports are best on the cayes. Boats depart Ambergris (p241) and Caulker (p235) on day and overnight voyages to the best spots. Many resorts on the smaller cayes offer all-inclusive weekly dive, snorkel and fishing packages. See the Northern Cayes (p229) and Southern Cayes (p287) sections for details.

ROOM TAX INCREASE

At the time of writing, a 7% room tax was added to the price of all rooms listed in this book (but often waived in cheaper hotels). This tax is due to increase to 9% in mid-2005. Room tax is separate from the service charge (usually 10%) and other extras that top-end hotels often tack on.

Horseback riding, canoeing and kayaking, hiking, bird-watching and archaeology are all possibilities in the Cayo District of western Belize (p269).

BOOKS

Lonely Planet's *Diving & Snorkeling Belize* by Franz O Meyer provides detailed descriptions of dive sites and extensive photos of underwater wildlife. Lonely Planet also offers *Belize*, a title solely devoted to the country.

13 Chapters in the History of Belize by Belizean historian Assad Shoman is a detailed account of the history of the country and tends not to glamorize the colonial past as some other studies do.

Warlords and Maize Men – A Guide to the Maya Sites of Belize by Byron Foster is recommended for its descriptions of the lives of the Maya.

Snapshots of Belize: An Anthology of Short Fiction published in Belize by Cubola Productions features short stories of past and present Belize.

Conch Shell by José Sánchez features some excellent poetry by this emerging Belizean writer. Sanchez writes about the streets, people and history of Belize, often mixing Kriol with English.

BUSINESS HOURS

Banking hours vary, but most banks are open 8am to 1:30pm Monday to Thursday and 8am to 4:30pm Friday. Most banks and many businesses and shops close on Wednesday afternoon. Shops are usually open 8am to noon Monday to Saturday and 1pm to 4pm Monday, Tuesday, Thursday and Friday. Some shops have evening hours from 7pm to 9pm on those days as well. Most businesses, offices and city restaurants close on Sunday. Note that in smaller towns, the popular Belizean restaurants usually close before 6pm. Otherwise, a general guide to restaurant hours goes something like this: breakfast 7am to 10am, lunch noon to about 3pm and dinner 6pm to 9pm or 10pm.

DANGERS & ANNOYANCES

Petty theft is the greatest danger (and annoyance) to travelers in Belize. Take care not to show obvious signs of wealth. Keep a close eye on camera equipment, don't leave valuables in plain view in cars and try to watch your bags when you're on a bus. Belize City has a bad reputation, mostly a hangover from the past, but you should still exercise normal precautions. If you're driving, be extra careful – Belize is renowned for road accidents. Wear your seat belt, and be aware of what's going on around you.

EMBASSIES & CONSULATES
Belize Embassies & Consulates
Belize's overseas diplomatic affairs are generally handled by British embassies and consulates.

Canada (Consulate; ☎ 416-865-7000; c/o McMillan Binch, Suite 3800, South Tower, Royal Bank Plaza, Toronto, Ontario M5J 2JP)

Guatemala (☎ 2334-5531; embelguate@guat.net; Edificio El Reformador, Suite 803, 8th fl, Av Reforma 1-50, Zone 9, Guatemala City)

Mexico (☎ 5520-1274; embelize@prodigy.net.mx; 215 Calle Bernardo de Galvez, Col Lomas de Chapultepec, Mexico DF 11000)

UK (High Commission; ☎ 020-7499-9728; 22 Harcourt House 19, Cavendish Sq, London W1G 0PL)

USA (☎ 202-332-9636; 2535 Massachusetts Ave NW, Washington, DC 20008)

For more information, check www.embassy world.com/embassy/belize.htm.

Embassies & Consulates in Belize
EMBASSIES
Guatemala (Map p217; ☎ 223-3150; 8 A St, Belize City)

Honduras (Map pp220-1; ☎ 224-5889; 22 Gabourel Lane, Belize City)

Mexico (Map pp220-1; ☎ 223-0193/4; 18 North Park St, Belize City)

UK (Map p266; ☎ 822-2146; PO Box 91, Belmopan)

USA (Map pp220-1; ☎ 227-7161; cnr Gabourel Lane & Hutson St, Belize City)

CONSULATES
Canada (Map pp220-1 ☎ 223-1060, fax 223-0060; 83 N Front St, Belize City)

France (Map pp220-1; ☎ 223-2708, fax 223-2416; 109 New Rd, Belize City)

Germany (Map p217; ☎ 222-4371, fax 222-4375; 3.5 miles Western Hwy, Belize City)

Italy (Map pp220-1; ☎ 227-8449, fax 223-0385; 18 Albert St, Belize City)

Netherlands (Map p217; ☎ 227-3227; cnr Baymen Ave & Calle al Mar, Belize City)

FESTIVALS & EVENTS
The following list describes the major holidays and festivals in Belize; they may well be celebrated for several days around the actual date:

Fiesta de Carnival (February; Sunday to Tuesday before the beginning of Lent) Celebrated in northern Belize.

Holy Week (April; the week leading up to Easter Sunday) Various services and processions.

Cashew Festival (first weekend in May) Crooked Tree (p250).

Feast of San Pedro (June; date varies) San Pedro, Ambergris Caye (p239).

Lobster Season start (June; dates vary) Placencia (p292), Caye Caulker (p233) and San Pedro (p239) have lobster festivals on successive weekends in June and early July, after the season officially opens, usually the first or second weekend of June.

Benque Viejo Festival (July; dates vary) Benque Viejo del Carmen (p275).

Feast of San Luis (August; dates vary) San Antonio (p298).

Costa Maya Festival (August; date varies) San Pedro, Ambergris Caye (p239) – a celebration of Mayan coastal culture with participants from Belize and the Yucatán.

Garifuna Settlement Day (November 19) Dangriga (p284) and Hopkins (p288).

GAY & LESBIAN TRAVELERS
Unfortunately, the rules for gay and lesbian travelers in Belize seem to be the same as those in most Central American countries – keep it low key, and look but don't touch. While it's an incredibly tolerant society, underlying Latino machismo and traditional religious beliefs combine to make public displays of same-sex affection a pretty bad idea. Gay men in Belize use the word 'fish' as a codeword (as in 'are you a fish?' and 'I'm looking for some fish').

More cosmopolitan destinations (San Pedro, p239 in particular) are more gay-friendly. In fact, some Belizeans say they dislike San Pedro because there are 'too many gays there', but at the time of writing the gay scene was decidedly low-key.

A number of gay- and lesbian-oriented tour operators offer package tours and cruises throughout Central America – check out the Out and About website (www.out andabout.com) for details.

Further information on gay and lesbian travel can be obtained through the offices of the International Gay & Lesbian Travel Association (www.iglta.com).

HOLIDAYS

Many of Belize's holidays are of historical or political interest. On major holidays, banks, offices and other services are closed.

New Year's Day (January 1)
Baron Bliss Day (March 9) Honors the memory of one of the great benefactors of Belize.
Labor Day (May 1)
Commonwealth Day (May 25)
National Day (September 10) Also called St George's Caye Day.
Independence Day (September 21)
Pan-American Day (October 12) Also called Columbus Day.
Christmas Day (December 25)
Boxing Day (December 26)

INTERNET RESOURCES

Belize Arts Council (www.belizemall.com/bac) Information about Belizean culture and contact information for the various ethnic councils.
Belize by Naturalight (www.belizenet.com) Covers just about everything visitors might want to know.
Belize District (www.belizedistrict.com)
Belize Forums (www.belizeforum.com) Online discussion groups covering all aspects of Belize – an excellent resource for on-the-ground, up-to-date information.
Belize Net (www.belize.net) A search engine for all things Belize.
Belize Tourism Board (www.travelbelize.org) Comprehensive tourist information.
Belize Web (www.belizeweb.com) Links to newspapers, radio and an online telephone directory.
Simply Belize (www.simplybelize.org) A transcription of the 13-part TV series of the same name that deals with Belize's fascinating cultural history in great detail.

MAPS

If you're driving, pick up a copy of Emory King's annual *Driver's Guide to Beautiful Belize*, sold in bookstores and gift shops in Belize City. The guide has basic maps and detailed route descriptions – they're helpful since road markers in Belize are few and far between.

The various British Ordnance Survey maps (1:750,000 to 1:1000) are the most detailed and accurate of the country. In North America, order them from **OMNI Resources** (☎ +1-336-227-8300; www.omnimap.com; PO Box 2096, Burlington, NC 27216) or **Map Link** (☎ +1-805-692-6777; www.maplink.com; Unit 5, 30 South Patera Lane, Santa Barbara, CA 93117).

More readily accessible in Belize is the Belize Facilities Map issued by the **Belize**

Tourism Board (BTB; Map pp220-1; ☎ 223-1913; btbb@btl.net; PO Box 325, Belize City). Derived from the Ordnance Survey maps, it has plans of all major towns in Belize, a road map, plans of the archaeological sites at Altun Ha and Xunantunich and a list of facts about Belize. If you write to the Board in advance you may be able to get one free; in Belizean shops the map is sold for US$4.

MONEY
ATMs

ATMs are the easiest way of getting cash, but at the time of writing, only First Caribbean Bank machines in Belize City, Belmopan and Dangriga and Belize Bank machines (in all major towns) accepted foreign cards. The only problem with using Belize Bank machines is that they only let you withdraw US$250 at a time, and if your bank charges outrageously per overseas transaction (as most do) this can get very expensive.

Credit Cards

Credit cards are useful, particularly when buying cash from a bank. Visa and MasterCard are the most widely accepted. Some tour operators and higher-end hotels and restaurants accept cards, but it's always best to have a good supply of the folding stuff on hand.

Currency

The Belizean dollar (BZ$) is divided into 100 cents. Coins come in denominations of one, five, 10, 25 and 50 cents, and one dollar; bills (notes) are all of the same size but differ in color and come in denominations of two, five, 10, 20, 50 and 100 dollars. Be sure to have small denominations if you're heading off the tourist trail.

Prices are generally quoted in Belizean dollars, written as '$30 BZ,' though you will also occasionally see '$15 US.' To avoid surprises, be sure to confirm with service providers whether they are quoting prices in US or Belizean dollars.

Exchanging Money

Most businesses accept US currency in cash without question. They usually give change in Belizean dollars, though they may return US change if you ask for it. Many also accept US-dollar traveler's checks.

BELIZE

Canadian dollars and UK pounds sterling are exchangeable at any bank, although non-US-dollar traveler's checks are not consistently accepted by Belizean banks. It is difficult if not impossible to exchange other foreign currencies in Belize.

Moneychangers around border-crossing points will change your US cash for Belizean dollars legally at the current standard rate (which has not changed for years) of US$1=BZ$2. If you change money or traveler's checks at a bank, you may get only US$1=BZ$1.97; they may also charge a fee of BZ$5 (US$2.50) to change a traveler's check.

POST

By airmail to Canada or the USA, a postcard costs BZ$0.30, a letter BZ$0.60. To Europe it's BZ$0.40 for a postcard and BZ$0.75 for a letter.

To claim poste restante mail, present a passport or other identification; there's no charge. Address poste restante (general delivery) mail as follows:

Tom JONES (last name in capitals)
c/o Poste Restante
(Town)
BELIZE

TELEPHONE

The country's telephone system is operated by Belize Telecommunications Ltd (BTL), with offices in major cities. Local calls cost BZ$0.25. Telephone debit cards are sold in denominations of BZ$10, BZ$20 and BZ$50. The country code is ☎ 501.

TOURIST INFORMATION

The government-run **Belize Tourism Board** (BTB; ☎ 223-1913; www.travelbelize.org) maintains tourist offices in most larger towns. They are generally underfunded, but staffed by friendly folks who usually do what they can to answer your questions.

Also of great help is the **Belize Audubon Society** (Map pp220-1; ☎ 223-5004; www.belizeaudubon .org; 12 Fort St, Belize City). It provides information on national parks and wildlife reserves throughout the country.

VISAS

Citizens of many countries (among them Australia, Canada, France, Germany, Ireland, Italy, Mexico, New Zealand, the UK, the USA and many Caribbean nations) do not need to obtain a Belizean visa in advance, provided they have a valid passport and an onward or round-trip airline ticket (with a departure from Belize or any other country). A visitor's permit valid for 30 days will be stamped in their passport at a border crossing or at the airport. Visitor's permits can usually be extended with minimal fuss for around US$15 for 30 days from any immigration office, but it's best to do it in Belize City. You won't need a working visa for volunteer work. Details on visa requirements are available from any Belizean embassy or consulate (see p302).

WOMEN TRAVELERS

Men in Belize can be forward and at times aggressive with comments about women's appearance. This can be uncomfortable and embarrassing, but shouldn't be considered threatening (although common-sense rules for women travelers should be followed). Do as your mother probably told you in elementary school: ignore them, and they'll go away. And (you may have heard this from mom, too), the more modestly you're dressed, the less attention you'll receive.

WORK

Officially you need a resident's visa to get a job in Belize. You might, however, pick up some work on the Cayes or in Placencia working in bars, but the pay isn't likely to be anything to get excited about. For volunteering opportunities, see listings in the Environment section (p39) and also the Regional Directory (p446).

TRANSPORTATION IN BELIZE

GETTING THERE & AWAY

Air

Belize City has two airports. All international flights use **Goldson International Airport** (BZE; ☎ 225-3412), 9 miles (16km) northwest of the city center.

Airlines flying to and from Belize:
American Airlines (☎ 223-2522; www.americanair.com, airline code AA; hubs in Dallas/Fort Worth, Chicago, Miami)

Continental Airlines (☎ 227-8309; www.continental
.com, airline code CO; hubs in Houston, Newark and
Cleveland)
Grupo TACA (☎ 227-7363; www.grupotaca.com;
airline code TA; hub in San Salvador)
Maya Island Air (☎ 223-1140; www.mayaairways
.com; airline code MW; hub in Belize City)
Tropic Air (☎ 226-2012; www.tropicair.com; airline
code PM; hub in Belize City)

Grupo TACA also offers direct flights
between Belize City and Guatemala City
(Guatemala), San Salvador (El Salvador),
and Roatán and San Pedro Sula (Honduras), as well as connecting flights from
Panama, Nicaragua and Costa Rica. Maya
Island Air and Tropic Air offer daily flights
to Flores (Guatemala). Departure taxes and
airport fees of US$35 are levied on non-
Belizean travelers departing Goldson International Airport in Belize City for foreign
destinations.

Land
Several companies operate direct buses from
Chetumal (Mexico) to Belize City. Novelo's
runs between Belize City and Benque Viejo
del Carmen on the Guatemalan border, connecting with Guatemalan buses headed for
Flores. Daily luxury buses also leaves Belize
City's Marine terminal for Flores, Guatemala (US$15 to US$20) – see p228 for details. There are also shuttles between Belize
City and Flores that originate in Chetumal
(p350) in Mexico. Exit tax at Belizean land
border crossing points is US$18.

Sea
The *Gulf Cruza* runs between Belize City
and Puerto Cortés (Honduras), with stops
in Placencia (p296) and Big Creek, every
Friday, returning Monday morning. Scheduled boats and occasional small passenger
boats ply the waters between Punta Gorda
in southern Belize and Lívingston and
Puerto Barrios in eastern Guatemala. See
p298 for details. These boats can usually be
hired for special trips between countries,
and if enough passengers split the cost, the
price can be reasonable.
Exit tax from Belize by sea is US$3.75.

GETTING AROUND
It's a small country, and most roads that you
are likely to be traveling on have now been

paved, so even the most hellish chicken-
bus experience isn't likely to last too long
(patience, grasshopper).

Air
People *do* fly within Belize, but then people
do all sorts of crazy stuff. If you're going
to the cayes, it's a lot more fun (and, in a
certain guidebook writer's opinion, a lot
less scary) to grab a boat rather than blow
your dough on a light plane which takes
about the same time.
Belize's two domestic carriers are **Maya
Island Air** (Belize City ☎ 223-1140, US & Canada
☎ 1800-225-6732; www.mayaairways.com) and **Tropic
Air** (☎ 226-2012, US & Canada ☎ 1800-422-3435; www
.tropicair.com).
There are two principal domestic air
routes: Belize City–Caye Caulker–San
Pedro–Corozal, and Belize City–Dangriga–
Placencia–Punta Gorda.
Sometimes planes will not stop at a
particular airport if they have no passengers to drop off or pick up, so be sure to
reserve your seat in advance whenever
possible. Tickets for both airlines can be
booked through most of the hotels and tour
agencies within the country. Sample fares
include Belize City–San Pedro US$26 and
Belize City–Punta Gorda US$76.
Note: flying domestically from the international airport costs US$15 to US$20
more than departing from the domestic
terminal.

Bicycle
Around town, Belizeans are big bike rid-
ers. Out on the highways you're likely to
see a few lycra-clad enthusiasts, but not
many. Either way, if you're pedaling yourself around, remember that the law of the
jungle is in full effect out on the roads, and
the larger vehicle always has right of way
(despite what the road rules may say). Policemen take particular glee in busting tourists riding without lights at night – strap a
flashlight on somewhere and you'll be immune from these sorts of shenanigans.

Boat
Fast motor launches zoom between Belize
City, Caye Caulker and Ambergris Caye
frequently every day.
Be sure to bring sunscreen, a hat and
clothing to protect you from the sun and

BELIZE

the spray. If you sit in the bow, there's less spray, but you bang down harder when the boat goes over a wave. Sitting in the stern will give you a smoother ride, but you may get dampened.

Due to the high cost of gasoline in Belize, private motor boat hire can be prohibitively expensive. Expect to pay at least US$100 for a one-hour ride with captain, with minor discounts available for longer trips. The best places to hook up with motor or sail boats are Placencia, Dangriga and the Northern Cayes.

Bus

Bus is the mode of transportation for most Belizeans, so departures are frequent – there's no real need to book ahead, but it *is* wise to turn up early and snag yourself a seat.

Most Belizean buses are used US school buses, although a few 1st-class (relatively speaking) services are available. The larger companies operate frequent buses along the country's three major roads. Smaller village lines tend to be run on local work and school schedules: buses run from a smaller town to a larger town in the morning, and then they return in the afternoon. Fares average about US$1.50 per hour's ride.

Each major bus company has its own terminals. Outside Belize City, bus drivers will usually pick up and drop off passengers at undesignated stops if requested.

Visit www.belizecentral.net/bus_schedule /schedule for an automated bus schedule.

Pilferage of luggage has been a problem, particularly on the Punta Gorda route. Give your luggage only to the bus driver or conductor, and watch as it is stored. Be there when the bus is unloaded and retrieve your luggage at once. See p228 for details of bus companies and their routes.

Car & Motorcycle

DRIVER'S LICENSE

Visitors to Belize can use their driver's license from home – it's not necessary to get an international one.

FUEL & SPARE PARTS

Plenty of fuel stations are available in the larger towns and along the major roads. At last report, leaded gasoline was going for about US$3.80 per US gallon (US$1 per liter). You can gas up with regular, premium (unleaded) and diesel fuel throughout Belize.

HIRE

Just in case you were starting to think that Belize was somehow normal, check this out: it's cheaper to hire a taxi with driver (US$60 per day, not including gas, or less if you bargain hard) than it is to hire a car (around US$70 per day, not including gas, insurance or 9% sales tax) and drive yourself. Car-hire rates are notorious for their fluctuations, so you might want to check those figures.

Generally, renters must be at least 25 years old, have a valid driver's license and pay by credit card or leave a large cash deposit. Most rental agencies will not allow you to take a rental out of the country without first signing a release. The release allows you to leave Belize, but be forewarned that your insurance will not cover you or the car in other countries.

For details on car-rental companies, see p228.

Note that you won't need to rent a car for travel on any of the cayes. Bicycles and electric golf carts, available for rent on Ambergris Caye and Caye Caulker, are sufficient.

INSURANCE

Liability insurance is required in Belize, and you must have it for the customs officer to approve the temporary importation of your car into the country. You can usually buy the insurance from booths at the border for about US$1 per day. The booths are generally closed Sunday, meaning no insurance is sold that day and no temporary import permits are issued. If you're crossing the border with a car, try to do it on a weekday morning.

Insurance is automatically added to the price of rental cars – you can't rent a car without using the company's insurance.

ROAD CONDITIONS

Belize has three good asphalt-paved two-lane roads: the Northern Hwy between the Mexican border near Corozal and Belize City; the Western Hwy between Belize City and the Guatemalan border near Benque Viejo del Carmen; and the Hummingbird

Hwy from Belmopan to Dangriga. Most other roads are narrow one- or two-lane dirt roads; many are impassable after heavy rains. The Southern Hwy is paved in patches but remains slow going.

Anyone who drives a lot in Belize has a 4WD vehicle or a high-clearance pickup truck. But if you plan on sticking to the main roads and you're traveling during the dry season, you will be fine renting a car, which will cost about US$20 a day less than a 4WD.

Sites off the main roads are often accessible only by 4WD vehicles, especially during the rainy season between May and November. After heavy rains in Belize, you can get profoundly stuck in floodwaters or mud even with a 4WD, and getting winched out is expensive. Wet conditions aren't the only challenge; in mountain regions the dry soil is loose and rocky, making it hard to keep traction on steep roads.

Watch out for sudden changes in road conditions, especially in the south; an overly quick transition from pavement to dirt could cause you to lose control of your vehicle. Be prepared to slow down for double speed-control bumps (called 'sleeping policemen') along the approaches to towns and intersections.

All paved roads in Belize are two-lane (one in each direction), except for some one-way roads in towns, and you'll soon learn that Belizeans aren't timid about passing, even on busy stretches of road. Next you'll learn that if you want to get anywhere, you're going to have to play the passing game, too. Major roads are used by vehicles of all sizes and speeds – from lumbering sugarcane trucks to swift new SUVs.

Mileposts and highway signs record distances in miles and speed limits in miles per hour (mph), although many vehicles have odometers and speedometers that are calibrated in kilometers.

mph	km/h
10mph	16km/h
20mph	32km/h
30mph	48km/h
40mph	64km/h
50mph	80km/h

ROAD RULES
Although Belize is a former British colony, cars drive on the right side of the road here. Road signs pointing the way to towns and villages are often few and far between. Keep track of your mileage so you know when your turnoff is approaching, and don't be afraid to ask people for directions.

Be safe by using your turn signals when you're ready to pass, always heeding no-passing zones (double solid lines) and keeping an eye out for fast-approaching vehicles behind you. If you are in doubt about whether you have room to pass, don't take a risk – there will be other opportunities.

Use of seat belts is required outside of city limits. If you're caught on the highway not wearing one, the fine can be upwards of US$50.

If you want to make a left turn on the highway, you must pull over to the verge and let traffic behind you pass before turning.

Left turners have the right of way over right turners at a crossroads, but if you're facing up against a logging truck coming full steam, it may pay to be flexible and courteous.

The maximum blood alcohol content in Belize is 0.07%, which generally translates to two drinks in the first hour, then one drink every hour after that for men and one drink per hour for women, but don't take our word for it.

Petty theft can be an issue – keep your vehicle locked at all times and do not leave valuables in it, especially not in plain view.

Hitching
Hitchhiking is never 100% safe and caution should be exercised at all times. That said, if you're out in the middle of nowhere in the baking sun without a bus in sight and a pickup slows down, you may be tempted to hitch.

Plenty of Belizeans do. Off the main roads, where buses are infrequent if they exist at all, hitching is an integral part of the transport network, and you can flag down a passing pickup (drivers with enclosed vehicles will be much less likely to offer you a ride) the way you would a taxi. Otherwise, the international gesture of the outstretched thumb and hopeful smile is widely understood.

Clamber into the back. It could be crowded (most drivers will either stop for nobody or everybody). It will be dusty. Chances are that you'll be rolling around with a couple of very sharp machetes, but with the wind in your hair and a spare tire as a seat, it's a fine way to see the countryside.

Some drivers expect you to pay. Most barely give you time to get out before they roar off. If you do want to offer something, the equivalent fare for the journey on a bus is a good guide.

Taxi

Except for in Belize City, you're never really going to need a taxi (unless you are incredibly drunk, lazy, or both). The towns just aren't that big. In Belize City, the fixed fare is US$2.50 in the daytime, within the city. At night, the price gets a bit more flexible (in an upwards direction). Offer what you think is fair, based on the day rates, and don't get too het up over a dollar's difference.

Yucatán Peninsula, Tabasco & Chiapas

Yucatán Peninsula, Tabasco & Chiapas

The Yucatán Peninsula and the states of Tabasco and Chiapas are some of the most exciting regions within the Mayan world. Dig this: the region as a whole boasts more (around 1400 more!) and bigger Mayan archaeological sites than Guatemala and Belize combined. Within Mexico itself, the area attracts more foreigners with its spectacular ruins, world-class resorts (did someone say Cancún?), white-sand beaches, premier diving sites and highland villages than nearly anywhere else.

When it comes to Mayan architecture, Bonampak, Chichén Itzá, Cobá, Palenque, Uxmal, Yaxchilán and other sites are equaled only by the great cities of Caracol in Belize, Tikal in Guatemala and Copán in Honduras. As for diving and snorkeling, well, simply float on the fact that the corral reefs of Cozumel have been one of the world's top dive destinations ever since Jacques Cousteau took them to television in 1961. That's without mentioning Isla Mujeres, Playa del Carmen and the bizarre inland cenotes (limestone sinkholes that make for some *triiiippy* diving).

Cancún is famed for its Caribbean location as much as its debauchery, and while it's the easiest place to fly into, you can escape (if you wish) to more tranquil resorts like Tulum and Isla Mujeres. Then wander into highland Chiapas for a break from the sea, and experience modern Mayan cultures, which are basically an extension of those found in Guatemala's highlands.

Don't forget the cities of Campeche, Mérida and Valladolid, which all have their particular charms and cultural attractions to keep you rejoicing in the fact that you *are* in Mexico.

YUCATÁN PENINSULA, TABASCO & CHIAPAS

FAST FACTS

- **Area** Yucatán Peninsula 181,300 sq km; Tabasco 25,338 sq km; Chiapas 74,211 sq km
- **Capital** Mexico City (not covered in this book)
- **Country Code** ☎ 52
- **Departure Tax** US$25 by air, free by land and sea
- **Languages** Spanish, Mayan languages
- **Money** Pesos (US$=M$11.49)
- **Phrases (slang)** *chela* (beer), *pachanga* (party), *chamaco/a* (guy/girl), *¿mande?* (what? as in 'come again?')
- **Population** 8.02 million (Yucatán Peninsula, Tabasco & Chiapas)
- **Visas** North American and most European citizens need only a valid passport

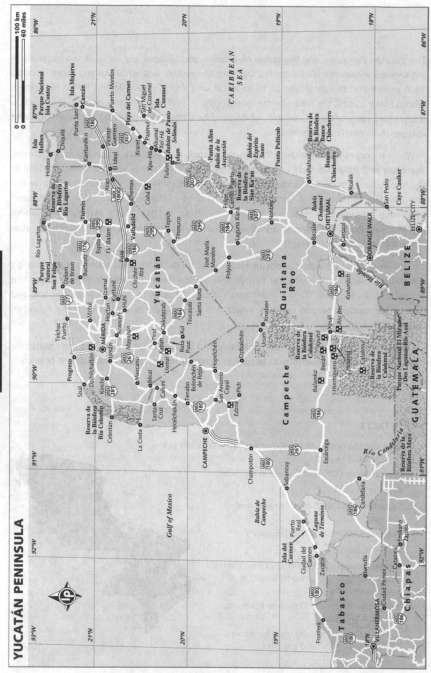

YUCATÁN PENINSULA

YUCATÁN PENINSULA, TABASCO & CHIAPAS

TABASCO & CHIAPAS

HIGHLIGHTS

- Dance the salsa with the locals on the streets of **Mérida** (p351) on any given Sunday afternoon.
- Admire **Palenque** (p408): wow, now that's a Maya site. Then again, **Chichén Itzá** (p368), **Cobá** (p345) and **Uxmal** (p358) are stunning too.
- Strap on ye ol' mask and flippers to play Jacques Cousteau in the coral reefs off **Cozumel** (p337), **Isla Mujeres** (p331) and **Playa del Carmen** (p339).
- Enjoy the tranquil highland atmosphere, Mayan culture and arts scene of colonial **San Cristóbal de Las Casas** (p392).
- Stray from the beaten track and head to remote rain forest lake of **Laguna Miramar**

(p405) where you'll wake to the morning chorus of howler monkeys.

ITINERARIES

- **Three days** Fly into Cancún, take a deep breath and head south (the same day) to Playa del Carmen or, even better, Tulum to log some serious hours on the beach. From Tulum, buzz over to the spectacular Maya site of Cobá for a day and return to Cancún for a night on the town before the next day's flight home (you will sleep better).
- **One week** Fly into Cancún or Mérida and hit the Maya sites of Chichén Itzá, Cobá and Uxmal. You'll still have time for a day on the Caribbean coast.

Two weeks Follow the one week itinerary, adding the San Cristóbal de Las Casas area and heading into Guatemala for a few days.

One month With this much time, you are really styled; visit all three countries (p19).

CLIMATE & WHEN TO GO

The Yucatán Peninsula and Tabasco state are *always* hot; temperatures often hit 40°C (104°F). From May to October, the rainy season creates humidity to boot. During the dry season (October to May), violent but brief storms called *nortes* can roll in any afternoon, their black clouds, high winds and torrents of rain followed within an hour by bright sun and utterly blue sky.

Mountainous central Chiapas can get lots of rain in summer, but at least it's cool at the higher altitudes. Around San Cristóbal de Las Casas, mornings and evenings are usually chilly (a thrill after the sticky heat of Palenque!) and the nights downright cold.

Tourist high season is roughly mid-December through March with a peak around Semana Santa (Easter week). During these times prices and crowd factors skyrocket everywhere except in Tabasco.

HISTORY
Yucatán Peninsula

Geographically removed from the heart of Mexico, the colonists of the Yucatán Peninsula participated little in Mexico's War

---

HOW MUCH?

- **Five-hour 1st-class bus ride** US$23
- **One-person hammock** US$15
- **Internet access per hour** US$1
- **Major archaeological site** US$4
- **Comfortable double room with bathroom** US$25-35

LP INDEX

- **Liter of gas (petrol)** US$0.60
- **1.5L of bottled water** US$0.80
- **Bottle of Bohemia** US$2
- **Souvenir T-shirt** US$8
- **Street taco** US$0.50-1

---

of Independence (1810–21). Even though the Yucatán joined liberated Mexico, the peninsula's long isolation gave it a strong sense of independence, and this Mayan region desired little subsequent interference from Mexico City.

Not long after gaining freedom from the Spanish (1821), the Yucatecan ruling classes were again dreaming of independence, this time from Mexico, and perhaps union with the USA. With these goals in mind, and in anticipation of an invasion from Mexico, the *hacendados* (landowners) made the mistake of arming and training their Maya peons as local militias. The Maya then boldly rebelled against their Yucatecan masters.

The War of the Castes began in 1847 in Valladolid, a city known for its particularly strict and oppressive laws. The Maya were forbidden to enjoy the main plaza or the prominent streets and had to keep to the backstreets and the outskirts. The Maya rebels quickly gained control of the city in an orgy of killing, looting and vengeance. Supplied with arms and ammunition by the British through Belize, they spread relentlessly across the peninsula.

In little more than a year the Maya revolutionaries had driven their oppressors from every part of the peninsula except Mérida and the walled city of Campeche. Seeing the whites' cause as hopeless, the region's governor was about to abandon Mérida when the rebels saw the annual appearance of the winged ant. In Mayan mythology, corn (the staff of life) must be planted at the first sighting of the winged ant. If the sowing is delayed, Chac, the rain god, will be affronted and respond with a drought. The rebels abandoned the attack and went home to plant the corn. This gave the whites and mestizos time to regroup and receive aid from their erstwhile adversary, the government in Mexico City.

The counterrevolution against the Maya was without quarter and vicious in the extreme. Between 1848 and 1855 the indigenous population of the Yucatán was halved. Some Maya combatants sought refuge in the jungles of southern Quintana Roo. There they were inspired to continue fighting by a religious leader working with a ventriloquist, who in 1850 at Chan Santa Cruz made a sacred cross 'talk' (the cross was an important Mayan religious symbol long before the coming of Christianity). The talking cross convinced them that their gods had made them invincible, and they continued to fight for decades.

The governments in Mexico City and Mérida largely ignored the Maya rebels of Chan Santa Cruz until the beginning of the 20th century, when Mexican troops with modern arms subdued the region. The shrine of the talking cross at Chan Santa Cruz was destroyed, and the town was renamed Felipe Carrillo Puerto in honor of a progressive Yucatecan governor, but the local Maya were allowed a good deal of autonomy. Nonetheless, resistance lasted into the 1920s. The Yucatán was declared a Mexican 'territory' only in 1936 and did not become a state until 1974. Today, if you travel to Felipe Carrillo Puerto (p347), you can visit the restored shrine of the talking cross above a cenote (limestone sinkhole) in what is now a city park.

Tabasco

La Venta, the second great Olmec center (after San Lorenzo, Veracruz) was in western Tabasco. Olmec religion, art, astronomy and architecture deeply influenced all later pre-Hispanic civilizations in Mexico. The Chontal Maya who followed the Olmecs built a great ceremonial city called Comalcalco in northwest Tabasco.

Hernán Cortés, who disembarked on the Tabasco coast in 1519, initially defeated the Maya and founded a settlement called Santa María de la Victoria. The Maya regrouped and offered stern resistance until they were defeated by Francisco de Montejo, around 1540. Later, pirate attacks forced the original settlement to be moved inland from the coast, and it was renamed Villahermosa de San Juan Bautista.

After Mexico won independence from Spain, various local land barons tried to assert their power over the area, causing considerable strife. The economy languished until after the Mexican Revolution (1910–20), when exports of cacao, bananas and coconuts started to increase.

In the 20th century, US and British petroleum companies discovered oil, and Tabasco's economy began to revolve around the resource. During the 1970s Villahermosa became an oil boomtown, and profits from agricultural exports added to the good times. This prosperity has brought a feeling of sophistication that cuts right through the tropical heat, stamping Tabasco as different from neighboring Chiapas and Campeche.

Chiapas

Chiapas' colonial history is quite distinct – for most of the Spanish era it was administered from Guatemala. Central Chiapas was brought under Spanish control by the 1528 expedition of Diego de Mazariegos, who defeated the dominant, warlike Chiapa people, many of whom jumped to their death in the Cañón del Sumidero rather than be captured. New diseases arrived with the Spaniards, and an epidemic in 1544 killed about half its indigenous people.

The remoteness of Chiapas from Guatemala meant there was little check on the excesses of the colonists against its native people. However, some church figures, particularly Bartolomé de Las Casas (1474–1566), the first bishop of Chiapas, did fight for indigenous rights.

A small military force under General Vicente Filísola managed to persuade Chiapas to join the Mexican union, which was approved by a referendum in 1824.

After the Mexican Revolution, a succession of governors appointed by Mexico City, along with local landowners, maintained an almost feudal control over Chiapas. Periodic uprisings and protests bore witness to bad governance, but the world took little notice until January 1, 1994, when the Zapatistas briefly occupied San Cristóbal de Las Casas and nearby towns by military force. Fighting for a fairer deal for indigenous peoples, the rebel army won widespread support, but few concessions. From remote jungle bases they campaigned for democratic change and indigenous rights, though Mexico's National Congress twice watered down progressive new legislation. (see p391).

THE CULTURE
The National Psyche

Mexicans will not easily be pinned down. They love fun, music and a fiesta, yet in many ways are deeply serious. They work hard but relax to the max in their time off. They're hospitable and warm to guests, yet are most truly themselves only within their family group. They will laugh at death, but have a profound vein of spirituality. You may read about anti-gringo sentiment in the media, but Mexicans will treat you, as a visitor to their country, as an individual and with refreshing warmth and courtesy. Ask for help or information and people will go out of their way to give it.

Geographically removed from the heart of Mexico, the Yucatán has always been culturally distinct from the rest of the country. It, along with Chiapas, is distinctly Mayan. Thanks to the continuation of their unique cultural identity, the Maya are proud without being arrogant, confident without the machismo seen so frequently elsewhere in Mexico, and kind without being servile. And, with the exception of those who have become jaded by the tourist hordes of Cancún, many Maya retain a sense of humor.

Lifestyle

Around three-quarters of Mexicans now live in cities and towns, and this percentage continues to increase as rural folk are sucked in by the hope of raising their standard of living. Most urban dwellers inhabit crowded, multi-generational family homes on tightly packed streets in built-up neighborhoods with few parks or open spaces.

More affluent neighborhoods in inner cities may have blocks of relatively spacious, well-provided apartments. In the wealthiest quarters, imposing detached houses with well-tended gardens and satellite dishes sit behind high walls with strong security gates.

Out in the villages, people often work the land and have homes comprising a yard surrounded by few separate small buildings for members of an extended family.

The contrasts between poor and rich couldn't be greater: while kids from rich families go out nightclubbing in flashy cars and attend private universities, poor villagers may dance only at village fiestas and be lucky to complete primary education.

Gender roles are relaxing among the middle class, with young women getting educations and jobs. Women now hold 41% of the country's professional and technical jobs.

Mexico is more broad-minded about sexuality than you might expect. Gays and lesbians tend to keep a low profile but rarely attract open discrimination or violence. Relatively open gay scenes exist in major

coastal resorts, such as Cancún. (See p426 for more information.)

Population

Over millennia, the Maya of the Yucatán and Chiapas have intermarried with neighboring peoples, especially those of central Mexico. During the 20th century they have also intermarried, to some degree, with the descendants of the conquering Spanish. People of mixed Mayan and Spanish blood are called mestizos. Most of Mexico's population is mestizo, but the Yucatán Peninsula has an especially high proportion of pure-blooded Maya. In many areas of the Yucatán and Chiapas, Mayan languages prevail over Spanish, or Spanish may not be spoken at all.

SPORTS

No sport ignites Mexicans' passions as much as *fútbol* (soccer). Attending a game is fun, and rivalry between opposing fans is generally good-humored. Mexico's national team, known as El Tri (short for Tricolor, the name for the national flag), reached the last 16 of the World Cup in 1994, 1998 and 2002.

Bullfighting, called the *corrida de toros* or *fiesta brava*, is another Mexican passion, though less widespread than soccer. Fights take place chiefly in the larger cities, often during local festivals.

THE BALL GAME, THEN & NOW

Probably all pre-Hispanic Mexican cultures played some version of the Mesoamerican ball game, the world's first-ever team sport. Over 500 ball courts have survived at archaeological sites around Mexico and Central America. The game seems to have been played between two teams, and its essence was apparently to keep a rubber ball off the ground by flicking it with hips, thighs and possibly knees or elbows. The vertical or sloping walls alongside the courts were probably part of the playing area. The game had, at least sometimes, a deep religious significance. It perhaps served as an oracle, with the result indicating which of two courses of action should be taken. Games could be followed by the sacrifice of one or more of the players – whether winners or losers, no one is sure.

Baseball is wildly popular throughout Mexico, including the Yucatán. The Mexican League season runs from April to early September, and among its teams are the Campeche Pirates, Cancún Langosteros (Lobstermen) and Yucatán Leones (Lions, of Mérida).

Mexico has produced many world champions in boxing, supreme among them being Julio César Chávez, who achieved an amazing 90 consecutive wins after turning pro in 1980, and won five world titles at three different weights. The highly popular *lucha libre* (wrestling) is more showbiz than sport.

RELIGION
Roman Catholicism
Nearly 90% of Mexicans profess Catholicism. The Mexican church's most binding symbol is Nuestra Señora de Guadalupe (www.interlupe.com.mx), the dark-skinned manifestation of the Virgin Mary who appeared to an Aztec potter, Juan Diego, on a hill near Mexico City in 1531. The Virgin of Guadalupe became a crucial link between Catholic and indigenous spirituality, and as Mexico grew into a mestizo society she became the most potent symbol of Mexican Catholicism. Today she is the country's patron, her blue-cloaked image is ubiquitous, and her name is invoked in religious ceremonies, political speeches and literature.

Around 7% of Mexicans profess other varieties of Christianity. Many have been converted since the 1970s by a wave of American Pentecostal, evangelical, Mormon, Jehovah's Witness and Seventh-Day Adventist missionaries. These churches have gained millions of converts, particularly among the rural and indigenous peoples of southeast Mexico, sometimes leading to serious strife with Catholics, notably in and around San Juan Chamula (p401) in Chiapas.

Indigenous Religions
As in Guatemala, the missionaries of the 16th and 17th centuries won the indigenous people over to Catholicism by grafting it onto pre-Hispanic religions. Often old gods were simply renamed as Christian saints, and the old festivals continued to be celebrated much as they had been in pre-Hispanic times, but on the nearest saint's day. Acceptance of the new religion was greatly helped by the appearance of the Virgin of Guadalupe in 1531.

Today, despite modern inroads into indigenous life, indigenous Christianity is still fused with more ancient beliefs. In some remote regions Christianity is only a veneer at most. Among peoples such as the Tzotzil in highland Chiapas, drunkenness is an almost sacred element at festival times.

ARTS
The arts and crafts scene in the Yucatán and Chiapas is enormously rich and varied. The influence of the Mayan or Spanish cultures (or both) appears in almost every facet of regional art, from dance and music to clothing such as *huipiles*, the colorfully embroidered white cotton tunic-dresses Mayan women have been wearing for centuries, and *panamás* (panama hats), which were being woven in the state of Campeche long before their famous namesake received worldwide acclaim as stylish and practical headgear for the tropics. The Tzotzil weavers of Chiapas are some of the most skilled and imaginative in Mexico.

Pre-Hispanic Art
Mexico's first civilization, the Olmecs of the Gulf Coast, produced remarkable stone sculptures, depicting deities, animals and wonderfully lifelike human forms. Most awesome are the huge Olmec heads – such as those at Parque-Museo La Venta (p384) in Villahermosa – that combine the features of human babies and jaguars.

The Classic Maya of southeast Mexico, at their cultural height from about AD 250 to 800, were perhaps ancient Mexico's most artistically gifted people. They left countless beautiful stone sculptures of complicated design but possessing an easily appreciable delicacy of touch. Subjects are typically rulers, deities and ceremonies. The Classic Veracruz civilization (about AD 400 to 900) left a wealth of pottery and stone sculpture.

Architecture
The ancient civilizations of Mexico produced some of the most spectacular, eye-pleasing architecture ever built. At sites such as Chichén Itzá and Uxmal you can still see fairly intact pre-Hispanic cities. Their spectacular ceremonial centers were designed to impress, with great stone pyramids, palaces

and ball courts. Pyramids usually functioned as the bases for small shrines on their summits.

There were many differences in style between Mexico's pre-Hispanic civilizations: while Teotihuacán, Monte Albán and Aztec buildings were relatively simple in design, intended to awe by their grand scale, Mayan architecture paid more attention to aesthetics, with intricately patterned facades, delicate 'combs' on temple roofs and sinuous carvings. Buildings at Mayan sites such as Uxmal, Chichén Itzá and Palenque are among the most beautiful examples. Most Mayan roofcombs, formed by gridlike arrangements of stone with multiple gaps, were originally taller than what remains of them today. The Maya's buildings are also characterized by the corbeled vault, their version of the arch: two stone walls leaning toward one another, nearly meeting at the top and surmounted by a capstone.

Music

Latin jazz, Caribbean reggae and English- and Spanish-language rock 'n' roll is often performed in the tourist haunts of Cancún, Mérida and Playa del Carmen, while the latest popular dance music fills the dance halls from Mérida to Chetumal. These days *música tropical*, including salsa, merengue, mambo and the galumphing *cumbia*, is quite the rage.

The deepest-rooted Mexican folk music is *son* (literally 'sound'), a broad term covering a range of country styles that grew out of the fusion of indigenous, Spanish and African musical cultures (but not related to the traditional Cuban style of the same name). *Son* is essentially guitars plus harp or violin, often played for a foot-stamping dance audience, with witty, frequently improvised lyrics. Particularly celebrated brands of Mexican *son* come from four areas of Mexico, one of them Veracruz. Called *son jarocho*, Veracruz *son* is particularly African-influenced. To hear traditional Yucatecan music you must attend one of the folkloric shows put on for tourists in Cancún, or a *vaquería* (traditional Yucatecan parties where couples dance in unison to a series of songs). *Vaquerías* are held every Monday night in front of Mérida's Palacio Municipal.

Jarana music is generally provided by an orchestra consisting of at least two trumpets, two trombones, violins, kettledrums and a guiro (a percussion instrument made out of a gourd that is played by rasping its rough surface with a drumstick). A *jarana* orchestra always ends its performances with the traditional *torito*, a vivacious song that evokes the fervor of a bullfight. If you're in Mérida for a *vaquería*, be sure to stay until the very end.

Dance

The Spanish influence on Mayan culture is quite evident in the *jarana*, a dance Yucatecans have been performing for centuries. In this dance, the men and women move separately, facing each other in two lines. At different stages of the *jarana*, the couples raise their arms and snap their fingers. The dancers move in precision to the music, with their torsos held rigid and a formal distance separating men from women.

Textiles

Women throughout the Yucatán traditionally wear straight, white cotton dresses called *huipiles*, the bodices of which are embroidered. These tunics generally fall just below the knee. *Huipiles* are never worn with a belt, which would defeat its airy, cool design. The *huipiles* of Chiapas are beautifully colorful, like in Guatemala.

In addition to *huipiles*, Mayan women throughout the Yucatán and Chiapas are known for weaving lovely sashes, shawls, tablecloths and napkins.

Wooden Crafts

In handicraft shops of the Yucatán and Tabasco, you'll come across beautiful wooden crafts, such as carved wooden panels and wooden galleons.

The ancient Maya made wooden carvings of their many gods, just as they carved the images of their deities in stone. The skill and techniques associated with the artistry survive to this day. The wooden panels are often a meter or more in height and feature a strange-looking character of unmistakably Mayan imagination – the image will resemble figures you've seen at Mayan ruins. If the carved image is one of a heavily adorned man raising a chalice, most likely you're looking at a representation of Itzamná, lord of the heavens; he's a popular figure on the wooden panels of contemporary Maya.

Mayans, impressed with the Spanish galleons that arrived on their shores, have been making wooden galleons for generations. Today, the galleons that used to haul cargoes of hardwood back to Europe are gone, but the craft of galleon model-making is alive and well in the Yucatán.

You can usually find carved wooden sailfish, turtles and parrots at the same craft shops where you find the lovely models of galleons. Campeche is the state most associated with such items, but they are made by artisans in the states of Yucatán and Quintana Roo as well.

ENVIRONMENT
The Land

The Mexican Mayan lands include cool pine-clad volcanic mountain country, hot and dry tropical forest, dense forest, broad grassy savannas and sweltering coastal plains.

YUCATÁN PENINSULA

The Yucatán Peninsula is one vast, flat limestone shelf rising only a few meters above sea level. The shelf extends outward from the shoreline for several kilometers under water. If you approach the peninsula or Belize by air, you should have no trouble seeing the barrier reef that marks the limit of the limestone shelf. It's the longest in the Northern Hemisphere, extending from southern Belize to Isla Mujeres off the northern coast of Quintana Roo.

The underwater shelf makes the coastline wonderful for aquatic sports, keeping the waters warm and the marine life (fish, crabs, lobsters, tourists) abundant.

The only anomaly in the flat terrain of the Yucatán Peninsula is the low range of the Puuc Hills, near Uxmal, which attain heights of several hundred meters.

Because of their geology, the northern and central portions of the peninsula have no aboveground rivers and very few lakes. The people there have traditionally drawn their fresh water from cenotes – limestone sinkholes that serve as natural cisterns. Rainwater, which falls between May and October, collects in the cenotes for use during the dry season. South of the Puuc Hills, in the Chenes region, there are few cenotes, and the inhabitants there traditionally have resorted to drawing water from limestone pools deep within the earth. These *chenes* (wells) give the region its name.

The peninsula is covered in a blanket of dry thorny forest, which the Maya have traditionally cleared to make space for planting crops and, more recently, pasturing cattle.

TABASCO & CHIAPAS

West of the peninsula along the Gulf Coast is the state of Tabasco – low, well-watered and humid country that is mostly covered in equatorial rain forest. The relative humidity in some places averages 78%. The lush rain forest is endangered by farmers and cattle ranchers who slash and burn it to make way for more crops and cattle. Besides its agricultural wealth, Tabasco is one of Mexico's most important regions of petroleum production.

Chiapas is a huge state comprising several distinct topographical areas. The northern part of the state is lowland with low hills similar to those of Tabasco, and is well watered and sparsely populated.

The central and south-central area is mountainous and volcanic, rising from several hundred meters in the west to more than 3900m in the southeast, near the Guatemalan border. Annual rainfall varies from less than 40cm at Tuxtla Gutiérrez, the state capital, to more than 200cm on the mountain slopes facing the Pacific Ocean. The high country around San Cristóbal de Las Casas is known locally as the *tierra fría* (cold country) because of its altitude and many cloudy days. The mountains in this area are covered in forests of oak and pine.

The Continental Divide follows the ridge of the Sierra Madre, which towers above the Pacific littoral. South and west of the ridge is the Pacific slope of the mountains. Rainfall along the coastal plain (which is known as the Soconusco) is abundant.

Wildlife

The dazzling sight and chilling roars of howler monkeys will likely be your most impressive experience with animals. If you make it out to Laguna Miramar (p405) in Chiapas, you'll surely hear (and probably even see) these magnificent creatures. They also inhabit the forests surrounding the temples of Yaxchilán (p415) and Bonampak (p414). Squirrel monkeys are also commonly spotted.

NATIONAL PARKS OF YUCATÁN

Protected Area	Features	Activities	Best Time to Visit	Page
Parque Marino Nacional Arrecifes de Cozumel	coral reefs, clear waters, awesome variety of marine life, beaches	diving, snorkeling	year-round	p335
Parque Nacional Cañón del Sumidero	800m-deep flooded canyon	boat trips, adventure sports	year-round	p391
Parque Nacional Lagunas de Montebello	temperate forest, 59 lakes, 2 archaeological zones	hiking, biking, swimming, camping	year-round	p417
Parque Nacional Tulum	seaside Maya ruins, spectacular beaches, cenotes	snorkeling, swimming, lounging	year-round	p343
Reserva de la Biósfera Banco Chinchorro	largest coral atoll in the Northern Hemisphere	diving, snorkeling	summer	p348
Reserva de la Biósfera Calakmul	rain forest with major Mayan ruins	visiting ruins, wildlife observation	year-round	p380
Reserva de la Biósfera El Triunfo	cloud forests, many rare birds incl resplendent quetzal	guided hiking & birding	Nov-Apr	p420
Reserva de la Biósfera Montes Azules	tropical jungle, lakes, rivers, jungle wildlife	hikes, kayaking, wildlife-watching	year-round	p405
Reserva de la Biósfera Ría Celestún	large flamingo colony	flamingo tours	Mar-Sep	p365
Reserva de la Biósfera Ría Lagartos	mangrove-lined estuary, largest flamingo colony in Mexico, sea turtles and crocodiles	wildlife tours	year-round; May-Sep for sea turtles	p374
Reserva de la Biósfera Sian Ka'an	Caribbean coastal jungle, wetlands & islands with incredibly diverse wildlife	snorkeling, bird-watching & nature tours, mostly by boat	year-round	p347
Reserva Ecológica Huitepec	oak woods and cloud forest, medicinal plants	self-guided or guided hikes	year-round	p401

In Quintana Roo, the Reserva de la Biósfera Sian Ka'an (p347) is home to howler monkeys, anteaters, foxes, ocelots, pumas, crocodiles, eagles, raccoons, tapirs, peccaries, giant land crabs and jaguars, as well as hundreds of bird species.

Speaking of birds, Yucatán state boasts two world-famous flamingo colonies: Celestún (p365) and Río Lagartos (p374). The latter is also a swimming ground for crocodiles.

The Caribbean coast is internationally famous for its diving and snorkeling, and the number of tropical fish you'll see (such as the bright yellow coney grouper, redband parrot fish, butterfly fish and yellow stingray) is truly staggering.

National Parks & Reserves

There are several national parks on the Yucatán Peninsula, some scarcely larger than the ancient Mayan cities they contain – Parque Nacional Tulum (p343) is a good example of this. National biosphere reserves covering thousands of hectares, surround Río Lagartos (p374), Celestún (p365) and Banco Chinchorro (p348). Even more impressive are the two vast Unesco-designated biosphere reserves: Reserva de la Biósfera Calakmul (p380) and Reserva de la Biósfera Sian Ka'an (p347).

In Chiapas, Parque Nacional Lagunas de Montebello (p417) comprises temperate forest along the Guatemalan border and is named for its 59 stunning lakes. The cloud forest setting of Reserva de la Biósfera El Triunfo (p420), also in Chiapas, will dazzle bird lovers and plant fanatics alike with its stunning array of birds, orchids, bromeliads and epiphytes. The Reserva Ecológica Huitepec (p401), near San Cristóbal de Las Casas, provides easy access to rare cloud forest. The remote rain forest reserve Reserva de la Biósfera Montes Azules (p405) protects Laguna Miramar, one of Mexico's most isolated and exquisite lakes.

Environmental Issues

Pollution, poaching, illegal traffic of rare species and the filling in of coastal areas for yet another resort are taking an enormous toll on the Yucatán's wildlife. However, the biggest killer of all is deforestation. Since 1960, more than five million hectares of forest have been felled in the Yucatán. The lives of all the plants and animals that depend on the forest have also passed to another world. Species on the peninsula that are threatened with extinction include five species of cat, four sea turtle species, the manatee, the tapir and hundreds of bird species, including the harpy eagle, the red flamingo and the jabiru stork.

FOOD & DRINK

Mexicans traditionally eat three meals each day. *Desayuno* (breakfast) hits the table sometime between about 7am and 10am. It consists of anything from coffee and *pan tostado* (toast) or *pan dulce* (delicious 'sweet breads') to the ever-present *huevos rancheros*, a large selection of omelettes filled with everything from squash blossoms to *chorizo* (a Mexican-style sausage). You will also find *chilaquiles*, a breakfast favorite made by heating red or green chili sauce with tortilla chips, and topping it with cheese and often a fried egg. They may be served *con pollo* (with chicken), which is usually shredded and mixed in. Tropical fruits, yogurt and granola are also popular for breakfast.

The *comida* (lunch) is the main meal of the day, and is usually eaten between about 1:30pm and 4pm. Along with their usual menu, restaurants often offer a *comida corrida* (set meal), which is usually a far better deal than the normal menu items. It usually consists of an appetizer; soup or salad; a main course of meat, poultry or seafood; rice and/or beans; and steaming hot tortillas. From the menu you'll usually encounter favorites including enchiladas (cheese, chicken or beef rolled in corn tortillas and smothered in red or green chili sauce) and *chiles rellenos* (mild, lightly battered chilies stuffed with cheese and covered in red sauce). A popular dish is *mole poblano*, a dark, rich sauce made with chilies, fruits, nuts, spices and chocolate! It's usually served with chicken.

Dessert can be anything from pastry or flan to fresh fruit.

The *cena* (supper) in Mexico usually consists of a light meal, perhaps some soup or a few tacos around 8pm or 9pm. Mexicans all have their favorite *taquería* (taco restaurant) or taco stand where they can grab a light bite in the evening. The varieties of tacos are endless; be sure to try as many as you can. Most restaurants are happy to serve the larger dinner that so many visitors desire, throughout the normal evening hours.

Yucatán Specialties

Because of the Yucatán's long-time isolation from the rest of Mexico, the peninsula's cuisine derived its own distinct character. The food, simply put, is divine. Sinking your teeth into Yucatecan favorites is one of the highlights of traveling the peninsula. Some of the classics include:

Achiote A paste ground from annatto seeds and mixed with lemon juice and spices.

Frijol con puerco Yucatecan-style pork and beans, topped with a sauce made with grilled tomatoes.

Huevos motuleños 'Eggs Motul style'; fried eggs atop a tortilla, garnished with beans, peas, chopped ham, sausage, grated cheese and a certain amount of spicy chili.

Papadzules Tortillas stuffed with chopped hard-boiled eggs and topped with a sauce made with squash or cucumber seeds.

Pavo relleno Slabs of turkey meat layered with chopped, spiced beef and pork and served in a rich, dark sauce.

Pibil Meat wrapped in banana leaves, flavored with *achiote*, garlic, sour orange, salt and pepper, traditionally baked in a barbecue pit called a *pib*; the two main varieties are *cochinita pibil* (suckling pig) and *pollo pibil* (chicken).

Poc-chuc Tender pork strips marinated in sour orange juice, grilled and served topped with pickled onions.

Puchero A stew of pork, chicken, carrots, squash, potatoes, plantains and chayote (vegetable pear), spiced with radish, fresh cilantro and sour orange.

Salbutes Yucatán's favorite snack: a handmade tortilla fried then topped with shredded turkey, onion and slices of avocado.

Sopa de lima 'Lime soup'; chicken broth with bits of shredded chicken, tortilla strips, lime juice and chopped lime.

Venado Venison, a popular traditional dish, might be served as a *pipián* (a dish made with a thick chili sauce), flavored with a sauce of ground squash seeds, wrapped in banana leaves and steamed.

QUINTANA ROO

The state of Quintana Roo, Mexico's only Caribbean real estate, stretches north from the border with Belize to the extreme northeastern tip of the Yucatán Peninsula. Its barrier reef – the world's second largest – runs almost this entire distance, ending at Isla Mujeres. This and the other reefs along the coast, all bathed in crystal-clear Caribbean waters teeming with tropical fish, provide a profusion of excellent diving and snorkeling sites that are ranked among the world's best. Quintana Roo is also home to several impressive Mayan ruins and to resorts of every size and flavor.

CANCÚN

☎ 998 / pop 457,000

Famous for its spring break debauchery, Cancún is Mexico's most visited resort. It was built from scratch on an idyllic, deserted sand spit just offshore from the little fishing village of Puerto Juárez, on the peninsula's eastern shore. It merits a day or two's exploration, if only to shake your groove thang in one of the discos until the sun comes up.

Orientation

Cancún is actually made up of two very distinct areas: the downtown area (Ciudad Cancún) and the hotel zone (Zona Hotelera). The two sections have little in common. Very few locals, except those who work in the service industry, spend time in the Zona Hotelera, and few tourists venture beyond the resorts to visit downtown.

On the mainland lies **Ciudad Cancún**, a planned city founded as the service center of the resort industry. The area of interest to tourists is referred to as *el centro* ('downtown').

Those who are content to trundle out to the beach by bus or taxi can save pots of money by staying downtown in one of the smaller, low- to medium-priced hotels, many of which have swimming pools.

The sandy spit of an island, Isla Cancún, is usually referred to as the **Zona Hotelera** (*so-na oh-te-le-ra*). Blvd Kukulcán, a four-lane divided avenue, leaves Ciudad Cancún and goes eastward out on the island for several kilometers, passing condominium developments, several moderately priced hotels, some expensive larger ones and several shopping complexes, to **Punta Cancún** (Cancún Point). At Punta Cancún it follows the island south before turning west back to the mainland.

Information

BOOKSTORES

Librería Dalí (Map p324; 2nd fl, Kukulcán Plaza) Thousands of books in Spanish and English.

Fama (Map p326; ☎ 884-56-86; Av Tulum 105) Great selection of international newspapers, magazines, and Mexican road maps and atlases.

EMERGENCY

Fire & Police (☎ 060)

Red Cross (☎ 884-16-16)

IMMIGRATION

Instituto Nacional de Migración (Map p326; ☎ 884-14-04; Av Náder at Av Uxmal) This office handles visa and tourist-card extensions.

INTERNET ACCESS

Vikings del Caribe (Map p326; Av Uxmal at Pino; per hr US$1.20) They also have good international phone rates.

YUCATÁN PENINSULA

The Yucatán Peninsula, comprising three Mexican states – Quintana Roo, Yucatán and Campeche – is unlike any area of Mexico. Isolated from the rest of the country for centuries, the region developed its own identity, its own cuisine, its own proud character. The still insular world of the Yucatán Peninsula is the world of the Maya. The majority of people living in the peninsula today are direct descendants of the great empire builders of the past and many preserve the customs of their ancestors, including language, dress and religion. Though Yucatecans are known for a certain reserve, you'll find that the warmth you extend is returned exponentially.

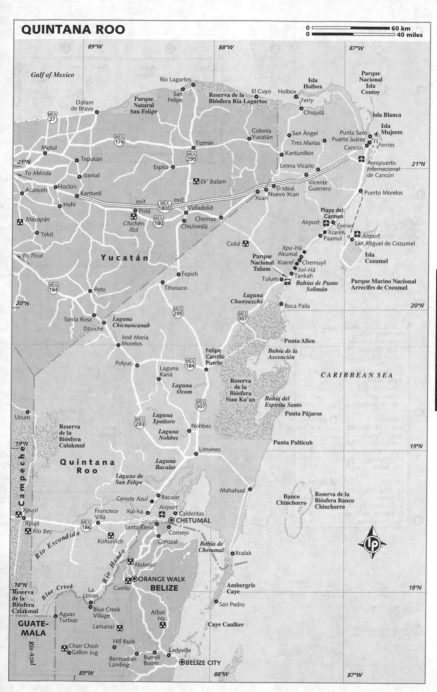

QUINTANA ROO

0 _____ 60 km
0 _____ 40 miles

Gulf of Mexico

Río Lagartos
San Felipe
Reserva de la Biósfera Ría Lagartos
El Cuyo
Holbox
Isla Holbox
Ferry
Chiquilá
Parque Nacional Isla Contoy

Dzilam de Bravo
MEX 27
Parque Natural San Felipe
Colonia Yucatán
San Ángel
Tres Marías
Punta Sam
Puerto Juárez
Cancún
Isla Blanca
Isla Mujeres
Ferries

Motul
Tepakán
Tizimín
MEX 176
MEX 295
Kantunilkin
Leona Vicario
Aeropuerto Internacional de Cancún

21°N
To Mérida
Izamal
Espita
Ek' Balam
Vicente Guerrero
Puerto Morelos
21°N

Acanceh
Hoctún
Kantunil
El Ideal
Nuevo Xcan
Xcan
Playa del Carmen

Huhí
exit
exit
MEX 180D
Valladolid
Airport
Xcaret
Ferries

Mayapán
Pisté
Chichén Itzá
MEX 180
Chemax
Chichimilá
Xcaret
Paamul
Airport
San Miguel de Cozumel

Tekit
Cobá
Parque Nacional Tulum
Xpu-Há
Akumal
Xcacel
Chemuyil
Xel-Há
Tankah
Isla Cozumel

Yucatán
Tepich
Tihosuco
Tulum
Bahías de Punto Solimán
Parque Marino Nacional Arrecifes de Cozumel

MEX 184
Peto
MEX 295
Laguna Chunyaxché
Boca Paila

20°N
Santa Rosa
Dzuiché
Laguna Chicancanab
MEX 307
Punta Allen
20°N

José María Morelos
Felipe Carrillo Puerto
Bahía de la Ascensión
CARIBBEAN SEA

Polyuc
Laguna Kaná
MEX 184
Reserva de la Biósfera Sian Ka'an
Bahía del Espíritu Santo

Laguna Ocom
MEX 307
Punta Pájaros

Ucum
MEX 293
Laguna Xpaitoro
Nohbec
Laguna Nohbec
Punta Pulticub

19°N
Reserva de la Biósfera Calakmul
Limones
19°N

Campeche
Quintana Roo
Laguna Bacalar

Laguna de San Felipe
Mahahual
Banco Chinchorro
Reserva de la Biósfera Banco Chinchorro

Cenote Azul
Bacalar
Xpujil
Francisco Villa
Xúl-ha
Airport
Calderitas

Xpujil
Río Bec
MEX 186
Santa Elena
CHETUMAL
Consejo

Kohunlich
Corozal
Bahía de Chetumal
Xcalak

18°N
Reserva de la Biósfera Calakmul
Nohmul
ORANGE WALK
BELIZE
Ambergris Caye
18°N

GUATE-MALA
La Unión
Cuello
Blue Creek
Blue Creek Village
Lamanai
Altun Ha
San Pedro

Aguas Turbias
Chan Chich
Gallon Jug
Hill Bank
Bermudian Landing
Burrell Boom
Caye Caulker

Río Azul
Ladyville
BELIZE CITY

CANCÚN

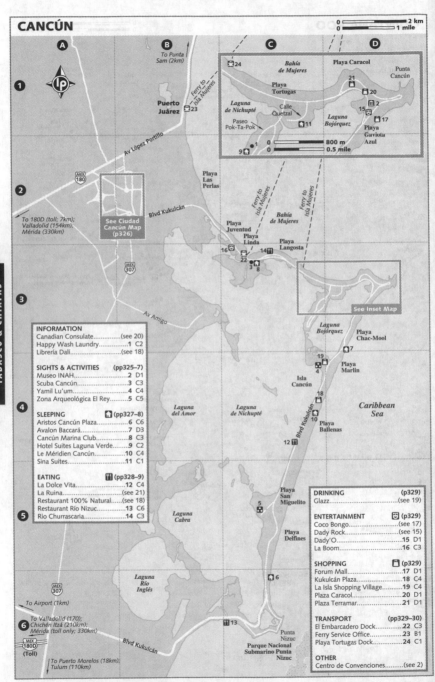

0 _____ 2 km
0 _____ 1 mile

A **B** **C** **D**

1

To Punta
Sam (2km)

**Puerto
Juárez**

23

*Bahía
de Mujeres*

24

*Playa
Tortugas*

Playa Caracol

21

Punta
Cancún

20

15 2

17

*Laguna
de Nichupté*

Calle
Quetzal

Paseo
Pok-Ta-Pok

11

*Laguna
Bojórquez*

*Playa
Gaviota
Azul*

9

0 _____ 800 m
0 _____ 0.5 mile

Av López Portillo

MEX
180

2

To 180D (toll; 7km);
Valladolid (154km);
Mérida (330km)

See Ciudad
Cancún Map
(p326)

Blvd Kukulcán

*Playa
Las
Perlas*

Ferry to
Isla Mujeres

Ferry to
Isla Mujeres

*Bahía
de Mujeres*

*Playa
Juventud*
*Playa
Linda*

*Playa
Langosta*

16

22
3 8

14

MEX
307

3

Av Amigo

*Laguna
Bojórquez*

*Playa
Chac-Mool*

See Inset Map

19

7

4

*Playa
Marlin*

**Isla
Cancún**

18

10

*Playa
Ballenas*

12

*Caribbean
Sea*

*Laguna
del Amor*

*Laguna
de Nichupté*

Blvd Kukulcán

4

*Playa
San
Miguelito*

5

*Playa
Delfines*

*Laguna
Cabra*

*Laguna
Río
Inglés*

MEX
307

To Airport (1km)

To Valladolid (170);
Chichén Itzá (210km);
Mérida (toll only; 330km)

MEX
180D
(Toll)

To Puerto Morelos (18km);
Tulum (110km)

Blvd Kukulcán

13

6

Punta
Nizuc

**Parque Nacional
Submarino Punta
Nizuc**

5

6

Soft Jazz (Map p326; ☎ 887-31-68; Av Tulum; per hr US$1.20)

LAUNDRY
Happy Wash Laundry (Map p326; Paseo Pok-Ta-Pok)
Lava y Seca (Map p326; Crisantemos 20)

MEDICAL SERVICES
Hospital Americano (Map p326; ☎ 884-61-33; Calle Viento 15; ☒ 24hr) Emergency service and English-speaking staff.

MONEY
The shopping malls in the Zona Hotelera all have major bank branches with money exchange services and ATMs (many of which dispense US dollars as well as pesos). ATMs are common downtown, and there are several banks on Av Tulum between Avs Cobá and Uxmal. (See map for some locations.) There are currency-exchange booths in the Mercado Municipal Ki-Huic. The best place to change money at the airport is the Bital bank just outside the domestic arrivals and departures area.

POST
Main Post Office (Map p326; cnr Avs Sunyaxchén & Xel-Ha)

TOURIST INFORMATION
Cancún Convention & Visitors Bureau (Map p326; ☎ 884-65-31; Av Cobá at Av Tulum; ☒ 9am-2pm & 4-7pm Mon-Fri)
State Tourist Office (Map p326; ☎ 884-80-73; Calle Pecari 23; ☒ 9am-9pm Mon-Fri)

Dangers & Annoyances
Cancún has a reputation for being safe, and the Zona Hotelera is particularly well policed and secure; however, it is always best not to leave valuables unattended in your hotel room or beside your beach towel.

Vehicular traffic on Blvd Kukulcán, particularly as it passes between the malls, bars and discotheques at Punta Cancún is a serious concern. Drivers (often drunk) hit pedestrians (often drunk) on a frighteningly regular basis.

Cancún's ambulance crews respond to as many as a dozen near-drownings per week. The most dangerous beaches seem to be Playa Delfines and Playa Chac-Mool.

Though the surf is usually gentle, undertows can be powerful, and sudden storms – called *nortes* – can blacken the sky and

sweep in at any time without warning. The local authorities have devised a system of colored pennants to warn beachgoers of potential dangers:
Blue Normal, safe conditions.
Yellow Use caution, changeable conditions.
Red Unsafe conditions; use a swimming pool instead.

Sights & Activities
MAYAN RUINS   Map p324
There are two sets of Mayan ruins in the Zona Hotelera, and though neither is particularly impressive, both are worth a look if time permits. In the **Zona Arqueológica El Rey** (admission US$3; ☒ 8am-5pm), on the west side of Blvd Kukulcán between Km 17 and Km 18, are a small temple and several ceremonial platforms. The other, much smaller, site is **Yamil Lu'um** (admission free), atop a beachside knoll on the parklike grounds separating the Sheraton Cancún and Pirámides Cancún towers. To reach the site visitors must pass through either of the hotels flanking it or approach it from the beach – there is no direct access from the boulevard.

MUSEO INAH   Map p324
This **archaeological museum** (☎ 883-03-05; admission US$3.50; ☒ 9am-8pm Tue-Fri, 10am-7pm Sat & Sun) is on the south side of the Centro de Convenciones in the Zona Hotelera. Most of the items – including jewelry, masks and intentionally deformed skulls – are from the Postclassic period (AD 1200–1500).

BEACHES   Map p324
Under Mexican law you have the right to walk and swim on every beach in the country except those within military compounds. In practice, it is difficult to approach many stretches of beach without walking through the lobby of a hotel, particularly in the Zona Hotelera. However, unless you look suspicious or unless you look like a local (the hotels tend to discriminate against locals, particularly the Maya), you'll usually be allowed through.

Starting from Ciudad Cancún in the northwest, all of Isla Cancún's beaches are on the left-hand side of the road (the lagoon is on your right). The first beaches are **Playa Las Perlas**, **Playa Juventud**, **Playa Linda**, **Playa Langosta**, **Playa Tortugas** and **Playa Caracol**; after rounding Punta Cancún, the beaches to the south offer wonderful views:

CIUDAD CANCÚN

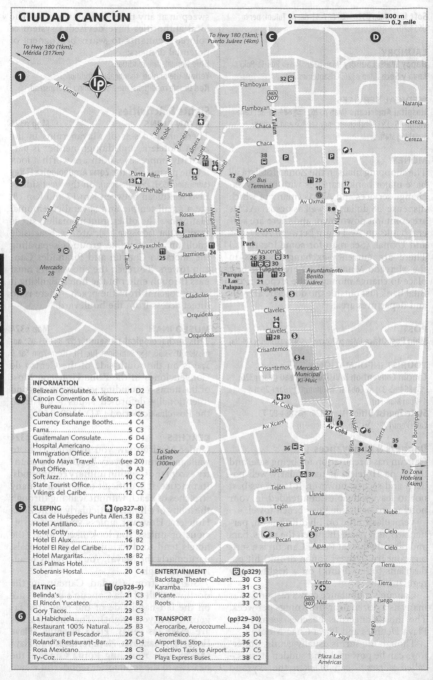

0 ———————— 300 m
0 ———————— 0.2 mile

A **B** **C** **D**

1

To Hwy 180 (1km);
Mérida (317km)

To Hwy 180 (1km);
Puerto Juárez (4km)

Av Uxmal

Flamboyan   32

Flamboyan

Naranja

Cereza

Cereza

Chaca
Chaca

38

19

Robbie
Robbie
Palmera
Palmera
Laurel
Laurel
Av Yaxchilán

Punta Allen
13
Nicchehabi

22
16
15
12 @ Pino
Bus
Terminal

P

P

1

29
10 @
Av Uxmal

17

8

Av Náder

2

Punta
Yoquen
Av Xel-Ha

Mercado
28

9

Rosas

Rosas
18

Margaritas
Margaritas

Azucenas

Av Sunyaxchén
Jazmines
Jazmines
25   24

Park
Azucenas
26 33
21   31
30
Tulipanes
23

5

Ayuntamiento
Benito
Juárez

Parque
Las
Palapas

Tulipanes

Claveles
14
Claveles
28

3

Tauch

Gladiolas

Gladiolas

Orquídeas

Orquídeas

Crisantemos

Crisantemos
4

Mercado
Municipal
Ki-Huic

20
Av Cobá

Av Xcaret

27
2
Av Cobá

Av Náder
6

Brisa
Sierra
Nube

35

Av Bonampak

To Sabor
Latino
(300m)

36
Av Tulim

Jaleb

Tejón

37

To Zona
Hotelera
(4km)

4

INFORMATION
Belizean Consulates...............1 D2
Cancún Convention & Visitors
  Bureau.............................2 D4
Cuban Consulate....................3 C5
Currency Exchange Booths....4 C4
Fama..................................5 C3
Guatemalan Consulate...........6 D4
Hospital Americano................7 C6
Immigration Office.................8 D2
Mundo Maya Travel.........(see 20)
Post Office..........................9 A3
Soft Jazz............................10 C2
State Tourist Office..............11 C5
Vikings del Caribe................12 C2

Tejón

Lluvia

Pecari
11
3
Pecari

Lluvia

Agua

Agua

Nube

Cielo

Cielo

5

SLEEPING   (pp327–8)
Casa de Huéspedes Punta Allen.13 D2
Hotel Antillano...................14 C3
Hotel Cotty.......................15 B2
Hotel El Alux.....................16 B2
Hotel El Rey del Caribe.........17 D2
Hotel Margaritas.................18 B2
Las Palmas Hotel.................19 B1
Soberanis Hostal.................20 C4

Viento

Viento
7
Mar

Tierra

Tierra

Fuego

6

EATING   (pp328–9)
Belinda's...........................21 C3
El Rincón Yucateco..............22 B2
Gory Tacos........................23 C3
La Habichuela.....................24 B3
Restaurant 100% Natural.......25 B3
Restaurant El Pescador.........26 B3
Rolandi's Restaurant-Bar......27 D4
Rosa Mexicano....................28 C3
Ty-Coz............................29 C2

ENTERTAINMENT   (p329)
Backstage Theater-Cabaret....30 C3
Karamba............................31 C3
Picante.............................32 C1
Roots...............................33 C3

TRANSPORT   (pp329–30)
Aerocaribe, Aerocozumel.......34 D4
Aeroméxico.......................35 D4
Airport Bus Stop..................36 C4
Colectivo Taxis to Airport.....37 C5
Playa Express Buses..............38 C2

Av Sayil

Plaza Las
Américas

Nube

Cielo

Cielo

Tierra

Tierra

Fuego

Fuego

Playa Gaviota Azul, **Playa Chac-Mool**, **Playa Marlin**, the long stretch of **Playa Ballenas** and, finally, at Km 17, **Playa Delfines**. Tortugas and Chac-Mool are popular spots, though rough waves can be a feature of the latter, and at the less-crowded Ballenas. Marlin is another one where you'll find some breathing room.

WATER SPORTS

For decent **snorkeling**, you need to travel to one of the nearby reefs. Resort hotels, travel agencies and various tour operators in the area can book you on day-cruise boats that take snorkelers to the barrier reef, as well as to other good sites within 100km of Cancún. To see the sparse aquatic life off Cancún's beaches, you can rent snorkeling equipment for about US$10 a day from most luxury hotels.

For a variety of dive options, try **Scuba Cancún** (Map p324; ☎ 849-75-08; www.scubacancun .com.mx; Blvd Kukulcán Km 5).

Cancún for Children

Couples usually come here before they have children or forget to bring them along once they do have them, but Cancún actually has a lot to offer kids – mainly the beach, sun and surf. The ocean playground here is endless and the waters are calm and shallow enough that even young children can be introduced to snorkeling.

Tours

Most hotels and travel agencies work with companies that offer tours to surrounding attractions. **Mundo Maya Travel** (Map p326; ☎ 884-45-64; www.mayaworld.com; Av Cobá 5) operates out of the lobby of Soberanis Hostal downtown. They offer professional tours at some of the lowest rates available.

Sleeping

Rates at most Cancún hotels change with the tourist seasons. Generally, Cancún's high season is from mid-December through March, with a peak during Semana Santa (Easter week). Prices quoted here are for high season unless specified. Bargain during low season.

If you're after a deluxe, all-inclusive resort experience, a little Internet research will yield huge results; most of the following hotels are independently owned.

> ### GAY & LESBIAN CANCÚN
>
> Cancún is well known for its lively gay and lesbian scene (though there's more for gay men than women), meaning there's plenty to do most nights. Here's but a pinch of what's out there.
>
> **Backstage Theater-Cabaret** (Map p326; ☎ 887-91-06; Tulipanes 30) Backstage features drag shows, strippers (male and female), fashion shows and musicals. Terrific ambiance, joyful crowd.
>
> **Karamba** (Map p326; ☎ 884-00-32; cnr Azucenas & Av Tulum; ☸ 10:30pm-6am Tue-Sun) Above the Ristorante Casa Italiana, this nightclub is popular among cross-dressers and lesbians, and famous for its frequent drink specials.
>
> **Picante** (Map p326; Plaza Galeria shopping mall) Picante is mainly for talkers, not dancers.

BUDGET   Map p326

All budget accommodations can be found downtown.

Soberanis Hostal (☎ 884-45-64, 800-101-01-01; www.soberanis.com.mx; Av Cobá 5; dm/d US$12/40; 🔀 🖳) The Soberanis is excellent value. All rooms have strong air-con, comfortable beds, tile floors and cable TV. It is primarily a hotel, with one four-bed dorm room available. Breakfast is included.

Casa de Huéspedes Punta Allen (☎ 884-02-25; www.puntaallen.da.ru; Punta Allen 8; d US$33-37; 🔀) The ample rooms at this family-run guesthouse have bathrooms and air-con. Breakfast is included.

Las Palmas Hotel (☎ 884-25-13; Palmera 43; d US$28; 🔀) Las Palmas has clean, cool rooms with comfy beds and TV. Good, cheap meals are also available.

Hotel El Alux (☎ 884-66-13; Av Uxmal 21; s/d US$28/37; 🔀) The Alux has 35 spacious (though slightly dark) air-conditioned rooms, each with hot shower, phone and TV.

MID-RANGE

'Mid-range' in Cancún is a two-tiered category; the downtown area is much cheaper than the Zona Hotelera and only a short bus ride away from the Zona's beaches.

Hotel El Rey del Caribe (Map p326; ☎ 884-20-28; www.reycaribe.com; cnr Avs Uxmal & Náder; s/d US$50/60; 🅿 🔀 🖳 ⊠) Do yourself and the environment a favor and stay at this oasis of calm in the heart of the city. El Rey is a true eco-tel that composts, uses solar collectors and cisterns, gardens with gray water and even has a few composting toilets. The 25 suites have fully equipped kitchenettes, good showers, comfy beds, cable TV and phones. There's a lush courtyard, a lovely small pool and a Jacuzzi. The shoes-off garden café serves healthy fruit-filled breakfasts and organic coffee.

Hotel Cotty (Map p326; ☎ 884-05-50; Av Uxmal 44; www.hotelcotty.com; s/d US$34/38; P ⊠) Each of the 38 rooms here has a shower, air-con, cable TV, phone and two comfortable double beds. Breakfast is included.

Hotel Antillano (Map p326; ☎ 884-11-32; www .hotelantillano.com; Claveles 1; d US$65; ⊠ ⊑) Just off Av Tulum near the bus terminal, this pleasant hotel has 48 light and airy guestrooms with comfortable beds, telephones and cable TV.

Hotel Margaritas (Map p326; ☎ 884-93-33; cnr Av Yaxchilán & Jazmines; d US$85; ⊠ ⊑) This cheerful, friendly hotel has 100 bright and clean guestrooms all with phones and cable TV. There is a sunny pool patio and very good restaurant/bar.

Aristos Cancún Plaza (Map p324; ☎ 885-33-33; www.aristoshotels.com; Blvd Kukulcán Km 20.5; r US$90; P ⊠ ⊑) Considering its beachfront location and amenities, this place offers among the best value of the Zona's moderately priced digs. All rooms have marble floors, cable TV and balconies with sea or lagoon views. The hotel also has a restaurant and two pools.

Hotel Suites Laguna Verde (Map p324; ☎ 883-34-14; http://hotel-suites-laguna-verde-cancun.world -hotel-network.com; Paseo Pok-Ta-Pok Km 1; d US$80; P ⊠ ⊑) The spacious, clean comfortable rooms are equipped with kitchenettes, dining tables and a couch. There's a good restaurant. Though the hotel is not on the beach, guests have access to the nearby Fat Tuesday beach club.

Sina Suites (Map p324; ☎ 883-10-17; Quetzal 33; ste US$106-143) Each of the 33 spacious suites here has a kitchen, 1.5 baths, two double beds, a separate living room (with a sofa bed) and satellite TV. Other amenities include a bar and restaurant.

Cancún Marina Club (Map p324; ☎ 849-49-99; Blvd Kukulcán Km 5.5; r US$110; P ⊠ ⊑) This popular hotel has a water-sports center, a very inviting pool and a pleasant restaurant-bar overlooking the lagoon.

TOP END   Map p324
The following resorts are located on the Caribbean coastline.

Avalon Baccará (☎ 883-20-77; www.avalonvacations .com; Blvd Kukulcán Km 11.5; r from US$185; P ⊠ ⊠ ⊑) This is Cancún's only boutique hotel and the only real choice for intimate accommodations on the beach. Each of the 34 rooms is beautifully decorated with Mexican furnishings, art and textiles, and each has a kitchenette, living room, dining area and balcony with Jacuzzi.

Le Méridien Cancún (☎ 881-22-00; US ☎ +1-800-543-4300; www.meridiencancun.com.mx; Blvd Kukulcán Km 14; r from US$365; P ⊠ ⊑ ⊑) This is one of the classiest hotels in Cancún and smaller (relatively) than the other cruise ship–sized resorts in the Zona Hotelera. Each room is warm and elegant and features a marble tiled bathroom with separate tub and walk-in shower. The onsite European spa offers an array of exotic treatments.

Eating

Downtown, rather than the Zona Hotelera, has the best selection of budget and mid-range eats. All chain hotels have upscale restaurants.

Belinda's (Map p326; Tulipanes 23; breakfast US$3-4, mains US$4-5) This friendly café is the place to go for a delicious big breakfast. The Yucatecan lunches and dinners are tasty too.

El Rincón Yucateco (Map p326; Av Uxmal 24; meals US$3.50) Across from the Hotel Cotty, this place serves excellent yet inexpensive Yucatecan food, with good *comidas corridas*.

Ty-Coz (Map p326; ☎ 884-60-60; Av Tulum; sandwiches US$3-4; ⊗ closed Sun) The specialties here are stuffed baguette or croissant sandwiches. The espresso drinks are good too.

La Ruina (Map p324; Plaza Terramar; mains US$6.25) Pop in here for delicious traditional Mexican food.

Restaurant Río Nizuc (Map p324; mains US$5-8) At the end of a short, nameless road near Blvd Kukulcán Km 22, this outdoor restaurant is a nice place to settle into a chair under a *palapa* (a palm-leaf–roofed shelter) and watch convoys of snorkelers pass by. Fresh octopus, conch and fish are served in various ways.

Rosa Mexicano (Map p326; ☎ 884-63-13; Claveles 4; mains from US$10) A long-standing favorite, this is the place to go for unusual Mexican dishes in a pleasant hacienda atmosphere. Try the squid sautéed with three chilies or the shrimp in a *pipián* sauce (made of ground pumpkin seeds and spices).

Restaurant El Pescador (Map p326; ☎ 884-26-73; Tulipanes 28; mains US$7-12) Many locals insist this is the best seafood place in town. Expect to wait for a table.

Rolandi's Restaurant-Bar (Map p326; ☎ 883-25-27; Av Cobá 12; mains US$7-10) This attractive Italian eatery, between Avs Tulum and Náder just off the southern roundabout, serves elaborate pizzas, spaghetti plates and more substantial dishes of veal and chicken.

Gory Tacos (Map p326; Tulipanes 26; mains US$4-8) Don't let the name spoil your appetite; this *taquería* serves excellent tacos, burgers and vegetarian meals.

Restaurant 100% Natural (Map p324 & p326; ☎ 884-36-17; Av Sunyaxchén; mains US$4-10; 🕭) This Mexican franchise serves good juices, baked goods, yogurt/fruit/vegetable combinations and pasta, fish and chicken dishes. There's another **branch** (☎ 885-29-04; Kukulcán Plaza, Paseo Kukulcán Km 13) in town.

Rio Churrascaria (Map p324; ☎ 849-90-40; Blvd Kukulcán Km 3.5; mains US$8-15; 🕭) This Brazilian-style grill serves fresh-off-the-skewer charcoal-grilled meat. There is also an extensive salad bar.

La Habichuela (Map p326; ☎ 884-31-58; Margaritas 25; mains US$12-30; 🕭) The dimly lit courtyard is full of romantic ambiance. The house specialty, *habichuela* (string bean) soup is excellent, as is the shrimp in tequila sauce. Save room for dessert.

La Dolce Vita (Map p324; ☎ 885-01-61; Blvd Kukulcán Km 14.8; mains US$12-30; 🅿 🕭) Overlooking the lagoon, this is one of Cancún's fanciest Italian restaurants.

Drinking & Entertainment

Much of the Zona Hotelera's nightlife is aimed toward a young crowd and is loud and booze-oriented (often with an MC urging women to display body parts). Most of the dance clubs charge around US$12 admission (some have open-bar nights for about US$25); some don't open their doors before 10pm, and few get hopping before midnight.

Coco Bongo (Map p324; ☎ 883-50-61; Forum Mall) is a favorite with spring breakers. (It is often a featured venue for MTV spring break coverage.) The party starts early here with live entertainment (celebrity impersonators, clowns, dancers) and continues all night.

Dady'O (Map p324; Blvd Kukulcán Km 9) Opposite the Forum mall, this is one of Cancún's hottest dance clubs. The setting is a five-level, black-walled faux cave with a two-level dance floor and zillions of laser beams and strobes.

La Boom (Map p324; Blvd Kukulcán Km 3.8) A varied and relatively sophisticated selection of danceable tunes are featured here, all played at mega decibels.

Sabor Latino (Map p326; ☎ 892-19-16; cnr Avs Xcaret & Tankah) Dance all night and into the morning at this ever-lively salsa club.

Roots (Map p326; ☎ 884-24-37; Tulipanes 26; 🕭 closed Sun) This relaxed venue features live jazz, reggae, salsa, rock and occasionally flamenco performers.

Also recommended:

Glazz (Map p324; La Isla Shopping Village) A sleek, hip cocktail lounge.

Dady Rock (Map p324; Blvd Kukulcán Km 3.8) A steamy rock 'n' roll club with live music.

Shopping

Bargains are few. For last-minute purchases before flying out of Cancún, try the **Mercado Municipal Ki-Huic** (Map p326; Av Tulum), north of Av Cobá, a warren of stalls and shops carrying a wide variety of souvenirs and handicrafts. It's 100% tourist trap, so even hard bargaining may not avail.

Getting There & Away
AIR

Cancún's international airport (Map p324; ☎ 886-00-49), about 8km south of the city center, is the busiest in southeastern Mexico.

Between Mexicana and its subsidiaries Aerocaribe and Aerocozumel there is at least one flight daily to each of the following: Mexico City (US$120), Oaxaca (US$180), Tuxtla Gutiérrez (US$225), Villahermosa (US$175) and Veracruz (US$217). The airlines have a total of two flights daily to Chetumal (US$145) and Mérida (US$115), as well as daily flights to Cozumel (US$75). They also fly twice daily to Havana, Cuba (US$290).

BOAT

Puerto Juárez (Map p324), the port for passenger ferries to Isla Mujeres, is about 3km north of the center. Punta Sam, the dock for the slower car ferries to Isla Mujeres, is about 7km north of the center. See p334 for details about getting to Isla Mujeres.

BUS

Cancún's bus terminal (Map p326) occupies the wedge where Avs Uxmal and Tulum meet. Services are 2nd-class, 1st-class and any of several luxury flavors. Across Pino from the bus terminal, a few doors from Av Tulum, is the ticket office and mini-terminal of **Playa Express** (Map p326; Pino), which runs shuttle buses down the Caribbean coast to Tulum and Felipe Carrillo Puerto at least every 30 minutes until early evening, stopping at major towns and points of interest along the way.

Following are some of the major routes serviced daily:

Chetumal (5½-6½hr; many buses, US$14-17)

Chichén Itzá (3-4hr; 1 Riviera bus at 9am, US$11; hourly Oriente buses 5am-5pm, US$7.50)

Felipe Carrillo Puerto (3½-4hr; 8 Riviera buses, US$11; hourly 2nd-class Mayab buses, US$9)

Mérida (4-6hr; 15 deluxe & 1st-class UNO, ADO GL & Super Expresso buses, US$20; hourly 2nd-class Oriente buses 5am-5pm, US$12)

Mexico City (Terminal Norte; 24hr; 1 1st-class ADO bus, US$80)

Mexico City (TAPO; 24hr; 1 1st-class ADO bus, US$80; 2 deluxe ADO GL, US$88)

Playa del Carmen (45min-1¼hr; 1st-class Riviera buses every 15min 5am-midnight, US$3.50; many 2nd-class buses, US$2.50)

Puerto Morelos (40min; Playa Express bus every 30min to 4:30pm, numerous others, US$1.50-2)

Ticul (6hr; 6 2nd-class Mayab buses, US$17)

Tizimín (3-4hr; 9 2nd-class Noreste & Mayab buses, US$7)

Tulum (2-2½hr; 7 1st-class Riviera buses, US$6; 2nd-class Playa Express, US$5, every 30min, numerous others)

Valladolid (2-3hr; many 1st-class ADO buses, US$8; 2nd-class Oriente buses, US$6)

Villahermosa (12hr; 11 1st-class buses, US$45)

CAR & MOTORCYCLE

Alamo (☎ 886-01-79), **Avis** (☎ 886-02-22), **Budget** (☎ 886-00-26), **Dollar** (☎ 886-01-79), **Hertz** (☎ 886-01-50) and **Thrifty** (☎ 886-03-93), among others, have counters (at the airport. You can often receive better rates if you reserve ahead of time.

Getting Around

TO/FROM THE AIRPORT

If you don't want to pay US$40 for a taxi ride into town, there are a few options. Comfortable shared vans charging US$9 per person leave from the curb in front of the international terminal about every 15 minutes. They

head into town after the island, but it can take up to 45 minutes to get downtown. If volume allows, however, they will separate passengers into downtown and Zona groups. To get downtown more directly and cheaply, exit the terminal and pass the parking lot to a smaller dirt lot between the Budget and Executive car rental agencies. There is a ticket booth there for buses (US$5) that leave the lot every 20 minutes or so between 5:30am and midnight. They travel up Av Tulum. One of the most central stops is across from the Chedraui supermarket on Av Cobá (confirm your stop with the driver as there are two Chedrauis in town). There is now bus service between the airport and the main bus terminal (US$1.50).

If you follow the access road out of the airport and past the traffic-monitoring booth (a total of about 300m), you can often flag down a taxi leaving the airport empty that will take you for US$5 to US$7.

To get to the airport you can catch the airport bus on Av Tulum just south of Av Cobá, outside the Es 3 Café, or a colectivo taxi from the stand in the parking area a few doors south. These operate between 6am and 9pm, charge US$3 per person and leave when full. The official rate for private taxis from town is US$15.

Riviera runs 11 express 1st-class buses from the airport to Playa del Carmen (p339) between 7am and 7:30pm (45 minutes to one hour, US$7.25). Tickets are sold at a counter in the international section of the airport.

BUS

To reach the Zona Hotelera from downtown, catch any bus with 'R1,' 'Hoteles' or 'Zona Hotelera' displayed on the windshield as it travels south along Av Tulum or east along Av Cobá. The fare each way is US$0.60.

To reach Puerto Juárez or Punta Sam and the Isla Mujeres ferries, catch a Ruta 13 ('Pto Juárez' or 'Punta Sam', US$0.40) bus at the stop in front of Cinemas Tulum, on Av Tulum north of Av Uxmal.

TAXI

Cancún's taxis do not have meters. There is a sign listing official fares on the northeast outside wall of the bus terminal; if you can't refer to it you'll probably have to haggle. From downtown to Punta Cancún is US$8, to Puerto Juárez US$3.

ISLA MUJERES

☎ 998 / pop 12,000

Isla Mujeres (Island of Women) has a reputation as a backpackers' Cancún. Though not as true today (thanks to the boatloads of tourists arriving on day trips from Cancún), Isla Mujeres continues to offer good value, a popular sunbathing beach and plenty of dive and snorkel sites in its warm, Windex-blue waters.

Orientation

The island is 8km long, 300m to 800m wide and 11km off the coast. The town of Isla Mujeres is at the island's northern tip, and the ruins of a Mayan temple are at the southern tip; the two are linked by Av Rueda Medina, a loop road that hugs the coast. Between them are a handful of small fishing villages, several saltwater lakes, a string of westward-facing beaches, a large lagoon and a small airport.

The best snorkeling sites and some of the best swimming beaches are on the island's southwest shore; the eastern shore is washed by the open sea, and the surf there is dangerous. The ferry docks, the town and the most popular sand beach (Playa Norte) are at the northern tip of the island.

Information

Cosmic Cosas (Matamoros 82, just north of Hidalgo; 🖳) Buys, sells and trades mostly English-language books. You can also check your email here for US$1.50 per hour.

Lavandería Automática Tim Phó (Juárez at Abasolo) Wash, dry and fold 3kg of laundry for about US$3.

Medical Center (Av Guerrero btwn Madero & Morelos)

Post Office (Guerrero at López Mateos)

Tourist Information Office (☎ 877-07-67; Av Rueda Medina btwn Madero & Morelos; 🕙 8am-8pm Mon-Fri, 9am-2pm Sat & Sun)

There are several banks within a couple of blocks of the ferry dock; most exchange currency and have ATMs.

Sights & Activities

TORTUGRANJA (TURTLE FARM)

Three species of sea turtle lay eggs in the sand along the island's calm western shore. Although they are endangered, sea turtles are still killed throughout Latin America for their eggs and meat, considered a delicacy. In the 1980s efforts by a local fisherman led to the founding of the **Isla Mujeres Tor-**tugranja (☎ 877-05-95; Carr Sac Bajo Km 5; admission US$2; 🕙 9am-5pm), which protects the turtles' breeding grounds and places wire cages around their eggs to protect against predators. The main draw here is several hundred sea turtles, ranging in weight from 150g to more than 300kg. Tours are available in Spanish and English. The facility is easily reached by taxi (about US$3). If you're driving, biking or walking, bear right at the unsigned 'Y' south of town.

MAYAN RUINS

At the south end of the island lie the severely worn remains of a temple dedicated chiefly to Ixchel, Mayan goddess of the moon and fertility. Francisco Hernández de Córdoba's expedition came upon this temple in 1517. The conquistadors found various clay female figures here; whether they were all likenesses of Ixchel or represented several goddesses is unclear. The ruins are beyond the lighthouse, just past Playa Garrafón. From downtown, a taxi costs about US$5.

BEACHES

Walk west along Calle Hidalgo or Guerrero to reach the town's principal beach, **Playa Norte**, sometimes called Playa Los Cocos or Cocoteros. The slope of the beach is gradual, and the transparent and calm waters are only chest-high even far from shore. Playa Norte is well supplied with bar/restaurants and can get crowded at times.

About 5km south of town is **Playa Lancheros**, the southernmost point served by local buses. The beach is less attractive than Playa Norte, but it sometimes has free musical festivities on Sunday. A taxi ride to Lancheros is US$2.

Another 1.5km south of Lancheros is **Playa Garrafón**, with translucent waters, colorful fish and little sand. Unfortunately the reef here has been heavily damaged by hurricanes and careless visitors. The water can be very choppy, sweeping you into jagged areas, so it's best to stay near the shore.

DIVING & SNORKELING

Within a short boat ride of the island are a handful of lovely reef dives, such as Barracuda, La Bandera, El Jigueo and Manchones. A popular nonreef dive is the one to a sunken cargo ship resting in 30m of

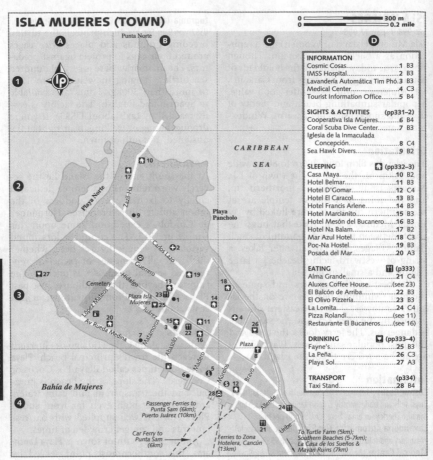

ISLA MUJERES (TOWN)

water 90 minutes by boat northeast of Isla Mujeres.

At all the reputable dive centers you need to show your certification card and you will be expected to have your own gear, though any piece of scuba equipment is usually available for rent. One reliable shop is **Coral Scuba Dive Center** (☎ 877-07-63; www.coralscubadivecenter.com; cnr Matamoros & Av Rueda Medina). They offer dives for US$30 to US$100 and snorkel trips for US$15. Another reliable place is friendly **Sea Hawk Divers** (☎ 877-02-96; abarran@prodigy.net.mx; Carlos Lazo).

The fishermen of Isla Mujeres have formed a cooperative that offers snorkeling tours of various sites from US$14. Book through their office, **Cooperativa Isla Mujeres** (☎ 877-02-74; Av Rueda Medina) in a *palapa* just steps away from the dock.

Sleeping
Prices here are the high season, when places book solid by midday (earlier during Semana Santa).

BUDGET
Poc-Na Hostel (☎ 877-00-90; www.pocna.com; cnr Matamoros & Carlos Lazo; campsites US$6.50, dm US$9-12.50, d US$26-36; ✗ 🖳) Located on 100m of beachfront property, this is the Club Med of hostels. There is a full beach restaurant/bar and a big, bright, airy *palapa*-roofed communal space, plus a billiard and game

room. Breakfast is included. Tents are provided for those who want to camp. Lots of extras.

Hotel El Caracol (☎ 877-01-50; Matamoros btwn Hidalgo & Guerrero; d with fan/air-con US$25/35; 🔲) El Caracol offers 18 clean, well-furnished rooms with insect screens and tiled bathrooms.

Hotel Marcianito (☎ 877-01-11, Abasolo 10; r US$30-35) The 'Little Martian' is a neat, tidy hotel offering 13 comfortably furnished, fan-cooled rooms.

Hotel D'Gomar (☎ 877-05-41; Av Rueda Medina btwn Morelos & Bravo; d with fan/air-con US$35/45; 🔲) A friendly place facing the ferry dock, the D'Gomar has four floors of attractive, amply sized rooms with double beds, air-con and large tiled bathrooms.

MID-RANGE
Casa Maya (☎ 877-00-45; www.kasamaya.com.mx; Calle Zazil-Ha 129; d from US$60; 🔲) This cheerful place has rooms and cabañas of different sizes and configurations (some with air-con, some with fans), but all are clean and comfortable and most are bright and breezy. Best of all is the location on Playa Secreto lagoon.

Hotel Mesón del Bucanero (☎ 877-02-10; www .bucaneros.com; Hidalgo btwn Abasolo & Madero; d US$30-75; 🔲) Above Restaurante El Bucanero, the charming rooms (most with air-con) all have TV and come with various combinations of beds, balcony, tub and fridge.

Hotel Francis Arlene (☎ 877-03-10; Guerrero 7; r with fan/air-con US$45/50; 🔲) This homey hotel offers good-sized, comfortable rooms with fan and fridge. Rooms have balconies, many with sea views.

Hotel Belmar (☎ 877-04-30; Hidalgo btwn Abasolo & Madero; d US$55-95; 🔲) All rooms are comfy and well kept and have cable TV and good air-con.

Mar Azul Hotel (☎ 877-01-20; Madero; d US$60; 🔲 🔳) A block north of Guerrero right on the eastern beach, this hotel has a restaurant and 91 nice, sizable rooms on three floors. All have balconies and most have wonderful sea views.

Posada del Mar (☎ 877-00-44; Av Rueda Medina 15; d US$70-85; 🔲 🔳) One of the island's first inns, Posada del Mar is simple, quiet and comfortable and just a block from the beach. The rooms in the main building have sea views and air-con.

TOP END
Hotel Na Balam (☎ 877-02-79; www.nabalam.com; Calle Zazil-Ha; r from US$170; 🔲 🖳) This hotel is situated on an ideal section of Playa Norte near the northern tip of the island. Most of the accommodations face the beach, while a few other thatched-roof units are located across the street surrounding a garden with pool. All have terraces or balconies with hammocks. The hotel offers yoga and meditation classes, two bars and an acclaimed restaurant.

La Casa de los Sueños (☎ 877-06-51; www.casa delossuenosresort.com; Carr El Garrafón; d US$110-275; 🔲 ⊠) The nine-room 'Dream House' is pretty much that. This secluded B&B is nestled away on the south end of the island atop a bluff overlooking Bahía de Mujeres. The terraced rooms have breathtaking views. Most spectacular is the cliffside pool, which appears to seamlessly merge with the sea. Breakfast is included.

Eating
Most places to eat on the island are casual and relatively inexpensive, and the seafood of course is fresh and delicious.

Alma Grande (Av Rueda Medina btwn Allende & Uribe; mains US$6-8) The Alma is a tiny, colorfully painted shack dishing up delicious seafood cocktails, ceviche and seafood soups.

La Lomita (Juárez btwn Allende & Uribe; mains US$4-6) 'The Little Hill' serves good, inexpensive Mexican food. Seafood and chicken dishes predominate.

El Balcón de Arriba (Hidalgo at Abasolo; mains US$5-9) Airy, casual 2nd-floor eatery popular with tourists.

Restaurante El Bucaneros (☎ 877-01-26; Hidalgo btwn Abasolo & Madero; mains US$3-12) El Bucaneros serves a variety of alcoholic and nonalcoholic tropical shakes and drinks. For food the best deal is the US$7 *menú ejecutivo* (daily special).

Aluxes Coffee House (Matamoros btwn Guerrero & Hidalgo; sandwiches US$4-5) Friendly Aluxes serves bagels with cream cheese, croissants, muffins, sandwiches and espresso drinks.

Both **El Olivo Pizzería** (Matamoros btwn Guerrero & Hidalgo; pizza slices US$1.50) and **Pizza Rolandi** (Hidalgo btwn Abasolo & Madero, mains US$7-10, pizzas US$6-10) serve good pizza.

Drinking
Fayne's (Hidalgo at Matamoros) features live reggae, salsa and lots of dancing. The English-

run **La Peña** (Guerrero btwn Morelos & Bravo) has a fun atmosphere and great music.

Hotel Na Balam (Calle Zazil-Ha) boasts a popular beach bar and dancing, while **Playa Sol** (Playa Norte) is a happening spot, day and night.

Getting There & Away

There are five main points of embarkation to reach Isla Mujeres. The following description starts from the northernmost port and progresses southeast. (See the Cancún map, p324.)

Punta Sam, located about 8km north of central Cancún, provides the only vehicle-carrying service to Isla Mujeres. The car ferries, which also carry passengers, take about an hour to reach the island. There are five departures daily in both directions. Walk-ons and vehicle passengers pay US$1.50; cars cost US$19 and bicycles US$6, one-way.

About 4km north of central Cancún is **Puerto Juárez**, from which express boats head to Isla Mujeres every 30 minutes from 6am to 8pm (US$4 one-way, 25 minutes), with a final departure at 9pm. Slower boats (US$2 one-way, 45 minutes) run roughly every hour from 5am to 5:30pm.

From **El Embarcadero** a shuttle departs at Playa Linda in the Zona Hotelera approximately five times daily between 9:30am and 4:15pm, returning from Isla Mujeres at 12:30pm, 3:30pm and 5:15pm. Non-express ferries take 40 minutes to one hour to reach the island. The roundtrip fare is US$15 and includes soft drinks on board. Show up at the terminal at least 20 minutes before departure so you'll have time to buy your ticket and get a good seat on the boat. It's the beige building between the Costa Real Hotel and the channel, on the mainland side of the bridge (Blvd Kukulcán Km 4).

The **Isla Shuttle** (Playa Tortugas) leaves the Zona Hotelera from the dock near Fat Tuesday's on Playa Tortugas beach (Blvd Kukulcán Km 6.35) at 9:15am, 11:30am, 1:45pm and 3:45pm, returning from Isla Mujeres at 10:15am, 12:30pm, 3:30pm and 6:30pm. The fare is US$9 one-way. Non-express ferries take 40 to 60 minutes to reach the island.

Getting Around
BUS & TAXI

By local (and infrequent) bus from the market or dock, you can get within 1.5km of Playa Garrafón; the terminus is Playa

Lancheros. Unless you're pinching pennies, you're better off taking a taxi – the most expensive one-way trip on the island is under US$4.

SCOOTER & BICYCLE

If you rent a scooter or 50cc Honda 'moped,' shop around for the best deal and best machine. The cost per hour is usually US$8 with a two-hour minimum, or US$28 all day. Shops away from the busiest streets tend to have better prices. Try a golf cart if you dare.

Cycling is an excellent way to get around the island. A number of shops rent out bicycles for about US$2/7 per hour/day; most will ask for a deposit of about US$10.

PARQUE NACIONAL ISLA CONTOY

From Isla Mujeres it's possible to take an excursion by boat to tiny, uninhabited Isla Contoy, a national park and bird sanctuary 25km north. There is good snorkeling both en route to and just off Contoy, which sees about 1500 visitors a month. Bring mosquito repellent. Daily visits to Isla Contoy are offered by the **Cooperativa Isla Mujeres** (☎ 877-02-74; Av Rueda Medina; US$40).

ISLA HOLBOX
☎ 984 / pop 1600

Isla Holbox (hol-*bosh*) is a pristine beach site not yet overwhelmed by foreigners, though guesthouses and hotels (mostly Italian- and Majorcan-owned) are going up at a rapid pace. The island has seemingly endless beaches, tranquil waters and a galaxy of shells in various shapes and colors.

From April to October over 400,000 flamingoes visit the island. Dolphins are a common sight year-round and during the summer months enormous, gentle whale sharks swim the waters here. Bring repellent and be prepared to stay inside for a couple of hours each evening.

The town of Holbox has sand streets and few vehicles. Everything is within walking distance of the central plaza ('el Parque') and locals will graciously direct visitors. There are no banks on the island and few places accept credit cards.

Sleeping & Eating

From budget to top end, Holbox offers a variety of accommodations. Rates given here are for high season.

Note: some of the hotels pay taxi drivers to bring guests to them; don't let a driver's suggestion on where to stay sway you.

Posada Los Arcos (☎ 875-20-43; Juárez; d with fan/air-con US$20/30; ✜) This is the best budget option in town.

Posada d'Ingrid (☎ 875-20-70; d with fan/air-con US$25/35; ✜) All rooms have hot water and TV. Good value.

The following accommodations (all sans air-con) are located on the beach.

Hotelito Casa Las Tortugas (☎ 875-21-19; www.holboxcasalastortugas.com; d US$45) Nestled between palms and flourishing bougainvillea, these lovely *palapa* units are bright, airy and clean. Some units have kitchenettes. There is a small café and a great shared common space with expansive sea views.

Resort Xaloc (☎ 875-21-60; www.holbox-xaloc resort.com; d US$120; ✚) This intimate eco-resort comprises 18 individual palm-roofed cabañas. Each is rustic and romantic, and all have porches with hammocks. There are two swimming pools, a restaurant and bar, plus a small library and games room. Breakfast is included.

Villas Chimay (☎ 875-22-20; www.holbox.info/; d US$75) This Swiss-owned eco-getaway is located 1km west of town on a secluded section of beach. There are seven cheery *palapa*-topped bungalows and a good bar/restaurant.

Villas Delfines (☎ 884-86-06; www.holbox.com; d US$100) This charming place is an eco-tel that composts waste, catches rainwater and uses solar power. Its large beach bungalows are built on stilts, fully screened and fan-cooled. Meal plans are available.

The specialty on the island is seafood in general and lobster in particular. Most restaurants are around the plaza. The restaurants in the beach hotels tend to be good but pricey; an exception is the restaurant at **Hotel Faro Viejo**, which has a good menu and a prime right-on-the-beach location.

Getting There & Away

A launch ferries passengers (US$3.50, 25 minutes) to Holbox from the mainland port village of Chiquilá eight times a day from 5am to 6pm in winter, and 6am to 7pm in summer. Three 2nd-class buses (two Mayab, one Noreste) leave Cancún daily for Chiquilá (US$6, 3½ hours) at 8am, 12:30pm and 1:45pm. There are also Oriente buses from

Valladolid (US$6, 2½ hours) at 1:30pm. Another way to go is to take a 2nd-class bus traveling between Mérida and Cancún to El Ideal, on Hwy 180 about 73km south of Chiquilá. From there you can take a cab (about US$20) or catch one of the Chiquilá-bound buses coming from Cancún, which pass through El Ideal at around 10:30am and 3:30pm. All schedules are subject to change; verify ahead of time.

If you're driving, you can either park your car in Chiquilá (US$2.50 per day) or try to catch the infrequent car ferry to Holbox. It doesn't run on a daily schedule, and you won't have much use for a car once you arrive.

COZUMEL

☎ 987 / pop 70,000

Cozumel, 71km south of Cancún, is a teardrop-shaped coral island ringed by crystalline waters. Lying within the **Parque Marino Nacional Arrecifes de Cozumel**, it is Mexico's only Caribbean island and, measuring 53km by 14km, it is also the country's largest. Called Ah-Cuzamil-Peten (Island of Swallows) by its earliest inhabitants, Cozumel has been a favorite destination for divers since 1961, when a Jacques Cousteau documentary on its glorious reefs first appeared on TV. Today, no fewer than 100 world-class dive sites have been identified within 5km of Cozumel, and no fewer than a dozen of them are shallow enough for snorkeling.

Mayan settlement here dates from AD 300. During the Postclassic period, Cozumel flourished as a trade center and, more importantly, a ceremonial site. Every Maya woman on the Yucatán Peninsula and beyond was expected to make at least one pilgrimage here to pay tribute to Ixchel, the goddess of fertility and the moon, at a temple erected in her honor at San Gervasio, near the center of the island.

It is easy to make your way on foot around the island's only town, San Miguel de Cozumel.

Information

Centro Médico de Cozumel (☎ 872-35-45; cnr Calle 1 Sur & Av 50 Nte) Medical Center.

Express Lavandería (Calle Dr Adolfo Rosado Salas btwn Avs 5 & 10 Sur; US$6) Laundry.

Fama (Av 5 Nte btwn Av Juárez & Calle 2 Nte) Bookstore with books in English and Spanish.

YUCATÁN PENINSULA, TABASCO & CHIAPAS

SAN MIGUEL DE COZUMEL

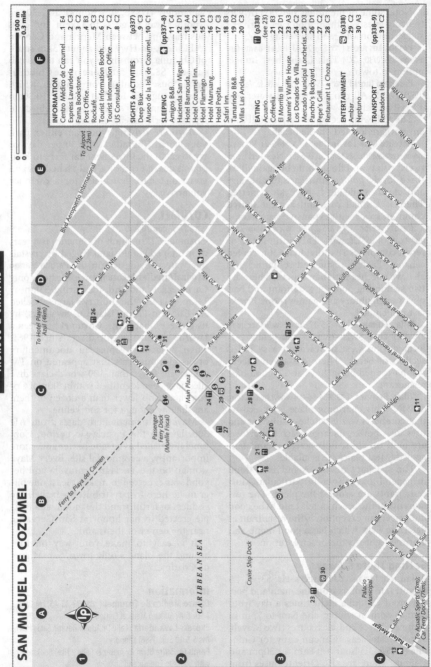

INFORMATION
Centro Médico de Cozumel.........1 E4
Express Lavandería......................2 C3
Fama Bookstore...........................3 C2
Post Office...................................4 B3
Rockafé..5 C3
Tourist Information Booth............6 C2
Tourist Information Office............7 C2
US Consulate................................8 C2

SIGHTS & ACTIVITIES   (p337)
Deep Blue....................................9 C3
Museo de la Isla de Cozumel.....10 C1

SLEEPING   (pp337-8)
Amigos B&B................................11 C4
Hacienda San Miguel.................12 D1
Hotel Barracuda.........................13 A4
Hotel Cozumel Inn......................14 C2
Hotel Flamingo...........................15 D1
Hotel Marruang..........................16 C3
Hotel Pepita...............................17 C3
Safari Inn....................................18 B3
Tamarindo B&B...........................19 D2
Villas Las Anclas........................20 C3

EATING   (p338)
Acuario...................................(see 23)
Coffeelia....................................21 B3
El Morrito III...............................22 D1
Jeannie's Waffle House...............23 A3
Los Dorados de Villa..................24 C2
Mercado Municipal Loncherías...25 D3
Pancho's Backyard.....................26 D1
Pepe's Grill................................27 C3
Restaurant La Choza..................28 C3

ENTERTAINMENT   (p338)
Ambar..29 C2
Neptuno.....................................30 A3

TRANSPORT   (pp338-9)
Rentadora Isis............................31 C2

Post Office (Calle 7 Sur at Av Melgar)
Rockafé (Calle Dr Adolfo Rosado Salas btwn Avs 15 & 20 Sur; per hr US$2) Internet access.
Tourist Information Booth (ferry dock; ⊗ 8am-4pm Mon-Sat)
Tourist Information Office (☎ 872-75-63; Plaza del Sol, main plaza; ⊗ 9am-3pm Mon-Fri)
Tourist Police Kiosk (main plaza; ⊗ 9am-11:30pm)

For currency exchange, try any of the banks near the main plaza (shown on the map). Many have ATMs.

Sights

In order to see most of the island you will have to rent a bicycle, moped or car, or take a taxi. The following route will take you south from San Miguel, then counterclockwise around the island. There are some places along the way to stop for food and drink, but it's good to bring water.

Before you explore the island, check out **Museo de la Isla de Cozumel** (Av Rafael Melgar btwn Calles 4 & 6 Nte; admission US$3; ⊗ 9am-6pm), which presents a clear and detailed picture of the island's flora, fauna, geography, geology and ancient Mayan history.

Parque Chankanaab (admission US$10; ⊗ 6am-6pm), on the bay of the same name, is a very popular snorkeling spot, though there's not a lot to see in the water beyond brightly colored fish and some deliberately sunken artificial objects. The beach is a beauty, though, and 50m inland is a limestone lagoon teeming with iguanas and turtles. A taxi from town costs about US$10 one-way.

Playa Palancar, about 17km south of town, is one of the island's nicest publicly accessible beaches. There's a beach club that rents hydro bikes, kayaks, snorkel gear and sailboats, plus a restaurant and a dive operation. Nearby **Arrecife Palancar** (Palancar Reef) has some very good diving and snorkeling.

Cozumel's **eastern shoreline** is the wildest part of the island and highly recommended for its beautiful seascapes. Unfortunately, except at Punta Chiqueros, Playa Chen Río and Punta Morena, swimming is dangerous on Cozumel's east coast because of riptides and undertows. There are a few small restaurants along the road serving seafood; most are expensive, but have great views of the sea.

Beyond where the east coast highway meets the Carretera Transversal, intrepid travelers may opt to take a poorly maintained, infrequently traveled road toward **Punta Molas**, the island's northeast point, accessible only by 4WD or on foot. About 17km down the road are the Mayan ruins known as **El Castillo Real**, and a few kilometers further is **Aguada Grande**. Both sites are quite far gone, their significance lost to time. In the vicinity of Punta Molas are some fairly good beaches and a few more minor ruins. The best camping spot along the road is **Playa Bonita**.

Diving & Snorkeling

Cozumel is one of the most popular diving destinations in the world. Its diving conditions are unsurpassed for many reasons, chief among them the fantastic year-round visibility (50m and greater) and a jaw-droppingly awesome variety of marine life.

There are scores of dive centers on Cozumel and dozens more in Playa del Carmen (p339). Prices vary, but in general expect to pay about US$70 for a two-tank dive (less if you bring your own BCD and regulator), US$60 for an introductory 'resort' course and about US$350 for PADI open-water-diver certification.

There are dozens of dive shops and instructors in Cozumel. The most reputable are **Acuatic Sports** (☎ 872-06-40; www.scubacozumel .com; Av 15 Sur & Calle 21 Sur) and **Deep Blue** (☎ 872-56-53; www.deepbluecozumel.com; Av 10 Sur at Calle Dr Adolfo Rosado Salas).

Snorkelers: all of the best sites are reached by boat. A half-day tour will cost US$30 to US$50, but you'll do some world-class snorkeling. You can save on the boat fare by walking into the gentle surf at Playa La Ceiba, Bahía Chankanaab, Playa San Francisco and elsewhere.

Sleeping

All hotel rooms come with private bathroom and fan. Prices in all categories are high season rates and may be much lower at other times of year.

BUDGET

Hotel Pepita (☎ 872-00-98; Av 15 Sur btwn Calle 1 Sur & Calle Dr Adolfo Rosado Salas; d US$30; ⊠) This is a friendly place with well-maintained rooms grouped around a garden. All have two double beds, refrigerators and air-con.

Hotel Marruang (☎ 872-16-78; Dr Adolfo Rosado Salas 440; r US$28) Across from the municipal

YUCATÁN PENINSULA, TABASCO & CHIAPAS

market, the Marruang is simple and clean with well-screened, fan-cooled rooms.

Hotel Cozumel Inn (☎ 872-03-14; Calle 4 Nte btwn Avs Rafael Melgar & 5 Nte; d with fan/air-con US$30/37; 🍴 💷) The Cozumel has 30 decent rooms and a small swimming pool.

Safari Inn (☎ 872-01-01; www.aquasafari.com; Av Rafael Melgar at Calle 5 Sur; d US$45; 🍴) This simple, clean and friendly hotel above the Aqua Safari Dive Shop has big beds, warm showers and cool air-con.

MID-RANGE & TOP END

Tamarindo B&B (☎ 872-36-14; www.cozumel.net/bb /tamarind; Calle 4 Nte 421 at Av 20 Nte; d from US$40) Five blocks from downtown, this is an out-of-the-way (and well worth finding) B&B. A big breakfast is included and there's a kitchenette and barbecue for guest use.

Amigo's B&B (☎ 872-38-68; www.bacalar.net; Calle 7 Sur btwn Avs 25 Sur & 30 Sur; d US$70; 🍴 💷) It's worth the hike from the center to enjoy one of the three well-appointed, cottage-style rooms here. All have air-con and full kitchenettes. Book ahead.

Villas Las Anclas (☎ 872-61-03; www.lasanclas .com; Av 5 Sur btwn Calles 3 Sur & 5 Sur; d US$75; 🍴) Lovely, roomy two-story suites with air-con and kitchenettes are clustered around a leafy garden. Excellent complimentary breakfasts are served in your suite.

Hotel Flamingo (☎ 872-12-64; www.hotelflamingo .com; Calle 6 Nte btwn Avs Rafael Melgar & 5 Nte; d US$40-60; 🍴) Colorful, charming and friendly. Spacious rooms surround a leafy courtyard where you can eat breakfast or have a drink.

Hacienda San Miguel (☎ 872-19-86; www.hacienda sanmiguel.com; Calle 10 Nte btwn Rafael Melgar & Av 5 Nte; r US$70; 🍴) Built and furnished to resemble an old hacienda, this hotel seems a little out of place in its island habitat but has a lot of charm nonetheless.

Hotel Barracuda (☎ 872-00-02; www.cozumel -hotels.net/barracuda; Av Melgar 628; d US$75; 🍴 💷) On the beach five blocks south of downtown, the Barracuda is a good spot for divers, snorkelers or anyone who wants to enjoy the water. Most of the 52 rooms have sea views.

The big luxury resort hotels begin several kilometers south of town. One nice option is **Hotel Playa Azul** (☎ 872-0199; www.playa-azul .com; Carr a San Juan Km 4; d/ste from US$185/220; 🍴 💷) where all rooms have ocean view balconies and guests can golf for free at a nearby course.

Eating

Los Dorados de Villa (☎ 872-01-97; Calle 1 Sur at Av 5 Sur; mains US$4-10) The menu here is Mexican with an emphasis on regional dishes from Mexico City.

Restaurant La Choza (☎ 872-09-58; cnr Dr Adolfo Rosado Salas & Av 10 Sur; mains US$8-12) Excellent restaurant specializing in authentic regional cuisine.

Pepe's Grill (Av Rafael Melgar at Dr Adolfo Rosado Salas; mains US$20-25) This is traditionally considered Cozumel's finest restaurant. Mains are mostly meat, plus charcoal-broiled lobster. Flambé desserts are a house specialty.

Pancho's Backyard (☎ 872-21-41; cnr Av Rafael Melgar & Calle 8 Nte; mains US$10-17) Intimate restaurant set in a handsomely decorated courtyard. The food (mostly seafood) is as good as the ambiance.

El Morrito III (☎ 876-01-07; Calle 6 Nte btwn Avs Rafael Melgar & 5 Nte; mains US$4-10) This family-run joint serves good Mexican dishes, breakfasts and *licuados* (blended fruit drinks).

Coffeelia (Calle 5 Sur btwn Avs Rafael Melgar & 5 Sur; breakfast US$3-5) This is a relaxed meeting place for Cozumel's art community. The menu includes quiches, good salads, vegetarian dishes and premium organic coffee.

Jeannie's Waffle House (☎ 872-60-95; Av Rafael Melgar at Calle 11 Sur; breakfast US$3-7, sandwiches US$5-6) Jeannie's serves waffles (of course), hash browns, egg dishes, sandwiches and other light fare accompanied by great views. By late afternoon, Jeannie's becomes **Acuario**, a romantic dining spot.

Cheapest of all eating places are the little *loncherías* (lunch stalls) next to the **Mercado Municipal** on Calle Dr Adolfo Rosado Salas between Avs 20 and 25 Sur.

Entertainment

Ambar (Av 5 Sur btwn Calles 1 Sur & Dr Adolfo Rosado Salas; 🌙 closed Wed) This artistically decorated bar and lounge has a lovely garden, DJ-spun lounge and house music, and live music on Saturdays.

Neptuno (cnr Av Rafael Melgar & Calle 11 Sur; 🌙 nights Thu-Sat). The only disco in town worth the title; it's huge.

Getting There & Away

AIR

There are some direct flights from the US, but European flights are usually routed via the US or Mexico City. **Continental** (☎ 800-

900-50-00, US ☎ +1-800-231-0856; www.continental
.com) has direct flights from Newark and
Houston. **Mexicana** (☎ 872-02-63) flies direct
to Mexico City on Saturday and Sunday.

Aerocozumel (☎ 872-09-28), with offices at
the airport, flies a few times daily between
Cancún and Cozumel for US$75 one-way.

BOAT
Passenger ferries run from Playa del Carmen
(see p341 for details). A vehicle ferry departs
most days at 5am from the town of **Puerto
Morelos**, 33km south of Cancún, though it's
hardly worth shipping a car over.

Getting Around
TO/FROM THE AIRPORT
The airport is about 2km north of town. You
can take a van from the airport into town
for about US$5 (slightly more to the hotels
south of town), but you'll have to take a taxi
(US$4.50 from town, US$9 to US$20 from
southern hotels) to return to the airport.

BICYCLE
Bicycles typically rent for US$5 to US$10
for 24 hours and can be a great way to get
to Bahía Chankanaab and other spots on
this flat island.

CAR & MOTORCYCLE
Rates for rental cars usually run from US$35
to US$50 per day, all inclusive, though you'll
pay more during late December and January. There are plenty of agencies around the
main plaza. **Rentadora Isis** (☎ 872-33-67; Av 5 Nte
btwn Calles 2 Nte & 4 Nte) rents cars, bicycles and
scooters.

Motorbikes are one-way to tour the island on your own, and rental opportunities
abound. The standard price is US$30 a day
(US$20 in the low season), with gas, insur-
ance and tax included. The best time to rent
is first thing in the morning, when all the
machines are there.

TAXI
Fares in and around town are US$2 per
ride; luggage may cost extra. Carry exact
change. There is no bus service.

PLAYA DEL CARMEN
☎ 984 / pop 50,000
Only a decade ago Playa was still a relatively
small fishing village. As Cancún's popularity

grew over the years, however, the number
of travelers stopping here increased dramatically, as did the number and range of
hotels and restaurants serving them. Today
Playa is the fastest-growing city in Mexico,
and rivals Cancún as a preferred vacation
destination.

What's to do in Playa? Hang out. Swim.
Dive. Shop. Eat. Drink. Walk the beach. Get
some sun. Listen to beach bands. Dance in
the clubs.

Nudity is tolerated on at least three
beaches north of the town center. Never
leave valuables unattended.

Orientation
Playa is laid out on an easy grid. The pedestrian stretch of Quinta Av (Fifth Ave) is the
most happening street in town, especially
along the pedestrian stretch.

The **Terminal del Centro** – the older bus terminal – is opposite the main plaza at the intersection of Quinta Av and Av Juárez. The
newer **Terminal ADO** is several blocks north
on 20 Av near Calle 12.

Information
Centro de Salud (15 Av at Av Juárez) Medical Center.
Cibernet (Calle 8; per hr US$1.50) Internet access.
Police & Fire (☎ 060)
Post office (cnr 15 Av & Av Juárez)
Tourist Information Office (☎ 873-28-04; Av Juárez
at 15 Av; ☉ 9am-9pm Mon-Sat, 9am-5pm Sun)
Tourist Police Kiosk (☎ 873-02-91; main plaza)

There are many banks with ATMs around
town. (See the map for some locations.)

Diving & Snorkeling
Playa is one of the best places on the coast to
dive and snorkel. While you can do both from
the beach, the most spectacular underwater
sites are at the offshore reefs. The following
dive centers offer both scuba and snorkeling
trips, including night excursions:
Abyss (☎ 873-21-64; www.abyssdiveshop.com; Blue
Parrot Inn, Calle 12)
Dive Mike (☎ 873-09-69; www.divemike.com; Calle
8 btwn Quinta Av & beach)
Phocéa Caribe (☎ 873-12-10; www.phoceacaribe
dive.com; 1 Av btwn Calles 10 & 12)

Sleeping
Room prices here are for the winter tourist
season (roughly January to March). Prices

PLAYA DEL CARMEN

0 — 300 m
0 — 0.2 mile

INFORMATION		
Centro de Salud	1	A3
Cibernet	2	C2
Post Office	3	A3
Tourist Information Office	4	A3
Tourist Police Kiosk	5	B4

SIGHTS & ACTIVITIES		(p339)
Abyss	(see 8)	
Dive Mike	6	C2
Phocéa Caribe	7	C2

SLEEPING		(pp339–41)
Blue Parrot Inn	8	C2
Camping-Cabañas La Ruina	9	B3
Hostel Playa	10	A2
Hotel Azul	11	C2
Hotel Balam Nah	12	A4
Hotel Casa Tucán	13	B3
Mosquito Blue	14	C2
Pancho's Hotel	15	C2
Posada Barrio Latino	16	B3
Treetops Hotel	17	B2
Villa Catarina	18	C2

EATING		(p341)
Babe's	19	C2
Club Náutico Tarraya	20	B3
Coffee Press	21	B3
Hot	22	C1
Java Joe's	23	C2
Sur	24	C2
Yaxché	25	B2

DRINKING		(p341)
Dragon Bar	(see 8)	

ENTERTAINMENT		(p341)
Apasionado	26	C1

TRANSPORT		(pp341–2)
Colectivo Vans to Tulum	27	A3
Terminal ADO	28	B1
Terminal del Centro	29	B3

CARIBBEAN
SEA

To Hotel
Quinto Sol
(300m)

To Gas Station (250m);
Hwy 307 (300km);
El Alux (600m);
Tulum (63km);
Cancún (68km)

Main Plaza

Airstrip

Ferry to
Cozumel

YUCATÁN PENINSULA,
TABASCO & CHIAPAS

can drop by 40% outside these months and rise by 40% between December 20 and January 5.

BUDGET

Posada Barrio Latino (☎ 873-23-84; www.posada barriolatino.com; Calle 4 btwn Avs 10 & 15; d with fan/air-con US$35/43; P ⊠) This hotel offers 16 clean, pleasant rooms with good ventilation, tiled floors, ceiling fans and hammocks (in addition to beds). The friendly Italian owners speak English and Spanish and maintain strict security.

Hotel Casa Tucán (☎ 873-02-83; Calle 4 btwn Avs 10 & 15; d from US$25; ☑) This German/Texan-run hotel features 29 fan-cooled rooms. The restaurant is set in a tropical garden.

Hostel Playa (☎ 879-39-28; www.hostelworld.com; cnr Av 25 & Calle 8; dm/d US$9.50/20) This new hostel is very well run, extremely clean and unusually quiet. There is a large communal kitchen and a comfy common area.

Camping-Cabañas La Ruina (☎ 873-04-05; Calle 2; tents & hammocks per person US$6, d with shared bathroom US$18-25, with private bathroom US$30-38; ⊠) Aptly named, this place is sort of a ruin, but it is the only place to (officially) camp in Playa. The rooms in the hotel are worn but clean. Pitch a tent or hang a hammock (they're available for rent) in a large lot on the beach.

MID-RANGE

Treetops Hotel (☎ 873-14-95; www.treetopshotel.com; Calle 8 at Quinta Av; d US$45-75; ⊠ ☑) Treetops is small, quiet and the air-conditioned spacious rooms are surrounded by jungle vegetation. The upstairs rooms are nestled in the (surprise!) treetops.

Hotel Quinto Sol (☎ 873-32-92; www.hotelquintosol.com; Quinta Av 330 at Calle 28; d US$75; ✗ ✗) Located at the quiet north end of Quinta Av, Quinto Sol has a Mediterranean feel with spacious, air-conditioned rooms. Dig the rooftop Jacuzzi and easy access to the beach.

Villa Catarina (☎ 873-20-98; Calle Privada Norte btwn Calles 12 & 14; d US$75) Set amid a flowering tropical garden, this cozy beachside hotel offers a variety of rooms, from cabañas to *palapa* towers.

Pancho's Hotel (☎ 873-22-22; www.panchoshotel.com; Quinta Av 217 at Calle 12; d US$70; ✗ ✗) Situated at the decadent heart of Quinta Av, Pancho's invokes a revolutionary-chic mood. Irony aside, the rooms are spacious and tastefully furnished.

Hotel Balam Nah (☎ 873-21-17; www.hotelbalamnah.com; Calle 1 btwn Avs Quinta & 10; d with fan/air-con US$40/50; ✗) Rooms in this three-story hotel surround a cool, green courtyard. Each is very clean with good beds, nice baths and tile floors; most have a small fridge.

Hotel Azul (☎ 873-05-62; www.hotel-azul.com; Quinta Av btwn Calles 10 & 12; d US$55; ✗) The rooms at this friendly hotel are simple but very clean and comfortable. Some have air-con and all have TV. For the location – the heart of Quinta Av – the price is right.

TOP END

Blue Parrot Inn (☎ 873-00-83, US ☎ +1-888-854-4498; www.blueparrot.com; Calle 12; cabaña/d US$75/145; ✗ ✗ ✗) This is the place most people wish they were staying when they wander up the beach and discover it. Many of its charming rooms have terraces or sea views. The inn's very popular beachfront bar, the Dragon Bar, has the occasional live band.

Mosquito Blue (☎ 873-12-45; www.mosquitoblue.com; Quinta Av at Calle 12; d US$140; ✗ ✗ ✗) Rooms in this luxurious hideaway are sumptuously furnished in rich mahogany with thick-pillowed sofas and beds. There are two cloistered interior courtyards with a bar, restaurant and designer swimming pools. There is also a library with billiards table.

Eating

Yaxché (☎ 873-25-02; Calle 8 at Quinta Av; mains US$10-25; ✗) The cuisine here is authentically

Mayan. Everything is exquisitely seasoned and the seafood dishes are delicious.

Sur (☎ 873-803-32-85; Quinta Av btwn Calles 12 & 14; lunch US$8-15, dinner US$10-25) This relaxed but refined Argentinean restaurant serves delicious grilled delicacies including meat and seafood.

Club Náutico Tarraya (Calle 2; mains US$4-7) This eatery at the beach is one of the few in town that dates from the 1960s. Good food, decent prices.

Babe's (Calle 10 btwn Avs Quinta & 10; mains US$5-9) Babe's serves fabulous Thai food.

Two great all-day coffee shops are **Java Joe's** (Quinta Av btwn Calles 8 & 12; breakfast US$2-3) and the **Coffee Press** (Calle 2 at Quinta Av; breakfast US$3-4, lunch US$4). **Hot** (☎ 876-43-70; Calle 14 btwn Avs Quinta & 10; breakfast US$4) serves up scrumptious baked goods, omelets and coffee.

Drinking & Entertainment

Bet you've never boozed it up anywhere like **El Alux** (☎ 803-07-13; Av Juárez). It's in a cave – a real cave – replete with stalactites, stalagmites and natural fresh water pools.

There's a party scene along Quinta Av most nights. For Latin jazz, hit **Apasionado** (☎ 803-11-00; cnr Quinta Av & Calle 14). The Blue Parrot Inn's legendary open-sided **Dragon Bar** (Calle 12), at the beach, is a true swingers' bar (you sit in swings instead of bar stools).

Getting There & Away

BOAT

Ferries to Cozumel run nearly every hour on the hour from 6am to 11pm (US$8 one-way, 30 to 45 minutes).

BUS

Playa has two bus terminals. The **Terminal ADO** (20 Av), just east of Calle 12, is where 1st-class buses arrive and depart. A taxi to the main plaza from this bus station will cost about US$1.25.

The older terminal, **Terminal del Centro** (cnr Avs Juárez & Quinta) gets all the 2nd-class service. All Riviera buses leave from this station. Buses to Cancún and its airport have a separate ticket counter, on the Av Juárez side of the terminal.

Cancún (US$3.50; 1hr; Riviera buses every 10min)
Cancún International Airport (US$7; 45min-1hr; 9 direct Riviera buses, 7am-7:30pm)
Chetumal (5-5½hr; 12 Riviera buses, US$15; 11 2nd-class Mayab buses, US$14)

Chichén Itzá (3½hr; 1 Riviera bus, 7:30am, US$15.50)
Cobá (1½hr; 1 Riviera bus, 7:30am, US$4.50)
Mérida (5-8hr; 9 1st-class Super Expresso buses, US$20)
Palenque (10hr; 3 1st-class buses, US$33-40)
San Cristóbal de Las Casas (16hr; 3 1st-class buses, US$40-50)
Tulum (1hr; several Riviera & Mayab buses, US$3)
Valladolid (2½-3½hr; various Riviera & Mayab buses, US$6.25-10.50)

CAR & MOTORCYCLE
Located 68km south of Cancún, just of Hwy 307, Playa del Carmen is an easy and direct drive from Cancún and its airport. Other points south along the well-paved Hwy 307 (including Tulum, 63km) are also easily reached from Playa. Many of the major car-rental agencies have cars in Playa.

COLECTIVO VANS
Shared vans head south to Tulum (US$2, 45 minutes) from Calle 2 near 20 Av about every 15 minutes from 5am to 10pm daily.

PLAYA DEL CARMEN TO TULUM
Xpu-Há
Pronounced 'shpoo-*ha*', this beach area about 95km south of Cancún extends for several kilometers. It's reached by numbered access roads (most of them private).

At the end of X-4 (Xpu-Há access road 4), **Hotel Villas del Caribe** (☎ 984-873-21-94; cafe delmarxpuha@yahoo.com.mx; cabaña/r US$45/55) is a slightly weathered, very laid-back place on a lovely stretch of beach whose northern reaches are nearly empty. The personable owners offer massage, yoga and meditation classes.

Akumal
Famous for its beautiful beach, Akumal (Place of the Turtles) does indeed see some sea turtles crawl ashore to lay their eggs in summer, although fewer arrive each year because of resort development. Akumal is one of the Yucatán Peninsula's oldest resorts, and consists primarily of pricey hotels and condominiums on nearly 5km of wide beach bordering four consecutive bays. Diving remains the area's primary attraction.

Bahías de Punto Solimán
These two protected bays are one of the best-kept secrets on the coastline. Located 123km south of Cancún and 11km north of

Tulum (turn off Hwy 307 at the big white signed exit reading: Oscar y Lalo's), this area offers good wildlife watching, kayaking, excellent snorkeling and long, white swaths of palm-shaded beach. On the north bay sits **Oscar y Lalo's** (☎ 984-804-69-73; mains US$7-15), a spacious restaurant overlooking the water.

On the south bay (also known as Bahía de San Francisco), private homes – many very luxurious – line the road. **Casa Nah Uxibal** (www.locogringo.com; per night from US$90) rents four lovely beachfront units. Artistically furnished **Casa del Corazón** (www.locogringo.com; per night from US$150) rents three cozy bungalows. There is a three-night minimum.

Cenotes
On the west side of the highway south of **Paamul** are several cenotes (limestone sinkholes/caverns filled with water) you can visit (and usually swim in) for a price. A few kilometers south of **Akumal** is the turnoff for Cenote Dos Ojos, which provides access to the **Nohoch Nah Chich** cave system, the largest underwater cave system in the world. You can take guided snorkel and dive tours of some amazing underwater caverns, floating past illuminated stalactites and stalagmites in an eerie wonderland.

Contact the American-run **Hidden Worlds** (☎ 984-877-85-35; www.hiddenworlds.com.mx) for three-hour snorkeling tours (US$40), and one- and two-tank dive tours (US$50 and US$80).

TULUM
☎ 984 / pop 7000
Some 130km to the south of Cancún, Tulum means Mayan ruins, beautiful beaches and a profusion of cabañas for rent, all at the ocean's edge.

Orientation & Information
Approaching from the north the first thing you reach is **Tulum Crucero**, the junction of highway 307 and the old access road to the ruins. The new access road is 400m further south and leads another 600m to the ruins themselves. Another 1.5km south on the highway brings you to the Cobá junction; turning right (west) takes you to Cobá. The road to the left leads about 3km to the north-south road servicing the **Zona Hotelera**, the string of waterfront lodgings

extending 10km south from the ruins. This road eventually enters the Reserva de la Biósfera Sian Ka'an, continuing some 50km past Boca Paila to Punta Allen.

The town, sometimes referred to as **Tulum Pueblo**, flanks the highway (called Av Tulum through town) south of the Cobá junction. It has Telmex pay phones, numerous currency-exchange booths and one Bital bank with ATM. The Weary Traveler hostel (p344) has fast Internet access (US$1.50 per hour), travelers' information, free storage and a book exchange.

Tulum Ruins

The **ruins** (admission US$4; ☀ 7am-5pm) of Parque Nacional Tulum, though well preserved, would hardly merit rave reviews if it weren't for their setting. Even on dark, stormy days, the majestic cliff-top ruins overlooking vast stretches of pristine beach are fit for a guidebook cover. The buildings here, decidedly Toltec in influence, were the product of a Mayan civilization in decline. The city was abandoned about 75 years after the Spanish conquest.

Tulum is a prime destination for tour buses. To best enjoy the ruins, visit them either early in the morning or late in the afternoon. Parking costs US$3, and the optional shuttle to the site (about a seven-minute walk) is US$2 per roundtrip.

THE SITE

The two-story **Templo de Las Pinturas** was constructed in several stages around AD 1400–50. Its decoration was among the most elaborate at Tulum and included relief masks and colored murals on an inner wall. The murals have been partially restored but are nearly impossible to make out.

Overlooking the Caribbean is Tulum's tallest building, a watchtower appropriately named **El Castillo** (the Castle) by the Spaniards. Note the Toltec-style serpent columns at the temple's entrance.

The **Templo del Dios Descendente** (Temple of the Descending God) is named for the relief figure above the door – a diving figure, partly human, that may be related to the Maya's reverence for bees.

YUCATÁN PENINSULA, TABASCO & CHIAPAS

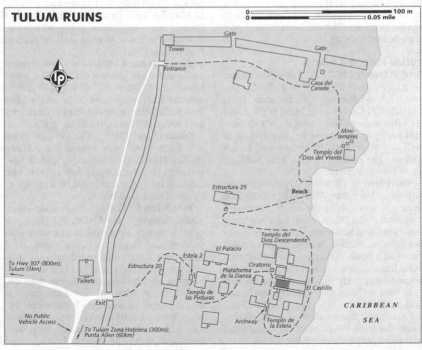

TULUM RUINS

The restored **Templo de la Estela** (Temple of the Stela) is also known as the Temple of the Initial Series. If you're anxious for a look at the sea, go through the corbeled arch to the right of the temple and turn left.

El Palacio (the Palace) features a beautiful stucco carving of a diving god over its main doorway. The **Templo del Dios del Viento** (Temple of the Wind God) provides the best views of El Castillo juxtaposed with the sea below.

Tours

Cenote Dive Center (☎ 871-22-32; www.cenotedive .com; Av Tulum) specializes in guided cavern tours and cave dives as well as cenote and cavern snorkeling trips.

Sian Ka'an Info Tours (☎ 871-24-99; www.sian kaan.org; Tulum Crucero), adjacent to Hotel El Crucero, is a professional eco-tour operation offering guided tours to Sian Ka'an Biosphere Reserve.

Sleeping & Eating

Hotels in town and Crucero Ruinas are the logical place to stay if you're just passing through or only want to visit the ruins. If it is the beach you're after, the Zona Hotelera is a better choice. The following listings give high-season lodging rates.

TULUM PUEBLO & NORTH

Hotel El Crucero (☎ 871-26-10; www.el-crucero.com; Tulum Crucero; dm/d/r US$7.50/35/50; ⓟ ⌧ ⌨) Located just a limestone's throw away from the ruins, El Crucero's location is ideal and its value unbeatable. There is an excellent and very popular restaurant/bar on site as well as a professional dive shop and an art gallery. The beach is just a long walk or short bike ride away.

Weary Traveler (☎ 871-24-61; www.intulum.com; Av Tulum; s/d beds in dorm US$7.50/13.50, r US$20) The Weary is across from the bus terminal and one block south. Dorm rooms have two bunk beds, a fan, and bathroom with shower. There is a relaxing, shaded courtyard, Internet access and a book exchange. The hostel provides free shuttle service to the beach and is home to very lively Sunday-night barbecues.

La Nave (Av Tulum; mains US$5; ✎ closed Sun) If you come here for breakfast, you'll be back for lunch and dinner. It's that good. Really. From the fresh baked bread to wood-fired pizza and ceviche, everything is tops.

El Tacontento (Av Tulum; mains US$3-6) Located on the corner a couple of blocks south from La Nave, this Mexican restaurant serves very tasty tacos, ceviche and fresh fish dishes.

ZONA HOTELERA

Along the coastal road leading to Punta Allen (Carretera Tulum Ruinas–Boca Paila), which begins less than 1km south of the ruins, is a string of cabaña hotels. A few cater primarily to backpackers, and nearly all have simple restaurants but no telephones. Of those places that have electricity, many shut it off at 9pm or 10pm.

The cheapest way to sleep here is to have your own hammock and mosquito net; if you don't, several of the inexpensive places rent them. Bring repellent. Few of the flimsy, primitive cabañas can be reliably secured.

The following places are ordered north to south. As a rule, the further south you travel, the more expensive (and secure) accommodations become. Listed are just a few of over 40 establishments.

Cabañas El Mirador (☎ 879-60-19; cabaña with hammock/bed US$10/20; ⓟ) Closest to the ruins, El Mirador has 28 cabañas (half with sand floors), most with beds, some with hammocks. The beach is wide and the restaurant has excellent views.

Hotel Diamante K (☎ 871-23-76; www.diamantek .com; r with shared bathroom US$25-55, with private bathroom US$60-200; ⓟ) This eco-tel's lovely cabañas have suspended beds and a table for candles (the solar-generated electricity goes off at 11:30pm). It fills up quickly.

Cabañas Copal (☎ 871-24-81; www.cabanascopal .com; d with shared/private bathroom from US$35/65; ⓟ ⌨) This long-time budget spot is now a chakra-cleansing, New Age retreat. The cabañas are lovely and overlook a clothing-optional stretch of beach.

Nohoch Tunich (☎ 871-22-71; cabaña with shared/ private bathroom US$35/45, r US$45-65; ⓟ) This place offers both tidy, appealing hotel rooms with porches and electricity (until 11pm), and handsome thatch-and-board cabañas with wooden floors, very near the beach.

Zamas (US ☎ +1-415-387-9806; www.zamas.com; d US$80-145; ⓟ) Zamas' romantic cabañas all have terraces with two hammocks, a 24-hour light, purified drinking water, big private bathrooms and two comfy beds with mosquito nets. The regionally acclaimed restaurant, **Que Fresco**, overlooks the rocks, sea and beach.

Posada Margherita (www.posadamargherita.com; d US$70-140; P) This beautiful eco-friendly hotel has something virtually unheard of in the Yucatán: complete wheelchair access. Most impressive is the dive shop, which offers scuba for those with limited mobility. The six rooms here are tiled and bright with verandas or balconies. Many locals consider the beachfront restaurant the best around.

Nueva Vida (☎ 877-20-92; www.tulumnv.com; d US$110-260; P ☒) This secluded, tranquil eco-retreat fronts a spectacular, vast, sugary beach. The seven rustic cabañas are spread out in the lush jungle back from the shore and elevated on stilts. All rooms have good beds, strong fans and warm showers. There's round-the-clock electricity.

Getting There & Around

You can walk from Tulum Crucero to the ruins (800m). The cabañas begin about 600m south of the ruins and can be reached by taxi from Tulum Pueblo; fares are fixed and cheap. At the center of town you'll see the large sign of the Sindicato de Taxistas, on which the rates are posted. To the ruins it's US$3, and to most of the cabañas US$5.

The bus terminal is toward the southern end of town (look for the two-story building with 'ADO' painted on it in huge letters). When leaving Tulum, you can also wait at Tulum Crucero for a Playa Express or regular intercity bus. Here are some distances, travel times and prices for buses leaving Tulum:

Cancún (US$5-6, 2hr)
Chetumal (US$9-11, 3½-4hr)
Chichén Itzá (US$7.25, 3hr)
Cobá (US$2.25, 45min)
Felipe Carrillo Puerto (US$4-5, 1¾hr)
Mérida (US$14, 7hr)
Playa del Carmen (US$3, 1hr)
Valladolid (US$4-5, 2hr)

If you are headed for Valladolid, be sure that your bus is traveling the short route through Chemax, not via Cancún.

COBÁ

Among the largest of Mayan cities, Cobá, 50km northwest of Tulum, offers the chance to explore mostly unrestored antiquities set deep in tropical jungle.

Cobá was settled much earlier than Chichén Itzá or Tulum, and construction reached its peak between AD 800 and 1100. Archaeologists believe this city once covered 50 sq km and held 40,000 Maya.

Cobá's architecture is a mystery; its towering pyramids and stelae resemble the architecture of Tikal, several hundred kilometers away, rather than the much nearer sites of Chichén Itzá and the northern Yucatán Peninsula.

Some archaeologists theorize that an alliance with Tikal was made through marriage to facilitate trade between the Guatemalan and Yucatecan Maya. Stelae appear to depict female rulers from Tikal holding ceremonial bars and flaunting their power by standing on captives. These Tikal royal females, when married to Cobá's royalty, may have brought architects and artisans with them.

Archaeologists are also baffled by the extensive network of *sacbeob* (stone-paved avenues) in this region, with Cobá as the hub. The longest runs nearly 100km from the base of Cobá's great pyramid Nohoch Mul to the Mayan settlement of Yaxuna.

Archaeologists estimate that Cobá contains some 6500 structures, of which just a few have been excavated and restored.

Orientation & Information

The small village of Cobá, 2.5km west of the Tulum–Nuevo Xcan road, has a small, cheap hotel and several small, simple and low-cost restaurants. At the lake, turn left for the ruins, right for the upscale Villas Arqueológicas Cobá hotel.

The **archaeological site** (admission US$4; ☉ 7am-6pm) has a parking lot charging US$1.50 per passenger car.

Be prepared to walk several kilometers on paths, depending on how much you want to see. Bring insect repellent and water; the shop next to the ticket booth sells both at reasonable prices, but there are no drinks stands within the site. Avoid the midday heat if possible.

A short distance inside, at the Grupo Cobá, are bicycles renting at US$2.50 for the day. These are useful if you really want to get around the further reaches, and the breeze they create is cooling.

Sights

GRUPO COBÁ

Walking just under 100m along the main path from the entrance and turning right brings you to the **Templo de las Iglesias** (Temple of the Churches), the most prominent structure in the Cobá Group. It's an enormous pyramid, but climbing it is forbidden.

Back on the main path, you pass through the **juego de pelota** (ball court), 30m further along.

GRUPO MACANXOC

About 500m beyond the **juego de pelota**, the path forks. Going straight gets you to the Grupo Macanxoc, a group of stelae that bore reliefs of royal women who are thought to have come from Tikal. They are badly eroded, and it's a 1km walk; the flora along the way is interesting, however.

CONJUNTO DE LAS PINTURAS

Though it's signed to the left at the fork, if you're on foot you can reach the Conjunto de las Pinturas (Group of Paintings) by heading toward the Grupo Macanxoc a very short distance and turning left. The temple here bears traces of glyphs and frescoes above its door and remnants of richly colored plaster inside.

You approach the temple from the southeast. Leave by the trail at the northwest (opposite the temple steps) to see several stelae. Continue along the path past another badly weathered stela and a small temple to rejoin the Nohoch Mul path and turn right.

NOHOCH MUL

A walk of 800m more brings you to Nohoch Mul (Big Mound), also known as the Great Pyramid, built on a natural hill. Along the way is another ball court, at whose north end lie weathered stelae; the track then bends between piles of stones – a ruined temple – before passing Templo 10 and Stela 20. The exquisitely carved stela bears a picture of a ruler standing imperiously over two captives. Eighty meters beyond stands the **Great Pyramid**.

At 42m high, the Great Pyramid is the tallest Mayan structure on the Yucatán Peninsula. There are two diving gods carved over the doorway of the temple at the top (built in the Postclassic period, AD 1100–1450), similar to the sculptures at Tulum. The view is spectacular!

Sleeping & Eating

There's no organized campsite, but you can try finding a place along the shore of the lake, which is inhabited by crocodiles (local children can show you a safe swimming spot).

Hotel y Restaurant El Bocadito (☎ 985-852-00-52; r US$8-10) The hotel has very simple fan-cooled rooms with private bathrooms. The restaurant is very well run and serves a great *menú* (set meal). They'll store luggage while you visit the ruins. El Bocadito also serves as Cobá's bus terminal and *colectivo* taxi terminus.

Villas Arqueológicas Cobá (☎ 998-858-15-27, US ☎ +1-800-258-2633; d US$70) This Club Med hotel next to the lake has a swimming pool and mediocre restaurant to complement the air-conditioned rooms. It's a nice place to relax and the best value among the Villas Arqueológicas on the Yucatán Peninsula.

Restaurant Las Pirámides (mains US$5) A few doors down from the Villas Arqueológicas, this restaurant has good lake views and friendly service.

There are several small restaurants by the site parking lot, including **Restaurant El Faisán** and **Restaurant El Caracol**, both of which serve inexpensive meals.

Getting There & Away

There are six to eight buses daily between Tulum and Cobá (US$2.50); six of these also serve Playa del Carmen (US$4.50, 1½ hours). Combis between Cobá and Tulum charge US$5 per person. There is also bus service to Valladolid (US$2.50, one hour), Chichén Itzá (US$5, 1½ hours) and Mérida (US$11, 3½ hours).

A more comfortable but expensive way to reach Cobá is by taxi from Tulum Crucero. Find some other travelers interested in the trip and split the cost, about US$50 per roundtrip, including two hours at the site.

The 31km road from Cobá to Chemax is arrow-straight and in good shape. If you're driving to Valladolid or Chichén Itzá this is the way to go.

PUNTA ALLEN

Although it suffered considerable damage from the ferocious winds of Hurricane

Gilbert in 1988, Punta Allen still sports a laid-back ambiance reminiscent of the Belizean cayes. There is also a healthy reef 400m from shore that offers snorkelers and divers wonderful sights.

The area is known primarily for its bonefishing, and for that many people come a long way. The guides listed on right, as well as cooperatives in town, do fishing trips for about US$200, including lunch.

Tres Marías (d US$25) is a set of locally run, simple cabañas in the middle of town.

Fully furnished cabañas at **Posada Sirena** (☎ 984-878-77-95; www.casasirena.com; d US$30-40) have kitchens and hot-water showers.

The accommodations at **Cuzan Guest House** (☎ 983-834-03-58; www.flyfishmx.com; d US$40-80) are rustic but offer all the amenities you could need.

Getting There & Away

Punta Allen is at the end of a narrow stretch of land that reaches south nearly 40km from its start just below Tulum. There are some charming beaches along the way, with plenty of privacy, and most of the spit is within the protected, wildlife-rich Reserva de la Biósfera Sian Ka'an.

There are two ways to reach Punta Allen from Tulum. One is to take the unpaved, muffler-busting coastal road that goes directly to Punta Allen; the other is to go to the pier in Playón where boats leave regularly for Punta Allen.

If you are taking public transportation to Punta Allen, you have a couple of options. A van (weather and road permitting) makes the trip from the taxi cooperative in the middle of Tulum Pueblo to Punta Allen at around 11:30am, taking 1½ to three hours (US$12). Alternatively you can take a bus to Felipe Carrillo Puerto and then a shared van from there to the pier in Playón (US$9, three hours). Water taxis from Playón (about US$3) run between 9am and 5pm – again, weather permitting.

By car the most direct way – when the road is open – to get to Punta Allen is on the coastal road. Though Punta Allen is only 40km away, the crater-sized potholes will slow you down considerably. No fuel is available on the beach road route.

To reach Playón by car take the 'Vigía Chico' exit off Hwy 307 (about 42km south of Tulum) and drive another 42km (on an unpaved road, about two hours) to the boat landing.

RESERVA DE LA BIÓSFERA SIAN KA'AN

Over 5000 sq km of tropical jungle, marsh, mangroves and islands on Quintana Roo's coast have been set aside by the Mexican government as a large biosphere reserve, and recognized by Unesco in 1987 as a World Heritage Site.

Sian Ka'an (Where the Sky Begins) is home to howler monkeys, anteaters, foxes, ocelots, pumas, crocodiles, eagles, raccoons, tapirs, peccaries, giant land crabs, jaguars and hundreds of bird species, including roseate spoonbills and some flamingos. There are no hiking trails through the reserve; it's best explored with a professional guide.

Three Punta Allen locals with training in English, natural history, interpretation and birding conduct bird-watching, snorkeling and nature tours, mostly by boat, for about US$110 for five to six people: **Baltazar Madera** (☎ 984-871-20-01), **Marcos Nery** (local telephone office ☎ 984-871-24-24) and **Chary Salazar** (enquire in town). The latter two are experts on endemic and migratory bird species, and Chary also does walking tours when she's around.

A new eco-tel, **Boca Paila Camps** (☎ 984-871-24-99; www.siankaan.org; dm/d US$25/$65) recently opened about 4km from the entrance of the reserve on the Tulum-Punta Allen road. The hotel, run by the Tulum-based ecology group Centro Ecológico Sian Ka'an (CE-SiaK), has 15 elevated, low-environmental-impact (solar power, compost toilets) *palapa* units. There is a restaurant and the staff offers tours of the surrounding reserve as well as kayak and bike rentals.

FELIPE CARRILLO PUERTO

☎ 983 / pop 21,000

Now named for a progressive governor of Yucatán, this crossroads town 95km south of Tulum was once known as Chan Santa Cruz, the rebel headquarters during the War of the Castes.

Carrillo Puerto offers the visitor little in the way of attractions, but it's a transit hub and the first town of consequence if you are arriving from the Mérida/Ticul/Uxmal area. There is a gas station on the highway, where you also can find inexpensive, air-conditioned accommodations.

For sleeps try **Hotel Esquivel** (☎ 834-03-44; Calle 65 No 746; d with fan/air-con US$17/22), around the corner from the plaza and bus terminal, or **El Faisán y El Venado** (834-07-02; Av Juárez 7812; d US$22).

Most buses serving Carrillo Puerto are *de paso* ('in passing'; they don't originate there) to/from Cancun (US$8 to US$10.50, four hours), Chetumal (US$6 to US$7.75, two to three hours), Mérida (US$12, 5½ hours), Playa del Carmen (about US$7, 2½ hours), Ticul (US$9, 4½ hours) and Tulum (US$4 to US$4.75, 1¾ hours)

COSTA MAYA

The coast south of the Reserva de la Biósfera Sian Ka'an to the small fishing village of Xcalak (shka-*lak*) is often referred to as the Costa Maya. Development of the area has been in fits and starts, and Mahahual and Xcalak remain relatively primitive parts of Mexico.

Mahahual

This precious beach town faces slow but steady exploitation, but for the time being Mahahual retains its tranquility and charm and is one of the most peaceful enclaves on the coast.

The diving is superb. The friendly and seasoned professional, Douglas Campell-Smith at **Blue Ha diving Center** (☎ 983-753-58-21; www .bluehadiving.com; Km 2.7), offers a variety of diving and snorkeling classes and excursions.

There are a few places to stay right in town, but the best accommodations are at the beachside cabañas south of town, including the gorgeous **Balamku Inn** (☎ 983-838-00-83; www .balamku.com; Km 5.7; d US$65; 🖵) and **Kohun Beach** (http://kohunbeach.o-f.com, Km 7; d US$35). **Travel'in** (Km 5.8; dm US$7) is the perfect spot to pitch your tent, hang a hammock or enjoy a comfortable dorm bed. German-run **Casa del Mar** (Km 2; breakfast, mains US$3-5) serves breakfast, yummy baked goods and vegetarian dishes.

Xcalak

Xcalak's appeal lies in its quiet atmosphere, Caribbean-style wooden homes, swaying palms and pretty beaches. Another draw is the little-explored **Reserva de la Biósfera Banco Chinchorro**, the largest coral atoll in the Northern Hemisphere, 40km northeast.

Xcalak to Chinchorro (XTC) Dive Center (☎ 983-831-04-61; www.xcalak.com.mx), about 300m north

of town on the coast road, offers dive and snorkel trips to the wondrous barrier reef just offshore.

SLEEPING & EATING

Hotel Caracol (d US$11) is a six-room hotel with decent rooms with fan and cold-water private bathroom. Electricity is available from 6pm to 10pm. Look for the owner, Señora Mauricia Garidio, next door to the hotel. Ask Alan, the owner of **Restaurant Bar Xcalak Caribe**, about a possible new **campground**.

The following places are among a handful on the old coastal road leading north from town (most run by Americans or Canadians); rates given are the higher winter prices. All listed have purified drinking water, ceiling fans, 24-hour electricity (from solar or wind with generator backup), bikes and/or sea kayaks for guests' use, and private hot-water bathrooms. They all have lovely beaches and docks from which to swim or snorkel.

Hotel Tierra Maya (☎ 983-831-04-04; www.tier ramaya.net; d US$85-95) This is a modern beachfront hotel 2km north of town.

Casa Carolina (☎ 983-831-04-44; www.casacaro lina.net; d US$85), just up the road from Hotel Tierra Maya, boasts four guestrooms with large balconies facing the sea.

Playa Sonrisa (☎ 983-838-18-72; www.playason risa.com; d US$75-95) 'All you need is a smile' is the motto here... Many guests wear little else. The six guest rooms are bright and comfortable and the restaurant/bar is particularly homey.

Grocery trucks service the coast road, and there are a few small restaurants near the center of Xcalak, keeping sporadic hours.

Getting There & Around

From Hwy 307, take the signed turnoff for Mahahual. The turnoff is 68km south of Felipe Carrillo Puerto (1km south of Limones), and 46km north of Bacalar. About 55km east, a few kilometers before Mahahual, turn right (south) and follow the signs to Xcalak (another 60km).

Rickety Sociedad Cooperativa del Caribe buses depart Chetumal's main bus terminal for Xcalak (US$5.50, 200km, five hours) daily at 5am and 3pm. From Felipe Carrillo Puerto catch a bus to Limones; from there buses to Xcalak (US$4.25) depart at around 6:30am and 4:30pm.

LAGUNA BACALAR

A large, clear, turquoise freshwater lake with a bottom of gleaming white sand, Laguna Bacalar comes as a surprise in this region of tortured limestone and scrubby jungle.

The small, sleepy town of **Bacalar**, east of the highway, 125km south of Felipe Carrillo Puerto, is noted for its Spanish fortress and its popular *balneario* (swimming facility).

About two blocks south of the fort, **Casita Carolina** (☎ 983-834-23-34; www.casitacarolina.com; d US$25-45) is a delightful place near the lake with five rooms and a deluxe *palapa*. Kayaks are available for guests.

Costera Bacalar is the road that winds south along the lakeshore to **Cenote Azul**, a 90m-deep natural pool. There's a **restaurant** (meals US$6-10) overlooking the cenote.

You can camp on the lakeshore at **Los Coquitos** (per person US$4.50), about 700m south of Hotel Laguna along the Costera. Bring your own food and water.

Southbound buses will usually drop you in Bacalar – ask first.

From Chetumal's minibus terminal (p350), buses leave about hourly from 5am to 9pm (45 minutes, US$1.75).

CHETUMAL

☎ 983 / pop 130,000

Chetumal is the gateway to Belize. With the peso so low against the neighboring currency, Belizean shoppers come here frequently.

Despite Chetumal's sprawling layout, the city center is easily manageable on foot, and it contains several hotels and restaurants.

A **tourist information kiosk** (☎ 832-36-63; ⏱ 9am-2pm & 6-9pm Mon-Sat) is on Av de los Héroes right in the center of town.

The **post office** (☎ 832-00-57) is at the corner of Plutarco Elías Calles and Av 5 de Mayo. The **immigration office** (☎ 832-63-53; ⏱ 9am-11pm Mon-Fri) is on Av de los Héroes on the left about four blocks north of Av Insurgentes (and the bus terminal). There are several **banks** and ATMs around town.

Sights

The **Museo de la Cultura Maya** (☎ 823-68-38; Av de los Héroes btwn Colón & Av Gandhi; admission US$5.50; ⏱ 9am-7pm Tue-Thu & Sun, 9am-8pm Fri & Sat) is the city's claim to fame – a bold showpiece drawing visitors from as far away as Cancún.

The museum is organized into three levels, mirroring Mayan cosmology. The main floor represents this world, the upper floor the heavens, and the lower floor the underworld. Though the museum is short on artifacts, the various exhibits (labeled in Spanish and English) cover all of the lands of the Maya and seek to explain their way of life, thought and belief. The museum's **courtyard** (admission free) has salons for temporary exhibits of modern artists and paintings reproducing Mayan frescoes. Just walk past the ticket window.

Sleeping

Holiday Inn Chetumal Puerta Maya (☎ 835-04-00; www.holiday-inn.com; Av de los Héroes 171; d US$110; 🅿 🔁) The Holiday Inn is two blocks north of Los Cocos along Av de los Héroes, near the tourist information kiosk. Its comfortable rooms overlook a small courtyard with a swimming pool. It's the best in town.

The cheapest in town is the youth hostel, **Instituto Quintanarroense de la Juventud** (☎ 832-05-25; Heroica Escuela Naval; dm US$4, campsites per person US$2), off Calzada Veracruz just past the eastern end of Av Obregón.

Other good hotels include:

Hotel Caribe Princess (☎ 832-09-00; Av Álvaro Obregón 168; d US$40; 🅿 🔁)

Hotel Los Cocos (☎ 832-05-44; cnr Av de los Héroes & Calle Héroes de Chapultepec; d with air-con & TV US$68; 🅿 🔁 🔁)

Hotel María Dolores (☎ 832-05-08; Av Álvaro Obregón 206; d US$18; 🅿)

Hotel Ucum (☎ 832-07-11, 832-61-86; Av Mahatma Gandhi 167; d with fan/air-con US$20/25; 🅿 🔁 🔁)

Eating & Drinking

Café-Restaurant Los Milagros (Calle Ignacio Zaragoza btwn Avs 5 de Mayo & de los Héroes; breakfast US$3-4, mains US$4-5) A favorite with Chetumal's student and intellectual set.

Café Espresso (cnr 22 de Enero & Av Miguel Hidalgo; breakfast US$3-4, mains US$6-9) Good for breakfast and dinner.

Sergio's Pizzas (Av Álvaro Obregón 182; pizza US$4-18, mains US$5-15) Great for pizza and beer.

Restaurant Sosilmar (Av Álvaro Obregón 206; mains US$4-6) Beneath the Hotel María Dolores, it serves filling platters of fish or meat.

For juicy roasted chicken, hit **Pollo Brujo** (Av Álvaro Obregón btwn Avs de los Héroes & Benito Juárez; chicken US$4), and for vegetarian fare try **Restaurant Vegetariano La Fuente** (Lázaro Cárdenas 222; meals US$4-5; ⏱ closed Sun) or **Euro Buffet** (Blanco btwn Avs Benito Juárez & Independencia; ⏱ closed Sat & Sun).

YUCATÁN PENINSULA, TABASCO & CHIAPAS

CHETUMAL

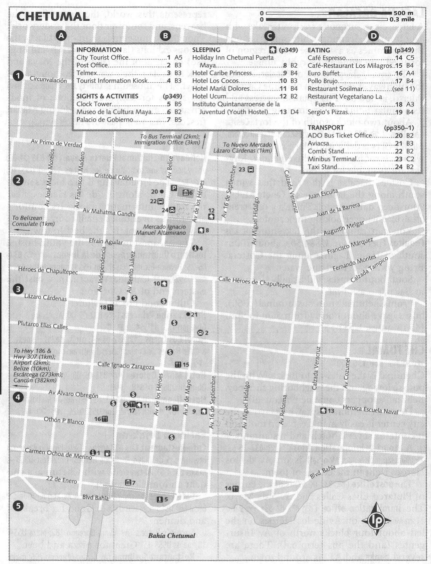

INFORMATION
City Tourist Office..................1 A5
Post Office................................2 B3
Telmex....................................3 B3
Tourist Information Kiosk.........4 B3

SIGHTS & ACTIVITIES   (p349)
Clock Tower.............................5 B5
Museo de la Cultura Maya.......6 B2
Palacio de Gobierno.................7 B5

SLEEPING   (p349)
Holiday Inn Chetumal Puerta
  Maya.....................................8 B2
Hotel Caribe Princess...............9 B4
Hotel Los Cocos.....................10 B3
Hotel Mariá Dolores...............11 B4
Hotel Ucum..........................12 B2
Instituto Quintanaroense de la
  Juventud (Youth Hostel)......13 D4

EATING   (p349)
Café Espresso.........................14 C5
Café-Restaurant Los Milagros..15 B4
Euro Buffet.............................16 A4
Pollo Brujo.............................17 B4
Restaurant Sosilmar..............(see 11)
Restaurant Vegetariano La
  Fuente.................................18 A3
Sergio's Pizzas.......................19 B4

TRANSPORT   (pp350–1)
ADO Bus Ticket Office...........20 B2
Aviacsa...................................21 B3
Combi Stand..........................22 B2
Minibus Terminal...................23 C2
Taxi Stand..............................24 B2

Getting There & Away

AIR

Chetumal's small airport is less than 2km northwest of the city center along Av Álvaro Obregón.

Aviacsa (☎ 832-77-65, airport ☎ 832-77-87) flies to Mexico City. Its in-town office is on Av Lázaro Cárdenas at Av 5 de Mayo.

For flights to Belize City (and on to Tikal) or to Belize's cayes, cross the border into Belize and fly from Corozal.

BUS

The bus terminal is about 2km north of the center near the intersection of Avs Insurgentes and Belice. The terminal has lockers, a bus information kiosk, ATM, shops and other services.

Many local buses, and those bound for Belize, begin their runs from the Nuevo Mercado Lázaro Cárdenas, on Calzada Veracruz at Confederación Nacional Campesina (also called Segundo Circuito) about 10 blocks north of Av Primo de Verdad. From this market, some Belize-bound buses continue to the long-distance terminal and depart from there 15 minutes later. Tickets can be purchased at the market, on board the buses or at the main terminal.

The **minibus terminal** (cnr Avs Primo de Verdad & Hidalgo) has services to Bacalar and other nearby destinations. Departures listed below are from the main terminal unless otherwise noted.

Bacalar (45min, many Mayab buses, US$1.50 from the minibus terminal, US$1.75 from the main terminal)

Belize City (Belize) (3-4hr; 20 Novelo's & Northern buses, US$5.50-7, 4:30am-6pm) Departing from Nuevo Mercado.

Campeche (6½-9hr; 1 1st-class ADO bus, US$20, noon; 2 2nd-class buses, US$16)

Cancún (5½-6½hr; regular buses, US$14.50-17)

Corozal (Belize) (1hr with border formalities; 2nd-class, US$2.25) See Belize City schedule.

Escárcega (4-6hr; 9 buses, 4:15am-10:30pm, US$10.50-12.50)

Felipe Carrillo Puerto (2-3hr; regular buses, US$6-7)

Flores, Guatemala (for Tikal) (8hr; 5 1st-class Servicio San Juan & Mundo Maya buses, US$36, 6:20am-2:30pm)

Mahahual (4hr; 3 2nd-class buses, 4am, 6am & 3:15pm, US$4)

Mérida (6-8hr; US$15.50-US$19)

Orange Walk (Belize) (2¼hr; US$3-3.50) See Belize City listing, above.

Playa del Carmen (4½-6hr; regular buses, US$12-14.50)

Ticul (6hr; 6 buses, US$12.50)

Tulum (3½-4hr; regular buses, US$12)

Valladolid (6hr; 2 2nd-class buses, US$11.50)

Veracruz (16hr; 2 1st-class buses, US$49)

Villahermosa (7-9hr; 5 buses, US$26)

Xcalak (5hr; 3 2nd-class buses, 4am, 6am & 3:15pm, US$5.50)

Xpujil (2-3hr; 9 buses, US$4.75-5.75)

Getting Around

Taxis from the stand at the bus terminal charge US$1.25 to the center (agree on the price before getting in). To reach the terminal, head for the combi and taxi stands on Av Belice behind the Museo de la Cultura Maya. By combi, ask to be dropped off at the *glorieta* (traffic circle) at Av Insurgentes. Head west to reach the terminal.

YUCATÁN STATE

The state of Yucatán is a pie slice at the top of the Yucatán Peninsula. Until the development of Cancún in neighboring Quintana Roo, it was the peninsula's economic engine. While the tourist-driven economy of Quintana Roo has surpassed Yucatán's in recent years, historically and culturally Yucatán remains paramount. Here you'll find the peninsula's most impressive Mayan ruins (Chichén Itzá and Uxmal), its finest colonial cities (Mérida and Valladolid) and two coastal communities internationally famous for their wild red flamingoes.

A high-speed highway served by numerous 1st-class buses links Cancún and Mérida, and the trip to one of Mexico's oldest cities following a visit to one of its most modern resorts is highly recommended.

MÉRIDA

☎ 999 / pop 690,000

Mérida, once the Mayan city of T'hó, has been the dominant metropolitan center in the Yucatán region since the Spanish Conquest. Today the capital of the state of Yucatán is a prosperous city of narrow streets, colonial buildings and shady parks. Mérida is the cultural center of the peninsula, and every night of the week some engaging event takes place. The city center is especially delightful on weekends when the streets are blocked off to all but pedestrians. Mérida makes a good base for excursions around the region.

Orientation

The Plaza Grande, as *meridanos* (people from Mérida) call the main square, has been the city's center since Mayan times. Most services you'll need lie within five blocks of the square.

Information
BOOKSTORES

Arte Maya (Calle 57 btwn Calles 60 &62) Buy or trade used books here.

Librería Dante (☎ 928-26-11; on the main square next to the Olimpio; also a smaller location on Calle 59) Sells paperbacks and guidebooks in English.

EMERGENCY

Fire (☎ 924-92-42)
Police (☎ 925-20-34)

MÉRIDA

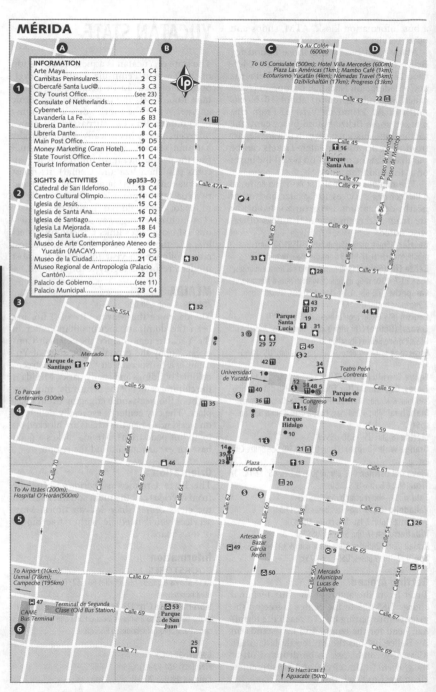

Ⓐ **Ⓑ** **Ⓒ** **Ⓓ**

INFORMATION
Arte Maya......................................	**1** C4
Cambitas Peninsulares....................	**2** C3
Cibercafé Santa Luci@....................	**3** C3
City Tourist Office..........................	(see 23)
Consulate of Netherlands...............	**4** C2
Cybernet..	**5** C4
Lavandería La Fe...........................	**6** B3
Librería Dante...............................	**7** C4
Librería Dante...............................	**8** C4
Main Post Office............................	**9** D5
Money Marketing (Gran Hotel).......	**10** C4
State Tourist Office........................	**11** C4
Tourist Information Center.............	**12** C4

SIGHTS & ACTIVITIES (pp353–5)
Catedral de San Ildefonso..............	**13** C4
Centro Cultural Olimpio..................	**14** C4
Iglesia de Jesús.............................	**15** C4
Iglesia de Santa Ana......................	**16** D2
Iglesia de Santiago........................	**17** A4
Iglesia La Mejorada.......................	**18** E4
Iglesia Santa Lucía........................	**19** C3
Museo de Arte Contemporáneo Ateneo de	
Yucatán (MACAY).......................	**20** C5
Museo de la Ciudad.......................	**21** C4
Museo Regional de Antropología (Palacio	
Cantón)......................................	**22** D1
Palacio de Gobierno......................	(see 11)
Palacio Municipal...........................	**23** C4

To Av Colón (600m)

To US Consulate (500m); Hotel Villa Mercedes (600m);
Plaza Las Américas (1km); Mambo Café (1km);
Ecoturismo Yucatán (4km); Nómadas Travel (5km);
Dzibilchaltún (17km); Progreso (33km)

Calle 43 22

Calle 45 16

Parque Santa Ana

Calle 47 Calle 47

Calle 47A 4

Calle 49

Paseo de Montejo

Calle 56A

41

Calle 62 Calle 60 Calle 58 Calle 56

30 33 Calle 51

28

Calle 53

Calle 55A 32 43 37 44

Parque Santa Lucía 19 31

6 3@ 29 27 45
2

Mercado 24
Parque de Santiago 17

34 Teatro Peón Contreras

To Parque Centenario (300m)

Calle 59 Universidad de Yucatán 1 42 12 38 48 5 Calle 57
40 Congreso Parque de la Madre
35 36 15

8

Parque Hidalgo 10

14 39 7 21 13
23 Plaza Grande

20

Calle 66A Calle 66 Calle 64 Calle 62 Calle 60 Calle 58 Calle 56 Calle 54

To Av Itzáes (200m); Hospital O'Horán (500m)

Calle 68 46

Calle 63

Calle 70

9 Calle 65
Artesanías Bazar García Rejón 49

26
Calle 54A

To Airport (10km); Uxmal (78km); Campeche (195km)

Calle 67 50 Mercado Municipal Lucas de Gálvez 51

47 Terminal de Segunda Clase (Old Bus Station) Calle 69 53
CAME Bus Terminal Parque de San Juan

Calle 67

25

Calle 71 Calle 69

To Hamacas El Aguacate (50m)

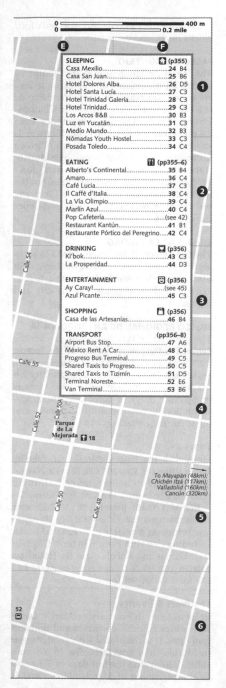

SLEEPING   (p355)
Casa Mexilio	24 B4
Casa San Juan	25 B6
Hotel Dolores Alba	26 D5
Hotel Santa Lucía	27 C3
Hotel Trinidad Galería	28 C3
Hotel Trinidad	29 C3
Los Arcos B&B	30 B3
Luz en Yucatán	31 C3
Medío Mundo	32 B3
Nómadas Youth Hostel	33 C3
Posada Toledo	34 C4

EATING   (pp355–6)
Alberto's Continental	35 B4
Amaro	36 C4
Café Lucía	37 C3
Il Caffé d'Italia	38 C4
La Vía Olimpio	39 C4
Marlín Azul	40 C4
Pop Cafetería	(see 42)
Restaurant Kantún	41 B1
Restaurante Pórtico del Peregrino	42 C4

DRINKING   (p356)
Ki'bok	43 C3
La Prosperidad	44 D3

ENTERTAINMENT   (p356)
Ay Caray!	(see 45)
Azul Picante	45 C3

SHOPPING   (p356)
Casa de las Artesanías	46 B4

TRANSPORT   (pp356–8)
Airport Bus Stop	47 A6
México Rent A Car	48 C4
Progreso Bus Terminal	49 C5
Shared Taxis to Progreso	50 C5
Shared Taxis to Tizimín	51 D5
Terminal Noreste	52 E6
Van Terminal	53 B6

Parque de La Mejorada 18

To Mayapán (48km);
Chichén Itzá (117km);
Valladolid (160km);
Cancún (320km)

Red Cross (☎ 924-98-13)
Tourism Police (☎ 930-32-00)

INTERNET ACCESS
Internet cafés are ubiquitous. Try:
Cibercafé Santa Lucí@ (cnr Calles 62 & Calle 55)
Cybernet (Calle 57A btwn Calles 58 & 60)

LAUNDRY
Lavandería La Fe (Calle 64 No 470 btwn Calles 55 & 57;
per 3kg load US$4)

MEDICAL SERVICES
Hospital O'Horán (☎ 924-4800; Av Itzáes; Parque
Centenario)

MONEY
Banks and ATMs are scattered throughout
the city, especially along Calle 65, one block
south of the Plaza Grande (see map for locations). *Casas de cambio* give good rates and
have faster service. Try:
Cambistas Peninsulares (Calle 60 btwn Calles 55 & 57)
Money Marketing (Gran Hotel on Parque Hidalgo)

POST
Central Post Office (cnr Calles 65 & 56)

TOURIST INFORMATION
City Tourist Office (☎ 928-20-20; Calle 62 on Plaza
Grande; ⏰ 8am-8pm)
State Tourist Office (☎ 930-31-03; Calle 61 on Plaza
Grande; ⏰ 8am-9pm)
Tourist Information Center (☎ 924-9290; cnr Calles
60 & 57A; ⏰ 8am-8pm) At the northeast edge of Parque
de la Madre.

TRAVEL AGENCIES
Nómadas Travel (☎ 948-11-87; www.nomadastravel
.com in Spanish; Prolongacíon Paseo de Montejo No 370)
Student discount tickets and ISIC (international student
identity cards) available.

Dangers & Annoyances
Guard against pickpockets in the market
district and in any crowd, such as at a performance. The area around the bus station
is not safe at night for women alone, nor
are the hotels in that neighborhood (none
of which are listed below).

Sights
PLAZA GRANDE
This large but at times surprisingly intimate
square is the most logical place to start a

tour of Mérida. Also known as 'El Centro' (as in the center of town) or the Plaza Principal, the Plaza Grande was the religious and social center of the ancient Mayan city T'hó. The plaza is surrounded by some of the city's most impressive and harmonious colonial buildings, and its carefully tended laurel trees provide welcome shade. On Sunday hundreds of *meridanos* take their *paseo* (stroll) here. Various events take place around the plaza on weekly schedules.

On the plaza's east side, on the former site of a Mayan temple, is one of Mexico's oldest churches: **Catedral de San Ildefonso** (1561-88; ☺ 6am-noon & 4-7pm). Be certain to step inside to see the towering crucifix, Cristo de la Unidad (Christ of Unity), behind the altar. In the small chapel to the left of the altar is a replica of Mérida's most famous religious artifact, a statue called Cristo de las Ampollas (Christ of the Blisters).

South of the cathedral, housed in the former archbishop's palace, is the **Museo de Arte Contemporáneo Ateneo de Yucatán** (MACAY; ☎ 928-31-91; admission US$2.50; ☺ 10am-6pm Wed-Mon), which holds permanent exhibits of Yucatán's most famous painters and sculptors.

Across the square from the cathedral is Mérida's **Palacio Municipal** (1542; City Hall). Adjoining it to the north is the **Centro Cultural Olimpo**, Mérida's municipal cultural center. On the north side of the plaza, the **Palacio de Gobierno** (1892; admission free; ☺ 8am-9pm) houses the state of Yucatán's executive government offices (and tourist information office).

CALLE 60

A block north of the Plaza Grande, just beyond shady Parque Hidalgo, rises the 17th-century **Iglesia de Jesús**, also called Iglesia de la Tercera Orden. It was built by the Jesuits in 1618 using stones of a destroyed Mayan temple. On the west wall facing Parque Hidalgo, you can see two stones still bearing Mayan carvings.

North of the church is the large and lavish Italian-designed **Teatro Peón Contreras** (cnr Calles 60 & 57), built between 1900 and 1908, during Mérida's henequen heyday.

At the intersection of Calles 60 and 55 is pretty little **Parque Santa Lucía**, with arcades on the northern and western sides. The **Bazar de Artesanías**, the local handicrafts market, is held here at 11am on Sunday.

To reach the Paseo de Montejo walk four blocks north and two east.

PASEO DE MONTEJO

The Paseo de Montejo was an attempt by Mérida's 19th-century city planners to create a wide boulevard similar to the Paseo de la Reforma in Mexico City or the Champs-Élysées in Paris. Though more modest than its predecessors, the Paseo de Montejo is still a beautiful, long, wide swath of green in an otherwise urban conglomeration of stone and concrete. Most tourists don't venture beyond the downtown area, but the Paseo de Montejo is where life for many *meridanos* (especially the middle and upper class) begins.

MUSEO DE LA CIUDAD

The **City Museum** (Calle 61 btwn Calles 58 & 60; admission free; ☺ 10am-2pm & 4-8pm Tue-Fri, 10am-2pm Sat & Sun) is small but worthwhile, with artifacts, exhibits and good photos of the city and region.

MUSEO REGIONAL DE ANTROPOLOGÍA

The great white Palacio Cantón houses the **Regional Anthropology Museum of the Yucatán** (1909-11; cnr Paseo de Montejo & Calle 43; admission US$3; ☺ 8am-8pm Tue-Sat, 8am-2pm Sun). Exhibits on Mayan culture include explanations (many in Spanish only) of forehead-flattening – which was done to beautify babies – and other cosmetic practices.

Tours

Housed in the Palacio Municipal, the **City Tourist Office** (☎ 928-20-20; Calle 62 on Plaza Grande) offers free daily walking tours of the historic center. They begin out front at 9:30am.

Nómadas Youth Hostel (☎ 924-52-23; www.nomadastravel.com; Calle 62 No 433 at Calle 51) offers low prices on a variety of organized tours, including Celestún Flamingo tour, Chichén Itzá, Uxmal and Kabah. Also try **Ecoturismo Yucatán** (☎ 920-27-72; www.ecoyuc.com; Calle 3 No 235) for a variety of tours.

Festivals & Events

Prior to Lent, in February or March, **Carnaval** features colorful costumes and nonstop festivities. It is celebrated with greater vigor in Mérida than anywhere else in Yucatán state. Also during the last days of February or the beginning of March (dates vary) is

Kihuic, a market that fills the Plaza Grande with handicrafts artisans from all over Mexico.

Between September 22 and October 14, *gremios* (guilds or unions) venerate the **Cristo de las Ampollas** (Christ of the Blisters) statue in the cathedral with processions.

Another big religious tradition is the **Exposición de Altares**, held the night of November 1, when the Maya welcome the spirits of their ancestors with elaborate dinners outside their homes.

Sleeping

High season runs roughly mid-December through March. Wherever possible, high-season rates have been given.

Nómadas Youth Hostel (☎ 924-52-23; www.noma dastravel.com; Calle 62 No 433 at Calle 51; hammock or tent US$4, dm US$6, r with shared bathroom US$13) This spacious, clean, extremely well-run hostel boasts a kitchen, hot showers and hand-laundry facilities. Breakfast is included. Nómadas also has live Trova (folk music) Tuesdays and Fridays, and free salsa dance classes the rest of the week.

Hotel Trinidad Galería (☎ 923-24-63; Calle 60 No 456; s/d US$22/25; ⊠) Funky, fun and downright silly, the Trinidad Galería boasts spacious patios and a palm-shaded poolside (which make up for the smallish, dark rooms).

Hotel Trinidad (☎ 923-20-33; www.hoteltrinidad .com; Calle 62 No 464 btwn Calles 55 & 57; dm US$8, r with private/shared bathroom US$30/25; ⊠) This 19-room hotel centers on two lovely courtyards. Each unit is uniquely furnished with an artist's eye for decor and ambiance.

Medio Mundo (☎ 924-54-72; www.hotelmedio mundo.com; Calle 55 No 533; r with fan US$45-55, with fan & air-con US$60-65) Every detail here, from the quiet air-con to comfy beds, has been attended to. What's it missing? Distractions: no phone, no TV, no noise. Healthy breakfasts (US$8) and organic coffee to boot.

Luz en Yucatán (☎ 924-00-35; US ☎ www.luzenyucatan .com; Calle 55 No 499; r US$40-60; ⊠ ⊠) Two beers on arrival is the delightfully eccentric owner's policy. Each of the seven rooms that surround the courtyard and small pool is an original work dedicated to comfort and coziness.

Casa Mexilio (☎ 928-25-05; US ☎ +1-800-538-6802; www.casamexilio.com; Calle 68 No 495 btwn Calles 57 & 59; r US$47-83; ⊠ ⊠) Housed in a beautifully deco-rated 19th-century townhouse, Casa Mexilio boasts eight attractively adorned rooms and a courtyard with pool and Jacuzzi.

Posada Toledo (☎ 923-16-90; Calle 58 No 487 at Calle 57; d with fan/air-con US$35/45; ⓟ ⊠) This former mansion retains its regal air, and much of the furnishings (don't worry, not the beds) are straight out of the 19th century.

Casa San Juan (☎ 986-29-37; www.casasanjuan .com; Calle 62 No 545A btwn Calles 69 & 71; d US$45-55; ⓟ ⊠) This pensión is housed in a lovingly restored colonial home. Some of the seven large rooms have air-con, and all have mile-high ceilings and original woodwork. Breakfast is included.

Los Arcos B&B (☎ 928-02-14; www.losarcosmerida .com; Calle 66 btwn Calles 49 & 53; s/d US$ 65/85; ⊠ ⊠) This gay-friendly B&B only has the three rooms, so as a guest you virtually have this whole gorgeous home to yourself. There's a stunning garden and pool area too.

Hotel Dolores Alba (☎ 928-56-50, 800-849-50-60; www.doloresalba.com; Calle 63 btwn Calles 52 & 54; r with/ without air-con US$40/35; ⓟ ⊠ ⊠) The Dolores Alba, with courtyards and a pool, is a Mérida institution and an excellent value.

Hotel Santa Lucía (☎ 928-26-72; www.hotel santalucia.com.mx; Calle 55 No 508 btwn Calles 60 & 62; s/d US$36/40; ⊠ ⊠) This pastel pink colonial hotel across the street from Parque Santa Lucía is understandably a favorite among travelers. It has a small pool, and all 51 rooms are clean and have TV and telephone.

Hotel Villa Mercedes (☎ 924-90-00; www.hotelvilla mercedes.com.mx; Av Colón 500 at Calle 60; r from US$110; ⓟ ⊠ ⊠ ⊠) This refurbished mansion has been restored to its original Art Nouveau splendor. It's smaller (84 rooms) and more intimate (as mansions go) than Mérida's other top-end hotels. There's a pool, gym and business center.

Eating

Pop Cafetería (☎ 928-61-63; Calle 57 btwn Calles 60 & 62; breakfast US$3-5, mains US$4-6; ⊠) Tasty, cheap breakfast combinations and a good variety of Mexican dishes.

Marlín Azul (Calle 62 No 488 btwn Calles 51 & 53; mains US$5) Frequented by locals but rarely tourists, this small place serves cheap and yummy sea food; the *ceviche mixto* (mixed ceviche) is excellent.

Amaro (☎ 928-24-52; Calle 59 btwn Calles 60 & 62; mains US$6-10) Very romantic, especially at night, Amaro serves Yucatecan food and a good variety of vegetarian plates.

Café Lucia (☎ 928-07-40; Calle 60 No 474 btwn Calles 55 & 53; mains US$8-10; ✷) Chic gallery/restaurant with impressive artwork and very good seafood, steak and pasta dishes.

Restaurant Kantún (☎ 923-44-93; Calle 45 btwn Calles 64 & 66; mains US$6-8; ✪ Thu-Sun) This family-run place serves some of the best seafood in town.

Il Caffè d'Italia (☎ 925-94-52; Calle 57A btwn Calles 58 & 60; mains US$ 5-8) Good breakfasts, strong coffee, and reasonable Italian fare for lunch and dinner.

La Vía Olimpio (☎ 923-58-43; Calle 62 btwn Calles 61 & 63; breakfast US$5, mains US$5-8) This trendy restaurant-café facing Plaza Grande is open practically 24-7 (closed only between 11pm Monday and 7am Tuesday). Soups, salads, sandwiches and breakfasts complete the menu.

Alberto's Continental (☎ 928-53-67; Calle 64 at Calle 57; mains US$10-20) Housed in a 1727 colonial home, Alberto's is rich in atmosphere, and the cuisine is mostly Middle Eastern (and completely delicious!).

Restaurante Pórtico del Peregrino (☎ 928-61-63; Calle 57 btwn Calles 60 & 62; meals US$12-20; ✷) Yucatecan dishes are the forte here, especially the *pollo pibil*.

Mercado Municipal Lucas de Gálvez (Calle 56A) A bustling market full of small, cheap eateries.

Jugos California (Plaza Mayor) Perfect place for a tall glass of cool fruit juice.

Entertainment
CULTURAL EVENTS
Mérida's cultural life is thriving, and every night of the week offers an opportunity to take in a different musical or theatrical performance. Pick up a copy of *Yucatán Today* (available at any tourist office and most hotels) to check the schedule of current events.

Ballet Folklórico de la Universidad de Yucatán (University of Yucatán, Calle 60 at Calle 57; ✪ show 9pm; US$2), the university's folk dance troupe, puts on an impressive and authentic performance of regional dances every Friday night.

Centro Olimpio (☎ 928-20-20; Plaza Grande) has something interesting – from films to concerts to art installations – scheduled nearly every night of the week. **Teatro Peón Contreras** (cnr Calle 60 & 57) features Mexican and international musical and dance performances.

Mérida en Domingo (Mérida on Sunday; ✪ 9am-9pm Sun) is a lively fair that takes place when the main plaza and Calle 60 are closed to cars. From about 11am onwards, bands play in front of the Palacio del Gobierno on the plaza. Live salsa music and dancing kick in around 7pm in Parque Hidalgo.

NIGHTCLUBS & DISCOS
Ay Caray! (Calle 60 btwn Calles 55 & 57) is a loud trendy bar with live music most nights. **La Prosperidad** (☎ 924-14-07; Calle 56 at Calle 53) is a big *palapa* bar featuring live rock, lots of beer and tasty *botanas* (snacks).

At labyrinthine café/bar **Ki'bok** (☎ 928-55-11; Calle 60 btwn 55 & 53), you may need to leave a trail of breadcrumbs to find your way back to the front door. The always-crowded **Mambo Café** (☎ 987-75-33; Plaza Las Américas Shopping Mall) has live salsa bands on weekends and DJ-spun disco, house and pop other nights.

Azul Picante (Calle 60 btwn Calles 55 & 57) features live salsa and dance lessons.

Shopping
Mérida is a fine place for buying Yucatecan handicrafts. Purchases to consider include traditional Mayan clothing such as the colorful embroidered *huipiles*, panama hats, and the wonderfully comfortable Yucatecan hammocks.

Mercado Municipal Lucas de Gálvez (Calle 56A) southeast of Plaza Grande, is Mérida's main market.

Casa de las Artesanías (Calle 63 btwn Calles 64 & 66; ✪ 9am-8pm Mon-Sat, 10am-2pm Sun) is a government-supported market for local artisans selling just about everything. Prices are fixed but reasonable.

The best place in town to buy hammocks is **Hamacas El Aguacate** (☎ 928-64-69; Calle 58 at Calle 73). If you want to venture out of town you can go to the nearby village of Tixkokob (Map p359; buses run from the Progreso bus station) and watch hammock makers at work. It is also a good place to find a well-crafted hammock at a fair price.

Getting There & Away
AIR
Mérida's airport is a 10km, 20-minute ride southwest of the Plaza Grande off Hwy 180 (Av Itzáes). It has car rental desks, an ATM, currency exchange and a tourist office.

Most international flights to Mérida are connections through Mexico City or Cancún. Nonstop international services are provided by **Aeroméxico** (Los Angeles and Miami) and **Continental** (Houston). Scheduled domestic flights are operated mostly by smaller regional airlines, with a few flights by **Aeroméxico** and **Mexicana**.

BUS
Mérida is the bus transport hub of the Yucatán Peninsula. Watch your gear on night buses and those serving popular tourist destinations (especially 2nd-class buses); Lonely Planet has received many reports of theft on the night runs to Chiapas and of a few daylight thefts on the Chichén Itzá route.

Mérida has a variety of **bus terminals**, and some lines operate out of (and stop at) more than one terminal. Tickets for departure from one terminal can often be bought at another, and destinations overlap greatly among lines. Following are some of the stations, bus lines operating out of them and areas served.

Parque de San Juan (Calle 69 btwn Calles 62 & 64) is the terminus for vans and Volkswagen combis going to Dzibilchaltún Ruinas, Muna, Oxkutzcab, Petó, Sacalum, Tekax and Ticul.

Terminal CAME (☎ 924-83-91; Calle 70 btwn Calles 69 & 71) is Mérida's main terminal, located seven blocks southwest of the Plaza Grande. Come here for (mostly 1st-class) buses to points around the Yucatán Peninsula and beyond.

Second-class buses depart from **Terminal de Segunda Clase** (Calle 69 btwn Calles 68 & 70) to points in the state and around the peninsula.

Terminal Noreste (Calle 67 btwn Calles 50 & 52) is the Noreste bus line's terminal. Buses run from here to many small towns in the northeast part of the peninsula, including Tizimín and Río Lagartos, as well as frequent service to Cancún and points along the way, and small towns south and west of Mérida, including Celestún, Ticul and Oxkutzcab.

Destinations served from Mérida include the following:

Campeche (via Bécal, 2½-3½hr; frequent 1st-class ADO buses, US$8; 2nd-class ATS buses every 30min to 7pm, US$7)

Campeche (via Uxmal, 4hr; 5 2nd-class SUR buses, 6am & 5pm, US$7.50)

Cancún (4-6hr; 16 2nd-class Oriente buses, US$12; 20 Super Expresso deluxe buses, US$17) And many other buses.

Celestún (2hr; 15 2nd-class buses, US$3.50)

Chetumal (6-8hr; 8 deluxe Omnitur del Caribe & Super Expresso buses, US$19; 3 2nd-class Mayab buses, US$16)

Chichén Itzá (2-2½hr; 3 Super Expresso & 16 2nd-class Oriente buses, US$5) Some Cancún-bound buses stop at Chichén Itzá during the day, and at night in nearby Pisté.

Cobá (3½hr; 1 deluxe Super Expresso bus, 1pm, US$11; 1 Oriente bus, 5:15am, US$8)

Escárcega (5½hr; 1 1st-class Altos bus, US$14; 5 1st-class ADO bus, US$16; many 2nd-class Sur buses, US$13)

Felipe Carrillo Puerto (5½hr; 7 2nd-class Mayab buses, US$12; 5 2nd-class TRP buses, US$12.50)

Izamal (1½hr; frequent 2nd-class Oriente buses, US$3)

Mayapán Ruinas (2hr; 15 2nd-class LUS buses, US$1.50) From Terminal Noreste.

Mexico City (Norte, 19hr; 1st-class ADO bus, 12:05pm, US$77)

Mexico City (TAPO, 20hr; 4 1st-class ADO buses, 10am-9:15pm, US$75)

Palenque (8-9hr; 1 deluxe Maya de Oro bus, US$29; 3 1st-class ADO buses, US$26; 1 Altos, US$24)

Playa del Carmen (5-7hr; 10 deluxe Super Expresso buses, US$20)

Río Lagartos (3-4hr; 3 1st- & 2nd-class Noreste buses, from 9am, US$6-8)

Ticul (2hr; frequent 2nd-class Mayab buses, US$3.50; frequent minibuses, US$2.75) The minibuses leave from Parque de San Juan.

Tizimín (2½-4hr; several 1st- & 2nd-class Noreste buses, US$7-8)

Tulum (via Cobá, 4hr; deluxe Super Expresso, 6:30am, 11am & 1pm, US$13) There is 2nd-class service to Tulum, but it costs more and takes twice as long.

Tuxtla Gutiérrez (13-16hr; 1 deluxe Maya de Oro bus, 9:30pm, US$45; 1 Altos bus, 7:15pm, US$37) Or change at Palenque or Villahermosa.

Valladolid (2½-3½hr; deluxe Super Expresso buses, US$8.50; 2nd-class Oriente & ATS buses, US$6.50) Many more buses.

Villahermosa (8-9hr; 10 1st-class ADO buses, US$30; 2 superdeluxe UNO buses, 9:30pm & 11pm, US$50; 1 ADO GL bus, 5:30pm, US$48)

CAR & MOTORCYCLE
The optimal way to tour the many archaeological sites south of Mérida is by car; however, getting around town is definitely better done with public transportation or on foot.

México Rent A Car (☎ 923-36-37; Calle 57A btwn 58 & 60) offers rates the big-name agencies often can't touch, especially if you're paying cash.

It's sometimes possible to get a VW Beetle for as little as US$25 a day, and long-term rentals can bring prices lower than that.

Several other agencies have branches at the airport as well as on Calle 60 between Calles 55 and 57.

Getting Around

TO/FROM THE AIRPORT

Bus 79 ('Aviación') travels between the airport and the city center every 15 to 30 minutes until 9pm, with occasional service until 11pm. The half-hour trip (US$0.50) goes via a very roundabout route; the best place to catch the bus is on Calle 70 just south of Calle 69, near the corner of the CAME terminal.

Transporte Terrestre (☎ 946-15-29) provides speedy service between the airport and the center, charging US$11 per carload (same price for hotel pick-up). A taxi from the center to the airport should cost you about US$8.

BUS

City buses are cheap at US$0.40, but most parts of Mérida that you'll want to visit are within five or six blocks of the Plaza Grande and are thus accessible on foot.

TAXI

Taxis in Mérida are not metered. Rates are fixed, with an outrageous US$3 minimum fare, which will get you from the bus terminals to all downtown hotels. Costs of most rides within city limits do not exceed US$5.50.

SMALL WONDER

The Irish have leprechauns, Scandinavians have elves and Snow White has her dwarfs. In Mayan mythology the equivalent big-spirited, small-bodied inhabitants of the forest are called *aluxes* (a-*loosh*-es). These very clever, often mischievous little people are said to live in caves and make themselves seen only occasionally and usually to small children. *Aluxes* hold an important position in Maya legend and are attributed with power for both assisting those who believe in them and wreaking havoc for those who don't.

SOUTH OF MÉRIDA

Mayapán

These **ruins** (admission US$3; ☉ 8am-5pm) are some 50km southeast of Mérida, on Yucatán state Hwy 18. Though far less impressive than many Mayan sites, Mayapán is historically significant. Its main attractions are clustered in a compact core, and visitors usually have the place to themselves.

According to legend, Mayapán was founded by Kukulcán (Quetzalcóatl) in AD 1007. His dynasty, the Cocom, organized a confederation of city-states that included Uxmal, Chichén Itzá and many other notable cities.

The city of Mayapán was large, with a population estimated at 12,000; it covered 4 sq km, all surrounded by a great defensive wall. In the early 1950s and early '60s, archaeologists mapped over 3500 buildings, 20 cenotes and traces of the city wall.

Don't confuse the ruins of Mayapán with the Mayan village of the same name, some 40km southeast of the ruins, past the town of Teabo.

The ruins of Mayapán are just off Hwy 18, a few kilometers southwest of the town of Telchaquillo. LUS runs 15 2nd-class buses between 5:30am and 8:00pm from the Terminal Noreste in Mérida (US$1.50, two hours) that will let you off near the entrance of the ruins.

Uxmal

Some visitors rank **Uxmal** (admission US$9, Sun & holidays US$4; ☉ 8am-5pm) among the top Mayan archaeological sites. It certainly is one of the most harmonious and peaceful. Fascinating, well-preserved structures made of pink-hued limestone cover the wide area. Adding to its appeal is Uxmal's setting in the hilly Puuc region, which lent its name to the architectural patterns in this area. *Puuc* means 'hills,' and these, rising to about 100m, are the only ones in the northwest region of the otherwise flat peninsula.

Uxmal (oosh-*mahl*) was an important city, and its dominance extended to the nearby towns of Sayil, Kabah, Xlapak and Labná. Although Uxmal means 'Thrice Built' in Mayan, it was actually constructed five times.

First settled about AD 600, Uxmal was influenced by highland Mexico in its architecture, most likely through contact fostered by trade. This influence is reflected in

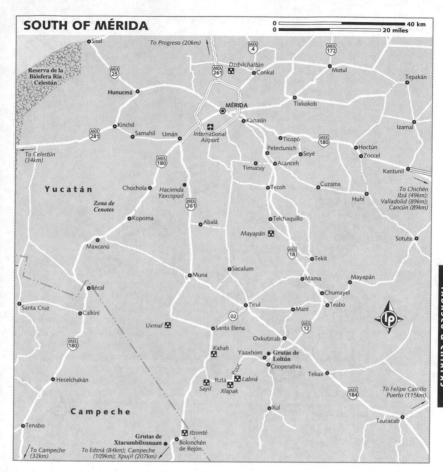

SOUTH OF MÉRIDA

0 _____ 40 km
0 _____ 20 miles

Reserva de la Biósfera Ría Celestún

Sisal

To Progreso (20km)

MEX 4

MEX 172

MEX 25

MEX 261

Dzibilchaltún
Conkal

Motul

Tepakán

Hunucmá

MÉRIDA

Tixkokob

MEX 281

Kinchil

Samahil   Umán

International Airport

Kanasín

Izamal

To Celestún (34km)

MEX 180

Timucuy

Petectunich
Ticopó
Seyé

MEX 180

Hoctún
Zoccel

Acanceh

Kantunil

Yucatán

Chochola
Hacienda Yaxcopoil

Tecoh

Cuzama

To Chichén Itzá (49km);
Valladolid (89km);
Cancún (89km)

Zona de Cenotes

MEX 261

Abalá

Telchaquillo

Huhí

Kopoma

Mayapán

Sotuta

Maxcanú

MEX 18

Tekit

Bécal

Muna

Sacalum

Mama

Mayapán

Santa Cruz

Calkiní

Uxmal

Ticul

Maní

Teabo

Chumayel

02

Santa Elena

Oxkutzcab

MEX 12

Kabah

Yaaxhom

Grutas de Loltún

Hecelchakán

Puuc

Cooperativa

Tekax

To Felipe Carrillo Puerto (115km)

MEX 180

Ruta

Labná

Sayil   Xlapak

MEX 184

Campeche

Xul

Tenabo

Grutas de Xtacumbilxunaan

Itzimté

Bolonchén de Rejón

Tzucacab

To Campeche (32km)

To Edzná (84km); Campeche (109km); Xpujil (207km)

the town's serpent imagery, phallic symbols and columns. The well-proportioned Puuc architecture was strongly influenced by the slightly earlier Río Bec and Chenes styles.

The scarcity of water in the region meant that Chac-Mool – the rain god or sky serpent – was supreme in importance. His image is ubiquitous at the site in the form of stucco masks protruding from facades and cornices.

INFORMATION
Parking is US$1 per car. The site is entered through the modern Unidad Uxmal building, which holds an air-conditioned restaurant, a small museum, shops selling souvenirs and crafts, an auditorium and

bathrooms. Also here is Librería Dante, a bookstore that stocks an excellent selection of travel and archaeological guides and general-interest books on Mexico in English, Spanish, German and French.

The price of admission, if you retain the wristband-ticket, includes a 45-minute light and sound show, beginning nightly at 8pm in summer and 7pm in winter. It's in Spanish, but you can rent translation devices (for English, French, German or Italian) for US$2.75.

SIGHTS
Decorated in elaborate Chenes style (which originated further south), the main doorway to the 39m-high temple of **Casa del**

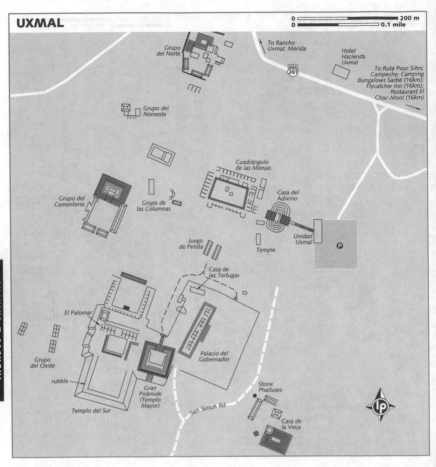

UXMAL

Adivino (the Magician's House) forms the mouth of a gigantic Chac-Mool mask.

Directly west of the Casa del Adivino stands the sprawling 74-room **Cuadrángulo de las Monjas** (Nuns' Quadrangle). The long-nosed face of Chac-Mool appears everywhere on the facades of the four separate temples that form the quadrangle. Passing through the corbeled arch in the middle of the south building of the quadrangle and continuing down the slope takes you through the **Juego de Pelota** (ball court).

Climb the stairs to the right of the ball court to see the **Casa de las Tortugas** (House of the Turtles), which takes its name from the turtles carved on the cornice. The Maya associated turtles with Chac-Mool. Accord-ing to Mayan myth, when the people suffered from drought so did the turtles, and both prayed to Chac-Mool to send rain.

The **Palacio del Gobernador** (Governor's Palace), with its magnificent facade, has been called 'the finest structure at Uxmal and the culmination of the Puuc style' by Mayanist Michael D Coe. The lower part of the facade is plain, and the upper part festooned with stylized Chac-Mool faces and geometric designs. Other elements of Puuc style are decorated cornices, rows of half-columns (as in the House of the Turtles) and round columns in doorways.

Though it's adjacent to the Governor's Palace, to reach the 32m-high **Gran Pirámide** (Great Pyramid) without disobeying any signs you must retrace your route down the hillside and turn left before reaching the ball court.

West of the Great Pyramid sits **El Palomar**, a structure whose roofcomb is latticed with a pattern reminiscent of the Moorish pigeon houses built into walls in Spain and northern Africa – hence the building's name (the Dovecote, or Pigeon House).

SLEEPING & EATING
There is no town at Uxmal – only the archaeological site and several top-end hotels, so for cheap food you must head up or down the road a ways.

Camping Bungalows Sacbé (☎ 985-858-12-81; sacbebungalow@hotmail.com; campsites per person US$3; dm with/without HI card US$6/6.50, d US$14-16; P) A quiet, well-kept HI affiliate on the south side of Santa Elena village, 16km southeast of Uxmal and 8km north of Kabah. To get here, catch a southbound bus from Uxmal and ask the driver to let you off at the *campo de béisbol* (baseball field) beyond the Santa Elena turnoff.

Flycatcher Inn (www.mexonline.com/flycatcherinn .htm; d US$40; P) This lovely B&B on the southeastern edge of Santa Elena offers three spacious, comfortable rooms. Breakfast is included.

Rancho Uxmal (☎ 997-972-62-54; d US$25; P ⊠) Twenty-three basic, serviceable guestrooms with good ventilation, a swimming pool and a welcoming restaurant.

Hotel Hacienda Uxmal (☎ 997-976-20-12, US ☎ +1-800-235-4079; www.mayaland.com; d with/without air-con US$100/40; P ⊠ ⊠) This is a Mayaland Resort operation, 500m from the ruins, across the highway. It's an exceptionally comfortable place to stay.

Restaurant El Chac-Mool (☎ 996-20-25; mains US$4) At the south entrance of Santa Elena, El Chac-Mool serves generous helpings of Yucatecan food with vegetarian alternatives.

GETTING THERE & AWAY
Uxmal is 80km (1½ hours) from Mérida. The inland route between Mérida and Campeche passes Uxmal, and most buses coming from either city will drop you there, or at Kabah or the Ruta Puuc turnoff.

When you want to leave, though, passing buses may be full (especially Saturday and Monday).

ATS buses depart Mérida's Terminal de Segunda Clase at 8am daily on a whirlwind excursion (US$10) to the Ruta Puuc sites, Kabah and Uxmal, heading back from Uxmal's parking lot at 2:30pm. This 'tour' is transportation only; you pay all other costs. The time spent at each site is enough to get only a nodding acquaintance.

Organized tours of Uxmal and other sites can be booked in Mérida (p354).

If you are going from Uxmal to Ticul, then first take a northbound bus to Muna (US$0.50, 20 minutes), then catch one of the frequent buses from there to Ticul (US$0.80, 30 minutes).

Kabah
After Uxmal, Kabah (AD 750–950) was the most important city in the region. The **ruins of Kabah** (admission US$3; ☾ 8am-5pm), just over 23km southeast of Uxmal, are right astride Hwy 261. The guard shack/souvenir shop (selling snacks and cold drinks) and the bulk of the restored ruins are on the east side of the highway.

On entering, head to your right to climb the stairs of the structure closest to the highway, **El Palacio de los Mascarones** (Palace of Masks). The facade is an amazing sight, covered in nearly 300 masks of Chac-Mool, the rain god or sky serpent. Most of their huge curling noses are broken off; the best intact beak is at the building's south end. These curled up noses may have given the palace its modern Mayan name, Codz Pop (Rolled Mat).

Once you're up to your ears in noses, head around back to check out the two restored **atlantes** (an atlas – plural 'atlantes' – is a male figure used as a supporting column). These are especially interesting as they're among the very few three-dimensional human figures you'll see at a Mayan site.

Descend the steps near the atlantes and turn left, passing the small **Pirámide de los Mascarones**, to reach the plaza containing **El Palacio**. The Palace's columned doorways and the decorative *columnillas* (little columns) on the upper part of the facade are characteristics of the Puuc architectural style.

Steps on the north side of El Palacio's plaza put you on a path leading a couple of hundred meters through the jungle to the **Templo de las Columnas**.

KABAH

0 ———— 200 m
0 ———— 0.1 mile

To Santa Elena (6km);
Uxmal (14km); Mérida (65km)

MEX 261

Office

Templo de
las Columnas

P

El Palacio

To Arch
& Gran
Pirámide

Pirámide de
los Mascarones

Atlantes

MEX 261

To Sayil (6km);
Ruta Puuc;
Campeche

El Palacio
de los Mascarones
(Codz Pop)

YUCATÁN PENINSULA,
TABASCO & CHIAPAS

West of El Palacio, across the highway, a path leads up the slope and passes to the south of a high mound of stones that was once the **Gran Pirámide** (Great Pyramid). The path curves to the right and comes to a large restored **monumental arch**. It's said that the *sacbé*, or cobbled and elevated ceremonial road, leading from here goes through the jungle all the way to Uxmal, terminating at a smaller arch; in the other direction it goes to Labná. Once, all of the Yucatán Peninsula was connected by these marvelous 'white roads' of rough limestone.

There's good, affordable lodging about 8km north of Kabah at **Camping Bungalows Sacbé** and the **Flycatcher Inn**; see p361.

Kabah is 101km from Mérida, a ride of about two hours. See p361 for details on transport. Kabah gets particularly short shrift from the ATS excursion bus; you'll have only 25 minutes or so to look around.

Buses will usually make flag stops at the entrance to the ruins. Hitching from the ruins may be possible.

Ruta Puuc

Just 5km south of Kabah on Hwy 261, a road branches off to the east and winds past the ruins of Sayil, Xlapak and Labná, ending at the Grutas de Loltún. This is the Ruta Puuc, and its sites offer some marvelous architectural detail and a deeper acquaintance with the Puuc Mayan civilization, which flourished roughly between AD 750 and 950.

See p361 for details on the ATS excursion bus, the only regularly scheduled public transport on the route. During the busy winter season it's usually possible to hitch rides from one site to the next; however, the best way year-round to appreciate the sites is by rental car.

SAYIL & XLAPAK
The ruins of **Sayil** (admission US$3; 8am-5pm) are 4.5km from the junction of the Ruta Puuc with Hwy 261.

Sayil is best known for **El Palacio**, the huge three-tiered building with a facade some 85m long reminiscent of the Minoan palace on Crete. The distinctive columns of Puuc architecture are used here over and over, as supports for the lintels, as decoration between doorways and as a frieze above them, alternating with huge stylized Chac-Mool masks and 'descending gods.'

From the entrance gate at Sayil, it's 6km east to the entrance gate at **Xlapak** (shla-pak; admission US$2.50; 8am-5pm) The name means 'Old Walls' in Mayan and was a general term among local people for ancient ruins.

LABNÁ
If you only hit one Ruta Puuc site, make it **Labná** (admission US$3; 8am-5pm). Archaeologists believe that at one point in the 9th century, some 3000 Maya lived at Labná. To support such numbers in these arid hills, water was collected in *chultunes* (cisterns). At Labná's peak there were some 60 *chultunes* in and around the city; several are still visible. From the entrance gate at Xlapak, it's 3.5km east to the gate at Labná.

El Palacio, the first building you come to at Labná, is one of the longest in the Puuc region. On the west corner of the main structure's facade, straight in from the big tree near the center of the complex, is a serpent's head with a human face peering out from between its jaws, the symbol of the planet Venus. From the upper level, the view of the site and the hills beyond is stunning.

From the Palace a limestone-paved *sacbé* leads to **El Arco Labná**, which is best known for its magnificent arch. The corbeled structure, 3m wide and 6m high, is well preserved, and the reliefs decorating its upper facade are exuberantly Puuc in style.

Standing on the opposite side of the arch and separated from it by the *sacbé* is

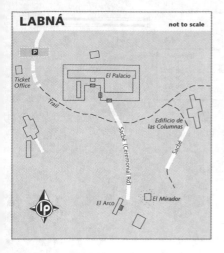

LABNÁ   not to scale

P

Ticket
Office

Trail

El Palacio

*Edificio de
las Columnas*

Sacbé (Ceremonial Rd)

Sacbé

El Arco

El Mirador

LP

a pyramid known as **El Mirador**, topped by
a temple.

GRUTAS DE LOLTÚN

Fifteen kilometers northeast of Labná, an
overgrown sign points out the left turn to
the Grutas de Loltún, 5km further northeast.

The **Loltún Caverns** (admission US$5.25; ⏰ 9am-
5pm), one of the largest and most interesting
cave systems on the Yucatán Peninsula, has
provided a treasure trove of data for archaeologists. Carbon dating of artifacts reveals
that humans used the caves 2500 years ago.
Chest-high murals of hands, faces, animals and geometric motifs were apparent
as recently as 20 years ago, but so many
people have touched them that scarcely a
trace remains. To explore the labyrinth,
you must take a scheduled guided tour
at 9:30am, 11am, 12:30pm, 2pm, 3pm or
4pm, but they may depart early if enough
people are waiting, or switch languages if
the group warrants it. The services of the
English-speaking guides are included in the
admission price.

At the time of writing, LUS had tem-
porarily discontinued its service from the
Noreste terminal in Mérida to the Grutas.
Other buses run frequently between Mérida
and Oxkutzcab (osh-kootz-*kahb*) via Ticul.
Loltún is 7km southwest of Oxkutzcab,
and there is usually some transportation
along the road. *Camionetas* (pickups) and
camiones (trucks) charge around US$1 for

a ride. A taxi from Oxkutzcab may charge
about US$6 one-way.

If you're driving from Loltún to Labná,
turn right out of the Loltún parking lot
and take the next road on the right, which
passes Restaurant El Guerrero's driveway.
Do not take the road marked for Xul. After
5km turn right at the T intersection to join
the Ruta Puuc west.

Ticul

☎ 997 / pop 27,000

Ticul, 30km east of Uxmal and 14km northwest of Oxkutzcab, is the largest town in
this ruin-rich region. It has decent hotels
and restaurants, and good transportation.
Although there is no public transportation
to the Ruta Puuc from Ticul, it is possible
to stay the night here and take an early
morning bus to Muna, arriving there in
time to catch a tour bus to the Ruta Puuc
ruins; see below. Ticul is also a center for
fine *huipil* weaving, and ceramics made
here from the local red clay are renowned
throughout the Yucatán Peninsula. While
here, be sure to see Ticul's **Iglesia de San
Antonio de Padua**, which dates from the late
16th century.

A **post office** faces the plaza, as do two
banks with ATMs. The bus terminal is about
100m away.

Hotel Plaza (☎ 972-04-84; www.hotelplazayucatan
.com; cnr Calles 23 & 26; r with fan/air-con US$30/35;
P ✗) is considered the nicest hotel in
town, although the newer **Hotel San Antonio**
(☎ 927-19-83; cnr Calles 25A & 26; s/d US$24/30; P ✗)
is a better value.

Restaurant Los Almendros (Calle 23 No 207 btwn
Calles 26A & 28; mains US$5-8) specializes in hearty
Yucatecan food. Try the *poc-chuc* (pork
with tomatoes and onions in a sour-orange
sauce).

GETTING THERE & AWAY

Ticul's **bus terminal** (Calle 24) is behind the massive church. Mayab runs frequent 2nd-class
buses between Mérida and Ticul (US$3.50,
two hours) from 4:30am to 9:45pm. There
are 11 buses to Felipe Carrillo Puerto
(US$9, 4½ hours), frequent buses to Oxkut-
zcab (US$0.70), in addition to five a day to
Chetumal (US$12.50, 6½ hours). There are
also seven Mayab buses to Cancún each day
(US$17), three of which also serve Tulum
(US$12) and Playa del Carmen (US$15).

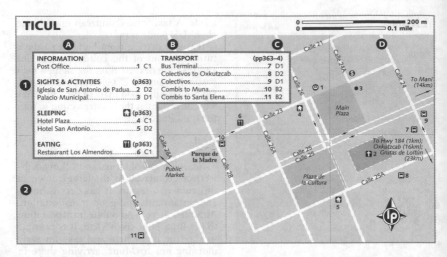

TICUL

INFORMATION	
Post Office....................................1 C1	

SIGHTS & ACTIVITIES	(p363)
Iglesia de San Antonio de Padua....2 D2	
Palacio Municipal...........................3 D1	

SLEEPING	(p363)
Hotel Plaza....................................4 C1	
Hotel San Antonio.........................5 D2	

EATING	(p363)
Restaurant Los Almendros............6 C1	

TRANSPORT	(pp363–4)
Bus Terminal..................................7 D1	
Colectivos to Oxkutzcab................8 D2	
Colectivos.......................................9 D1	
Combis to Muna...........................10 B2	
Combis to Santa Elena.................11 B2	

Super Expresso has less frequent 1st-class service to some of these destinations.

Colectivos (vans) depart from the intersection of Calles 24 and 25 between 5am and 7pm to Mérida (US$1, 1½ hours). To Oxkutzcab (US$0.80, 30 minutes) they leave from Calle 25A on the south side of the church between 7am and 8:30pm.

Combis (vans or cars) going to Santa Elena (US$0.80), the village between Uxmal and Kabah, depart from Calle 30 just south of Calle 25 between 6:15am and 7:45pm. They take Hwy 02 and drop you to catch another bus northwest to Uxmal (15km) or south to Kabah (3.5km). You can also take a combi or bus to Muna on Hwy 261 and another south to Uxmal (16km).

Ruta Puuc–bound travelers can catch one of the early-morning buses from Ticul to Muna and pick up the ATS tour bus (US$5) for Labná, Sayil, Xlapak, Kabah and Uxmal at 9am on its way from Mérida. It returns to Muna at 3pm. Any of the buses leaving Ticul between 6am and 8am for Muna (US$1) will get you there in time to catch the Ruta Puuc bus (all 2nd-class Mérida-bound buses stop in Muna). Combis for Muna (US$1) leave from in front of Lonchería Mary on Calle 23 near Calle 28.

Those headed east to Quintana Roo and the Caribbean coast by car can take Hwy 184 from Ticul through Oxkutzcab to Tekax, Tzucacab and José María Morelos. At Polyuc, 130km from Ticul, a road turns left (east), which ends after 80km in Felipe

Carrillo Puerto, 210km from Ticul. The right fork of the road goes south to the region of Laguna Bacalar.

DZIBILCHALTÚN

Lying about 17km due north of downtown Mérida, **Dzibilchaltún** (Place of Inscribed Flat Stones; admission US$6; ☺ 8am-5pm) was the longest continuously utilized Mayan administrative and ceremonial city, serving the Maya from 1500 BC or earlier until the European conquest in the 1540s. At the height of its greatness, Dzibilchaltún covered 15 sq km. Some 8500 structures were mapped by archaeologists in the 1960s; few of these have been excavated and restored.

Enter the site along a nature trail that terminates at the modern, air-conditioned **Museo del Pueblo Maya** (☺ 8am-4pm Tue-Sun), featuring artifacts from throughout the Mayan regions of Mexico.

The **Templo de las Siete Muñecas** (Temple of the Seven Dolls), which got its name from seven grotesque dolls discovered here during excavations, is a 1km walk from the central plaza. The **Cenote Xlacah**, now a public swimming pool, is more than 40m deep. South of the cenote is **Estructura 44**; at 130m, it's one of the longest Mayan structures in existence.

Parking costs US$1. Minibuses and *colectivo* taxis depart frequently from Mérida's Parque de San Juan (p356) for the village of Dzibilchaltún Ruinas (US$0.80, 30 minutes), just over 1km from the museum.

CELESTÚN

☎ 988 / pop 6200

Celestún is in the middle of a wildlife sanctuary, **Reserva de la Biósfera Ría Celestún**, which abounds with resident and migratory waterfowl, with flamingos the star attraction. It makes a good beach-and-bird day trip from Mérida, and it's also a great place to kick back for a few days. Fishing boats dot the white-sand beach that stretches to the north for kilometers.

Calle 11 is the road into town (due west from Mérida), ending at Calle 12, the dirt road paralleling the beach along which lie most of the restaurants and hotels.

Flamingo Tours

The 591-sq-km Reserva de la Biósfera Ría Celestún is home to a huge variety of animal life, including a large flamingo colony. The best months to see the flamingos are from March to September. The best time to see birds is in the morning.

Depending on the tide, the hour and the season, you may see hundreds or thousands of the colorful birds. Don't encourage your captain to approach them too closely; a startled flock taking wing can result in injuries and deaths (for the birds). In addition to taking you to the flamingoes, the captain will wend through a 200m mangrove tunnel and go to one or both (as time and inclination allow) of the freshwater cenote/springs welling into the saltwater of the estuary, where you can take a refreshing dip.

There are two places to hire a boat for bird-watching – from the bridge on the highway into town (about 1.5km from the beach), and from the beach itself.

Tours from the beach last 2½ to three hours and begin with a ride south along the coast for several kilometers. Asking price is US$100 per boatload (up to six passengers). Boats depart from several beachside spots, including from outside Restaurant Celestún, at the foot of Calle 11.

Tours from the bridge, where there is a parking lot, ticket booth, English speaking guides-for-hire and a place to wait for fellow passengers, are cheaper (US$40 per boat, up to six passengers, plus US$2 per passenger).

Sleeping & Eating

Except for the first listing below, Celestún's hotels are all on Calle 12, within a short walk of one another. Try to book ahead if you want a sea view, especially on weekends.

Eco-Paraíso Xixim (☎ 916-21-00; www.mexonline.com/eco-paraiso.htm; d US$175; P ⬛) This remote ecoresort is at the end of a dirt road 9km north of Celestún. Fifteen individual, lovely *palapas* are nestled between miniature coconut palms along a private three-mile stretch of virgin beach. It could be considered just another luxury joint, but its eco-centric policies set it apart.

In town, try: the recently built **Eco Hotel Flamingos Playa** (in Mérida ☎ 999-929-57-08; d US$28; ⬛ ⬛ ⬛); the bright and airy **Ría Celestún Hostel** (☎ 916-21-70; cnr Calles 12 & 13; dm US$7; ⬛); or the beachfront **Hotel María del Carmen** (☎ 916-21-70; Calle 12 south of Calle 11; d with fan/air-con US$22/30; ⬛).

Celestún's specialties are crab, octopus and, of course, fresh fish.

Dutch-owned **El Lobo** (breakfast & mains US$4-7), on the southwest edge of the plaza, serves good espresso drinks, breakfast, pizza and pasta. For large portions of fresh seafood, try **La Playita** (mains US$5-7), just north of the foot of Calle 11.

Getting There & Away

Buses from Mérida head for Celestún (US$3.75, two hours) 15 times daily between 5am and 8pm from the Terminal Noreste (p357). The route terminates at Celestún's plaza, a block inland from Calle 12. Returning to Mérida, buses run from 5am to 8pm.

Nómadas Youth Hostel (p354) books day trips to see the flamingoes for around US$40.

By car from Mérida, the best route to Celestún is via the new road out of Umán.

IZAMAL

☎ 988 / pop 14,500

Less than 70km east of Mérida, Izamal is a quiet, colonial gem of a town, nicknamed La Ciudad Amarilla (the Yellow City) for the yellow paint that brightens the walls of most buildings. It is easily explored on foot and makes a great day trip from Mérida.

In ancient times, Izamal was a center for the worship of the supreme Mayan god, Itzamná, and the sun god, Kinich-Kakmó. A dozen temple pyramids were devoted to these and other gods. It was probably these bold expressions of Mayan religiosity that inspired the Spaniards to build the enormous Franciscan monastery that stands today at the heart of this town.

When the Spaniards conquered Izamal, they destroyed the major Mayan temple, the Ppapp-Hol-Chac pyramid, and in 1533 began to build from its stones one of the first monasteries in the Western Hemisphere. Work on **Convento de San Antonio de Padua** (admission free; ☯ 6am-8pm) was finished in 1561.

Three of the town's original 12 Mayan **pyramids** have been partially restored so far. The largest is the enormous Kinich-Kakmó, three blocks north of the monastery.

Sleeping & Eating

Macan-Ché B&B (☎ 954-02-87; www.macanche.com; Calle 22 No 305; d US$28-55; 😵) About three long blocks east of the monastery, this charming B&B has a cluster of cottages in a jungle setting, with 12 pretty rooms in all.

Hotel Canto (d US$15) The Canto's location – directly in front of the monastery – and price make it a good value.

Restaurant Kinich-Kakmó (☎ 954-08-89; Calle 27 btwn Calles 28 & 30; mains US$4-8) This restaurant is casual and extremely friendly, offering fan-cooled patio dining beside a garden. Portions are huge.

Getting There & Away

Oriente operates frequent buses between Mérida and Izamal (US$2.75, 1½ hours) that leave from the 2nd-class terminal. There are buses from Valladolid (US$3, two hours) as well. Coming from Chichén Itzá you must change buses at Hóctun. Izamal's bus terminal is just one block west of the monastery.

Other services from Izamal include buses to Tizimín (US$5, 2½ hours) and Cancún (US$9, six hours).

Driving by car from the west, turn north at Hóctun to reach Izamal; from the east, turn north at Kantunil.

CHICHÉN ITZÁ

The most famous and best restored of the Yucatán Peninsula's Mayan sites, **Chichén Itzá** (Mouth of the Well of the Itzáes; admission US$9.50; ☯ 8am-6pm) will awe even the most jaded visitor. Many mysteries of the Mayan astronomical calendar are made clear when one understands the design of the 'time temples' here. Other than a few minor passageways, El Castillo is now the only structure at the site you're allowed to climb or enter.

At the vernal and autumnal equinoxes (March 20 to 21 and September 21 to 22), the morning and afternoon sun produces a light-and-shadow illusion of the serpent ascending or descending the side of El Castillo's staircase. Chichén is mobbed on these dates, however, making it difficult to get close enough to see, and after the spectacle, parts of the site are sometimes closed to the public. The illusion is almost as good in the week preceding and following each equinox, and is re-created nightly in the light and sound show year-round.

Heat, humidity and crowds can be fierce; try to spend the night nearby and do your

---

DEEP MYSTERY

In a cataclysmic collision 65 million years ago, a huge meteor struck the area that is now the Yucatán Peninsula, leaving a 284-kilometer wide crater on the land's surface. Millions of years later cracks formed just below the limestone surface of the crater's perimeter and rainwater began filling the cavities that these fissures created. Eventually the surface layer around the underground chambers began to erode and crumble, revealing the intricate vascular system of underground rivers and cenotes (pools, sinkholes) that lay beneath.

According to Mayan cosmology there are three levels of existence: heaven (which itself has several strata); earth; and the nine-tiered underworld of Xibalbá. The Maya viewed cenotes as entranceways into the after-worlds and they believed that anyone who was sacrificed to the cenotes as an offering to the gods would avoid Xibalbá and go directly to heaven.

In 2002 INAH (National Institute of Anthropology and History) in Mexico City began a six-year study of some of the Yucatán's nearly 3000 cenotes. The marine anthropologists are finding that not only subjects of sacrifice (usually virgins or captured enemy warriors) were thrown into the cenotes' depths but that as a sendoff to the other worlds, many dead – from the regal in full funerary finery to commoners – were also deposited in the watery graves of cenotes.

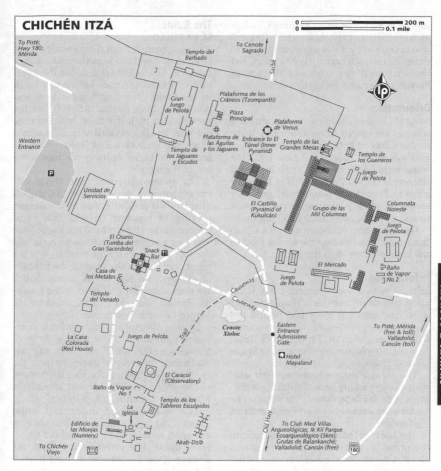

CHICHÉN ITZÁ

exploration of the site (especially climbing El Castillo) either early in the morning or late in the afternoon.

History

Most archaeologists agree that the first major settlement at Chichén Itzá, during the late Classic period, was pure Mayan. In about the 9th century, the city was largely abandoned for reasons unknown. It was resettled around the late 10th century, and Mayanists believe that shortly thereafter it was invaded by the Toltecs, who had migrated from their central highlands capital of Tula, north of Mexico City. Toltec culture was fused with that of the Maya, incorporating the cult of Quetzal-cóatl (Kukulcán, in Mayan). Throughout the city, you will see images of both Chac-Mool, the Mayan rain god, and Quetzal-cóatl, the plumed serpent.

The substantial fusion of highland central Mexican and Puuc architectural styles makes Chichén Itzá unique among the Yucatán Peninsula's ruins. The fabulous El Castillo and the Plataforma de Venus are outstanding architectural works built during the height of Toltec cultural input.

The warlike Toltecs contributed more than their architectural skills to the Maya. They elevated human sacrifice to a near obsession, and there are numerous carvings of the bloody ritual in Chichén demonstrating this. After a Maya leader moved his political capital to Mayapán while keeping Chichén as his religious capital, Chichén Itzá fell into decline. Why it was subsequently abandoned in the 14th century is a mystery, but the once-great city remained the site of Mayan pilgrimages for many years.

Orientation

Most of Chichén's lodgings, restaurants and services are ranged along 1km of highway in the village of **Pisté**, to the western (Mérida) side of the ruins. It's 1.5km from the ruins' main (west) entrance to the first hotel (Pirámide Inn) in Pisté, or 2.5km from the ruins to Pisté village plaza. Buses generally stop at the plaza; you can make the hot walk to and from the ruins in 20 to 30 minutes.

On the eastern (Cancún) side, it's 1.5km from the highway along the access road to the eastern entrance to the ruins.

Information

Filming with a video camera costs US$3 extra; tripods are forbidden. Hold onto your wristband ticket; it gives you in-and-out privileges and admission to that evening's light-and-sound show. Parking costs US$1. Explanatory plaques are displayed in Spanish and English.

The main entrance is the western one, with a large parking lot and entrance building, the **Unidad de Servicios** (⏰ 8am-10pm). The Unidad has a small but worthwhile **museum** (⏰ 8am-5pm).

The **Auditorio Chilam Balam**, located next to the museum, sometimes has video shows about Chichén and other Mexican sites. In the central space of the Unidad stands a scale model of the archaeological site, and off toward the toilets is an exhibit on excavations of the Sacred Cenote. Facilities include: two bookstores with a good assortment of guides and maps; a currency-exchange desk; and, around the corner from the ticket desk, a free *guardaequipaje* where you can leave your belongings while you explore the site.

The 45-minute **sound and light show**, performed beneath El Castillo, begins each evening at 8pm in summer and 7pm in winter. Cost is US$3 if you don't have a ruins ticket, and it's applicable toward admission price the following day. Translation devices (English, French, German and Italian) rent for US$2.50.

The Ruins

EL CASTILLO

As you approach from the turnstiles at the Unidad de Servicios into the archaeological zone, El Castillo (also called the Pyramid of Kukulcán) rises before you in all its grandeur. The first temple here was pre-Toltec, built around AD 800, but the present 25m-high structure, built over the old one, has the plumed serpent sculpted along the stairways and Toltec warriors represented in the doorway carvings at the top of the temple.

The pyramid is actually the Mayan calendar formed in stone. Each of El Castillo's nine levels is divided in two by a staircase, making 18 separate terraces that commemorate the 18 months of the Vague Year. The four stairways have 91 steps each; add the top platform and the total is 365, the number of days in the year. On each facade of the pyramid are 52 flat panels, which are reminders of the 52 years in the Calendar Round. (For more information on the Mayan calendar system, see p50.)

During the spring and autumn equinoxes, light and shadow form a series of triangles on the side of the north staircase that mimic the creep of a serpent (note the carved serpent's heads flanking the bottom of the staircase). The serpent ascends in March and descends in September.

The older pyramid inside El Castillo boasts a red jaguar throne with inlaid eyes and spots of jade, and it also holds a Chac-Mool figure. The entrance to **El Túnel**, the passage up to the throne, is at the base of El Castillo's north side; it's open only from 11am to 3pm and 4pm to 4:45pm.

GRAN JUEGO DE PELOTA

The great ball court, the largest and most impressive in Mexico, is only one of the city's eight courts, indicative of the importance the games held here. The court is flanked by temples at either end and bounded by towering parallel walls with stone rings cemented up high.

There is evidence that the ball game may have changed over the years. Some carvings show players with padding on their elbows and knees, and it is thought that they played a soccerlike game with a hard rubber ball, the use of hands forbidden. Other carvings show players wielding bats; it appears that if a player hit the ball through one of the stone hoops, his team was declared the winner. It may be that during the Toltec period the losing captain, and perhaps his teammates as well, were sacrificed. Along the walls of the ball court are stone reliefs, including scenes of decapitations of players.

The court's acoustics are amazing – a conversation at one end can be heard 135m away at the other, and a clap produces multiple loud echoes.

TEMPLO DE LOS JAGUARES Y ESCUDOS
The Temple of the Jaguars and Shields, built atop the southeast corner of the ball court's wall, has some columns with carved rattlesnakes and tablets with etched jaguars. Inside are faded mural fragments depicting a battle.

PLATAFORMA DE LOS CRÁNEOS
The Platform of Skulls (*tzompantli* in Náhuatl) is between the Templo de los Jaguares and El Castillo. You can't mistake it, because the T-shaped platform is festooned with carved skulls and eagles tearing open the chests of men to eat their hearts. In ancient days this platform held the heads of sacrificial victims.

PLATAFORMA DE LAS ÁGUILAS Y LOS JAGUARES
Adjacent to the *tzompantli*, the carvings on the Platform of the Eagles and Jaguars depict those animals gruesomely grabbing human hearts in their claws. It is thought that this platform was part of a temple dedicated to the military legions responsible for capturing sacrificial victims.

CENOTE SAGRADO
A 300m rough stone road runs north (a five-minute walk) to the huge sunken well that gave this city its name. The Sacred Cenote is an awesome natural well, some 60m in diameter and 35m deep. The walls between the summit and the water's surface are ensnared in tangled vines and other vegetation.

GRUPO DE LAS MIL COLUMNAS
Comprising the **Templo de los Guerreros** (Temple of the Warriors), **Templo de Chac-Mool** (Temple of Chac-Mool) and **Baño de Vapor** (Sweat House or Steam Bath), this group

behind El Castillo takes its name (Group of the Thousand Columns) from the forest of pillars stretching south and east.

EL CARACOL
Called El Caracol (the Snail) by the Spaniards for its interior spiral staircase, this observatory is one of the most fascinating and important of all the Chichén Itzá buildings. Its circular design resembles some central highlands structures, although, surprisingly, not those of Toltec Tula. In a fusion of architectural styles and religious imagery, there are Mayan Chac-Mool rain-god masks over four external doors facing the cardinal directions. The windows in the observatory's dome are aligned with the appearance of certain stars at specific dates. From the dome the priests decreed the times for rituals, celebrations, corn planting and harvests.

EDIFICIO DE LAS MONJAS
Thought by archaeologists to have been a palace for Mayan royalty, the so-called Edificio de las Monjas (Nunnery), with its myriad rooms, resembled a European convent to the conquistadors, hence their name for the building. The construction is Mayan rather than Toltec, although a Toltec sacrificial stone stands in front of the building.

AKAB-DZIB
On the path east of the Nunnery, the Puuc-style Akab-Dzib is thought by some archaeologists to be the most ancient structure excavated here. The central chambers date from the 2nd century. The name means 'Obscure Writing' in Maya and refers to the south-side annex door, whose lintel depicts a priest with a vase etched with hieroglyphics that have never been translated.

Sleeping
No matter what you plan to spend on a bed, don't hesitate to haggle in the off-season (May, June, September and October). Prices here are for high season.

Hwy 180 is known as Calle 15A on its way through Pisté.

Pirámide Inn (☎ 985-851-01-15; www.piramideinn .com; Calle 15A No 30; campsite per person US$4; d US$45; P ⊠ ⊠) An agreeable hotel on the west side of Pisté that allows you to pitch a tent or hang a hammock under a *palapa*. You also get to enjoy the pool and satellite TV.

Posada Olalde (☎ 985-851-00-86; Calle 6 btwn Calles 15 & 17; s/d US$15/20) Two blocks south of the highway by Artesanías Guayacán, this is the best of Pisté's several small pensiones, offering seven clean, quiet and attractive rooms.

Club Med Villas Arqueológicas (☎ 985-851-00-34, US ☎ +1-800-258-2633, in France ☎ +33-801 802 803; www.clubmed.com; d US$75; P ⊠ ⚐) This is the only mid-range priced hotel located next to the ruins, only 300m from the east entrance.

Hotel Dolores Alba (☎ 985-858-15-55; www.doloresalba.com; Hwy 180 Km 122; d US$40; P ⊠ ⚐) This hotel is across the highway from Cenote Ik Kil (p371), just over 3km east of the eastern entrance to the ruins and 2km west of the Grutas de Balankanché. Its 40 air-conditioned rooms are simple but pleasingly decorated and face two inviting swimming pools.

A good choice in town is **Hotel Chichén Itzá** (☎ 985-851-00-22; www.mayaland.com; Calle 15A No 45; d US$40-60; P ⊠ ⚐), on the west side of Pisté.

Hotel Mayaland (☎ 998-887-24-50; US ☎ 1-800-235-4079; www.mayaland.com; d US$150, bungalows from US$200; P ⊠ ⚐) Less than 100m from the ruins' main entrance, this hotel was built around 1923 and is the most gracious in Chichén's vicinity.

Eating

The highway through Pisté is lined with more than 20 small restaurants. The cheapest are the market eateries on the main plaza opposite the huge tree. The others are arranged along the highway from the town square to the Pirámide Inn. **El Carrousel** (mains US$4-6) and **Restaurant y Cocina Económica Chichén Itzá** (mains US$3-4) are both good.

Getting There & Away

A modern airport lies about 14km east of Pisté. At the time of writing it had yet to receive other than local charter flights.

When all goes well, Oriente's 2nd-class buses pass through Pisté bound for Mérida (US$4.50, 2½ hours) hourly between 7:30am and 9:30pm. Hourly Oriente buses to Valladolid (US$1.50, 50 minutes) and Cancún (US$7, 4½ hours) pass between 7:30am and 8:30pm. One bus for Chiquilá (to reach Isla Holbox; US$7, four hours) passes at 1:30am.

First-class buses depart for: Mérida (US$6.25, 1¾ hours) at 2:30pm and 5pm; Cancún (US$12, 2½ hours) at 4:30pm; and Cobá (US$5, 1½ hours), Tulum (US$7.50, 2½ hours) and Playa del Carmen (US$15, 3½ hours) at 8am and 4:30pm.

Shared vans to Valladolid (US$1.75, 40 minutes) pass through town regularly.

Getting Around

Buses passing through Pisté stop near the east and west sides of town; during Chichén Itzá's opening hours they also stop at the ruins (check with the driver), and they will take passengers from town for about US$0.60 when there's room. For a bit more, 2nd-class buses will also take you to the Grutas de Balankanché (be sure to specify your destination when buying your ticket).

There's a taxi stand near the west end of town; the going one-way rate is US$2.75. There are sometimes cabs at Chichén's parking lot, but make advance arrangements if you want to be sure of a ride.

AROUND PISTÉ
Grutas de Balankanché

In 1959 a guide to the Chichén ruins was exploring a cave on his day off when he came upon a narrow passageway. He followed the passageway for 300m, meandering through a series of caverns. In each cavern, perched on mounds amid scores of glistening stalactites, were hundreds of ceremonial treasures the Maya had placed there 800 years earlier. In the years following the discovery, the ancient ceremonial objects were removed and studied. Eventually most of them were returned to the caves, placed exactly where they were found.

The **caverns** (admission US$5; ☽ 9am-5pm) are 5km east of the ruins of Chichén Itzá and 2km east of the Hotel Dolores Alba on the highway to Cancún. Second-class buses heading east from Pisté toward Valladolid and Cancún will drop you at the Balankanché road. The entrance to the caves is 350m north of the highway.

Compulsory 40-minute tours (minimum six people, maximum 30) are accompanied by a recorded narration. English is at 11am, 1pm and 3pm; Spanish is at 9am, noon, 2pm and 4pm; and French is at 10am.

The cave is unusually hot, and ventilation is poor in its further reaches. The lack of oxygen makes it difficult to draw a full breath until you're outside again.

Cenote Ik Kil

A little more than 3km east of the eastern entrance to the ruins is **Ik Kil Parque Ecoarqueológico** (☎ 985-851-00-00; adult/child US$4/2; 9am-5pm), whose cenote has been developed into a divine swimming spot. Small cascades of water plunge from the high limestone roof, which is ringed by greenery. A good buffet lunch runs an extra US$5. Get your swim in by no later than 1pm to beat the tour groups.

VALLADOLID

☎ 985 / pop 56,776

Valladolid is relatively small, manageable and affordable, with an easy pace of life, many handsome colonial buildings and several good hotels and restaurants. It's a fine place to stop and spend a day or two getting to know the real Yucatán, and it makes a good base from which to visit the surrounding area, including Chichén Itzá.

Valladolid was once the Mayan ceremonial center of Zací (sah-*kee*).

Orientation & Information

The old highway passes through the center of town, though all signs urge motorists toward the toll road (Hwy 180) north of town. To follow the old highway eastbound, take Calle 41; westbound, take Calle 39.

Most hotels are on the main plaza, called Parque Francisco Cantón Rosado, or within a block or two of it. The **tourist office** (☎ 856-18-65; 9am-8pm) is on the east side of the plaza. It has maps and information. A few doors north is the **main post office**. Various **banks**, most with ATMs, are near the center of town (see map for some locations). Most Internet places in town charge about US$1.50 an hour. One reliable place is **@lbert's PC** (Calle 43 No 200G), which charges US$1.20 per hour for fairly fast connections. **Hospital Valladolid** (☎ 856-28-83; cnr Calles 49 & 52), near the Convento de Sisal, handles emergencies 24 hours a day.

Sights & Activities

To take a dip in a cenote, head to **Cenote Dzitnup** (Xkeken; admission US$2; 7am-6pm), 7km west of the plaza. It's artificially lit, and a massive limestone formation dripping with stalactites hangs from its ceiling. Dzitnup has a restaurant and drinks stand.

Across the road and a couple hundred meters closer to town is **Cenote Samulá** (admission US$1), a lovely cavern pool with *álamo* (poplar) roots stretching down many meters from the middle of the ceiling.

Pedaling a rented bicycle to the cenotes takes about 20 minutes. By bike from the center of town take all-colonial Calle 41A (Calzada de los Frailes), which leads past the Templo de San Bernardino and the convent. Keep them to your left as you skirt the park, then turn right on Calle 49. This opens into tree-lined Av de los Frailes and hits the old highway. Turn left onto the *ciclopista* (bike path) paralleling the road to Mérida. Turn left again at the sign for Dzitnup and continue for just under 2km; Samulá is off this road to the right and Dzitnup a little further on the left.

Paulino Silva (Calle 44 btwn Calles 39 & 41; bike rental per hour US$0.50) is among a few places that rent out bikes. The rental price includes a lock and map.

Sleeping & Eating

El Mesón del Marqués (☎ 856-20-73; Calle 39 No 203; d US$50;) Long considered the best hotel in town, El Mesón has two colonial courtyards, a pool, a good restaurant and guestrooms with air-con, ceiling fans and cable TV. Its restaurant, **Hostería del Marqués** (mains US$4-6), is the best in town. Try the Yucatecan sampler dish for a taste of a variety of regional specialties.

Hotel María de la Luz (☎ 856-20-71; www.maria delaluzhotel.com; Calle 42 No 193; d US$33;) The best value in town, this colonial house has comfortable rooms all with air-con and TV. The restaurant has breezy tables overlooking the plaza and serves a tasty and bountiful breakfast, and very good seafood for lunch and dinner.

Hotel Zací (☎ 856-21-67; Calle 44 No 191; d with fan/air-con US$30/35;) This well-kept place has 48 rooms with mock colonial decor and TVs, all situated around a quiet courtyard with a bar.

Hotel San Clemente (☎ 856-22-08; www.hotelsan clemente.com.mx; Calle 42 No 206; d US$35;) The San Clemente has a pool and 64 rooms with air-con, cable TV and decor nearly identical to Zací's (or vice vera). It's on the corner of the plaza, across from the cathedral.

VALLADOLID

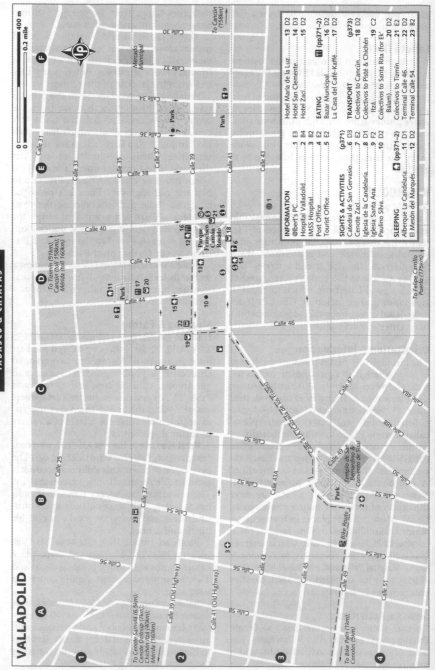

INFORMATION	
@lbert's PC.................................**1** E3
Hospital Valladolid........................**2** B4
IMSS Hospital...............................**3** B2
Post Office...................................**4** E2
Tourist Office...............................**5** E2

SIGHTS & ACTIVITIES	(p371)
Catedral de San Gervasio...........**6** D3
Cenote Zací..................................**7** E2
Iglesia de la Candelaria................**8** D1
Iglesia Santa Ana.........................**9** F2
Paulino Silva...............................**10** D2

SLEEPING	(pp371–2)
Alberque La Candelaria................**11** D1
El Mesón del Marqués..................**12** D2

Hotel María de la Luz..................**13** D2
Hotel San Clemente....................**14** D3
Hotel Zací..................................**15** D2

EATING	⊞ (pp371–2)
Bazar Municipal..........................**16** D2
La Casa del Café-Kaffé................**17** D2

TRANSPORT	(p373)
Colectivos to Cancún..................**18** D2
Colectivos to Pisté & Chichén	
Itzá..**19** C2
Colectivos to Santa Rita (for Ek'	
Balam)..................................**20** D2
Colectivos to Tizimín..................**21** E2
Terminal Calle 46.......................**22** D2
Terminal Calle 54.......................**23** B2

Albergue La Candelaria (☎ 856-22-67, 800-800-26-25; Calle 35 No 201F; dm with/without HI card US$7/7.50, d US$17) This HI affiliate is in a classic old house on the north side of the park across from Iglesia de la Candelaria. It has a full kitchen, self-service laundry area and a serene back area.

La Casa del Café-Kaffé (☎ 856-28-79; Calle 44; mains US$2-4) The best espresso in town is served here.

Bazar Municipal (cnr Calles 39 & 40; set meals US$2-3) This is a collection of market-style cookshops at the plaza's northeast corner, popular for their big, cheap breakfasts. At lunch and dinner there are *comidas corridas* (set meals).

Getting There & Around
BUS
Valladolid has two bus terminals: the convenient **Terminal 46** (Calle 39 at Calle 46), two blocks from the plaza; and **Terminal 54** (Calle 37 at Calle 54) five blocks further northwest. All buses going through town stop at both. Many 1st-class buses running between Cancún and Mérida don't go into town at all but drop passengers near the toll road's off-ramp. Free shuttles then take passengers into town.

The principal services are Oriente, Mayab and Expresso (2nd-class) and ADO and Super Expresso (1st-class).

Cancún (2-3hr; many buses, 8:30am-9:30pm, US$6-8)

Chetumal (6hr; 5 2nd-class Mayab buses, US$12)

Chiquilá (for Isla Holbox, 2½hr; 2nd-class bus, 1:30am, US$6)

Chichén Itzá/Pisté (45min; 17 Oriente Mérida-bound buses, 7:30am-6pm, US$1.75) Buses stop near the ruins during the day.

Cobá (1hr; 3 1st-class buses, US$4; 3 2nd-class buses, US$2.50)

Izamal (2hr; 3 2nd-class buses, US$3.50)

Mérida (2-3hr; many buses, US$6-8)

Playa del Carmen (3-3½hr; 3 1st-class buses, US$11; 5 2nd-class buses, US$6.25)

Tizimín (1hr; 12 buses, US$2)

Tulum (1hr; 3 1st-class buses, US$5; 3 2nd-class buses, US$4.50)

To get to Cenote Dzitnup you can hop aboard a westbound bus; ask the driver to let you off at the Dzitnup turnoff, then walk the final 2km (20 minutes) to the site.

COLECTIVO
Often faster, more reliable and more comfortable than buses are *colectivos*, which are shared vans that leave for various points as soon as their seats are filled. Direct services to **Mérida** (from Calle 39 just east of Calle 46, US$5) and **Cancún** (from in front of the cathedral, US$6) take two hours – confirm that the route is nonstop. *Colectivos* for **Pisté** and **Chichén Itzá** (US$1.50, 40 minutes) leave from Calle 46, north of Calle 39, and for **Tizimín** from the east side of the plaza.

TAXI
Taxis from Valladolid's main plaza charge US$1 for the roundtrip excursion to Dzitnup and Samulá, with an hour's wait (this is the locals' price; your rate may vary).

EK' BALAM
The turnoff for this fascinating **archaeological site** (admission US$2.50; ⊙ 8am-5pm) is north of Valladolid, 17km along the road to Tizimín. Ek' Balam is another 10.5km east. There is usually someone at the site willing to act as a guide; tips are appreciated.

Most impressive is the **main pyramid** – a massive, towering structure sporting a huge jaguar mouth with 360-degree dentition. From the top of the pyramid you can see pyramids at Chichén Itzá and Cobá.

It's possible to catch a *colectivo* from Calle 44 between Calles 35 and 37 in Valladolid for the village of Santa Rita (US$1), a 2km walk from Ek' Balam. A roundtrip taxi ride from Valladolid with an hour's wait at the ruins will cost around US$20. Albergue La Candelaria in Valladolid can arrange tours.

TIZIMÍN
☎ 986 / pop 41,000
Travelers bound for Río Lagartos change buses in Tizimín, a ranching center. There is little to warrant an overnight stay, but the tree-filled Parque Principal is pleasant, particularly at sundown.

Two great colonial structures – **Parroquia Los Santos Reyes de Tizimín** (Church of the Three Wise Kings) and its former **Franciscan monastery** (the ex-convent) – are worth a look.

The **Posada María Antonia** (☎ 863-23-84; Calle 50 No 408; r US$20), just south of the church, has 12 fairly basic air-conditioned rooms accommodating up to four people.

Oriente (shared with Mayab, both 2nd-class only) and Noreste (1st- and 2nd-class) share a terminal on Calle 47 between Calles 46 and 48. Noreste's 1st- and 2nd-class terminal is around the corner on Calle 46.

Cancún (3-3½hr; Mayab & Noreste buses btwn 3am & 8pm, US$7-8)

Izamal (2½hr; Oriente bus at 5:15am, 11:20am & 4pm, US$5.25)

Mérida (2¼hr; 10 1st-class Noreste btwn 4:30am & 6:30pm, US$7.50)

Río Lagartos (1hr; 8 Noreste btwn 6am & 7:45pm, US$1)

Valladolid (1hr; 7 Oriente btwn 5:30am & 7pm, US$2)

RÍO LAGARTOS

☎ 986 / pop 2200

The largest and most spectacular flamingo colony in Mexico makes a trip to this fishing village well worth while. The mangrove-lined estuary is also home to numerous other bird species and a small number of the crocodiles that gave the town its name (Alligator River). Río Lagartos lies within the **Reserva de la Biósfera Ría Lagartos**, 103km north of Valladolid and 52km north of Tizimín.

The Maya knew the place as Holkobén and used it as a rest stop on their way to the nearby lagoons (Las Coloradas) from which they extracted salt.

Flamingo Tours

The brilliant orange-red birds can turn the horizon fiery when they take wing. For their well-being, however, please ask your boat captain not to frighten the birds into flight. You can generally get to within 100m of flamingoes before they walk or fly away. Depending on your luck, you'll see either hundreds or thousands of them.

The four primary haunts, in increasing distance from town, are **Punta Garza**, **Yoluk**, **Necopal** and **Nahochín** (all flamingo feeding spots named for nearby mangrove patches). Prices vary with boat, group size (maximum five) and destination. The lowest you can expect to pay is around US$40; a full boat to Nahochín runs as much as US$65.

Ismael Navarro (☎ 826-00-00) and **Diego Núñez Martínez** (☎ 862-02-02) are licensed guides with formal training both as guides and naturalists. They offer extensive day tours as well as night excursions. (Crocodiles are a common nocturnal sight, and from May through September sea turtles are easily spotted.) To reach them follow the signs for Restaurante-Bar Isla Contoy; ask for either of them at the restaurant.

Alternatively, you can negotiate with one of the eager men in the waterfront kiosks near the entrance to town. They speak English and will connect you with a captain (who usually doesn't).

Sleeping & Eating

Most residents aren't sure of the town's street names, and signs are few. The road into town is north–south Calle 10, which ends at the waterfront Calle 13.

Cabañas Dos Hermanos (☎ 862-01-46; cabaña US$20) Located near the school at the east edge of town, this comfortable place has four spacious cabañas with fans.

Hotel Villas de Pescadores (☎ 862-00-20; Calle 14; d US$35) This hotel is near the water's edge and offers 12 very clean rooms, each with good cross-ventilation (all face the estuary), two beds and a fan. The owner rents out bicycles and canoes.

Restaurante-Bar Isla Contoy (Calle 19 at waterfront; mains US$4-6) This is a good place to meet other travelers and form groups for the boat tours.

Getting There & Away

Several buses run between Tizimín (US$2), Mérida (US$7; three to four hours) and Cancún (US$7; three to four hours). There are buses to the seldom-visited fishing village of San Felipe (US$1; 20 minutes) several times a day.

CAMPECHE STATE

Campeche, the least visited of the Yucatán Peninsula's three states, is proudly preparing to take its place among Mexico's top tourist destinations as rapid excavation and restoration continue at many archaeological sites throughout the state. Visitors can enjoy the uncrowded Mayan archaeological sites of Edzná (p379), Calakmul (p380) in Mexico's largest biosphere reserve, and Chicanná (p381), plus the impressive walled city of Campeche (p375), with its colonial fortifications and architecture.

The state is largely flat, like other parts of the peninsula, but instead of light forest and brush, 30% of Campeche is covered with jungle. Marshlands, ponds and inlets are common along the state's coastline, which faces the dark and generally uninviting waters of the Gulf of Mexico.

CAMPECHE
☎ 981 / pop 198,000

In 1999 Unesco added the famous walled city of Campeche to its list of World Heritage Sites. *Campechanos* are rightly proud of this and are doing an excellent job of improving the colonial heart of the city while retaining the best of the old.

Two segments of the city's famous wall have survived the times, as have seven of the *baluartes* (bastions or bulwarks) that were built into it.

Adding to Campeche's charm is its location on the Gulf of Mexico. Though the water is murky, the broad waterfront boulevard provides the perfect place for sunset-watching; add a thunderstorm rolling in off the Gulf and you have a sound and light show nonpareil.

History

Campeche was once a Mayan trading village called Ah Kin Pech (Lord Sun Tick, as in fleas) and was ruled by its fearless leader, Moch-Couoh. A Spanish expedition landed in 1517, and Moch-Couoh granted the parched sailors water, but warned them not to stay. When they didn't obey, Moch-Couoh and his men attacked the Spanish ship, killing everyone aboard. Over the next two decades other Spaniards attempted to conquer Moch-Couoh's kingdom, but met with the same success as their predecessors.

It wasn't until 1540 – after Moch-Couoh's death – that the Conquistadors gained enough control over the region to establish a surviving settlement. They named it Villa de San Francisco de Campeche.

The small city soon flourished and became the major port of the Yucatán Peninsula. Its growing wealth did not escape the notice of pirates, however, who terrorized Campeche for two centuries. The Spanish monarchy finally took preventive action and built a 2.5km hexagon wall with eight strategically placed bastions around the city. It took 18 years to build.

Orientation

Though the bastions still stand, the city walls themselves have been mostly razed and replaced. Today Av Circuito Baluartes rings the city center just as the walls once did. Many of the streets making up the circuit are paved with stone taken from the demolished wall.

According to the compass, Campeche is oriented with its waterfront to the northwest, but be aware that locals giving directions usually follow tradition and convenience, which dictate that the water is to the west, inland is east.

A multilane boulevard with bicycle and pedestrian paths on its seaward side extends several kilometers in either direction along Campeche's shore, changing names a few times. The stretch closest to the city center is named Av Adolfo Ruiz Cortínez and is commonly referred to as *el malecón* (the seafront drive).

Information

EMERGENCY
Ambulance, Fire & Police (☎ 060)
Police (☎ 816-36-35)
Red Cross (☎ 065)

INTERNET ACCESS
Café Internet (cnr Calles 10 & 61; per hr US$2) Air-conditioned with fast connections.

LAUNDRY
Lavandería Campeche (Calle 55 btwn Calles 12 & 14) Charges US$4 for a large load and has good, fast service.

MEDICAL SERVICES
IMSS Hospital (☎ 816-52-02; cnr Av Circuito Baluartes Este & Av Central)

MONEY
Banks with ATMs can be found near the main square. See the map for locations.

POST
Post Office (☎ 816-21-34; cnr Av 16 de Septiembre & Calle 53)

TOURIST INFORMATION
Secretaría de Turismo (☎ 816-67-67; 🕘 9am-3pm & 6-9pm) In Plaza Moch-Couoh off Av Adolfo Ruiz Cortínez.
City tourist desk (Calle 57 No 6; 🕘 9am-3:30pm & 6-9pm Mon-Fri) At Centro Cultural Casa Número 6, southwest of the cathedral.

Sights

Most of Campeche's historic sites are contained in the old city within the city walls and are easily accessible on foot.

CAMPECHE

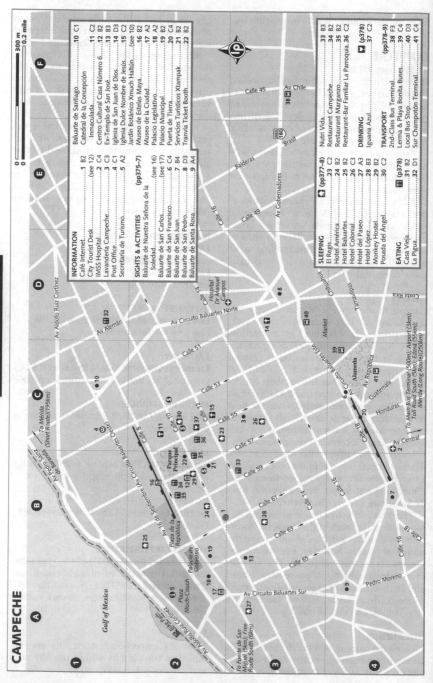

OLD CITY CENTER

The **Baluarte de Nuestra Señora de la Soledad** (Calle 8 at Calle 57) holds the **Museo de Estelas Maya** (admission US$2.50; ⊗ 8am-7:30pm Tue-Sun) featuring some badly weathered Mayan artifacts.

Parque Principal, Campeche's main plaza, is the center of town and a pleasant place to sit and do what the locals do (sit, think, chat, smooch, plot, snooze etc). Construction of the grand **Catedral de la Concepción Inmaculada** (northeast side of the main plaza) began in 1650 but wasn't finished until two centuries later in 1850.

The 18th-century **Centro Cultural Casa Número 6** (admission free; ⊗ 9am-9pm) is furnished with lovely period pieces; once inside it's easy (and fun) to imagine how the city's high society lived back then.

The **Baluarte de Santiago** (admission free; ⊗ 9am-3pm & 5-8pm Mon-Fri, 9am-1pm & 4-8pm Sat, 9am-1pm Sun) houses a minuscule yet lovely tropical garden, the **Jardín Botánico Xmuch Haltún** with 250 species of tropical plants.

The **Baluarte de San Pedro** (admission free; ⊗ 9am-3pm & 5-9pm) is in the middle of a complex traffic intersection at the beginning of Av Gobernadores. Within the bulwark is the **Exposición Permanente de Artesanías**, a regional crafts sales center.

Puerta de Tierra (Calle 59 at Av Circuito Baluartes; admission free; ⊗ 8am-9pm) is a great stone fortress, built in 1732. It remains virtually intact – even the massive wooden door is original. There is an interesting little museum with an early 18th-century five-ton canon in the entryway.

Baluarte de San Carlos (Calle 8 at Av Circuito Baluartes Sur; admission free; ⊗ 9am-2pm Mon, 8am-8pm Tue-Sat, 8am-2pm Sun) contains the modest **Museo de la Ciudad** (City Museum). You can visit the dungeon, or escape to the roof for a breathtaking view of the sea.

The **Ex-Templo de San José** (cnr Calles 10 & 63) is an absolute visual delight. The Jesuits built this baroque church in 1756. Its block-long facade is covered in striking blue and yellow Talavera tiles, and one spire is topped by a lighthouse complete with weather vane.

FUERTE DE SAN MIGUEL

Four kilometers southwest of Plaza Moch-Couoh, a road turns left off the *malecón* and climbs for about 600m to the **Fuerte de San Miguel** (admission US$2.50; ⊗ 9am-7pm Tue-Sat, 9am-noon Sun). This colonial fortress is now home to an excellent archaeological museum, where you can see objects found at the ancient Mayan sites of Calakmul, Edzná and Jaina, an island north of the city once used as a burial site for Mayan aristocracy. The fort is itself a thing of beauty, and the views are stellar.

Tours

Three different tours by motorized *tranvía* (trolley) depart from the Parque Principal daily; all cost US$8 and last about 45 minutes. Hourly between 9am and 9pm, the **Tranvía de la Ciudad** heads off on a tour of the principal neighborhoods of the historic town center. On the same schedule, **El Guapo** goes to the Fuerte de San Miguel and its twin on the north side of the city, the Fuerte de San José, which contains a modest maritime museum. You don't get enough time to take in the archaeological museum; if it's your goal, just use the tram to get there, then walk down the hill. The third tour departs at 9am and 5pm to the Fuerte de San José.

Servicios Turísticos Xtampak (☎ 812-64-85; xtampak@elfoco.com; Calles 57 btwn Calles 10 & 12) offers archaeological tours to Edzná, Calakmul and the various sites around Xpujil in eastern Campeche.

Monkey Hostel (see below) offers shuttle services to: Mayan sites Edzná and Kin-Há; Calakmul, Becán, Chicanná and Xpuhil; and the Ruta Puuc sites (p362).

Sleeping

Monkey Hostel (☎ 811-65-00; www.hostalcampeche.com; cnr Calles 10 & 57; dm US$8; 🖳) This deluxe hostel occupies the upstairs of a grand old building directly overlooking the Parque Principal, and has a rooftop terrace with a bar and superb views of the park and cathedral. Perks include lockers, kitchen and laundry facilities, book exchange, high-speed Internet access (US$1.50 per hour), and inexpensive bike rentals. Breakfast is included.

Hotel Colonial (☎ 816-22-22; Calle 14 No 122; r with/without air-con US$28/20; 🟦) Rooms in this former mansion ooze character. The showers are hot and the place is popular.

Hotel América (☎ 816-45-88; Calle 10 No 252; r with/without air-con US$42/35; P 🟦 🖳) Simple elegance characterizes this converted colonial home. The rooms are spacious and comfortable, and those with balconies are especially inviting (albeit noisy). Perks include breakfast and free Internet.

Hotel del Paseo (☎ 811-01-00; www.hoteldel paseo.8k.com; Calle 8 No 215; d US$48; ☒) The 48 like-new rooms here are very reasonably priced. All have air-con, cable TV and phone. There is a restaurant and bar as well.

Hotel López (☎ 816-33-44; lopezh@elsitio.com; Calle 12 No 189; r US$40; ☒) The López has clean, comfortable (though small) rooms that surround three tranquil courtyards.

Posada del Ángel (☎ 816-77-18; Calle 10 No 307; d with fan/air-con US$27/35; ☒) This 14-room hotel is great value and is centrally located across from the cathedral.

El Regis (☎ 816-31-75; Calle 12 No 148; r US$33; ☒) This two-story former colonial home has seven large, clean rooms with air-con and non-cable TV. The convenient central location makes this an excellent deal.

Hotel Baluartes (☎ 816-39-11; www.baluartes.com .mx; Av 16 de Septiembre 128; d US$62; P ☒ ☐ ☒) You can't tell from its office building facade, but this place is pretty stylish inside. Rooms are modern, beds are comfy, bathrooms are tiled and the air-con is strong.

Eating & Drinking

Most restaurants are located in the city center, a close walk from any downtown hotel. While in town, be sure to try the regional specialty *pan de cazón* (dogfish, a small shark) cooked between layers of tortillas in a dark sauce. Another regional specialty is *camarones al coco* (shrimp rolled in ground coconut and fried).

La Pigua (☎ 811-33-65; Av Alemán 179A; mains US$7-13; ☾ noon-6pm) The bright blue entrance leads you into this pretty little restaurant considered by locals to be the best restaurant in town – no argument here. The seafood menu is extensive and every item fresh and seasoned with regional flair.

Casa Vieja (☎ 811-13-11; Calle 10 No 319; mains US$8-12) The food is a good reason to dine here, but its location over the plaza is an even better one. Casa Vieja specializes in authentic Cuban cuisine as well as Campechean favorites.

Restaurant Marganzo (☎ 811-38-98; Calle 8 btwn Calles 57 & 59; breakfast US$3-5, mains US$5-10) Facing the Baluarte de Nuestra Señora, this popular restaurant serves good breakfasts and juices, plus espresso drinks, and has an extensive seafood menu.

Restaurant Campeche (☎ 816-21-28; Calle 57; mains US$5-9; ☾ dinner) Large selection, very popular and convenient for early-morning and late-night eats.

Restaurant-Bar Familiar La Parroquia (Calle 55 No 8; breakfast US$4.50-5, mains US$5-7; ☾ 24hr) La Parroquia is the complete family restaurant-café-hangout. Traditional and regional lunches and dinners are all tasty.

Nutri Vida (Calle 12 No 167; ☾ closed Sun) Hit this health food store/restaurant for soy burgers and the like.

El Mercado (main market) is located just north of downtown, outside the wall. You'll find fresh produce and lots of food stands selling tasty treats like fresh fish tacos.

The best place to enjoy a drink is in the lush patio at **Iguana Azul** (Calle 55) or at the bar at **Casa Vieja** (☎ 811-13-11; Calle 10 No 319).

Entertainment

Wednesday through Sunday nights there is always something going on in the Parque Principal, be it jazz, rock, marimba groups or the Banda del Estado (State Band). There's no cost to attend any of these festive performances.

Getting There & Away

AIR

The tiny **airport** is at the end of Av López Portillo (reached by Av Central), which is 3.5km southeast from Plaza Moch-Couoh. **Aeroméxico** (☎ 816-66-56) flies to Mexico City twice daily.

BUS

Campeche's **main bus terminal** (commonly referred to as the ADO) is located on the corner of Av Patricio Trueba (also known as Av Central) and Av Casa de la Justicia, about 20 blocks south of Av Circuito Baluartes Este. At the time of writing the 2nd-class bus station was still located on the corner of Av Gobernadores and Av Chile. 1.7km east of Plaza Moch-Couoh, or about 1.5km from most hotels (it may move to the same location as the main bus terminal).

Though most of its buses leave from the main terminal, Sur has a terminal for buses to Champotón on Av República across from the Alameda (south of the market). Rural buses for Edzná and other parts depart from here as well.

There have been reports of theft on night buses, especially to Chiapas; keep a close eye on your bags.

Daily buses from Campeche:

Bolonchén de Rejón (3-4hr; 4 buses, US$5)

Cancún (6-7hr; 2 direct 1st-class buses, US$27; 1 2nd-class via Mérida, US$22)

Chetumal (7-9hr; 1 1st-class bus, noon, US$20; 2 2nd-class buses, 8:15am & 10pm, US$17)

Edzná (1½hr; US$2) Buses leave from the Sur Champotón terminal at 6am and 10am, then roughly hourly until 6pm; see p379 for more information.

Escárcega (2½hr; 5 1st-class buses, US$8; many 2nd-class buses, US$6)

Hopelchén (2hr; several 2nd-class buses, US$3.50)

Mérida (via Bécal; 2½-3hr; 1st-class buses, hourly, US$10; 2nd-class buses, every 30min to 7pm, US$8)

Mérida (via Uxmal; 4hr; 5 2nd-class buses, 6am-5pm, US$7.50)

Mexico City (TAPO; 18hr; 4 1st-class buses, 1 deluxe, US$65-78)

Palenque (5hr; 1 deluxe bus, midnight; 3 1st-class buses, US$17-23) Some Villahermosa-bound buses can drop you at Catazajá (the Palenque turnoff), 27km north of Palenque town.

San Cristóbal de Las Casas (14hr; 1 deluxe bus, midnight, US$33)

Villahermosa (6hr; 8 1st-class buses, US$24)

Xpujil (6-8hr; 1 1st-class, noon, US$15; 4 2nd-class buses incl 1 via Hopelchén, US$12)

CAR & MOTORCYCLE

Whether you're heading for Edzná, the long route to Mérida, or the *cuota* (toll road) going south, take Av Central and follow signs for the airport and Edzná. For the free (slower) route south you can just head down the *malecón*.

For the non-toll route to Mérida, head north on the *malecón* – it curves to the right eventually and hits the highway at a Pemex station.

Getting Around

Local buses all originate at the market. Most charge US$0.35 and go at least partway around the Av Circuito Baluartes counterclockwise before heading to their final destinations. Ask a local where along the Circuito you can catch the bus you want.

Taxis have set prices for destinations on a sign posted in the back seat, but agree on a price with the driver before you go. By the hour they are US$7.75. The fare between the bus terminal and the center is

around US$2.50. Between the airport and the center should be US$7. *Colectivo* taxis from the airport charge about US$3 per person.

To get to Fuerte de San Miguel, take a 'Lerma' or 'Playa Bonita' bus (US$0.50), which depart from the market (at the northeast edge of the center) and travel counterclockwise most of the way around the Circuito before heading down the *malecón*. Tell the driver you're going to the Fuerte de San Miguel. To avoid the strenuous walk from the coastal road up the hill (about 700m), you can take a taxi or the *tranvía* (see Tours, p377).

CAMPECHE TO MÉRIDA
Hwy 180 (Short Route)

The *ruta corta* (short route) is the fastest way to get between the two cities, and it's the road traveled by most buses. If you'd like to stop at one of the towns along the short route, catch a 2nd-class bus.

From Campeche it's 109km to **Bécal**, a center of the Yucatán Peninsula's panama hat trade just inside the border of Campeche state. Townsfolk have been making the soft, pliable hats, called *jipis*, in backyard caves (to avoid humidity) since the mid-19th century. From Bécal it's 85km to Mérida.

Hwy 261 (Long Route)

If you'd prefer to go the long way via Kabah and Uxmal, ask for a seat on one of the less-frequent long-route buses. Most travelers take the long route from Campeche to Mérida in order to visit the various ruin sites on the way. It's often referred to as 'la Ruta Chenes,' for the *chenes* (wells) that give the region its name.

The closest major ruins to Campeche are at **Edzná** (admission US$4; ☯ 8am-5pm), about 53km to the southeast. Covering more than 17 sq km, Edzná was inhabited very early, from approximately 600 BC to the 15th century. Most of the visible carvings date from AD 550 to 810. Though it's a long way from such Puuc Hills sites as Uxmal and Kabah, some of the architecture here has elements of the Puuc style. What led to Edzná's decline and gradual abandonment remains a mystery.

From Campeche, dilapidated rural buses leave from outside the Sur Champotón terminal at 6am and 10am, then roughly hourly until 6pm (US$2, 1½ hours, 55km). Most drop you about 200m from the site entrance; ask before boarding. The last bus returning to Campeche passes near the site at about 2pm, so if you're coming here on a day trip from the city you'll want to catch one of the two early buses leaving Campeche. The bus schedules can vary slightly, so check the day before.

Coming from the north and east, get off at **San Antonio Cayal** and catch a bus 20km south to Edzná. If you're headed north on leaving Edzná, you'll have to depend on the occasional bus to get you to San Antonio Cayal, where you can catch a Chenes Route bus north to Hopelchén, Bolonchén de Rejón and ultimately Uxmal.

Forty kilometers east of San Antonio Cayal is **Hopelchén**, where Hwy 261 turns north. The next town to appear out of the lush countryside is **Bolonchén de Rejón**, after 34km. Its local festival of Santa Cruz is held each year on May 3.

Hwy 261 continues north into Yucatán state to **Uxmal** (p358), with a side road leading to the ruins along the Ruta Puuc (p362).

ESCÁRCEGA TO XPUJIL

Hwy 186 heads eastwards across southern-central Campeche state, from Escárcega through jungle to Chetumal in Quintana Roo, a 261km ride. It passes several fascinating Mayan sites and through the ecologically diverse and archaeologically rich **Reserva de la Biósfera Calakmul**. The largest settlement between Escárcega and Chetumal – and the only one with accommodations – is Xpujil (see opposite), on Hwy 186 about 20km west of the Campeche–Quintana Roo border. The only gasoline station on the same stretch is about 5km east of Xpujil.

Many of the numerous archaeological sites between Escárcega and Xpujil are being restored. The most significant historically is Calakmul, which is also one of the most difficult to reach (60km and no buses). It, and most of the other sites in this section, can be visited by taxis hired in Xpujil or tours booked either through hotels in Xpujil or Campeche (p377).

The predominant architectural styles of the region's archaeological sites are Río Bec and Chenes. The former is characterized by long, low buildings that look as though

they're divided into sections, each with a huge serpent or 'monster' mouth door. The facades are decorated with smaller masks, geometric designs (with many X forms) and columns. At the corners of the buildings are tall, solid towers with extremely small, steep, nonfunctional steps and topped by small false temples. Many of these towers have roofcombs. The Chenes style shares most of these characteristics except for the towers.

Balamkú

Sixty kilometers west of Xpujil (88km east of Escárcega) lies **Balamkú** (admission US$3; ☼ 8am-5pm). Discovered in 1990, this small site's attractions are its frescoes, and an exquisite, ornate stucco frieze. Amazingly, much original color is still visible on both the frescoes and the frieze. You'll notice toads dominate the designs at Balamkú. These amphibians, not only at home on land and water, were considered to move easily between this world and the next as well. The toad was a revered spirit guide that helped humans navigate between earth and the underworld.

Calakmul

Lying at the heart of the vast, untrammeled Reserva de la Biósfera Calakmul, **Calakmul** (admission US$3; ☼ 8am-5pm) was first discovered by outsiders in 1931. Mayanists consider the site to be of vital archaeological significance. Calakmul (Adjacent Mounds) was once the seat of a nearly unrivaled superpower, even further-reaching in size – and often influence – than neighboring Tikal (p179) in Guatemala.

From about AD 250 to 695, Calakmul was the leading city in a vast region known as the Kingdom of the Serpent's Head. Its perpetual rival was Tikal, and its decline began with the power struggles and internal conflicts that followed the defeat by Tikal of Calakmul's king Garra de Jaguar (Jaguar Paw). As at Tikal, there are indications that construction occurred over a period of more than a millennium.

The ruins (only a fraction of which have been cleared) are surrounded by rain forest, which is best viewed from the top of one of the several pyramids.

The turnoff to Calakmul is 59km west of Xpujil, and the site is 59km further south on a paved road. A toll of US$4 per car (more for heavier vehicles) and US$1.50 per person is levied at the turnoff from Hwy 186 to fund the constant road maintenance. From the parking lot to the ruins is a 500m walk.

At the Semarnat post 20km from the highway, rangers allow **camping**; please pay a donation if you use the shower and toilets.

Villas Puerta Calakmul (puertacalakmul@hotmail .com; cabaña US$60-80) has 15 tastefully decorated, fan-cooled cabañas. The restaurant serves generous meals at low prices.

Chicanná

Buried in the jungle almost 12km west of Xpujil and 500m south of the highway, **Chicanná** (House of the Snake's Jaws; admission US$3; ☺ 8am-5pm) is a mixture of Chenes and Río Bec architectural styles. The city was occupied from about AD 300 to 1100.

Enter through the modern *palapa* admission building, then follow the rock paths through the jungle to **Grupo D** and Estructura XX (AD 830), which features not one but two monster-mouth doorways, one above the other, topped by a roofcomb.

A five-minute walk along the jungle path brings you to **Grupo C**, with two low buildings – Estructuras X and XI – on a raised platform; the temples bear a few fragments of decoration.

The buildings in **Grupo B** (turn right when leaving Grupo C) have some intact decoration as well, and there's a good roofcomb on Estructura VI.

Shortly beyond is Chicanná's most famous building, Estructura II (AD 750–770) in **Grupo A**, with its gigantic Chenes-style monster-mouth doorway, believed to depict the jaws of the god Itzamná, lord of the heavens, creator of all things. If you photograph nothing else here, you'll want a picture of this, best taken in the afternoon.

Nearby, the charming and super eco-friendly **Río Bec Dreams** (☎ 983-871-60-57; www .riobecdreams.com; Hwy 186 Km 142; cabaña US$25-50) offers rustic 'jungalows' surrounded by bromeliads and orchids, a restaurant, bar and gift shop.

Becán

Among the largest and most elaborate archaeological sites in the area, **Becán** (admission US$3.50; ☺ 8am-5pm) lies 8km west of Xpujil, atop a rock outcrop. A 2km moat snakes its way around the entire city to protect it from attack. (Becán, literally 'path of the

snake,' is also the Mayan word for 'canyon' or 'moat.') Seven causeways crossed the moat, providing access to the city. Becán was occupied from 550 BC until AD 1000.

The first thing you'll come to on arrival is a plaza. Keep it to your left and you'll pass through a rock-walled passageway and beneath a corbeled arch. You will reach a huge twin-towered temple with cylindrical columns at the top of a flight of stairs. This is **Estructura VIII**, dating from about AD 600 to 730. The view from the top of this temple has become partially obscured by the trees, but on a clear day you can still see structures at the Xpujil ruins to the east.

Northwest of Estructura VIII is Plaza Central, ringed by 30m-high **Estructura IX** (the tallest building at the site) and the more interesting **Estructura X**.

In the jungle to the west are more ruins, including the **Plaza Oeste**, which is surrounded by low buildings and a ball court. Much of this area is still being excavated and restored, so it's open to the public only intermittently.

Loop back east, through the passageway again, to the plaza; cross it diagonally to the right, climbing a stone staircase to the **Plaza Sureste**. To exit, you can go around the plaza counterclockwise and descend the stone staircase on the southeast side or go down the southwest side and head left.

XPUJIL

The hamlet of Xpujil (shpu-*heel*) lies at the junction of east–west Hwy 186 and Campeche Hwy 261 (not to be confused with Mexico Hwy 261), which leads north to Hopelchén and eventually Mérida. A good base from which to explore the area's sites, Xpujil is growing rapidly in anticipation of a tourist boom. But it still has no bank or laundry, and the nearest gasoline station is 5km east of town. Several restaurants, a couple of hotels and a taxi stand are near the bus depot.

From the junction, the Xpuhil ruins are less than 1km west, Becán is 8km west, Chicanná is 11.5km west and Balamkú is 60km west.

Sights

Xpuhil (admission US$3; ☺ 8am-5pm), 'Place of the Cattails' in Mayan, flourished during the late Classic period from AD 400 to 900, though there was a settlement here much earlier. The site's entrance is on the west edge of town on the north side of Hwy 186, at the turnoff for the airport, less than 1km west of the junction.

One large building and three small ones have been restored. **Estructura I** in Grupo I, built about AD 760, is a fine example of the Río Bec architectural style, with its lofty towers. The three towers (rather than the usual two) have traces of the impractically steep ornamental stairways reaching nearly to their tops, and several fierce jaguar masks (go around to the back of the tower to see the best one). About 60m to the east is Estructura II, once an elite residence.

Sleeping & Eating

About 350m west of the junction, **Hotel y Restaurant Calakmul** (☎ 983-871-60-29; cabaña with shared bathroom US$22, d with fan & private bathroom US$40) offers large, modern rooms and a **restaurant** (⏰ 6am-midnight).

About 1km west of the junction, **El Mirador Maya** (☎ 983-871-60-05; bungalow/r US$25/35) has eight bungalows, two rooms and a **restaurant** (⏰ dinner).

Getting There & Around

Stopping in Xpujil are eleven buses daily to Escárcega (US$6), five to Campeche (US$14) and five to Chetumal (US$6). No buses originate in Xpujil, so you have to score a vacant seat on one passing through. The bus terminal is just east of the Xpujil junction.

The Xpuhil ruins are within walking distance of Xpujil junction. Hitch or hire a cab for Becán, Chicanná, Balamkú and other sites.

HORMIGUERO

This **site** (admission US$3; ⏰ 8am-5pm) is reached by heading 14km south from Xpujil junction, then turning right and heading another 8km west on a shoddily paved road. Hormiguero (Spanish for 'anthill') is an old site, with some buildings dating as far back as AD 50. Hormiguero has one of the most impressive buildings in the region.

RÍO BEC

The entrance to the collective farm **Ejido 20 de Noviembre** is 10km east of the Xpujil junction and signed 'Río Bec.' The unpaved

road leads 5km south to the collective itself and its **U'lu'um Chac Yuk Nature Reserve**. Look for the small store on the left side of the road, and ask there for guides to show you the various sites, which are about 13km further down the very rough road. Río Bec is the designation for an agglomeration of small sites, 17 at last count, in a 50-sq-km area southeast of Xpujil. It gave its name to the prevalent architecture style in the region. Of these many sites, the most interesting is certainly **Grupo B**, followed by **Grupos I and N**.

The road in is passable only when dry, and even then you need a high-clearance vehicle. The way is unsigned as well; you're best off hiring a guide whether you have a 4WD or not. A taxi to the *ejido* (communal landholding) will charge around US$5 for drop-off service; negotiate waiting time. Though it looks closer on the map, access to Río Bec from the road to Hormiguero is all but impossible.

TABASCO

Tabasco is not the most immediately appealing Mexican state, though if you are passing through there are a few interesting diversions, particularly Parque-Museo La Venta (p384) in Villahermosa and the acrópolis in Comalcalco (p385).

VILLAHERMOSA

☎ 993 / pop 348,000 / elevation 12m

Villahermosa is anything but the 'beautiful city' that its name implies, but it's an important gateway and a key provincial center. The pedestrianized Zona Luz (the city center) is an enjoyable place to explore, and its busy lanes – full of salsa-blaring clothes stores – buzz with life. The Zona Luz extends from the Plaza de Armas in the south to Parque Juárez in the north, and is roughly bounded by Calle Hidalgo and the banks of the Río Grijalva.

The bus station is a 20-minute walk from the Zona Luz.

Information

INTERNET ACCESS

Cybercafés are plentiful. Try:
Millenium (Sáenz 130)
Multiservicios (Aldama 621C)

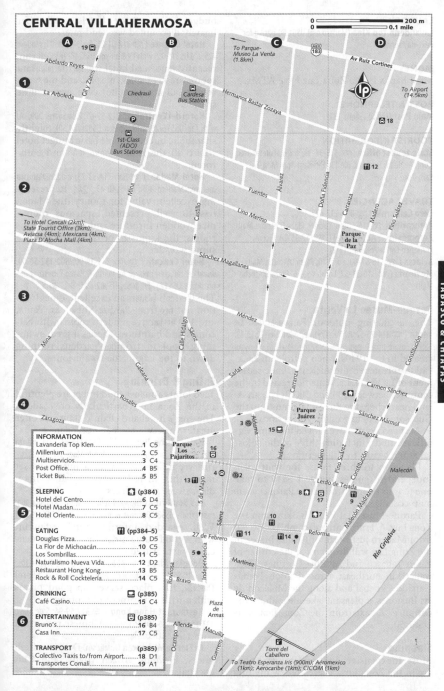

CENTRAL VILLAHERMOSA

0 ————— 200 m
0 ————— 0.1 mile

A 19 📮

Abelardo Reyes

Gil y Sáenz

1 La Arboleda

Chedraui

B

📮 Cardesa Bus Station

📮 1st-Class (ADO) Bus Station

P

To Parque-Museo La Venta (1.8km)

C

MEX 183

Hermanos Bastar Zozaya

Av Ruíz Cortines

To Airport (14.5km)

🚕 18

🏨 12

D

2 Fuentes

Mina

Castillo

Lino Merino

Juárez

Doña Fidencia

Carranza

Madero

Pino Suárez

To Hotel Cencali (2km);
State Tourist Office (3km);
Aviacsa (4km); Mexicana (4km);
Plaza D'Atocha Mall (4km)

Parque de la Paz

Sánchez Magallanes

3 Mina

Calle Hidalgo

Sáenz

Méndez

Carranza

Galeana

Sarlat

Constitución

Rosales

Carmen Sánchez

4 Zaragoza

Rosales

6 🏨

Parque Juárez

Sánchez Mármol

Zaragoza

Madero

Pino Suárez

Constitución

Malecón

3 @

15 💻

Juárez

INFORMATION

Lavandería Top Klen...........................1 C5
Millenium...2 C5
Multiservicios....................................3 C4
Post Office...4 B5
Ticket Bus..5 B5

Parque Los Pajaritos

16 🏨

5 de Mayo

13 🍴

4 @

@2

8 🏨

17

9

Lerdo de Tejada

Malecón Madrazo

Río Grijalva

SLEEPING 🏨 (p384)
Hotel del Centro.................................6 D4
Hotel Madan......................................7 C5
Hotel Oriente.....................................8 C5

EATING 🍴 (pp384–5)
Douglas Pizza.....................................9 D5
La Flor de Michoacán.........................10 C5
Los Sombrillas...................................11 C5
Naturalismo Nueva Vida.....................12 D2
Restaurant Hong Kong........................13 B5
Rock & Roll Coctelería........................14 C5

DRINKING 💻 (p385)
Café Casino.......................................15 C4

ENTERTAINMENT 🎬 (p385)
Bruno's...16 B4
Casa Inn...17 C5

TRANSPORT (p385)
Colectivo Taxis to/from Airport........18 D1
Transportes Comali...........................19 A1

5 10 🍴

7 🏨

11 🍴

14 🍴 1

Reforma

27 de Febrero

Sáenz

5

Independencia

Martínez

Rovirosa

Bravo

Vásquez

Plaza de Armas

Allende

Ocampo

Macuiliz

Guerrero

Torre del Caballero

To Teatro Esperanza Iris (900m); Aeromexico
(1km); Aerocaribe (1km); CICOM (1km)

6

LAUNDRY
Lavandería Top Klen (Madero s/n) US$1.50 per kg for
next-day service.

MONEY
Most banks in the Zona Luz have ATMs.

POST & TELEPHONE
Main Post Office (Sáenz 131)

TOURIST INFORMATION
State tourist office (☎ 316-36-33; www.visitetabasco
.com; Av de los Ríos at Calle 13; ☼ 8am-9pm Mon-Fri,
8am-1pm Sat)

TRAVEL AGENCIES
Aero California (☎ 800-237-6225)
Aerocaribe (☎ 316-50-46; Local 9, Plaza D'Atocha Mall)
Aeroméxico & Aerolitoral (☎ 312-15-28; Cicom,
Periférico Carlos Pellicer 511-2)
Aviacsa (☎ 316-57-00; Local 10, Plaza D'Atocha Mall)
Mexicana (☎ 316-31-32; Locales 5 & 6, Plaza D'Atocha
Mall)

Parque-Museo La Venta
The fascinating outdoor **Parque-Museo La
Venta** (☎ 314-16-52; Av Ruíz Cortines; admission US$2.75;
☼ sculpture trail & zoo 8am-4pm, zoo closed Mon) was
created in the 1940s, when petroleum excavation threatened the ancient Olmec settlement of La Venta. La Venta flourished in the
centuries between 900 and 500 BC on an island near where the Río Tonalá runs into the
Gulf some 130km west of Villahermosa.

Archaeologists have moved the most significant finds, including three of the colos-
sal stone heads, to Villahermosa.

Plan two to three hours for your visit.
Independent guides charge US$16 to take
one to four people around the Parque; a site
map costs US$1.

Parque-Museo La Venta is 3km from the
Zona Luz. A 'Fracc Carrizal' combi (US$0.50)
from Madero just north of Parque Juárez in
the Zona Luz will drop you at the corner of
Paseo Tabasco and Av Ruíz Cortines. Then
walk 1km northeast across Parque Tomás
Garrido Canabal and along the Malecón de
las Ilusiones, a pleasant lakeside path, to the
entrance. A taxi from the Zona Luz costs
US$1.50.

Sleeping
Most inexpensive and mid-range hotels
are in the Zona Luz. There are few inviting

budget options. Pricier hotels usually offer
heavily discounted weekend rates.

Hotel Oriente (☎ 312-01-21; fax 312-11-01; Madero
425; s/d US$15/22, with TV & air-con US$23/29) Well run,
recently renovated hotel where the pleasant
rooms are kept spick 'n' span, and the bathrooms (all are en suite) even have a little
sparkle.

Hotel del Centro (☎ 312-59-61; Pino Suárez 209; s/d
with fan US$16/20, with air-con US$20/24.50) Slightly
shambolic but acceptable basic budget hotel
where all the rooms have TV and bathroom.

Hotel Madan (☎ /fax 314-33-73; madan@intrasur
.net.mx; Madero 408; r US$40-43; ☒) Represent-
ing excellent value for money, the Madan
has 40 well presented, spacious rooms,
nice wooden furniture and attractive bathrooms; the king-size beds are ample for a
sumo wrestler.

Hotel Cencali (☎ /fax 315-19-99, 800-112-50-00;
www.cencali.com.mx; cnr Av Juárez & Paseo Tabasco; r incl
breakfast US$121, Fri & Sat US$62; ☒ ☒ ☒ ☐ ℗)
The Cencali boasts an excellent, quiet location not far from Parque-Museo La Venta,
and 120 attractive modern rooms with balconies and bathtubs. There's a great swimming pool in tropical gardens running
down to the Laguna de las Ilusiones.

Eating & Drinking
Taco joints and fast-food fryers are plentiful
in the Zona Luz, particularly on Madero.
The area's hotel and chain restaurants offer
greater variety – for a few pesos more.

Naturalismo Nueva Vida (☎ 312-81-98; Carranza
318; comida corrida US$3; ☼ lunch Mon-Fri) Family-
run veggie *comedor* with a nutritious set
menu that includes soup, salad, a main
dish, sweet and a drink.

Los Sombrillas (Howard Johnson Hotel, Aldama 404;
pasta from US$3.50, meat & fish mains from US$6; ☒)
Well regarded, informal hotel restaurant
with a good-value menu that includes delicious pasta Alfredo.

Douglas Pizza (☎ 312-76-76; Lerdo de Tejada 105;
pizzas US$5-12; ☼ dinner; ☒) Opposite Hotel
Pakaal, this place serves up good pizzas
with a wide assortment of toppings.

Restaurant Hong Kong (☎ 312-59-96; 5 de Mayo
433; mains US$6-10) Popular Chinese restaurant
with tasty specials.

La Flor de Michoacán (Juárez s/n) Delicious fresh
juices, *licuados*, frozen yogurt and fruit
cocktails.

Rock & Roll Cocktelería (☎ 312-05-93; Reforma 307; seafood cocktails US$6-12) Scruffy-looking place – a maelstrom of heat, swirling fans, a thumping jukebox and hard-drinking punters. Everyone's here for the *cócteles* (fish or seafood, tomato sauce, lettuce, onions and a lemon squeeze) and the cheap beer.

Coffee bar culture is sweeping the Zona Luz, but you'll find the best brew at the venerable **Café Casino** on Juárez where Villahermosa's chattering classes gather to discuss the political issues of the day.

Entertainment

Nightlife in the Zona Luz is very limited and pretty staid, with most of the 'action' confined to the hotels. On Madero, there's often live music in the bars inside the **Casa Inn** (☎ 358-01-02, 800-201-09-09; www.casainn.ws in Spanish; Madero 418) and **Hotel Madan** (opposite). For more of an alternative feel try **Bruno's** (cnr 5 de Mayo & Lerdo de Tejada), which is popular with artists, musicians and students.

Teatro Esperanza Iris (☎ 314-42-10; Periférico Carlos Pellicer), just north of Cicom, often stages folkloric dance, theater, cinema and music performances.

Getting There & Away

AIR

Villahermosa's **Aeropuerto Rovirosa** (☎ 356-01-57) is 13km east of the center on Hwy 186. Nonstop or one-stop direct flights to/from Villahermosa include the following:

Cancún Aerocaribe daily.
Houston, Texas Continental 4 days weekly.
Mérida Aviacsa daily.
Mexico City 8 flights daily between Aeroméxico, Mexicana, Aviacsa and Aero California.
Veracruz Aeroméxico and Aerolitoral both twice daily.

BUS

The 1st-class (ADO) **bus station** (☎ 312-76-92; Mina 297) is about 12 blocks north of the city center. It has a **luggage room** (per hour US$0.40; ⏰ 7am-11pm) and a selection of cafés. Deluxe and 1st-class UNO, ADO and Cristóbal Colón buses run from here, as well as a few 2nd-class services. Though Villahermosa is an important transportation point, many buses serving it are *de paso* (en route), so buy your onward ticket as early as possible. Few destinations in Tabasco are served by this bus station; most local services leave from small independent bus and minibus terminals.

It's also possible to book 1st-class bus tickets in the city center at **Ticket Bus** (☎ 312-12-60; Independencia 309; ⏰ 9am-9pm Mon-Sat), just north of the Plaza de Armas. They charge a commission of US$0.50 per ticket. Daily departures (most in the evening) include:

Campeche (6hr; 17 buses, US$17-22)
Cancún (12hr; 10 buses, US$40-60)
Chetumal (8hr; 8 buses, US$24)
Mérida (9hr; 17 buses, US$24-44)
Mexico City (TAPO; 11hr; 31 buses, US$43-63)
Palenque (2½hr; 12 buses, US$5-6.50)
Playa del Carmen (12hr; 8 buses, US$38)
San Cristóbal de Las Casas (7hr; 3 buses, US$13-14)
Tuxtla Gutiérrez (6hr; 6 buses, US$13-14)
Veracruz (8hr; 16 buses, US$22-35)

CAR & MOTORCYCLE

Most rental companies have desks at the airport.
Dollar Paseo Tabasco (☎ 315-80-88; Torre Empresarial, Paseo Tabasco 1203); Hotel Best Western (☎ 314-44-66; inside Hotel Best Western Maya Tabasco)

Getting Around

A taxi from city to airport costs US$10 to US$13 (from airport to city US$15) and takes about 25 minutes. Alternatively, go to the road outside the airport parking lot and pick up a *colectivo* taxi into the city for US$1 per person. These terminate on Carranza half a block south of Av Ruíz Cortines, about 1km north of the Zona Luz. Take a 'Dos Montes' vehicle from there to return to the airport.

To get from the ADO bus station to the Zona Luz, take a 'Centro' combi (US$0.50) or a taxi (US$1.25). Alternatively it's a 15- to 20-minute walk via Lino Merino, Parque de la Paz and Carranza. From the Zona Luz to the ADO bus station, take a 'Chedraui' bus or combi north on Malecón Madrazo. Chedraui is a big store just north of the bus station.

COMALCALCO

The Chontal Mayan city of **Comalcalco** (admission incl museum US$2.50; ⏰ 10am-4pm), 3km northeast of Comalcalco town, flourished during the late-Classic period, between AD 500 and 900. Comalcalcans traded the cacao bean with other Mayan settlements, and it is still the chief local cash crop.

Somewhat resembling Palenque in architecture and sculpture, Comalcalco is unique because it is built of bricks made from clay, sand and, ingeniously, oyster shells. Mortar was made with lime from the oyster shells. The **acrópolis** complex soars over the entire site with views from its summit over a panoply of palm trees to the Gulf of Mexico. All the site's buildings have information panels in Spanish and English.

Getting There & Away

Air-conditioned minibuses operated by Transportes Comali leave from their office on Gíl y Zaens in Villahermosa, three blocks north of the main ADO bus terminal, every 20 minutes between 5am and 9pm; they return from their private terminal in Comalcalco town two blocks west of the central plaza. The 55km journey takes about an hour and costs US$2.25.

The ruins are about 3km from Comalcalco town. You can cover the distance either by taxi (US$2.50) or by a Paraíso-bound combi. A few combis go right to the ruins, but most drop you at the entrance, from where it's a 1km walk.

TO GUATEMALA VIA RÍO SAN PEDRO

It's possible to travel from Tabasco into Guatemala via the town of Tenosique and a river route along the Río San Pedro, though there are no longer any scheduled boat services. Most travelers opt for the quicker, cheaper route via Frontera Corozal in Chiapas (see p415), which passes close to the impressive ruins of Yaxchilán.

If you do decide to travel via Tenosique, there are 10 buses a day (US$8.50, 3½ hours) from Villahermosa's ADO bus station. From Tenosique, regular *colectivo* taxis (US$2) and combis (US$1.75) go to the village of La Palma (45 minutes) from where you'll have to charter a boat (around US$80, four hours) to El Naranjo in Guatemala. Minibuses leave El Naranjo every half hour (four hours) until 3pm for Santa Elena, near Flores.

CHIAPAS

Chiapas is Mexico's most enigmatic state. It almost seems over-endowed, with mist-wrapped mountains, pine-forested peaks and extensive jungle reserves. But above all, Mexico's Chiapas is defined by the culture and customs of the Maya, both ancient and modern, for the descendants of the pyramid-builders remain in the region and give Chiapas a uniquely colorful indigenous identity.

San Cristóbal de Las Casas is a tranquil, hill-country colonial town surrounded by deeply traditional Maya villages. North of here are the spectacular turquoise Agua Azul waterfalls, and the evocative jungle-clad Maya temples of Toniná and Palenque. In the east of Chiapas is the Selva Lacandona, Mexico's largest rain forest, which envelopes a breathtaking lake, Laguna Miramar. Its forests fringe the Maya temples of Yaxchilán and Bonampak where you have a good chance of encountering toucans and howler monkeys.

Most *chiapanecos* (people from Chiapas) are very poor, and wealth is concentrated among a small oligarchy.

Dangers & Annoyances

Since the 1994 Zapatista uprising, the army has been present in big numbers in Chiapas. Though the security situation has been volatile at times in parts of the state, things were generally much calmer by early 2004. You'll almost certainly see large number of troops on the move as you travel around Chiapas, but violent incidents have been extremely rare and have not involved tourists.

There are regular checkpoints on some routes, particularly the Carretera Fronteriza. Make sure your tourist card and passport are in order. In some remote areas outside San Cristóbal de Las Casas, unknown outsiders could be at risk because of local politico-religious conflicts. Similarly, some Zapatista-aligned villages (particularly around the fringes of the Montes Azules reserve) have ideologically opposed ecotourism trips in their region. (See p39 and p391 for more on this issue.) Take local advice about where not to go. Unpleasant incidents of any kind affecting travelers have been extremely rare, and you are most unlikely to have anything other than a trouble-free time in Chiapas.

TUXTLA GUTIÉRREZ

☎ 961 / pop 456,000 / elevation 532m

Chiapas' state capital is a fairly mundane, modern city, though there are a couple of things worth stopping to see, particularly the nearby jungle-clad 800m-deep Cañón del Sumidero (p391).

Orientation

The city center is the Plaza Cívica, with the cathedral on its south side. The main east–west street, here called Av Central, runs past the north side of the cathedral. As it enters the city from the west, this same street is Blvd Dr Belisario Domínguez; to the east it becomes Blvd Ángel Albino Corzo.

East–west streets are called Avenidas and are named Norte or Sur depending whether they're north or south of Av Central. North–south streets are Calles and are called Poniente (Pte) or Oriente (Ote) depending whether they're west or east of Calle Central. Each street name also has a suffix indicating whether it is east (Oriente, Ote), west (Poniente, Pte), north (Nte) or south (Sur) of the intersection of Av Central and Calle Central. So the address 2a Av Nte Pte 425 refers to No 425 on the western (Pte) half of 2a Av Norte.

Information

EMERGENCY
Ambulance, Fire & Police (☎ 060)

INTERNET ACCESS
Cibercafé Prodinet (2a Calle Pte Sur; ☺ 9am-8pm Mon-Sat, noon-7pm Sun; per hour US$0.75; ▨)
Login (2a Av Sur Ote 540B; ☺ 8am-11pm Mon-Sat, 10am-7pm Sun; per hour US$0.50; ▨)

LAUNDRY
Lavandería Zaac (2a Av Nte Pte; per 3kg US$2.75)

MONEY
Bancomer (cnr Av Central Pte & 2a Calle Pte Nte; ☺ 9am-3pm Mon-Fri) Has ATMs.
Bital (west side of Plaza Cívica; ☺ 9am-3pm Mon-Fri) Has ATMs.
Western Union (Calle Central Nte; ☺ 9am-9pm) In the store Elektra. Does money transfers.

POST & TELEPHONE
Plenty of card phones are scattered around the plaza.
Main post office (1a Av Nte Ote) Just off Plaza Cívica.

TOURIST INFORMATION
Airport (☺ 7:30am-5pm)
Turismo Municipal (City Tourism Office; ☎ 612-55-11 ext 214; Calle Central Nte & 2a Av Nte Ote; ☺ 8am-8pm

Mon-Fri, 8am-4pm Sat) In the underpass at the northern end of Plaza Cívica.
Sectur (State Tourism Office; ☎ 800-280-35-00; Blvd Belisario Domínguez 250; ☺ 9am-9pm Mon-Fri, 9am-4pm Sat & Sun) 1.6km west of the center.

TRAVEL AGENCIES
Aerocaribe City (☎ 602-56-49; Blvd Belisario Domínguez 1748); airport (☎ 615-15-30)
Aviacsa City (☎ 611-20-00; Av Central Pte 160); airport (☎ 671-52-46)
Mexicana City (☎ 602-57-71; Blvd Belisario Domínguez 1748); airport (☎ 671-52-18)

Sights

The heart of the city, around the Plaza Cívica, is the liveliest part of town in the day. Most attractions are scattered around the suburbs.

Tuxtla's broad, lively main **Plaza Cívica** occupies two blocks and is flanked by an untidy array of concrete civic and commercial structures. At its southern end, across Av Central, is the whitewashed modern **Catedral de San Marcos**. The cathedral's clock tower tinkles out a tune on the hour to accompany a kitsch merry-go-round of apostles' images that emerge from one of the structure's upper levels.

A museum-theater-park area known as **Parque Madero** lies 1.25km northeast of the city center. If you don't want to walk there, take a *colectivo* along Av Central to Parque 5 de Mayo, then another *colectivo* north along 11a Calle Ote.

At Parque Madero, the modern **Museo Regional de Chiapas** (☎ 612-04-59; Calz de los Hombres Ilustres s/n; US$3; ☺ 9am-4pm Tue-Sun) has archaeological and colonial history exhibits, and costume and craft collections, all from Chiapas, plus temporary exhibitions. Parque Madero also contains the **Jardín Botánico** (Botanical Garden; admission free; ☺ 9am-6pm Tue-Sun).

Sleeping

Budget hotels congregate around the plaza. Most luxury and mid-range hotels are west of the center, and periodically offer discounted rates.

Hotel Posada Chiapas (☎ 612-33-54; 2a Calle Pte Sur 243; s/d US$9/16; [P]) An excellent budget choice, with small but attractive, brightly decorated rooms all with good beds, bathroom and fan, set around a courtyard.

TUXTLA GUTIÉRREZ

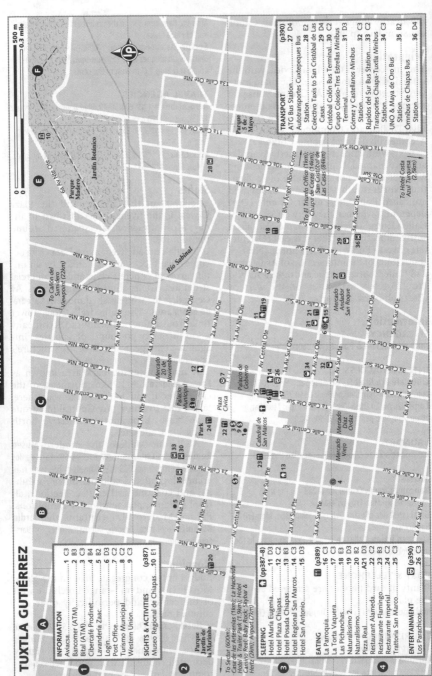

INFORMATION
Aviacsa.....................................	1 C3
Bancomer (ATM).......................	2 B3
Bital (ATM)..............................	3 C3
Cibercafé Prodinet...................	4 B4
Lavandería Zaac.......................	5 B2
Login......................................	6 D3
Post Office..............................	7 C2
Turismo Municipal...................	8 C2
Western Union.........................	9 C3

SIGHTS & ACTIVITIES (p387)
Museo Regional de Chiapas......10	E1

SLEEPING (pp387–8)
Hotel María Eugenia................11	D3
Hotel Plaza Chiapas.................12	C2
Hotel Posada Chiapas...............13	B3
Hotel Regional San Marcos......14	D3
Hotel San Antonio...................15	D3

EATING (p389)
La Parroquia............................16	C3
La Torta Vaquera.....................17	E3
Las Pichanchas........................18	D3
Naturalíssimo 2........................19	D2
Naturalíssimo..........................20	B2
Pizza Real................................21	D3
Restaurant Alameda.................22	A21
Restaurante Flamingo..............23	B3
Restaurante Imperial...............24	C3
Trattoria San Marco.................25	C3

ENTERTAINMENT (p390)
Los Parachicos........................26	C3

TRANSPORT (p390)
ATG Bus Station......................27	D4
Autotransportes Cuxtepeques Bus	
Station.................................28	E2
Colectivo Taxis to San Cristóbal de Las	
Casas...................................29	D4
Cristóbal Colón Bus Terminal....30	C2
Grupo Colosio-Tres Estrellas Minibus	
Terminal...............................31	D3
Gómez y Castellanos Minibus	
Station.................................32	C3
Rápidos del Sur Bus Station......33	C2
Transportes Chiapa-Tuxtla Minibus	
Station.................................34	C3
UNO & Maya de Oro Bus	
Station.................................35	B2
Ómnibus de Chiapas Bus	
Station.................................36	D4

Parque Jardín de la Marimba

To Sectur (600m);
Casa de las Artesanías (1km); La Hacienda
Hotel & Trailer Park (1.9km); Hotel
Camino Real; Baby Rock; Skybar &
Hertz (2km); Airport (7km)

To Cañón del
Sumidero
Viewpoint (22km)

Río Sabinal

Parque
Madero

Jardín Botánico

Parque
5 de
Mayo

To El Triunfo Office (1km);
Chiapa de Corzo (14km);
San Cristóbal de
Las Casas (84km)

Blvd Angel Albino Corzo

To Hotel Costa
Azul Turquesa
(2.5km)

Mercado
20 de
Noviembre

Palacio
Municipal

Plaza
Cívica

Catedral de
San Marcos

Palacio de
Gobierno

Mercado
Viejo

Mercado
Díaz
Ordaz

Mercado
Andador
San Roque

0   500 m
0   0.3 mile

Hotel San Antonio (☎ 612-27-13; 2a Av Sur Ote 540; s/d US$8.50/14; **P**) Hotel San Antonio is run by friendly people, is well located for the San Cristóbal minibus terminal and has clean, good-value rooms with fan and bathroom.

La Hacienda Hotel & Trailer Park (☎ 612-78-32; Blvd Belisario Domínguez 1197; trailer sites for 2 people US$12, extra person US$3.50, s/d with fan US$38/46, with air-con US$53/62; **P** **P**) This place is 3km west of Plaza Cívica, and has comfortable, spacious rooms, friendly management, all hookups, a coffee shop and a tiny pool, but the park area is small and somewhat blighted by traffic noise.

Hotel Plaza Chiapas (☎ 613-83-65; 2a Av Nte Ote 229; s/d US$14/16, with TV US$19/21) This place has a shiny lobby and a small restaurant. The rooms, all with fan and some with balcony, are clean and represent fair value.

Hotel Regional San Marcos (☎ 613-19-40; san marcos@chiapas.net; 2a Calle Ote Sur 176; s/d US$20/23, with air-con US$25/29; **P**) A minute's walk from Plaza Cívica, this hotel has medium-sized, fairly pleasant rooms with TV and private bathroom.

Hotel Costa Azul Turquesa (☎ 611-34-85; Libramiento Sur Ote 3722; r/ste US$42/61; **P** **P**) Located on the southeast edge of the town with fine vistas of Chiapas' central valley, this elegant new hotel is set in spacious leafy grounds. Good-value stylish rooms, and the suites all have Jacuzzis.

Hotel María Eugenia (☎ 613-37-67; heugenia@ prodigy.net.mx; Av Central Ote 507; r US$63-71; **P** **P**) This is the most comfortable downtown hotel, and has a good restaurant. The 83 airy, light rooms all have either two double beds or a huge king-size, cable TV, and many have great views.

Hotel Camino Real (☎ 617-77-77; www.caminoreal .com/tuxtla; Blvd Belisario Domínguez 1195; r US$195; **P** **P** **P** **P**) The five-star Camino Real boasts a spectacular interior, with a pool and waterfall in a large, verdant inner courtyard full of free-flying tropical birds. Commodious rooms come with all mod cons, and have wheelchair access. Facilities include a spa, tennis courts and a gym. Special rates sometimes offer doubles with breakfast for US$120.

Eating

There's plenty of choice in Tuxtla, though little in way of gourmet cuisine. Local specialties include *chipilín* (a corn-based cheesy soup).

The first three places listed all have outdoor tables, and offer a peaceful setting behind the cathedral to enjoy your meal.

Trattoria San Marco (☎ 612-69-74; Callejón Ote Sur, Local 5; mains US$3.25-5.75, pizzas US$4-10.50) Snack on a sub, baguette or salad, or delve into the extensive pizza menu.

La Parroquia (☎ 600-11-97; Callejón Ote Sur, Local 6; mains US$4-9) Next door to Trattoria San Marco, the Parroquia specializes in *parrillada* (grills), from bacon to filet mignon and chorizo.

La Torta Vaquera (☎ 613-20-94; Callejón Ote Sur; snacks from US$0.50) This place is popular for coffee, tacos and *quesadillas* (heated tortilla filled with cheese).

Restaurante Imperial (Calle Central Nte; snacks US$1-2, mains US$2.50-3, comida corrida US$3) Popular, efficient place facing the west side of Plaza Cívica and close to the 1st-class bus station. Offers a wholesome two-course *comida corrida* with lots of choices. Full breakfast menu too.

Restaurant Alameda (☎ 612-25-06; 1a Av Nte Pte 133; snacks US$1-2.25, mains US$2.50-3) Family-run place that's a great choice for inexpensive Mexican meals.

Naturalíssimo (breakfast US$3-4.50, antojitos US$2-3.25, lunch US$4.50) Calle Pte Nte (☎ 613-53-43; 6a Calle Pte Nte 124); Av Central Ote (☎ 613-96-48 Av Central Ote 525) Bright, cheery vegetarian Naturalíssimo offers healthy breakfasts, Mexican dishes like whole-wheat *tortas* and *chilaquiles* and a tasty three-course lunch.

Restaurante Flamingo (☎ 612-09-20; 1a Calle Pte Sur 17; mains US$4-11, comida corrida US$5.50; **P**) Located along a passage off a downtown street, this is a pleasingly formal restaurant. Dig into a full hotcakes breakfast, a filling set lunch, or meat and fish dishes.

Pizza Real (☎ 614-71-51; 2a Av Sur Ote 557; comida corrida US$1) Opposite Hotel San Antonio, this *comedor* does a bargain-priced lunchtime set meal including rice and two other dishes. No pizzas though!

Las Pichanchas (☎ 612-53-51; Av Central Ote 837; mains US$3-8; ☺ lunch & dinner) Courtyard restaurant, located six blocks east of Plaza Cívica with a long menu of local specialties. Try the tasty tamales, or *chipilín*, and leave room for the dessert *chimbos*, made from egg yolks and cinnamon. There's live marimba music, and Chiapas folkloric dance in the evening too.

YUCATÁN PENINSULA, TABASCO & CHIAPAS

Entertainment

Downtown there's little action after dark, but the bar **Los Parachicos** (☎ 613-19-40; cnr 1a Av Sur Ote & 2 Calle Ote Sur) is fine for a beer and, occasionally, live music. The bar above **Trattoria San Marco** (p389) also has live music.

Popular, free marimba concerts are held from 7pm to 10pm on Saturday and Sunday (and sporadically on other evenings when the weather's fine) in the **Parque Jardín de la Marimba**, a pleasant park beside Av Central Pte, eight blocks west of Plaza Cívica.

Clubbers congregate in the 'Zona Dorada,' west of the center along the Blvd Domínguez, where **Baby Rock** (☎ 615-14-28; Calz Emiliano Zapata 207) and **Skybar** (☎ 615-29-57; Blvd Las Fuentes 101) both play Latin and western dance hits.

Shopping

Casa de las Artesanías de Chiapas (☎ 602-65-65; Blvd Belisario Domínguez 2035; ☺ 10am-8pm Mon-Sat, 10am-3pm Sun) This place, though an unhandy 2km west of Plaza Cívica, sells a good range of Chiapas crafts.

Getting There & Away

AIR

Tuxtla's **Aeropuerto Francisco Sarabia** (☎ 612-29-20), also called Aeropuerto Terán, is 3km south of Hwy 190 from a signposted turnoff 5km west of Plaza Cívica. A taxi from the center to the airport costs US$6.

Aerocaribe flies to/from Mexico City, Oaxaca, Villahermosa, Veracruz, Tapachula, Palenque, Mérida, Cancún at least once daily. Aviacsa and Mexicana fly several times daily to/from Mexico City (US$174).

BUS

There are numerous bus stations. The main terminal, **Cristóbal Colón** (☎ 612-51-22; 2a Av Nte Pte 268) is two blocks west of the main plaza: Colón, Altos and ADO all operate from here. The 2nd-class line Rápidos del Sur (RS) is next door, and UNO and Maya de Oro deluxe services are across the street. There's no left luggage, but the Turismo Municipal (see p387) will look after your gear, as will some stores on 2a Av Nte Pte: look for 'Se guardan maletas' or 'Se guardan equipaje' signs.

A new bus station has been planned for a site east of the center near the Central de Abastos Libramiento Sur (Libramiento Sur Market) for years, but it may not come into operation during the lifetime of this book.

Most 2nd-class companies' terminals are east of the center.

Autotransportes Cuxtepeques (10a Calle Ote Nte at Av 3a Nte Ote)
Autotransportes Tuxtla Gutiérrez (ATG; 3a Av Sur Ote 712)
Fletes y Pasajes (FYPSA; 9a Av Sur Ote 1882)
Grupo Colosio-Tres Estrellas (2a Av Sur Ote 521)
Ómnibus de Chiapas (OC; 3a Av Sur Ote 884)

Daily departures from Tuxtla include:
Comitán (3½hr; 5 Maya de Oro buses, US$8; 3 Colón buses, US$7; 16 Cuxtepeques buses, US$5)
Mérida (13hr; 1 Maya de Oro bus, US$41; 1 Colón bus, US$36; 2 ATG buses, US$27)
Mexico City (most to TAPO, a few to Norte; 17hr; 1 UNO bus, US$80; 4 Maya de Oro buses, US$58; 8 Colón/ADO buses, US$51)
Oaxaca (10hr; 1 Maya de Oro bus, US$26; 3 Colón buses, US$22; 8 FYPSA buses, US$18)
Palenque (6hr; 2 Maya de Oro buses, US$12; 7 Colón buses, US$8-11; 4 ATG buses, US$9)
Puerto Escondido (11½hr; 2 Colón buses, US$23)
San Cristóbal de Las Casas (1-1½hr; 9 Maya de Oro/UNO buses, US$4.25-5.50; 7 Colón buses, US$3.50; 6 ATG buses, US$3; frequent Colosio-Tres Estrellas minibuses, US$3.25; OC minibuses every 20min 6am-6pm, US$2.75; frequent *colectivo* taxis from 3a Av Sur Ote 847, US$3.75)
Tapachula (7½hr; 1 UNO bus, US$26; 6 Maya de Oro buses, US$19; 14 Colón buses, US$16; 31 RS buses, US$13)
Villahermosa (7hr; 2 Maya de Oro buses, US$14; 4 Colón buses, US$13; 3 ATG buses, US$9)

CAR & MOTORCYCLE

These rental companies also have desks at the airport.
Budget (☎ 615-06-83; Blvd Belisario Domínguez 2510)
Hertz (☎ 615-53-48; Hotel Camino Real, Blvd Belisario Domínguez 1195)

Getting Around

All *colectivos* (US$0.40) on Blvd Belisario Domínguez–Av Central–Blvd Albino Corzo run at least as far as the Hotel Bonampak and state tourist office in the west, and 11a Calle Ote in the east. Official stops are marked by 'parada' signs but they'll sometimes stop for you elsewhere. Taxi rides within the city cost US$1.75 to US$2.

CHIAPA DE CORZO

☎ 961 / pop 31,000 / elevation 450m
Chiapa de Corzo is an attractive colonial town, with an easy-going provincial air. Situated on the north bank of the broad Río

THE ZAPATISTAS

On January 1, 1994, the day of the North American Free Trade Agreement's (Nafta) initiation, a previously unknown leftist guerrilla army, the Ejército Zapatista de Liberación Nacional (EZLN), emerged from the woods to occupy San Cristóbal de Las Casas and other towns in Chiapas. Linking anti-globalization rhetoric with Mexican revolutionary slogans, the Zapatistas' (as they are better known) declared goal was to overturn a wealthy local oligarchy's centuries-old hold on land, resources and power and to fight to improve the wretched living standards of Mexico's indigenous people.

The Mexican army evicted the Zapatistas within days (most of the 150 people killed in the fight were Zapatistas) and the rebels retreated to hideouts on the fringes of the Selva Lacandona. Here they launched a propaganda blitz – mainly fought via the Internet rather than direct military engagement. The Zapatistas' charismatic pipe-puffing Subcomandante Marcos (actually a former university professor named Rafael Guillén) rapidly became a cult figure. International supporters flocked to Zapatista headquarters at La Realidad, 85km southeast of Ocosingo. Zapatista-aligned peasants took over hundreds of farms and ranches in Chiapas.

In 1996 an agreement on indigenous rights was reached between Zapatista and government negotiators, though the government never turned the accords into law. Zapatistas later ousted local governing officials (affiliated with the ruling PRI party) and created 'autonomous municipalities.' In 1997, right-wing paramilitaries responded by massacring 45 people in the village of Acteal.

By 1999 an estimated 21,000 Zapatista-aligned villagers had fled their homes after the Mexican army soldiers (aided and abetted by paramilitaries) launched a campaign of intimidation.

Hopes of a fresh start rose in 2000 when two new non-PRI politicians were elected: Presidente Vicente Fox; and, in Chiapas, state governor Pablo Salazar. Two attempts to make the necessary constitutional changes failed, however, as Congress watered down EZLN proposals. After the second impasse in September 2002, the Zapatistas refused to participate in further talks and a period of silence ensued.

Parts of the Chiapas countryside remained tense, and occasional incidents propelled the unresolved conflict onto the news agenda, such as the Zapatista seizure of American-owned hotel Rancho Esmeralda near Ocosingo in February 2003. The Zapatistas also loudly denounced the concept of ecotourism, and detained kayakers in the south of the state.

In September 2003, signs of a more pragmatic, patient strategy appeared to be evident. Relatively low-key plans to celebrate the 10th anniversary of the 1994 uprising were announced, concentrating on raising money through raffles, dances and concerts, rather than headline-grabbing political statements. And as the Zapatista leadership acknowledged: 'For 500 years the authorities have refused to listen to us. We have time on our side.'

The main Zapatista-affiliated website is www.ezln.org, with further background available at www.globalexchange.org and http://flag.blackened.net/revolt/mexico.html.

Grijalva, it's 12km east of Tuxtla Gutiérrez, and is the main starting point for trips to the Parque Nacional Cañón del Sumidero.

Everything revolves around, or just off, Chiapa's vast central plaza. The **Banamex** (🕙 9am-2pm Mon-Fri, 9am-3pm Sat), on the west side of the plaza, has an ATM.

Chiapa's annual fiesta (January 9 to 21), the **Fiesta de Enero**, is one of the country's most extraordinary spectacles, with nightly dances involving cross-dressing young men, known as Las Chuntá. These blond-wigged, mask-toting Parachicos (actually conquistador-impersonators) parade on January 15, 17

and 20. A canoe battle and firework extravaganza follows on the final day.

Parque Nacional Cañón del Sumidero

This spectacular canyon, now filled by a 25km reservoir, lies just east of town. Most people see it by boat. **Motorboats** (US$11; 🕙 8am-4pm) driven by throttle-happy captains speed through the canyon's towering sheer rock walls during the two-hour tour. They leave from the Chiapa *embarcadero* (boat launch), two blocks south of the plaza along 5 de Febrero, the street on the plaza's west side.

Sleeping & Eating

Hotel Los Ángeles (☎ 616-00-48; fax 616-02-65; Plaza Albino Corzo; s/d with bathroom & fan US$16/18, with air-con US$21/23; P) This hotel, at the southeast corner of the plaza, has spotless rooms with hot water and TV; those on the upper level are more spacious.

Hotel La Ceiba (☎ 616-07-73; www.prodigyweb .net.mx/hotellaceiba in Spanish; Av Domingo Ruíz 300; s/d US$42/47; ⚇ ⚏ P) La Ceiba, located two blocks west of the plaza, has an inviting pool and extensive gardens, and the 91 attractive rooms have fans and cable TV.

The **restaurants** on the plaza are your best bet for convenient, reliable food. Those near the *embarcadero* are slightly overpriced, but the views over the river are enjoyable. Cruise over to the market, across from the Museo de la Laca, to find the ultra-cheap market *comedores* (eateries).

Getting There & Away

Minibuses from Tuxtla Gutiérrez to Chiapa de Corzo are run by Gómez y Castellanos, at 3a Av Sur Ote 380, and Transportes Chiapa-Tuxtla, on 2a Av Sur Ote at 2a Calle Ote Sur. Both depart every few minutes from 5:30am to 10:30pm for the 20-minute, US$0.60 trip. Buses and minibuses to and from Tuxtla stop on the north side of the central plaza.

Buses to/from San Cristóbal de Las Casas don't pass through central Chiapa de Corzo, but most will stop at a gas station on Hwy 190 on the northeast edge of town. Microbuses (US$0.40) run between this gas station and the top end of Chiapa's plaza.

SAN CRISTÓBAL DE LAS CASAS

☎ 967 / pop 121,000 / elevation 2163m

San Cristóbal (cris-*toh*-bal) has been a favorite travelers' haunt for decades. It's a pleasure to spend time here: exploring the cobbled streets and markets, visiting nearby indigenous villages and absorbing the unique, relaxed ambience. San Cristóbal has a bohemian, artsy, floating community of Mexicans and foreigners, a lively bar and music scene and wonderfully clear highland light. There's a terrific selection of accommodations at all price levels, and a cosmopolitan array of cafés and restaurants. All in all it's easy to see why San Cristóbal is many people's favorite Mexican town.

The city of San Cristóbal was catapulted into the limelight on January 1, 1994, when Zapatista rebels selected it as one of four places in which to launch their revolution (see The Zapatistas, p391).

Orientation

San Cristóbal is easy to walk around, with straight streets that ramble over several gentle hills. A long *andador* (pedestrianized walkway) starts at the Templo Santo Domingo in the north, passes the cathedral and finishes at the Torre del Carmen. The Pan-American Hwy (190) runs through the southern part of town. Officially named Blvd Juan Sabines, it's more commonly called 'El Bulevar.'

Nearly all transportation terminals are on or just off the Pan-American. From the Cristóbal Colón bus terminal, it's six blocks north up Insurgentes to the central square, Plaza 31 de Marzo.

Information
BOOKSTORES

La Pared (Hidalgo 2; lapared9@hotmail.com) Superb choice of new and used books in English, as well as travel guides.

Librería Chilam Balam (Utrilla 33) Mexican history, anthropology and literature in Spanish.

IMMIGRATION

Instituto Nacional de Migración (☎ 678-02-92; Diagonal El Centenario 30) On a corner with Pan-American Hwy, 1.2km west of the Cristóbal Colón bus station.

INTERNET ACCESS

Cybercafés are everywhere. Most charge US$0.50 to US$0.90 per hour.

Tr@vel Net (Paniagua 29A)

Crosan Estación (Av Belisario Domínguez s/n; ◷ 7am-11pm)

LAUNDRY

Lavomart (Real de Guadalupe 70A) US$3.50 wash and dry.

Lavandería La Rapidita (Insurgentes 9) Service within 2½ hours, or wash your own for less.

MEDICAL SERVICES

Dr Roberto Lobato (☎ 678-77-77; Belisario Domínguez 17; per consultation US$23)

Hospital (☎ 678-07-70; Insurgentes)

MONEY

Banamex (Plaza 31 de Marzo; ◷ 9am-5:30pm Mon-Sat)

Bital (Mazariegos s/n; ◷ 8am-7pm Mon-Sat, 10am-2pm Sun)

Outside bank hours (but at worse rates) you can use:

Lacantún Money Exchange (Real de Guadalupe 12A)
Viajes Chincultik (Casa Margarita, Real de Guadalupe 34)

TELEPHONE & POST
One of the cheapest places to call abroad is **La Pared** (see opposite)
Main post office (Ignacio Allende 5B)

TOURIST INFORMATION
Municipal tourist office (☎ 678-06-65; Palacio Municipal, Plaza 31 de Marzo; ☺ 8am-8pm Mon-Sat, 9am-3pm Sun)
Sectur (☎ 678-65-70; Hidalgo 1B; ☺ 9am-8pm Mon-Sat, 9am-2pm Sun) Best bet.

Sights

PLAZA 31 DE MARZO
The graceful main **plaza**, or *zócalo*, is surrounded by elegant colonial buildings and is a fine place to take in San Cristóbal's unique, unhurried highland atmosphere. Shoeshiners, newspaper vendors and *ambulantes* (walking vendors) gather around an elaborate iron bandstand.

The **cathedral**, on the north side of the plaza, was begun in 1528 but completely rebuilt in 1693.

The **Hotel Santa Clara**, on the plaza's southeast corner, was the house of Diego de Mazariegos, the Spanish conqueror of Chiapas. It is one of the few secular examples of plateresque style in Mexico.

TEMPLO & EX-CONVENTO DE SANTO DOMINGO
North of the center on 20 de Noviembre, the **Templo de Santo Domingo** is the most beautiful of San Cristóbal's many churches, especially when its pink facade catches the late-afternoon sun. The church and adjoining monastery were built between 1547 and 1560. The church's baroque frontage – on which can be seen the double-headed Hapsburg eagle, symbol of the Spanish monarchy in those days – was added in the 17th century.

The Ex-Convento (Ex-Monastery) attached to Santo Domingo contains two interesting exhibits. One is the showroom of **Sna Jolobil** (20 de Noviembre s/n; ☺ 9am-2pm & 4-6pm Mon-Sat), a cooperative of 800 indigenous women weavers from the Chiapas highlands. Prices on woven items range from a few dollars for smaller items to over

US$1000 for the best *huipiles* and ceremonial garments.

Also in the Ex-Convento buildings, the **Centro Cultural de los Altos** (20 de Noviembre s/n; admission US$3, free Sun & holidays; ☺ 10am-5pm Tue-Sun) houses a moderately interesting museum, dedicated primarily to regional history and Maya ceramics.

Chamulan women and bohemian types from all over the world conduct a supercolorful daily crafts market around Santo Domingo and the neighboring **Templo de La Caridad** (built in 1712). You'll find local and Guatemalan textiles, woolen rugs and blankets, leather bags and belts, Zapatista dolls, hippie jewelry, *animalitos* from Amatenango del Valle and more.

TORRE, TEMPLO & CENTRO CULTURAL DEL CARMEN
The **Torre del Carmen**, at the southern end of the *andador* on Hidalgo, was once the city's gateway. Built in Mudéjar style, the white arched structure, topped with a double bell tower, dates from 1680 and remains a city landmark. The baroque facade adjoining the tower to the east belongs to the **Templo del Carmen**, whose relatively sober interior contains hardwood paneling and a neoclassical altar.

Just west of the tower is an ex-convent building, now the **Centro Cultural El Carmen** (admission free; ☺ 9am-6pm Tue-Sun) which hosts art and photography exhibitions, and the odd musical event in a wonderful colonial building with large, peaceful gardens. There's a small café here too.

MERCADO MUNICIPAL
To get a real flavor of the region's indigenous character visit San Cristóbal's busy municipal **market** (☺ 7am-5pm) eight blocks north of the main plaza between Utrilla and Belisario Domínguez. It's an amazing assault on the senses.

CENTRO DE DESARROLLO DE LA MEDICINA MAYA
The **Maya Medicine Development Center** (Cedemm; ☎ 678-54-38; www.laneta.apc.org/omiech; Av Salomón González Blanco 10; admission US$1.75; ☺ 10am-6pm Mon-Fri, 10am-5pm Sat & Sun) was founded by Omiech, the Organization of Indigenous Doctors of Chiapas, which focuses on traditional Maya medicine. For these

SAN CRISTÓBAL DE LAS CASAS

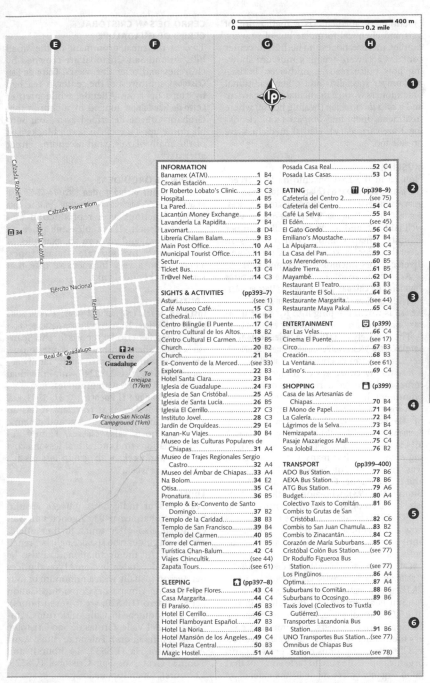

0
0   400 m
0.2 mile

INFORMATION
Banamex (ATM)..........................1 B4
Crosan Estación.........................2 C4
Dr Roberto Lobato's Clinic..........3 C3
Hospital....................................4 B5
La Pared...................................5 B4
Lacantún Money Exchange........6 B4
Lavandería La Rapidita..............7 B4
Lavomart..................................8 D4
Librería Chilam Balam................9 B3
Main Post Office......................10 A4
Municipal Tourist Office...........11 B4
Sectur....................................12 B4
Ticket Bus..............................13 C4
Tr@vel Net.............................14 C3

SIGHTS & ACTIVITIES   (pp393–7)
Astur....................................(see 1)
Café Museo Café.....................15 C3
Cathedral...............................16 B4
Centro Bilingüe El Puente.........17 C4
Centro Cultural de los Altos.......18 B2
Centro Cultural El Carmen........19 B5
Church...................................20 B2
Church...................................21 B4
Ex-Convento de la Merced.......(see 33)
Explora..................................22 B3
Hotel Santa Clara...................23 B4
Iglesia de Guadalupe...............24 F3
Iglesia de San Cristóbal...........25 A5
Iglesia de San Lucía................26 B5
Iglesia El Cerrillo.....................27 C3
Instituto Jovel........................28 C3
Jardín de Orquídeas................29 E4
Kanan-Ku Viajes.....................30 B4
Museo de las Culturas Populares de
  Chiapas...............................31 A4
Museo de Trajes Regionales Sergio
  Castro..................................32 A4
Museo del Ámbar de Chiapas....33 A4
Na Bolom...............................34 E2
Otisa.....................................35 C4
Pronatura...............................36 B5
Templo & Ex-Convento de Santo
  Domingo..............................37 B2
Templo de la Caridad...............38 B3
Templo de San Francisco..........39 B4
Templo del Carmen.................40 B5
Torre del Carmen....................41 B5
Turística Chan-Balum..............42 C3
Viajes Chincultik...................(see 44)
Zapata Tours.........................(see 61)

SLEEPING   (pp397–8)
Casa Dr Felipe Flores...............43 C4
Casa Margarita........................44 C4
El Paraíso...............................45 B3
Hotel El Cerrillo.......................46 C3
Hotel Flamboyant Español........47 B3
Hotel La Noria.........................48 B4
Hotel Mansión de los Ángeles...49 C4
Hotel Plaza Central..................50 B3
Magic Hostel...........................51 A4

Posada Casa Real.....................52 C4
Posada Las Casas.....................53 D4

EATING   (pp398–9)
Cafetería del Centro 2.............(see 75)
Cafetería del Centro.................54 C4
Café La Selva.........................55 B4
El Edén.................................(see 45)
El Gato Gordo.........................56 C4
Emiliano's Moustache..............57 B4
La Alpujarra...........................58 C4
La Casa del Pan......................59 C3
Los Merenderos......................60 B5
Madre Tierra..........................61 B5
Mayambé..............................62 D4
Restaurant El Teatro...............63 B3
Restaurante El Sol..................64 B6
Restaurante Margarita............(see 44)
Restaurante Maya Pakal..........65 C4

ENTERTAINMENT   (p399)
Bar Las Velas.........................66 C4
Cinema El Puente.................(see 17)
Circo.....................................67 B3
Creación................................68 B3
La Ventana...........................(see 61)
Latino's................................69 C4

SHOPPING   (p399)
Casa de las Artesanías de
  Chiapas...............................70 B4
El Mono de Papel....................71 B4
La Galería..............................72 B4
Lágrimos de la Selva...............73 B4
Nemizapata...........................74 C4
Pasaje Mazariegos Mall...........75 C4
Sna Jolobil............................76 B2

TRANSPORT   (pp399–400)
ADO Bus Station.....................77 B6
AEXA Bus Station...................78 B6
ATG Bus Station......................79 A6
Budget..................................80 A4
Colectivo Taxis to Comitán.......81 B6
Combis to Grutas de San
  Cristóbal.............................82 C6
Combis to San Juan Chamula....83 B2
Combis to Zinacantán.............84 C2
Corazón de María Suburbans....85 C6
Cristóbal Colón Bus Station.....(see 77)
Dr Rodulfo Figueroa Bus
  Station..............................(see 77)
Los Pingüinos.........................86 A4
Optima..................................87 A4
Suburbans to Comitán.............88 B6
Suburbans to Ocosingo............89 B6
Taxis Jovel (Colectivos to Tuxtla
  Gutiérrez)............................90 B6
Transportes Lacandonia Bus
  Station.................................91 B6
UNO Transportes Bus Station..(see 77)
Ómnibus de Chiapas Bus
  Station.............................(see 78)

practitioners, medicine is a matter not of pills and chemical formulae but of prayers, candles, incense, bones and herbs. The center contains an award-winning museum showing how pulse readers, midwives, herbalists, prayer specialists and other traditional practitioners work; a medicinal plant garden; and a *casa de curación* (healing house) where treatments including *limpias* (soul cleansings) are carried out. Herbal medicines are on sale too.

MUSEUMS

Housed in the Ex-Convento de la Merced, the **Museo del Ámbar de Chiapas** (Chiapas Amber Museum; Mazariegos s/n; www.museodelambar.com.mx; admission US$0.90; ☽ 10am-2pm & 4-7pm Tue-Sun) is very well laid out, and has some excellent amber exhibits. Chiapas amber, which comes in several shades, is known for its clarity and diverse colors (including green and red).

Across the road, the **Museo de las Culturas Populares de Chiapas** (Popular Cultures Museum; Mazariegos 37; admission by donation; ☽ 9am-2pm & 5-8pm Tue-Sat) is worth popping into for its temporary painting and photography exhibits.

The privately run **Museo de Trajes Regionales Sergio Castro** (Museum of Regional Costumes; ☎ 678-42-89; Guadalupe Victoria 38; admission by donation) houses a fascinating collection of indigenous costumes and assorted curios. Visit only by appointment, best made the day before.

A visit to the lovely 19th-century house of **Na Bolom** (☎ 678-14-18; www.nabolom.org; Guerrero 33; house US$3, 1½hr tour in English or Spanish US$4.50; ☽ tours 11:30am & 4:30pm) is an intriguing experience. For many years Na Bolom was the home of Swiss anthropologist and photographer Gertrude (Trudy) Duby-Blom (1901–93), who along with her Danish archaeologist husband Frans Blom (1893–1963) bought the house in 1950. It is now a museum and institute for the study and preservation of Chiapas' indigenous cultures.

Café Museo Café (Coffee Museum Café; ☎ 678-78-76; http://members.es.tripod.de/cafemuseocafe in Spanish; MA Flores 10; admission free; ☽ 9am-9pm Mon-Sat, 4-9pm Sun) is a venture of Coopcafé, a group of 15,000 small-scale, mainly indigenous, Chiapas coffee growers. The museum covers the history of coffee and its cultivation in Chiapas, indigenous coffee growing and organic coffee. Be sure to taste some of that good organic coffee made in the café.

CERRO DE SAN CRISTÓBAL & CERRO DE GUADALUPE

Two of the most prominent of the small hills around San Cristóbal are crowned by churches and offer fine views. **Cerro de San Cristóbal**, southwest of the center, is reached by steps up from Allende, while prettier **Cerro de Guadalupe**, topped by a church that Graham Greene described as a 'soapbubble dome upon a rock,' is seven blocks east of the main plaza. Avoid ascending either after dark.

JARDÍN DE ORQUÍDEAS

This pleasant **orchid garden** (☎ 674-62-52; Real de Guadalupe 153; admission by donation; ☽ 10am-6pm Tue-Sun) functions as a reproduction and resource center. It's a pleasant place to stroll around, and you can see examples of orchids from five separate climate zones. There's also a very inexpensive café that serves snacks and drinks.

Courses

Instituto Jovel (☎ /fax 678-40-69; www.instituto jovel.com; MA Flores 21; individual/group classes per hour US$11/7) Excellent reader reports for this Spanish school, where most tuition is one-to-one. Five days' tuition and seven days' family accommodation costs US$240 with individual lessons, or US$185 with group lessons.

Centro Bilingüe El Puente (☎ 678-37-23; Real de Guadalupe 55) Aimed at travelers, it has an attached café, Internet access and cinema, and also hosts salsa classes. Family accommodations and individual lessons cost US$175 per week; with group lessons it's US$160 per week.

Tours

For tours of indigenous villages around San Cristóbal see p403. Agencies in San Cristóbal also offer tours further afield, often with guides who speak English, French or Italian. All the destinations can also be reached independently. Some typical prices per person (usually with a minimum of four people) are: Chiapa de Corzo and Cañón del Sumidero (US$20, six to seven hours); Lagos de Montebello, Chinkultic ruins, Amatenango del Valle, Grutas de San Cristóbal (US$23, nine hours); Palenque ruins, Agua Azul, Misol-Ha (US$33, 14 hours); and Toniná, Grutas de San Cristóbal (US$25, 12 hours). Operators include:

ERIC L WHEATER

Mayan girls

JOHN ELK III

Chac-Mool masks on the Cuadrángulo de las Monjas (Nuns' Quadrangle, p360), Uxmal

SCOTT DOGGETT

A carved stone Olmec head in the jungle of Cozumel (p335)

A carving at the Mayan ruins of Edzná (p379)

SCOTT DOGGETT

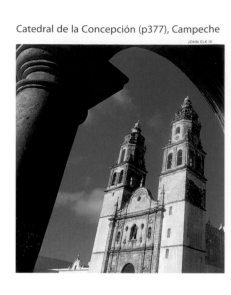

Catedral de la Concepción (p377), Campeche

JOHN ELK III

SCOTT DOGGETT

Fuerte de San Miguel (p377),
Campeche

Cenote Dzitnup (p371)

SCOTT DOGG

Astur (☎ 678-39-17; Portal Oriente B, Plaza 31 de Marzo)

Kanan-Ku Viajes (☎ 678-61-01; Niños Héroes 2C)

Otisa (☎ 678-19-33; www.otisatravel.com; Real de Guadalupe 3C)

Turística Chan-Balum (☎ 678-76-56; Real de Guadalupe 26G)

Viajes Chincultik (☎ 678-09-57; agchincultik@prodigy .net.com; Real de Guadalupe 34)

Zapata Tours (☎ 674-51-52; www.zapatatours.com; above Restaurant Madre Tierra, Insurgentes 19)

Explora (☎ 678-42-95; www.ecochiapas.com; 1 de Marzo 30; 4-6 day jeep, raft & kayak trips per person US$195-375) Explora offers excellent adventure trips in remote areas of Chiapas for groups of three to 12 people, stopping at Maya ruins en route. Combined jeep and kayak trips involve overnight stays at remote eco-lodges on the fringes of Selva Lacandona. Rafting trips follow the Lacanjá river (February to May) and La Venta river (July to October).

Festivals & Events

Semana Santa sees the crucifixion acted out on Good Friday in the Barrio de Mexicanos in the northwest part of town. The Saturday afternoon is the start of the annual town fair, the Feria de la Primavera y de la Paz (Spring and Peace Fair), with parades, bullfights and so on. Sometimes the celebrations of the anniversary of the town's founding (March 31) fall in the midst of it all too!

Also look out for events marking the feast of San Cristóbal (July 17 to 25).

Sleeping

BUDGET

You'll find most budget hotels are surprisingly pleasant.

Hotel Plaza Central (☎ 674-51-25; hostal_plaza central@latinmail.com; Paniagua 2; s/d US$4.50/11; 🖳) Great new budget place set in a historic house in the center of town. There are 30 large pleasant rooms, most with private bathrooms; shared facilities are spotless too. There are a sun terrace and bar area to boot.

Casa Margarita (☎ 678-09-57; agchincultik@prodigy .com; Real de Guadalupe 34; s/d US$15/19; 🖳) This ever-popular travelers' haunt offers 28 tastefully presented rooms set off by a pretty courtyard.

Posada Las Casas (☎ 678-28-82; Madero 81; pege deoro@hotmail.com; dm/s/d with shared bathroom US$3.50/ 7/11, with private bathroom & TV US$11/15) Family-owned posada offering large clean rooms on two floors along an open-air courtyard. There is a sun terrace and a kitchen for guests.

Posada Casa Real (☎ 678-13-03; Real de Guadalupe 51; s/d US$4.50/9) Friendly, quiet place, popular with women travelers. The eight clean rooms have shared bathrooms. Doors lock at 11pm.

Magic Hostel (☎ 674-70-34; marquelia50@hotmail .com; Guadalupe Victoria 47; dm/s/d US$3.75/7.50/9) Excellent hostel, with a sociable atmosphere and clean, spacious six- to eight-person dorms set round a large courtyard, plus six cabañas. There's a well-equipped kitchen, laundry, Internet access and safe.

Rancho San Nicolás (☎ 678-00-57; campsite per person US$3.50, trailer site for 2 people US$12; P) This camping and trailer park, nearly 2km east of the center on an eastward extension of León, is a friendly place with grassy lawns, tall trees, clean bathrooms, laundry and a central fireplace.

MID-RANGE

El Paraíso (☎ 678-00-85; 5 de Febrero 19; s/d US$32/42) This colonial-style hotel set around a lovely courtyard has real character. Ten large, elegantly decorated rooms have high ceilings and splendid bathrooms.

Na Bolom (☎ 678-14-18; www.nabolom.org; Guerrero 33; s/d with bathroom US$40/49) This museum/ research institute (p396) has 14 stylish guest rooms, all with real period character, and some with log fires. Diego Rivera stayed in the Harvard room. Meals are served in the house's stately dining room. Its location, about 1km from the plaza, is a drawback however.

Hotel La Noria (☎ 678-68-78; www.hotel-lanoria .com in Spanish; Insurgentes 18A; s/d US$26/35) La Noria has 30 comfortable, brightly decorated, carpeted rooms, with attractive tiled bathrooms and cable TV.

Hotel El Cerrillo (☎ /fax 678-12-83; Belisario Domínguez 27; r with 1 bed US$23-28, with 2 beds US$36-39; P) Friendly El Cerrillo has a flowery glass-covered courtyard and good-size, prettily painted, carpeted rooms with bathroom and cable TV. Roof terrace, restaurant and bar, too.

Hotel Mansión de los Ángeles (☎ 678-11-73; Madero 17; s/d with TV & bathroom US$37/42; P) Colonial-style building with 20 pleasant rooms around two patios. Indigenous costume prints add an attractive touch, and one patio contains a wood-and-glass-roofed restaurant.

TOP END

Hotel Flamboyant Español (☎ 678-00-45; www .hotelesflamboyant.com.mx; 1 de Marzo 15; s/d/ste US$52/ 59/81; P) Large hotel set in a historic building with comfortable rooms, all with smart bathrooms, heating and TV. There is a pretty garden with lots of trees, flowers and birds. Graham Greene stayed here in the 1930s.

Casa Dr Felipe Flores (☎ 678-39-96; www.felipe flores.com; JF Flores 36; r with bathroom US$75-90 incl breakfast) Wonderfully tranquil colonial guesthouse with five immaculate guest rooms, all with fireplaces, set off two flowery courtyards. The American owners have decorated the house with local artwork and furnishings, and the Mexican staff are welcoming and attentive. There are some terrific books to browse through in the commodious lounge area.

Eating

San Cristóbal's international blend of restaurants offers a break from purely Mexican cuisine (if such a desire is possible).

Mayambé (☎ 674-62-78; Real de Guadalupe 66; mains US$3-5; ☽ breakfast, lunch & dinner) Superb, very fairly priced courtyard restaurant with a highly innovative menu, developed by the well-traveled Mexican Sikh owners. Dig into delicious Indian and Thai curries, Greek and Lebanese treats including falafel and to-die-for lassis and juices.

Cafetería del Centro (Real de Guadalupe 15; mains US$4.50) Two friendly branches offering filling portions and decent breakfasts. Beers are a buck a pop. The other branch is at Pasaje Mazariegos mall off Real de Guadalupe.

Restaurante Margarita (☎ 678-09-57; Real de Guadalupe 34A; mains US$4-8) The broad choice of dependable meals, though a little pricey, have been satisfying travelers for decades.

Madre Tierra (☎ 678-42-97; Insurgentes 19; mains US$2.25-6, breakfast US$2-3.50; ☽ breakfast, lunch & dinner) Madre Tierra offers a lovely patio and atmospheric dining room setting for an eclectic and appetizing vegetarian menu: wholesome soups, great sandwiches, salads and jacket potatoes. Breakfasts are also superb.

Restaurante El Sol (Insurgentes 71; breakfast US$2.25-3, mains US$4) El Sol is a small, unpretentious restaurant serving economical breakfasts, a good-value *comida corrida* and tasty chicken and beef dishes.

El Gato Gordo (☎ 678-04-99; Madero 28; breakfast & veg comida US$2-2.25; ☽ lunch & dinner Wed-Mon) Bargain-priced Gato Gordo rightly attracts budget travelers in droves. There's an unbeatable set menu, and excellent pasta, *crepas*, *tortas* and a great choice of beers.

Restaurante Maya Pakal (☎ 678-59-11; Madero 21A; mains US$2.75-4; ☽ breakfast, lunch & dinner) Of the cluster of restaurants on Madero, Maya Pakal's likely the best. The Mexican dishes are popular, and the three-course *comida* (US$3.75) and cheap breakfasts are good value.

La Alpujarra (☎ 632-20-20; Madero 24; snacks US$1-1.50, pizzas US$2.75-7; ☽ breakfast, lunch & dinner) Excellent little café run by an industrious Mexican Muslim team. The menu includes flavorsome pastry *rollitos*, terrific *tortas*, pizzas and juicy juices.

Emiliano's Moustache (☎ 678-72-46; Crescencio Rosas 7; breakfast & snacks US$1.75-3.50, mains US$3.50-6.50; ☽ lunch & dinner) This large, enjoyable place specializes in tacos. Meat *filetes* also excel, and vegetarian possibilities exist too (including veggie tacos, pasta with pesto and quiche). The set menu is only average however.

El Edén (☎ 678-00-85; El Paraíso hotel, 5 de Febrero 19; mains US$7-9) Classy, comfortable hotel restaurant with a tempting European and Mexican menu that includes *sopa azteca* (a soup) and succulent meat dishes. The signature dish (Swiss-style fondue) is ample for three.

Restaurant El Teatro (☎ 678-31-49; 1 de Marzo 8; set menu US$6, mains US$4.50-9; ☽ dinner Tue-Sun) The venerable old-fashioned Teatro's European-based menu includes chateaubriand, crêpes, fresh pasta and generous desserts, plus a few Mexican dishes.

Café La Selva (☎ 678-72-43; Crescencio Rosas 9; baguettes & snacks US$2.50-4) Attractive, slightly bijou café, with an open courtyard where you can choose from 39 different types of organic, indigenous-grown Chiapas coffee.

La Casa del Pan (☎ 678-58-95; Dr Navarro 10; snacks & mains US$2.75-5.50; ☽ breakfast, lunch & dinner Tue-Sun) Attractive bakery-cum-restaurant that offers lots of vegetarian fare.

Los Merenderos (Insurgentes s/n; mains US$1.75-2) The food stalls around the Mercado de Dulces y Artesanías serve up some of the cheapest meals in town.

Entertainment

Live music is big in San Cristóbal, with reggae the most popular genre. Clubs tend to play a very eclectic mix of Latin dance, electro pop, rock, reggae and commercial techno.

Creación (☎ 678-66-64; 1 de Marzo; ☺ 9:30am-11pm Mon-Sat) Perhaps the hippest bar in town, with modish Latin dance, chill-out sounds and live music most nights. Happy hour offers 2-for-1 beers and cocktails, and there's a daytime food menu (mains US$3), Internet access and films upstairs.

Circo (☎ 678-56-63; 20 de Noviembre 7; admission free, weekends US$2; ☺ 8pm-3am Mon-Sat) Bar-cum-club where the city's *salseros* (salsa dancers) gather to groove. There's live music after 10pm.

Latino's (☎ 678-99-27; Madero 23; admission free; ☺ closed Sun) The live Latin music here attracts a slightly older crowd; there's space to dance, and reasonably priced food.

Bar Las Velas (Madero 14; admission US$1.25; ☺ 9pm-3am) This club attracts young locals and travelers alike, with Latin house, ska and reggae and a live band about 1am.

Several places show movies. For arthouse, alternative, Latin and some Hollywood films try **La Ventana** (Insurgentes 19; admission US$1.25), **Cinema El Puente** (☎ 678-37-23; Real de Guadalupe 55; US$1.25), or **Creación** (above).

Shopping

The outstanding local *artesanías* (handicrafts) are textiles such as *huipiles*, blouses and blankets: Tzotzil weavers are some of the most skilled and inventive in Mexico.

The heaviest concentration of **craft shops** is on Real de Guadalupe and along the *andador*, but there's also a huge range of wares at good prices at the busy daily **crafts market** around Santo Domingo and La Caridad churches. Next to Santo Domingo the showroom/shop of **Sna Jolobil** (p393) has some of the finest textiles in Mexico. The **Casa de las Artesanías de Chiapas** (cnr Niños Héroes & Hidalgo) also sells a good range of Chiapas crafts.

Another Chiapas specialty is amber, sold in numerous San Cristóbal shops. You'll find fine quality amber at fair prices at **Lá-grimos de la Selva** (Hidalgo 1C) and **El Árbol de La Vida** (Guadalupe 27). For jewelry, **La Galería** (Hidalgo 3) has a great selection in turquoise, amber, silver, gold and more. The **House of Jade** (16 de Septiembre No 16) is another classy jeweler's shop.

For Zapatista-made crafts and souvenirs head to **Nemizapata** (Real de Guadalupe 45). Subcomandante Marcos dolls in little black balaclavas and T-shirts are commonplace all over town. Several shops sell Zapatista videos, including **El Mono de Papel** (Libertad s/n).

Getting There & Away

AIR

San Cristóbal **airport** is about 15km out of town on the Palenque road. At the time of research the only passenger flight was to/from Mexico City daily by **Aeromar** (airport ☎ 674-30-03). One-way fares start around US$180: **Kanan-Ku Viajes** (☎ 678-61-01; Niños Héroes 2C) is one agency selling tickets. There are many more flights from Tuxtla Gutiérrez (p390). A taxi to Tuxtla airport costs around US$35 and takes about 1¼ hours via the toll highway.

BUS, SUBURBAN & TAXI

From Tuxtla Gutiérrez to San Cristóbal you'll either travel the via serpentine Hwy 190, or a fast new toll highway that cuts the 85km trip from two hours to one.

There are around a dozen bus terminals, with all of them on or just off the Pan-American Hwy, except for a few serving nearby villages (see p400).

The **main bus terminal** for deluxe and 1st-class services (Cristóbal Colón, ADO, Altos, UNO) and 2nd-class Transportes Dr Rodulfo Figueroa (TRF) buses are at the corner of Insurgentes and the Pan-American. Tickets for buses on all these lines are for sale at **Ticket Bus** (☎ 678-86-03; Belisario Domínguez 8C) in the center of town.

Transportes Lacandonia (TL), 2nd-class, is 150m west of Colón along the highway, and Autotransportes Tuxtla Gutiérrez (ATG), also 2nd-class, is just north of the highway on Allende.

AEXA (1st-class) and Ómnibus de Chiapas (2nd-class, OC) have a joint terminal on the south side of the highway, and various Suburban-type vans and *colectivo* taxi services have their depots on the highway nearby. The Suburbans and *colectivos* run all day from 6am or earlier and leave when the vehicle is full. See the map for departure locations.

Daily departures from San Cristóbal include the following:

Cancún (16hr; 4 buses, US$42-50; 2 ATG, US$34) From Colón terminal.

Chiapa de Corzo (1¼hr) Take a 2nd-class bus, van or *colectivo* heading for Tuxtla Gutiérrez, but check first that it will let you off in Chiapa de Corzo.

Ciudad Cuauhtémoc (Guatemalan border; 2½hr; 6 Altos buses, US$6.25) Leave early if you want to get any distance into Guatemala the same day.

Comitán (1-1½hr; 11 buses from Colón terminal, US$3.50-4.50; other buses & Suburbans, US$3, & *colectivo* taxis, US$3.50, from south side of Pan-American Hwy)

Mérida (via Campeche; 11hr; 2 buses, US$33-37) From Colón terminal.

Mexico City (TAPO; 19hr; 7 buses from Colón terminal, US$50-87; 1 ATG bus, US$44)

Ocosingo (2hr; 10 buses from Colón terminal, US$3.25-4.25; 4 AEXA buses, US$2.75; 4 ATG buses, US$3; 1 TL bus, US$1.75; *colectivo* taxis, US$3.75, & Suburbans, US$2.75, from north side of Pan-American Hwy)

Palenque (5hr; 10 buses from Colón terminal, US$6.50-9; 4 ATG buses, US$7; 3 AEXA buses, US$6.25)

Tuxtla Gutiérrez (1-1½hr; 18 buses from Colón terminal, US$3.50-5.50; 8 ATG buses, US$3; 3 AEXA buses, US$3; OC buses every 20min, 6am-6pm, US$2.75; Taxis Jovel *colectivos*, US$3.75; Corazón de María & Tojtic Ocotal Suburbans, 4am-9pm, US$2.75)

Villahermosa (7hr; 2 buses from Colón terminal, US$13-14; 4 ATG buses, US$11)

Buses of various classes from the Colón terminal also run to Tapachula, Bahías de Huatulco, Campeche, Chetumal, Playa del Carmen, Pochutla, Tulum and Veracruz.

For Guatemala, **Viajes Chincultik** (☎ 678-09-57; agchincultik@prodigy.net.com; Real de Guadalupe 34) runs a convenient shuttle service (on Tuesday and Friday) to La Mesilla (US$20, 2½ hours), Quetzaltenango (US$40, 5½ hours), Panajachel (US$50, 7½ hours) and Antigua (US$60, 9½ hours).

CAR & MOTORCYCLE
Car rental companies in San Cristóbal include the following:

Optima (☎ 674-54-09; optimacar1@hotmail.com; Mazariegos 39-1) VW Beetles for US$42 per day or US$240 per week including unlimited kilometers, insurance and taxes.

Budget (☎ 678-31-00; Hotel Mansión del Valle, Mazariegos 39) VW Beetles for US$52 per day on the same basis as Optima.

Getting Around
Combis go up Crescencio Rosas from the Pan-American Hwy to the town center. **Taxis** cost US$1.50 within town (after 11pm US$1.75).

Los Pingüinos (☎ 678-02-02; Ecuador 4B; www .bikemexico.com; office ☒ 10am-2:30pm & 3:30-7pm Mon-Sat), rents out decent quality mountain bikes with lock and maps for three hours (US$6), 24 hours (US$8.50) or per week (US$41). You need to deposit some security, such as your passport, with them. Staff can advise on good and safe routes; they also conduct guided bicycle tours (p403).

AROUND SAN CRISTÓBAL
The inhabitants of the beautiful Chiapas highlands are descended from the ancient Maya and maintain some unique customs, costumes and beliefs.

Dangers & Annoyances
Many of the conservative, traditional indigenous pueblos around San Cristóbal have remained tense since the Zapatista uprising in 1994. If you do decide to explore this region, be sure to be especially respectful of local customs. Some of the more remote villages are extremely close-knit and can be suspicious of outsiders.

San Juan Chamula, Zinacantán, Amatenango del Valle and San Andrés Larraínzar (a center of strong Zapatista support) were considered safe to visit at the time of writing. If you're going independently, make prior inquiries about security, and make sure you get back to San Cristóbal well before dark. Daylight excursions should not be risky, but avoid wandering into unfrequented areas or down isolated tracks.

In some villages cameras are at best tolerated – and sometimes not even that. Photography is banned completely in the church and during rituals at San Juan Chamula, and in the church and churchyard at Zinacantán. You may put yourself in physical danger if you take photos without permission. If in any doubt at all, ask before taking a picture.

Markets & Festivals
Weekly markets at the villages are nearly always on Sunday. Proceedings start very early – with people arriving from outlying

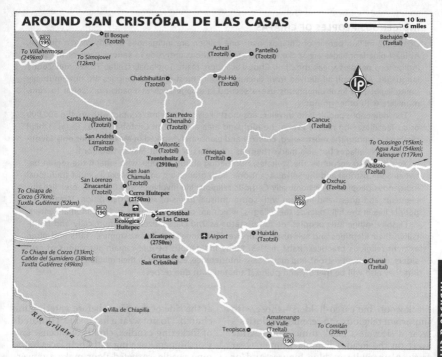

AROUND SAN CRISTÓBAL DE LAS CASAS

settlements as early as dawn – and wind down by lunchtime.

Festivals often give the most interesting insight into indigenous life, and there are plenty of them. Occasions like **Carnaval** (end of February), for which Chamula is famous, **Semana Santa**, **Día de Muertos** (November 2) and the **Día de la Virgen de Guadalupe** (December 12) are celebrated almost everywhere. At some of these fiestas locals drink *posh* (an alcoholic drink made from sugarcane) and there are barrages of firecrackers. During Carnaval, groups of minstrels stroll the roads in tall, pointed hats with long, colored tassels, strumming guitars and chanting.

Reserva Ecológica Huitepec

The entrance to **Reserva Ecológica Huitepec** (trail US$1.50; 9am-3pm Tue-Sun) is about 3.5km from San Cristóbal, on the road to San Juan Chamula. Set on the slopes of 2750m Cerro Huitepec, the reserve covers terrain rising from evergreen oak woods to rare cloud forest rich with bromeliads, and has some 60 resident bird species and over 40 winter visitors. The self-guided trail is 2.5km long.

If you're interested in plants, it's well worth taking a four-hour guided tour with the Tzotzil guide, Javier, who speaks some English and focuses on the medical and spiritual properties of plants. This tour costs US$9 per person (up to eight people) and you need to book one day beforehand at **Pronatura** (Map pp394-5; 967-678-50-00; www.pronatura-chiapas.org in Spanish; Hidalgo 9) in San Cristóbal. Javier also gives four-hour early-morning bird tours.

San Juan Chamula

pop 3100 / elevation 2200m

The Chamulans are a fiercely independent people, and their village **San Juan Chamula**, 10km northwest of San Cristóbal, is the center for some unique religious practices. They put up strong resistance to the Spaniards in 1524 and launched a famous rebellion in 1869, attacking San Cristóbal. Today they are one of the largest subgroups of the Tzotzil people, about 80,000 strong.

Local costume is highly distinctive. Most men wear loose homespun tunics of white wool (sometimes, in cool weather, thicker

---

INDIGENOUS PEOPLES OF CHIAPAS

Of the 4.2 million people of Chiapas, over one million are indigenous (mostly Mayan groups). At least nine languages are spoken in the state. In the countryside in various parts of the state, indigenous peoples speak the Chol, Chuj, Lacandón, Mam, Tojolabal, Tzeltal, Tzotzil and Zoque languages. Although all derived from ancient Mayan, most of these tongues are now mutually unintelligible, so local inhabitants use a second language such as Spanish or Tzeltal to communicate with other groups.

The indigenous people who travelers are most likely to come into contact with are the 500,000 or so Tzotziles, who mainly live in the highland area around San Cristóbal de Las Casas. Tzotzil clothing is among the most varied, colorful and elaborately worked in Mexico. It not only identifies wearers' villages but also marks them as inheritors of ancient Mayan traditions.

You may also encounter the Tzeltales, numbering about 500,000, who inhabit the region between San Cristóbal and the Selva Lacandona. Both groups are among Mexico's most traditional indigenous peoples. Their nominally Catholic religious life involves some distinctly pre-Hispanic elements and goes hand in hand with some unusual forms of social organization. Most of the people live in the hills outside the villages, which are primarily market and ceremonial centers.

Despite indigenous peoples' de facto status as 2nd-class citizens (economically and politically), their identities and self-respect survive. Traditional festivals, costumes, crafts and often ancient religious practices assist in this. Many indigenous people remain suspicious of outsiders (not without reason), and may resent interference, especially in their religious observances. But they also will be friendly and polite if treated with due respect.

---

black wool), but cargo-holders – those with important religious and ceremonial duties – wear a sleeveless black tunic and a white scarf on the head. Chamula women wear fairly plain white or blue blouses and/or shawls and woolen skirts.

Outsiders are free to visit Chamula, though it's essential to respect local traditions. A big sign at the entrance to the village strictly forbids photography in the village church or anywhere rituals are being performed. Nearby, around the shell of an older church, is the village graveyard, with black crosses for people who died old, white for the young, and blue for others. There's a small village museum, **Ora Ton** (admission US$0.60; ☾ 9am-6pm) near this old church too.

Starting at dawn on Sunday, people from the hills stream into San Juan Chamula for the weekly market and to visit the church. Busloads of tourists also stream in, so you might prefer to come another day (though avoid Wednesday when the church is often all but deserted due to local superstitions). *Artesanías* (mainly textiles) are sold every day for the passing tourist trade.

The **Templo de San Juan**, Chamula's main church, is white with a colorfully painted door arch and stands beside the main plaza. A sign tells visitors to obtain tickets (US$0.90) at the **tourist office** (☾ 9am-6pm),

at the side of the plaza, before entering the church. Do not wear a hat inside. Hundreds of flickering candles, clouds of incense and worshippers kneeling with their faces to the pine needle–carpeted floor make a powerful impression. Chanting *curanderos* (traditional indigenous healers) may be rubbing patients' bodies with eggs or bones. Images of saints are surrounded with mirrors and dressed in holy garments. Chamulans revere San Juan Bautista (St John the Baptist) above Christ, and his image occupies a more important place in the church.

Christian festivals are interwoven with older ones here: the important Carnaval celebrations also mark the five 'lost' days of the ancient Mayan Long Count calendar, which divided time into 20-day periods (18 of these make 360 days, leaving five to complete a year).

San Lorenzo Zinacantán
pop 3700 / 2558m

The road to the orderly village of **San Lorenzo Zinacantán**, about 11km northwest of San Cristóbal, forks left off the Chamula road before descending into a valley. This is the main village of the Zinacantán municipality (population 45,000). Zinacantán people are Tzotzil, and the men of Zinacantán have distinctive pink tunics embroidered with flower motifs and may sport flat, round, ribboned palm hats. Zinacantán women wear pink or purple shawls over richly embroidered blouses.

A small market is held on Sundays until noon and during fiesta times. The most important celebrations are for the festival of **La Virgen de la Candelaria** (August 7-11) and **San Sebastián** (January 19-22).

Amatenango del Valle
pop 3400 / elevation 1869m

The women of this Tzeltal village, by the Pan-American Hwy 37km to the southeast of San Cristóbal, are renowned potters. Amatenango women wear fine white *huipiles* with red and yellow embroidery, wide red belts and blue skirts. Pottery here is still fired by a pre-Hispanic method, building a wood fire around the pieces rather than putting them in a kiln. In addition to everyday pots and jugs that the village has turned out for generations, young girls now find a ready tourist market with *animalitos* – little animal figures that are inexpensive but fragile. If you visit the village, expect to be surrounded within minutes by children selling these.

Tours

Exploring the region with a good guide can open up doors and give you a feel for indigenous life and customs you could never gain alone. The following all offer well-received daily trips to local villages, usually San Juan Chamula and Zinacantán.

The friendly English-, German- and Spanish-speaking people at **Los Pingüinos** (☎ 678-02-02; Ecuador 4B; www.bikemexico.com; office ✆ 10am-2:30pm, 3:30-7pm Mon-Sat) operate guided mountain-bike tours of 20km to 42km. Most trips are to little-visited, scenic country areas east of San Cristóbal, passing through cloud forests; one 25km route (US$20, four hours) crosses a limestone bridge. The trails are predominantly off-road but without long, hard gradients. Book one day or more ahead.

Other operators include:

Alex and Raúl (☎ 967-678-37-41; alexraultours@yahoo.com.mx; 5hr tours per person US$9) Enjoyable and informative English or Spanish minibus tours. Alex, Raúl and/or their colleague César wait by San Cristóbal's cathedral at 9:30am daily. Tuesday and Sunday trips to Tenejapa; visits to San Andrés Larráinzar (US$14) can also be arranged.

Viajes Chincultik (☎ 967-678-09-57; agchincultik@prodigy.net.com; Real de Guadalupe 34, San Cristóbal; 5hr trip US$10, with extension to San Andrés Larráinzar US$14) Viajes Chincultik has received good reports. Educative trips are led by an English-, Spanish- and Tzotzil-speaking sociologist member of the family that runs the Casa Margarita.

Mercedes Hernández Gómez (5-6hr trips US$9) Mercedes waits just before 9am daily near the kiosk in San Cristóbal's main plaza, twirling a colorful umbrella. Her tours, traveling by minibus and on foot, have been popular for years. A fluent English-speaker who grew up in Zinacantán, she's a strong character and a knowledgeable (and loquacious) guide. On occasions she chastises participants for not concentrating properly.

Further village tours are offered by agencies including Astur, Kanan-Ku Viajes and Zapata Tours (see p397).

Getting There & Away

Transportation to most villages leaves from points around the Mercado Municipal in San Cristóbal. Check the latest return times before you set out: some services wind down by lunchtime. Combis to San Juan Chamula (US$0.60) leave from Calle Honduras fairly frequently from 5am up to about 6pm; for Zinacantán, combis (US$0.80) and *colectivo* taxis (US$1) go at least hourly, 6am to 5pm, from a yard off Robledo.

From San Cristóbal, take a Comitán-bound bus or combi.

OCOSINGO
☎ 919 / pop 29,000 / elevation 900m

Around the halfway mark of the 180km journey from San Cristóbal to Palenque, a trip that takes you down from cool, misty highlands to steamy lowland jungle, is the agreeable town of Ocosingo, a busy market hub. Ocosingo is only a few kilometers from the impressive Mayan ruins of Toniná, and also a jumping-off point for beautiful Laguna Miramar.

Ocosingo saw the bloodiest fighting during the 1994 Zapatista rebellion, with about 50 rebels killed here by the Mexican army.

Orientation & Information

The market area, three blocks east (downhill) from the pleasant main plaza, is the liveliest part of town.

Most hotels, restaurants and services are within a few blocks of the plaza. **Serfin** bank, on Calle Central Nte, which runs off the plaza beside Hotel Central, changes US dollars and traveler's checks and has an ATM. There are three **cybercafés** on Calle Central Nte just off the plaza; all charge US$0.90 per hour.

Sleeping & Eating

Hospedaje Esmeralda (☎ 673-00-14; www.ranchoesmeralda.net; Calle Central Nte 14; s/d US$11/18, with bathroom US$13/22; **P**) This welcoming guesthouse has five attractive rooms, good home-style cooking and a snug bar area, plus excellent horse-riding excursions (US$20).

Hotel Central (☎ 673-00-24; Av Central 5; s/d US$12/16; **P**) This very neat little hotel has a prime location on the north side of the main plaza, and simple, spotless rooms with fan, bathroom and TV.

Ocosingo is known for its *queso amarillo* (yellow cheese), indeed the town's nickname is 'Los Quesos.' There are six main types, including 'de Bola' that comes in 1kg balls with an edible wax coating and a crumbly, whole-fat center. For a taste check out **Fábrica de Quesos Santa Rosa** (☎ 673-00-09; 1 Ote Nte 1).

Grab a *comida corrida* for US$1.50 at *comedores* in the **mercado** (Av Sur Ote).

Las Delicias (☎ 673-00-24; Av Central 5; mains US$4-6.50) Set on the Hotel Central's veranda overlooking the plaza, this is a reliable restaurant that serves big portions and good breakfasts.

Restaurant Los Portales (Av Central 19; mains US$2.50-4.50; ☯ breakfast & lunch) A few doors east of Las Delicias, this is a straightforward place serving hearty soups, chicken, *milanesas* (breaded, fried meat cuts) and egg dishes at good prices.

Getting There & Away

The company **Servicios Aéreos San Cristóbal** (☎ 673-01-88; sasc_ocosingo@hotmail.com) does small-plane charters from Ocosingo's airstrip, about 4km out of town along the Toniná road. Possible destinations include day trips to Bonampak and Yaxchilán (around US$140 a person for a roundtrip flight) or San Quintín near Laguna Miramar (p405; one-way per person US$45). Prices are based on four paying passengers.

The bus terminals are near each other on Hwy 199, 600m west of the plaza. Departures include: Palenque (US$4.50 to US$6.50, 2¾ hours), San Cristóbal de Las Casas (US$2.75 to US$4.50, two hours), Tuxtla Gutiérrez (US$5 to US$7.50, 3½ hours) and Toniná (p405).

TONINÁ

elevation 900m

The Mayan ruins of **Toniná** (ruins & museum US$3; ruins ☯ 9am-4pm; museum ☯ 9am-5pm, closed Mon), 14km east of Ocosingo, overlook a verdant pastoral valley and form an expansive and intriguing site. Built into a steep hillside, Toniná's towering ceremonial core comprises one of the Maya world's most imposing temple complexes. The city has an interesting history, which is well explained in the neat site museum.

The prelude to Toniná's heyday was the inauguration of the Snake Skull-Jaguar Claw dynasty in AD 688. The new rulers contested control of the region with Palenque. In alliance with Calakmul (p380), they constantly harassed their rival state from around AD 690, and captured at least three Palenque leaders.

Toniná was at its most powerful in the decade after it devastated Palenque in 730. Around AD 900 Toniná was rebuilt in a simpler, austere style. But Jaguar Serpent, in 903, was the last Toniná ruler of whom any record has been found. Classic Mayan civilization was ending here, as elsewhere, and Toniná has the distinction of having the last ever recorded Long Count date – AD 909.

Some explanatory signs (in Spanish) near the site entrance explain Toniná's history and background.

The path from the entrance and museum crosses a stream and climbs to the broad, flat **Gran Plaza**. At the south end of the Gran Plaza is the **Templo de la Guerra Cósmica** (Temple of Cosmic War), with five altars in front of it. Off a side of the plaza is a **ball court**, which was inaugurated around 780 under the rule of female regent Smoking Mirror.

To the north rises the ceremonial core of Toniná, a semi-natural hillside terraced into a number of platforms, rising to a height of 80m above the Gran Plaza. At the right-hand end of the steps rising from the first to the second platform is the entry to a **ritual labyrinth** of passages.

Higher up on the right-hand side is the **Palacio de las Grecas y de la Guerra** (Palace of the Grecas and War). The *greca* referred to here is a zigzag X-shape, possibly representing Quetzalcóatl.

Higher again is Toniná's most remarkable sculpture, the **Mural de las Cuatro Eras** (Mural of the Four Eras). Created some time between AD 790 and 840, this stucco relief of four panels (the first, from the left end, has been lost) represents the four suns, or four eras of human history, in Maya belief. At the center of each panel is the upside-down head of a decapitated prisoner. Blood spurting from the prisoner's neck forms a ring of feathers and, at the same time, a sun. In one panel, a dancing skeleton holds a decapitated head with its tongue out. To the left of the head is a lord of the underworld, who resembles an enormous rodent. This mural was created at a time when a wave of destruction was running through the Maya world. The people of Toniná believed themselves to be living in the fourth sun, that of winter, mirrors, the direction north and the end of human life.

Near the middle of the same level you'll find a tomb with a stone sarcophagus. Up the next steps is the seventh level, with remains of four temples. Behind the second temple from the left, steps descend into the very narrow **Tumba de Treinta Metros** (Thirty-Meter Tomb).

Above here is the **acropolis**, the abode of the rulers of Toniná and site of its eight most important temples – four on each of two levels. The right-hand temple on the lower level, the **Templo del Monstruo de la Tierra** (Temple of the Earth Monster), has Toniná's best-preserved roofcomb, built around AD 713.

The topmost level has four more temples. The tallest is the **Templo del Espejo Humeante** (Temple of the Smoking Mirror).

Getting There & Away

Combis to Toniná (US$1.25) leave from opposite the Tianguis Campesino in Ocosingo every 45 minutes from the early morning. The last one returns around 5pm.

LAGUNA MIRAMAR
elevation 400m

Ringed by rain forest, pristine Laguna Miramar, 130km west of Ocosingo, is one of Mexico's most remote and exquisite lakes. Thanks to a successful ecotourism project, it's possible to stay in a village, **Ejido Emiliano Zapata**, near its western shore.

Frequently echoing with the roars of howler monkeys, the 16-sq-km lake, located within the **Reserva de la Biósfera Montes Azules**, has a beautiful temperature all year and is virtually unpolluted. Ejido life in Emiliano Zapata – a poor but well-ordered Maya community – is fascinating too. It is forbidden to bring alcohol or drugs into the community.

Miramar is not an easy place to get to. At the time of writing there were no organized tours to the lake. If you do decide to go, try to visit outside the rainy period, which is from late August to the end of October, when land access can be more difficult and foot trails muddy.

When you reach Emiliano Zapata, ask for the Presidente de la Laguna. Through him you must arrange and pay for the services you need – per day a guide is US$9, the overnight fee is US$3 and a canoe is US$20. The village is a spread-out place of huts and a few concrete communal buildings, on a gentle slope running down to the Río Perlas – a beautiful bathing place.

The 7km walk from village to lake takes about 1½ hours. Apart from the incessant growls of howler monkeys (*saraguatos*), you may hear jaguars at night. It takes about 45 minutes to canoe across to Isla Lacan-Tun, an island rich in overgrown ruined remains of a pre-Hispanic settlement. The Chol-Lacantún people who survived here were unconquered by the Spanish until the 1580s. As the island is looked after by another village, you could be asked to pay an additional fee if you want to visit it.

Sleeping & Eating

At the lakeshore you can camp or sling a hammock under a *palapa* shelter. A small guest house next to the Río Perlas in Ejido Emiliano Zapata, **Posada Zapata** (☎ 55-5150-5618; per bed US$5, hammock US$2.50) has six rooms, a hammock area, showers and lockers. Breakfast and dinner is available in villagers' homes.

Food supplies in Emiliano Zapata's stores are very basic; there are slightly better stocks and simple *comedores* in neighboring San Quintín.

Getting There & Away

At the time of writing the only option was to get there yourself via Ocosingo: either in a

YUCATÁN PENINSULA, TABASCO & CHIAPAS

tiny Cessna plane or by truck along a rough track to San Quintín. From the bus stop in San Quintín, walk five minutes along the airstrip and turn down a dirt road to the right, opposite a complex of military buildings. From here it's a 15- or 20-minute walk to the middle of Ejido Emiliano Zapata.

AIR
Servicios Aéreos San Cristóbal (☎ 673-01-88; sasc _ocosingo@hotmail.com) planes leave Ocosingo most mornings for San Quintín. If you're at the airstrip by 9:30am you should get a place. The one-way fare is US$45, based on four passengers. Return flight times are less reliable, but there's one most days.

BUS & TRUCK
From Ocosingo, four or five buses, microbuses or passenger-carrying trucks run between 9am and 11am daily to San Quintín from just south of the Tianguis Campesino. The 130km trip costs US$6.50 and takes around six hours (longer in the rainy season) through an area known as Las Cañadas de Ocosingo, a Zapatista stronghold. Your documents might be checked at Mexican army (and possibly Zapatista village) checkpoints as you travel through; keep your passport and tourist card handy.

Vehicles head back from San Quintín to Ocosingo at 8am, 2pm and midnight.

AGUA AZUL, AGUA CLARA & MISOL-HA
These three stunning attractions – the turquoise cascades of **Agua Azul** (admission US$1.50), serene **Río Shumulhá** and the spectacular waterfall of **Misol-Ha** (admission US$1.50) – are all short detours off the Ocosingo–Palenque road.

At Misol-Ha, you can catch your zzzs at the inviting **Centro Turístico Ejidal Cascada Misol-Ha** (☎ 5553-290-995 ext 7006; cabaña US$15, with kitchen US$30). There's also a **restaurant** close by.

All three of these places are most easily visited in an organized day tour from Palenque, though it's possible, but not necessarily cheaper, to go independently. (Note that during the rainy season, the sites may be less than stunning, as the water gets murky.)

Tours to Misol-Ha and Agua Azul generally cost US$11 to US$13 and last between seven and nine hours, spending 30 to 60 minutes at Misol-Ha and two to three hours at Agua Azul.

To do it independently, take a *camioneta* (pickup) from Cárdenas, off Juárez a block west of the Colón/ADO bus station in Palenque, or any 2nd-class bus along Hwy 199; they will drop you off at any of the three intersections.

The distances from the highway to Misol-Ha and Agua Clara are manageable on foot. For the 4.5km between the Agua Azul *crucero* (junction) and Agua Azul itself, there are *camionetas* for US$1. Check out times of *camionetas* going back to the *crucero*, as it's uphill in that direction.

A taxi from Palenque to Misol-Ha with a one-hour wait costs around US$25; to Agua Azul with a two-hour wait should be US$55.

In the past, the road between Ocosingo and Palenque has been scene of highway robberies, though no incidents have been reported recently. However, it's not advisable to be waiting around for transportation on Hwy 199 after about 5pm.

PALENQUE
☎ 916 / pop 33,000 / elevation 80m
The ancient Mayan city of Palenque, with its superb jungle setting and exquisite architecture and decoration, is one of the marvels of Mexico. Modern Palenque town, a few kilometers to the east, is a sweaty, humdrum place with little attraction except as a base for visiting the ruins. El Panchán, just down the road, is not for everyone, but it's a well-known traveler hangout.

History
The name Palenque (Palisade) is Spanish and has no relation to the city's ancient name, which according to current theories was probably B'aakal (Bone). Palenque was first occupied around 100 BC, and flourished from around AD 630 to around 740. The city rose to prominence under K'inich Janaab' Pakal (generally known just as Pakal), who reigned from AD 615 to 683. Archaeologists have determined that Pakal is represented by hieroglyphics of sun and shield, and he is also referred to as Sun Shield (Escudo Solar in Spanish). He lived to the age of 80.

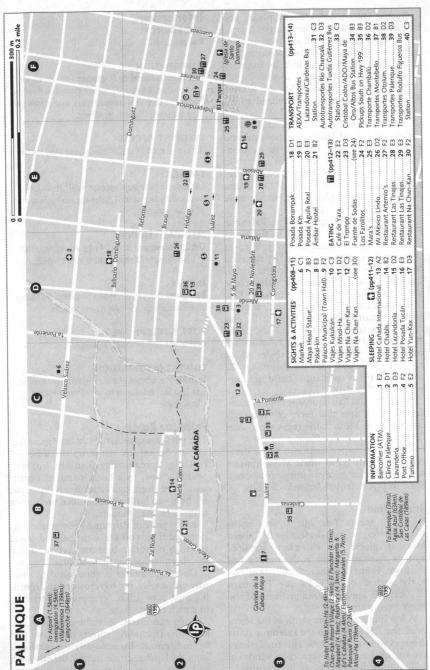

PALENQUE

300 m
0.2 mile

To Airport (1.5km);
Immigration (4.5km);
Villahermosa (139km);
Campeche (364km)

To Hotel Villas Kin-Ha (2.4km);
Chan-Kah Resort Village (2.9km); El Panchán (4.1km)
Mayabell (4.6km); Xibalba (4.3km); Margarita &
Ed's Cabañas (4.4km); Elementos Naturales (5.7km)
Palenque Ruins (7.2km);
Misol-Ha (19km)

To Palenque (3km);
Agua Azul (63km);
San Cristóbal de
Las Casas (189km)

LA CAÑADA

Glorieta de la
Cabeza Maya

Iglesia de
Santo
Domingo

Parque

During Pakal's reign, many plazas and buildings, including the superlative Templo de las Inscripciones (Pakal's own mausoleum), were constructed in Palenque. The structures were characterized by mansard roofs and very fine stucco bas-reliefs.

Pakal was succeeded by his son K'inich Kan B'alam II, who is symbolized in hieroglyphics by the jaguar and the serpent (and also called Jaguar Serpent II). Kan B'alam continued Palenque's political and economic expansion, and artistic development. He completed his father's crypt in the Templo de las Inscripciones and presided over the construction of the Grupo de la Cruz temples, placing sizable narrative stone stelae within each.

During Kan B'alam II's reign, Palenque extended its zone of control to the western bank of the Usumacinta river, but was challenged for regional control by the rival Maya city of Toniná, 65km to the south. Toniná's hostility was probably the major factor in Palenque's brief hiatus after Kan B'alam's death in 702. Kan B'alam's brother and successor, K'an Hoy Chitam II, was captured by forces from Toniná and probably executed there. However, Palenque recovered to enjoy a resurgence under Ahkal Mo' Naab' III, who took the throne in 721 and added many substantial buildings during a rule of perhaps 15 years.

After AD 900 Palenque was largely abandoned. In an area that receives the heaviest rainfall in Mexico, the ruins were soon overgrown.

The city remained unknown to the western world until 1746 when Maya hunters revealed the existence of a jungle palace to a Spanish priest named Antonio de Solís.

Orientation

Hwy 199 meets Palenque town's main street, Juárez, at the Glorieta de la Cabeza Maya, an intersection with a large statue of a Maya chieftain's head, at the west end of the town. From here Juárez heads 1km east to the central square, El Parque. The main bus stations are on Juárez just east of the Maya head statue.

A few hundred meters south of the Maya head, the 7.5km road to the Palenque ruins diverges west off Hwy 199. This road passes the site museum after 6km, then winds on 1.5km to the main entrance to the ruins.

Information

EMERGENCY
Police (☎ 066)

IMMIGRATION
Instituto Nacional de Migración (☎ 345-07-95; ☽ 8am-2pm & 6-8pm) 6km north of town on Hwy 199. Transportes Otolum or Transportes Palenque combis run there from their terminals on Allende.

INTERNET ACCESS
There are over a dozen cybercafés in town.

LAUNDRY
Lavandería (5 de Mayo opposite Hotel Kashlan). Will wash and dry 3kg for US$4. Same-day service if you drop off in the morning.

MEDICAL SERVICES
Clínica Palenque (☎ 345-15-13; Velasco Suárez 33; ☽ 9am-5pm) Dr Alfonso Martínez speaks English.

MONEY
Bancomer (Juárez s/n; ☽ 9am-noon Mon-Fri) Changes US dollars cash and US-dollar traveler's checks.

POST & TELEPHONE
Post office (Independencia at Bravo)

TOURIST INFORMATION
Turismo (cnr Juárez & Abasolo; ☽ 9am-9pm Mon-Sat, 9am-1pm Sun) Reliable for town and transportation information.

Palenque Ruins

The **ruins** (admission US$4; ☽ site 8am-5pm, museum 9am-4pm Tue-Sun) are made up of some 500 buildings spread over 15 sq km, but only relatively few, in a fairly compact central area, have been excavated. Everything you see here was built without metal tools, pack animals or the wheel.

At the peak of Palenque's power, the gray stone edifices you see were painted blood red with elaborate blue and yellow stucco details embellishing their facades.

Opening time is a good time to visit, when it's cooler, not too crowded and morning mist may still be wrapping the temples in a picturesque haze.

Bring sunscreen. Refreshments, hats and souvenirs (including quivers of arrows sold by indigenous Lacandones) are available from the hawker circus outside the entrance, and there are cafés here and at the museum.

PALENQUE RUINS

SIGHTS & ACTIVITIES   (pp408–11)
Ball Court (Juego de Pelota)..............**1**	C2
Casa de las Artesanías de	
Chiapas...**2**	D1
Grupo XVI...**3**	C3
Museo de Sitio.....................................**4**	D1
Templo de la Calavera (Templo	
XII)...**5**	A3
Templo de la Cruz Foliada........**6**	C4
Templo del Bello Relieve...........**7**	B4
Templo del Conde.......................**8**	B2
Templo del Sol.............................**9**	B3
Templo X..**10**	B2
Templo XI.......................................**11**	B3
Templo XIII....................................**12**	B3
Templo XIV....................................**13**	B3
Templo XVII..................................**14**	C4
Templo XIX....................................**15**	B4
Templo XX.....................................**16**	B4
Templo XXI....................................**17**	B4
Templo XXII..................................**18**	B4
Templo XXIV.................................**19**	A4
Tomb of Alberto Ruz Lhuillier...**20**	B3

EATING	🍴 (pp412–13)
Café...(see 2)	
Restaurant...................................**21**	A3

OTHER
Drink & Souvenir Stalls............**22**	A3
Guías e Interpretes Mayas.......**23**	A3
Lower Entrance/Exit...................**24**	C1
Main (Upper) Entrance...............**25**	A3
Official Guide Kiosk....................**26**	A3

YUCATÁN PENINSULA, TABASCO & CHIAPAS

Official site **guides** (2hr tour for up to 7 people US$32) are available by the entrance. A Maya guide association, **Guías e Interpretes Mayas**, also have a desk here and offer informative two-hour jungle tours (two people minimum, per person US$9) in Spanish that take in the outlying Templo Olvidado (Forgotten Temple).

An excellent place to read up on Palenque is the official website of some of the archaeologists who are working here (www.mesoweb.com/palenque).

TEMPLO DE LAS INSCRIPCIONES GROUP
As you emerge through the trees from the entrance, a line of temples rising in front of the jungle on your right comes into view.

The first of these is Templo XII, called the **Templo de la Calavera** (Temple of the Skull) for the relief sculpture of a rabbit or deer skull at the foot of one its pillars. The second temple has little interest. Third is **Templo XIII**, containing a tomb of a female skeleton, colored red as a result of treatment with cinnabar. You can enter this 'Tumba de la Reina Roja' (Tomb of the Red Queen) to see her sarcophagus. With the skeleton were found a malachite mask and about 1000 pieces of jade, but no inscriptions to tell who the 'queen' was. Some speculate, from resemblances to Pakal's tomb next door, that she was his wife.

This line of temples culminates with the **Templo de las Inscripciones** (Temple of the

Inscriptions), perhaps the most celebrated burial monument in the Americas, and the tallest and most stately of Palenque's buildings. Owing to inevitable damage to its murals from the humidity exuded by hordes of visitors, this temple is now only open on a restricted basis. Free permits can be obtained from the site museum and it's only possible to view Pakal's tomb after 3pm.

Constructed on eight levels, the Templo de las Inscripciones has a central front staircase rising 25m to a series of small rooms. The tall roofcomb that once crowned it is long gone, but between the front doorways are stucco panels with reliefs of noble figures. On the interior rear wall are the three panels with a long Mayan inscription, after which Ruz Lhuillier named the temple. The inscription, dedicated in AD 692, recounts the history of Palenque and the temple. Also at the top is the access to the slippery stairs leading down into the tomb of Pakal. A carved slab depicts Pakal's rebirth as the Maize god, encircled by serpents, mythical monsters and glyphs recounting his reign. Stucco figures on the walls represent the nine lords of the underworld. Between the crypt and the staircase, a snakelike hollow ventilation duct connected Pakal with the realm of the living.

EL PALACIO
Diagonally opposite the Templo de las Inscripciones is the **Palace**, a large, complex structure divided into four main courtyards, with a maze of corridors and rooms. Its tower, restored in 1955, has remnants of fine stucco reliefs on the walls, but is not open to visitors. Archaeologists believe the tower was constructed so that Mayan royalty and priests could observe the sun falling directly into the Templo de las Inscripciones during the winter solstice.

GRUPO DE LA CRUZ
Pakal's son Kan B'alam II was a prolific builder, who soon after the death of his father started designing the three temples of the **Grupo de la Cruz** (Group of the Cross). All three pyramid-shaped structures face inwards towards an artificial elevated plaza, just southeast of the Templo de las Inscripciones. They were all dedicated in 692 as a spiritual focal point for Palenque's triad of patron deities. The 'cross' carvings here

symbolize the ceiba tree, which in Maya belief held up the universe.

The **Templo del Sol** (Temple of the Sun) on the west side of the plaza has the best-preserved roofcomb at Palenque.

Steep steps climb to the **Templo de la Cruz** (Temple of the Cross), the largest and most elegantly proportioned in this group. On the **Templo de la Cruz Foliada** (Temple of the Foliated Cross), the corbeled arches are fully exposed, revealing how Palenque's architects designed these buildings.

AROUND ACRÓPOLIS SUR
In the jungle south of the Grupo de la Cruz is the **Southern Acropolis**.

Templo XVII, between the Cruz group and the Southern Acropolis, contains a reproduction carved panel depicting a standing figure bearing a spear, probably Kan B'alam, with a bound captive kneeling before him.

In 1999, close to **Templo XIX**, archaeologists made the most important Palenque find for decades: an 8th-century limestone platform with stunning carvings of seated figures and lengthy hieroglyphic texts that detail Palenque's origins. A reproduction has been placed inside Templo XIX. In **Templo XX**, a tomb of an unknown personage, with many murals, was found in 1999.

NORTH & NORTHEASTERN GROUPS
North of El Palacio are a **ball court** and the handsome buildings of the **Grupo Norte** (Northern Group). East of the Grupo Norte, the main path crosses Arroyo Otolum. Some 70m beyond the stream, a right fork will take you to **Grupo C**, a set of jungle-covered buildings and plazas on different levels, thought to have been lived in from about AD 750 to 800.

If you stay on the main path, you'll find it descends steep steps to a group of low, elongated buildings, thought to have been occupied residentially around AD 770 to 850. The path goes alongside the Arroyo Otolum, which here tumbles down a series of small falls known as the **Baño de la Reina** (Queen's Bath). Bathing is not permitted here anymore.

The path continues to another residential quarter, the **Grupo de los Murciélagos** (Bat Group), then crosses the **Puente Murciélagos** (Bat Bridge), a suspension footbridge across Arroyo Otolum.

Across the bridge and a bit further downstream, a path goes west to **Grupos I and II**, a short walk uphill. These ruins, only partly uncovered, are in a beautiful jungle setting. The main path continues downriver to the road, where the museum is along to the right a short distance.

MUSEO DE SITIO
Palenque's Site Museum does a fine job of displaying finds from the site and interpreting Palenque's history. It includes a copy of the lid of Pakal's sarcophagus and recent finds from Templo XIX. Next door are a pleasant café and a handicraft shop. The museum is closed on Mondays.

GETTING THERE & AWAY
Most people take a combi or taxi to the main (upper) entrance, see the major structures and a few outlying buildings, and then walk downhill to the museum, visiting minor ruins along the way. However, if you want to view Pakal's tomb (access inside the Templo de las Inscripciones is restricted) consider stopping first at the site museum and getting a permit early in the day.

Transporte Chambalú (Allende at Hidalgo) and **Transportes Palenque** (Allende at 20 de Noviembre) operate combis to the ruins about every 15 minutes from around 6am to 6pm daily (US$0.70 one-way). The vehicles will pick you up anywhere along the town-to-ruins road. A taxi from town to the ruins costs US$4.50.

El Panchán
About 4.4km along the road to the ruins from Palenque town, **El Panchán** (www.elpanchan.com) is a near-legendary travelers' hangout set in a patch of dense rain forest; the trippy epicenter of Palenque's alternative scene, and home to a bohemian bunch of Mexican and Western residents and wanderers. Once ranchland, the area has been reforested by the remarkable Morales family, one of whom heads the team of archaeologists working at Palenque ruins.

Tours
Several agencies in Palenque offer transportation packages to Agua Azul, Agua Clara and Misol-Ha (p406), to Bonampak (p414) and Yaxchilán (p415), and to Flores in Guatemala via Frontera Corozal.

Agencies include the following:
Pakal-kin (☎ 345-11-97; viajespakal_kin@hotmail.com; 5 de Mayo 7)
Transporte Chambalú (☎ 345-08-67; Hidalgo at Allende)
Transportes Palenque (Allende at 20 de Noviembre)
Viajes Kukulcan (☎ 345-15-06; www.dtcmexico.com/kukulcan; Juárez s/n)
Viajes Misol-Ha (☎ 345-22-71; www.palenquemx.com/viajesmisolha; Juárez 148)
Viajes Na Chan Kan (☎ 345-21-54; rosita_palenque@yahoo.com.mx) Two locations, on Hidalgo at Jiménez and on Juaréz (s/n).
Viajes Shivalba (☎ 345-04-11; www.palenquemx.com/shivalva; Merle Green 9, La Cañada)

Sleeping
The first choice to make is whether you want to stay in Palenque town, or at one of the places (including campgrounds) outside. Most places out of town are along the 7.5km road to the ruins, including El Panchán. Palenque town is scruffy and not particularly attractive, but if you stay here you'll have plenty of restaurants and services (like cybercafés and travel agents) close at hand.

Prices given here are for the high season, which at most establishments is from mid-July to mid-August, mid-December to early January, and Semana Santa.

IN TOWN
Posada Kin (☎ 345-17-14; Abasolo 1; s/d US$13/16) Welcoming posada with four floors of clean, light, decent-sized rooms; all have good beds, bathroom and ceiling fan. Breakfast is available for US$1.25.

Posada Bonampak (☎ 345-09-25; Belisario Domínguez 33; s/d US$5/6) This family-run place is a good budget bet. It has a quiet location, and basic but tidy, reasonable-sized rooms with fan. The attached tiled bathrooms have no hot water.

Hotel Yun-Kax (☎ 345-07-25; Corregidora 87; s/d with fan US$11/14, with air-con US$16/23) The Yun-Kax, between the bus stations and town center, has clean rooms with shower, arranged around a little patio. There's free water for guests.

Ámbar Hostel (☎ 345-10-08; ambarhostel2001@hotmail.com; Merle Green s/n; dm/s/d US$6/18/27) Set in the quiet, leafy La Cañada area, Ámbar has a couple of screened dorms with bunks and rooms with fan and bathroom. There's a kitchen, table tennis and a bar.

Hotel Lacandonía (☎ 345-00-57; Juárez at Allende; s/d US$22/33; ✖) A new hotel smack in the center of town, whose tastefully presented light, airy accommodations all have stylish furnishings including wrought-iron beds, reading lights and cable TV.

Hotel Posada Tucán (☎ 345-18-59; merisuiri@ hotmail.com; 5 de Mayo 5; r with fan/air-con US$23/31) Posada Tucán has a breezy upstairs location and attractive, clean and fair-sized rooms with fan, TV and nicely tiled bathrooms. Prices drop by 30% outside high season.

Posada Águila Real (☎ /fax 345-00-04; 20 de Noviembre s/n; s/d with bathroom & fan US$23/28, with air-con US$30/35) Six attractive, well-priced spotless rooms with good quality beds and TV set around a little patio. There's a small café/restaurant and lounge area too.

Hotel Cañada Internacional (☎ /fax 345-20-93; Juárez 1; r US$24-43; P ✖ ☎) The Cañada Internacional has comfortable rooms on four stories all with two beds (at least one a double) and TV. The more expensive rooms are bigger, newer and air-conditioned.

Hotel Chablis (☎ 345-08-70; Merle Green 7; r with 1/2 beds US$40/43; ✖ P) The Chablis enjoys a quiet location and offers well-presented, spacious rooms all with air-con or fan, TV and balcony.

OUTSIDE TOWN

There are some wonderful places on the road to the ruins, many in El Panchán. All of Panchán's accommodations are signposted and between 100m and 300m from the road.

Margarita & Ed Cabañas (☎ 341-00-63; edcab anas@yahoo.com; El Panchán; single cabaña US$11, double cabaña US$12-14, r with fan & bathroom US$12-23, with air-con US$27; P) Margarita and Ed, a welcoming Mexican/US couple, defy the odds and maintain scrupulously clean rooms in middle of the Panchán jungle. The rustic screened cabañas are also pleasant, and come with reading lights and private bathrooms. There's free drinking water for all.

Mayabell (☎ 345-01-25; mayabell82@hotmail.com; Carr Palenque-Ruinas Km 6; hammock space/campsite per person US$2.75, hammock to rent US$1.25, small vehicle without hookups US$1, vehicle site with hookups US$12, treehouse US$8, r with bathroom & fan US$16-22, with air-con US$37; P ☎) This spacious grassy site is just 400m from the site museum and has a plethora of different accommodation options, and a large heat-busting pool. Happy

campers and hammock heads share clean toilet and shower blocks. Rooms with air-con are very homey and comfortable, those with fan are basic. In the pleasant restaurant few items cost more than US$3.50. Lockers are US$0.90 a day, and a Maya-style steam bath is US$2.75. A taxi from town is US$3.25 by day and US$4.50 at night.

Rakshita's (www.rakshita.com; El Panchán; hammock & dm US$2.75, cabaña US$8-13) Rakshita's has a decent five-person dorm with shared bathroom facilities and simple cabañas (some have bathrooms) with fans and mosquito-netted windows. Guests can use the kitchen and plunge pool, and there's a meditation center and an inexpensive vegetarian restaurant (menú del día US$3).

Elementos Naturales (Carr Palenque-Ruinas Km 5; dm US$5.25, double cabaña US$13; P) It's 700m further from El Panchán to this calm spot with cabañas and palapa shelters scattered around grassy grounds. The dorms and cabañas have fan and electric light, the bathrooms are clean. Breakfast is included and they will look after your valuables at the desk.

Hotel Villas Kin-Ha (☎ 345-05-33; Carr Palenque-Ruinas Km 2.7; r US$52-59; ✖ P ☎) Kin-Ha offers pleasant thatched air-con casitas (little houses), with one king or two double beds, in pretty gardens that have a pool and open-sided palapa restaurant.

Chan-Kah Resort Village (☎ 345-11-00; Carr Palenque-Ruinas Km 3.2; r/ste US$105/263 ✖ P ☎) This resort on the road to the ruins, 4.5km from town, has handsome, well-spaced wood-and-stone cottages with generous bathrooms, ceiling fans and air-conditioning. However, it's the stupendous Eden-esque 70m stone-lined swimming pool and lush jungle gardens that are the real draws. Service can be distracted however, and it's rarely busy, except when tour groups block-book the place.

Eating & Drinking

Palenque is definitely not the gastronomic capital of Mexico, but there's an improving dining scene and prices are fair. The cheapest places are the taquerías along the eastern side of El Parque. Try **Los Farolitos** or neighboring **Fuente de Sodas** for a plate of tacos at around US$2.75.

Restaurant Las Tinajas (2 branches on 20 de Noviembre; mains US$4-7.50; ☺ breakfast, lunch & dinner) The gargantuan portions and home-style cooking make Las Tinajas a perennial travelers' favorite. A new branch next door has more upmarket pretensions, concentrating on fish and seafood.

Don Mucho's (☎ 341-48-46; El Panchán; mains US$3-4, snacks US$1.50-2.75) Ever popular Don Mucho's in El Panchán has a very good-value menu, with sandwiches and salads, and silly but tasty themed breakfasts. The epic pizzas must be the finest this side of Naples. There's live music here most nights.

El Trompo (☎ 345-18-81; Av Juárez s/n; tacos US$0.60-1.25, mains US$4-5.50) This refurbished, informal restaurant has a fish- and meat-based menu and also pulls 'em in with a 2-for-1 cocktail happy hour (5pm to 7pm).

Mi México Lindo (☎ 341-63-52; Av Hidalgo s/n; mains US$4.50-7; ☺ breakfast, lunch & dinner) Large, recently opened restaurant that serves some of the most authentic Mexican food in town, including great *mojarra al ajillo* (perch cooked with garlic).

Mara's (☎ 345-15-76; Juárez 1; mains US$5-8; ☺ breakfast, lunch & dinner) Mara's has a prime location facing El Parque, some sidewalk tables and an abundance of whirring fans inside. The Mexican cuisine here is reliable.

Restaurant Na Chan-Kan (☎ 345-02-63; cnr Hidalgo & Jiménez; set meals US$2.75-4.50) Opposite the northeast corner of El Parque, Na Chan-Kan serves tasty two-course meals (soup, main dish and drink) and *sincronizadas* (tortillas stuffed with cheese and other items and heated). Beers are US$1 each.

Restaurant Artemio's (☎ 345-02-63; Hidalgo 14; mains US$3-6.50) Family-run Artemio's serves pizzas, set menus from US$3 to US$4.50, breakfasts and a big range of *antojitos* (traditional Mexican snacks or small meals).

Café de Yara (☎ 345-02-69; Hidalgo 66; snacks & breakfast US$2-4, mains US$4-6; ☺ breakfast, lunch & dinner) Efficient and modern café that's good for breakfasts, spaghetti and salads. Also serves fine organic Chiapas coffee, with espresso, cappuccino and latte available.

Getting There & Away

Palenque's **airport**, 2km north of the Maya head statue along Hwy 199, was undergoing renovations and was closed at the time of writing. However it is likely that services will resume to Mérida, Tuxtla Gutiérrez, Cancún, Flores in Guatemala and possibly Mexico City.

There have been occasional reports of theft on buses serving Palenque, especially night buses to and from Mérida.

Westernmost of the main bus terminals on Juárez is the joint Cristóbal Colón/ADO/ Maya de Oro/Altos 1st-class terminal. A block east is Autotransportes Tuxtla Gutiérrez (ATG, 2nd-class), and half a block further east, at Juárez 159, is the joint AEXA (1st-class), Transportes Lacandonia (TL, 2nd-class) and Cárdenas (2nd-class) terminal; Transportes Rodulfo Figueroa (TRF) is opposite.

It's a good idea to buy your outward ticket a day in advance. Daily departures include the following:

Campeche (5hr; 4 buses from Colón terminal, US$15-20; 1 ATG bus, US$14)

Cancún (13hr; 5 buses from Colón, US$34-41; 1 ATG bus, US$28)

Mérida (8hr; 4 buses from Colón, US$23-24; 1 ATG bus, US$18)

Mexico City (TAPO & Norte; 16hr; 3 ADO buses, US$50)

Ocosingo (2¾hr; 9 buses from Colón, US$4.50-6.50; 4 TRF buses, US$4.50; 4 ATG buses, US$4; 5 AEXA buses, US$4.50)

Playa del Carmen (12hr; 4 buses from Colón, US$31-37)

San Cristóbal de Las Casas (5hr; 9 buses from Colón, US$6.50-9; 4 TRF buses, US$6.50; 4 ATG buses, US$6; 5 AEXA buses, US$6.50)

Tulum (11hr; 2 buses from Colon, US$31-35)

Tuxtla Gutiérrez (6½hr; 9 buses from Colón, US$8-12; 4 ATG buses, US$9; 4 TRF buses, US$9; 5 AEXA buses, US$9)

Villahermosa (2½hr; 12 buses from Colón, US$5-6.50)

Autotransportes Río Chancalá at 5 de Mayo 120 in Palenque runs combis to Frontera Corozal (US$4.50, three hours) five times daily between 6am and 3pm, and to Benemérito (US$5, three hours) 13 times between 4:30am and 4:15pm. Transportes Montebello, on Velasco Suárez two blocks west of Palenque market, runs buses to Frontera Corozal (US$4.50, four hours) at noon, to Benemérito (US$5, four hours) nine times daily, and around the Carretera Fronteriza to Comitán (US$14, 11 hours) four times per day. Both these companies,

---

WATCH THE CLOCK

The Márquez de Comillas area of southeastern Chiapas does not observe daylight saving time, so you should triple-check all transportation schedules!

like the region they travel to but unlike the rest of Palenque, tend to ignore daylight saving time in summer – meaning that by Palenque time, departures during that period are one hour after posted times.

Most services stop at San Javier (US$3.75, 2¼ hours), 140km from Palenque, where a side road branches to Bonampak and Lacanjá Chansayab. They also stop at Crucero Corozal, the intersection for Frontera Corozal, where there are *comedores*.

Numerous military checkpoints are dotted along the Carretera Fronteriza.

Getting Around
In town, taxis wait at the northeast corner of El Parque and at the Colón/ADO bus station; they charge US$2 to the airport.

BONAMPAK
Bonampak's setting in dense jungle hid it from the outside world until 1946. The **ruins** (admission US$3; ☾ 8am-5pm) are spread over 2.4 sq km, but all the main ruins stand around the rectangular **Gran Plaza**.

Bonampak was never a major city, and spent most of the Classic period under Yaxchilán's sphere of influence. The most impressive surviving monuments were built under Chan Muwan II, who took the throne in AD 776. He was a nephew of the Yaxchilán ruler Itzamnaaj B'alam II and was married to Yaxchilán royalty.

Bonampak gets its fame – and its name – from the astonishing frescoes inside the modest **Templo de las Pinturas** (Edificio 1) on the Acrópolis steps. Bonampak means 'Painted Walls' in Yucatecan Maya. The murals were never completely finished, however, because Bonampak was abandoned during the implosion of Classic Maya civilization.

Sleeping
Camping Margarito (campsite per person US$1, hammock site US$2, rented tent/hammock per person US$2/3.25) This Lacandón-run camp ground, 9km from Bonampak at Lacanjá Chansayab turnoff, is the closest you can stay to the ruins. There's a grassy campsite and a *palapa* for hammocks. Meals are available.

You can also stay in one of several local *campamentos* (camping areas) in the sprawling nearby village of Lacanjá Chansayab, 12km from Bonampak. **Campamento Río La-**

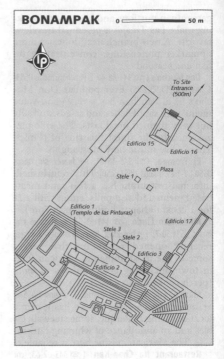

BONAMPAK   0 —— 50 m

To Site Entrance (500m)

Edificio 15
Edificio 16
Gran Plaza
Stele 1
Edificio 1 (Templo de las Pinturas)
Edificio 17
Stele 3
Stele 2
Edificio 3
Edificio 2

canjá (☎ 55-5329-0995 ext 8055; 2km south of village entrance; cabaña US$6.50, casitas US$30; meals US$3-4) is about the best and has a restaurant.

Lacanjá Chansayab is 6.5km by paved road from San Javier on the Carretera Fronteriza. A taxi is US$5 (US$1.25 *colectivo*) but you might have to walk or hitch.

Getting There & Away
Bonampak is 12km from San Javier, a junction on the Carretera Fronteriza (and 148km by road from Palenque). For information on getting to San Javier, see p414. The first 3km from San Javier, to the Lacanjá Chansayab turnoff, is paved; the rest is good gravel/dirt road through the forest. Just past the start of the gravel/dirt section is the entrance to the Monumento Nacional Bonampak protected zone: here you can rent bicycles for US$0.90 an hour or take a combi to the ruins for US$7.50 roundtrip.

A taxi from San Javier to Bonampak ruins and back, with time to visit the ruins, costs around US$12. You may have to wait a while at San Javier before one turns up, however. Hitching is possible.

FRONTERA COROZAL

pop 5200 / elevation 200m

This riverside frontier town (formerly called Frontera Echeverría) is 16km by paved road from Crucero Corozal junction on the Carretera Fronteriza. The broad Usumacinta river, flowing swiftly between jungle-covered banks, forms the Mexico–Guatemala border here. Frontera Corozal is an essential stepping-stone both to the ruins of Yaxchilán (see p416) and for onward travel into Guatemala.

Long, outboard-powered launches come and go from the river *embarcadero*, below a cluster of wooden buildings that includes a few inexpensive *comedores*. Almost everything you'll need is on the paved main street leading inland from here – including the local immigration office, where you should hand in your tourist card if you're leaving for Guatemala, or obtain one if you're arriving from Guatemala.

Sleeping & Eating

Escudo Jaguar (☎ 5532-900-993 ext 8059; www.chiapas tours.com.mx/escudojaguar; small cabaña US$12-18, larger cabaña with private bathroom US$26-39; P) This place, 100m back from the embarcadero, has 15 spotless thatched cabañas with fans and mosquito nets, and a good if slightly pricey **restaurant** (mains US$4.50-6.50).

Nueva Alianza (☎ 55-5329-0995 ext 8061; per person US$4.50; P) About 250m from the embarcadero, this is an excellent new budget place with rooms in well-constructed wood cabañas that have fans, mosquito nets and lights. There are also hammocks with nets (US$2.25), clean shared bathrooms and a decent **restaurant** (mains US$4).

Getting There & Away

If you can't get a bus or combi direct to Frontera Corozal, get off at Crucero Corozal, 20 minutes' southeast of San Javier on the highway, where taxis (US$2 per person for a *colectivo*, US$5.50 otherwise) and occasional buses can take you through to Frontera Corozal.

At the time of writing, combis left Frontera Corozal for Palenque at about 5am, 9am, midday and 3pm, and a Transportes Montebello bus left at 3am. The last daily Palenque-bound combi goes past Crucero Corozal about 5pm. For more information, see p414.

TO/FROM GUATEMALA

Fast river *lanchas* (launches) go to Bethel, on the Guatemalan bank of the Usumacinta 40 minutes upstream, and to La Técnica which is directly opposite Frontera Corozal. It's best to check timetables first at the *lancha* offices in the Escudo Jaguar, or at the Cooperativa Tikal Chilam (further up the main street from the *embarcadero*) where they also know the departure times of onward Guatemalan buses.

A boat to Bethel for up to six people costs US$40; for seven to 10 people it's about US$50. The launches can carry bicycles and even motorcycles. Buses from Bethel leave for Santa Elena (p169), near Flores, at 5am, noon, 2pm and 4pm (US$3.50, four hours).

Bethel's **Posada Maya** (☎ 502-801-1799; s/d US$9/18) has camping, hammock space and cabañas on the banks of the Usumacinta.

Lanchas to La Técnica cost US$0.70 per person, from where buses leave at 4am and 11am (US$4, five hours) for Flores (p169).

YAXCHILÁN

Shrouded in jungle, **Yaxchilán** (admission US$3; ☼ 8am-4:45pm) has a terrific setting above a horseshoe loop in the Usumacinta. This position and its ability to control commercial trade enabled the city to prosper in Classic Maya times. Archaeologically, Yaxchilán is famed for its ornamented building facades and roofcombs, and impressive stone lintels carved (often on their undersides) with conquest and ceremonial scenes. A flashlight (torch) is a help in exploring the site.

Another feature of these ruins is the howler monkeys that come to feed in some of the tall trees here. You'll almost certainly hear their roars, and you stand a good chance of seeing some.

Conquests and alliances made Yaxchilán one of the most important pre-Hispanic cities in the Usumacinta region. It peaked in power and splendor between AD 681 and 800, and was abandoned around AD 810.

As you walk toward the ruins, a signed path to the right leads up to the **Pequeña Acrópolis**, a group of ruins on a small hilltop – you can visit this later. Staying on the main path, you soon reach the mazy passages of **El Laberinto** (Edificio 19), built between AD 742 and 752. From this complicated two-level building you emerge at the northwest end of the Gran Plaza.

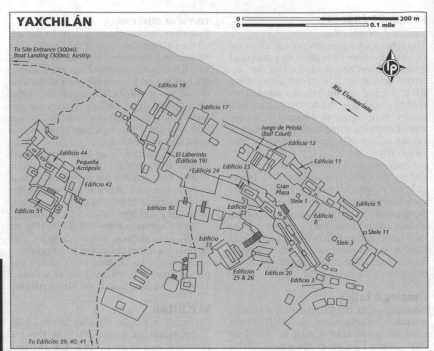

YAXCHILÁN

To Site Entrance (300m);
Boat Landing (300m); Airstrip

Río Usumacinta

Edificio 18

Edificio 17

Juego de Pelota
(Ball Court)

Edificio 12

Edificio 44

El Laberinto
(Edificio 19)

Edificio 11

Pequeña
Acrópolis

Edificio 23

Edificio 24

Gran
Plaza

Edificio 42

Stela 1

Edificio 5

Edificio 51

Edificio 30

Edificio
22

Edificio
8

Stele 11

Edificio
33

Stele 3

Edificios
25 & 26

Edificio 20

Edificio 3

To Edificios 39; 40; 41

YUCATÁN PENINSULA,
TABASCO & CHIAPAS

Though it's hard to imagine anyone here ever wanting to be hotter than they already were, **Edificio 17** was apparently a sweathouse. About halfway along the plaza, **Stela 1**, flanked by weathered sculptures of a crocodile and a jaguar, shows Pájaro Jaguar IV in a ceremony that took place in 761. **Edificio 20**, from the time of Itzamnaaj B'alam III, was the last significant structure built at Yaxchilán.

An imposing stairway climbs from Stela 1 to **Edificio 33**, the best-preserved temple at the site, with half of its roofcomb intact.

From the clearing behind Edificio 33, a path leads into the trees. About 20m along this, fork left uphill. Go left at another fork after about 80m, and in 10 minutes – mostly uphill – you reach three buildings on a hilltop, **Edificios 39, 40** and **41**. You can climb to the top of Edificio 41 for great views of the distant Guatemalan mountains.

Getting There & Away

You can reach Yaxchilán by chartered plane from places including Ocosingo (see p404) or by boat from Bethel (p187) or Frontera Corozal. The latter take 40 minutes from

Frontera Corozal, and one hour to return. A round trip, including about three hours at the ruins, costs US$55 for up to four people, and US$88 for up to 10 with either company. Lanchas leave frequently until 1:30pm or so, and you should be easily able to hook up with other travelers to share costs.

BENEMÉRITO DE LAS AMÉRICAS TO LAGUNAS DE MONTEBELLO

South of Frontera Corozal you soon enter the area of far eastern Chiapas known as Marqués de Comillas. Benemérito de las Américas is the main town, located on the west bank of the Río Salinas, which forms the Mexico–Guatemala border here. It's a pretty forlorn place.

There are a few budget **hotels** and **restaurants** in town, but Benemérito has no immigration post; you must pick up or hand in Mexican tourist cards at Frontera Corozal.

For Guatemala, you can hire a *lancha* for around US$150 to take you up the Río Salinas and Río de la Pasión to Sayaxché (Guatemala, p187) in three to four hours. An alternative is to take a *lancha* a short distance downriver to Laureles on the Guatemalan side (colectivo US$1.50, especial US$10). From Laureles buses leave for El Subín (US$2.50, 2½ hours) where you could change for Sayaxché and Flores.

South of Benemérito, the Carretera Fronteriza heads 60km south before turning west for the 150km stretch to the Lagunas de Montebello (p417). It's a slow but interesting ride (with army checkpoints every 50km or so) that crosses several huge rivers and villages, some settled by Guatemalan refugees. West of Ixcán you climb more than 1000m up to the cooler, pine-forested highlands around the Lagunas de Montebello.

For information on transportation along the Carretera Fronteriza, see the Getting There & Away sections under Bonampak (p414), Yaxchilán (opposite) and Comitán (p419). For information on how to get to Benemérito, see p413.

PARQUE NACIONAL LAGUNAS DE MONTEBELLO

The temperate forest along the Guatemalan border southeast of Comitán is dotted with 59 small lakes of varied colors, the Lagunas (lakes or lagoons) de Montebello. The area is very picturesque, refreshing and peaceful, and there's good swimming, hiking and biking. At the western edge of the lake district are the Mayan ruins of Chinkultic.

The paved road to Montebello turns east off Hwy 190 just before the town of **La Trinitaria**, 16km south of Comitán. It passes Chinkultic after 30km, and enters the forest and the Parque Nacional Lagunas de Montebello 5km beyond. At the park entrance (no fee) the road splits. One road continues 3km north to end at **Laguna Bosque Azul**. The other heads east to the village of **Tziscao** (9km), beyond which it becomes the Carretera Fronteriza, continuing east to Ixcán and ultimately Palenque (see p406).

Chinkultic

Worth a visit, these dramatically sited **ruins** (admission US$2.75; ☺ 10am-5pm) lie 2km north of La Trinitaria–Montebello road. The access road is paved.

Chinkultic was a minor power that rose during the Classic Maya period, from around AD 591 to 897. From the **Acrópolis** you have remarkable views over the surrounding lakes and forests and down into a cenote 50m below – into which the Maya used to toss offerings of pottery, beads, bones and obsidian knives.

The Lakes

From the park entrance gateway, one road heads straight ahead, passing the **Lagunas de Colores** – five lakes whose vivid hues range from turquoise to deep green. Following the other road from the gateway, after about 3km a track leads 200m left to **Laguna de Montebello**, one of the bigger lakes. Three kilometers further along the Tziscao road another track leads left to the **Cinco Lagunas** (Five Lakes). Only four are visible from the road, but the second, **La Cañada**, on the right after about 1.5km, is one of the most beautiful Montebello lakes. The track eventually reaches the village of San Antonio.

One kilometer further toward Tziscao from the Cinco Lagunas turnoff, a track leads 1km north to cobalt blue **Laguna Pojoj**, which has an island in the middle. **Laguna Tziscao**, on the Guatemalan border, comes into view on the right, 1km beyond the Laguna Pojoj turnoff. The junction for Tziscao village, a pleasant, spread-out place, is a little further along, again on the right.

Sleeping & Eating

El Pino Feliz (☎ 963-102-10-89; Carr La Trinitaria-Lagos de Montebello Km 31.5; cabaña per person US$4) The roadside 'Happy Pine' has simple wood cabañas, reliable hot water and also provides excellent meals.

Albergue Turístico (☎ 963-633-52-44; campsite per person US$1.75, r & cabaña with bathroom per person US$6) In Tziscao village, 2km from the highway turnoff, Albergue Turístico is also known as 'Hotel Tziscao.' It has a peaceful position right by the lakeside, with extensive grounds, a sandy beach and terrific views of the lake. Meals cost US$2.25 to US$3.25.

Getting There & Away

You can make a day trip to Chinkultic and the lakes from Comitán (see p418) or from San Cristóbal de Las Casas (see p396) either by public transpotation or as part of a tour. All of the buses and combis services will drop you off at the turnoffs for the above accommodation.

The last vehicles back to Comitán from Tziscao leave around 5pm, and from Laguna Bosque Azul around 5:30pm.

COMITÁN

☎ 963 / pop 75,600 / elevation 1635m

Comitán is an agreeable, orderly town with real colonial character and what must be the cleanest streets in Mexico. Most travelers bypass the place on their way to or from Guatemala, but with a few minor but interesting museums and archaeological sites (and the Lagunas de Montebello an hour away) you could easily spend an enjoyable couple of days based here.

Orientation & Information

Comitán is set on hilly terrain, with a beautiful broad main plaza. Hwy 190 passes through the west of town.

The **tourist office** (☎ 632-40-47; ☺ 8am-4pm), on the north side of the plaza, has fairly well-informed staff. **Bancomer** (☺ 9am-5pm Mon-Fri) on the southeast corner of the main plaza, does currency exchange and has an ATM. There's a central **post office** (Av Central Sur 45; ☺ Mon-Fri 9am-3pm) and card phones are dotted around the plaza's fringes.

Most cybercafés charge US$0.90 per hour. **Cyber@dicts** (Local 13B) and **Inter Net** (Local 12; ☺ 9am-2pm & 4-9pm), both on Pasaje Morales, have quick connections.

The laundry **Lavandería Montebello** (Av Central Nte 13A) charges US$1.50 per kilo for next-day service.

Sights

MUSEUMS

The **Casa de la Cultura**, on the southeast corner of the plaza, includes an exhibition gallery as well as an auditorium. Behind it you'll find the **Museo Arqueológico de Comitán** (☎ 632-06-24; 1a Calle Sur Ote; admission free; ☺ 10am-5pm Tue-Sun), which has artifacts from the region's archaeological sites.

Two blocks south of the main plaza, a neat little art museum, the **Museo de Arte Hermila Domínguez de Castellanos** (☎ 632-20-82; Av Central Sur 53; admission US$0.50; ☺ 10am-2pm & 4-6pm Mon-Fri, 10am-4pm Sat, 10am-1pm Sun) houses paintings by many leading 20th-century Mexican artists, including Rufino Tamayo, Francisco Toledo and José Guadalupe Posada.

TENAM PUENTE

This minor Maya **archaeological site** (admission free; ☺ 9am-4pm), 14km to the south of town, features three ball courts and a 20m tiered pyramid and other structures rising from a terraced, wooded hillside. It has a pleasant rural setting and good long-distance views from the topmost structures. Transportes Francisco Sarabia buses leave every 45 minutes from 3a Av Pte Sur 8 between 9am and 6pm (US$0.90) to the site, or the village of Francisco Sarabia, 2km before Tenam Puente. The last bus returns at 4pm from the ruins. A taxi costs US$11 roundtrip with an hour at the ruins.

Tours

Agencia de Viajes Tenam (☎ 632-16-54; www.viajes tenam.com in Spanish; Pasaje Morales 8A) has tours to Tenam Puente, Chinkultic and Lagunas de Montebello for US$18 per head (three-person minimum) and should also offer car hire by the time you read this.

Sleeping & Eating

Hospedaje Primavera (☎ 632-20-41; Calle Central Pte 4; s/d with shared bathroom US$6.50/8) This is one of Comitán's better cheap posadas with small, plain, but clean rooms.

Hospedaje Montebello (☎ 632-35-72; 1a Calle Nte Pte 10; f_montebello@prodigy.net.mx; s/d with shared bathroom US$4.50/9, with private bathroom US$5.50/11) Welcoming cheapie with large, tiled, clean rooms around a courtyard. There is free drinking water.

Hotel Internacional (☎ 632-01-10; fax 632-01-12; Av Central Sur 16; r US$28-39; Ⓟ) A block from the plaza, this excellent downtown hotel is great value considering the comfort levels and stylish decor offered. All the large rooms have two double beds, TV and attractive bathrooms, and there's a decent café/restaurant.

Hotel Posada del Virrey (☎ 632-18-11; hotel _delvirrey@hotmail.com; Av Central Nte 13; s/d with TV US$22/25) The Virrey has 19 characterful, though smallish rooms with reading lights and spotless tiled bathrooms around a pretty courtyard.

La Alpujarra (☎ 632-20-00; Av Central Sur 3; snacks US$0.90-2.50, pizzas US$2.75-7) Excellent place on the west side of the plaza with very flavorsome snacks, including pastries, homemade soups, good coffee and cakes, and terrific pizzas.

Helen's Enrique Restaurant (☎ 632-17-30; Av Central Sur 9; mains US$4-6.50 ☺ breakfast, lunch & dinner) This long-running place near the plaza is good for meat dishes: try the *brochete de*

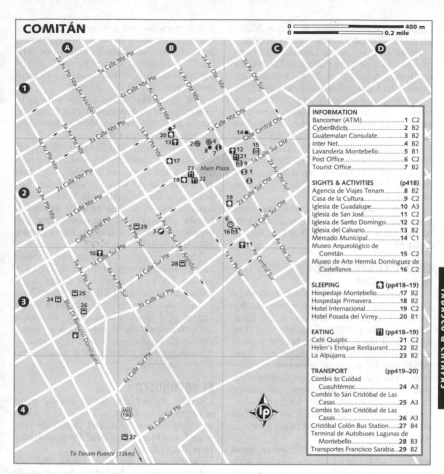

COMITÁN

INFORMATION	
Bancomer (ATM)......................1	C2
Cyber@dicts..........................2	B2
Guatemalan Consulate...........3	B2
Inter Net.............................4	B2
Lavandería Montebello...........5	B1
Post Office...........................6	C2
Tourist Office........................7	B2

SIGHTS & ACTIVITIES	(p418)
Agencia de Viajes Tenam.........8	B2
Casa de la Cultura..................9	C2
Iglesia de Guadalupe..............10	A3
Iglesia de San José................11	C2
Iglesia de Santo Domingo.......12	C2
Iglesia del Calvario................13	B2
Mercado Municipal................14	C1
Museo Arqueológico de	
Comitán...........................15	C2
Museo de Arte Hermila Domínguez de	
Castellanos.......................16	C2

SLEEPING	(pp418–19)
Hospedaje Montebello............17	B2
Hospedaje Primavera..............18	B2
Hotel Internacional................19	B2
Hotel Posada del Virrey..........20	B1

EATING	(pp418–19)
Café Quiptic.........................21	C2
Helen's Enrique Restaurant......22	B2
La Alpujarra.........................23	B2

TRANSPORT	(pp419–20)
Combis to Ciudad	
Cuauhtémoc.......................24	A3
Combis to San Cristóbal de Las	
Casas...............................25	A3
Combis to San Cristóbal de Las	
Casas...............................26	A3
Cristóbal Colón Bus Station....27	B4
Terminal de Autobuses Lagunas de	
Montebello.......................28	B3
Transportes Francisco Sarabia..29	B2

To Tenam Puente (13km)

YUCATÁN PENINSULA, TABASCO & CHIAPAS

carne con salsa de champiñones (beef kebabs with mushroom sauce).

Café Quiptic (632-04-00; 1a Av Ote Sur s/n; breakfasts US$3, mains US$3.75-5.50) On the other side of the plaza, the elegant Quiptic serves pricey but filling breakfasts plus superb organic coffee, *tortas*, salads, desserts and other light eats.

Getting There & Around

Comitán is 90km to the southeast of San Cristóbal along the Pan-American Hwy, and 83km from the Guatemalan border. The Cristóbal Colón bus station (deluxe, 1st class and 2nd class) is located on the Pan-American Hwy, here named Blvd Dr Belisario Domínguez and called simply 'El Bulevar.' Minibuses and Suburban vans depart when full, approximately every 20 to 30 minutes.

Daily Colón bus terminal departures include the following:

Ciudad Cuauhtémoc (1-1¼hr; 6 buses, US$3.50; minibuses, US$3.25) The minibuses leave from El Bulevar between 1a and 2a Calle Sur Pte.

Mexico City (TAPO & Norte; 20hr; 7 buses, US$54-67)

San Cristóbal de Las Casas (1-1½hr; 10 buses, US$3.50-4.50; Suburban vans, US$3) The Suburban vans leave from El Bulevar between 1a and 2a Calle Sur Pte.

Tapachula (via Motozintla; 5½hr; 7 buses, US$9.50)

Tuxtla Gutiérrez (3-3½hr; 7 buses, US$7-8; minibuses, US$6.50) The minibuses leave from El Bulevar between 1a and 2a Calle Sur Pte.

Colón also serves Oaxaca, Palenque, Villahermosa, Playa del Carmen and Cancún.

Buses and combis to Lagunas de Montebello and along the Carretera Fronteriza go from a terminal at 2a Av Pte Sur 23. Combis to Laguna Bosque Azul (US$1.75, one hour) run about every 20 minutes from 5:30am to 5:30pm. Other combis and buses (also leaving from the terminal at 2a Av Pte Sur 23) head to Tziscao (US$2, 1¼ hours, 20 or more daily), Ixcán (US$5, three hours, about 12 daily), Benemérito de las Américas (US$9, seven hours, four daily) and even Palenque (US$12, 11 hours, two daily).

'Centro' microbuses, across the road from the Colón bus station, will take you to the main plaza for US$0.40. A taxi is US$1.50.

CIUDAD CUAUHTÉMOC
☎ 963 / pop 2200

This 'city' amounts to not much more than a few houses and a *comedor* or two, but it's the last/first place in Mexico on the Pan-American Hwy (190). Comitán is 83km north, and the Guatemalan border post is 4km south at La Mesilla. *Colectivo* taxis (US$0.50) ferry people between the two sides. There's a bank on the Guatemalan side of the border, and plenty of money changers loiter with intent on both sides. Guatemalan officials often ask for unofficial entry fees of a dollar or two to get through the border.

If you do get stuck at this border, **Hotel Mily's** at La Mesilla has decent doubles with fan, cable TV and bathroom for around US$15.

Frequent buses and combis run to and from Comitán (p419) and fairly regularly to and from San Cristóbal (p400).

From La Mesilla, buses leave for Huehuetenango (US$1.50, two hours, p122) and Quetzaltenango (US$4, 3½ hours, p111) at least 20 times per day between 5:45am and 6pm. If there's no bus to your destination, take one to Huehuetenango, where you may be able to get an onward connection.

RESERVA DE LA BIÓSFERA EL TRIUNFO

The luxuriant cloud forests high in the remote El Triunfo Biosphere Reserve in the Sierra Madre de Chiapas are a bird-

lovers' paradise and a remarkable world of trees and shrubs festooned with epiphytes, ferns, bromeliads, mosses and vines. The cool cloud forest is formed by moist air rising from the hot, humid lowlands to form clouds and rain on the uplands.

The Sierra Madre de Chiapas is home to more than 30 bird species that are nonexistent or rare elsewhere in Mexico, including the resplendent quetzal.

Visits are controlled fairly strictly. Avoid the May-to-October wet season. For a permit and arrangements, contact – at least one month in advance – Jorge Uribe, Coordinador del Programa de Visitas Guiadas, Ecoturismo, **Reserva de la Biósfera El Triunfo** (☎ 961-612-1394; eco-triunfo@hotmail.com, jorgeuribe@hotmail.com; Av 4a Nte 143, Colonia El Centro, 29000 Tuxtla Gutiérrez, Chiapas).

There's a minimum group size of four, and a minimum cost of about US$180 per person. For that you get four nights at the basic Campamento El Triunfo, 1850m high in the heart of the reserve, guides who are expert bird-spotters and some assistance with transportation from/to the nearest town, Jaltenango, which is served by Autotranportes Cuxtepeques buses from Tuxtla Gutiérrez.

EL SOCONUSCO

Chiapas' steamy and fertile coastal plain is called the Soconusco. This strip – 15km to 35km wide – is hot and sweaty all year round, with serious rainfall from mid-May to mid-October.

Southwest of the town **Tonalá**, the seaside town of **Puerto Arista** has a broad, sandy beach that's popular with weekending *chiapanecos* (people from Chiapas). Initial impressions of the place can be bleak, but once you're on the beach itself, gazing at the Pacific surf breaking onto an infinite expanse of sweeping gray sands, Puerto Arista's appeal becomes evident.

Both Tonalá and Puerto Arista have simple hotels and restaurants. In Puerto Arista, try **José's Camping Cabañas** (☎ 600-90-48; campsite per person US$2, s/d with shared showers US$7/11, r with bathroom US$18; P ☒).

Tonalá is three to four hours by bus from Tapachula (opposite; US$9.50 to US$11), near the Guatemalan border, and four hours by bus from Tuxtla Gutiérrez (p386; US$7.50 to US$8).

From Tonalá, microbuses leave regularly for Puerto Arista (US$0.80, 20 minutes) from the corner of Juárez and 5 de Mayo, one block to the east of the market.

TAPACHULA
☎ 962 / pop 192,000 / elevation 96m
Mexico's bustling southernmost city is a busy commercial center, but has very limited appeal – other than as a gateway to Guatemala.

The city's main plaza, the Parque Hidalgo, is its focal point. Here you'll find the tourist office, banks, cathedral and museum. Bus stations and hotels are scattered around the central area.

Information
The **immigration office** (☎ 626-91-02; Carr del Antiguo Aeropuerto Km 1.5; ✆ 9am-4:30pm Mon-Fri) is about 2.5km south of the center. **Banorte** (8a Nte 28; ✆ 9am-4pm Mon-Fri) has an ATM and **Centro Cambiario Casa Santa** (2a Nte 6, ✆ 8:30am-5:30pm Mon-Fri, 8:30am-3pm Sat) changes money. The **City Tourist Office** (☎ 626-14-85 ext 116; 8a Nte s/n; ✆ 8am-4pm Mon-Fri & 9am-noon Sat) is on west side of Parque Hidalgo.

Sleeping
All hotels listed here have attached bathrooms.

Hospedaje Las Américas (☎ 626-27-57; 10a Nte 47; s US$5.50, d US$7.50-9) This pleasant cheapie has clean rooms with fan situated around a leafy patio.

Hospedaje Chelito (☎ 626-24-28; 1a Nte 107; s/d with fan & TV US$15/17, with air-con US$20/24) A short walk from the Cristóbal Colón bus station, Chelito has good-value clean, spacious rooms.

Galerías (☎ 626-44-48; 4a Nte 21; s/d US$33/40; 🍽 🅿 🖳) Smart, new place with eight large, comfortable air-con rooms, all with modem access and attractive bathrooms. There's a café here, too.

Hotel Tapachula (☎ 626-60-60; www.hotel tapachula.com in Spanish; 9a Pte 17; s/d/ste US$56/65/69; 🅿 🍽 🖳) This new glass-fronted luxury hotel is the best sleepery in town. There is a good restaurant and a small pool.

Hotel Esperanza (☎ /fax 625-91-35; 17a Ote 8; s/d incl breakfast US$23/28; 🍽) Opposite the Colón bus station, the Esperanza offers smallish, fairly modern rooms that have a TV and air-conditioning.

Eating
There's a good choice of places around the central plaza.

El Molcajete Taco (2a Nte 95; tacos US$0.50; ✆ breakfast & lunch), near the Colón terminal, has 26 different types of tacos. Wow! **Restaurante Los Jarrones** (☎ 626-11-43; 1a Pte 18; breakfast US$3.50-6.75, mains US$5.75-11.50; 🍽), in Hotel Don Miguel, is perennially popular.

Of the several restaurants on the south side of Parque Hidalgo, **Los Comales Grill** (☎ 626-24-05; Portal Pérez; mains US$4.25-8; ✆ 24hr) is the best.

Getting There & Around
AIR
Aviacsa (☎ 626-14-39; Central Nte 18) and **Aeroméxico** (☎ 800-021-40-10; Central Ote 4) both fly at least twice daily to/from Mexico City. One-way tickets cost around US$160.

Tapachula's airport is 20km southwest of the city off the Puerto Madero road. **Transporte Terrestre** (☎ 625-12-87; 2a Sur 68), charges around US$5 per person from the airport to any hotel in the city, or vice versa.

BUS
The **Cristóbal Colón terminal** (☎ 626-28-81; 17a Oriente), 1km northeast of Parque Hidalgo, operates deluxe and 1st-class buses. The main 2nd-class bus stations are Rápidos del Sur (RS) at 9a Pte 62, and Ómnibus de Tapachula (OT) at 7a Pte 5.

Departures include:
Comitán (via Motozintla; 6hr; 7 buses from Colón, US$9.50)
Escuintla (1hr; 7 buses from Colón, US$3.25; 32 RS buses, US$1.50; 50 OT buses, US$1.50)
Mexico City (TAPO or Norte; 18hr; 12 buses from Colón, US$57-88)
Oaxaca (12hr; 3 buses from Colón, US$22-25)
San Cristóbal de Las Casas (7hr; 3 buses from Colón, US$12)
Tonalá (4hr; 9 buses from Colón, US$9.50-11.50; 32 RS buses, US$7)
Tuxtla Gutiérrez (7hr; 19 buses from Colón, US$16-26; 32 RS buses, US$13)

Buses from the Colón station also go twice daily to Palenque, and daily to Bahías de Huatulco, Pochutla, Puerto Escondido, Cancún, Villahermosa and Veracruz.

TO/FROM GUATEMALA
Two companies run bus services from the Colón station to Guatemala City (and on to

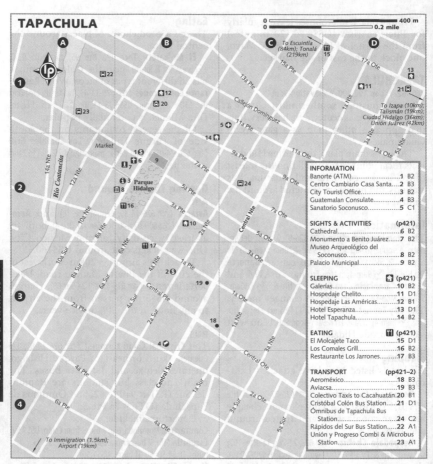

TAPACHULA

other main Central American cities). **Transportes Galgos** (www.transgalgosinter.com.gt in Spanish) goes to/from Guatemala City (US$17, six hours, three daily). **Tica Bus** (www.ticabus.com) leaves at 7am for Guatemala City (US$13, six hours).

For destinations in western Guatemala including Quetzaltenango it's best to get a bus from the border (see below).

CIUDAD HIDALGO & TALISMÁN BRIDGE

It is 37km from Tapachula to the international border at **Ciudad Hidalgo**, opposite Ciudad Tecún Umán in Guatemala, the busier (and more chaotic) of the two border crossings.

The other entry point is closer, 20km from Tapachula, at the **Talismán bridge** opposite El Carmen in Guatemala. Both crossings are open 24 hours and have money-changing facilities. The Guatemalan officials may ask for various (illegal) small charges as you go through.

Getting There & Away

Combis run by Ómnibus de Tapachula head to Ciudad Hidalgo from 7a Pte 5 in Tapachula every 10 minutes between 5:30am and 8:40pm (US$0.90, 30 minutes). Rápidos del Sur buses from 9a Pte 62 in Tapachula cover the same route, leaving every 20 minutes from 5:40am to 6:30pm (US$1). In the opposite direction, combis and bus services run from 7am to around 9pm.

Unión y Progreso combis leave for Talismán from 5a Pte 53 in Tapachula every few minutes, 5:30am to 10:30pm (US$0.80).

You can also catch combis to either border crossing from the street outside the Cristóbal Colón bus station as they leave town. A taxi from Tapachula to Talismán takes 20 minutes and costs around US$7.

Frequent buses leave Ciudad Tecún Umán for Guatemala City (about five hours away) by the coastal slope route through Retalhuleu and Escuintla. From El Carmen there's a *colectivo* taxi service to Malacatán, on the road to Quetzaltenango (Xela, p111). If you are heading for Lago de Atitlán (p89) or Chichicastenango (p105), you need to get to Quetzaltenango first, for which you can get buses at Retalhuleu or Malacatán.

Talismán is also convenient for Quetzaltenango in western Guatemala, with direct buses until around 4pm, but other services here are less frequent.

MEXICO DIRECTORY

This Directory is designed to give you the basics on travel in Mexico, including information on accommodations, activities, Mexican business hours, and embassy and consulate locations. You will also find information on national holidays, media, money, telephone and tips for gay and lesbian travelers.

For information on weights and measures, video systems, electricity and more on photography, see this book's Regional Directory (p433).

ACCOMMODATIONS

Accommodations in Mexico range from hammocks and huts to hotels of every imaginable standard and world-class luxury resorts. Prices are higher in the Yucatán Peninsula than they are in neighboring Tabasco and Chiapas, and they're highest of all in coastal resorts such as Cancún, Playa del Carmen and Cozumel. High season is from December through mid-March with a peak around Semana Santa (Easter Week). Low-season rates are often negotiable and are regularly 25% to 40% lower than tourist

season rates. Wherever possible, high season rates are quoted in this chapter.

During high season, in popular destinations like Cancún, Tulum or Playa del Carmen, it's best to reserve a room in advance or arrive early in the day.

Most organized campgrounds are actually trailer parks, set up for RVs (camper vans) and trailers (caravans), but they're open to tent campers at lower rates. Along the Caribbean coast, you can often rent a hammock and a place to hang it for anywhere from US$4 to US$10.

Cheap and congenial accommodations are often to be found at a *casa de huéspedes*, which are usually family-run with a relaxed, friendly atmosphere.

Mexico specializes in good mid-range hotels where two people can get a room with private bathroom, TV and perhaps air-con for US$30 to US$60. B&Bs, where they exist, are generally attractive, upmarket guesthouses, often aimed at North American tourists. They can be comfortable and enjoyable places to stay.

Room nomenclature can be a bit confusing, especially when you're trying to explain what you'd like to reserve over the phone. A *sencilla* is a room with one double, queen- or king-size bed meant for one or two people. Both the bed and the room are also called *matrimonial* (you can guess the meaning). If you want a room with two beds you need to ask for a *doble* (double). *Dobles* are for two and sometimes four people, yet are priced differently depending on the number of people in the room.

Many showers in cheaper hotels throughout Chiapas use an electrical attachment to the showerhead to heat the water. To avoid electrical shock (and it happens) don't touch the showerhead or the metal pipe to the head and wear rubber-soled sandals so you're not grounded.

ACTIVITIES

The Caribbean is world-famous for its wonderful reefs and clear waters. Great diving locations include Isla Mujeres (p331), Playa del Carmen (p339), Cozumel (p337) and Punta Allen (p346). All of these places are excellent for snorkeling, too. Inland you can dive some of the Yucatán's famed cenotes (limestone sinkholes) near Akumal (p342).

YUCATÁN PENINSULA, TABASCO & CHIAPAS

The Federacion Mexicana de Actividades Subacuaticas (FMAS) is the internationally recognized Mexican equivalent of PADI and NAUI. Other popular watersports along the Caribbean include hydro biking (jet skiing), kayaking and sailing.

Horseback riding to remote villages is popular from San Cristóbal de Las Casas (p396) in Chiapas.

Bird-watching and wildlife viewing are excellent in the region's national parks and biosphere reserves. See p320 for specific information on where to go and what you might see.

BOOKS

Lonely Planet also publishes *Yucatán*, which provides much more in-depth coverage of the three Yucatán Peninsula states. If you are going to be doing some diving or snorkeling, get Lonely Planet's Pisces guide *Diving & Snorkeling Cozumel* – it has beautiful, full-color underwater shots and detailed accounts of the possible dives and dive outfitters. *Caribbean Reef Ecology* (Lonely Planet) brims with bright color photos and introduces its subject with lively text. It's not easy to find, but usually available through online used-book dealers.

John L. Stephen's *Incidents of Travel in Yucatán* is a fascinating account of his travels in the peninsula. First published in 1843, it's still a remarkable read.

BUSINESS HOURS

Stores generally open from 9am to 2pm, close for siesta, then reopen from 4pm to 7pm Monday to Saturday. In particularly hot locales, such as Mérida and Chetumal, stores sometimes take a longer siesta but stay open later in the evening. Some may not open Saturday afternoon.

Most churches are in frequent use and therefore frequently are open. Archaeological sites are usually open 8am to 5pm daily. Most museums have one closing day a week, typically Monday. On Sunday, nearly all archaeological sites and museums are free, and the major ones can get very crowded.

Banks are open Monday to Friday 9am to 1:30pm, though many have begun to keep longer hours and some are open Saturday. For post office hours, see p427.

Many offices and businesses close during major national festivals (opposite and p426).

Typical restaurant hours are 7am or 8am to 10pm, 11pm or midnight. If a restaurant has a closing day, it's usually Sunday, Monday or Tuesday. Cafés typically open from 8am, 9am or 10am to 8pm, 9pm or 10pm daily.

EMBASSIES & CONSULATES

Many Mexican embassies and consulates and foreign embassies in Mexico City have websites. Links to most of them can be found on www.mexicoweb.com.mx in Spanish.

Two particularly useful sites, which have tourist information and data on Mexican visas and tourist permits, are those of the Mexican embassy in Washington, DC (www .embassyofmexico.org) and the Mexican consulate in New York (www.consulmex ny.org).

Mexican Embassies & Consulates

Unless otherwise noted, details are for embassies or their consular sections.

Australia (☎ 02-6273-3963; www.embassyof mexicoinaustralia.org; 14 Perth Ave, Yarralumla, ACT)

Belize (☎ 223-0193; www.embamexbelize.gob.mx; 18 North Park St, Belize City)

Canada Ottawa (☎ 613-233-8988; www.embamexcan .com; 45 O'Connor St, Suite 1500, ON); Consulate Montreal (☎ 514-288-2502; www.consulmex.qc.ca; 2055 rue Peel, bureau 1000, QC); Consulate Toronto (☎ 416-368-2875; www.consulmex.com; Commerce Court West, 199 Bay St, Suite 4440, ON); Consulate Vancouver (☎ 604-684-3547; www.consulmexvan.com; 710-1177 West Hastings St, BC)

France Paris (☎ 01 53 70 27 70; www.sre.gob.mx /francia; 9 rue de Longchamp, 75116); Consulate Paris (☎ 01 42 86 56 20; 4 rue Notre Dame des Victoires, 75002)

Germany Berlin (☎ 030-269-323-332; www.embamex .de; Klingelhöferstrasse 3, 10785 Berlin); Consulate Frankfurt-am-Main (☎ 069-299-8750; Taunusanlage 21, 60325)

Guatemala Guatemala City (☎ 5420-3433; www.sre.gob .mx/guatemala in Spanish; 2a Av 7-57, Zona 10); Consulate Quetzaltenango (☎ 7767-5542; mexicog@yahoo.com .mx; 21a Av 8-64, Zona 3); Consulate Ciudad Tecún Umán (☎ 7776-8181; comexteu@terra.com.gt; 1a Av 4-01, Zona 1)

Ireland (☎ 01-260-0699; www.sre.gob.mx/irlanda; 43 Ailesbury Rd, Ballsbridge, Dublin)

Netherlands (☎ 070-360 2900; www.embamex-nl
.com; Burgemeester Patijnlaan 1930, The Hague)
New Zealand (☎ 04-472-0555; www.mexico
.org.nz; Level 8, 111 Customhouse Quay,
Wellington)
UK (☎ 020-7235-6393; www.embamex.co.uk; 8 Halkin
St, London)
USA Washington, DC (☎ 202-728-1600; www.sre.gob
.mx/eua; 1911 Pennsylvania Ave NW); Consulate Washington, DC (☎ 202-736-1000; consulwas@aol.com; 2827
16th St NW) There are Mexican consulates in many other
US cities, especially in the border states. Check www
.embassyofmexico.org for details.

Embassies & Consulates in Mexico

Embassies are in Mexico City. The follow-
ing is a list of foreign consulates and con-
sular agencies in the Yucatán.
Belize Chetumal (Map p350; ☎ 983-832-18-03;
Av Armada de México 91, Colonia Campestre); Cancún
(Map p326; ☎ 998-887-84-17; Av Náder 34 503B,
Super-Manzana 2A) Belize has a vice consul in Mérida
at the UK's consular office; see UK in this list.
Canada (Map p324; ☎ 983-33-60; fax 983-32-32;
Plaza Caracol No 330, Cancún)
Cuba (Map p326; ☎ 884-3423; cubacancun@prodigy
.net.mx; Calle Pecari 17, Super Manzana 20, Cancún)
France Cancún (☎ 985-29-24; Casa Turquesa, Blvd
Kukulcán Km 13.5); Mérida (☎ 925-28-86; fax 925-
70-09; Calle 33B No 528 btwn Calles 62 & 64)
Germany Cancún (☎ 984-18-98; Punta Conoco 36);
Mérida (☎ 981-29-76; Calle 7 No 217 btwn Calles 20
& 20A, Colonia Chuburna de Hidalgo)
Guatemala Cancún (Map p326; ☎ 883-82-96; Av
Nader 148); Chetumal (☎ 9-832-30-45; Retorno 4,
Casa 8, Fraccionamiento Bahía); Comitán (Map p419;
☎ 9-632-04-91; 1a Calle Sur Pte 26); Tapachula (Map
p422; ☎ 9-626-12-52; 2a Oriente 33); Ciudad Hidalgo
(☎ 969-698-01-84; 5a Calle Ote btwn 1a & 3a Nte)
Netherlands Cancún (☎ 983-02-00; Presidente
Inter-Continental, Blvd Kukulcán Km 7); Mérida
(Map p352; ☎ 924-31-22, ☎ /fax 924-41-47;
pixan@diario1.sureste.com; Calle 64 No 418, btwn
Calles 47 & 49)
UK Cancún (☎ 985-01-00; fax 985-12-25; Royal Caribbean, Blvd Kukulcán Km 16.5); Mérida (☎ 928-61-52;
fax 928-39-62; Calle 58 No 450 at Calle 53, Fraccionamiento del Norte) You can also get information about
travel in Belize in Mérida.
USA Cancún (☎ 983-02-72; fax 983-13-73; 3rd fl, Plaza
Caracol Two, No 320-323, Blvd Kukulcán Km 8.5); Cozumel
(Map p336; ☎ 872-61-52; Villa Mar Mall btwn Avs Rafael
Melgar & 5 Nte); Mérida (☎ 925-50-11, after-hours emergency ☎ 947-22-85; fax 925-62-19; Paseo de Montejo
453 at Av Colón)

FESTIVALS & EVENTS

Mexico's many fiestas are full-blooded,
highly colorful affairs that often go on for
several days and add much spice to everyday life. In addition to the national festivals listed below, each town adds a range
of local saints' days, regional fairs, arts festivals and so on (see individual sections for
information on local festivals). There's also
a national public holiday just about every
month (see p426), often the occasion for yet
further partying.

January
Día de los Reyes Magos (Three Kings' Day or Epiphany;
January 6) This is the day that Mexican children traditionally receive gifts, rather than at Christmas (but some get
two loads of presents!).

February/March
Carnaval (late February or early March) Carnaval, a big
bash preceding the 40-day penance of Lent, takes place
during the week or so before Ash Wednesday (which
falls 46 days before Easter Sunday); it's celebrated most
festively in Mérida.

March/April
Semana Santa Holy Week starts on Palm Sunday
(Domingo de Ramos); most of Mexico seems to be on the
move at this time, especially to the coastal resorts.

September
Día de la Independencia (September 16) Independence Day commemorates the start of Mexico's war for
independence from Spain.

November
Día de Todos los Santos (All Saints' Day; November
1) & **Día de Muertos** (Day of the Dead; November 2)
Every cemetery in the country comes alive as families visit
graveyards to commune with their dead on the night of
November 1–2 and the day of November 2, when the souls
of the dead are believed to return to earth. The souls of
dead children (*angelitos*, little angels) are celebrated the
previous day, All Saints' Day.

December
Día de Nuestra Señora de Guadalupe (December
12) A week or more of celebrations throughout Mexico
leads up to the Day of Our Lady of Guadalupe, the national
religious patron (p317).
Posadas (December 16–24) Nine nights of candlelit
parades reenact the journey of Mary and Joseph to
Bethlehem; more important in small towns than
big cities.

Christmas (December 25) Día de Navidad is traditionally celebrated with a feast in the early hours of December 25, after midnight mass.

GAY & LESBIAN TRAVELERS

Mexico is more broad-minded about sexuality than you might expect, and Cancún has one of the most lively gay scenes in the country. Gays and lesbians do not generally maintain a high profile, but rarely attract open discrimination or violence. Discrimination based on sexual orientation has been illegal since 1999 and can be punished with up to three years in prison.

A good source of information on the Internet is **Gay Mexico Network** (www.gaymexico.net). It includes information on gay-friendly hotels and tours in Mexico. **Sergay** (www.sergay.com.mx) is a Spanish-language magazine and website, focused on Mexico City, but with bar, disco and cruising-spot listings for the whole country. Also worth a look is **PlanetOut** (www.planetout.com). *Gay Mexico: The Men of Mexico*, by Eduardo David, is a portrait of gay culture in Mexico.

HOLIDAYS

The chief Mexican holiday periods are Christmas to New Year, Semana Santa and mid-July to mid-August. Transport and tourist accommodations get heavily booked at these times. Banks, post offices, government offices and many shops throughout Mexico are closed on the following national holidays:

Año Nuevo (January 1) New Year's Day.
Día de la Constitución (February 5) Constitution Day.
Día de la Bandera (February 24) Day of the National Flag.
Día de Nacimiento de Benito Juárez (March 21) Anniversary of Benito Juárez' birth.
Día del Trabajo (May 1) Labor Day.
Cinco de Mayo (May 5) Anniversary of Mexico's 1862 victory over the French at Puebla.
Día de la Independencia (September 16) Commemorates the start of Mexico's war for independence from Spain.
Día de la Raza (October 12) Commemorates Columbus' discovery of the New World and the founding of the mestizo (mixed-ancestry) Mexican people.
Día de la Revolución (November 20) Anniversary of the 1910 Mexican Revolution.
Día de Navidad (December 25) Christmas Day.

At Easter, businesses close usually from Good Friday (Viernes Santo) to Easter Sunday (Domingo de Resurrección).

INTERNET ACCESS

Visiting an Internet café is the easiest way to get online in Mexico. Only the smallest of villages lacks a café, so you'll rarely have trouble finding one.

Going online with your laptop means you will have to hunt down a hotel room with a telephone jack or find a café that offers access or wireless connections. Mid-range and top-end hotels usually have telephone lines in the room, but remember that your portable's modem may not work once you leave your home country (p442).

Only rooms in the most expensive hotels have direct Internet access lines into the rooms. Many B&B or boutique-type hotels have a computer where you can go online for free.

MONEY

Mexico's currency is the peso, usually denoted by the '$' sign. The peso is divided into 100 centavos. Coins come in denominations of five, 10, 20 and 50 centavos and one, two, five, 10 and 20 pesos, and there are notes of 20, 50, 100, 200 and 500 pesos.

The most convenient form of money in Mexico is a major international credit card or debit card. Cards such as Visa, American Express and MasterCard can be used to obtain cash easily from ATMs and are accepted for payment by most airlines, car rental companies, travel agents, many top-end and upper mid-range hotels, and some restaurants and shops. When making a purchase by credit card, you'll normally have to pay a 'foreign exchange' transaction fee of around 2.5%. Be aware that acceptance of cards is erratic in Mexico – American Express cards in particular are not accepted for payment by significant numbers of Mexican businesses. Visa, AmEx or MasterCard stickers on an establishment's door or window in Mexico do not necessarily mean that these cards will be accepted for payment there.

As a backup to credit or debit cards, it's best also to take some traveler's checks and a little cash. US dollars are still the most easily exchangeable foreign currency in Mexico. Euros, British pounds and Canadian dollars, in cash or as traveler's checks, are now accepted by most banks and some *casas de cambio* (exchange houses), but procedures may be a little more time-consuming and acceptance is less certain if you are away from main cities and tourist centers. Your traveler's checks should be a major brand such as American Express or Visa. American Express is recognized everywhere.

PHOTOGRAPHY

Most types of film (with the general exception of Kodachrome slide film) are available in larger cities and resorts. A 36-exposure 100-ASA print film generally costs around US$5 to buy and about the same to process. Processing is usually suitable for snapshots, but you're probably better off waiting to develop your photos until you get home if you're at all finicky.

Many indigenous people, especially in Chiapas, are opposed to having their picture taken. In the town of San Juan Chamula (p401) photography is completely banned inside the church and anywhere in town during rituals. It's also not allowed in the church and churchyard at Zinacantán (p402). You may put yourself in physical danger if you take photos without permission. If in any doubt at all, ask before taking a picture.

POST

An airmail letter or postcard weighing up to 20g costs US$0.80 to north America, US$1 to Europe or South America and US$1.10 to the rest of the world. Items weighing between 20g and 50g cost US$1.30, US$1.50 and US$1.80 respectively. *Certificado* (registered) service costs an extra US$1.50. Delivery times are elastic. Mark airmail items 'Vía Aérea.' An airmail letter from Mexico to the USA or Canada should take somewhere between four and 14 days to arrive. Mail to Europe may take between one to two weeks; to Australasia it's two to three weeks.

Post offices *(oficinas de correos)* are typically open from 8am or 9am to 4pm, 5pm or 6pm Monday to Friday, and 9am to 1pm Saturday. Some post offices that open on Saturdays do so only to sell stamps. You can receive letters and packages care of a post office if they're addressed to the post office's Lista de Correos (Mail List). To claim your mail, present your passport or other identification. Have the sender address the letter as follows:

Tom JONES (last name in capitals)
Lista de Correos
Correo Central
Cancún
Quintana Roo 00000 (post code)
MEXICO

TELEPHONE

Local calls are cheap (about US$0.05 per minute). International calls can be expensive, but needn't be if you call from the right place at the right time.

Internet telephony (calls carried through an Internet server line instead of a telephone line) has made an appearance at some cybercafés in Mexico and can be a lot cheaper than regular phone calls, at around US$0.20 per minute to the USA or US$0.30 a minute to Canada or Europe, though line quality can be very patchy. Internet telephony aside, there are two main types of public telephone service, with broadly similar costs: public card phones, and call offices *(casetas de teléfono* or *casetas telefónicas)* where an on-the-spot operator connects the call for you. A third option is to call from your hotel, but hotels can, and do, charge what they like for this service. It's nearly always cheaper to go elsewhere.

Public card phones are common. Local calls cost about US$0.05 per minute. Calls to another area code within Mexico cost about US$0.40 per minute, while calls to the US and Canada cost about US$0.50. A call to Europe costs approximately US$2 per minute, and to Australia about US$2.50 per minute. The most affordable card phones are those marked with the name of the country's biggest phone company, Telmex. To use a Telmex card phone you need a phone card known as a *tarjeta Ladatel.* These are sold at kiosks and shops everywhere. The cards come in denominations ranging from 10 pesos (about US$0.90) to 500 pesos (US$46).

In some parts of Mexico frequented by foreign tourists you may notice a variety of phones that advertise that they accept credit cards or that you can make easy collect calls to the USA on them. While some of these phones offer fair value, there are others on which very high rates are charged. Be very sure about what you will have to pay before making a call on a non-Telmex phone.

Costs in *casetas de teléfono* (call offices) are broadly similar to those Telmex card phones, and they have the advantages that they eliminate street noise and you don't need a phone card to use them.

Calling Cards

Some calling cards from other countries can be used for calls from Mexico by dialing special access numbers:

AT&T (US ☎ +1-800-462-4240, 01-800-288-2872)
Bell Canada (US ☎ +1-800-123-0200, 01-800-021-1994)
BT Charge Card (UK) (US ☎ +1-800-123-02-44, 01-800-021-6644)
MCI (US ☎ +1-800-674-7000, 01-800-021-1000)
Sprint (US ☎ +1-800-877-8000)

Cellular Phones

The most widespread cellular (mobile) phone system in Mexico is **Telcel** (www.telcel .com in Spanish), with coverage virtually everywhere that has significant population. Telcel has roaming partnerships with systems from many countries, though using a phone from another country in Mexico can be expensive. For information, contact your service provider or visit www.gsm coverage.co.uk.

Many top-end hotels have cell phone rental booths in their lobbies. To purchase a typical new phone with some air time costs around US$200 to US$250. Telcel cards for additional air time are fairly widely available from newsstands and mini-marts.

Prefixes & Codes

If you're calling a number in the town or city you're in, simply dial the local number. To call another town or city in Mexico, dial the long-distance prefix (☎ 01), followed by the area code and then the local number.

For international calls, dial the international prefix (☎ 00), followed by the country code, area code and local number.

To call a number in Mexico from another country, dial your international access code, then the Mexico country code (☎ 52), then the area code and number.

Toll-free & Operator Numbers

Mexican toll-free numbers – all ☎ 800 followed by seven digits – always require the ☎ 01 prefix. You can call these and the ☎ 060 emergency number from Telmex pay phones without inserting a telephone card.

For a Mexican domestic operator, call ☎ 020; for an international operator, call ☎ 090. You can make a collect call *(llamada por cobrar)* through these numbers. For Mexican directory information, call ☎ 040.

TOURIST INFORMATION

Just about every town of touristic interest in Mexico has a state or municipal tourist office. They are generally helpful with maps, brochures and questions, and often some staff members speak English.

You can call the **Mexico Tourism Board** (☎ 55-5250-0123, 800-903-92-00, in US & Canada ☎ +1-800-446-3942; www.visitmexico.com) at any time – 24 hours a day, seven days a week – for information or help in English or Spanish.

Local tourist offices in Mexico are listed in the Information sections of each city or town.

VISAS

All visitors to Mexico should have a valid passport. Citizens of the USA, Canada, the 15 EU countries (pre-EU expansion in 2004), Australia, New Zealand, the Czech Republic, Hungary, Iceland, Israel, Japan, Norway, Poland, South Africa and Switzerland are among those who do *not* require visas to enter Mexico as tourists. The list changes from time to time – check well ahead of travel with your local Mexican embassy or consulate. Visa procedures, for those who need them, can take up to a month.

Those who do not need a visa require only the easily obtained Mexican government tourist card, officially called the Forma Migratoria para Turista (FMT). This is a brief card document that you must fill out and get stamped by Mexican immigration when you enter Mexico and must keep until you leave. It's available at official border crossings, international airports and ports, and often from airlines, travel agencies and Mexican consulates. At

A coconut-juice stand, Cozumel (p335)

The cathedral (p393) in San Cristóbal de Las Casas

Old cannons line the waterfront in Campeche (p375)

Convento de San Antonio de Padua (p366), Izamal

Sailing past a pier in Cancún (p322)

Girls on their way to school, Mérida (p351)

Campeche (p375)

Ballet Folklórico dancers (p351), Mérida.

the US–Mexico border you won't usually be given one automatically; you have to ask for it. The card is valid for up to 180 days, depending on the number the immigration officer gives you upon entering. Be sure you get more than the number of days you plan to stay in the country.

If the number of days given on your tourist card is less than the 180-day maximum, its validity may be extended one or more times, up to the maximum. To get a card extended you have to apply to the Instituto Nacional de Migraciones (INM or immigrations), which has offices in many towns and cities. The procedure will cost around US$20. You'll need your passport, tourist card, photocopies of the important pages of these documents, and, at some offices, evidence of 'sufficient funds.' A major credit card is usually OK for the latter, or an amount in traveler's checks anywhere from US$100 to US$1000, depending on the office.

Because the regulations can sometimes change, it's a good idea to confirm them at a Mexican embassy or consulate before you go. Several Mexican embassies and consulates, and foreign embassies in Mexico, have websites with useful information on tourist permits, visas, travel with minors and so on (see p424), but they don't all agree with each other, so you should back up any Internet findings with some phone calls. The **Lonely Planet website** (www.lonelyplanet.com) has links to updated visa information.

WORK

Mexicans themselves need jobs, and people who enter Mexico as tourists are not legally allowed to take employment. The many expats working in Mexico have usually been posted there by their companies or organizations with all the necessary papers.

English-speakers (and a few German or French speakers) may find teaching jobs in language schools, *preparatorias* (high schools) or universities, or can offer personal tutoring.

A foreigner working in Mexico normally needs a permit or government license, but a school will often pay a foreign teacher in the form of a *beca* (scholarship), and thus circumvent the law, or the school's administration will procure the appropriate papers.

Opportunities exist for unpaid volunteer work (or work that you pay to do) in Mexico, short-term or longer.

The **Council on International Educational Exchange** (www.ciee.org), the **Alliance of European Voluntary Service Organisations** (www.alliance-network.org) and Unesco's **Coordinating Committee for International Voluntary Service** (www.unesco.org/ccivs) all have further information on volunteer programs in Mexico.

For volunteer work in Chiapas, check out **Global Exchange** (www.globalexchange.org) and **Sipaz** (www.sipaz.org). Both do very interesting human rights and peace work in the region, but do require its volunteers to speak Spanish.

TRANSPORTATION IN MEXICO

GETTING THERE & AWAY

Following is general information for the Yucatán region. For specific information on each town or city, see the individual sections. For detailed information on flights and other transport options to and from Cancún, see p448.

Air

Cancún's international airport is unquestionably the busiest airport in the region, with the most local and international flights.

Aerocaribe, Mexicana's regional airline, covers destinations in the Yucatán Peninsula and beyond in a fleet of small and medium-size planes. Some domestic and international flights to or from Cancún stop at Cozumel as well, giving it excellent air service.

Most international flights to Mérida are connections through either Mexico City or Cancún; there is no nonstop international service, except for Aeroméxico's two daily flights from Miami. Domestic service includes half a dozen Aerocaribe/Mexicana flights daily from Mexico City to Mérida, and one or two by Aeroméxico as well. Bonanza has flights to Cancún, Mérida, Palenque, Tuxtla Gutiérrez and Villahermosa.

The small town of Palenque now receives scheduled flights by Aerocaribe from

Bahías de Huatulco, Oaxaca, Tuxtla Gutiérrez, Cancún and Mérida.

Aviacsa, the Chiapan regional airline, has several daily nonstop flights between Tuxtla Gutiérrez and Mexico City, and also makes a daily nonstop run to Tapachula. The major airport for the Tabasco and Chiapas region, however, is at the Tabascan capital of Villahermosa, which has good domestic air links to Mérida, Cancún, Tuxtla Gutiérrez and Mexico City. Grupo TACA flies daily between Cancún and Flores near Tikal.

Land
The most popular and easily accessible entry points to Mexico from Guatemala are at Tecún Umán/Ciudad Hidalgo (p422), entering the Soconusco region of Chiapas from Guatemala's Pacific Slope, and at La Mesilla/Ciudad Cuauhtémoc (p420), entering highland Chiapas from the southwestern highlands of Guatemala. More adventurous routes take you by country bus and riverboat from El Petén, Guatemala, down the Río Usumacinta or the Río de la Pasión to Yaxchilán in Chiapas. For information on these routes, see p187 and p453. Flores to Chetumal (via Belize City) is a popular route in the other direction. For a list of bus lines see p455.

There are almost no international bus lines; usually you take one company's bus to the border, then change to the bus of another company. The exception is Chetumal, which receives buses from Belize, and the special fast service from Flores (Guatemala), near Tikal. See p455 for more on bus travel.

GETTING AROUND
Air
There are some domestic flights that both originate and end within the region of the Yucatán Peninsula, Tabasco and Chiapas (such as Villahermosa to Cancún). The following airlines fly to and from Belize or Guatemala, and from within southern Mexico:

Aerocaribe (in Cancún ☎ 884-20-00; www.aerocaribe .com; airline code QA; hub Cancún)

Aeroméxico (in Cancún ☎ 884-10-97; www.aero mexico.com; airline code AM; hub Mexico City)

Aviacsa (in Cancún ☎ 887-42-11, 800-006-22-00; www.aviacsa.com.mx; airline code 6A; hub Mexico City)

Mexicana (in Cancún ☎ 881-90-90, 800-502-20-00; www.mexicana.com; airline code MX; hub Mexico City)

Aeroméxico and Mexicana are the country's two major airlines. Nearly all of their flights connect through Mexico City, allowing you to fly from most major cities in Mexico, via the capital, to major cities throughout the Yucatán Peninsula, Tabasco and Chiapas. Between the two biggies, their subsidiaries and smaller airlines you can connect to Mexico City from: Cancún (p329), Cozumel (p338), Chetumal (p350), Mérida (p356), Campeche (p378), Villahermosa (p385), Tuxtla Gutiérrez (p390), San Cristóbal de Las Casas (p399) and Tapachula (p421).

Bus
The best way around is generally not by air but overland. In Mexico the buses range from luxury-class air-conditioned cruisers to shabby but serviceable village buses. The various companies offer different levels of comfort and service, usually determined by price: the more you pay, the more comfortable the bus and the faster the trip. Luxury service is available on the busiest long-haul routes.

Except for short runs, it's usually not worth the savings to travel by 2nd-class bus when 1st-class service is available, unless you're really pinching pennies. That said, 2nd-class buses are a great place to soak up local atmosphere (including pitches for health products of dubious value) and they pass through lots of towns that the 1st-class buses blow by.

A general rule of thumb is that 1st class costs about 30% more and takes about a third less time. The price differential can be even smaller; the big differences are in comfort, security and time.

Here's a quick rundown on some of the bus lines of the Yucatán and the destinations they serve:

ADO (Autobuses de Oriente) Long-haul 1st-class routes between Mérida, Campeche, Palenque, Villahermosa, Veracruz, Mexico City and beyond.

ATS (Autotransportes del Sur) Services primarily within the southern peninsula, including frequent buses from Mérida to Cancún and Campeche. It also runs buses to Bolonchén de Rejón, Celestún, Chiquilá, Ciudad del Carmen, Emiliano Zapata, Hecelchakán, Hopelchén, Izamal, Ocosingo, Palenque, Playa del Carmen,

San Cristóbal de Las Casas, Tizimín, Tulum and Valladolid.

Mayab Mostly 2nd-class services between Mérida and Cancún, the Costa Maya, Chetumal, Felipe Carrillo Puerto and many small towns on the peninsula.

Noreste Services to many small towns in the northeastern part of the peninsula, including Río Lagartos and Tizimín.

Omnitur del Caribe (Caribe) Deluxe services between Mérida and Chetumal via Felipe Carrillo Puerto.

Oriente (Autotransportes de Oriente) Frequent buses between Mérida and Cancún, stopping at Chichén Itzá and Valladolid; buses between Mérida and Cobá, Izamal, Playa del Carmen and Tulum.

Super Expresso Deluxe services between Mérida, Cancún, Chetumal and Ticul.

UNO Superdeluxe services on major routes, such as Mérida to Cancún and Mérida to Villahermosa and Mexico City.

Boat

If you plan to head to any of the Caribbean islands, you'll most likely travel by boat. Ferries from Cancún to Isla Mujeres (p334) are cheap (about US$2 per passenger) and quick. Passenger ferries also run hourly from Playa del Carmen (p341) and Cancún to Cozumel (p339), while vehicle ferries run to the island from nearby Puerto Morelos (p339).

Occasionally, boats serve as alternatives to land routes, such as that between Tulum and Punta Allen (p347).

Some of the Caribbean's best snorkeling and dive sites are reachable only by boat, usually as a tour. Similarly, water-based nature tours and tours to visit flamingos at places like Río Lagartos (p374) and Celestún (p365) mean traveling by boat. These trips are often in *pangas* (open fiberglass fishing skiffs), which may or may not have shade canopies. Either way, you should always prepare for an excursion by *panga* by loading on the sunscreen and bringing protection from spray, wind and sun.

Car & Motorcycle

FUEL

At the time of writing fuel costs in Mexico were US$2.04 and US$2.24 per US gallon (US$0.54 and US$0.60 per liter) for the two grades of unleaded gas, Pemex Magna and Pemex Premium. Gasoline prices rise almost on a monthly basis, which is a baffling phenomenon given the fact that Pemex is a government-run enterprise in a country with huge oil reserves.

HIRE

Renting a car is a viable option for getting around the Yucatán if you are visiting some of the more out-of-the-way archaeological sites, especially if you have two or more people to share costs. Assume you will pay a total of US$40 to US$60 per day (tax, insurance and gas included) for the cheapest car offered, usually a bottom-of-the-line Volkswagen or Nissan.

You can book vehicles through the agencies listed in this chapter, or through the foreign offices of the big-name international agencies. Doing the latter can sometimes get you lower rates, but be aware that most of these offices are only affiliated with the companies whose names they bear. In the event of a dispute, the big-name agency may bow out and leave you to try to settle with the Mexican firm.

Here are toll-free (Mexican) telephone numbers for some of the international firms that have offices in Yucatán:

Avis (☎ 01-800-288-88-88)
Budget (☎ 01-800-700-17)
Dollar (☎ 01-800-900-10)
Hertz (☎ 01-800-709-50-00)
National (☎ 01-800-003-95)
Thrifty (☎ 01-800-018-59)

INSURANCE

It is foolish to travel without Mexican liability insurance. If there is an accident and you cannot show a valid insurance policy, you will be arrested and not permitted to leave the locale of the accident until all claims are settled, which could be weeks or months. Mexico's legal system follows the Napoleonic model, in which all persons involved in an incident are required to prove their innocence; trial is by a court of three judges, not by a jury. Your embassy can do little to help you in such a situation, except to tell you how stupid you were to drive without local insurance.

Mexican insurance is sold in US, Guatemalan and Belizean towns near the Mexican border. At the busiest border-crossing points (Tijuana, Mexicali, Nogales, Agua Prieta, Ciudad Juárez, Nuevo Laredo and Matamoros) there are insurance offices that open 24 hours a day.

Prices for Mexican policies are set by law in Mexico, so bargain-hunting isn't easy. Instead of discounts (which cannot be offered), insurance offices offer incentives such as free guidebooks and/or maps, connections to automobile clubs and other treats.

Mexican motor-vehicle insurance policies are priced so as to penalize the short-term buyer with extremely high rates. You may pay almost as much for a one-month policy (which is approximately US$200, on average) as you would for a full year's policy.

Regional Directory

CONTENTS

What exciting things can I do? Where will I sleep? What can I flush? This Regional Directory answers these general questions and more, but for ATMs in Belize, dangers in Guatemala or fiestas in Mexico, see the individual Directories (Guatemala p190; Belize p301; Mexico p423). Also see the title pages of each country for useful 'fast facts' such as country telephone codes and visa requirements.

ACCOMMODATIONS

Where to lay your head is a daily travel challenge involving everything from money and transport connections to climate control and whose company you keep. We've simplified things slightly by arranging accommodation listings from budget to top end, with the top recommendations or most important places leading. In this book, budget means a room for two people ('double')

PRACTICALITIES

- Electrical current and plugs are the same as in the US and Canada: 110V (Mexico and Belize) or 115V to 125V (Guatemala), 60Hz in outlets accepting two flat-pronged plugs.

- Guatemala and Mexico officially use the metric system, but you may find that *onzas* (ounces), *libras* (pounds), *pies* (feet), *millas* (miles) and *galones* (US gallons) are used informally. In Belize, both systems are used – and confused. For example, your rental car odometer and speedometer will be in kilometers and kilometers per hour, but the few road signs indicate distances in miles. When you see quarts and gallons, they are the smaller American measure, not the larger British Imperial measure. For conversion information, see the inside front cover.

- The English-language *Mexico City News* is distributed throughout Mexico wherever tourists gather. US dailies the *New York Times*, *USA Today* and *Miami Herald* (with better coverage of Latin America than most) are usually available in luxury hotels throughout the region, plus bookstores in bigger Yucatán towns like Cancún and Mérida. Where these newspapers are sold, you'll likely stumble across current issues of *Newsweek* and *Time* magazines as well. *Belize First* magazine (www.belizefirst.com) has information of interest to travelers.

- If your hotel room has a television, you'll likely have cable with access to channels like CNN, HBO, MTV, ESPN and the major US networks. Preachers, Madonna, merengue, reggae, salsa and the latest sugar pop/rock from the US is all found on the radio dial here; in Spanish in Guatemala and Mexico, English in Belize.

- Almost all prerecorded videos sold in the region use the NTSC image registration system, incompatible with the PAL and Secam systems.

for under US$30, mid-range is a double for US$30 to US$80 and top end is anything more than US$80 a double; ranges are a bit higher in resort areas like Cancún.

At basic and some mid-range places, reservations will be hard to secure, no matter if it's by fax, phone or email. Don't worry: except for Semana Santa and around Christmas and New Year's Eve, you probably won't need them. Keep in mind that a price spike (from a manageable 10% to an obscene 100% in some cases!) happens during these peak seasons, and again during July and August. Hot destinations like Antigua, Guatemala or San Cristóbal de Las Casas in Chiapas are particularly prone to price hikes.

Speaking of prices, please remember that they change. Use the rates in this book only as a gauge – accommodation owners complain to us all the time about travelers crying for prices listed in the book, as if they're etched in stone. In fact, flashing prices listed here is a far less successful tactic for getting a discount than simply asking for one. Speaking of which, do ask (¿hay una oferta/promoción?). Off season, stays of more than three days, or arriving just to crash overnight before an early morning bus connection, are all opportunities for reduced room rates. Bargaining is less common in Belize than in Guatemala or Mexico.

Camping

The best of fairly limited camping opportunities will be along the Yucatán and Belize coasts, and in parks and reserves throughout the region. Sites usually cost from US$3 to US$7. Sparking conversation and friendship with landowning locals is another way to secure a camping spot. Rare is the individual who will deny you space to camp if asked politely and respectfully. Regardless of where you pitch camp, you should be prepared to do it yourself: carry all your own gear (rentals are rare); bring a stove or rely on raw foods; provision for potable water; and slather on the bug repellent. Choose your spot carefully, as remote camping carries risks. Always be aware of your surroundings and don't leave belongings unattended. Please clean up after yourself.

Hammocks & Cabañas

Hammocks are a comfortable, cheap way to get a good night's sleep out of doors:

bring your own or rent on site. Renting a thatch-covered space and hammock at guesthouses or beach restaurants will cost anywhere between US$2 and US$10, with bathroom and perhaps shower or kitchen use included. The Belizean Cayes, along the Mexican coast and Tikal are all popular spots for hammock hanging. Remember that the trick to spending a comfortable night in a hammock is to lie diagonally; a mosquito net will bring you immeasurable happiness as you snooze out of the bloodsuckers' reach.

At their most basic, cabañas are palm-thatched huts with dirt or sand floors and bunk or twin beds, and may not have electricity or screens. These are popular along Mexican beaches and in Belize and cost anywhere from US$10 to US$35. On the flip side, cabañas in rain-forest reserves and resorts are often deluxe digs done out in honeymoon style with mosquito nets flowing over canopied king-sized beds, refrigerator and mini-bar, plus a porch slung with hammocks overlooking your own slice of jungle.

Homestays

Many students studying Spanish in Guatemala or the Yucatán (Mérida is popular) choose to stay with a local family. Homestays are a guaranteed cross-cultural experience and can be economical – prices in Guatemala, for instance, start at US$35 a week including three meals a day except Sunday. Not all homestays are created alike, however: do your research, paying particular attention to the foreigner-to-family ratio, as some homestays are more like hostels, with many students under one roof.

Hostels & Hotels

Hostels here share those basic characteristics we've come to love (or hate!) the world over: dormitory rooms outfitted with several bunk beds may be single sex or coed, bathrooms and kitchen facilities are shared and there's usually a garden or common room for hanging out. A bunk bed costs US$3 to US$10, depending on where you are. Locking valuables is essential in hostels, as you can't always trust other travelers, no matter how cool they seem; use the lockers provided or padlock your pack zippers. Two or more people traveling together may find it cheaper and more comfortable to stay in a budget hotel rather than a hostel. Alternatively, many hostels also have a few private rooms, if you want the international traveler's scene without a stranger snoring next to you. Only in Mexico will you find hostels associated with Hostelling International.

Budget hotels in the region are called *hospedajes*, *casas de huéspedes*, *posadas* or pensiones. These can range from simple and clean to simply disgusting and cost anywhere from US$6 to US$30 per double. At the lower end, you can expect a sparse but serviceable room with shared bathrooms – always peek at the room and the *baño* (bathroom) especially, when considering a room at rock-bottom prices. Higher-end budget hotels usually offer bigger rooms with private bathroom and fan and might have hammocks, flowering gardens or other atmospheric perks.

Mid-range hotels and motels, often with colonial ambience and architecture, have reliably clean, spacious rooms with aircon or fan. Bonuses like a swimming pool, restaurant or free purified drinking water might also be available.

Top-end accommodation is found in Mexican resorts like Cancún and Cozumel and bigger cities like Villahermosa, Guatemala City and Belize City. Some of the Belizean rain-forest resorts and those on the cayes are positively sybaritic, with prices to match (doubles start at US$80 and soar beyond US$250). If you want to relax in the lap of luxury without paying through the nose, cruise the websites of top-end resorts and hotels for online deals.

ACTIVITIES

Let your travel fantasies guide you to the scads of activities here; for more practical guidance, see individual country directories (Guatemala p190; Belize p301; Mexico p423).

Climbing, Trekking & Hiking

Guatemala's 30 volcanoes offer loads of hiking opportunities, from easy day trips to multiday summit treks. Around Lago de Atitlán (p89), the Cuchumatanes range (accessed from Todos Santos, p125) and the Ixil Triangle (accessed from Nebaj, p110) are other hiking hot spots. In Mexico, the best opportunities are around the Chiapas highlands, near San Cristóbal de Las Casas

(p392). Belize's Mountain Pine Ridge Forest Reserve (p276) offers challenging hiking and some nice trails are cut in the Cockscomb Basin Wildlife Sanctuary (p290). Jungle hikes, some fierce, go to El Mirador, El Perú and other remote Mayan sites in El Petén (p189).

Cycling

Hike and bike tours are popular in and around the Guatemalan highlands, particularly from Antigua (p83), Lago de Atitlán (p83 and p94) and Quetzaltenango (p115), and mountain biking is growing in popularity around San Cristóbal de Las Casas (p396) and western Belize. Your cycling opportunities here are limited only by your stamina and schedule, as the region has lots of good road – and bad drivers, so be careful out there!

Diving & Snorkeling

The best diving – in the world, according to some – is along the barrier reef flanking the shores of Cozumel (p337) and the Belizean cayes (p229 and p287). All types of specialist dives (cenotes, nighttime, shark etc) are also on offer here and snorkelers can jump on dive boats for a cut rate. Cancún (p327) has diving opportunities, though with longer travel times to dive sites than from more atmospheric Cozumel. The Guatemala coast is not good for diving or snorkeling, though you can get certified (including for high-altitude dives) in Lago de Atitlán (p104).

Divers should bring their certification and always check over rental equipment carefully before setting out. Before embarking on a scuba diving, skin diving or snorkeling trip, carefully consider the following points to ensure a safe and enjoyable experience:

- Possess a current diving certification card from a recognized scuba diving instructional agency (if scuba diving).
- Be sure you are healthy and feel comfortable diving.
- Obtain reliable information about physical and environmental conditions at the dive site (eg from a reputable local dive operation).
- Be aware of local laws, regulations and etiquette about marine life and the environment.

CONSIDERATIONS FOR RESPONSIBLE DIVING

The popularity of diving is placing immense pressure on many sites. Please consider the following tips when diving, and help preserve the ecology and beauty of reefs:

■ Do not use anchors on the reef and take care not to ground boats on coral. Encourage dive operators and regulatory bodies to establish permanent moorings at popular dive sites.

■ Avoid touching living marine organisms with your body or dragging equipment across the reef. Polyps can be damaged by even the gentlest contact. Never stand on corals, even if they look solid and robust. If you must hold on to the reef, only touch exposed rock or dead coral.

■ Be conscious of your fins. Even without contact, the surge from heavy fin strokes near the reef can damage delicate organisms. When treading water in shallow reef areas, take care not to kick up clouds of sand. Settling sand can easily smother the delicate organisms of the reef.

■ Practice and maintain proper buoyancy control. Major damage can be done by divers descending too fast and colliding with the reef. Make sure that you are correctly weighted and that your weight belt is positioned so that you stay horizontal. If you have not dived for a while, do a practice dive in a pool before taking to the reef. Be aware that buoyancy can change over the period of an extended trip: Initially, you may breathe harder and need more weight; a few days later, you may breathe more easily and need less weight.

■ Take great care in underwater caves. Spend as little time within them as possible, as your air bubbles may be caught within the roof and thereby leave previously submerged organisms high and dry. Taking turns to inspect the interior of a small cave lessens the chances of damaging contact.

■ Resist the temptation to collect or buy corals or shells. Aside from the ecological damage, taking home marine souvenirs depletes the beauty of a site and spoils the enjoyment of others. The same goes for marine archaeological sites (mainly shipwrecks). Respect their integrity; some sites are even protected from looting by law.

■ Ensure that you take home all your rubbish and any litter you may find as well. Plastics in particular are a serious threat to marine life. Turtles can mistake plastic for jellyfish and eat it.

■ Resist the temptation to feed fish. You may disturb their normal eating habits, encourage aggressive behavior or feed them food that is detrimental to their health.

■ Minimize your disturbance of marine animals. In particular, do not ride on the backs of turtles, as this causes them great anxiety.

■ Dive only at sites within your realm of experience; if available, engage the services of a competent, professionally trained dive instructor or dive master.

■ Be aware that underwater conditions vary significantly from one region, or even site, to another. Seasonal changes can significantly alter any site and dive conditions. These differences influence the way divers dress for a dive and what diving techniques they use.

■ Ask about the environmental characteristics that can affect your diving and how local trained divers deal with these considerations.

Spelunking

Guatemala's Verapaces region is a wonder world of underground caves and rivers,

providing stellar spelunking opportunities in a beautiful setting (p142). Belize is run through with caves, several with wild adventures awaiting you, like tube-caving, overnighting or swimming in a cave near Blue Hole National Park (p282), or hiking to caves in the Mountain Pine Ridge area (p277). 'Speliotourism' is particularly big in Belize, where caves serve as living museums and many of the artifacts and skeletal remains are left as found. Most caves are open to the general public, with no special training required to explore them.

Water Sports

Choices for getting on the water are many. Paddle a kayak provided free by your Cancún resort, white-water raft in the Guatemalan highlands near Cobán (p191), command a canoe along jungle-clad waterways near Río Dulce and Lívingston (p164), or go tubing in the wilds of western Belize (p273). Swimming, sailing, fishing, waterfall romping and hot-spring soaking opportunities also abound. Surfers will be disappointed here: leave the board at home.

Wildlife- & Bird-Watching

The parks, refuges, biosphere reserves and other protected areas throughout the region facilitate independent, world-class wildlife- and bird-watching. Prime places to spot wildlife include the jungle around Tikal (p179) and Palenque (p406), the barrier reef off Belize (p229), the bird colonies of the Yucatán (p374) and Bocas del Polochic (p158), the Cockscomb Basin Wild-

life Sanctuary (p290), and the Río Bravo Conservation Area in Belize (p252). To see manatees or hawksbill turtles, head to Gales Point (p281), also in Belize. Early morning and late afternoon are the best times to watch for wildlife activity anywhere. For more on wildlife viewing, see p10.

CHILDREN

Many big travelers start small and this is a great region to introduce kids to exotic cultural and natural landscapes. Not only will they be received enthusiastically wherever they go, children have the ability to leap across or disregard boundaries many adults find inhibiting. When planning your itinerary, remember to mix in lots of kid-friendly spots (eg Parque Acuático

---

KIDDIE LIT

Traveling with a few region-specific books will help children contextualize their trip and better comprehend the different cultures and customs they're experiencing. Many of the following titles are also available as books on tape: a wonderful diversion on long bus or car rides.

- A new classic in the cross-cultural children's genre, *The Most Beautiful Place in the World*, by Ann Cameron, unflinchingly describes the hardship of a poor boy growing up on Lago de Atitlán. A humanistic tale realistically illustrated, travelers with kids aged six to nine headed to Lago de Atitlán will want to take this along.

- Bringing to life Mayan myths and motifs using stunning cut-paper illustrations, the *Rain Player*, by David Wisniewski, is the story of a young Yucatán superhero doing battle with the gods; ages five to nine.

- The *Corn Grows Ripe*, by Dorothy Rhoads and illustrated by Jean Charlot, is an inspiring tale of how a young Mayan boy overcomes life's adversity in the Yucatán; ages seven to 10.

- For a charming interpretation of a classic folktale that helps explain the Mayan world vision, check out *Maya Moon*, by Marianne Mitchell. The illustrations by Z John Martinez complement the story well; ages five to seven.

- *Abuela's Weave*, by Guatemalan writer Omar S Castaneda, is a simple story that addresses complex issues in modern indigenous life including maintaining traditions, handmade vs machine-made weavings and the importance of family in the community; ages four to eight.

- *Trouble Dolls: A Guatemalan Legend*, written by Suzanne Simons and vibrantly illustrated by Diego Isaias Hernández Méndez, is a terrific introduction to Guatemalan customs for small travelers. A Maya pronunciation guide, recipes and how to use those ubiquitous trouble dolls are sure to engage; ages nine to 12.

- A fable that draws on concepts from the *Popol Vuh*, Jan Wahl's *Once When the World Was Green* will excite kids with its fabulously rich illustrations, rendered by Fabricio Vandenbroeck; ages seven to 10.

- Part myth and part moral, the *Hummingbird King*, by Palacios, weaves an interesting tale about the Maya belief system and how otherworldly elements are easily incorporated into contemporary life; ages nine to 12.

- The youngest travelers can familiarize themselves with indigenous gods, games and dances while keeping entertained with *A Coloring Book of Incas, Aztecs and Mayas*.

Xocomil in Guatemala, p129, the zoo at Parque-Museo La Venta near Villahermosa, p384, or tubing or horseback riding near San Ignacio, p269), as the ruin circuit can elicit big yawns from young 'uns after a while. Sticking around a town for a spell, giving kids time to acclimatize and make friends, is another itinerary idea; most Spanish schools have instruction for kids, plus culture classes like dance or weaving.

Main attractions are bound to excite kids and their imaginations, including snorkeling in the Belizean cayes, horseback riding in the Chiapas highlands, a jungle-river ride in Guatemala, or spotting toucans or macaws in a wildlife sanctuary. Cancún (p322) and similar resort areas are chock full of stuff for kids to do. Other activities like shopping at colorful markets, visiting a Mayan ritual site (eg caves or where Maximón calls home, p98), and partaking of festivals like the one featuring giant kites (p193) or men flying around atop a tall pole (p108), both in Guatemala, will prove unforgettable.

Practicalities

Cribs, cots and high chairs will be available at most mid-range and top-end places, but budget travelers will have to play it by ear, being ready to improvise if need be. Put some thought into how you'll move about the region: eg renting from an international car agency if you'll need a car seat, splitting long bus journeys over two days and mixing boat and/or plane travel with bus trips to break monotonous hauls. Diapers (nappies) are widely available in coastal Mexico and Belize, less so in Guatemala and more rugged parts of Mexico, so you should stock up in major cities in these areas. Bring from home any specific products you rely on, such as creams, sunblock, nonperishable snacks or medicine. Public breastfeeding is best done discreetly.

Children usually qualify for discounts on airfares, bus tickets and sometimes site admission. It's always worth asking.

Pay careful attention to heat-related health issues, making sure your children stay hydrated and wear sunblock and hats; for more, see p468. Lonely Planet's *Travel With Children* contains a wealth of first-hand practical experience, sprinkled with on-the-road anecdotes.

CLIMATE CHARTS

Thanks to altitude variations and micro-climates, you can usually find patches of agreeable weather somewhere no matter the time of year, but be mindful of hurricane season, which officially runs from June to November. The worst storms usually make landfall in October and November. For more weather planning tips, see p13.

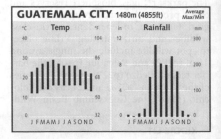

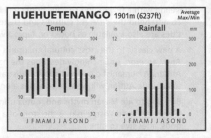

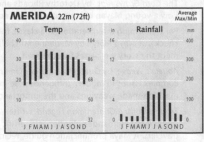

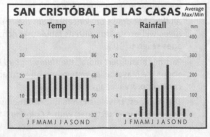

COURSES

Guatemala is one of the Western Hemisphere's top spots to learn Spanish. There are hundreds of schools, classes are cheap, and you can tailor a program to suit your needs and even connect with volunteer work through your school. What's more, you can choose from several locations including ever (some say over) popular Antigua (p84), Quetzaltenango (p115), around Lago de Atitlán (p101), near Flores (p171), or in the mountain town of Todos Santos (p125). The last is the place to go to take courses in Mam, the Mayan language spoken up this way. More expensive Spanish courses are also offered in Playa del Carmen, Mérida and San Cristóbal de Las Casas (the last is fast becoming a traveler favorite, p396), if you prefer to study in Mexico.

Most schools also offer a wide variety of cultural courses (eg traditional weaving, dance or cooking classes) and can arrange homestays and provide volunteer opportunities. The combination of learning and doing good is increasingly popular among travelers wishing to immerse themselves in the culture, make new friends and give something back to the host country. See the Guatemala Directory (p191) for more information on Spanish courses in that country.

CUSTOMS

Most travelers won't have to think twice about customs, as there are only a few things which excite border officials: drugs and paraphernalia, weapons, fruits, vegetables and plants, large amounts of currency, artifacts, automobiles and other expensive items that might be sold while you are in the country. Don't carry illegal drugs or any sort of firearms across any of the region's borders.

Normally, customs officers won't look seriously in your luggage and may not look at all. Some will hedge for a 'tip' so as to spare you the delay and hassle of a search. Valuable items like expensive cameras, electronic gizmos or jewelry may be seen as leverage or be deemed as liable for duty at the discretion of the customs officer. Be prepared and be firm but flexible. Whatever you do, keep it all formal and polite. Anger, surliness or rudeness can get you thrown out of the country, into jail, or worse.

Duty free limits are as follows:

- Guatemala – 80 cigarettes or 99 grams of tobacco; 1.5L of alcohol
- Belize – 200 cigarettes, 250 grams of tobacco or 50 cigars; 1L of alcohol
- Mexico – 400 cigarettes, 250 grams of tobacco or 50 cigars; 3L of alcohol

DANGERS & ANNOYANCES

Traveling in the region demands caution, particularly in Guatemala and border areas. The 36-year-long guerrilla war in Guatemala is over, but that danger has been replaced by an alarming rise in the general crime rate. There have been incidents of rape, robbery, carjacking and even murder of foreign tourists. While these incidents occur at random and are not predictable, in 2004 the Guatemalan government established a 'red zone map', identifying the riskiest areas for tourists and beefing up the police presence in those zones. The tourist police force was increased from 325 to 800 and concentrated in Guatemala City (the international airport and Zona Viva), on the highway to Antigua and around Volcán de Fuego, on the roads to Tikal, Lago de Atitlán and Río Dulce and on the borders shared with Mexico, El Salvador and Honduras. There has also been episodic violence (carjackings and rape recently) on the Belizean side in the Cayo district. Hiking around Lago de Atitlán is another high-risk area; verify local conditions before deciding to set out.

Pickpocketing, bag slashing and other types of robberies are another danger here, as is nighttime bus travel, which is generally not worth the risk. Your best defense against crime is prevention. Talking to other travelers, inquiring at local tourist offices and participating on the Thorn Tree, Lonely Planet's virtual travel community (www.lonelyplanet.com), will be your best source of up-to-date information. Your country's foreign affairs department carries updates and warnings as well, though they can make it sound scarier than it actually is: **Australia** (☎ 1300 139 281; www.dfat .gov.au); **Canada** (☎ 800-267-8376; www.dfait-maeci .gc.ca); **UK** (☎ 0870-606-0290; www.fco.gov.uk); **USA** (☎ 202-647-5225; http://travel.state.gov). Heed your intuition and revamp your itinerary if, in your opinion, the risk outweighs the reward. Female travelers might consider taking a self-defense course, which will serve at home as well as on the road.

While you listen to the awful things that have befallen travelers in this region, remember that hundreds of thousands of people travel here annually without incident. Chances are you will too.

Robbery & Theft

Robbery, pickpocketing and camera- or purse-snatching is a danger in Guatemala City, Antigua, Chichicastenango, Belize City, Mérida and beach areas. Foreign tourists are particularly singled out for theft as they are presumed to be carrying cash and valuables. If you are a robbery victim, you'll likely have to present a police report to your insurance company (see p442). Tell Spanish-speaking officers: 'Yo quisiera poner una acta de un robo' (I'd like to report a robbery). This should make it clear that you merely want a piece of paper and aren't going to ask the police to do anything active.

Taking these commonsense precautions will minimize risk:

- Only hit the streets, beach etc with the money, documentation and valuables that you'll be in immediate need of. Leave the rest in a sealed, signed envelope in your hotel's safe, and obtain a receipt for the envelope. If your hotel doesn't have a safe, secrete your money and valuables in several different stashes among your locked luggage (an airtight baggy in the toilet tank works too) in your room, rather than carrying them with you.
- A bag or purse in plain sight is a slash target; at ticket counters, phone booths and anywhere you need to put your bag down, place it between your feet.
- Wear a money belt or a neck pouch underneath your clothing with your valuables. A small amount of ready money in a pocket or bag serves for small purchases.
- Don't flaunt jewelry, expensive-looking watches or cameras.
- Be aware of current scams like the soiling-your-clothes ploy whereby pickpockets (sometimes in teams) distract the victim by 'accidentally' soiling him or her (with mustard, ice cream or the like), then help clean the victim off and out. In a variation, a setup person will spit at, sneeze on or throw a noxious substance (eg dog shit) on you while the other nicks your wallet.
- Do not wander alone down empty city streets or in isolated areas, particularly at night. Above all, steer clear of lonely beaches.
- When using ATMs (cash machines), keep alert to people nearby. Don't accept help from strangers when using ATMs.
- Do not leave any valuables visible in your vehicle when you park in a city.
- On buses, keep valuables on your person and stay vigilant.
- Take extreme care when camping on beaches and in the countryside, as lonely campsites are a target; try to verify where it's safe(r) to pitch camp.
- When paying for something, wait until all of the change has been counted out before picking it up. A favorite ruse of dishonest ticket clerks is to hand over the change slowly, bit by bit, in the hope that you'll pick it up and go before you have it all.
- Credit-card fraud, like double billing and sticky fingers among hotel personnel with access to safe-deposit boxes, does happen. Travelers report this type of scam happening in Guatemala City. Check credit-card records carefully upon returning home.

DISABLED TRAVELERS

This is a challenging destination for disabled travelers, especially those with mobility problems One great place for the mobility challenged is Posada Margherita near Tulum (p345). Hotel Camino Real (p389) in Tuxtla Gutiérrez also has wheelchair access. The classic layout of Mayan cities, with large, grassy expanses and buildings spread over several kilometers, makes getting around difficult. Colonial towns with cobblestone streets, plus crowded, uneven or nonexistent sidewalks and the paucity of ramps (Antigua, Cancún and central Mérida being the notable exceptions), compound the problem. Public transportation will be untenable for all but the hardiest travelers in wheelchairs, as many buses are uncomfortable and crowded and boats may be narrow or rickety; traveling with a buddy helps or renting a car (and driver if need be).

Mobility International USA (www.miusa.org) advises disabled travelers on mobility issues, offers exchange programs (in Guatemala,

Belize and Mexico) and publishes some useful books. In the UK, try the **Royal Association for Disability and Rehabilitation** (www .radar.org.uk) and in Australia/New Zealand, the **National Information Communication Awareness Network** (www.nican.com.au). Also worth consulting are **Access-Able Travel Source** (www .access-able.com) and **Accessible Journeys** (www .disabilitytravel.com). The **Council on International Educational Exchange** (CIEE; US ☎ +1-888-268-6245, +1-212-822-2600; www.ciee.org) can help disabled people interested in working, studying or volunteering outside their home countries.

For a list of services available to disabled travelers by airline, go to www.everybody .co.uk/airindex.htm.

EMBASSIES & CONSULATES

Please reference the individual country directories for embassy and consulate lists for Guatemala (p193), Belize (p302) and Mexico (p424). General embassy information can be found at www.embassyworld.com.

It's important to realize what your own country's embassy can and can't do if you get into trouble while visiting a foreign country. Generally, it won't be much help in emergencies where you're remotely at fault. Remember, you are bound by the laws of the country you are in. Your embassy will not be sympathetic if you end up in jail after committing a crime locally, even if such actions are legal in your own country.

In genuine emergencies, you might get some assistance. For example, if all your money and documents are stolen, it might assist with getting a new passport, but a loan for onward travel is out of the question. Most embassies and consulates, however, can help you by contacting relatives or friends, or by suggesting reliable doctors, clinics etc. If you plan to travel in unstable areas or to stay in a country longer than a month or two, it's a good idea to register with your consulate so that they can warn you of dangers if necessary or contact your family should something go seriously awry.

GAY & LESBIAN TRAVELERS

News flash: this part of Latin America isn't too keen on the gay scene. While anything goes in Cancún, the rest of the region blends machismo, religious beliefs, and ignorance and fear regarding HIV and AIDS to make it pretty unwelcoming for gay, let alone transgender, folks. Men, especially, should err on the side of caution, enjoying themselves discreetly and privately; public displays of affection are out, guys. How sad to have to write that, but the possibility of harassment, verbal and physical, against homosexuals is real. Lesbians generally fall under the antigaydar and should have an easier time of things.

Scenes

You'll find at least one gay bar in bigger cities, which usually serves as a meeting and greeting space for the entire community. Cancún is the Christopher St of Mexico, with gay bars, discos, plus a cabaret with drag shows; gay nightlife in Playa del Carmen swirls around Quinta Avenida and the gay beaches are a 40-minute walk north of the town center. In Guatemala, your choices for gay nightlife are in Guatemala City or Antigua. For a gay time out in Belize, head to…Cancún. More detailed information on each destination can be found in the Guatemala (p193), Belize (p302) and Mexico (p426) Directories.

Resources

Cancún notwithstanding, websites and magazines devoted to gay travel are slim on region-specific information. In this regard, travel agencies catering to the gay community might be your best bet. Some good websites include the following:

www.outandabout.com Links on Cancún, Playa del Carmen and Guatemala; information on gay tours, plus gay guides, including the *International Gay Phrase Book*.

www.thegully.com Politically charged gay zine in English and Spanish, with interesting Central America coverage (for lesbians too!) on its Americas link.

www.rainbownetwork.com Travel section has a gay guide to Cancún, plus a useful forum with informative, searchable posts from travelers who have been around.

www.gay.com Its travel page has limited info on Belize, better stuff on Guatemala and oodles of useful tidbits on Cancún and Mérida.

www.indiana.edu/~arenal/ingles.html Arenal Lesbigay homepage, in English and Spanish, has news stories and country-by-country reports of Latin American countries.

Additional general information on gay and lesbian travel in Latin America can be obtained through the US or Australian offices of the **International Gay & Lesbian Travel Association** (IGLTA; www.iglta.com), an organization of over 1200 companies that serves travelers worldwide.

Another useful resource is the **International Gay & Lesbian Human Rights Commission** (IGLHRC; www.iglhrc.org), which addresses human-rights violations worldwide.

HOLIDAYS

Major holiday periods to consider when trip planning include Semana Santa (Easter Week; Palm Sunday to Easter Sunday in March or April), Christmas to New Year's, and July and August. At these times, prices rise, hotels fill up and tourist density reaches a maximum. Consider making reservations ahead of time if you'll travel during these periods. For holiday hours and closures in each country, see the individual directories.

INSURANCE

A travel insurance policy to cover theft, loss and medical problems is a good idea. Some policies specifically exclude dangerous activities, which can include scuba diving, motorcycling, even trekking.

You may prefer a policy that pays doctors or hospitals directly rather than you having to pay on the spot and claim later. If you have to claim later, ensure you keep all documentation. Check that the policy covers ambulances or an emergency flight home.

See also the information on insurance on p461 and p457.

INTERNET ACCESS

In big to medium towns, Internet cafés are ubiquitous and cheap (US$1 to US$2 an hour), so you'll rarely have a problem connecting here. Smaller towns are the exception and far-off places like the Cayes charge an arm and a leg – up to US$12 an hour – so plan accordingly.

Most travelers make constant use of internet cafés and free Web-based email such as Yahoo (www.yahoo.com) or Hotmail (www.hotmail.com). Another option for collecting mail through cybercafés is to open a free ekit web-based email account online at www.lonelyplanet.ekit.com.

To access a specific account of your own, you'll need to know your incoming (POP or IMAP) mail server name, your account name and your password. Get these from your Internet service provider (ISP) or network supervisor.

If you're traveling with a notebook or handheld computer, be aware that your modem may not work once you leave your home country. The safest option is to buy a reputable 'global' modem before you leave home, or buy a local PC-card modem if you're spending an extended time in any one country. A second issue is the plug: all countries here use 110V to 125V, two-pronged, flat plugs like those found in the US. Thirdly, unless you're sporting a completely wireless system, you'll have to hunt down a hotel room with a phone jack to plug into – or find a jack you can use somewhere else.

If you're hell-bent on traveling with a laptop, consider using a local ISP (both Guatemala and Mexico have reliable services, see p194), unless you already subscribe to an ISP with local access numbers like AOL or CompuServe. For more information on traveling with a portable computer, see www.teleadapt.com. See Internet Resources in the Getting Started chapter (p16) for some interesting regional websites to start on.

LEGAL MATTERS

Police officers in these countries are often part of the problem rather than the solution, so the less you have to do with local law enforcement, the better.

As a gateway to the great market to the north, illegal drugs float around this region with regularity and you would be smart to 'just say no.' Don't buy, sell, use or carry drugs or associate with people who do. Penalties are severe throughout the region, even for possession of small amounts (a few joints can land you in a Mexican jail for 10 years. Now *that's* a buzz kill!). Foreigners, seen as easy, lucrative marks, are sometimes set up by dealers, cops or the two in collusion in hopes of attaining a bribe. If you are caught holding, using, buying or selling, suggesting to 'work things out' with some financial stimulation might be your best first defense.

If arrested, you have the right to contact your embassy or consulate. Consular officials can tell you your rights, provide lists of local lawyers, monitor your case, make sure you are treated humanely, and notify your relatives or friends – but they can't get you out of jail. Any doubts? See the film *Midnight Express* – grossly exaggerated, perhaps, but it gives you an idea.

MAPS

International Travel Maps (US ☎ +1-604-879-3621; www.itmb.com) publishes a series of useful titles for the region including *Guatemala* (1:500,000), which also covers portions of neighboring Chiapas, Tabasco, Belize and Honduras; *Yucatán Peninsula* (1:1,000,000), which extends to Tabasco, Chiapas, Belize and El Petén (northern Guatemala); and *Belize* (1:350,000). If you're not a preplanner, not to worry: these are widely sold in tourist shops throughout the region for about US$10. Also see individual country directories (Guatemala p194, Belize p303 and Mexico p428).

MONEY

Due to the tendency for local currencies to fluctuate from mildly to wildly, all prices in this book are quoted in US dollars.

Your best strategy for paying your way around the region is to carry a debit and/or credit card, a backup of traveler's checks to be safe and some cash dollars for the unexpected. See p57, p205 and p314 for sample costs and general budget considerations. For ideas on saving money, see p15. Tips on concealing (and keeping) your money safe are in the Dangers & Annoyances section (p439).

ATMs

Except for small towns and out of the way places, ATMs on the Visa/Plus or MasterCard/Cirrus networks are plentiful. Withdrawing money from an ATM (cash machine or *cajero automático*) is usually the easiest and most reliable way of getting cash. It can also be the most economical.

If you rely on ATMs, bring two cards in case one is lost or stolen and keep an emergency phone number for your bank in a separate place. Many issuing banks charge a fee for international transactions; check the policy before leaving home.

To check out worldwide MasterCard/Cirrus ATM locations, visit www.mastercard.com; for Visa/Plus ATM locations, see www.visa.com.

Cash

The wise traveler always has some US dollars tucked away just in case. Cash is king if a national holiday takes you by surprise, the ATM is out of money or you're stranded at a crossroads. It can be changed virtually anywhere, making it particularly handy at borders where bank facilities might not be available. Some businesses, especially in Belize, accept cash dollars no questions asked. Always carry enough cash when heading into remote areas, where smaller notes in local currency are preferred as change is hard to come by.

Credit Cards

Plastic money – generally Visa or MasterCard – is useful for several reasons when traveling. First, you can use it to get cash advances at banks and even some ATMs. Second, it can be used in emergencies, for splurges or to purchase big-ticket items like air tickets. Third, it can be shown to demonstrate 'sufficient funds' when entering a country. Last, since the amount you actually pay your credit-card company depends on when they bill you and the current exchange rate (rather than when you made the purchase), you can save some money with a little micro-leveraging.

Now the down side. International credit-card transactions usually carry fees (typically 1% to 3%) and the bank giving you a cash advance might also charge a fee. Some businesses pass on fees to consumers in the form of higher prices (25% higher is not unheard of), so it can be costlier to pay for goods and services by credit card instead of cash. Some places in the region are still not comfortable with credit-card technology and transactions can be slow. Fraud is another potential pitfall (see p439).

Exchanging Money

Money is exchanged at banks everywhere and also at *casas de cambio* (exchange houses) in Mexico. For practical purposes, US dollars are the currency to carry, as only Belize and touristy Mexico know a euro from a pound sterling or Canadian dollar. Make sure you have enough money to make it through Sundays, holidays and across borders. Big hotels are a safe bet for exchanging money when banks are closed, but the exchange rate won't be as good.

Changing money on the street really only happens at border crossings, where you'll be mobbed by changers angling for your business. Stay cool, try to know the official exchange rate when you open negotiations, double-check the math (even if the person is using a calculator, as they're sometimes fixed) and always count every bill before concluding business. When crossing borders, try to leave one country with as little of its currency as possible, as it will be hard to change and devaluate immediately when you cross into the next country.

International Transfers

It happens: you're on the road and you run out of money. To arrange a wire transfer in 24 hours or less, you can use **Western Union** (in the US ☎ +1-800-325-6000; www.westernunion.com). They charge a 5% to 10% fee, but it's super convenient to arrange either online or at one of their thousands of offices worldwide. Electronic money transfers from bank to bank are also possible but take longer and involve cumbersome bureaucracy.

Tipping & Bargaining

In most restaurants a 10% tip is expected. In Cancún and Cozumel, 15% is more the going rate and in cheaper eateries like *cafeterías* and *comedores*, tipping is optional, though you might follow the local lead and leave some spare change. If you've stayed three nights or more in the same digs, tipping the person who kept your room clean (assuming they did!) is good form. Again, 10% of your room bill is about right. Tour guides should be tipped, especially on longer trips; 10% is appropriate.

From *hamacas* to *huipiles*, bargaining is big sport in the markets here. Sellers expect shoppers to bargain, and with some skill and good humor, you might slash the original price by half or even two-thirds. Artist cooperatives however, where the money ostensibly stays in the community, usually have set prices. Except in Guatemala, hotel prices are generally fixed, though you can angle for a deal out of season; for other money-saving ideas see p15.

Traveler's Checks

Traveler's checks in US dollars, especially American Express, Visa or Thomas Cook, will be the easiest to change. This can be a time-consuming process, so don't leave it until moments before the bus departure. As with almost everything in Latin America, tending to bank and other official business on weekday mornings is sound strategy.

The inherent utility of traveler's checks is that they can be replaced in case of loss or theft. Keep a separate transaction record and receipts to facilitate replacement.

PHOTOGRAPHY & VIDEO

Film stores, pharmacies and hotels all sell film, though you may not find the brand or type you like without a hunt. B&W and *diapositiva* (slide film) is hard, but not impossible, to find. Expect to pay a dollar or two more than you would in North America or Europe for film. There are quick processing labs in the main cities, though quality can vary, so you might consider waiting until you return home to develop your shots.

Videos for sale in the region conform to the NTSC image registration system. VHS and mini DV tapes are sold in film stores and some pharmacies in main cities and heavily touristed areas. Many archaeological sites charge a 'video fee' for folks wishing to film their visit; expect to shell out up to US$20 for the right.

Etiquette & Restrictions

Most people in the region won't mind having their picture taken – if you ask first. Increasingly, you will be asked to pay for the photo. This is especially true in areas that see heavy tourist traffic. Many locals have grown tired of being treated like living art or zoo animals and want to be compensated for being 'framed.'

If you intend to take lots of people pictures, consider bringing a Polaroid camera along with your main unit. Presenting strangers with photos of themselves can ease the tension they may feel about being photographed. Digital cameras, with their instant gratification, will bring rounds of smiles too.

Common sense and decency are the rule of the day. Ask permission before snapping away at anything military, religious or close up and personal. And keep in mind that there are a few locations where photography is forbidden, like the village of San Juan Chamula (p401) outside San Cristóbal de Las Casas, other villages nearby, the church of Santo Tomás (p107) in Chichicastenango and many Mayan ritual sites. If local people make any sign of being offended, you should put your camera away and apologize immediately, both out of decency and for your own safety.

It is illegal to take pictures in Mexican airports and of police stations and penal institutions. Also, many police officers do not like being photographed, and they have the authority to arrest you for photographing them without authorization. When in doubt, it's best to ask before you shoot.

SOLO TRAVELERS

There are always good parts and bad parts about traveling solo and that's the story here. The good part is there are so many interesting things to do, you won't get bored. Studying Spanish, volunteer work, hostel arrangements, beach culture and lively social scenes along the Gringo Trail mean you won't have problems meeting other people should you want to either.

The not-so-good news is the safety situation, which requires travelers to be on their toes at all times. Since much of the crime is opportunistic, a solo traveler is viewed as an easier mark, and indeed, has no one watching their back (or their pack). Be especially vigilant in crowds, in lonelier parts and whenever your travel savvy is less than optimum: after long bus trips, orienting yourself in a strange city, leaving a bar or at night. Because single rooms cost more per person than doubles or triples, soloists looking to save cash will need to sleep dormitory-style or hook up with others to cut costs.

TELEPHONE

Reliable local and international telephone service is available regionwide. Street pay phones, call centers, hotels and Internet cafés are the most common places to make calls. Internet telephony (where calls are carried over an Internet server line not a phone line) has debuted in Mexico and Guatemala and is supercheap: about half the price of a normal telephone call, but it's about half as reliable. Phone rates are usually cheaper during nights and weekends; you can also cut your costs by calling collect (reverse charge) or making a quick international call to give your party a number where they can call you back. Each country has its specific wackiness when it comes to calling in, out or around. Please see individual Directories for all the details (Guatemala p195; Belize p304; Mexico p427).

You can rent mobile phones in Guatemala (p195), Belize or Mexico (p428) for reason-

able rates. Fax service is also widely available in bigger towns; look for the 'Fax' sign.

Country codes are Guatemala ☎ 502, Belize ☎ 501 and Mexico ☎ 52.

TIME

North American central standard time (GMT/UTC minus six hours) is the basis of time throughout the region. Belize and Guatemala, plus Yucatán villages around Felipe Carrillo Puerto and the Marqués de Comillas area of eastern Chiapas, do not observe daylight saving (or 'summer') time. The rest of Mexico does, turning clocks ahead one hour in April and back an hour in October. See the World Time Zones map (p469).

TOILETS

To paraphrase WC Fields, never pass up the opportunity to use a toilet; you don't know when you might next get the chance. Hotels, restaurants, museums and bus stations are all prime potty spots (sometimes charging US$0.15 or so). Toilet paper is rarely provided and travelers in this part of the world know to carry it in their daily kit – some learn the hard way.

You can't flush anything, including toilet paper, down Guatemalan toilets (and some Mexican ones too) – that's what the wastebasket by your side is for. If not, drop it on the floor like those who preceded you. You can flush in Belize, where the toilets are usually nice, modern affairs.

TOURIST INFORMATION

Each country has a national tourism board providing information and assistance. In Mexico, it's **Sectur** (☎ 800-903-92-00; www.visit mexico.com), with a 24-hour help line in English and Spanish and offices around the country; in Belize it's the **Belize Tourism Board** (BTB; ☎ 223-1913; www.travelbelize.org), with offices in most large towns; and in Guatemala it's **INGUAT** (☎ 801-464-8281; www.mayaspirit.com .gt), also with a 24-hour assistance line and several offices countrywide. In Mexico and Guatemala, these resources may be complemented by regional, municipal or private-enterprise tourism agencies.

VISAS

If you attend to one bureaucratic detail before you hit the road, it should be making sure your passport is not soon to expire (all travelers, except those from the US or Canada, must have at least six months until their passport expires to enter Mexico, for example) and verifying what visas, if any, you'll need to move among Ruta Maya countries. Visitors from Australia, Canada, the EU, New Zealand and the US do not need visas to enter any of the countries covered in this book, including Honduras. At the time of writing, visitors from pre-expansion EU countries still needed visas. Swiss and Japanese visitors need visas to enter Belize. Please see the individual directories for visa specifics, length-of-stay regulations and extension options (Guatemala p196; Belize p304; Mexico p428).

WOMEN TRAVELERS

Though in great part gracious and endearing, the land of the Maya occasionally feels like the land of the Macho. Indigenous areas see less machismo in general, but attempts to chat you up, catcalls and come-ons are part of the scenario here, and can become tiresome. This is especially true for women traveling solo who have to shoulder the burden alone and are somehow seen as lacking (a man, a husband, a friend); why else would they be on their own? Compounding the problem is the general perception that foreign women are easy. While uninvited attention leads to interesting conversation or friendship once in a while, there are steps you can take to minimize those out-of-the-blue chats, leaving you to choose with whom you'd like to speak:

- **Avoid eye contact** – meeting eyes can be an invitation to talk; wear sun glasses if that makes you more comfortable.
- **Move with confidence** – projecting a degree of self-assurance is important for well-being as well as safety, but don't confuse confidence with aggression.
- **Dress modestly** – we're not talking convent wear here, but donning a bra is a very good idea and unwanted come-ons should drop proportionately with your hem line.
- **Just say no** – this little word, spoken coolly, confidently and consistently, can deflect or derail guileful intentions.
- **Invent a husband, brother, lover or friend** – female travelers can wear wedding bands to indicate they're unavailable (though some men couldn't care and will carry on any-

way). If things get uncomfortable, speak of a brother, lover or male friend who is just about to make an appearance.
- **Observe local gender guidelines** – don't challenge a man's masculinity, allowing men to 'save face,' especially in public; don't go drinking alone in a *cantina*; avoid isolated beaches; and skip the hitchhiking.
- **Watch your drink** – instances of drugging drinks, snacks, cigarettes and gum with the odorless drug scopolamine (*burandanga* or *borachera* in Spanish) have been reported in Belize. Always mind your drink and don't accept food or beverages from strangers.
- **Watch out for your traveling sisters** – sometimes other travelers are your best (or only) allies. Be alert to funky, untoward or dangerous-looking situations. Stick around, sidle over or step in to assess if someone needs help.

WORK

With every corner of the world already visited, mapped, travelogued and web blogged, adventure travel in the 21st century often means going deeper, rather than further. Volunteering is a purposeful way to combine travel and exploration, not only of a country but of a culture, language and context. To begin to understand a foreign reality, you have to live it and that's what, above all else, volunteering offers.

Most, but by no means all, volunteer positions require a minimum time commitment. From one month to three is typical, though organizations realize that there are many altruistic travelers who only have two or three weeks to vacation and are looking to spend it doing good. Consequently, shorter-term opportunities are becoming more available; several programs in Belize and Guatemala have such volunteer positions and connecting through your Spanish school is another option. In Mexico and Guatemala, there may be a Spanish-language requirement and some positions ask you to pay for room and board.

From observing human-rights progress in Chiapas and counting manatees in Belize to working with orphans, rescued animals or recovering addicts in Guatemala, there is no shortage of positions or variety in the region. Do your research before committing, read the fine print associated with different positions and talk to past volunteers. Some people prefer to wait until they're in a country to connect with volunteer opportunities; this is completely realistic in Guatemala, and a little bit more difficult (but not impossible) in Belize and Mexico. You can begin narrowing your search by poring over the following:

AmeriSpan (www.amerispan.com) Offers a range of volunteer opportunities in Mexico and Guatemala; participants should expect to pay around US$2000 for a two-month program.

Australian Volunteers International (www .australianvolunteers.com) Places volunteers from Australia and New Zealand in year-long (or even longer) volunteer positions, mostly in Guatemala.

Council on International Educational Exchange (www.ciee.org) Has shorter-term volunteer opportunities in Chiapas and Guatemala, usually during the summer, with no language requirement.

Earthwatch (www.earthwatch.org) With offices in the USA, Britain, Australia and Japan, Earthwatch runs environmental projects in Mexico, Belize and Guatemala. Volunteers usually pay around US$1000 per week.

Entre Mundos (www.entremundos.org) Fat, searchable database of volunteer opportunities in Guatemala is also an invaluable resource tool for how to choose and connect with a suitable and rewarding position. Novices might start here.

International Volunteer Programs Association (www.volunteerinternational.org) Collects many volunteer positions like working with Garifuna children in Belize, building schools on the Caribbean coast and tagging turtles in Guatemala. Also has good general resources and internships.

Peace Brigades International (www.peacebrigades .org) Promotes human-rights initiatives in the developing world; most volunteer positions involve accompanying human-rights activists in Guatemala or Chiapas.

Servicio Internacional Para la Paz (Sipaz) (International Service for Peace; www.sipaz.org) International peace-building coalition working in Chiapas to heighten visibility, accountability and nonviolent resolution of local problems needs Spanish-speaking volunteers; minimum one-year commitment.

Transitions Abroad (www.transitionsabroad.com) Excellent resource for finding paid work, contacts and volunteer positions, from planting mangroves on the Yucatán coast to educating sex workers in Guatemala.

Trekforce International (www.trekforce.org.uk) Arranges interesting positions in Belize, building schools, cutting trails, teaching Spanish or working with wildlife.

Volunteer Abroad (www.volunteerabroad.com) Scores of volunteer, study abroad and internship opportunities listed by country, plus many useful resources. Paid teaching jobs and opportunities for high-school students also available.

Transportation in Guatemala, Belize & Yucatán

CONTENTS

GETTING THERE & AWAY

Most visitors reach the region by air, or overland via the US and Mexico or points south in Central America.

ENTRY REQUIREMENTS

With your passport in hand, plus visa if necessary (see p445), entering Mexico, Guatemala or Belize should be a breeze: You fill out the normal forms, immigration officials flick through your passport and stamp it with frightening vigor, and you're on your way. You should not have to pay anything. Be patient and polite, even – or especially – if it's taking longer than you might like.

If you're going to encounter false fees or other such border-crossing scams, there's a greater chance of it happening at land or river crossings than at the international airports. Guatemala has a certain fame for this. To determine whether the fees are legitimate, you can ask for *un recibo* (a receipt). You may find that the 'fee' is dropped, or

you may watch as the officer cannibalizes yesterday's newspaper to invent a receipt. When in doubt, try to observe what, if anything, other travelers are paying before it's your turn. For more advice, see p452.

AIR

The international airport at Cancún (see p329) is unquestionably the most convenient, and often the cheapest, access point to the region. There are direct flights from Canada, the USA, Europe and Latin America and buses and shuttles run constantly from the Cancún bus terminal to most places you might want to go: Tulum, Playa del Carmen, Mérida, Campeche, the Belizean border at Chetumal and further afield such as Villahermosa in Chiapas. Time it right and you can push straight from Cancún onto San Cristóbal de Las Casas (via Villahermosa), the Belizean Cayes or Flores in Guatemala (both via Chetumal/Corozal on the Mexico-Belize border, p261).

Guatemala City (with buses ready to take you to Mexico, El Salvador or beyond) is another possible entry point, though with fewer flights and higher fares, especially from North America. Ditto Belize City. Regional airports receiving international flights (mostly from the USA with connections from Canada) include Campeche, Chetumal, Cozumel, Mérida and Villahermosa, all in Mexico. International flights from Cancún and Belize City are also received in Santa

---

THINGS CHANGE...

The information in this chapter is particularly vulnerable to change. Check directly with the airline or a travel agent to make sure you understand how a fare (and ticket you may buy) works and be aware of the security requirements for international travel. Shop carefully. The details given in this chapter should be regarded as pointers and are not a substitute for your own careful, up-to-date research.

Elena/Flores (see p175). Once you're on the ground, you can call the airports directly:
Belize City (☎ 225-2249)
Cancún (☎ 998-886-03-40)
Guatemala City (☎ 2334-7680, 2331-7241/3, 2334-7689)

Airlines

Carrier choice from anywhere in the Western Hemisphere is extensive. You may have to fly through a gateway city, especially coming from Canada, the Caribbean or South America, but connections are frequent. Travelers from Europe have many options to Cancún, including nonstop and direct flights; most service to Guatemala or Belize, however, connects through the USA. Fewer flight options, with the same gateway scenario, exist from Australia as well.

Mexicana and Aeroméxico are Mexico's national airlines; Aerocaribe is the regional arm of Mexicana. Their safety records are similar to major US and European airlines: Mexicana has had only one fatal crash in about two million flights since 1970, while Aeroméxico has suffered only one fatal event since 1986. Aviateca, the Guatemalan national airline, hasn't fared as well according to the US Federal Aviation Administration: it lists Aviateca as Category 2, which means they are not in compliance with international aviation safety standards. Aviateca is part of the important regional consortium of airlines called Grupo TACA, along with Taca (El Salvador), Nica (Nicaragua) and Lacsa (Costa Rica). Belize's Maya Island Air and Tropic Air fly daily between Belize City and Flores.

Contact information for carriers to the region:

Aerocaribe (Mexico ☎ 800-502-20-00; www.aerocaribe.com in Spanish; airline code QA; hub Cancún)
Aeroméxico (Mexico ☎ 800-021-40-00, 800-021-40-00; www.aeromexico.com; airline code AM; hub Mexico City)
Air Canada (Mexico ☎ 800-719-28-27; www.aircanada.ca; airline code AC; hub Toronto)
Air Europa (Mexico ☎ 998-898-22-55; www.aireuropa.com; airline code UX; hub Madrid)
Air France (Mexico ☎ 800-006-77-00; www.airfrance.com; airline code AF; hub Paris)
American Airlines (Guatemala ☎ 2337-1177, Belize ☎ 223-2522, Mexico ☎ 800-904-60-00; www.aa.com; airline code AA; hub Dallas)
America West (Mexico ☎ 800-235-92-92; www.americawest.com; airline code HP; hub Phoenix)

ATA Airlines (Mexico ☎ 800-883-52-28; www.ata.com; airline code TZ; hub Chicago)
Aviateca See Grupo TACA
British Airways (Mexico ☎ 55-5387-0300; www.britishairways.com; airline code BA; hub Heathrow Airport, London)
Continental Airlines (Guatemala ☎ 2366-9985, Belize ☎ 227-8309, Mexico ☎ 800-900-50-00; www.continental.com; airline code CO; hub Houston)
Copa Airlines (Guatemala ☎ 2385-5500, Mexico ☎ 800-265-26-72; www.copaair.com; airline code CM; hub Panama City)
Cubana (Guatemala ☎ 2367-2288/89, Mexico ☎ 998-887-72-10; www.cubana.cu; airline code CU; hub Havana)
Delta Airlines (Guatemala ☎ 1-800-300-0005, Mexico ☎ 800-902-21-00; www.delta.com; airline code DL; hub Atlanta)
Grupo TACA (Guatemala ☎ 5470-8222, Belize ☎ 227-7363, Mexico ☎ 998-887-4110; www.taca.com; airline code TA; hub San Salvador)
Iberia (Guatemala ☎ 2331-1012, Mexico ☎ 55-5130-3030; www.iberia.com; airline code IB; hub Madrid)
Japan Airlines (Mexico ☎ 800-024-01-50; www.jal.co.jp/en; airline code JL; hub Tokyo)
KLM (Mexico ☎ 800-907-4700; www.klm.com; airline code KL; hub Amsterdam)
Lacsa See Grupo TACA
Lan-Chile (Mexico ☎ 800-700-67-00; www.lanchile.com; airline code LA; hub Santiago de Chile)
Lloyd Aereo Boliviano (LAB; Mexico ☎ 998-810-21-59; www.labairlines.com; airline code LB; hub La Paz)
Lufthansa (Mexico ☎ 55-5230-0000; www.lufthansa.com; airline code LH; hub Frankfurt)
Martinair (Mexico ☎ 998-887-44-44; www.martinair.com; airline code MPH; hub Amsterdam)
Maya Island Air (Guatemala ☎ 7926-3386, in Belize ☎ 223-1140; www.mayaairways.com; airline code MW; hub Belize City)
Mexicana (Guatemala ☎ 2333-6001, Mexico ☎ 800-502-20-00; www.mexicana.com; airline code MX; hub Mexico City)
Northwest Airlines (Mexico ☎ 800-907-4700; www.nwa.com; airline code NW; hubs Detroit, Minneapolis/St Paul, Memphis)
Spirit Airlines (www.spiritair.com; airline code NK; hub Fort Lauderdale)
Sun Country Airlines (www.suncountry.com; airline code SY; hub Minneapolis/St Paul)
Tropic Air (Guatemala ☎ 7926-0348, Belize ☎ 226-2012; www.tropicair.com; airline code PM; hub Belize City)
United Airlines (Guatemala ☎ 2336-9923/4/5, Mexico ☎ 800-003-0777; www.united.com; airline code UA; hub Los Angeles)
US Airways (www.usairways.com; airline code US; hub Philadelphia)

Varig (Guatemala ☎ 2334-0043, Mexico ☎ 998-887-4377; www.varig.com.br; airline code RG; hub São Paulo)

Tickets

Many flights into the region from the rest of the world pass through a handful of 'hub' cities including Dallas/Fort Worth, Houston, Los Angeles, Miami, Mexico City or Panama City. If you are flying from Australia or Europe, chances are you will receive a free stopover in one of these gateways – a splendid opportunity to screen Hollywood or cruise South Beach. Ask when buying your ticket.

If you are checking out La Ruta Maya as part of a bigger Latin American trip or if you want to minimize backtracking, the best ticket may be an open jaw (where you fly into one place and out of another, covering the intervening distance by land). The Cancún–Guatemala City combination works especially well and is not prohibitively expensive: at the time of writing a New York–Cancún outbound with a Guatemala City–New York return ticket cost US$595.

If you are coming from Australasia, a round-the-world (RTW) ticket could work out only slightly more expensive than a return ticket to Mexico or Guatemala, while greatly broadening your travel options.

Everyone wants to fly cheap or at least brag about it. Start your research early, play with your dates (try to avoid the high seasons: Semana Santa, July, August, and mid-December to mid-January), consider secondary airports as departure and/or arrival points and visit the websites of airlines which often run special deals.

DEPARTURE TAXES

The following departure taxes are levied on international outbound air passengers at airport check-in. You must pay it in cash – either in local currency or US dollars.

- Belize – US$35
- Guatemala – US$30
- Mexico – US$25; the departure tax is usually included in the price of your ticket; look for the code XD on your ticket or ask your travel agent.

Australia & New Zealand

There are no direct flights from this part of the world. While the cheapest routings usually go via Japan and the USA, it's also possible to go through South America. From Sydney during the low season, you will pay around A$2300 return to Cancún or Guatemala City via Dallas/Fort Worth, LA or San Francisco. At peak travel times, you can expect to pay A$300 to A$400 more. If you've got the travel bug and time to indulge it, check out RTW fares, which may be only slightly more expensive. Japan Airlines, United, American and Qantas have service from Australia.

From Auckland to Cancún, an off-season return flight costs NZ$2445 with Air New Zealand or Mexicana; to Guatemala City you can fly with United, American or Qantas airlines, but you'll pay NZ$2785.

The following are well-known agents for cheap fares, including RTW, with branches throughout both countries:

Flight Centre Australia (☎ 1300 133 133; www.flightcentre.com.au); New Zealand (☎ 0800 243 544; www.flightcentre.co.nz)

STA Travel Australia (☎ 1300 733 035; www.statravel.com.au); New Zealand (☎ 0508 782 872; www.statravel.co.nz)

Try these websites for online fares: www.travel.com.au and www.travel.co.nz.

Canada

Air Canada, Continental, Northwest Airlines, American, Aeroméxico and Mexicana have direct flights from Toronto and Montreal to Cancún at around C$540 and C$600 return, respectively. Mérida is served by Air Canada, Continental and Mexicana. Travelers to other destinations, including Belize City, Guatemala City and Cozumel, are routed through the US. **Travel Cuts** (☎ 800-667-2887; www.travelcuts.com) is Canada's national student travel agency. For online bookings try www.expedia.ca and www.travelocity.ca.

Central America & Cuba

Central America is well connected via air thanks to Grupo TACA, which has service from San Salvador, Tegucigalpa (Honduras), Managua and San José to Guatemala City, Cancún and Belize City. Additionally, Grupo TACA flies between Belize City and Roatán and San Pedro Sula in Honduras.

Mexicana, American and Continental serve the San José–Cancún route, while United, Copa and Lacsa fly between San José and Guatemala City. Taca flies from San José to Belize City, via El Salvador. Tropic Air and Maya Island Air both fly daily from Belize City to Flores and back for around US$90 each way. Cancún to Flores costs about double that with Grupo TACA.

When planning to fly within Central America, be aware that fares can fluctuate wildly, so you might play with arrival cities and consider traveling at least part of the way overland. Round trips almost always come out cheaper than one way. Here are some example return fares at the time of writing:

- San José–Cancún US$534
- San José–Guatemala City US$186
- San José–Belize City US$440
- San Pedro Sula–Belize City US$430

Mexicana and Cubana connect Cancún to Havana daily (return fares with Cubana cost US$275); Cubana also flies between Havana and Guatemala City twice weekly (return fares hover around US$350); Lacsa and Copa have even more frequent flights. A recommended agency for buying tickets online is www.cubalinda.com.

The best place to buy flight tickets in Guatemala is Antigua (p81), where many agencies peddle competitive fares.

Europe

The cheapest flights from many European cities are usually with Iberia or Air Europa via Madrid, but you also might try Martinair or KLM from Amsterdam or American Airlines or British Airways through London. Iberia flies direct from Europe to Guatemala, while Delta, Air France, Lufthansa, United and Mexicana connect through Paris, Mexico City or Miami. American Airlines, Iberia, Continental, US Airways, KLM and Martinair all fly to Cancún; the last offers nonstop service four times a week. The most direct way to reach Belize is with American Airlines or British Airways from London.

In the off-season, you can expect to pay between £545 and £650 round trip from London to Guatemala City or Cancún and €810 between Cancún or Guatemala City and Frankfurt return.

An alternative is to fly with a US airline or alliance partner, changing planes in the USA. Open-jaw or multi-stopover tickets are options if the Mayan lands are just part of a larger Latin American trip.

To search online for budget flights, try www.dialaflight.com and www.lastminute .com. Recommended agencies in Europe include the following:

FRANCE
Nouvelles Frontières (☎ 0825 000 747; www .nouvelles-frontieres.fr)
OTU Voyages (☎ 0 820 817 817; www.otu.fr) Student and youth travel specialist.
Voyageurs du Monde (☎ 01 40 15 11 15; www.vdm .com)

GERMANY
Expedia (www.expedia.de)
Just Travel (☎ 089 747 3330; www.justtravel.de)
STA Travel (☎ 01805 456 422; www.statravel.de) For travelers aged under 26.

ITALY
CTS Viaggi (☎ 06-462 0431, www.cts.it) A specialist in student and youth travel.

NETHERLANDS
AirFair (☎ 020-620 5121; www.airfair.nl)

SCANDINAVIA
Kilroy Travels (www.kilroytravels.com)

SPAIN
Viajes Zeppelin (☎ 902 384 253; www.v-zeppelin.es)

UK
Journey Latin America (☎ 020-8747 3108; www .journeylatinamerica.co.uk)
Flight Centre (☎ 0870 890 8099; www.flightcentre .co.uk)
Flightbookers (☎ 0870 010 7000; www.ebookers.com)
STA Travel (☎ 0870 160 0599; www.statravel.co.uk) For travelers under the age of 26.
Trailfinders (☎ 020-7937 1234; www.trailfinders .co.uk)

South America

Lacsa (with transfers in San José, Costa Rica) and Copa (with transfers in Panama City) both fly to Guatemala City from Bogotá, Caracas, Quito and Lima. Copa, American, Mexicana and Continental connect Quito with Cancún (via Mexico City), while Lloyd

Aereo Boliviano flies between La Paz and Cancún. Further south, Lan-Chile flies direct to Cancún from Santiago de Chile, with decent fares at around US$680 return. It also connects Buenos Aires with Cancún through Miami. Varig flies daily to Cancún from Brazil.

Flights to Belize connect through Central American capital cities or Miami. Caracas is one of the cheapest South American gateways.

Recommended agencies include:

ASATEJ (☎ 54-011 4114-7595; www.asatej.com) In Argentina.

IVI Tours (☎ 0212-993 6082; www.ividiomas.com) In Venezuela.

Student Travel Bureau (☎ 3038 1555; www.stb.com .br) In Brazil.

Viajo.com (www.viajo.com) Online and telephone bookings from several countries.

USA

You can fly direct to Cancún on a major scheduled airline from any of the following American cities: Atlanta, Boston, Charlotte, Chicago, Cincinnati, Dallas/Fort Worth, Houston, Los Angeles, Memphis, Miami, Minneapolis, New Orleans, Newark, New York, Philadelphia, Phoenix, Pittsburgh and Tampa/St Petersburg. You can choose from Aeroméxico, Air Canada, America West, American, Continental, Mexicana, Northwest, Sun Country and United Airlines. There are departures from many of these same cities to Guatemala City.

Airlines serving Belize City include American (from Miami or Dallas), Continental (from Houston) and Grupo TACA (from Los Angeles). Secondary airports in the region connected with the USA and Canada include Campeche, Chetumal, Cozumel, Mérida and Villahermosa.

Sample low-season, round-trip fares:

from	to Guatemala City	to Cancún	to Belize City
Chicago	US$385	US$295	US$380
Dallas/Fort Worth	US$560	US$285	US$350
Los Angeles	US$510	US$315	US$380
Miami	US$265	US$245	US$375
New York	US$355	US$375	US$365

The following agencies are recommended for online bookings:

- www.cheaptickets.com
- www.expedia.com
- www.itn.net
- www.lowestfare.com
- www.orbitz.com
- www.smarterliving.com
- www.sta.com (for travelers under the age of 26)
- www.travelocity.com

LAND
Border Crossings

The most common and hassle-free mode of arrival at the region's land borders is by bus. Typically you have to alight from the bus, walk a few hundred meters at most to immigration, attend to entry formalities and connect with ongoing bus service on the other side. Rental cars usually require special permission from the agency to cross borders: if, for example, quick side trips to the ruins at Copán, Honduras (see the boxed text for specifics, p153) or the barrier reef in Belize are on your itinerary, be sure to clear it with the rental agency first.

If you arrive in a car or motorcycle, have your paperwork in order (see p453). Even with all your bureaucratic details well in hand, there's always the chance of getting a crafty immigration official with designs on a bribe (called *la mordida*, or the bite). You should only have to pay an overland departure tax from Belize (US$18); if you're asked to pay leaving Guatemala or Mexico, there's either a new regulation since this book was written or it's a scam.

First, always act respectfully and deferentially. Keep everything formal, never raise your voice or curse out an official, maintaining your cool while trying to ascertain whether it's a scam or not. Are there departure taxes posted at the immigration post? Are other travelers paying a tax (pay special attention to Latinos or locals)? Talk to other travelers, particularly the closer you get to the border. What's the latest? You can ask for a receipt in an effort to ferret out the bogus fee, but after several Lonely Planet editions carrying this advice, officials are hip to it and are creating some very convincing facsimiles thereof.

If you really like to play the game (at your own risk), offer some weird currency such as Thai baht or Norwegian kroner. At the sight of strange money the officer may drop the request. If the unusual currency is acceptable, inflate its value; tell the officer a low note is actually worth big bucks.

Below are the main land border crossings between the countries in the region; see also river and sea crossings on this page. Onward bus connections are usually well coordinated.

Guatemala–Belize Melchor de Mencos/Benque Viejo del Carmen (p275 and p187)

Guatemala–El Salvador From south to north: Ciudad Pedro de Alvarado/La Hachadura (p75); Valle Nuevo/Las Chinamas (p76); San Cristóbal/San Cristóbal; Anguiatú/Metapán (p146)

Guatemala–Honduras Esquipulas/Agua Caliente (p148); El Florido/Copán Ruinas (p153); Entre Ríos/Corinto (p162)

Mexico–Belize Chetumal/Corozal (p261)

Mexico–Guatemala From south to north: Ciudad Hidalgo/Ciudad Tecún Umán (p127 and p422); Talismán/El Carmen (p128 and p422); Ciudad Cuauhtémoc/La Mesilla (p127 and p420)

Car & Motorcycle

Bringing your own vehicle from Canada or the US is possible and lots of people do it, but there is significant paperwork and loads of liability involved. Since each country has it's own vehicular and customs laws, the rigmarole is unique at each border crossing. At the very least, each country requires a permit for temporary importation of a vehicle, plus locally purchased insurance; see the individual Transport sections for rules (Guatemala p197; Belize p306; Mexico p431). For more information on car insurance, see p431.

While you won't save money traveling with your own wheels (think tolls, gas, insurance, parking lot and border fees to start), you will certainly create memories to last a lifetime. For some other considerations regarding bringing your own vehicle, see p456. Buying a car in Mexico or Guatemala is complicated.

A few other pretrip considerations:

- Obtain a valid driver's license or International Driving Permit (IDP) from your home country.
- Preliminary paperwork you'll need includes title, registration and temporary vehicle-import permit (also obtainable at most borders).
- Be sure that the shock absorbers and suspension are in good shape for bumpy roads.

- A spare fuel filter and other spare parts could be invaluable.
- A sedan with trunk (boot) provides safer storage than a van, hatchback or station wagon.
- If traveling south, keep in mind that there are no roads connecting Central and South America.
- Rules on bringing a car into Mexico change frequently – call the **Mexican Tourist Board** (US ☎ +1-800-446-3942) or visit the website of the **American Automobile Association** (www.aaa.com) for information.

RIVER

To spice up your border-crossing experiences, consider jumping between Mexico and Guatemala on jungle-fringed rivers. On most routes, the transport is reasonably reliable and the scenery is wonderful to behold.

Options for river crossings include:

Mexico–Guatemala on the Río de la Pasión Benemérito de las Américas/Sayaxché (p187); no scheduled passenger service, but boat hire is possible.

Mexico–Guatemala on the Río San Pedro La Palma/El Naranjo (p187); no scheduled passenger service, but boat hire is possible.

Mexico–Guatemala on the Río Usumacinta Frontera Corozal/La Técnica or Bethel (p187); packages available from Flores to Palenque incorporate this crossing.

SEA

The following sea crossings have decent transport and connections:

Belize–Honduras Belize City (via Placencia & Big Creek)/Puerto Cortés (p296 and p305)

Guatemala–Belize Puerto Barrios/Punta Gorda (p161); Lívingston/Punta Gorda (p165)

Guatemala–Honduras Lívingston/Omoa (p165)

GETTING AROUND

AIR

Flying can be good value if you have more money than time or if you just can't stand more chicken-bus jostling. Each country covered in this book has a domestic airline industry and certain flights (eg Guatemala City–Flores or Cancún–Villahermosa) can save you buckets of time you would otherwise spend on the road. There are also several handy regional routes like Belize

City–Flores or Cancún–Guatemala City that can maximize itinerary options if you want to cover ground fast.

Airlines in Guatemala, Belize & Mexico

Mexico has many carriers covering the entire region. Guatemala has several airlines, all serving just one domestic route: Guatemala City to Flores. Belize's airline industry relies on smaller planes (de Havilland Twin Otters, Cessnas etc) to zip people around the country and over to Flores in Guatemala. To check on the safety record of the local carriers in the accompanying box, visit www.airsafe.com. For specific schedules, see individual country chapters (Guatemala p198; Belize p305; Mexico p429).

Air Passes

Unless you really want to cover a lot of ground fast or are designing a trip that links North, Central and/or South America, an air pass probably won't prove good value. Still, for those frequent flyers there's the Mexi-Pass International, which offers flight passes on North, Central and South American routes served by Mexicana and Aeroméxico (you must purchase a minimum of three flights); similarly, Grupo TACA has an AirFlex pass. To travel between Central and South America, you might consider COPA's Hop-Over Pass, which requires you purchase at least two flights.

A good source for current flight-pass deals is Journey Latin America (www.journeylatinamerica.co.uk).

BICYCLE

The Guatemalan highlands and the cayes of Belize are cycling hot spots and rentals are easily arranged. Mexico as a whole has less of a biking tradition, which is reason enough for hardy cyclists to tackle the terrain around Chiapas and in the southeast. Bicycle tours, especially of the mountain-bike variety, are gaining popularity throughout the region (see Tours in the Regional Directory, p198). For country-by-country details, see the individual Transportation sections (Guatemala p198; Belize p305).

BOAT

Canoe, fishing skiff, ferry or dive boat: chances are you'll shove off in one or the other during your trip. Motorboats are efficient modes of transportation all over the region, especially around Lago de Atitlán, Río Dulce, Lívingston and Puerto Barrios in Guatemala (see p198). In the Yucatán,

Airline	Local Telephone	Website	Areas Served
Aerocaribe	☎ 800-502-20-00	www.aerocaribe.com	Mérida, Cancún, Chetumal, Tuxtla Gutiérrez, Villahermosa
Aerocozumel	☎ 800-502-20-00	www.mexicana.com	Yucatán Peninsula
Aeroméxico	☎ 800-021-40-00	www.aeromexico.com	over 50 cities nationwide
Grupo TACA	☎ 5470-8222	www.taca.com	Guatemala City–Flores
Jungle Flying Tours	☎ 2339-0502		Guatemala City–Flores
Líneas Aéreas Azteca	☎ 800-229-83-22	www.aazteca.com.mx	Cancún, Mexico City, north and west Mexico
Magnicharters	☎ 55-5566-8199	www.magnicharters.com in Spanish	Mérida, Mexico City, coastal resorts
Maya Island Air	☎ 223-1140	www.mayaairways.com	Belize City, Caye Caulker, San Pedro, Corozal, Dangriga, Placencia, Punta Gorda, Flores (Guatemala)
Mexicana	☎ 800-502-20-00	www.mexicana.com	over 50 cities nationwide
Racsa	☎ 2361-5703/4		Guatemala City–Flores
TAG	☎ 2360-3038		Guatemala City–Flores
Tikal Airlines (Tikal Jets)	☎ 2334-6855	www.tikaljets.com	Guatemala City–Flores
Tropic Air	☎ 226-2012	www.tropicair.com	Belize City, Caye Caulker, San Pedro, Corozal, Dangriga, Placencia, Punta Gorda, Flores (Guatemala)

ferries connect the mainland to Isla de Mujeres and Cozumel (see p431). In Belize, the choppy waters between the Cayes and Belize City are plied by launches all day long (see p305).

Exciting river trips – to the ruins at Lamanai (p254) or through the Cañon del Sumidero (p391), among others – are also in the offing.

BUS

The bus network here is extensive, reliable and economical. Most roads are in good repair, especially in Belize and on major regional routes, making this a prime destination to explore on public transporta-tion. Indeed, you can travel the length of Central America by bus and even the most remote spots are usually reachable with a bus-pickup combo. You'll find all manner of safety and comfort on buses here, from dangerously full shuttle vans whizzing around blind curves to luxury coaches with movies and food service. These plush buses usually ply longer routes or those connecting big cities (see Classes, p456).

Old school buses known colloquially as chicken buses (for their fowl cargo) are ubiquitous in Guatemala. Colorful, cheap and crowded, these buses connect big and small towns and are the source of many a funny or unforgettable travel tale. Chicken

Bus Company	Local Telephone	Website	Areas Served
ADO	☎ 800-702-80-00	www.ado.com.mx in Spanish	Mérida, Campeche, Palenque, Villahermosa Veracruz State, Mexico City
ATS (Autotransportes del Sur)	☎ 800-702-80-00		Mérida, Cancún, Campeche, Celestún, Ocosingo, Palenque, Playa del Carmen, San Cristóbal de Las Casas
Cristóbal Colón (OCC)	☎ 800-702-80-00	www.cristobalcolon .com.mx in Spanish	Yucatán, Chiapas, Mexico City
Fortaleza del Sur	☎ 2230-3390		Guatemala City, Ciudad Tecún Umán/ Ciudad Hidalgo, El Carmen/Talismán (Mexican border), Retalhuleu
Fuente del Norte	☎ 2251-3817		Guatemala City, Flores, Sayaxché, Poptún, Río Dulce, Melchor de Menos (Belize)
Hedman Alas	☎ 2362-5072/3/4	www.hedmanalas.com	Guatemala City–Copán Ruinas–San Pedro Sula–La Ceiba–Tegucigalpa, Honduras
Línea Dorada	☎ 2232-5506, ☎ 5201-2710	www.lineadorada.com	Guatemala City–Flores, Belize City–Flores, Chetumal–Flores, Guatemala City–Tapachula
Maya de Oro	☎ 800-702-80-00	www.mayadeoro .com.mx	Mexico City, Chiapas, Campeche, Mérida, Quintana Roo
Novelo's	☎ 207-2025		Belize City, San Ignacio, Benque Viejo del Carmen, Orange Walk, Corozal, Chetumal, Dangriga, Placencia, Punta Gorda
Omnitur del Caribe (Caribe)	☎ 832-8001		Mérida, Chetumal
Oriente (Autotran-sportes de Oriente)	☎ 884-1365		Mérida, Chichén Itzá, Valladolid, Cobá, Playa del Carmen, Tulum, Cancún
Super Expresso	☎ 800-702-80-00		Mérida, Cancún, Chetumal, Ticul
Tica Bus	☎ 2331-4279, ☎ 2361-1773	www.ticabus.com	Guatemala City, San Salvador, Tegucigalpa, Managua, San José, Panama City, Tapachula
Transportes Velásquez	☎ 2221-1084		Guatemala City, Huehuetenango, La Mesilla/Ciudad Cuauhtémoc
UNO	☎ 800-702-80-00	www.uno.com.mx	Mérida, Villahermosa, San Cristóbal de Las Casas, Tapachula, Cancún, Mexico City

TRANSPORTATION

buses are also a fixture in rural Belize. More expensive, faster shuttle services designed to zip tourists along popular routes are an alternative to the chicken buses and are convenient for border-crossing trips (see p458). Still, some travelers favor chicken buses over tourist shuttles since the latter are prime highway-robbery targets.

Highway robbery is a risk in Guatemala and parts of Mexico, and nighttime bus travel is generally not recommended for a whole host of reasons, ranging from bad lighting to drunk drivers.

Classes
In Mexico, the best, most luxurious and fastest bus service is called *de lujo* or *ejecutivo* (deluxe). In Guatemala, it's known as Pullman or *especial* services; in Belize, express or premier. Legroom, reclining seats, air conditioning, on-board toilets, movies and food service typify these buses, which make few or no stops. Most people find the added comfort and speed are worth the extra dollar or two.

First-class buses, called *primera* or *1a clase* in Mexico and Guatemala, are entirely adequate and efficient and usually have air-conditioning and maybe a toilet on board. Mexican second-class buses *(segunda* or *2a clase)* and chicken buses in Guatemala and Belize connect smaller villages and towns and are mostly recycled US school buses. Slow, cramped and chaotic, these babies can get you off the beaten track and save you from the side of the road – they'll stop almost anywhere for anyone and all you have to do is flag one down.

In Mexico and Guatemala, another transportation alternative are small buses called microbuses, which run short routes. See individual Transportation sections for more bus details (Guatemala p198; Belize p306; Mexico p430).

Costs
In Mexico, superdeluxe buses (eg UNO) cost around US$6.50 for each 70km to 80km of travel, while deluxe cost US$4.50 for the same distance. First-class buses are typically 10% to 20% cheaper (ie US$3.50 to US$4) and second-class buses 10% or 20% than first class. In Guatemala, the cheapest chicken buses typically cost US$1 for each 50km of travel; the most luxurious buses

cost nearly double that. Tourist shuttles can cost five to fifteen times the cost of a bus. In Belize, you'll pay about US$1.50 for each 80km of travel.

Reservations
Not only are reservations generally not required, sometimes they're not even possible. More often than not, you can just show up at the bus terminal, buy a ticket and get on board. Still, you should consider making reservations a day or two in advance if you'll be traveling great distances, on a route with infrequent service, on a popular tourist route or during a big holiday period like Semana Santa.

In Mexico, you can make reservations and buy tickets with many bus companies over the Internet, by telephone or in the offices of **Ticketbus** (☎ 5133-2424, 800-702-80-00; www.ticketbus.com.mx). Consider this handy alternative if you'll be traveling with UNO, Maya de Oro, ADO, Cristóbal Colón, Altos, Sur, Mayab, AU or Rápidos del Sur lines.

CAR & MOTORCYCLE
Driving in Guatemala, Belize or Mexico allows you to go where you want to go, when you want to go and it is this convenience, coupled with the allure of reaching remote spots, that has many travelers driving around the region. Whether you bring your own vehicle (see p453) or hire one upon arrival, it's worth thinking about some of the following to determine whether driving here is for you (and remember, buses are generally safe, economical and efficient):

Are you traveling alone? Cost, liability issues and endurance limits tip the scales against driving for most solo travelers.

Do you have language or mechanical facility? Spanish-speaking drivers will be better able to resolve problems in Guatemala and Mexico, while any off-the-beaten-track breakdown will likely require some repair work by you. Bikers, especially, should know how to fix their ride.

Are you traveling during the rainy season? Flooding and washouts are common in Belize from May to November and roads to more isolated spots are often in disrepair any time of year. Consider renting a 4WD.

Do you have gear? Anything unwieldy like a kayak, photo equipment or surfboard may make driving a car the most convenient alternative.

Are you at least 25 years old? In Belize and Guatemala, the person renting a vehicle usually has to be at least 25. Mexico is more flexible, often renting to people 21 or over.

Do you have a major credit card? Rental agencies usually require a credit card or large cash deposit. Folks driving their own vehicles will want one too, for that 'oh shit!' scenario.

Will you be crossing borders? Rental agencies usually require you to sign a release if you take their car into another country; insurance policies typically don't translate across borders.

Driver's License

Your home driver's license is sufficient to drive and rent a car in any of the countries covered in this book, but carry an International Driving Permit (IDP) as well, just in case.

Fuel & Spare Parts

Unleaded gasoline (*petrol* in Spanish) and diesel are widely available in Guatemala, Belize and Mexico and you'll have no problem finding a service station, except in very far-flung places; fill up before heading into the boondocks.

In Mexico, spare parts are more readily available for Volkswagen, Nissan, General Motors and Ford models because there are domestic manufacturing and assembly plants and dealerships. In Guatemala, where modern vehicles with problems can illicit much head scratching, old Toyota pickup trucks are everywhere and so are the mechanics that can fix them.

Motorcycle parts and mechanics are harder to come by. Bikers should know their cycle and pack a decent toolkit. The parts you'll most easily find will be for Kawasaki, Honda and Suzuki bikes.

Hire

To rent a car or motorcycle you will need your passport, a valid driver's license and major credit card (sometimes a cash deposit in the neighborhood of US$250 works in lieu of plastic). Many agencies will only rent to travelers 25 years or older, though this is more flexible in Mexico, where 21 is usually the minimum age requirement. Most agencies offer either a per-kilometer or unlimited-kilometer deal; if you're going to be hitting the road in any serious manner, the latter will probably work out better. International agencies sometimes offer Internet deals, but local agencies may be cheaper in general.

Here is a list of the bigger local and international players on the car rental scene with their local phone numbers:

BELIZE
Avis (☎ 225-2385; www.avis.com)
Budget Rent-A-Car (☎ 223-2435; www.budget-belize.com)
Crystal Auto Rental (☎ 223-1600; www.crystal-belize.com)
Thrifty Car Rental (☎ 225-2436; www.thrifty.com)

GUATEMALA
Ahorrent (☎ 2361-5661; www.ahorrent.com in Spanish)
Avis (☎ 2339-3249; www.avisenlinea.com in Spanish)
Dollar (☎ 2332-7525; www.dollar.com)
Hertz (☎ 2331-1711, 2339-2631; www.hertz.com.gt)
Tabarini (☎ 2331-6108; www.tabarini.com)
Tally Renta Autos (☎ 2332-6063; www.tallyrentaautos.com)
Thrifty (☎ 2333-7444; www.thrifty.com)

MEXICO
Alamo (☎ 55-1101-1100; www.alamo.com)
Avis (☎ 800-288-88-88; www.avis.com)
Budget (☎ 800-700-17-00; www.budget.com)
Dollar (☎ 33-3825-5080; www.dollar.com)
Europcar (☎ 800-201-20-84; www.europcar.com)
Hertz (☎ 800-709-50-00; www.hertz.com)
National (☎ 55-5661-5000; www.nationalcar.com)
Thrifty (☎ 55-5207-1100; www.thrifty.com)

Insurance

Whether you bring your own car (see p453) or rent one, you need insurance. Rental cars are accompanied by insurance policies (sometimes called a Loss Damage Waiver), but read the fine print: some policies only cover 90% of damage or theft costs, while others won't cover 'partial theft' (eg tires, mirrors, taillights) at all. Your insurance will not be valid in Mexico if you are involved in an incident while driving under the influence of alcohol or drugs.

If you're bringing in your own vehicle, you have to buy local insurance as foreign policies are not honored in Mexico and Central America. It's available at many border towns, especially between the US and Mexico. (Approaching the border from the US, you will see billboards advertising offices selling Mexican policies.) Rates start around US$15 a day (cheaper in Belize), but long hauls will do better with an annual policy. Texas-based **Sanborn's Insurance** (US

TRANSPORTATION

TRANSPORTATION

☎ +1-800-222-0158; www.sanbornsinsurance.com) sells coverage for Mexico and Central America and has a 24-hour emergency hotline in Mexico. It has close to 20 US offices near the border and one in San Miguel de Allende, Mexico. You can prepurchase policies here.

Try not to cross borders with your car on a Sunday as insurance agents often close.

Road Conditions

Major highways in the region are generally in good repair and should present nothing dramatic in terms of road conditions. Anywhere else, however, you may encounter potholes, speed bumps, iguanas, kids on bikes, men on horses, women hauling wood, poor signage, blind curves and lots of loud honking. Sometimes many of these things can be happening at once, other times they can come suddenly or without warning; stay alert behind the wheel. Motorcyclists, especially, will have to be on their guard.

Driving at night is not recommended due to low visibility, increased risk of robbery and tired or drunk drivers. Speed bumps (*topes* in Mexico, *túmolos* in Guatemala) are common at the entrances to cities and towns. Road signage isn't what it might be and drivers will be happy they invested in a good road map (see p443).

Road Rules

In the countries covered in this book, driving is on the right-hand side of the road. While seat belts are obligatory, they are not always used (in Belize you can get fined for not wearing one) and while speed limits are posted, they're not always observed. As a general rule, speed limits are 100km/h on the highway, 40km/h in populated areas. On one-lane roads, cars coming uphill always have the right of way. Signaling when passing and honking on blind curves lets other drivers know how you're coming and going.

If you are involved in an accident that causes injury or death, you may be taken into custody until authorities can ascertain who is responsible.

HITCHING

Hitchhiking (thumb out by the side of the road, looking for a free ride) is not practiced here as it is not safe. However, in rural and remote places not served by buses, pickup trucks and other private or commercial vehicles supplement traditional public transport, picking up passengers along the side of the road. Just hold out your arm and drivers will stop. This is especially true in Belize and Guatemala, where you will probably have to pay for the lift; something equivalent to the (chicken) bus fare is typical. Prepare for very crowded (and, in the case of open-air trucks, windy) conditions.

Hitchhiking is never entirely safe in any country in the world and travelers who decide to hitch should understand that they are taking a potentially serious risk. People who do choose to hitch will be safer if they travel in pairs and let someone know where they are planning to go. Women traveling alone should be especially alert and wary and should not hitchhike in Mexico; even two women hitchhiking together is not advisable there.

LOCAL TRANSPORTATION
Bicycle

Peddling around smaller cities and towns is a great way to better appreciate the landscape and provides an independence of movement that is not available on buses (mopeds and motorcycles offer similar advantages). Isla de Mujeres, Cozumel and San Cristóbal de Las Casas are only a few of the places with bike rentals in Mexico, while Campeche and Valladolid even have bike paths. Rentals are available in Panajachel, Antigua and Quetzaltenango in Guatemala, and cycling is a popular mode of local transport throughout Belize, especially on the cayes.

Boat

Boat travel is likely to enter into the travel picture when venturing to outlying islands (eg Isla de Mujeres or Caye Caulker) or to remote beaches, around Lago de Atitlán or along rivers like the Río Dulce in Guatemala.

Bus

Local buses are handy if you'll be spending more than a few days in bigger, spread-out cities (eg Guatemala City, Quetzaltenango or Villahermosa) or want to reach nearby villages from an urban base. For short stints, however, the dollar or so savings involved

TRANSPORTATION

CRUISIN' THE CAYES

There's no scarcity of options here. From self-sail to water taxi, the Caribbean is not a hard place to get around. Island hopping is surely one of life's great pleasures – being out in the middle of all that beautiful warm clear water, cruising from one sandy paradise to the next, diving, snorkeling and fishing on spectacular reefs along the way.

Those evil twins, time and money, are pretty much the only restrictions and depending on how much you have of both, you've got a (watery) world of options at your disposal.

You can get to Caye Caulker in under an hour from Belize City on a water taxi (see p227). From San Pedro, you can hire a boat with or without skipper (see p242) to cruise around the Cayes at a leisurely pace and end up in Placencia a week or so later. Ragamuffin Tours (p236) on Caye Caulker offers an excellent, reasonably priced sailing trip around the Cayes that also ends up in Placencia to connect with the *Gulf Cruza* (see p296), a motorboat that goes direct to Honduras. Water taxis in Dangriga (p287) zoom out to a variety of cayes, but unless you're going on a scheduled run, these can get expensive (like US$200 per hour).

From tiny Hopkins (see p289), you can learn to sail your own 18ft catamaran while cruising around the Cayes on a week-long diving, snorkeling, fishing and hammocking trip.

And for those who really like a workout, Deb & Dave's Last Resort in Placencia (see p293) has four-day kayaking trips around the southern cayes, with luxury camping out on Silk Caye.

---

in waiting, catching and riding on a local bus won't be worth it to most travelers – take a taxi instead.

Mopeds & Motorcycles

Mopeds ('scooters') are available for rent at Yucatán hot spots like Cozumel, Isla de Mujeres and Cancún, and in Guatemala City, Antigua, Panajachel and Quetzaltenango, where you can also rent motorcycles proper. The use of proper safety gear like a helmet, gloves and long pants is highly recommended.

Taxi

Plentiful and reasonably priced, taxis are a realistic way to get about larger towns in Mexico and Guatemala. Most taxis in Mexico use *taxímetros* (meters) and cost around US$1 per kilometer. In Guatemala taxis don't use meters, but you can expect to pay about US$3 for a 10-minute ride. Always be ready to haggle with hacks, who know a money-making opportunity when they see it; settle on a price *before* getting in, if possible, and be prepared to walk away if you smell a scam. Taxis can be very handy for day trips to archaeological or natural sites; with a small group, a round-trip excursion plus waiting time can work out pretty economically.

Smaller towns, plus cheap, efficient buses, mean travelers will find less of a need for taxis in Belize.

SHUTTLE

Shuttles are a popular, easy way to reach the most visited towns on the tourist circuit. Usually minivans carrying 10 people – while they cost more than buses (from five to 15 times more) – they are faster and often the most direct option. But some travelers feel they are a beacon for thieves. Indeed, incidents of highway robbery consistently involve these shuttles, though that doesn't mean chicken buses are exempt. It's best to check local conditions once you arrive. At the time of writing, shuttle routes included:

- Antigua–Chichicastenango
- Antigua–Copán Ruinas, Honduras
- Antigua–Panajachel
- Antigua–Río Dulce
- Flores–Chetumal, Mexico (via Belize City)
- Flores–Palenque, Mexico
- Flores–Tikal
- Guatemala City Airport–Antigua
- San Cristóbal de Las Casas–La Mesilla, Quetzaltenango, Panajachel and Antigua

TOURS

Organized tours take the strain out of travel planning and are especially worth considering if you have limited time, or you don't have a travel partner, or you shrink at exploring solo. A knowledgeable and enthusiastic guide can add much to your understanding and enjoyment of a place, and group trips can also be a practical way of getting access to remote attractions. Outdoor-adventure tours are a challenging way to discover new places – within the region and yourself.

Here are some outfitters:

Adventure Center (US ☎ +1-800-228-8747; www .adventurecenter.com; Suite 200, 1311 63rd St, Emeryville, CA, USA) Ecologically conscious, community-focused small-group camping and hotel trips taking in the best of La Ruta Maya; family trips and longer adventures the length of Central America available.

Ecocolors (☎ 998-884-3667; www.ecotravelmexico .com; Calle Cameron 32, Smza 27, Cancún, Mexico) Small-group tours through the Mayan world; kayak, snorkel, dive, bird-watch, mountain-bike, research the jaguar in the Reserva de la Biósfera Sian Ka'an or motorcycle to Mayan sites in the Yucatán. Tours in English, German or French.

Ecoturismo Yucatán (☎ 999-920-2772; www.ecoyuc .com; Calle 3 No 325, Mérida, Mexico) Ecotours in Mexico, Guatemala and Honduras including biking, caving, kayaking, birding and trekking, concentrating on culture and archaeology. Also jungle tours to Biósfera Calakmul.

Explore Worldwide (in the UK ☎ +44-01252-760000; www.explore.co.uk; 1 Frederick St, Aldershot, Hampshire, UK) Small-group land trips with interesting itineraries and departures year-round.

Gap Adventures Canada (☎ +1-800-465-5600, www.gap.ca; Suite 401, 19 Duncan St, Toronto, ON); USA (☎ +1-805-985-0922; 567 W Channel Islands, Blvd 346, Port Hueneme, CA) Small-group tours throughout Maya lands, mainly using local transportation and simple accommodation like homes and hostels.

Journey Latin America (in the UK ☎ +44-020-8747-3108; www.journeylatinamerica.co.uk; 12 & 13 Heathfield Terrace, Chiswick, London, UK) Organized outfit offering three-week tours on a budget or more comfy basis, taking in Guatemala, Belize and Mexico.

Mayatours (US ☎ +1-800-392-6292; www.mayatour .com; 3412 Leigh Rd, Pompano Beach, FL, USA) Shorter tours and travel services to Mexico and Central America emphasizing Maya archaeology, ecology and diving; accommodations in four-star hotels or jungle lodges on request.

Health Dr David Goldberg

Travelers to Central America and Mexico need to be concerned about food- and mosquito-borne infections. Most are not life-threatening, but they can certainly ruin your trip. Besides getting the proper vaccinations, it's important that you pack a good insect repellent and exercise great care in what you eat and drink.

BEFORE YOU GO

INSURANCE

If your health insurance does not cover you for medical expenses abroad, consider supplemental insurance. Check the Subway section of the Lonely Planet website (www .lonelyplanet.com/subwwway) for more information. See also the US State Department website (www.travel.state.gov/medical .html) for a list of medical evacuation and travel-insurance companies.

Find out in advance if your insurer will pay providers directly or reimburse you later for overseas health expenditures. You may prefer a policy that pays doctors or hospitals directly rather than requiring you to pay up front and claim later. If you have to claim later, keep all documentation. Some policies ask you to call collect to a center in your home country, where an immediate assessment of your problem is made. Check that the policy covers ambulances and an emergency flight home. Some policies offer lower and higher medical-expense options; the higher ones are chiefly for countries such as the USA, which have extremely high medical costs. There is a wide variety of policies available, so check the small print.

RECOMMENDED VACCINATIONS

Since most vaccines don't produce immunity until at least two weeks after they're given, visit a physician four to eight weeks before departure. Ask your doctor for an International Certificate of Vaccination (also known as a yellow booklet), which will list all the vaccinations you've received. This is mandatory for countries that require proof of yellow-fever vaccination upon entry, but it's a good idea to carry it wherever you travel.

Note that some of the recommended vaccines are not approved for use by children and pregnant women; check with your physician.

The only required vaccine for Guatemala, Belize and the Yucatán is yellow fever, and that's only if you're arriving from a yellow fever–infected country in Africa or South America. However, a number of vaccines are recommended; see the box on next page.

MEDICAL CHECKLIST

It is a very good idea to carry a medical and first-aid kit with you, to help yourself in the case of minor illness or injury. Following is a list of items you should consider packing:

- antibiotics
- antidiarrheal drugs (eg loperamide)
- acetaminophen/paracetamol (Tylenol) or aspirin
- anti-inflammatory drugs (eg ibuprofen)
- antihistamines (for hay fever and allergic reactions)
- antibacterial ointment (eg Bactroban) for cuts and abrasions
- steroid cream or cortisone (for poison ivy and other allergic rashes)
- bandages, gauze, gauze rolls
- adhesive or paper tape

vaccine	recommended for	dosage	side effects
chickenpox	travelers who've never had chickenpox	2 doses 1 month apart	fever; mild case of chickenpox
hepatitis A	all travelers	one dose before trip with booster 6-12 months later	soreness at injection site: head aches; body aches
hepatitis B	long-term travelers in close contact with the local population	3 doses over a 6 month period	soreness at injection site: low grade fever
measles	travelers born after 1956 who've had only 1 measles vaccination	1 dose	fever; rash; joint pain; allergic reaction
tetanus-diphtheria	all travelers who haven't had a booster within 10 years	1 dose lasts 10 years	soreness at injection site
typhoid	all travelers	4 capsules by mouth, 1 taken every other day	pain; abdominal nausea; rash
yellow fever	required for travelers arriving from yellow fever–infected areas in Africa or South America	1 dose lasts 10 years	headaches; body aches: severe reactions are rare severe

- scissors, safety pins, tweezers
- thermometer
- pocket knife
- DEET-containing insect repellent for the skin
- permethrin-containing insect spray for clothing, tents and bed nets
- sunblock
- oral rehydration salts
- iodine tablets (for water purification)
- syringes and sterile needles

Bring medications in their original containers, clearly labeled. A signed, dated letter from your physician describing all medical conditions and medications, including generic names, is also a good idea. If carrying syringes or needles, be sure to have a physician's letter documenting their medical necessity.

INTERNET RESOURCES

There is a wealth of travel health advice on the Internet. The Lonely Planet website at www.lonelyplanet.com is a good place to start. The World Health Organization publishes a superb book, *International Travel and Health*, which is revised annually and is available free online at www.who.int/ith.

It is a good idea to consult your government's travel health website before your departure:

Australia www.dfat.gov.au/travel
Canada www.hc-sc.gc.ca/pphb-dgspsp/tmp-pmv /pub_e.html

United Kingdom www.doh.gov.uk/traveladvice /index.htm
United States www.cdc.gov/travel

FURTHER READING

For more information, see Lonely Planet's *Healthy Travel Central & South America*. If you're traveling with children, Lonely Planet's *Travel with Children* may be useful. *ABC of Healthy Travel,* by Eric Walker et al, and *Medicine for the Outdoors,* by Paul S Auerbach, are other valuable resources.

IN TRANSIT

DEEP VEIN THROMBOSIS (DVT)

Blood clots may form in the legs (DVT) during plane flights, chiefly because of prolonged immobility. The longer the flight, the greater the risk. Though most blood clots are reabsorbed uneventfully, some may break off and travel through the blood vessels to the lungs, where they could cause life-threatening complications.

The chief symptom of DVT is swelling or pain of the foot, ankle or calf, usually but not always on just one side. When a blood clot travels to the lungs, it may cause chest pain and difficulty breathing. Travelers with any of these symptoms should immediately seek medical attention.

To prevent the development of DVT on long flights, you should walk about the cabin, perform isometric compressions of the leg muscles (ie contract the leg muscles while sitting), drink plenty of fluids and avoid alcohol.

JET LAG & MOTION SICKNESS

Jet lag is common when crossing more than five time zones and causes insomnia, fatigue, malaise or nausea. To avoid jet lag, drink plenty of fluids (non-alcoholic) and eat light meals. Upon arrival, get exposure to natural sunlight and readjust your schedule (for meals, sleep etc) as soon as possible.

Antihistamines such as dimenhydrinate (Dramamine) and meclizine (Antivert, Bonine) are usually the first choice for treating motion sickness. Their main side effect is drowsiness. A herbal alternative is ginger, which works like a charm for some people.

IN GUATEMALA, BELIZE & YUCATÁN

AVAILABILITY & COST OF HEALTH CARE

Most doctors and hospitals in the region expect payment in cash, regardless of whether you have travel health insurance. If you develop a life-threatening medical problem, you'll probably want to be evacuated to a country with state-of-the-art medical care. Since this may cost tens of thousands of dollars, be sure you have insurance to cover this before you depart.

Many pharmacies in the region are well supplied, but important medications may not be consistently available. Be sure to bring along adequate supplies of all prescription drugs.

In Guatemala, good medical care is available in Guatemala City, but options are limited elsewhere in the country. In general, private hospitals are more reliable than public facilities, which may experience significant shortages of equipment and supplies. Many travelers use **Hospital Herrera Llerandi** (☎ 2334-5959; www.herrerallerandi.com; 6a Av 8-71, Zona 10).

Medical facilities in Belize are extremely limited, and the number of doctors is quite small. Routine care is readily obtainable in Belize City and the larger towns, but facilities for complicated problems may be diffi-cult to find. In rural areas, medical care may be unavailable. In Belize City, there are two private hospitals that provide generally good care, **Belize Medical Associates** (☎ 223-0302/3/4) and **Universal Health Services** (☎ 223-5865). In San Ignacio, **La Loma Luz Hospital** (☎ 824-2087) offers primary care as well as 24-hour emergency services. For divers, there is a hyperbaric chamber on Ambergris Caye.

Most prescription medications are available in Belize, but may be relatively expensive. You can obtain prescriptions from general practitioners, who will provide this service for a small fee. Some pharmacists, especially in smaller pharmacies, will dispense medications without a prescription.

In Belize, the phone number for an ambulance is ☎ 90, but this service is not available in many communities. For a private ambulance in Belize City, call ☎ 223-3292.

In the Yucatán, adequate medical care is available in the major cities, but facilities in rural areas may be limited. Mexican pharmacies are identified by a green cross and a 'Farmacia' sign. Most are well supplied and the pharmacists well trained. Reliable pharmacy chains include Sanborns, Farmacia Guadalajara, Benavides and Farmacia Fenix. Some medications requiring a prescription in the US may be dispensed in Mexico without a prescription. To find an after-hours pharmacy, look in local newspapers, ask your hotel concierge, or check the front door of a local pharmacy, which will often post the name of a nearby after-hours pharmacy.

INFECTIOUS DISEASES
Chagas' Disease

Chagas' disease is a parasitic infection transmitted by triatomine insects (reduviid bugs), which inhabit crevices in the walls and roofs of traditional housing in South and Central America. In Guatemala, Belize and Mexico, Chagas' disease occurs in rural areas. The triatomine insect lays its feces on human skin as it bites, usually at night. A person becomes infected when he or she unknowingly rubs the feces into the bite wound or an open sore. Chagas' disease is extremely rare in travelers. However, if you sleep in a poorly constructed house, especially one made of mud, adobe or thatch, you should be sure to protect yourself with a bed net and a good insecticide.

HEALTH

Cholera

Cholera outbreaks occur periodically in Guatemala, but the disease is rare among travelers. No cases of cholera have been reported in Belize since 2000, and only a handful of cases have been reported in southern Mexico.

Dengue Fever

Dengue fever is a viral infection found throughout Central America and transmitted by aedes mosquitoes, which bite mostly during the daytime and are usually found close to human habitations, often indoors. They breed primarily in artificial water containers such as jars, barrels, cans, cisterns, metal drums, plastic containers and discarded tires. As a result, dengue is especially common in densely populated, urban environments.

Dengue usually causes flu-like symptoms, including fever, muscle aches, joint pains, headaches, nausea and vomiting, often followed by a rash. The body aches may be quite uncomfortable, but most cases resolve uneventfully in a few days. Severe cases usually occur in children under the age of 15 who are experiencing their second dengue infection.

Though relatively uncommon in Belize, thousands of cases occur each year in Guatemala, and all the Mexican states covered in this book suffered outbreaks after the 2002 rainy season. The risk in the Yucatán is greatest from July to September.

There is no treatment for dengue fever except to take analgesics such as acetaminophen/paracetamol (Tylenol) and drink plenty of fluids. Severe cases may require hospitalization for intravenous fluids and supportive care. There is no vaccine. The cornerstone of prevention is protection against insect bites (see p467).

Hepatitis A

Hepatitis A occurs throughout Central America. It's a viral infection of the liver that is usually acquired by ingestion of contaminated water, food or ice, though it may also be acquired by direct contact with infected persons. The illness occurs all over the world, but the incidence is higher in developing nations. Symptoms may include fever, malaise, jaundice, nausea, vomiting and abdominal pain. Most cases resolve uneventfully, though hepatitis A occasionally causes severe liver damage. There is no treatment.

The vaccine for hepatitis A is extremely safe and highly effective. If you get a booster six to 12 months later, it lasts for at least 10 years. It is recommended for travelers visiting Guatemala, Belize or Mexico. Because the safety of hepatitis A vaccine has not been established for pregnant women or children under age two, they should instead be given a gamma-globulin injection.

Hepatitis B

Like hepatitis A, hepatitis B is a liver infection that occurs worldwide but is more common in developing nations. Unlike hepatitis A, the disease is usually acquired by sexual contact or by exposure to infected blood, generally through blood transfusions or contaminated needles. The vaccine is recommended only for long-term travelers (on the road more than six months) who expect to live in rural areas or have close physical contact with the local population. Additionally, the vaccine is recommended for anyone who anticipates sexual contact with local people or the need for medical, dental or other treatments while abroad, especially transfusions or injections.

Hepatitis B vaccine is safe and highly effective. However, three injections are necessary to establish full immunity. Several countries added hepatitis B vaccine to the list of routine childhood immunizations in the 1980s, so many young adults are already protected.

Leishmaniasis

Leishmaniasis occurs in the mountains and jungles of Guatemala, Belize and the Yucatán. The infection is transmitted by sand flies. To protect yourself, follow the same precautions for mosquitoes (p467), except that netting must be finer (at least 18 holes to the linear inch), and you should stay indoors during the early evening. There is no vaccine.

In Belize, the disease is generally limited to the skin, causing slow-growing ulcers over exposed parts of the body; less commonly, it may disseminate to the bone marrow, liver and spleen.

In Guatemala, most cases of cutaneous leishmaniasis are reported from the northern parts of the country at elevations less than 1000m. The greatest risk occurs in the forested areas of El Petén. The disseminated form may occur in the semiarid valleys and foothills in the east central part of the country.

The disseminated form is rare in the Yucatán.

Leptospirosis

Leptospirosis is acquired by exposure to water contaminated by the urine of infected animals. The disease is reported throughout the region. Outbreaks may occur as a result of flooding, when sewage overflow contaminates water sources. The initial symptoms, which resemble a mild flu, usually subside uneventfully in a few days, with or without treatment, but a minority of cases are complicated by jaundice or meningitis. There is no vaccine. You can minimize your risk by staying out of bodies of fresh water that may be contaminated by animal urine. If you're engaging in high-risk activities in an area where an outbreak is in progress, you can take 200mg of doxycycline once weekly as a preventative measure. If you develop leptospirosis, the treatment is 100mg of doxycycline twice daily.

Malaria

Malaria occurs in every country in Central America. It's transmitted by mosquito bites, which usually occur between dusk and dawn. The main symptom is high, spiking fevers, which may be accompanied by chills, sweats, headache, body aches, weakness, vomiting or diarrhea. Severe cases may involve the central nervous system and lead to seizures, confusion, coma and death.

For Belize, malaria pills are recommended for travel to all areas except Belize City. The risk is highest in the western and southern regions.

In Guatemala, taking malaria pills is strongly recommended for all rural areas, except at altitudes higher than 1500m (4900ft). Risk is high in the departments of Alta Verapaz, Baja Verapaz, Petén and San Marcos, and moderate in the departments of Escuintla, Huehuetenango, Izabal, Quiché, Retalhuleu, Suchitepéquez and Zacapa. Transmission is greatest during the rainy season (June through November). There is no risk in Antigua or Lago de Atitlán.

In the Yucatán region, malaria is a recurring problem. Taking malaria pills is strongly recommended when visiting rural areas in the states of Chiapas, Tabasco, Quintana Roo and Campeche.

The malaria pill of choice is chloroquine, taken once weekly in a dosage of 500mg, starting one to two weeks before arrival and continuing during the trip and for four weeks afterwards. Chloroquine is safe, inexpensive and highly effective. Side effects are typically mild and may include nausea, abdominal discomfort, headache, dizziness, blurred vision or itching. Severe reactions are uncommon.

Since no pills are 100% effective, protecting yourself against mosquito bites (p467) is just as important as taking malaria pills.

You may not have access to medical care while traveling, so you should bring additional pills for emergency self-treatment, which you should take if you can't reach a doctor and you develop symptoms that suggest malaria, such as high, spiking fevers. One option is to take four tablets of Malarone once daily for three days. If you start self-medication, you should try to see a doctor at the earliest possible opportunity.

If you develop a fever after returning home, see a physician, as malaria symptoms may not occur for months.

Onchocerciasis (River Blindness)

Onchocerciasis is caused by a roundworm that may invade the eye, leading to blindness. The infection is transmitted by black flies, which breed along the banks of rapidly flowing rivers and streams.

In Guatemala, the disease occurs in heavily forested areas between 500m and 1500m in elevation, chiefly the Pacific slope of the Sierra Madre and in Escuintla along the Verde and Guachipilín rivers. In Mexico, the disease is reported from highland areas in Chiapas. This disease is not a problem in Belize.

Rabies

Rabies is a viral infection of the brain and spinal cord that is almost always fatal. The rabies virus is carried in the saliva of infected animals and is typically transmitted through an animal bite, though contamination of any break in the skin with infected saliva may result in rabies.

Rabies occurs in all Central American countries. The greatest risk is in the triangle where Guatemala, Belize and the Yucatán

HEALTH

region meet. Most cases are related to bites from dogs or bats.

Rabies vaccine is safe, but requires three injections and is quite expensive. Those at high risk for rabies, such as spelunkers (cave explorers), should certainly be vaccinated. The treatment for a possibly rabid bite consists of vaccine with immune globulin. It's effective, but must be given promptly. Most travelers don't need to be vaccinated against rabies.

All animal bites and scratches must be promptly and thoroughly cleansed with large amounts of soap and water and local health authorities contacted to determine whether or not further treatment is necessary (see right).

Rocky Mountain Spotted Fever

This fever is a tick-borne infection characterized by fever, headache and muscle aches, followed by a rash. Complications may include pneumonia, meningitis, gangrene and kidney failure, and may be life threatening. Cases have been reported in the Yucatán Peninsula.

Typhoid Fever

Typhoid fever is caused by ingestion of contaminated food or water. Outbreaks often occur at times of flooding, when sewage overflow may contaminate water sources. The initial symptoms, which resemble a mild flu, usually subside uneventfully in a few days, with or without treatment, but a minority of cases are complicated by jaundice or meningitis. Fever occurs in virtually all cases. Other symptoms may include headache, malaise, muscle aches, dizziness, loss of appetite, nausea and abdominal pain, and either diarrhea or constipation. There is no vaccine.

The drug of choice for typhoid fever is usually a quinolone antibiotic such as ciprofloxacin (Cipro) or levofloxacin (Levaquin), which many travelers carry for treatment of travelers' diarrhea. If you self-treat for typhoid fever, however, you may also need to self-treat for malaria, since the symptoms of the two diseases may be indistinguishable.

Unless you expect to take all your meals in major hotels and restaurants, vaccination for typhoid is a good idea. It's usually given orally, but is also available as an injection.

Neither vaccine is approved for use in children under age two.

Yellow Fever

Yellow fever no longer occurs in Central America, but Guatemala, Belize and Mexico require yellow-fever vaccination before entry *only* if you're arriving from an infected country in Africa or South America. Yellow-fever vaccine is given only in approved yellow-fever vaccination centers, which provide validated International Certificates of Vaccination ('yellow booklets'). The vaccine should be given at least 10 days before departure and remains effective for approximately 10 years. Reactions to the vaccine are generally mild and may include headaches, muscle aches, low-grade fevers or discomfort at the injection site. Severe, life-threatening reactions are extremely rare.

TRAVELERS' DIARRHEA

To prevent diarrhea, avoid tap water unless it has been boiled, filtered or chemically disinfected (with iodine tablets); only eat fresh fruit or vegetables if cooked or peeled; be wary of dairy products that might contain unpasteurized milk; and be highly selective when eating food from street vendors.

If you develop diarrhea, be sure to drink plenty of fluids, preferably an oral rehydration solution containing salt and sugar. A few loose stools don't require treatment, but if you start having more than four or five stools a day, you should start taking an antibiotic (usually a quinolone drug) and an antidiarrheal agent (such as loperamide). If diarrhea is bloody, persists for more than 72 hours or is accompanied by fever, shaking chills or severe abdominal pain, you should seek medical attention.

ENVIRONMENTAL HAZARDS
Animal Bites

Do not attempt to pet, handle or feed any animal, with the exception of domestic animals known to be free of infectious diseases. Most animal injuries occur when people attempt to touch or feed animals.

Any bite or scratch by a mammal, including bats, should be promptly and thoroughly cleansed with large amounts of soap and water, and an antiseptic such as iodine or alcohol applied. The local health authorities should be contacted immediately for possible post-exposure rabies treatment, whether or not you have been immunized against rabies. It may also be advisable to take antibiotics, since wounds caused by animal bites and scratches frequently become infected. One of the newer quinolones, such as levofloxacin (Levaquin), which many travelers carry in case of diarrhea, would be an appropriate choice.

Mosquito Bites

To prevent mosquito bites, wear long sleeves, long pants, hats and shoes (rather than sandals). Pack a good insect repellent, preferably one containing DEET, which should be applied to exposed skin and clothing, but not to eyes, mouth, cuts, wounds or irritated skin. Products containing lower concentrations of DEET are as effective, but for shorter periods of time. In general, adults and children over 12 should use preparations containing 25% to 35% DEET, which usually lasts about six hours. Children between two and 12 years of age should use preparations containing no more than 10% DEET, applied sparingly, which will usually last about three hours. Neurologic toxicity has been reported from DEET, especially in children, but appears to be extremely uncommon and is generally related to overuse. DEET-containing compounds should not be used on children under age two.

Insect repellents containing certain botanical products, including eucalyptus and soybean oil, are effective but last only 1½ to two hours. DEET-containing repellents are preferable for areas where there is a high risk of malaria or yellow fever. Products based on citronella are not effective.

For additional protection, you can apply permethrin to clothing, shoes, tents and bed nets. Permethrin treatments are safe and remain effective for at least two weeks, even when items are laundered. Permethrin should not be applied directly to skin.

Don't sleep with windows open unless there is a screen. If sleeping outdoors or in accommodations that allow entry of mosquitoes, use a bed net, preferably treated with permethrin, with the edges tucked in under the mattress. The mesh size should be less than 1.5mm. If the sleeping area is not otherwise protected, use a mosquito coil, which will fill the room with insecticide through the night. Repellent-impregnated wristbands are not effective.

Snake Bites

Snakes are a hazard in these areas of Central America. The chief concern is *Bothrops asper*, the Central American or common lancehead, also called the fer-de-lance and known locally as *barba amarilla* (yellow beard) or *terciopelo* (velvet skin). This heavy-bodied snake reaches up to 2m (6.5ft) in length and is found especially in the northern provinces. It has a broadly triangular head with a pattern of Xs and triangles on its back. Others to watch out for are the brightly striped coral snake and the tropical rattlesnake. All three snakes are deadly dangerous, though the coral snake is shyer than the 'irritable' rattlesnake.

In the event of a venomous snake bite, place the victim at rest, keep the bitten area immobilized, and move the victim immediately to the nearest medical facility. Avoid the use of tourniquets, which are no longer recommended.

Sun

To protect yourself from excessive sun exposure, you should stay out of the midday sun, wear sunglasses and a wide-brimmed hat, and apply sunscreen with SPF 15 or higher, with both UVA and UVB protection. Sunscreen should be generously applied to all exposed parts of the body approximately 30 minutes before sun exposure and should be reapplied after swimming or vigorous activity. Travelers should also drink plenty of fluids and avoid strenuous exercise when it's hot. Dehydration and salt deficiency can cause heat exhaustion, which can then progress to heatstroke. Symptoms of this serious condition include a general feeling of unwellness, not sweating very much (or not at all) and a high body temperature (39°C to 41°C, or 102°F to 106°F). Severe, throbbing headaches and lack of coordination can also occur. Hospitalization is essential, but in the interim get victims out of the sun, remove their clothing, cover them with a wet sheet or towel and fan continually. Give fluids if they are conscious.

Tick Bites

To protect yourself from tick bites, follow the same precautions as for mosquitoes,

HEALTH

except that boots are preferable to shoes, with pants tucked in. Be sure to perform a thorough tick check at the end of each day. You'll generally need the assistance of a friend or a mirror for a full examination. Remove ticks with tweezers, grasping them firmly by the head. Insect repellents based on botanical products (p467) have not been adequately studied for insects other than mosquitoes and cannot be recommended to prevent tick bites.

Water
Tap water is not safe to drink in any of the three countries. Vigorous boiling for one minute is the most effective means of water purification. At altitudes greater than 2000m (6500ft), boil for three minutes.

Another option is to disinfect water with iodine pills. Follow the enclosed instructions carefully. Alternatively, you can add 2% tincture of iodine to one quart or liter of water (five drops to clear water, 10 drops to cloudy water) and let stand for 30 minutes. If the water is cold, longer times may be required. The taste of iodinated water may be improved by adding vitamin C (ascorbic acid). Iodinated water should not be consumed for more than a few weeks. Pregnant women, those with a history of thyroid disease and those allergic to iodine should not drink iodinated water.

Water filters with smaller pores (reverse osmosis filters) provide the broadest protection, but they are relatively large and are readily plugged by debris. Those with some-

what larger pores (microstrainer filters) are ineffective against viruses, although they remove other organisms. Follow manufacturers' instructions carefully.

Safe, inexpensive *agua pura* (purified water) is widely available in hotels, shops and restaurants.

CHILDREN & PREGNANT WOMEN
In general, it's safe for children and pregnant women to go to Guatemala, Belize and the Yucatán. However, because some of the vaccines listed above are not approved for use in children and during pregnancy, these travelers should be particularly careful not to drink tap water or consume any questionable food or drink. Also, when traveling with children, make sure they're up to date on all routine immunizations. It's sometimes appropriate to give children some of their vaccines a little early before visiting a developing nation – discuss this with your pediatrician. If pregnant, you should bear in mind that should a complication such as premature labor develop while abroad, the quality of medical care may not be comparable to that in your home country.

Since yellow-fever vaccine is not recommended for pregnant women or children less than nine months old, these travelers, if arriving from a country with yellow fever, should obtain a waiver letter, preferably written on letterhead and bearing the stamp used by official immunization centers to validate the international certificate of vaccination.

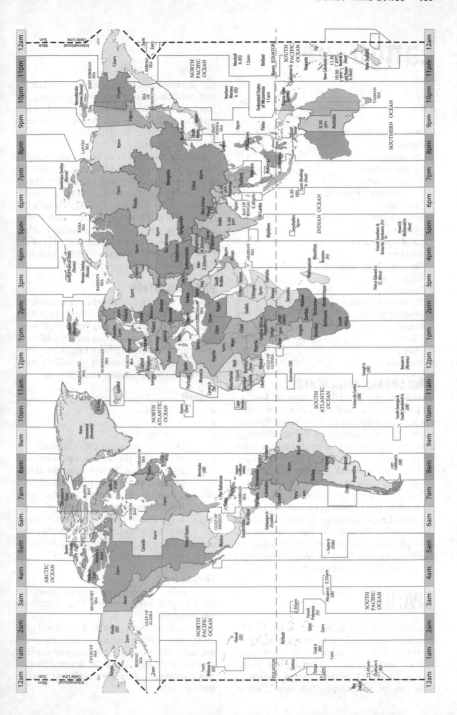

Language

CONTENTS

WHO SPEAKS WHAT WHERE?

Spanish is the official language of Mexico and Guatemala, and the most commonly spoken language on La Ruta Maya. English is the official language of Belize, although Spanish, Garifuna and a local creole are also widely spoken. Groups of people throughout the region speak various Mayan languages and dialects.

For a more comprehensive guide to the Spanish of the region, get a copy of Lonely Planet's *Latin American Spanish* or *Mexican Spanish Phrasebook*. For a few words and phrases plus general information on Garifuna and the Modern Mayan languages Mam and Quiché, see pp476–8.

SPANISH

Studying at home before you leave for the Mayan region might get you up to speed in Spanish, but for learning the language quickly and well there's nothing like studying in your destination country. Not only will you be sure to pick up local idioms,

you'll also absorb the cultural intricacies that provide context for the proper usage of your new knowledge. Many schools offer programs that allow you to stay with a local family while you study – the ultimate in total immersion.

Language schools can be found throughout Guatemala and the Yucatán, but several towns are especially well known for them. In Guatemala these are Antigua (p84), Cobán (p139), Flores (p171), Panajachel (p94), Quetzaltenango (p115), San Pedro La Laguna (p101) and Todos Santos Cuchamatán (p126). In Mexico these are Playa del Carmen (p339), Mérida (p351) and San Cristóbal de Las Casas (p396).

PRONUNCIATION

Spanish spelling is phonetically consistent, meaning that there's a clear and consistent relationship between what you see in writing and how it's pronounced. In addition, most Spanish sounds have English equivalents, so English speakers shouldn't have too much trouble being understood.

Vowels

a	as in 'father'
e	as in 'met'
i	as in 'marine'
o	as in 'or' (without the 'r' sound)
u	as in 'rule'; the 'u' is not pronounced after **q** and in the letter combinations **gue** and **gui**, unless it's marked with a diaeresis (eg *argüir*), in which case it's pronounced as English 'w'
y	at the end of a word or when it stands alone, it's pronounced as the Spanish **i** (eg *ley*); between vowels within a word it's as the 'y' in 'yonder'

Consonants

As a rule, Spanish consonants resemble their English counterparts. The exceptions are listed below.

While the consonants **ch**, **ll** and **ñ** are generally considered distinct letters, **ch** and **ll** are now often listed alphabetically under **c** and **l** respectively. The letter **ñ** is still treated as a separate letter and comes after **n** in alphabetical listings.

b	similar to English 'b,' but softer; referred to as 'b larga'
c	as in 'celery' before **e** and **i**; otherwise as English 'k'
ch	as in 'church'
d	as in 'dog,' but between vowels and after **l** or **n**, the sound is closer to the 'th' in 'this'
g	as the 'ch' in the Scottish *loch* before **e** and **i** ('kh' in our guides to pronunciation); elsewhere, as in 'go'
h	invariably silent. If your name begins with this letter, listen carefully if you're waiting for public officials to call you.
j	as the 'ch' in the Scottish *loch* (written as 'kh' in our guides to pronunciation)
ll	as the 'y' in 'yellow'
ñ	as the 'ni' in 'onion'
r	as in 'run', but strongly rolled, especially in words with **rr**
rr	very strongly rolled
v	similar to English 'b,' but softer; referred to as 'b corta'
x	usually pronounced as **j** above; as in 'taxi' in other instances. Note that in Mayan words **x** is pronounced like English 'sh'
z	as the 's' in 'sun'

Word Stress

In general, words ending in vowels or the letters **n** or **s** have stress on the next-to-last syllable, while those with other endings have stress on the last syllable. Thus *vaca* (cow) and *caballos* (horses) both carry stress on the next-to-last syllable, while *ciudad* (city) and *infeliz* (unhappy) are both stressed on the last syllable.

Written accents will almost always appear in words that don't follow the rules above, eg *sótano* (basement), *América* and *porción* (portion).

GENDER & PLURALS

In Spanish, nouns are either masculine or feminine, and there are rules to help determine gender (there are of course some exceptions). Feminine nouns generally end with **-a** or with the groups **-ción**, **-sión** or **-dad**. Other endings typically signify a masculine noun. Endings for adjectives also change to agree with the gender of the noun they modify (masculine/feminine **-o/-a**).

Where both masculine and feminine fo are included in this language guide, they a. separated by a slash, with the masculine form first, eg *perdido/a*.

If a noun or adjective ends in a vowel, the plural is formed by adding **s** to the end. If it ends in a consonant, the plural is formed by adding **es** to the end.

ACCOMMODATIONS

I'm looking for ...	*Estoy buscando ...*	e·stoy boos·kan·do ...
Where is ...?	*¿Dónde hay ...?*	don·de ai ...
a hotel	*un hotel*	oon o·tel
a boarding house	*una pensión/ residencial/ un hospedaje*	oo·na pen·syon/ re·see·den·syal/ oon os·pe·da·khe
a youth hostel	*un albergue juvenil*	oon al·ber·ge khoo·ve·neel

Are there any rooms available?

¿Hay habitaciones libres?	ay a·bee·ta·syon·es lee·bres

MAKING A RESERVATION

(for phone or written requests)

To ...	*A ...*
From ...	*De ...*
Date	*Fecha*
I'd like to book ...	*Quisiera reservar ...* (see the list under 'Accommodations' for bed and room options)
in the name of ...	*en nombre de ...*
for the nights of ...	*para las noches del ...*
credit card ...	*tarjeta de crédito ...*
number	*número*
expiry date	*fecha de vencimiento*
Please confirm ...	*Puede confirmar ...*
availability	*la disponibilidad*
price	*el precio*

I'd like a room.	*Quisiera una habitación ...*	kee·sye·ra oo·na a·bee·ta·syon ...
double	*doble*	do·ble
single	*individual*	een·dee·vee·dwal
twin	*con dos camas*	kon dos ka·mas

How much is it per ...?	*¿Cuánto cuesta por ...?*	kwan·to kwes·ta por ...
night	*noche*	no·che
person	*persona*	per·so·na
week	*semana*	se·ma·na

	baño privado/	ba·nyo pree-va·do/
	ompartido	kom·par·tee·do
	·sión	pen·syon
	·mpleta	kom·ple·ta
~~expensive~~	demasiado caro	de·ma·sya·do ka·ro
cheaper	más económico	mas e·ko·no·mee·ko
discount	descuento	des·kwen·to

Does it include breakfast?
  ¿Incluye el desayuno? een·kloo·ye el de·sa·yoo·no

May I see the room?
  ¿Puedo ver la pwe·do ver la
  habitación? a·bee·ta·syon

I don't like it.
  No me gusta. no me goos·ta

It's fine. I'll take it.
  OK. La alquilo. o·kay la al·kee·lo

I'm leaving now.
  Me voy ahora. me voy a·o·ra

CONVERSATION & ESSENTIALS

In their public behavior, Central Americans are very conscious of civilities, sometimes to the point of ceremoniousness. Never approach a stranger for information without extending a greeting, and use only the polite form of address, especially with the police and public officials. Young people may be less likely to expect this, but it's best to stick to the polite form unless you're quite sure you won't offend by using the informal mode. The polite form is used in all cases in this guide; where options are given, the form is indicated by the abbreviations 'pol' and 'inf.'

Saying *por favor* (please) and *gracias* (thank you) are second nature to most Central Americans and a recommended tool in your travel kit. The three most common Spanish greetings are often shortened to simply *buenos* (for *buenos días*) and *buenas* (for *buenas tardes* and *buenas noches*).

Hello.	Hola.	o·la
Good morning.	Buenos días.	bwe·nos dee·as
Good afternoon.	Buenas tardes.	bwe·nas tar·des
Good evening/ night.	Buenas noches.	bwe·nas no·ches
Goodbye.	Adiós.	a·dyos (rarely used)
Bye/See you soon.	Hasta luego.	as·ta lwe·go
Yes.	Sí.	see
No.	No.	no
Please.	Por favor.	por fa·vor
Thank you.	Gracias.	gra·syas
Many thanks.	Muchas gracias.	moo·chas gra·syas

You're welcome.	De nada.	de na·da
Pardon me.	Perdón.	per·don
Excuse me.	Permiso.	per·mee·so
(used when asking permission)		
Forgive me.	Disculpe.	dees·kool·pe
(used when apologizing)		

How are things?
  ¿Qué tal? ke tal

What's your name?
  ¿Cómo se llama? ko·mo se ya·ma (pol)
  ¿Cómo te llamas? ko·mo te ya·mas (inf)

My name is ...
  Me llamo ... me ya·mo ...

It's a pleasure to meet you.
  Mucho gusto. moo·cho goos·to

The pleasure is mine.
  El gusto es mío. el goos·to es mee·o

Where are you from?
  ¿De dónde es/eres? de don·de es/er·es (pol/inf)

I'm from ...
  Soy de ... soy de ...

Where are you staying?
  ¿Dónde está alojado? don·de es·ta a·lo·kha·do (pol)
  ¿Dónde estás alojado? don·de es·tas a·lo·kha·do (inf)

May I take a photo?
  ¿Puedo sacar una foto? pwe·do sa·kar oo·na fo·to

DIRECTIONS

How do I get to ...?
  ¿Cómo puedo llegar a ...? ko·mo pwe·do ye·gar a ...

Is it far?
  ¿Está lejos? es·ta le·khos

Go straight ahead.
  Siga/Vaya derecho. see·ga/va·ya de·re·cho

Turn left.
  Voltée a la izquierda. vol·te·e a la ees·kyer·da

Turn right.
  Voltée a la derecha. vol·te·e a la de·re·cha

I'm lost.
  Estoy perdido/a. es·toy per·dee·do/a

SIGNS	
Entrada	Entrance
Salida	Exit
Información	Information
Abierto	Open
Cerrado	Closed
Prohibido	Prohibited
Comisaria	Police Station
Servicios/Baños	Toilets
Hombres/Varones	Men
Mujeres/Damas	Women

LANGUAGE

| nuts | *las fruta secas* | las *froo*·tas *se*·kas |
| penicillin | *la penicilina* | la pe·nee·see·*lee*·na |

I'm ...	*Soy ...*	soy ...
asthmatic	*asmático/a*	as·*ma*·tee·ko/a
diabetic	*diabético/a*	dya·*be*·tee·ko/a
epileptic	*epiléptico/a*	e·pee·*lep*·tee·ko/a

I have ...	*Tengo ...*	*ten*·go ...
a cough	*tos*	tos
diarrhea	*diarrea*	dya·*re*·a
a headache	*un dolor de*	oon do·*lor* de
	cabeza	ka·*be*·sa
nausea	*náusea*	*now*·se·a

LANGUAGE DIFFICULTIES

Do you speak (English)?
¿Habla/Hablas (inglés)? a·bla/*a*·blas (een·*gles*) (pol/inf)
Does anyone here speak English?
¿Hay alguien que hable ai al·*gyen* ke *a*·ble
inglés? een·*gles*
I (don't) understand.
Yo (no) entiendo. yo (no) en·*tyen*·do
How do you say ...?
¿Cómo se dice ...? *ko*·mo se *dee*·se ...
What does ... mean?
¿Qué quiere decir ...? ke *kye*·re de·*seer* ...

Could you	*¿Puede ..., por*	*pwe*·de ... por
please ...?	*favor?*	fa·vor
repeat that	*repetirlo*	re·pe·*teer*·lo
speak more	*hablar más*	a·*blar* mas
slowly	*despacio*	des·*pa*·syo
write it down	*escribirlo*	es·kree·*beer*·lo

NUMBERS

1	*uno*	*oo*·no
2	*dos*	dos
3	*tres*	tres
4	*cuatro*	*kwa*·tro
5	*cinco*	*seen*·ko
6	*seis*	says
7	*siete*	*sye*·te
8	*ocho*	*o*·cho
9	*nueve*	*nwe*·ve
10	*diez*	dyes
11	*once*	*on*·se
12	*doce*	*do*·se
13	*trece*	*tre*·se
14	*catorce*	ka·*tor*·se
15	*quince*	*keen*·se
16	*dieciséis*	dye·see·*says*
17	*diecisiete*	dye·see·*sye*·te
18	*dieciocho*	dye·see·*o*·cho
19	*diecinueve*	dye·see·*nwe*·ve
20	*veinte*	*vayn*·te

EMERGENCIES

Help!	*¡Socorro!*	so·*ko*·ro
Fire!	*¡Incendio!*	een·*sen*·dyo
I've been robbed.	*Me robaron.*	me ro·*ba*·ron
Go away!	*¡Déjeme!*	*de*·khe·me
Get lost!	*¡Váyase!*	*va*·ya·se

Call ...!	*¡Llame a ...!*	*ya*·me a ...
an ambulance	*una ambulancia*	oo·na am·boo·*lan*·sya
a doctor	*un médico*	oon *me*·dee·ko
the police	*la policía*	la po·lee·*see*·a

It's an emergency.
Es una emergencia. es oo·na e·mer·*khen*·sya
Could you help me, please?
¿Me puede ayudar, me *pwe*·de a·yoo·*dar*
por favor? por fa·*vor*
I'm lost.
Estoy perdido/a. es·*toy* per·*dee*·do/a
Where are the toilets?
¿Dónde están los baños? *don*·de es·*tan* los *ba*·nyos

Can you show me (on the map)?
¿Me lo podría indicar me lo po·*dree*·a een·dee·*kar*
(en el mapa)? (en el *ma*·pa)

north	*norte*	*nor*·te
south	*sur*	soor
east	*este/oriente*	*es*·te/o·*ryen*·te
west	*oeste/occidente*	o·*es*·te/ok·see·*den*·te
here	*aquí*	a·*kee*
there	*allí*	a·*yee*
avenue	*avenida*	a·ve·*nee*·da
block	*cuadra*	*kwa*·dra
street	*calle/paseo*	*ka*·lye/pa·*se*·o

HEALTH

I'm sick.
Estoy enfermo/a. es·*toy* en·*fer*·mo/a
I need a doctor.
Necesito un médico. ne·se·*see*·to oon *me*·dee·ko
Where's the hospital?
¿Dónde está el hospital? *don*·de es·*ta* el os·pee·*tal*
I'm pregnant.
Estoy embarazada. es·*toy* em·ba·ra·*sa*·da
I've been vaccinated.
Estoy vacunado/a. es·*toy* va·koo·*na*·do/a

I'm allergic	*Soy alérgico/a*	soy a·*ler*·khee·ko/a
to ...	*a ...*	a ...
antibiotics	*los antibióticos*	los an·tee·*byo*·tee·kos

21	veintiuno	vayn·tee·oo·no
30	treinta	trayn·ta
31	treinta y uno	trayn·ta ee oo·no
40	cuarenta	kwa·ren·ta
50	cincuenta	seen·kwen·ta
60	sesenta	se·sen·ta
70	setenta	se·ten·ta
80	ochenta	o·chen·ta
90	noventa	no·ven·ta
100	cien	syen
101	ciento uno	syen·to oo·no
200	doscientos	do·syen·tos
1000	mil	meel
5000	cinco mil	seen·ko meel
10,000	diez mil	dyes meel
50,000	cincuenta mil	seen·kwen·ta meel

SHOPPING & SERVICES

I'd like to buy ...
Quisiera comprar ...   kee·sye·ra kom·prar ...
I'm just looking.
Sólo estoy mirando.   so·lo es·toy mee·ran·do
May I look at it?
¿Puedo mirarlo/la?   pwe·do mee·rar·lo/la
How much is it?
¿Cuánto cuesta?   kwan·to kwes·ta
That's too expensive for me.
Es demasiado caro   es de·ma·sya·do ka·ro
para mí.   pa·ra mee
Could you lower the price?
¿Podría bajar un poco   po·dree·a ba·khar oon po·ko
el precio?   el pre·syo
I don't like it.
No me gusta.   no me goos·ta
I'll take it.
Lo llevo.   lo ye·vo

Do you accept ...?	¿Aceptan ...?	a·sep·tan ...
American dollars	dólares americanos	do·la·res a·me·ree·ka·nos
credit cards	tarjetas de crédito	tar·khe·tas de kre·dee·to
traveler's checks	cheques de viajero	che·kes de vya·khe·ro
less	menos	me·nos
more	más	mas
large	grande	gran·de
small	pequeño/a	pe·ke·nyo/a
I'm looking for (the) ...	Estoy buscando ...	es·toy boos·kan·do
ATM	el cajero automático	el ka·khe·ro ow·to·ma·tee·ko
bank	el banco	el ban·ko

bookstore	la librería	la lee·bre·ree·a
embassy	la embajada	la em·ba·kha·da
exchange house	la casa de cambio	la ka·sa de kam·byo
general store	la tienda	la tyen·da
laundry	la lavandería	la la·van·de·ree·a
market	el mercado	el mer·ka·do
pharmacy/ chemist	la farmacia/ la droguería	la far·ma·sya/ la dro·ge·ree·a
post office	los correos	los ko·re·os
supermarket	el supermercado	el soo·per·mer·ka·do
tourist office	la oficina de turismo	la o·fee·see·na de too·rees·mo

What time does it open/close?
¿A qué hora abre/cierra? a ke o·ra a·bre/sye·ra
I want to change some money/traveler's checks.
Quiero cambiar dinero/   kye·ro kam·byar dee·ne·ro/
cheques de viajero.   che·kes de vya·khe·ro
What is the exchange rate?
¿Cuál es el tipo de   kwal es el tee·po de
cambio?   kam·byo
How many quetzals per dollar?
¿Cuántos quetzales   kwan·tos ket·za·les
por dólar?   por do·lar
I want to call ...
Quiero llamar a ...   kye·ro lya·mar a ...

airmail	correo aéreo	ko·re·o a·e·re·o
letter	carta	kar·ta
registered mail	certificado	ser·tee·fee·ka·do
stamps	estampillas	es·tam·pee·lyas

TIME & DATES

What time is it?	¿Qué hora es?	ke o·ra es
It's one o'clock.	Es la una.	es la oo·na
It's seven o'clock.	Son las siete.	son las sye·te
midnight	medianoche	me·dya·no·che
noon	mediodía	me·dyo·dee·a
half past two	dos y media	dos ee me·dya
now	ahora	a·o·ra
today	hoy	oy
tonight	esta noche	es·ta no·che
tomorrow	mañana	ma·nya·na
yesterday	ayer	a·yer
Monday	lunes	loo·nes
Tuesday	martes	mar·tes
Wednesday	miércoles	myer·ko·les
Thursday	jueves	khwe·ves
Friday	viernes	vyer·nes
Saturday	sábado	sa·ba·do
Sunday	domingo	do·meen·go

LANGUAGE

January	enero	e·ne·ro
February	febrero	fe·bre·ro
March	marzo	mar·so
April	abril	a·breel
May	mayo	ma·yo
June	junio	khoo·nyo
July	julio	khoo·lyo
August	agosto	a·gos·to
September	septiembre	sep·tyem·bre
October	octubre	ok·too·bre
November	noviembre	no·vyem·bre
December	diciembre	dee·syem·bre

TRANSPORT
Public Transport

What time does	¿A qué hora ...	a ke o·ra ...
... leave/arrive?	sale/llega?	sa·le/ye·ga
the bus	el autobus	el ow·to·boos
the plane	el avión	el a·vyon
the ship	el barco/buque	el bar·ko/boo·ke
airport	el aeropuerto	el a·e·ro·pwer·to
bus station	la estación de	la es·ta·syon de
	autobuses	ow·to·boo·ses
bus stop	la parada de	la pa·ra·da de
	autobuses	ow·to·boo·ses
luggage check	guardería/	gwar·de·ree·a/
room	equipaje	e·kee·pa·khe
ticket office	la boletería	la bo·le·te·ree·a

I'd like a ticket to ...
Quiero un boleto a ... kye·ro oon bo·le·to a ...

What's the fare to ...?
¿Cuánto cuesta hasta ...? kwan·to kwes·ta a·sta ...

student's	de estudiante	de es·too·dyan·te
1st class	primera clase	pree·me·ra kla·se
2nd class	segunda clase	se·goon·da kla·se
single/one-way	ida	ee·da
return/round trip	ida y vuelta	ee·da ee vwel·ta
taxi	taxi	tak·see

Private Transport

I'd like to	Quisiera	kee·sye·ra
hire a/an ...	alquilar ...	al·kee·lar ...
bicycle	una bicicleta	oo·na bee·see·kle·ta
car	un auto/	oon ow·to/
	un coche	oon ko·che
4WD	un todo terreno	oon to·do te·re·no
motorbike	una moto	oo·na mo·to
pickup (truck)	camioneta	ka·myo·ne·ta
truck	camión	ka·myon
hitchhike	hacer dedo	a·ser de·do

Is this the road to ...?
¿Se va a ... por se va a ... por
esta carretera? es·ta ka·re·te·ra

Where's a petrol station?
¿Dónde hay una don·de ai oo·na
gasolinera/un grifo? ga·so·lee·ne·ra/oon gree·fo

Please fill it up.
Lleno, por favor. ye·no por fa·vor

I'd like (20) liters.
Quiero (veinte) litros. kye·ro (vayn·te) lee·tros

diesel	diesel	dee·sel
leaded (regular)	gasolina con	ga·so·lee·na kon
	plomo	plo·mo
petrol (gas)	gasolina	ga·so·lee·na
unleaded	gasolina sin	ga·so·lee·na seen
	plomo	plo·mo

(How long) Can I park here?
¿(Por cuánto tiempo) (por kwan·to tyem·po)
Puedo aparcar aquí? pwe·do a·par·kar a·kee

Where do I pay?
¿Dónde se paga? don·de se pa·ga

I need a mechanic.
Necesito un ne·se·see·to oon
mecánico. me·ka·nee·ko

The car has broken down (in ...).
El carro se ha averiado el ka·ro se a a·ve·rya·do
(en ...). (en ...)

The motorbike won't start.
No arranca la moto. no a·ran·ka la mo·to

I have a flat tyre.
Tengo un pinchazo. ten·go oon peen·cha·so

I've run out of petrol.
Me quedé sin gasolina. me ke·de seen ga·so·lee·na

I've had an accident.
Tuve un accidente. too·ve oon ak·see·den·te

LANGUAGE

TRAVEL WITH CHILDREN

I need ...	Necesito ...	ne·se·see·to ...
Do you have ...?	¿Hay ...?	ai ...
a car baby seat	un asiento de seguridad para bebés	oon a·syen·to de se·goo·ree·da pa·ra be·bes
a child-minding service	un servicio de cuidado de niños	oon ser·vee·syo de kwee·da·do de nee·nyos
a children's menu	una carta infantil	oona kar·ta een·fan·teel
a creche	una guardería	oo·na gwar·de·ree·a
(disposable) diapers/nappies	pañoles (de usar y tirar)	pa·nyo·les de oo·sar ee tee·rar
an (English-speaking) babysitter	una niñera (de habla inglesa)	oo·na nee·nye·ra (de a·bla een·gle·sa)
formula (milk)	leche en polvo	le·che en pol·vo
a highchair	una trona	oo·na tro·na
a potty	una pelela	oo·na pe·le·la
a stroller	un cochecito	oon ko·che·see·to

Do you mind if I breast-feed here?

¿Le molesta que dé de pecho aquí?	le mo·les·ta ke de de pe·cho a·kee

Are children allowed?

¿Se admiten niños?	se ad·mee·ten nee·nyos

MODERN MAYAN

Since the Classic period, the two ancient Mayan languages, Yucatecan and Cholan, have subdivided into 35 separate Mayan languages (such as Yucatec, Chol, Chortí, Tzeltal, Tzotzil, Lacandón, Mam, K'iche' and Kaqchiquel), some of them unintelligible to speakers of others, some not. Indigenous languages are seldom written, but when they are, the Roman alphabet is used. Most literate Maya will only be able to read and write Spanish, the language of government, schools, the church and the media – they may not be literate in Mayan.

PRONUNCIATION

There are several rules to remember when pronouncing Mayan words and place names. Mayan vowels are pretty straightforward, but consonants can be tricky.

c	always hard, as in 'cat'
j	an aspirated 'h' sound, eg *jipijapa* is

pronounced 'hee-pee-haa-pah' and *abaj* is pronounced 'ah-bahh'; to get the 'ah' sound, imagine the 'h' sound from 'half' at the end of a word

u	as in 'prune', except when it occurs at the beginning or end of a word, in which case it is like English 'w'; thus *baktun* is 'bahk-toon,' but *Uaxactún* is 'wah-shahk-toon' and *ahau* is 'ah-haw'
x	as English 'sh'

Mayan glottalized consonants (indicated by an apostrophe: **b', ch', k', p', t'**) are similar to normal consonants, but are pronounced more forcefully and 'explosively.' An apostrophe following a vowel signifies a glottal stop (like the momentary stop between the syllables in 'oh-oh'), not a more forceful vowel.

Another rule to remember is that in most Mayan words the stress falls on the last syllable. Sometimes this is indicated by an acute accent, and sometimes not. The following place names are useful guides to pronunciation:

Abaj Takalik	a·bah ta·ka·leek
Acanceh	a·kan·keh
Ahau	a·haw
Kaminaljuyú	ka·mee·nal·hoo·yoo
Pop	pope
Tikal	tee·kal
Uaxactún	wa·shak·toon

K'ICHE'

K'iche' is widely spoken throughout the Guatemalan Highlands, from around Santa Cruz del Quiché to the area adjacent to Lake Atitlán and around Quetzaltenango. There are estimated to be around 2 million K'iche' Maya living in Guatemala.

Greetings & Civilities

These are great icebreakers, and even if you're not completely and accurately understood, there'll be goodwill and smiles all around just for making the effort.

Good morning.	Saqarik.
Good afternoon.	Xb'eqij.
Good evening/night.	Xokaq'ab'.
Goodbye.	Chab'ej.
Bye. See you soon.	Kimpetik ri.
Thank you.	Uts awech.

Excuse me.	*Kyunala.*
What's your name?	*Su ra'b'i?*
My name is ...	*Nu b'i ...*
Where are you from?	*Ja kat pewi?*
I'm from ...	*Ch'qap ja'kin pewi ...*

Useful Words & Phrases

Where is (a/the) ...?	*Ja k'uichi ri ...?*
bathroom	*b'anb'al chulu*
hotel	*jun worib'al*
police station	*ajchajil re tinamit*
doctor	*ajkun*
bus stop	*tek'lib'al*

Do you have ...?	*K'olik ...?*
coffee	*kab'e*
boiled water	*saq'li*
copal	*kach'*
a machete	*choyib'al*
rooms	*k'plib'al*

We have it.	*K'olik.*
We don't have it.	*K'otaj.*

vegetables	*ichaj*
blanket	*k'ul*
soap	*ch'ipaq*
good	*utz*
bad	*itzel*
open	*teb'am*
closed	*tzapilik*
hot	*miq'in*
cold	*joron*
sick	*yiwab'*
north (white)	*saq*
south (yellow)	*k'an*
east (red)	*kaq*
west (black)	*k'eq*

Numbers

1	*jun*
2	*keb'*
3	*oxib'*
4	*kijeb'*
5	*job'*
6	*waq'ib'*
7	*wuqub'*
8	*wajxakib'*
9	*b'elejeb'*
10	*lajuj*
11	*julajuj*
12	*kab'lajuj*
13	*oxlajuj*
14	*kajlajuj*
15	*o'lajuj*

16	*waklajuj*
17	*wuklajuj*
18	*wajxaklajuj*
19	*b'elejlajuj*
20	*juwinak*
30	*lajuj re kawinak*
40	*kawinak*
50	*lajuj re oxk'al*
60	*oxk'al*
70	*lajuj re waqk'al*
80	*waqk'al*
90	*lajuj re o'k'al*
100	*o'k'al*
200	*lajuj k'al*
400	*omuch'*

MAM

Mam is spoken in the department of Huehuetenango, in the western portion of Guatemala. This is the indigenous language you'll hear in Todos Santos Cuchumatán, which is nestled among the Cuchumatanes mountains.

Greetings & Civilities

Luckily, in Mam you only need two phrases for greeting folks, no matter what time of day it is.

Good morning/	*Chin q'olb'el teya.*
afternoon/evening.	(informal singular)
	Chin q'olb'el kyeyea.
	(informal plural)
Goodbye.	*Chi nej.*
Bye. See you soon.	*Chi nej. Ak qli qib'.*
Thank you.	*Chonte teya.*
How are you?	*Tzen ta'ya?*
Excuse me.	*Naq samy.*
What's your name?	*Tit biya?*
My name is ...	*Luan bi ...*
Where are you from?	*Jaa'tzajnia?*
I'm from ...	*Ac tzajni ...*

Useful Words & Phrases

Where is (a/the) ...?	*Ja at ...?*
bathroom	*bano*
hotel	*hospedaje*
doctor	*medico/doctor*

Many words in Mam have been in disuse for so long that the Spanish equivalent is now used almost exclusively.

Where is the bus	*Ja nue camioneta?* (literally,
stop?	where does the bus stop?)

How much is the fruits & vegetables?	Je te ti lobj?

Do you have ...?	At ...?
coffee	café
boiled water	kqa'
rooms	cuartos

Is there somewhere we can sleep?	Ja tun kqta'n?
We have it.	At.
We don't have it.	Nti'.
I'm cold.	At xb'a'j/choj.
I'm sick.	At yab'
good	banex/g'lan
bad	k'ab'ex/nia g'lan
open	jqo'n
closed	jpu'n
hard	kuj
soft	xb'une
hot	kyaq
north (white)	okan
south (yellow)	eln
east (red)	jawl
west (black)	kub'el

Numbers

The numbers from one to 10 are the same as in K'iche' (p477). For numbers higher than 10, Mam speakers use the Spanish equivalents.

GARIFUNA

Until 1993 the Garifuna language had no standardized written form. The publication of the *People's Garifuna Dictionary* (National Garifuna Council of Belize, 1993) was a part of an ongoing effort to preserve a language that has been slowly dying, as it is not generally taught in schools, and most Garinagu use Kriol (the local creole) or English as their first language.

It's not necessary to learn Garifuna – every Garifuna speaker will almost certainly have a better command of English than non-Garifuna will ever have of Garifuna, but we have included some handy phrases to use as ice-breakers or just to make a big impression on the locals.

The language itself is a mixture of Arawak, Yoruba, Swahili, Bantu, Spanish, English and French. For more on the Garifuna language and people, see the Garínagu

boxed text (p296). You can also check out the books *Garifuna History, Language and Culture of Belize, Central America and the Caribbean* (Cayetano, 1993) and the bilingual (English/Garifuna) *Marcella Our Legacy* (Lewis, 1994), both of which may be available from Angelus Books (p218) or through the National Garifuna Council of Belize (see www.belizemall.com/bac for contact details).

Pronunciation

Consonants are pronounced as they are in English (**g** is always hard as in 'gum', and vowels are similar to those in Spanish (see Pronunciation on p470). Stress is usually placed on the first syllable of two-syllable words and the second syllable in longer words.

Greetings & Conversation

Hello.	Mabuiga.
Good morning.	Buiti binafi.
Good afternoon.	Buiti amidi.
Good evening.	Buiti raba weyu.
Good night.	Buiti gunyon.
How are you?	Ida biangi?
I'm well.	Magadietina.
How about you?	Angi buguya?
Have a good day.	Buidi lamuga buweyuri.
Thank you.	Seremein, nian bun.
Thank you very much.	Owembu seremein na bun.
What is your name?	Ka biri?
My name is ...	... niribei.
Where do you come from?	Halia giendibu sa?
I come from ...	... giendina.
I was born in America.	Meriga naguruwa.
Where are you going?	Halion badibu?
I'm going to ...	Neibuga ...
I want to learn Garifuna.	Buseintina nafureinderu Garifuna.
Teach me a little Garifuna.	Arufudahaba murusu Garifuna nu.
What's this called in Garifuna?	Ka liri le lidan Garifuna.
This is ... in Garifuna.	... le lidan Garifuna.
I don't understand.	Uwati gufaranda nanibu.
Tell me again.	Arienga ya bei nu.
Do you like it?	Hiseinti bun?
I like it.	Hisienti nun.
I don't like it.	Misienti.
It's nice.	Semeti.
It's not nice.	Mesemeti.
It's good.	Buiti.
It's bad.	Wuribati.

LANGUAGE

Glossary

abrazo – embrace, hug; in particular, the formal, ceremonial hug between political leaders

aceite de frenos – brake fluid

almuerzo – two- or three-course set meal served at lunchtime, usually the cheapest option (Guatemala); see also *comida corrida* and *menú del día*

alux (aluxes) – Mayan for gremlin, leprechaun, benevolent 'little people'

Ángeles Verdes – 'Green Angels'; bilingual (Spanish and English) mechanics in green trucks who patrol major highways, offering breakdown assistance in Mexico

antojitos – literally 'little whims', these are snacks or light dishes such as burritos, *chiles rellenos*, *chuchitos*, enchiladas, quesadillas , tacos and tamales; eaten at any time, on their own or as part of a larger meal in Guatemala and Chiapas

Apartado Postal – post-office box, abbreviated Apdo Postal

Ayuntamiento – town council or city hall, often seen as 'H Ayuntamiento' *(Honorable Ayuntamiento)*, translated as 'Municipal Government'; see *Palacio Municipal*

barato/a – cheap

barrio – district, neighborhood

billete – banknote (unlike in Spain, where it's a ticket)

boleto – ticket (bus, train, museum etc)

bolo – Guatemalan term for a drunk

caballeros – literally 'horsemen,' but corresponds to 'gentlemen' in English; look for it on toilet doors

cacique – Mayan chief; also used to describe provincial warlord or strongman

cafetería – literally 'coffee shop,' it refers to any informal restaurant with waiter service; it does not usually mean a self-service restaurant, as it does in North America

cajero automático – automated bank-teller machine (ATM)

callejón – alley or small, narrow (or very short) street

camión – truck, bus

camioneta – bus or pickup truck; see also *picop*

campechanos – citizens of Campeche

campesinos – country folk, farm workers

cardamomo – cardamom; a spice grown extensively in the Verapaces of Guatemala and used as a flavor enhancer for coffee, particularly in the Middle East

caro/a – expensive

casa de cambio – currency exchange office; offers exchange rates comparable to banks, but with faster service

caseta de larga distancia – long-distance telephone station, often shortened to *caseta*; see also *larga distancia*

casita – little house (from *casa*)

cazuela – clay cooking pot, usually sold in a nested set

cenote – large, natural limestone sinkhole or cave, often used as a water source (or for ceremonial purposes) in the Yucatán

cerveza – beer

Chac – Mayan god of rain

chac-mool – Mayan sacrificial stone sculpture

chapín – a citizen of Guatemala; Guatemalan

charro – cowboy

chicle – chewing gum; also a substance processed from the sap of the sapodilla tree, used to make chewing gum

chiclero – a person who extracts chicle from the sapodilla tree

Chinka' – a small, non-Maya indigenous group living on Guatemala's Pacific Slope

chuchitos – corn dough filled with spicy meat and served in a corn husk

chuchkajau – Mayan prayer leader

chuj – a traditional Mayan sauna; see also *tuj*

chultún – artificial Mayan cistern found at Puuc archaeological sites south of Mérida

cigarillo – cigar

cigarro – cigarette

cocina – kitchen; also used for a small, basic, woman-run restaurant, often located in or near a municipal market; also seen as *cocina económica* (economical kitchen) or *cocina familiar* (family kitchen)

cofradía – in Guatemala, refers to a religious brotherhood

colectivo – literally 'shared'; a car, van or minibus that picks up and drops off passengers along its set route; also known as *taxi colectivo*

comal – hot griddle used to cook tortillas

combi – a catch-all term used in Mexico for taxi, van or minibus services regardless of van type

comedor – a basic and cheap eatery, usually with a limited menu

comida corrida – two- or three-course set meal served at lunchtime, usually the cheapest option (Mexico); also see *almuerzo* and *menú del día*

completo – full up, as in no vacancy at a hotel

conquistador – any of the Spanish explorer-conquerors of Latin America

copal – a tree resin used as incense in Mayan ceremonies

correos – post office

corte – Mayan wrap-around skirt (Guatemala); see also *enredo*

costumbre – traditional Mayan rites

criollos – people of Spanish ancestry born in the New World

cruce – a crossroads, usually where you make bus connections; see also *entronque*

cuota – toll road (Mexico)

curandero – traditional indigenous healer

damas – ladies; the usual sign on toilet doors

derecha – right

derecho – straight ahead

DNI – Derecho para No Inmigrante; nonimmigrant fee charged to all foreign tourists and business travelers visiting Mexico

dzul (dzules) – Mayan for foreigners or 'townfolk,' ie not Maya from the rural countryside

ejido – in Mexico, communally owned indigenous land once taken over by landowners but returned to the local people under a program started by President Lázaro Cárdenas

embarcadero – boat dock, pier or launch

encomienda – Spanish colonial practice of putting indigenous people under the 'guardianship' of landowners, practically akin to medieval serfdom

enredo – Mayan wrap-around skirt (Mexico); also see *corte*

entronque – a crossroads where you make bus connections; see also *cruce*

faja – Mayan waist sash or belt

feria – fair or carnival, typically occurring during a religious holiday

ferrocarril – railroad

finca – estate, ranch, farm

frenos – brakes

galón (galones) – US gallon (3.79L); gallons are sometimes used as a measurement in Belize and Guatemala

glyph – a symbolic character or figure, usually engraved or carved in relief

gringo/a – term applied to a male/female visitor from North America; sometimes applied to any visitor of European heritage; can be used pejoratively, but usually is simply a statement of fact

gruta – cave

guardaequipaje – room for storing luggage (eg in a bus terminal)

hacendado – landowner

hacienda – country estate, ranch; also 'Treasury,' as in Departamento de Hacienda (Treasury Department)

hamaca – hammock

hay – pronounced like 'eye,' meaning 'there is' or 'there are'; you're equally likely to hear *no hay* ('there isn't' or 'there aren't')

henequen – the fibers of an agave plant (grown particularly around Mérida), used to make rope; also the plant itself

hombre(s) – man/men

huipil – woven Mayan woman's tunic, often very colorful and elaborately embroidered

iglesia – church

invierno – literally winter; signifies the rainy season (May to November)

IVA – *impuesto al valor agregado* or '*ee*-vah'; a value-added tax that can be as high as 15% and is added to many items in Mexico

Ixchel – Mayan goddess of the moon and fertility

izquierda – left

kaperraj – Mayan woman's all-purpose cloth, used as a head covering, baby sling, produce sack, shawl and more

Kukulcán – Mayan name for the Aztec-Toltec plumed serpent Quetzalcóatl

ladino – a person of mixed indigenous and European race (Guatemala); see also *mestizo*

ladrón (ladrones) – robber(s) or thief/thieves

lancha – motor boat used to transport passengers; it's driven by *lancheros*

larga distancia – long-distance telephone, abbreviated as Ladi; see also *caseta de larga distancia*

lavadero – a cement sink for washing clothes; see also *pila*

lavandería – laundry; a *lavandería automática* refers to a coin-operated laundry (Laundromat)

leng – colloquial Mayan term for coins (Guatemalan highlands)

libra – pound (0.45kg); pounds are used as a measurement in Belize and sometimes in Guatemala

lista de correos – general delivery in Mexico; literally 'mail list,' the list of addressees for whom mail is being held, displayed in the post office

llantas – tires

lleno – full (can apply to fuel tank)

lonchería – from the English 'lunch'; a simple restaurant that may serve meals all day, not just lunch (often seen near municipal markets)

machismo – maleness, masculine virility or bravura

malecón – waterfront boulevard

manglar – mangrove

manzana – apple; also a city block
mariachi – small group of street musicians featuring string instruments, trumpets and often an accordion
marimba – Guatemala's xylophone-like national instrument
más o menos – more or less, somewhat
matrimonial – double bed; a matrimonial room has one bed for two people
mecapal – a forehead tumpline made of thick leather; still used by rural Maya as a means of carrying heavy loads
menú del día – two- or three-course set meal served at lunchtime, usually the cheapest option (Guatemala); see also *almuerzo* and *comida corrida*
meridanos – citizens of Mérida
mestizo – a person of mixed indigenous and European blood; the word now more commonly means 'Mexican' (see also *ladino*)
metate – flattish stone on which corn is ground with a cylindrical stone roller
milla – mile (1.6km); miles are used as a measurement in Belize and sometimes in Guatemala
mirador – lookout, vista point
mochila – backpack
mochilero/a – backpacker
Montezuma's revenge – Mexican/Guatemalan version of 'Delhi belly' or travelers' diarrhea
mordida – 'bite', or small bribe, paid to keep the wheels of bureaucracy turning; traffic cops are frequent recipients
mudéjar – Moorish architectural style
mujer(es) – woman/women

Nte – abbreviation for *norte* (north), used in street names

oferta – promotional deal or discount
onza – ounce (28.35g); ounces are used as a measurement in Belize and sometimes in Guatemala
Ote – abbreviation for *oriente* (east), used in street names in Mexico

pachete – loofa; a squash-type vegetable used as shower scrubbies
Palacio de Gobierno – building housing the executive offices of a state or regional government
Palacio Municipal – City Hall, seat of the municipal government
palapa – thatch-roofed shelter with open sides
parada – bus stop, usually for city buses
petrol – unleaded gasoline
picop – pickup truck (Guatemala); see also *camioneta*
pie (pies) – foot (a length equal to 0.3m); feet are used as a measurement in Belize and sometimes in Guatemala
pila – a sink for washing clothes; see also *lavadero*

pisto – colloquial Mayan term for money, quetzals (Guatemalan highlands)
Plateresque – describes buildings constructed in a 16th-century Spanish architectural style using elaborate decoration reminiscent of silverwork
Popol Vuh – painted Mayan book containing sacred legends and stories; similar to the Bible
PRI – Institutional Revolutionary Party, the controlling force in Mexican politics for more than half a century
propino (propina) – a tip, different from a *mordida*
Pte – abbreviation for *poniente* (west) used in street names in Mexico
punta – sexually suggestive dance enjoyed by the Garífuna of the Caribbean coast
puro – cigar

Quetzalcóatl – plumed serpent god of the Aztecs and Toltecs

rebozo – long woolen or linen scarf covering the head or shoulders
recibo – receipt
refacciones – simple snacks; literally refreshments
refago – Mayan wrap-around skirt
retablo – ornate, often gilded altarpiece; also a small painting on tin, wood, cardboard, glass etc, placed in a church to give thanks for answered prayers or other divine intercession
retorno – 'return'; used on traffic signs to indicate a U-turn or turn around
robo – robbery
roofcomb – a decorative stonework lattice atop a Mayan pyramid or temple
rutelero – jitney

sacbé (sacbeob) – ceremonial limestone avenue or path between or within great Mayan cities
sacerdote – priest
sanatorio – hospital, particularly a small private one
sanitario – literally 'sanitary'; usually means toilet
secadora – clothes dryer
Semana Santa – Holy Week running from Palm Sunday to Easter Sunday; falls in March or April
serape – traditional woolen blanket
stela (stelae) – standing stone monument(s), usually carved
supermercado – supermarket, ranging from a small corner store to a large, American-style supermarket
Sur – south, used in street addresses in Mexico

taller – shop, workshop or studio; a *taller mecánico* is a mechanic's shop, usually for cars, while a *taller de artesanía* is a crafts shop or studio

teléfono comunitario – community telephone found in the smallest towns

templo – temple, also a church (anything from a wayside chapel to a cathedral)

tepezcuintle – edible jungle rodent the size of a rabbit

tequila – clear, distilled liquor produced, like pulque and *mezcal*, from the maguey cactus

tienda – small store that may sell anything from candles and chickens to aspirin and bread

típico – typical or characteristic of a region; particularly used to describe food

tocoyal – Mayan head covering

topes – speed bumps found in many Mexican towns, sometimes indicated by a highway sign bearing a row of little bumps

traje – traditional clothing worn by the Maya

tuj – a traditional Mayan sauna; see also *chuj*

túmulos – speed bumps (Guatemala)

tzut – Mayan man's equivalent of a *kaperraj*

verano – literally summer; means the dry season (November to May)

viajero/a – traveler

vulcanizadora – automobile tire-repair shop (Mexico)

War of the Castes – bloody Mayan uprising that took place in the Yucatán during the mid-19th century

xate – a low-growing palm native to Guatemala's Petén region and exported for use in floral arrangements, particularly in the US

xateros – men who collect *xate*

Xibalbá – in Mayan religious belief, the secret world or underworld

xtabentún – a traditional Mayan spirit in the Yucatán; an anise-flavored liqueur made by fermenting honey

zócalo – Aztec for 'pedestal' or 'plinth,' but now used to refer to a town's main plaza (Mexico)

zotz – bat (the mammal) in many of the Mayan languages

Behind the Scenes

THIS BOOK

The front and back chapters of this 5th edition were written by coordinating author Conner Gorry. Lucas Vidgen wrote the Guatemala and Belize chapters, and Danny Palmerlee wrote the Yucatán chapter based on text by Suzanne Plank. Dr Allen J Christenson contributed the Ancient Mayan Culture chapter, and Dr David Goldberg wrote the Health chapter. The previous edition, *Belize, Guatemala & Yucatán 4* was written by Ben Greensfelder, Carolyn Miller, Conner Gorry and Sandra Bao.

THANKS from the Authors

Conner Gorry I had the pleasure of working with some fine folks on this project. Most important, *muchísimas gracias* is due my coauthors Danny Palmerlee and Lucas Vidgen who did a terrific job under some extraordinary circumstances. The knowledge of regional experts and authors John Noble and Susan Forsyth was especially helpful, while Lily Suárez provided insight into the Chiapas region, helping me understand the complex situation with the Zapatistas and their struggle. Supporting me in *my* struggle were Teresita with her unsurpassed *potajes*, Asli Pelit and Fidelito Pérez Cabrera ('El Mago'). Unless you're married to a Lonely Planet writer, you have no idea what a working hell home can be. Thanks to Joel Suárez, mine is (mostly) heaven. *Te quiero con tres pares...*

Lucas Vidgen Firstly, thanks to nearly every Belizean I ever met for making traveling in your country such a joy. Specifically, to Sherilee Rivero of the BTB, for endless patience and the supply of obscure (but useful!) information. To Diane Wade of the Belize Audubon Society, for the lowdown on Chalillo, to Marion Nolberto and Modesta Palacio of the National Garífuna Council and Peace Corps worker Rachel Hockfield for help in compiling the Garifuna language section and Silvana Woods of the Kriol Council for supplying the Kriol phrases. Also to Gerard 'Mr Organization' the Dread the best taxi driver I never got a ride from – and Junior – the boat driver in Dangriga – for fun and laughs and that jacket when things got choppy. Guatemala wouldn't have been the same without the tips and friendship of a whole stack of travelers and locals, the biggies being America Hernandez, Brenda Orantes, Mario Rivera and Greg, Andrew, Claire, Erica and Nicholas in Xela – I haven't forgotten your surnames, guys; I never knew them in the first place! Thanks also to my family for love, support and, most importantly, storage space – I'll be back one day, I promise!

Danny Palmerlee First and foremost, my deepest thanks (and hugest of hugs) to Rebecca 'Sugarbutt' Santana for letting me take over her apartment while writing this thing. You rule! Alex Hershey, I can't thank you enough for your help and rapid responses to all my frantic questions. Conner Gorry, 'twas fun once again, no? Of course, thanks to David Zingarelli for involving me in this project in the first place.

CREDITS

This title was commissioned and developed in Lonely Planet's Oakland office by David Zingarelli. Alex Hershey and Erin Corrigan followed as commissioning editors. Cartography for this guide was developed by Alison Lyall.

Barbara Delissen was the coordinating editor, assisted by Pete Cruttenden, Charlotte Harrison, Thalia Kalkipsakis, Anne Mulvaney and Simon Sellars. Coordinating cartographer Jack Gavran was assisted by Lyndell Stringer. The book was laid out by John Shippick and Tamsin Wilson. Project managers Glenn van der Knijff and Sally Darmody kept the production of this title on track. Thanks to Gerard Walker and Ryan Evans in LPI, to James Hardy for designing the cover and to Quentin Frayne for the language chapter. And of course a big thank you to authors Conner Gorry, Lucas Vidgen, Danny Palmerlee, Dr Allen J Christenson and Dr David Goldberg.

THANKS from Lonely Planet

Many thanks to the following travellers who used the last edition and wrote to us with helpful hints, useful advice and interesting anecdotes.

A Johannes Abeling, Harm Aben, Bruce Aisthorpe, Natasha Aisthorpe, Igor Ajdisek, Sanne L Albrectsen, Nick Ambridge, Henrik Andersen, Eve Astrid Andersson, Ervin Andrino, Beata Antal, Linda Anzalone, Enrique Araoz, Shawna Archa, Sue Arnold, Santiago Ash, Christine Astaniou, Jörg Ausfelt, Judy Avisar, Arturo Azcarraga **B** Klaus Bajohr-Mau, Jacki & Percy Balon, E Baltus, Marco Balzarini, Pashiera Barkhuysen, Jenny Barnes, Alec Beardsell, Laresa Beck, Chuck Behrens, Jean Jacques Beletan, Mike & Daphne Bell, Kathy Benavides, Nick Bennett, Andrew Bergmann, Harald Berninger, Eliza Berries, Christophe Bevilacqua, Ernst Biebl, Hilmar Bijma, Tom Billings, Liz Bissett, Mike Bissett, Mark Bixler, Vashti Blacker, Erica Boas, Norbert Bolis, Laetitia Bonnet, Maaike Bosschart, Nancy Bouchard, George Boutilier, Richard Bovenschen, Sue Bowling, Hank Bragg, Jan Brascamp, Michael Brasier, Charlotte Brauer, Jason Braun, Will Braun, Liesbeth Breesch, Michael Brennan, Graeme Brooks, Corina Browne, Linda Bufton, Sam Bull, Simon Burchell, Stephanie Burke, Steven J Burris, Ian Burton, Mark Burton, Ute Buscher, Janey Byrne **C** Rebecca Cague, Ben Campbell, Alan & Clare Cannon, Ben Capell, Giovanni Capellini, Denny Carhart, Kimber Carhart, Peggy Carlson, Kristen Carney, Graham Carr, Luis Carreras, Olivia Carrescia, Gaetano Carubia, Eva Casas, Sophia Castillo, Daniela Cellino, Marco Ceschi, Fred Chevre, Chungwah Chow, Mike & Trena Christensen, Weihaw Chuang, Simon Cloutier Gagne, Geoffery Clover, Chris Coates, Philip Coebergh, Francis & Maite Coke, Roger Conant, Gerald Conrad, Monica Contini, Cam Cooper, Richard Cooper, Sue Corby, Catherine Corry, Paolo Cotta-Ramusino, Chris Courtheyn, Andrew Cox, Olivia Cozzolino, Mick Creedon, Filip Crombez, Jai Cross, Martin Crossland, Emma Curnow **D** Gail D'Alessio, Jan-Hendrik Damerau, Emma Darley, Serge Dauvillier, Hannah Dawson, Dennis de Graaf, Niels de Greef, Serjos de Groot, Elma de Jong, Maria de Keyser, Fatima de la Fuente, Jose de Leon Guzman, Elio De Meo, Martin de Ruiter, Emily Dean, Dan Dennis, IA Dickie, Neil Dickinson, Irene Dijkstra, Mads Dippel Rasmussen, Rena Distasio, Andrew Dix, Andrew Doak, Pat Dobie, Sue Doherty, Danielle Douglas, Roberta Downing, Glo-Ann D'Souza, Monique du Pau, Alejandra Duarte, Catherine Duclos, Stephanie Dula, Jean-Marc Dumont, Hamish Duncan **E** Andreas Eberl, Lisbeth Edelmann Nyborg, Caroline Edwards, Jay Edwards, Simone Egger, Peter Ehrenkranz, Anne-Marie Elbe, Jerry Eldred, Antonieta & Petronio Elias, Demetre Eliopoulos, Jocelyn Elliot, Nick Ellis, Thomas Ellis, Miriam Engeln, Patrik Eqvist, Tandi Erlmann, Litza Escobar, Mark Esposito, Nory Esteban, Robert Ettinger, Melissa Evanson, Will Everett **F** Roi Faust, Greg Feather, Stacy Fehlenberg, Tom & Suzanne Fell, Alexander Fenske, Enrique Fernandez, Joseph Fette, Chuck Fields, Cromez Filip, Pamela Firchow, Gary Fishman, Dorothee Flaig, Annelies Florquin, Ben Flynn, Yannick Foing, Lucas Fortini, Kathy Fournier, Brian Fowler, Cara Frankel, Heather Frankel, Amy Frappier, Jacob Frederiksen, Lee Freedom, David Frier, Tina Fridrich, Karen Fu, Andreas Funke, Tammo Funke **G** Katerina Gaita, Mary Collette Gallagher, Christian Gandara, Dario Garcia, Jennifer Garcia, Richard Garcia, Stuart Gardiner, Marcelo Garza, Raymond Gaudart, Robert Gehrung, Martina Gempp, Sandra Gennai, Elain Genser, Brian Gentis, Ann George, Rose George, Roger Gerritzen, Rachel Gibbs, Andrew Gill, Mark Goettel, Wendy Gonsalves, Nicolas Gonze, Jenny Goodall, Lisa Goodlin, Caroline Goodman, Anette Gram Madsen, Nancy Grant, Dave Graves, Lisa Graybill, Alvaro Greene, Carol Greenough, Lisa Greenspan, Sheryl Griffith, Victor Gruber, Maria Guasch, Oliver Guba, Shamir Gurfinkel **H** Christof Haars, Wolfgang Haertel, A Hafferty, Marita Hagen, Chrystal Hagerty, Peter Hahn, Aaron Hall, Evan Hall, Sarah Haller, Lisa Hamilton, Brain Hammond, Kelly Hammond, Jon Hampson, Kim Haney, Kim Hannah, Angie Harding, Keith Harding, Jill Harmer, Daniel Haug, Ian Haynes, Liselotte Hedegaard, Jacob Hegner, Larry Heinlein, David Henry, Gerlinde Hensel, Simon Heuking, John Richard Hewitt, Jeff Hicks, David Higgs, Greg Hill, Sirpa Hillberg, Michiel Hillenius, Matthias Hillenkamp, Sara Hillman, Camilla Hinde, Andrea Hindinger, Rakhee Hindocha, Justin Hines, Ana María Hintermann-Villamil, Bernhard Hofbauer, Krista Hoffs, Moshe & Ruti Hofsetter, Natalie Hohmann, Mary Ann Hollebeck, Sophia Holtz, Marco Hopstaken, Olivia Horgan, Martin Howard, Celina & Mirek Hrabanek, Jayne Husband, Tasneem Hussain **I** Eran Inbar, Dave Ingram, Nadler Ishay, Shamim Islam, Marko Istenic **J** Dave Jackaman, Gasper Jakopin, Marjolaine Janvier-Houde, Jan Jasiewicz, Magali Jean, Marije Jeltes, Alex Jensen, Erick Johns, Carlisle Johnson, Helen Johnson, Ken Johnson, Tahirah Johnson, Judy Johnson Flaherty, Georgina Jones, Jennifer Jones, Justin Jones, Margreet Joosen, Tammy Jorgensen, Vince Jorgensen, Isabelle Jost, Greg Juhl **K** Thomas Kaeslin, Ofer Kashtan, Christian Kasprzyk, Suli Katainen, Rupert

Kaufmann, Judy King, Julie King, Trevor King, Gregory Kipling, Joanne Kitson, Ariane Klein, Vincent Kleinekorte, Marit & Timo Kleinow, Elizabeth Knell, Linda Knight, Dave Knipe, Meike Kolb, Jeannette Koller, Greg Kondrak, Bart Konings, Leo Kooi, Mil Kooyman, Rastko Kozlevcar, Aarnoud Kraan, Alon Kramer, Julie Kramer, Diane Kremer, Hans Baekke Kristensen, Katrin Krueger, Astrid Kueffer, Kristen Kurczak, Martha Kvaal **L** Joanna Lake, Tab Lamoureux, Jean-Pierre Lamure, Giobatta Lanfranco, Kyle Langlois, José Larios, Shirley Larsen, Jenny Lau, Harriet Lavender, Annette Lavers, Eve Lavigne, Viviane Le Courtois, Danisa Lederer, Michelle Legere, Ruben Lehnert, Andre Lehovich, Diane Leighton, Nicolai Leymann, T Liljeberg, Morten Lind, Jeff Linwood, Marc & Ilse Litjens, Karin Lock, Lluis Lopez Bayona, Elizabeth Lorimer, Andreas Lots, Stephen Lowe, Judith Lumb, Elsbeth Luning **M** Campbell Macdonald, Renee MacDonald, Zoe Macfarlane, Paul M Mack, Leslie MacKay, Jan Maes, Charles Maliszewski, Uwe Mall, Richard Mallett, Gabriella Malnati, Casper Maltha, Marsh Marcus, Mercedes Marin, Birgit Maris, Marcus Marsden, Kathy Martens, Nicky Martens, David Martin, Itziar Martin, Luis Martinez, Annabel Mary, Andrea Masnata, Corine Massicot, Francois Maurice, Joanne Mauro, Michael B McClellan, Sherry McCarnan, Tristan McCoy, Robin McCutcheon, Emily McDonald, Dan McDougall, Sarah McKinnon, Kimberly McLaughlin, Amy McLeod, Roger McNellie, Seán McNulty, Michael Meallem, Andrea Medovarski, Jan Meerman, Toni Meier, Guadalupe Mendoza, Joseph Mendoza, Aditya Menon, Nick Menzies, Andrea Merschilz, Bruce Meyer, Heidi Meyer, Monika Meyer, Fred Midtgaard, Stephanie Mignacca, David Miller, Gretchen Miller, John Miller, Michelle Miranda, Kjell Mittag, Kari & Anne Molden, Guillemette Moreau, Steffi Morgner, Diane Morrison, Susanne & Christian Moskob, Connie Mosquera, Sonja Munnix, David Murray, Donna Murray **N** Ingrid Naden, Nicola Wendy Nelson, Spencer & Mary Beth Nelson, Dori Neubronner, Kars Neven, Gillian Newell, Brigitte Niemeijer, Dennis Nilsson, Sander Nolles, Morten Norjordet, Katharina Nothelfer, Ippolita Novali, Norberto Nunez, Soren Nyegaard, Nadja Nys **O** Richard Oas, Brent Ohata, Katye Oliver, Emanuele Olivero, Grejon Olivier, David Olson, Caprice Olsthoorn, Celia Ortega, Conor Oshea, Donal O'Sullivan, Pascal Otten **P** Jennifer Pacourek, Kristen Page, Leigh Paris, Gina Parise, Mark Parkes, Elena Parlanti, Marije Paternotte, Ludovica & Pierpaolo Patroncini, Sheri Patterson, Ariane & Moran Pazeller, Karin Pedersen, Monique Peeters, Sabina Pensek, Rebecca Perez, Al Perry, Matthew Peters, Tim Peterson, Stephanie Petit, Severine Peudupin, Jason Pielemeier, Melissa Pike, Anthony Pirro, Jennifer Pittman, Leonard Plompen, Claire Plumridge, Elisabeth Poetscher-Maerky, Steve Pogue, Ryan Pohl, Martin Polajnar, Cheri Powell, Dimitri Prybylski, Juli Puryear **Q** Shahreen Quazi **R** Andre Racine, Jurgen Rahmer, Paul Reeves, M Rehorst, John P Reid, Scott Reilly, Karina Reindlmeier, Neal Reiter, Diana Renard, Jean Claude Rey, Pamela Rey, Julia Rhodes, Shelly-Marie Rios, Romolo & Gessica Ripini, Alex Robertson, Eric Robette, Jo Robinson, Mike Rodgers, Ruth Rodgers, Deborah Rodrigo, Filipe Rodrigues, Jane Roehl, Hilde Roelofsen, James Rogers, Elisabeth Rogolsky, Matt Roque, Jane Rose, Jessica Rosien, Pierre Ross, Marion & Michael Roszak, Francoise Roux, Joan Rubin, Floren Rudy, Rachel Rumsey,

Sarah Russell, Paul Rutten, Krzysztof Rybak, Katie Ryde, Claire Ryder **S** Rahni Sadler, Rajasi Saha, Esther Sanders, Marilyn Sanders, Stephen Sandlos, Edwina Sassoon, Jen Savage, Laura Sawyer, Thomas Schaffner, Lex Schaling, Gernot Scharf, Christian Schild, Angela Schleiniger, Treya Marie Schmitt, Laura Schmulewitz, Wendy Schneider, Patrick Schnell, Doris Schoch, Susanne Schoenauer, Marianne Schrotter, Tim Schultz, David Scott, Terry Scott, Seth Seiderman, Julia Seiders, Elke Selter, Gavin Sexton, Alexander Sharman, Cynthia Sharon, Daniel Sher, Noa Sher, Paul Sheridan, Caesar Sherrard, Ian Sherriff, Amy Shindler, Amit Irit Shwartz, Nadine Sicard, Alen Silva, Jason Simard, Michael Simone, Evita Sips, Luca Sita, Karen Skibo, Emma Slater, Dorkas Sloth, Erica Smith, James Smith, Jason Smith, Joseph Smith, Matthew Smith, Samuel Smith, Timothy J Smith, Todd Smith, Tom Sobhani, Vic Sofras, Claudine Solin, Simone Sommer, Susan Sommer, Heike Sonnberger, Loes Sparwer, Will Staler, Sally Stanley, Peggy Stauffer, Cara Stauss, Sander Steijnis, Hendrik Steringa, Mary Kay Stine, Andy Stock, Helen Stohlman, Katarina Stoltz, Cecilia Stranneby, Ursula Strauss, Beat Stueber, Thomas Stutzer, Melissa Sulivan, Caroline Sutherland, Amelia Swan Baxter, Tom Sweeney **T** Achim Talmon, Robert Taylor, Paul Templeman, Jeroen Thijs, Nick Thomas, Eltjo Timmerman, Edward Timpson, Julia Timpson, Markus Toepler, Karen Toohey, Andrew Trout, Magnus Trovik, David Truman, Christine Tuhy **U** PM Ullman, BL Underwood **V** Mauro Valentini, James Valenzuela, Annet van de Kreke, Maurits van den Boorn, Judith van den Hengel, Thomas van der Lijke, Ilse van der Veer, Wendy van Driel, Eelco van Geene, Marly van Horck, Wim van Immerzeel, Peter van

---

SEND US YOUR FEEDBACK

We love to hear from travellers – your comments keep us on our toes and help make our books better. Our well-travelled team reads every word on what you loved or loathed about this book. Although we cannot reply individually to postal submissions, we always guarantee that your feedback goes straight to the appropriate authors, in time for the next edition. Each person who sends us information is thanked in the next edition – and the most useful submissions are rewarded with a free book.

To send us your updates – and find out about LP events, newsletters and travel news – visit our award-winning website: **www.lonelyplanet.com**.

Note: We may edit, reproduce and incorporate your comments in Lonely Planet products such as guidebooks, websites and digital products, so let us know if you don't want your comments reproduced or your name acknowledged. For a copy of our privacy policy visit www.lonelyplanet.com/privacy.

Nes, Jan van Opstal, Rutger van Otterlo, Max van Riel, Martine van Rijn, Ron van Rooijen, Leonie van Rossum, Michel van Rossum, Lianne van Someren, Judy van Veen, Carl Johan van Vugt, Diederik Vanderburg, Todd Varness, Petra Veenman, Frits Verbeek, Didier Verbruggen, Bart Verlinden, Yves Vervaet, Richard Veul, Jesus Villen, Marcella Vinciguerra, Rolf von Behrens, Kirsten Vroombout, Veronique Vuylsteke **W** Petra Waeckens, Kelsey Wagner, Thomas Wagner, Chow Chung Wah, David Wahl, Katrin Wanner, Helena Warren, Gwynn Watkins, Katherine Watson, Gabriel Wechter, Dan & Martha Weese, David Weibel, Andreas Weichert, Melissa Weiss, Mark Weitz, Peggy Wenrick, Sascha Wenzel, Kirsten Wheeler, Jason White, Natalie White, Philip Wiebe, Martin Wielecki, Ellen

Wijnand, Krista Willeboer, Jason Williams, Martin Williams, Steve Wilson, Christopher & Tanda Wilson-Clarke, Ralph Winkelmolen, Margaret Winn, Jennifer Winter, Emma Wise, Stephan Wolde, Stephen Wollmer, Young-Jee Won, Liz Woolmington, Cornelius Wright, Ben Wrigley, Marisa Wyatt **Y** Todd Youngs, Maria Yule **Z** Dennis Zijlstra, Heidi Zotter, Alexandra Zum Felde

ACKNOWLEDGMENTS

Many thanks to the following for the use of their content:

Globe on back cover © Mountain High Maps 1993 Digital Wisdom, Inc.

Index

000 Map pages
000 Location of colour photographs

000 Map pages
000 Location of colour photographs

500

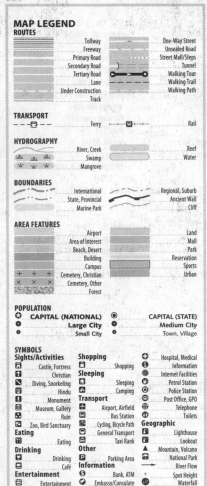

MAP LEGEND

ROUTES

Tollway
Freeway
Primary Road
Secondary Road
Tertiary Road
Lane
Under Construction
Track

One-Way Street
Unsealed Road
Street Mall/Steps
Tunnel
Walking Tour
Walking Trail
Walking Path

TRANSPORT

Ferry
Rail

HYDROGRAPHY

River, Creek
Swamp
Mangrove

Reef
Water

BOUNDARIES

International
State, Provincial
Marine Park

Regional, Suburb
Ancient Wall
Cliff

AREA FEATURES

Airport
Area of Interest
Beach, Desert
Building
Campus
Cemetery, Christian
Cemetery, Other
Forest

Land
Mall
Park
Reservation
Sports
Urban

POPULATION

✪	**CAPITAL (NATIONAL)**	◉	**CAPITAL (STATE)**
●	**Large City**	◎	**Medium City**
●	Small City	○	Town, Village

SYMBOLS

Sights/Activities
Castle, Fortress
Christian
Diving, Snorkeling
Hindu
Monument
Museum, Gallery
Ruin
Zoo, Bird Sanctuary

Eating
Eating

Drinking
Drinking
Café

Entertainment
Entertainment

Shopping
Shopping

Sleeping
Sleeping
Camping

Transport
Airport, Airfield
Bus Station
Cycling, Bicycle Path
General Transport
Taxi Rank

Other
Parking Area

Information
Bank, ATM
Embassy/Consulate

Hospital, Medical
Information
Internet Facilities
Petrol Station
Police Station
Post Office, GPO
Telephone
Toilets

Geographic
Lighthouse
Lookout
Mountain, Volcano
National Park
River Flow
Spot Height
Waterfall

LONELY PLANET OFFICES

Australia
Head Office
Locked Bag 1, Footscray, Victoria 3011
☎ 03 8379 8000, fax 03 8379 8111
talk2us@lonelyplanet.com.au

USA
150 Linden St, Oakland, CA 94607
☎ 510 893 8555, toll free 800 275 8555
fax 510 893 8572, info@lonelyplanet.com

UK
72–82 Rosebery Ave,
Clerkenwell, London EC1R 4RW
☎ 020 7841 9000, fax 020 7841 9001
go@lonelyplanet.co.uk

France
1 rue du Dahomey, 75011 Paris
☎ 01 55 25 33 00, fax 01 55 25 33 01
bip@lonelyplanet.fr, www.lonelyplanet.fr

Published by Lonely Planet Publications Pty Ltd
ABN 36 005 607 983

© Lonely Planet 2004

© photographers as indicated 2004

Cover photographs: El Castillo, Chichén Itzá, Yucatán, Angelo Cavalli/
Getty Images (front); Man with pig, Guatemala, Eric L Wheater/
Lonely Planet Images (back). Many of the images in this guide are
available for licensing from Lonely Planet Images: www.lonelyplanet
images.com.

Printed through SNP SPrint Singapore Pte Ltd at
KHL Printing Co Sdn Bhd, Malaysia